**Contemporary American literature is a living record of an age
that challenges our skill, our strength, our beliefs.**

ADVENTURES IN AMERICAN LITERATURE

TO

His Eminence

FRANCIS CARDINAL SPELLMAN

untiring in his devotion to God and Country

REWEY BELLE INGLIS
FORMERLY UNIVERSITY HIGH SCHOOL
MINNEAPOLIS, MINNESOTA

MARY RIVES BOWMAN
EAST TEXAS STATE TEACHERS COLLEGE
COMMERCE, TEXAS

JOHN GEHLMANN
OAK PARK HIGH SCHOOL
OAK PARK, ILLINOIS

WILBUR SCHRAMM
DEAN, DIVISION OF COMMUNICATIONS
UNIVERSITY OF ILLINOIS, URBANA, ILLINOIS

MERCURY EDITION

Harcourt, Brace and Company   NEW YORK . CHICAGO

Adventures in AMERICAN LITERATURE

SISTER MARIE THERESA, S.C.
SUPERVISOR OF SCHOOLS, SISTERS OF CHARITY,
MOUNT ST. VINCENT, NEW YORK

BROTHER BASILIAN RICHARD, F.S.C.
CHAIRMAN, ENGLISH DEPARTMENT, LA SALLE ACADEMY,
NEW YORK CITY

SISTER ANNA MERCEDES, S.C.
CHAIRMAN, ENGLISH DEPARTMENT, CATHEDRAL HIGH
SCHOOL, NEW YORK CITY

THE REVEREND LEO F. HALPIN
CHAIRMAN, ENGLISH DEPARTMENT, CARDINAL HAYES
HIGH SCHOOL, NEW YORK CITY

CARDINAL NEWMAN EDITION

*The photograph which appears on the cover and on the title page is
from Ewing Galloway. It shows the mission at Santa Barbara,
California, which was founded in 1786 by the Franciscan Fathers.
The present building dates from 1820 and is one of the best preserved
of all the Spanish missions.*

*The endpaper kodachromes show a New England town scene with
its colonial church, photographed by David Corson from Devaney;
and the Golden Gate Bridge, San Francisco, photographed by Fred
Lyon from Rapho-Guillumette.*

Drawings by Edwin Schmidt

Acknowledgments for permissions and illustrations are covered
by the present copyright for this edition as well as copyrights for
the 1930, 1936, 1941, 1947, 1949, and 1952 editions of *Adventures
in American Literature.*

Contents

PART ONE:
MODERN AMERICAN LITERATURE

Modern Fiction

v

Modern Nonfiction

Modern Poetry

CONTENTS

Modern Drama

PART TWO:
THE GROWTH OF AMERICAN LITERATURE

The Colonial Time

The Making of a Nation

The Flowering of the East, Part One

The Flowering of the East, Part Two

The Westward Movement

PIONEER LIFE AND LITERATURE

THE WAR BETWEEN THE STATES

Time of Change

NEW DIRECTIONS IN POETRY

SOCIAL CONSCIOUSNESS AND THE RISE OF REALISM

American Literature in the Modern World

PART ONE

Modern American Literature

MODERN FICTION

MODERN NONFICTION

MODERN POETRY

MODERN DRAMA

Modern Fiction

EVERYONE enjoys a good story. At six we clamor for stories at bedtime; at sixteen we call for them around the campfire; at sixty we count on them to pass our armchair evenings. Primitive man had his wonder tales, the tired businessman has his mystery stories. The story belongs to all ages and climes and is a common link in the literature of all languages. Yet we say that the short story belongs especially to American literature. How can that be? Because the *short* story has come to have a special meaning as a type of writing: as such, it was first defined by an American, Edgar Allan Poe. It has had its most rapid and varied development through American magazines. It is probably more widely written and read in America than anywhere else in the world.

The stories in this section have all been written by Americans in the twentieth century. They picture many different parts of our land — the settled East, the open country of the West, the North, and the South. The characters in these stories reveal something of the variety of people in our nation. Some of them come from " old stock "; others are immigrants. Some speak standard English; others use local dialects. Some are sly or cruel; most are fine and honorable. During the reading of these stories you will come to know intimately some kinds of Americans you may never have met before.

Of course you have already read many short stories in magazines and books, and will be reading many more during your lifetime. You have already discovered that anyone's prime purpose in reading fiction is getting pleasure, not information. However, you also gain deep insight into human nature from well-drawn characters. You can learn about yourself and about your relations with other people by watching the problems, the actions, the thoughts of characters in stories. Toward this end, the editorial questions for each story are designed to help you read stories more skillfully. With your eyes open and your senses alert to the fine points you might otherwise miss, the stories you read here will bring you greater satisfaction and pleasure.

THE SHORT STORY

RICHARD CONNELL
1893–1949

The Most Dangerous Game

At the age of ten Richard Connell was covering baseball games for his father's newspaper at ten cents a game. At sixteen he became city editor of this same paper. At Harvard he worked on two college publications. During World War I he edited *Gas Attack*, a camp paper. From 1919 until his death he was a free-lance writer of fiction, with the remarkable record of more than three hundred stories published in magazines. He never cared to write novels, but rather devoted himself entirely to the short story. His originality of plot and his mastery of suspense were never better shown than in the following story. A remote, mysterious setting — a diabolical character — a dangerous match of wits between skillful men. You can't put it down!

"OFF there to the right — somewhere — is a large island," said Whitney. "It's rather a mystery —"

"What island is it?" Rainsford asked.

"The old charts call it 'Ship-Trap Island,'" Whitney replied. "A suggestive name, isn't it? Sailors have a curious dread of the place. I don't know why. Some superstition —"

"Can't see it," remarked Rainsford, trying to peer through the dank tropical night that was palpable as it pressed its thick warm blackness in upon the yacht.

"You've good eyes," said Whitney, with a laugh, "and I've seen you pick off a moose moving in the brown fall bush at four hundred yards, but even you can't see four miles or so through a moonless Caribbean night."

"Nor four yards," admitted Rainsford. "Ugh! It's like moist black velvet."

"It will be light enough in Rio," promised Whitney. "We should make it in a few days. I hope the jaguar guns have come from Purdey's. We should have some good hunting up the Amazon. Great sport, hunting."

"The best sport in the world," agreed Rainsford.

"For the hunter," amended Whitney. "Not for the jaguar."

"Don't talk rot, Whitney," said Rainsford. "You're a big-game hunter, not a philosopher. Who cares how a jaguar feels?"

"Perhaps the jaguar does," observed Whitney.

"Bah! They've no understanding."

"Even so, I rather think they understand one thing — fear. The fear of pain and the fear of death."

"Nonsense," laughed Rainsford. "This hot weather is making you soft, Whitney. Be a realist. The world is made up of two classes — the hunters and the huntees. Luckily, you and I are hunters. Do you think we've passed that island yet?"

"I can't tell in the dark. I hope so."

"Why?" asked Rainsford.

"The place has a reputation — a bad one."

"Cannibals?" suggested Rainsford.

"Hardly. Even cannibals wouldn't live in such a God-forsaken place. But it's got into sailor lore, somehow. Didn't you notice that the crew's nerves seemed a bit jumpy today?"

"They were a bit strange, now you mention it. Even Captain Nielsen —"

"Yes, even that tough-minded old Swede, who'd go up to the devil himself and ask him for a light. Those fishy blue eyes held a look I never saw there before. All I could get out of him was: 'This place has an evil name among seafaring men, sir.' Then he said to me, very gravely: 'Don't you feel anything?' — as if the air about us was actually poisonous. Now, you mustn't laugh when I tell you this — I did feel something like a sudden chill.

"There was no breeze. The sea was as flat as a plate-glass window. We were drawing near the island then. What I felt was a — a mental chill; a sort of sudden dread."

"Pure imagination," said Rainsford. "One superstitious sailor can taint the whole ship's company with his fear."

"Maybe. But sometimes I think sailors have an extra sense that tells them when they are in danger. Sometimes I think evil is a tangible thing — with wave lengths, just as sound and light have. An evil place can, so to speak, broadcast vibrations of evil. Anyhow, I'm glad we're getting out of this zone. Well, I think I'll turn in now, Rainsford."

"I'm not sleepy," said Rainsford. "I'm going to smoke another pipe up on the after deck."

"Good night, then, Rainsford. See you at breakfast."

"Right. Good night, Whitney."

There was no sound in the night as Rainsford sat there but the muffled throb of the engine that drove the yacht swiftly through the darkness, and the swish and ripple of the wash of the propeller.

Rainsford, reclining in a steamer chair, indolently puffed on his favorite brier. The sensuous drowsiness of the night was on him. "It's so dark," he thought, "that I could sleep without closing my eyes; the night would be my eyelids —"

An abrupt sound startled him. Off to the right he heard it, and his ears, expert in such matters, could not be mistaken. Again he heard the sound, and again. Somewhere, off in the blackness, someone had fired a gun three times.

Rainsford sprang up and moved quickly to the rail, mystified. He strained his eyes in the direction from which the reports had come, but it was like trying to see through a blanket. He leaped upon the rail and balanced himself there, to get greater elevation; his pipe, striking a rope, was knocked from his mouth. He lunged for it; a short, hoarse cry came from his lips as he realized he had reached too far and had lost his balance. The cry was pinched off short as the blood-warm waters of the Caribbean Sea closed over his head.

He struggled up to the surface and tried to cry out, but the wash from the speeding yacht slapped him in the face and the salt water in his open mouth made him gag and strangle. Desperately he struck out with strong strokes after the receding lights of the yacht, but he stopped before he had swum fifty feet. A certain coolheadedness had come to him; it was not the first time he had been in a tight place. There was a chance that his cries could be heard by someone aboard the yacht, but that chance was slender, and grew more slender as the yacht raced on. He wrestled himself out of his clothes, and shouted with all his power. The lights of the yacht became faint and ever-vanishing fireflies; then they were blotted out entirely by the night.

Rainsford remembered the shots. They had come from the right, and doggedly he swam in that direction, swimming with slow, deliberate strokes, conserving his strength. For a seemingly endless time he fought the sea. He began to count his strokes; he could do possibly a hundred more and then —

Rainsford heard a sound. It came out of the darkness, a high screaming sound, the sound of an animal in an extremity of anguish and terror.

He did not recognize the animal that made the sound; he did not try to; with fresh vitality he swam toward the sound. He heard it again; then it was cut short by another noise, crisp, staccato.

"Pistol shot," muttered Rainsford, swimming on.

Ten minutes of determined effort brought another sound to his ears — the most welcome he had ever heard — the muttering and growling of the sea breaking on a rocky shore. He was almost on the rocks before he saw them; on a night less calm he would have been shattered against them. With his remaining strength he dragged himself from the swirling waters. Jagged crags appeared to jut up into the opaqueness; he forced himself upward, hand over hand. Gasping, his hands raw, he reached a flat place at the top. Dense jungle came down to the very edge of the cliffs. What perils that tangle of trees and underbrush might hold for him did not concern Rainsford just then. All he knew was that he was safe from his enemy, the sea, and that utter weariness was on him. He flung himself down at the jungle edge and tumbled headlong into the deepest sleep of his life.

When he opened his eyes he knew from the position of the sun that it was late in the afternoon. Sleep had given him new vigor; a sharp hunger was picking at him. He looked about him, almost cheerfully.

"Where there are pistol shots, there are men. Where there are men, there is food," he thought. But what kind of men, he wondered, in so forbidding a place? An unbroken front of snarled and ragged jungle fringed the shore.

He saw no sign of a trail through the closely knit web of weeds and trees; it was easier to go along the shore, and Rainsford floundered along by the water. Not far from where he had landed, he stopped.

Some wounded thing, by the evidence, a large animal, had thrashed about in the underbrush; the jungle weeds were crushed down and the moss was lacerated; one patch of weeds was stained crimson. A small, glittering object not far away caught Rainsford's eye and he picked it up. It was an empty cartridge.

"A twenty-two," he remarked. "That's odd. It must have been a fairly large animal too. The hunter had his nerve with him to tackle it with a light gun. It's clear that the brute put up a fight. I suppose the first three shots I heard was when the hunter flushed his quarry and wounded it. The last shot was when he trailed it here and finished it."

He examined the ground closely and found what he had hoped to find — the print of hunting boots. They pointed along the cliff in the direction he had been going. Eagerly he hurried along, now slipping on a rotten log or a loose stone, but making headway; night was

General Zaroff lived in " a palatial château . . . set on a high bluff . . . on three sides of it cliffs dived down to where the sea licked greedy lips . . ."
(*Ewing Galloway*)

beginning to settle down on the island.

Bleak darkness was blacking out the sea and jungle when Rainsford sighted the lights. He came upon them as he turned a crook in the coast line, and his first thought was that he had come upon a village, for there were many lights. But as he forged along he saw to his great astonishment that all the lights were in one enormous building — a lofty structure with pointed towers plunging upward into the gloom. His eyes made out the shadowy outlines of a palatial château; it was set on a high bluff, and on three sides of it cliffs dived down to where the sea licked greedy lips in the shadows.

"Mirage," thought Rainsford. But it was no mirage, he found, when he opened the tall spiked iron gate. The stone steps were real enough; the massive door with a leering gargoyle [1] for a knocker was real enough; yet above it all hung an air of unreality.

He lifted the knocker, and it creaked up stiffly, as if it had never before been used. He let it fall, and it startled him with its booming loudness. He thought he heard steps within; the door remained closed. Again Rainsford lifted the heavy knocker, and let it fall. The door opened then, opened as suddenly as if it were on a spring, and Rainsford stood blinking in the river of glaring gold light that poured out. The first thing Rainsford's eyes discerned was the largest man Rainsford had ever seen — a gigantic creature, solidly made and black-bearded to the waist. In his hand the man held a long-barreled revolver, and he was pointing it straight at Rainsford's heart.

Out of the snarl of beard two small eyes regarded Rainsford.

"Don't be alarmed," said Rainsford, with a smile which he hoped was disarming. "I'm no robber. I fell off a

[1] **gargoyle** (gär′goil): a grotesquely carved head, animal or human, originally used as a waterspout on the outside of a building.

yacht. My name is Sanger Rainsford of New York City."

The menacing look in the eyes did not change. The revolver pointed as rigidly as if the giant were a statue. He gave no sign that he understood Rainsford's words, or that he had even heard them. He was dressed in uniform, a black uniform trimmed with gray astrakhan.

"I'm Sanger Rainsford of New York," Rainsford began again. "I fell off a yacht. I am hungry."

The man's only answer was to raise with his thumb the hammer of his revolver. Then Rainsford saw the man's free hand go to his forehead in a military salute, and he saw him click his heels together and stand at attention. Another man was coming down the broad marble steps, an erect, slender man in evening clothes. He advanced to Rainsford and held out his hand.

In a cultivated voice marked by a slight accent that gave it added precision and deliberateness, he said: "It is a very great pleasure and honor to welcome Mr. Sanger Rainsford, the celebrated hunter, to my home."

Automatically Rainsford shook the man's hand.

"I've read your book about hunting snow leopards in Tibet, you see," explained the man. "I am General Zaroff."

Rainsford's first impression was that the man was singularly handsome; his second was that there was an original, almost bizarre quality about the general's face. He was a tall man past middle age, for his hair was a vivid white; but his thick eyebrows and pointed military mustache were as black as the night from which Rainsford had come. His eyes, too, were black and very bright. He had high cheek bones, a sharp-cut nose, a spare, dark face, the face of a man used to giving orders, the face of an aristocrat. Turning to the giant in uniform, the general made a sign.

The giant put away his pistol, saluted, withdrew.

"Ivan is an incredibly strong fellow," remarked the general, "but he has the misfortune to be deaf and dumb. A simple fellow, but, I'm afraid, like all his race, a bit of a savage."

"Is he Russian?"

"He is a Cossack," said the general, and his smile showed red lips and pointed teeth. "So am I.

"Come," he said, "we shouldn't be chatting here. We can talk later. Now you want clothes, food, rest. You shall have them. This is a most restful spot."

Ivan had reappeared, and the general spoke to him with lips that moved but gave forth no sound.

"Follow Ivan, if you please, Mr. Rainsford," said the general. "I was about to have my dinner when you came. I'll wait for you. You'll find that my clothes will fit you, I think."

It was to a huge, beam-ceilinged bedroom with a canopied bed big enough for six men that Rainsford followed the silent giant. Ivan laid out an evening suit, and Rainsford, as he put it on, noticed that it came from a London tailor who ordinarily cut and sewed for none below the rank of duke.

The dining room to which Ivan conducted him was in many ways remarkable. There was a medieval magnificence about it; it suggested a baronial hall of feudal times with its oaken panels, its high ceiling, its vast refectory tables where twoscore men could sit down to eat. About the hall were the mounted heads of many animals — lions, tigers, elephants, moose, bears; larger or more perfect specimens Rainsford had never seen. At the great table the general was sitting, alone.

"You'll have a cocktail, Mr. Rainsford," he suggested. The cocktail was surpassingly good; and, Rainsford noted, the table appointments were of the finest — the linen, the crystal, the silver, the china.

They were eating borsch, the rich, red soup with whipped cream so dear to Russian palates. Half apologetically General Zaroff said: "We do our best to preserve the amenities of civilization here. Please forgive any lapses. We are well off the beaten track, you know. Do you think the champagne has suffered from its long ocean trip?"

"Not in the least," declared Rainsford. He was finding the general a most thoughtful and affable host, a true cosmopolite. But there was one small trait of the general's that made Rainsford uncomfortable. Whenever he looked up from his plate he found the general studying him, appraising him narrowly.

"Perhaps," said General Zaroff, "you were surprised that I recognized your name. You see, I read all books on hunting published in English, French, and Russian. I have but one passion in my life, Mr. Rainsford, and it is the hunt."

"You have some wonderful heads here," said Rainsford as he ate a particularly well cooked *filet mignon*.[1] "That Cape buffalo is the largest I ever saw."

"Oh, that fellow. Yes, he was a monster."

"Did he charge you?"

"Hurled me against a tree," said the general. "Fractured my skull. But I got the brute."

"I've always thought," said Rainsford, "that the Cape buffalo is the most dangerous of all big game."

For a moment the general did not reply; he was smiling his curious, red-lipped smile. Then he said slowly: "No. You are wrong, sir. The Cape buffalo is not the most dangerous big game." He sipped his wine. "Here in my preserve on this island," he said in the same slow tone, "I hunt more dangerous game."

Rainsford expressed his surprise. "Is there big game on this island?"

The general nodded. "The biggest."

"Really?"

[1] *filet mignon* (fē-lĕ′ mē-nyÔN′): a round piece of tenderloin steak.

"Oh, it isn't here naturally, of course. I have to stock the island."

"What have you imported, general?" Rainsford asked. "Tigers?"

The general smiled. "No," he said. "Hunting tigers ceased to interest me some years ago. I exhausted their possibilities, you see. No thrill left in tigers, no real danger. I live for danger, Mr. Rainsford."

The general took from his pocket a gold cigarette case and offered his guest a long black cigarette with a silver tip; it was perfumed and gave off a smell like incense.

"We will have some capital hunting, you and I," said the general. "I shall be most glad to have your society."

"But what game — " began Rainsford.

"I'll tell you," said the general. "You will be amused, I know. I think I may say, in all modesty, that I have done a rare thing. I have invented a new sensation. May I pour you another glass of port?"

"Thank you, general."

The general filled both glasses, and said: "God makes some men poets. Some He makes kings, some beggars. Me He made a hunter. My hand was made for the trigger, my father said. He was a very rich man with a quarter of a million acres in the Crimea, and he was an ardent sportsman. When I was only five years old he gave me a little gun, specially made in Moscow for me, to shoot sparrows with. When I shot some of his prize turkeys with it, he did not punish me; he complimented me on my marksmanship. I killed my first bear in the Caucasus when I was ten. My whole life has been one prolonged hunt. I went into the army — it was expected of noblemen's sons — and for a time commanded a division of Cossack cavalry, but my real interest was always the hunt. I have hunted every kind of game in every land. It would be impossible for me to tell you how many animals I have killed."

The general puffed at his cigarette.

"After the debacle [1] in Russia I left the country, for it was imprudent for an officer of the Tsar to stay there. Many noble Russians lost everything. I, luckily, had invested heavily in American securities, so I shall never have to open a tea room in Monte Carlo or drive a taxi in Paris. Naturally, I continued to hunt — grizzlies in your Rockies, crocodile in the Ganges, rhinoceroses in East Africa. It was in Africa that the Cape buffalo hit me and laid me up for six months. As soon as I recovered I started for the Amazon to hunt jaguars, for I had heard they were unusually cunning. They weren't." The Cossack sighed. "They were no match at all for a hunter with his wits about him, and a high-powered rifle. I was bitterly disappointed. I was lying in my tent with a splitting headache one night when a terrible thought pushed its way into my mind. Hunting was beginning to bore me! And hunting, remember, had been my life. I have heard that in America businessmen often go to pieces when they give up the business that has been their life."

"Yes, that's so," said Rainsford.

The general smiled. "I had no wish to go to pieces," he said. "I must do something. Now, mine is an analytical mind, Mr. Rainsford. Doubtless that is why I enjoy the problems of the chase."

"No doubt, General Zaroff."

"So," continued the general, "I asked myself why the hunt no longer fascinated me. You are much younger than I am, Mr. Rainsford, and have not hunted as much, but you perhaps can guess the answer."

"What was it?"

"Simply this: hunting had ceased to be what you call 'a sporting proposition.' It had become too easy. I always got my quarry. Always. There is no

---

[1] **debacle** (de·bä'k'l): a violent disruption. In this case, the Bolshevik Revolution in 1917, which overthrew the tsarist government.

greater bore than perfection."

The general lit a fresh cigarette.

"No animal had a chance with me any more. That is no boast; it is a mathematical certainty. The animal had nothing but his legs and his instinct. Instinct is no match for reason. When I thought of this it was a tragic moment for me, I can tell you."

Rainsford leaned across the table, absorbed in what his host was saying.

"It came to me as an inspiration what I must do," the general went on.

"And that was?"

The general smiled the quiet smile of one who has faced an obstacle and surmounted it with success. "I had to invent a new animal to hunt," he said.

"A new animal? You're joking."

"Not at all," said the general. "I never joke about hunting. I needed a new animal. I found one. So I bought this island, built this house, and here I do my hunting. The island is perfect for my purposes — there are jungles with a maze of trails in them, hills, swamps — "

"But the animal, General Zaroff?"

"Oh," said the general, "it supplies me with the most exciting hunting in the world. No other hunting compares with it for an instant. Every day I hunt, and I never grow bored now, for I have a quarry with which I can match my wits."

Rainsford's bewilderment showed in his face.

"I wanted the ideal animal to hunt," explained the general. "So I said: 'What are the attributes of an ideal quarry?' And the answer was, of course: 'It must have courage, cunning, and, above all, it must be able to reason.'"

"But no animal can reason," objected Rainsford.

"My dear fellow," said the general, "there is one that can."

"But you can't mean — " gasped Rainsford.

"And why not?"

"I can't believe you are serious, General Zaroff. This is a grisly joke."

"Why should I not be serious? I am speaking of hunting."

"Hunting? Hunting? General Zaroff, what you speak of is murder."

The general laughed with entire good nature. He regarded Rainsford quizzically. "I refuse to believe that so modern and civilized a young man as you seem to be harbors romantic ideas about the value of human life. Surely your experiences in the war — "

"Did not make me condone cold-blooded murder," finished Rainsford stiffly.

Laughter shook the general. "How extraordinarily droll you are!" he said. "One does not expect nowadays to find a young man of the educated class, even in America, with such a naïve, and, if I may say so, Mid-Victorian point of view. It's like finding a snuffbox in a limousine. Ah, well, doubtless you had Puritan ancestors. So many Americans appear to have had. I'll wager you'll forget your notions when you go hunting with me. You've a genuine new thrill in store for you, Mr. Rainsford."

"Thank you, I'm a hunter, not a murderer."

"Dear me," said the general, quite unruffled, "again that unpleasant word. But I think I can show you that your scruples are quite ill-founded."

"Yes?"

"Life is for the strong, to be lived by the strong, and, if need be, taken by the strong. The weak of the world were put here to give the strong pleasure. I am strong. Why should I not use my gift? If I wish to hunt, why should I not? I hunt the scum of the earth — sailors from tramp ships — lascars,[1] blacks, Chinese, whites, mongrels — a thoroughbred horse or hound is worth more than a score of them."

"But they are men," said Rainsford hotly.

[1] lascars (lăs'kẽrz): East Indian native sailors.

"Precisely," said the general. "That is why I use them. It gives me pleasure. They can reason, after a fashion. So they are dangerous."

"But where do you get them?"

The general's left eyelid fluttered down in a wink. "This island is called Ship Trap," he answered. "Sometimes an angry god of the high seas sends them to me. Sometimes, when Providence is not so kind, I help Providence a bit. Come to the window with me."

Rainsford went to the window and looked out toward the sea.

"Watch! Out there!" exclaimed the general, pointing into the night. Rainsford's eyes saw only blackness, and then, as the general pressed a button, far out to sea Rainsford saw the flash of lights.

The general chuckled. "They indicate a channel," he said, "where there's none; giant rocks with razor edges crouch like a sea monster with wide-open jaws. They can crush a ship as easily as I crush this nut." He dropped a walnut on the hardwood floor and brought his heel grinding down on it. "Oh, yes," he said, casually, as if in answer to a question, "I have electricity. We try to be civilized here."

"Civilized? And you shoot down men?"

A trace of anger was in the general's black eyes, but it was there for but a second, and he said, in his most pleasant manner: "Dear me, what a righteous young man you are! I assure you I do not do the thing you suggest. That would be barbarous. I treat these visitors with every consideration. They get plenty of good food and exercise. They get into splendid physical condition. You shall see for yourself tomorrow."

"What do you mean?"

"We'll visit my training school," smiled the general. "It's in the cellar. I have about a dozen pupils down there now. They're from the Spanish bark *San Lucar* that had the bad luck to go on the rocks out there. A very inferior lot, I regret to say. Poor specimens and more accustomed to the deck than to the jungle."

He raised his hand, and Ivan, who served as waiter, brought thick Turkish coffee. Rainsford, with an effort, held his tongue in check.

"It's a game, you see," pursued the general blandly. "I suggest to one of them that we go hunting. I give him a supply of food and an excellent hunting knife. I give him three hours' start. I am to follow, armed only with a pistol of the smallest caliber and range. If my quarry eludes me for three whole days, he wins the game. If I find him" — the general smiled — "he loses."

"Suppose he refuses to be hunted?"

"Oh," said the general, "I give him his option, of course. He need not play that game if he doesn't wish to. If he does not wish to hunt, I turn him over to Ivan. Ivan once had the honor of serving as official knouter to the Great White Tsar, and he has his own ideas of sport. Invariably, Mr. Rainsford, invariably they choose the hunt."

"And if they win?"

The smile on the general's face widened. "To date I have not lost," he said. Then he added, hastily: "I don't wish you to think me a braggart, Mr. Rainsford. Many of them afford only the most elementary sort of problem. Occasionally I strike a tartar. One almost did win. I eventually had to use the dogs."

"The dogs?"

"This way, please. I'll show you."

The general steered Rainsford to a window. The lights from the windows sent a flickering illumination that made grotesque patterns on the courtyard below, and Rainsford could see moving about there a dozen or so huge black shapes; as they turned toward him, their eyes glittered greenly.

"A rather good lot, I think," observed the general. "They are let out at seven every night. If anyone should try to get into my house — or out of it — something extremely regrettable would occur to him." He hummed a snatch of song from the *Folies Bergères.*

"And now," said the general, "I want to show you my new collection of heads. Will you come with me to the library?"

"I hope," said Rainsford, "that you will excuse me tonight, General Zaroff. I'm really not feeling well."

"Ah, indeed?" the general inquired solicitously. "Well, I suppose that's only natural, after your long swim. You need a good, restful night's sleep. Tomorrow you'll feel like a new man, I'll wager. Then we'll hunt, eh? I've one rather promising prospect — " Rainsford was hurrying from the room.

"Sorry you can't go with me tonight," called the general. "I expect rather fair sport — a big, strong black. He looks resourceful — Well, good night, Mr. Rainsford; I hope you have a good night's rest."

The bed was good, and the pajamas of the softest silk, and he was tired in every fiber of his being, but nevertheless Rainsford could not quiet his brain with the opiate of sleep. He lay, eyes wide open. Once he thought he heard stealthy steps in the corridor outside his room. He sought to throw open the door; it would not open. He went to the window and looked out. His room was high up in one of the towers. The lights of the château were out now, and it was dark and silent, but there was a fragment of sallow moon, and by its wan light he could see, dimly, the courtyard; there, weaving in and out in the pattern of shadow, were black, noiseless forms; the hounds heard him at the window and looked up, expectantly, with their green eyes. Rainsford went back to the bed and lay down. By many methods he tried to put himself to sleep. He had achieved a doze when, just as morning began to come, he

heard, far off in the jungle, the faint report of a pistol.

General Zaroff did not appear until luncheon. He was dressed faultlessly in the tweeds of a country squire. He was solicitous about the state of Rainsford's health.

"As for me," sighed the general, "I do not feel so well. I am worried, Mr. Rainsford. Last night I detected traces of my old complaint."

To Rainsford's questioning glance the general said: "Ennui. Boredom."

Then, taking a second helping of crêpes suzette, the general explained: "The hunting was not good last night. The fellow lost his head. He made a straight trail that offered no problems at all. That's the trouble with these sailors; they have dull brains to begin with, and they do not know how to get about in the woods. They do excessively stupid and obvious things. It's most annoying. Will you have another glass of Chablis, Mr. Rainsford?"

"General," said Rainsford firmly, "I wish to leave this island at once."

The general raised his thickets of eyebrows; he seemed hurt. "But, my dear fellow," the general protested, "you've only just come. You've had no hunting —"

"I wish to go today," said Rainsford. He saw the dead black eyes of the general on him, studying him. General Zaroff's face suddenly brightened.

He filled Rainsford's glass with venerable Chablis from a dusty bottle.

"Tonight," said the general, "we will hunt — you and I."

Rainsford shook his head. "No, general," he said. "I will not hunt."

The general shrugged his shoulders and delicately ate a hothouse grape. "As you wish, my friend," he said. "The choice rests entirely with you. But may I not venture to suggest that you will find my idea of sport more diverting than Ivan's?"

He nodded toward the corner to where the giant stood, scowling, his thick arms crossed on his hogshead of chest.

"You don't mean —" cried Rainsford.

"My dear fellow," said the general, "have I not told you I always mean what I say about hunting? This is really an inspiration. I drink to a foeman worthy of my steel — at last." The general raised his glass, but Rainsford sat staring at him.

"You'll find this game worth playing," the general said enthusiastically. "Your brain against mine. Your woodcraft against mine. Your strength and stamina against mine. Outdoor chess! And the stake is not without value, eh?"

"And if I win —" began Rainsford huskily.

"I'll cheerfully acknowledge myself defeated if I do not find you by midnight of the third day," said General Zaroff. "My sloop will place you on the mainland near a town." The general read what Rainsford was thinking.

"Oh, you can trust me," said the Cossack. "I will give you my word as a gentleman and a sportsman. Of course you, in turn, must agree to say nothing of your visit here."

"I'll agree to nothing of the kind," said Rainsford.

"Oh," said the general, "in that case — But why discuss that now? Three days hence we can discuss it over a bottle of *Veuve Cliquot*, unless —"

The general sipped his wine.

Then a businesslike air animated him. "Ivan," he said to Rainsford, "will supply you with hunting clothes, food, a knife. I suggest you wear moccasins; they leave a poorer trail. I suggest, too, that you avoid the big swamp in the southeast corner of the island. We call it Death Swamp. There's quicksand there. One foolish fellow tried it. The deplorable part of it was that Lazarus followed him. You can imagine my feelings, Mr. Rainsford. I loved Lazarus;

he was the finest hound in my pack. Well, I must beg you to excuse me now. I always take a siesta after lunch. You'll hardly have time for a nap, I fear. You'll want to start, no doubt. I shall not follow till dusk. Hunting at night is so much more exciting than by day, don't you think? Au revoir, Mr. Rainsford, au revoir." General Zaroff, with a deep, courtly bow, strolled from the room.

From another door came Ivan. Under one arm he carried khaki hunting clothes, a haversack of food, a leather sheath containing a long-bladed hunting knife; his right hand rested on a cocked revolver thrust in the crimson sash about his waist.

Rainsford had fought his way through the bush for two hours. "I must keep my nerve. I must keep my nerve," he said through tight teeth.

He had not been entirely clearheaded when the château gates snapped shut behind him. His whole idea at first was to put distance between himself and General Zaroff, and, to this end, he had plunged along, spurred on by the sharp rowels of something very like panic. Now he had got a grip on himself, had stopped, and was taking stock of himself and the situation. He saw that straight flight was futile; inevitably it would bring him face to face with the sea. He was in a picture with a frame of water, and his operations, clearly, must take place within that frame.

"I'll give him a trail to follow," muttered Rainsford, and he struck off from the rude path he had been following into the trackless wilderness. He executed a series of intricate loops; he doubled on his trail again and again, recalling all the lore of the fox hunt, and all the dodges of the fox. Night found him leg-weary, with hands and face lashed by the branches, on a thickly wooded ridge. He knew it would be insane to blunder on through the dark, even if he had the strength. His need for rest was imperative and he thought: "I have played the fox, now I must play the cat of the fable." A big tree with a thick trunk and outspread branches was nearby, and, taking care to leave not the slightest mark, he climbed up into the crotch, and stretching out on one of the broad limbs, after a fashion, rested. Rest brought him new confidence and almost a feeling of security. Even so zealous a hunter as General Zaroff could not trace him there, he told himself; only the devil himself could follow that complicated trail through the jungle after dark. But, perhaps the general was a devil —

An apprehensive night crawled slowly by like a wounded snake, and sleep did not visit Rainsford, although the silence of a dead world was on the jungle. Toward morning when a dingy gray was varnishing the sky, the cry of some startled bird focused Rainsford's attention in that direction. Something was coming through the bush, coming slowly, carefully, coming by the same winding way Rainsford had come. He flattened himself down on the limb, and through a screen of leaves almost as thick as tapestry, he watched. . . . That which was approaching was a man.

It was General Zaroff. He made his way along with his eyes fixed in utmost concentration on the ground before him. He paused, almost beneath the tree, dropped to his knees and studied the ground. Rainsford's impulse was to hurl himself down like a panther, but he saw that the general's right hand held something metallic — a small automatic pistol.

The hunter shook his head several times, as if he were puzzled. Then he straightened up and took from his case one of his black cigarettes; its pungent incenselike smoke floated up to Rainsford's nostrils.

Rainsford held his breath. The general's eyes had left the ground and were traveling inch by inch up the tree. Rainsford froze there, every muscle tensed for a spring. But the sharp eyes of the hunter stopped before they reached the limb where Rainsford lay; a smile spread over his brown face. Very deliberately he blew a smoke ring into the air; then he turned his back on the tree and walked carelessly away, back along the trail he had come. The swish of the underbrush against his hunting boots grew fainter and fainter.

The pent-up air burst hotly from Rainsford's lungs. His first thought made him feel sick and numb. The general could follow a trail through the woods at night; he could follow an extremely difficult trail; he must have uncanny powers; only by the merest chance had the Cossack failed to see his quarry.

Rainsford's second thought was even more terrible. It sent a shudder of cold horror through his whole being. Why had the general smiled? Why had he turned back?

Rainsford did not want to believe what his reason told him was true, but the truth was as evident as the sun that had by now pushed through the morning mists. The general was playing with him! The general was saving him for another day's sport! The Cossack was the cat; he was the mouse. Then it was that Rainsford knew the full meaning of terror.

"I will not lose my nerve. I will not."

He slid down from the tree, and struck off again into the woods. His face was set and he forced the machinery of his mind to function. Three hundred yards from his hiding place he stopped where a huge dead tree leaned precariously on a smaller, living one. Throwing off his sack of food, Rainsford took his knife from its sheath and began to work with all his energy.

The job was finished at last, and he threw himself down behind a fallen log a hundred feet away. He did not have to wait long. The cat was coming again to play with the mouse.

Following the trail with the sureness of a bloodhound came General Zaroff. Nothing escaped those searching black eyes, no crushed blade of grass, no bent twig, no mark, no matter how faint, in the moss. So intent was the Cossack on his stalking that he was upon the thing Rainsford had made before he saw it. His foot touched the protruding bough that was the trigger. Even as he touched it, the general sensed his danger and leaped back with the agility of an ape. But he was not quite quick enough; the dead tree, delicately adjusted to rest on the cut living one, crashed down and struck the general a glancing blow on the shoulder as it fell; but for his alertness, he must have been smashed beneath it. He staggered, but he did not fall; nor did he drop his revolver. He stood there, rubbing his injured shoulder, and Rainsford, with fear again gripping at his heart, heard the general's mocking laugh ring through the jungle.

"Rainsford," called the general, "if you are within sound of my voice, as I suppose you are, let me congratulate you. Not many men know how to make a Malay man-catcher. Luckily, for me, I too have hunted in Malacca. You are proving interesting, Mr. Rainsford. I am going now to have my wound dressed; it's only a slight one. But I shall be back. I shall be back."

When the general, nursing his bruised shoulder, had gone, Rainsford took up his flight again. It was flight now, a desperate, hopeless flight, that carried him on for some hours. Dusk came, then darkness, and still he pressed on. The ground grew softer under his moccasins; the vegetation grew ranker, denser; insects bit him savagely. Then, as he stepped forward, his foot sank into the ooze. He tried to wrench it back, but the muck sucked viciously at his foot as if it were a giant leech. With a violent effort, he tore his feet loose. He knew where he was now. Death Swamp and its quicksand.

His hands were tight closed as if his nerve were something tangible that someone in the darkness was trying to tear from his grip. The softness of the earth had given him an idea. He stepped back from the quicksand a dozen feet or so and, like some huge prehistoric beaver, he began to dig.

Rainsford had dug himself in in France when a second's delay meant death. That had been a placid pastime compared to his digging now. The pit grew deeper; when it was above his shoulders, he climbed out and from some hard saplings cut stakes and sharpened them to a fine point. These stakes he planted in the bottom of the pit with the points sticking up. With flying fingers he wove a rough carpet of weeds and branches and with it he covered the mouth of the pit. Then, wet with sweat and aching with tiredness, he crouched behind the stump of a lightning-charred tree.

He knew his pursuer was coming; he heard the padding sound of feet on the soft earth, and the night breeze brought him the perfume of the general's cigarette. It seemed to Rainsford that the general was coming with unusual swiftness; he was not feeling his way along, foot by foot. Rainsford, crouching there, could not see the general, nor could he see the pit. He lived a year in a minute. Then he felt an impulse to cry aloud with joy, for he heard the sharp crackle of the breaking branches as the cover of the pit gave way; he heard the sharp scream of pain as the pointed stakes found their mark. He leaped up from his place of concealment. Then he cowered back. Three feet from the pit a man was standing, with an electric torch in his hand.

"You've done well, Rainsford," the voice of the general called. "Your Burmese tiger pit has claimed one of my best dogs. Again you score. I think, Mr. Rainsford, I'll see what you can do against my whole pack. I'm going home for a rest now. Thank you for a most amusing evening."

At daybreak Rainsford, lying near the swamp, was awakened by a sound that made him know that he had new things to learn about fear. It was a distant sound, faint and wavering, but he knew it. It was the baying of a pack of hounds.

Rainsford knew he could do one of two things. He could stay where he was and wait. That was suicide. He could flee. That was postponing the inevitable. For a moment he stood there, thinking. An idea that held a wild chance came to him, and, tightening his belt, he headed away from the swamp.

The baying of the hounds drew nearer, then still nearer, nearer, ever nearer. On a ridge Rainsford climbed a tree. Down a watercourse, not a quarter of a mile away, he could see the bush moving. Straining his eyes, he saw the lean figure of General Zaroff; just ahead of him Rainsford made out another figure whose wide shoulders surged through the tall jungle weeds; it was the giant Ivan, and he seemed pulled forward by some unseen force; Rainsford knew that Ivan must be holding the pack in leash.

They would be on him any minute now. His mind worked frantically. He thought of a native trick he had learned in Uganda. He slid down the tree. He caught hold of a springy young sapling and to it he fastened his hunting knife, with the blade pointing down the trail; with a bit of wild grapevine he tied back the sapling. Then he ran for his life. The hounds raised their voices as they hit the fresh scent. Rainsford knew now how an animal at bay feels.

He had to stop to get his breath. The baying of the hounds stopped abruptly, and Rainsford's heart stopped too. They must have reached the knife.

He shinned excitedly up a tree and looked back. His pursuers had stopped. But the hope that was in Rainsford's brain when he climbed died, for he saw in the shallow valley that General Zaroff was still on his feet. But Ivan was not. The knife, driven by the recoil of the springing tree, had not wholly failed.

Rainsford had hardly tumbled to the ground when the pack took up the cry again.

" Nerve, nerve, nerve! " he panted, as he dashed along. A blue gap showed between the trees dead ahead. Ever nearer drew the hounds. Rainsford forced himself on toward that gap. He reached it. It was the shore of the sea. Across a cove he could see the gloomy gray stone of the château. Twenty feet below him the sea rumbled and hissed. Rainsford hesitated. He heard the hounds. Then he leaped far out into the sea. . . .

When the general and his pack reached the place by the sea, the Cossack stopped. For some minutes he stood regarding the blue-green expanse of water. He shrugged his shoulders. Then he sat down, took a drink of brandy from a silver flask, lit a cigarette, and hummed a bit from *Madame Butterfly.*

General Zaroff had an exceedingly good dinner in his great paneled dining hall that evening. With it he had a bottle of Pol Roger and half a bottle of Chambertin. Two slight annoyances kept him from perfect enjoyment. One was the thought that it would be difficult to replace Ivan; the other was that his quarry had escaped him; of course the American hadn't played the game — so thought the general as he tasted his after-dinner liqueur. In his library he read, to soothe himself, from the works of Marcus Aurelius. At ten he went up to his bedroom. He was deliciously tired, he said to himself, as he locked himself in. There was a little moonlight, so, before turning on his light, he went to the window and looked down at the courtyard. He could see the great hounds, and he called, "Better luck another time," to them. Then he switched on the light.

A man, who had been hiding in the curtains of the bed, was standing there.

"Rainsford!" screamed the general. "How in God's name did you get here?"

"Swam," said Rainsford. "I found it quicker than walking through the jungle."

The general sucked in his breath and smiled. "I congratulate you," he said. "You have won the game."

Rainsford did not smile. "I am still a beast at bay," he said, in a low, hoarse voice. "Get ready, General Zaroff."

The general made one of his deepest bows. "I see," he said. "Splendid! One of us is to furnish a repast for the hounds. The other will sleep in this very excellent bed. On guard, Rainsford."

He had never slept in a better bed, Rainsford decided.

For Discussion of Connell

1. What feeling does the opening conversation between Rainsford and Whitney arouse in you? What is the importance of the remarks about the jaguars?

2. What details lead you to mistrust the general even before you know his evil practice? Characterize the general and Ivan — how are they alike or different?

3. How does Rainsford live up to the general's opinion of him? What kind of man is he?

4. How many times before the end does the story come to a critical point? Using this story as an illustration, how would you define the term *suspense*?

5. Does the story leave any unanswered questions in your mind? What are they? Carry events a step further, beginning with Rainsford's awakening the next day.

For Your Vocabulary

GETTING MEANING FROM CONTEXT: After a questioning glance from Rainsford, General Zaroff says that his "old complaint" is "ennui." And immediately he defines *ennui* for us by adding, "boredom." Thus the context (the passage or phrase preceding or following a word) helps us to understand the meaning of a difficult word. Similarly, note how *thick* and *warm* help to give meaning to *palpable* on page 4. On page 9, also, what word helps you arrive at the meaning of *amenities*? Find other unfamiliar words in this story and try to discover their meanings from context.

The Pacing Goose

JESSAMYN WEST

Jessamyn West is a new star on the literary horizon. Her first novel, *The Witch-Diggers*, was not published until the 1950's and her stories have appeared only since the forties. The unusual quality of her stories has already made them modern "classics" of their kind, appearing several times in the annual collections of *Best American Short Stories* and the *O. Henry Memorial Award Prize Stories*. Jessamyn West was

born in Indiana of Quaker parentage. Of
this background she has made good use in
her stories, which often center about a
Quaker farm family of a century ago. The
character of Eliza in the following story
is based on her own grandmothers, both
of whom were Quaker preachers. Throughout the story you will find the quiet humor,
the good will, and the quaint language that
we associate with the older Quakers. The
characters come alive as distinct personalities. You will like Eliza particularly.

J ESS sat in the kitchen at the long table
by the west window where in winter
he kept his grafting tools: the thin-
bladed knife, the paper sweet with the
smell of beeswax and the resin, the
boxes of roots and scions.[1] Jess was a
nurseryman and spring meant for him
not only spirits flowering — but the
earth's. A week more of moderating
weather and he'd be out, still in gum
boots, but touching an earth that had
thawed, whose riches were once again
fluid enough to be sucked upward, toward those burgeonings which by summer would have swelled into Early Har-
vests, Permains, and Sweet Bows.[2]

Spring's a various season, Jess
thought, no two years the same: comes
in with rains, mud deep enough to swallow horse and rider; comes in cold,
snow falling so fast it weaves a web;
comes in with a warm wind blowing
about thy ears and bringing a smell of
something flowering, not here, but
southaways, across the Ohio, maybe, in
Kentucky. Nothing here now but a
smell of melting snow — which is no
smell at all, but a kind of prickle in the
nose, like a bygone sneeze. Comes in
so various, winter put by and always so
welcome.

"And us each spring so much the
same."

"Thee speaking to me, Jess?"

"Nothing thee'd understand, Eliza."

Spring made Jess discontented with
the human race — and with women, if
anything more than men. It looked as
if spring put them all in the shade: the
season so resourceful and they each
year meeting it with nothing changed

from last year, digging up roots from
the same sassafras thicket, licking sulfur and molasses[3] from the big-bowled
spoon.

Behind him the table was set for
supper, plates neatly turned to cover
the bone-handled knives and forks,
spoon vase aglitter with steel well
burnished by brick dust, dishes of jam
with more light to them than the sun,
which was dwindling away, peaked
and overcast, outside his window.

"Spring opening up," he said, "and
nobody in this house so much as putting down a line of poetry."

Eliza, who was lifting dried-peach
pies from a hot oven, said nothing. She
set the four of them in a neat row on
the edge of her kitchen cabinet to cool,
and slid her pans of cornbread into the
oven. Then she turned to Jess, her
cheeks red with heat, and her black
eyes warm with what she had to say.
"Thee'd maybe relish a nice little rhyme
for thy supper, Jess Birdwell."

Jess sighed, then sniffed the pies, so
rich with ripe peach flavor that the
kitchen smelled like a summer orchard,
nothing lacking but the sound of bees.
"Now, Eliza," he said, "thee knows I
wouldn't have thee anyways altered.
Thee . . ."

"Thee," Eliza interrupted him, "is
like all men. Thee wants to have thy
poetry and eat it too."

Jess wondered how what he'd felt
about spring, a season with the Lord's
thumbprint fresh on it, could've led to
anything so unspringlike as an argument about a batch of dried-peach
pies.

---

[1] **scions** (sī′ŭnz): shoots prepared for grafting.
[2] **Early ... Bows:** varieties of apples.

[3] **sulfur and molasses:** an old-time "spring
tonic."

"Eliza," he said firmly, "I didn't mean thee. Though it's crossed my mind sometimes as strange that none of the boys have ever turned, this time of year, to rhyming."

"Josh writes poems," Eliza said.

"Thee ever read what Josh writes, Eliza?"

Eliza nodded.

Ah, well, Jess thought, no use at this late date to tell her what's the difference.

Eliza looked her husband over carefully. "Jess Birdwell," she said, "thee's full of humors. Thy blood needs thinning. I'll boil thee up a good cup of sassafras tea."

Jess turned away from the green and gold sunset and the patches of snow it was gilding and fairly faced the dried-peach pies and Eliza, who was dropping dumplings into a pot of beans.

"That's just it, Eliza," he said. "That's just the rub."

Eliza gave him no encouragement, but he went on anyway. "Earth alters, season to season, spring comes in never two times the same, only us pounding on steady as pump bolts and not freshened by so much as a grass blade."

"Jess, thee's got spring fever."

"I could reckon time and temperature, each spring, by the way thee starts honing [1] for geese. 'Jess, don't thee think we might have a few geese?' It's a tardy spring," Jess said. "Snow still on the ground and not a word yet from thee about geese."

Eliza pulled a chair out from the table and sat. "Jess, why's thee always been so set against geese?"

"I'm not set against geese. It's geese that's set against farming. They can mow down a half acre of sprouting corn while thee's trying to head them off — and in two minutes they'll level a row of pie plant it's taken two years to get started. No, Eliza, it's the geese that's

---

[1] **honing**: yearning.

against me."

"If thee had tight fences . . ." Eliza said.

"Eliza, I got tight fences, but the goose's never been hatched that'll admit fences exist. And an old gander'd just as soon go through a fence as hiss — and if he can't find a hole or crack in a fence he'll left the latch."

"Jess," said Eliza flatly, "thee don't like geese."

"Well," said Jess, "I wouldn't go so far's to say I didn't like them, but I will say that if there's any meaner, dirtier animal, or one that glories in it more, I don't know it. And a thing I've never been able to understand about thee, Eliza, is what thee sees in the shifty-eyed birds."

"Geese," said Eliza, with a dreaminess unusual to her, "march along so lordly like . . . they're pretty as swans floating down a branch . . . in fall they stretch out their necks and honk to geese passing overhead as if they's wild. My father never had any trouble raising geese and I've heard him say many a time that there's no better food for a brisk morning than a fried goose egg."

Jess knew, with spring his topic, he'd ought to pass over Eliza's father and his fried goose egg but he couldn't help saying, "A fried goose egg always had a kind of bloated look to me, Eliza " — but then he went on fast. "The season's shaping up," he said. "I can see thee's all primed to say, 'Jess, let's get a setting of goose eggs.'"

Eliza went over to the bean kettle and began to lift out dumplings. "It's a forwarder season than thee thinks, Jess," she said. "I got a setting under a hen now."

Jess looked at his wife. He didn't know what had made him want spring's variety in a human being — nor Eliza's substituting doing for asking. And speaking of it just now, as he had, made opposition kind of ticklish.

" When'd thee set them? " he asked finally.

" Yesterday," said Eliza.

" Where'd thee get the eggs? "

" Overbys'," said Eliza. The Overbys were their neighbors to the south.

" Well, they got enough for a surety," Jess said, " to give a few away."

" The Overbys don't give anything away, as thee knows. I paid for them. With my own money," Eliza added.

" How many? " Jess asked.

" Eight," Eliza said.

Jess turned back to his window. The sun had set, leaving a sad green sky and desolate black and white earth. " Five acres of corn gone," he calculated.

" Thee said," Eliza reminded him, " that what thee wanted was a little variety in me. 'Steady as a pump bolt,' were thy words."

" I know I did," Jess admitted glumly, " I talk too much."

" Draw up thy chair," Eliza said placidly, not contradicting him; " here's Enoch and the boys."

Next morning after breakfast Jess and Enoch left the kitchen together. The sun was the warmest the year had yet produced and the farm roofs were steaming; south branch, swollen by melting snow, was running so full the soft lap of its eddies could be heard in the barnyard; a rooster tossed his voice into the bright air, loud and clear as if aiming to be heard by every fowl in Jennings County.

" Enoch," said Jess to his hired man, " what's thy feeling about geese? "

Enoch was instantly equipped, for the most part, with feelings on every subject. Geese was a homelier topic than he'd choose himself to enlarge upon, not one that could be much embellished nor one on which Mr. Emerson,[1] so far's

he could recall, had ever expressed an opinion. " In the fall of the year," he said, " long about November or December, there's nothing tastier on the table than roast goose."

" Goose on the table's not what I mean," Jess said. " I was speaking of goose on the hoof. Goose nipping off a stand of corn, Enoch, goose roistering round, honking and hissing so's thee can't hear thyself think, goose eying thee like a snake on stilts."

Enoch gazed at his employer for a few seconds. " Mr. Birdwell," he said, " I think that if they's an ornery bird, it's a goose. Ornery and undependable."

" I'm glad we's so like minded about them," Jess said. " Otherwise, I'd not like to ask thee to do this little job." He pulled a long darning needle from beneath the lapel of his coat.

Enoch eyed it with some mistrust. " I can't say's I've ever been handy with a needle, Mr. Birdwell."

" Thee'll be handy enough for this," Jess said with hearty conviction. " To come to it, Enoch, Eliza's set eight goose eggs. Next year with any luck she'd have two dozen. And so on. More and more. Feeling the way thee does, Enoch, about geese, it's no more'n fair to give thee a chance to put a stop to this before it goes too far. One little puncture in each egg with this and the goose project's nipped in the bud and Eliza none the wiser."

" I'm mighty awkward with my hands," said Enoch, " doing fine work. Ticklish job like this I might drop an egg and break it."

" Enoch," said Jess, " thee's not developing a weakness for geese, is thee? "

" It ain't the geese," said Enoch frankly, " it's your wife. She's been mighty clever [2] to me and if she's got her heart set on geese, it'd go against the grain to disappoint her. Whyn't you do it, Mr. Birdwell? "

---

[1] **Mr. Emerson:** Ralph Waldo Emerson, American philosopher. For a short account of his life see page 551. Some of his writings are presented on pages 555–565.

[2] **clever:** kind, good-natured. This is a local use of the word.

"Same reason," said Jess, "only more of them — and if Eliza ever asks if I tampered with that setting of eggs I figure on being able to say No." Jess held the needle nearer Enoch, who looked at it but still made no motion to take it.

"Likely no need to do a thing," Enoch said. "Two to one those eggs'll never hatch anyways. Overbys're such a fox-eared tribe they more'n likely sold her bad eggs to begin with."

"Thee's knowed about this," Jess asked, "all along?"

"Yes," Enoch said.

"Here's the needle," Jess said.

"You look at this," Enoch inquired, "not so much as a favor asked as a part of the day's work with orders from you?"

"Yes," Jess said, "that's about the way I look at it."

Enoch took the needle, held it somewhat gingerly, and with the sun glinting across its length walked slowly toward the chicken house.

It takes thirty days for a goose egg to hatch, and the time, with spring work to be done, went fast. The hen Eliza had picked was a good one and kept her mind strictly on her setting. Eliza kept her mind on the hen, and Jess and Enoch found their minds oftener than they liked on Eliza and her hoped-for geese.

At breakfast on the day the geese were due to break their shells Jess said, "If I's thee, Eliza, I wouldn't bank too much on them geese. I heard Enoch say a while back he wouldn't be surprised if not an egg hatched. Thought the eggs were likely no good."

Enoch was busy pouring coffee into a saucer, then busy cooling it, but Eliza waited until he was through. "Did thee say that, Enoch?"

Enoch looked at Jess. "Yes," he said, "I kind of recollect something of the sort."

"What made thee think so, Enoch?"

"Why," said Jess, for Enoch was busy with his coffee again, "it was the Overbys. Enoch's got a feeling they's kind of unreliable. Fox-eared, I think thee said, Enoch, didn't thee?"

Enoch's work took him outside almost at once and Jess himself said, "If thee'll just give me a little packet of food, Eliza, I won't trouble thee for anything at noon. I'm going to be over'n the south forty and it'll save time coming and going."

Eliza was surprised, for Jess'd usually come twice as far for a hot dinner at midday, but she made him fried ham sandwiches and put them and some cold apple turnovers in a bag.

"It's a pity thee has to miss thy dinner," she told him, but Jess only said, "Press of work, press of work," and hurriedly departed.

Jess came home that evening through the spring twilight, somewhat late, and found a number of things to do at the barn before he went up to the house. When he entered the kitchen nothing seemed amiss — lamps ruddy, table set, stove humming, and beside the stove a small box over which Eliza was bending. Jess stopped to look — and listen; from inside the box was coming a kind of birdlike peeping, soft and not unpleasant. Reluctantly he walked to Eliza's side. There, eating minced boiled egg, and between bites lifting its beak to Eliza, it seemed, and making those chirping sounds he'd heard, was a gray-gold gosling.

Eliza looked up pleasantly. "Enoch was right," she said. "The eggs were bad. Only one hatched. I plan to call it Samantha," she told Jess. "It's a name I've always been partial to."

"Samantha," said Jess without any enthusiasm whatever for either name or gosling. "How's thee know it's a she?"

"I don't," said Eliza, "but if it's a gander it's a name easily changed to Sam."

Enoch came in just then with a load of wood for the kitchen woodbox. "Enoch," asked Jess, "has thee seen Samantha — or Sam?"

Enoch mumbled but Jess understood him to say he had.

"It was my understanding, Enoch, that thy opinion was that all those eggs were bad."

"Well, Mr. Birdwell," said Enoch, "a man could make a mistake. He could count wrong."

"A man ought to be able to count to eight without going astray," said Jess.

Eliza was paying no attention to either of them; she was making little tweeting sounds herself, bending over the chirping gosling. "Does thee know," she asked Jess, "that this is the first pet I ever had in my life?"

"Thee's got Ebony," Jess said.

"I don't mean a caged pet," Eliza said, "but one to walk beside thee. I'm reconciled the others didn't hatch. With eight I'd've had to raise geese for the table. With one only I can make Samantha a pure pet."

A pure pet was what she made of her: Samantha ate what the family ate, with the exception of articles which Eliza thought might be indigestible and would risk on humans but not on her goose. Cake, pie, corn-on-the-cob, there was nothing too good for Samantha. From a big-footed, gold-downed gosling she swelled, almost at once, like a slack sail which gets a sudden breeze, into a full-rounded convexity.

"Emphasis on the vexity," Jess said when he thought of this. Samantha was everything he'd disliked in the general run of geese, with added traits peculiar to herself, which vexed him. Because she was fed at the doorstep, she was always underfoot. No shout, however loud, would move her before she's ready to move. If she's talked to too strong she'd flail you with her wings and pinch the calf of your leg until for some days it would look to be mortifying. She'd take food out of children's hands, and the pansies Jess had planted in a circle at the base of the Juneberry tree she sheared so close that there was not a naked stem left to show for all his work. And when not being crossed in any way, Jess simply looking at her and meditating, trying to fathom Samantha's fascination for Eliza, the goose would suddenly extend her snakelike neck, and almost touching Jess, hiss with such a hint of icy disapprobation that Jess would involuntarily recoil.

But she was Eliza's pure pet, no two ways about that, and would lift her head for Eliza to scratch, and walk beside her with the lordly roll of the known elect.

"There was some goddess," Enoch remembered, "who always had a big bird with her." Jess supposed Enoch was thinking of Juno and her peacock, but the reference didn't convince him that a goose was a suitable companion for any goddess — let alone Eliza, and he couldn't honestly feel much regret when one evening toward the end of November Eliza told him Samantha was missing. "She'll turn up," Jess said. "That bird's too ornery to die young."

Eliza said nothing, but next evening she proved Jess was right. "Samantha's over at Overbys'," she said.

"Well, did thee fetch her home?" Jess asked.

"No," said Eliza with righteous indignation, "they wouldn't let me. They said they had forty geese — and forty's what they got now, and they don't think Samantha's there. They provoked me so, Jess, I told them they'd sold me seven bad eggs and now they try to take the eighth away from me."

Jess felt a little abashed at this, but

he asked, "How can thee be so sure Samantha's there? She might've been carried off by a varmint."

Eliza was scornful. "Thee forgets I hand-raised Samantha from a gosling. I'd know her among four hundred — let alone forty."

"Whyn't thee buy her back then," Jess asked, "if that's the only way?"

"After what I said about their eggs," Eliza answered sadly, "the Overbys say they don't want any more dealings with me."

Eliza mourned so for the lost Samantha that first Enoch and then Jess went over to the Overbys' but no one there would admit the presence of a visiting goose — forty they had, and forty you could see by counting was what they had now. Short of force there didn't seem any way of getting Samantha home again.

When Eliza heard the Overbys were going to sell geese for Christmas eating she was frantic. "Jess," she said, "I just can't bear to think of Samantha, plucked naked and resting on a table waiting to be carved. She used to sing as sweet as any bird when she was little, and she'd walk by my side taking the air. She's the only goose I ever heard of," Eliza remembered mournfully, "who'd drink tea."

In Jess's opinion a goose'd eat anything at either end of the scale, but he didn't suppose this was a suitable time to mention it to Eliza. "Eliza," he said, "short of me and Enoch's going over there and using force on old man Overby — or sneaking over at night and breaking into their chicken pen, I don't know how in the world we're going to get Samantha back for thee."

"We could sue," said Eliza.

"Thee mean go to law?" Jess asked, astounded. Quakers stayed out of courts, believing in amicable settlements without recourse to law.

"Yes," said Eliza. "I'd do it for Samantha. I'd think it my duty. Going to law'd be a misery for us . . . but not so lasting a misery as being roasted would be for Samantha."

Jess couldn't deny this, but he said, "I'd have to think it over. I've never been to law yet in my life and suing for a gone goose don't seem to me a very likely place to start."

Next morning Eliza served a good but silent breakfast, not sitting herself to eat with the rest of her family.

"Thee feeling dauncy,[1] Eliza?" Jess asked.

"I just can't eat," she said, "for thinking of Samantha."

Labe and Mattie had tears in their eyes. Little Jess was mournfully bellowing. Enoch looked mighty glum. Jess felt ashamed to be swallowing victuals in the midst of so much sorrow. Eliza stood at the end of the stove where the gosling's box had rested for the first few weeks of its life, looking down, as if remembering how it had sung and lifted its beak to her.

Jess couldn't stand it. "Eliza," he said, "if thee wants to go through with it I'll go to Vernon and fee a lawyer for thee. Thee'll have to go to court, be on the witness stand — and even then I misdoubt thee'll ever get thy goose back. Does thee still want me to do it?"

Eliza came to the table and stood with her hand on Jess's shoulder. "Yes, Jess," she said, "I want thee to do it."

Jess went to Vernon, fee'd a lawyer, had a restraining order put on the Overbys so they couldn't sell or kill the goose Eliza said was Samantha, and awaited with misgivings the day of the trial. It came in mid-December.

Eliza, Jess, and Enoch rode to the trial through a fall of light, fresh snow. Brilliant sunlight, crisp air, glittering snow, and Rome's[2] spirited stepping made the occasion, in spite of its purpose, seem festive. Eliza made it seem

---

[1] **dauncy:** ill.

[2] **Rome:** the Birdwell's carriage horse.

"At heart she was a pacer, and what two legs could do in that line, Samantha accomplished." (*Ewing Galloway*)

festive. Jess, who did not forget its purpose, regarded her with some wonder. He couldn't say what it was about her — dress and bonnet appeared to be simply her First Day [1] best — but she had a holiday air.

He considered it his duty to warn her. "Eliza," he said, "thee understands thee's not going to Meeting? [2] They're not going to sit silent while thee tells them how much thee loves Samantha and how she sang when young and drank tea. Old man Overby'll have his say and he's got a lawyer hired for no other purpose than to trip thee up."

Eliza was unimpressed. "What's our lawyer fee'd for, Jess?" she asked.

Jess took another tack. "Eliza," he told her, "I don't figger thee's got a chance in a thousand to get Samantha back."

"This is a court of justice, isn't it?" Eliza asked.

"Yes," Jess said.

"Then there's no need for thee to fash [3] thyself, Jess Birdwell. I'll get Samantha back."

Not getting Samantha back wasn't what fashed Jess — he reckoned he could bear up under that mighty well. What fashed him was the whole shooting match . . . In some few cases, matters of life and death, going to court might be necessary, and he could imagine such. But a suit over a goose named Samantha wasn't one of them. And poor Eliza. Law to her was all Greek and turkey tracks . . . and here she was bound for court as chipper as if she was Chief Justice Taney [4] himself. Jess sighed and shook his head. Getting shut of Samantha would be no hardship for him, but he was downcast for Eliza's sake and the way she'd have to turn homeward empty-handed.

In the courtroom, hard clear light reflected upward from the snow fell onto what Jess thought were hard faces: courthouse hangers-on; farmers whose slackening work made the diversion of a trial an inviting possibility; lovers of oddity who figured a tilt between a Quaker female, preacher to boot, and an old sinner like Milt Overby over the ownership of a goose ought to produce some enlivening quirks. They stared at Eliza, exchanged salutes with Milt Overby and inspected Samantha, who in her crate awaited the court's decision.

The two lawyers, Jess considered to be on a par. Nothing fancy, either one . . . old roadsters both, gone gray in service and with a knowledge of their business. The circuit judge was something else, unaccountably young, jug-eared and dressed more sprightly than a groom for his own wedding. A city whipper-snapper, born and trained north of the Mississinewa, [5] and now, in Jess's opinion, setting a squeamish foot in backwoods provinces, and irked to find himself trying so trifling a case. Didn't know a goose from a guinea hen, like as not, and would consider tossing a coin a more suitable manner of settling such a matter — just as near right in the end — and his valuable time saved.

Eliza, Jess saw, was of no such opinion. She, too, was scanning the young judge, and Jess, who knew her, saw from the look on her face that she was taken by him. A neat, thin, pious boy — far from home — he looked, no doubt to her; a young man who could do with better cooking and more regular eating.

The young man rapped the court to order. Spitting and shuffling slackened and in a high, precise voice he read, "Birdwell versus Overby. Charge, petty larceny. Appropriation and willful withholding of goose named Samantha."

---

[1] **First Day**: Quaker term for Sunday.

[2] **Meeting**: The Quaker church practice, in which the congregation meets to pray.

[3] **fash**: vex.

[4] **Taney** (tô′nĭ): Roger B. Taney was Chief Justice of the Supreme Court (1836–1864).

[5] **Mississinewa** (Mĭs·ĭs·sĭn′ê·wà): a small river flowing into the Wabash River in Indiana.

The name Samantha seemed to somewhat choke him, but he got it out.

"Ready for Birdwell," said Mr. Abel Samp, Eliza's lawyer.

"Ready for Overby," said the defendant's lawyer.

Eliza was the first witness on the stand. Jess sometimes forgot what a good-looking woman Eliza was, but the interest shown on lifted faces all about him refreshed his memory.

"Swear the plaintiff in," the judge said.

Eliza, in her sweet voice, spoke directly to the judge. "I don't swear," she said.

The judge explained that profanity was not asked for. "I understood," said Eliza, "that thee wasn't asking for profanity. No one would think that of thee. But we Quakers do not take oaths in court. We affirm."

"Permit Mrs. Birdwell to affirm," said the judge. Eliza affirmed.

Mr. Samp then proceeded to question Eliza as to Samantha's birth and habits.

"Judge," Eliza began.

"Address the judge," Mr. Samp said, "as Your Honor."

"We Quakers," Eliza told the judge, gently, "do not make use of such titles. What is thy name? I think thee'll go far in our state and thy name's one I'd like to know."

The judge appeared somewhat distraught, undecided as to whether to make the tone of the court brisk and legal (if possible) or to follow Eliza's lead of urbane sociability.

"Pomeroy," he said and made a slight bow in Eliza's direction.

Eliza returned the bow, deeper and with more grace. "Friend Pomeroy," she said, "it is indeed a pleasure to know thee."

Samantha's story as Eliza told it to Friend Pomeroy was surprisingly terse. Affecting, and losing nothing by Eliza's telling, but to the point.

"Mrs. Birdwell," said Samp, "how long have you had an acquaintanceship with geese and their habits?"

"Since I was a child," Eliza said. "My father was a great fancier of geese."

"And you think you could identify this goose Samantha, which you admit in looks was similar to the defendant's?"

"I could," Eliza said with much authority.

Mr. Samp, to Jess's surprise, left the matter there. "Take the witness," he said to Overby's lawyer — but the counsel for the defendant was in no hurry to cross-examine Eliza. Instead he put his client on the stand.

"Farewell, Samantha," Jess said to Enoch.

"You relieved?" Enoch asked.

"Putting Eliza first," Jess said, "as I do, no."

Milt Overby, whose natural truculence was somewhat stimulated by a nip he'd had to offset snappy weather, bellowed his way through his testimony. At one juncture he set the judge aright when he asked some elementary questions concerning the habits and configurations of geese. "Where in tarnation you from?" he snorted. "What they mean sending us judges down here who don't know Toulouse from Wyandotte,[1] or goose from gander?"

The young judge used voice and gavel to quiet the guffawing which filled the courtroom and the trial proceeded. A number of witnesses for both sides were brought to the stand and while it was shown that Overbys had maybe eaten a goose or two and neglected out of pure fondness for the creatures to count them as among the departed, still nobody had been able to positively identify Samantha.

Mr. Overby's lawyer seemed somewhat loath to cross-examine Eliza, but he put her on the stand. She'd said she

---

[1] **Toulouse** (to͞o·lo͞oz′) . . . **Wyandotte** (wī′ăn-dŏt): breeds of fowl.

knew geese and her testimony had been direct and positive. "Mrs. Birdwell," he said, "how can you be so sure your goose was with my client's geese?"

Eliza's black eyes rested confidingly upon the judge. "Friend Pomeroy," she said, "I raised Samantha from a gosling."

Jess sighed. "Here it comes," he said, "how that goose could sing and drink tea."

Eliza continued, "And there's one thing about her that always set her apart from every other goose."

"Yes, Mrs. Birdwell," said Judge Pomeroy, who was inclined to forget, with Eliza on the stand, that he was in a courtroom.

"Samantha," said Eliza, with much earnestness, "from the day she was born had a gait unlike any other goose I ever saw and one that set her apart from all her Overby connections. I picked her out at once when I went over there, because of it. Thee couldn't-'ve missed it, Friend Pomeroy."

"Yes, Mrs. Birdwell," said the judge with interest in his voice.

"Samantha," said Eliza, "was a born pacer. Thee knows what a pacer is?"

"Certainly," said Judge Pomeroy. "A pacer," he repeated with no surprise — and with obvious pleasure that Eliza'd hit upon so clear and differentiating an aspect of her goose and one that made identification possible.

A titter was mounting through the courtroom — Judge Pomeroy lifted his head. He had no desire to be further instructed as to the history, habits, and breeds of geese, and he liked to see a trial settled by some such little and too often overlooked subtlety. Judge Pomeroy brought down his gavel. "The court awards decision in favor of the plaintiff. Case dismissed." While the silence that followed on his words still prevailed Judge Pomeroy stepped briskly and with obvious pleasure out through the rear door.

Jess was also brisk about departure. No use lingering until friend Pomeroy had been more thoroughly informed as to gaits in general and geese in particular. Mid-afternoon's a quiet time in any season. In winter with snow on the ground, no leaves to rustle and bare limbs rigid as rock against a cloudless sky, the hush is deepest of all. Nothing broke that hush in the surrey, except the squeak of leather and snow, the muffled footfalls of Rome Beauty. Jess and Eliza, on the front seat, rode without speaking. Enoch, in the back, seemed to meditate. Even Samantha in her crate at Enoch's feet was silent.

Maple Grove Nursery was in sight before Jess spoke. "Eliza," he said, "would thee mind telling me — did thee ever see a trotting goose?"

Enoch ceased to meditate and listened. He had been wondering about this himself.

"Certainly not," said Eliza. "Thee knows as well as I, Jess Birdwell, an animal can't trot without hind feet and forefeet."

"So far, Eliza," Jess said, "we see eye to eye. Now maybe thee'd tell me — did thee ever see a goose that didn't pace?"

Eliza was truly amazed, it seemed. "Why, Jess," she said, "an ordinary goose just walks — but Samantha paces."

Jess was silent for a spell. "What'd thee say the difference is?"

"It's the swing, Jess Birdwell," said Eliza, "same as in a horse that nature's formed for a pacer . . . it's the natural bent, the way the spirit leads the beast to set his feet down. Samantha's a natural pacer."

That seemed as far as they'd likely get on the subject and Jess joined Enoch in meditation. In the barnyard, before she went up to the house, Eliza said, like an old hand at the business, "Attending court whettens the appetite. It's a little early but I thought if thee'd relish it" — and she looked at

Jess and Enoch, never sparing a glance for Samantha, as if her menfolk's welfare was her sole concern — "I'd stir us up a bite to eat. Hot tea and fresh sweetcakes, say. Might fry a little sausage and open some cherry preserves. If thee'd relish it," she repeated.

Jess wasn't taken in, but he'd relish it, and so would Enoch, and they both said so. They hustled with the unhitching so they could uncrate Samantha and note her progress with eyes newly instructed as to what made a pacer. Jess dumped her in the snow, and Enoch tapped her with his hat. Samantha made for the back door.

"By sugar," said Jess, "Eliza's right. She paces." Samantha had the smooth roll of a racker [1] — there were no two ways about it. At heart she was a pacer, and what two legs could do in that line, Samantha accomplished.

"With four legs," Enoch said, "you could enter her in any county fair — rack on," he cried with enthusiasm. As they followed Samantha to the house, Enoch, for whom any event existed chiefly in its after aspects as a cud for rumination, asked, "How you feel in respect of court trials, now, Mr. Birdwell?"

"I'm still against them," Jess said, "though they's three things this trial's taught me I might never otherwise have learned. Two's about women."

Enoch revered all knowledge and he had a notion that information on this subject might have a more than transcendental [2] value. "What's the two things you learned about women, Mr. Birdwell?"

"Well, Enoch, I learned first, dependability's woman's greatest virtue. Steady as a pump bolt, day in, day out. When thee finds a woman like that, Enoch, don't try to change her. Not

[1] **racker:** a horse that paces or single-foots.
[2] **transcendental:** The philosophy of Emerson, in whom Enoch was interested, is often called transcendental.

even in spring."

"No, sir," said Enoch, "I won't."

"Second, when it's a case of woman and the law — thee don't need to waste any worry on the woman."

"No, sir," said Enoch again.

When they reached the back steps, Enoch asked, "I understood you to say you'd learned three things, Mr. Birdwell. What's the third about?"

"Hired men," said Jess.

Enoch was taken aback, but he'd asked for it. "Yes, Mr. Birdwell," he said.

"Never hire one," Jess told him, "till thee finds out first if he can count to eight. Save thyself a lot of trouble that way, Enoch."

"How's I to know the eighth'd turn out to be Samantha?" Enoch asked.

Samantha herself, who was waiting at the doorstep for an expected tidbit, reached out and, unhampered by either boots or work pants, nipped Enoch firmly through his thin Sunday best.

"Thee say something, Enoch?" Jess asked.

Enoch had but he didn't repeat it. Instead he said, "Pacer or no pacer, that's Samantha," and the two of them stepped out of the snow into the warm kitchen, scented with baking sweetcakes and frying sausage.

For Discussion of West

1. Both the chief and minor characters in this story are presented with skillful touches that build up distinct personalities. Let's look at them more closely:

   a. In what ways are Jess and Eliza alike? How do they differ, aside from their attitude toward geese? What evidence do you find of warm affection between them? Find good examples of Jess's troubled conscience, of Eliza's poise and self-possession.

   b. Enoch is something of a diplomat. How is this revealed in the story? How do you know he is a wide reader?

   c. How does Judge Pomeroy differ from the usual conception of a judge? Why are Eliza's tactics in court more likely to appeal to him than Overby's? Explain whether you think the Judge was "taken in" by Eliza's description of Samantha as a "pacer."

2. The humor of this story lies in both the situation itself and in its manner of telling. Pick out passages and phrases you think are particularly amusing, like Jess's remark about "vexity" on page 23. Do you come away with mental pictures of scenes in the story that would be funny if put on a movie screen? Describe one or two.

For Your Vocabulary

DIALECT: Much of the charm of "The Pacing Goose" comes from its local color, that is, its picturing of people and scenes in a particular community. Local color stories often depend heavily on a skillful use of dialect. Point out examples of Quaker speech and local farm expressions in the story. What is the difference between *dialect* and *accent?* between *dialect* and *slang?* Does your community have a dialect? Draw up a list of words and phrases that are peculiar to your part of the country.

Guide to Reading Short Stories

We like to read short stories because we like to know people. We like to watch them in action. We want to know what they do and say to each other, how life treats them, and how they try to turn events to their own purposes. Of course, the people in stories are not "real" in the ordinary sense of the word; a story is not, like a biography, a factual record of an actual person's life. Yet fiction can seem more realistic and believable than fact, oftentimes, and a good writer can tell us many truths about life. Moreover, a piece of fiction can call upon the free play of the author's imagination, and hold our interest with suspense or humor. The writer's hand is always behind the story, arranging events, causing things to happen, beckoning the reader on to the end. A skillful reader soon learns to recognize the clever ways in which a story is created.

The Opening of the Story

If you were reading a newspaper account of some situation, you would find, baldly stated in the first sentence or two, all the important facts of time, place, and persons involved. Not so in

a short story. This information is never hurled at you all at once. You will receive it gradually, and often by suggestion rather than directly. The mention of frost on the windowpane may be the only hint that the story is laid in a cold climate. A powdered wig may suggest that the story takes place in the eighteenth century; a television set thrusts you right into the present time.

Similarly, do not expect to learn everything about the characters immediately. You may find only slight clues to the personalities of the characters in the opening conversation. The storyteller is rarely so blunt as to declare that this character is surly, troublesome, and unlikable, while another is genial and happy. He expects you to draw such conclusions from the many details and suggestions throughout the story. For example, in "The Pacing Goose," there are no general introductory statements about the characters of Eliza and Jess, yet you soon recognize them as distinct personalities. Even without complete information, the beginning of a story thus tells you the setting and introduces the characters.

The opening paragraphs also tell you the *point of view* from which the story will be told. In "The Pacing Goose," the point of view is that of the all-seeing, all-knowing author, who seems to stand in the clouds looking down on the characters, seeing everything and everybody at once.

Besides observing the outer action of the story, we may also be allowed to dip into the minds of different characters and know what they are thinking. Some stories, though told in the third person, concentrate on the point of view of one character. "The Most Dangerous Game" is told from Rainsford's point of view throughout; we see and feel only what Rainsford sees and feels. When a story is told in the first person, it is quite obvious whose point of view is being followed, and you will probably identify yourself, temporarily at least, with the "I" in the story. This person may be the main character in the story, but is not necessarily so — perhaps he is just an observer watching the action. Still another point of view developed in modern stories is the "stream of consciousness" method by which you, the reader, *become* the main character by being admitted to all the ideas that pass through the mind of that person. Many of his thoughts may be broken, disconnected bits that seem, for the moment, off the subject, yet they help to build up a remarkably vivid total impression.

Besides introducing the place, characters, and point of view, the opening of a story also serves to set its mood. Edgar Allan Poe's famous definition of the short story laid great emphasis on the value of the opening sentences to establish the right mood. The two stories you have just read are good illustrations. In the first, a tropical night and a mysterious island prepare the way for unguessed dangers and a grim struggle. In the second, a bright spring day on a well-run farm makes you feel cheerful and gay and prepares you for a warmhearted, humorous tale. Once

you have discovered the mood the author seeks to establish, co-operate with him. Try to put yourself in this mood and accept the story on its own grounds. You can hardly enjoy a funny situation if you are worrying about a forthcoming history test, or be moved by the ruin of a man's life if you are listening to dance music on the radio. Give the story a chance.

The Action of the Story

Every story must have action; otherwise it becomes an essay or a character sketch. Near the beginning of the story something happens that starts the action rolling. Two characters are in disagreement, serious or otherwise, over some matter; or within the mind of a single character there is some indecision, some doubt troubling him. There is, in other words, some kind of conflict or problem. You learn about the problem at the start of the story, and then you are curious to see how it will be worked out. In "The Most Dangerous Game," the action begins immediately when Rainsford falls from his ship and must find his way to safety, but the main problem comes later, of course. In "The Pacing Goose" the action begins with the conflict between Eliza and Jess over the raising of geese, and once again, this gives way later in the story to a still larger conflict.

After the action is once started, the events fall into place. "The plot thickens," we often say, meaning that the characters get more and more involved in a particular situation. Since the plot is based on struggle, it must have suspense. You will be uncertain of the outcome and eager to reach it. If you can guess the end too easily or if you feel little interest in the characters, there will be little suspense in the story for you. But usually you will find yourself engrossed in the turn of events. Because we all tend to identify ourselves with a character in a short story, we tend to "choose sides" in the problem or conflict presented. We want the character to win out in his struggle against nature (a storm, for example) or against another person; or if the struggle is in his own mind, we want him to choose wisely and make the right decision.

The breaking point in a story — the point where something is bound to happen one way or another to end the conflict or solve the problem — is called the climax. In a short story the climax usually comes and goes quickly. There is not much room for a long and complicated plot; because the story is brief, so is the action. After the climax, the tenseness is relieved. You know the best or the worst; the outcome is certain. There are two major questions that you are likely to ask yourself — often unconsciously — upon completing a story. First, was I surprised by the ending? Not all stories have a "surprise ending," but you will feel a certain pleasant tingle when you run across one. O. Henry was a master of the "surprise ending," as you will discover in reading "Mammon and the Archer." Of course, the ending is never completely a surprise. A good writer gives you hints as to the outcome, and a good reader recognizes these, so that he half expects the ending before it is reached.

The second question you may well ask yourself is: did the ending satisfy me? Now, if you are the kind of person who always wants a happy ending, you will be disappointed in a large part of modern literature. Many modern writers, convinced that the bitter and the gloomy are the usual outcomes of life, conscientiously produce only wry endings. Of course, if the characters were bound to come to a tragic end because of some weakness they displayed or because they were overwhelmed by stronger forces, then don't look for some quick reversal of events to make the story end happily. On the other hand, it's not the things that happen to people, but the way that people respond to the things that happen which makes life a success or failure — and this holds for fiction, too.

The People in the Story

A brief word needs to be said about characters in fiction. You know from reading plays and novels and short stories that the best way to obtain a rounded picture of a character is to watch three things: what the character says, what he does, and what is said about him by others. This information you gather easily if you read attentively, but you will want to go a step further and try to *understand* the feelings and thoughts of a character. Rarely do you meet a character in fiction exactly like yourself. If you are young the character may be old; if you are poor, he may be rich; if you are farm-bred, he may be from a city; and so forth. Thus, you will find it necessary to step outside of your own narrow circle of experience and place yourself in another frame of mind. Try to imagine what life must be like in a different place, under different circumstances. If you are successful, you enjoy stories all the more for having understood the characters in them.

And this is, finally, the great reward that short stories will offer you — taking you into different places, introducing you to new and different kinds of people, facing you with different but "real" problems that you have never encountered before. Short stories can be like windows on the world, if you will but sit by them and give your attention entirely to what they show.

O. HENRY
1862–1910

ear mark.

Mammon and the Archer

O. Henry was such a successful pen name that today it completely overshadows the writer's real name — William Sydney Porter. Aside from literature his life was not always successful. Threatened by tuberculosis in his youth, Porter left his North Carolina birthplace for a Texas ranch. Later as a bank clerk in Austin he was involved in a charge of embezzlement. To escape it he fled to Central America, but the critical illness of his wife, who had remained in Texas, brought him back to face trial and imprisonment. It was afterward shown that the bank's careless system of accounting was responsible for the loss rather than any intentional dishonesty on his part. In prison he wrote many of his stories that have settings in the South and in the revolution-ridden republics of Central America. When, in later life, he went to live in New York City he found his richest source of fiction. His best-known collection of stories is *The Four Million*. The title was chosen in contrast to the select "Four Hundred" of New York society, and illustrates the kind of story O. Henry loved to write — about the daily dramas of people in a great city.

Although O. Henry was never financially successful as a writer, his name became famous among newspaper and magazine readers as a guarantee of clever stories. The earmarks of an O. Henry story are brevity, wit, and amazing sense of plot. He was the master of the surprise ending.

Yet O. Henry offered more than just that. He was a distinctive stylist with humorous, many-syllabled words, and a warm human sympathy underlies the surface gaiety of his style. You will find all these qualities in "Mammon and the Archer," which pictures, for a change, the Four Hundred, rather than the Four Million, of New York City. Mammon, incidentally, is the ancient god of wealth, and the Archer is, of course, Cupid, the god of love.

O LD Anthony Rockwall, retired manufacturer and proprietor of Rockwall's Eureka Soap, looked out the library window of his Fifth Avenue mansion and grinned. His neighbor to the right — the aristocratic clubman, G. Van Schuylight Suffolk-Jones [1] —

came out to his waiting motorcar, wrinkling a contumelious nostril, as usual, at the Italian renaissance sculpture of the soap palace's front elevation.

"Stuck-up old statuette of nothing doing!" commented the ex-Soap King.

[1] **G. Van Schuylight Suffolk-Jones:** Notice the way in which the author makes fun of this snobbish member of aristocratic society. Old Dutch and English families are prominent in New York aristocracy; therefore, he turns the Dutch name Schuyler (skī'lẽr) into Schuylight (skylight), and makes use of the first initial and hyphenated surname common among British aristocracy.

" The Eden Musée'll [1] get that old frozen face yet if he don't watch out. I'll have this house painted red, white, and blue next summer and see if that'll make his Dutch nose turn up any higher."

And then Anthony Rockwall, who never cared for bells, went to the door of his library and shouted " Mike! " in the same voice that had once chipped off pieces of the welkin on the Kansas prairies.

" Tell my son," said Anthony to the answering menial, " to come in here before he leaves the house."

When young Rockwall entered the library the old man laid aside his newspaper, looked at him with a kindly grimness on his big, smooth, ruddy countenance, rumpled his mop of white hair with one hand and rattled the keys in his pocket with the other.

" Richard," said Anthony Rockwall, " what do you pay for the soap that you use? "

Richard, only six months home from college, was startled a little. He had not yet taken the measure of this sire of his, who was as full of unexpectedness as a girl at her first party.

" Six dollars a dozen, I think, Dad."

" And your clothes? "

" I suppose about sixty dollars, as a rule."

" You're a gentleman," said Anthony, decidedly. " I've heard of these young bloods spending twenty-four dollars a dozen for soap, and going over the hundred mark for clothes. You've got as much money to waste as any of 'em, and yet you stick to what's decent and moderate. Now I use the old Eureka — not only for sentiment, but it's the purest soap made. Whenever you pay more than ten cents a cake for soap you buy bad perfumes and labels. But fifty cents is doing very well for a young man in

your generation, position, and condition. As I said, you're a gentleman. They say it takes three generations to make one. They're off. Money'll do it as slick as soap grease. It's made you one. By hokey! it's almost made one of me. I'm nearly as impolite and disagreeable and ill-mannered as these two old Knickerbocker [2] gents on each side of me that can't sleep of nights because I bought in between 'em."

" There are some things that money can't accomplish," remarked young Rockwell, rather gloomily.

" Now, don't say that," said old Anthony, shocked. " I bet my money on money every time. I've been through the encyclopedia down to Y looking for something you can't buy with it; and I expect to have to take up the appendix next week. I'm for money against the field. Tell me something money won't buy."

" For one thing," answered Richard, rankling a little, " it won't buy one into the exclusive circles of society."

" Oho! won't it? " thundered the champion of the root of evil. " You tell me where your exclusive circles would be if the first Astor [3] hadn't had the money to pay for his steerage passage over? "

Richard sighed.

" And that's what I was coming to," said the old man, less boisterously. " That's why I asked you to come in. There's something wrong with you, boy. I've been noticing it for two weeks. Out with it. I guess I could lay my hands on eleven millions within twenty-four hours, besides the real estate. If it's your liver, there's the *Rambler* down in the bay, coaled, and ready to steam down to the Bahamas in two days."

[1] **The Eden Musée** (ē'děn mūs·ā'): a new York museum once famous for its Chamber of Horrors, with lifelike wax figures of notorious criminals.

[2] **Knickerbocker** (nĭk'ēr·bŏk'ēr): a term for members of the Dutch aristocracy, made famous by Washington Irving. See page 473.

[3] **Astor**: John Jacob Astor, a German immigrant who came to New York in 1784, made a great fortune, and founded one of the most influential families of that city.

"Not a bad guess, Dad; you haven't missed it far."

"Ah," said Anthony, keenly; "what's her name?"

Richard began to walk up and down the library floor. There was enough comradeship and sympathy in this crude old father of his to draw his confidence.

"Why don't you ask her?" demanded old Anthony. "She'll jump at you. You've got the money and the looks, and you're a decent boy. Your hands are clean. You've got no Eureka soap on 'em. You've been to college, but she'll overlook that."

"I haven't had a chance," said Richard.

"Make one," said Anthony. "Take her for a walk in the park, or a straw ride, or walk home with her from church. Chance! Pshaw!"

"You don't know the social mill, Dad. She's part of the stream that turns it. Every hour and minute of her time is arranged for days in advance. I must have that girl, Dad, or this town is a blackjack swamp forevermore. And I can't write it — I can't do that."

"Tut!" said the old man. "Do you mean to tell me that with all the money I've got you can't get an hour or two of a girl's time for yourself?"

"I've put it off too late. She's going to sail for Europe at noon day after tomorrow for a two years' stay. I'm to see her alone tomorrow evening for a few minutes. She's at Larchmont now at her aunt's. I can't go there. But I'm allowed to meet her with a cab at the Grand Central Station tomorrow evening at the eight-thirty train. We drive down Broadway to Wallack's [1] at a gallop,[2] where her mother and a box party will be waiting for us in the lobby. Do you think she would listen to a declaration

¹ **Wallack's**: a theater named for its manager, a well-known actor of the eighties.

² **at a gallop**: Remember that cabs at the time of this story were horse-drawn.

from me during that six or eight minutes under those circumstances? No. And what chance would I have in the theater or afterward? None. No, Dad, this is one tangle that your money can't unravel. We can't buy one minute of time with cash; if we could, rich people would live longer. There's no hope of getting a talk with Miss Lantry before she sails."

"All right, Richard, my boy," said old Anthony, cheerfully. "You may run along down to your club now. I'm glad it ain't your liver. But don't forget to burn a few punk sticks in the joss house to the great god Mazuma from time to time. You say money won't buy time? Well, of course, you can't order eternity wrapped up and delivered at your residence for a price, but I've seen Father Time get pretty bad stone bruises on his heels when he walked through the gold diggings."

That night came Aunt Ellen, gentle, sentimental, wrinkled, sighing, oppressed by wealth, in to brother Anthony at his evening paper, and began discourse on the subject of lovers' woes.

"He told me all about it," said brother Anthony, yawning. "I told him my bank account was at his service. And then he began to knock money. Said money couldn't help. Said the rules of society couldn't be bucked for a yard by a team of ten-millionaires."

"Oh, Anthony," sighed Aunt Ellen, "I wish you would not think so much of money. Wealth is nothing where a true affection is concerned. Love is all-powerful. If he only had spoken earlier! She could not have refused our Richard. But now I fear it is too late. He will have no opportunity to address her. All your gold cannot bring happiness to your son."

At eight o'clock the next evening Aunt Ellen took a quaint old gold ring from a moth-eaten case and gave it to Richard.

"Wear it tonight, nephew," she

begged. "Your mother gave it to me. Good luck in love she said it brought. She asked me to give it to you when you had found the one you loved."

Young Rockwall took the ring reverently and tried it on his smallest finger. It slipped as far as the second joint and stopped. He took it off and stuffed it into his vest pocket, after the manner of man. And then he phoned for his cab.

At the station he captured Miss Lantry out of the gadding mob at eight thirty-two.

"We mustn't keep Mamma and the others waiting," said she.

"To Wallack's Theater as fast as you can drive!" said Richard loyally.

They whirled up Forty-second to Broadway,[1] and then down the white-starred lane that leads from the soft meadows of sunset to the rocky hills of morning.

At Thirty-fourth Street young Richard quickly thrust up the trap [2] and ordered the cabman to stop.

"I've dropped a ring," he apologized, as he climbed out. "It was my mother's, and I'd hate to lose it. I won't detain you a minute — I saw where it fell."

In less than a minute he was back in the cab with the ring.

But within that minute a cross-town car had stopped directly in front of the cab. The cabman tried to pass to the left, but a heavy express wagon cut him off. He tried the right, and had to back away from a furniture van that had no business to be there. He tried to back out, but dropped his reins and swore dutifully. He was blockaded in a tangled mess of vehicles and, horses.

One of those street blockades had occurred that sometimes tie up commerce and movement quite suddenly in the big city.

"Why don't you drive on?" said Miss Lantry, impatiently. "We'll be late."

Richard stood up in the cab and looked around. He saw a congested flood of wagons, trucks, cabs, vans, and streetcars filling the vast space where Broadway, Sixth Avenue, and Thirty-fourth Street cross one another as a twenty-six-inch maiden fills her twenty-two-inch girdle. And still from all the cross streets they were hurrying and rattling toward the converging point at full speed, and hurling themselves into the struggling mass, locking wheels and adding their drivers' imprecations to the clamor. The entire traffic of Manhattan seemed to have jammed itself around them. The oldest New Yorker among the thousands of spectators that lined the sidewalks had not witnessed a street blockade of the proportions of this one.

"I'm very sorry," said Richard, as he resumed his seat, "but it looks as if we are stuck. They won't get this jumble loosened up in an hour. It was my fault. If I hadn't dropped the ring we — "

"Let me see the ring," said Miss Lantry. "Now that it can't be helped, I don't care. I think theaters are stupid, anyway."

At eleven o'clock that night somebody tapped lightly on Anthony Rockwall's door.

"Come in," shouted Anthony, who was in a red dressing gown, reading a book of piratical adventures.

Somebody was Aunt Ellen, looking like a gray-haired angel that had been left on earth by mistake.

"They're engaged, Anthony," she said softly. "She has promised to marry our Richard. On their way to the theater there was a street blockade, and it was two hours before their cab could get out of it.

"And oh, brother Anthony, don't ever boast of the power of money again.

---

[1] **Broadway:** famous as the theater center of New York.

[2] **trap:** In the old-fashioned horse cab the driver sat on an elevated seat at the back and could be addressed only through a little trap door in the roof of the cab.

A little emblem of true love — a little ring that symbolized unending and unmercenary affection — was the cause of our Richard finding his happiness. He dropped it in the street, and got out to recover it. And before they could continue, the blockade occurred. He spoke to his love and won her there while the cab was hemmed in. Money is dross compared with true love, Anthony."

" All right," said old Anthony. " I'm glad the boy has got what he wanted. I told him I wouldn't spare any expense in the matter if — "

" But, brother Anthony, what good could your money have done? "

" Sister," said Anthony Rockwall, " I've got my pirate in a devil of a scrape. His ship has just been scuttled, and he's too good a judge of the value of money to let drown. I wish you would let me go on with this chapter."

The story should end here. I wish it would as heartily as you who read it wish it did. But we must go to the bottom of the well for truth.

The next day a person with red hands and a blue polka-dot necktie, who called himself Kelly, called at Anthony Rockwall's house, and was at once received in the library.

" Well," said Anthony, reaching for his checkbook, " it was a good bilin' of soap. Let's see — you had five thousand dollars in cash."

" I paid out three hundred more of my own," said Kelly. " I had to go a little above the estimate. I got the express wagons and cabs mostly for five dollars, but the trucks and two-horse teams mostly raised me to ten. The motormen wanted ten, and some of the loaded teams twenty. The cops struck me hardest — fifty dollars I paid two, and the rest twenty and twenty-five. But didn't it work beautiful, Mr. Rockwall? I'm glad William A. Brady [1] wasn't on to that little outdoor vehicle mob scene. I

[1] **William A. Brady:** a well-known theatrical producer and director of that day.

wouldn't want William to break his heart with jealousy. And never a rehearsal, either! The boys was on time to the fraction of a second. It was two hours before a snake could get below Greeley's statue." [2]

" Thirteen hundred — there you are, Kelly," said Anthony tearing off a check. " Your thousand, and the three hundred you were out. You don't despise money, do you Kelly? "

" Me? " said Kelly. " I can lick the man that invented poverty."

Anthony called Kelly when he was at the door.

" You didn't notice," said he, " anywhere in the tie-up, a kind of a fat boy without any clothes on shooting arrows around with a bow, did you? "

" Why, no," said Kelly, mystified. " I didn't. If he was like you say, maybe the cops pinched him before I got there."

" I thought the little rascal wouldn't be on hand," chuckled Anthony. " Goodby, Kelly."

For Discussion of O. Henry

1. In reading the first five paragraphs of the story, what clues do you find to the appearance, personality, and background of Anthony Rockwall? You should be able to find at least five, and probably more. Is his name one of them? Do you like him? Why or why not? Do you have any reason for changing your first impression of Anthony Rockwall as the story goes on?

2. Line all the characters up to show on which team they are playing — that of Mammon or that of the Archer. How does the author make you think that one side is winning and then reverse the decision? In what sense did both sides win? At what point is Rockwall's scheme first revealed? Why didn't he tell his sister about it when she gloated over him?

3. Was the traffic-jam scheme really possible, or does it strike you as a clever trick on the part of the author to surprise

[2] Meaning Greeley Square, where the statue stands, at Thirty-fourth Street and Broadway, below Times Square.

you? What is the value of the final question Rockwall puts to Kelly?

4. Point out several bits of local color that would place this story in New York City even if you did not know the setting beforehand. What details in the story show that the time of the action is much earlier than the present? About what date would you place it?

5. Prove that this story does or does not illustrate the earmarks of an O. Henry story as given on page 33.

For Your Vocabulary

HUMOROUS LANGUAGE: Humor is sometimes created by the use of ridiculously high-flown language. A good example in this story is " wrinkling a contumelious nostril," a humorous way of saying that one turns up one's nose scornfully. Another instance is the use of *welkin*, a fancy substitute for *sky*. This archaic word is scarcely ever heard today except in the expression " to make the welkin ring." How is the word used humorously on page 34? Still another example of extravagant language for humorous effect is Anthony's advice to Richard, " But don't forget to burn a few punk sticks in the joss house to the great god Mazuma from time to time." In simple but unhumorous language this means, " Burn incense in the temple to the god Money." Find other examples of high-flown language you consider particularly humorous in this story.

To Build a Fire

JACK LONDON
1876–1916

Jack London's own adventures are more varied and amazing than those of the hero in many an imaginary thriller. As a street waif he played and fought on the waterfront at Oakland, California, and became the leader of a gang that robbed the oyster beds. At seventeen he had his first cruise on a sailing vessel on the North Pacific. The next year he became a tramp, roamed over much of the United States and Canada and was jailed for vagrancy in Niagara. By this time he had decided that his life was going the wrong way and could only be righted by education. Back at Oakland he performed the surprising feat of covering the whole high school course in three months of study. He enrolled at the University of California, but after a few months there left to go seeking a fortune in Alaska. The gold rush to the Klondike was then at its height, but the fortune did not materialize for Jack London. After a

year he sailed back to San Francisco — nineteen hundred miles in an open boat. Then followed several years of struggle to make ends meet, until the novels and stories he had been working on all this time began to pay. At thirty, he built a schooner, the *Snark,* in which he and his wife sailed the South Seas during much of the remaining decade of his life. He lived dangerously and furiously, and when he died at forty, he had written forty-eight volumes in less than twenty years.

It was in Hawaii that London wrote " To Build a Fire," considered by many his greatest story. It was obviously based on his experience in Alaska. " To Build a Fire " will strike you as quite different from any of the stories you have read so far. There is only one human being in it. But what an opponent he takes on! You meet the opponent even before the man, but, like the man, you must go on to ap-

"To Build a Fire," from *Lost Faces,* by Jack London. Reprinted by permission of The Macmillan Company, publishers.

preciate its terrific power. Try to read this story when no interruption will break your absorption in the struggle — one menace conquered, then a new menace —

Day had broken cold and gray, exceedingly cold and gray, when the man turned aside from the main Yukon trail and climbed the high earth bank, where a dim and little-traveled trail led eastward through the fat spruce timberland. It was a steep bank, and he paused for breath at the top, excusing the act to himself by looking at his watch. It was nine o'clock. There was no sun or hint of sun, though there was not a cloud in the sky. It was a clear day, and yet there seemed an intangible pall over the face of things, a subtle gloom that made the day dark, and that was due to the absence of sun. This fact did not worry the man. He was used to the lack of sun. It had been days since he had seen the sun, and he knew that a few more days must pass before that cheerful orb, due south, would just peep above the sky line and dip immediately from view.

The man flung a look back along the way he had come. The Yukon lay a mile wide and hidden under three feet of ice. On top of this ice were as many feet of snow. It was all pure white, rolling in gentle undulations where the ice jams of the freeze-up had formed. North and south, as far as his eye could see, it was unbroken white, save for a dark hairline that curved and twisted from around the spruce-covered island to the south, and that curved and twisted away into the north, where it disappeared behind another spruce-covered island. This dark hairline was the trail — the main trail — that led south five hundred miles to the Chilkoot Pass, Dyea, and salt water; and that led north seventy miles to Dawson, and still on to the north a thousand miles to Nulato, and finally to St. Michael on Bering Sea, a thousand miles and half a thousand more.

But all this — the mysterious, far-reaching hairline trail, the absence of sun from the sky, the tremendous cold, and the strangeness and weirdness of it all — made no impression on the man. It was not because he was long used to it. He was a newcomer in the land, a cheechako, and this was his first winter. The trouble with him was that he was without imagination. He was quick and alert in the things of life, but only in the things, and not in the significances. Fifty degrees below zero meant eighty-odd degrees of frost. Such fact impressed him as being cold and uncomfortable, and that was all. It did not lead him to meditate upon his frailty as a creature of temperature, and upon man's frailty in general, able only to live within certain narrow limits of heat and cold, and from there on it did not lead him to the conjectural field of immortality and man's place in the universe. Fifty degrees below zero stood for a bite of frost that hurt and that must be guarded against by the use of mittens, ear flaps, warm moccasins, and thick socks. Fifty degrees below zero was to him just precisely fifty degrees below zero. That there should be anything more to it than that was a thought that never entered his head.

As he turned to go on, he spat speculatively. There was a sharp, explosive crackle that startled him. He spat again. And again, in the air, before it could fall to the snow, the spittle crackled. He knew that at fifty below spittle crackled on the snow, but his spittle had crackled in the air. Undoubtedly it was colder than fifty below — how much colder he did not know. But the temperature did not matter. He was bound for the old claim on the left fork of Henderson Creek, where the boys were already. They had come over across the divide from the Indian Creek country, while he had come the roundabout way to take a look at the possibilities of getting out logs in the spring from the islands in the Yukon. He would be into camp by six o'clock; a bit after dark, it was true, but the boys would be there, a fire would be going, and a hot supper would be ready. As for lunch, he pressed his hand against the protruding bundle under his jacket. It was also under his shirt, wrapped up in a handkerchief and lying against the naked skin. It was the only way to keep the biscuits from freezing. He smiled agreeably to himself as he thought of those biscuits, each cut open and sopped in bacon grease, and each enclosing a generous slice of fried bacon.

He plunged in among the big spruce trees. The trail was faint. A foot of snow had fallen since the last sled had passed over, and he was glad he was without a sled, traveling light. In fact, he carried nothing but the lunch wrapped in the handkerchief. He was surprised, however, at the cold. It certainly was cold, he concluded, as he rubbed his numb nose and cheekbones with his mittened hand. He was a warm-whiskered man, but the hair on his face did not protect the high cheekbones and the eager nose that thrust itself aggressively into the frosty air.

At the man's heels trotted a dog, a big native husky, the proper wolf dog, gray-coated and without any visible or temperamental difference from its brother, the wild wolf. The animal was depressed by the tremendous cold. It knew that it was no time for traveling. Its instinct told it a truer tale than was told to the man by the man's judgment. In reality, it was not merely colder than fifty below zero; it was colder than sixty below, than seventy below. It was seventy-five below zero. Since the freezing point is thirty-two above zero, it meant that one hundred and seven degrees of frost obtained. The dog did not know anything about thermometers. Possibly in its brain there was no sharp consciousness of a condition of very cold such as was in the man's brain. But the brute had its instinct. It experienced a vague but menacing apprehension that subdued it and

made it slink along at the man's heels and that made it question eagerly every unwonted movement of the man, as if expecting him to go into camp or to seek shelter somewhere and build a fire. The dog had learned fire, and it wanted fire, or else to burrow under the snow and cuddle its warmth away from the air.

The frozen moisture of its breathing had settled on its fur in a fine powder of frost, and especially were its jowls, muzzle, and eyelashes whitened by its crystaled breath. The man's red beard and mustache were likewise frosted, but more solidly, the deposit taking the form of ice and increasing with every warm, moist breath he exhaled. Also, the man was chewing tobacco, and the muzzle of ice held his lips so rigidly that he was unable to clear his chin when he expelled the juice. The result was that a crystal beard of the color and solidity of amber was increasing its length on his chin. If he fell down it would shatter itself, like glass, into brittle fragments. But he did not mind the appendage. It was the penalty all tobacco chewers paid in that country, and he had been out before in two cold snaps. They had not been so cold as this, he knew, but by the spirit thermometer at Sixty Mile he knew they had been registered at fifty below and at fifty-five.

He held on through the level stretch of woods for several miles, crossed a wide flat of niggerheads, and dropped down a bank to the frozen bed of a small stream. This was Henderson Creek, and he knew he was ten miles from the forks. He looked at his watch. It was ten o'clock. He was making four miles an hour, and he calculated that he would arrive at the forks at half-past twelve. He decided to celebrate that event by eating his lunch there.

The dog dropped in again at his heels, with a tail drooping discouragement, as the man swung along the creek bed. The furrow of the old sled trail was plainly visible, but a dozen inches of snow cov-

the marks of the last runners. In a month no man had come up or down that silent creek. The man held steadily on. He was not much given to thinking, and just then particularly he had nothing to think about save that he would eat lunch at the forks and that at six o'clock he would be in camp with the boys. There was nobody to talk to; and, had there been, speech would have been impossible because of the ice muzzle on his mouth. So he continued monotonously to chew tobacco and to increase the length of his amber beard.

Once in a while the thought reiterated itself that it was very cold and that he had never experienced such cold. As he walked along he rubbed his cheekbones and nose with the back of his mittened hand. He did this automatically, now and again changing hands. But rub as he would, the instant he stopped his cheekbones went numb, and the following instant the end of his nose went numb. He was sure to frost his cheeks; he knew that, and experienced a pang of regret that he had not devised a nose strap of the sort Bud wore in cold snaps. Such a strap passed across the cheeks, as well, and saved them. But it didn't matter much, after all. What were frosted cheeks? A bit painful, that was all; they were never serious.

Empty as the man's mind was of thought, he was keenly observant, and he noticed the changes in the creek, the curves and bends and timber jams, and always he sharply noted where he placed his feet. Once, coming around a bend, he shied abruptly, like a startled horse, curved away from the place where he had been walking, and retreated several paces back along the trail. The creek, he knew, was frozen clear to the bottom — no creek could contain water in that arctic winter — but he knew also that there were springs that bubbled out from the hillsides and ran along under the snow and on top of the ice of the creek. He knew that the coldest snaps never froze these springs, and he knew likewise their danger. They were traps. They hid pools of water under the snow that might be three inches deep, or three feet. Sometimes a skin of ice half an inch thick covered them, and in turn was covered by the snow. Sometimes there were alternate layers of water and ice skin, so that when one broke through he kept on breaking through for a while, sometimes wetting himself to the waist.

That was why he had shied in such panic. He had felt the give under his feet and heard the crackle of a snow-hidden ice skin. And to get his feet wet in such a temperature meant trouble and danger. At the very least it meant delay, for he would be forced to stop and build a fire, and under its protection to bare his feet while he dried his socks and moccasins. He stood and studied the creek bed and its banks, and decided that the flow of water came from the right. He reflected a while, rubbing his nose and cheeks, then skirted to the left, stepping gingerly and testing the footing for each step. Once clear of the danger, he took a fresh chew of tobacco and swung along at his four-mile gait.

In the course of the next two hours he came upon several similar traps. Usually the snow above the hidden pools had a sunken, candied appearance that advertised the danger. Once again, however, he had a close call; and once, suspecting danger, he compelled the dog to go on in front. The dog did not want to go. It hung back until the man shoved it forward, and then it went quickly across the white, unbroken surface. Suddenly it broke through, floundered to one side, and got away to firmer footing. It had wet its forefeet and legs, and almost immediately the water that clung to it turned to ice. It made quick efforts to lick the ice off its legs, then dropped down in the snow and began to bite out the ice that had formed between the toes. This was a matter of instinct. To permit the ice to remain would mean sore feet. It did not know this. It merely obeyed the mysterious prompting that arose from the deep crypts of its being. But the man knew, having achieved a judgment on the subject, and he removed the mitten from his right hand and helped tear out the ice particles. He did not expose his fingers more than a minute, and was astonished at the swift numbness that smote them. It certainly was cold. He pulled on the mitten hastily, and beat the hand savagely across his chest.

At twelve o'clock the day was at its brightest. Yet the sun was too far south on its winter journey to clear the horizon. The bulge of the earth intervened between it and Henderson Creek, where the man walked under a clear sky at noon and cast no shadow. At half-past twelve, to the minute, he arrived at the forks of the creek. He was pleased at the speed he had made. If he kept it up, he would certainly be with the boys by six. He unbuttoned his jacket and shirt and drew forth his lunch. The action consumed no more than a quarter of a minute, yet in that brief moment the numbness laid hold of the exposed fingers. He did not put the mitten on, but, instead, struck the fingers a dozen sharp smashes against his leg. Then he sat down on a snow-covered log to eat. The sting that followed upon the striking of his fingers against his leg ceased so quickly that he was startled. He had had no chance to take a bite of biscuit. He struck the fingers repeatedly and returned them to the mitten, baring the other hand for the purpose of eating. He tried to take a mouthful, but the ice muzzle prevented. He had forgotten to build a fire and thaw out. He chuckled at his foolishness, and as he chuckled he noted the numbness creeping into the exposed fingers. Also he noted that the stinging which had first come to his toes when he sat down was already passing away. He wondered whether the toes were warm or numb. He moved them inside the moccasins and decided that they were numb.

He pulled the mitten on hurriedly and stood up. He was a bit frightened. He stamped up and down until the stinging returned into the feet. It certainly was cold, was his thought. That man from Sulfur Creek had spoken the truth when telling how cold it sometimes got in the country. And he had laughed at him at the time! That showed one must not be too sure of things. There was no mistake about it, it *was* cold. He strode up and down, stamping his feet and threshing his arms, until reassured by the returning warmth. Then he got out matches and proceeded to make a fire. From the undergrowth, where high water of the previous spring had lodged a supply of seasoned twigs, he got his firewood. Working carefully from a small beginning, he soon had a roaring fire, over which he thawed the ice from his face and in the protection of which he ate his biscuits. For the moment the cold of space was outwitted. The dog took satisfaction in the fire, stretching out close enough for warmth and far enough away to escape being singed.

When the man had finished, he filled his pipe and took his comfortable time over a smoke. Then he pulled on his mittens, settled the ear flaps of his cap firmly about his ears, and took the creek trail up the left fork. The dog was disappointed and yearned back toward the fire. This man did not know cold. Possibly all the generations of his ancestry had been ignorant of cold, of real cold, of cold one hundred and seven degrees below freezing point. But the dog knew; all its ancestry knew, and it had inherited the knowledge. And it knew that it was not good to walk abroad in such fearful cold. It was the time to lie snug in a hole in the snow and wait for a curtain of cloud to be drawn across the face of outer space whence this cold came. On the other hand, there was no keen intimacy between the dog and the man.

The one was the toil-slave of the other, and the only caresses it had ever received were the caresses of the whiplash and of harsh and menacing throat sounds that threatened the whiplash. So the dog made no effort to communicate its apprehension to the man. It was not concerned in the welfare of the man; it was for its own sake that it yearned back toward the fire. But the man whistled, and spoke to it with the sound of whiplashes, and the dog swung in at the man's heels and followed after.

The man took a chew of tobacco and proceeded to start a new amber beard. Also, his moist breath quickly powdered with white his mustache, eyebrows, and lashes. There did not seem to be so many springs on the left fork of the Henderson, and for half an hour the man saw no signs of any. And then it happened. At a place where there were no signs, where the soft, unbroken snow seemed to advertise solidity beneath, the man broke through. It was not deep. He wet himself halfway to the knees before he floundered out to the firm crust.

He was angry, and cursed his luck aloud. He had hoped to get into camp with the boys at six o'clock, and this would delay him an hour, for he would have to build a fire and dry out his footgear. This was imperative at that low temperature — he knew that much; and he turned aside to the bank, which he climbed. On top, tangled in the underbrush about the trunks of several small spruce trees, was a high-water deposit of dry firewood — sticks and twigs, principally, but also larger portions of seasoned branches and fine, dry, last year's grasses. He threw down several large pieces on top of the snow. This served for a foundation and prevented the young flame from drowning itself in the snow it otherwise would melt. The flame he got by touching a match to a small shred of birch bark that he took from his pocket. This burned even more readily than paper. Placing it on the foundation,

he fed the young flame with wisps of dry grass and with the tiniest dry twigs.

He worked slowly and carefully, keenly aware of his danger. Gradually, as the flame grew stronger, he increased the size of the twigs with which he fed it. He squatted in the snow, pulling the twigs out from their entanglement in the brush and feeding directly to the flame. He knew there must be no failure. When it is seventy-five below zero a man must not fail in his first attempt to build a fire — that is, if his feet are wet. If his feet are dry, and he fails, he can run along the trail for half a mile and restore his circulation. But the circulation of wet and freezing feet cannot be restored by running when it is seventy-five below. No matter how fast he runs, the wet feet will freeze the harder.

All this the man knew. The old-timer on Sulfur Creek had told him about it the previous fall, and now he was appreciating the advice. Already all sensation had gone out of his feet. To build the fire, he had been forced to remove his mittens, and the fingers had quickly gone numb. His pace of four miles an hour had kept his heart pumping blood to the surface of his body and to all the extremities. But the instant he stopped, the action of the pump eased down. The cold of space smote the unprotected tip of the planet, and he, being on that unprotected tip, received the full force of the blow. The blood of his body recoiled before it. The blood was alive, like the dog, and like the dog it wanted to hide away and cover itself up from the fearful cold. So long as he walked four miles an hour, he pumped that blood, willy-nilly, to the surface; but now it ebbed away and sank down into the recesses of his body. The extremities were the first to feel its absence. His wet feet froze the faster, and his exposed fingers numbed the faster, though they had not yet begun to freeze. Nose and cheeks were already freezing, while the skin of all his body chilled as it lost its blood.

But he was safe. Toes and nose and cheeks would be only touched by the frost, for the fire was beginning to burn with strength. He was feeding it with twigs the size of his finger. In another minute he would be able to feed it with branches the size of his wrist, and then he could remove his wet footgear, and, while it dried, he could keep his naked feet warm by the fire, rubbing them at first, of course, with snow. The fire was a success. He was safe. He remembered the advice of the old-timer on Sulfur Creek, and smiled. The old-timer had been very serious in laying down the law that no man must travel alone in the Klondike after fifty below. Well, here he was; he had had the accident; he was alone; and he had saved himself. Those old-timers were rather womanish, some of them, he thought. All a man had to do was to keep his head, and he was all right. Any man who was a man could travel alone. But it was surprising the rapidity with which his cheeks and nose were freezing. And he had not thought his fingers could go lifeless in so short a time. Lifeless they were, for he could scarcely make them move together to grip a twig, and they seemed remote from his body and from him. When he touched a twig he had to look and see whether or not he had hold of it. The wires were pretty well down between him and his finger ends.

All of which counted for little. There was the fire, snapping and crackling and promising life with every dancing flame. He started to untie his moccasins. They were coated with ice; the thick German socks were like sheaths of iron halfway to the knees; and the moccasin strings were like rods of steel all twisted and knotted as by some conflagration. For a moment he tugged with his numb fingers, then, realizing the folly of it, he drew his sheath knife.

But before he could cut the strings it happened. It was his own fault, or, rather, his mistake. He should not have built the fire under the spruce tree. He should have built it in the open. But it had been easier to pull the twigs from the bush and drop them directly on the fire. Now the tree under which he had done this carried a weight of snow on its boughs. No wind had blown for weeks, and each bough was fully freighted. Each time he had pulled a twig he had communicated a slight agitation to the tree — an imperceptible agitation, so far as he was concerned, but an agitation sufficient to bring about the disaster. High up in the tree one bough capsized its load of snow. This fell on the boughs beneath, capsizing them. This process continued, spreading out and involving the whole tree. It grew like an avalanche, and it descended without warning upon the man and the fire, and the fire was blotted out! Where it had burned was a mantle of fresh and disordered snow.

The man was shocked. It was as though he had just heard his own sentence of death. For a moment he sat and stared at the spot where the fire had been. Then he grew very calm. Perhaps the old-timer on Sulfur Creek was right. If he had only had a trailmate he would have been in no danger now. The trailmate could have built the fire. Well, it was up to him to build the fire over again, and this second time there must be no failure. Even if he succeeded, he would most likely lose some toes. His feet must be badly frozen by now, and there would be some time before the second fire was ready.

Such were his thoughts, but he did not sit and think them. He was busy all the time they were passing through his mind. He made a new foundation for a fire, this time in the open, where no treacherous tree could blot it out. Next he gathered dry grasses and tiny twigs from the high-water flotsam. He could not bring his fingers together to pull them out, but he was able to gather them by the handful. In this way he got many rotten twigs and bits of green

A man in the far north country has always an enemy at his back — lurking, destroying cold. (Ewing Galloway)

moss that were undesirable, but it was the best he could do. He worked methodically, even collecting an armful of the larger branches to be used later when the fire gathered strength. And all the while the dog sat and watched him, a certain yearning wistfulness in its eyes, for it looked upon him as the fire provider, and the fire was slow in coming.

When all was ready, the man reached in his pocket for a second piece of birch bark. He knew the bark was there, and, though he could not feel it with his fingers, he could hear its crisp rustling as he fumbled for it. Try as he would, he could not clutch hold of it. And all the time, in his consciousness, was the knowledge that each instant his feet were freezing. This thought tended to put him in a panic, but he fought against it and kept calm. He pulled on his mittens with his teeth, and threshed his arms back and forth, beating his hands with all his might against his sides. He did this sitting down, and he stood up to do it; and all the while the dog sat in the snow, its wolf brush of a tail curled around warmly over its forefeet, its sharp wolf ears pricked forward intently as it watched the man. And the man, as he beat and threshed with his arms and hands, felt a great surge of envy as he regarded the creature that was warm and secure in its natural covering.

After a time he was aware of the first faraway signals of sensation in his beaten fingers. The faint tingling grew stronger till it evolved into a stinging ache that was excruciating, but which the man hailed with satisfaction. He stripped the mitten from his right hand and fetched forth the birch bark. The exposed fingers were quickly going numb again. Next he brought out his bunch of sulfur matches. But the tremendous cold had already driven the life out of his fingers. In his effort to separate one match from the others, the whole bunch fell in the snow. He tried to pick it out of the snow, but failed. The dead fingers could neither touch nor clutch. He was very careful. He drove the thought of his freezing feet, and nose, and cheeks, out of his mind, devoting his whole soul to the matches. He watched, using the sense of vision in place of that of touch, and when he saw his fingers on each side of the bunch, he closed them — that is, he willed to close them, for the wires were down, and the fingers did not obey. He pulled the mitten on the right hand, and beat it fiercely against his knee. Then, with both mittened hands, he scooped the bunch of matches, along with much snow, into his lap. Yet he was no better off.

After some manipulation he managed to get the bunch between the heels of his mittened hands. In this fashion he carried it to his mouth. The ice crackled and snapped when by a violent effort he opened his mouth. He drew the lower jaw in, curled the upper lip out of the way, and scraped the bunch with his upper teeth in order to separate a match. He succeeded in getting one, which he dropped on his lap. He was no better off. He could not pick it up. Then he devised a way. He picked it up in his teeth and scratched it on his leg. Twenty times he scratched before he succeeded in lighting it. As it flamed he held it with his teeth to the birch bark. But the burning brimstone went up his nostrils and into his lungs, causing him to cough spasmodically. The match fell into the snow and went out.

The old-timer on Sulfur Creek was right, he thought in the moment of controlled despair that ensued: after fifty below, a man should travel with a partner. He beat his hands, but failed in exciting any sensation. Suddenly he bared both hands, removing the mittens with his teeth. He caught the whole bunch between the heels of his hands. His arm muscles, not being frozen, enabled him to press the hand heels tightly against the matches. Then he scratched the bunch along his leg. It flared into flame, seventy sulfur matches at once! There was no wind to blow them out. He kept his head to one side to escape the strangling fumes, and held the blazing bunch to the birch bark. As he so held it, he became aware of sensation in his hand. His flesh was burning. He could smell it. Deep down below the surface he could feel it. The sensation developed into pain that grew acute. And still he endured it, holding the flame of the matches clumsily to the bark that would not light readily because his own burning hands were in the way, absorbing most of the flame.

At last, when he could endure no more, he jerked his hands apart. The blazing matches fell sizzling into the snow, but the birch bark was alight. He began laying dry grasses and the tiniest twigs on the flame. He could not pick and choose, for he had to lift the fuel between the heels of his hands. Small pieces of rotten wood and green moss clung to the twigs, and he bit them off as well as he could with his teeth. He cherished the flame carefully and awkwardly. It meant life, and it must not perish. The withdrawal of blood from the surface of his body now made him begin to shiver, and he grew more awkward. A large piece of green moss fell squarely on the little fire. He tried to poke it out with his fingers, but his shivering frame made him poke too far, and he disrupted the nucleus of the little fire, the burning grasses and tiny twigs separating and scattering. He tried to poke them together again, but, in spite of the tenseness of the effort, his shivering got away with him, and the twigs were hopelessly scattered. Each twig gushed a puff of smoke and went out. The fire provider had failed. As he looked apathetically about him, his eyes chanced on the dog, sitting across the ruins of the fire from him, in the snow, making restless, hunching movements, slightly lifting one forefoot and then the other,

shifting its weight back and forth on them with wistful eagerness.

The sight of the dog put a wild idea into his head. He remembered the tale of the man, caught in a blizzard, who killed a steer and crawled inside the carcass, and so was saved. He would kill the dog and bury his hands in the warm body until the numbness went out of them. Then he could build another fire. He spoke to the dog, calling it to him; but in his voice was a strange note of fear that frightened the animal, who had never known the man to speak in such way before. Something was the matter, and its suspicious nature sensed danger — it knew not what danger, but somewhere, somehow, in its brain arose an apprehension of the man. It flattened its ears down at the sound of the man's voice, and its restless, hunching movements and the liftings and shiftings of its forefeet became more pronounced; but it would not come to the man. He got on his hands and knees and crawled toward the dog. This unusual posture again excited suspicion, and the animal sidled mincingly away.

The man sat up in the snow for a moment and struggled for calmness. Then he pulled on his mittens, by means of his teeth, and got upon his feet. He glanced down at first in order to assure himself that he was really standing up, for the absence of sensation in his feet left him unrelated to the earth. His erect position in itself started to drive the webs of suspicion from the dog's mind; and when he spoke peremptorily with the sound of whiplashes in his voice, the dog rendered its customary allegiance and came to him. As it came within reaching distance, the man lost his control. His arms flashed out to the dog, and he experienced genuine surprise when he discovered that his hands could not clutch, that there was neither bend nor feeling in the fingers. He had forgotten for the moment that they were frozen and that they were freezing more and more. All this happened quickly, and before the animal could get away, he encircled its body with his arms. He sat down in the snow, and in this fashion held the dog, while it snarled and whined and struggled.

But it was all he could do, hold its body encircled in his arms and sit there. He realized that he could not kill the dog. There was no way to do it. With his helpless hands he could neither draw nor hold his sheath knife nor throttle the animal. He released it, and it plunged wildly away, with tail between its legs, and still snarling. It halted forty feet away and surveyed him curiously, with ears sharply pricked forward. The man looked down at his hands in order to locate them, and found them hanging on the ends of his arms. It struck him as curious that one should have to use his eyes in order to find out where his hands were. He began threshing his arms back and forth, beating the mittened hands against his sides. He did this for five minutes, violently, and his heart pumped enough blood up to the surface to put a stop to his shivering. But no sensation was aroused in the hands. He had an impression that they hung like weights on the ends of his arms, but when he tried to run the impression down, he could not find it.

A certain fear of death, dull and oppressive, came to him. This fear quickly became poignant as he realized that it was no longer a mere matter of freezing his fingers and toes, or of losing his hands and feet, but that it was a matter of life and death, with the chances against him. This threw him into a panic, and he turned and ran up the creek bed along the old dim trail. The dog joined in behind and kept up with him. He ran blindly, without intention, in fear such as he had never known in his life. Slowly, as he plowed and floundered through the snow, he began to see things again — the banks of the creek, the old timber jams, the leafless aspens,

and the sky. The running made him feel better. He did not shiver. Maybe, if he ran on, his feet would thaw out; and, anyway, if he ran far enough, he would reach the camp and the boys. Without doubt he would lose some fingers and toes and some of his face; but the boys would take care of him, and save the rest of him when he got there. And at the same time there was another thought in his mind that said he would never get to the camp and the boys; that it was too many miles away, that the freezing had too great a start on him, and that he would soon be stiff and dead. This thought he kept in the background and refused to consider. Sometimes it pushed itself forward and demanded to be heard, but he thrust it back and strove to think of other things.

It struck him as curious that he could run at all on feet so frozen that he could not feel them when they struck the earth and took the weight of his body. He seemed to himself to skim along above the surface, and to have no connection with the earth. Somewhere he had once seen a winged Mercury, and he wondered if Mercury felt as he felt when skimming over the earth.

His theory of running until he reached camp and the boys had one flaw in it: he lacked the endurance. Several times he stumbled, and finally he tottered, crumpled up, and fell. When he tried to rise, he failed. He must sit and rest, he decided, and next time he would merely walk and keep on going. As he sat and regained his breath, he noted that he was feeling quite warm and comfortable. He was not shivering, and it even seemed that a warm glow had come to his chest and trunk. And yet, when he touched his nose or cheeks, there was no sensation. Running would not thaw them out. Nor would it thaw out his hands and feet. Then the thought came to him that the frozen portions of his body must be extending. He tried to keep this thought down, to forget it, to think of something else; he was aware of the panicky feeling that it caused, and he was afraid of the panic. But the thought asserted itself, and persisted, until it produced a vision of his body totally frozen. This was too much, and he made another wild run along the trail. Once he slowed down to a walk, but the thought of the freezing extending itself made him run again.

And all the time the dog ran with him, at his heels. When he fell down a second time, it curled its tail over its forefeet and sat in front of him, facing him, curiously eager and intent. The warmth and security of the animal angered him, and he cursed it till it flattened down its ears appeasingly. This time the shivering came more quickly upon the man. He was losing in his battle with the frost. It was creeping into his body from all sides. The thought of it drove him on, but he ran no more than a hundred feet, when he staggered and pitched headlong. It was his last panic. When he had recovered his breath and control, he sat up and entertained in his mind the conception of meeting death with dignity. However, the conception did not come to him in such terms. His idea of it was that he had been making a fool of himself, running around like a chicken with its head cut off — such was the simile that occurred to him. Well, he was bound to freeze anyway, and he might as well take it decently. With this new-found peace of mind came the first glimmerings of drowsiness. A good idea, he thought, to sleep off to death. It was like taking an anesthetic. Freezing was not so bad as people thought. There were lots worse ways to die.

He pictured the boys finding his body next day. Suddenly he found himself with them, coming along the trail and looking for himself. And, still with them, he came around a turn in the trail and found himself lying in the snow. He did not belong with himself any more, for even then he was out of himself standing with the boys and looking at himself in the snow. It certainly was cold, was his thought. When he got back to the States, he could tell the folks what real cold was. He drifted on from this to a vision of the old-timer on Sulfur Creek. He could see him quite clearly, warm and comfortable, and smoking a pipe.

"You were right, old hoss; you were right," the man mumbled to the old-timer of Sulfur Creek.

Then the man drowsed off into what seemed to him the most comfortable and satisfying sleep he had ever known. The dog sat facing him and waiting. The brief day drew to a close in a long, slow twilight. There were no signs of a fire to be made, and, besides, never in the dog's experience had it known a man to sit like that in the snow and make no fire. As the twilight drew on, its eager yearning for the fire mastered it, and with a great lifting and shifting of forefeet, it whined softly, then flattened its ears down in anticipation of being chidden by the man. But the man remained silent. Later, the dog whined loudly. And still later it crept close to the man and caught the scent of death. This made the animal bristle and back away. A little longer it delayed, howling under the stars that leaped and danced and shone brightly in the cold sky. Then it turned and trotted up the trail in the direction of the camp it knew, where were the other food providers and fire providers.

For Discussion of London

1. Very little is said about "the man" in this story; you are not even told his name. Yet the few pieces of information revealed about him are very important. Illustrate this with specific mention of passages from the story.

2. Is the man's lack of imagination a help or hindrance to him in his particular situation? Discuss whether a literal, matter-of-fact mind stands a person in better stead during a crisis than an imaginative, far-roving mind. Try to cite actual occur-

rences to prove your point, or write a story that uses this question as a theme.

3. Suspense depends on uncertainty of outcome. What circumstances at the beginning gave the man confidence that he could make the trip safely? What warnings in the natural surroundings did he fail to heed? At what point does his confidence begin to weaken? At what point in the story are you sure of the outcome? Is it a satisfactory outcome? (Review the matter of story endings in the Guide on page 32.)

4. The dog stands midway between the man and impersonal nature. How does the author use the dog to increase your sense of danger? What does the story suggest about animal instinct as opposed to human instinct? Do you think this conclusion is scientifically sound? Describe the relationship between the dog and the man. Had the dog trusted the man more, would the story have ended differently?

5. Struggle against cold is a particularly dramatic and dangerous part of human existence. How does this story suggest that cold makes a man his own enemy, especially as he nears death? Try to find other stories, both true and fictional, that deal with this subject. Other Jack London stories that show men pitted against the forces of nature can be found in *Children of the Frost, The Call of the Wild,* and *The Sea-Wolf.*

For Your Vocabulary

EXACT MEANING: Having a general idea of the meaning of a word is a help to understanding, but knowing its exact meaning gives you the full power of the word in reading — and the power to use it confidently yourself. Two sensations of the man in London's story are described with words that are particularly expressive, *excruciating* (p. 46) and *poignant* (p. 48). An intensely sharp physical pain is said to be excruciating, or like being crucified. But *poignant,* which literally means " piercing," is used to describe intense emotions more often than physical feeling. Another difference is that although *poignant* is often used of painful feelings, like regret and fear, it can also be used of keenly pleasant feelings, such as *poignant* delight. *Pungent* and *piquant* are two words whose meanings are similar to that of *poignant.* Just how do the *exact* meanings of these three words differ? What is the exact pronunciation of each?

Footfalls

WILBUR DANIEL STEELE
1886–

Wilbur Daniel Steele has probably covered more territory in his life than any other writer represented in this book. Different positions held by his father, a college professor, account for the fact that Wilbur was born in Greensboro, North Carolina, went to kindergarten in Berlin, and attended grade school in Denver. As a young man he had a strong bent toward painting, which took him to Boston, Paris, and New York for study. Then he joined the artists' colony in Provincetown, Massachusetts, at the tip of Cape Cod. This area is the scene of many of his best stories, including " Footfalls." World War I took Steele far afield as a war correspondent — to the coast of the British Isles and France, to Bermuda and North Africa. At the close of the war he began to write stories that won him immediate recognition. In 1922 the O. Henry Memorial Award committee gave him a special prize for having produced the best short fiction in the United States between 1919 and 1921. During the 1920's he was an acknowledged master of the short story in America; in more recent times he has turned to novel writing. "Footfalls" is a typical Steele story, its plot wound tightly like a string, its main character an unforgettable human being.

THIS is not an easy story; not a road for tender or for casual feet. Better the meadows. Let me warn you, it is as hard as that old man's soul and as sunless as his eyes. It has its inception in catastrophe, and its end in an act of almost incredible violence; between them it tells barely how one long blind can become also deaf and dumb.

He lived in one of those old Puritan sea towns where the strain has come down austere and moribund, so that his act would not be quite unbelievable. Except that the town is no longer Puritan and Yankee. It has been betrayed; it has become an outpost of the Portuguese islands.

This man, this blind cobbler himself, was a Portuguese from St. Michael, in the Western Islands, and his name was Boaz Negro.

He was happy. An unquenchable exuberance lived in him. When he arose in the morning he made vast, as it were, uncontrollable, gestures with his stout arms. He came into his shop singing. His voice, strong and deep as the chest from which it emanated, rolled out through the doorway and along the street, and the fishermen, done with their morning work and lounging and smoking along the wharves, said, " Boaz is to work already." Then they came up to sit in the shop.

In that town a cobbler's shop is a club. One sees the interior always dimly thronged. They sit on the benches watching the artisan at his work for hours, and they talk about everything in the world. A cobbler is known by the company he keeps.

Boaz Negro kept young company. He would have nothing to do with the old. On his own head the gray hairs set thickly.

He had a grown son. But the benches in his shop were for the lusty and valiant young, men who could spend the night drinking, and then at three o'clock in the morning turn out in the rain and dark to pull at the weirs, sing songs, buffet one another among the slippery fish in the boat's bottom, and make loud jokes about the fundamental things, love and birth and death. Hearkening to their boasts and strong prophecies, his breast heaved and his heart beat faster. He was a large, full-blooded fellow, fashioned for exploits; the flame in his darkness burned higher even to hear of them.

It is scarcely conceivable how Boaz Negro could have come through this much of his life still possessed of that unquenchable and priceless exuberance; how he would sing in the dawn; how, simply listening to the recital of deeds in gale or brawl, he could easily forget himself a blind man, tied to a shop and a last; easily make of himself a lusty young fellow breasting the sunlit and adventurous tide of life.

He had had a wife, whom he had loved. Fate, which had scourged him with the initial scourge of blindness, had seen fit to take his Angelina away. He had had four sons. Three, one after another, had been removed, leaving only Manuel, the youngest. Recovering slowly, with agony, from each of these recurrent blows, his unquenchable exuberance had lived. And there was another thing quite as extraordinary. He had never done anything but work, and that sort of thing may kill the flame where an abrupt catastrophe fails. Work in the dark. Work, work, work! And accompanied by privation, an almost miserly scale of personal economy. Yes, indeed, he had "skinned his fingers," especially in the earlier years. When it tells most.

How he had worked! Not alone in the daytime, but also sometimes, when orders were heavy, far into the night. It was strange for one, passing along that deserted street at midnight, to hear issuing from the black shop of Boaz Negro the rhythmical tap-tap-tap of hammer on wooden peg.

Nor was that sound all: no man in town could get far past that shop in his nocturnal wandering unobserved. No more than a dozen footfalls, and from the darkness Boaz's voice rolled forth, fraternal, stentorian, "Good night, Antone!" "Good night to you, Caleb Snow!"

To Boaz Negro it was still broad day.

Now, because of this, he was what might be called a substantial man. He owned his place, his shop, opening on the sidewalk, and behind it the dwelling-house with trellised galleries upstairs and down.

And there was always something for his son, a "piece for the pocket," a dollar, five, even a ten-dollar bill if he had "got to have it." Manuel was "a good boy." Boaz not only said this; he felt that he was assured of it in his understanding, to the infinite peace of his heart.

It was curious that he should be ignorant only of the one nearest to him. Not because he was physically blind. Be certain he knew more of other men and of other men's sons than they or their neighbors did. More, that is to say, of their hearts, their understandings, their idiosyncrasies, and their ultimate weight in the balance pan of eternity.

His simple explanation of Manuel was that Manuel "wasn't too stout." To others he said this, and to himself. Manuel was not indeed too robust. How should he be vigorous when he never did anything to make him so? He never

worked. Why should he work, when existence was provided for, and when there was always that "piece for the pocket"? Even a ten-dollar bill on a Saturday night! No, Manuel "wasn't too stout."

In the shop they let it go at that. The missteps and frailties of everyone else in the world were canvassed there with the most shameless publicity. But Boaz Negro was a blind man, and in a sense their host. Those reckless, strong young fellows respected and loved him. It was allowed to stand at that. Manuel was "a good boy." Which did not prevent them, by the way, from joining later in the general condemnation of that father's laxity — "the ruination of the boy!"

"He should have put him to work, that's what."

"He should have said to Manuel, 'Look here, if you want a dollar, go earn it first.'"

As a matter of fact, only one man ever gave Boaz the advice direct. That was Campbell Wood. And Wood never sat in that shop.

In every small town there is one young man who is spoken of as "rising." As often as not he is not a native, but "from away."

In this town Campbell Wood was that man. He had come from another part of the state to take a place in the bank. He lived in the upper story of Boaz Negro's house, the ground floor now doing for Boaz and the meager remnant of his family. The old woman who came in to tidy up for the cobbler looked after Wood's rooms as well.

Dealing with Wood, one had first of all the sense of his incorruptibility. A little ruthless perhaps, as if one could imagine him, in defense of his integrity, cutting off his friend, cutting off his own hand, cutting off the very stream flowing out from the wellsprings of human kindness. An exaggeration, perhaps.

He was by long odds the most eligible young man in town; good-looking in a spare, ruddy, sandy-haired Scottish fashion; important, incorruptible, "rising." But he took good care of his heart. Precisely that; like a sharp-eyed duenna [1] to his own heart. One felt that here was the man, if ever was the man, who held his destiny in his own hand. Failing, of course, some quite gratuitous and unforeseeable catastrophe.

Not that he was not human, or even incapable of laughter or passion. He was, in a way, immensely accessible. He never clapped one on the shoulder; on the other hand, he never failed to speak. Not even to Boaz.

Returning from the bank in the afternoon, he had always a word for the cobbler. Passing out again to supper at his boarding place, he had another, about the weather, the prospects of rain. And if Boaz were at work in the dark when he returned from an evening at the Board of Trade, there was a "Good night, Mr. Negro!"

On Boaz's part, his attitude toward his lodger was curious and paradoxical. He did not pretend to anything less than reverence for the young man's position; precisely on account of that position he was conscious toward Wood of a vague distrust. This was because he was an uneducated fellow.

To the uneducated the idea of large finance is as uncomfortable as the idea of the law. It must be said for Boaz that, responsive to Wood's unfailing civility, he fought against this sensation of dim and somehow shameful distrust.

Nevertheless his whole parental soul was in arms that evening, when, returning from the bank and finding the shop empty of loungers, Wood paused a moment to propose the bit of advice already referred to.

"Haven't you ever thought of having Manuel learn the trade?"

A suspicion, a kind of premonition, lighted the fires of defense.

"Shoemaking," said Boaz, "is good enough for a blind man."

"Oh, I don't know. At least it's better than doing nothing at all."

Boaz's hammer was still. He sat silent, monumental. Outwardly. For once his unfailing response had failed him, "Manuel ain't too stout, you know." Perhaps it had become suddenly inadequate.

He hated Wood; he despised Wood; more than ever before, a hundredfold more, quite abruptly, he distrusted Wood.

How could a man say such things as ·Wood had said? And where Manuel himself might hear!

Where Manuel *had* heard! Boaz's other emotions — hatred and contempt and distrust — were overshadowed. Sitting in darkness, no sound had come to his ears, no footfall, no infinitesimal creaking of a floor plank. Yet by some sixth uncanny sense of the blind he was aware that Manuel was standing in the dusk of the entry joining the shop to the house.

Boaz made a Herculean effort. The voice came out of his throat, harsh, bitter, and loud enough to have carried ten times the distance to his son's ears.

"Manuel is a good boy!"

"Yes — h'm — yes — I suppose so."

Wood shifted his weight. He seemed uncomfortable.

"Well. I'll be running along, I — ugh! Heavens!"

Something was happening. Boaz heard exclamations, breathings, the rustle of sleeve cloth in large, frantic, and futile graspings — all without understanding. Immediately there was an impact on the floor, and with it the unmistakable clink of metal. Boaz even heard that the metal was minted, and that the coins were gold. He understood. A coin sack, gripped not quite carefully enough for a moment under the other's over-

[1] **duenna** (dü·ĕn′á): chaperon.

coat, had shifted, slipped, escaped, and fallen.

And Manuel had heard!

It was a dreadful moment for Boaz, dreadful in its native sense, as full of dread. Why? It was a moment of horrid revelation, ruthless clarification. His son, his link with the departed Angelina, that " good boy " — Manuel, standing in the shadow of the entry, visible alone to the blind, had heard the clink of falling gold, and — *and Boaz wished that he had not!*

There, amazing, disconcerting, destroying, stood the sudden fact.

Sitting as impassive and monumental as ever, his strong, bleached hands at rest on his work, round drops of sweat came out on Boaz's forehead. He scarcely took the sense of what Wood was saying. Only fragments.

" Government money, understand — for the breakwater workings — huge — too many people know here, everywhere — don't trust the safe — tin safe — 'Noah's Ark' — give you my word — Heavens, no! "

It boiled down to this — the money, more money than was good for that antiquated " Noah's Ark " at the bank — and whose contemplated sojourn there overnight was public to too many minds — in short, Wood was not only incorruptible, he was canny. To what one of those minds, now, would it occur that he should take away that money bodily, under casual cover of his coat, to his own lodgings behind the cobbler shop of Boaz Negro? For this one, this important night!

He was sorry the coin sack had slipped, because he did not like to have the responsibility of secret sharer cast upon anyone, even upon Boaz, even by accident. On the other hand, how tremendously fortunate that it had been Boaz and not another. So far as that went, Wood had no more anxiety now than before. One incorruptible knows another.

" I'd trust you, Mr. Negro " (that was one of the fragments which came and stuck in the cobbler's brain), " as far as I would myself. As long as it's only you. I'm just going up here and throw it under the bed. Oh, yes, certainly."

Boaz ate no supper. For the first time in his life food was dry in his gullet. Even under those other successive crushing blows of Fate the full and generous habit of his functionings had carried on unabated; he had always eaten what was set before him. Tonight, over his untouched plate, he watched Manuel with his sightless eyes, keeping track of his every mouthful, word, intonation, breath. What profit he expected to extract from this catlike surveillance it is impossible to say.

When they arose from the supper table Boaz made another Herculean effort: " Manuel, you're a good boy! "

The formula had a quality of appeal, of despair, and of command.

" Manuel, you should be short of money, maybe. Look, what's this? A tenner? Well, there's a piece for the pocket; go and enjoy yourself."

He would have been frightened had Manuel, upsetting tradition, declined the offering. With the morbid contrariness of the human imagination, the boy's avid grasping gave him no comfort.

He went out into the shop, where it was already dark, drew to him his last, his tools, mallets, cutters, pegs, leather. And having prepared to work, he remained idle. He found himself listening.

It has been observed that the large phenomena of sunlight and darkness were nothing to Boaz Negro. A busy night was broad day. Yet there was a difference; he knew it with the blind man's eyes, the ears.

Day was a vast confusion, or rather a wide fabric, of sounds; great and little sounds all woven together, voices, footfalls, wheels, far-off whistles and foghorns, flies buzzing in the sun. Night was another thing. Still there were voices and footfalls, but rarer, emerging from the large, pure body of silence as definite, surprising, and yet familiar entities.

Tonight there was an easterly wind, coming off the water and carrying the sound of waves. So far as other fugitive sounds were concerned it was the same as silence. The wind made little difference to the ears. It nullified, from one direction at least, the other two visual processes of the blind, the sense of touch and the sense of smell. It blew away from the shop, toward the living-house.

As has been said, Boaz found himself listening, scrutinizing with an extraordinary attention, this immense background of sound. He heard footfalls. The story of that night was written, for him, in footfalls.

He heard them moving about the house, the lower floor, prowling here, there, halting for long spaces, advancing, retreating softly on the planks. About this aimless, interminable perambulation there was something to twist the nerves, something led and at the same time driven like a succession of frail and indecisive charges.

Boaz lifted himself from his chair. All his impulse called him to make a stir, join battle, cast in the breach the reinforcement of his presence, authority, good will. He sank back again; his hands fell down. The curious impotence of the spectator held him.

He heard footfalls, too, on the upper floor, a little fainter, borne to the inner rather than the outer ear, along the solid causeway of partitions and floor, the legs of his chair, the bony framework of his body. Very faint indeed. Sinking back easily into the background of the wind. They, too, came and went, this room, that, to the passage, the stairhead, and away. About them, too, there was the same quality of being led and at the same time of being driven.

Time went by. In his darkness it seemed to Boaz that hours must have passed. He heard voices. Together with the footfalls, that abrupt, brief, and (in view of Wood's position) astounding interchange of sentences made up his history of the night. Wood must have opened the door at the head of the stair; by the sound of his voice he would be standing there, peering below perhaps; perhaps listening.

"What's wrong down there?" he called. "Why don't you go to bed?"

After a moment, came Manuel's voice, "Ain't sleepy."

"Neither am I. Look here, do you like to play cards?"

"What kind? Euchre! I like euchre all right. Or pitch."

"Well, what would you say to coming up and having a game of euchre then, Manuel? If you can't sleep?"

"That'd be all right."

The lower footfalls ascended to join the footfalls on the upper floor. There was the sound of a door closing.

Boaz sat still. In the gloom he might have been taken for a piece of furniture, of machinery, an extraordinary lay figure, perhaps, for the trying on of the boots he made. He seemed scarcely to breathe, only the sweat starting from his brow giving him an aspect of life.

He ought to have run, and leaped up that inner stair and pounded with his fists on that door. He seemed unable to move. At rare intervals feet passed on the sidewalk outside, just at his elbow, so to say, and yet somehow, tonight, immeasurably far away. Beyond the orbit of the moon. He heard Rugg, the policeman, noting the silence of the shop, muttering, "Boaz is to bed tonight," as he passed.

The wind increased. It poured against the shop with its deep, continuous sound of a river. Submerged in its body, Boaz caught the note of the town bell striking midnight.

Once more, after a long time, he

heard footfalls. He heard them coming around the corner of the shop from the house, footfalls half swallowed by the wind, passing discreetly, without haste, retreating, merging step by step with the huge, incessant background of the wind.

Boaz's muscles tightened all over him. He had the impulse to start up, to fling open the door, shout into the night, "What are you doing? Stop there! Say! What are you doing and where are you going?"

And as before, the curious impotence of the spectator held him motionless. He had not stirred in his chair. And those footfalls, upon which hinged, as it were, that momentous decade of his life, were gone.

There was nothing to listen for now. Yet he continued to listen. Once or twice, half arousing himself, he drew toward him his unfinished work. And then relapsed into immobility.

As has been said, the wind, making little difference to the ears, made all the difference in the world with the sense of feeling and the sense of smell. From the one important direction of the house. That is how it could come about that Boaz Negro could sit, waiting and listening to nothing in the shop and remain ignorant of disaster until the alarm had gone away and come back again, pounding, shouting, clanging.

"Fire!" he heard them bawling in the street. "Fire! Fire!"

Only slowly did he understand that the fire was in his own house.

There is nothing stiller in the world than the skeleton of a house in the dawn after a fire. It is as if everything living, positive, violent, had been completely drained in the one flaming act of violence, leaving nothing but negation till the end of time. It is worse than a tomb. A monstrous stillness! Even the footfalls of the searchers cannot disturb it, for they are separate and superficial. In its presence they are almost frivolous.

Half an hour after dawn the searchers found the body, if what was left from that consuming ordeal might be called a body. The discovery came as a shock. It seemed incredible that the occupant of that house, no cripple or invalid but an able man in the prime of youth, should not have awakened and made good his escape. It was the upper floor which had caught; the stairs had stood to the last. It was beyond calculation. Even if he had been asleep!

And he had not been asleep. This second and infinitely more appalling discovery began to be known. Slowly. By a hint, a breath of rumor here; there an allusion, half taken back. The man, whose incinerated body still lay curled in its bed of cinders, had been dressed at the moment of disaster; even to the watch, the cuff buttons, the studs, the very scarf pin. Fully clothed to the last detail, precisely as those who had dealings at the bank might have seen Campbell Wood any weekday morning for the past eight months. A man does not sleep with his clothes on. The skull of the man had been broken, as if with a blunt instrument of iron. On the charred lacework of the floor lay the leg of an old andiron with which Boaz Negro and his Angelina had set up housekeeping in that new house.

It needed only Mr. Asa Whitelaw, coming up the street from that gaping "Noah's Ark" at the bank, to round out the scandalous circle of circumstance.

"Where is Manuel?"

Boaz Negro still sat in his shop, impassive, monumental, his thick, hairy arms resting on the arms of his chair. The tools and materials of his work remained scattered about him, as his irresolute gathering of the night before had left them. Into his eyes no change could come. He had lost his house, the visible monument of all those years of "skinning his fingers." It would seem that he had lost his son. And he had

lost something incalculably precious —
that hitherto unquenchable exuberance
of the man.

"Where is Manuel?"

When he spoke his voice was unaccented and stale, like the voice of a man
already dead.

"Yes, where is Manuel?"

He had answered them with their
own question.

"When did you last see him?"

Neither he nor they seemed to take
note of that profound irony.

"At supper."

"Tell us, Boaz; you knew about this
money?"

The cobbler nodded his head.

"And did Manuel?"

He might have taken sanctuary in a
legal doubt. How did he know what
Manuel knew? Precisely! As before, he
nodded his head.

"After supper, Boaz, you were in the
shop? But you heard something?"

He went on to tell them what he had
heard: the footfalls, below and above,
the extraordinary conversation which
had broken for a moment the silence of
the inner hall. The account was bare,
the phrases monosyllabic. He reported
only what had been registered on the
sensitive tympanums of his ears, to the
last whisper of footfalls stealing past
the dark wall of the shop. Of all the
formless tangle of thoughts, suspicions,
interpretations, and the special and personal knowledge given to the blind
which moved in his brain, he said nothing.

He shut his lips there. He felt himself
on the defensive. Just as he distrusted
the higher ramifications of finance (his
house had gone down uninsured), so
before the rites and processes of that
inscrutable creature, the Law, he felt
himself menaced by the invisible and
the unknown, helpless, oppressed; in an
abject sense, skeptical.

"Keep clear of the Law!" they had
told him in his youth. The monster his
imagination had summoned up then
still stood beside him in his age.

Having exhausted his monosyllabic
and superficial evidence, they could
move him no farther. He became deaf
and dumb. He sat before them, an image cast in some immensely heavy stuff,
inanimate. His lack of visible emotion
impressed them. Remembering his exuberance, it was only the stranger to
see him unmoving and unmoved. Only
once did they catch sight of something
beyond. As they were preparing to leave
he opened his mouth. What he said was
like a swan song to the years of his exuberant happiness. Even now there was
no color of expression in his words,
which sounded mechanical.

"Now I have lost everything. My
house. My last son. Even my honor.
You would not think I would like to live.
But I go to live. I go to work. That
cachorra, one day he shall come back
again, in the dark night, to have a look.
I shall go to show you all. That *cachorra!*"

(And from that time on, it was noted,
he never referred to the fugitive by any
other name than *cachorra,* which is a
kind of dog. "That *cachorra!*" As if he
had forfeited the relationship not only
of the family, but of the very genus, the
very race! "That *cachorra!*")

He pronounced this resolution without passion. When they assured him
that the culprit would come back again
indeed, much sooner than he expected,
"with a rope around his neck," he shook
his head slowly.

"No, you shall not catch that *cachorra* now. But one day —"

There was something about its very
colorlessness which made it sound oracular. It was at least prophetic. They
searched, laid their traps, proceeded
with all their placards, descriptions, rewards, clues, trails. But on Manuel Negro they never laid their hands.

Months passed and became years. Boaz Negro did not rebuild his house. He

might have done so, out of his earnings, for upon himself he spent scarcely anything, reverting to his old habit of almost miserly economy. Yet perhaps it would have been harder after all. For his earnings were less and less. In that town a cobbler who sits in an empty shop is apt to want for trade. Folk take their boots to mend where they take their bodies to rest and their minds to be edified.

No longer did the walls of Boaz's shop resound to the boastful recollections of young men. Boaz had changed. He had become not only different, but opposite. A metaphor will do best. The spirit of Boaz Negro had been a meadowed hillside giving upon the open sea, the sun, the warm, wild winds from beyond the blue horizon. And covered with flowers, always hungry and thirsty for the sun and the fabulous wind and bright showers of rain. It had become an intrenched camp, lying silent, sullen, verdureless, under a gray sky. He stood solitary against the world. His approaches were closed. He was blind, and he was also deaf and dumb.

Against that what can young fellows do who wish for nothing but to rest themselves and talk about their friends and enemies? They had come and they had tried. They had raised their voices even higher than before. Their boasts had grown louder, more presumptuous, more preposterous, until, before the cold separation of that unmoving and as if contemptuous presence in the cobbler's chair, they burst of their own air, like toy balloons. And they went and left Boaz alone.

There was another thing which served, if not to keep them away, at least not to entice them back. That was the aspect of the place. It was not cheerful. It invited no one. In its way that fire-bitten ruin grew to be almost as great a scandal as the act itself had been. It was plainly an eyesore. A valuable property, on the town's main thoroughfare — and an eyesore! The neighboring owners protested.

Their protestations might as well have gone against a stone wall. That man was deaf and dumb. He had become, in a way, a kind of vegetable, for the quality of a vegetable is that, while it is endowed with life, it remains fixed in one spot. For years Boaz was scarcely seen to move foot out of that shop that was left him, a small, square, blistered promontory on the shores of ruin.

He must indeed have carried out some rudimentary sort of domestic program under the debris at the rear (he certainly did not sleep or eat in the shop). One or two lower rooms were left fairly intact. The outward aspect of the place was formless; it grew to be no more than a mound in time; the charred timbers, one or two still standing, lean and naked against the sky, lost their blackness and faded to a silvery gray. It would have seemed strange, had they not grown accustomed to the thought, to imagine that blind man, like a mole, or some slow slug, turning himself mysteriously in the bowels of that gray mound — that time-silvered " eyesore."

When they saw him, however, he was in the shop. They opened the door to take in their work (when other cobblers turned them off), and they saw him seated in his chair in the half-darkness, his whole person, legs, torso, neck, head, as motionless as the vegetable of which we have spoken — only his hands and his bare arms endowed with visible life. The gloom had bleached the skin to the color of damp ivory, and against the background of his immobility they moved with a certain amazing monstrousness, interminably. No, they were never still. One wondered what they could be at. Surely he could not have had enough work now to keep those insatiable hands so monstrously in motion. Even far into the night. Tap-tap-tap! Blows continuous and powerful. On

what? On nothing? On the bare iron
last? And for what purpose? To what
conceivable end?

Well, one could imagine those arms,
growing paler, also growing thicker and
more formidable with that unceasing labor; the muscles feeding themselves,
omnivorously on their own waste, the
cords toughening, the bone tissues revi-
talizing themselves without end. One
could imagine the whole aspiration of
that mute and motionless man pouring
itself out into those pallid arms, and the
arms taking it up with a kind of blind
greed. Storing it up. Against a day!

" That *cachorra!* One day — "

What were the thoughts of this man?
What moved within that motionless cra-
nium covered with long hair? Who can
say? Behind everything, of course, stood
that bitterness against the world — the
blind world — blinder than he would
ever be. And against " that *cachorra*."
But this was no longer a thought; it was
the man.

Just as all muscular aspiration flowed
into his arms, so all the energies of his
senses turned to his ears. The man had
become, you might say, two arms and
two ears. Can you imagine a man listening, intently, through the waking hours
of nine years?

Listening to footfalls. Marking with
a special emphasis of concentration the
beginning, rise, full passage, falling
away, and dying of all footfalls. By day,
by night, winter and summer and winter again. Unraveling the skein of footfalls passing up and down the street!

For three years he wondered when
they would come. For the next three
years he wondered if they would ever
come. It was during the last three that
a doubt began to trouble him. It gnawed
at his huge moral strength. Like a hidden seepage of water, it undermined (in
anticipation) his terrible resolution. It
was a sign, perhaps of age, a slipping
away of the reckless infallibility of
youth.

Supposing, after all, that his ears
should fail him. Supposing they were
capable of being tricked, without his
being able to know it. Supposing that
that *cachorra* should come and go, and
he, Boaz, living in some vast delusion,
some unrealized distortion of memory,
should let him pass unknown. Supposing precisely this thing had already happened!

Or the other way around. What if he
should hear the footfalls coming, even
into the very shop itself? What if he
should be as sure of them as of his own
soul? What, then, if he should strike?
And what then, if it were not that *cachorra* after all? How many tens and
hundreds of millions of people were
there in the world? Was it possible for
them all to have footfalls distinct and
different?

Then they would take him and hang
him. And that *cachorra* might then come
and go at his own will, undisturbed.

As he sat there sometimes the sweat
rolled down his nose, cold as rain.

Supposing!

Sometimes, quite suddenly, in broad
day, in the booming silence of the night,
he would start. Not outwardly. But beneath the pale integument of his skin
all his muscles tightened and his nerves
sang. His breathing stopped. It seemed
almost as if his heart stopped.

What was it? Were those the feet,
there emerging faintly from the distance? Yes, there was something about
them. Yes! Memory was in travail. Yes,
yes, yes! No! How could he be sure? Ice
ran down into his empty eyes. The footfalls were already passing. They were
gone, swallowed up already by time and
space. Had that been that *cachorra?*

Nothing in his life has been so hard
to meet as this insidious drain of distrust in his own powers; this sense of a
traitor within the walls. His iron-gray
hair had turned white. It was always
this now, from the beginning of the day
to the end of the night: how was he to

know? How was he to be inevitably, unshakably, sure?

Curiously, after all this purgatory of doubts, he did know them. For a moment at least, when he had heard them, he was sure. It was on an evening of the winter holidays, the Portuguese festival of *Menin' Jesus*. Christ was born again in a hundred mangers on a hundred tiny altars; there was cake and wine; songs went shouting by to the accompaniment of mandolins and tramping feet. The wind blew cold under a clear sky. In all the houses there were lights; even in Boaz Negro's shop a lamp was lit just now, for a man had been in for a pair of boots which Boaz had patched. The man had gone out again. Boaz was thinking of blowing out the light. It meant nothing to him.

He leaned forward, judging the position of the lamp chimney by the heat on his face, and puffed out his cheeks to blow. Then his cheeks collapsed suddenly, and he sat back again.

It was not odd that he had failed to hear the footfalls until they were actually within the door. A crowd of merrymakers was passing just then; their songs and tramping almost shook the shop.

Boaz sat back. Beneath his passive exterior his nerves thrummed; his muscles had grown as hard as wood. Yes! Yes! But no! He had heard nothing; no more than a single step, a single foot-pressure on the planks within the door. Dear God! He could not tell!

Going through the pain of an enormous effort, he opened his lips.

" What can I do for you? "

" Well, I — I don't know. To tell the truth — "

The voice was unfamiliar, but it might be assumed. Boaz held himself. His face remained blank, interrogating, slightly helpless.

" I am a little deaf," he said. " Come nearer."

The footfalls came halfway across the intervening floor, and there appeared to hesitate. The voice, too, had a note of uncertainty.

" I was just looking around. I have a pair of — well, you mend shoes? "

Boaz nodded his head. It was not in response to the words, for they meant nothing. What he had heard was the footfalls on the floor.

Now he was sure. As has been said, for a moment at least after he had heard them he was unshakably sure. The congestion of his muscles had passed. He was at peace.

The voice became audible once more. Before the massive preoccupation of the blind man it became still less certain of itself.

" Well, I haven't got the shoes with me. I was — just looking around."

It was amazing to Boaz, this miraculous sensation of peace.

" Wait! " Then, bending his head as if listening to the winter wind, " It's cold tonight. You've left the door open. But wait! " Leaning down, his hand fell on a rope's end hanging by the chair. The gesture was one continuous, undeviating movement of the hand. No hesitation. No groping. How many hundreds, how many thousands of times, had his hand schooled itself in that gesture!

A single strong pull. With a little *bang* the front door had swung to and latched itself. Not only the front door. The other door, leading to the rear, had closed, too, and latched itself with a little *bang*. And leaning forward from his chair, Boaz blew out the light.

There was not a sound in the shop. Outside, feet continued to go by, ringing on the frozen road; voices were lifted; the wind hustled about the corners of the wooden shell with a continuous, shrill note of whistling. All of this outside, as on another planet. Within the blackness of the shop the complete silence persisted.

Boaz listened. Sitting on the edge of his chair, half crouching, his head, with its long, unkempt, white hair, bent slightly to one side, he concentrated upon this chambered silence the full power of his senses. He hardly breathed. The other person in that room could not be breathing at all, it seemed.

No, there was not a breath, not the stirring of a sole on wood, not the infinitesimal rustle of any fabric. It was as if, in this utter stoppage of sound, even the blood had ceased to flow in the veins and arteries of that man, who was like a rat caught in a trap.

It was appalling even to Boaz; even to the cat. Listening became more than a labor. He began to have a fight against a growing impulse to shout out loud, to leap, sprawl forward without aim in that unstirred darkness — do something. Sweat rolled down from behind his ears, into his shirt collar. He gripped the chair arms. To keep quiet he sank his teeth into his lower lip. He would not! He would not!

And of a sudden he heard before him, in the center of the room, an outburst of breath, an outrush from lungs in the extremity of pain, thick, laborious, fearful. A coughing up of dammed air.

Pushing himself from the arms of the chair, Boaz leaped.

His fingers, passing swiftly through the air, closed on something. It was a sheaf of hair, bristly and thick. It was a man's beard.

On the road outside, up and down the street for a hundred yards, merrymaking people turned to look at one another. With an abrupt cessation of laughter, of speech. Inquiringly. Even with an unconscious dilation of the pupils of their eyes.

" What was that? "

There had been a scream. There could be no doubt of that. A single, long-drawn note. Immensely high-pitched. Not as if it were human.

" Did you hear! What was it? Where'd it come from? "

Those nearest said it came from the cobbler shop of Boaz Negro.

They went and tried the door. It was closed; even locked, as if for the night. There was no light behind the window shade. But Boaz would not have a light. They beat on the door. No answer.

But from where, then, had that prolonged, as if animal, note come?

They ran about, penetrating into the side lanes, interrogating, prying. Coming back at last, inevitably, to the neighborhood of Boaz Negro's shop.

The body lay on the floor at Boaz's feet, where it had tumbled down slowly after a moment from the spasmodic embrace of his arms; those ivory-colored arms which had beaten so long upon the bare iron surface of the last. Blows continuous and powerful. It seemed incredible. They were so weak now. They could not have lifted the hammer now.

But that beard! That bristly, thick, square beard of a stranger!

His hands remembered it. Standing with his shoulders fallen forward and his weak arms hanging down, Boaz began to shiver. The whole thing was incredible. What was on the floor there, upheld in the vast gulf of darkness, he could not see. Neither could he hear it; smell it. Nor (if he did not move his foot) could he feel it. What he did not hear, smell, or touch did not exist. It was not there. Incredible!

But that beard! All the accumulated doubtings of those years fell down upon him. After all, the thing he had been so fearful of in his weak imaginings had happened. He had killed a stranger. He, Boaz Negro, had murdered an innocent man!

And all on account of that beard. His deep panic made him lightheaded. He began to confuse cause and effect. If it were not for that beard, it would have been that *cachorra*.

On this basis he began to reason with a crazy directness. And to act. He went and pried open the door into the entry. From a shelf he took down his razor. A big, heavy-heeled strop. His hands began to hurry. And the mug, half full of soap. And water. It would have to be cold water. But after all, he thought (lightheadedly), at this time of night —

Outside, they were at the shop again. The crowd's habit is to forget a thing quickly, once it is out of sight and hearing. But there had been something about that solitary cry which continued to bother them, even in memory. Where had it been? Where had it come from? And those who had stood nearest the cobbler shop were heard again. They were certain now, dead certain. They could swear!

In the end they broke down the door. If Boaz heard them he gave no sign. An absorption as complete as it was monstrous wrapped him. Kneeling in the glare of the lantern they had brought, as impervious as his own shadow sprawling behind him, he continued to shave the dead man on the floor.

No one touched him. Their minds and imaginations were arrested by the gigantic proportions of the act. The unfathomable presumption of the act. As throwing murder in their faces to the tune of a jig in a barbershop. It is a fact that none of them so much as thought of touching him. No less than all of them, together with all other men, shorn of their imaginations — that is to say, the expressionless and imperturbable creature of the Law — would be sufficient to touch that ghastly man.

On the other hand, they could not leave him alone. They could not go away. They watched. They saw the damp, lather-soaked beard of that victimized stranger falling away, stroke by stroke of the flashing, heavy razor. The dead denuded by the blind!

It was seen that Boaz was about to speak. It was something important he was about to utter; something, one would say, fatal. The words would not come all at once. They swelled his cheeks out. His razor was arrested.

Lifting his face, he encircled the watchers with a gaze at once of imploration and of command. As if he could see them. As if he could read his answer in the expressions of their faces.

"Tell me one thing now. Is it that *cachorra?* "

For the first time those men in the room made sounds. They shuffled their feet. It was as if an uncontrollable impulse to ejaculation, laughter, derision, forbidden by the presence of death, had gone down into their boot soles.

"Manuel? " one of them said. "You mean *Manuel?* "

Boaz laid the razor down on the floor beside its work. He got up from his knees slowly, as if his joints hurt. He sat down in his chair, rested his hands on the arms, and once more encircled the company with his sightless gaze.

"Not Manuel. Manuel was a good boy. But tell me now, is it that *cachorra?* "

Here was something out of their calculations; something for them, mentally, to chew on. Mystification is a good thing sometimes. It gives to the brain a fillip, stirs memory, puts the gears of imagination in mesh. One man, an old, tobacco-chewing fellow, began to stare harder at the face on the floor. Something moved in his intellect.

"No, but look here now, do you — "

He had even stopped chewing. But he was forestalled by another.

"Say now, if it don't look like that fellow Wood, himself. The bank fellow — that was burned — remember? Himself."

"That *cachorra* was not burned. Not that Wood. You darned fool! "

Boaz spoke from his chair. They hardly knew his voice, emerging from its long silence: it was so didactic and arid.

"That *cachorra* was not burned. It was my boy that was burned. It was that *cachorra* called my boy upstairs. That *cachorra* killed my boy. That *cachorra* put his clothes on my boy, and he set my house on fire. I knew that all the time. Because when I heard those feet come out of my house and go away, I knew they were the feet of that *cachorra* from the bank. I did not know where he was going to. Something said to me — you better ask him where he is going to. But then I said, you are foolish. He had the money from the bank. I did not know. And then my house was on fire. No, it was not my boy that went away; it was that *cachorra* all the time. You darned fools! Did you think I was waiting for my own boy?

"Now I show you all," he said at the end. "And now I can get hanged."

No one ever touched Boaz Negro for that murder. For murder it was in the eye and letter of the Law. The Law in a small town is sometimes a curious creature; it is sometimes blind only in one eye.

Their minds and imaginations in that town were arrested by the romantic proportions of the act. Simply, no one took it up. I believe the man, Wood, was understood to have died of heart failure.

When they asked Boaz why he had not told what he knew as to the identity of that fugitive in the night, he seemed to find it hard to say exactly. How could a man of no education define for them his own but half-defined misgivings about the Law, his sense of oppression, constraint, and awe, of being on the defensive, even, in an abject way, his skepticism? About his wanting, come what might, to "keep clear of the Law"?

He did say this, "You would have laughed at me."

And this, "If I told folks it was Wood went away, then I say he would not dare come back again."

That was the last. Very shortly he began to refuse to talk about the thing at all. The act was completed. Like the creature of fable, it had consumed itself. Out of that old man's consciousness it had departed. Amazingly. Like a dream dreamed out.

Slowly at first, in a makeshift, piece-at-a-time, poor man's way, Boaz commenced to rebuild his house. That "eyesore" vanished.

And slowly at first, like the miracle of a green shoot pressing out from the dead earth, that priceless and unquenchable exuberance of the man was seen returning. Unquenchable, after all.

For Discussion of Steele

1. "Footfalls" is a masterpiece of close-knit storytelling. How closely did you follow the development of character and the clues to the action?

a. Where did you run across the phrase "unquenchable exuberance" in the story? What is the meaning of the phrase as applied to Boaz Negro?

b. In what way do you learn that Boaz recognizes people by their footfalls? Why is this fact important to the story?

c. What is your first impression of Wood? What word is several times applied to Wood? Considering Wood's real character, why does the author overemphasize this word?

d. Notice that at a certain point you begin to learn of the events of the story chiefly through Boaz's hearing. What is the first instance of Boaz's hearing a sound that is important? How does the author explain the failure of Boaz to realize that the house was on fire? Why is this a necessary element in the story?

e. Why did Boaz give a brief and inadequate account of Manuel's disappearance to the townspeople? What is the effect of his always using the word *cachorra* to refer to the culprit?

f. Were you prepared for the ending? If you thought that Manuel was guilty, what led you to this opinion?

2. "Footfalls" lends itself well to dramatizing as a radio script. Parcel out assignments of writing, directing, and acting for presentation of the story before the school assembly.

3. Define from context the following words in the story: *moribund* (p. 51), *weirs* (p. 51), *stentorian* (p. 52), *fillip* (p. 62), *perambulation* (p. 55).

Two Soldiers

WILLIAM FAULKNER
1897–

Since childhood William Faulkner has lived in the town of Oxford, Mississippi, which appears under the name "Jefferson" in many of his stories. He comes from a wealthy old Southern family that was left in comparative poverty for several generations after the War between the States. Consequently his schooling was irregular and his only advanced education was an occasional course at the University of Mississippi at Oxford. When World War I broke out, he joined the Canadian Air Force and saw action in France. On his return he wrote a novel that no publisher would accept because of its involved style and unusual method of jumbling the characters' thoughts as if they were constantly thinking aloud without any particular direction. This was the "stream of consciousness" technique which was later acclaimed as an exciting way of telling a story, but Faulkner was ahead of his time.

Gradually his novels won readers, though Faulkner was, and still is, severely criticized by some for his emphasis on violence and social decay. Many critics have long considered him America's leading novelist, but only recently has he been recognized widely. In 1951 he became the fifth American to receive the Nobel Prize for Literature.

"Two Soldiers" is a typical Faulkner story in some ways: it is laid in the Mississippi farm country, and it is written in the language of uneducated characters. Telling the story from the point of view of a young boy is a favorite device of this author. There is little opening description or explanation by the author. You are plunged at once into action. And while the story has its harsh side, it affirms, as do most Faulkner stories, that courage and loyalty are two of the qualities that make life worth living.

ME AND Pete would go down to Old Man Killegrew's and listen to his radio. We would wait until after supper, after dark, and we would stand outside Old Man Killegrew's parlor window, and we could hear it because Old Man Killegrew's wife was deaf, and so he run the radio as loud as it would run, and so me and Pete could hear it plain as Old Man Killegrew's wife could, I reckon, even standing outside with the window closed.

And that night I said, "What? Japanese? What's a pearl harbor?" and Pete said, "Hush."

And so we stood there, it was cold, listening to the fellow in the radio talking, only I couldn't make no heads nor tails out of it. Then the fellow said that would be all for a while, and me and Pete walked back up the road to home, and Pete told me what it was. Because he was nigh twenty and he had done finished the Consolidated [1] last June and he knowed a heap: about them Japanese dropping bombs on Pearl Harbor and that Pearl Harbor was across the water.

[1] **Consolidated:** the consolidated high school.

"Across what water?" I said. "Across that Government reservoy up at Oxford?"

"Naw," Pete said. "Across the big water. The Pacific Ocean."

We went home. Maw and pap was already asleep and me and Pete laid in bed, and I still couldn't understand where it was, and Pete told me again — the Pacific Ocean.

"What's the matter with you?" Pete said. "You're going on nine years old. You been in school now ever since September. Ain't you learned nothing yet?"

"I reckon we ain't got as fer as the Pacific Ocean yet," I said.

We was still sowing the vetch [1] then that ought to been all finished by the fifteenth of November, because pap was still behind, just like he had been ever since me and Pete had knowed him. And we had firewood to git in, too, but every night me and Pete would go down to Old Man Killegrew's and stand outside his parlor window in the cold and listen to his radio; then we would come back home and lay in bed and Pete would tell me what it was. That is, he would tell me for a while. Then he wouldn't tell me. It was like he didn't want to talk about it no more. He would tell me to shut up because he wanted to go to sleep, but he never wanted to go to sleep.

He would lay there, a heap stiller than if he was asleep, and it would be something, I could feel it coming out of him, like he was mad at me, or like he was worried about something, and it wasn't that neither, because he never had nothing to worry about. He never got behind like pap, let alone stayed behind. Pap give him ten acres when he graduated from the Consolidated, and me and Pete both reckoned pap was durn glad to get shut of at least ten acres, less to have to worry about himself; and Pete had them ten acres all

[1] **vetch:** a plant of the same family as peas and beans, used as a winter cover crop.

sowed to vetch and busted out and bedded for the winter, and so it wasn't that. But it was something. And still we would go down to Old Man Killegrew's every night and listen to his radio, and they was at it in the Philippines now, but General MacArthur was holding um. Then we would come back home and lay in the bed, and Pete wouldn't tell me nothing or talk at all. He would just lay there still as an ambush and when I would touch him, his side or his leg would feel hard and still as iron, until after a while and I would go to sleep.

Then one night — it was the first time he had said nothing to me except to jump on me about not chopping enough wood at the wood tree where he was cutting — he said, "I got to go."

"Go where?" I said.

"To that war," Pete said.

"Before we even finish gettin' in the firewood?"

"Firewood, heck," Pete said.

"All right," I said. "When we going to start?"

But he wasn't even listening. He laid there, hard and still as iron in the dark. "I got to go," he said. "I jest ain't going to put up with no folks treating the Unity States that way."

"Yes," I said. "Firewood or no firewood, I reckon we got to go."

This time he heard me. He laid still again, but it was a different kind of still.

"You?" he said. "To a war?"

"You'll whup the big uns and I'll whup the little uns," I said.

Then he told me I couldn't go. At first I thought he just never wanted me tagging after him, like he wouldn't leave me go with him when he went sparking them girls of Tull's. Then he told me the Army wouldn't leave me go because I was too little, and then I knowed he really meant it and that I couldn't go nohow noways. And somehow I hadn't believed until then that he was going himself, but now I knowed he was and that he wasn't going to leave me go with him a-tall.

"I'll chop the wood and tote the water for you-all then!" I said. "You got to have wood and water!"

Anyway, he was listening to me now. He wasn't like iron now.

He turned onto his side and put his hand on my chest because it was me that was laying straight and hard on my back now.

"No," he said. "You got to stay here and help pap."

"Help him what?" I said. "He ain't never caught up nohow. He can't get no further behind. He can sholy take care of this little shirttail of a farm while me and you are whupping them Japanese. I got to go too. If you got to go, then so have I."

"No," Pete said. "Hush now. Hush." And he meant it, and I knowed he did. Only I made sho from his own mouth. I quit.

"So I just can't go then," I said.

"No," Pete said. "You just can't go. You're too little, in the first place, and in the second place —"

"All right," I said. "Then shut up and leave me to go to sleep."

So he hushed then and laid back. And I laid there like I was already asleep, and pretty soon he was asleep and I knowed it was the wanting to go to the war that had worried him and kept him awake, and now that he had decided to go, he wasn't worried any more.

The next morning he told maw and pap. Maw was all right. She cried.

"No," she said, crying, "I don't want him to go. I would rather go myself in his place, if I could. I don't want to save the country. Them Japanese could take it all and keep it, so long as they left me and my family and my children alone. But I remember my brother Marsh in that other war. He had to go to that one when he wasn't but nineteen and our mother couldn't understand it then any more than I can now. But she

told Marsh if he had to go, he had to go. And so, if Pete's got to go to this one, he's got to go to it. Jest don't ask me to understand why."

But pap was the one. He was the feller. "To the war?" he said. "Why I don't see a bit of use in that. You ain't old enough for the draft, and the country ain't being invaded. Our President in Washington, D.C., is watching the conditions and he will notify us. Besides, in that other war your ma just mentioned, I was drafted and sent clean to Texas and was held there nigh eight months until they finally quit fighting. It seems to me that that, along with your Uncle Marsh who received a actual wound on the battlefields of France, is enough for me and mine to have to do to protect the country, at least in my lifetime. Besides, what'll I do for help on the farm with you gone? It seems to me I'll get mighty far behind."

"You been behind as long as I can remember," Pete said. "Anyway I'm going. I got to."

"Of course he's got to go," I said. "Them Japanese —"

"You hush your mouth!" maw said, crying. "Nobody's talking to you! Go and get ma a armful of wood! That's what you can do!"

So I got the wood. And all the next day, while me and Pete and pap was getting in as much wood as we could in that time because Pete said how pap's idea of plenty of wood was one more stick laying against the wall that maw ain't put on the fire yet, maw was getting Pete ready to go. She washed and mended his clothes and cooked him a shoe box of vittles. And that night me and Pete laid in the bed and listened to her packing his grip and crying, until after a while Pete got up in his night-shirt and went back there, and I could hear them talking, until at last maw said, "You ought to go, and so I want you to go. But I don't understand it, and I won't never, and so don't expect me to." And Pete come back and got into bed again and laid again still and hard as iron on his back, and then he said, and he wasn't talking to me, he wasn't talking to nobody: "I got to go. I just got to."

"Sho you got to," I said. "Them Japanese —" He turned over hard, he kind of surged over onto his side, looking at me in the dark.

"Anyway, you're all right," he said. "I expected to have more trouble with you than with all the rest of them put together."

"I reckon I can't help it neither," I said. "But maybe it will run a few years longer and I can get there. Maybe someday I will jest walk in on you."

"I hope not," Pete said. "Folks don't go to wars for fun. A man don't leave his maw crying just for fun."

"Then why are you going?" I said.

"I got to," he said. "I just got to. Now you go on to sleep. I got to ketch that early bus in the morning."

"All right," I said, "I hear tell Memphis is a big place. How will you find where the Army's at?"

"I'll ask somebody where to go to join it," Pete said. "Go on to sleep now."

"Is that what you'll ask for? Where to join the Army?" I said.

"Yes," Pete said. He turned onto his back again. "Shut up and go to sleep."

We went to sleep. The next morning we et breakfast by lamplight because the bus would pass at six o'clock. Maw wasn't crying now. She jest looked grim and busy, putting breakfast on the table while we et it. Then she finished packing Pete's grip, except he never wanted to take no grip to the war, but maw said decent folks never went nowhere, not even to a war, without a change of clothes and something to tote them in. She put in the shoe box of fried chicken and biscuits and she put the Bible in, too, and then it was time to go. We didn't know until then that maw wasn't going to the bus. She jest brought Pete's cap and overcoat, and still she didn't cry no more, she jest stood with her hands on Pete's shoulders and she didn't move, but somehow, and just holding Pete's shoulders, she looked as hard and fierce as when Pete had turned toward me in the bed last night and tole me that anyway I was all right.

"They could take the country and keep the country, as long as they never bothered me and mine," she said. Then she said, "Don't never forget who you are. You ain't rich and the rest of the world outside of Frenchman's Bend never heard of you. But your blood is good as any blood anywhere, and don't you never forget it."

Then she kissed him, and then we was out of the house, with pap toting Pete's grip whether Pete wanted him to or not. There wasn't no dawn even yet, not even after we had stood on the highway by the mailbox, awhile. Then we seen the lights of the bus coming and I was watching the bus until it come up and Pete flagged it, and then, sho enough, there was daylight — it had started while I wasn't watching. And now me and Pete expected pap to say something else foolish, like he done before, about how Uncle Marsh getting wounded in France and that trip to Texas pap had taken in 1918 ought to be enough to save the Unity States in 1942, but he never. He done all right too. He jest said, "Good-by, son. Always remember what your ma told you and write her whenever you find the time." Then he shaken Pete's hand, and Pete looked at me for a minute and put his hand on my head and rubbed my head durn nigh hard enough to wring my neck off and jumped into the bus, and the feller wound the door shut and the bus begun to hum; then it was moving, humming and grinding and whining louder and louder; it was going fast, with two little red lights behind it that never seemed to get no littler, but jest seemed to be running together until pretty soon they would touch and jest be one light. But they never did, and then the bus was gone, and even like it was, I could have pretty nigh busted out crying, nigh to nine years old and all.

Me and pap went back to the house. All that day we worked at the wood tree, and so I never had no good chance until about middle of the afternoon. Then I taken my slingshot and I would have liked to took all my bird eggs, too, because Pete had give me his collection and he holp me with mine, and he would like to git the box out and look at them as good as I would, even if he was nigh twenty years old. But the box was too big to tote a long ways and have to worry with, so I just taken the shike-poke egg, because it was the best un, and wropped it up good into a match-box and hid it and the slingshot under the corner of the barn. Then we et supper and went to bed, and I thought then how if I would 'a' had to stayed in that room and that bed like that even for one more night, I jest couldn't 'a' stood it. Then I could hear pap snoring, but I never heard no sound from maw, whether she was asleep or not, and I don't reckon she was. So I taken my shoes and drapped them out the window, and then I clumb out like I used to watch Pete do when he was still jest seventeen and pap wouldn't leave him out, and I put on my shoes and went to the barn and got the slingshot and the shikepoke egg and went to the highway.

It wasn't cold, it was jest durn confounded dark, and that highway stretched on in front of me like, without nobody using it, it had stretched out half again as fer just like a man does when he lays down, so that for a time it looked like full sun was going to ketch me before I had finished them twenty-two miles to Jefferson. But it didn't. Daybreak was jest starting when I walked up the hill into town. I could smell breakfast cooking in the cabins

and I wished I had thought to brought me a cold biscuit, but that was too late now. And Pete had told me Memphis was a piece beyond Jefferson, but I never knowed it was no eighty miles. So I stood there on that empty square, with daylight coming and coming and the street lights still burning and that Law [1] looking down at me, and me still eighty miles from Memphis, and it had took me all night to walk jest twenty-two miles, and so, by the time I got to Memphis at that rate, Pete would 'a' done already started for Pearl Harbor.

"Where do you come from?" the Law said. And I told him again. "I got to git to Memphis. My brother's there."

"You mean you ain't got any folks around here?" the Law said. "Nobody but that brother? What are you doing way off down here and your brother in Memphis?"

And I told him again, "I got to git to Memphis. I ain't got no time to waste talking about it and I ain't got time to walk it. I got to git there today."

"Come on here," the Law said.

We went down another street. And there was the bus, jest like when Pete got into it yestiddy morning, except there wasn't no lights on it now and it was empty. There was a regular bus dee-po like a railroad dee-po, with a ticket counter and a feller behind it, and the Law said, "Set down over there," and I set down on the bench, and the Law said, "I want to use your telephone," and he talked into the telephone a minute and put it down and said to the feller behind the ticket counter, "Keep your eye on him. I'll be back as soon as Mrs. Habersham can arrange to get herself up and dressed." He went out. I got up and went to the ticket counter.

"I want to go to Memphis," I said.

"You bet," the feller said. "You set down on the bench now. Mr. Foote will be back in a minute."

[1] **Law:** policeman.

A long walk on a country road. (Armstrong Roberts)

"I don't know no Mr. Foote," I said. "I want to ride that bus to Memphis."

"You got some money?" he said. "It'll cost seventy-two cents."

I taken out the matchbox and unwropped the shikepoke egg. "I'll swap you this for a ticket to Memphis," I said.

"What's that?" he said.

"It's a shikepoke egg," I said. "You never seen one before. It's worth a dollar. I'll take seventy-two cents fer it."

"No," he said, "the fellers that own that bus insist on a cash basis. If I started swapping tickets for bird eggs and livestock and such, they would fire me. You go and set down on the bench now, like Mr. Foote —"

I started for the door, but he caught me, he put one hand on the ticket counter and jumped over it and caught up with me and reached his hand out to ketch my shirt. I whupped out my pocketknife and snapped it open.

"You put a hand on me and I'll cut it off," I said.

I tried to dodge him and run at the door, but he could move quicker than any grown man I ever see, quick as Pete almost. He cut me off and stood with his back against the door and one foot raised a little, and there wasn't no other way to get out. "Get back on that bench and stay there," he said.

And there wasn't no other way out. And he stood against the door. So I went back to the bench. And then it seemed like to me that dee-po was full of folks. There was that Law again, and there was two ladies in fur coats and their faces already painted. But they still looked like they had got up in a hurry and they still never liked it, a old one and a young one, looking down at me.

"He hasn't got an overcoat!" the old one said. "How in the world did he ever get down here by himself?"

"I ask you," the Law said. "I couldn't get nothing out of him except his brother is in Memphis and he wants to get back up there."

"That's right," I said. "I got to git to Memphis today."

"Of course you must," the old one said. "Are you sure you can find your brother when you get to Memphis?"

"I reckon I can," I said. "I ain't got but one and I have knowed him all my life. I reckon I will know him again when I see him."

The old one looked at me. "Somehow he doesn't look like he lives in Memphis," she said.

"He probably don't," the Law said. "You can't tell though. He might live anywhere, overhalls or not. This day and time they get scattered overnight from hope to breakfast; boys and girls, too, almost before they can walk good. He might have been in Missouri or Texas either yestiddy, for all we know. But he don't seem to have any doubt his brother is in Memphis. All I know to do is send him up there and leave him look."

"Yes," the old one said.

The young one set down on the bench by me and opened a hand satchel and taken out a artermatic writing pen and some papers.

"Now, honey," the old one said, "we're going to see that you find your brother, but we must have a case history for our files first. We want to know you name and your brother's name and where you were born and when your parents died."

"I don't need no case history neither," I said. "All I want is to git to Memphis. I got to git there today."

"You see?" the Law said. He said it almost like he enjoyed it. "That's what I told you."

"You're lucky, at that, Mrs. Habersham," the bus feller said. "I don't think he's got a gun on him, but he can open that knife fast enough to suit any man."

But the old one just stood there looking at me.

"Well," she said. "Well. I really don't know what to do."

"I do," the bus feller said. "I'm going to give him a ticket out of my own pocket, as a measure of protecting the company against riot and bloodshed. And when Mr. Foote tells the city board about it, it will be a civic matter and they will give me a medal too. Hey, Mr. Foote?"

But nobody paid him no mind. The old one still stood looking down at me. She said "Well," again. Then she taken a dollar from her purse and give it to the bus feller. "I suppose he will travel on a child's ticket, won't he?"

"Wellum," the bus feller said, "I just don't know what the regulations would be. Likely I will be fired for not crating him and marking the crate Poison. But I'll risk it."

Then they were gone. Then the Law come back with a sandwich and give it to me.

"You're sure you can find that brother?" he said.

"I ain't yet convinced why not," I said. "If I don't see Pete first, he'll see me. He knows me too."

Then the Law went out for good, too, and I et the sandwich. Then more folks come in and bought tickets, and then the bus feller said it was time to go, and I got into the bus just like Pete done, and we were gone.

I seen all the towns. I seen all of them. When the bus got to going good, I found out I was jest about wore out for sleep. But there was too much I hadn't never saw before. We run out of Jefferson and run past fields and woods, then we would run into another town and out of that un and past fields and woods again, and then into another town with stores and gins [1] and water tanks, and we run along by the railroad for a spell and I seen the signal arm move, and then some more towns, and I was jest about

plumb wore out for sleep, but I couldn't resk it. Then Memphis begun. It seemed like, to me, it went on for miles. We would pass a patch of stores and I would think that was sholy it and the bus would even stop. But it wouldn't be Memphis yet and we would go on again past water tanks and smokestacks on top of the mills, and if they was gins and sawmills, I never knowed there was that many and I never seen any that big, and where they got enough cotton and logs to run um I don't know.

Then I seen Memphis. I knowed I was right this time. It was standing up into the air. It looked like about a dozen whole towns bigger than Jefferson was set up on one edge in a field, standing up into the air higher than ara [2] hill in all Yoknapatawpha County. Then we was in it, with the bus stopping every few feet, it seemed like to me, and cars rushing past on both sides of it and the streets crowded with folks from ever'-where in town that day, until I didn't see how there could 'a' been nobody left in Mis'sippi a-tall to even sell me a bus ticket, let alone write out no case histories. Then the bus stopped. It was another bus dee-po, a heap bigger than the one in Jefferson. And I said, "All right. Where do folks join the Army?"

"What?" the bus feller said.

And I said it again, "Where do folks join the Army?"

"Oh," he said. Then he told me how to get there. I was afraid at first I wouldn't ketch on how to do in a town as big as Memphis. But I caught on all right. I never had to ask but twice more. Then I was there, and I was durn glad to git out of all them rushing cars and shoving folks and all that racket fer a spell, and I thought, it won't be long now, and I thought how if there was any kind of a crowd there that had done already joined the Army, too, Pete would likely see me before I seen him. And so I walked into the room.

[1] gins: machines for separating cotton lint from the seeds.

[2] ara: any.

And Pete wasn't there.

He wasn't even there. There was a soldier with a big arrerhead on his sleeve, writing, and two fellers standing in front of him, and there was some more folks there, I reckon. It seems to me I remember some more folks there.

I went to the table where the soldier was writing, and I said, "Where's Pete?" and he looked up and I said, "My brother. Pete Grier. Where is he?"

"What?" the soldier said. "Who?"

And I told him again. "He joined the Army yestiddy. He's going to Pearl Harbor. So am I. I want to ketch him. Where you-all got him?" Now they were all looking at me, but I never paid them no mind. "Come on," I said. "Where is he?"

The soldier had quit writing. He had both hands spraddled out on the table. "Oh," he said. "You're going, too, hah?"

"Yes," I said. "They got to have wood and water. I can chop it and tote it. Come on. Where's Pete?"

The soldier stood up. "Who let you in here?" he said. "Go on. Beat it."

"Durn that," I said. "You tell me where Pete —"

I be dog if he couldn't move faster than the bus feller even. He never come over the table, he come around it, he was on me almost before I knowed it, so that I jest had time to jump back and whup out my pocketknife and snap it open and hit one lick, and he hollered and jumped back and grabbed one hand with the other and stood there cussing and hollering.

One of the other fellers grabbed me from behind, and I hit at him with the knife, but I couldn't reach him.

Then both of the fellers had me from behind, and then another soldier come out of a door at the back. He had on a belt with a britching strop [1] over one

---

[1] **britching strop:** part of a rude harness — the boy's impression of a Sam Browne belt.

shoulder.

"What's this?" he said.

"That little son cut me with a knife!" the first soldier hollered. When he said that I tried to git at him again, but both them fellers was holding me, two against one, and the soldier with the backing strop said, "Here, here. Put your knife up, feller. None of us are armed. A man don't knife-fight folks that are bare-handed." I could begin to hear him then. He sounded jest like Pete talked to me. "Let him go," he said. They let me go. "Now what's all the trouble about?" And I told him. "I see," he said. "And you come up to see if he was all right before he left."

"No," I said. "I came to —"

But he had already turned to where the first soldier was wropping a handkerchief around his hand.

"Have you got him?" he said. The first soldier went back to the table and looked at some papers.

"Here he is," he said. "He enlisted yestiddy. He's in a detachment leaving this morning for Little Rock." He had a watch stropped on his arm. He looked at it. "The train leaves in about fifty minutes. If I know country boys, they're probably all down there at the station right now."

"Get him up here," the one with the backing strop said. "Phone the station. Tell the porter to get him a cab. And you come with me," he said.

It was another office behind that un, with jest a table and some chairs. We set there while the soldier smoked, and it wasn't long; I knowed Pete's feet soon as I heard them. Then the first soldier opened the door and Pete come in. He never had no soldier clothes on. He looked jest like he did when he got on the bus yestiddy morning, except it seemed to me like it was at least a week, so much had happened, and I had done had to do so much traveling. He come in and there he was, looking at me like he hadn't never left home, except that here we was in Memphis, on the way to Pearl Harbor.

"What in durnation are you doing here?" he said.

And I told him, "You got to have wood and water to cook with. I can chop it and tote it for you-all."

"No," Pete said. "You're going back home."

"No, Pete," I said. "I got to go too. I got to. It hurts my heart, Pete."

"No," Pete said. He looked at the soldier. "I jest don't know what could have happened to him, lootenant," he said. "He never drawed a knife on anybody before in his life."

He looked at me. "What did you do it for?"

"I don't know," I said. "I jest had to. I jest had to git here. I jest had to find you."

"Well, don't you never do it again, you hear?" Pete said. "You put that knife in your pocket and you keep it there. If I ever again hear of you drawing it on anybody, I'm coming back from wherever I am at and whup the fire out of you. You hear me?"

"I would pure cut a throat if it would bring you back to stay," I said. "Pete," I said. "Pete."

"No," Pete said. Now his voice wasn't hard and quick no more, it was almost quiet, and I knowed now I wouldn't never change him. "You must go home. You must look after maw, and I am depending on you to look after my ten acres. I want you to go back home. To-day. Do you hear?"

"I hear," I said.

"Can he get back home by himself?" the soldier said.

"He come up here by himself," Pete said.

"I can get back, I reckon," I said. "I don't live in but one place. I don't reckon it's moved."

Pete taken a dollar out of his pocket and give it to me. "That'll buy your bus ticket right to our mailbox," he said. "I want you to mind the lootenant. He'll send you to the bus. And you go back home and you take care of maw and look after my ten acres and keep that durn knife in your pocket. You hear me?"

"Yes, Pete," I said.

"All right," Pete said. "Now I got to go." He put his hand on my head again. But this time he never wrung my neck. He just laid his hand on my head a minute. And then I be dog if he didn't lean down and kiss me, and I heard his feet and then the door, and I never looked up and that was all, me setting there, rubbing the place where Pete kissed me and the soldier throwed back in his chair, looking out the window and coughing. He reached into his pocket and handed something to me without looking around. It was a piece of chewing gum.

"Much obliged," I said. "Well, I reckon I might as well start back. I got a right fer [1] piece to go."

"Wait," the soldier said. Then he telephoned again and I said again I better start back, and he said again, "Wait. Remember what Pete told you."

So we waited, and then another lady come in, old, too, in a fur coat, too, but she smelled all right, she never had no artermatic writing pen nor no case history neither. She come in and the soldier got up, and she looked around quick until she saw me, and come and put her hand on my shoulder light and quick and easy as maw herself might 'a' done it.

"Come on," she said. "Let's go home to dinner."

"Nome," [2] I said. "I got to ketch the bus to Jefferson."

"I know. There's plenty of time. We'll go home and eat dinner first."

[1] fer: far.
[2] "Nome": contraction of "no ma'am."

She had a car. And now we was right down in the middle of all them other cars. We was almost under the busses, and all them crowds of people on the street close enough to where I could have talked to them if I had knowed who they was. After a while she stopped the car. "Here we are," she said, and I looked at it, and if all that was her house, she sho had a big family. But all of it wasn't. We crossed a hall with trees growing in it and went into a little room without nothing in it but a Negro dressed up in a uniform a heap shinier than them soldiers had, and the Negro shut the door, and then I hollered, "Look out!" and grabbed, but it was all right; that whole little room jest went right on up and stopped and the door opened and we was in another hall, and the lady unlocked a door and we went in, and there was another soldier, an old feller, with a britching strop, too, and a silver-colored bird on each shoulder.

"Here we are," the lady said. "This is Colonel McKellogg. Now, what would you like for dinner?"

"I reckon I'll jest have some ham and eggs and coffee," I said.

She had done started to pick up the telephone. She stopped. "Coffee?" she said. "When did you start drinking coffee?"

"I don't know," I said. "I reckon it was before I could remember."

"You're about eight, aren't you?" she said.

"Nome," I said. "I'm eight and ten months. Going on eleven months."

She telephoned then. Then we set there and I told them how Pete had jest left that morning for Pearl Harbor and I had aimed to go with him, but I would have to go back home to take care of maw and look after Pete's ten acres, and she said how they had a little boy about my size, too, in a school in the East. Then a Negro, another one, in a short kind of shirttail coat, rolled a kind

of wheelbarrer in. It had my ham and eggs and a glass of milk and a piece of pie, too, and I thought I was hungry. But when I taken the first bite I found out I couldn't swallow it, and I got up quick.

"I got to go," I said.

"Wait," she said.

"I got to go," I said.

"Just a minute," she said. "I've already telephoned for the car. It won't be but a minute now. Can't you drink the milk even? Or maybe some of your coffee?"

"Nome," I said. "I ain't hungry. I'll eat when I git home." Then the telephone rung. She never even answered it.

"There," she said. "There's the car." And we went back down in that 'ere little moving room with the dressed-up Negro. This time it was a big car with a soldier driving it. I got into the front with him. She give the soldier a dollar. "He might get hungry," she said. "Try to find a decent place for him."

"O.K., Mrs. McKellogg," the soldier said.

Then we was gone again. And now I could see Memphis good, bright in the sunshine, while we was swinging around it. And the first thing I knowed, we was back on the same highway the bus run on this morning — the patches of stores and them big gins and sawmills, and Memphis running on for miles, it seemed like to me, before it begun to give out. Then we was running again between the fields and woods, running fast now, and except for that soldier, it was like I hadn't never been to Memphis a-tall. We was going fast now. At this rate, before I knowed it we would be home again, and I thought about me riding up to Frenchman's Bend in this here big car with a soldier running it, and all of a sudden I begun to cry. I never knowed I was fixing to, and I couldn't stop it. I set there by that soldier, crying. We was going fast.

For Discussion of Faulkner

1. In this story we see everything through the boy's eyes, but as older persons we can interpret what he sees in our own terms. For instance, who were the ladies in the bus depot who tried to get his case history? What sort of home did the lady who invited him to dinner in Memphis live in? What was the little room that went up? Can you give other examples of your seeing over and above the boy's understanding?

2. List the boy's chief traits. Do you find him likable? Is he typical of small boys you have observed, or is he in any way unique? Is the relation between the boy and his older brother natural or forced? What point of character does the boy have in common with Boaz Negro in " Footfalls "?

3. What difference was there in the way the older brother said good-by at home and in Memphis? What was the reason for this difference? What kind of person is the older brother?

4. Think back on your own childhood and recall an incident when you rebelled against the ways of the grown-up world. Write an account of the incident as it seemed to you then, without bringing in your later understanding of the situation.

Split Cherry Tree

JESSE STUART
1907–

Both his personal sincerity and his knowledge of his native Kentucky impress the readers of Jesse Stuart's stories. He came from a farm family, none of whom had ever had a high-school education. But Jesse, who always wanted to be a writer, made every sacrifice to attend school and college. He even lived at times on one meal a day, and worked variously as a steel laborer, quarryman, and hired farm hand. Upon graduation, he took over the management of a county school system, which he found was involved in innumerable lawsuits.

Life was far from easy for him, but he gathered power from his difficulties. His poems, some of which were first composed on scraps of paper and tobacco leaves while he was plowing, and his many stories of Kentucky farmers and hunters make him one of America's leading regional writers. His *Taps for Private Tussie* sold a half-million copies and introduced a new type of humor into American fiction. In the recent autobiographical novel *The Thread That Runs So True*, he tells of his early career as a schoolteacher, when he was actually younger than some of his students. " Split Cherry Tree " is partly autobiographical, too. The boy and Professor Herbert might both be Stuart himself, at different ages.

I DON'T mind staying after school," I says to Professor Herbert, " but I'd rather you'd whip me with a switch and let me go home early. Pa will whip me anyway for getting home two hours late."

"You are too big to whip," says Professor Herbert, " and I have to punish you for climbing up in that cherry tree. You boys knew better than that! The other five boys have paid their dollar each. You have been the only one who has not helped pay for the tree. Can't you borrow a dollar?"

"I can't," I says. "I'll have to take the punishment. I wish it would be quicker punishment. I wouldn't mind."

Professor Herbert stood and looked at me. He was a big man. He wore a gray suit of clothes. The suit matched his gray hair.

"You don't know my father," I says to Professor Herbert. "He might be called a little old-fashioned. He makes us mind him until we're twenty-one years old. He believes: 'If you spare the rod you spoil the child.' I'll never be able to make him understand about the cherry tree. I'm the first of my people to go to high school."

"You must take the punishment," says Professor Herbert. "You must stay two hours after school today and two hours after school tomorrow. I am allowing you twenty-five cents an hour. That is good money for a high-school student. You can sweep the schoolhouse floor, wash the blackboards, and clean windows. I'll pay the dollar for you."

I couldn't ask Professor Herbert to loan me a dollar. He never offered to loan it to me. I had to stay and help the janitor and work out my fine at a quarter an hour.

I thought as I swept the floor, "What will Pa do to me? What lie can I tell him when I go home? Why did we ever climb that cherry tree and break it down for anyway? Why did we run crazy over the hills away from the crowd? Why did we do all of this? Six of us climbed up in a little cherry tree after one little lizard! Why did the tree split and fall with us? It should have been a stronger tree! Why did Eif Crabtree just happen to be below us plowing and catch us in his cherry tree? Why

wasn't he a better man than to charge us six dollars for the tree?"

It was six o'clock when I left the schoolhouse. I had six miles to walk home. It would be after seven when I got home. I had all my work to do when I got home. It took Pa and me both to do the work. Seven cows to milk. Nineteen head of cattle to feed, four mules, twenty-five hogs, firewood and stove-wood to cut, and water to draw from the well. He would be doing it when I got home. He would be mad and wondering what was keeping me!

I hurried home. I would run under the dark, leafless trees. I would walk fast uphill. I would run down the hill. The ground was freezing. I had to hurry. I had to run. I reached the long ridge that led to our cow pasture. I ran along this ridge. The wind dried the sweat on my face. I ran across the pasture to the house.

I threw down my books in the chipyard. I ran to the barn to spread fodder on the ground for the cattle. I didn't take time to change my clean school clothes for my old work clothes. I ran out to the barn. I saw Pa spreading fodder on the ground to the cattle. That was my job. I ran up to the fence. I says, "Leave that for me, Pa. I'll do it. I'm just a little late."

"I see you are," says Pa. He turned and looked at me. His eyes danced fire. "What in th' world has kept you so? Why ain't you been here to help me with this work? Make a gentleman out'n one boy in th' family and this is what you get! Send you to high school and you get too onery fer th' buzzards to smell!"

I never said anything. I didn't want to tell why I was late from school. Pa stopped scattering the bundles of fodder. He looked at me. He says, "Why are you gettin' in here this time o' night? You tell me or I'll take a hickory withe to you right here on th' spot!"

I says, "I had to stay after school." I

couldn't lie to Pa. He'd go to school and find out why I had to stay. If I lied to him it would be too bad for me.

"Why did you haf to stay atter school?" says Pa.

I says, "Our biology class went on a field trip today. Six of us boys broke down a cherry tree. We had to give a dollar apiece to pay for the tree. I didn't have the dollar. Professor Herbert is making me work out my dollar. He gives me twenty-five cents an hour. I had to stay in this afternoon. I'll have to stay in tomorrow afternoon!"

"Are you telling me th' truth?" says Pa.

"I'm telling you the truth," I says. "Go and see for yourself."

"That's jist what I'll do in th' mornin'," says Pa. "Jist whose cherry tree did you break down?"

"Eif Crabtree's cherry tree!"

"What was you doin' clear out in Eif Crabtree's place?" says Pa. "He lives four miles from th' county high school. Don't they teach you no books at that high school? Do they jist let you get out and gad over th' hillsides? If that's all they do I'll keep you at home, Dave. I've got work here fer you to do!"

"Pa," I says, "spring is just getting here. We take a subject in school where we have to have bugs, snakes, flowers, lizards, frogs, and plants. It is biology. It was a pretty day today. We went out to find a few of these. Six of us boys saw a lizard at the same time sunning on a cherry tree. We all went up the tree to get it. We broke the tree down. It split at the forks. Eif Crabtree was plowing down below us. He ran up the hill and got our names. The other boys gave their dollar apiece. I didn't have mine. Professor Herbert put mine in for me. I have to work it out at school."

"Poor man's son, huh," says Pa. "I'll attend to that myself in th' mornin'. I'll take keer o' 'im. He ain't from this county nohow. I'll go down there in th' mornin' and see 'im. Lettin' you leave your books and galavant all over th' hills. What kind of a school is it nohow! Didn't do that, my son, when I's a little shaver in school. All fared alike too."

"Pa, please don't go down there," I says, "just let me have fifty cents and pay the rest of my fine! I don't want you to go down there! I don't want you to start anything with Professor Herbert!"

"Ashamed of your old Pap are you, Dave," says Pa, "atter th' way I've worked to raise you! Tryin' to send you to school so you can make a better livin' than I've made.

"I'll straighten this thing out myself! I'll take keer o' Professor Herbert myself! He ain't got no right to keep you in and let the other boys off jist because they've got th' money! I'm a poor man. A bullet will go in a professor same as it will any man. It will go in a rich man same as it will a poor man. Now you get into this work before I take one o' these withes and cut the shirt off'n your back!"

I thought once I'd run through the woods above the barn just as hard as I could go. I thought I'd leave high school and home forever! Pa could not catch me! I'd get away! I couldn't go back to school with him. He'd have a gun and maybe he'd shoot Professor Herbert. It was hard to tell what he would do. I could tell Pa that school had changed in the hills from the way it was when he was a boy, but he wouldn't understand. I could tell him we studied frogs, birds, snakes, lizards, flowers, insects. But Pa wouldn't understand. If I did run away from home it wouldn't matter to Pa. He would see Professor Herbert anyway. He would think that high school and Professor Herbert had run me away from home. There was no need to run away. I'd just have to stay, finish foddering the cattle, and go to school with Pa the next morning.

I would take a bundle of fodder, remove the hickory-withe band from around it, and scatter it on rocks, clumps of green briers, and brush so the cattle wouldn't tramp it under their feet. I would lean it up against the oak trees and the rocks in the pasture just above our pigpen on the hill. The fodder was cold and frosty where it had set out in the stacks. I would carry bundles of the fodder from the stack until I had spread out a bundle for each steer. Pa went to the barn to feed the mules and throw corn in the pen to the hogs.

The moon shone bright in the cold March sky. I finished my work by moonlight. Professor Herbert really didn't know how much work I had to do at home. If he had known he would not have kept me after school. He would have loaned me a dollar to have paid my part on the cherry tree. He had never lived in the hills. He didn't know the way the hill boys had to work so that they could go to school. Now he was teaching in a county high school where all the boys who attended were from hill farms.

After I'd finished doing my work I went to the house and ate my supper. Pa and Mom had eaten. My supper was getting cold. I heard Pa and Mom talking in the front room. Pa was telling Mom about me staying in after school.

"I had to do all th' milkin' tonight, chop th' wood myself. It's too hard on me atter I've turned ground all day. I'm goin' to take a day off tomorrow and see if I can't remedy things a little. I'll go down to that high school tomorrow. I won't be a very good scholar fer Professor Herbert nohow. He won't keep me in atter school. I'll take a different kind of lesson down there and make 'im acquainted with it."

"Now, Luster," says Mom, "you jist stay away from there. Don't cause a lot o' trouble. You can be jailed fer a trick like that. You'll get th' Law atter you. You'll jist go down there and show off and plague your own boy Dave to death in front o' all th' scholars!"

"Plague or no plague," says Pa, "he don't take into consideration what all I haf to do here, does he? I'll show 'im it ain't right to keep one boy in and let the rest go scot free. My boy is good as th' rest, ain't he? A bullet will make a hole in a schoolteacher same as it will anybody else. He can't do me that way and get by with it. I'll plug 'im first. I aim to go down there bright and early in the mornin' and get all this straight! I aim to see about bug larnin' and this runnin' all over God's creation huntin' snakes, lizards, and frogs. Ransackin' th' country and goin' through cherry orchards and breakin' th' trees down atter lizards! Old Eif Crabtree ought to a-poured th' hot lead to 'em instead o' chargin' six dollars fer th' tree! He ought to a-got old Herbert th' first one!"

I ate my supper. I slipped upstairs and lit the lamp. I tried to forget the whole thing. I studied plane geometry. Then I studied my biology lesson. I could hardly study for thinking about Pa. "He'll go to school with me in the morning. He'll take a gun for Professor Herbert! What will Professor Herbert think of me! I'll tell him when Pa leaves that I couldn't help it. But Pa might shoot him. I hate to go with Pa. Maybe he'll cool off about it tonight and not go in the morning."

Pa got up at four o'clock. He built a fire in the stove. Then he built a fire in the fireplace. He got Mom up to get breakfast. Then he got me up to help feed and milk. By the time we had our work done at the barn, Mom had breakfast ready for us. We ate our breakfast. Daylight came and we could see the bare oak trees covered white with frost. The hills were white with frost. A cold wind was blowing. The sky was clear. The sun would soon come out and melt the frost. The afternoon would be warm with sunshine and the frozen ground with thaw. There would be mud on the hills again. Muddy water would then run down the little ditches on the hills.

"Now, Dave," says Pa, "let's get ready fer school. I aim to go with you this mornin' and look into bug larnin', frog larnin', lizard and snake larnin', and breakin' down cherry trees! I don't like no sicha foolish way o' larnin' myself!"

Pa hadn't forgot. I'd have to take him to school with me. He would take me to school with him. We were going early. I was glad we were going early. If Pa pulled a gun on Professor Herbert there wouldn't be so many of my classmates there to see him.

I knew that Pa wouldn't be at home in the high school. He wore overalls, big boots, a blue shirt and a sheepskin coat and a slouched black hat gone to seed at the top. He put his gun in its holster. We started trudging toward the high school across the hill.

It was early when we got to the county high school. Professor Herbert had just got there. I just thought as we walked up the steps into the schoolhouse, "Maybe Pa will find out Professor Herbert is a good man. He just doesn't know him. Just like I felt toward the Lambert boys across the hill. I didn't like them until I'd seen them and talked to them. After I went to school with them and talked to them, I liked them and we were friends. It's a lot in knowing the other fellow."

"You're th' Professor here, ain't you?" says Pa.

"Yes," says Professor Herbert, "and you are Dave's father."

"Yes," says Pa, pulling out his gun and laying it on the seat in Professor Herbert's office. Professor Herbert's eyes got big behind his black-rimmed glasses when he saw Pa's gun. Color came into his pale cheeks.

"Jist a few things about this school I want to know," says Pa. "I'm tryin' to make a scholar out'n Dave. He's the only one out'n eleven youngins I've sent to high school. Here he comes in late and leaves me all th' work to do! He said you's all out bug huntin' yesterday and broke a cherry tree down. He had to stay two hours atter school yesterday and work out money to pay on that cherry tree! Is that right?"

"Wwwwy," says Professor Herbert, "I guess it is."

He looked at Pa's gun.

"Well," says Pa, "this ain't no high school. It's a bug school, a lizard school, a snake school! It ain't no school nohow!"

"Why did you bring that gun?" says Professor Herbert to Pa.

"You see that little hole," says Pa as he picked up the long blue forty-four and put his finger on the end of the barrel, "a bullet can come out'n that hole that will kill a schoolteacher same as it will any other man. It will kill a rich man same as a poor man. It will kill a man. But atter I come in and saw you, I know'd I wouldn't need it. This maul o' mine could do you up in a few minutes."

Pa stood there, big, hard, brown-skinned, and mighty beside of Professor Herbert. I didn't know Pa was so much bigger and harder. I'd never seen Pa in a schoolhouse before. I'd seen Professor Herbert. He'd aways looked big before to me. He didn't look big standing beside of Pa.

"I was only doing my duty," says Professor Herbert, "Mr. Sexton, and following the course of study the state provided us with."

"Course o' study," says Pa, "what study, bug study? Varmint study? Takin' youngins to th' woods and their poor old Ma's and Pa's at home a-slavin' to keep 'em in school and give 'em a education! You know that's dangerous, too, puttin' a lot o' boys and girls out together like that!"

Students were coming into the schoolhouse now.

Professor Herbert says, "Close the door, Dave, so others won't hear."

I walked over and closed the door. I

was shaking like a leaf in the wind. I thought Pa was going to hit Professor Herbert every minute. He was doing all the talking. His face was getting red. The red color was coming through the brown, weather-beaten skin on Pa's face.

"I was right with these students," says Professor Herbert. "I know what they got into and what they didn't. I didn't send one of the other teachers with them on this field trip. I went myself. Yes, I took the boys and girls together. Why not?"

"It jist don't look good to me," says Pa, "a-takin' all this swarm of youngins out to pillage th' whole deestrict. Breakin' down cherry trees. Keepin' boys in atter school."

"What else could I have done with Dave, Mr. Sexton?" says Professor Herbert. "The boys didn't have any business all climbing that cherry tree after one lizard. One boy could have gone up in the tree and got it. The farmer charged us six dollars. It was a little steep, I think, but we had it to pay. Must I make five boys pay and let your boy off? He said he didn't have the dollar and couldn't get it. So I put it in for him. I'm letting him work it out. He's not working for me. He's working for the school!"

"I jist don't know what you could a-done with 'im," says Pa, "only a-larruped 'im with a withe! That's what he needed!"

"He's too big to whip," says Professor Herbert, pointing at me. "He's a man in size."

"He's not too big fer me to whip," says Pa. "They ain't too big until they're over twenty-one! It jist didn't look fair to me! Work one and let th' rest out because they got th' money. I don't see what bugs has got to do with a high school! It don't look good to me no-how!"

Pa picked up his gun and put it back in its holster. The red color left Profes-sor Herbert's face. He talked more to Pa. Pa softened a little. It looked funny to see Pa in the high-school building. It was the first time he'd ever been there.

"We were not only hunting snakes, toads, flowers, butterflies, lizards," says Professor Herbert, "but, Mr. Sexton, I was hunting dry timothy grass to put in an incubator and raise some protozoa."

"I don't know what that is," says Pa. "Th' incubator is th' new-fangled way o' cheatin' th' hens and raisin' chickens. I ain't so sure about th' breed o' chickens you mentioned."

"You've heard of germs, Mr. Sexton, haven't you?" says Professor Herbert.

"Jist call me Luster, if you don't mind," says Pa, very casual-like.

"All right, Luster, you've heard of germs, haven't you?"

"Yes," says Pa, "but I don't believe in germs. I'm sixty-five years old and I ain't seen one yet!"

"You can't see them with your naked eye," says Professor Herbert. "Just keep that gun in the holster and stay with me in the high school today. I have a few things I want to show you. That scum on your teeth has germs in it."

"What," says Pa, "you mean to tell me I've got germs on my teeth!"

"Yes," says Professor Herbert. "The same kind as we might be able to find in a living black snake if we dissect it!"

"I don't mean to dispute your word," says Pa, "but I don't believe it. I don't believe I have germs on my teeth!"

"Stay with me today and I'll show you. I want to take you through the school anyway! School has changed a lot in the hills since you went to school. I don't guess we had high schools in this county when you went to school!"

"No," says Pa, "jist readin', writin', and cipherin'. We didn't have all this bug larnin', frog larnin', and findin' germs on your teeth and in the middle o' black snakes! Th' world's changin'."

"It is," says Professor Herbert, "and we hope all for the better. Boys like your own there are going to help change it. He's your boy. He knows all of what I've told you. You stay with me today."

"I'll shore stay with you," says Pa. "I want to see th' germs off'n my teeth. I jist want to see a germ. I've never seen one in my life. 'Seein' is believin',' Pap allus told me."

Pa walks out of the office with Professor Herbert. I just hoped Professor Herbert didn't have Pa arrested for pulling his gun. Pa's gun has always been a friend to him when he goes to settle disputes.

The bell rang. School took up. I saw the students when they marched in the schoolhouse look at Pa. They would grin and punch each other. Pa just stood and watched them pass in at the schoolhouse door. Two long lines marched in the house. The boys and girls were clean and well dressed. Pa stood over in the schoolyard under a leafless elm, in his sheepskin coat, his big boots laced in front with buckskin, and his heavy socks stuck above his boot tops. Pa's overalls legs were baggy and wrinkled between his coat and boot tops. His blue work shirt showed at the collar. His big black hat showed his gray-streaked black hair. His face was hard and weather-tanned to the color of a ripe fodder blade. His hands were big and gnarled like the roots of the elm tree he stood beside.

When I went to my first class I saw Pa and Professor Herbert going around over the schoolhouse. I was in my geometry class when Pa and Professor Herbert came in the room. We were explaining our propositions on the blackboard. Professor Herbert and Pa just quietly came in and sat down for a while. I heard Fred Wurts whisper to Glenn Armstrong, "Who is that old man? Lord, he's a rough-looking scamp." Glenn whispered back, "I think he's Dave's Pap." The students in geometry looked at Pa. They must have wondered what he was doing in school.

Before the class was over, Pa and Professor Herbert got up and went out. I saw them together down on the playground. Professor Herbert was explaining to Pa. I could see the prints of Pa's gun under his coat when he'd walk around.

At noon in the high-school cafeteria Pa and Professor Herbert sat together at the little table where Professor Herbert always ate by himself. They ate together. The students watched the way Pa ate. He ate with his knife instead of his fork. A lot of the students felt sorry for me after they found out he was my father. They didn't have to feel sorry for me. I wasn't ashamed of Pa after I found out he wasn't going to shoot Professor Herbert. I was glad they had made friends. I wasn't ashamed of Pa. I wouldn't be as long as he behaved. He would find out about the high school as I had found out about the Lambert boys across the hill.

In the afternoon when we went to biology Pa was in the class. He was sitting on one of the high stools beside the microscope. We went ahead with our work just as if Pa wasn't in the class. I saw Pa take his knife and scrape tartar from one of his teeth. Professor Herbert put it on the lens and adjusted the microscope for Pa. He adjusted it and worked awhile. Then he says: "Now Luster, look! Put your eye right down to the light. Squint the other eye!"

Pa put his head down and did as Professor Herbert said. "I see 'im," says Pa. "Who'd a ever thought that? Right on a body's teeth! Right in a body's mouth. You're right certain they ain't no fake to this, Professor Herbert?"

"No, Luster," says Professor Herbert. "It's there. That's the germ. Germs live in a world we cannot see with the naked eye. We must use the microscope. There are millions of them in our bodies. Some are harmful. Others are helpful."

Pa holds his face down and looks

through the microscope. We stop and watch Pa. He sits upon the tall stool. His knees are against the table. His legs are long. His coat slips up behind when he bends over. The handle of his gun shows. Professor Herbert pulls his coat down quickly.

"Oh, yes," says Pa. He gets up and pulls his coat down. Pa's face gets a little red. He knows about his gun and he knows he doesn't have any use for it in high school.

"We have a big black snake over here we caught yesterday," says Professor Herbert. "We'll chloroform him and dissect him and show you he has germs in his body, too."

"Don't do it," says Pa. "I believe you. I jist don't want to see you kill the black snake. I never kill one. They are good mousers and a lot o' help to us on the farm. I like black snakes. I jist hate to see people kill 'em. I don't allow 'em killed on my place."

The students look at Pa. They seem to like him better after he said that. Pa with a gun in his pocket but a tender heart beneath his ribs for snakes, but not for man! Pa won't whip a mule at home. He won't whip his cattle.

"Man can defend hisself," says Pa, "but cattle and mules can't. We have the drop on 'em. Ain't nothin' to a man that'll beat a good pullin' mule. He ain't got th' right kind o' a heart!"

Professor Herbert took Pa through the laboratory. He showed him the different kinds of work we were doing. He showed him our equipment. They stood and talked while we worked. Then they walked out together. They talked louder when they got out in the hall.

When our biology class was over I walked out of the room. It was our last class for the day. I would have to take my broom and sweep two hours to finish paying for the split cherry tree. I just wondered if Pa would want me to stay. He was standing in the hallway watching the students march out. He looked lost among us. He looked like a leaf turned brown on the tree among the treetop filled with growing leaves.

I got my broom and started to sweep. Professor Herbert walked up and says, "I'm going to let you do that some other time. You can go home with your father. He is waiting out there."

I laid my broom down, got my books, and went down the steps.

Pa says, "Ain't you got two hours o' sweepin' yet to do?"

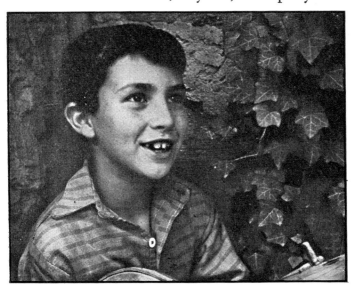

Kentucky mountain boy singing himself a song. (From Holiday, copyright 1951 by the Curtis Publishing Co.)

I says, "Professor Herbert said I could do it some other time. He said for me to go home with you."

"No," says Pa. "You are goin' to do as he says. He's a good man. School has changed from my day and time. I'm a dead leaf, Dave. I'm behind. I don't belong here. If he'll let me I'll get a broom and we'll both sweep one hour. That pays your debt. I'll hep you pay it. I'll ast 'im and see if he won't let me hep you."

"I'm going to cancel the debt," says Professor Herbert. "I just wanted you to understand, Luster."

"I understand," says Pa, "and since I understand, he must pay his debt fer th' tree and I'm goin' to hep 'im."

"Don't do that," says Professor Herbert. "It's all on me."

"We don't do things like that," says Pa, "we're just and honest people. We don't want somethin' fer nothin'. Professor Herbert, you're wrong now and I'm right. You'll haf to listen to me. I've larned a lot from you. My boy must go on. Th' world has left me. It changed while I've raised my family and plowed th' hills. I'm a just and honest man. I don't skip debts. I ain't larned 'em to do that. I ain't got much larnin' myself but I do know right from wrong atter I see through a thing."

Professor Herbert went home. Pa and I stayed and swept one hour. It looked funny to see Pa use a broom. He never used one at home. Mom used the broom. Pa used the plow. Pa did hard work. Pa says, "I can't sweep. Durned if I can. Look at th' streaks o' dirt I leave on th' floor! Seems like no work a-tall fer me. Brooms is too light 'r somethin'. I'll jist do th' best I can, Dave. I've been wrong about th' school."

I says, "Did you know Professor Herbert can get a warrant out for you for bringing your pistol to school and showing it in his office! They can railroad you for that!"

"That's all made right," says Pa. "I've made that right. Professor Herbert ain't goin' to take it to court. He likes me. I like 'im. We jist had to get together. He had the remedies. He showed me. You must go on to school. I am as strong a man as ever come out'n th' hills fer my years and th' hard work I've done. But I'm behind, Dave. I'm a little man. Your hands will be softer than mine. Your clothes will be better. You'll allus look cleaner than your old Pap. Jist remember, Dave, to pay your debts and be honest. Jist be kind to animals and don't bother th' snakes. That's all I got agin th' school. Puttin' black snakes to sleep and cuttin' 'em open."

It was late when we got home. Stars were in the sky. The moon was up. The ground was frozen. Pa took his time going home. I couldn't run like I did the night before. It was ten o'clock before we got the work finished, our suppers eaten. Pa sat before the fire and told Mom he was going to take her and show her a germ sometime. Mom hadn't seen one either. Pa told her about the high school and the fine man Professor Herbert was. He told Mom about the strange school across the hill and how different it was from the school in their day and time.

For Discussion of Stuart

1. What is the real conflict in this story? Is it between personalities or something else? What is the outcome of the conflict? The pistol is Pa's weapon; what is Professor Herbert's? Explain how each is a good symbol for its side of the conflict.

2. What are the weak points in Pa's character? What are the good points? Why was he so unjust to the school before he visited it?

3. How does Stuart's treatment of Professor Herbert show that Stuart himself has had teaching experience? Where does the Professor show his shrewdness in handling a difficult person?

4. How would you describe the boy's attitude toward his father? Do you admire him for it, or not?

JAMES FARL POWERS

1917–

The Old Bird, a Love Story

James Farl Powers graduated from Quincy College Academy in Quincy, Illinois, in 1935. He worked as a salesman in Marshall Field's store in Chicago, bought himself a typewriter, traveled through the South and Southwest as a chauffeur, and decided that he was to be a writer.

While he was working in Chicago, he studied English at Northwestern University, and later he taught at St. John's University, Collegeville, Minnesota, and at Marquette University in Milwaukee. In 1948 Mr. Powers received a fellowship in creative writing from the Guggenheim Foundation and a grant from the National Institute of Arts and Letters. His short stories have appeared in national magazines.

As a writer, J. F. Powers has a rare insight, as well as vast powers of characterization. He creates an atmosphere in his stories that matches exactly the thoughts and feelings of the characters. His people are always concerned, consciously or subconsciously, with the spiritual challenge of life. The following story is a luminous tale of success and failure that very nearly encompasses the total beauty of the nuptial vow "till death do us part."

UNEMPLOYED and elderly Mr. Newman sensed there were others, some of them, just as anxious as he was to be put on. But he was the oldest person in the room. He approached the information girl, and for all his show of business, almost brusqueness, he radiated timidity. The man in front of him asked the girl a question, which was also Mr. Newman's.

"Are they doing any hiring today?"

The girl gave the man an application, a dead smile, and told him to take a seat after he had filled it out.

An answer, in any event, ready on her lips, she regarded Mr. Newman. Mr. Newman thought of reaching for an application and saying, "Yes, I'll take a seat," making a kind of joke out of the coincidence — the fellow before him looking for a job, too — only he could see from the others who had already taken seats it was no coincidence. They all had that superior look of people out of work.

"Got an application there for a retired millionaire?" Mr. Newman said, attempting jauntiness. That way it would be easier for her to refuse him. Perhaps it was part of her job to weed out applicants clearly too old to be of any use to the company. Mr. Newman had a real horror of butting in where he wasn't wanted.

The girl laughed, making Mr. Newman feel like a regular devil, and handed him an application. The smile she gave him was alive and it hinted that things were already on a personal basis between him and her and the company.

"You'll find a pen at the desk," she said.

Mr. Newman's bony old hand clawed

at his coat pocket and unsnapped a large ancient fountain pen. "I carry my own! See?" In shy triumph he held up the fountain pen, which was orange. He unscrewed it, put it together, and fingered it as though he were actually writing.

But the girl was doing her dead smile at the next one.

Mr. Newman went over to the desk. The application questioned him: Single? Married? Children of your own? Parents living? Living with parents? Salary (expect)? Salary (would take)? Mr. Newman made ready with his fountain pen and in the ensuing minutes he did not lie about his age, his abilities, or past earnings. The salary he expected was modest. He was especially careful about making blots with his pen, which sometimes flowed too freely. He had noted before he started that the application was one of those which calls for the information to be printed. This he had done. Under "DO NOT WRITE BELOW THIS LINE" he had not written.

Mr. Newman read the application over and rose to take it to the information girl. She pointed to a bench. Hesitating for a moment, Mr. Newman seemed bent on giving it to her. He sat down. He got up. His face distraught, he walked unsteadily over to the girl.

Before she could possibly hear him, he started to stammer, "I wonder . . . maybe it will make a difference," his voice both appealing for her mercy and saying it was out of the question — indeed he did not desire it — that she should take a personal interest in him. Then he got control, except for his eyes, which, without really knowing it, were searching the girl's face for the live smile, like the first time.

"I used green ink," he said limply.

"Let's see." The girl took the application, gave both sides a darting scrutiny, looking for mistakes.

"Will it make any difference? If it does and I could have another application, I could —" Mr. Newman had his

orange fountain pen out again, as though to match the green on its tip with the ink on the application and thus fully account for what had come about.

"Oh no, I think that'll be all right," the girl said, finally getting the idea. "We're not that fussy." Mr. Newman, however, still appeared worried. "No, that's fine — and neat, too," the girl said. "Mr. *Newman.*" She had spoken his name and there was her live smile. Mr. Newman blushed, then smiled a little himself. With perspiring fingers he put the fountain pen together and snapped it in his pocket.

The girl returned the application. Mr. Newman, lingering on, longed to confide in her, to tell her something of himself — why, for instance, he always used green ink; how famous and familiar a few years ago the initials "C. N." in green had been at the old place. Like his friend Jack P. Ferguson (died a few years back, it was in the papers) and the telegram. "Telegram" Ferguson, he was called, because he was always too busy to write. Green ink and telegrams, the heraldry of business. He wanted to tell her of the old days — the time he met Elbert Hubbard and Charley Schwab at a banquet.

Then on this side of the old days he saw a busy girl, busy being busy, who could never understand, and he forced himself to give up hope.

"I thank you," he said, going quickly back to his place on the bench to wait. He sat there rereading his application. Under "DO NOT WRITE BELOW THIS LINE" were some curious symbols. He guessed at their significance: CLN (Clean?); DSPN (Disposition?); PRSNLTY (Personality, no doubt about that one); PSE (Poise?); FCW (?); LYL (Loyal?); PSBLE LDR (Possible Leader); NTC (?). His fingers were damp with perspiration, and for fear he would present an untidy application, he laid it on his lap and held his hands open at his sides, letting them get cool and dry in case he had to shake hands with the interviewer.

When they were ready to see him, Mr. Newman hustled into a small glass office and stood before a young man. A sign with wooden letters indicated that he was Mr. Shanahan. Mr. Shanahan was reading a letter. Mr. Newman did not look directly at Mr. Shanahan: it was none of Mr. Newman's business — Mr. Shanahan's letter — and he did not want to seem curious or expectant of immediate attention. This was their busy season.

Mr. Shanahan, his eyes still reading the letter, noiselessly extended a hand toward Mr. Newman. A moment later he moved his head and it was then that Mr. Newman saw the hand. Mr. Newman paled. Caught napping! A bad beginning. He hastened to shake Mr. Shanahan's hand, recoiled in time. Mr. Shanahan had only been reaching for the application. Mr. Newman handed it to Mr. Shanahan and said, "Thank you," for some reason.

"Ah, yes. Have a seat." Mr. Shanahan rattled the application in one hand. "What kind of work did you want to do?" Evidently he expected no answer, for he went on to say, "I don't have to tell you, Mr. Newman, there's a labor shortage, especially in non-defense industries. That, and that alone, accounts for the few jobs we have to offer. We're an old-line house."

"Yes," Mr. Newman said.

"And there aren't any office jobs," Mr. Shanahan continued. "That's the kind of work you've always done?"

"Yes, it is," Mr. Newman said. Mr. Shanahan sucked a tooth sadly.

Mr. Newman was ready now for the part about the company letting him know later.

"How'd you like a temporary job in our shipping room?" Mr. Shanahan said, his eyes suddenly watchful.

For an instant Mr. Newman succeeded in making it plain that he, like any man of his business experience, was meant for better things. A moment later, in an interesting ceremony which took place in his heart, Mr. Newman surrendered his well-loved white collar. He knew that Mr. Shanahan, with that dark vision peculiar to personnel men, had witnessed the whole thing.

"Well . . ." he said.

Mr. Shanahan, the game bagged and bumping from his belt, got cordial now. "How are you, pretty handy with rope?"

He said it in such a flattering way that Mr. Newman trembled under the desire to be worthy. "Yes, I am," he said.

"But can you begin right away?" It was the final test.

"Yes, I can!" Mr. Newman said, echoing some of Mr. Shanahan's spirit. "You bet I can!"

"Well then, follow me!"

Mr. Shanahan guided Mr. Newman through a maze of departments. On an elevator, going down, he revealed what the job paid to start. Mr. Newman nodded vigorously that one could not expect too much to start. Mr. Shanahan told him that he didn't have to tell him that they were a firm known far and wide for fair dealing and that if (for any reason) Mr. Newman ever left them, it should be easy to get another position, and . . . Out of the elevator and in the lower depths, Mr. Shanahan said he would like to make sure Mr. Newman understood the job was only temporary. After the Christmas holidays things were pretty slow in their line. Otherwise, they would be glad to avail themselves of his services the year round. However, the experience Mr. Newman would get here might very well prove invaluable to him in later life. Mr. Newman nodded less vigorously now.

They came to a long table, flat against a wall, extending around a rafterish room fitted out for packing: tough twine and hairy manila rope on giant spools, brown paper on rollers, sticking tape bearing the company's name, crest, and slogan: "A modern house over 100 years *young*."

Several men were packing things. Mr. Shanahan introduced Mr. Newman to one of them.

"This is your boss, Mr. Hurley. This is Mr. Newman. Mr. Newman's pretty handy with rope. Ought to make an A-1 packer."

"Well . . ." Mr. Newman said, embarrassed before the regular packers.

He shook Mr. Hurley's hard hand.

"I sure hope so," Mr. Hurley said grimly. "This is our busy season."

When Mr. Shanahan had gone Mr. Hurley showed Mr. Newman where he could hang his coat. He told him what he would have to do and what he would be held responsible for. He cited the sad case of the shipment sent out last week to Fargo, North Dakota. The company had lost exactly double the amount of the whole sale, to say nothing of good will. Why? Faulty packing! He urged Mr. Newman to figure it out for himself. He told Mr. Newman that haste made waste, but that they were expected to get incoming orders out of the house on the same day. Not tomorrow. Not the next day. The same day. Finally Mr. Hurley again brought up the case of the shipment sent to Fargo, and seemed pleased with the reaction it got. For Mr. Newman frowned his forehead all out of shape and rolled his head back and forth like a sad old bell, as if to say, "Can such things be?"

"All right, Newman, let's see what you can do!" Mr. Hurley slapped him on the shoulder like a football coach sending in a substitute. Mr. Newman, gritting his false teeth, tackled his first assignment for the company: a half-dozen sets of poker chips, a box of rag dolls, 5,000 small American flags, and a boy's sled going to Waupaca, Wisconsin.

Mr. Newman perspired . . . lost his breath, caught it, tried to break a piece of twine with his bare hands, failed, cut his nose on a piece of wrapping paper, bled, barked his shin on an ice skate, tripped, said a few cuss words to himself . . . perspired.

"We go to lunch at twelve in this section," Mr. Hurley told him in a whisper a few minutes before that time. "If you want to wash up, go ahead now."

But Mr. Newman waited until the whistle blew before he knocked off. He had a shipment he wanted to get off. It was ten after twelve when he punched out.

There was no crowd at the time clock and he had a chance to look the thing over. He tried to summon up a little interest, but all he felt with any intensity was the lone fact that he'd never had to punch a clock before. It had always been enough before that he live by one.

On his lunch hour he did not know where to go. The company had a place where you could eat your lunch, but Mr. Newman had neglected to bring one. Quite reasonably he had not anticipated getting a job and starting on it the same day. After the usual morning of looking around, he had expected to go home and eat a bite with Mrs. Newman.

He walked past a lunch stand twice before he could make certain, without actually staring in the window at the menu painted on the wall, that hamburgers were ten cents and coffee five. He entered the place, then, and ordered with assurance that he would not be letting himself in for more than he could afford. He did not have any money to spare. Would it be better, he wondered, to have payday come soon and get paid for a few days' work, or could he hold out for a week or so and really have something when he did get paid? Leaving the lunch stand, he walked in the direction of the company, but roundabout so he would not get back too soon. Say about fifteen minutes to one. That would give him time to go to the washroom.

"Where did you eat your lunch?" Mr. Hurley asked him the first thing. "I didn't see you in the lunchroom."

"Oh, I ate out," Mr. Newman said, gratified that he'd been missed until he saw that he had offended Mr. Hurley by eating out. "I didn't bring my lunch today," he explained. "Didn't think I'd be working so soon."

"Oh." But Mr. Hurley was still hurt.

"I heard they let you eat your lunch in the building," Mr. Newman said, giving Mr. Hurley his chance.

Mr. Hurley broke down and told Mr. Newman precisely where the employees' lunchroom was, where it wasn't, how to get there from the shipping room, how not to. There were two ways to get there, he said, and he guessed, as for him, he never went the same way twice in a row.

"You know how it is," Mr. Hurley laughed, tying it in with life.

In the end Mr. Newman was laughing with Mr. Hurley, "Well, I guess so." Talking with Mr. Hurley gave Mr. Newman a feeling of rare warmth. It was man-to-man or nothing with Hurley. He hoped there would be other lunch hours like this one. He went back to work at four minutes to one.

During the afternoon Mr. Newman worked up a dislike for the fat fellow next to him, but when they teamed up on a big shipment of toys the fat fellow made some cynical remarks about the company and Mr. Newman relaxed. His kind were harmless as rivals. Mr. Newman thought the company would be better off with employees like himself. And then he was ashamed, for at bottom he admired the fat fellow for his independence. Mr. Newman regretted that he was too old to be independent.

Toward the end of the day he was coming from getting a drink of water when he overheard Mr. Hurley talking with Mr. Shanahan.

"Yeah," Mr. Hurley said, "when you said the old bird was handy with rope I thought, boy, he's old enough to think about using some on himself. Shanahan, if this keeps up we'll have to draft them

from the old people's home."

Mr. Newman, feeling indecently aged, unable to face them, went for another drink of water. He had to keep moving. When he returned to the shipping room they were all working and Mr. Shanahan was not there.

Just before quitting time, Mr. Hurley came over and congratulated him on his first day's work. He said he thought Mr. Newman would make out all right, and showed him an easier way to cut string. When he suggested that Mr. Newman wash up before the whistle blew, Mr. Newman did not have the faith to refuse. He could not look Mr. Hurley in the eye now and say something about wanting to finish up a shipment. Any extraordinary industry on his part, he knew now, was useless. He was too old. All they could see when they looked at him was an old man. That was the only fact about him. He was an old bird.

"All right, Charley, see you in the morning," Mr. Hurley said.

Mr. Newman slowly brought himself to realize he was "Charley" to Mr. Hurley. He had never before been "Charley" to anyone on such short acquaintance. Probably he would be "Old Charley" before long, which reminded him that Christmas was coming. There was no meaning beyond Christmas in all this sweat and humiliation, but that was enough. He would stick it out.

Mr. Newman was impressed again with the vaultlike solemnity of the washroom. Young here, he luxuriated. Still he was sensible about it. He would not knowingly abuse a privilege. He read a notice concerning a hospitalization service the company offered the employees. The sensibleness of such a plan appealed strongly to Mr. Newman. He thought he would have to look into that, completely forgetting that he was only temporary.

At the sound of the five-o'clock whistle Mr. Newman hurried out and took his place in the line of employees at the

" There was enough snow on the sidewalk to ease his swollen feet . . ."
(*Armstrong Roberts*)

time clock. When his turn came to punch out, clutching his time card, he was shaking all over. The clock would jam, or stamp the time in the wrong place, or at the last moment, losing confidence in the way he was holding the card, after all his planning, he would somehow stick it in the wrong way. Then there would be shouts from the end of the line, and everybody would know it was all on account of an old bird trying to punch out.

Mr. Newman's heart stopped beating, his body followed a preconceived plan from memory in the lapse, and then his heart started up again. Mr. Newman, a new friend to the machine, had punched out smoothly. One of the mass of company employees heading for home, Mr. Newman, his old body at once tired and tingling, walked so briskly he passed any number of younger people in the corridors. His mood was unfamiliar to him, one of achievement and crazy gai-

ety. He recognized the information girl ahead of him, passed her, and said over his shoulder:

" Well, good night! "

She smiled in immediate reflex, but it was sobering to Mr. Newman, though she did say good night, that she did not seem to remember him very well, for it had not been the live smile.

At the outside door it was snowing. Mr. Newman bought a newspaper and let the man keep the two cents change. He meant to revive an old tradition with him by reading the paper on the streetcar. There was enough snow on the sidewalk to ease his swollen feet.

It was too crowded on the streetcar to open his paper and he had to stand all the way. His eyes on a placard, he considered the case of a man from Minneapolis who had got welcome relief. Hanging there on a strap, rocking with the elemental heave of the streetcar, he felt utterly weary, a gray old thing.

What mattered above all else, though — getting a job — he had accomplished. This he told himself over and over until it became as real as his fatigue and mingled itself with the tortured noise of the streetcar.

His wife met him at the door. One glimpse of his face, he thought, was all she needed and she would know how to treat him tonight. Already she knew something was up and had seen the scratch on his nose. She only said:

"You stayed downtown all day, Charley."

"Yes, I did," he said.

She went to hang up his coat, hat, and scarf. He stepped across the familiar rug to the radiator. He stood there warming his hands and listening to her moving things in the kitchen. He could not bring himself to go there, as he did on any other night before supper, to talk of nothing important or particular, to let the water run till it got cold, to fill their glasses. He had too much to tell her tonight. He had forgotten to remove his rubbers.

"Come on now, Charley."

He took a few steps, hesitated a second, and went straight into the kitchen. He was immediately, as he knew he would be, uneasy. He could think of nothing insignificant to say. His eyes were not meeting hers. The glasses were filled with water. Suddenly he had to look at her. She smiled. It was hard to bear. He *did* have news. But now, he felt, she expected too much.

He bit his lips in irritation and snapped, "Why didn't you let me get the water?" That was beside the point, of course, but it gave him leeway to sit down at the table. He made a project of it. Trying to extend the note of normalcy, he passed things to her. He involved her subtly in passing them back. He wanted her to know there was a time and place for everything and now it was for passing. He invented an un-

precedented interest in their silverware. His knife, fork, and spoon absorbed him.

"Where did we get this spoon?" he asked crossly.

It was all wasted. She had revamped her strategy. She appeared amused, and there was about her a determination deeper than his to wait forever. Her being so amused was what struck him as insupportable. He had a dismaying conviction that this was the truest condition of their married life. It ran, more or less, but always present, right through everything they did. She was the audience — that was something like it — and he was always on stage, the actor who was never taken quite seriously by his audience, no matter how heroic the role. The bad actor and his faithful but not foolish audience. Always! As now! It was not a hopeless situation, but only because she loved him.

She *did* love him. Overcome by the idea, he abandoned his silence. He heard himself telling her everything. Not exactly as it was, naturally, but still everything. Not at first about his being handy with rope, nothing about being "Charley" and an old bird, but quite frankly that he was working in the shipping room instead of the office. About Mr. Shanahan, the interviewer — how nice he was, in a way. About the information girl who seemed to take quite an interest in him and who, to his surprise, had said good night to him. Mr. Hurley, his department head, and how to get to the employees' lunchroom. The washroom, plenty of soap and towels, a clean place — clean as her kitchen; she should see it. Where he had lunch, not much of a place. The fat fellow next to him at the table, not exactly loyal to the company, but a very likeable chap . . . and here — he dug into his shirt pocket — was a piece of their sticking tape, as she could see, with their name and trademark.

" ' A modern house,' " she read, " ' over 100 years young ' — *young* — well, that's pretty clever."

" Oh, they're an old-line firm," Mr. Newman said.

" I'll have to pack you a lunch then, Charley," she said. She had finally got into the adventure with him.

" I bought a paper tonight," he said. " It's in the other room."

With a little excited movement she parted the organdy curtain at the window. " My, Charley, just look at that! " Snowflakes tumbled in feathery confusion past the yellow light burning in the court, wonderfully white against the night, smothering the whole dirty, roaring, guilty city in innocence and silence and beauty.

Mr. Newman squirmed warm inside the thought of everything he could think of — the snow falling, the glow in the kitchen, landing the job, Christmas coming, her . . .

Their supper got cold.

She let the curtain fall together, breathing, " My! "

Reluctantly Mr. Newman assumed the duty he had as husband and only provider — not to be swept away by dreams and snowflakes. He said with the stern wisdom of his generation:

" Keeps up much longer it'll tie up transportation."

" But do you like that kind of work, Charley? "

He assured her most earnestly that he did, knowing she knew he'd do anything to get into an office again. He caught himself on the verge of telling her that working in the shipping room was just the way the company, since it was so old and reliable, groomed its new employees for service in the office. But that sounded too steep and ultimately disastrous. He had to confess it was only temporary work. This pained her, he could see, and he tried to get her mind on something else.

" I'll bet you had no idea your husband was so handy with rope."

He told her how it came on big spools, like telegraph wire. But she did not think this important.

" The people," he said, " the ones I've met at least — well, they all seem very nice."

" Then, maybe they'll keep you after Christmas, Charley! "

He looked sharply at her and could tell she was sorry she said that. She understood what must follow. He opened his mouth to speak, said nothing, and then, closing his eyes to the truth, he said:

" Yes. You know, I think they will. I'm sure of it."

He coughed. That was not the way it was at all. It had happened again. He was the bad actor again. His only audience smiled and loved him.

For Discussion of Powers

1. What impressions of Mr. Newman's character do you get from the opening paragraphs? Why was he so observant of the information girl? of the people around him? What hints about Mr. Newman do the fountain pen, the green ink, and the carefully filled application provide?

2. What do you think Mr. Shanahan's first impressions might have been? Do you think he was aware of all Mr. Newman felt when offered the job?

3. How was Mr. Newman affected by the conversation he overheard? Why did he dread punching the time clock?

4. Pick out indications of Mr. Newman's gallant spirit on his way home. What other feeling did he have as he rode home?

5. What did the Newmans' reactions to the snowstorm indicate? What kind of married life had they had? How much of the whole situation did Mrs. Newman understand?

6. When did you first become aware of the inclusiveness of the title? Write in one

sentence what you think is the theme of the story, and compare it with your classmates' answers. Discuss what you mean by love, success, self-respect, understanding.

For Your Vocabulary

DESCRIPTIVE PHRASES: J. F. Powers is especially expert in choosing exact details to build a picture of a character or create an atmosphere for his story. For example, he says that Mr. Newman "radiated timidity," and that the girl gave a "dead smile" and a "live smile." What do these descriptive phrases tell you about the characters? Go through the story noticing the use of small but significant details depicting the characters' attitudes and feelings. How do they add to your deeper understanding of the people in the story?

ALBERT EISELE
1897–1951

Farmer at Forty Hours

Albert Eisele wrote his love for the soil and the common man into every line of his starkly beautiful short stories. Born in Metamora, Illinois, his only formal education was at the Whittemore, Iowa, grade school. The Sisters who taught him lent him books to read while he worked his father's farm, and encouraged him to keep studying. All his literary background he acquired himself. He kept thousands of notes, all indexed, and never used the same note twice.

He farmed throughout his life, mostly at Blue Earth, Minnesota, where his wife, Susan Frawley Eisele, still lives. Also a writer, she produces a Countryside column that appears in twenty-six Midwest dailies and weeklies.

Eisele was uncompromising, believing that Catholic writers should strive above all for the truth. His stories have appeared in *America, Catholic World, Commonweal,* and other Catholic magazines.

PETER GREBNER rose at dawn and went to bring in the cows. He felt too tired to tie his shoes; and so he walked with unlaced footgear across the dewy pasture. He felt a sort of disinterested pleasure in the clear November morning. He brought the cows home and milked them, hurried through breakfast, and soon, with his wife and

their daughter Mary, was on the way to Mass.

It was Monday, and very unusual for them to be going to Mass on this first of the weekdays, but the Forty Hours was beginning, and the Grebners always made the Forty Hours. Mass was at 6:30, and they were not late. As the sun burst over the clouds, the interior of the

"Farmer at Forty Hours" by Albert Eisele. Reprinted by permission of *The Ave Maria.*

church lit up as from a sudden flame. The rays shining through the windows projected patches of color on the opposite wall.

A railingful of people received Holy Communion. These were the ones who had received yesterday. The main body of the parish would go to confession tonight, following the evening services, and they would receive on Tuesday and Wednesday.

The priest in charge entered the pulpit. It was not good old Father Finnegan, the pastor, but a strange priest, slight of build, and mild-mannered. He made some announcements, and followed these with a short discourse on Catholic doctrine. The main sermon of the day would be tonight. Soon church was out and the Grebners went home.

Peter Grebner had finished husking his corn, but there was still much other work to be done before winter came. All afternoon he hauled fodder.

In the evening the Grebners went to church again. First there was the Rosary, and then the sermon by the visiting priest. The sermon was scholarly and kindly, but Peter Grebner from where he sat could see four parishioners in familiar sleep. The sermon progressed. Old Grandfather Kissner arose in his pew; Grandmother Kissner, who was sitting beside him, pulled hastily at his coat and he sat down again. Grandfather Kissner was childish, but grandmother always brought him to church with her, and for some reason he was always getting it into his head that Mass was over. He always wanted to go, go, go.

The sermon drew gracefully to a close and Peter Grebner felt grateful, for his feet were beginning to hurt. His Sunday shoes were not exactly new, but they hurt his feet if he wore them too often.

The penitents lined up for confession. There was a long line before both confessionals. In one sat Father Finnegan, in the other the visiting priest. Peter Grebner, for a change, chose the latter.

The confessions went on, with the strange priest hearing them almost as fast as Father Finnegan. That was unusual, for whenever there was a strange confessor, he usually drew the more sorely afflicted. And to shrive the sorely afflicted took somewhat more time, which seemed natural enough. But tonight the strange priest was turning out the sheep. And Peter felt grateful for that. For it seemed that the strange priest had a deep understanding of country people who, worn by the day's toil and often with many miles to go, were wont to become physically wearied with standing in line.

At last it was Peter's turn. He found the visiting priest gentle and understanding and pastorly. Peter said his penance, found his wife and daughter waiting, and they went home.

It was a relief to get out of his Sunday shoes. He fell asleep. But it seemed he had been asleep only a minute when his wife woke him, saying, " Peter! Mass is at 6:30; it's time to get up! "

He went out. The tree by the hen house was white with roosting Leghorns. The birds caught the gleam of the moon, low in the west and still bright, and they shone like silver. Why did Leghorns always roost in trees? It was November, and time for all chickens to be housed.

He set out for the cows. One of his old shoes had lost its string, and he paused by the strawstack for a sheaf twine. Around the strawstack the frost was heavy and sparkled in the moonlight. Peter selected a twine that had its knot in the exact middle, because no twine knot could be run through the eyelets.

They went to Mass, and received. The visiting priest gave a short homily on Catholic doctrine, but Peter's mind wandered. Catholic doctrine did not bother Peter, what bothered him was getting his pew rent paid and his fall work done. In the afternoon, Peter and his wife worshiped before the Blessed Sacrament from 3:00 to 3:15.

They reached home late in the afternoon, did their chores, and then set out again. "The gas and oil and everything cost us a dollar every time we go to church," Peter complained. His feet hurt, too. Sore feet from Sunday shoes was a sign of a lot of church.

The sermon was like the one on the evening previous, polished and kindly. Chronic sleepers dropped off almost immediately. Grandfather Kissner got up to go; his wife grabbed him by the coat and yanked him down again.

The collection was for the visiting priest. One had to be as generous as possible. But Peter Grebner was pinched for money. He didn't have his pew rent for the year paid yet. He knew that he ought to put in a dollar at least. But he had only a nickel handy, so he put that in. The spiritual riches which one obtained from the Forty Hours couldn't be paid for in silver anyway.

They drove home. The sky clouded over and it was turning colder.

Wednesday was the final day of the Forty Hours, so the Grebners got up early again. It had snowed in the night, a wet snow, one that striped the trunks of the farmstead trees; and the striped trunks leaped into the air as Peter approached with his lantern. In his dilapidated shoes his feet became wet and cold.

They attended Mass. There was the usual short talk, and a brief appearance by Father Finnegan, who said, "Those who have not yet made their contribution for the officiating priest may do so tonight."

"Peter, you made your contribution last night, didn't you?" asked Mrs. Grebner, as they drove home.

"Yes," said Peter. But he did not tell her that he had given only a miserable nickel. "Where is he from, I wonder?"

"From a little place up north, in the drought district," said Mrs. Grebner. "I forget the name of the town, but it is just a small parish, and a poor one, and somebody said that Father Finnegan felt sorry for this priest and had him come here so he could add a dollar or two to his scanty income."

When he had changed clothes, Peter hunted up his four-buckle overshoes. He needed new work shoes, but could not afford them until he sold his hogs. If the sun came out, the light snow would go, and then perhaps the old shoes would do for another week or so.

Peter had a two-wheel trailer. He pumped its tires and ran it to the granary, where he shoveled it full of oats. He hauled the oats to town. It was a small load, but it brought over $7. Now he had a little money. One had to have money to work with.

In the evening the little church was crowded. Everyone had turned out for the closing services of the Forty Hours. Peter was just able to squeeze into his own pew. He left his hat in the aisle, but on second thought brought it inside — one time an awkward boy had squashed it with a genuflection.

Grandfather Kissner was in his pew. During the sermon he arose to go, but his watchful wife jerked him back by his worn coattails.

The sermon ended; the priest left the sanctuary, and the altar boys came out to light the additional candles for Benediction. The collectors appeared. Grandfather Kissner arose once more; his wife yanked him back; and there were those who maintained (those who sat behind him) that Grandfather Kissner was acting entirely normal.

Sometimes Peter had thought that the business of money should not be mixed up with the business of religion. Tonight, however, as he saw the thin visiting priest, he found himself won-

For a farmer there are always daily chores to do . . . (Black Star)

dering if he got enough to eat. That would be bad, not enough to eat!

Peter took out a dollar bill, folded it a little, and put it in the collection box. That was for the visiting priest. The visiting priest was his own brother in Christ and his brother in poverty.

The Forty Hours came to a close with the hymn "Holy God, We Praise Thy Name." Peter joined with the singing, though he was never much for singing. But that was such a wonderful song. His eyes misted until all the Benediction tapers had golden lines running up and down from them.

For Discussion of Eisele

1. What kind of person is Peter Grebner? his wife? Describe the Grebner farm as you think it looked in the November dawn. Select effective phrases that give you a picture of the village church.

2. Pick out the homely details of daily living in the story. How do these elements add to the story's effectiveness?

3. What did Peter Grebner think of the visiting priest? What does the author mean by "the strange priest was turning out the sheep"? Why was Peter grateful? What caused Peter to change his mind about his offering?

4. What similarities and differences do you find in Forty Hours services as described here and in your own parish church?

For Your Vocabulary

STYLE: Albert Eisele strives to catch the beauty of everyday life. Study "Farmer at Forty Hours" to see how the short, direct sentences seem to match our simplest thinking. Pick out the details, like the recurring mention of Peter's shoes, that make the situation real to you.

Using the style of this story as a model, write of a church incident you recall. Describe a Saturday night confession line; the congregation at novena service; the scattered faithful at a 6:30 weekday Mass. Choose ordinary details to make your writing concrete, and aim throughout for a terse effect.

STEPHEN VINCENT BENÉT
1898–1943

The Devil and Daniel Webster

Stephen Vincent Benét belonged to a family that is noted for the number of excellent writers within its small circle. At Yale University, Stephen showed his creative gift by publishing two volumes while still an undergraduate. Later he studied at the Sorbonne, Paris, where he was married. His wife Rosemary also has literary ability, and the two collaborated on a series of verse narratives based on American themes.

"The Devil and Daniel Webster" from *Selected Works of Stephen Vincent Benét*, published by Rinehart & Company, Inc. Copyright, 1936, by Stephen Vincent Benét.

Benét early decided to make writing his lifework, and so, unlike many of the authors in this book, he practiced no other profession. It is not often that an author wins almost equal laurels in both poetry and short fiction. Because Benét has this double distinction you will find additional information about him in the Poetry section on page 305. In fiction he shows his poetic bent by tending away from a realistic picture of life toward the fantastic and the symbolical. Combine with this tend-ency his ardent Americanism, and the result is a series of remarkable stories based on American history. Among these " The Devil and Daniel Webster " has become a modern American classic.

This story is definitely a fantasy; that is, the events as narrated could not have taken place, yet they seem real because of the author's skill in the telling. The dramatic quality of the tale has caused it to be made into a motion picture, a one-act play, and a grand opera.

I T's a story they all tell in the border country, where Massachusetts joins Vermont and New Hampshire.

Yes, Dan'l Webster's dead — or, at least, they buried him. But every time there's a thunderstorm around Marshfield,[1] they say you can hear his rolling voice in the hollows of the sky. And they say that if you go to his grave and speak loud and clear, " Dan'l Webster — Dan'l Webster! " the ground'll begin to shiver and the trees begin to shake. And after a while you'll hear a deep voice saying, " Neighbor, how stands the Union? " Then you better answer the Union stands as she stood, rock-bottomed and copper-sheathed, one and indivisible, or he's liable to rear right out of the ground. At least, that's what I was told when I was a youngster.

You see, for a while, he was the biggest man in the country. He never got to be President, but he was the biggest man. There were thousands that trusted in him right next to God Almighty, and they told stories about him and all the things that belonged to him that were like the stories of patriarchs and such. They said when he stood up to speak stars and stripes came right out in the sky, and once he spoke against a river and made it sink into the ground. They said when he walked the woods with his fishing rod, Killall, the trout would jump out of the streams right into his pockets, for they knew it was no use putting up a fight against him; and, when he argued a case, he could turn on the harps of the blessed and the shaking of the earth underground. That was the kind of man he was, and his big farm up at Marshfield was suitable to him. The chickens he raised were all white meat down through the drumsticks, the cows were tended like children, and the big ram he called Goliath[2] had horns with a curl like a morning-glory vine and could butt through an iron door. But Dan'l wasn't one of your gentlemen farmers; he knew all the ways of the land, and he'd be up by candlelight to see that the chores got done. A man with a mouth like a mastiff, a brow like a mountain, and eyes like burning anthracite — that was Dan'l Webster in his prime. And the biggest case he argued never got written down in the books, for he argued it against the devil, nip and tuck, and no holds barred. And this is the way I used to hear it told:

There was a man named Jabez Stone, lived at Cross Corners, New Hampshire. He wasn't a bad man to start with, but he was an unlucky man. If he planted corn, he got borers; if he planted potatoes, he got blight. He had good-enough land, but it didn't prosper him;

[1] **Marshfield:** a small town south of Boston, where Webster had a farm, and where he spent most of his private life.

[2] **Goliath** (gṓ·lī′ăth): a famous giant in the Bible (I Samuel 17), slain by David.

he had a decent wife and children, but the more children he had, the less there was to feed them. If stones cropped up in his neighbor's field, boulders boiled up in his; if he had a horse with the spavins,[1] he'd trade it for one with the staggers [2] and give something extra. There's some folks bound to be like that, apparently. But one day Jabez Stone got sick of the whole business.

He'd been plowing that morning and he'd just broke the plowshare on a rock that he could have sworn hadn't been there yesterday. And, as he stood looking at the plowshare, the off horse began to cough — that ropy kind of cough that means sickness and horse doctors. There were two children down with the measles, his wife was ailing, and he had a whitlow [3] on his thumb. It was about the last straw for Jabez Stone. " I vow," he said, and he looked around him kind of desperate — " I vow it's enough to make a man want to sell his soul to the devil! And I would, too, for two cents! "

Then he felt a kind of queerness come over him at having said what he'd said; though, naturally, being a New Hampshireman, he wouldn't take it back. But, all the same, when it got to be evening and, as far as he could see, no notice had been taken, he felt relieved in his mind, for he was a religious man. But notice is always taken, sooner or later, just like the Good Book says. And, sure enough, the next day, about suppertime, a soft-spoken, dark-dressed stranger drove up in a handsome buggy and asked for Jabez Stone.

Well, Jabez told his family it was a lawyer, come to see him about a legacy. But he knew who it was. He didn't like the looks of the stranger, nor the way he smiled with his teeth. They were white teeth, and plentiful — some

say they were filed to a point, but I wouldn't vouch for that. And he didn't like it when the dog took one look at the stranger and ran away howling, with his tail between his legs. But having passed his word, more or less, he stuck to it, and they went out behind the barn and made their bargain. Jabez Stone had to prick his finger to sign, and the stranger lent him a silver pen. The wound healed clean, but it left a little white scar.

After that, all of a sudden, things began to pick up and prosper for Jabez Stone. His cows got fat and his horses sleek, his crops were the envy of the neighborhood, and lightning might strike all over the valley, but it wouldn't strike his barn. Pretty soon, he was one of the prosperous people of the county; they asked him to stand for selectman,[4] and he stood for it; there began to be talk of running him for state senate. All in all, you might say the Stone family was as happy and contented as cats in a dairy. And so they were, except for Jabez Stone.

He'd been contented enough, the first few years. It's a great thing when bad luck turns; it drives most other things out of your head. True, every now and then, especially in rainy weather, the little white scar on his finger would give him a twinge. And once a year, punctual as clockwork, the stranger with the handsome buggy would come driving by. But the sixth year, the stranger lighted, and, after that, his peace was over for Jabez Stone.

The stranger came up through the lower field, switching his boots with a cane — they were handsome black boots, but Jabez Stone never liked the look of them, particularly the toes. And, after he'd passed the time of day, he said, " Well, Mr. Stone, you're a hummer! It's

[1] **spavins:** a disease of the leg bone that causes a horse to limp.
[2] **staggers:** a disease that causes a horse to reel or fall down.
[3] **whitlow:** an inflamed sore.

[4] **selectman:** one of a board of officers chosen annually in some New England towns to transact public business.

a very pretty property you've got here, Mr. Stone."

"Well, some might favor it and others might not," said Jabez Stone, for he was a New Hampshireman.

"Oh, no need to decry your industry!" said the stranger, very easy, showing his teeth in a smile. "After all, we know what's been done, and it's been according to contract and specifications. So when — ahem — the mortgage falls due next year, you shouldn't have any regrets."

"Speaking of that mortgage, mister," said Jabez Stone, and he looked around for help to the earth and the sky, "I'm beginning to have one or two doubts about it."

"Doubts?" said the stranger, not quite so pleasantly.

"Why, yes," said Jabez Stone. "This being the U.S.A. and me always having been a religious man." He cleared his throat and got bolder. "Yes, sir," he said, "I'm beginning to have considerable doubts as to that mortgage holding in court."

"There's courts and courts," said the stranger, clicking his teeth. "Still, we might as well have a look at the original document." And he hauled out a big black pocketbook, full of papers. "Sherwin, Slater, Stevens, Stone," he muttered. "I, Jabez Stone, for a term of seven years — Oh, it's quite in order, I think."

But Jabez Stone wasn't listening, for he saw something else flutter out of the black pocketbook. It was something that looked like a moth, but it wasn't a moth. And as Jabez Stone stared at it, it seemed to speak to him in a small sort of piping voice, terrible small and thin, but terrible human.

"Neighbor Stone!" it squeaked. "Neighbor Stone! Help me! I beg you, help me!"

But before Jabez Stone could stir hand or foot, the stranger whipped out a big bandanna handkerchief, caught the creature in it, just like a butterfly, and started tying up the ends of the bandanna.

"Sorry for the interruption," he said. "As I was saying — "

But Jabez Stone was shaking all over like a scared horse.

"That's Miser Stevens' voice!" he said, in a croak. "And you've got him in your handkerchief!"

The stranger looked a little embarrassed.

"Yes, I really should have transferred him to the collecting box," he said with a simper, "but there were some rather unusual specimens there and I didn't want them crowded. Well, well, these little contretemps [1] will occur."

"I don't know what you mean by contertan," said Jabez Stone, "but that was Miser Stevens' voice! And he ain't dead! You can't tell me he is! He was just as spry and mean as a woodchuck, Tuesday!"

"In the midst of life — " [2] said the stranger, kind of pious. "Listen!" Then a bell began to toll in the valley, and Jabez Stone listened, with the sweat running down his face. For he knew it was tolled for Miser Stevens and that he was dead.

"These long-standing accounts," said the stranger with a sigh; "one really hates to close them. But business is business."

He still had the bandanna in his hand, and Jabez Stone felt sick as he saw the cloth struggle and flutter.

"Are they all as small as that?" he asked hoarsely.

"Small?" said the stranger. "Oh, I see what you mean. Why, they vary." He measured Jabez Stone with his eyes, and his teeth showed. "Don't worry,

---

[1] contretemps (kôn′trĕ·täN): an embarrassing situation. Note Stone's pronunciation of the word in the next paragraph.

[2] The remainder of this quotation is "we are in death." It is part of the burial service in the *Book of Common Prayer*.

Mr. Stone," he said. "You'll go with a very good grade. I wouldn't trust you outside the collecting box. Now, a man like Dan'l Webster, of course — well, we'd have to build a special box for him, and even at that, I imagine the wing spread would astonish you. He'd certainly be a prize. I wish we could see our way clear to him. But, in your case, as I was saying — "

"Put that handkerchief away!" said Jabez Stone, and he began to beg and to pray. But the best he could get at the end was a three years' extension, with conditions.

But till you make a bargain like that, you've got no idea of how fast four years can run. By the last months of those years, Jabez Stone's known all over the state and there's talk of running him for governor — and it's dust and ashes in his mouth. For every day, when he gets up, he thinks, "There's one more night gone," and every night when he lies down, he thinks of the black pocketbook and the soul of Miser Stevens, and it makes him sick at heart. Till, finally, he can't bear it any longer, and, in the last days of the last year, he hitches up his horse and drives off to seek Dan'l Webster. For Dan'l Webster was born in New Hampshire, only a few miles from Cross Corners, and it's well known that he has a particular soft spot for old neighbors.

It was early in the morning when he got to Marshfield, but Dan'l was up already, talking Latin to the farm hands and wrestling with the ram, Goliath, and trying out a new trotter and working up speeches to make against John C. Calhoun.[1] But when he heard a New Hampshireman had come to see him, he dropped everything else he was doing, for that was Dan'l's way. He gave Jabez Stone a breakfast that five men couldn't eat, went into the living history of ev-

ery man and woman in Cross Corners, and finally asked him how he could serve him.

Jabez Stone allowed that it was a kind of mortgage case.

"Well, I haven't pleaded a mortgage case in a long time, and I don't generally plead now, except before the Supreme Court," said Dan'l, "but if I can, I'll help you."

"Then I've got hope for the first time in ten years," said Jabez Stone, and told him the details.

Dan'l walked up and down as he listened, hands behind his back, now and then asking a question, now and then plunging his eyes at the floor, as if they'd bore through it like gimlets. When Jabez Stone had finished, Dan'l puffed out his cheeks and blew. Then he turned to Jabez Stone, and a smile broke over his face like the sunrise over Monadnock.[2]

"You've certainly given yourself the devil's own row to hoe, Neighbor Stone," he said, "but I'll take your case."

"You'll take it?" said Jabez Stone, hardly daring to believe.

"Yes," said Dan'l Webster. "I've got about seventy-five other things to do and the Missouri Compromise[3] to straighten out, but I'll take your case. For if two New Hampshiremen aren't a match for the devil, we might as well give the country back to the Indians."

Then he shook Jabez Stone by the hand and said, "Did you come down here in a hurry?"

"Well, I admit I made time," said Jabez Stone.

"You'll go back faster," said Dan'l Webster, and he told 'em to hitch up Constitution and Constellation to the carriage. They were matched grays with one white forefoot, and they

---

[1] **Calhoun:** the great orator for the South, as Webster was for the North.

[2] **Monadnock** (mŏ·năd′nŏk): a mountain in New Hampshire. How does the comparison effect a contrast to the smile of the devil?

[3] **Missouri Compromise:** An act passed by Congress in 1820 in an attempt to settle the North-South dispute about slave territory.

" He stood there for a moment, his black eyes burning like anthracite. And then he began to speak." Edward Arnold dominates a scene in the movie The Devil and Daniel Webster. (*RKO Radio Pictures*)

stepped like greased lightning.

Well, I won't describe how excited and pleased the whole Stone family was to have the great Dan'l Webster for a guest, when they finally got there. Jabez Stone had lost his hat on the way, blown off when they overtook a wind, but he didn't take much account of that. But after supper he sent the family off to bed, for he had most particular business with Mr. Webster. Mrs. Stone wanted them to sit in the front parlor, but Dan'l Webster knew front parlors and said he preferred the kitchen. So it was there they sat, waiting for the stranger, with a jug on the table between them and a bright fire on the hearth — the stranger being scheduled to show up on the stroke of midnight, according to specification.

Well, most men wouldn't have asked for better company than Dan'l Webster and a jug. But with every tick of the clock Jabez Stone got sadder and sadder. His eyes roved round, and though he sampled the jug you could see he couldn't taste it. Finally, on the stroke of 11:30 he reached over and grabbed Dan'l Webster by the arm.

"Mr. Webster, Mr. Webster!" he said, and his voice was shaking with fear and a desperate courage. "For God's sake, Mr. Webster, harness your horses and get away from this place while you can!"

"You've brought me a long way, neighbor, to tell me you don't like my company," said Dan'l Webster, quite peaceable, pulling at the jug.

"Miserable wretch that I am!" groaned Jabez Stone. "I've brought you a devilish way, and now I see my folly. Let him take me if he wills. I don't hanker after it, I must say, but I can stand it. But you're the Union's stay and New Hampshire's pride! He mustn't get you, Mr. Webster! He mustn't get you!"

Dan'l Webster looked at the distracted man, all gray and shaking in the firelight, and laid a hand on his shoulder.

"I'm obliged to you, Neighbor Stone," he said gently. "It's kindly thought of. But there's a jug on the table and a case in hand. And I never left a jug or a case half finished in my life."

And just at that moment there was a sharp rap on the door.

"Ah," said Dan'l Webster, very coolly, "I thought your clock was a trifle slow, Neighbor Stone." He stepped to the door and opened it. "Come in!" he said.

The stranger came in — very dark and tall he looked in the firelight. He was carrying a box under his arm — a black, japanned[1] box with little air holes in the lid. At the sight of the box, Jabez Stone gave a low cry and shrank into a corner of the room.

"Mr. Webster, I presume," said the stranger, very polite, but with his eyes glowing like a fox's deep in the woods.

"Attorney of record for Jabez Stone," said Dan'l Webster, but his eyes were glowing too. "Might I ask your name?"

"I've gone by a good many," said the stranger carelessly. "Perhaps Scratch will do for the evening. I'm often called that in these regions."

Then he sat down at the table and poured himself a drink from the jug. The liquor was cold in the jug, but it came steaming into the glass.

"And now," said the stranger, smiling and showing his teeth, "I shall call upon you, as a law-abiding citizen, to assist me in taking possession of my property."

Well, with that the argument began — and it went hot and heavy. At first, Jabez Stone had a flicker of hope, but when he saw Dan'l Webster being forced back at point after point, he just sat scrunched in his corner, with his eyes on that japanned box. For there wasn't any doubt as to the deed or the signature — that was the worst of it. Dan'l Webster twisted and turned and thumped his fist on the table, but he

---

[1] japanned: lacquered.

couldn't get away from that. He offered to compromise the case; the stranger wouldn't hear of it. He pointed out the property had increased in value, and state senators ought to be worth more; the stranger stuck to the letter of the law. He was a great lawyer, Dan'l Webster, but we know who's the King of Lawyers, as the Good Book tells us, and it seemed as if, for the first time, Dan'l Webster had met his match.

Finally, the stranger yawned a little. "Your spirited efforts on behalf of your client do you credit, Mr. Webster," he said, "but if you have no more arguments to adduce, I'm rather pressed for time — " and Jabez Stone shuddered.

Dan'l Webster's brow looked dark as a thundercloud. "Pressed or not, you shall not have this man!" he thundered. "Mr. Stone is an American citizen, and no American citizen may be forced into the service of a foreign prince. We fought England for that in '12 [1] and we'll fight all hell for it again!"

"Foreign?" said the stranger. "And who calls me a foreigner?"

"Well, I never yet heard of the dev — of your claiming American citizenship," said Dan'l Webster with surprise.

"And who with better right?" said the stranger, with one of his terrible smiles. "When the first wrong was done to the first Indian, I was there. When the first slaver put out for the Congo, I stood on her deck. Am I not in your books and stories and beliefs, from the first settlements on? Am I not spoken of, still, in every church in New England? 'Tis true the North claims me for a Southerner, and the South for a Northerner, but I am neither. I am merely an honest American like yourself — and of the best descent — for, to tell the truth, Mr. Webster, though I don't like to boast of it, my name is older in this country than yours."

"Aha!" said Dan'l Webster, with the veins standing out in his forehead. "Then I stand on the Constitution! I demand a trial for my client!"

"The case is hardly one for an ordinary court," said the stranger, his eyes flickering. "And, indeed, the lateness of the hour — "

"Let it be any court you choose, so it is an American judge and an American jury!" said Dan'l Webster in his pride. "Let it be the quick [2] or the dead; I'll abide the issue!"

"You have said it," said the stranger, and pointed his finger at the door. And with that, and all of a sudden, there was a rushing of wind outside and a noise of footsteps. They came, clear and distinct, through the night. And yet, they were not like the footsteps of living men.

"In God's name, who comes by so late?" cried Jabez Stone, in an ague of fear.

"The jury Mr. Webster demands," said the stranger, sipping at his boiling glass. "You must pardon the rough appearance of one or two; they will have come a long way."

And with that the fire burned blue and the door blew open and twelve men entered, one by one.

If Jabez Stone had been sick with terror before, he was blind with terror now. For there was Walter Butler, the loyalist, who spread fire and horror through the Mohawk Valley in the times of the Revolution; and there was Simon Girty, the renegade, who saw white men burned at the stake and whooped with the Indians to see them burn. His eyes were green, like a catamount's, and the stains on his hunting shirt did not come from the blood of the deer. King Philip [3] was there, wild and proud as

---

[1] '12: The War of 1812 was partially caused by the impressing of Americans into the British navy.

[2] quick: living.

[3] King Philip: an Indian chief who organized an uprising against the white settlers in 1675, and was himself killed the following year.

he had been in life, with the great gash in his head that gave him his death wound, and cruel Governor Dale,[1] who broke men on the wheel. There was Morton of Merry Mount, who so vexed the Plymouth Colony, with his flushed, loose, handsome face and his hate of the godly. There was Teach, the bloody pirate, with his black beard curling on his breast. The Reverend John Smeet, with his strangler's hands and his Geneva gown,[2] walked as daintily as he had to the gallows. The red print of the rope was still around his neck, but he carried a perfumed handkerchief in one hand. One and all, they came into the room with the fires of hell still upon them, and the stranger named their names and their deeds as they came, till the tale of twelve was told. Yet the stranger had told the truth — they had all played a part in America.

"Are you satisfied with the jury, Mr. Webster?" said the stranger mockingly, when they had taken their places.

The sweat stood upon Dan'l Webster's brow, but his voice was clear.

"Quite satisfied," he said. "Though I miss General Arnold from the company."

"Benedict Arnold is engaged upon other business," said the stranger, with a glower. "Ah, you asked for a justice, I believe."

He pointed his finger once more, and a tall man, soberly clad in Puritan garb, with the burning gaze of the fanatic, stalked into the room and took his judge's place.

"Justice Hathorne is a jurist of experience," said the stranger. "He presided at certain witch trials once held in Salem. There were others who repented of the business later, but not he."

"Repent of such notable wonders and undertakings?" said the stern old justice. "Nay, hang them — hang them all!" And he muttered to himself in a way that struck ice into the soul of Jabez Stone.

Then the trial began, and, as you might expect, it didn't look anyways good for the defense. And Jabez Stone didn't make much of a witness in his own behalf. He took one look at Simon Girty and screeched, and they had to put him back in his corner in a kind of swoon.

It didn't halt the trial, though; the trial went on, as trials do. Dan'l Webster had faced some hard juries and hanging judges in his time, but this was the hardest he'd ever faced, and he knew it. They sat there with a kind of glitter in their eyes, and the stranger's smooth voice went on and on. Every time he'd raise an objection, it'd be "Objection sustained," but whenever Dan'l objected, it'd be "Objection denied." Well, you couldn't expect fair play from a fellow like this Mr. Scratch.

It got to Dan'l in the end, and he began to heat, like iron in the forge. When he got up to speak he was going to flay that stranger with every trick known to the law, and the judge and jury too. He didn't care if it was contempt of court or what would happen to him for it. He didn't care any more what happened to Jabez Stone. He just got madder and madder, thinking of what he'd say. And yet, curiously enough, the more he thought about it, the less he was able to arrange his speech in his mind.

Till, finally, it was time for him to get up on his feet, and he did so, all ready to bust out with lightnings and denunciations. But before he started he looked over the judge and jury for a moment, such being his custom. And he noticed the glitter in their eyes was twice as strong as before, and they all leaned forward. Like hounds just before they get the fox, they looked, and the blue mist of evil in the room thickened as he watched them. Then he saw what he'd

---

[1] **Dale:** English Deputy-Governor of Virginia, 1611–1616, whose severe laws caused the colonists to call these the "years of slavery."

[2] **Geneva gown:** minister's robe.

been about to do, and he wiped his forehead, as a man might who's just escaped falling into a pit in the dark.

For it was him they'd come for, not only Jabez Stone. He read it in the glitter of their eyes and in the way the stranger hid his mouth with one hand. And if he fought them with their own weapons, he'd fall into their power; he knew that, though he couldn't have told you how. It was his own anger and horror that burned in their eyes; and he'd have to wipe that out or the case was lost. He stood there for a moment, his black eyes burning like anthracite. And then he began to speak.

He started off in a low voice, though you could hear every word. They say he could call on the harps of the blessed when he chose. And this was just as simple and easy as a man could talk. But he didn't start out by condemning or reviling. He was talking about the things that make a country a country, and a man a man.

And he began with the simple things that everybody's known and felt — the freshness of a fine morning when you're young, and the taste of food when you're hungry, and the new day that's every day when you're a child. He took them up and he turned them in his hands. They were good things for any man. But without freedom, they sickened. And when he talked of those enslaved, and the sorrows of slavery, his voice got like a big bell. He talked of the early days of America and the men who had made those days. It wasn't a spread-eagle speech, but he made you see it. He admitted all the wrong that had ever been done. But he showed how, out of the wrong and the right, the suffering and the starvations, something new had come. And everybody had played a part in it, even the traitors.

Then he turned to Jabez Stone and showed him as he was — an ordinary man who'd had hard luck and wanted to change it. And, because he'd wanted to change it, now he was going to be punished for all eternity. And yet there was good in Jabez Stone, and he showed that good. He was hard and mean, in some ways, but he was a man. There was sadness in being a man, but it was a proud thing too. And he showed what the pride of it was till you couldn't help feeling it. Yes, even in hell, if a man was a man, you'd know it. And he wasn't pleading for any one person any more, though his voice rang like an organ. He was telling the story and the failures and the endless journey of mankind. They got tricked and trapped and bamboozled, but it was a great journey. And no demon that was ever foaled could know the inwardness of it — it took a man to do that.

The fire began to die on the hearth and the wind before morning to blow. The light was getting gray in the room when Dan'l Webster finished. And his words came back at the end to New Hampshire ground, and the one spot of land that each man loves and clings to. He painted a picture of that, and to each one of that jury he spoke of things long forgotten. For his voice could search the heart, and that was his gift and his strength. And to one, his voice was like the forest and its secrecy, and to another like the sea and the storms of the sea; and one heard the cry of his lost nation in it, and another saw a little harmless scene he hadn't remembered for years. But each saw something. And when Dan'l Webster finished he didn't know whether or not he'd saved Jabez Stone. But he knew he'd done a miracle. For the glitter was gone from the eyes of judge and jury, and, for the moment, they were men again, and knew they were men.

"The defense rests," said Dan'l Webster, and stood there like a mountain. His ears were still ringing with his speech, and he didn't hear anything else till he heard Judge Hathorne say, " The jury will retire to consider its verdict."

Walter Butler rose in his place and his face had a dark, gay pride on it.

"The jury has considered its verdict," he said, and looked the stranger full in the eye. "We find for the defendant, Jabez Stone."

With that, the smile left the stranger's face, but Walter Butler did not flinch.

"Perhaps 'tis not strictly in accordance with the evidence," he said, "but even the damned may salute the eloquence of Mr. Webster."

With that, the long crow of a rooster split the gray morning sky, and judge and jury were gone from the room like a puff of smoke and as if they had never been there. The stranger turned to Dan'l Webster, smiling wryly. "Major Butler was always a bold man," he said. "I had not thought him quite so bold. Nevertheless, my congratulations, as between two gentlemen."

"I'll have that paper first, if you please," said Dan'l Webster, and he took it and tore it into four pieces. It was queerly warm to the touch. "And now," he said, "I'll have you!" and his hand came down like a bear trap on the stranger's arm. For he knew that once you bested anybody like Mr. Scratch in fair fight, his power on you was gone. And he could see that Mr. Scratch knew it too.

The stranger twisted and wriggled, but he couldn't get out of that grip. "Come, come, Mr. Webster," he said, smiling palely. "This sort of thing is ridic — ouch! — is ridiculous. If you're worried about the costs of the case, naturally, I'd be glad to pay —"

"And so you shall!" said Dan'l Webster, shaking him till his teeth rattled. "For you'll sit right down at that table and draw up a document, promising never to bother Jabez Stone nor his heirs or assigns nor any other New Hampshireman till doomsday! For any hades we want to raise in this state, we can raise ourselves, without assistance from strangers."

"Ouch!" said the stranger. "Ouch! Well, they never did run very big to the barrel, but — ouch! — I agree!"

So he sat down and drew up the document. But Dan'l Webster kept his hand on his coat collar all the time.

"And, now, may I go?" said the stranger, quite humble, when Dan'l'd seen the document was in proper and legal form.

"Go?" said Dan'l, giving him another shake. "I'm still trying to figure out what I'll do with you. For you've settled the costs of the case, but you haven't settled with me. I think I'll take you back to Marshfield," he said, kind of reflective. "I've got a ram there named Goliath that can butt through an iron door. I'd kind of like to turn you loose in his field and see what he'd do."

Well, with that the stranger began to beg and to plead. And he begged and he pled so humble that finally Dan'l, who was naturally kindhearted, agreed to let him go. The stranger seemed terrible grateful for that and said, just to show they were friends, he'd tell Dan'l's fortune before leaving. So Dan'l agreed to that, though he didn't take much stock in fortunetellers ordinarily.

But, naturally, the stranger was a little different. Well, he pried and he peered at the lines in Dan'l's hands. And he told him one thing and another that was quite remarkable. But they were all in the past.

"Yes, all that's true, and it happened," said Dan'l Webster. "But what's to come in the future?"

The stranger grinned, kind of happily, and shook his head. "The future's not as you think it," he said. "It's dark. You have a great ambition, Mr. Webster."

"I have," said Dan'l firmly, for everybody knew he wanted to be President.

"It seems almost within your grasp," said the stranger, "but you will not attain it. Lesser men will be made President and you will be passed over."

"And, if I am, I'll still be Daniel Webster," said Dan'l. "Say on."

"You have two strong sons," said the stranger, shaking his head. "You look to found a line. But each will die in war and neither reach greatness."

"Live or die, they are still my sons," said Dan'l Webster. "Say on."

"You have made great speeches," said the stranger. "You will make more."

"Ah," said Dan'l Webster.

"But the last great speech you make will turn many of your own against you," said the stranger. "They will call you Ichabod;[1] they will call you by other names. Even in New England some will say you have turned your coat and sold your country, and their voices will be loud against you till you die."

"So it is an honest speech, it does not matter what men say," said Dan'l Webster. Then he looked at the stranger and their glances locked.

"One question," he said. "I have fought for the Union all my life. Will I see that fight won against those who would tear it apart?"

"Not while you live," said the stranger, grimly, "but it will be won. And after you are dead, there are thousands who will fight for your cause, because of words that you spoke."

"Why, then, you long-barreled, slab-sided, lantern-jawed, fortunetelling note-shaver!" said Dan'l Webster, with a great roar of laughter, "be off with you to your own place before I put my mark on you! For, by the thirteen original colonies I'd go to the Pit itself to save the Union!"

And with that he drew back his foot for a kick that would have stunned a

[1] **Ichabod** (ĭk′á·bŏd): the title of Whittier's poem criticizing Webster's speech of March 7, 1850, in which he denounced the Abolitionists. Because of this speech many Northerners considered Webster a traitor. Ichabod is a Hebrew name meaning "where is the glory?" or, as it is usually translated, "the glory is departed."

horse. It was only the tip of his shoe that caught the stranger, but he went flying out of the door with his collecting box under his arm.

"And now," said Dan'l Webster, seeing Jabez Stone beginning to rouse from his swoon, "let's see what's left in the jug, for it's dry work talking all night. I hope there's pie for breakfast, Neighbor Stone."

But they say that whenever the devil comes near Marshfield, even now, he gives it a wide berth. And he hasn't been seen in the state of New Hampshire from that day to this. I'm not talking about Massachusetts or Vermont.

For Discussion of Benét

1. Point out some of the details in the beginning that make Webster almost a mythical figure. What has this picture of Webster in common with such folk heroes as Paul Bunyan and John Henry?

2. What caused the stranger to appear? What is ironical about the way he is described? What details confirmed the suspicion of Stone as to the man's identity?

3. How was Stone's life affected by his secret compact with the stranger? What means did he use to try to dodge the compact? Why did he fail? What is the meaning of the butterfly episode?

4. On what grounds did the stranger claim American citizenship? What criticism of some American policies of the past is implied? Is it justified? In what other ways is the case made to go against Webster at first?

5. How is suspense increased by the entrance of the jury? Only seven of the twelve jurors are mentioned. What evil characters in American history would you suggest for the remaining five? Give reasons for each. Why did Webster mention Benedict Arnold? Why was the judge particularly well chosen for the stranger's side of the case? What indicates that the court procedure was unfair?

6. What made Webster change the tone of his final speech? In what way was it a masterpiece of appeal to such a jury? How

were they affected? From your knowledge of American history, tell how Scratch's prophecy about Webster's future was fulfilled.

7. On page 475 there is a story by Washington Irving on the same general theme. When you have read both stories, you will want to compare them.

For Your Vocabulary

FIGURATIVE USE OF WORDS: A sure way to improve your command of language is to learn new words. An equally certain way to achieve effective speech is to use familiar words vividly, with imagination. By now, you have studied figures of speech and know the effectiveness of comparisons: " gone from the room like a puff of smoke," " as contented as cats in a dairy "; and of exaggeration: when he spoke, " stars and stripes came right out in the sky."

Look at the way Benét puts life into his story with figures of speech. The story is full of them. Let's narrow it down to his picturing of eyes. Daniel Webster had eyes " burning like anthracite." Simon Girty, the renegade, had eyes " green, like a catamount's." The devil had eyes " glowing like a fox's deep in the woods." Now those are all similes, expressed comparisons with *like* for a label. But Benét uses single verbs figuratively for the look in these men's eyes. He describes Webster as " *plunging* his eyes at the floor, as if they'd bore through it like gimlets." The devil's eyes were *flickering.* Justice Hathorne had " the *burning* gaze of the fanatic." Not one of these words is used literally, yet each one gives you the impression more clearly than a detailed realistic description. Find other examples of figurative language in this story. Compare your list with those of your classmates.

The Scoundrel

JOHN FANTE
1911–

John Fante learned things the hard way. Born in Denver, Colorado, of Italian parentage, he attended Regis High School in Denver and the University of Colorado, and by his own admission, " hated school all the time." He left college without a degree to take odd jobs as a hotel and grocery clerk and a stevedore, and failed at all of them. Later, he began to write short

stories, and suddenly met success. *American Mercury, The Atlantic, Story,* and *The Woman's Home Companion* published his work, and he now writes for the movies.

" The Scoundrel " strikes a familiar note for Catholic students. No doubt you'll substitute different names, but most of us have met Sister Agnes, Father Cooney, and Sister Thomas before. Enjoy the reunion!

SISTER MARY AGNES had been my principal for eight years at St. Vincent's. She knew more about me than my mother. But Mama was like that.

For instance, it was Sister Agnes who

got me out of jail for breaking street lamps. The police sergeant called Mama, but Mama didn't believe him. Sergeant Corelli had caught Jack Jenson and me red-handed. I was standing right there when Sergeant Corelli telephoned Mama. I could hear her voice in the receiver.

"There must be some mistake," she said, "my son Jimmy would never do a thing like that."

"I tell you this is your boy," Sergeant Corelli said, "he's right here. James Kennedy."

"Oh no," Mama said, "I know you've made a mistake. There are lots of Kennedys in this world. My Jimmy isn't like that."

She hung up. Sergeant Corelli shook his head.

"You've sure got her buffaloed," he said. Then he asked me where I went to school.

I told him I was in the eighth grade at St. Vincent's. He telephoned Sister Mary Agnes because she was principal and Sister Superior. She hopped into a cab and came right down to the city hall.

Jack Jenson's father got there about the same time. We didn't get along, Mr. Jenson and I. He shook his finger at me. "You're responsible for this."

"I broke two lamps," I said, "Jack broke the other two."

"That's a lie," Jack said, "I got that one on the corner of Ninth and Pine, and you know it. You only got one. I got three."

"I don't know who busted what," Sergeant Corelli said, "All I know is — four lamps is broke. City property."

Sister Agnes clucked like a hen. "It's scandalous," she said to me, "perfectly scandalous. To think that you, a Catholic boy, of Catholic parents, educated in a Catholic school, should go around destroying public property. James, if I've warned you once, I've warned you a thousand times — stay away from bad company."

Mr. Jenson's mouth and eyes popped open. "Now wait a minute, miss," he said, "you can't call my boy 'bad company.' You may be a holy lady, miss, but I'm not going to stand here and let you call my boy a criminal."

"I didn't *say* he was a criminal," Sister Agnes said.

"Let's quit arguing and get to the bottom of this," Sergeant Corelli said. "Now then: Why did you kids do it?"

Jack looked at me. "Go ahead and tell him."

"To settle a bet," I said.

Sister Agnes took a deep breath. "Why, James Kennedy. Gambling too. You know gambling is a sin."

"Not a very big sin," I said. "We were gambling for small stakes."

"What was the bet?" Sergeant Corelli asked.

Jack told him: "I bet him a couple of cigars against a pack of cigarettes that I could bust more lamps than him."

"Cigars!" Mr. Jenson said. "So that's where my cigars been going."

"Cigarettes!" Sister Agnes said. "So you've been smoking again."

We didn't say anything. We were being honest, but nobody seemed to pay the least attention or to appreciate it at all.

"There you are," Sergeant Corelli said. "They admit everything. Now — what's to be done with these kids?"

Mr. Jenson opened his mouth and his teeth were like wolf fangs. "I know what *I'm* going to do," he said.

Jack swallowed and rolled his eyes around.

"And I think I can handle this young man," Sister Agnes said.

Jack left the city hall on tiptoe. Mr. Jenson had a strong grip on his left ear. I felt sorry for poor Jack. Mr. Jenson was foreman of a construction gang with the state highway.

"I'm taking you to see Father Cooney," Sister Agnes said to me. She asked Sergeant Corelli to call a taxi. The sergeant picked up the phone. Sister Agnes and I sat on a bench in front of the window and waited. I was, slumped forward, trying to think of something pleasant to say. Sister Agnes kissed the crucifix at the end of the brown beads which hung from her belt and began to say the Rosary.

"Sit up straight," she whispered.

I sat up and folded my arms.

"Aren't you going to pray?" she asked. "You ought to be grateful to Almighty God that you're not behind bars. You should be on your knees, offering up thanks and begging Him to forgive you for this day."

"Right here?" I asked. "In the police station?"

"At least pray in your heart," she said closing her eyes.

I closed my eyes and thought out a prayer: Dear Lord, thanks a lot for getting me out of this mess. I think the whole thing is a bluff and they can't do much to me because I'm only fourteen. But things could have been a lot worse. So thanks again. And please, dear Savior, try to fix it up so Sister Agnes won't phone my old man. Please, Lord. If you ever did a fellow a favor, please, please, don't let her tell my old man.

Bill Callen owned the Boulder Taxi Company. He drove it up to the curb and we went outside and down the city hall steps. A long time before, Bill had been one of Sister Agnes' pupils. He opened the cab door and helped her inside.

"Anything wrong, Sister?" he said. "Anything I can do?"

"Nothing, Bill," Sister smiled. "Nothing at all. Just take us back to the convent, if you please."

"Him too?"

She smiled again.

I got in beside Sister Agnes. Bill looked at me and said it all over again — "If there's anything I can do, Sister, just any little thing at all, just let me know."

"Thank you, Bill."

"What are we going to do now, Sister?" I asked.

"First I'm going to take you to Father Cooney."

That wasn't bad. Father Cooney didn't deliver very good sermons but he was a sucker for penitence. All you had to do was hold your head down and make a sad face, and he'd give you the shirt off his back.

"Father Cooney'll be very disappointed in me," I said.

"It's my duty to report this," she said.

"I know. I'm awfully ashamed. Poor Father Cooney."

"And then of course I must tell your father."

"My father? You mean, my father?"

"Your father."

Father Cooney was one thing, but my father was something else again. My father was the strong silent type. He was mostly strong and he liked to throw his weight around. He wasn't particularly silent, either. Something else: he lacked imagination. There was only one way he dealt with situations of this kind. It was very unpleasant to think about.

"I'll phone him tonight," she said.

I laughed. Not a loud laugh. Softly.

She glanced at me. "Why are you laughing?"

"It's kinda funny," I said shaking my head. "Just a little while ago I said a prayer to Our Lord. I asked Him to please not let my father know about this. And now you're going to tell him."

"Of course I am."

"I know," I said. "You have to. It's your duty. It wouldn't be right if you didn't tell him. Still, at the same time, the catechism says that all things come to him who prays. I know you have to tell my father. I know that. But still, it only goes to show that sometimes the things you learn in the catechism don't work out in real life."

She watched me with her big blue eyes. I curled my mouth and slouched down in the seat and smiled like a man who is sad but not afraid, and ready for anything. Now and then she bit her lip and looked at me.

Father Cooney was eating supper. He told his housekeeper, Mrs. Hanley, she could be excused. Sister Mary Agnes and I watched her go away. Father Cooney had started his dessert, which was chocolate cake. He was a tall heavy man with a bald spot on the top of his head. He pointed to the other chairs around the table.

"Sit down," he said, "please do. You like chocolate cake, Jimmy?"

"Boy — do I!"

Sister Agnes did not sit down. Father Cooney took up the cake knife and cut off a big slab for me.

"After what this young man has done," Sister Agnes said, "I don't think he should be rewarded with a piece of chocolate cake."

"Indeed?" Father Cooney said looking at me. "What's this, Jimmy? What've you done?"

"I got into trouble."

"Trouble? What kind of trouble?"

I hung my head and didn't say anything. Father Cooney put the piece of cake on a dish in front of me. Sister Agnes folded her arms. The look on her face said: Leave the cake alone. I sneaked down into the chair and sat with my hands in my lap. Father Cooney was watching us. I lifted my hand from under the table and picked up a fork. The cake was devil's food, with about a foot of chocolate icing. I took one quick look at Sister Agnes. She was daring me to try it. When I moved the fork toward the cake she stepped up to the table and put her hand on my arm.

"You haven't told Father Cooney why you're here," she said.

I didn't put down the fork but I hung my head in shame. "I was arrested, Father. Another kid and me got picked up for busting street lamps."

"Indeed," Father Cooney said.

I told him how it had happened.

"He wasn't a Catholic boy," I said. "I should of known better than to associate with him."

"There's no reason why you shouldn't associate with non-Catholics," Father said, "provided they're good boys."

"He wasn't exactly a bad boy," I said. "Only thing is, he said he could break more lamps than any Catholic kid in town."

"Who won?" Father said.

"It was a tie. Two apiece."

"Humph."

He ate another mouthful of cake and sipped some coffee. He was thinking it over. I moved my fork toward the dish again. This time Sister Agnes didn't stop me. The cake melted in my mouth. I sat back and tasted the thick sweet chocolate on my teeth and tongue, tasted it all the way down into my stomach.

Father Cooney tried again to make Sister Agnes sit down.

"Do try this cake," he said. "It's marvelous."

"No thank you, Father. My own supper is waiting for me at the convent. I brought this young man here because I feel he should be reprimanded. Destroying public property is a very serious offense."

"It *is* a serious offense," Father Cooney said. "It most certainly is. And I intend to punish him severely."

"I shall phone Mr. Kennedy immediately," Sister Agnes said.

"A splendid idea," Father said.

All at once the cake had a flat taste. I couldn't swallow any more. Sister Agnes said good-by to Father Cooney. At the door she stopped to say she wanted to see me before I went home. I felt better after she was gone. Father Cooney got me a glass of milk, and he gave me another piece of cake. For a long time we ate without talking. Then I finished my cake and sat back. Father Cooney lit a cigar.

"Last night I was reading the life of

St. Paul," he said. " A wonderful man — truly wonderful."

It was coming. It was going to be a sermon about St. Paul and everybody in the parish agreed that Father Cooney's sermons were the worst of any priest in the whole diocese.

" The Apostle Paul believed in the doctrine not of faith alone, but of faith by good works. Not mere lip service to our Blessed Savior, but piety as well, and good works; setting a fine example among the early Christians as well as the heathen."

" Yes, Father."

He tipped the ash off his cigar and leaned forward. " Let me put it this way, my boy: How would it have been if, in the early days of the struggling young Church, the blessed apostle instead of setting an example by good works, had gone about the countryside breaking street lights? What chance would Christianity have had? "

" Not a chance," I said.

" Indeed not."

" Did they have street lights in those days, Father? "

" Perhaps they did, and perhaps not. Nevertheless the Light of Faith in Christ shone in the hearts of St. Paul and his loyal followers. They were willing and even glad to brave persecution and death in His name. Everywhere they traveled, they set an example that endeared them to God and man. It was not the light of destructiveness, of breaking things. It was the light of faith, of gentleness, of human brotherhood. You see what I mean, son? "

" Yes, Father."

" Good. Fine. More cake? "

" No thanks, Father."

He pushed back his chair and stood up. " You may go now."

He put his hand on my shoulder and walked to the door with me. " I'll check with the Bureau of Power and Light, and see about the damage. But promise me you won't do it again."

" I promise."

He shook hands with me just like I was a man. " Good night, Jim."

" Good night, Father. Thanks for the cake."

It was almost six o'clock. The nuns lived in the west wing of the school building. I still had to see Sister Agnes, so I decided to go to the back door. At that hour it was most unusual to be seen knocking at the front door of the convent. It could only mean that a fellow was in some kind of mess. Besides, Sister Mary Thomas was in the convent kitchen. She did the cooking for the nuns. She was always good for a cooky or a piece of pie.

" I have to see Sister Agnes," I said.

" You always have to see Sister Mary Agnes. Little man, what now? "

" Nothing much."

" Of course not. Just some trifle like bank robbery or something. And you probably wouldn't like a piece of apple pie, either."

" Just a very small piece."

" I know," she said, " just a very small piece."

I sat down at the end of the long table that ran the length of the room. On the table were six hot steaming French apple pies. Sister Thomas cut me almost half a pie.

" We have some strawberry ice cream," she said, " But I don't suppose you want any; not very much, at any rate."

" Just a bit."

The pie was so hot that the ice cream melted and the pink cream filtered through the cinnamon and apples. It was wonderful. Sister Mary Thomas waited until I was almost finished before she called Sister Agnes on the house telephone.

I put the last bite of pie in my mouth just as Sister Agnes came into the kitchen.

" What's the meaning of this? " she

said.

"He looked hungry," Sister Thomas said.

"Hungry? He always looks hungry — the scoundrel."

I stood up and wiped my mouth with the back of my hand.

"Sister Mary Thomas," she said, "I've forbidden you to feed these boys. I've told you repeatedly: Stop — feeding — the boys. How in heaven's name can I hope to have any discipline in this school if they're rewarded instead of punished? I repeat it for the last, the very last time: Stop — feeding — the boys!"

Sister Agnes swung around and faced me. She took off her glasses and scowled.

"You," she said. "You scoundrel. You reprobate. After all the disgrace you've heaped upon your immortal soul — after all the humiliation you've brought down upon your church and your city — you have the sheer unmitigated audacity to stand there facing me, gorged with chocolate cake and apple pie." She looked down at my plate. "And strawberry ice cream."

I moved my feet a little but I didn't talk.

"Well — what have you to say for yourself?"

"Nothing, I guess." I figured I'd better do something quick. So I hung my head and began to sob.

"What did Father Cooney say to you?" she asked.

I didn't say anything. I just stood there looking down at my shoes and crying softly.

"So now you're crying," she said.

I threw myself into a chair and buried my face and sobbed. I could hear my own big sobs filling the kitchen. For some time nothing was said.

Then Sister Agnes spoke. "At least there appears to be some scrap of human decency left in him."

I howled.

"You'd better go home now," she said.

I kept my face covered and dragged myself toward the door. "Good night, Sister Thomas," I said.

"Good night, James."

"Thanks for the pie," I choked.

As I opened the door Sister Agnes came toward me. "One moment," she said. She put her hand on my shoulder and she was smiling — a sweet beautiful smile. "I really believe you're sorry for what happened today."

"I feel terrible," I said keeping my head down. "All those street lights. All that pie and cake. I feel awful."

She lifted my face with the tip of her finger. "I'm sorry it happened too," she said. "But since you've shown such sincere sorrow, we'll all try to forget it." She smiled again. "About your father, you won't have to worry. I won't telephone him."

I said, "Gee, Sister. Thanks!"

"And now, go home as fast as you can. And don't throw any rocks — at anything."

I hurried away and cut across the lawn. Except that I had eaten too much, I felt pretty good. The long cool shadows from the maple trees fell across the lawn. The rim of the big gold sun was sagging behind the mountains and the mountains were a dark blue. I walked very fast for a couple of blocks and when I thought of what would have happened if my father had found out, it made me stop and take a deep breath.

Then I remembered my little prayer to God, asking Him not to let my father know. It filled me up. I leaned against one of the maple trees on Tenth Street and started to cry. Not the same kind of a cry I had in Sister Thomas' kitchen. This was a real cry that shook me all over, until I thought I would break into pieces. I couldn't stop. I peeled some bark from the tree and cried for a long time. Then I started for home again.

For Discussion of Fante

1. In what ways is James typical of his age? What can you tell about his parents from his attitudes toward them?

2. Contrast Sister Mary Agnes and Father Cooney. What was the relationship between James and Father Cooney?

3. Why did James go into the convent by the back door? Describe Sister Mary Thomas.

4. Do you think James fooled Sister Agnes? Does he fear her? Why did she change her mind about calling his father? What made him cry on the way home?

5. Is this episode a common experience in the life of an adolescent?

Sixteen

*MAUREEN DALY
1921–

It is not unusual for a writer to begin creative work in the teens or even younger. What *is* unusual is for nationwide recognition to come to anyone at so young an age. Maureen Daly was only sixteen herself when she wrote the short story " Sixteen." It brought her first place in a *Scholastic* contest and the distinction of being the youngest author ever to be included in the O. Henry Memorial collection. This story and her later novel, *Seventeenth Summer*, deal with youth, its hurts and joys, its defeats and triumphs.

Maureen was born in Ireland, but her family moved soon after to Fond du Lac, Wisconsin, where her writing career began at the local high school. After college she turned to journalism and now conducts a newspaper column for teen-agers and the " Sub-Deb" department of *The Ladies' Home Journal*.

Of " Sixteen," the author says, " It wasn't meant to be a short story at all, but rather I just wanted to get the experience down on paper to relieve the tense, hurt feelings inside of me."

Now don't get me wrong. I mean, I want you to understand from the beginning that I'm not really so dumb. I know what a girl should do and what she shouldn't. I get around. I read. I listen to the radio. And I have two older sisters. So you see, I know what the score is. I know it's smart to wear tweedish skirts and shaggy sweaters with the sleeves pushed up and pearls and ankle socks and saddle shoes that look as if they've seen the world. And I know that your hair should be long, almost to your shoulders, and sleek as a wet seal, just a little fluffed on the ends, and you should wear a campus hat or a dink or else a peasant hankie if you've that sort of face. Properly, a peasant hankie should make you think of edelweiss,[1] mist and sunny mountains, yodeling and Swiss cheese. You know, that kind of peasant. Now, me, I never wear a hankie. It makes my face

[1] **edelweiss** (ā'dĕl·vīs): a white mountain flower growing high up in the rocks of the Alps.

seem wide and Slavic and I look like a picture always in one of those magazine articles that run — "And Stalin says the future of Russia lies in its women. In its women who have tilled its soil, raised its children — " Well, anyway. I'm not exactly too small-town either. I read Winchell's column. You get to know what New York boy is that way about some pineapple princess on the West Coast and what Paradise pretty is currently the prettiest, and why someone, eventually, will play Scarlett O'Hara.[1] It gives you that cosmopolitan feeling. And I know that anyone who orders a strawberry sundae in a drugstore instead of a lemon coke would probably be dumb enough to wear colored ankle socks with high-heeled pumps or use Evening in Paris with a tweed suit. But I'm sort of drifting. This isn't what I wanted to tell you. I just wanted to give you the general idea of how I'm not so dumb. It's important that you understand that.

You see, it was funny how I met him. It was a winter night like any other winter night. And I didn't have my Latin done, either. But the way the moon tinseled the twigs and silver-plated the snowdrifts, I just couldn't stay inside. The skating rink isn't far from our house — you can make it in five minutes if the sidewalks aren't slippery — so I went skating. I remember it took me a long time to get ready that night because I had to darn my skating socks first. I don't know why they always wear out so fast — just in the toes, too. Maybe it's because I have metal protectors on the toes of my skates. That probably *is* why. And then I brushed my hair — hard, so hard it

[1] **Scarlett O'Hara:** At the time of this story preparations were being made to produce *Gone with the Wind* as a movie and there was much discussion as to the most suitable actress for the coveted role of the heroine. Vivien Leigh was finally chosen.

clung to my hand and stood up around my head in a hazy halo.

My skates were hanging by the back door all nice and shiny, for I'd just got them for Christmas and they smelled so queer — just like fresh smoked ham. My dog walked with me as far as the corner. She's a red chow, very polite and well mannered, and she kept pretending it was me she liked when all the time I knew it was the ham smell. She panted along beside me and her hot breath made a frosty little balloon balancing on the end of her nose. My skates thumped me good-naturedly on my back as I walked and the night was breathlessly quiet and the stars winked down like a million flirting eyes. It was all so lovely.

It was all so lovely I ran most of the way and it was lucky the sidewalks had ashes on them or I'd have slipped surely. The ashes crunched like crackerjack and I could feel their cindery shape through the thinness of my shoes. I always wear old shoes when I go skating.

I had to cut across someone's back garden to get to the rink and last summer's grass stuck through the thin ice, brown and discouraged. Not many people came through this way and the crusted snow broke through the little hollows between corn stubbles frozen hard in the ground. I was out of breath when I got to the shanty — out of breath with running and with the loveliness of the night. Shanties are always such friendly places. The floor all hacked to wet splinters from skate runners and the wooden wall frescoed with symbols of dead romance. There was a smell of singed wool as someone got too near the glowing isinglass grin of the iron stove. Girls burst through the door laughing, with snow on their hair, and tripped over shoes scattered on the floor. A pimply-faced boy grabbed the hat from the frizzled head of an eighth-grade blonde and stuffed it into an empty galosh to prove his love and then hastily bent to examine his skate strap with innocent unconcern.

It didn't take me long to get my own skates on and I stuck my shoes under the bench — far back were they wouldn't get knocked around and would be easy to find when I wanted to go home. I walked out on my toes and the shiny runners of my new skates dug deep into the sodden floor.

It was snowing a little outside — quick, eager little Luxlike flakes that melted as soon as they touched your hand. I don't know where the snow came from, for there were stars out. Or maybe the stars were in my eyes and I just kept seeing them every time I looked up into the darkness. I waited a moment. You know, to start to skate at a crowded rink is like jumping on a moving merry-go-round. The skaters go skimming round in a colored blur like gaudy painted horses and the shrill musical jabber re-echoes in the night from a hundred human calliopes. Once in, I went all right. At least after I found out exactly where that rough ice was. It was "round, round, jump the rut, round, round, round, jump the rut, round, round — "

And then he came. All of a sudden his arm was around my waist so warm and tight and he said very casually, "Mind if I skate with you?" and then he took my other hand. That's all there was to it. Just that and then we were skating. It wasn't that I'd never skated with a boy before. Don't be silly. I told you before I get around. But this was different. He was a smoothie! He was a big shot up at school and he went to all the big dances and he was the best dancer in town except Harold Wright, who didn't count because he'd been to college in New York for two years! Don't you see? This was different.

I can't remember what we talked about at first; I can't even remember if we talked at all. We just skated and

skated and laughed every time we came to that rough spot and pretty soon we were laughing all the time at nothing at all. It was all so lovely.

Then we sat on the big snowbank at the edge of the rink and just watched. It was cold at first even with my skating pants on, sitting on that hard heap of snow, but pretty soon I got warm all over. He threw a handful of snow at me and it fell in a little white shower on my hair and he leaned over to brush it off. I held my breath. The night stood still.

The moon hung just over the warming shanty like a big quarter slice of muskmelon and the smoke from the pipe chimney floated up in a sooty fog. One by one the houses around the rink twinked out their lights and somebody's hound wailed a mournful apology to a star as he curled up for the night. It was all so lovely.

Then he sat up straight and said, "We'd better start home." Not "Shall I take you home?" or "Do you live far?" but "We'd better start home." See, that's how I know he wanted to take me home. Not because he *had* to but because he *wanted* to. He went to the shanty to get my shoes. "Black ones," I told him. "Same size as Garbo's." And he laughed again. He was still smiling when he came back and took off my skates and tied the wet skate strings in a soggy knot and put them over his shoulder. Then he held out his hand and I slid off the snowbank and brushed off the seat of my pants and we were ready.

It was snowing harder now. Big, quiet flakes that clung to twiggy bushes and snuggled in little drifts against the tree trunks. The night was an etching in black and white. It was all so lovely I was sorry I lived only a few blocks away. He talked softly as we walked, as if every little word were a secret. "Did I like Wayne King, and did I plan to go to college next year, and had I a cousin who lived in Appleton and knew his

Winter evening in Wisconsin — the setting of Maureen Daly's "Sixteen."
(Ewing Galloway)

brother?" A very respectable Emily Post sort of conversation, and then finally "how nice I looked with snow in my hair and had I ever seen the moon so – close?" For the moon was following us as we walked and ducking playfully behind a chimney every time I turned to look at it. And then we were home.

The porch light was on. My mother always puts the porch light on when I go away at night. And we stood there a moment by the front steps and the snow turned pinkish in the glow of the colored light and a few feathery flakes settled on his hair. Then he took my skates and put them over my shoulder and said, "Good night now. I'll call you." "I'll call you," he said.

I went inside then and in a moment he was gone. I watched him from my window as he went down the street. He was whistling softly and I waited until the sound faded away so I couldn't tell if it was he or my heart whistling out there in the night. And then he was gone, completely gone.

I shivered. Somehow the darkness seemed changed. The stars were little hard chips of light far up in the sky and the moon stared down with a sullen yellow glare. The air was tense with sudden cold and a gust of wind swirled his footprints into white oblivion. Everything was quiet.

But he'd said, "I'll call you." That's what he said – "I'll call you." I couldn't sleep all night.

And that was last Thursday. Tonight is Tuesday. Tonight is Tuesday and my homework's done, and I darned some stockings that didn't really need it, and I worked a crossword puzzle, and I listened to the radio, and now I'm just sitting. I'm just sitting because I can't think of anything else to do. I can't think of anything, anything but snowflakes and ice skates and yellow moons and Thursday night. The telephone is sitting on the corner table with its old black face turned to the wall so I can't see its leer. I don't even jump when it rings any more. My heart still prays, but my mind just laughs. Outside the night is still, so still I think I'll go crazy, and the white snow's all dirtied and smoked into grayness and the wind is blowing the arc light so it throws weird, waving shadows from the trees onto the lawn – like thin, starved arms begging for I don't know what. And so I'm just sitting here and I'm not feeling anything; I'm not even sad, because all of a sudden I know. All of a sudden I know. I can sit here now forever and laugh and laugh and laugh while the tears run salty in the corners of my mouth. For all of a sudden I know, I know what the stars knew all the time – he'll never, never call – never.

For Discussion of Daly

1. You do not understand until the end why the opening of the story emphasizes the point, "I'm not so dumb." Why did the girl feel the need to make this point clear?

2. The girl experiences four successive moods. Show how the descriptions of the scene change to suit each mood.

3. When did the girl first get the feeling that this happy interlude had ended? Why did she keep up her hope that it was only a beginning? Why did she laugh at the end?

4. Was the ending a surprise to you? Would you have had the story end differently? Why, or why not? If you were the girl, would you prefer to miss the happy evening rather than suffer the later disappointment? Boys in the class may wish to write a short story, or sketch, giving the reverse side of "Sixteen," showing the thoughts and feelings of the boy who didn't call.

5. Search your memory for some experience that you felt keenly, whether merry or fearful or exciting or sad, and tell it with descriptions of the scene that bring out the mood. Let your descriptions of outside things – people around or the natural setting – reflect what your emotions were,

rather than stating them directly.

That is what Maureen Daly does — what makes the story remarkable. She conveys her feelings not by describing them but by describing things about her. (For the outside world is a mirror that reflects our moods.) Follow the changing look of the night in this story to share the emotions that turn a series of simple happenings into a moving story.

For Your Vocabulary

FIGURATIVE USE OF WORDS: This story gains a large part of its charm from its vividness. And its vividness is the result of expressed comparisons and figurative use of single words. Some comparisons are easy to spot, from the key words *like* and *as:*

hair sleek as a wet seal
stars winked like flirting eyes
ashes crunched like crackerjack
the moon like a big quarter slice of muskmelon.

Did you notice the implied comparisons in single words used figuratively to just as good effect?

the moon *tinseled* the twigs and *silver-plated* the snowdrifts
the dog's hot breath made a frosty little *balloon balancing* on the end of her nose
the shrill musical jabber (of the skaters) re-echoes from a hundred human *calliopes*
a hound wailed a mournful *apology* to a star
a very respectable *Emily Post* sort of conversation
the telephone's black *face* turned to the wall so I can't see its *leer*

Apply this method on the narrative suggested in question 5, or choose a place where you have a particularly good time, and write a short description which gives its feeling as well as its appearance. Don't say anything *was* thus and so. Use nouns and verbs figuratively for the impressions, and go easy on *like* phrases.

JAMES THURBER
1894–

The Secret Life of Walter Mitty

The creator of Walter Mitty is almost as well known for his cartoons and illustrations as for his writings. James Thurber's humorous drawings of flop-eared dogs, dominant-looking females, and discontented males appear regularly in *The New Yorker* magazine, of which he was once general editor and is now a staff writer. In recent years it has become increasingly difficult for him to draw because of failing eyesight; as a boy in Columbus, Ohio, he lost the sight of one

eye. Thurber has described his boyhood days and his career at Ohio State University in a series of hilarious autobiographical sketches. After working as a newspaperman in Columbus and New York, he joined *The New Yorker* and began to publish the stories and essays that make him a leading American humorist and prose stylist. He has collaborated with E. B. White (see p. 176), and with his former college classmate, the actor Elliott Nugent, in writing the play *The Male Animal*. Most recently he has written fairy tales for grownups, *The White Deer* and *The Thirteen Clocks*.

" The Secret Life of Walter Mitty " is probably the most popular short story of the last twenty years. First published in 1943, it has been reprinted many times and made into a movie. During World War II our airmen formed several " Walter Mitty " clubs and the phrase " pocketa-pocketa " became a byword on airfields scattered over the globe. Walter Mitty appeals to anyone who has ever daydreamed — and that includes about everybody!

W E'RE going through! " The Commander's voice was like thin ice breaking. He wore his full-dress uniform, with the heavily braided white cap pulled down rakishly over one cold gray eye. " We can't make it, sir. It's spoiling for a hurricane, if you ask me." " I'm not asking you, Lieutenant Berg," said the Commander. " Throw on the power lights! Rev her up to 8,500! We're going through! " The pounding of the cylinders increased: ta-pocketa-pocketa-pocketa-*pocketa-pocketa*. The Commander stared at the ice forming on the pilot window. He walked over and twisted a row of complicated dials. " Switch on No. 8 auxiliary! " he shouted. " Switch on No. 8 auxiliary! " repeated Lieutenant Berg. " Full strength in No. 3 turret! " shouted the Commander. " Full strength in No. 3 turret! " The crew, bending to their various tasks in the huge, hurtling eight-engined navy hydroplane, looked at each other and grinned. " The Old Man'll get us through," they said to one another. " The Old Man ain't afraid of hell! . . ."

" Not so fast! You're driving too fast! " said Mrs. Mitty. " What are you driving so fast for? "

" Hmm? " said Walter Mitty. He looked at his wife, in the seat beside him, with shocked astonishment. She seemed grossly unfamiliar, like a strange woman who had yelled at him in a crowd. " You were up to fifty-five," she said. " You know I don't like to go more than forty. You were up to fifty-five." Walter Mitty drove on toward Waterbury in silence, the roaring of the SN-202 through the worst storm in twenty years of navy flying fading in the remote, intimate airways of his mind. " You're tensed up again," said Mrs. Mitty. " It's one of your days. I wish you'd let Dr. Renshaw look you over."

Walter Mitty stopped the car in front of the building where his wife went to have her hair done. " Remember to get those overshoes while I'm having my hair done," she said. " I don't need overshoes," said Mitty. She put her mirror back into her bag. " We've been all through that," she said, getting out of the car. " You're not a young man any longer." He raced the engine a little. " Why don't you wear your gloves? Have you lost your gloves? " Walter Mitty reached in a pocket and brought out the gloves. He put them on, but after she had turned and gone into the building and he had driven on to a red light, he took them off again. " Pick it up, brother! " snapped a cop as the light changed, and Mitty hastily pulled on his gloves and lurched ahead. He drove around the streets aimlessly for a time, and then he drove past the hospital on his way to the parking lot.

. . . " It's the millionaire banker, Wellington McMillan," said the pretty nurse. " Yes? " said Walter Mitty, removing his gloves slowly. " Who has the case? " " Dr. Renshaw and Dr. Benbow, but there are two specialists here, Dr. Remington from New York and Dr. Pritchard-Mitford from London. He flew over." A door opened down a long cool corridor and Dr. Renshaw came out. He looked distraught and haggard. " Hello, Mitty," he said. " We're having the devil's own time with McMillan, the millionaire banker and close personal friend of Roosevelt. Obstreosis of the ductal tract. Tertiary. Wish you'd take a look at him." "Glad to," said Mitty.

In the operating room there were whispered introductions: "Dr. Remington, Dr. Mitty. Dr. Pritchard-Mitford, Dr. Mitty." "I've read your book on streptothricosis," said Pritchard-Mitford, shaking hands. "A brilliant performance, sir." "Thank you," said Walter Mitty. "Didn't know you were in the States, Mitty," grumbled Remington. "Coals to Newcastle, bringing Mitford and me up here for a tertiary." "You are very kind," said Mitty. A huge, complicated machine, connected to the operating table, with many tubes and wires, began at this moment to go pocketa-pocketa-pocketa. "The new anesthetizer is giving away!" shouted an intern. "There is no one in the East who knows how to fix it!" "Quiet, man!" said Mitty, in a low, cool voice. He sprang to the machine, which was now going pocketa-pocketa-queep-pocketa-queep. He began fingering delicately a row of glistening dials. "Give me a fountain pen!" he snapped. Someone handed him a fountain pen. He pulled a faulty piston out of the machine and inserted the pen in its place. "That will hold for ten minutes," he said. "Get on with the operation." A nurse hurried over and whispered to Renshaw, and Mitty saw the man turn pale. "Coreopsis has set in," said Renshaw nervously. "If you would take over, Mitty?" Mitty looked at him and at the craven figure of Benbow, who drank, and at the grave, uncertain faces of the two great specialists. "If you wish," he said. They slipped a white gown on him; he adjusted a mask and drew on thin gloves; nurses handed him shining . . .

"Back it up, Mac! Look out for that Buick!" Walter Mitty jammed on the brakes. "Wrong lane, Mac," said the parking-lot attendant, looking at Mitty closely. "Gee. Yeh," muttered Mitty. He began cautiously to back out of the lane marked "Exit Only." "Leave her sit there," said the attendant. "I'll put her away." Mitty got out of the car. "Hey, better leave the key." "Oh," said Mitty, handing the man the ignition key. The attendant vaulted into the car, backed it up with insolent skill, and put it where it belonged.

They're so darn cocky, thought Walter Mitty, walking along Main Street; they think they know everything. Once he had tried to take his chains off, outside New Milford, and he had got them wound around the axles. A man had had to come out in a wrecking car and unwind them, a young, grinning garageman. Since then Mrs. Mitty always made him drive to a garage to have the chains taken off. The next time, he thought, I'll wear my right arm in a sling; they won't grin at me then. I'll have my right arm in a sling and they'll see I couldn't possibly take the chains off myself. He kicked at the slush on the sidewalk. "Overshoes," he said to himself, and he began looking for a shoe store.

When he came out into the street again, with the overshoes in a box under his arm, Walter Mitty began to wonder what the other thing was his wife had told him to get. She had told him twice before they set out from their house for Waterbury. In a way he hated these weekly trips to town — he was always getting something wrong. Kleenex, he thought, Squibb's, razor blades? No. Tooth paste, toothbrush, bicarbonate, carborundum, initiative and referendum? He gave it up. But she would remember it. "Where's the what's-its-name?" she would ask. "Don't tell me you forgot the what's-its-name." A newsboy went by shouting something about the Waterbury trial.

. . . "Perhaps this will refresh your memory." The District Attorney suddenly thrust a heavy automatic at the quiet figure on the witness stand. "Have you ever seen this before?" Walter Mitty took the gun and examined it expertly. "This is my Webley-Vickers 50.80," he said calmly. An excited buzz ran around the courtroom. The Judge rapped for order. "You are a crack shot with any sort of firearms, I believe?" said the District Attorney, insinuatingly. "Objection!" shouted Mitty's attorney. "We have shown that the defendant could not have fired the shot. We have shown that he wore his right arm in a sling on the night of the fourteenth of July." Walter Mitty raised his hand briefly and the bickering attorneys were stilled. "With any known make of gun," he said evenly, "I could have killed Gregory Fitzhurst at three hundred feet *with my left hand.*" Pandemonium broke loose in the courtroom. A woman's scream rose above the bedlam and suddenly a lovely, dark-haired girl was in Walter Mitty's arms. The District Attorney struck at her savagely. Without rising from his chair, Mitty let the man have it on the point of the chin. "You miserable cur!". . .

"Puppy biscuit," said Walter Mitty. He stopped walking and the buildings of Waterbury rose up out of the misty courtroom and surrounded him again. A woman who was passing laughed. "He said 'Puppy biscuit,'" she said to her companion. "That man said 'Puppy biscuit' to himself." Walter Mitty hurried on. He went into an A & P, not the first one he came to but a smaller one farther up the street. "I want some biscuit for small, young dogs," he said to the clerk. "Any special brand, sir?" The greatest pistol shot in the world thought a moment. "It says 'Puppies Bark for It' on the box," said Walter Mitty.

His wife would be through at the hairdresser's in fifteen minutes, Mitty saw in looking at his watch, unless they had trouble drying it; sometimes they had trouble drying it. She didn't like to get to the hotel first; she would want him to be there waiting for her as usual. He found a big leather chair in the lob-

by, facing the window, and he put the overshoes and the puppy biscuit on the floor beside it. He picked up an old copy of *Liberty* and sank down into the chair. "Can Germany Conquer the World Through the Air?" Walter Mitty looked at the pictures of bombing planes and of ruined streets.

. . . "The cannonading has got the wind up in young Raleigh, sir," said the sergeant. Captain Mitty looked at him through tousled hair. "Get him to bed," he said wearily, "with the others. I'll fly alone." "But you can't, sir," said the sergeant anxiously. "It takes two men to handle that bomber and the Archies are pounding hell out of the air. Von Richtman's circus is between here and Saulier." "Somebody's got to get that ammunition dump," said Mitty. "I'm going over. Spot of brandy?" He poured a drink for the sergeant and one for himself. War thundered and whined around the dugout and battered at the door. There was a rending of wood, and splinters flew through the room. "A bit of a near thing," said Captain Mitty carelessly. "The box barrage is closing in," said the sergeant. "We only live once, Sergeant," said Mitty, with his faint, fleeting smile. "Or do we?" He poured another brandy and tossed it off. "I never see a man could hold his brandy like you, sir," said the sergeant. "Begging your pardon, sir." Captain Mitty stood up and strapped on his huge Webley-Vickers automatic. "It's forty kilometers through hell, sir," said the sergeant. Mitty finished one last brandy. "After all," he said softly, "what isn't?" The pounding of the cannon increased; there was the rat-tat-tatting of machine guns, and from somewhere came the menacing pocketa-pocketa-pocketa of the new flame-throwers. Walter Mitty walked to the door of the dugout humming "Auprès de Ma Blonde." He turned and waved to the sergeant. "Cheerio!" he said. . . .

Something struck his shoulder. "I've

been looking all over this hotel for you," said Mrs. Mitty. "Why do you have to hide in this old chair? How did you expect me to find you?" "Things close in," said Walter Mitty vaguely. "What?" Mrs. Mitty said. "Did you get the what's-its-name? The puppy biscuit? What's in that box?" "Overshoes," said Mitty. "Couldn't you have put them on in the store?" "I was thinking," said Walter Mitty. "Does it ever occur to you that I am sometimes thinking?" She looked at him. "I'm going to take your temperature when I get you home," she said.

They went out through the revolving doors that made a faintly derisive whistling sound when you pushed them. It was two blocks to the parking lot. At the drugstore on the corner she said, "Wait here for me. I forgot something. I won't be a minute." She was more than a minute. Walter Mitty lighted a cigarette. It began to rain, rain with sleet in it. He stood up against the wall of the drugstore, smoking. . . . He put his shoulders back and his heels together. "Forget about the handkerchief," said Walter Mitty scornfully. He took one last drag on his cigarette and snapped it away. Then, with that faint, fleeting smile playing about his lips, he faced the firing squad; erect and motionless, proud and disdainful, Walter Mitty the Undefeated, inscrutable to the last.

For Discussion of Thurber

1. Like most Thurber writings, the humor in this story is edged with seriousness. Why do you think Walter Mitty daydreams so much? What makes you sympathize with him at the same time that you laugh at him?

2. Select passages in the story you particularly enjoyed. How would you film this story if you were a movie director? Which scenes would you emphasize? If you needed more episodes to make a longer movie, what others could you devise that would fit into the mood and spirit of the story?

3. Walter's daydreams are exciting, dramatic, and romantic. What kind of daydreams have you had? Write a short sketch of one of your daydreams, placing it in a real-life setting, like a classroom or bus or library. Arrange a panel discussion or debate on the question of whether daydreaming is good or bad for a person. Your librarian may be able to obtain reference material on the subject.

4. For other Thurber stories, see his book *The Thurber Carnival.* "University Days," in *My Life and Hard Times,* is one of his most familiar autobiographical pieces.

For Further Reading of Short Stories

OTHER STORIES IN THIS BOOK

By reading the short stories in Part Two of this book you can trace the history of the short story from Irving (whose "Rip Van Winkle," written in 1819, was the first American short story) to the moderns. (See reading lists on pp. 547, 683, and 751.)

Irving, Washington, "The Devil and Tom Walker" (p. 475)

Hawthorne, Nathaniel, "Dr. Heidegger's Experiment" (p. 533)

Poe, Edgar Allan, "The Pit and the Pendulum" (p. 515), "The Tell-Tale Heart" (p. 526)

Harte, Bret, "The Outcasts of Poker Flat" (p. 663)

Garland, Hamlin, "Under the Lion's Paw" (p. 715)

Aldrich, Thomas Bailey, "A Struggle for Life" (p. 743)

STORIES IN MAGAZINES

Current magazines contain many short stories, ranging from poor to excellent. Since most of us do not have time to read more than a small fraction of these stories, we welcome any guidance we can find to the better ones. To this end two annual anthologies are most helpful: *The Best American Short Stories of 19—* (a series which began in 1915, formerly edited by Edward J. O'Brien, and since his death edited by Martha Foley), and the *O. Henry Memorial Award Prize Stories of 19—* (the first volume in this series appeared in 1919).

A study of these anthologies indicates that many of the best American short stories are published in the following magazines:

The Atlantic
Commonweal
Harper's Magazine
The New Yorker
The Saturday Evening Post

Several magazines, such as *The Saturday Evening Post* and *The New Yorker,* issue collections of stories from their pages.

COLLECTIONS

(Only those having a large proportion of American stories are given.)

Becker, M. L., *Golden Tales of Our America* (Dodd, Mead, 1929), and other series of *Golden Tales*

Becker, M. L., *Growing Up with America* (Stokes, 1941)

Brunini, J. G. and F. X. Connolly, *Stories of Our Century by Catholic Authors* (Lippincott, 1949)

Burrell, J. A. and Bennett Cerf, *The Bedside Book of Famous American Stories* (Random House, 1939)

Canby, H. S. and R. Bailey, *The Book of the Short Story* (Appleton, 1948)

Cerf, Bennett, *Modern American Short Stories* (World, 1945)

Collison, T., *This Winged World* (Longmans, 1943)

Conklin, G., *The Best of Science Fiction* (Crown, 1946)

Conklin, G., *A Treasury of Science Fiction* (Crown, 1948)

Curtin, Mary A., *Pilgrims All* (Bruce, 1943)

Daly, M., *My Favorite Stories* (Dodd, Mead, 1948)

Eaton, H. T., *Short Stories for Study and Enjoyment* (Odyssey, 1945)

Fabricant, N. D. and H. Werner, *A Caravan of Music Stories* (Fell, 1947)

Flanagan, John T., *America Is West* (University of Minnesota Press, 1945

Gable, Sister Mariella, *They Are People* (Sheed and Ward, 1942)

Gable, Sister Mariella, *Our Father's House* (Sheed and Ward, 1945)

Goodman, J., *The Fireside Book of Dog Stories* (Simon and Schuster, 1943)

Goodspeed, C. E., *A Treasury of Fishing Stories* (Barnes, 1946)

Havighurst, W., *Masters of the Modern Short Story* (Harcourt, Brace, 1945)

Hitchcock, A. J., *The Fireside Book of Suspense* (Simon and Schuster, 1947)

Holman, Mabel, *Short Story Parade* (Harcourt, Brace, 1940)

Jessup, Alexander, *Representative Modern Short Stories* (Macmillan, 1944)

Kielty, B., *A Treasury of Short Stories* (Simon and Schuster, 1947)

Maule, H. E., *Great Tales of the American West* (Random House, 1945)

Moore, R. A. and W. Wyatt, *Stories of the Forties* (Nicholson, 1945)

Oberfirst, R., *Short Short Stories* (Humphries, 1948)

Owen, Frank, *Teen-Age Baseball Stories* (Lantern Press, 1948), and other collections of stories for teen-agers

Pence, R. W., *Short Stories by Present Day Authors* (Macmillan, 1934)

Schramm, Wilbur, *Great Short Stories* (Harcourt, Brace, 1950)

Schweikert, H. C., *Short Stories* (enlarged ed.) (Harcourt, Brace, 1947)

Shaw, H. L. and R. Davis, *Americans One and All* (Harper, 1947)

Wagenknecht, E., *The Fireside Book of Christmas Stories* (Bobbs-Merrill, 1945)

Williams, B. C., *New Narratives* (Appleton, 1944)

Wood, W. R., *Short Short Stories* (Harcourt, Brace, 1951)

World's Great Humor Stories (World, 1944)

INDIVIDUAL AUTHORS

Aldrich, Thomas Bailey, *Marjorie Daw and Other Stories*

Benét, Stephen Vincent, *Twenty-Five Short Stories* (Sun Dial, 1943)

Bierce, Ambrose, *In the Midst of Life*

Brown, Alice, *Meadow-Grass*

Buck, Pearl, *First Wife and Other Stories* (John Day, 1933)

Bunner, Henry Cuyler, *The Stories of H. C. Bunner* (Scribner, 1916)

Cable, George W., *Old Creole Days*

Canfield, Dorothy, *Four-Square* (Harcourt, Brace, 1949)

Cather, Willa, *Youth and the Bright Medusa* (Knopf, 1920)

Cobb, Irvin S., *The Escape of Mr. Trim* (Doran, 1913)

Cobb, Irvin S., *Old Judge Priest* (Doran, 1916)

Cohen, Octavus Roy, *Carbon Copies* (Appleton, 1932)

Connell, Richard, *Apes and Angels* (Minton, Balch, 1924)

Connolly, James Brendan, *Gloucestermen* (Scribner, 1930)

Craddock, C. E. (Mary N. Murfree), *In the Tennessee Mountains*

Davis, Richard Harding, *From "Gallegher" to "The Deserter"; the Best Stories of Richard Harding Davis* (Scribner, 1927)

Deland, Margaret, *Old Chester Tales* (Harper, 1919)

Edmonds, Walter D., *Mostly Canallers* (Little, Brown, 1934)

Faulkner, William, *Knight's Gambit* (Random House, 1949)

Ferber, Edna, *Roast Beef Medium* (Grosset, 1915)

Fitch, George H., *At Good Old Siwash*

Freeman, Mary E. Wilkins, *Best Stories*, ed. by H. W. Lanier (Harper, 1927)

Gale, Zona, *Friendship Village*

Hale, Edward Everett, *The Man Without a Country*

Harris, Joel Chandler, *Uncle Remus, His Songs and Sayings*

Hemingway, Ernest, *The Fifth Column and the First Forty-Nine Stories* (Modern Library, 1942)

Henry, O., *Best Stories of O. Henry*, sel. by Bennett Cerf and Van H. Cartwell (Sun Dial, 1945)

Horgan, Paul, *The Devil in the Desert* (Longmans, 1952)

James, Henry, *Short Stories*, sel. by Clifton Fadiman (Modern Library, 1948)

Jewett, Sarah Orne, *A White Heron* (Houghton Mifflin, 1925)

Jewett, Sarah Orne, *Best Stories of Sarah Orne Jewett*, ed. by Willa Cather (Houghton Mifflin, 1925)

Johnson, Owen, *The Tennessee Shad*

Kantor, MacKinlay, *Author's Choice* (Coward-McCann, 1944)

La Farge, Oliver, *All the Young Men* (Houghton Mifflin, 1935)

Lardner, Ring, *Round Up* (Scribner, 1929)

Lewis, Sinclair, *Selected Short Stories of Sinclair Lewis* (Doubleday, 1935)

London, Jack, *Best Stories of Jack London* (Sun Dial, 1945)

Montague, Margaret Prescott, *England to America* (Doubleday, 1920)

Page, Thomas Nelson, *In Ole Virginia*

Parker, Dorothy, *Here Lies: the Collected Stories of Dorothy Parker* (Viking, 1939)

Ready, William, *The Great Disciple and Other Stories* (Bruce, 1951)

Rinehart, Mary Roberts, *The Amazing Adventures of Letitia Carberry* (Bobbs-Merrill, 1911)

Runyon, Damon, *The Best of Runyon* (Stokes, 1938)

Saroyan, William, *My Name Is Aram* (Harcourt, Brace, 1940)

Schramm, Wilbur, *Windwagon Smith and Other Yarns* (Harcourt, Brace, 1947)

Steele, W. D., *The Best Stories of Wilbur Daniel Steele* (Doubleday, 1946)

Stockton, Frank R., *The Lady, or the Tiger?*

Street, James, *Oh, Promised Land* (Dial, 1940)

Stuart, Jesse, *Tales from the Plum Tree Hills* (Dutton, 1946)

Stuart, Ruth M., *Sonny*

Suckow, Ruth, *Country People* (Knopf, 1924)

Suckow, Ruth, *Iowa Interiors* (Knopf, 1926)

Suckow, Ruth, *Children and Older People* (Knopf, 1931)

Thurber, James, *The Beast in Me and Other Animals* (Harcourt, Brace, 1948)

Twain, Mark, *The Celebrated Jumping Frog of Calaveras County, and Other Sketches*

Van Dyke, Henry, *The Blue Flower*

Van Dyke, Henry, *The Other Wise Man*

West, Jessamyn, *The Friendly Persuasion* (Harcourt, Brace, 1945)

Weston, Christine, *There and Then: Stories of India* (Scribner, 1950)

Wharton, Edith, *Xingu* (Scribner, 1916)

White, Stewart Edward, *Blazed Trail Stories* (Garden City, 1926)

White, William Allen, *The Court of Boyville*

Williams, Ben Ames, *Fraternity Village* (Houghton Mifflin, 1949)

Yezierska, Anzia, *Hungry Hearts* (Houghton Mifflin, 1920)

THE NOVEL

It is easy enough to see why there is no complete novel in this book. There is not space for one along with all the other selections that are needed to give you a good view of American literature. But it would be a mistake for you to omit the reading of novels from your course in American literature, for they are among the most important and most popular of our nation's writings.

Choosing Your Novel

On page 129 is a list of recommended novels from which you will want to choose at least one, and probably more, for reading at home. The annotation under each title and your teacher's advice will help you select those that especially appeal to you. Remember that novels have a slower pace and are often slower in their openings than short stories. It would be unwise to prejudice yourself against a book because the first few pages failed to interest you. On the other hand, if after sampling three or four chapters you are sure that reading this book will be merely an unpleasant chore, it is better to try to find another more to your taste. But don't look just for highly exciting or light, amusing stories. There are few greater satisfactions than to read a fine novel that challenges you, stretches your thinking to new limits, and gives you worth-while new experiences.

Reporting on Your Novel

The kind of report you make on your reading will depend largely on the methods recommended by your particular teacher and school. Some of the most commonly used are:

1. Brief records of your reading under designated headings put in a card catalogue or special notebook.

2. An interview with your teacher in which you discuss the book informally.

3. A rather complete report in essay form to show the teacher how well you have understood the book and how you reacted toward it.

4. An oral presentation of the book before your classmates.

The last form of report, because it involves an audience, requires you to be certain of your purpose. If you liked the book, you may wish to " sell " it to the class — to get as many others as possible to read it. Then be sure not to spoil the story by revealing too much. Keep your classmates guessing as to its outcome. If you wish to give a critical evaluation, that is, to show why the book is good or unsatisfactory, consider it in the light of the following discussion of the novel and compare it with others you have read. If several students have read the same book, and you wish to avoid monotonous duplication for the class, you might plan a panel discussion, by which each can present a different aspect of the book, with an opportunity for informal comments and questions afterward.

If you report on a novel which you have also seen as a film, include some comparison of the two. The class will enjoy hearing your answers to such questions as these: How closely did the screen version follow the original? Did changes improve or spoil the story? Did the actors' interpretations of the characters satisfy your mental picture of them as derived from the novel? Were the characters and the setting exaggerated or unrealistic?

Making a Critical Estimate

If you wish to try your hand at a critical estimate, which is the most valuable and mature form of report, try one of the two following procedures:

1. Open with a brief statement of the author's position in the history of our literature: when he lived, where he lived, what sort of reputation he has as a writer. Next, place the particular book you have read by telling whether it is one of the author's early or later books and whether it is considered one of his best.

Then make your main statement an answer — fortified with incidents and quotations cited from the book — to these two questions: What was the author's purpose in writing the story? How well did he succeed in carrying out his purpose?

Among the many purposes for writing novels are the following: to give the reader an escape from reality by means of fantasy or thrilling adventure; to entertain by presenting humorous incidents or characters; to present a picture of life and thought in a given place at a given time; to present a study of a specific character; to teach some great truth; to present propaganda for a cause; to satirize some social situation or a particular group. As your experience with novels increases, you will find truer enjoyment in those books that emphasize character or theme, rather than merely plot.

2. Since novels, like short stories, are made up of action, characters, and setting, you will find it helpful to report on one of these elements, or each of them in turn. The Guide to Reading the Novel which follows will enable you to recognize the important differences between a novel and a short story. This information should help you not only in reading novels intelligently but also in forming judgments and in talking about novels.

Guide to Reading the Novel

The difference between the short story and the novel is especially clear in the matter of plot complication. Unlike the short story, the novel is likely to have subplots, introduced to give contrast, richness, or variety to the main plot. Some subplots may be so fully developed that the author seems to be weaving several stories at once. He leaves one set of characters, for chapters at a time, while he narrates the actions of another set. Gradually these strands are brought together into a unified pattern. Suspense heightens and leads to a climax. Sometimes in an action story there is a series of climaxes, each a little more exciting than the one before. Once the main climax is reached, moreover, the novel cannot close as quickly as the short story, for there are more characters to dispose of, more loose ends to tie up.

Reading a novel requires your close attention on this score alone; with a complicated plot the reader must make sure to "keep the story straight."

In a novel the list of characters is likely to be much longer than in a short story, especially if there are subplots or if the main character moves about from one locality or another. You may sometimes find it profitable to keep a list of characters as you read and jot notations after the names which you wish to use later in a report. Sort out the major characters from the minor ones. Though minor characters play a less important part in the plot, they are not necessarily of minor interest. Some authors are noted for their ability to make minor characters stand out as individuals in spite of their brief appearances on the scene.

If there is a single major character, give him special attention in your reading. Watch for hints that build up a picture of his personality and disposition. Observe particularly what causes his character to change — for better or worse. Try to decide whether the changes grow logically out of the situations in the story. Finally, notice whether the persons in the story act consistently. If any of them seem to you definitely " out of character " at some point, you will have a legitimate reason for feeling the author has played a trick on the reader.

The extended length of the novel gives its setting an added meaning over that in a short story. You travel farther and stay longer in a novel. A more lasting impression is made on your mind by the setting. You learn from some books how lives can be permanently shaped by the mountains or the plains or the sea. You come to know how the pinch of poverty on a run-down farm can shrivel the spirit, or how unlimited wealth in a great metropolis may corrupt it. On the other hand, you may have a demonstration of how a strong soul can triumph over whatever handicap his environment offers. Study the setting in a novel as a key to the author's interpretation of his characters.

Development of the American Novel

Although American literature began in the early part of the seventeenth century, no novelist of importance appeared in America before 1800. One reason is that few novels had been written anywhere before this time. As a distinct form of prose writing, the novel did not develop fully in England until after 1750. A more important reason, perhaps, is that for two centuries the American colonists were too busy conquering the wilderness and founding a new nation to have much time for such luxuries as art, music, and literature.

During the early years of the nineteenth century, James Fenimore Cooper became our first important novelist. Cooper's reputation rests primarily upon the five romantic adventure novels about the early American frontier which compose the famous Leatherstocking series. Somewhat later, two other important novelists appeared: Nathaniel Hawthorne and Herman Melville. Hawthorne lifted the American novel above the plane of mere entertainment and made of it an artistic vehicle for the teaching of profound moral truths. His novels are four in number. Of these *The Scarlet Letter* and *The House of the Seven Gables* are the most famous; the former has been called the greatest American novel. Herman Melville's most important book, *Moby Dick*, the saga of the white whale, is not only a vivid picture of the whaling industry painted on a vast canvas, but an allegorical presentation of man's struggle with nature and his own soul. Although it was neglected until the twentieth century, critics today acclaim it a masterpiece. (A selection from *Moby Dick* appears on page 541.)

In contrast to the romantic tales of Cooper, Hawthorne, and Melville, the fiction of the last quarter of the nineteenth century turned realistic, and the novel has remained predominantly so ever since. The two leaders in this movement toward realism were William Dean Howells and Henry James. Howells's realism was not of the harsh kind to come later; he did not stress the unpleasant or grim side of life. Yet in novels like *The Rise of Silas Lapham* he did try to picture the thoughts and habits of " real " people — ordinary people living in commonplace surroundings with nothing strange or " romantic " about them. Henry James, on the other hand, is especially known as the forerunner of modern novelists who are interested in the psychology of character.

A great novelist of this time who stands by himself is the best of American humorists, Mark Twain, whose sense of humor made the most of the awkward age of a growing nation. In

The Adventures of Huckleberry Finn, the epic of the Mississippi River vagabond, the American humorous novel reaches its highest point.

In the last decade of the century several novelists pushed realism a step beyond Howells and James by revealing the disagreeable, sordid, brutal phases of life. These writers are sometimes called "naturalists" because they tried to write in a completely natural, lifelike way, to depict all the details in a scene, all the information about a character. The result was novels that dwelt often on tragedy and failure in life. Stephen Crane wrote of the deadening fear of war in *The Red Badge of Courage,* and Frank Norris wrote of "little" people crushed by big forces, like railroads and banks, in *The Octopus.* (A selection from Norris appears on page 736.)

After World War I, American fiction became an exceptionally exciting and varied kind of writing. Willa Cather wrote of the timeless values and their impact on ordinary human beings in her stories of the Nebraska prairies. A later regional writer, Paul Horgan, has built a solid reputation on his stories of New Mexico. Sinclair Lewis, in novels set in the Midwest, like *Arrowsmith,* turned a hard bright light on certain American manners and alternately irritated and fascinated readers with his satire.

Ernest Hemingway popularized a prose style distinguished by short clipped sentences, and unfailingly real dialogue. He represented the "lost generation" of the twenties, a group of young writers who were disillusioned by the war and saw no hopeful meaning in modern life. Hemingway has become a master craftsman, as his recent novelette, *The Old Man of the Sea,* verifies, but has settled in a neo-stoic philosophy of life that prizes endurance above hope. William Faulkner puzzled readers with an involved, intricate style, abnormal characterization, and powerful, gloomy tales of perversity.

In recent years, novels have not fallen into easily defined categories. Several young writers have concentrated on the problems and feelings of adolescents. Carson McCullers is a sensitive portrayer of teen-age characters. Leo Brady has produced a psychological study of aberration and repentance in *The Edge of Doom.* Another group, the "documentary novelists," have borrowed techniques from journalism, and created closely detailed "factual" novels. One of the best known of these writers is John Hersey, author of *The Wall,* a story about the devastation of the Warsaw ghetto in World War II.

The American novel, with its rich tradition, will continue to be engrossing, varied, and memorable. When appraising novels, you will do well to remember a basic principle of good literature — fidelity to the truth of human nature and circumstances, which always places first in importance the supernatural realities of man, and never fails to show that man, by spiritual power, can rise above any material or physical disaster.

For Reading of Novels

The following novels have proved their value over a period of years in adding to the total picture of America.

THE NINETEENTH CENTURY

Cooper, James Fenimore, *The Deerslayer* (1841 [1])
This "Leatherstocking Tale" carries the young woodsman Natty Bumppo through the exciting adventures of his youth from 1740 to 1745, when central New York State was a wilderness.

Cooper, James Fenimore, *The Last of the Mohicans* (1826)
"Hawkeye" the scout (Natty Bumppo as an older man) and two friendly Indians repeatedly rescue the colonel's

[1] The original date of publication is given for older novels. They have been reissued at various times by more than one publisher.

daughter from hostile Indians. The younger Mohican, Uncas, gives the title to the story.

Crane, Stephen, *The Red Badge of Courage* (1896)

This story traces the feelings of a young soldier in the War between the States through the stages of impatience to get into action, terror during his first battle, shame at his frightened retreat, and final triumph over his inner weakness.

Eggleston, Edward, *The Hoosier Schoolmaster* (1870)

Through his pluck and humor, Ralph Hartsook, a young Indiana schoolmaster (when that state was still a frontier) withstands the efforts of his rough pupils to oust him.

Hawthorne, Nathaniel, *The House of the Seven Gables* (1851)

This old Salem house, said to have a curse upon it, is the home of a brother and sister who are persecuted by their cousin, Judge Pyncheon, to conceal his own misdeeds.

(Hawthorne's *The Scarlet Letter* is also recommended for mature students.)

Howells, William Dean, *The Rise of Silas Lapham* (1885)

The family of Silas Lapham, a forceful, uneducated man who has built up a great fortune, is brought into contact with an old aristocratic Boston family. The results range from the humorous to the heartbreaking, from realism to romance.

James, Henry, *The American* (1877)

A successful American businessman is defeated in love by the French social code.

Melville, Herman, *Moby Dick* (1851)

This remarkable tale of the sworn enmity of Captain Ahab for the great white whale, Moby Dick, is noted for its vivid descriptions of the sea and life on a whaling vessel.

Stowe, Harriet Beecher, *Uncle Tom's Cabin* (1852)

This propaganda novel, a northern abolitionist's view of slavery, caused Lincoln to refer to the conflict as " Mrs. Stowe's war."

Twain, Mark, *The Adventures of Huckleberry Finn* (1884)

" Huck," Tom Sawyer, and Negro Jim float down the Mississippi on a raft, having remarkable and highly amusing adventures along the way.

Twain, Mark, *The Adventures of Tom Sawyer* (1876)

Tom's brain is full of plans which get him and his friends in and out of trouble in a most laughable way.

Twain, Mark, *A Connecticut Yankee in King Arthur's Court* (1889)

A fantastic story of how a modern Yankee, after a blow on the head, wakes to find himself in England back in King Arthur's time. He applies modern methods to ancient situations with astounding results.

Wallace, Lew, *Ben-Hur* (1880)

In the first century a young Jewish aristocrat is falsely accused of murdering a Roman officer and is sent to the galleys. The long feud between him and his Roman accuser comes to a climax in the famous chariot race.

THE TWENTIETH CENTURY

Aldrich, Bess Streeter, *A Lantern in Her Hand* (Appleton, 1928)

Abbie Deal's hard life on the frontier epitomizes the enduring spirit of the pioneer woman.

Boyd, James, *Drums* (Scribner, 1925)

A story of a young man of North Carolina during the American Revolution. An exciting part of the tale gives his experience with John Paul Jones on the *Bonhomme Richard,* during one of its marauding expeditions.

Cather, Willa, *Death Comes for the Archbishop* (Knopf, 1927)

This story of New Mexico and Arizona in the late nineteenth century is based on the experiences, full of dangers and privations, of two actual priests, though their identity is concealed by fictitious names.

Cather, Willa, *My Ántonia* (Houghton Mifflin, 1918)

A young Bohemian girl, a member of an immigrant family in a Nebraska town, shows her all-round strength of character under trying circumstances.

Churchill, Winston, *The Crisis* (Macmillan, 1901)

In St. Louis just before the War between the States, Stephen Brice, a Northerner, falls in love with Virginia Carvel, an ardent Southerner.

Clark, Walter Van Tilburg, *The Ox-Bow Incident* (Random House, 1940)
A masterpiece of suspense in which a posse tracks down some innocent men. Nevada, 1885.

Cozzens, James Gould, S.S. *San Pedro* (Harcourt, Brace, 1931)
An exciting tale of a crash at sea, with deeper meanings, as in *Moby Dick,* underlying the dramatic action.

Edmonds, Walter D., *Drums along the Mohawk* (Little, Brown, 1936)
A vivid and authentic story of how settlers in central New York State in the days of the American Revolution are forced to defend themselves against the British and the Indians.

Ferber, Edna, *So Big* (Grosset, 1924)
The indomitable courage of Selina, a Midwestern country schoolteacher, contrasts sharply with the superficiality of her son Dirk.

Fisher, Dorothy Canfield, *The Bent Twig* (Holt, 1917)
This life story of the daughters of a college professor proves that " as the twig is bent . . ."

Hersey, John, *The Wall* (Knopf, 1950)
The " wall " was built around the Warsaw ghetto by the Nazis. This is the story of the lives and deaths of the Jews who lived behind it.

Lane, Rose Wilder, *Let the Hurricane Roar* (Longmans, 1935)
A young couple brave and conquer the terrors of the Dakotas during the homesteading 1870's.

Lewis, Sinclair, *Arrowsmith* (Harcourt, Brace, 1925)
A young doctor, Martin Arrowsmith, goes through successive experiences in general practice, public health, and research, with many struggles and disillusionments, but finally finds the niche in which he belongs.

Nordhoff, Charles B., and James N. Hall, *Mutiny on the Bounty* (Little, Brown, 1932)
Based on an actual mutiny of 1787, this story reflects the thrills, the heroism, the brutalities, and the tragedies of sea life on old sailing vessels.

Page, Elizabeth, *The Tree of Liberty* (Farrar and Rinehart, 1939)
The Howard family of Virginia witness the birth pangs of American democracy, as the aristocratic ideas of Hamilton clash with the democratic dream of Jefferson.

Rawlings, Marjorie Kinnan, *The Yearling* (Scribner, 1938)
A beautifully told story of the warm affection and understanding between Jody Baxter and his father, in the Florida scrub country. Jody's pet fawn is the means through which the boy himself matures into a " yearling."

Richter, Conrad, *The Trees, The Fields, and The Town* (Knopf, 1940, 1946, and 1950)
This trilogy recounts how the towering forests of the Midwest were subdued and transformed into typically American farm lands and towns.

Roberts, Kenneth, *Northwest Passage* (Doubleday, 1937)
Part I is a thrilling story of an expedition into Canada made by Rogers' Rangers during the French and Indian War. Part II shows Rogers in later years, slowly degenerating from the heroic qualities of his earlier manhood.

Tarkington, Booth, *Alice Adams* (Grosset, 1937)
The pathetic struggle of a high-school girl to keep up with the Joneses.

Wharton, Edith, *Ethan Frome* (Scribner, 1938)
A short, grim tragedy, set in New England, of three frustrated people. It has become a minor classic.

Wilder, Thornton, *The Bridge of San Luis Rey* (Boni, 1929)
In the days when Peru was a Spanish colony, the most famous bridge in that country collapsed and five travelers were killed. The novel reconstructs the life of each of the five, showing how death came at a critical point in the life of every one of them.

Wister, Owen, *The Virginian* (Macmillan, 1902)
This well-worn romantic yarn of the six-shooter West has added a striking phrase to our language — " When you call me that, smile! "

Devaney

Modern Nonfiction

ONLY a few years ago popular magazines in America filled more than half their columns with short stories and serialized novels. But the tide has been shifting steadily to nonfiction, until now the general magazines contain considerably more articles than fiction. The change is true of books, too. At one time most of the current best-sellers were novels, but now biographies and informational books of all kinds are as frequently found among the leaders. Perhaps the movies and radio and television drama have largely satisfied the appetite for stories, and people want a different sort of fare when they settle down to read. Perhaps our twentieth century is producing so many new developments in every field of human activity — science, communication, transportation, amusements, government, and international relations — that people are hungry for facts to help them keep up with the changes. Whatever the reason, we turn to nonfiction not only for enjoyment, as in all reading, but also for information and ideas that may help us to understand our complicated and rapidly changing world.

It would be hard to imagine greater variety in writing than we find in nonfiction. Nonfiction may be narration or discussion or description or argument. It includes such familiar types as essays, magazine articles, newspaper articles, book and drama reviews, speeches, editorials, and biographies. Since it is almost impossible to make exact distinctions between these many types, in the following pages you will find the selections arranged in two main groups: essays and articles, and biographies.

The subjects of nonfiction are as varied as the types. Just about everything that interests people can be found in this division of literature. A writer once remarked that there are no uninteresting subjects — there are only uninterested people. Judging from the range of nonfiction, there are plenty of people interested in everything under the sun. That is good news for you, the reader. It means that you can find good reading about any special interest you may have — from your favorite radio star to the United Nations, from football formations to atomic energy. Even more important, the time you spend in reading nonfiction opens up new interests and builds up your store of information and understanding. It makes you a well-informed person, good company for your friends and for yourself.

Try a sample and see if you don't agree.

ESSAYS AND ARTICLES

Do you like people and ideas? Are you curious about the world that lies beyond the reach of your own eyes and ears? Then essays and articles will provide you with many an hour of satisfaction and pleasure.

There was a time when the word *essay* usually meant a serious discussion of a serious subject. But the lighter, informal essay is the kind that you will find most often in modern American writing. If you were making a list of the things you really enjoy doing, you would probably put near the top the simple, everyday pleasure of sitting down and chatting with good friends about things in general. Wherever people are thrown together for an hour's chat, in a train, hotel lobby, party, or picnic, you will hear little essays in progress on "The Weather," "What I Like to Eat," "The Best Make of Car," and so on. The best informal essays are like that: conversational, easy-going, sometimes humorous, designed to take you into the confidence of the writer. They are the literary form which is nearest to human friendship and its daily pleasures.

No one would like to have the job of making a clear-cut distinction between essays and articles. Many of the short pieces of nonfiction in American magazines would fall near the border line. As a matter of fact, the very first piece of nonfiction you will read in this book, " The U.S.A. from the Air," contains in-

teresting new information after the fashion of the article, as well as presenting the thoughts and reflections and comments of the writer, the characteristic material of the essay. It even resembles autobiography, for the writer is narrating events from his own life. It shows you at once why it would be difficult to put most short nonfiction pieces into definite classifications.

But while the typical essay relies on personality and ideas for its chief interest, the typical article is strong on information and facts. If you read regularly any of the better magazines you will find that you are steadily getting to know more about science, current events, interesting and important people, books, the theater, how people in other parts of the country live, national and international problems — the list could go on and on.

Fortunately, you do not have to sort out the essays from the articles and label them. Here you will find a wide assortment, just as you do in magazines. Some are fairly definite types, like the interview and the book review; others defy classification. Some will make you laugh and some will make you think seriously about important issues. You will range the country, climbing mountains on the West Coast, having a taste of ranch life in the Southwest, watching the making of a musical comedy for Broadway.

Let's be off!

WOLFGANG LANGEWIESCHE

1907–

The U.S.A. from the Air

This is the air age. Planes fly over every section of our land day and night, and the air view of the U.S.A. is becoming familiar to more Americans all the time. But even a veteran air traveler would get some new ideas about the landscape beneath him if he made a flight with such an observant pilot as Wolfgang Langewiesche.[1] A student of sociology, he came from Austria in 1930 to study at Columbia University and took up flying as a hobby. Every penny he could scrape together was spent

[1] **Wolfgang Langewiesche:** (wŏlf'gäng län'gĕ-vēsh'ĕ).

to rent planes. Once when planes rented for twenty-five cents a minute he sold his old car to buy five hours' flying time! Nearsightedness kept him from qualifying as a commercial pilot, but after a period as a college professor — still flying every time he could get a chance — he became a research pilot for an aircraft company. His love of flying shines from every page of his books, two of which are *I'll Take the High Road* and *A Flier's World*. Whether you have flown or not, there are new experiences in store for you in this sweeping view of America from the air.

I USED to think of the U.S.A. as one thinks of a golf course. It was simply terrain on which to practice your technique. The technique was "Cross-Country Flight"; XC for short, when you wrote it up afterward in your log book. Flight was *much* newer then, in the early nineteen-thirties. Merely to circle the airport still filled you, every last cubic inch of you, with a sensation that was like nothing else. And to quit circling, to head out straight cross-country — that was Flight, raised to the second power. Boy!

I used to look down, in those ancient days, and watch my fat little rubber tire hang idle over the depth. It went across somebody's roof: no jolt. Treetops; a highway; then a river. You flew out

from over land to over water: no sink. No coolness. Imagine that: walking on land and water like a god. What a machine! And what a pilot! — (me). Bring on your skyscrapers, so I can top them. Bring on your hills, so I can cross them. Bring on your distances, and I shall eat them up. Bring on your country, and I shall ignore it.

Well, you find out.

I remember my first flight over New England. Ignore it? I wished I could. Instead, I thought: "What horrible country!" You see, the thing about XC was — that fat little tire was always looking for a field to roll on. The engine might quit any time: that was official doctrine. It never did quit, even then — much less now. But the fear of it was carefully drilled into you. Any time at all, in the midst of the most delicate Figure 8, when you were trying to make some farmer's barn hold still off your wing-tip, bang! would come a tremendous silence as your instructor pulled back the throttle and said: "Forced landing!" Then you quickly picked a field (really, you were supposed to have one all picked out: "Always Have a Field in Mind") and you went gliding down in a long S-turn — through the "Key Position" — down across the trees — down into the field — down until the grass began to tickle your tires. Then he was kind enough to open the throttle for you and let you climb out. To shoot a good forced landing was considered about three-quarters of the art of flying. And so you judged country mostly by its fields.

New England rated low indeed. Those gloomy hills, all wooded. Those nasty little pastures, with the naked rock poking up right through the middle. Those ugly stone walls around every plot of land — just imagine you overshot and rolled into one of *those!* "Horrible country. Not a decent field in sight." Then I caught myself: "What *are* you saying, man? You are supposed to find this charming. Don't you have any education? This is the cradle. . . . You *know* it's charming. Look at that white steeple nestled in the green. Trouble with you, you can't take it; you're scared!" But of course I was right in the first place; it *was* a horribly tough country they picked to settle; there *was* no decent field, nor a flat place to put one. They themselves called it a howling wilderness, and it very nearly starved them to death. Besides, most of them left it, first chance they got, for points west.

How different North Dakota felt! I had spent a week flying in the canyons of Idaho — a mountainside off each wing-tip, a wild river below — with the thought of engine failure strictly repressed, of course: no use thinking about it where you simply can't afford one! I had flown down into North Dakota through night, a black night, with nothing visible but the beacons along the airway; and again the forced landing idea had been switched off — there are lots of badlands on that route. Toward morning, not to get too low on gas, I had sat down on an Auxiliary Field to wait for daylight. It was deserted. (Those fields are not built to serve a town, but to serve the airway — they sit there, every hundred miles or so, their boundaries outlined by lights, just in case.) Parked there under the beacon tower, I had fallen asleep right in the airplane.

I woke up, and it was daylight. I started her up, and took off. Still dull in mind, I cleared the fence. There it was: landings unlimited. You cleared the fence, and you had cleared everything. As far as the eye could see, big fields — flat as a table and bigger than airports. And smoothly cultivated: where farm machinery can roll, an airplane tire can also roll. It was fall, and most of them were stubble. The nice, combed-looking stubble of machine-sown wheat: a guaranteed surface, along with unlimited room.

"This," I thought, "is one hundred per cent okay. This is the rose without the thorn; this is the meal that is all dessert; this goes in easy." In fact, I swear I had a strong sensation as if I were a little boy again and had just been handed a dish of whipped cream with chocolate.

"I think I'll just roll my wheels on that one." I had only flown a minute, but why not? "I'll fly straight for exactly three minutes, and then close my throttle." Nothing to it — just glide straight ahead. I thought it would be fun to roll up to a fence and jump it and sit right down again, so I did. Why not? "I think I'll spiral up to 1,000 feet

and cut my ignition and stop my prop."
Done.

Now, I don't claim it is a red hot and
brand new idea that North Dakota is
different from New England. I tell it to
show you how a pilot reacts to the
country: he does react; he can't help it.
And not as a tourist; he is not ever
"just looking." He has business with
the country, and the country with him.

II

Now, flying has changed. You have
more speed, more radio, perhaps two
engines. Even with only one, the forced
landing obsession has faded out. You
try again to treat the country with contempt. You try to think of it as pure
expanse — graph paper, yours to make
lines on. But it still doesn't work out
that way. The country still makes itself
felt. In fact, speed sometimes makes you
feel it more. It's like a phonograph record: the needle has to slide to bring out
the tune.

I like to see East change to West. I
like that moment, on the New York–
Pittsburgh–St. Louis route, when you
get to the last ridge, called Laurel Ridge.
There, at the end, the dislikable Alleghenies are almost real mountains. On
the brow of the ridge, facing west,
there is a bald, stony strip, scoured clean
by the west winds and the sleet and the
rain. An airway beacon stands up there,
alone. Then the stuff falls steeply away
under you. You slide out across there,
and you enter the Middle West. It feels
different. It feels easy-like. Not that the
country turns nice right away. Right
around Pittsburgh, it is a tortuous jumble — small, steep hills, slag fields, deep-
cut railroad tracks, lots of smoke. But
you know it will calm down. A pilot
gets the habit of "thinking ahead of
the airplane." The Now and Here is no
longer so important in the faster airplane: now and here, the engine per-
colates, the weather is okay, the gadgets
work, you have lots of gas. What's

ahead is what matters. And so you study
cloud shapes, listen to weather reports,
and feel out the situation ahead. And
there, you know, comes flat country,
come open fields, come comfortable
cities, big airports, runways with clear
approaches. The squeeze, that makes
the Easterner elbowy and unfriendly,
squeezes also in flying. In the East, airports are small, obstructed by power
lines, hills, gas works, squeezed in between the cemeteries and the insane
asylums. West of the Alleghenies, they
give you room.

So now, if the ceiling is low, you can
stay under it and push on; you know
the terrain gets better all the time. Or
you can go on top of the overcast; you
know that when you want to get down,
no hills will stick up into a low ceiling.
And so you feel, ahead of time, way up
in the air, that certain ease and plenty
of the Middle West.

Presently, you pick up the section
lines. Now *that* is something. It is really
one of the odd sights of the world, and
it is strictly an air-sight: a whole country laid out in a mathematical gridwork,
in sections one mile square each; exact,
straight-sided, lined up in endless lanes
that run precisely — and I mean precisely — north-south and east-west. It makes
the country look like a giant real-estate
development: which it is. One section
has 640 acres. A quarter section, 160
acres, is the historical homestead. You
sold your goods, you crossed the sea
somehow, and they *gave* you *that!*
"Land-office business" used to be done
in this matter, and no wonder.

Get this right. These section lines are
not something that an attentive eye can
distinguish in the landscape. They *are*
the landscape. Compared to this gridwork, the natural landscape — flat here,
a little rolling there, a river valley, a
pond — just can't quite catch your attention. In fact, the natural landscape
has long fitted itself to this scheme. A
man has a wood lot, his neighbor a corn-

field; the boundary between woods and field is of course the fence line; but the fence line is part of the grid. More than people know, all their coming and going is channeled by that grid. Their roads — except for the biggest highways — run and jog along the grid. In fact, from the air, the lines are mostly marked by roads.

For flying, the section lines are wonderful. They make this country in reality just what a pilot wants country to be — graph paper. You can time your shadow with a stop watch across two lines, and get your exact speed. You can head the airplane down a section line and check your compass. But you hardly need a compass. You simply draw your course on the map and see what angle it makes. Then you cross the sections at the same angle. You can't miss. If you want to go exactly west, you get on a fence and follow it. The fence presently leaves off; the line becomes a highway. The highway curves off, but the line goes on as a fence again, as a lane between fields, as a farm road, then perhaps as the main street of a town, a highway again. It is easy on the brain.

It's true what the foreigners say — it all looks pretty much alike. A town comes out of the haze, moves through below you, falls back — only (you sometimes think) to run through some secret passageway and plant itself again in front of you!

Flying, you tell these towns apart as you tell stars — by constellation. This one, of about the fourth magnitude, with a smaller one to the north of it — that must be this one on the map. Those three-in-line, that's those.

What is it like, this American town? Well it isn't crowned by a castle, that's for sure; nor by a cathedral either. By an insurance skyscraper, more likely; or by a hotel, perhaps; but most likely by nothing. It is not fortified, and never was: no crowded Old Town, no ring-shaped boulevard where the walls used to be. Neither is it like a town I once saw in the South — a company town with a street-plan like this

☐ ⟨⟨⟨⟨⟨⟨⟨

with the mill at its head. And it is not a village.

It is always a small city. It is laid out with streets at right angles, and has at its center a little Downtown, perhaps only two streets crossing each other, perhaps a few blocks. In there, it's naked and stony; it achieves a certain business-like ugliness. There is a well-developed parking problem. And at night, that downtown core glows with bright lights and red neon signs, where the seller entertains the buyer and the boy the girl.

The rest is quiet streets with little houses and lots of trees. It fades out into the farmland in an indifferent way — streets and avenues already marked out on the ground, but still empty. You can tell — it expects to grow. Add a few blocks on the outskirts, and the downtown gets a bit more stony. Keep adding, and Farmerville becomes Bloomington, Bloomington becomes Springfield, Springfield becomes, say, Indianapolis.

There is always a Wrong Side of the Tracks to the town. In the thirties, when the price of paint made a bigger difference, this used to show up plainly. There is always a giant high school, and certain other standard furniture — a gasoline bulk plant, race track, " institution " (may be a veterans' hospital, may be a teachers' college, may be a county poorhouse). These things are marked on the flying maps, not because it is remarkable that a town should have them, but because it helps you tell the towns apart. This town has its high school at the east end. If this is the town I think it is, there should be an institution on the north edge. Sure, there it is.

Section lines in the Midwest — " a whole country laid out in a mathematical gridwork, in sections one mile square each . . ." (Ewing Galloway)

You make a pencil mark on the map and fly on.

Somewhere now, about a third of the way across the country, you notice something has changed. The fields are bigger; the air is clearer. Things have opened up. There is less junk around the landscape — I mean by junk, I guess, things of which a pilot cannot immediately see the sense and purpose: a clump of trees here, a different-colored patch of field there, an old abandoned factory building — that sort of thing. The landscape is tidier. Each farmhouse sits on its land as if it had just been set there; each fence shows straight and strong, as if it had just been strung. Each town seems to say: "Look, I am a town." Things have a sharper edge to them.

What's happened is that you have crossed the line between the forest and the prairie — the line that was there in Indian days. The white man has cleared the forest and plowed the prairie, and has made them both superficially alike — both farmland. But still the difference shows. Maybe it's the different color of the soil. Maybe it's that up to here, the country has been darkened by the last poor remnants of the old dark forests — a clump of trees, a wood lot — and here the trees leave off. Maybe it is simply the drier, clearer air. At any rate, you have moved one more notch west.

Here, in the less cluttered country, your map reading must change. A town may be so small that it would rate only a circle, o, further east: here, it gets the full treatment. The map shows it as a yellow area, shaped like the town's built-up area. A town may be so small that further east it wouldn't be on the map at all: here it gets at least an o, and a name. This, I like. It reminds you of the way each person counts for more out west. Go West, young man, and put yourself on the map.

And I like the names of those towns. It used to be that a prince would graciously call a town after himself — Wil-liamstown or Fredericksburg or Charles' Rest, or what not. Out here, the ordinary man sat himself down, founded himself a town, and named it, by gosh, after himself. I like to check them as I fly: here comes Charlie. Howdy, Riley. *Wie geht's,*[1] Hoehne. Hello, Kline. Landusky, Henderson, Milliken, Goessel, Weir, Swink, McPhee: how are you doing?

Or the man would name the town after a woman of his: Beulah, Maybell, Dolores. I had often flown over a town named Beatrice, Nebraska, and I had thought: "Poor Beatrice, whoever you were (farmer's wife? railroad president's daughter?) — that really wasn't much of a present to give a woman." It is a nice town and all that, but it isn't exactly — you know — it hasn't got *glamour,* out here in the sun-blasted country between Omaha and Wichita. (It hasn't got glamour if you were over Manhattan yesterday and will be over the Hollywood hills tomorrow.) Well, I came over Beatrice again one night. Now people don't know this, but a town at night is the most beautiful thing made by man in the past hundred years — especially an American town, where they don't spare the current. A brave sight, too, out there, where towns are far apart, with a lot of darkness in between. People went out into this vastness, built a home town here, and lit all those lights. A proud sight, just by being there. And I thought: "Beatrice, wherever you are now, you ought to be proud. It looks real nice."

Now, halfway across the country, come the Great Plains. It happens fast, in a matter of minutes. A grassy butte sticks up right through the fields. A bit of badlands shows up. The pattern of the farms opens up to detour around it and comes together again. A gully shows

[1] **Wie geht's** (vē gāts): an informal shortening of the German "How do you do?" Why does Langewiesche use the German phrase for this greeting?

up — Grand Canyon in miniature. You know the signs. You are getting west another notch. You hitch yourself up in your seat and take new notice.

Ahead, the country rises a step, and the step is a bluff: its face is eroded; it grins at you like the teeth of a skull. As you pass over, the farms fall back. The last you see of them is a mile-square wheat field draped over some hump, abandoned. It reminds you of a wrecked ship on a beach — tried to go where it should not be, and got in trouble. Ahead are the vast khaki plains, rising toward the West. There's nothing to see but vastness, clarity of air, distance. The sun glistens on a window of some ranch house, fifty miles away. A train, very far away, is a small black thing under a smoke plume, like a ship at sea.

You head straight out there, and the world fades out: badlands; the dry, bare hills. That fellow yammering about the " Lone Prairie " — he's been there. You suddenly remember you have no water aboard, no strong shoes, no big hat. You are lucky if you see a ranch, hidden deep down in some secret canyon, in a patch of green. More likely, you see next to nothing: a barbed-wire fence; some cattle; a windmill pumping beside a water hole.

You fall in line and follow the railroad. Everybody and everything else does, in that country; even the Civil Airways. Now the U.S.A. slenders down to a mere strip — river-plus-railroad-plus-highway. Along this strip are the irrigated fields, the towns, the airports. And the railroad is the great sight — doubly great by default of everything else. Its long straightaways and mathematical curves, the way it goes on and on through empty country up toward the West.

Finally these bright yellow-green plains rise under you like a wave about to break; over the crest comes a white spot that turns out to be snow. There, between two high mountains, is a gate-way, where the river comes out. Toward this gate you have been steering all along; so was the railroad; so was the highway; so were the radio beams along the airway. You go in through that gate, and East has changed to West.

III

The air view is an honest view: " You can't kid *me* " is your attitude as you look down. " So *that's* how it is." For example, the great famous dams — Hoover, Norris, Grand Coulee. In the ground view, the thing you marvel at is how big they are. The glamour photographs show them that way — small human figures, dwarfed by this gigantic wall behind them. Well, from the air, it's the other way round. It strikes you how *small* they are. Hoover Dam especially — it's actually hard to find! The eye sweeps all over the naked rock and the shores of Lake Mead before you find it — hidden down in a gulch. It makes you smile. Some boy has jammed a rock into this stream at just the right spot — and has managed to dam up a big lake. Small cause, big effect: clever little devil. And that, I'm sure, is the correct view. An engineer would say so. He would always try to build the smallest possible dam, not the biggest.

The foreground doesn't hide the background. Looking down at a place from the air, you see everything, literally, that's there. You may not notice everything; you may not understand the half of it; but at least you've seen it. What's this? Why does it look so odd? It's been amusing, for example, to watch the college campuses: the old fake Gothic, ivy-covered; the stadium with its vast parking space; the new research factory; the rows of Quonset huts. 'Tain't Oxford, brother. You run your own private census all the time. This thing — why do I see more and more of this? Not much can happen in the country that you don't notice, often ahead of the papers and magazines. For example, much will be written soon about our cities, how they have grown in area, not to say exploded; how the FHA town, way out on the potato fields, is taking the place of the tenement; and so on. Why sure: pilots have seen that grow for years.

The American landscape is a palimpsest.[1] Underneath what is written in it now, in concrete and barbed wire, there is older writing.

To bring out old writing, a man might photograph a document under trick light. The same in flying. Over the forests of New England, winter light is best. The trees must be bare, so the eye is not stopped at the treetop level. There must be snow on the forest floor, because that lights up the inside of the forest and makes it easier to look down into it.

Then you see, underneath the present-day forest, the farms of long ago. They did have decent fields there after all! Not decent to land on, but lovingly made, cleared out of the forest, carefully fenced by stone walls. Each rock once was picked up by hand, carried out of the field, carefully placed. It's said they made their children do that, to make them hard-working and God-fearing. Stern stuff. It's all under the forest. The forest is still only scrubby; but already it is full of dead trees helter-skelter, like virgin forest. The 1938 hurricane put them down, and nobody cares. History did a high-speed job here.

The second layer in this palimpsest is in strong plain writing: those section lines are the main part of it. About this, the main feature of the U.S. landscape, it is curiously hard to find anything in books. But I have often admired this scheme. Remember — it was drawn up on paper before the country had even been explored. The lines were run before the people came; so it was literally

[1] **palimpsest** (păl'ĭmp·sĕst): a parchment or tablet which has been used twice or three times, the earlier writing having been erased.

a blueprint for a future society — homestead by homestead, men would sit each in his own domain free and equal: each man's domain clearly divided from his neighbor's.

I mean, it wasn't the only way they could have parceled out the country. They could have gone out there with manor houses, each with a bunch of cottages around it. (You do see some of that in the South.) They could have built villages nestling around a commons and a church. They might have built forts. Today, I think, we would build a headquarters first. There would be a row of houses; a communal water tower, " housing " for bachelor workers, a hospital, a recreation area. Radiating out, I imagine, would be roads, and off the roads would be the fields. The whole " development " would be star-shaped, and right in the center would be of course the Administration Building.

But they picked the layout where every man is his own boss. Even now, this is the main feature of the American landscape: the square-cornered parcels, big in the West, small in the East, big in the country, small in the cities, of which each means a man. I realize they rent 'em, they are mortgaged, they grow the stuff by government subsidy, all that; but it is still true — the *design* of the landscape, seen from the air, is a design for independent men.

For Discussion of Langewiesche

1. Tell a new bit of information about flying that you picked up from this essay and that might make an interesting contribution to your conversation. Relate to the class a similar " overview " of the country or of your section of the country that you have experienced in traveling or reading. What distinguishing features would help you to identify your own home town from a plane? What is the origin of your town's name?

2. Which of his observations show that the writer has a European background?

Comment on the difference between the patterns of American and European towns. How does the "company town" fit into the American pattern? Has it some resemblance to European towns? Tell some of the things Langewiesche likes about American towns.

3. Why do the section lines of the plains please a flier? What deeper significance does Langewiesche see in the pattern of this landscape?

4. A writer as informal as this one is easy to get acquainted with. How do Langewiesche's sentences show that he takes a very personal attitude toward his reader? Find some words or phrases he uses that set an informal tone. Style reveals personality. What sort of person is the author? Which of his qualities do you like best?

5. Are you able to locate the places where Langewiesche notices a distinct change in the landscape as he flies west? Use a map to do this. How will a *topographical* map help?

For Your Vocabulary

A WORD FAMILY: Langewiesche says he used to think of the U.S.A. as "simply *terrain* on which to practice your technique." The word *terrain* has the root *terra* meaning "land," and it means just that. Many other English words have this same root. What is the meaning of *terrace, terra cotta, terra firma, terrestrial, Mediterranean?* (Note how knowledge of its root meaning helps you to spell this last word.) Why are some dogs called *terriers?*

Guide to Reading Nonfiction

There is no fixed pattern for reading nonfiction as a whole. The range is too great! Some of the specific types, like the book review and the interview, have distinctive features that you come to expect; and biography falls into fairly clear groups with definite characteristics. But most nonfiction has only two constant elements, style and content, or, to put it another way, the author's personality and what he has to tell you.

As you read "The U.S.A. from the Air," you came to know Langewiesche, an ardent flying fan with a friendly, informal manner. He is so full of his experiences aloft that he wants to tell you how America looks to a flier and what ideas the air view brings to his mind. The next article or essay you read, in this book or in one of the many magazines in your home or library, may bring you a quite different sort of person telling you about a quite different subject. These two ingredients of personality and content are the only ones you can count on finding in every piece of truly literary nonfiction you read.

Style: The Author's Personality

If a writer leads up to his main point gradually, like a graceful conversationalist, you may have to read a paragraph or two before you discover what subject he is going to talk about or just what ideas he is going to advance. But the first few sentences will give you an impression of his personality. It is his style of writing that portrays him. The style is the man himself.

Style is difficult to analyze but easy to recognize. Many elements contribute to the total effect — choice of words, sentence pattern, characteristic twists given to the expression of thoughts. Dignified phrasing and long, balanced sentences may give you a clue that the man who writes them is a serious person of stately manner. Short, chatty sentences and colloquial usage quickly give you the impression of an easygoing, friendly person. Any humor that the serious writer indulges in will probably be ironical and have a direct bearing on his subject. On the other hand, the informal writer will throw in little quips just for the fun of it. If you want to enjoy a writer fully, treat him as you would someone face to face. Fall in with his mood and manner, respond sympathetically to him, as you do in talking with a friend.

The best way to get acquainted with a writer rapidly is to respond to the tone he takes. The first few sentences will provide clues to the tone. For words have emotional color as well as meaning. They are bright and gay, or gloomy, or indignant, or solemnly serious. For example, you will read one little article which has the ominous word " death " in the first sentence. But in the next sentence you find the phrase " hooted at " where " objected to " would ordinarily have served. Then instead of saying that the girl could ride any horse, the writer quotes her as saying, " I'm always trying to hold 'em in my lap." By that time you realize that the writer intends to hold to a lighter tone, no matter how serious his subject. Hints such as these are always present to reveal the tone of the writer and to give you a glimpse of his personality.

Content: The Author's Purpose

The content of any piece of nonfiction is governed by the author's purpose in writing it. He may write to furnish information, or to present ideas, or simply to entertain. He may, for example, want to explain how important cattle brands are in ranch life, or how a song writer goes about fitting words to music. Or he may set out to convince you that Americans can and must stop the waste of our natural resources. Perhaps he wishes merely to share an amusing or thrilling or enlightening experience. Whatever his purpose, you will want to get as much as possible from what the author says. The best way to extract facts or ideas from a piece of nonfiction, you will find, is to follow the exact method by which the author presents them. This is not as important for essays of a chatty, conversational nature as for articles that are mainly informational in purpose and content.

Organizing Information

In a well-written informational article there are main divisions of thought with details to illustrate or support each one. Langewiesche, for example, started off with the early flier's view of the countryside in terms of possible emergency landing fields, and then contrasted New England and North Dakota by way of illustration. In reading, spot the major points as you come to them; then gather the minor bits that round out the picture and fit them in. A good writer has gone through the same steps in building an article, and has already attended to the arranging for you. He sets up signposts, too, to warn you that he is turning to a new main division. When Langewiesche moved up to modern flying, he marked his shift with, " Now, flying has changed," and without effort you skipped from the early thirties to 1950.

Recognizing such divisions, like making a mental outline of an article as you read, speeds up both reading and later recall. Gaining skill in this process will make you efficient in most of the reading you do for a serious purpose, such as studying lessons, or reading up on your own favorite interests and hobbies.

Examining Ideas

" On your guard! " is a good motto to follow when you find a writer seeking to persuade you of his own ideas. Propaganda is thick in the air these days. Never have people needed more urgently the ability to examine ideas and decide whether they are soundly based on reliable facts and clear thinking. A tremendous amount of the matter you encounter in casual reading or listening is designed to influence your opinions and attitudes. You do not want to be a mental tumbleweed, swayed this way and that by every wind that blows across your path.

Ideas are thoughts. They should appeal to your mind. But all too many writers and speakers try to win converts by appealing to feelings, especially prejudice. In reading, you need to decide, first of all, which method is used. If the appeal is emotional, you should be wary indeed of accepting the ideas advanced. If facts are given to bolster the ideas, examine them. If the facts are pertinent and sufficient, then the ideas will generally be sound and acceptable.

As you think through the reasoning a writer uses to support his ideas, you increase your ability to think clearly for yourself. You will read many articles in magazines and newspapers that are often conflicting in judgments and often opposed in purpose. Every time you read one article critically, bringing your intelligence to bear on the opinions expressed in it, you build up your defenses against the propaganda that surrounds us today. You take one more step on the road to true mental independence.

OSCAR HAMMERSTEIN II

1895–

Where the Song Begins

Broadway, which has been the scene of Oscar Hammerstein II's labors and his triumphs, is strong in the family blood. His grandfather, the great original Oscar Hammerstein, was a leading theater-builder and producer of his day; his father, William, managed the Victoria theater; and his uncle Arthur was a musical-comedy producer. William Hammerstein did not want his son to go into show business. Reluctantly, young Oscar took his law degree from Columbia University and spent a year in a law office, but the lure of the theater finally won. He persuaded his uncle to give him a job as assistant stage manager, but it was only with the condition that he should not try to write for the theater until he worked in it for a year and understood its special requirements.

That advice was evidently good, for Hammerstein has written the libretto for many a smash musical hit and has won every prize offered in the American theater. Some of his best-known productions are *Oklahoma!* and *South Pacific,* both of which have won a Pulitzer Prize, *Show Boat, Carousel,* and the recent *The King and I.* Together with his composer-collaborator, Richard Rodgers, Hammerstein has been the leading creator of a new kind of stage art: the musical play. Some critics have said that a play like *South Pacific* is an original American contribution to the theater, not so grand or ambitious as opera but also not so lacking in ideas as the usual musical comedy. Americans have so far not been very successful in writing opera, and perhaps in the musical play they have found their niche in music. In the following essay, you can listen to a man who is well qualified to explain how words are combined with music.

I T TOOK me years to learn that I did not play the piano very well. I so enjoyed my own playing. I tackled everything — Victor Herbert, Verdi, Leoncavallo, George Cohan. What expression I could put into their music! What exaltation I felt! My mother thought I had "a lovely touch," she told her friends. But when I became fifteen or sixteen my own friends began to express less sympathetic reactions, and it became clear to me that they were not hearing the same music I thought I was hearing when I played. Remembering this illuminating and disturbing experience, I have misgivings right now as I embark on a discussion of lyrics. I am going to love it, but will you? The hunter gloats reminiscently over the last saber-toothed tiger he has brought back alive. So does the song writer like to tell of how he has captured a refrain and imprisoned it safely behind thirty-two bars. Both are likely to overrate the spare time of their audience.

Almost every layman [1] I have ever met exhibits a real curiosity about songs and how they are written. It is a standing joke among authors and composers that when they meet people the first question asked of them is "Which comes first, the words or the music?" Perhaps it is high time that one of us stopped laughing at the classic query and provided a sensible answer to it. There is nothing foolish about the question. A song is a wedding of two crafts, and it is a natural thing to wonder how they meet

[1] **layman:** a term used by a professional person to mean anyone not belonging to that profession.

and live together.

There is, as a matter of fact, no invariable or inevitable method for writing songs. Sometimes the words are written first, sometimes the music. Sometimes two or more collaborators lock themselves in a room and write words and music at the same time. The kind of songs, the individuals involved, and the conditions under which they work dictate the process. Grand-opera scores are almost always set to texts already written by the librettists. In the case of the most famous of all comic-opera collaborations, it was the librettist, Gilbert, who wrote the words first. He would sometimes mail an entire act to Sullivan, who would then set music to his verses. On the other hand, the lyrics for most of the popular songs and musical comedies in our country today are written after the music. Up until my first collaboration with Richard Rodgers in 1943, I had always written this way. For twenty-five years, collaborating with Jerome Kern, Herbert Stothart, Sigmund Romberg, Rudolf Friml, and Vincent Youmans, I set words to their music. It would seem to most people — and I am one of them — that writing the words first would be a more logical procedure, music being the more flexible and less specific of the two mediums. Why then did I write in this upside-down manner for so long a time?

In the first decade of this century there were two factors which led song writers into the custom of writing words to music. The best musical plays of that time were being created in Vienna. When they were imported, American librettists had to write translations and adaptations for melodies that had been set to another language. In those days we imported not only plays from Middle Europe, but many of the composers themselves came over here, settled down, and became American citizens. They embraced our democratic philosophy, but they found it much more difficult to get used to our language. Lyric writers who submitted verses to be set were horrified by the abortive accents written to their words, and they soon found it less trying on their nerves to let the foreign musician have his say first and then write a lyric to fit his melody.

The second influence was not foreign at all. It was distinctly an American one — the broken rhythm. First came ragtime, then jazz. For the purpose of creating these eccentric deviations from orthodox meters, it was better to let the composer have his head. Concomitant with [1] the creation of these new rhythms came what we called, in 1911, "the dance craze." Dancing, once confined to ballrooms and performed mainly by the young, became a new international sport indulged in by all people of all ages in all kinds of restaurants and at all mealtimes, lunch, tea, dinner, and supper. The hit melodies of that time had to be good dance melodies. This being the most important consideration, it was better for the lyric writer to trail along after the composer and fit his words to a refrain written mainly to be danced to. Many lyrics of the period were about dancing. Irving Berlin wrote "Everybody's Doing It." (Doing what? The turkey trot!) People were also, in other songs, doing the bunny hug and the grizzly bear. Not satisfied with writing lyrics describing dances already established by leading teachers and famous

[1] Concomitant (kŏn·kŏm′ĭ·tănt) with: occurring at the same time as.

dancing teams, lyric writers set to work creating dances, giving them names, and hoping that the public would follow them.

I have conducted no exhaustive investigation of this subject, but these developments, as I remember them, seem to have been the chief influences which established the American song writer's habit of writing the music first and the words later. It is a strange habit, an illogical one, but not entirely without compensating virtues. Writing in this way, I have frequently fallen into the debt of my composers for words and ideas that might never have occurred to me had they not been suggested by music. If one has a feeling for music — and anyone who wants to write lyrics had better have this feeling — the repeated playing of a melody may create a mood or start a train of thought that results in an unusual lyric. Words written in this way are likely to conform to the spirit of the music. It is difficult to fit words into the rigid framework of a composer's meter, but this very confinement might also force an author into the concise eloquence which is the very essence of poetry. There is in all art a fine balance between the benefits of confinement and the benefits of freedom. An artist who is too fond of freedom is likely to be obscure in his expression. One who is too much a slave to form is likely to cripple his substance. Both extremes should be avoided, and no invariable laws or methods should be obeyed.

In our collaboration Mr. Rodgers and I have no definite policy except one of complete flexibility. We write songs in whatever way seems best for the subject with which we are dealing and the purposes of the song in the story which we are telling. Most often I write the words first, and yet in nearly all of our scores there are at least one or two songs in which he wrote the music first. When we first started to write together in 1943 we had no conversations on method. The first song we wrote was "Oh, What a Beautiful Mornin'," and the words were written first. I would like to tell you how this happened, because it furnishes a typical illustration of composer-author collaboration in the structure of a musical play.

Attacking the job of turning Lynn Riggs's *Green Grow the Lilacs* [1] into what eventually became *Oklahoma!* the first serious problem that faced us involved a conflict of dramaturgy [2] with showmanship. As we planned our version, the story we had to tell in the first part of the first act did not call for the use of a female ensemble. The traditions of musical comedy, however, demand that not too long after the rise of the curtain the audience should be treated to one of musical comedy's most attractive assets — the sight of pretty girls in pretty clothes moving about the stage, the sound of their vital young voices supporting the principals in their songs. Dick and I, for several days, sought ways and means of logically introducing a group of girls into the early action of the play. The boys were no problem. Here was a farm in Oklahoma with ranches nearby. Farmers and cowboys belonged there, but girls in groups? No. Strawberry festivals? Quilting parties? Corny devices! After trying everything we could think of, and rejecting each other's ideas as fast as they were submitted, after passing through phases during which we would stare silently at each other unable to think of anything at all, we came finally to an extraordinary decision. We agreed to start our story in the real and natural way in which it seemed to want to be told! This decision meant that the first act would be half over before a female chorus would make its entrance. We realized that such a course was experimental,

amounting almost to the breach of an implied contract with a musical-comedy audience. I cannot say truthfully that we were worried by the risk. Once we had made the decision everything seemed to work right and we had that inner confidence people feel when they have adopted the direct and honest approach to a problem.

Now, having met our difficulty by simply refusing to recognize its existence, we were ready to go ahead with the actual writing. We had agreed that we should start the play outside a farmhouse. The only character on the stage would be a middle-aged woman sitting at a butter churn. The voice of Curley, a cowboy, would be heard off stage, singing. Searching for a subject for Curley to sing about, I recalled how deeply I had been impressed by Lynn Riggs's description at the start of his play:

It is a radiant summer morning several years ago. The kind of morning which, enveloping the shapes of earth — men, cattle in the meadow, blades of the young corn, streams — makes them seem to exist now for the first time, their images giving off a visible golden emanation that is partly true and partly a trick of imagination, focusing to keep alive a loveliness that may pass away.

On first reading these words I had thought what a pity it was to waste them on stage directions. Only readers could enjoy them. An audience would never hear them. Yet, if they did, how quickly they would slip into the mood of the story. Remembering this reaction, I reread the description and determined to put it into song. "Oh, What a Beautiful Mornin'" opens the play and creates an atmosphere of relaxation and peace and tenderness. It introduces the lighthearted young man who is the center of the story. My indebtedness to Mr. Riggs's description is obvious. The cattle and the corn and the golden haze on the meadow are all there. I added some observations of my own based on my

---

[1] A play produced on Broadway in 1931.

[2] **dramaturgy** (drăm′á·tûr′jĭ): the art of dramatic composition.

The schoolroom scene from The King and I, *a Rodgers and Hammerstein musical version of the popular biography,* Anna and the King of Siam. *Gertrude Lawrence* (at left) *plays the role of the governess, Anna, who has come to educate the King's children.* (Vandamm)

experience with beautiful mornings, and I brought the words down to the more primitive poetic level of Curley's character. He is, after all, just a cowboy and not a playwright.

Let us take a case where the music was written first. The refrain of " People Will Say We're in Love " was a melody written by Richard Rodgers with the thought that it might serve well as a duet for the two lovers in *Oklahoma!* This procedure is the more usual approach to writing musical-comedy scores. The composer dreams up some melodies which suggest certain treatments. One might seem to him to be the love duet of the piece, the other a

good comedy song or a good tune to dance to. Almost all composers have a reservoir of melodies which come to them at different times and which they write down in what they call a sketchbook. When they start work on a new musical play, they play over these previously written melodies for their collaborator, and it is decided which ones can be used in this particular score. They then write additional melodies as required. Dick Rodgers, however, does not work in this way. He writes music only for a specific purpose. Ideas for tunes seldom come to him while he is walking down the street or riding in taxicabs, and he doesn't rush to his piano very often to write a tune just for the sake of writing a tune. I don't believe that either Dick or I would be very successful essentially as popular song writers — writers of song detached from plays. We can write words and music best when they are required by a situation or a characterization in a story.

In all I have been saying, it will be noted that the composer and author work in very close collaboration during the planning of a song and the story that contains the song. This is an important point. It must be understood that the musician is just as much an author as the man who writes the words. He expresses the story in his medium just as the librettist expresses the story in his. Or, more accurately, they weld their two crafts and two kinds of talent into a single expression. This is the great secret of the well-integrated musical play. It is not so much a method as a state of mind, or rather a state of two minds, an attitude of unity. Musical plays, then, are not " books " written by an author with songs later inserted by a composer and a lyric writer. They are often written this way, but it is not a good way to write them and such plays seldom have a very long life. They are sure to lack form, and they cannot sustain a story interest when it is interrupted continually by songs that are of little value to the plot.

Let me say a few words now about the actual writing of lyrics once the subject matter of the song has been determined, and once it has been placed in its proper spot in the telling of the story. I am often asked if I use a rhyming dictionary. I do. I find it a great help and a timesaver. The one I like best is Loring's *Rhymer's Lexicon*. A rhyming dictionary, however, should be used as a supplement to one's own ingenuity, and not a substitute for it. I do not open mine until I have exhausted my own memory and invention of rhymes for a word. Attractive combinations of words to make double and triple rhymes are not found in rhyming dictionaries, nor are modern words or colloquialisms which can be used with humorous effect in a song. A rhyming dictionary is of little use and may, in fact, be a handicap when one is writing a song which makes a feature of rhyming. If you would achieve the rhyming grace and facility of W. S. Gilbert or Lorenz Hart, my advice would be never to open a rhyming dictionary. Don't even own one. While I, on occasion, place a timid, encroaching foot on the territory of these two masters, I never carry my invasion very far. I would not stand a chance with either of them in the field of brilliant light verse. I admire them and envy them their fluidity and humor, but I refuse to compete with them. Aside from my shortcomings as a wit and rhymester — or, perhaps because of them — my inclinations lead me to a more primitive type of lyric. The longer I write, the more interested I become in expressing my own true convictions and feelings in the songs I write. When I was very much younger I thought that if ever I made all the money I needed out of writing musical comedy I would then sit back and turn to straight dramatic plays in which I could say whatever I wanted to say and state my reactions to the world I live in. Later on, however, I became convinced that whatever I wanted to say could be said in songs, that I was not confined necessarily to trite or light subjects, and that since my talent and training in the writing of lyrics are far beyond my attainments in other fields of writing, I had better use this medium.

If one has fundamental things to say in a song, the rhyming becomes a question of deft balancing. A rhyme should be unassertive, never standing out too noticeably. It should, on the other hand, not be a rhyme heard in a hundred other popular songs of the time, so familiar that the listener can anticipate it before it is sung. There should not be too many rhymes. In fact, a rhyme should appear only where it is absolutely demanded to keep the pattern of the music. If a listener is made rhyme-conscious, his interest may be diverted from the story of the song. If, on the other hand, you keep him waiting for a rhyme, he is more likely to listen to the meaning of the words.

After rhyming, I would place next in importance a study and appreciation of phonetics. Some words and groups of words that look beautiful in printed poetry are unavailable to one who is writing lyrics to be sung to music. There is an inexorable mathematics in music — so many measures in a refrain, so many beats in a measure, and they cannot be ignored. There is rhythm and tempo, and its continuity must be unbroken. The concessions with which a melody can favor words are limited. The larynxes of singers are limited. They must be given a chance to breathe after a certain number of words have been sung, and if they are building up to a high note at the finish, they must be given a good deep breath before they attack it. Both the lyric writer and the composer must worry about all these things. If a song is not singable, it is no song at all.

Lest at any point I seem to be laying down rigid rules, let me acknowledge quickly that there are no such things in my craft. Some of our most successful compositions stray far beyond the narrow borders that restrict the well-made refrain. " Star Dust " rambles and roams like a truant schoolboy in a meadow. Its structure is loose, its pattern complex. Yet it has attained the kind of long-lived popularity that few songs can claim. What has it got? I'm not certain. I know only that it is beautiful and I like to hear it. It is a mood-creating song. It has repose and wistfulness. It is something very special, all by itself. Anyone who tried to imitate it would be a fool.

" Begin the Beguine " is another rule-breaker — too long! It is what is known among professional song writers as " a tapeworm." It hasn't the cohesive and compact continuity of a popular song. But it *is* popular and has been for about twenty years. That's *very* popular. This is an " atmospheric " song. It transports you to places where palm trees wave across yellow moons and Spanish is spoken, which is exactly what Cole Porter wants it to do to you.

Songs like these, ignoring the orthodox principles, are freaks and anomalies. One doesn't learn much from anomalies. Common-sense solutions to normal problems are the first things to master. One very fundamental problem is the special use of certain words in songs. Some words, for instance, have lost their value through overuse. " Divine " is such a word. It occurs in " All the Things You Are." I didn't like this word when I submitted the song to Jerry Kern and, as I had anticipated, he didn't like it either. For many days I worked trying to find a substitute. I just couldn't. The last lines are: " Some day I'll know that moment divine, When all the things you are, are mine." I was trapped. " All the things you are," referred to poetically and romantically throughout the song, are certainly what I wish to be " mine." I could not surrender this finish. But it demands an " ine " rhyme. " Some day I'll know that moment . . ." What? Sign, line, fine, shine? Nothing served as well as the unwanted " divine." I never could find a way out. The song written in 1937 shows signs of being a long-lived standard ballad — but I shall never be happy with that word!

Rhyming, phonetics, semantics — all very important. But technique and professional polish do not make a song. They improve it and their absence might ruin it, but there is an element much less tangible that is the deciding factor in a song's life. The most important ingredient of a good song is sincerity. Let the song be yours and yours alone. However important, however trivial, believe it. Mean it from the bottom of your heart, and say what is on your mind as carefully, as clearly, as beautifully as you can.

This sounds like simple advice, but no one knows better than I how hard it is to follow. The basic rules are always the hardest ones to observe, even though they seem the easiest. No beginner on the golf course or the tennis courts questions the good sense of his first lesson when he is told to keep his eye on the ball. This seems such an obvious thing to do, and yet no matter how many years you play these games your chief mistake remains taking your eye off the ball. This tendency to skip over the fundamental things and grasp the superficial is the tragedy of man's history from the beginning of time. I used to write songs very quickly. A Long Island commuter, I prided myself that I could often write a refrain on one trip into New York, and the verse on the way back that night. Not many of these were good songs. I was too easily satisfied with my work. I was too often trying to emulate older and better lyric writers, saying things similar to the things they were saying. It would have been all right had I been content to imitate the forms of their songs, but the substance should have been mine and it was not. I know that insincerity held me back for several years, and I know that even after I'd had a period of success, it again handicapped me and caused me to have failures. Loathing all dishonest and sloppy work for the sorrows it has caused me, I loathe it in others as I would any poison, and if I can knock it out of anyone, I will.

For Discussion of Hammerstein

1. Check yourself to see how well you recall the information in this essay. See if you can tell without looking back: (a) Where *does* the song begin? (three answers); (b) Why are the words often written last? (two answers); (c) What does dramatic tradition demand early in the first act of a musical comedy, and why doesn't *Oklahoma!* have it? (d) Where did Hammerstein get the idea for " Oh, What a Beautiful Mornin' "? (e) What two popular songs seem to break the rules of songmaking?

2. Then check on how clearly you grasped the writer's ideas. What does he think about (a) having to write words to music, (b) rhyme in songs (three ideas), (c) the most important ingredient of a good song? Do you find his ideas convincing, or do you want to argue with him on some points?

3. In every personal essay you get an impression of the writer. What are some of Hammerstein's traits?

4. You can get some ideas of your own about song writing from comparing " Oh, What a Beautiful Mornin' " with the passage that suggested it. (Some classmate can supply all the words of the song.) See if you can tell how Hammerstein changed the original words to fit the character who sings the song.

5. If you are interested enough to try song writing yourself, take a bit of description from " Sixteen " (pp. 114–19) and work it into a verse pattern to fit some tune appropriate to the mood. Results will be interesting if the whole class works on the project as a group.

For Your Vocabulary

WORD ANALYSIS: Mr. Hammerstein calls attention to the importance of *phonetics* (the science of speech sounds) and also mentions *semantics* (the science of meanings). By analyzing these words we obtain clues to the meanings of other words, such as *telephone, phonograph, linguistics, semaphore*. Show how analysis of the parts of these words provides their meaning.

See if you can work out the meanings of the following words by using clues obtained from analyzing them in the order listed: *telegraph, orthography, orthodox, heterodox, heterogeneous, homogeneous, homonym.*

BERNARD DE VOTO

1897–

Restoration in the Wasatch

Bernard DeVoto, a native of Utah and historian of the West, writes a monthly feature called "The Easy Chair" for that venerable Eastern magazine, *Harper's*. The chair may be easy, but DeVoto does not loll in it. Some of the most vigorous essays to be found in America today appear under that deceptive heading.

After attending college in his native state and at Harvard, and serving as an infantry officer in World War I, DeVoto taught English at Northwestern University and Harvard before turning all his time to editing and writing. He is a hard-hitting critic of present-day affairs, but he is a critic with an ideal. His best-known books, *Mark Twain's America, The Year of Decision:* *1846,* and *Across the Wide Missouri* (winner of a Pulitzer Prize in 1948) remind Americans of their proud heritage.

The early days of the country beyond the Mississippi hold a special charm for DeVoto, but his interest in the West does not end with its romantic past. He is equally concerned with its present and its future, as you will observe in the following essay. Notice that the essay does not state its main theme at the beginning; almost as in a play, the essayist here first sets a scene and then tells a story. Telling a story is an effective way of getting an idea across to the reader. See how early in the reading you can discover what general subject the story illustrates.

M OST tourists who cross Utah by automobile travel the whole length of Davis County. Twenty-two miles long from south to north, the county lies between the two largest Utah towns, Salt Lake City and Ogden; the drive between them is spectacularly beautiful. To the east the Wasatch [1] Mountains thrust up a mile-high wall. To the west is Great Salt Lake, accurately described as "a desert of water." Its salt shore is blinding white in sunlight, its salt water an amazing sapphire blue.

From east to west the valley strip between the Wasatch and Great Salt Lake is nowhere more than fifteen miles wide; it averages barely five miles. There are fields of sugar beets, grains, alfalfa. There are truck gardens that supply the neighboring cities with vegetables, and even richer orchards. And the countryside is riotous with trees, which shade-thirsty men have planted against the desert sun. There are eight or nine villages, and here there is almost an explosion of trees, or lawns, or flower gardens.

It is the most intensively cultivated agricultural land in Utah. Few farms anywhere else in the state are as valuable as these, none more valuable. And part of its beauty on any summer morning is the water flowing in irrigation

[1] **Wasatch** (wô′săch).

"Restoration in the Wasatch" by Bernard DeVoto, from *The American Scholar*, Vol. 18, No. 4, Autumn 1949. Reprinted by permission of the author.

canals. Only water has made the farmland green. Without it there would be
no fields, no orchards, no crops, no villages.

For Davis County is a desert. In this
latitude it takes a minimum of twenty
inches of rainfall a year to grow crops.
On the valley floor the annual rainfall
averages fifteen. To the westward, beyond the Great Salt Lake, there are only four or five inches of rain a year, less
than the Sahara gets, and for hundreds
of miles the land is absolute desolation.
But the Wasatch Mountains provide the
water that gives life to land that would
be sterile without it. On the heights of
the Wasatch, rain and snow together
amount to between forty and fifty inches of water, the water that has made
twenty-two miles of level valley the
richest land in Utah.

It comes out of the mountains in
creeks that flow down canyons and de-
bouch on the foothills. From here it is
distributed over the farms by an irrigation system that has cost the labor and
wealth of generations. Downhill from
any lateral canal there is a rich, almost choked productivity: berries,
fruits, vegetables, trees, grass, flowers.
Take one step uphill from that same
lateral and you are in the vegetation of
the desert — cactus, sagebrush, rabbit-
bush, smokeweed. From barrenness to
civilization, from death to life, is only
a single step. And the step always has
to be taken across a ditch that is flowing water.

Water, the creator of life, can also
be a destroyer.

In Utah west of the Wasatch Mountains, summers are very dry, but usually
the drought is broken at intervals in
July or August by violent thunder-
storms. At the beginning of a storm the
rate of fall may be up to six and a half
inches an hour. For those few minutes
the rain is like a solid wall.

Such cloudbursts have been known
to the people of Utah ever since the

Mormon pioneers under Brigham Young
reached Salt Lake Valley (of which
Davis County is a part) in 1847. But
shortly after 1900, in some places they,
or rather their results, began to be different. People noticed that after summer cloudbursts the creeks rose much
higher than they used to, subsided
much sooner, were more turbid, carried more debris, did more damage —
though as yet the damage was slight
and marginal. A few understood what
was happening, but nothing is easier
than to remain unaware of gradual
processes.

Then abruptly Davis County rounded a turn that headed it straight back
toward the desert from which it had
been wrested. On August 14, 1923, a
cloudburst struck the western front of
the Wasatch. Within a few minutes after the storm broke, five of seven canyons above the narrowest part of the
valley floor poured out over the farms
floods immeasurably larger than Davis
County had ever seen. Moreover, they
were the most terrifying kind of mountain flood, the kind that is called a mud
flow. High up on a mountainside, a
slope of bare earth has collapsed under the sudden assault of the cloudburst. A torrent of fearful stuff that
looks like thick cement starts flowing
downhill. Every foot of slope gives it
more momentum, and it gets more still
as the collapsing mountainside behind
it shoves it on. When it reaches the bottom of the canyon, the narrow walls act
like the nozzle on a hose and multiply
its power many times.

The area struck that August day runs
northward from a village called Centerville past another called Farmington.
In a single hour, five floods or mud
flows spread over some of the richest
farms in Utah. They crushed houses,
barns, schools. They severed irrigation
canals and filled them with mud. They
broke railroad lines, telegraph and telephone lines, state highways, burying

them deep under rocks and mud. They killed six people. Over hundreds of acres of farmland they deposited mud, gravel, rocks, and giant boulders weighing up to 200 tons apiece. In some places this deposit was six feet deep — and wherever it is more than a few inches, it destroys the land's fertility. In many places it was so deep that no one could afford the cost of removing it.

Prompt public relief was provided for those who suffered in the floods of 1923. Few people realized even then that Davis County had entered a period of prolonged crisis. But every summer brought new floods from the canyons, though not on the same scale, until fear began to spread among the people of the Farmington–Centerville area, and economic decline set in. Farmers could not pay the interest on their mortgages, still less the principal. So banks refused to accept real estate as security for loans; it became harder to finance farming operations, and harder to keep irrigation systems in repair. Real estate agents refused to list farms for sale. Relief rolls lengthened, bank deposits dried up. Meanwhile the land itself deteriorated just as steadily.

In the summer of 1930, the wasting disease came to crisis. A July cloudburst brought mud flows out of all five canyons in the area that had flooded in 1923, on a greater scale than ever before, and out of a sixth canyon that had not previously flooded, this last one more destructive by far than any of the others. As the summer went on, there were more cloudbursts, and more floods came rushing out of canyons. Some streams poured four mud-rock flows apiece over the helpless land during that summer.

Davis County was poised on the brink of destruction, and the state of Utah was roused to a realization that much of its richest farmland — and so its whole economy and social structure — were in deadly peril. It was roused, too,

to a realization that the problem was not local, not confined to Utah, but Western and even national, and that all resources of knowledge must be focused on its solution. Relief agencies were put to work, and the power and purse of Congress were invoked.

At the direction of the legislature, the governor appointed a commission to study the causes of this destruction and to bring every kind of scientific, engineering, and practical knowledge to bear on the question of whether it could be halted. The commission made an exhaustive study and brought in a report. With that report, the way to the salvation of Davis County was made clear.

The report was the work of many hands. So was the drama that followed. Some of the actors stood out, but hundreds of people had a hand. Here was a concerted and co-operative drive to a common goal, an effort that can be truly called that of a whole community.

What had happened? What had caused these floods? Why was Davis County returning to the desert? The flood commission's study made it very clear that not nature, but the inhabitants of Davis County were responsible.

When rain falls or snow melts, the water must either sink into the ground or run off downhill. That which is absorbed by the ground nourishes vegetation and builds up the subterranean water supply. The soil is held in place and made absorbent by the vegetation that covers it. Trees, brush, shrubs, plants, grass, the litter of their fallen leaves and decayed stems — these are the great protectors of the soil. They hold it firm against wind and runoff. They break the force of falling rain and slow it up: slow-moving water is absorbed. They keep the soil granular and porous: it will take up more water. Their roots make branching channels to lead water deep into the ground. On a well-vegetated hillside, a heavy rain will be almost or fully absorbed; the ground may be soaked to the depth of a foot and a half. On bare patches of that same slope, almost all the water may run off, and the ground will be dry only an inch or so below the surface.

That is what had happened to the watersheds [1] of the creeks that flow down the Wasatch to the Davis County farms. The scanty timber of the west face of the mountains had been entirely logged off, but this was only a minor cause. A more important cause was a long series of brush and grass fires over the years that had destroyed the plant cover. Much more important was the fact that for many years the people of Davis County had grazed too many cattle and sheep on the slopes of the Wasatch and in their mountain meadows. Every area of grazing land has a capacity to feed so many livestock — a number that can be almost exactly calculated — without being harmed. If only the proper number graze it, the grass, herbage, and browse will completely reproduce themselves every year. But when more than the proper number graze any area, the nutritious and soil-preserving plants slowly thin and eventually disappear. Bare patches of hillside appear. They harden, and when they dry, the wind blows the soil away, and when rain falls it runs off, carrying the soil with it. The bare patches widen, gullies begin to form; every wind and every rain widen and deepen the gullies. The land will stand up under hard misuse for a long time; but when it begins to go, it goes fast.

On the watershed of every creek that had flooded Davis County, the experts found bare slopes of eroded earth. Some of them were small, only a few acres in extent; some of them were larger. In the Farmington area, all told, they added up to only 1,300 acres. But all the

[1] **watersheds:** regions contributing to the supply of rivers.

damage that had been done in that area originated on those 1,300 acres, about two square miles. When the terrific downpour of summer cloudbursts hit those patches of bare, hardened and gullied earth, the water rushed down to the creeks below, carrying the soil and gravel and boulders of the mountain-sides with it. Every storm widened those patches, and made certain that worse damage would ensue.

The lesson of land misuse thus shockingly made clear was highlighted just a little more than a mile to the south of the canyon that had produced the most destructive mud flow of all. Here there was another canyon, the seventh in the Farmington–Centerville area, and it had never had a flood of any kind. Every cloudburst that struck the six canyons immediately north of it also struck this one, but its creek has never overflowed. At the mouth of this stream is the village of Centerville, whose 600 inhabitants had interpreted the warning signs correctly and had acted on them. Using town funds, they had bought or leased the whole watershed above. Where the worn spots that mean overgrazing were beginning to show, they had ruled all livestock off till the grass and shrubs came back. Throughout the rest of the watershed, they had limited the cattle and sheep allowed to graze there to the numbers the experts decided were safe. And that was all. The sickening land had rapidly healed itself, grass grew plentifully, the soil stayed in place, the cloudbursts did no damage. Center-ville Creek ran clear; the town was secure from the desert threat, while its neighbors suffered.

Centerville had solved the problem before the rest of Davis County understood what the problem was. It had protected itself by its own efforts and at comparatively little cost. But to save the rest of Davis County was now an undertaking altogether beyond the power of local communities: it required help from both the state and the federal governments. Both co-operated, and the great project was entrusted to the United States Forest Service.

Two things were necessary. First, the causes that had produced the destruction of vegetation and the erosion of the land — fire and overgrazing — must be removed. So, small areas that were in the most critical condition were leased, and all grazing on them was prohibited. A special act of Congress authorized the Forest Service to use part of the fees received for grazing in the nearest National Forest to buy land in the mountains above Davis County. Year by year, it has done so, acquiring tracts in the order of worst condition, till by now almost all the mountain area of Davis County has been added to the Wasatch National Forest. This area is covered by the Forest Service's expert and scientific system of fire protection, and grazing on them has been prohibited until the areas that were the sources of floods are entirely restored.

There remained the direct attack on the exhausted lands. In the spring of 1934, under the direction of the Forest Service, 200 boys in the Civilian Conservation Corps [1] went to work on the Wasatch slopes. They worked there in force that year and the next, and some of them were kept at work there until 1940, when CCC funds ran out. They did the most spectacular job of restoring damaged land that the West has ever seen.

On all the bare spots where the floods had originated, and on all other slopes where erosion had begun, they built series of contour trenches. The function of these terracelike trenches was to break up the erosion gullies that had formed, and to catch the runoff from denuded

slopes and hold it back so that it could sink into the ground. At short intervals down the length of each trench a lower, cross-dam of earth was built, to make sure that only small portions could be destroyed at any one time. The CCC constructed as many of them as it could with tractor-driven bulldozers. On steep slopes and rocky outcrops it used horses and plows, and in a few almost vertical places it was necessary to dig the trenches by hand.

Terracing on the contour is an ancient way of protecting farm land from soil erosion, but never before had it been used as a measure of flood prevention on high Western mountainsides. It made a spectacular, inspiring, almost incredible sight. Wherever the slopes had been denuded, the trenches climbed them in twenty-five foot steps, straight up, sometimes all the way to the ridge, which might be 2,000 feet or more. The Forest Service planted them and the spaces between them with a mixture of grasses — some natives of the region, and some aliens, chosen because they spread rapidly or had unusually big root-systems to hold soil in place. Also, it planted tree seedlings.

The Forest Service calculated in 1934 that fifteen years would suffice to remove the threat of disastrous flood. (Some relief would begin at once; full restoration would take many years.) A spectacular, triumphant vindication of the treatment came on August 19, 1945, when the Davis County project was still four years short of completion. On that day the Forest Service methods of healing sick land were proved sound in the eyes of anyone who might care to look — and the entire West learned a lesson that will serve it from now on.

That day the most violent summer cloudburst ever recorded in Utah struck the west front of the Wasatch. Every creek in the restored watersheds of Davis County held to its banks; there were no floods; no damage was done in the

[1] Civilian Conservation Corps: A federal government "army" of young men who worked on conservation projects during the 1930's. Its primary object was to ease unemployment during the depression years.

areas that had been repeatedly damaged in 1930. But at Salt Lake City, just outside Davis County to the south, a small creek whose watershed had been impaired by fire and overgrazing came roaring out of its banks and caused $350,000 worth of damage in fifteen minutes. And at Ogden, just outside Davis County to the north, another overgrazed watershed poured a destructive mud flow to within two miles of the center of town.

That dramatic contrast produced action in Utah. Long-imperiled watersheds in the Wasatch are now receiving treatment and regulation that will save them. (Less drastic regulation and less expensive treatment than Davis County had to have, for the damage had not proceeded so far.) Public knowledge of the destructive forces at work has spread so widely that Utah, the Western state which has traveled farthest down the road back to the desert, is certainly going to save itself from the desert threat.

Meanwhile, Davis County has already been saved. True, the farm land that was actually destroyed will never be farm land again during the geological epoch in which we live, but there will be no more mud flows and no more floods. The creeks are secure. The farms have got back their fertility — and their monetary value. Production has been restored, the valley flourishes, many people have moved in. With the nonchalance of Westerners hardened to risk, some of them have built new houses directly below the mouths of canyons that nineteen years ago poured out death and destruction in ten-foot walls of mud.

For Discussion of DeVoto

1. What is the general problem stated in this essay? How does DeVoto use a specific area and specific incidents to illustrate the problem and to advance his ideas? In reading, how soon did you recognize the author's main theme in telling the story of Davis County?

2. Why does this problem concern all people in all sections of the country? Can you tell of other instances of similar damage and the measures taken to repair it? Is there a need for conservation in your own locality? How is it being dealt with?

3. Does DeVoto convince you that the methods used to combat the destructive floods were good ones? Trace his argument for terracing eroded slopes.

4. Why do some men ignore conservation rules? Why are there loud objections whenever laws are proposed to prevent overgrazing?

5. What was the chief difference between the people in Centerville and those in the rest of Davis County? Did the Centerville people have any information the others lacked?

6. A frequent subject for argument today is whether the world's farm lands, even if properly used, could produce adequate food for all the people on earth. What bearing does this essay have on the problem?

7. DeVoto serves on the Advisory Committee on Conservation to the Secretary of the Interior. Does this fact increase your respect for the ideas he advances in this essay? In reading a factual article or essay, how can one go about determining the author's competence or authority to speak on his subject?

For Your Vocabulary

SYNONYMS: *Synonyms* are words having the same, or almost the same, essential meaning. (What is an *antonym?*) The ability to discriminate in the use of synonyms — to choose just the right word from several which mean almost the same thing — is a mark of a good writer. DeVoto says that the land *deteriorated* (p. 155). *Degeneration* and *decadence* are synonyms of *deterioration*. What is the exact meaning of each of these three words? Why is *deteriorate* the best word for the context here? The writer also speaks of the "*nonchalance* of Westerners." Explain the difference between *nonchalant* and its synonyms, *cool, tranquil, imperturbable*.

J. FRANK DOBIE
1888–

The Heraldry of the Range

J. Frank Dobie once complained that in all his school life no one ever directed him to a piece of literature that dealt with life as he knew it in the Southwest. Early in his career as an English professor at the University of Texas, he proposed a course entitled " Literature of the Southwest." When his colleagues told him there was not enough literature of the Southwest to justify such a course, he suggested a course on " Life and Literature of the Southwest," claiming that there was plenty of life to make up for any lack in literature.

No one has done more than Dobie to prove there is interest in the life of the Southwest and to provide literature about it. In *Coronado's Children* and *Apache Gold and Yaqui Silver* he has retold the legends of the lost mines of the Spaniards and of the men who even today spend their lives with an old chart and a pickax in search of buried treasure. *A Vaquero of the*

Brush Country recounts the life of a great early cattleman of South Texas, where a thick growth of mesquite, chaparral, and cactus made ranching a very different business from what it was out on the open plains. In *The Longhorns* and *The Song of the Coyote* he has gathered the complete stories of the two animals most characteristic of the Southwestern plains. His latest book, *The Ben Lilly Legend*, follows the trail of a famous hunter of mountain lions in the Rockies.

One distinction of a skillful reader is the ability to keep up with the main divisions of a factual piece of writing such as an article or essay. As you read this article on cattle brands and the part they play in ranch life, you will find it easy to pick out the principal topics and to recognize how the author builds up a topic with supporting details before he moves on to a new phase of his subject.

THE other day a ranchman out in West Texas whose brand is T Half Circle announced that the United States Patent Office had registered it as a trade-mark. Since many cattle raisers nowadays sell their product by mail, the owner's brand on an animal being a guaranty of its standard breeding, other cowmen are likely to have their brands registered as trade-marks. A brand is just that – a trade-mark – though it is also much more, and to it is attached all

the sentiment and connotation once borne by coats of arms.

Primarily it is a means of identification, whether against thieves or among honest men, on the owner's home range or far away. If names and addresses were not so long, they would be branded on cattle. A brand is a seal that stands for a name; and somewhere, with name and address, every legal brand is recorded, just as with the purchaser's name are recorded the make and engine number of every automobile, some-where.

Just when brands were introduced into the world it would be difficult to say. The claim has often been made that Cortes, conqueror of Mexico, origi-nated branding in America. At Thebes, so it is said, a tomb twenty-five hundred years old has been uncovered bearing among other mural decorations the rep-resentation of a cow tied down and a man branding her with a geometric de-sign. The tomb must have been that of an Egyptian cattle king. When Chau-cer's pilgrims set out on their immortal journey from London to Canterbury more than five hundred years ago, some of them probably rode on rented horses. At least, horses kept for rent at that time were, says the great historian Jus-serand — who cites authority for the statement — "branded in a prominent manner, so that unscrupulous travelers should not be tempted to quit the road and appropriate the steeds." In 1643, before the cattle industry in the South-west was born, the New Haven, Con-necticut, code stipulated how horses should be branded in order to prevent trouble between rival claimants of "hor-ses running together in the woods."

But nowhere have brands been so im-portant to people or so interwoven with their lives as on the ranges of western America. A ranchboy often learns the language of brands earlier than he learns the language of books.

When George Asa was a very small boy living on a big ranch near the Rio Grande, his father began one day to teach him the letters of the alphabet, drawing them on paper with a pencil. He drew A, and George Asa learned it; then B, and George Asa learned it. But when he drew a C and called it, George Asa refused to accept it as a letter.

"Aw, Daddy," he exclaimed, "you're trying to tease me now! That's not a letter at all. That's Mr. Cox's brand."

Mr. Cox was a neighboring ranchman whose brand, a big C, was familiar to George Asa before he knew one letter from another. As a ranchboy he was learning to read brands before he learned his A B C's.

At a one-teacher school out in the mesquite the Friday-afternoon session usually closed with recitations. A fre-quent recitation began with the well-known injunction to the little star:

> Twinkle, twinkle, little star!
> How I wonder what you are,
> Up above the world so high
> Like a diamond in the sky.

One of the school urchins was the son of a rancher who ran the Diamond P brand — $\langle\!\!\!\!P\rangle$. That was the only diamond the lad knew, and he confesses now that he used to study the stars by the hour, trying to catch one of them as-suming the diamond shape so familiar to him on the sides of cows and at the hot end of a branding iron. He knew the language of brands better than he knew the language of jewels and poetry.

The brand gives its name to every-thing on the ranch. The chuck wagon of the Olmos — Elms — Ranch is seldom called the Olmos wagon, but is almost invariably referred to as the "A Dot wagon," Λ being the ranch brand. The "cow crowd" working on the Withers range is customarily referred to not as the Withers outfit but as the "Pig Pen outfit"; the Pig Pen — made thus, $\#$ — being the Withers brand. A cowboy rides a "Double Circle horse," which is branded $\circledcirc$. Another cowboy is "one of the Rocking Chair hands" because he works on the Rocking Chair — $\underline{\mathtt{H}}$ — Ranch.

A ranch may be named for its owner, as the Kokernut Ranch; it may be named after a creek that runs through it, as the San Francisco Ranch; it may take its name from some other feature of na-ture, as the Seven Oaks Ranch. But the greater number of ranches by far take their names simply from the ranch brand: the J A Ranch — $\mathcal{A}$ — the Pitchfork — Ψ — the Hundred and One — IOI. Sometimes after a brand is no longer in use some feature of the land keeps its name; although the great 7D outfit has quitted the Pecos forever, 7D Mountain keeps the brand as part of the language of the country.

The very owner of a ranch sometimes loses his name in his brand. There is "Diamond and a Half Hud" of the plains, who signs his checks as W. D. Hudson and gives $\Diamond$ as his brand. Colonel B. H. Campbell, a prominent cowman of the Indian Territory who for a time managed the great XIT Ranch of Texas, gave for his brand $\overline{BQ}$. It was read as "Barbeque," and "Barbeque Campbell" became known where B. H. Campbell had never been heard of.

As a means of identification the brand envelops all things else on the range. An incident related by Walter Billingsley, an old trail driver, well illustrates this fact.

In 1884 [he says] I took a herd of King Ranch steers from South Texas to Cheyenne, Wyoming. Everything went all right until we crossed the South Platte and reached Fort Sidney, Nebraska. While we held the herd a few miles out from town, I let a bunch of the boys go in to see the sights. Five of them laid out and did not report for work next morning. I rode in, found them, and fired them on the spot. I owed them one hundred and twenty dollars apiece. I had no money to pay them off, and I did not know a soul in Sidney.

My first move was to see the banker. Says I to him: "I'm trail boss for the King Ranch, owned by Captain Richard King and known from Canada to the Rio Grande. I've fired five of the sorriest cowboys that ever rode out of Texas. They are due six hundred dollars, and when they get it they will make you fine citizens and spend it all right here. I want to leave them with you, and I want to draw on Wright and Beverley at Dodge City for the six hundred dollars. Will you cash my draft?"

"Well," says the banker, "you look all right and I am satisfied you are all right, but can't you get someone to identify you?"

"I'm where I never was before and where I never expect to be again," I replied, "and I don't see a soul in town that I know."

The banker seemed awful anxious to accommodate me, and I sure did not want to hire those cowboys back just because I couldn't pay them off. I just wasn't going to give them the whip hand over me that way.

"Suppose you look around a little and see if you can't strike somebody you know," the banker concluded, "and then come back."

I went out. My mind was made up. I rounded up the men I'd fired and said, "Follow me and get your money."

We galloped to camp. "Load up and hitch up," I says to the cook, "and follow me."

Then I called the horse wrangler. "Drive up that *remuda* [1] of saddle horses," I says to him, "and follow the chuck wagon."

When we were all ready we struck a high trot for town, and a sight we must have made — me in the lead, those five sorry cowboys swinging after me, then the chuck wagon with six mules hitched to it, and then one hundred and fifty saddle horses with the *remudero* and a couple of other hands driving them. I drew up at the bank and the outfit halted.

"Come here!" I yelled to the banker, who was already at the door. "Come out here and look at my identification!"

He came a-laughing.

"Now," says I, "I guess you know what the King Ranch brand is — Running W on the side and K on the jaw. Well, there's one hundred and fifty saddle horses branded K W. There's a wagon with K W branded on the sideboards, branded on the chuck box, branded all over everything. Look at the cook's saddle on that near wheel mule, and you'll see K W on it. In fact, everything and everybody in this outfit is branded K W."

The banker was impressed all right. He shelled out the six hundred dollars right

[1] remuda (rê·mū′dà): all of the saddle horses belonging to the outfit.

away. I paid off the quitters; they unsaddled right there, turned their horses into the *remuda*, took their bedding out of the wagon, and the Running W outfit rolled its tail on for Cheyenne.

The average cow hand is so conscious of brands that in season and out of season, appropriately and inappropriately, consciously and unconsciously, he brands whatever he comes across. He whittles brands on sticks; he burns them into the planks of branding chutes, on pasture gates, on the anchor posts of windmill towers. He smears them with axle grease across the doors of barns and garages. He paints them with charcoal on the rock walls of canyons in which he has made a campfire. He carves them into his spur traps, leggings, and saddle — above all, into his boot tops. More pistols were etched with cattle brands than were ever notched for dead victims. Many a cook has stenciled the ranch coat of arms into the top crust of that gala-day treat — a wild-plum cobbler. Ranchboys are incorrigible when it comes to carving brands on their desks at school. They play ranch, and with bailing wire for running irons brand oak balls, the sawed-off tips of horns, spools, and other objects used to represent cattle and horses.

An old-time, dyed-in-the-wool cowman took pride in nothing more than in his memory for brands, and good cowmen still take the same pride. There are hotel clerks who never forget a face, scholars who never falter on a date, and automobile salesmen who hold in mind the engine number of every car sold or inspected. One must marvel with Mark Twain at the memory of a trained Mississippi River steamboat pilot. But the memory of a top brandman surpasses any other kind of memory I have ever met or heard of. It is more than memory; it is an instinct for cattle. Still riding the range are men who can count a hundred head of mixed cattle as they string along, and then from memory classify them and give every brand correctly.

Some of the cattle inspectors operating today in stockyards and on the range can recognize, with only an occasional reference to their brand books, literally thousands of brands. They say that Lod Calohan, head inspector for the Texas and Southwestern Cattle Raisers' Association at the Kansas City stockyards, can tell what brand an animal had on it by tasting the beef.

Deciphering and remembering the letters, figures, curves, and other configurations that make up brands is not enough. The thoroughgoing rangeman is a master of brand nomenclature, on the esoteric principles of which somebody ought to write a grammar. Generally, be it said, brands read from top to bottom and from left to right. A majority of the cattle brands in use are so simple that nearly anyone, once he has mastered a few principles, can " call " them properly. The brand H4 can be nothing else than " H Four "; H⊳ will easily be conceived to be the " H Triangle." But only the initiated denominate ⊥ as " Lazy H," or Ɛ as " Crazy Three." Any letter " too tired to stand up " is " lazy "; though if it is merely in an oblique position and not on its back, it is " tumbling." ⟙ or ⟊ is " Tumbling T."

A letter with curves at the end is often said to be " running." The most noted illustration of this principle is the " Running W " brand — ∿∿∫ — of the million-acre King Ranch. A letter or figure with " wings " to it is " flying " — thus, W is the " Flying W."

Brands " walk," " drag," " swing," and " rock " as well as they " run " or " fly." Ɛ is the " Walking F " and A is the " Walking A." The projection at the bottom of the figure makes 7 the " Drag Seven." L suspended from a curve — ⌒L — becomes the " Swinging L." Many

The heraldry of the range in the making (A. Devaney, Inc.)

brands are on rockers, as the " Rocking H " – ⨆. But if the rocker is unjoined, then it is a half or quarter circle; so ⨆ is " H Half Circle." One of the most historic brands of the West is the " Rocking Chair " – ⨆.

Sometimes a brand rests on a " bench," as ⅄, the " Y Bench." V-shaped prongs attached to some part of a letter make it forked. ⟋S is " Forked S," but ⊣⊦ is not " Forked N "; it is " Forked Lightning."

A straight mark is usually called a " bar "; but if it is very long or leaning at an angle to the normal horizontal position, it is apt to be called a " slash." The /\ is called " Cut and Slash." ⊢⟶ is " Bradded Dash." John Chisum, noted cowman of the Pecos, branded twenty thousand calves each year with a straight line running from shoulder to tail, and that " bar " was known all over the cattle country as the " Fence Rail." A brand burner added to it thus, ⟶ᴏ⟶, and the result was known both as " Knot on the Rail" and " Bug on the Rail." ᴏ⟶ᴏ might be " O Bar O," but it isn't. It is " Hobble O," for it resembles a pair of horse hobbles.

One time a rancher started a new brand made thus, (). Somebody asked him what he called it. " *Quién sabe?* " [1] (" Who knows?") he replied. And as the " Quién Sabe " brand it was known ever afterward and was placed on tens of thousands of cattle. Looking through a mixed herd of cattle or a brand book, one might note many brands of apparently a *quien sabe* nature; but somehow the rangemen have usually found a name for the most nameless device.

[1] *Quién sabe* (kyän sä′vå).

Fanciful designs frequently have fanciful names that could never be guessed even by good cowmen not familiar with the local interpretation of the brand. For instance, ⌒⌒ was known on the Colorado River in Texas as "Pot Hooks." When the owners moved their cattle to a new ranch several hundred miles to the southwest, the brand took the name of "Straddle Bug." A well-known brand was the "Gourd and Vine." It was run in this manner, ⌒⌒, so as to cover the whole side of an animal; and while everybody called it "Gourd and Vine," no stranger would at first sight of it ever guess the name.

Many owners use their initials in brands and sometimes even spell out their names. John M. Doak took DOK for his brand. With elegant simplicity Mrs. Katie Barr spelled out her whole name in KT, "KT Bar." Jack Barber approached the sound of his last name with B̄R̄. Pete Coffin had both his jest and his name in ℗. A man by the name of Hightower used HIℍ. Napoleon Daniel embodied in a brand his nickname –BONY. Ingenious but a little puzzling was Mr. Float's brand – Ⅎꝺ, which does spell FLOT.

Instead of telling the owner's name, a brand may suggest something of his biography. J. C. Studer was a blacksmith working for the Santa Fe Railroad when it was built across the Texas Panhandle. He fell in love with the country, invested his savings in land and cattle, and out of respect for his trade adopted an anvil – ⏛ – as his brand. One of the sea captains who used to sail in the Gulf of Mexico quit the sea for ranching; but he could not forget the old seafaring life, and his "Ship's Anchor" brand – ⟵⊹∘ – was a tribute to the memory.

There are legendary tales about brands, as there are about everything else with which man has had a vital connection. One of the most widely known of these legends tells how the "Four Sixes" – 6666 – originated.

Back in the early days a young cowboy by the name of Burk Burnett, who was just getting his start in cattle, rode into the village of Fort Worth one morning bent on indulging his skill in the favorite game of the range – poker. At one of the many gaming tables, then wide open to the public, he invested in a sombrero full of chips. At first he lost heavily; then the game became variable; about midnight his luck had changed, and by daylight he had a barrelful of money.

One of his opponents was desperate. "Burk," he said, "I'm broke, but I'll play my ranch and cattle against your pile."

"You've made a bet," was the reply.

On the deal Burk Burnett drew two sixes. He discarded three other cards, keeping the pair. Then he drew two more sixes. The four sixes won the ranch. Immediately, the story goes on, Burnett rebranded the cattle he had won with his lucky number – 6666. In time he increased his holdings until he had three hundred thousand acres in the Indian Territory stocked with Four Sixes cattle, besides an enormous ranch in North Texas. An oil field came in on his land and a boom city named Burkburnett sprang up. When his widow died, only a few years ago, she left several million dollars to Texas Christian University – probably the best poker hand that a Christian institution ever drew.

Whatever the facts, the poker story has fastened itself upon the imagination of thousands of recounters and will live for a long time.

No account of brands would be complete without consideration of the art of burning out brands. It was an art that reached the height of development during the days of open range, but it is by no means lost yet. Before the practice of counter-branding went out, a thief might void a brand by running a bar through it or by counterbranding the animal — as if it had been legitimately sold — and then putting his own brand on it. Again, he might rub out the owner's brand by taking a hot smoothing iron and burning all that part of an animal's hide covered by a brand. This was called blotching, or blotting. The result would be an enormous scar or blotch, through which the original lines were apt still to be visible. In any case, the blotch was evidence that the animal had been stolen, though not always could it be ascertained from whom stolen.

The most common practice by far was, and is yet, to run the original brand into something else.

One of the oldest chestnuts in the cow country is the "I See You Too" story. A ranchman somewhere started the **IC** brand. Before long he noticed that certain cattle in his herd wore the brand **ICU**. Not to be outdone, he did a little doctoring himself, and then the whole herd wore the **ICU2** brand. Then there was the fellow who started with **B4** for a brand. A Longhorn neighbor presently claimed that cattle branded **B4U** were his. The king of brand alterers then rode in, and presently nobody could find on the range anything that was not branded **B4U2**.

If brands could always be added to so easily and if they could be subtracted from as well as added to, the problem of the brand burner would be much simpler; but in brands, as in Scripture, what is writ is writ. In addition to adding a fresh figure or mark to an old device, the brand burner must try to cover up his alterations. For instance, one cattle company gave **7P** — "Seven P" — for a brand. A thief ran it into **7P** — "Seven Up." But expert rangemen can usually detect such mutilations. The new part never has the same look as the old part that has been reburned.

The classic story of brand burning has, fittingly, to do with the largest ranch the United States of America has known, the XIT, the three million acres of which were granted by the State of Texas to the Capitol Syndicate in exchange for the present granite capitol building at Austin. Wherever men talk of brands — and that is wherever range cattle graze — the story of the "Star Cross burn" is told.

Range rustlers had tried and tried to figure out a way to turn XIT into another brand that would not give itself away. At last, so the yarn goes, a clever range rider solved the problem. He revealed his secret to no one; he never blurred a brand. He was an artist. Nevertheless, he was finally brought to trial. The evidence was conclusive that he had built up from nothing a herd of cattle branded "Star Cross" —

— but the prosecuting attorney was unable to inform the jury how XIT could be altered into that symbol. So the rustler was freed. The XIT people were helpless. They offered him five thousand dollars if he would tell them how he achieved the Star Cross and would quit burning it on their cattle. Then the legendary rustler told his secret.

Among the thousands of calves branded each year on the XIT Ranch many of them had one or more of the letters imperfectly placed. The rustler looked for animals on which the T was slanting. When he found X|/ he easily ran it into

Many brand burners have been clever, but probably not one of them ever gained anything by his cleverness. After all, a great majority of the rangemen have always been honest men, and among them brands on cattle have served well the purpose for which they were designed; that is, to identify and maintain ownership. On ranches cattle are branded today by the millions, just as they were branded during the days of the open range.

If branding could be avoided it would be avoided. Humane societies have protested against the practice; experiments have been conducted with chemical compositions purporting to make an indelible but painless mark. But no substitute has been found for branding. Anyhow, branding is not unduly cruel, and the resultant pain is of short duration. As long as there are ranches, there will be brands — and that will be until millions and millions of acres of rocks and arid soil are made fertile and moist. The heraldry of the range is not obsolete; it is not even obsolescent.

For Discussion of Dobie

1. What are the main divisions in Dobie's discussion of cattle brands? List the topics and subtopics in order. After getting these divisions clearly in mind, pick out one or two topics and show how various details and illustrations are used to develop the topic.

2. What do you think is the writer's purpose in this article? Can you cite evidence that the life of the cattle ranch is still high in interest for the American people?

3. To understand better the phrase " The Heraldry of the Range," look up heraldry and find examples of coats of arms with symbols commemorating events or objects important in the history of a family.

4. Brands are often used as decorative motifs in buildings and house furnishings in the Southwest. Pick out some of the brands reproduced in this article that would make good decorative designs and suggest uses for them.

5. What other professions does Dobie compare with that of brandman, in the matter of memory? Can you think of professions in your own neighborhood that rely as heavily on trained memory?

Mary White

WILLAM ALLEN WHITE
1868–1944

If ever a literary man was identified through his whole life with a single town, that man was William Allen White, and the town was Emporia, Kansas. His birth, his schooling, and his long career as owner and editor of the Emporia *Gazette* forged such a strong link between his name and that of the town that one hardly thinks of one without the other. Through White's grasp of public affairs and his penetrating editorials, his " small town " newspaper attained a national reputation and White himself became an adviser and friend to several Presidents. He also wrote essays, short stories, biographies, and novels. His two best-known pieces of fiction are *The Court of Boyville* and *A Certain Rich Man*. Today his biographies of Woodrow Wilson and Calvin Coolidge, and his *Autobiography*, published posthumously in 1946, are more widely read than his fiction.

It is not, however, as an editor or a novelist that we see him in this editorial, but as a father. Perhaps no such remarkable obituary has ever appeared in a newspaper as the one he wrote for his own daughter. One of the things that make it remarkable is the tone White adopts in telling of his daughter's tragically short life. You will discover what this tone is almost from the start of the editorial.

THE Associated Press reports carrying the news of Mary White's death declared that it came as the result of a fall from a horse. How she would have hooted at that! She never fell from a horse in her life. Horses have fallen on her and with her — " I'm always trying to hold 'em in my lap," she used to say. But she was proud of few things, and one was that she could ride anything that had four legs and hair. Her death resulted not from a fall, but from a blow on the head which fractured her skull, and the blow came from the limb of an overhanging tree on the parking.

The last hour of her life was typical of its happiness. She came home from a day's work at school, topped off by a hard grind with the copy on the high-school *Annual,* and felt that a ride would refresh her. She climbed into her khakis, chattering to her mother about the work she was doing, and hurried to get her horse and be out on the dirt roads for the country air and the radiant fields of the spring. As she rode through the town at an easy gallop she kept waving at passers-by. She knew everyone in town. For a decade the little figure with the long pigtail and the red hair-ribbon has been familiar on the streets of Emporia, and she got in the way of speaking to those who nodded at her. She passed the Kerrs, walking the horse, in front of the Normal Library, and waved at them; passed another friend a few hundred feet farther on, and waved at her. The horse was walking, and as she turned into North Merchant Street she took off her cowboy hat, and the horse swung into a lope. She passed the Tripletts and waved her cowboy hat at them, still moving gaily north on Merchant Street. A *Gazette* carrier passed — a high-school boy friend — and she waved at him, but with her bridle hand; the horse veered quickly, plunged into the parking where the low-hanging limb faced her, and, while she still looked back, waving, the blow came. But she did not fall from the horse; she slipped off, dazed a bit, staggered, and fell in a faint. She never quite recovered consciousness.

But she did not fall from the horse, neither was she riding fast. A year or so ago she used to go like the wind. But that habit was broken, and she used the horse to get into the open to get fresh, hard exercise, and to work off a certain surplus energy that welled up in her and needed a physical outlet. That need has been in her heart for years. It was back of the impulse that kept the dauntless little brown-clad figure on the streets and country roads of this community and built into a strong, muscular body what had been a frail and sickly frame during the first years of her life. But the riding gave her more than a body. It released a gay and hardy soul. She was the happiest thing in the world. And she was happy because she was enlarging her horizon. She came to know all sorts and conditions of men. Charley O'Brien, the traffic cop, was one of her best friends. W. L. Holtz, the Latin teacher, was another. Tom O'Connor, farmer-politician, and the Rev. J. H. J. Rice, preacher and police judge, and Frank Beach, music master, were her special friends, and all the girls, black and white, above the track and below the track, in Pepville and Stringtown, were among her acquaintances. And she brought home riotous stories of her adventures. She loved to rollick; persiflage was her natural expression at home. Her humor was a continual bubble of joy. She seemed to think in hyperbole and metaphor. She was mischievous without malice, as full of faults as an old shoe. No angel was Mary White, but an easy girl to live with, for she never nursed a grouch five minutes in her life.

With all her eagerness for the out-of-doors, she loved books. On her table when she left her room were a book by Conrad, one by Galsworthy, *Creative Chemistry* by E. E. Slosson, and a Kipling book. She read Mark Twain, Dickens, and Kipling before she was ten — all of their writings. Wells and Arnold Bennett particularly amused and diverted her. She was entered as a student in Wellesley in 1922; was assistant editor of the high-school *Annual* this year, and in line for election to the editorship of the *Annual* next year. She was a member of the executive committee of the high-school Y.W.C.A.

Within the last two years she had begun to be moved by an ambition to draw. She began as most children do by scribbling, in her schoolbooks, funny pictures. She bought cartoon magazines and took a course — rather casually, naturally, for she was, after all, a child with no strong purposes — and this year she tasted the first fruits of success by having her pictures accepted by the high-school *Annual*. But the thrill of delight she got when Mr. Ecord, of the Normal *Annual*, asked her to do the cartooning for that book this spring, was too beautiful for words. She fell to her work with all her enthusiastic heart. Her drawings were accepted, and her pride — always repressed by a lively sense of the ridiculousness of the figure she was cutting — was a really gorgeous thing to see. No successful artist ever drank a deeper draft of satisfaction than she took from the little fame her work was getting among her schoolfellows. In her glory,

she almost forgot her horse — but never her car.

For she used the car as a jitney bus. It was her social life. She never had a "party" in all her nearly seventeen years — wouldn't have one; but she never drove a block in the car in her life that she didn't begin to fill the car with pickups! Everybody rode with Mary White — white and black, old and young, rich and poor, men and women. She liked nothing better than to fill the car full of long-legged high-school boys and an occasional girl, and parade the town. She never had a "date," nor went to a dance, except once with her brother Bill, and the "boy proposition" didn't interest her — yet. But young people — great spring-breaking, varnish-cracking, fender-bending, door-sagging carloads of "kids" — gave her great pleasure. Her zests were keen. But the most fun she ever had in her life was acting as chairman of the committee that got up the big turkey dinner for the poor folks at the county home; scores of pies, gallons of slaw; jam, cakes, preserves, oranges, and a wilderness of turkey were loaded in the car and taken to the county home. And, being of a practical turn of mind, she risked her own Christmas dinner by staying to see that the poor folks actually got it all. Not that she was a cynic; she just disliked to tempt folks. While there, she found a blind colored uncle, very old, who could do nothing but make rag rugs, and she rustled up from her school friends rags enough to keep him busy for a season. The last engagement she tried to make was to take the guests at the county home out for a car ride. And the last endeavor of her life was to try to get a rest room for colored girls in the high school. She found one girl reading in the toilet, because there was no better place for a colored girl to loaf, and it inflamed her sense of injustice and she became a nagging harpy to those

William Allen White with his two children — William Lindsay and Mary. (Culver)

who, she thought, could remedy the evil. The poor she had always with her and was glad of it. She hungered and thirsted for righteousness; and was the most impious creature in the world. She joined the Congregational Church without consulting her parents; not particularly for her soul's good. She never had a thrill of piety in her life, and would have hooted at a "testimony." But even as a little child she felt the Church was an agency for helping people to more of life's abundance, and she wanted to help. She never wanted help for herself. Clothes meant little to her. It was a fight to get a new rig on her; but eventually a harder fight to get it off. She never wore a jewel and had no ring but her high-school class ring, and never asked for anything but a wrist watch. She refused to have her hair up, though she was nearly seventeen. "Mother," she protested, "you don't know how much I get by with, in my braided pigtails, that I could not with my hair up." Above every other passion of her life was her passion not to grow up, to be a child. The tomboy in her, which was big, seemed to loathe to be put away forever in skirts. She was Peter Pan, who refused to grow up.

Her funeral yesterday at the Congregational Church was as she would have wished it; no singing, no flowers save the big bunch of roses from her brother Bill's Harvard classmen — heavens, how proud that would have made her! — and the red roses from the *Gazette* force — in vases at her head and feet. A short prayer, Paul's beautiful essay on " Love " from the thirteenth chapter of First Corinthians, some remarks about her democratic spirit by her friend, John H. J. Rice, pastor and police judge, which she would have deprecated if she could, a prayer sent down for her by her friend, Carl Nau, and, opening the service, the slow, poignant movement from Beethoven's " Moonlight Sonata," which she loved, and, closing the service, a cutting from the joyously melancholy first movement of Tchaikovsky's *Pathetic Symphony*, which she liked to hear in certain moods on the phonograph; then the Lord's Prayer by her friends in the high school.

That was all.

For her pallbearers only her friends were chosen: her Latin teacher, W. L. Holtz; her high-school principal, Rice Brown; her doctor, Frank Foncannon; her friend, W. W. Finney; her pal at the *Gazette* office, Walter Hughes; and her brother Bill. It would have made her smile to know that her friend, Charley O'Brien, the traffic cop, had been transferred from Sixth and Commercial to the corner near the church to direct her friends who came to bid her good-by.

A rift in the clouds in a gray day threw a shaft of sunlight upon her coffin as her nervous, energetic little body sank to its last sleep. But the soul of her, the glowing, gorgeous, fervent soul of her, surely was flaming in eager joy upon some other dawn.

For Discussion of White

1. What word gave you the first clue to the tone White intended to take in his editorial? What other details in the first paragraph confirmed this impression? Would the readers of the Emporia *Gazette* remember Mary more vividly and affectionately because her father took the tone he did in writing about her? Why?

2. Give some of the details of Mary White's appearance and interests and actions that make her seem like a real girl and not an idealized figure. Have you ever known anyone like her?

3. Would you have liked Mary as a classmate? Point out specific reasons for your answer. Do you think you could place her as a particular " type " of high-school girl?

4. How do her favorite authors compare with your own?

5. What was particularly appropriate about her funeral service?

For Your Vocabulary

WORD GROUP: *Cynic* is one of those valuable words for which we have no substitute except to explain the whole idea. A *cynical* person is one who doubts the worth, truth, or virtue of what other people have genuine faith in. Why does the writer pause to assure the reader that Mary was not a *cynic* (p. 168)? *Cynicism* is the attitude of mocking other people's faith in right and goodness, or doubting the honor and trustworthiness of human nature. Make a similar word group from *idealist* and *optimist*, which are opposite in meaning to *cynic*.

JAMES SAXON CHILDERS
1899–

A Boy Who Was Traded for a Horse

Except for his student days at Oberlin College, James Childers [1] has been identified with the South all his life. He was born in Birmingham, Alabama, was sent to Oxford as a Rhodes scholar from Atlanta, Georgia, and has spent most of his later life as professor of English at Birmingham Southern College, and literary editor of the Birmingham *News*. Having been an airforce pilot in World War I, he returned to that service in World War II with the rank of colonel. He has published many volumes of both fiction and nonfiction, including *War Eagles,* an account of the Army Air Forces abroad.

In this article, Childers reports an interview with a widely loved and honored American who also lived in Alabama, the great Negro scientist, George Washington Carver of Tuskegee [2] Institute. The interview, a popular type of article in modern periodicals, usually follows a fairly definite pattern: an introductory statement about the person who is interviewed; the interviewer's first impression on meeting him in person; an accumulation of detailed information and impressions as the interview proceeds; and a final summing-up impression. If you become familiar with this pattern you can speed your reading and comprehension of any interview or biographical sketch.

THE stooped old Negro shuffled along through the dust of an Alabama road at a curiously rapid rate. He was carrying an armful of sticks and wild flowers.

The sticks I could understand — he would use them for kindling — but I had never before seen an old black man ambling along a road at nine o'clock in the morning with swamp roses, wild geranium, and creeping buttercups mingled with a lot of dry sticks.

When I got a little closer to him I saw that he was wearing a saggy coat which originally might have been a green alpaca, but which the sun had faded until I couldn't be sure about the color; there were so many patches that

I couldn't even be certain about the material.

The old man was walking toward a large brick building, one of the buildings of Tuskegee Institute, the famous school for Negroes at Tuskegee, Alabama. His thin body bent by the years, his hair white beneath a ragged cap, he seemed pathetically lost on the campus of a great modern educational institution.

At the entrance of the building toward which we were both walking, the old Negro turned in. "He's probably the janitor," I told myself, "and I'm sincerely glad that they've given him a job of some kind."

I stepped into the hallway. I saw a

[1] **Childers** (chĭl′dĕrz).

[2] **Tuskegee** (tŭs·kē′gē̇).

"A Boy Who Was Traded for a Horse" by James Saxon Childers. Reprinted by permission of the author.

trim little secretary hurry toward the bent old Negro. I heard her say to him, "That delegation from Washington is waiting for you, Dr. Carver."

Dr. George Washington Carver, the very man I had come to see! Fantastic and unbelievable as it seemed, this old man with his armful of sticks and wild flowers was none other than the distinguished Negro scientist of Tuskegee Institute — a discoverer renowned far and wide for his chemical wizardry in creating useful new products from such stuff as peanut shells and fallen leaves, which most of us waste and throw away.

That saggy alpaca coat covered a Bachelor of Science, Master of Science, Honorary Doctor of Science; winner of the Spingarn Medal for Negro achievement; member of the Royal Society for the Encouragement of Arts, Manufactures, and Commerce of Great Britain.

Yet as I looked at him, studied his kindly face, and recalled what I had heard of the story of his life, I saw that the figure of the man himself was not half so fantastic or unbelievable as is the record of his achievement.

Dr. George Washington Carver started with nothing. He never had anything. Yet out of nothing he has created inestimable wealth for fellow human beings, to whom he has devoted his life.

Born a slave child, he began life without even so much as a name. He never knew his father. He never knew his mother. To this day [1] he doesn't know just when he was born, though he figures his age at somewhere close to seventy. Without a red cent he worked out his own early schooling, then his higher college education, then the postgraduate work for his Master of Science degree. All his life he has been joyously at work with common, everyday things, making something out of nothing or

next to nothing. During the thirty-six years in which he has been director of agricultural research at Tuskegee Institute, that has been his work. And out of it have come scientific marvels:

From wood shavings he has made synthetic marble.

From peanut shells he has made insulating walls for houses.

From the muck of swamps and the leaves of the forest floor he has made valuable fertilizers.

From cow dung he has made paint.

From the common, ordinary peanut he has made 285 useful products, including milk, butter, cheese, candies, instant coffee, pickles, sauces, oils, shaving lotions, wood stains, dyes, lard, linoleum, flour, breakfast foods, soap, stock foods, face powder, tan remover, shampoo, printer's ink, and even axle grease!

From the lowly sweet potato he has made 118 products, among them flour, meal, starch, library paste, vinegar, shoe blacking, ginger, ink, rubber compound, chocolate compound, dyes, molasses, wood filler, caramels.

From clays of the earth he has made nonfading paints and pigments.

From worn-out, sandy soil he has produced paying crops.

Something from nothing. And this is only a portion of his work. Experts say that he has probably done more than any other living man to rehabilitate agriculture in the South.

And more still. Dr. Carver is also an artist, especially skilled in painting flowers. His paintings have been exhibited at world fairs, and at least one is going to the Luxembourg Gallery in Paris after his death. He makes all his own paints, using Alabama clays. The paper he paints on he makes from peanut shells, and the frames for his pictures he makes out of cornhusks. His work in embroidery and crochet has won prizes in various exhibits. He has woven gorgeous rugs with fibers he had made from cotton stalks. He is a skilled mu-

---

[1] **to this day:** in 1934. Dr. Carver died in 1943.

From Dr. Carver's conviction that everything in nature has some use came many important discoveries. (Wide World)

sician, too — once he toured the Middle West as a concert pianist. And last, but not least, he is an expert cook. His recipes are used today in some of the leading hotels of the country.

All this does sound a bit incredible, doesn't it? I confess that when I set out for Tuskegee to see and talk with Dr. Carver I was more than skeptical of many of the stories I had heard about him. And so, after he had entertained the visiting delegation from Washington, I returned to see him, in his office in the big brick building, with many doubts lingering in my mind.

He was sitting behind a desk cluttered inches high with letters and papers. On top of the papers were the sticks and wild flowers that I had seen him carrying that morning. As I went in, he was looking through a microscope at the stem of a wild rose. "I beg your pardon," I said.

The old man raised his head and looked at me; then, taking hold of the edge of the desk to steady himself, he pushed himself up from his squeaky swivel chair. He wore a long canvas apron that was splotched and stained. His gold-rimmed spectacles rested far down on his nose. Standing there so tall despite his noticeable stoop, he peered over the tops of his spectacles and smiled at me.

"Good morning," he said, and the quiet tone of his voice blended with the gentle sincerity of his smile.

In slight confusion, then, I explained why I had called on him.

"Do you mind if I stay here awhile?" I asked. "I'd like to very much — that is, if I won't trouble you."

"It will be a pleasure, sir, a very great pleasure to me."

I was touched by his gentleness, and by an unmistakable spiritual quality in the glow of his face. Frankly, I was confused. To open the conversation, I remarked on the numerous Maxfield Parrish paintings that hang on his office walls. " Somehow they seem a little out of place in the office of a scientist," I said lamely.

" But can't a scientist be a lover of the beautiful? " he asked. " There is no one of the moderns who uses blue half so well as Maxfield Parrish uses it."

And then he was off. For forty-five minutes he shuffled about his office, showing me how Maxfield Parrish uses blue, and telling how the ancients used the color. Quietly, even humbly, he told how the Egyptians loved it, how they had adorned their homes and tombs with it.

Then he led me from his office across the hall into his laboratory, a room about thirty by twenty feet. It was filled with racks and shelves and tables, bottles and tubes and retorts. He picked up a jar and carried it to the window. " See " — and he held it to the sun.

And I saw the richest, the purest blue that I have ever seen.

Dr. Carver was talking quietly as he tilted the jar one way and the other, giving the sun its full chance to mate with the glorious color. " I believe," he went on, " that it's a rediscovery of the old Egyptian blue. A number of chemists have come to see it, and they agree with me. At present I'm working on the Egyptian purple; I believe that soon we shall have that too.

" I get my dyes," the old man continued, " from Alabama clays. You remember what the Bible says " — Dr. Carver has built his life on what the Bible says — " you remember that the Bible says, ' Look to the hills from whence cometh your help.' I did it; I looked to these Alabama hills, and I made these dyes from the clays that I found there. All these dyes and paints " — he waved toward thirty-six boards, each of which was colored differently — " all of them were made from Alabama clay — all," he added, " except this one; it was made from rotten sweet potatoes; and this one, which was made from cow dung; and this one, a much finer paint, was made from horse dung."

After I had been an hour in Dr. Carver's laboratory, after I had seen rope made from okra fiber; baskets from wistaria; and dyes from the dandelion, black oak, wood ashes, sweet gum, swamp maple, sweet potato, pomegranate, peanut, Osage orange, muscadine grape, onion, velvet bean, and tomato vine — after I had seen those discoveries, among a few hundred others, I was willing to believe almost anything possible to this kindly man to whom apparently bricks without straw [1] would be a simple problem.

" When you do the common things of life in an uncommon way," Dr. Carver once said to his students, " you will command the attention of the world." In that sentence lies the secret of his own achievement.

He was born in a rude slave cabin on the farm of Moses Carver near Diamond Grove, Missouri. Moses Carver owned his mother, and a neighbor owned his father. When he was a baby six months old, night riders swooped down on his master's plantation and carried away a number of slaves, among them the baby and his mother.

In their flight, the raiders took no care of the child; he developed whooping cough and was dying when emissaries sent out by Moses Carver arrived from Missouri to buy back the stolen slaves.

But the mother had already been disposed of; no one ever learned what became of her. Indeed, there is only one thing of hers that is left: in Dr. Carver's room in one of the dormitories at

---

[1] **bricks without straw:** When the Israelites were held as slaves by the Egyptians, they were commanded to make bricks without straw. The fifth chapter of Exodus tells the story.

Tuskegee is a battered old spinning wheel on which his mother spun flax when she was a slave. A friend of Dr. Carver's said to me, "I've seen him touch that wheel; he touches it like a priest reverently touching an altar. I sometimes feel that if I could be in his room when he retires, I should hear the old man say 'Good night' to that wheel."

The emissaries sent to ransom the stolen slaves finally struck a bargain with the night riders. The baby was evaluated and traded back to his owner; he was traded for a broken-down race horse worth about $300!

For Discussion of Childers

1. Does this article fit the interview pattern described on page 171? What part is not in the usual order? For what reason do you think Childers made this shift?
2. What previous knowledge of Dr. Carver did Childers have? How much of this information did *you* know before reading the article?
3. How well did the first impression of Dr. Carver fit his reputation? How well did the information gathered later in the interview fit it?

4. Try your hand at interviewing. Select an interesting person in your school or community, interview him (better make an appointment), and then write up the experience for your school or town paper.
5. You can read the whole story of the two great men of Tuskegee in Booker T. Washington's autobiography, *Up from Slavery,* and Rackham Holt's *George Washington Carver.*

For Your Vocabulary

NAMES OF FLOWERS: Dr. Carver made baskets from *wistaria.* Did you realize that *wistaria* is the correct spelling of the name (often spelled *wisteria*) of this beautiful flower? It was named for Caspar *Wistar,* an American scientist. The names of many flowers have interesting origins. The *nasturtium* is so called because of its pungency; the word means "nose twist." *Carnation* is derived from *carnis,* the Latin word for "flesh," and formerly meant "flesh color." The *poinsettia* was named after Joel R. Poinsett of South Carolina. *Daisy* is a contraction of *day's eye* (can you understand how this term originated?). *Tulip* comes from the Turkish word for "turban." What is the old Greek story of the origin of the *narcissus?* Look up the name of your favorite flower and report its origin to the class.

Two Book Reviews

Hundreds of book reviews appear weekly in newspapers and magazines all over the United States. Intelligent people everywhere read reviews not only to choose the books they want to read but also to keep up with major ideas and new developments in literature and other fields. These two benefits everyone can find in reviews, but the high-school or college student can gain another. During your school career, you will make many book reports, oral and written, and published book reviews will suggest new approaches and methods to improve your performance. Only the most

elementary reviews and reports stop with a mere summary of the book. The more possible topics for comment you accumulate from reading good reviews, the more you will notice as you read a book. The more you notice, the more good material you will have for your next report.

The prospect of profit alone, however, would never win millions of American readers to book reviews. We demand entertainment, and book reviews can be entertaining articles. A good book review can give you pleasure in many ways: in its style of writing, in its deft handling of information, in the provocative ideas it advances. The leading writers of America often turn their hands to reviewing. For example, the first of the reviews printed here is the work of E. B. White, staff writer for *The New Yorker* and probably the finest essayist in the United States today; and the second is from the pen of an experienced critic, Katherine Woods.

A comparison of the two reviews will show the basic pattern of this kind of article: first, information about the contents of the book; then, the reviewer's judgment of its merits. You will see, too, what different angles for specific emphasis reviewers may choose. One is largely concerned with the subject matter of the book and its relevance today. The other is concerned with the underlying spirit of a novel. But each tells you what is in the book, how good he thinks it is, and why. And the telling makes interesting reading!

E. B. WHITE
1899–

Journal of a Contaminated Man

(A review from *The New Yorker* of David Bradley's *No Place to Hide*)

A subtle writer like E. B. White can talk about one thing and at the same time suggest something else. In this review he discusses a diary that was kept by a young scientist during his work with the atomic bomb tests in the Pacific in 1946. Yet while White summarizes certain information in the book about radioactivity and its effects on machinery and nature, he is also suggesting something about modern warfare and its effects on men and society. The ships at Bikini [1] atoll in the Pacific were contaminated with radioactivity, and White implies that men themselves will be "contaminated" until they cure the disease of war.

AMONG the many who went out to Bikini in the spring of 1946 was a young doctor named David Bradley. He had boned up on radiation and was well equipped with instruments of detection. When the cloud from the first bomb had drifted away, he flew into the area of the explosion to sample the radioactive atmosphere. In the days that followed, he was one of the monitors whose job was to lead the crews back aboard the target fleet. Wearing galoshes, coveralls, a mask, gloves, and

---

[1] **Bikini** (bĕ·kē′nē): an atoll in the Marshall Islands, scene of the above- and below-water atom bomb tests.

"Journal of a Contaminated Man" by E. B. White from *The New Yorker*, December 4, 1948. Reprinted by permission of the publisher.

goggles, and carrying a black box that made a clicking noise in his earphones, he poked around in the lethal passageways of dying ships, followed by an uneasy band of navy brass and seamen, who had to be told what stanchion they might safely sit on, what fish they might safely eat. It now turns out that the most sensitive instrument Dr. Bradley had with him at the crossroads [1] was pencil-and-paper: he kept a log — a sort of diary of contamination, a notebook of the last days of an atoll. Excerpts from this log are available in a small book called "No Place to Hide," published by Atlantic–Little, Brown. It is no book to miss.

The days and nights of David Bradley, the monitor, in the strange summer of 1946 are like a chapter in a dream book. His laboratory was a paradise, and the experiment in which he was involved was an experiment in befouling the laboratory itself. All through June the ships of the doomed fleet swung to their anchors in the crowded lagoon, awaiting Able Day.[2] Dr. Bradley did his waiting on a small, treeless isle called Ebeye, a hundred and seventy-five miles away, near Kwajalein.[3] He speared fish from the barrier reef, wading about in the warm sea on nights of pure tropical enchantment. Rain squalls beat into his windowless Quonset hut, and the damp salt air kept shorting his instruments. "There is something about an approaching storm," he wrote on Tuesday, June 18th, "which gives warning though it cannot be seen: there is a new undertone to the surf, a sound not exactly ominous, but deep and persistent; the wind seems more restless and the darkness more black."

Before sunup on the morning of July 1st, Dr. Bradley arose with the others and flew toward Bikini and How Hour.[4] While he listened to background stuff coming in on his counters [5] (the theme song of the cosmos), a crewman of the seaplane cooked a steak in the galley. And when they sighted the white hospital ship Bountiful, the pilot dived sharply down and buzzed a nurse. The bomb went off on schedule. Not many ships were sunk. Boarding parties were operating soon after the cloud blew away. On Able Day plus one, Dr. Bradley wrote in his diary, "It would appear that at least for the time being we have escaped from the real threat of atomic weapons, namely the lingering poison of radioactivity." That was July 2nd.

Three weeks later, the underwater bomb went off. Again Bradley was in a navy plane several miles away. For twenty minutes after the blast, a cloud hung over the ships; then it gradually cleared, and the ships emerged; most of the fleet was still afloat. But when the reconnaissance planes, feeling their way along with Geiger counters, started their sweeps over the target area, they met intense radiation coming up from the ships and from the water. The counters clicked and screamed, and the needles went off scale.

"It always seemed a little strange to me," wrote Dr. Bradley, "that at such a time the pilot should be calmly looking down at the fleet, or glancing over his instrument panel. . . . Something was wrong. We should be able to feel this barrage of gamma rays [6] tearing

---

[1] crossroads: The official name for the tests was "Operation Crossroads." What deeper meaning does the author find in this name?

[2] Able Day: The day for the A or over-water test was called by the military signal code word for the letter A.

[3] Ebeye, Kwajalein (ĕ′bĕ·yĕ, kwôj′á·lĭn).

[4] How Hour: the hour set for the test. "How" is the navy signal code word for the letter H.

[5] counters: Geiger counters, instruments which detect the presence of radioactive substances, such as, here, a ship's deck subjected to the atomic blast.

[6] gamma rays: radiation similar to X-rays, emitted during nuclear fission, which occurs during the explosion of an atom bomb and is the source of atomic energy.

through our bodies. It was there. It was hot."

That is the burden of the book — people should feel the rays, and they don't. It's hard for anyone to believe in something he can't see or hear or feel. It was particularly hard for the navy, which had never before joined battle with a gamma ray and which is contemptuous of anything that isn't big and noisy and that refuses to come out in the open and fight.

On Baker Day plus one, miles from the dead fleet, Dr. Bradley's plane ran into a spot of intense radioactivity over an oil slick. The Geiger tubes jammed. On the whole, though, the sky over Bikini wasn't bad, and the navy felt confident that the target ships would soon be got under way. Skeleton crews on some of them awaited the signal to up-anchor. This was the navy's first major engagement with the products of atomic fission, and the navy vastly underrated its foe.

As the radioactivity in the air diminished, the water in the lagoon got steadily worse, presumably because stuff was still coming up from the bottom. By noon of July 9th, the radioactivity was so alarming that the so-called " live " fleet — ships that had not been directly exposed to the bomb — moved off to a safer distance, fearful lest their water intakes and evaporators pick up something. On most of the target ships it was possible for the crews to work below decks, but topside the radiation was greater and the men could work only in short shifts if they were to keep within the established limit of one-tenth of a roentgen [1] per day. Exasperated, the navy tried soap-and-water — the old ritual of " a clean sweepdown fore and aft." Suds seemed to make things worse, if anything. Even in ships of the live fleet, the evaporator tanks became hot,

[1] **roentgen** (rŭnt'gĕn): the international unit for measuring the quantity of X-rays.

their scaly linings acting as a sponge for radioactive particles. Toilets and fire lines showed that they had picked up fission products. The hulls of the ships became hot along their waterlines, because the algae clinging to them picked up the stuff and did not release it. Radiation from this marine growth penetrated the steel plates and stirred Geigers on the inside.

The oil slick, heavily charged, came back from sea, swept inshore over the reef, and left a gummy emulsion. Coral became radioactive, and so did fish. Some of the contaminated reef fish were eaten by bigger fish, and so passed their contamination on. In certain areas the coral turned from pink to white. Dr. Bradley, working with the U.S. Fisheries group, dredged up sand from the bottom. The first netful dumped on his boat proved to be so radioactive that it was immediately dumped overboard again. The calking in deck seams was hot. The rust spots in metalwork were hot. A seaman cut his thumb slightly on a radioactive cable, and there was a close decision as to whether his arm would have to be amputated. One experimentalist ripped up a deck plank and started planing it down to see how far he'd have to go before he struck harmless wood. He had to go almost a quarter of an inch. In laboratories, scientists sliced fish longitudinally, dried them, placed them on photographic plates, and discovered that a Bikini fish could produce a perfect radio-autograph — the long intestines bright with activity, the liver radiant, the gonads showing plainly.

" The whole business must seem like a very bad dream to the regular navy man: decks you can't stay on for more than a few minutes but which seem like other decks; air you can't breathe without gas masks but which smells like all other air; water you can't swim in, and good tuna and jacks you can't eat. It's a fouled-up world."

This diary belongs, of course, to the already large body of post-bomb literature in which men of science try to warn laymen of their new environment. Dr. Bradley's is a peculiarly effective book, I think. It is casual, personal, and written by a man who seems to have the training of a scientist, the eyes and ears of a poet. He probed the fringes of the hottest fire that has yet been lit and wrote down what he felt and what he wondered. Perhaps not all scientists will subscribe to his major conclusions, but few can challenge in any important respect his simple report.

It was a happy accident that caused the navy to set the Crossroads experiment in a tropic island, where life on earth has a sort of storied goodness — the fabulous South Seas that so many caged men have dreamed of, the warm Pacific water foaming over the barrier reefs, the trades blowing endlessly. Such a setting easily forms a symbol of man's close relationship to nature, to sea and land and sky; here people actually achieved a simplicity that for most of us is unattainable — sailing their canoes, spearing their fish. Bikini was, and still is, the perfect place to test the long-range intentions and the supreme ingenuity of human beings, the perfect proving ground for controlled contamination, deliberate destruction, and the ominous antics of a race whose genius has led it to an impasse. Dr. Bradley's conclusion is simple: in a society that still accepts war as a way of life, Bikini is the world in miniature; radioactivity is the disease that can knock it out.

In one place in his diary, Dr. Bradley describes a navy diver at work on a sunken hull at the bottom of the polluted lagoon — a man of almost comic-strip proportions, great lead shoes, great clumsy suit, escape valve throwing bubbles, all cluttered up with telephone lines and gadgets, including a water-tight Geiger counter that sent messages up to somebody on deck. He was the last word in sunken man, a regular paragon of a submerged individual. When the accomplice on deck suddenly heard a warning in his earphones, he had to phone down to the poor fellow below and tell him that he must be touching something he shouldn't. One wonders, reading this true atomic fairy tale, what has happened to the world to bring this man to such a pass, this watery sailor leaning against a radioactive stanchion at the bottom of a condemned lagoon.

Before Dr. Bradley left the Pacific, he went to Rongerik and paid a call on King Juda and the little bunch of Bikinese natives who were evicted from their beloved island when the navy took over. To a man, they wanted to return. They were running short of coconuts and were sick of eating nothing but fish. Through an interpreter, King Juda said he would like to ask when he and his people might go home. Dr. Bradley explained that things were pretty bad on Bikini — water no good, fish no good, whole place no good any more. It would be a long time, a long, long time, before they could go back.

"Oh," said the interpreter, respectfully. "We very sorry to hear this."

For Your Vocabulary

CONTEXT: Both this review and the next one by Katherine Woods provide you with an excellent opportunity to check your skill in defining unfamiliar words by their surroundings — their context. In this review there are a number of technical terms referring to the atomic experiment. The context helps somewhat, though you may need also to refer to a dictionary. Try your hand with the following words (some are not technical): *monitor* (p. 176), *hot* — not the ordinary meaning (p. 178), *live* — again, an unusual meaning (p. 178), *jacks* (p. 178), and *lethal* (p. 177).

KATHERINE WOODS
1886–

The Saint of Lourdes

A Review from *The New York Times Book Review*
of Franz Werfel's *The Song of Bernadette*

Many modern novelists have taken the lives of the saints as the basis of their plots. Few have been as successful as Franz Werfel in his *The Song of Bernadette*. The novel is unusual for two reasons: first, it is the result of a vow made by the author; second, it reveals a Catholic subject treated with understanding and reverence by a non-Catholic. To give a true and valued opinion of a book of this type, the reviewer must try to understand and appreciate the spirit of the author. Franz Werfel's treatment of Saint Bernadette is reverent and humble. Katherine Woods brings the same spirit to her review.

PERHAPS children might get silly notions of seeing dream ladies, Louise Soubirous [1] tried to reason, just because they never had quite enough to eat. Or perhaps the sight of something that didn't exist might be an illusion of any fourteen-year-old. This last was what one of the priests said, and what she told her daughter: "Just put it out of your mind. Life is far too hard," Louise Soubirous added, "to bother with things like that." But her husband, the former miller who was now a mere laborer out of work, let rage burst from embarrassment and self-pity. "Showing off — wanting to be important!" he rebuked his suddenly notorious child. "If you're going to invent lying stories you don't belong among respectable folk. You belong among jugglers."

The vicar said much the same thing,

[1] **Soubirous** (sōō′bē·rōō′).

in even more terrifying language. But at the Café Progrès, where the little town's leading citizens exchanged opinion and gossip, the political aspect of these "apparitions" was uppermost. And the Public Prosecutor spoke the extreme of denunciation: "The phenomena in question are directed personally against the Emperor."

Thus unsympathetically began, in the late winter of 1858, those strange experiences which were to set all France by the ears, arouse Christendom, make the name of Lourdes the synonym for the world's greatest pilgrimages, and reach the climax of the canonization of Bernadette Soubirous in 1933. And thus Bernadette — indifferent to applause and unshaken by persecution — becomes the heroine of a stirring, profound, and beautiful novel in which Franz Werfel makes his affirmation of universal faith.

"The Saint of Lourdes" by Katherine Woods from *The New York Times Book Review*, May 10, 1942. Reprinted by permission of the author and *The New York Times Book Review*.

When the author of *The Forty Days of Musa Dagh* was fleeing from his enemies after the defeat of the country where he had found refuge, he hid for a while in Lourdes. A Jew who had actively fought Nazism, he was one of the men proscribed by the Franco-German armistice, and now in bitter peril. And as in those weeks of 1940 he came to know the facts about Lourdes's nineteenth-century saint and the Lourdes healings, he was moved to a vow: if he escaped, he would write the song of Bernadette. With steadfastness and power as in his earlier masterpiece, and with a significance now as broad as humanity, that vow is here nobly fulfilled. And in his creative treatment of the events of Lourdes he has vivified historic fact with a force greater than that of literal statement, and far beyond controversy. *The Song of Bernadette* is a matter of record in its important happenings; it is no less a novel of compelling artistry, as its characters grow, its plot develops, its conflicts crystallize, its incandescent light shines clear. There is excitement here, great compassion, humor; and, always stronger and more luminous, the love of mankind.

When Bernadette first saw the lady in the grotto outside town, she couldn't keep her happiness to herself. Throngs gathered almost at once, growing larger until there were thousands of people to follow the child to a tryst only she could see. Some were merely curious, some scornful; most believed. What they believed was that the Blessed Virgin was here in person. But Bernadette herself did not make that claim.

There was nothing mystical about the hitherto inconspicuous little Soubirous girl. She was a literal-minded, unassuming child who did as she was told, suffered from chronic asthma, slept in a wretched room with five other people, and was hungry most of the time. Bernadette knew nothing about religious ecstasies. She knew little, indeed, about

The Grotto of Lourdes marks the place where the Most Blessed Virgin appeared in a vision to the young peasant girl, Bernadette. (Monkmeyer)

religion. She was, and seemed likely to remain, at the foot of her catechism class. What she did know was that a most beautiful lady came to the grotto and told her things she was to do, and was her friend. But what was quite simple to Bernadette was a cause of dismay to Church and State. And for this dismay she was cruelly made to suffer for years.

As that arrogantly self-sufficient freethinker, the poet Hyacinthe de Lafite, put it, " the true problem is offered not so much by the little visionary as by the great crowd that follows her." To the learned and logical she was merely a troublemaker, acting in delusion or fraud. And while the aristocratic nun who was her teacher scolded and

scoffed, the town police and the prosecutor threatened imprisonment of the
child and her family, the Mayor closed
the grotto, an *agent provocateur* was
sent to trap the girl into profit-making,
and when everything else failed — as everything did fail — the Prefect tried to
have her declared insane. But meanwhile the spring had gushed from the
rock, blind Bouriette could see again,
the paralyzed child had been cured, the
stern vicar and the progressive physician had become reluctant but honest
believers, and hard-headed workmen
threatened a general strike if " the interests " interfered with the child of the
people. In his official examination, as
before it, the Bishop made everything as
difficult as possible; for the Church must
protect itself against danger of deception or hysteria. The politicians, on the
other hand, wanted to placate public
opinion, suppress mob feelings, turn
whatever happened to their own advantage, and evade the perils of responsibility.

It is a witty novelist who thus follows
the self-expression of the local worthies
from the first café discussion to the climax of ironic comedy in the Mayor's
dream of Lourdes as a fashionable spa,
and who pursues the twisting paths of
opportunism to the boudoir of His Im-
perial Majesty Napoleon III. It is a master dramatist who keeps events and characters in confrontation through a cre-
scendo of acute and complex interest.
And Franz Werfel's searching realism is
not blurred but sharpened by his human
sympathy. But as the novel proceeds, its
significance is felt in more comprehen-
sive subtlety. Pride and humility oppose
each other, obviously; but there is much
more. " What have you thought of your
future, Bernadette? " the priest asks.
And the one impossible destiny is the
only one in her mind: like the other
girls' in the neighborhood; like anyone's
who is simple, and poor, and ordinary.
She was, they said, " commonplace."

She was never clever. She was wholly
natural. Her truth was matter-of-fact,
veracity untouched by argument and
thus unanswerable. Her courage was no
absence of fear, but concentration on
something beyond it. She cried with
pain and disappointment, yet surmounted failure with trust. In her singlemindedness there was no room for vanity, no picture of herself in the crowd's
eyes: she simply gave herself completely to the love of the goodness she saw.
Precisely so, she became the channel
that could communicate blessing to the
people, the key that could unlock —
though not always as they clamored for
it — the answer to their need. And so her
eventful human story becomes the exultant song of faith.

It is faith in goodness. In such truth
and love and oneness is Bernadette a
saint. But toward all these others, self-
seeking, blind, arrogant, there is yet no
complete condemnation; the miraculous
spring of goodness may still flow beneath the rocks of greed and pride.

This is a novel of magnificent completeness. Unfortunately the translation
is not wholly good. Clumsy phrases
(" love-filled consoledness," " cognition
of mystical coherences ") may jostle
modern colloquialisms in the narrative
(" had a hunch," " put on an act,"
" drapes " as noun). But the book's beauty is from within. In it is the fulfillment
not only of a single vow but of an earlier
consecration. It is the immanent and un-
dying beauty that can face the world's
cruelty and evil and still see the triumphant glory of the " holiness of man."

For Discussion of Book Reviews

1. What is the content of *No Place to
Hide?* What does the reviewer suggest is
the general or broad importance of such a
book, beyond its simple recording of a situation or experiment? What does White
mean by calling the Geiger counters' tick-

ing " the theme song of the cosmos "? In what sense does he use the word " contaminated "?

2. Tell what you learned about Dr. Bradley, the author of the book. Do the quotations from the book support the statement that the author has " the eyes and ears of a poet "?

3. What new details about radioactivity from the atomic bomb did you learn? What fact about it seemed queerest to Bradley himself?

4. What is the effect of the little story about the exiled Bikini natives? Why did White choose it to close his review?

5. Judging from the review, what would you say is the theme of *The Song of Bernadette?* Explain how Katherine Woods' review interests you and encourages you to read the book.

6. What qualities in the book does Katherine Woods point out which indicate that she considers *The Song of Bernadette* to be an outstanding novel? What are some of the characteristics of Saint Bernadette that she mentions?

7. Why were the parish priests and the bishop skeptical at the first reports of the apparitions? In this connection, why must the Church protect itself? Why did the town government object to the reaction of the people?

CLARENCE DAY

1874–1935

Father and His Hard-Rocking Ship

Clarence Day's family, a prominent and prosperous one, lived in a typical late nineteenth-century New York house with a brownstone front. The father, Clarence Day, Sr., son of the founder of the New York *Sun*, was a successful stockbroker. The mother had been a beautiful debutante before her marriage. The four little boys were brought up with all the advantages of that day. From without, the family would seem to inspire awe or envy, perhaps, but certainly not laughter. Yet seen through the eyes of the eldest son, this family has become a famous source of mirth for present-day Americans.

Clarence Day's mature life was a struggle against arthritis, which crippled him to such an extent that he spent much of the time on crutches, in a wheel chair, or in bed. But disease did not deter him from trying ranch life in Colorado, managing a glove business, making and losing money on the stock exchange, marrying a charming New England girl, and gaining a reputation as one of the wittiest conversationalists in New York. Although he wrote several other entertaining books, Day's enduring place in American literature has been won by three comparatively short books of sketches about his own family — *God and My Father, Life with Father,* and *Life with Mother.* Since the author's death, incidents and conversations from these books have been woven into a comedy called

"Father and His Hard-Rocking Ship" from *Life with Father* by Clarence Day. Reprinted by permission of Alfred A. Knopf, Inc.

Life with Father, one of the greatest successes in the history of our theater. The play has also been adapted for movies and television.

Some writers describe characters in general terms. Day simply pulls back a curtain and lets you watch and listen to their everyday routine. Your impressions accumulate until you form an opinion of each person as you would from knowing him in real life. You will find that you can identify the traits of Mother and Father Day as easily as you identify those of some of your friends.

FATHER said that one great mystery about the monthly household expenses was what made them jump up and down so. "Anyone would suppose that there would be some regularity after a while which would let a man try to make plans, but I never know from one month to another what to expect."

Mother said she didn't, either. Things just seemed to go that way.

"But they have no business to go that way, Vinnie," Father declared. "And, what's more, I won't allow it."

Mother said she didn't see what she could do about it. All she knew was that when the bills mounted up it didn't mean that she had been extravagant.

"Well, it certainly means that you've spent a devil of a lot of money," said Father.

Mother looked at him obstinately. She couldn't exactly deny this, but she said that it wasn't fair.

Appearances were often hopelessly against Mother, but that never daunted her. She wasn't afraid of Father or anybody. She was a woman of great spirit who would have flown at and pecked any tyrant. It was only when she had a bad conscience that she had no heart to fight. Father had the best of her there because he never had a bad conscience. And he didn't know that he was a tyrant. He regarded himself as a long-suffering man who asked little of anybody, and who showed only the greatest moderation in his encounters with unreasonable beings like Mother. Mother's one advantage over him was that she was quicker. She was particularly elusive when Father was trying to hammer her into shape.

When the household expenses shot up very high, Father got frightened. He would then, as Mother put it, yell his head off. He always did some yelling anyhow, merely on general principles, but when his alarm was genuine he roared in real anguish.

Usually this brought the total down again, at least for a while. But there were times when no amount of noise seemed to do any good and when every month for one reason or another the total went on up and up. And then, just as Father had almost resigned himself to this awful outgo, and just as he had eased up on his yelling and had begun to feel grim, the expenses, to his utter amazement, would take a sharp drop.

Mother didn't keep track of these totals; she was too busy watching small details, and Father never knew whether to tell her the good news or not. He always did tell her, because he couldn't keep things to himself. But he always had cause to regret it.

When he told her, he did it in as disciplinary a manner as possible. He didn't congratulate her on the expenses having come down. He appeared at her door, waving the bills at her with a threatening scowl, and said, "I've told you again and again that you could keep the expenses down if you tried, and this shows I was right."

Mother was always startled at such attacks, but she didn't lose her presence of mind. She asked how much less the amount was and said it was all due to her good management, of course, and Father ought to give her the difference.

At this point Father suddenly found

himself on the defensive, and the entire moral lecture that he had intended to deliver was wrecked. The more they talked, the clearer it seemed to Mother that he owed her that money. Only when he was lucky could he get out of her room without paying it.

He said that this was one of the things about her that was enough to drive a man mad.

The other thing was her lack of system, which was always cropping up in new ways. He sometimes looked at Mother as though he had never seen her before. " Upon my soul," he said, " I almost believe you don't know what system is. You don't even want to know, either."

He had at last invented what seemed a perfect method of recording expenses. Whenever he gave any money to Mother, he asked her what it was for and made a note of it in his pocket notebook. His idea was that these items, added to those in the itemized bills, would show him exactly where every dollar had gone.

But they didn't.

He consulted his notebook. " I gave you six dollars in cash on the twenty-fifth of last month," he said, " to buy a new coffeepot."

" Yes," Mother said, " because you broke your old one. You threw it right on the floor."

Father frowned. " I'm not talking about that," he answered. " I am simply endeavoring to find out from you, if I can — "

" But it's so silly to break a nice coffeepot, Clare, and that was the last of those French ones, and there was nothing the matter with the coffee that morning; it was made just the same as it always is."

" It wasn't," said Father. " It was made in a barbaric manner."

" And I couldn't get another French one," Mother continued, " because that little shop the Auffmordts told us about

has stopped selling them. They said the tariff wouldn't let them any more, and I told Monsieur Duval he ought to be ashamed of himself to stand there and say so. I said that if I had a shop I'd like to see the tariff keep me from selling things."

" But I gave you six dollars to buy a new pot," Father firmly repeated, " and now I find that you apparently got one at Lewis and Conger's and charged it. Here's their bill: ' One brown earthenware drip coffeepot, five dollars.' "

" So I saved you a dollar," Mother triumphantly said, " and you can hand it right over to me."

" Bah! What nonsense you talk! " Father cried. " Is there no way to get this thing straightened out? What did you do with the six dollars? "

" Why, Clare! I can't tell you now, dear. Why didn't you ask at the time? "

" Oh, great Scott! " Father groaned.

" Wait a moment," said Mother. " I spent four dollars and a half for that new umbrella I told you I wanted, and you said I didn't need a new one; but I did, very much."

Father got out his pencil and wrote " New Umbrella for V." in his notebook.

" And that must have been the week," Mother went on, " that I paid Mrs. Tobin for two extra days' washing, so that was two dollars more out of it, which makes it six-fifty. There's another fifty cents that you owe me."

" I don't owe you anything," Father said. " You have managed to turn a coffeepot for me into a new umbrella for you. No matter what I give you money for, you buy something else with it; and if this is to keep on, I might as well not keep account books at all."

" I'd like to see you run this house without having any money on hand for things," Mother said.

" I am not made of money," Father replied. " You seem to think I only have to put my hand in my pocket to get some."

In the film version of Life with Father, *William Powell played Father, and Irene Dunne was his charming, unpredictable wife.* (*Culver*)

Mother not only thought this, she knew it. His wallet always was full. That was the provoking part of it — she knew he had the money right there, but he tried to keep from giving it to her. She had to argue it out of him.

"Well, you can put your hand in your pocket and give me that dollar-fifty this minute," she said. "You owe me that, anyhow."

Father said that he didn't have a dollar-fifty to spare and tried to get back to his desk, but Mother wouldn't let him go till he paid her. She said she wouldn't put up with injustice.

Mother said it hampered her dreadfully never to have any cash. She was always having to pay out small amounts for demands that she had forgot to provide for, and in such emergencies the only way to do was to juggle things around. One result, however, of all these more or less innocent shifts was that in

this way she usually took care of all her follies herself. All the small ones, at any rate. They never got entered on Father's books, except when they were monstrous.

She came home one late afternoon in a terrible state. "Has it come yet?" she asked the waitress.

The waitress said nothing had come that she knew of.

Mother ran upstairs with a hunted expression and flung herself down on her bed. When we looked in, she was sobbing.

It turned out that she had gone to an auction, and she had become so excited that she had bought but not paid for a grandfather's clock.

Mother knew in her heart that she had no business going to auctions. She was too suggestible; and if a hypnotic auctioneer once got her eye, she was lost. Besides, an auction aroused all her worst instincts — her combativeness, her recklessness, and her avaricious love of a bargain. And the worst of it was that this time it wasn't a bargain at all. At least she didn't think it was now. The awful old thing was about eight feet tall, and it wasn't the one she had wanted. It wasn't half as nice as the clock that old Miss Van Derwent had bought. And inside the hood over the dial, she said, there was a little ship which at first she hadn't noticed, a horrid ship that rocked up and down every time the clock ticked. It made her ill just to look at it. And she didn't have the money, and the man said he'd have to send it this evening, and what would Father say?

She came down to dinner, and left halfway through. Couldn't stand it. But an hour or two later, when the doorbell rang, she bravely went to tell Father.

She could hardly believe it; but she found that luck was with her, for once. If the clock had come earlier, there might have been a major catastrophe; but Father was in a good mood, and he had had a good dinner. And though he never admitted it or spoke of it, he had a weakness for clocks. There were clocks all over the house, which he would allow no one to wind but himself. Every Sunday between breakfast and church he made the rounds, setting them at the right time by his infallible watch, regulating their speed, and telling us about every clock's little idiosyncrasies. When he happened to be coming downstairs on the hour, he cocked his ear, watch in hand, to listen to as many of them as he could, in the hope that they would all strike at once. He would reprove the impulsive pink clock in the spare room for striking too soon, and the big solemn clock in the dining room for being a minute too late.

So when Mother led him out in the hall to confess to him and show him what she had bought, and he saw it was a clock, he fell in love with it and made almost no fuss at all.

The letdown was too much for Mother. She tottered off to her room without another word and went straight to bed, leaving Father and the auctioneer's man setting up the new clock alongside the hatrack. Father was especially fascinated by the hard-rocking ship.

For Discussion of Day

1. What characteristics of Mother and Father are clear from even this short acquaintance with them? What was Mother's usual method of dealing with Father's attacks?

2. Whose side are you on in this family contest? What traits of each person do you like? Do you think the writer shared your attitude?

3. Would you call any one of these conversations a family quarrel? Could one of them have been treated seriously with tragic rather than comic effect? What is the essential difference between comic bickering and tragic quarreling?

4. Why is this narrative classed as an essay rather than a short story? Discuss differences between the two types as illustrated by the selections from Clarence Day and James Thurber (p. 119).

For Your Vocabulary

FIGURATIVE USE OF WORDS: It would be nearly impossible to picture the lively atmosphere of this home without figures of speech. The troublesome household expenses would " jump up and down " and sometimes they " shot up very high." Mother was a woman " who would have flown at and pecked any tyrant." To what is Mother compared? In addition to comparison, exaggeration is appropriately used to give the mood of the Day household. Father would " yell his head off " when the expenses indulged in their acrobatics. Such exaggeration is called *hyperbole* (look up the pronunciation of this word). It is a favorite figure of speech with young people. Did you ever say " I nearly died laughing " or " I waited ages for the phone to ring "? What are some of the common hyperboles in the conversation of your crowd?

BISHOP FULTON JAMES
SHEEN

1895–

Equity and Equality

Bishop Fulton James Sheen, outstanding television personality in 1952, has had a long and honorable career in broadcasting. He was the first priest to deliver the sermons on the Catholic Sunday Hour when it was inaugurated on the radio in 1930. He conducted the first religious service ever telecast, in 1940.

Born at El Paso, Illinois, he moved with his family to Peoria. He attended a Christian Brothers high school there and went to the College of St. Viator in Bourbonnais, Illinois. He took his B.A. degree in 1917 and his M.A. degree in 1919, in which year he was ordained priest. After receiving graduate degrees from St. Paul's Seminary and the Catholic University of America, he was awarded his Ph.D. in 1923 from the famous University of Louvain in Belgium. His writing had already won him honors, for Louvain awarded him the Cardinal Mercier prize in philosophy for his dissertation, *God and Intelligence*. In 1924, he earned his D.D. from the Angelico University, Rome, and a year later he taught dogmatic theology at St. Edmund's College, Ware, England.

Bishop Sheen returned to the United States to do parish work in Peoria for a year. He then went to teach the philosophy of religion at the Catholic University of America. He was made Papal Chamberlain in 1934, Domestic Prelate in 1935, and consecrated Auxiliary Bishop of New York in 1951. At present he is the national director of the Society for the Propagation of the Faith.

Over thirty-five books, many of which are compilations of sermons, testify to Bishop Sheen's zeal and scholarship. A tireless lecturer and preacher, he has been one of the greatest forces in fighting Communism in the United States since the 1930's. As his highly popular television broadcasts have shown, he has a special talent for rendering abstruse religious and ethical ideas into easily grasped language. His work in conversions has been singularly blessed. In the following essay, Bishop Sheen gives us a telling summary of the position of woman in modern society, pointing the way to a balanced life. As you read, notice how simple he can make a complicated subject, and how clear his solution appears.

T HE TWO basic errors of both Communism and Historical Liberalism [1] on the subject of women are: (1) that women were never emancipated until modern times, since religion particularly

[1] **Historical Liberalism:** that system of free enterprise that Adam Smith advocated in his *The Wealth of Nations*. Eventually it penetrated economic, social, and political thinking in the nineteenth century.

kept them in servitude; (2) that equality means the right of a woman to do a man's work.

It is not true that women began to be emancipated in modern times and in proportion to the decline of religion. Woman's *subjection* began in the seventeenth century, with the breakup of Christendom, and took on a positive form at the

"Equity and Equality " from *The World's First Love* by Fulton J. Sheen, published by McGraw-Hill Book Company. Reprinted by permission of the publisher.

time of the Industrial Revolution. Under the Christian civilization women enjoyed rights, privileges, honors, and dignities which have since been swallowed up by the machine age. No one has better dissipated the false idea than Mary Beard in her scholarly work, *Woman as Force in History*. She points out that, of eighty-five guilds in England during the Middle Ages, seventy-two had women members on an equal basis with men, even in such professions as barbers and sailors. They were probably as outspoken as men, for one of the rules of the guilds was that "the sistern as well as the brethren" may not engage in disorderly or contumacious debates. In Paris, there were fifteen guilds reserved exclusively for women, while eighty of the Parisian guilds were mixed. Nothing is more erroneous historically than the belief that it was our modern age which recognized women in the professions. The records of these Christian times reveal the names of thousands upon thousands of women who influenced society and whose names are now enrolled in the catalogue of saints — Catherine of Siena alone having left eleven large volumes of her writings. Up to the seventeenth century in England, women engaged in business, and perhaps even more so than today; in fact, so many wives were in business that it was provided by law that the husbands should not be responsible for their debts. Between 1553 and 1640, ten per cent of the publishing in England was done by women. Because the homes had their own weaving, cooking, and laundry, it has been estimated that women in preindustrial days were producing half the goods required by society. In the Middle Ages women were as well educated as men, and it was not until the seventeenth century that women were barred from education. Then, at the time of the Industrial Revolution, all the activities and freedom of women were curtailed, as the machine took over the business of production and

men moved into the factory.

This brings us to the second error in the bourgeois-capitalistic theory of women, namely, the failure to make a distinction between mathematical and proportional equality. Mathematical equality implies exactness of remuneration, for example, that two men who work at the same job at the same factory should receive equal pay. Proportional equality means that each should receive this pay according to his function. In a family, for example, all children should be cared for by the parents, but this does not mean that, because sixteen-year-old Mary gets an evening gown with an organdy trim, the parents should give seventeen-year-old Johnnie the same thing. Women, in seeking to regain some of the rights and privileges they had in Christian civilization, thought of equality in mathematical terms or in terms of sex. Feeling themselves overcome by a monster called "man," they identified freedom and equality with the right to do a man's job. All the psychological, social, and other advantages which were peculiar to women were ignored until the inanities of the bourgeois world reached their climax in Communism, under which a woman is emancipated the moment she goes to work in a mine. The result has been that woman's imitation of man and her flight from motherhood has developed neuroses and psychoses [1] which have reached alarming proportions. The Christian civilization never stressed equality in a mathematical sense, but only in the proportional sense, for equality is wrong when it reduces the woman to a poor imitation of a man. Once woman became man's mathematical equal, he no longer gave her a seat in a bus, and no longer took off his hat in an elevator.

Modern woman has been made equal with man, but she has not been made

---

[1] **neuroses and psychoses:** Neuroses are functional disorders of the nervous system; pyschoses are mental diseases.

happy. She has been "emancipated," like a pendulum removed from a clock and now no longer free to swing, or like a flower which has been emancipated from its roots. She has been cheapened in her search for mathematical equality in two ways: by becoming a victim to man and a victim to the machine. She became a victim to man by becoming only the instrument of his pleasure and ministering to his needs in a sterile exchange of egotisms. She became a victim to the machine by subordinating the creative principle of life to the production of nonliving things, which is the essence of Communism.

This is not a condemnation of a professional woman, because the important question is not whether a woman finds favor in the eyes of a man, but whether she can satisfy the basic instincts of womanhood. The problem of a woman is whether certain God-given qualities, which are specifically hers, are given adequate and full expression. These qualities are principally devotion, sacrifice, and love. They need not necessarily be expressed in a family, nor even in a convent. They can find an outlet in the social world, in the care of the sick, the poor, the ignorant — in the seven corporal works of mercy. It is sometimes said that the professional woman is hard. This may in a few instances be true, but if so, it is not because she is in a profession, but because she has alienated her profession from contact with human beings in a way to satisfy the deeper cravings of her heart.

The solution lies in a return to the Christian concept, wherein stress is placed not on *equality* but on *equity*. Equality is law. It is mathematical, abstract, universal, indifferent to conditions, circumstances, and differences. Equity is love, mercy, understanding, sympathy — it allows the consideration of details, appeals, and even departures from fixed rules which the law has not yet embraced. In particular, it is the ap-

plication of law to an individual person. Equity places its reliance on moral principles and is guided by an understanding of the motives of individual families which fall outside the scope of the rigors of law.

Applying this distinction to women, it is clear that *equity* rather than *equality* should be the basis of all the feminine claims. Equity goes beyond equality by claiming superiority in certain aspects of life. Equity is the perfection of equality, not its substitute. It has the advantages of recognizing the specific difference between man and woman, which equality does not have. As a matter of fact, men and women are not equal in sex; they are quite unequal, and it is only because they are unequal that they complement one another. Each has a superiority of function. Man and woman are equal, inasmuch as they have the same rights and liberties, the same final goal of life, and the same redemption by the Blood of Our Divine Savior — but they are different in function.

If women, in the full consciousness of their creativeness, say to the world: "It takes us twenty years to make a man, and we rebel against every generation snuffing out that manhood in war," such an attitude will do more for the peace of the world than all the covenants and pacts. Where there is equality there is justice, but there is no love. If man is the equal of woman, then she has rights — but no heart ever lived only on rights. All love demands inequality or superiority. The lover is always on his knees; the beloved must always be on a pedestal. Whether it be man or woman, the one must always consider himself or herself as undeserving of the other. Even God humbled Himself in His Love to win man, saying He "came not to be ministered unto, but to minister." And man, in his turn, approaches that loving Savior in Communion with the words: "Lord, I am not worthy."

As we said, professional careers do

not of themselves defeminize women; otherwise the Church would not have raised political women to sainthood, as in the cases of St. Elizabeth and St. Clotilde. The unalterable fact is that no woman is happy unless she has someone for whom she can sacrifice herself — not in a servile way, but in the way of love. Added to the devotedness is her love of creativeness. A man is afraid of dying, but a woman is afraid of not living. Life to a man is personal; life to a woman is otherness. She thinks less in terms of perpetuation of self and more in terms of perpetuation of others — so much so, that in her devotedness she is willing to sacrifice herself for others. To the extent that a career gives her no opportunity for either, she becomes defeminized. If these qualities cannot be given an outlet in a home and a family, they must nevertheless find other substitutions in works of charity, in the defense of virtuous living, and in the defense of right, as other Claudias [1] enlighten their political husbands. The woman's work as a money earner becomes a mere prelude and a condition for the display of equity, which is her greatest glory.

Christianity does not ask the modern woman to be exclusively a Martha or a Mary; the choice is not between a professional career and contemplation, for the Church reads the Gospel of Martha and Mary for Our Lady to symbolize that she combines both the speculative and the practical, the serving of the Lord and the sitting at His Feet. If woman wants to be a revolutionist, then *The Woman* is her guide, for she sang the most revolutionary song ever written — the Magnificat, the burden of which was the abolition of principalities and powers, and the exaltation of the humble. She breaks the shell of woman's isolation from the world and puts woman back into the wide ocean of humanity. She, who is the Cosmopolitan Woman,

St. Patrick's Cathedral, New York City, where Bishop Sheen has delivered many sermons. (A. Devaney)

[1] **Claudias:** Claudia, wife of Pontius Pilate, warned the Procurator not to condemn Christ.

gives us the Cosmopolitan Man, for which giving all generations shall call her blessed.

Great men we need, like Paul with a two-edged sword to cut away the bonds that tie down the energies of the world — and men like Peter, who will let the broad stroke of their challenge ring out on the shield of the world's hypocrisy — great men like John who, with a loud voice, will arouse the world from the sleek dream of unheroic repose. But we need women still more; women like Mary of Cleophas, who will raise sons to lift up white hosts to a Heavenly Father; women like Magdalene, who will take hold of the tangled skeins of a seemingly wrecked and ruined life and weave out of them the beautiful tapestry of saintliness and holiness; and women, above all, like Mary who will leave the lights and glamours of the world for the shades and shadows of the Cross, where saints are made. When women of this kind return to save the world with equity, then we shall toast them, we shall salute them, not as " the modern woman, once our superior and now our equal,"

but as the Christian woman closest to the Cross on Good Friday, and first at the Tomb on Easter morn.

For Discussion of Sheen

1. List the two basic modern errors concerning the position of women. Pick out the facts Bishop Sheen gives that refute the first error.

2. Why is it necessary to explain woman's position today? Why has " emancipation " failed to satisfy woman? Why should equity replace equality in defining woman's position?

3. Explain the difference between " mathematical and proportionate equality." Can you give another illustration of this?

4. Bishop Sheen states that " the subordination of the creative principle of life to the production of nonliving things " is the essence of Communism. Can you explain why?

5. Can you give any good reasons why women today should go into professions? When does a career liberate a woman? When does it frustrate her?

6. Why does Bishop Sheen consider Our Lady revolutionary? Pick out the outstanding characteristics of St. Peter, St. Paul, and St. John as they are listed in this essay.

Circus at Dawn

THOMAS WOLFE
1900–1938

During Thomas Wolfe's short life, arguments about his huge novels, *Look Homeward, Angel* and *Of Time and the River*, raged back and forth. Some readers hailed these books as new high marks in the attempt to express the struggle and yearning of human life. Others contended the

books were clumsily constructed and offensive in their use of autobiographical material. Like the central character of these two novels, Wolfe was born in a Southern town, Asheville, North Carolina, struggled to get a college education, which he finished at Harvard, taught school a few

"Circus at Dawn" from *From Death to Morning* by Thomas Wolfe. Reprinted by permission of Charles Scribner's Sons.

years, and then settled down to write. He spent his last years in a poor section of Brooklyn, where he felt he was in closer touch with real life than he could be mingling with the literary sophisticates of Manhattan. Pneumonia struck him down in 1938, before the publication of his third and fourth novels.

However critics may argue about the construction and the meaning of Wolfe's novels, many agree that he wrote "some of the noblest prose to come out of America." Like many passages in his novels, Wolfe's shorter pieces are more like poetry than ordinary prose. They reveal an intense emotional response to all that he sees and hears and smells and touches, coupled with a rare power to capture in words both feeling and sensation. In "Circus at Dawn," taken from a collection of sketches called *From Death to Morning*, he relives an experience of his youth that would hold special charm for any boy and was thrilling to one with Wolfe's keen senses. Fall in with the writer's mood to share his excited glimpses of a glamorous world.

THERE were times in early autumn — in September — when the greater circuses would come to town — the Ringling Brothers, Robinson's, and Barnum and Bailey shows, and when I was a route-boy on the morning paper, on those mornings when the circus would be coming in I would rush madly through my route in the cool and thrilling darkness that comes just before break of day, and then I would go back home and get my brother out of bed.

Talking in low excited voices we would walk rapidly back toward town under the rustle of September leaves, in cool streets just grayed now with that still, that unearthly and magical first light of day which seems suddenly to rediscover the great earth out of darkness, so that the earth emerges with an awful, a glorious sculptural stillness, and one looks out with a feeling of joy and disbelief, as the first men on this earth must have done, for to see this happen is one of the things that men will remember out of life forever and think of as they die.

At the sculptural still square where at one corner, just emerging into light, my father's shabby little marble shop stood with a ghostly strangeness and familiarity, my brother and I would "catch" the first streetcar of the day bound for the "depot" where the circus was — or sometimes we would meet someone we knew, who would give us a lift in his automobile.

Then, having reached the dingy, grimy, and rickety depot section, we would get out, and walk rapidly across the tracks of the station yard, where we could see great flares and steamings from the engines, and hear the crash and bump of shifting freight cars, the swift sporadic thunders of a shifting engine, the tolling of bells, the sounds of great trains on the rails.

And to all these familiar sounds, filled with their exultant prophecies of flight, the voyage, morning, and the shining cities — to all the sharp and thrilling odors of the trains — the smell of cinders, acrid smoke, of musty, rusty freight cars, the clean pine-board of crated produce, and the smells of fresh stored food — oranges, coffee, tangerines and bacon, ham and flour and beef — there would be added now, with an unforgettable magic and familiarity, all the strange sounds and smells of the coming circus.

The gay yellow sumptuous-looking cars in which the star performers lived and slept, still dark and silent, heavily and powerfully still, would be drawn up in long strings upon the tracks. And all around them the sounds of the unloading circus would go on furiously in the darkness. The receding gulf of lilac and departing night would be filled with the savage roar of the lions, the murderously sudden snarling of great jun-

gle cats, the trumpeting of the elephants, the stamp of the horses, and
with the musty, pungent, unfamiliar
odor of the jungle animals: the tawny
camel smells, and the smells of pan-
thers, zebras, tigers, elephants, and
bears.

Then, along the tracks, beside the circus trains, there would be the sharp
cries and oaths of the circus men, the
magical swinging dance of lanterns in
the darkness, the sudden heavy rumble
of the loaded vans and wagons as they
were pulled along the flats and gondo-
las, and down the runways to the
ground. And everywhere, in the thrilling mystery of darkness and awakening
light, there would be the tremendous
conflict of a confused, hurried, and yet
orderly movement.

The great iron-gray horses, four and
six to a team, would be plodding along
the road of thick white dust to a rattling
of chains and traces and the harsh cries
of their drivers. The men would drive
the animals to the river which flowed
by beyond the tracks, and water them;
and as first light came one could see the
elephants wallowing in the familiar river and the big horses going slowly and
carefully down to drink.

Then, on the circus grounds, the tents
were going up already with the magic
speed of dreams. All over the place
(which was near the tracks and the only space of flat land in the town that
was big enough to hold a circus) there
would be this fierce, savagely hurried,
and yet orderly confusion. Great flares
of gaseous circus light would blaze
down on the seared and battered faces
of the circus toughs as, with the rhythmic precision of a single animal — a
human riveting machine — they swung
their sledges at the stakes, driving a
stake into the earth with the incredible
instancy of accelerated figures in a motion picture. And everywhere, as light
came, and the sun appeared, there
would be a scene of magic, order, and

of violence. The drivers would curse
and talk their special language to their
teams, there would be the loud, gasping, and uneven labor of a gasoline engine, the shouts and curses of the bosses, the wooden riveting of driven stakes,
and the rattle of heavy chains.

Already in an immense cleared space
of dusty beaten earth, the stakes were
being driven for the main exhibition
tent. And an elephant would lurch pon-
derously to the field, slowly lower his
great swinging head at the command of
a man who sat perched upon his skull,
flourish his gray wrinkled snout a time
or two, and then solemnly wrap it
around a tent pole big as the mast of a
racing schooner. Then the elephant
would back slowly away, dragging the
great pole with him as if it were a stick
of matchwood. . . .

Meanwhile, the circus food-tent — a
huge canvas top without concealing
sides — had already been put up, and
now we could see the performers seated
at long trestled tables underneath the
tent, as they ate breakfast. And the savor of the food they ate — mixed as it
was with our strong excitement, with
the powerful but wholesome smells of
the animals, and with all the joy, sweetness, mystery, jubilant magic and glory
of the morning and the coming of the
circus — seemed to us to be of the most
maddening and appetizing succulence
of any food that we had ever known or
eaten.

We could see the circus performers
eating tremendous breakfasts, with all
the savage relish of their power and
strength: they ate big fried steaks, pork
chops, rashers of bacon, a half dozen
eggs, great slabs of fried ham and great
stacks of wheat cakes which a cook kept
flipping in the air with the skill of a jug-
gler, and which a husky-looking waitress kept rushing to their tables on
loaded trays held high and balanced
marvelously on the fingers of a brawny

A stolen glimpse of the fantastic circus world. (Ewing Galloway)

hand. And above all the maddening odors of the wholesome and succulent food, there brooded forever the sultry and delicious fragrance — that somehow seemed to add a zest and sharpness to all the powerful and thrilling life of morning — of strong boiling coffee, which we could see sending off clouds of steam from an enormous polished urn, and which the circus performers gulped down, cup after cup.

And the circus men and women themselves — these star performers — were such fine-looking people, strong and handsome, yet speaking and moving with an almost stern dignity and decorum, that their lives seemed to us to be as splendid and wonderful as any lives on earth could be. There was never anything loose, rowdy, or tough in their comportment. . . .

Rather, these people in an astonishing way seemed to have created an established community which lived an ordered existence on wheels, and to observe with a stern fidelity unknown in towns and cities the decencies of family life. There would be a powerful young man, a handsome and magnificent young woman with blond hair and the figure of an Amazon, and a powerfully-built, thickset man of middle age, who had a stern, lined, responsible-looking face and a bald head. They were probably the members of a trapeze team — the young man and woman would leap through space like projectiles, meeting the grip of the older man and hurtling back again upon their narrow perches, catching the swing of their trapeze in mid-air, and whirling thrice before they caught it, in a perilous and beautiful exhibition of human balance and precision.

But when they came into the breakfast tent, they would speak gravely yet courteously to other performers, and seat themselves in a family group at one of the long tables, eating their tremendous breakfast with an earnest concentration, seldom speaking to one another, and then gravely, seriously, and briefly.

And my brother and I would look at them with fascinated eyes; my brother would watch the man with the bald head for a while and then turn toward me, whispering:

"D-d-do you see that f-f-fellow there with the bald head? W-w-well, he's the heavy man," he whispered knowingly. "He's the one that c-c-c-catches them! That f-f-fellow's got to know his business! You know what happens if he m-m-misses, don't you?" said my brother.

"What?" I would say in a fascinated tone.

My brother snapped his fingers in the air.

"Over!" he said. "D-d-done for! W-w-why, they'd be d-d-d-dead before they knew what happened. Sure!" he said, nodding vigorously. "It's a f-f-f-fact! If he ever m-m-m-misses it's all over! That boy has g-g-g-got to know his s-s-s-stuff!" my brother said. "W-w-w-why," he went on in a low tone of solemn conviction, "it w-w-w-wouldn't surprise me at all if they p-p-p-pay him s-s-seventy-five or a hundred dollars a week! It's a fact!" my brother cried vigorously.

And we would turn our fascinated stares again upon these splendid and romantic creatures, whose lives were so different from our own, and whom we seemed to know with such familiar and affectionate intimacy. And at length, reluctantly, with full light come and the sun up, we would leave the circus grounds and start for home.

And somehow the memory of all we had seen and heard that glorious morning, and the memory of the food-tent with its wonderful smells, would waken in us the pangs of such a ravenous hunger that we could not wait until we got home to eat. We would stop off in town at lunchrooms and, seated on tall stools before the counter, we would devour ham-and-egg sandwiches, hot hamburgers red and pungent at their cores with coarse spicy sanguinary beef, coffee, glasses of foaming milk, and doughnuts, and then go home to eat up everything in sight upon the breakfast table.

For Discussion of Wolfe

1. What words early in the narrative convey the special sense of excitement and strangeness that pervades the whole sketch? What general impression of the town does Wolfe give as a contrasting setting to the circus grounds? What details does he use to create this impression?

2. Recall some of the activities going on in the circus world at dawn. Which seemed to you especially interesting?

3. Select for reading aloud descriptive phrases that have the rhythm and suggestive power of poetry.

4. In what ways does this glimpse into circus life change your preconceived ideas about circus people? What other people have you had wrong notions about before you became acquainted with them?

5. Have you had glimpses of a scene quite different from your usual daily round — as different as that of the circus? Try to recount one with the wealth of sight and sound and odor that Wolfe gets into this sketch.

For Your Vocabulary

WORD DISCRIMINATION: One of Wolfe's distinctions is the way he makes physical sensations vivid. Three words he uses of smell are richly descriptive. The *pungent* odor of jungle animals (p. 194) is piercing and strong. A *pungent* odor may be pleasant or unpleasant, but it is always stimulating. The *acrid* smell of smoke (p. 193) is sharp and penetrating, too strong, rather unpleasant. *Acrid* is often used of sharp and unpleasant remarks. *Savor* (p. 194) is used of the smell of foods, and it has an appetite-stirring quality. For *savor* is always pleasant, promising delicious taste.

The *succulence* of food (p. 195) appeals to feeling, for it means juiciness. A bit of gossip, as well as food, can be *succulent*.

What other sounds and sights and smells does the writer record with notable vivid-ness? Try to list, from Wolfe's writing, three or four adjectives describing each of these physical sensations, and give an exact definition for each. Then write sentences, using one of these words in each.

WILLIAM O. DOUGLAS
1898–

Two Boys on a Mountain

William O. Douglas's life is a fine example of the typical American success story. The son of an itinerant preacher, he grew up in the state of Washington, hitched his way east on freight cars to enter Columbia University, and earned his own living while going through college and law school. He rapidly became a law professor and then a member of the Securities and Exchange Commission, which regulates the activities of the stock market. At forty he had reached the pinnacle for an American law-yer, a seat on the United States Supreme Court.

From youth a lover of the outdoor life, Douglas still spends his vacations in a mountain cabin in Washington and in-dulges his love of horseback riding and mountain climbing. Recently he recounted his adventures in the latter sport in his first book of general interest, *Of Men and Mountains*. In the episode reprinted here, mountain-climbing fan Bill Douglas takes you along on a perilous ascent made in his youth. Use his words plus your imagina-tion to feel inside your very flesh the strain on bone and muscle and nerve as you toil up the sheer rock.

K LOOCHMAN ROCK stands on the southern side of the Tieton Basin in the Cascade Mountains of the state of Washington. It is an oval-shaped lava rock, running lengthwise northwest by southeast a half-mile or more. It rises 3,000 feet above the basin. A third or more of its elevation is gained through gentle slopes of pine and fir. Next are a few hundred yards of tumbled rock. Then there is the cliff rising to the sky,

1,500 feet or more — straight as the Washington Monument and over twice as high.

It was in 1913, when my friend Doug-las Corpron was nineteen and I was not quite fifteen, that the two of us climbed Kloochman. Walter Kohagen, Doug, and I were camped in the Tieton Basin at a soda spring. The basin was then in large part a vast rich bottom-land. We were traveling light, one blanket each. The night, I recall, was so bitter cold that we took turns refueling the campfire so that we could keep our backs warm enough to sleep. We rose at the first show of dawn, and cooked frying-pan bread and trout for breakfast. We had not planned to climb Kloochman, but somehow the challenge came to us as the sun touched her crest.

After breakfast we started circling the rock. There are fairly easy routes up Kloochman, but we shunned them. When we came to the southeast face (the one that never has been conquered, I believe) we chose it. Walter decided not to make the climb, but to wait at the base of the cliff for Doug and me. We started in midmorning. By then the July day was warm and cloudless. Doug led. The beginning was easy. For one hundred feet or so we found ledges six to twelve inches wide we could follow to the left or right. Some ledges ran up the rock ten feet or more at a gentle grade. Others were merely steps to another ledge higher up. Thus by hugging the wall we could either ease ourselves upward or hoist ourselves from one ledge to another.

When we were about one hundred feet up the wall, the ledges became narrower and the footwork more precarious. Doug suggested we take off our shoes. This we did, tying them behind us on our belts. In stocking feet we wormed up the wall, clinging like flies to the dark rock. The pace was slow. We gingerly tested each toehold and fingerhold for loose rock before putting our weight on it. At times we had to inch along sidewise, our stomachs pressed tightly against the rock, in order to gain a point where we could reach the ledge above us. If we got on a ledge that turned out to be a cul-de-sac, the much more dangerous task of going down the rock wall would confront us. So we picked our route with care and weighed the advantages of several choices which frequently were given us. At times we could not climb easily from one ledge to another. The one above might be a foot or so high. Then we would have to reach it with one knee, slowly bring the other knee up, and then, delicately balancing on both knees on the upper ledge, come slowly to our feet by pressing close to the wall and getting such purchase with our fingers as the lava rock permitted.

In that tortuous way we made perhaps eight hundred feet in two hours. It was late forenoon when we stopped to appraise our situation. We were in serious trouble. We had reached the feared cul-de-sac. The two- or three-inch ledge on which we stood ended. There seemed none above us within Doug's reach. I was longer-legged than Doug; so perhaps I could have reached some ledge with my fingers if I were ahead. But it was impossible to change positions on the wall. Doug was ahead and there he must stay. The problem was to find a way to get him up.

Feeling along the wall, Doug discovered a tiny groove into which he could press the tips of the fingers of his left hand. It might help him maintain balance as his weight began to shift from the lower ledge to the upper one. But there was within reach not even a lip of rock for his right hand. Just out of reach, however, was a substantial crevasse, one that would hold several men. How could Doug reach it? I could not boost him, for my own balance was insecure. Clearly, Doug would have to jump to reach it — and he would have but one jump. Since he was standing on a ledge only a few inches wide, he could not expect to jump for his handhold, miss it, and land safely. A slip meant he would go hurtling down some eight hundred feet onto the rocks. After much discussion and indecision, Doug decided to take the chance and go up.

He asked me to do him a favor. If he failed and fell, I might still make it, since I was longer-legged; would I give certain messages to his family in that event? I nodded.

"Then listen carefully. Try to remember my exact words," he told me. "Tell Mother that I love her dearly. Tell her I think she is the most wonderful person in the world. Tell her not to worry — that I did not suffer, that God willed it so. Tell Sister that I have been a mean little devil but I had no malice toward her. Tell Dad I was brave and died unafraid. Tell him I have always been very proud of him, that some day I had planned to be a doctor too. Tell Mother, Sister, and Dad I prayed for them."

Every word burned into me. My heart was sick, my lips quivered. I pressed my face against the rock so that Doug could not see.

All was silent. A pebble fell from the ledge on which I was squeezed. I counted seconds before it hit below with a faint, faraway tinkling sound. Would Doug drop through the same space? Would I follow? When you fall eight hundred feet do you die before you hit the bottom? Closing my eyes, I asked God to help Doug up the wall.

In a second Doug said in a cheery voice, "Well, here goes."

A false bravado took hold of us. I said he could do it. He said he would. He wiped first one hand then the other on his trousers. He placed both palms against the wall, bent his knees slowly, paused a split second, and jumped straight up. It was not much of a jump — only six inches or so. But that jump by one pressed against a cliff eight hundred feet in the air had daredevil proportions. I held my breath; my heart pounded. The suspense was over at once. Doug made the jump, and in a second was hanging by two hands from a strong, wide ledge. There was no toehold; he would have to hoist himself by his arms alone. He did just that. His body went slowly up as if pulled by some unseen winch. Soon he had the weight of his body above the ledge and was resting on the palms of his hands. He then put his left knee on the ledge, rolled over on his side, and chuckled as he said: "Nothing to it."

A greater disappointment followed. Doug's exploration of the ledge showed he was in a final cul-de-sac. There was no way up. There was not even a higher ledge he could reach by jumping. We were now faced with the nightmare of going down the sheer rock wall. We could not go down frontwards because the ledges were too narrow and the wall too steep. We needed our toes, not our heels, on the rock; and we needed to have our stomachs pressed tightly against it. Then we could perhaps feel our way. But as every rock expert knows, descent of a cliff without ropes is often much more difficult than ascent.

That difficulty was impressed on us by the first move. Doug had to leave the ledge he had reached by jumping. He dared not slide blindly to the skimpy ledge he had just left. I must help him. I must move up the wall and stand closer to him. Though I could not possibly hold his weight, I must exert sufficient pressure to slow up his descent and to direct his toe onto the narrow ledge from which he had just jumped.

I was hanging to the rock like a fly, twelve feet or more to Doug's left. So I inched my way toward him, first dropping to a lower ledge and then climbing to a higher one, using such toeholds as the rock afforded and edging my way crabwise.

When I reached him I said, "I'll help."

Doug lowered himself and hung by his fingers full length. His feet were about six inches above the ledge from which he had jumped. He was now my responsibility. If he dropped without aid or direction he was gone. He could not catch and hold to the scanty ledge. I had little space for maneuvering. The surface on which I stood was not more than three inches wide. My left hand fortunately found an overhead crevasse that gave a solid anchor in case my feet slipped.

I placed my right hand in the small of Doug's back and pressed upward with all my might. "Now you can come," I said.

He let go gently, and the full weight of his body came against my arm. My arm trembled under the tension. My left hand hung onto the crack in the rock like a grappling hook. My stomach pressed against the wall as if to find mucilage in its pores. My toes dug in as I threw in every ounce of strength.

Down Doug came — a full inch. I couldn't help glancing down and seeing the rocks far below.

Down Doug moved another inch, then a third. My left hand seemed paralyzed. The muscles of my toes were aching. My right arm shook. I could not hold much longer.

Down came Doug a fourth inch. I thought he was headed for destruction. His feet would miss the only toehold within reach. I could not possibly hold him. He would plunge to his death because my arm was not strong enough to hold him. The messages he had given me for his family raced through my mind. And I saw myself, sick and ashamed, standing before them, testifying to my own inadequacy, repeating his last words.

I wanted to pray again but there was no time for it.

"Steady, Doug. The ledge is a foot to your right." He pawed the wall with the toes of his foot, searching.

"I can't find it. Don't let go. The only hold I have is with my left hand and it's not much."

The crisis was on us. Even if I had been safely anchored, my cramped position would have kept me from help-ing him much more. I felt helpless. In a few seconds I would reach the physical breaking point and Doug would go hurtling off the cliff. I did not see how I could keep him from slipping through and yet maintain my own balance.

I will never know how I did it. But I tapped some reserve and directed his right foot onto the ledge from which he had earlier jumped. I did it by standing for a moment on my left foot alone and then using my right leg as a rod to guide his right foot to the ledge his swinging feet had missed.

His toes grabbed the ledge as if they were the talons of a bird. My right leg swung back to my perch.

"Are you okay?" I asked.

"Yes," said Doug. "Good work."

My right arm fell from him, numb and paralyzed. I shook from exhaustion and for the first time noticed that my face was wet with perspiration. We stood against the rock in silence for several minutes, relaxing and regaining our composure.

Doug said: "Let's throw our shoes down. It will be easier going." So we untied them from our belt and dropped them to Walter Kohagen, who was waiting at the rock field below us.

Our descent was painfully slow but uneventful. We went down backwards, weaving a strange pattern across the face of the cliff as we moved from one side to the other. It was perhaps mid-afternoon when we reached the bottom, retrieved our shoes, and started around the other side of the rock. We left the southeast wall unconquered.

II

But, being young, we were determined to climb the rock. So once more we started to circle. When we came to the northwest wall, we selected it as our route.

Here, too, is a cliff rising 1,500 feet like some unfinished pyramid. But close examination shows numerous toe- and fingerholds that make the start at least fairly easy. So we set out with our shoes on.

When we were part way up the rock, for a while Doug and I were separated. I worked laterally along a ledge to the south, found easier going, and in a short time was two hundred feet or more up the rock wall. I was above Doug, twenty-five feet or more, and fifty feet to his right. We had been extremely careful to test each toe- and fingerhold before putting our trust in it. Kloochman is full of treacherous rock. We often discovered thin ledges that crumbled under pressure and showered handfuls of rock and dust down below. Perhaps I was careless; but whatever the cause, the thin ledge on which I was standing gave way.

As I felt it slip, I grabbed for a hold above me. The crevasse I seized was solid. But there I was, hanging by my hands two hundred feet in the air, my feet pawing the rock. To make matters worse, my camera had swung between me and the cliff when I slipped. It was a crude and clumsy instrument, a box type that I carried on a leather strap across my shoulders. Its hulk was actually pushing me from the cliff. I twisted in an endeavor to get rid of it, but it was firmly lodged between me and the wall.

I yelled to Doug for help. He at once started edging toward me. It seemed hours, though it was probably not over a few minutes. He shouted: "Hang on. I'll be there."

Hang on I did. My fingers ached beyond description. They were frozen to the rock. My exertion in pawing with my feet had added to the fatigue. The ache of my fingers extended to my wrists and then along my arms. I stopped thrashing and hung like a sack, motionless. Every second seemed a minute, every minute an hour. I did not see how I could possibly hold.

"We picked our route with care and weighed the advantages of several choices . . ." In the challenge of a difficult climb lies a test of one's surefootedness, judgment, and patience — followed by the reward of reaching the summit and looking down over the world that has been conquered. (Black Star)

I would slip, I thought, slip to sure death. I could not look down because of my position. But in my mind's eye I saw in sharp outline the jagged rocks that seemed to pull me toward them. The camera kept pushing my fingers from the ledge. I felt them move. They began to give way before the pull of a force too great for flesh to resist.

Fright grew in me. The idea of hanging helpless two hundred feet above the abyss brought panic. I cried out to Doug but the words caught in my dry throat. I was like one in a nightmare who struggles to shout — who is then seized with a fear that promises to destroy him.

Then there flashed through my mind a family scene. Mother was sitting in the living room talking to me, telling me what a wonderful man Father was. She told me of his last illness and his death. She told me of his departure from Cleveland, Washington, to Portland, Oregon, for what proved to be a fatal operation. His last words to her were: " If I die, it will be glory. If I live, it will be grace."

The panic passed. The memory of those words restored reason. Glory to die? I could not understand why it would be glory to die. It would be glory to live. But as Father said, it might take grace to live, grace from One more powerful than either Doug or I.

And so again that day I prayed. I asked God to give me guts, to give me power to do the impossible.

My fingers were as numb as flesh that is full of novocain. They seemed detached from me, as if they belonged to someone else. My wrists, my shoulders, cried out for respite from the pain. It would be such welcome relief if they could be released from the weight that was on them.

Hang on? You can't hang on. You are a weakling — puny. The weaklings die in the woods.

Puny, eh? I'll show you. Weakling? I'll show you. How long must I hang on? All day? Okay, it's all day then. I'll hang on, I'll hang on. By God, I'll hang on. O God, dear God, help me hang on!

I felt someone pushing my left foot upward. It was Doug. As if through a dream his voice was saying, " Your feet are eighteen inches below your toehold." Doug found those toeholds for my feet.

I felt my shoes resting in solid cracks. I pulled myself up and rested on my elbows on the ledge to which my hands had been glued. I flexed my fingers and bent my wrists to bring life back.

Doug came up abreast of me and said, " We're even Stephen now."

" Even Stephen? "

" Today each of us has saved the other's life."

It was shortly above the point where Doug saved my life that we discovered a classic path up Kloochman. It is a three-sided chimney chute, a few feet wide, that leads almost to the top. There are several small chutes on Kloochman. In later years Cragg Gilbert and Louis Ulrich went up Devil's Chimney on the northeast face in a seven-hour, nerve-racking climb with ropes. Clarence Truitt and many others have gone up the chimney chute that Doug and I discovered. Then as now this chute was filled with loose rock that had to be cleared away. To negotiate the chute we took off our shoes and tied them to our belts. We climbed the chute in stocking feet, pressing our hands and feet against the opposing walls as we kept our backs to the abyss below us. This day we went up the chute with ease, stopping every eight feet or so to measure our progress.

The sun was setting when we reached the top. We were gay and buoyant. We talked about the glories of the scene in front of us. We bragged a bit about our skill in rock work — how we must be part mountain goat to have reached the top. We shouted and hallooed to the empty meadows far below us.

On Kloochman Rock that July afternoon both Doug and I valued life more because death had passed so close. It was wonderful to be alive, breathing, using our muscles, shouting, seeing.

We stayed briefly at the top. We went down as we came up, in stocking feet. We raced against darkness, propelled by the thought of spending the night on Kloochman's treacherous wall.

It was deep dusk when we rejoined Walter on the rock fields at the base.

III

I climbed Kloochman again in the summer of 1948. This time my steps were more cautious and measured than they had been in 1913. There was less dash, less abandon in this adult ascent. I took my ease, feeling my way with care. But the memories of the earlier trip were still fresh in my mind as if it had happened only the previous week instead of thirty-five years ago.

As I climbed, I realized how conservative man becomes in his physical endeavors as he passes his thirties. I was not thinking of wind or stamina, for mine were both good. I was thinking of the subtle forces that control the reflexes. It struck home why only young men make good fighter pilots — how it is that age fast takes the daredevil out of man. There was a thrill in this adult climb, but the reckless, carefree attitude of the earlier day had gone.

Yet I relived the experience of 1913. All the sensations of the earlier trip returned to me. There was the trembling excitement of the start. Doug's messages to his family raced once more through my mind, as if he had just uttered them. I saw Doug make his jump up the side of the cliff while he was eight hundred feet in the air. I saw him hanging on the ledge, doomed to die. I felt the weight of his body against my arm. I felt myself slipping slowly from the rock to destruction. It seemed once more that demons were pulling at my feet with a power too great for flesh and blood to resist. Once again little vestiges of the old fear passed through me.

Those, however, were fleeting sensations. When I came to the top a sense of calm came over me, a deep peace. I knew now what a boy could not know, that fear of death was the compound of all other fears. I knew that long years ago I had begun to shed on Kloochman's walls the great, overpowering fear. Kloochman became for me that day a symbol of adversity and challenge — of the forces that have drawn from man his greatest spiritual and physical achievements.

For Discussion of Douglas

1. How fully did you share the climb and the desperate tests of endurance? Tell physical sensations you actually felt as you read. In what way did the knowledge that this account is true and factual affect your reaction?

2. What did you learn from this narrative about the dangers and special techniques of mountain climbing? (See the vocabulary section that follows.) If there is a mountaineering enthusiast in the class, he can explain how ropes are used by climbers.

3. Which called for the greater courage, Doug's decision to jump for the ledge just out of reach, or the two boys' decision to try another route up the mountain after the first failure? On what reasoning do you base your answer?

4. State in your own words Douglas's idea about the relation of the fear of death to all other fears. Do you agree with him? What is the relation of this belief to his love of mountain climbing?

5. The literature of mountain climbing is a rich and exciting one. If you would like to explore it, try James Ullman's *The Kingdom of Everest* and his novel *The White Tower,* and Douglas's complete book *Of Men and Mountains.*

For Your Vocabulary

TECHNICAL TERMS: Every trade, profession, or business occupation has technical terms, words, or uses of words, peculiar to it. Every sport, also, has its technical terms. In mountain climbing one such term is *cul-de-sac* (kŏol'dē·săk'), a passage with only one outlet, a "blind alley." (This word comes directly from the French and means literally "the bottom of the bag.") *Purchase* (p. 198) means a mechanical advantage applied to the raising of bodies. A *crevasse* (krĕ·văs') is a deep crevice, or cleft. Do you recall any other mountain-climbing terms used by Mr. Douglas?

BIOGRAPHY

American biography has made great strides in the modern age. You can count on the fingers of one hand the great biographies in American literature before 1900 and have at least a thumb left over. In fact, you could easily start an argument about the merits of any book you named after Benjamin Franklin's *Autobiography*. But it would take all your fingers and all your toes to start checking off the notable biographies of the twentieth century. The upsurge is due not so much to a sudden wealth of writers as to new ways of writing biography that have attracted readers interested in the true stories of real people.

Older Types of Biography

In earlier times there were only two main types of biography: first, the scholarly but often dull collection of all the known facts about some important individual, and second, the hero-worshiper's chronicle of some human paragon without a single endearing fault. A familiar example of the second type is Parson Weems's notorious life of George Washington, containing many moral but purely invented tales like the one about the cherry tree. The reaction of readers to this kind of obviously distorted life-story led early in the new century to a wave of "debunking" biographies which, instead of glorifying the subject, went to the opposite extreme and stressed the evidence of his weaknesses and faults. But, like all extremes, this vogue was short-lived.

Distinguished Modern American Biographies

The most distinguished modern American biographers combine the scholar's painstaking care to collect all the known facts about his subject with the modern writer's care to organize his material effectively and tell his story interestingly. These two characteristics are found in such literary landmarks as Carl Sandburg's *Abraham Lincoln* and Douglas Southall Freeman's *R. E. Lee*. The thorough marshaling and careful weighing of evidence in such great works make them documents that will be treasured by future generations. Through them, the events and men of specific times are brought memorably alive. You will appreciate this quality when you read Sandburg's narrative of Lincoln's Gettysburg address (pp. 213–22).

Popular Biographies

Although these great biographies hold rich rewards, most people prefer the life-story told more rapidly. Many excellent one-volume biographies are available today. It is possible to find a good one on any famous American statesman or general or scientist or poet or inventor — in fact, on any American of note or special interest, from Babe Ruth to Einstein. Many of these books follow the general method of telling only what is well supported by reliable evidence. The desire to make the narratives real, however, has led to a recent development that has proved highly popular, the fictionalized biography, in which the author allows himself some of the privileges of the novelist in inventing minor incidents, conversation, feelings, and thoughts. When the biographer has studied all available information about his subject and then shapes it with fictional elements that are thoroughly consistent with the known character, the result is a particularly vivid portrait. *The Song of Bernadette* by Franz Werfel (which is reviewed on pp. 180–83) is an admirable example of this type of fictional biography.

Variety in Autobiography

At one time, only a famous person could expect to find many readers for his autobiography. Nowadays anyone who has an interesting life-story to tell and can tell it entertainingly will probably be read. The inside story of a successful career can be absorbing, as you will discover in reading Cornelia Otis Skinner's narrative of her early skirmishes with the theater (pp. 206–12) or Lincoln Steffens's account of his initiation into journalism (pp. 237–43).

In these troubled times autobiography which reveals a soul's search for truth and spiritual satisfaction is very popular. Frances Parkinson Keyes' "Along a Little Way" (pp. 229–36) is of this type. Still another type of modern autobiography is a collection of personal or reminiscent essays, similar to those by Clarence Day and Thomas Wolfe that you

have read. Thomas Merton's recollection of his first days in a Trappist abbey (pp. 223–29) well illustrates the style of the personal essay.

On Reading Biography

Your own reading of biography will gain in interest if you remember that the author's purpose will influence your own reactions. If you realize that a thorough student of the subject is presenting all the known evidence, you will not become impatient because the narrative proceeds slowly or be puzzled by the introduction of contradictory bits of evidence. If the story is presented with fictional trimmings, you will understand that some parts of the narrative do not pretend to be actual reports of happenings but are introduced only to make the people of the story more real and understandable. Similarly, in reading autobiography, prompt recognition of the author's purpose speeds reading and heightens enjoyment, whether the focus is on the building of a career, participation in significant events, intimate views of prominent people, or plain joy in living.

Recognizing and responding to the author's tone is as great a help in reading biography as in reading essays. Biography offers less variety of tone, because most of the good books in the field are committed to a serious presentation of the subject. But autobiography runs the whole gamut from gay mockery to intense earnestness. The purpose may determine the tone. An account of a year in a wartime concentration camp, for example, would naturally be serious in tone. But many writers prefer to take a light tone about their own experiences, even their trials and their triumphs. In that case, you will be reminded that entertainment of the reader is a major purpose of autobiography, whatever information or challenging ideas may be presented.

The Family Trade

CORNELIA OTIS SKINNER
1901–

Cornelia Otis Skinner's parents were both actors. Her mother gave up a promising career shortly after she married, and her father, Otis Skinner, enjoyed popular acclaim throughout his many years on the stage. It was natural that the daughter should turn to the theater. Under her father's guidance she received the best of training, climaxed by study in France at the Sorbonne and with members of the Comédie Française, a famous Parisian theatrical company.

But Cornelia was not content merely to follow in her father's footsteps. After performing for a few years in conventional plays she became interested in solo drama — short plays in which a single actor appears — and developed it to a stage of high artistry. She has delighted all America with programs of individual interpretations written and acted solely by herself. Like her " matinee idol " father, she is a real trouper and likes to cover the whole country and meet all kinds of people in her tours.

In recent years, Miss Skinner has made a new career of writing personal essays and reminiscences, which appear in many of our best magazines and have been collected in book form. *That's Me All Over* is a good volume to start with, and you would also enjoy *Our Hearts Were Young and Gay,* written in collaboration with her girlhood friend, Emily Kimbrough. The autobiographical *Family Circle,* from which the following is taken, is not only an account of her early life but also a delightful picture of a charming family. In reading Miss Skinner's own account of the first steps in her stage career, you will take special pleasure in noticing the attitudes she reveals toward her mother and her father, toward herself, and toward her future as an actress. Notice the pattern she uses in the opening paragraph. It is a nice trick of style that you can use yourself with good effect.

I T IS part of the autobiographical formula for an author to tell of the particular incident which gave him a clairvoyant vista of his future career — the politician and his class-day oration, the sculptor whose childish mud pie suddenly turned into a likeness of his mother, the physician as a barefoot lad spearing a worm with a fishhook and realizing his calling would be abdominal surgery. In regard to acting, I had no such moment of revelation. In spite of Mother's often repeated refrain of no, indeed, her daughter was never going on the stage, I always knew, privately and simply, that I was. I was neither stage-struck nor dazzled by any delusions of what theatrical life never turns out to be, and certainly I did not experience (and never have) that happy sense of dedication to ART which press agents like to convey to be the chronic emotional state of actresses. No supernatural voices bade me come save the spoken drama and I entertained no belief that my emergence into the theatrical arena

"The Family Trade" from *Family Circle* by Cornelia Otis Skinner. Reprinted by permission of Houghton Mifflin, publishers.

would cause Ethel Barrymore or Mrs. Fiske [1] any great uneasiness. I merely knew that I wanted to act.

My only chance for venting the urge was with the Baldwin School Dramatic Club which proved its earnest worth by giving one Shakespearean play a year. Mother, a good friend of the school and the adored of the faculty, was always asked to stage the annual production. She did it, of course, beautifully, cutting the text, designing the costumes, directing the performance, and generally reducing herself to a bundle of nerves. What nearly defeated her was correcting the heterogeneous accents of the cast which hailed from all over the U.S.A., gently informing the girl from Chattanooga that *can't* does not rhyme with *paint* and the girl from Philadelphia that a *garden* is much prettier when it's not a *gorrrden*. She must have written Father of her trials, for in one of his letters he indulgently chides her for wasting her time " plugging away at those little nasal Baldwin dubs — the daughters of the Great American R which gathers force as it rolls across the Midwestern plains."

Because I was tall and angularly shapeless and had access to Father's costume trunks, I was usually the leading man. As Petruchio [2] I strutted in Father's boots, periodically walking out of them. As Orlando,[3] a leather jerkin which had once belonged to Booth [4] was apprehensively placed upon me with strict instructions I was to take it off during the ice-cream party after the show. In that *As You Like It* production, the part of Charles the Wrestler was in the untried hands of my roommate, a big and genial Irish girl by the name of Lib

Donohue. Choosing her to play the Elizabethan Strangler Lewis was a case of type-casting only as far as her bulk was concerned, for her personality was anything but menacing. Her voice was extremely soft and high-pitched and she had an engaging grin which turned into an uncontrollable giggle whenever she started rehearsing her scene. Mother did her best with her, cut her speeches down to a single line, and the night of the performance achieved on her a triumph of costuming and make-up. Her amiable face was disguised with rustic tan grease paint, beetling eyebrows, and a bushy beard. A shaggy wig, many sizes too large for her, was fitted to her head with a tuck and a safety pin. Her legs were painted brown and she wore a tunic of burlap. A leopard skin swinging fiercely from her shoulders put the finishing Herculean touch to her savage aspect. She took one look at herself in the mirror and froze with fright. Her already gentle voice weakened into inaudibility. Lib's mother, sister, and aunt had journeyed over from Bound Brook, New Jersey, and were sitting in the front row awaiting her dramatic debut with happy anticipation.

The play went on. Lib made her entrance and none of the Donohue clan knew her. Nor did they recognize her when she spoke her one line, for although they were only a few feet away, not one of them could hear her. The wrestling match started and Lib, realizing she had not come through vocally, began to retrieve herself physically. Under the dubiously authoritative instruction of the gym teacher, we had practiced a few wrestling holds which Lib, now in a revolt of brave independence, completely disregarded. Seizing me by waist and shoulder, she flung me to one side, grabbed my wrist as I shot past as in a movement of a wild Virginia Reel, and hurtled me to the other side. I struggled frantically to remain upright. I pushed, I pinched, I tried to trip her, to

[1] **Ethel Barrymore, Mrs. Fiske:** famous actresses of that day. Miss Barrymore, sister of John and Lionel, is still active on the stage.

[2] **Petruchio** (pĕ·troo'kĭ·ō): hero of Shakespeare's *The Taming of the Shrew*.

[3] **Orlando:** the romantic hero of Shakespeare's *As You Like It*.

[4] **Booth:** Edwin Booth, a celebrated nineteenth-century Shakespearean actor.

tickle her — anything to make her let go. Finally, when she had got me clamped in a sort of bear hold, I managed to pant in her ear that she must let me pretend to throw her — the plot of the play hinged on it! — the reputation of the Dramatic Club! — the honor of Baldwin! This last appeal to her inner integrity worked, and with a certain amount of reluctance she disintegrated in a swift, backward collapse. At that moment, her wig flew off, soared over the footlights, and landed at the feet of Mrs. Donohue, who during the space of the audience's gasp of astonishment came out with a loud " Mercy! That man's Elizabeth! "

The selection of the play each year was made at the close of spring term by the forthcoming president. When I had been elected to that position of distinction, I settled on *Macbeth*. It seemed a quaint project for a girl's school, what with Lady Macbeth the only woman in the piece, Lady Macduff being usually cut, and the sex of the three witches being doubtful. But such obstacles in no way daunted me. I had a burning desire to play Lady Macbeth and I silenced any questions as to the incongruity of a cast of primitive Scot warriors being impersonated by a bunch of Junior Misses, with the smugly cultural observation that in Shakespeare's time Ophelia and Juliet had been played by boys. The role of tragedy's most sinister heroine fitted in with my exotic picture of myself. I would, I planned, dedicate the vacation months to a profound study of the part.

We spent that summer in Colorado at Enos Mills's Long's Peak Inn. Days I was not riding, I studied Lady Macbeth. Father, with patient indulgence, and, I suspect, a fair amount of carefully concealed amusement, helped coach me. For purposes of privacy we'd go a short distance from the Inn to a small steep hill on the summit of which was an ideal hide-out, a flat space, boulder-encircled, where there was no one to see or hear us except blue jays and chipmunks and

one beady-eyed old marmot. Sometimes I worked alone. Father had told me that a part must always be studied aloud, at full tone. His specific instructions were, " Take the pins out of your diaphragm, Kiddie, and let 'er rip! " And I obeyed him to the best of my vocal capacity, feeling very inspired indeed.

Macbeth was the big event of the following school year. It looked at one time as though the performance would have to be called off owing to the fact that twenty-four hours beforehand, the girl playing Macduff, a lass from Savannah, Georgia, who sounded less like the Thane of Fife than the Little Colonel, came down with mumps. But the day was saved by the young thing cast as the Bleeding Sergeant who rushed forth with the news that she knew the lines of Macduff and if anyone could take her place on the gory army cot, she'd go on in the part. The girl was short, plump, and pretty. Her eyes were a clear blue and her hair a shimmering mane of genuine platinum blond. She was hardly the ideal of a Highland war lord, but we camouflaged her as best we could with a horn-trimmed helmet, a bearskin hearth rug, and a Viking mustache. She was not only letter-perfect in the lines, but she gave evidence of great talent. One extraordinary thing about her was her voice, which she could turn from a tone soft, gentle, and low into a basso profundo [1] bellow. That night she unleashed its full diapason, her impersonation was remarkable, and she saved the situation for everyone. But in doing so she strained a vocal cord and claims it was the cause of a certain throatiness which is still one of her most attractive characteristics. The name of that girl is Ann Harding. [2]

---

[1] **basso profundo** (bàs'ō prŏ·fŭn'dō): a deep, heavy bass voice.

[2] **Ann Harding:** a star of the movies in the 1925–40 period and now occasionally seen on television, well known for her husky yet gentle voice.

Those happy amateur days! And that delirious amateur confidence! My Lady Macbeth must have been terrible, but at the time I was completely charmed with it. Long after the actual performance, I continued to recite the Sleepwalking scene at the drop of a hat, or even without that much encouragement. Julia Marlowe,[1] I felt, had better start looking to her laurels and I had better start preparing for the stage. I had yet to broach the family about it, but a performance of *Within the Law* with Helen Ware gave me the impulse to write Father about my ambitions. This was his reply:

Maiden Mine:

I rejoice that your week end brought you such joys as marshmallow breakfasts and *Within the Law.* Your question regarding Helen Ware startled me a little. Are you going to be an actress? I was hoping you *wouldn't.* But if you *are* there is a long time yet; and the one thing that will put you ahead of others on the stage will be the soundness of a good education, and the mental training your studies will give you. I have often regretted deeply that my own schooling was not more thorough: it would have made things much easier for me.

You speak of Helen Ware — she was a schoolteacher before she became an actress. The road from the bottom where she started up to her stellar position in *Within the Law* was a long and hard one.

If that is the road you are thinking to take, you must prepare yourself for it in these present years. Every bit of good work you do now will be of inestimable help. Your knowledge of languages will refine and render beautiful your use of English. Your history will enable you to estimate the subtleties of drama; even your abhorred algebra will give you a grip and a poise in your mental ability to meet the tough situations of character portrayal. It all *helps beyond words.*

Above everything, don't neglect your

[1] Julia Marlowe: a famous actress of the early twentieth century, who, with her husband, Edward Southern, often starred in Shakespearean plays.

voice. Start in just as soon as you read this and listen to every word you speak. Let your vocal teacher tell you where your voice comes from and how your tones are produced. If I had known these things in the beginning of my career it would have saved me thousands of dollars in doctor's bills. I have had to find out through the years, alone and unaided. I know *now,* but think what I could have saved by an early knowledge of vocalization.

And *sing!* Sing your little head off!!! You cannot realize, daughter mine, what wealth will be added to your speaking voice by a complete knowledge of singing even though your profession doesn't require you to sing a note. And know the *best* in music. Not the cheapest — know the best in literature. That is the sort of training the great ones of the French stage have gone through and the French are the greatest actors in the world today.

It was the *voix d'or*[2] of Sarah Bernhardt that gave her the mightiest asset of her career.

Your voice, first, last and always. YOUR VOICE!!

Your Daddy's love, dearest Daughter.

So, reluctantly, I resigned myself to trying a year of college, God willing and pushing me through the entrance exams. It would be pleasant to be able to say that I sailed into Bryn Mawr with flying colors. But when I finally managed to squeeze in, the only color I exhibited was a red failure mark in algebra, a subject which remained a condition throughout my brief academic career.

I am glad that I went to college, and glad that I stayed for only two years. It gave me much to be thankful for and quite a good deal which it took some time to get over. It would be untrue to say that the Bryn Mawr atmosphere in those days was one of intellectual snobbishness. But there was, among the Big Shots, a youthful assurance, a bland acceptance of the fact that they were the elect — of what, they themselves couldn't have said. We ourselves were somewhat

[2] *voix d'or* (vwä dôr): golden voice (French).

aware of this attitude, and one of our own popular campus songs satirically sung to a Gregorian chant expressed it to a nicety in its solemn refrain of "We are the Leaders." The standard ideal was to be athletic, studious (to a temperate degree), and splendidly clear-eyed. The improvement of our minds was no more important than that of our bodies or our souls, and scholarship went hand in hand with hockey and chapel. Miss Bryn Mawr was the wholesome American peach, good at studies and sports, determinedly fair-minded, and bravely guiltless of make-up. She was typified by the girl who, selected as the best all-round jolly-good person of the year was awarded a prize known, I regret to say, as the "Sunny Jim," a distinction rating as much local publicity as the European Fellowship given for academic excellence.

My brief college career was not brilliant. I was not the splendid all-round type. I avoided most rah-rah activities and I attended chapel only because I sang in the choir, a duty I found not only agreeable but remunerative, as it paid a salary of fourteen dollars a semester. I savagely loathed all organized exercise, a certain amount of which was compulsory, and wasted a lot of valuable hours trying resentfully and vainly to find my athletic niche. But Bryn Mawr offered plenty of other advantages far more agreeable than those of an Atalantean [1] nature. I found a number of amusing and stimulating acquaintances and made a few warm friendships which have lasted a lifetime. And best of all, there was, for me, a gradual coming to life in regard to matters of the mind. The dark clouds of adolescent mental apathy slowly began to disperse and there started to dawn the revelation of intel-

[1] **Atalantean** (ăt′á·lăn′tĕ·án): of the nature of Atalanta, a fleet-footed maiden in Greek mythology, who challenged her suitors to a footrace, with the suitors' lives staked against her hand in marriage.

lectual adventure. Not, God knows, that I ever became any sort of scholar, but I discovered that a world I had hitherto dismissed as pedantic and dull could be rich and exciting. Browsing amid the stacks in the library, or sitting comfortably in the great dim Gothic reading room, with a pile of books beside me, I realized the amenities of research. Having no intentions of graduating, I had postponed all required courses I considered unsympathetic until a junior year which I knew would never materialize, and went in solely for the studies I liked. What specifically I learned, I couldn't say, but I recall with grateful warmth my instructors and the subjects they imbued with such vitality.

And college offered opportunity for venting my yearning to act. There were class shows and varsity dramatics, and one spring the May Day Fete was held. The big festival that year was staged by my mother and I believe it was the loveliest and most imaginative production ever seen at Bryn Mawr.

I spent my sophomore year on bounds as punishment for having cut all classes the last few weeks of freshman term. It was a penance in which I rather gloried, for I had taken the cuts in order to fill my first theatrical engagement. It was only a four-week engagement (two of which were taken up by rehearsals), but it gave me an excuse for calling myself an actress, although it is doubtful if anyone else would have done so. George Tyler had taken the National Theatre in Washington in an experimental stock venture for trying out a number of new plays. As it was his intention to bring them into New York the following season, they were all pretty well finished productions with top-notch casts. A nucleus of competent actors was kept as a permanent company for supporting parts while the leads were played by a series of visiting stars — Helen Hayes, Emily Stevens, and oth-

*Cornelia Otis Skinner
and her famous actor
father (Wide World)*

ers. The Lunts [1] came there, too. Only they weren't the Lunts then. It was at this engagement that Miss Fontanne and Mr. Lunt met and soon afterward started that partnership which has proved so felicitous for the English-speaking world. They appeared in two of the try-outs in which I too was to be seen; that is, if one looked quickly enough.

In Richard Washburn Child's *Made of Money*, I was discovered at the rise of the first-act curtain, arranging some roses in a vase. A comedy butler, excellently done by Sidney Toller, entered, looking glum, and I spoke my only line, which was " What's the matter now? " He made some sort of reply after which I said " Oh," turned, and exited up-back-left. The " Oh " was my own gratuitous pad-

[1] **The Lunts:** Alfred and Lynn Fontanne Lunt, a renowned contemporary acting team.

ding of the part. This opening bit, of course, was over before half the audience had settled into their seats, but to judge by the earnestness with which I approached it, it might have been the big scene from *Zaza*.[2] I put my all into that single speech, elaborating it by preceding it with a humorous " Ho-hum! " and winding it up with a curious sound I endeavored to make into a ripple of laughter. I worked up fancy bits of business such as burying my nose in one of the roses and sniffing ecstatically. The dye in the cloth petals gave forth a vile smell and a deposit of property-room dust made me have to struggle not to sneeze, but in the service of Art such

[2] **Zaza:** a grand opera by Ruggiero Leoncavallo, produced in Milan in 1900, and also produced as a play. It is the story of Zaza, a music hall singer, and her tragic love affair with a married man.

slight discomforts were to be ignored. In an ensuing act laid in a beauty parlor, I came on as a manicurist and worked industriously on Lynn Fontanne's fingernails, while a hairdresser, a real one, gave her a genuine marcel. The only person to be impressed with my characterization was the hairdresser, who offered me a job in his salon across the street.

The next play, *A Young Man's Fancy*, in which Jeanne Eagels later starred, was a rather nice whimsy about a youth who falls in love with a dummy in a shop window. The curtain rose on a shallow set representing a pavement outside a store front which had a window display of sports clothes modeled by a number of wax ladies and gentlemen foregathered in what appeared to be a portion of a Country Club. Lynn was a wax lady and Alfred was the flesh-and-blood young man who, observing her through plate glass, fell in love with her. I too was a wax lady. Only no one fell in love with me. Not even a wax gentleman. I was one of the small group at the back standing about an undersized tea table. There was a short but uncomfortable scene during which Alfred, out on the pavement, confided his infatuation to a friend, while we dummies stood frozen in attitudes of quaking immobility; then the transparency lifted, the set widened out into a realistic lawn and porch, and we all, mercifully, came to life. I had some three or four lines. What they were, I have no recollection, but I still cherish the memory of the ad lib remark of an actor named Cushman who played one of the wax society men and who, having been directed at one point to stroll over to me, turn upstage, and engage me in polite *sotto-voce* [1] chitchat, always at each and every performance came out with the elegant observation, "About this time of the afternoon I always prefer a nut sundae."

[1] *sotto-voce* (sôt′tô-vō′chå): in an undertone.

My salary was thirty-five dollars a week. I was barely eighteen and Mother considered it necessary to go along with me. We took a minimum-rate room at the old Shoreham and ate our meals at a dairy-lunch counter, but my pay hardly sufficed, and Father, who was in California at the time, sent Mother a check " to defray the expense of our daughter earning her own living. Never fear," he goes on, " Father will stand the gaff! It is all very funny and too good to keep, so to the dozens of enquirers out here who daily ask me ' How is Mrs. Skinner and what is the Daughter doing?' I reply ' Doing? Why, doing Father of course!'"

For Discussion of Skinner

1. See how accurately you can state Miss Skinner's attitude toward her acting career. What is the pattern she uses in making it clear? Try using this pattern in explaining the modest aims of a high-school student going out for football or trying out for the orchestra.

2. What evidence did you find of Miss Skinner's appreciation of her mother? of her father? From which parent do you think she got her sense of humor? On what evidence in the autobiography do you base your choice?

3. What does the letter from her father contribute to your impression of him? Summarize his advice on training to be an actor.

4. How did the problems encountered in producing the Baldwin school plays compare with the ones encountered in your own school? What faults of pronunciation that plagued Mrs. Skinner are ones your group needs to guard against? What others would probably give trouble?

5. Does the picture of Miss Skinner's college days give you more or less desire to go to college? Weigh the evidence she gives for each side.

6. Describe her first professional roles and her attempt to make the most of them. How is her treatment of this experience typical of her attitude toward her achievements?

CARL SANDBURG
1878–

Lincoln Speaks at Gettysburg

Carl Sandburg, whose six-volume life of Lincoln is one of the greatest biographies in American literature, had already made his reputation as a poet (see pp. 278–84) before *Abraham Lincoln: The Prairie Years* appeared in 1926. In 1939 he completed the series with *Abraham Lincoln: The War Years.* Through his busy years as poet, journalist, lecturer, and ballad-collector, Sandburg had been steadily gathering all available information about Lincoln. In dealing with evidence he is as careful as any professor of history, but the interpre-

tative passages in his biography could have been written only by a poet.

As you read Sandburg's narrative of the events surrounding Lincoln's classic speech, you have an excellent opportunity to observe how bits of information from various sources are woven together into a smooth narrative. Do not be confused by occasional contradictory reports that are included here. Try to understand why the witnesses who are quoted received different impressions as they stood on the battlefield that day in November, 1863.

A PRINTED invitation came to Lincoln's hands notifying him that on Thursday, November 19, 1863, exercises would be held for the dedication of a National Soldiers' Cemetery at Gettysburg. The same circular invitation had been mailed to Senators, Congressmen, the governors of Northern states, members of the cabinet, by the commission of Pennsylvanians who had organized a corporation through which Maine, New Hampshire, Vermont, Massachusetts, Rhode Island, Maryland, Connecticut, New York, New Jersey, Pennsylvania, Delaware, West Virginia, Ohio, Indiana, Illinois, Michigan, Wisconsin, and Minnesota were to share the cost of a decent burying ground for the dust and bones of the Union and Confederate dead.

In the helpless onrush of the war, it

was known, too many of the fallen had lain as neglected cadavers rotting in the open fields or thrust into so shallow a resting place that a common farm plow caught in their bones. Now by order of Governor Curtin of Pennsylvania seventeen acres had been purchased on Cemetery Hill, where the Union center stood its colors on the second and third of July, and plots of soil had been allotted each state for its graves.

The sacred and delicate duties of orator of the day had fallen on Edward Everett. An eminent cultural figure, perhaps foremost of all distinguished American classical orators, he was born in 1794, had been United States Senator, Governor of Massachusetts, member of Congress, Secretary of State under Fillmore, minister to Great Britain, Phi Beta

Kappa poet at Harvard, professor of Greek at Harvard, president of Harvard.

The Union of States was a holy concept to Everett, and the slavery issue secondary, though when president of Harvard from 1846 to 1849 he refused to draw the color line, saying in the case of a Negro applicant, Beverley Williams, that admission to Harvard College depended on examinations. " If this boy passes the examinations, he will be admitted; and if the white students choose to withdraw, all the income of the college will be devoted to his education." Not often was he so provocative.

Serene, suave, handsomely venerable in his sixty-ninth year, a prominent specimen of Northern upper-class distinction, Everett was a natural choice of the Pennsylvania commissioners, who sought an orator for a solemn national occasion. When in September they notified him that the date of the occasion would be October 23, he replied that he would need more time for preparation, and the dedication was postponed till November 19.

Lincoln meanwhile, in reply to the printed circular invitation, sent word to the commissioners that he would be present at the ceremonies. This made it necessary for the commissioners to consider whether the President should be asked to deliver an address when present. Clark E. Carr, of Galesburg, Illinois, representing his state on the Board of Commissioners, noted that the decision of the board to invite Lincoln to speak was an afterthought.

The question was raised as to his ability to speak upon such a grave and solemn occasion. Besides, it was said that, with his important duties and responsibilities, he could not possibly have the leisure to prepare an address. In answer it was urged that he himself, better than anyone else, could determine as to these questions, and that, if he were invited to speak, he was sure to do what, under the circumstances, would be right and proper.

And so on November 2 David Wills of Gettysburg, as the special agent of Governor Curtin and also acting for the several states, by letter informed Lincoln that the several states having soldiers in the Army of the Potomac who were killed, or had since died at hospitals in the vicinity, had procured grounds for a cemetery and proper burial of their dead.

These grounds will be consecrated and set apart to this sacred purpose by appropriate ceremonies on Thursday, the 19th instant. I am authorized by the Governors of the various States to invite you to be present and participate in these ceremonies, which will doubtless be very imposing and solemnly impressive. It is the desire that after the oration, you, as Chief Executive of the nation, formally set apart these grounds to their sacred use by a few appropriate remarks.

Mr. Wills proceeded farther as to the solemnity of the occasion, and when Lincoln had finished reading the letter he understood definitely that the event called for no humor and that a long speech was not expected of him.

The invitation [wrote Clark E. Carr] was not settled upon and sent to Mr. Lincoln until the second of November, more than six weeks after Mr. Everett had been invited to speak, and but little more than two weeks before the exercises were held.

Lamon noted that Lincoln wrote part of his intended Gettysburg address at Washington, covered a sheet of foolscap paper with a memorandum of it, and before taking it out of his hat and reading it to Lamon he said that it was not at all satisfactory to him, that he was afraid he would not do himself credit nor come up to public expectation. He had been too busy to give it the time he would like to.

Various definite motives besides vague intuitions may have guided Lincoln in his decision to attend and speak even though half his cabinet had sent formal declinations in response to the printed circular invitations they had all received. Though the Gettysburg dedication was to be under interstate auspices, it had tremendous national significance for Lincoln because on the platform would be the state governors whose co-operation with him was of vast importance. Also a slander and a libel had been widely mouthed and printed that on his visit to the battlefield of Antietam nearly a year before he had laughed obscenely at his own funny stories and called on Lamon to sing a cheap comic song. Perhaps he might go to Gettysburg and let it be seen how he demeaned himself on a somber landscape of sacrifice.

His personal touch with Gettysburg, by telegraph, mail, courier, and by a throng of associations, made it a place of great realities to him. Just after the battle there, a woman had come to his office, the doorman saying she had been " crying and taking on " for several days trying to see the President. Her husband and three sons were in the army. On part of her husband's pay she had lived for a time, till money from him stopped coming. She was hard put to scrape a living and needed one of her boys to help.

The President listened to her, standing at a fireplace, hands behind him, head bowed, motionless. The woman finished her plea for one of her three sons in the army. He spoke. Slowly and almost as if talking to himself alone the words came and only those words:

" I have two, and you have none."

He crossed the room, wrote an order for the military discharge of one of her sons. On a special sheet of paper he wrote full and detailed instructions where to go and what to say in order to get her boy back.

In a few days the doorman told the President that the same woman was again on hand crying and taking on. "Let her in," was the word. She had found doors opening to her and officials ready to help on seeing the President's written words she carried. She had located her boy, camp, regiment, company. She had found him, yes, wounded at Gettysburg, dying in a hospital, and had followed him to the grave. And, she begged, would the President now give her the next of her boys?

As before he stood at the fireplace, hands behind him, head bent low, motionless. Slowly and almost as if talking to himself alone the words came and as before only those words:

" I have two, and you have none."

He crossed the room to his desk and began writing. As though nothing else was to do she followed, stood by his chair as he wrote, put her hand on the President's head, smoothed his thick and disorderly hair with motherly fingers. He signed an order giving her the next of her boys, stood up, put the priceless paper in her hands as he choked out the one word, " There! " and with long quick steps was gone from the room with her sobs and cries of thanks in his ears.

Thus the Kentuckian, James Speed, gathered the incident and told it. By many strange ways Gettysburg was to Lincoln a fact in crimson mist.

When Lincoln boarded the train for Gettysburg on November 18, his best chum in the world, Tad, lay sick abed and the doctors were not sure what ailed him. The mother still remembered Willie [1] and was hysterical about Tad. But the President felt imperative duty called him to Gettysburg.

Provost Marshal General James B. Fry as a War Department escort came to the White House, but the President was late in getting into the carriage for the drive to the station. They had no time to lose, Fry remarked. Lincoln said he felt like an Illinois man who was going to be hanged and as the man passed along the road on the way to the gallows the crowds kept pushing into the way and blocking passage. The condemned man

---

[1] **Willie:** a son who had died in 1862.

at last called out, "Boys, you needn't be in such a hurry to get ahead; there won't be any fun till I get there."

Flags and red-white-and-blue bunting decorated the four-car special train. Aboard were the three cabinet members, Nicolay and Hay, army and navy representatives, newspapermen, the French and Italian ministers and attachés. The rear third of the last coach had a drawing room, where from time to time the President talked with nearly everyone aboard as they came and went. Henry Clay Cochrane, lieutenant of marines, noted:

I happened to have a New York *Herald* and offered it to Mr. Lincoln. He took it and thanked me, saying, "I like to see what they say about us." The news was about Burnside at Knoxville, Grant and Sherman at Chattanooga, and Meade on the Rapidan, all expecting trouble. He read for a little while and then began to laugh at some wild guesses of the paper about pending movements. It was pleasant to see his sad face lighted up. He was looking sallow, sunken-eyed, thin, careworn, and very quiet. He returned the paper, remarking among other things that when he had first passed over that road on his way to Congress in 1847 he noticed square-rigged vessels up the Patapsco River as far as the Relay House and now there seemed to be only small craft.

At the Calvert Street Station, Secretary Seward began to get uneasy as we approached Baltimore. Upon reaching the Calvert Street Station in Baltimore all was quiet, less than two hundred people assembled, among them women with children in arms. They called for the President. He took two or three of the babies up and kissed them, which greatly pleased the mothers. General Schenck and staff joined us and soon after the President went forward in the car and seated himself with a party of choice spirits, among whom was Major Frederick W. Lincoln of Boston, not a kinsman. They told stories for an hour or so, Mr. Lincoln taking his turn and enjoying it. Approaching Hanover Junction, he arose and said, "Gentlemen, this is all very pleasant, but the people will expect me to say something to them tomorrow, and I must give the matter some thought." He then returned to the rear room of the car.

At sundown the train pulled into Gettysburg and Lincoln was driven to the Wills residence, Seward to the Harper home fronting on the public square. A sleepy little country town of 3,500 was overflowing with human pulses again. Private homes were filled with notables and nondescripts. Hundreds slept on the floors of hotels. Military bands blared till late in the night serenading whomsoever. The weather was mild and the moon up for those who chose to go a-roaming. When serenaders called on the President for the speech, he made again one of those little addresses saying there was nothing to say. "In my position it is sometimes important that I should not say foolish things. [A voice: "If you can help it."] It very often happens that the only way to help it is to say nothing at all. Believing that is my present condition this evening, I must beg of you to excuse me from addressing you further."

The crowd didn't feel it was much of a speech. They went next door with the band and blared for Seward. He spoke so low that Hay could not hear him, but he opened the stopgaps of patriotic sentiment, saying in part, "I thank my God for the hope that this is the last fratricidal war which will fall upon the country which is vouchsafed to us by Heaven — the richest, the broadest, the most beautiful, the most magnificent, and capable of a greater destiny than has ever been given to any part of the human race." What more could a holiday crowd ask for on a fair night of moonlit November? Seward gave them more and closed: "Fellow citizens, good night." It was good night for him but not for them. They serenaded five other speakers.

At dinner in the Wills home that evening Lincoln met Edward Everett, a guest under the same roof, and Governor Curtin and others. About ten o'clock he was in his room, with paper and pencil ready to write, when he sent a colored servant down for Judge Wills to come up. Still later, about eleven o'clock, he sent the colored servant down again for Judge Wills, who came up and heard Lincoln request to see Mr. Seward. Judge Wills offered to go and bring Seward from next door at the Harpers'. "No, I'll go and see him," said Lincoln, who gathered his sheets of paper and went for a half-hour with his Secretary of State.

Whether Seward made slight or material alterations in the text on the sheets was known only to Lincoln and Seward. It was midnight or later that Lincoln went to sleep, probably perfectly clear in his mind as to what his speech would be the next day. The one certainty was that his "few appropriate remarks," good or bad, would go to an immense audience. Also he slept better for having a telegram from Stanton reporting there was no real war news and "On inquiry Mrs. Lincoln informs me that your son is better this evening."

Fifteen thousand, some said thirty thousand or fifty thousand people were on Cemetery Hill for the exercises the next day when the procession from Gettysburg arrived afoot and horseback representing the United States Government, the army and navy, governors of states, mayors of cities, a regiment of troops, hospital corps, telegraph-company representatives, Knights Templar, Masonic Fraternity, Odd Fellows, and other benevolent associations, the press, fire departments, citizens of Pennsylvania and other states. They were scheduled to start at ten o'clock, and at that hour on the clock Lincoln in a black suit, high silk hat, and white gloves came out of the Wills residence and mounted a horse. A crowd was on hand and he held a reception on horseback. At eleven the parade began to move. The President's horse seemed small for him, as some looked at it. Clark E. Carr, just be-

hind the President, believed he noticed that the President sat erect and looked majestic to begin with and then got to thinking so that his body leaned forward, his arms hung limp, and his head bent far down.

A long telegram sent by Stanton at ten o'clock from Washington had been handed him. Burnside seemed safe though threatened at Knoxville, Grant was starting a big battle at Chattanooga, and "Mrs. Lincoln reports your son's health as a great deal better and he will be out today."

The march of the procession of military and civic bodies began. "Mr. Lincoln was mounted upon a young and beautiful chestnut horse, the largest horse, the largest in the Cumberland Valley," wrote Lieutenant Cochrane. This seemed the first occasion that anyone had looked at the President mounted with a feeling that just the right horse had been picked to match his physical length. "His towering figure surmounted by a high silk hat made the rest of us look small," thought Cochrane.

Minute guns spoke while the procession moved along Baltimore Street to the Emmittsburg Road, then by way of the Taneytown Road to the cemetery, where troop lines stood in salute to the President.

The march was over in fifteen minutes. But Mr. Everett, the orator of the day, had not arrived. Bands played till noon. Mr. Everett arrived.

The United States House chaplain, the Reverend Thomas H. Stockton, offered a prayer while the thousands stood with uncovered heads.

Benjamin B. French, officer in charge of buildings in Washington, introduced the Honorable Edward Everett, orator of the day, who rose, bowed low to Lincoln, saying, "Mr. President." Lincoln responded, "Mr. Everett."

The orator of the day then stood in silence before a crowd that stretched to limits that would test his voice. Beyond and around were the wheat fields, the meadows, the peach orchards, long slopes of land, and five and seven miles farther the contemplative blue ridge of a low mountain range. His eyes could sweep them as he faced the audience. He had taken note of it in his prepared and rehearsed address.

Overlooking these broad fields now reposing from the labors of the waning year, the mighty Alleghenies dimly towering before us, the graves of our brethren beneath our feet, it is with hesitation that I raise my poor voice to break the eloquent silence of God and Nature. But the duty to which you have called me must be performed; — grant me, I pray you, your indulgence and your sympathy. [Everett proceeded] It was appointed by law in Athens [and gave an extended sketch of the manner in which the Greeks cared for their dead who fell in battle. He spoke of the citizens assembled to consecrate the day.] As my eye ranges over the fields whose sods were so lately moistened by the blood of gallant and loyal men, I feel, as never before, how truly it was said of old that it is sweet and becoming to die for one's country.

Northern cities would have been trampled in conquest but for "those who sleep beneath our feet," said the orator. He gave an outline of how the war began, traversed decisive features of the three days' battles at Gettysburg, discussed the doctrine of state sovereignty and denounced it, drew parallels from European history, and came to his peroration quoting Pericles on dead patriots: " The whole earth is the sepulcher of illustrious men." The men of nineteen sister states had stood side by side on the perilous ridges. " Seminary Ridge, the Peach Orchard, Cemetery, Culp, and Wolf Hill, Round Top, Little Round Top, humble names, henceforward dear and famous — no lapse of time, no distance of space, shall cause you to be forgotten." He had spoken for an hour and fifty-seven minutes, some said a trifle over two hours, repeating almost word for word an address that occupied nearly two newspaper pages, as he had written it and as it had gone in advance sheets to many newspapers.

Everett came to his closing sentence without a faltering voice: " Down to the latest period of recorded time, in the glorious annals of our common country there will be no brighter page than that which relates THE BATTLES OF GET-TYSBURG." It was the effort of his life and embodied the perfections of the school of oratory in which he had spent his career. His erect form and sturdy shoulders, his white hair and flung-back head at dramatic points, his voice, his poise, and chiefly some quality of inside goodheartedness, held most of his audience to him, though the people in the front rows had taken their seats three hours before his oration closed.

The Baltimore Glee Club sang an ode written for the occasion by Benjamin B. French, who had introduced Everett to the audience. The poets Longfellow, Bryant, Whittier, Lowell, George Boker, had been requested but none found time to respond with a piece to be set to music. The two closing verses of the ode by French immediately preceded the introduction of the President to the audience.

Having read Everett's address, Lincoln knew when the moment drew near for him to speak. He took out his own manuscript from a coat pocket, put on his steel-bowed glasses, stirred in his chair, looked over the manuscript, and put it back in his pocket. The Baltimore Glee Club finished singing the ode by French. Ward Hill Lamon introduced the President of the United States. He rose, and holding in one hand the two sheets of paper at which he occasionally glanced, he delivered the address in his high-pitched and clear-carrying voice. The Cincinnati *Commercial* reporter wrote: " The President rises slowly, draws from his pocket a paper, and, when commotion subsides, in a sharp, unmusical treble voice, reads the brief and pithy remarks." Hay wrote in his diary: "The President, in a firm, free way, with more grace than is his wont, said his half dozen words of consecration." Charles Hale of the Boston *Advertiser*, also officially representing Governor Andrew of Massachusetts, had notebook and pencil in hand, took down the slow-spoken words of the President, as follows: [1]

Fourscore and seven years ago, our fathers brought forth upon this continent a new nation, conceived in liberty and dedicated to the proposition that all men are created equal.

Now we are engaged in a great civil war, testing whether that nation — or any nation, so conceived and so dedicated — can long endure.

We are met on a great battlefield of that war. We are met to dedicate a portion of it as the final resting place of those who have given their lives that that nation might live.

It is altogether fitting and proper that we should do this.

But, in a larger sense, we cannot dedicate, we cannot consecrate, we cannot hallow, this ground. The brave men, living and dead, who struggled here, have consecrated it, far above our power to add or to detract.

The world will very little note nor long remember what we say here; but it can never forget what they did here.

It is for us, the living, rather, to be dedicated, here, to the unfinished work that they have thus far so nobly carried on. It is rather for us to be here dedicated to the great task remaining before us; that from these honored dead we take increased devotion to that cause for which they here gave the last full measure of devotion; that we here high-

[1] The speech as here recorded has some slight variations in wording from the standard version, which appears among the Lincoln writings on page 644.

ly resolve that these dead shall not have died in vain; that the nation shall, under God, have a new birth of freedom, and that government of the people, by the people, for the people, shall not perish from the earth.

In a speech to serenaders just before the battle of Gettysburg four and a half months before, Lincoln had referred to the founding of the republic as taking place "eighty odd years since." Then he had hunted up the exact date, which was eighty-seven years since, and phrased it "Fourscore and seven years ago" instead of "Eighty-seven years since."

In the written copy of his speech from which he read, Lincoln used the phrase "our poor power." In other copies of the speech which he wrote out later, he again used the phrase "our poor power." So it was evident that he meant to use the word "poor" when speaking to his audience, but it escaped him. Also in the copy held in his hands while facing the audience he had not written the words "under God," though he did include those words in later copies which he wrote. Therefore, the words "under God" were decided upon after he wrote the text the night before at the Wills residence.

The New York *Tribune* and many other newspapers indicated "[Applause]" at five places in the address and "[Long continued applause]" at the end. The applause, however, according to most of the responsible witnesses, was formal and perfunctory, a tribute to the occasion, to the high office, to the array of important men of the nation on the platform, by persons who had sat as an audience for three hours. Nine sentences had been spoken in five minutes, and some were surprised that it should end before the orator had really begun to get his outdoor voice.

A photographer had made ready to

record a great historic moment, had bustled about with his dry plates, his black box on a tripod, and before he had his head under the hood for an exposure, the President had said "by the people, for the people" and the nick of time was past for a photograph.

The New York *Times* reporter gave his summary of the program by writing:

The opening prayer by Reverend Mr. Stockton was touching and beautiful, and produced quite as much effect upon the audience as the classic sentences of the orator of the day. President Lincoln's address was delivered in a clear loud tone of voice, which could be distinctly heard at the extreme limits of the large assemblage. It was delivered (or rather read from a sheet of paper which the speaker held in his hand) in a very deliberate manner, with strong emphasis, and with a most businesslike air.

The Philadelphia *Press* man, John Russell Young, privately felt that Everett's speech was the performance of a great actor whose art was too evident, that it was "beautiful but cold as ice." The New York *Times* man noted:

Even while Mr. Everett was delivering his splendid oration, there were as many people wandering about the fields, made memorable by the fierce struggles of July, as stood around the stand listening to his eloquent periods. They seemed to have considered, with President Lincoln, that it was not what was *said* here, but what was *done* here, that deserved their attention. In wandering about these battlefields, one is astonished and indignant to find at almost every step of his progress the carcasses of dead horses which breed pestilence in the atmosphere. I am told that more than a score of deaths have resulted from this neglect in the village of Gettysburg the past summer; in the house in which I was compelled to seek lodgings, there are now two boys sick with typhoid fever attributed to this cause. Within a stone's throw of the whitewashed hut occupied as the headquarters of General Meade, I counted yesterday no less than ten carcasses of dead horses, lying on the ground

where they were struck by the shells of the enemy.

The audience had expected, as the printed program stipulated, "Dedicatory Remarks, by the President of the United States." No eloquence was promised. Where eloquence is in flow the orator must have time to get tuned up, to expatiate and expand while building toward his climaxes, it was supposed. The New York *Tribune* man and other like observers merely reported the words of the address, with the one preceding sentence: "The dedicatory remarks were then delivered by the President." These reporters felt no urge to inform their readers about how Lincoln stood; what he did with his hands; how he moved, vocalized; or whether he emphasized or subdued any parts of the address. Strictly, no address as such was on the program for him. He was down for just a few perfunctory "dedicatory remarks."

According to Lamon, Lincoln himself felt that about all he had given the audience was ordinary garden-variety dedicatory remarks, for Lamon wrote that Lincoln told him just after delivering the speech that he had regret over not having prepared it with greater care. "Lamon, that speech won't *scour*. It is a flat failure and the people are disappointed." On the farms where Lincoln grew up as a boy, when wet soil stuck to the moldboard of a plow they said it didn't "scour."

The nearby *Patriot and Union* of Harrisburg took its fling:

The President succeeded on this occasion because he acted without sense and without constraint in a panorama that was gotten up more for the benefit of his party than for the glory of the nation and the honor of the dead. We pass over the silly remarks of the President; for the credit of the nation we are willing that the veil of oblivion shall be dropped over them and that they shall no more be repeated or thought of.

This expressive head sculptured by Gutzon Borglum is on Lincoln's tomb in Springfield, Illinois. (Armstrong Roberts)

Everett's opinion of the speech he heard Lincoln deliver was written in a note to Lincoln the next day and was more than mere courtesy: " I should be glad if I could flatter myself that I came as near to the central idea of the occasion in two hours as you did in two minutes." Lincoln's immediate reply was: " In our respective parts yesterday, you could not have been excused to make a short address, nor I a long one. I am pleased to know that, in your judgment, the little I did say was not entirely a failure."

The ride to Washington took until midnight. Lincoln was weary, talked little, stretched out on one of the side seats in the drawing room, and had a wet towel laid across his eyes and forehead.

He had stood that day, the world's foremost spokesman of popular government, saying that democracy was yet worth fighting for. He had spoken as one in mist who might head on deeper yet into mist. He incarnated the assurances and pretenses of popular government, implied that it could and might perish from the earth. What he meant by " a new birth of freedom " for the nation could have a thousand interpretations. The taller riddles of democracy stood up out of the address. It had the dream touch of vast and furious events epitomized for any foreteller to read what was to come. He did not assume that the drafted soldiers, substitutes, and bounty-paid privates had died willingly under Lee's shot and shell, in deliberate consecration of themselves to the Union cause. His cadences sang the ancient song that where there is freedom men have fought and sacrificed for it, and that freedom is worth men's dying for. For the first time since he became President he had on a dramatic occasion declaimed, howsoever it might be read, Jefferson's proposition which had been a slogan of the Revolutionary War — "All men are created equal" — leaving no other inference than that he regarded the Negro slave as a man. His outwardly smooth sentences were inside of them gnarled and tough with the enigmas of the American experiment.

Back at Gettysburg the blue haze of the Cumberland Mountains had dimmed till it was a blur in a nocturne. The moon was up and fell with a bland golden benevolence on the new-made graves of soldiers, on the sepulchers of old settlers, on the horse carcasses of which the onrush of war had not yet permitted removal. The New York *Herald* man walked amid them and ended the story he sent his paper: "The air, the trees, the graves are silent. Even the relic hunters are gone now. And the soldiers here never wake to the sound of reveille."

In many a country cottage over the land, a tall old clock in a quiet corner told time in a ticktock deliberation. Whether the orchard branches hung with pink-spray blossoms or icicles of sleet, whether the outside news was seedtime or harvest, rain or drouth, births or deaths, the swing of the pendulum was right and left and right and left in a ticktock deliberation.

The face and dial of the clock had known the eyes of a boy who listened to its ticktock and learned to read its minute and hour hands. And the boy had seen years measured off by the swinging pendulum, and grown to man size, had gone away. And the people in the cottage knew that the clock would stand there and the boy never again come into the room and look at the clock with the query, "What is the time?"

In a row of graves the unidentified boy would sleep long in the dedicated final resting place at Gettysburg. Why he had gone away and why he would never come back had roots in some mystery of flags and drums, of national fate in which individuals sink as in a deep sea, of men swallowed and vanished in a man-made storm of smoke and steel.

The mystery deepened and moved with ancient music and inviolable consolation because a solemn Man of Authority had stood at the graves of the unidentified and spoken the words "We cannot consecrate — we cannot hallow — this ground. The brave men, living and dead, who struggled here, have consecrated it far above our poor power to add or detract. . . . From these honored dead we take increased devotion to that cause for which they gave the last full measure of devotion."

To the backward and forward pendulum swing of a tall old clock in a quiet corner they might read those cadenced words while outside the windows the first flurry of snow blew across the orchard and down over the meadow, the beginnings of winter in a gun-metal gloaming to be later arched with a star-flung sky.

For Discussion of Sandburg

1. Did you notice any conflicting reports by witnesses of these events? What explanation can you offer for the differing impressions? Why did Sandburg present both views in such cases?

2. Which of the contemporary reactions to Lincoln's remarks came nearest to the opinion most Americans hold today?

3. Recount some minor parts of this narrative that give it depth and the feeling of reality. Which passages would you select to illustrate Sandburg's poetic style?

4. What is added by the inclusion of the story of the woman who had lost her son? by the daily reports on Tad's health and the progress of the war?

5. Contrast the style of Lincoln's address with that of Everett's as indicated by the excerpts included here. Judge some recent speeches by public figures against the simplicity of Lincoln's style.

My New Freedom

THOMAS MERTON
1915–

Thomas Merton (Father Louis, O.C.S.O.) was born in southern France. His formal education was broadened by travel. He attended high school in England and studied at Cambridge for one year. In 1930 he came to this country and completed his college education at Columbia University, where he stayed on to undertake graduate work in English. During this time he read the works of Catholic philosophers and poets, becoming imbued with Catholic culture and thought, and before he finished his studies for the M.A. degree he was received into the Church. After receiving his degree, he taught English at St. Bonaventure College for one year.

Having made a retreat at the famous Trappist Abbey in Gethsemani, Kentucky, he later returned and sought admission as a member. Thomas Merton is like the scribe mentioned in the Gospel parable. He displays some of the immense treasures of the kingdom of God, treasures exchanged for what Christ-lovers would call the frivolous things of this world. To those who are merely curious as well as those who long to know what Trappist spirituality is like, Father Merton simply and beautifully illumines the scene.

In the excerpt that follows, he describes his entry into Gethsemani and his acceptance as a postulant. Merton, now more the man than the poet, relates his anxiety to please God and do His will. Silence consoles him, but he does not condemn speech. One cannot fail to appreciate the religious beauty and Catholic thought of Merton's writings as he bids adieu to the world and turns to kiss the bright hand of his Father in heaven.

WHEN I finally got off in Bardstown, I was standing across the road from a gas station. The street appeared to be empty, as if the town were asleep. But presently I saw a man in the gas station. I went over and asked where I could get someone to drive me to Gethsemani. So he put on his hat and started his car and we left town on a straight road through level country, full of empty fields. It was not the kind of landscape that belonged to Gethsemani, and I could not get my bearings until some low, jagged, wooded hills appeared ahead of us, to the left of the road, and we made a turn that took us into rolling, wooded land.

Then I saw that high familiar spire.

I rang the bell at the gate. It let fall a dull, unresonant note inside the empty court. My man got in his car and went away. Nobody came. I could hear somebody moving around inside the Gatehouse. I did not ring again. Presently, the window opened, and Brother Matthew looked out between the bars, with his clear eyes and graying beard.

"Hullo, Brother," I said.

He recognized me, glanced at the suitcase and said: "This time have you come to stay?"

"Yes, Brother, if you'll pray for me," I said.

Brother nodded, and raised his hand to close the window.

"That's what I've been doing," he said, "praying for you." . . .

So Brother Matthew locked the gate behind me and I was enclosed in the four walls of my new freedom.

And it was appropriate that the beginning of freedom should be as it was. For I entered a garden that was dead and stripped and bare. The flowers that had been there last April were all gone. The sun was hidden behind low clouds and an icy wind was blowing over the gray grass and the concrete walks.

In a sense my freedom had already begun, for I minded none of these things. I did not come to Gethsemani for the flowers, or for the climate — although I admit that the Kentucky winters were a disappointment. Still, I had not had time to plan on any kind of a climate. I had been too busy with the crucially important problem of finding out God's will. And that problem was still not entirely settled.

There still remained the final answer: would I be accepted into this monastery? Would they take me into the novitiate, to become a Cistercian? [1]

Father Joachim, the guest master, came out the door of the monastery and crossed the garden with his hands under his scapular and his eyes fixed on the cement walk. He only raised them when he was near me and then he grinned.

" Oh, it's you," he said. I suppose he had been doing some praying for me too.

I did not give him a chance to ask if I had come to stay. I said: " Yes, Father, this time I want to be a novice [2] — if I can."

He just smiled. We went into the house. The place seemed very empty. I put the suitcase down in the room that had been assigned to me, and hastened to the church. . . .

That evening at supper I found that there was another postulant [3] — an ancient, toothless, gray-haired man hunched up in a huge sweater. He was a farmer from the neighborhood who had lived in the shadow of the abbey for years and had finally made up his mind to enter it as a lay brother. [4] However, he did not stay.

The next day I found out there was still a third postulant. He arrived that morning. He was a fat bewildered youth from Buffalo. Like myself, he was applying for the choir. [5] Father Joachim put the two of us to work together washing dishes and waxing floors, in silence. We were both absorbed in our own many thoughts, and I dare say he was no more tempted to start a conversation than I was.

In fact every minute of the day I was secretly congratulating myself that conversations were over and done with — provided always I was accepted.

I could not be quite sure whether someone would call me and tell me to go down for an interview with the Father Abbot, or whether I was expected to go down to him on my own initiative, but that part of the problem was settled for me toward the end of the morning work.

I went back to my room and started puzzling my head over the copy of the *Spiritual Directory* that Father Joachim had brought me. Instead of settling down quietly and reading the chapter that directly concerned me, the one that said what postulants were supposed to do while they were waiting in the Guest House, I started leafing through the two thin volumes to see if I could not discover something absolutely clear and

---

[1] Cistercian (sĭs·tûr'shăn): the Trappists' official name is The Cistercians of the Strict Observance.

[2] novice: one undergoing a period of probation with the object of testing his vocation to a religious order or institute.

[3] postulant (pŏs'tu̇·lănt): one who seeks to enter a religious order or institute and undergoes a period of probation before receiving the religious habit.

[4] lay brother: a religious who performs the manual tasks in a monastery. He does not aspire to the priesthood.

[5] choir: choir monk, one who is required to say the Divine Office in choir, hence a priest.

definite as to what the Cistercian vocation was all about. . . .

As I was laying aside the *Directory* to take up another small volume of pidgin English, someone knocked on the door.

It was a monk I had not seen before, a rather burly man with white hair and an extremely firm jaw, who introduced himself as the Master of Novices. I took another look at the determination in that jaw and said to myself: " I bet he doesn't take any nonsense from novices, either."

But as soon as he started to talk I found that Father Master was full of a most impressive simplicity and gentleness and kindness and we began to get along together very well from that hour. He was not a man that stood on ceremony and he would have nothing to do with the notorious technique of elaborately staged humiliations which have given La Trappe [1] a bad name in the past. By those standards he should have walked into the room and slammed the door with an insult and then asked me if I were entering the monastery in order to get away from the police.

But he just sat down and said: " Does the silence scare you? "

I almost fell over myself in my eagerness to assure him that the silence not only did not scare me but that I was entranced with it and already felt myself to be in heaven.

" Aren't you cold in here? " he asked. " Why don't you shut the window? Is that sweater warm enough? "

I assured him with consummate bravery that I was as warm as toast but he made me shut the window anyway.

Of course, what had happened was that Brother Fabian, who worked in the Guest House that year, had been feeding me with horror stories about how cold it was when you got up in the morning and went creeping down to choir with

your knees knocking together and your teeth chattering so loud that you could hardly hear the prayers. So I was trying to get myself in trim for the ordeal by sitting with the windows open, without a coat on.

" Have you ever learned any Latin? " asked Father Master. I told him all about Plautus and Tacitus.[2] He seemed satisfied.

After that we talked about many other things. Could I sing? Did I speak French? What made me want to become a Cistercian? . . .

It was such a pleasant conversation that I was getting to be more and more unwilling to unload the big shadowy burden that still rested on my conscience, and tell this good Trappist all the things about my life before my conversion that had once made me think I could not possibly have a vocation to the priesthood. However, I finally did so in a few sentences.

" How long is it since you were baptized? " said Father Master.

" Three years, Father."

He did not seem to be disturbed. He just said that he liked the way I had told him all that there was to be told, and that he would consult Father Abbot about it. And that was all.

I was still half expecting to be called down for a cross-examination by the First Superior, but that never came. The Fat Boy from Buffalo and I waxed floors for the next couple of days, and went down to church and knelt at the benches in front of St. Joseph's altar while the monks chanted the Office,[3] and then came back to the Guest House to eat our scrambled eggs and cheese and milk. At what Brother Fabian would have described as our " last meal," he slipped us each a bar of Nestle's chocolate, and

---

[1] **La Trappe:** first abbey of The Cistercians of the Strict Observance, founded in 1140 in France.

[2] **Plautus** (plô'tŭs): Roman comic dramatist, 254?–184 B.C. **Tacitus** (tăs'ĭ·tŭs): Roman historian, orator, and politician, 55?–117? A.D.

[3] **Office:** the Divine Office which must be said daily by priests. It is sung by the Trappists.

afterwards whispered to me:

"Tom, I think you are going to be very disappointed with what you see on the table when you go into the refectory this evening . . ."

That evening? It was the Feast of St. Lucy and a Saturday. I went back to the room and nibbled on the chocolate and copied out a poem I had just written by way of a farewell to Bob Lax and Mark Van Doren.[1] Father Joachim came in and hid his face behind his hands to laugh when I told him what I was doing.

"A *poem?* " he said, and hastened out of the room.

He had come to get me to wax the floors some more, so presently the Fat Boy from Buffalo and I were on our knees again in the hall, but not for very long. Father Master came up the stairs and told us to get our things together and follow him.

So we put on our coats and got our bags and started downstairs, leaving Father Joachim to finish waxing the floor by himself.

The noise of our footsteps resounded in the great stair well. Down at the bottom of the flight, by the door, under the sign that said " God Alone " there were half a dozen local farmers standing around with their hats in their hands. They were waiting to go to confession. It was a kind of an anonymous, abstract delegation bidding us farewell in the name of civil society. As I passed one of them, a solemn polite old man with a four days' growth of beard, I suddenly got a somewhat melodramatic impulse and leaned over toward him whispering: " Pray for me."

He nodded gravely that he was willing to do that, and the door closed behind us leaving me with the sense that my last act as a layman in the world still smacked of the old Thomas Merton who had gone around showing off all over

[1] **Bob Lax:** friend of the author at Columbia; **Mark Van Doren:** Merton's English professor at Columbia University.

two different continents.

The next minute we were kneeling by the desk of the man who had absolute temporal and spiritual authority over the monastery and everybody in it. This priest, who had been a Trappist for nearly fifty years, looked much younger than he was because he was so full of life and nervous energy. They had been fifty years of hard work which, far from wearing him out, had only seemed to sharpen and intensify his vitality.

Dom Frederic was deep in a pile of letters which covered the desk before him, along with a mountain of other papers and documents. Yet you could see that this tremendous volume of work did not succeed in submerging him. He had it all under control. Since I have been in the monastery I have often had occasion to wonder by what miracle he manages to *keep* all that under control. But he does.

In any case, that day Father Abbot turned to us with just as much ease and facility as if he had nothing else whatever to do but to give the first words of advice to two postulants leaving the world to become Trappists.

"Each one of you," he said, "will make the community either better or worse. Everything you do will have an influence upon others. It can be a good influence or a bad one. It all depends on you. Our Lord will never refuse you grace . . ."

We kissed his ring as he blessed us both, and went out again. His parting shaft had been that we should be joyful but not dissipated, and that the Names of Jesus and Mary should always be on our lips.

At the other end of the long dark hall we went into a room where three monks were sitting at typewriters, and we handed over our fountain pens and wrist watches and our loose cash to the Treasurer, and signed documents promising that if we left the monastery we would not sue the monks for back wages for our hours of manual labor.

And then we passed through the door into the cloister.

Now I began to see the part of the monastery I had never seen — the long wing beyond the cloister, in the back of the building, where the monks actually live, where they gather in the intervals.

It was a contrast to the wide-open frigid formality of the cloister itself. To begin with, it was warmer. There were notice boards on the walls, and there was a warm smell of bread coming from the bakery which was somewhere in those parts. Monks moved about with their cowls over their arms, waiting to put them on when the bell rang for the end of work. We stopped in the tailor shop and were measured for our robes, and then passed through the door to the novitiate.

Father Master showed us where the novitiate chapel was, and we knelt a moment before the Blessed Sacrament in that plain, whitewashed room. I noticed a statue of my friend St. Joan of Arc on one side of the door, and on the other was, of course, the Little Flower.

Then we went down to the basement where all the novices were milling around in the clatter of washbasins, groping for towels with their eyes full of soap and water.

Father Master picked the one who seemed to be the most badly blinded by suds and I heard him tell him to take care of me when we got to church.

"That's your guardian angel," Father explained, and added: "He used to be a Marine." . . .

Now I saw the monastery from within, from the church floor, so to speak, not from the visitor's gallery. I saw it from the novitiate wing, not from the shiny and well-heated Guest House. Now I was face to face with monks that belonged not to some dream, not to some medieval novel, but to cold and inescapable reality. The community which I had seen functioning as a unity, in all

the power of that impressive and formal liturgical anonymity which clothes a body of men obscurely in the very personality of Christ Himself, now appeared to me broken up into its constituent parts, and all the details, good and bad, pleasant and unpleasant, were there for me to observe at close range.

By this time God had given me enough sense to realize at least obscurely that this is one of the most important aspects of any religious vocation: the first and most elementary test of one's call to the religious life — whether as a Jesuit, Franciscan, Cistercian, or Carthusian — is the willingness to accept life in a community in which everybody is more or less imperfect. . . .

The house was full of people, men hidden in white cowls and brown capes, some with beards, the lay brothers, others with no beards but monastic crowns. There were young men and old men, and the old ones were in the minority. At a rough guess, with all the novices we have in the house now I think the average age of the community cannot be much over thirty.

There was, I could see, something of a difference between the community proper and the novices. The monks and the professed brothers were more deeply absorbed in things that the novices had not yet discovered. And yet looking around at the novices there was a greater outward appearance of piety in them — but you could sense that it was nearer the surface.

It can be said, as a general rule, that the greatest saints are seldom the ones whose piety is most evident in their expression when they are kneeling at prayer, and the holiest men in a monastery are almost never the ones who get that exalted look, on feast days, in the choir. The people who gaze up at Our Lady's statue with glistening eyes are very often the ones with the worst tempers. . . .

You felt that the best of them were

the simplest, the most unassuming, the ones who fell in with the common norm without fuss and without any special display. They attracted no attention to themselves, they just did what they were told. But they were always the happiest ones, the most at peace. . . .

On Monday morning I went to confession. It was Ember week, and the novices all went to their extraordinary confessor,[1] who was Father Odo that year. I knelt at the little open confessional and confessed with deep contrition that when Father Joachim had told me, one day in the Guest House, to go and tell the Fat Boy from Buffalo to go down to the church for the canonical office of None,[2] I had failed to do so. Having unburdened my soul of this and other similar offenses, I got so mixed up at the unfamiliar Cistercian ritual that I was all ready to leave the confessional and run away as soon as Father Odo had finished the first prayer and before he had given me any absolution.

In fact I was already on my feet and about to walk away when he started talking to me so I thought I had better stay.

I listened to the things he had to say. He spoke very kindly and simply. And the burden of it was this:

"Who knows how many souls are depending on your perseverance in this monastery? Perhaps God has ordained that there are many in the world who will only be saved through your fidelity to your vocation. You must remember them if you are ever tempted to leave. And you probably will be tempted to leave. Remember all those souls in the world. You know some of them. Others you may never know until you meet them in heaven. But in any case, you did not come here alone . . ."

The next morning Father Master called me in at the end of work and gave me an armful of white woolen garments, telling me to put them on. Postulants used to receive the oblate's [3] habit a few days after their admission — one of those anomalous customs that grow up in isolated houses. It survived at Gethsemani until one of the recent visitations. And so within three days of my admission to the novitiate I was out of my secular clothing and glad to get rid of it for ever.

It took me a few minutes to figure out the complications of the fifteenth-century underwear that Trappists wear under their robes, but soon I was out of the cell in a white robe and scapular, and a white cloth band tied around my waist, with the white, shapeless oblate's cloak around my shoulders. And I presented myself to Father Master to find out my name.

I had spent hours trying to choose a name for myself when I thought I was going to become a Franciscan — and now I simply took what I got. In fact, I had been too busy to bother with such trivial thoughts. And so it turned out that I was to be called Frater Louis. The Fat Boy from Buffalo was Frater Sylvester. I was glad to be Louis rather than Sylvester, although I would probably never have dreamed of choosing either name for myself. . . .

I went immediately into the scriptorium and took a piece of paper and printed on it "FRATER MARIA LU-DOVICUS"[4] and stuck it on the front of the box that was to represent all the privacy I had left: one small box, in which I would keep a couple of notebooks full of poems and reflections, and a volume of St. John of the Cross and Gilson's *Mystical Theology of St. Ber-*

---

[1] **extraordinary confessor:** a priest, not the regular confessor, appointed four times a year to hear the confessions of members of religious communities.

[2] **None** (nōn): a section of the Divine Office.

[3] An **oblate** (ŏb'lāt) is one who offers himself to God. Here it is used with the same meaning as postulant.

[4] **FRATER MARIA LUDOVICUS:** Brother Mary Louis.

nard,[1] and the letters I would receive from John Paul [2] at his R.A.F. camp in Ontario, and from Mark Van Doren and from Bob Lax.

I looked out the window at the narrow rocky valley beyond the novitiate parapet, and the cedar trees beyond and the bare woods on the line of jagged hills. *Haec requies mea in saeculum saeculi, hic habitabo quoniam elegi eam!* [3]

For Discussion of Merton

1. Many people, even Catholics, have difficulty understanding the Trappist mode of life. Father Odo, Thomas Merton's confessor, explains the purpose of the Trap-

[1] **St. John of the Cross** (1542–1591): Spanish poet, theologian, and mystic, an authority on higher forms of prayer and meditation. **Gilson** (zhēl′sôn′), Étienne: a French writer on medieval philosophy, currently professor at the Medieval Institute, University of Toronto.
[2] **John Paul:** Merton's younger brother, who was later killed in action.
[3] *Haec . . . elegi eam!* Here is my home forever and ever, I will dwell here since I have selected it.

pist life. Look up his statement and then explain it to your classmates.

2. After entering Gethsemani, Thomas Merton writes, " I was enclosed in the four walls of my new freedom." What did he understand to be his new freedom? What figure of speech is found in this statement?

3. What difference did the author notice in the conduct of the professed members and the conduct of the novices? What does he think of the novices whose piety was most evident? Who were the happiest among the novices? What do you think was the purpose of the insults directed at those who sought admission to La Trappe?

For Your Vocabulary

RELIGIOUS TERMS: In this selection you came across many terms relating to the religious life. Can you give the difference in meaning between the paired terms in the following list? Some are new, others are from the selection.

abbey — monastery
postulant — novice
novice — scholastic
temporary profession — final profession
religious clergy — diocesan clergy

FRANCES PARKINSON KEYES

1885–

Along a Little Way

Frances Parkinson Keyes,[4] one of the most popular novelists of our times, was born in Virginia. Her father was John Henry Wheeler, professor of Greek at the University of Virginia. Mrs. Keyes was educated in private schools, both here and abroad.

Instead of living in an ivory tower, where many writers spend their days, she has lived in the busy center of social and political life. Her husband was Governor

[4] **Keyes** (kīz).

of New Hampshire and later represented his state in the United States Senate from 1919 to 1937.

Few modern authors have written with such distinction in such widely divergent fields. Almost yearly a book comes from her prolific and talented pen. Few American novelists can equal her list of best sellers. She has written biographies of Saint Bernadette of Lourdes and Saint Theresa, " The Little Flower." Her best-selling novels include *All That Glitters, Crescent Carnival, The River Road, Came a Cavalier,* and her recent success, *Steamboat Gothic.*

In September, 1946, she was awarded the Siena Medal by the Theta Phi Alpha Sorority. This award is made each year to a Catholic woman who has made a distinctive contribution to Catholic life in America.

Mrs. Keyes' early religious training was Protestant. Both her parents were Congregationalists, as was her husband. Her conversion to Catholicism, unlike that of many converts, was the result of a long and gradual process. In fact, from her early teens she seemed to be attracted to the Church. The following selection is an account of her pilgrimage from Protestantism to Catholicism.

I HAVE recently taken a step that seems to me momentous. I have not taken it hastily. Indeed, I have been considering it for nearly twenty years, and for ten I have known that someday I should do so. It is momentous to me personally, both because it represents one of the most significant decisions of my life and because it is inconsistent, in a way, with my background, traditions, and training. And it may seem momentous within the sphere of my personal influence because, as a writer, I reach out to thousands of persons whom I never see, and whose own mental image of me may be suddenly shattered. These persons have a right to understand what I am doing, whether they approve of it or not. Many of them have honored me with their confidence. The time has come when I feel that I should try to honor them with mine. I do not want them to feel bewildered when they read an announcement which I know is bound to amaze them. I do not want them to say to themselves and to each other, " So Frances Parkinson Keyes has become a Catholic! *But why?* "

Here is the answer, in so far as I can express it:

Perhaps it may seem a simple, even an inconsequential one. I was not drawn toward Catholicism, in the beginning, by any turmoil of spirit or any dogmatic dissension. I am one of those fortunate human beings who was born with religious faith, and who, with the passage of years, has found this faith increasingly strong and sustaining. I use the word " fortunate " advisedly, for it has always seemed to me that a person who does not possess it should elicit sympathy; it is not easy to acquire and maintain when it is not indigenous. And I use the word " religious " in its general sense, which may be wholly undenominational, or connected with any denomination, as the case may be. In other words, I have always found prayer a refuge, a solace, and a power; many of my prayers have been answered, and in most cases where they have not, I have lived to be thankful that this was so. I have always found worship a privilege and an inspiration, and it has been possible for me to test the truth of this under all sorts of conditions, in many parts of the world. I have always possessed, for a lay woman, a fair knowledge of the Scriptures. At the age of four I was taught to read out of the Bible by my paternal grandmother, who was one of the most learned, courageous, and devout women whom I have ever known. I would no more think of traveling without a Bible than without a toothbrush, and after fifty years of close acquaintance with it I constantly find new meaning and new values in it.

With so generally soul-satisfying a basis, it is natural to ask why I should have striven to change its form in any way. If I may be permitted to say so, without seeming to cast the slightest reflection on any kind of faith, so long as this is sincere, it has not been so much a question of strife as of growth. My paternal grandfather was a Congregational clergyman and all the members of my family, on both sides, were members of the Congregational Church. I went to church as a matter of course, to Sunday school, and to Christian Endeavor meetings. I went willingly and contentedly. But by the time I was nine years old, when the question first arose as to whether I myself should "join the church," I did not want to do so. I was conscious of a lack of completeness, for me, in the services I was attending and the doctrine I heard expounded. I did not know just what was lacking, but I felt that there was something.

I recently heard a story which illustrates my own frame of mind at that time, as far as I can interpret this. In Washington a large Presbyterian church and a large Catholic church stand almost side by side, and the little girls who attend a parochial school directly behind them are encouraged to undertake frequent devotion. Two of them, becoming slightly confused as to direction, wandered into the Presbyterian church by mistake and, upon looking up to the place where they expected to see the altar, beheld only a formidable array of organ pipes. They immediately arose from their knees and hastened to the door, where they met the pastor to whom I am indebted for this story and who happened to be going through the vestibule. Observing their manifest distress, he asked if there were anything he could do to help them. "Oh sir!" one of them exclaimed. "We wanted to talk to God, but we don't find Him!"

I believe that this little girl's bewilderment was akin to my own childish perplexity. I have said before that I am a great believer in prayer. As time went on, I found it urgent, for various reasons, to pray with increasing frequency. I was not wholly satisfied, or sufficiently sustained, when I did so only at stated hours, on certain days. I earnestly desired and desperately needed to find a way of praying at any hour, on any day; and very often, when I attempted to enter the church of which I was a member, I found it locked. The result was that I sought out one that was open, and this was a Catholic church. . . .

There have been many middays when, after excited shopping along the Faubourg St. Honoré,[1] I have dropped in at the Madeleine[2] to give thanks because I had been able to earn the money to pay for the pretty dresses and chic hats I had bought. There have been many midnights — in Manila, in Santiago, in Freiburg,[3] in Washington itself — when I have gone to one beautiful candlelighted church after another to give thanks for God's Greatest of all Gifts to men. In Manila it is customary — or at least it used to be — to leave the fashionable ball at Tiro el Blanco,[4] add a mantilla and an all-enveloping cloak to one's evening dress, and go to Christmas Mass, returning, after this was over, to the ball again. In nobody's mind was there any idea that it was unsuitable to mingle secular and sacred joy in this way.

I was profoundly impressed by this

[1] **Faubourg St. Honoré** (fō'bŏōr' săɴ' tŏ-nō·rā'): a district of Paris, where there are many luxury shops.

[2] **Madeleine** (mȧ'dlĕn'): the Church of St. Mary Magdalene, often called "Church of the Americans," since Americans frequent it.

[3] **Santiago** (săn'tǐ·ä'gō): the capital of Chile; **Freiburg** (frī'bŏōrg): a city in Germany.

[4] **Tiro el Blanco:** a sport and social club no longer in existence.

fact. The more I traveled about, the more it was borne home to me that no Catholic with whom I came in contact seemed to consider that any reasonable pleasure was in itself an evil thing. It could be converted into evil, of course. But that was entirely different. Enjoyment of life, in all its normal phases, was regarded as natural and desirable.

I heard this viewpoint embodied in a charming old Spanish legend. St. Peter, so the story ran, was accustomed to ask suppliants at the gates of heaven whether they had taken advantage of all the earthly joys made available to them through the goodness of God. If they admitted that they had not, he shook his head sadly. "Alas, my child!" he then said in a somber tone, "how can you expect to be ready for celestial joys if you have not prepared yourself for them through the medium of terrestrial joys? I shall be obliged to send you away unless and until you learn better." Recognizing that St. Peter would probably have many other peccadilloes with which to reproach me, I decided that he should never do so on this particular score!

The change in my own viewpoint, of which I had hardly been conscious, was brought home to me in full force for the first time when I was spending a week end in Boston. One of my sons was then at the Harvard Law School, another at Harvard College, and the third at Milton Academy. I suggested that after church, to which we all went together, each bring a boy who was far from home to a midday dinner at the quiet hotel where I was staying with my secretary; after dinner we would make up two tables of bridge. I recall that one of the boys invited was a member of the Soong family, a brother of two charming women, each of whom has been the wife of a president of China.

They lingered so long that I was late for a supper engagement with an aunt. By way of explanation I laughingly said that I had been playing bridge all the afternoon with a group of youngsters, who had had such a good time that they did not know when to stop. I shall never forget the chilly silence with which this announcement was greeted. I was conscious of reproving eyes all around the family board. For an instant I could not imagine what was the matter. Then I realized that in the opinion of my relatives I had not been creating a harmonious and helpful atmosphere for my sons and their friends; instead I had been breaking the Sabbath Day and encouraging the young in bad habits. In my own turn, I was frozen with horror that such a construction could be put on "a source of innocent merriment." I felt then that I was nearing a parting of the ways.

I felt still more certain of this parting after a gloomy Sunday which I spent alone in London. At four in the afternoon I went through the pouring rain to vespers at Westminster Abbey. After the service was over I wandered down the nave to look at the tomb of the Unknown Soldier, which I really wanted to see. But almost instantly a severe verger appeared at my side and in a somber tone ordered me to pass on out, as the abbey was about to be closed. "But surely you keep it open for prayer and meditation," I protested. "Not on Sunday, madam," he informed me in a voice of finality, and I went forth into the rain again.

At the same time that I was absorbing the essential joyousness of Catholicism as contrasted to the essential austerity of Puritanism, I was also observing the unswerving policy of the Catholic Church in regard to what, for lack of a better expression, might be called basic decency. With this, so I discovered, it never compromised. In the midst of a confused and chaotic world it remained steadfast in its attitude not only toward the famous Seven Deadly Sins, but toward degeneracy and depravity in any form.

All this roused my admiration and challenged my courage. I had been brought up to set stern standards for myself, but all around me I saw these standards slipping; I had begun to wonder whether they really mattered so much after all. At that stage I had never written a best-seller, and it is the natural desire of every author to achieve one; I felt that perhaps if I wrote a different type of book I should be more successful. All around me I saw disrupted families which were apparently getting along very well; I thought it was perhaps not worth while to insist on the maintenance of an unsevered circle.

It was the attitude of the Catholic Church, with which by this time I had become thoroughly familiar, that made me realize, more than any other one thing, that the old standards were not all gone, that they did still matter, that they were vital and essential, and that they always would be.

As I continued to go, with increasing frequency, into Catholic churches, I did this with a mounting sense of naturalness and of joy. . . . I went to church in Portugal, in Spain, in Italy, in France, in the Azores, the Canaries,[1] Cuba, and Puerto Rico; to small chapels and great cathedrals, to the cloisters where nuns knelt in seclusion behind the grille, and to the sanctuaries where the scum of the pavements found refuge. I went to church in all the major and many of the minor cities of South America, including Magallanes,[2] which is the southernmost city of the world. And finally, one snowy silent afternoon in midwinter, I went to the shrine of St. Anne de Beaupré, in Canada.

[1] **Azores** (á·zōrz′): an island group in the North Atlantic forming a part of Portugal; **Canaries** (ká·nâr′ĭz): a group of mountainous islands in the Atlantic Ocean off the northwest coast of Africa.
[2] **Magallanes** (mä′gä·yä′näs): a city in Chile, also called Punta Arenas.

It was not a time of pilgrimage. There was not a soul in the church besides the friend who was with me, and myself. I dipped my fingers in holy water as I entered, knelt down, and crossed myself, in the same way that I had done hundreds of times already, first merely because it seemed courteous to follow prevalent custom in the house of God, as one would in the house of a friend, and later because this had become instinctive. Then I raised my eyes to the lighted altar, and in one blinding flash, my whole life was transformed.

I did not know exactly what to do next. As a matter of fact, the first thing I did, when I returned to my hotel room, was to sit down and write a sonnet addressed to St. Anne, or rather to permit my fingers to form the words of one that flowed without effort from my mind.

Anyone who has ever written verse at all knows that the sonnet is one of the most difficult types to achieve, and I have often spent days in trying to perfect one; yet on this occasion the words were all on paper within twenty minutes. Just as I finished writing, the friend who had been with me at the shrine came into my room. I read the sonnet aloud to her, and when I finished I saw that her eyes were full of tears. "I am glad I was with you when this happened," she said, and nothing more. When I reached my own home it came about that my eldest son, who has always been exceptionally close to me in spirit, was the first person I saw. He had hardly looked at me when he said, "So it has happened at last! I have known that someday it inevitably would!"

For a long time no one besides these two persons had certain knowledge of what had taken place. But there were some who had begun to guess that I had "Catholic leanings," and the forms which the opposition to these assumed ranged all the way from the sublime to the ridiculous and back again. The most laughable objection raised was that they would "injure my social position"; the most serious that "no woman of my intelligence could possibly subscribe to blind beliefs." . . .

As to the charge that no woman of my intelligence could believe blindly, I have never laid claim to remarkable intelligence, but still I found that my usual reply did not bring back a convincing counter-retort. "There are two miracles which I am sure you do accept," I ventured to say; "one is the miracle of birth and the other is the miracle of death. Both are universal and eternal. But as far as I know, they have never been logically explained. Can you do so?" There would be a moment's silence and then I would go on. "Well, in that case, why should it be hard to accept other occurrences which seem phenomenal?"

My work took me, to an increasing degree, into Catholic countries, and finally the way opened, through no initiative of my own, for me to write the life of St. Thérèse of Lisieux.[1] While I did so, I lived at Notre Dame du Pré, the Abbaye des Bénédictines[2] where she was educated; and I was also in close and constant communication with Carmel[3] of Lisieux, where she spent her cloistered life, where one of her sisters is still prioress and two others members of the Community.

Long before, when I had been on the point of starting on a journey which took me to remote places, a great statesman had said to me: "Remember that no matter where you go, you will always find two gentlemen: the British vice-consul and the Catholic priest. If you get into any kind of a jam, go to one or the other. He will be able and glad to help you." I have never got into any kind of a jam, but on the other hand I have had many occasions to observe the astuteness of the great statesman's estimate. My mind reverted to it frequently, during my first sojourn at Lisieux, and eventually I decided to have a talk with the bishop. I knew that, as a gentleman, he would give me every consideration, even though he might feel it his duty, as a churchman, to discourage me. I told him everything that I have put down here on paper, and much besides. When I had finished, without asking a single question, he told me that he would be glad to arrange for my reception into the Church at any time. Then he blessed me. It was as natural and as simple as that.

There is a beautiful story of a mother who took her child with her when she was received in private audience with the Pope — Pius X, I think it was, though I am not sure. As she was leaving, the Holy Father said to her, "Bring your little boy back with you tomorrow. I will confirm him." Somewhat startled, she asked, "But isn't he too young to know what that means?" The Pope placed his hand gently under the child's chin and looked into his eyes. "Do you know what God is, my son?" he asked. "Yes," the child answered, "God is love." "You see," remarked the Holy Father to the child's mother.

I thought of this story after my first talk with the bishop, not once but many times. It was two years before I talked with him privately again. In the meantime I had twice thought that the moment was at hand when I might make a public declaration of faith, and twice I had been thwarted, or so it seemed to me.

I went to see the bishop a second time. "Monseigneur," I said, "I hoped that last year I might come and ask you to fulfill your promise of receiving me into the Church and I could not do so.

[1] St. Thérèse (tā'râz') of Lisieux (lē'zyû'): (1873–1897), popularly known as "The Little Flower." Lisieux is a city in Normandy.

[2] Notre Dame du Pré (nô'tr' dàm' dü prā'): Our Lady of the Field; Abbaye des Bénédictines (à·bā' dā bā·nā·dēk'tēn'): Benedictine Abbey.

[3] Carmel: any Carmelite monastery, usually of nuns.

Now in a sense I am free. And yet in another sense I feel that I am not." I told him what I meant by this and his answer came unhesitatingly.

" I think that you are right, my daughter," he said. " If this week had ended on a note of war instead of on a note of peace, I might not advise you in this way.[1] I might tell you that in spite of what you had said, I believed it would be best for you to enter the Church now, since you wish to perform this act in Lisieux and since it might not be possible for you to return to France next year. But under the circumstances I think it best that you should go home now and return to us later. I shall have one more talk with you, when you come back, to finally examine the state of your soul. But I am not disturbed about this, and I beseech you not to let anyone else trouble your peace of mind. I know that in the interval before I see you again you will pray a great deal. I assume that you will also ponder, read, and study. God has given you great faith. Rejoice in it. Do not ever permit it to seem like a burden and never doubt that you will return to us. And now my daughter, let me bless you again before you go." . . .

I tried to put my house in order, both figuratively and literally. I did my work, which was heavy, for I wrote a long novel outside editorial office hours, and went on several long lecture tours. And " when spring rolled round again next year," I began my preparations to return to Lisieux.

I am not using a figure of speech when I say that a royal welcome awaited me there. The nuns never neglected an opportunity to impress me with the spiritual aspects of the experience that awaited me.

[One week after her return to Lisieux, Mrs. Keyes was received into the Church in the chapel of the Benedictine nuns where

[1] This was immediately after the Munich Conference.

the " Little Flower " made her First Communion.]

The portion of the chapel encircling the chancel and sanctuary, which is open to the public, was filled to overflowing; I had not realized that I had made so many friends during my quiet summers in Normandy. . . . Beyond the sanctuary, the curtains had been folded back from the grille. I could see them all, those sixty nuns who had waited and watched so long for this day. " We have prayed for you a great deal! " — this had been the greeting of each and every one whom I had seen during that final week. Well, their prayers had been answered. And to show that this was a great day for them too, they had withdrawn the veil from the tabernacle, they had revealed themselves to the world which only on the rarest occasions is permitted to gaze upon them.

Somebody gave a slight signal. It was time for me to go into the sanctuary myself, with my acting godmother at my side. Madame de Laboulaye, the wife of the former French Ambassador to the United States, had expected to act as my sponsor on this occasion. At the last moment a telegram had arrived from her, stating that her son-in-law had been mobilized and that she could not leave her daughter and newborn grandchild. So it was Katharine McKiever, who had been my " good companion " through this latest of European journeyings who went with me to the altar steps.

Most of the ceremonial was familiar to me. I had rehearsed it with care: mentally, that I might be sure, beyond any shadow of doubt, that I understood both the spirit and the letter of it, and that I could wholeheartedly subscribe to these; orally, lest my tongue might slip in the pronunciation of words, the meaning of which was clear, but the usage unfamiliar. But neither the bishop, with whom I had been twice in conference during the week, nor the Mère

Hôtelière,[1] who had spent many hours interpreting the Catechism to me, had warned me that I would be asked to recite the Creed, the Lord's Prayer, or the Hail Mary. When one of the officiating clergy suddenly told me to do so, I was startled. I had never said them in French, for the occasion had not arisen, and my Latin is very rusty.

"May I recite them in English?" I stammered, under my breath. It was the first hard moment, and it was the bishop who made it easy for me, as simply and naturally as he had assuaged many others.

"Of course," he told me in an answering whisper, "God understands every language as well as every heart." I believe it was this statement which sounded the keynote of that day, and of all the days which have followed.

"Simplify your life," said the bishop, "do not keep on taxing your strength and your spirit to the breaking point. When you learn to distinguish better between essentials and nonessentials, you will gain in repose what you lose in excitement, and life is always bound to be a thrilling adventure for you. There is no need that you yourself should strive to make it so. You have a pleasing penchant for laughter. Share it with those to whom it comes less easily. The good God is not a harsh master but a gentle Father. He rejoices in the happiness of His children. Go often to Communion. And your work is important. Do not minimize it in your own eyes. The printed page reaches thousands who can be reached in no other way. The spoken word reaches thousands more. Testify to the faith that is in you. Let your light so shine before men . . ."

Perhaps the bishop had more confidence in me than I deserve. Perhaps the

---

[1] **Mère Hôtelière** (mâr' ô·tĕl·yâr'): Mother Guest Mistress.

ends he outlined are too great for me to meet. Perhaps my "way" will always be a little one, though it may widen and lengthen after all. It is too soon to tell. I can tread it only a step at a time, and those steps are slow. But often, in the past, I have thought — materially speaking — that my path was not only rough but obscure, that it led nowhere. Then suddenly, without warning, I found that it had taken me by a devious route to a broad and beautiful highway. I learned that whatever else I had to face, life held no blind alleys for me; there was always a way out. I think that — spiritually speaking — a similar experience may be in store for me, that this time the obscure path will lead upward as well as onward. I have no reason to doubt that this is so. I have every reason to believe it.

For Discussion of Keyes

1. At the start of the selection Mrs. Keyes writes, "I was not drawn toward Catholicism, in the beginning, by any turmoil of spirit or any dogmatic dissension." What is the meaning of this quotation? Later on, she reveals that she became dissatisfied with the attitude of Protestantism on moral problems. Do you think this suggests dogmatic turmoil? Explain your answer.

2. What is the Church's attitude toward pleasure? What is the Puritan attitude toward pleasure (see p. 413)? How did the Church's attitude play a part in the conversion of the author?

3. After her baptism, the bishop reminded the author of the mission of the written word. How is your daily life affected by what you read? Can the written word be an influence for great evil? In what ways may the written word accomplish great good?

4. Make a listing of the events and influences that led Mrs. Keyes into the Church. As the narrative progresses, do you notice any important change in these influences and events? What is the change?

I Become a Reporter

LINCOLN STEFFENS
1866–1936

During the first decade of this century everyone was reading Lincoln Steffens's exposures of political corruption, which appeared first in *McClure's* magazine and later in book form as *The Shame of the Cities*. These set the style for a great period of "muckraking," as President Theodore Roosevelt called it. The details of these exposures are matters of the past, but the experiences of Steffens himself have become a permanent part of our literature. When Lincoln Steffens's *Autobiography* appeared in 1931, it captured the fancy of the public at once and was hailed as one of the great American autobiographies. The author's long journalistic experience enabled him to write with an easy yet exciting style. It is the kind of book that is as fascinating as a novel and at the same time opens up innumerable problems of our modern life. The frankness which made his early articles breathtaking is characteristic of this book also, whether he is discussing himself or others.

Steffens tells the story of his return to New York (after a long period of study in Europe) in a straight narrative fashion, with one event following after another. Yet this is not a mere recital of what he did day by day or month by month. Look for threads in the narrative that reveal to you something about Steffens as a reporter as well as a man coming into contact with many different people.

WHEN my ship sailed into New York harbor, my father's agent brought down to quarantine a letter which I still remember, word perfect, I think.

My dear Son: When you finished school you wanted to go to college. I sent you to Berkeley. When you got through there, you did not care to go into my business; so I sold out. You preferred to continue your studies in Berlin. I let you. After Berlin it was Heidelberg; after that Leipzig. And after the German university you wanted to study at the French universities in Paris. I consented, and after a year with the French, you had to have half a year of the British Museum in London. All right. You had that too.

By now you must know about all there is to know of the theory of life, but there's a practical side as well. It's worth knowing. I suggest that you learn it, and the way to study it, I think, is to stay in New York and hustle.

Enclosed please find one hundred dollars, which should keep you till you can find a job and support yourself.

This letter made me feel as if the ship were sinking under me; I had to swim. I did not know how, not in those waters, but it was not fear that hit me so hard. Nor disappointment. I had no plans to be disturbed. My vague idea was to go home to California and "see" what chance there was, say, at some college, to teach or lecture on the theories of ethics while making a study of morals: the professional ethics and the actual conduct of men in business, politics, and the professions. I could get no academic position in the East, where I was not known, but I might carry on my research as an insider in business just as well as I could as an observer. My wife asked me how I was going to go about getting a job in business and how meanwhile we were to live. For the first time, I think, I realized that I was expected to support my wife and that meanwhile my wife expected my father to help us. And my father would have done it. He said afterward that if he had known that I was married, he would not have thrown me off as he did — for my good, "just to see what you could do for yourself," he said. My wife was for telling him then and there, but I could not. I declared that I would never ask my father for another cent, and I didn't. The next money transaction between us was a loan I made to him.

No, my father was putting me to a test, I said, and I would show him. And my mother-in-law, Mrs. Bontecou,[1] backed me up. She said she would see us through with her little money. Josephine was angry, and, in brief, ours was a gloomy landing party. I alone was cheerful, secretly; I had an idea. I would write.

At the small hotel Josephine knew, I took pencil and paper and I wrote a short story, "Sweet Punch." That was a Saturday. I did it that day and rewrote and finished it on Sunday. Louis Loeb called that night. He was illustrating for *Harper's Magazine,* and he said he would offer them my story the next day. He sold it to them for fifty dollars. I sat me down to calculate. That story was done and sold in three days. Call it a week. I could make fifty dollars a week, which multiplied by fifty-two was, say, twenty-five hundred dollars a year. Enough to live on. But I didn't do another story that week nor the next. Too busy looking for a job, I excused; but

[1] **Mrs. Bontecou** (bŏn'tē·cōō): The name is French, but the Bontecous were Americans whom Steffens met while they were traveling abroad.

the fact was that I couldn't do another for a month, and then the second story was rejected. It was years before I got into the magazines again.

It was weeks before I found a job. I was amazed at the difficulty. There I was, all dressed up in my beautiful morning coat with top hat, answering ads, any ads for anything, from an editorship to errand boy. Literally. The juvenile literature I had read as a boy, about lads who began at the bottom and worked up, had stuck. Here I was, what I had once grieved that I was not, a poor but willing young fellow, without parents, friends, or money, seeking a start in life, just a foothold on the first rung of the ladder; I would, like my boy heroes, attend to the rest. And I couldn't get the chance! I couldn't understand it.

The most urgent ads came from the water front, and I would go into one of those shabby little dirty, dark shops, where they dealt in ship furnishings or produce — dressed like a dude, remember; especially careful to be in my best to make a good first impression — and showing the clipping from the paper, ask for an opening. The shopkeeper would throw himself back in his chair and stare at me and sputter, "But — but do you think you can do the work? It's hard work and — and — are you — qualified? What has been your experience?" And I answered that I had studied at Berkeley, Berlin, Heidelberg, the Sorbonne! And for some reason that seemed to end it.

Those were the days when businessmen were prejudiced against a college education. My father's partners had the prejudice. They warned him that his course with me would ruin me, and I think that it was they who advised him to drop me in New York and see who was right, he or they. Businessmen have learned since that college does not unfit average young men for anything but an intellectual career; they take them on and will tell you that the colleges are the best source in the world for cheap labor. But in my day, next to my clothes and general beautifulness, the heaviest handicap I had was my claim to a college education, and not only one college, but — five. Some employers dropped their hands and jaw and stared me silently out of their sight; others pushed me out, and others again — two I remember vividly — called in all hands to " see this college graduate that wants to clean the windows and run errands."

My father was right. As I went home to my wife and mother-in-law to describe life as I found it and businessmen as they found me, I had to confess that I was learning something, that life wasn't what I had expected from my reading. My money was all gone, all the one hundred and also the fifty dollars, and I was paying for myself alone. Mrs. Bontecou paid for her daughter, and soon she was paying for her son-in-law too. I became desperate. My father had given me a letter from the supervising editor of all the Southern Pacific Railroad publications, the monthly magazines, weeklies, and daily newspapers that " the Road " owned or subsidized, to an editor of the *Century Magazine*. I had not used it, because I preferred not to apply " pull." I was for getting my start in life on merit alone. Mrs. Bontecou was with me on that; Josephine was impatient and practical. She pressed me to deliver the letter of introduction, and I did. I asked Mr. Robert Underwood Johnson to give me an editorial position on the *Century*.

He read the letter, pondered, asked me questions, and sized me up. Seeing through my clothes and my story, I guess, he very cautiously asked me if I would be willing to start — just for the practice — to begin my editorial career as — a — reporter. Would I? I certainly would; I would have laid off my top hat to be a copy boy. That cleared the air for him; maybe it stripped off my English clothes. Anyway he offered to get me on either the *Tribune* or the *Evening*

Post, and I went home, happy and proud, to discuss with my family the choice I had between those two New York papers.

I can't recall what decided us, but I think it was only that the *Evening Post* was an evening paper; I could be home at night and so have time to do some literary work. However it was, I took a note from Mr. Johnson to Joseph B. Bishop, an editorial writer on the *Post*. Bishop frowned, but he led me out to the city room and introduced me to Henry J. Wright, the city editor, who looked helplessly at me and, I thought, resentfully at Bishop.

" I don't need any more reporters," he said to Bishop, " but," to me, " you can come in next Monday and sit down out there with the reporters, and as I get a chance, I'll try you out — on space."

I didn't know what that meant, but I didn't care. I had a job. As I described it to my wife and her mother, Josephine was not elated as her mother was, and the next Monday when I sat out there in the city room, ignored, while all the world seemed to be in a whirl, I was not elated either. The next day I saw " Larry " Godkin, the editor who wrote the leaders I read and reread, admiring; he passed by the city door. Bishop nodded to me once, but neither Wright nor the other reporters looked my way. Interesting fellows they seemed to be; they must know all the mysteries of a great city. They did not talk much, but I overheard enough to infer that they were familiar and bored with sport, politics, finance, and society. I was awed by the way they would, upon a few words from the city editor, dart or loaf out of the room, be gone an hour or so, come in, report briefly, and then sit down, write, turn in their copy carelessly, and lie back and read, idly read, newspapers.

One afternoon about one o'clock Mr. Wright came into the room, and seeing no one there but me, exclaimed impatiently and went out. A moment later he came back and right up to me.

"See here," he said, "there's a member of a stockbrokerage firm missing. Disappeared utterly. Something wrong. Go and see his partner and find out why the man is gone, whether there's funds missing too."

He handed me a memorandum giving the firm name and address in Wall Street. An assignment! I was to report. I darted out of the office into the elevator, and asking anybody for directions, found my way to Wall Street — Wall Street! — and the office of the lost broker. His partner rebuffed me. "No, I don't know why he skipped. No idea. No, nothing missing. How should there be?" But I wasn't going to fail on my first chance; so I persisted, asking questions, all about the missing man, his character, antecedents, habits, and when that caused only irritation, I asked about Wall Street. The broker soon was talking; we moved into his private office, sat down, and I told him the story of my life; he told me his, and I was thinking all the time how I could write something interesting about the ethics of a stockbroker; I had long since been convinced that the missing broker was innocent of anything more than a drink or an escapade with a woman, when all of a sudden the partner sprang up and said:

"Well, you are the most persistent son of a gun I ever met in all my life, and you win. I'll give you what you seem so sure of anyhow. My partner has not only skipped, I don't know where; he has taken every cent there was in the office, in the banks, and — then some." He named the amount, and I, astonished by the revelation, but satisfied that I had a front-page sensation, ran back to the office, where I astonished my city editor.

"Really?" he said. "You are sure? It's libel, you know, if it's wrong. He told you himself, the partner did? Sure? Umh — Well, write it, and we'll see."

I had pencils all sharpened — sharpened every day — ready for this moment, and I went to work. It was easy enough to report the facts, but I felt I must write this big news as the news was written. That I had studied in my idle hours, the newspaper style, and that was not easy. I labored till the city editor darted out to see what I was doing; he saw; he read over my shoulder the writes and rewrites of my first paragraph, and picking up one, said, "This is enough." And away he went with it. All I had to do was to lie back in a chair and wait to read my stuff in print, a long wait, perhaps half an hour, till three o'clock, when the last edition went to press, and then twenty minutes before the paper came down. And then when it came down, the damp, smelly paper, my paragraph wasn't in it! I searched again and again, with anxiety, hope, dread. I did not care for the money; the space was too short to count, but I felt that my standing as a reporter was at stake, and so, when I was at last convinced that my "story" was left out, I got up and dragged home, defeated and in despair. I told Mrs. Bontecou about it, not my wife, and was comforted some. If I failed at journalism, the old lady argued, there still was literature.

The facts of my story appeared in the morning newspapers, but they were better, more neatly, briefly stated, than I had put them; perhaps I had failed, not as a reporter, but as a writer. And this conclusion was confirmed at the office, where the city editor said "Good morning" to me and, after all the other reporters were gone out, gave me an assignment to ask the superintendent of schools something. One more chance.

Braced to make the most of it, I gave that official a bad hour. He had to answer, not only the question the city editor asked, but others, many others. He found himself telling me all about the schools, education and its problems, and his policy. I had some ideas on that subject, and he got them; and he had to accept or refute them. He became so interested that, when he had to break off, I was invited to come back another day to "continue our conversation." Good. I returned to the office and wrote a column interview, beginning with the city editor's question and the answer. This time, when the paper came out it had my story, but cut down to the first question and answer, rewritten as an authoritative statement of fact. My reporting was all right; my writing was not. The next day, a Friday, I had to go out, confirm a reported suicide, and telephone the news, which another reporter took down and wrote.

That afternoon I saw reporters clipping from the cut files of the *Post*. I asked what it was for, and one of them said he was making up his bill. He cut out his own stories, stuck them together in a long strip, and measuring them with a foot rule, reckoned up the amount of space and charged for it so much a column. I did the same, and my poor little bill of earnings for my first week of practical life was something like two dollars and ten cents. And I was not ashamed of it; I was reassured, if not proud.

Nor was that all. As I was finishing this task the city editor called me up to his desk and bade me rewrite as a separate story for the Saturday paper the interview I had had with the superintendent of schools during the week. He suggested the idea or theme to write it around, and I, elated, stayed there in the office till closing time, grinding out my first long "story." And the next day I had the deep gratification of reading it at full length, the whole thing as I had written it. I measured it, secretly, and it came to four dollars plus — a fine start for my next week.

That Sunday was a bore; I could hardly wait for Monday to go on with my reporting, and talking with my wife and her mother, I developed ideas and plans. There were several promising questions to put to the superintendent of schools; the news suggested other

men to see and talk to, and no doubt now the city editor himself would ask me to do more. When I walked into the office on Monday morning, eager and confident, I was dashed by the way I was ignored. No greetings from anybody, and as the morning wore on and the other reporters were sent off on assignments, I realized heavily that I was not to be used. I took my hat and told the city editor I would like to go out on a quest of my own. He nodded consent, and I went and had with the superintendent of schools a long interview which I wrote and handed in. It did not appear in the paper, and for two days I was ignored and got nothing out of my assignments. The men I tried to see were not in or would not see me. I had the experience so common for reporters of being defeated, and in an obscure way, too. Toward the end of the week I was sent out to see a rapid-transit commissioner and got some news which pleased the city editor: a formal, printed statement, which was printed. That was all. My space bill was about six dollars. But on Saturday, too late to be included, appeared my interview with the superintendent of schools.

With this to start with again, I could live over Sunday and was ready to dive on Monday into my journalism. I had to be my own city editor, but I could be, now. I got another school story, which was printed; it was news; and another which was held, I knew now, for Saturday. I called again on the rapid-transit commissioner, and he gave me a brief interview which I used to tempt the other commissioners to answer. That was news and appeared right away. So was a statement by the mayor which I went for all by myself. Somebody had said something in print that was critical in a small way of some department, and his office being open to the public I walked in and talked to him about it. My bill that week was something like fifteen dollars.

My system was working, and, I learned afterward, was amusing the staff and interesting the city editor, who described it as I could not have described it. It was a follow-up system, well known in journalism but unknown to me as a method. Every time I was sent to or met a man in a position to furnish news, I cultivated him as a source and went back repeatedly to him for more news or more general views on the news. If there was a news story in the papers, and not too big, I would read it through for some angle overlooked and slip out to the persons involved and ask some questions. My contribution often appeared as a part of some other reporter's story, usually at the end, but several times as the lead. And always there were school-news articles from my superintendent, who was talking policy to me weekly and letting me visit and write about schools. These articles brought letters to the editor, which showed that we were tapping a field of interest. I had a free hand here till, later, there was an education department which included the universities and private schools, and so brought in advertising. But there was the art museum, too, to " cover " and report; rapid transit with its plans, not only for transportation in the city, but for real estate, park, and street development. Every time the city editor sent me into a field for a bit of news I got what he wanted and went back for more general reports. He used me very little, however, leaving me to my own devices; and his reason came out when, after a few months, my bills were running up to fifty, sixty, and more dollars a week, and the other reporters were taking rather unfriendly notice of me.

One Friday, as I was making out my bill, William G. Sirrene, a fine Southern boy who was one of the star reporters, looked over my shoulder and exclaimed, " What's that? Seventy-two dollars! Why, that's nearly three times what I'm getting on salary."

He called out to the others the amount of my bill, and when they also exclaimed, he explained, " Why, you are the best-paid man on the staff! "

I felt like exclaiming myself. It was news to me. I had no knowledge of salaries or earnings on the paper; all I knew was that I was supporting myself and my wife at last, saving a little each week, and driving on for more, and more. And I would have given it all to be a regular reporter like Sirrene or the others, and that is what I was asked to do. I think now that some of the reporters, not Sirrene, " kicked " to the city editor that I, a new man, was being paid more than they were, the veterans. Anyway he sent for me and, explaining that my bills were running too high, asked me if I would be changed from space to a salary, the best salary they paid the ordinary reporter, thirty-five dollars a week.

" Then," he said, " I can use you more myself on more important news."

I not only consented, I was dazed with the implication of my triumph. All became clear in that short talk with my chief. I had not been sent off on assignments because I was making too much money on my own and I had " made good." Even my first disappointment, the failure to print my news of the defalcation of the missing broker, was to my credit. The city editor did not dare print the report, by a new and untried man, of a piece of libelous news; he had sent an old reporter down to confirm it, and the broker who had talked to me not only repeated what he told me; he had spoken well of me. But by the time the confirmation was delivered, it was too late, the paper was gone to press. I was " reliable, quick, and resourceful," the city editor said, as he made me a regular reporter.

In a word I was a success, and though I have never since had such a victory and have come to have some doubt of the success of success, I have never since failed to understand successful men; I know, as I see them, how they feel inside.

For Discussion of Steffens

1. At the beginning of this account what was Steffens's main concern? What is his mood at the end of the account? Trace the main steps in his climb to success as a reporter. Why was he happy to become a "regular," even though his earnings decreased?

2. Did you sympathize with Steffens's father in his decision to put his son on his own? In what ways was the decision a wise one? What evidence of real affection for the son did you find?

3. How did Steffens's original vague plan for finding a job fit in with the career he actually made for himself?

4. Two other main threads of interest should have caught your attention: the relationship between Steffens and his mother-in-law, and Steffens's curiosity and constructive interest in business and civic operations, which made him not merely a successful but a great reporter. The strong human interest of the mother-in-law situation makes it appeal to almost any reader, but the second element would catch the attention of only an alert, thoughtful reader. See how many details on each topic you can recall without actually rereading the selection.

5. Point out examples of Steffens's frankness in writing of himself and of the other people who had some part in his life.

6. Write an account of any experience you have had in looking for a job. Try to see yourself as you appeared to your prospective employer. If you have never had such an experience, select a job you might reasonably expect to get right now, and concentrate on making the account realistic and convincing.

For Your Vocabulary

TECHNICAL AND GENERAL MEANINGS: The meaning of the legal term *libel*, which played an important part in the handling of Steffens's first news story, should be quite clear from the context. *Libel* is the printing or public pronouncement of damaging opinions or facts, and the injured person may take legal action to collect damages. How do you pronounce *libeled* and *libelous?* How does libel differ from *slander?*

Charles Phillips

RICHARD SULLIVAN
1908–

Charles Phillips crowded a variety of experience into his fifty-three years. He was editor of the San Francisco *Monitor*, an active welfare worker in Poland after World War I, and author of a dozen books of fiction, poetry, and plays. And yet he will probably be best remembered as Professor of Literature at Notre Dame during the period from 1924 to 1933. It may come as a mild surprise to some students that Notre Dame has other traditions besides football; at any rate, "Charlie" Phillips himself is now a Notre Dame tradition. His courses in literature had a wide following, including students who had no special interest in the subject, precisely because he could attract people and catch up their enthusiasm in his own. His special contribution, however, was in the small group of young authors whom he influenced and directed into a career of writing. In that way, he left a permanent mark on the Catholic literary scene.

The author of this essay, Richard Sullivan, is one of his disciples. He was born in Kenosha, Wisconsin, and he took his degree at Notre Dame in 1930. For a time his interest was divided equally between painting and writing, but a preference for literature won out. His first novel, *Summer After Summer*, demonstrated an ability to write about simple people bringing the power of Catholic belief into the quiet heroism of their lives. Since then he has published two other novels and contributed stories to *The Atlantic, The Catholic World, Scribner's, Cosmopolitan,* and other magazines. In 1936 he returned to Notre Dame to teach playwriting and poetry.

The following selection is not so much a biography of Charles Phillips as an account of the impressions that a teacher made on one of his students. It is unquestionably true that a teacher influences his pupils more by what he is than by what he says. Long after we have forgotten much of what we call the "facts" of a subject, we will be impressed by the way it was presented or by the personality of the teacher. Every teacher will have influenced you in a subtle manner; a few will have touched you in a special way by their great learning, pleasant manner, or unique methods, and forever afterwards be numbered among your own "unforgettable characters." In this selection, see if you can detect the intangible qualities that made "Charlie" Phillips one of the best-loved professors at Notre Dame.

WHEN I first saw Charlie Phillips, in late September of 1926, he was lugging a huge armchair with a flowery cretonne slipcover out of a room in Sorin Hall; he beamed at me over the top of it, a round-faced and — I thought at the time — elderly man with thick glasses, thin hair, and a remarkably springy way of bouncing around with furniture. My dentist at home, a remote cousin of his, had given me a letter to present. Dutifully — but with acute embarrassment, because in my first week here I had heard the name of Phillips spoken with such admiration among students that I was honestly somewhat scared of meeting the man — I presented the letter. Charlie was almost oriental in the lavish politeness and ceremony with which he read it and then shook both my hands. But I had caught him at the moment when he was moving into the third-floor tower of Sorin, into the pair of rooms which to this day seems to me his home; a couple of seniors were bustling in and out helping him carry his belongings down the corridor; he was a man who accumulated belongings; he had a lot of them; the seniors shouted intricate questions at him; he beamed, turned his good ear, nodded, and said, "Fine! That's right! Good, Bill! Just anywhere at all!" He shook both my hands and explained how profoundly sad he was that on this day of all days, when I had come to see him, he should be involved — as no doubt I saw? — in the ridiculous, frantic, unspeakable business of moving. I would forgive him, he knew. He trusted me to come back. Carefully he folded my dentist's letter and stuck it into a carton of books. Instantly one of the seniors seized the carton and waddled past me with it. Charlie patted my shoulder. "Come back," he said. He picked up a great silver coffee urn and handed it carefully to the other senior: "Guard it with your life!" To me he added: "Remember, next time you come I'll be living in the tower!" I didn't understand in any way, though I did notice and still remember clearly, the pride with which he spoke of his future address.

This happened at the time when I was still out for football, before I had been grounded. I must have been an extraordinarily ungracious youth. Despite the cordiality of Charlie's greeting and what I know now was his thoroughly sincere invitation to return, I didn't go back for almost three years. Partly, I think, it was because of his very warmth that I didn't go back: I don't think I quite trusted him, because he was so kind to me at first sight. Partly it was the excited and natural preoccupation with other constantly shifting interests. Partly it was a continued awe; because he was a tremendously popular teacher, and I didn't like to play up to him by reason of a dentist's letter.

It was late in my junior year that a friend brought me up to Charlie's third-floor tower in Sorin Hall. I had by this time become an English major. Although I had flunked the four-hour exam by which candidates for this program were screened, I was squeezed in on condition that I show improvement in composition. My friend took me to Charlie to make arrangements for my getting into his playwriting course, which was open only to students personally approved by the teacher.

The big tower room had bookcases running around most of its wall space; there was a davenport in the middle, and a desk at one end of it; the ceiling hung a good fifteen feet above the half dozen throw rugs that covered the worn carpet, and the high walls were loaded with signed photographs, water colors, icons [1] in silvery frames. On the window sills stood little figurines, on the bookshelves Mexican vases, on the radiator tops stacks of manuscript; everywhere there were more photographs. A huge wooden mantelpiece — a fake —

---

[1] **icons** (ī′kŏnz): flat paintings which take the place of statues in the Eastern churches.

sat against one wall, its fire-hole full of stacked magazines and a couple of pairs of rubbers; a day bed stretched under a window; beyond the half-open door to the bedroom, at one end, peeked a white wash bowl, with some bookcases beyond it merging into gloom. But in the big room the great long windows behind monkscloth drapes opened up on tree tops; and in the rounding bay in the corner, in the windowed curve of the tower, sitting in an armchair with a lapboard across his middle, scribbling passionately in red ink on the margin of a student paper, one cigarette in his mouth and another one burning forgotten in the ash tray beside him, sat Charlie.

He never heard you come in. What had been his better ear had been permanently closed off in a railroad wreck in Poland, and his once bad ear was now his good one. You could call to him in an ordinary voice from the door and he wouldn't hear you. Nobody ever knocked; you simply walked in — if the door was locked the keys were always lying above it on the transom ledge; but of course if they were there, he wasn't — you walked in and moved diagonally across the room toward him in his corner. Usually he glanced up at once; he seemed to catch movement; but there were times later on when I found him so engrossed that I had to go over and tap him on the shoulder to let him know I was there. When he saw you he made a great ceremony of welcome. When I think of it carefully, though, it was not a great ceremony at all; it merely seemed like one. Because he was a person so honestly pleased at seeing people, so fervently delighted at seeing friends, so truly flattered that his friends would come to see him, that he became radiant in his greetings. You felt the effect of elaborate and ceremonious excitement in his manner. Actually all he might do was beam and beckon and say: "I just read that paper of yours on Plautus. Beautiful! But now *look* — "

He was the kind of teacher who was constantly bowled over by his students' achievements. You'd turn in a crude first draft of the first act of a play to him at nine o'clock in the morning; at eight-thirty that night he'd tramp across the campus and bang on your door. "I've been reading this first act. *Tremendous!* But now look — !" He'd have the manuscript in his topcoat pocket; he'd sit on your bed and explain to you the marvelous subtleties of your work, its power and glory; you'd feel paralyzed by your own accomplishment; then he'd say: "But now *look* — !" And for three quarters of an hour, with the sheets of the manuscript lying all over the bed, he'd go through your first act and tell you charmingly, ingratiatingly, what was the matter with it. You saw the Theatre Guild [1] getting farther and farther away as he spoke. Only he made it seem just a trifling matter of reconceiving the whole thing — which was wonderful despite its faults, mind you! — and the Theatre Guild was waiting outside the door again. You could in fact see the whole play, reconceived, the first act rewritten, the second and third already done. And Charlie would say, dropping ashes on your pillow and beating them on to the floor, six pages flying: "Remember this — what I've said here isn't *my* idea at all! It's *yours!* I got it from what *you* wrote! And this thing is going to be terrific! How soon can you get it done?"

Before God, he was a wonderful teacher. He knew things, and he had integrity and grace and enthusiasm.

Another night at half-past eight he'd pound on your door. "I saw your light. You're working like a bloody fool. Why do you work so hard? You're too young. Come on out and take a walk." He'd pull you off along the gravel path to town and tell you stories about the moon.

I got to know him well in my senior year and in the few years afterward. From things he said, never very much at one time, but little bits dropped now and again, I came to know a little about his life. Not in any detailed way, but in the large sequence.

He was born in 1880 in Richmond, Wisconsin, up in the northwest corner of the State. De La Salle College, Georgetown, and St. Mary's College of Oakland, California, were schools he attended; but when and for what period he was at each I don't know. He had an honorary degree from the University of Krakow, given in recognition of his work in war relief in Poland. When he was in his early twenties he was writing poetry and doing magazine pieces. He edited newspapers in St. Paul, in Washington, D.C., and in San Francisco.

Some place along the line he got stage-struck. His feeling for the theater was a permanent, fierce, and contagious excitement which affected any number of persons thereafter. Dimly I connect, without certainty, his passion for the theater with his permanent, fierce, romantic attitude toward the great Polish actress, Modjeska.[2] Possibly as a newspaperman he met her; I don't know; I seem to remember most hazily that he did. Anyhow, he was in love with her, very truly, very chivalrously, all his life. You could tell by the way he talked. When he was in San Francisco he wrote a poetic play called *The Divine Friend*; Margaret Anglin [3] appeared in it in 1915; ever afterward, very truly, very chivalrously, Charlie was in love with her. You could again tell by the way he talked.

He was, while I am on the subject,

[1] **Theatre Guild:** an organization that regularly produces plays in the New York theaters.

[2] **Modjeska** (mô·jĕs′kȧ), Helena (1840–1909). She toured the United States in plays during the 1880's and 1890's.

[3] **Margaret Anglin:** a noted American actress (1876–   ). Notre Dame awarded her the Laetare Medal in 1926.

also in love with the country of Poland and with the *terza rima* of Dante.[1] Using the phrase " in love " I am not being intemperate or inexact or figurative: in addition to the recipients mentioned a considerable number of other persons and things were the objects of his very definite, concentrated, intense, personal, and unwavering affection.

I am not sure when he married; he spoke to me of his marriage only once, though afterwards he sometimes referred to it as something I knew about and understood. I remember that he jerked his head contemptuously in the direction of the silver coffee urn, which always stood on a special table in his tower room. " I didn't always live here! " he said. " *That* belonged in my home! You didn't know I had a home one time, did you? " For an instant he was quite bitter, querulous, practically accusing. I was startled. We had just been talking. I don't know now what had brought up the matter of homes or coffee urns. But then he relaxed; he told me, almost by way of apology for an outburst, that a long time ago he had married a woman who shortly afterward lost her mind. She was still alive, in a sanitarium. (It may be that at the date of this writing she is still alive.) Either I have lost the date or I never knew; but I'd guess that he married in the San Francisco period, about the time the play was produced. My impression is that it was the collapse of his domestic life that sent him off to war in 1918. He went as some sort of official in a Catholic relief mission. After the armistice he switched to the Red Cross, and worked in Poland until 1922. But telling me in 1930 about his marriage he did not say or imply that he stayed in Europe for intimate private reasons; he didn't say or imply that he dreaded to come home: that is something I read into his story.

Most people here knew him as a bachelor. He kept the story of his marriage generally secret. No doubt he found that the easiest way to live without self-pity. If he talked much about the thing he would have had to acknowledge the personal disaster. He was a man built for marriage, home, sons and daughters. As a Catholic he of course could not remarry. But he did not choose to dwell upon these aspects. So he supported his wife and let himself be known as an aging celibate. He shut up about the whole thing.

As a bachelor he fitted into a pattern which seems to me peculiarly a Notre Dame one. I don't know; I've made no survey of American universities on this or any other question. But a good and gifted friend and present colleague of mine, who has taught at several universities, a man not a Catholic, pointed out to me lately the special role which, it seemed to him, was played here by the unmarried lay faculty. I'm convinced that his observation is a true one. At Notre Dame as long as I have known the place, and earlier by record, there have always been a small number of bachelors living on the campus and doing work there which has never been officially recognized nor publicly saluted. Personally, with St. Paul, I feel that marriage is a great sacrament; and I have at moments felt sorry for some of my colleagues who — without entering into the vowed celibacy of any religious community — nevertheless have foregone the human satisfactions and apprehensions of family life. But naming no names, I know men now living among students on the campus who — not by formal counsel or by self-conscious example, but simply by being themselves, naturally, richly,

[1] *terza rima* (tĕr′tsä rē′mä): a scheme of continuous verse arranged in three-line units, in which the second line of each rhymes with the first and third lines of the next; **Dante** (dăn′tĕ): Italian poet (1265–1321), author of the *Divine Comedy*.

and fully — have effected amazing things among their younger fellow-residents in the halls. Students whom no priest could reach, and certainly no teacher like myself, living in town, could possibly get close to and understand, will confide in and share desperations with these unmarried hall-laymen, and will emerge from the confidence curiously enlightened, straightened out. "There are many ministries." I'm inclined, privately, to believe that under providence there may be a special ministry for the Notre Dame faculty bachelors. And I'm inclined to regard them as extraordinary figures in the educational structure of this place. Charlie Phillips was one of them, one of the best.

Only he was not very happy here, I think, when he came to Notre Dame in 1924, about two years after his return from Europe. His book *The New Poland* had been published in London the year before; he had been lecturing a bit; he was still unsettled, unlocated; he came here as a venture into stability; he was immediately troubled by the newness, the strangeness, of teaching; he was doubtful about it as a way of life for himself, uncertain about his own talent for it. It took him months, maybe it took him a year or so, to settle in and feel assured. I think that it was not until he moved to the tower that he felt himself permanently at home here. And despite his rare, irritable awareness that this was not the home he had originally chosen, the tower room did mean to him, for the first time in years, a permanent place, a fixed spot, a center in which to live. He saw it as his own. He was immensely proud of it. He probably did not realize how much he needed it, when he set up the coffee urn and hung his pictures, arranged his photographs to stay.

That coffee urn. Once a former student of his was married in the Log Chapel. There was a need to hurry

after trains and a boat to catch in New York. Charlie improvised a quick wedding breakfast. Orange juice, the wedding cake, and coffee, of course, out of the silver urn. A hygienic friend of the groom, knowing Charlie, undertook privately to inspect the urn just before breakfast; found it full of the gray dust curls of years; scoured it hastily but thoroughly; the coffee which came out was thus strong, fine, and clear. Charlie never knew about the crusty inside of his cherished pot or about the last-minute purging. I know: it was my wedding.

He might have been hurt if he had ever suspected that people who knew him well had learned to watch out for such things as dust inside his precious silver. He had a quick sensitivity; he could quite easily be cut; yet he had learned to guard somewhat against this sort of pain by steadily making fun of himself. At deafness in general — most of all at his own deafness, which must have been a constant embarrassment, handicap, and torment — he always jeered. He had a fine, expanding repertoire of jokes about the subject, and seemed to enjoy them all immensely. The telephone in his room was rigged up so that it blinked a light which was supposed to attract his attention. (He could hear quite well over the telephone or when riding in a car. "The vibration," he used to explain, solemnly. "I own one slightly vibrant eardrum.") But when the phone rang he of course never heard it, and when the light blinked he usually was much too occupied to notice it. So for safety's sake a bell also rang on an extension in the room of a colleague and close friend of his, down the corridor. This friend answered all calls; when Charlie was wanted the friend dashed down the hall, into the tower room, shouting and pointing at the faithfully blinking but unacknowledged bulb on the far wall. Charlie always found this routine up-

Charles Phillips' rooms at Notre Dame were on the third floor of the tower of this building, Sorin Hall. (Notre Dame University)

roariously amusing. Or he pretended to find it so. I honestly don't know. I've talked just lately to the friend who used to answer the phone and he honestly doesn't know either. Charlie could be deceptive. He used to sign letters with a funny little caricature of himself, round faced, with three hairs showing on his scalp, and a hand up to a huge extended ear.

He was such a practiced and effective talker that in his classes nobody was ever very much aware that if a question was asked in a normal tone he'd never hear it; because he talked as if he were answering all individual questions all the time, as he went along, so much in accord with his hearers that he anticipated their collective curiosities. But once, I remember, an unthinking man in his World Literature class did raise his hand and ask a question in class. Charlie ran down off the platform, cupped a hand round his good ear.

Everybody in the room — seventy-five of us; he drew big classes — hated the questioner, who in embarrassment repeated his words in a shout. And Charlie said, "Oh, yes, yes, a *very* good question." And answered beautifully and at length.

In his World Lit class when he was trying to give us the feel and fever of Spain, while we were reading a bit of Cervantes and a dab of Calderon,[1] Charlie put on a bullfight. He was a teacher who, thank God, let himself get carried away once in a while. No educator; a teacher pure and simple. He was telling us about Spain. He was going to give us the reality of the Spanish soul as he knew it. Something suggested bullfight to him; I will swear he had not prepared this part of his lec-

[1] **Cervantes** (sĕr·văn′tēz): Spanish novelist (1547–1616), author of *Don Quixote;* **Calderon** (kôl′dĕr·ŏn): Spanish dramatist and poet (1600–1681), educated by Jesuits in Madrid.

ture, because it had the wonder and life of the impromptu; it was the expression of the unrehearsable. The six-inch-high wooden platform at the front end of the classroom ran wall to wall; it made a stage; and on this stage, from window at one edge to desk at the other Charlie became in turn — and sometimes simultaneously — picador, matador,[1] bull, and howling crowd. From horseback he leaned heavily on his lance, pic-ing the bull; he pawed and whirled; he stamped the boards; steam came from his nostrils; poising, he placed the banderillas;[2] holding an invisible cape and sword he waited, thrust, killed, and was killed; as crowd he cheered. Watching him we goggled in captivation; because it was art — a re-creation: a bullfight here and now — but Charlie too, putting it on all by himself in a tempest of spontaneous excitement; and he was good. When the performance was over, in say five minutes, he tied it right into his lecture, and went on, a bit breathlessly at first, about Don Quixote freeing the galley slaves and then being beaten by them. That linked up somehow with the bullfight, though I can't remember what connection he established. He was getting on to fifty that year.

Once in Chicago in the dead of winter, the year after I graduated, I met him for half an hour as he was passing through; we went to a sandwich joint. He asked me what I was going to have. Used to talking loud to his good ear I yelled "Swiss on rye!" and the man behind the counter yelled "Swiss on rye!" and down in the entrails of the place, where construction was carried on, a voice echoed "Swiss on rye!" Everybody along the counter gawked at us. But Charlie never heard a word outside my original answer. "I think I'll have ham," he said, and kept right on telling me about the rector who the day before had slipped and sat down hard on the ice outside Walsh Hall. Charlie, just behind him, hurried along to help the rector to his feet. "Remember, Father, there's a divinity that shapes our ends," said Charlie. "Rough-hew them how we will," said the priest, rubbing his sore spots. And then the waitress slid our sandwiches down the marble counter; and I kept shouting questions and Charlie went on posting me on Notre Dame.

He always did a lot of dashing back and forth between Chicago and South Bend. Often it was to see plays; very often it was on a lecture job: he booked more lectures than were good for him, ignoring the nervous drain in favor of the honorarium. Like most of us, he generally could use money. He had his private high family expenses, which he kept quiet about; he also helped support at least two members of his immediate lateral kin; and he was anything but parsimonious in his personal spending. Because he needed money — yet I'm convinced out of simple habit, too — he worked like a dog. He put so much energy into teaching, into writing red-ink essays on the margins and backs of class papers, into conferring at appointed hours and at unappointed hours, for literally hours, with students, that it is now to me a wonder that he got any other work done. But in the time I knew him — which at the most was about seven years; at the least less than five — he published a book of poems, a book of essays about teaching, a novel, and — posthumously[3] by just a short while — a biography of Pader-

---

[1] picador (pĭk'à·dōr): in a bullfight, a horseman who enrages the bull by prodding it with a lance; matador (măt'à·dōr): the star performer, the one who tries to kill the bull after enraging it with elaborate motions of his cape.

[2] *banderillas* (bän'dä·rēl'yäz): barbed darts thrust into the neck or shoulder of the bull to weaken it before the final sword thrust of the matador.

[3] posthumously (pŏs'tṹ·mŭs·lĭ): published after the death of its author.

ewski.[1] I know that in addition to these published works he did at least one play and a full book about the young Lincoln, both of which are presumably somewhere in manuscript right now. And he wrote innumerable reviews, stray pieces for magazines; he was always sneaking off sonnets in odd hours; each week for it seems to me fifty dollars, though I'm not sure, he turned out half a page of Sunday comment for a now defunct South Bend newspaper. One afternoon a week he exiled himself (not leaving the keys up over the transom) to do this job. I can't remember which afternoon it was. Wednesday afternoons he exiled himself to prepare his Dante class, which was taught each Wednesday night. But I remember the pressure and tension with which he always talked of the weekly newspaper routine. The fifty dollars, or whatever it was, seemed exceedingly important to him; he had a place for it, all right. He worked like a dog, teaching, writing, lecturing.

I used to be amazed at his power to get so much done. I remember telling him one time that I didn't see how it was possible to set aside an afternoon to do an article and then simply do it, in the allotted period. That seemed to me an impossible procedure at the time. He said that it was just a routine you sort of got used to. He also told me that it was a bad thing for a writer to talk much about what he was writing or planning to write, because he could crystallize it, give it its form orally instead of on paper; and once a thing had got crystallized and settled in its form there was no changing it. He was of course precisely right.

Not long ago, in a book of his which I was looking through, I found a loose clipping of a piece he did — " A Note on Passion Plays " — for the drama section of the Sunday New York *Times*. The

date has been cut off; from play advertisements on the reverse side — *The Green Pastures*,[2] *Three's a Crowd*, Walter Hampden and Fay Bainter reviving *The Admirable Crichton*, *Girl Crazy* with Ginger Rogers, *Private Lives* reopening with Gertrude Lawrence and Noel Coward — I'd guess the time was spring, 1931. The couple of thousand words by Charles Phillips very neatly sum up fifty years of American theater in a given field, with excursions to Oberammergau,[3] Tokyo, Indochina, France, and England. It is exactly the kind of pleasant, informative, documented thing which Charlie, making notes on the back of an envelope for twenty minutes, could write in an hour and a half; I can't imagine him looking up or even checking on the fact that Eugene O'Neill's father played Our Lord in the Salmi Morse Passion Play produced in the Grand Opera House, San Francisco, in 1880: that was the kind of fact he simply knew, by the thousands, with absolute certainty. But what struck me most forcibly in this little piece was its beginning: " Running through some old files the other day I came across a letter of Charles Warren Stoddard's,[4] a letter written originally to my old friend, now dead many years, Elizabeth Gray Lightner. Mrs. Lightner was Isadora Duncan's aunt and lived with Isadora through some of the famous dancer's stormiest years . . ."

That is pure Charlie. He not only knew everybody: he knew everybody's aunt as well. Into all his talk there was threaded a long line of reference to personalities he had somewhere or other,

---

[1] **Paderewski** (păd′ĕ·rĕf′skĕ): Polish pianist and composer, premier of Poland in 1919.

[2] *The Green Pastures:* a play by Marc Connelly that won the Pulitzer Prize in 1930. The other plays and actors mentioned here were all in the news during the 1920's and 1930's.

[3] **Oberammergau** (ō′bĕr·äm′ĕr·gou): village in Upper Bavaria, Germany, where a famous Passion Play is presented every tenth year.

[4] **Charles Warren Stoddard:** American short-story writer and essayist (1843–1909).

somehow or other, encountered; and he managed, by being himself, to link them all together in some sort of fantastical intimacy — Papini and William Butler Yeats, Modjeska and Chesterton,[1] Isadora and at least three Popes, Paderewski and God knows who; I can't remember them all.

He may very well have written — it would indeed have been quite like him to write — the longhand draft of the Passion Play piece with Charles Warren Stoddard's pen; I think it was Stoddard's pen he kept on his desk and prized; somebody's pen, surely. Anyhow, Stoddard — who taught here for a year or so in the mid-eighties — was a character whose minor eccentricities (a man of letters who, by his own spelling, smoked "sigarettes" but never "chowed") Charlie admired with reservations.

He might have written with Stoddard's pen (if I'm right about it's being Stoddard's pen he kept on the desk) because he had a lot of sentiment in him; and it would have seemed to him remarkably appropriate, even touching, to connect in this way the man whose letter gave rise to the article with the very instrument which, possibly, had written that letter. He liked to tie things together; he liked to wrap them up.

It occurs to me as I write that my knowledge of Stoddard and his pen is as vague as most people's knowledge of Charlie. Today at Notre Dame his name is almost universally unknown. Students sometimes see it on the bookplate of a library book that once belonged to him and had a place in the tower room. They wonder who he was. I've asked them; I know. They wonder casually and respectfully what *Ex Libris* [2] — *Charles Phillips* signifies.

Men who knew him during the not quite ten years he was here remember him as a great and gifted teacher, not formally trained for his work but temperamentally endowed for it: which is, perhaps, even better. Teaching fulfilled him. It seems to me unquestionably what he was made for. His work here, I think, was what his whole life pointed toward. I know how easy it is to make big statements out of an after-view, and out of affection. But I think Charlie's years at Notre Dame were both his personal consummation and his rich destiny.

He died — suddenly, unexpectedly — during the Christmas holidays of 1933, on December 29, in Minneapolis. Some of us used to arrange each year on the anniversary of his death to have a Mass said for him; we would go to Communion for his intention at it, and afterward we'd talk about him at breakfast in the cafeteria. But during the Christmas holidays a lot of us are away, necessarily. We don't do it anymore.

Once when I was a student I went up to his room late on a Wednesday afternoon. It was his time for preparing the Dante class, but I was sure he'd be through by half-past five, and I had to see him briefly about something I thought was important. Peering up over the lapboard he looked wretched and bleary. "Dante!" he said. There were books and papers all over everywhere. He started to shake his finger at me. "You know what Dante could do? Hate! He could hate! That man had a power for hating! And you know what the trouble with *me* is? You know why I'm a bum poet? Well, I'll tell you — sit down — you want a cigarette? — I haven't got any hate in me! All I do is *love* everything, no matter what, all the time. All the *time!* "

That was probably his real trouble.

<hr/>

[1] **Papini** (pä·pē′nê), Giovanni: Italian biographer (1881–   ); **William Butler Yeats** (yāts): Irish poet and playwright (1865–1939); **Chesterton,** Gilbert Keith: English poet, essayist, novelist, and critic (1874–1936).

[2] *Ex Libris:* from the library.

I suppose there may somewhere have existed greater, surer, more learned, and definitely more renowned teachers than he was. But of all I have ever myself known he was the best.

For Discussion of Sullivan

1. List the qualities you consider desirable in a teacher. Check your list against this selection and see how many of the qualities you can find in Charles Phillips.

2. "Great heroism is often silent heroism." How does this statement apply to Charles Phillips? Give examples of silent heroism in people you know. Do you recall any literary personalities to whom this statement can be applied?

3. Mr. Sullivan pays tribute to the unmarried laymen on the Notre Dame faculty. What is their particular contribution to the students at the University?

4. One of the achievements of Professor Phillips was the encouragement he gave to young writers who have enriched the American literary scene. Explain the ways in which he gave this encouragement.

5. "I haven't got any hate in me! All I do is *love* everything, no matter what, all the time." This is a quotation from Charles Phillips. Do you think this love was the secret of his success as a teacher? How did it affect his dealings with his students?

For Your Vocabulary

MODIFIERS: The clear picture Richard Sullivan gives you of his friend and teacher results largely from his ability to use words effectively. The following are a few examples of his use of modifying words in order to give an exact and vivid meaning: *honestly* pleased, *fervently* delighted, *elaborate* and *ceremonious* excitement. A cursory reading of the selection will reveal other examples. In your own writing try imitating Sullivan's effective use of modifiers.

Of Charles Phillips the author writes, "He had *integrity, grace,* and *enthusiasm*." Look up the meanings of these words,

then show how each quality was evident in the life of Mr. Phillips.

For Further Reading of General Nonfiction

TO UNDERSTAND AMERICA

Adams, James Truslow, *The American; the Making of a New Man* (Scribner, 1943)

Allen, F. L., *Only Yesterday* (Harper, 1931)

Allen, F. L., *Since Yesterday* (Blue Ribbon Books, 1943)

Benét, Stephen Vincent, *America* (Farrar and Rinehart, 1944)

Bruckberger, Raymond L., *One Sky to Share* (Kenedy, 1952)

De Voto, Bernard, *Across the Wide Missouri* (Houghton Mifflin, 1947)

Gunther, John, *Inside U.S.A.* (Harper, 1947)

Johnson, Gerald, *Incredible Tale: The Odyssey of the Average American in the Last Half Century* (Harper, 1950)

LaFarge, Oliver, *As Long as the Grass Shall Grow* (Alliance Book Corp., 1940)

Perry, George Sessions, *Families in America* (Whittlesey House, 1949)

Rawlings, Marjorie Kinnan, *Cross Creek* (Grosset, 1945)

Rienow, Robert, *Calling All Citizens* (Houghton Mifflin, 1947)

Shippen, Katherine L., *Passage to America* (Harper, 1951)

Stewart, George R., *Names on the Land* (Random House, 1945)

White, E. B., *Here Is New York* (Harper, 1950)

Book Series: The Rivers of America (Rinehart), American Customs (Vanguard)

ENTERTAINING PEOPLE

Benchley, Robert C., *Inside Benchley* (Harper, 1942)

Benchley, Robert C., *Chips Off the Old Benchley* (Harper, 1949)

Broun, Heywood, *Seeing Things at Night* (Harcourt, Brace, 1921)

Day, Clarence, *Clarence Day Omnibus* (Sun Dial, 1945). Includes *Life with Father, Life with Mother,* and *God and My Father.*

Forbes, Kathryn, *Mama's Bank Account* (Harcourt, Brace, 1943)

Gilbreth, Frank B., and Ernestine Gilbreth Carey, *Cheaper by the Dozen* (Crowell, 1948)

Kimbrough, Emily, *It Gives Me Great Pleasure* (Dodd, Mead, 1948)

Leacock, Stephen, *Literary Lapses* (Penguin, 1939)

Linscott, Robert N., ed., *Comic Relief, an Omnibus of American Humor* (Blue Ribbon Books, 1942)

Ross, Leonard Q., *The Education of Hyman Kaplan* (Harcourt, Brace, 1941)

Skinner, Cornelia Otis, and Emily Kimbrough, *Our Hearts Were Young and Gay* (Dodd, Mead, 1942)

Thurber, James, *The Thurber Carnival* (Harper, 1945)

Thurber, James, *The Beast in Me and Other Animals* (Harcourt, Brace, 1948)

Toombs, Alfred, *Raising a Riot* (Crowell, 1949)

White, E. B., *One Man's Meat* (Harper, 1944)

NATURE AND SCIENCE

Andrews, Roy Chapman, *Under a Lucky Star* (Viking, 1943)

Beebe, William, *Half Mile Down* (Harcourt, Brace, 1934)

Bendik, Jeanne, *Television Works Like This* (McGraw-Hill, 1949)

Bromfield, Louis, *Pleasant Valley* (Harper, 1945)

Bromfield, Louis, *Out of the Earth* (Harper, 1950)

Carson, Rachel, *The Sea Around Us* (Oxford, 1951)

DeKruif, Paul, *Microbe Hunters* (Harcourt, Brace, 1939)

DeKruif, Paul, *Hunger Fighters* (Harcourt, Brace, 1939)

Ditmars, Raymond L., *The Fight to Live* (Stokes, 1938)

Dobie, J. Frank, *The Voice of the Coyote* (Little, Brown, 1949)

Montgomery, Elizabeth Rider, *The Story Behind Great Inventions* (Dodd, Mead, 1944)

Peattie, Donald Culross, *Flowering Earth* (Phoenix House, 1948)

Sanderson, Ivan, *Animal Tales* (Knopf, 1946)

Skilling, Hugh H., *Exploring Electricity* (Ronald, 1949)

White, Stewart Edward, *The Forest* (Nelson, 1933)

MODERN PROBLEMS

Bennett, Hugh H., and William Pryor, *This Land We Defend* (Longmans, 1942)

Hersey, John, *Hiroshima* (Knopf, 1946)

Peattie, Donald Culross, *American Heartwood* (Houghton Mifflin, 1950)

Tead, Ordway, *The Case for Democracy* (Association Press, 1938)

Welles, Sumner, *We Need Not Fail* (Houghton Mifflin, 1948)

TRAVEL AND ADVENTURE

Banning, Margaret Culkin, *Salud! A South American Journal* (Harper, 1941)

Byrd, Richard E., *Discovery: The Story of the Second Byrd Antarctic Expedition* (Putnam)

Ellsberg, Edward, *Men Under the Sea* (Dodd, Mead, 1939)

Halliburton, Richard, *Royal Adventure* (Bobbs-Merrill, 1947). Includes *The Royal Road to Romance* and *The Glorious Adventure.*

Johnson, Martin, *Congorilla* (Harcourt, Brace, 1939)

London, Jack, *The Cruise of the Snark* (Macmillan, 1928)

Marshall, Edison, *Shikar and Safari* (Farrar, Straus, 1947)

Ullman, James R., *High Conquest* (Lippincott, 1941)

COLLECTIONS OF ESSAYS

Brown, Sharon, *Essays of Our Times* (Gage, 1939)

Chamberlain, Essie, *Essays Old and New* (Harcourt, Brace, 1948)

Gehlmann, John, *The Challenge of Ideas* (Odyssey, 1950)

Johnson, Burges, *Essaying the Essay* (Little, Brown, 1927)

Lester, John A., *Essays of Yesterday and Today* (Harcourt, Brace, 1943)

Morley, Christopher, *Modern Essays for Schools* (Harcourt, Brace, 1921)

Walter, E. A., *Essay Annual* (a series beginning in 1933) (Appleton)

Wood, W. R., *Fact and Opinion* (Heath, 1945)

For Further Reading of Biography

LEADERS AND PATHFINDERS

Daugherty, Sonia, *The Way of an Eagle* (Jefferson) (Oxford, 1941)

Eaton, Jeanette, *Leader by Destiny* (Washington) (Harcourt, Brace, 1938)

Harlow, Alvin Fay, *Theodore Roosevelt, Strenuous American* (Messner, 1943)

Horn, Stanley F., *The Boys' Life of Robert E. Lee* (Grosset, 1948)

James, Marquis, *Andrew Jackson* (Bobbs-Merrill, 1937)

Magaret, Helene, *Father de Smet* (Bruce, 1940)

Rourke, Constance, *Davy Crockett* (Harcourt, Brace, 1934)

Stone, Irving, *Immortal Wife* (Jessie Benton Frémont) (Doubleday, 1944)

White, Stewart Edward, *Daniel Boone, Wilderness Scout* (Doubleday, 1946)

NOTABLE ACHIEVEMENTS

DeForrest, Lee, *Father of Radio* (Wilcox and Follett, 1950)

Embree, E. R., *13 Against the Odds* (outstanding Negroes) (Viking, 1944)

Forbes, Esther, *Paul Revere and the World He Lived In* (Houghton Mifflin, 1942)

Keller, Helen, *The Story of My Life* (Doubleday, 1947)

Kelly, Fred C., *The Wright Brothers* (Harcourt, Brace, 1943)

Merton, Thomas, *The Seven Storey Mountain* (Harcourt, Brace, 1948)

Repplier, Agnes, *Mère Marie of the Ursulines* (Doubleday, 1931)

Washington, Booker T., *Up from Slavery* (Oxford, 1945)

AMERICANS FROM OTHER LANDS

COLUMBIA. Ybarra, T. R., *Young Man of Caracas* (Washburn, 1941)

DENMARK. Riis, Jacob A., *The Making of an American* (Macmillan, 1943)

JAPAN. Matsui, Haru, *Restless Wave* (Modern Age, 1940)

NETHERLANDS. Bok, Edward W., *The Americanization of Edward Bok* (Scribner, 1923)

RUMANIA. Ravage, Marcus Eli, *An American in the Making* (Harper, 1936)

RUSSIA. Papashvily, George and Helen, *Anything Can Happen* (Harper, 1945)

SCOTLAND. Muir, John, *The Story of My Boyhood and Youth* (Houghton Mifflin, 1913)

SYRIA. Rizk, Salom, *Syrian Yankee* (Doubleday, 1943)

YUGOSLAVIA. Pupin, Michael I., *From Immigrant to Inventor* (Scribner, 1925)

INTERESTING JOBS AND CAREERS

Addams, Jane, *Forty Years at Hull House*, reissue (Macmillan, 1935)

Andrews, Roy Chapman, *Under a Lucky Star; a Lifetime of Adventure* (Viking, 1943)

Bartlett, Robert M., *Sky Pioneer: The Story of Igor Sikorsky* (aeronautical engineer) (Scribner, 1947)

Chase, Mary Ellen, *A Goodly Heritage* (Holt, 1932)

Day, Dorothy, *The Long Loneliness* (Harper, 1952)

De Mille, Agnes, *Dance to the Piper* (Little, Brown, 1952)

Ferber, Edna, *A Peculiar Treasure* (World, 1947)

Garst, Shannon, *Jack London, Magnet for Adventure* (Messner, 1944)

Garwood, Darrell, *Artist in Iowa* (Grant Wood) (Norton, 1944)

Heiser, Victor, *An American Doctor's Odyssey* (Grosset, 1941)

Mack, Connie, *My Sixty-Six Years in the Big Leagues* (Winston, 1950)

Pace, Mildred M., *Clara Barton* (Scribner, 1941)

Partridge, Bellamy, *The Country Lawyer* (Grosset, 1941)

Rak, Mary Kidder, *A Cowman's Wife* (Houghton Mifflin, 1934)

Rinehart, Mary Roberts, *My Story; A New Edition and Seventeen New Years* (Rinehart, 1948)

Wald, Lillian D., *The House on Henry Street* (Little, Brown, 1934)

Williams, William W., *The Quiet Lodger of Irving Place* (O. Henry) (Dutton, 1936)

Devaney

Modern Poetry

POETRY is next to impossible to define. Much poetry has rhyme and meter, it is true, but rhyme and meter alone add up to only doggerel verse like

"Thirty days hath September,
April, June, and November."

Moreover, blank verse (the form of our greatest English poetry, including Shakespeare's plays) has no rhyme; and free verse (the form of much modern poetry) has neither rhyme nor regular metrical rhythm. Rhyme and meter are not the essentials of poetry. Then what are?

First, poetry stirs the emotions. Emily Dickinson said, "If I read a book and it makes my whole body so cold no fire can ever warm me, I know it is poetry." Carl Sandburg puts it this way, "Poetry is a language that tells us, through a more or less emotional reaction, something that cannot be said."

What stimulates the emotions? So far as poetry is concerned it is largely the imagination. The poet may start out with the rough clay of ordinary things seen every day; but before he has finished molding it, mental vision has far outstripped the merely physical. He has touched the imagination. With the magic spell of words he has clothed an idea with beauty. To realize this, we need only take some poem that really moves us, state the same subject or idea in plain prose, and then compare the two versions. Shorn of its wings, the prose version simply confronts us with a fact or a principle; it has lost its power to thrill or sway or uplift us.

Granting that stirring the emotions through appeal to the imagination is one of the essentials of poetry, what more can we discover? Again a direct answer eludes us, but we may say that without *rhythm* there can be no poetry. Rhythm need not be systematically arranged and measured in a fixed pattern or meter, but a more or less regular arrangement of accented and unaccented syllables must be present. Rhythm is essential to music, and its presence in poetry suggests that music and poetry are allied arts. The poet uses the *sounds* of language, by arranging words in rhythmic patterns.

Poetry, we may conclude, is the expression of a feeling or idea or story in rhythmical language; it stirs the emotions by stimulating the imagination.

Guide to Reading Poetry

How can you most enjoy your reading of poetry? First of all, you must not expect to get the meaning of a poem from one rapid reading. In most poems the thought is compressed; every line, every word, counts. Indeed, some of what the poet wishes to say is not actually expressed in words at all, but is suggested in the overtones of the poem, or is found " between the lines." Moreover, many poems are written in some traditional pattern (such as the sonnet), and to fit the thought to the pattern the poet packs his lines and phrases with much heavier loads of meaning than does a prose writer. You cannot hope to get the meaning of many lines of poetry without several readings and considerable thought. You would not expect, in a single reading, to catch the full import of Edwin Arlington Robinson's lines from " An Old Story ":

> But cursed him for the ways he had
>   To make me see
> My envy of the praise he had
>   For praising me.

Practically no poem comes clear in a single reading.

Much of the charm of poetry is in its music. Therefore, to read poetry rapidly for thought alone is to lose one of its most important pleasures. You must learn to read poetry so as to get the full effect of its rhythms and rhymes (and other musical elements). This means that you should take the time to read poetry aloud. At the very least, you must read it to yourself slowly enough so

that in your " mind's ear " you can actually hear it. Read these lines from Elinor Wylie's " Pretty Words " rapidly to yourself as you would read prose:

> I love smooth words, like gold-enameled fish
> Which circle slowly with a silken swish.

Now read them again, out loud, and see what has been added by actually hearing the words. Poetry must be heard to be appreciated.

A third way in which you can develop skill in reading poetry is to remember that you must keep your imagination alert and on the job. Most poems are attempts on the part of the poet to make you *feel* something. He often uses figures of speech and symbols to stimulate your emotions. You will miss all this unless your imagination is alert and active. " Life has loveliness to sell," says Sara Teasdale, and she wants you to *feel* that life is full of lovely things: " climbing fire that sways and sings," " music like a curve of gold," " scent of pine trees in the rain." But to feel this loveliness, you must, in your imagination, see the fire, hear the music, smell the pine trees. All this sensuous beauty will pass you by if you let your imagination go to sleep.

As you read the poems of this section, keep in mind the three aids to better reading which have been suggested here: read each poem several times; read aloud to hear the music in the poetry; keep your imagination alert so that your mind and senses respond as the poet intends.

Edwin Arlington Robinson
1869–1935

Edwin Arlington Robinson was a creator of portraits in verse. Wherever he was, he explored the lives of those around him, seeking answers to his questions about man's nature and destiny. As we turn the pages of his books, a whole gallery of men is revealed to our eyes, or better yet, to our imaginations. Sometimes their whole souls are laid open to us; often we catch only a suggestion. Sometimes they are treated earnestly, sometimes half cynically, sometimes with whimsical tenderness. And always these portraits in verse are made very real, very human.

Robinson found much of his material in the Maine town where he spent his boyhood, among his associates during two years at Harvard, and in New York, where he once struggled to earn a living checking loads of stone for the subway. Success came to him late, though he won the Pulitzer Prize three times and is today considered one of the great American poets. Besides studying modern men, he turned his attention to the Arthurian legends, and in his long works *Merlin, Lancelot,* and *Tristram,* wrote the most extensive poems based on these stories since Tennyson. While the English poet dwelt mainly on the colorful pageantry and romance of King Arthur's court, Robinson typically explored the dark, hidden faults in human character that led to the decline and fall of the knights of the Round Table.

RICHARD CORY

In his exploration of human character, Robinson found many puzzles and contradictions. In some of his poems he suggests an explanation of human behavior, but in "Richard Cory," probably his best-known poem, he leaves it to you to resolve the mystery.

Whenever Richard Cory went downtown,
  We people on the pavement looked at him:
He was a gentleman from sole to crown,
  Clean-favored, and imperially slim.

And he was always quietly arrayed, 5
  And he was always human when he talked;

But still he fluttered pulses when he said,
  "Good morning," and he glittered when he walked.

And he was rich — yes, richer than a king —
  And admirably schooled in every grace: 10
In fine, we thought that he was everything
  To make us wish that we were in his place.

So on we worked, and waited for the light,
  And went without the meat, and cursed the bread;

"Richard Cory" by Edwin Arlington Robinson. Reprinted by permission of Charles Scribner's Sons.

And Richard Cory, one calm summer
　　night,　　　　　　　　　　　　15
　　Went home and put a bullet through
　　　his head.

MINIVER CHEEVY

Miniver Cheevy is a very different person from Richard Cory, and the poet's picture of him is also different in tone. Don't
miss the humor in this devastating portrait.

Miniver Cheevy, child of scorn,
　　Grew lean while he assailed the sea-
　　　sons;
He wept that he was ever born,
　　And he had reasons.

Miniver loved the days of old　　　5
　　When swords were bright and steeds
　　　were prancing;
The vision of a warrior bold
　　Would set him dancing.

Miniver sighed for what was not,
　　And dreamed, and rested from his
　　　labors;　　　　　　　　　　　10
He dreamed of Thebes° and Camelot,°
　　And Priam's° neighbors.

Miniver mourned the ripe renown
　　That made so many a name so fra-
　　　grant;
He mourned Romance, now on the
　　town,　　　　　　　　　　　　15
　　And Art, a vagrant.

11. **Thebes** (thēbz): a famous city of ancient
Greece. (Notice the circle after the word *Thebes*.
This sign is used in the poetry sections of this
book to call your attention to each word that
is explained in a footnote.) **Camelot** (kăm'ĕ·lŏt):
the city of King Arthur and the knights of the
Round Table. 12. **Priam** (prī'ăm): the king of
Troy during the time the Greeks were besieging
it.

Miniver loved the Medici,°
　　Albeit he had never seen one;
He would have sinned incessantly
　　Could he have been one.　　　　20

Miniver cursed the commonplace
　　And eyed a khaki suit with loathing;
He missed the medieval grace
　　Of iron clothing.

Miniver scorned the gold he sought,　25
　　But sore annoyed was he without it;
Miniver thought, and thought, and
　　thought,
　　And thought about it.

Miniver Cheevy, born too late,
　　Scratched his head and kept on think-
　　　ing;　　　　　　　　　　　　30
Miniver coughed, and called it fate,
　　And kept on drinking.

17. **Medici** (mĕd'ê·chê): a highly cultivated
but often unprincipled ruling family of Florence,
Italy, in the fifteenth and sixteenth centuries.

BEWICK FINZER

Bewick Finzer is a failure in a different
way from Miniver Cheevy and Richard
Cory. He is a sad picture of the man who
had achieved his dream, that of wealth,
and cracked under the strain of losing it.
To get the full meaning of some lines (such
as the last two) you will need to read them
several times — and think them over.

Time was when his half-million drew
　　The breath of six per cent;
But soon the worm of what-was-not
　　Fed hard on his content;
And something crumbled in his brain　5
　　When his half-million went.

Time passed, and filled along with his
　　The place of many more;
Time came, and hardly one of us

"Miniver Cheevy" by Edwin Arlington Robinson. Reprinted by permission of Charles Scribner's Sons.
"Bewick Finzer" from *Collected Poems*, by Edwin Arlington Robinson. Reprinted by permission of The Macmillan Company, publishers.

Had credence to restore,   10
From what appeared one day, the man
  Whom we had known before.

The broken voice, the withered neck,
  The coat worn out with care,
The cleanliness of indigence,   15
  The brilliance of despair,
The fond imponderable dreams
  Of affluence — all were there.

Poor Finzer, with his dreams and
  schemes,
  Fares hard now in the race,   20
With heart and eye that have a task
When he looks in the face
Of one who might so easily
  Have been in Finzer's place.

He comes unfailing for the loan   25
  We give and then forget;
He comes, and probably for years
  Will he be coming yet —
Familiar as an old mistake,
  And futile as regret.   30

AN OLD STORY

This poem describes a certain relationship between two persons. The clue to the speaker's jealousy of his friend lies in the second stanza. Do not be misled by the simple words into thinking this is an easy stanza to understand. It will become clear if you start at the end of the stanza and work back.

Strange that I did not know him then,
  That friend of mine!
I did not even show him then
  One friendly sign;

But cursed him for the ways he had   5
  To make me see
My envy of the praise he had
  For praising me.

I would have rid the earth of him
  Once in my pride! . . .   10
I never knew the worth of him
  Until he died.

CALVARY

No verse form in English is more neatly adapted to expressing a single idea than the sonnet. If you can recognize the *pattern* of a poem like a sonnet, your enjoyment is increased by watching how skillfully the poet compresses and shapes his thought. Before reading " Calvary " turn to page 262 and learn more about the sonnet form. Then, as you read the poem, note that Robinson uses the first eight lines to sketch a situation " nineteen hundred years ago," and the last six lines to make a comment about today, " after nineteen hundred years." Be able to make a clear summary of each part of the poem.

Friendless and faint, with martyred
  steps and slow,
Faint for the flesh, but for the spirit
  free,
Stung by the mob that came to see the
  show,
The Master toiled along to Calvary;
We gibed him, as he went, with hound-
  ish glee,   5
Till his dimmed eyes for us did overflow;
We cursed his vengeless hands thrice
  wretchedly, —
And this was nineteen hundred years
  ago.
But after nineteen hundred years the
  shame
Still clings, and we have not made good
  the loss   10
That outraged faith has entered in his
  name.
Ah, when shall come love's courage to
  be strong!

Tell me, O Lord — tell me, O Lord, how
  long
Are we to keep Christ writhing on the
  cross!

For Discussion of Robinson

Richard Cory

1. What are possible causes for Richard's suicide? Why do you suppose Robinson did not himself supply the reason for Cory's desperate act?

2. What bit of philosophy about life does this poem suggest to your mind? What does Richard Cory's fate suggest about people's inner and outer lives?

3. Give in your own words the meaning of the first two lines of the last stanza.

Miniver Cheevy

1. Point out the lines in this poem that you found particularly amusing.

2. What is the real trouble with Miniver? What kinds of people do you know who spend their energies longing for " the good old days "?

Bewick Finzer

1. Point out lines or phrases in this poem which meant little to you on first reading, but which in successive readings came to be meaningful and memorable.

2. Which of the three men, Cory, Cheevy, and Finzer, do you consider most pathetic? Why?

An Old Story

1. What is the significance of the title?

2. Explain in your own words the reason for the speaker's jealousy. Try to put into exact language your reasons for disliking someone. Discuss whether your reasons reveal something about you yourself as well as something about the object of your dislike.

Calvary

1. What human failing keeps Christ " writhing on the cross "? The hint is in line 12. What is the meaning of the word *love* in this line?

2. Compare your summary of the two parts of the poem with those of your classmates. Select the best summary for each part and then put them together. In what

ways does the sonnet pattern make an idea seem more impressive?

Types of Poetry

THE SONNET: Poetry falls naturally into three great classes: *narrative, dramatic,* and *lyric.* The first two both tell stories, the narrative resembling in method the short story or novel, the dramatic being a play, or at least a dialogue, in verse. Lyric poetry expresses thought or feeling, and is usually personal in tone. Though a lyric poem may suggest a story, it does not tell it outright.

A *sonnet* is a lyric poem of highly restricted metrical form. It is limited to fourteen lines. Its rhythm is always te TUM, te TUM, te TUM, te TUM, te TUM. (This is " iambic pentameter." See p. 274.) In the so-called Italian sonnet there is a break in the thought between the first eight and the last six lines (called the *octave* and the *sestet*), and an intricate rhyme scheme. The Shakespearean sonnet is more flexible, usually in alternate rhyme, with a couplet at the end. Perhaps because of this very challenge to ingenuity, the sonnet has been a great favorite with poets of all times. Besides " Calvary," other sonnets appear on pages 296 and 304. To fix the form in your mind, you might choose one of these sonnets and commit it to memory.

For Your Vocabulary

FIGURATIVE LANGUAGE — SYMBOLS: When Robinson says, in " Richard Cory," that *people on the pavement* went without the *meat* and cursed the *bread,* he uses symbols. A symbol is something that stands for something else. *People on the pavement* or *in the street* is a symbol for " people in general " or the average man. *Meat* and *bread* are often used as symbols for food in general. Here *meat* stands for the more desirable things of life, as *bread* stands for bare necessities. Think of other ways in which both can be used symbolically. Try transferring the ideas into other symbols. If we use *velvet* to symbolize luxuries, what would symbolize bare necessities? What would symbolize actual want?

Amy Lowell
1874–1925

Amy Lowell was a remarkable woman. A member of the renowned Lowell family of Cambridge, Massachusetts — James Russell Lowell was a cousin of her grandfather — she was born to wealth and social position. Miss Lowell was widely known as a "bluestocking" — woman intellectual — in her youth. A large, vigorous person, given to eccentric dress and habits, she delighted in shocking genteel New England society with her candid manner. But she also won for herself a secure place in American literary history by spearheading a poetic movement known as "Imagism."

The Imagists were a group of American and English poets attempting a new style in poetry. The most debated techniques of the Imagists were the "pure image" or picture ("hard and clear, never blurred or indefinite") and "new rhythms" (which included free verse). Not much of this was really new, but Amy Lowell was a determined crusader, and she not only organized the publication of works by other Imagists, but also wrote several volumes of poetry applying Imagist principles.

A LADY

You are beautiful and faded
Like an old opera tune
Played upon a harpsichord;
Or like the sun-flooded silks
Of an eighteenth-century boudoir.   5
In your eyes
Smolder the fallen roses of outlived minutes,
And the perfume of your soul
Is vague and suffusing,
With the pungence of sealed spice jars.   10
Your half tones delight me,
And I grow mad with gazing
At your blent colors.
My vigor is a new-minted penny,
Which I cast at your feet.   15
Gather it up from the dust,
That its sparkle may amuse you.

For Discussion of Amy Lowell

1. In "A Lady" point out the hard, clear images. What does the poet make you hear, see, and smell?

2. What kind of person is suggested by a "new-minted penny"?

3. Try writing an "image" that compares one sense — sight, sound, smell, or touch — with another, as here Amy Lowell compares the lady's looks to a tune on a harpsichord.

Louise Guiney
1861–1920

Louise Guiney wanted "to emigrate to some hamlet that smells strongly of the Middle Ages." Born in Boston, she grew up loving studies, nature, and her hero-soldier-father, General Patrick R. Guiney of Civil War fame. A cavalier sense of honor and exploit marked her approach to life and letters. She spent the last twenty years of her life in England, where she edited the works of the Recusant poets — those who remained true to the Old Faith (Roman Catholic) in the days of the Protestant Revolt. A staunch Catholic, she shows her spiritual appreciation in all her work.

In "The Wild Ride" she weaves into ringing lines of verse her love for the heroic, her sense of the challenge in life, and her faith in the Providence of God.

THE WILD RIDE

I hear in my heart, I hear in its ominous pulses
All day, on the road, the hoofs of invisible horses,
All night, from their stalls, the importunate pawing and neighing.

Let cowards and laggards fall back! but alert to the saddle,
Weatherworn and abreast, go men of our galloping legion,   5
With a stirrup cup each to the lily of women that loves him.

The trail is through dolour and dread, over crags and morasses;
There are shapes by the way, there are things that appall or entice us:
What odds? We are Knights of the Grail, we are vowed to the riding.

Thought's self is a vanishing wing, and joy is a cobweb,   10
And friendship a flower in the dust, and glory a sunbeam:
Not here is our prize, nor, alas! after these our pursuing.

A dipping of plumes, a tear, a shake of the bridle,
A passing salute to this world and her pitiful beauty:
We hurry with never a word in the track of our fathers.   15

(I hear in my heart, I hear in its ominous pulses
All day, on the road, the hoofs of invisible horses,
All night, from their stalls, the importunate pawing and neighing.)

We spur to a land of no name, outracing the stormwind;
We leap to the infinite dark like sparks from the anvil.   20
Thou leadest, O God! All's well with Thy troopers that follow.

For Discussion of Guiney

1. In "The Wild Ride" why does the poet speak of "ominous pulses"? What does the phrase suggest? What is the galloping legion she refers to? What is a stirrup cup?

2. Explain the third and fourth stanzas. What is the "track of our fathers"? Where are the knights going? How do we know that all is well?

3. Write a brief paragraph summarizing the ideal embodied in the poem.

For Your Vocabulary

WORDS THAT CREATE IMAGES: "The Wild Ride" is predominantly a sight and sound poem. Louise Guiney chose words that will sharpen the reader's impressions. Pick out the sight and sound words. Notice how the rhythm suits the idea of the poem. What sound does it suggest? If you were to see these riders, how do you imagine they would be dressed? Explain the absence of any sense of time or season in the poem.

Charles L. O'Donnell, C.S.C.

1884–1934

Except for a brief year during World War I when he was chaplain of the famous Sixty-Ninth regiment with Father Duffy, Father O'Donnell's adult life was spent at Notre Dame. Born at Greenfield, Indiana, he attended school at Kokomo, and at the age of fourteen, presented himself at Notre Dame as a candidate for the Congregation of Holy Cross. After finishing college at Notre Dame, he studied theology for four years at the Holy Cross College, Washington, D.C., and was ordained in 1910. He was professor of English at Notre Dame until 1928 when he was made president of the University.

His first volume of poetry, *Dead Musician and Other Poems,* appeared in 1916, with subsequent volumes in 1922 and 1928. In 1942, in honor of the Notre Dame Centenary, his nephew, Charles Carey, C.S.C., edited his works under the title, *The Collected Poems of Charles L. O'Donnell.* Many of Father O'Donnell's lyrics are concerned with the beauties of God in nature. His penetrating love of God and Our Lady are evident in the poems that follow.

COMPASSION

Our Lady's part in the Redemption has been honored by the Church, as the beautiful Sequence, *Stabat Mater,* indicates.

Father O'Donnell here commemorates the pain of her human motherhood on the first Good Friday.

She was not very old the day He died —
So young she was the night that gave Him birth —
But when the spear withdrew that pierced His side,
No one was quite so old in all the earth.

"Compassion" from *The Collected Poems of Charles L. O'Donnell.* Reprinted by permission of University of Notre Dame Press, Notre Dame, Indiana.

O Lady, for the tears that you have shed,   5
I would make a song as evening hushed and dim,
Could you forget one hour that He is dead
And to your breast, a Baby, gather Him.

SENTRY

Here we are given some brief idea why
Christ chose poverty during His mortal life.

The wolf was at the door
    Of a house in Galilee,
The prowler that men know
    And fear as Poverty.

And oftentimes the Child   5
    Crept from His cozy bed
To steal out in the cold
    And stroke its hungry head.

" Be you to these," He spoke,
    " A guard by night and day,   10
By My beloved prized
    For what you keep away."

TRANSFORMATION

I kept a beggar's hut till Love
    Knocked at my sullen door;
I knew not what a spirit then
    Footed that earthen floor.

No lights were in his tangled hair,   5
    His bare feet bled with cold,
But all his frail hands chanced upon
    Flamed into sudden gold.

THE SPINNER

Mary the Mother of Jesus,
    A lady of high degree,
Sat by her cottage spinning
    In Nazareth of Galilee.

A light fell over her shoulder   5
    As she sat in the plane-tree's shade,
While a delicate lace of shadows
    The sun and the green leaves made.

Busy her foot on the treadle,
    And her wheel busily whirled   10
As a Child looked out from the doorway,
    A Child who had made the world.

Deftly she handled the distaff,
    And happily whirred her wheel
As the Child came down from the
        doorway   15
    And ran to her side to kneel.

" Mother," He said as He watched her
    There while she sat and spun,
" Some things are more fair than I
        dreamed them
    The day that I made the sun.   20

" And you are My heart of all beauty,
    My star of all seas, of all lands —"
" Hush, Child," whispered Mary His
        Mother,
    Her tears falling down on His hands.

For Discussion of O'Donnell

1. Explain why Father O'Donnell used
" Compassion " as the title of his poem.
About how old was Our Lady when Christ
died? What does line 4 mean?

2. Do you think " Sentry " is a good title
for this poem? Why? How can poverty be
a guardian in this world? What things does
it exclude? Who are the " beloved " mentioned in the last stanza? Recall the Beati-
tude that refers to poverty.

3. What did Love look like in " Transformation "? Why is he pictured as frail?
To what does the transformation refer?

4. In " The Spinner " what things might
have looked " more fair " to the Boy
Christ? Is the appraisal of Mary in the last
stanza exact? What is her position in
Heaven? Why does she weep in the poem?

"Sentry," "Transformation," and "The Spinner" from *The Collected Poems of Charles L. O'Donnell*. Reprinted by permission of University of Notre Dame Press, Notre Dame, Indiana.

Robert Frost
1875–

Robert Frost's paternal ancestors lived in Massachusetts for eight generations. Though he was born in San Francisco and spent his first eleven years there, until his father died, he has been identified ever since with New England, particularly with the farm life of New Hampshire, which state he once declared to be "one of the two best states in the Union" (the other being Vermont). Both in his person and his poetry Frost is a typical New England rugged individualist. While in high school at Lawrence, Massachusetts, he worked as a farm hand, played on the football team, and graduated at the head of his class. But the next years were restless and mostly unsuccessful ones for Robert Frost. He entered Dartmouth College but left almost immediately to work in a mill; and later, after he was married, he enrolled at Harvard, but quit again, this time to become a cobbler, teacher, and newspaper editor in quick succession. Finally his grandfather bought him a farm in New Hampshire, where he struggled against witch grass and sheep laurel, trying to wrest a living from the barren soil. All the while he was working far into the night writing poetry, for which he could find practically no market in America.

At thirty-seven, Frost sold his farm and moved with his family to England. Here he published two books of poetry, *North of Boston* and *A Boy's Will*. Three years later, in 1915, he returned to America to find himself famous. Since then he has won the Pulitzer Prize four times, and been acclaimed the most distinguished living American poet. Over the years he has combined occasional teaching (at Amherst and Harvard) with farming and writing. In 1950, at the age of seventy-five, he published his *Complete Poems*.

Both in subject matter and style Frost's poetry is deceptively simple. At first glance he seems to be relating rather obvious facts about New England farm life, and he uses the plain, direct language of everyday speech. But by more careful reading one discovers magical insights and mature wisdom, and the technical discipline of a true artist.

THE PASTURE

"The Pasture" was printed as a motto at the beginning of *North of Boston,* and may well serve as an invitation to the reader to become acquainted with the work of Robert Frost.

I'm going out to clean the pasture
  spring;
I'll only stop to rake the leaves away

(And wait to watch the water clear, I
  may):
I shan't be gone long — You come too.

I'm going out to fetch the little calf   5
That's standing by the mother. It's so
  young,
It totters when she licks it with her
  tongue.
I shan't be gone long — You come too.

"The Pasture" from *Poems* by Robert Frost. Reprinted by permission of Henry Holt and Company, Inc.

STOPPING BY WOODS ON A SNOWY EVENING

In a recent (1950) feature article on Robert Frost, the editors of *Time* magazine called this " one of the loveliest poems ever written." Notice how the last stanza endows a seemingly commonplace incident with impressive significance. Frost's ability to express serious thought in simple terms is also illustrated in " A Minor Bird," which follows.

Whose woods these are I think I know.
His house is in the village though;
He will not see me stopping here
To watch his woods fill up with snow.

My little horse must think it queer   5
To stop without a farmhouse near
Between the woods and frozen lake
The darkest evening of the year.

He gives his harness bells a shake
To ask if there is some mistake.   10
The only other sound's the sweep
Of easy wind and downy flake.

The woods are lovely, dark, and deep,
But I have promises to keep,
And miles to go before I sleep,   15
And miles to go before I sleep.

A MINOR BIRD

I have wished a bird would fly away,
And not sing by my house all day;

Have clapped my hands at him from the
        door
When it seemed as if I could bear no
        more.   4

The fault must partly have been in me.
The bird was not to blame for his key.

And of course there must be something
        wrong
In wanting to silence any song.

MENDING WALL

The meanings behind simple things are evident to the imagination of Robert Frost. Here we have an ordinary task in New England, where low stone walls are the common boundaries between farms. Two farmers move along either side of the wall repairing the winter's ravages. One is a practical, unimaginative man who thinks only conventionally as he has been taught in the past: " Good fences make good neighbors." The other has a lively fancy and a questioning mind: "*Why* do they make good neighbors? "

Something there is that doesn't love a
        wall,
That sends the frozen ground swell un-
        der it,
And spills the upper boulders in the
        sun;
And makes gaps even two can pass
        abreast.
The work of hunters is another thing: 5
I have come after them and made re-
        pair
Where they have left not one stone on
        a stone,
But they would have the rabbit out of
        hiding,
To please the yelping dogs. The gaps I
        mean,
No one has seen them made or heard
        them made,   10
But at spring mending time we find
        them there.
I let my neighbor know beyond the hill;
And on a day we meet to walk the
        line
And set the wall between us once again.
We keep the wall between us as
        we go.
To each the boulders that have fallen
        to each.   16
And some are loaves and some so near-
        ly balls

We have to use a spell to make them balance:
"Stay where you are until our backs are turned!"
We wear our fingers rough with handling them.   20
Oh, just another kind of outdoor game,
One on a side. It comes to little more:
There where it is we do not need the wall:
He is all pine and I am apple orchard.
My apple trees will never get across 25
And eat the cones under his pines, I tell him.
He only says, "Good fences make good neighbors."
Spring is the mischief in me, and I wonder
If I could put a notion in his head:
"*Why* do they make good neighbors? Isn't it   30
Where there are cows? But here there are no cows.
Before I built a wall I'd ask to know
What I was walling in or walling out,
And to whom I was like to give offense.
Something there is that doesn't love a wall,   35
That wants it down." I could say "Elves" to him,
But it's not elves exactly, and I'd rather
He said it for himself. I see him there
Bringing a stone grasped firmly by the top
In each hand, like an old stone savage armed.   40
He moves in darkness as it seems to me,
Not of woods only and the shade of trees.
He will not go behind his father's saying,
And he likes having thought of it so well
He says again, "Good fences make good neighbors."   45

THE ROAD NOT TAKEN

All the mystery of how fate affects human lives is suggested in this little episode of a walk in the woods. Frost does not put a "moral tag" at the end of his poems as the older writers were inclined to do. That is, he does not say bluntly: "This is the lesson to be found here." Instead, his whole poem becomes a symbol of a great truth. The reader must make out what the symbol stands for and follow up the idea in his own mind.

Two roads diverged in a yellow wood,
And sorry I could not travel both
And be one traveler, long I stood
And looked down one as far as I could
To where it bent in the undergrowth; 5

Then took the other, as just as fair,
And having perhaps the better claim,
Because it was grassy and wanted wear;
Though as for that the passing there
Had worn them really about the same,

And both that morning equally lay 11
In leaves no step had trodden black.
Oh, I kept the first for another day!
Yet knowing how way leads on to way,
I doubted if I should ever come back.

I shall be telling this with a sigh 16
Somewhere ages and ages hence:
Two roads diverged in a wood, and I —
I took the one less traveled by,
And that has made all the difference. 20

FIRE AND ICE

The two poems which follow are Robert Frost's recent comments on the end of the world. Although they are very short, they may teach you something about poetry. Asked his opinion about the fate in store for this planet, someone might say, "I think probably some day the earth will get too near the sun and burn up. Or, perhaps, the sun will burn out, and life on earth will end for lack of heat." Not a very impressive answer. Now see how a poet expresses the same opinion.

Some say the world will end in fire,
Some say in ice.
From what I've tasted of desire
I hold with those who favor fire.
But if it had to perish twice,   5
I think I know enough of hate
To say that for destruction ice
Is also great
And would suffice.

IT BIDS PRETTY FAIR

In this quatrain, Frost does not mention the end of the world at all. The " play," " actors," and " lighting " are all symbols of something more important than any mere theatrical production. The key word is " sun " in line 3.

The play seems out for an almost indefinite run.
Don't mind a little thing like the actors fighting.
The only thing I worry about is the sun.
We'll be all right if nothing goes wrong with the lighting.

THE DEATH OF THE HIRED MAN

This is the best of Frost's longer narrative poems. While it tells a story, definite and tragic, there is no action; merely a conversation between a New England farmer and his wife. As always in Frost's work, there are graphic pictures which enhance the setting and in this poem help to soften the sting of the tragedy. Although so much of his poetry concerns the Yankee farmer, Frost never uses dialect.

Mary sat musing on the lamp flame at the table,
Waiting for Warren. When she heard his step,
She ran on tiptoe down the darkened passage
To meet him in the doorway with the news
And put him on his guard. " Silas is back."   5
She pushed him outward with her through the door
And shut it after her. " Be kind," she said.
She took the market things from Warren's arms
And set them on the porch, then drew him down   9
To sit beside her on the wooden steps.

" When was I ever anything but kind to him?
But I'll not have the fellow back," he said.
" I told him so last haying didn't I?
' If he left then,' I said, ' that ended it.'
What good is he? Who else will harbor him   15
At his age for the little he can do?
What help he is there's no depending on.
Off he goes always when I need him most.
' He thinks he ought to earn a little pay,
Enough at least to buy tobacco with,   20
So he won't have to beg and be beholden.'
' All right,' I say, ' I can't afford to pay
Any fixed wages, though I wish I could.'
' Someone else can.' ' Then someone else will have to.'   24
I shouldn't mind his bettering himself
If that was what it was. You can be certain,
When he begins like that, there's someone at him
Trying to coax him off with pocket money —

In haying time, when any help is scarce.
In winter he comes back to us. I'm
done."   30

"Sh! not so loud: he'll hear you," Mary
said.

"I want him to: he'll have to soon or
late."

"He's worn out. He's asleep beside the
stove.
When I came up from Rowe's I found
him here,
Huddled against the barn door fast
asleep,   35
A miserable sight, and frightening,
too —
You needn't smile — I didn't recognize
him —
I wasn't looking for him — and he's
changed.
Wait till you see."

        "Where did you say he'd been?"

"He didn't say. I dragged him to the
house,   40
And gave him tea, and tried to make
him smoke.
I tried to make him talk about his
travels.
Nothing would do: he just kept nodding off."

"What did he say? Did he say anything?"

"But little."

        "Anything? Mary, confess   45
He said he'd come to ditch the meadow
for me."

"Warren!"

        "But did he? I just want to know."

"Of course he did. What would you
have him say?
Surely you wouldn't grudge the poor
old man

Some humble way to save his self-re-
spect.   50
He added, if you really care to know,
He meant to clear the upper pasture,
too.
That sounds like something you have
heard before?
Warren, I wish you could have heard
the way
He jumbled everything. I stopped to
look   55
Two or three times — he made me feel
so queer —
To see if he was talking in his sleep.
He ran on Harold Wilson — you remem-
ber —
The boy you had in haying four years
since.
He's finished school, and teaching in his
college.   60
Silas declares you'll have to get him
back.
He says they two will make a team for
work:
Between them they will lay this farm as
smooth!
The way he mixed that in with other
things.
He thinks young Wilson a likely lad,
though daft   65
On education — you know how they
fought
All through July under the blazing sun,
Silas up on the cart to build the load,
Harold along beside to pitch it on."

"Yes, I took care to keep well out of
earshot."   70

"Well, those days trouble Silas like a
dream.
You wouldn't think they would. How
some things linger!
Harold's young college boy's assurance
piqued him.
After so many years he still keeps finding
Good arguments he sees he might have
used.   75

I sympathize. I know just how it feels
To think of the right thing to say too
     late.
Harold's associated in his mind with
     Latin.
He asked me what I thought of Har-
     old's saying
He studied Latin like the violin   80
Because he liked it — that an argument!
He said he couldn't make the boy be-
     lieve
He could find water with a hazel
     prong° —
Which showed how much good school
     had ever done him.
He wanted to go over that. But most of
     all   85
He thinks if he could have another
     chance
To teach him how to build a load of
     hay — "

" I know, that's Silas' one accomplish-
     ment.
He bundles every forkful in its place,
And tags and numbers it for future ref-
     erence,   90
So he can find and easily dislodge it
In the unloading. Silas does that well.
He takes it out in bunches like big birds'
     nests.
You never see him standing on the hay
He's trying to lift, straining to lift him-
     self."   95

" He thinks if he could teach him that,
     he'd be
Some good perhaps to someone in the
     world.
He hates to see a boy the fool of books.
Poor Silas, so concerned for other folk,
And nothing to look backward to with
     pride,   100

And nothing to look forward to with
     hope,
So now and never any different."

Part of a moon was falling down the
     west,
Dragging the whole sky with it to the
     hills,
Its light poured softly in her lap. She
     saw   105
And spread her apron to it. She put out
     her hand
Among the harplike morning-glory
     strings,
Taut with the dew from garden bed to
     eaves,
As if she played unheard the tenderness
That wrought on him beside her in the
     night.   110
" Warren," she said, " he has come home
     to die:
You needn't be afraid he'll leave you
     this time."

" Home," he mocked gently.

               " Yes, what else but home?
It all depends on what you mean by
     home.
Of course he's nothing to us, any more
Than was the hound that came a stran-
     ger to us   116
Out of the woods, worn out upon the
     trail."

" Home is the place where, when you
     have to go there,
They have to take you in."

               " I should have called it
Something you somehow haven't to de-
     serve."   120

Warren leaned out and took a step or
     two,
Picked up a little stick, and brought it
     back
And broke it in his hand and tossed it
     by.
" Silas has better claim on us, you think,

---

83. **find water with a hazel prong:** a farm
superstition that a proper location for a well can
be ascertained by walking around holding a
branch in front of one. The branch is supposed
to bend down at the point where water is to be
found under the surface.

Than on his brother? Thirteen little
 miles 125
As the road winds would bring him to
 his door.
Silas has walked that far no doubt today.
Why didn't he go there? His brother's
 rich,
A somebody — director in the bank."

" He never told us that."

" We know it though." 130

" I think his brother ought to help, of
 course.
I'll see to that if there is need. He ought
 of right
To take him in, and might be willing
 to —
He may be better than appearances.
But have some pity on Silas. Do you
 think 135
If he'd had any pride in claiming kin
Or anything he looked for from his
 brother,
He'd keep so still about him all this
 time? "

" I wonder what's between them."

" I can tell you.
Silas is what he is — we wouldn't mind
 him — 140
But just the kind that kinsfolk can't
 abide.
He never did a thing so very bad.
He don't know why he isn't quite as
 good
As anyone. He won't be made ashamed
To please his brother, worthless though
 he is." 145

" I can't think Si ever hurt anyone."

" No, but he hurt my heart the way he
 lay
And rolled his old head on that sharp-
 edged chair back.
He wouldn't let me put him on the
 lounge.

You must go in and see what you can
 do. 150
I made the bed up for him there tonight.
You'll be surprised at him — how much
 he's broken.
His working days are done; I'm sure of
 it."

" I'd not be in a hurry to say that."

" I haven't been. Go, look, see for yourself. 155
But, Warren, please remember how it
 is:
He's come to help you ditch the meadow.
He has a plan. You mustn't laugh at
 him.
He may not speak of it, and then he
 may.
I'll sit and see if that small sailing
 cloud 160
Will hit or miss the moon."

It hit the moon.
Then there were three, making a dim
 row,
The moon, the little silver cloud, and
 she.

Warren returned — too soon, it seemed
 to her,
Slipped to her side, caught up her hand
 and waited. 165

" Warren? " she questioned.

" Dead," was all he answered.

For Discussion of Frost

Short Poems

1. What significance do you read into the
apparently simple incident in " Stopping by
Woods on a Snowy Evening "? What effect
does the repetition of the last line have?

2. What is the meaning of the word
minor in the title " A Minor Bird "? What
is meant when Frost says, " The bird was
not to blame for his *key* "?

3. In "Mending Wall" what makes the poet suddenly see his neighbor as "an old stone savage"? How would you describe the personalities of these two men?

4. Apply the ideas of the two men in "Mending Wall" to the international situation. Write a short dialogue between two nations concerning the "wall" between them.

5. Of what is "the road not taken" a symbol? Of what is "the one less traveled by" a symbol? Which sort of person do you admire more — the one who conforms to the fashion of the day, or the "rugged individualist" who takes the road "less traveled by"? Defend your choice.

6. Show several ways in which the poem "Fire and Ice" is superior to the prose statement preceding it. Why does the poet choose fire over ice? From your own experience, observation, and reading, give some examples of the destructive powers of "desire" and hate. What do you think Frost means by "desire"?

7. Try to state a fact in symbolic language (as is done in "It Bids Pretty Fair"), choosing a subject like "growing older" or "seeking success" or "going out into the world." Phrase it clearly so that the class will understand your meaning.

8. Look up in Shakespeare's *As You Like It*, the famous speech, "All the world's a stage" (Act II, Scene vii). What mood pervades this speech? What mood would you say pervades Frost's "It Bids Pretty Fair"? If you were going to compare life to a play on a stage, what sort of play would you choose for comparison, a comedy or a tragedy?

The Death of the Hired Man
1. In the second stanza, lines 11–30, remember that Warren is saying all this to his wife. Which two people are speaking in the conversation that he quotes?

2. Study the two definitions of home (ll. 118–20). Which do you prefer?

3. What does the discussion about the rich brother (ll. 124–45) add to our understanding of Silas? Quote Mary's four-line summary of the tragedy of Silas's life.

4. What makes the end of the poem especially impressive?

5. Let two well-qualified students dramatize "The Death of the Hired Man" before the class. Be careful to maintain the quiet pathos of the poem.

6. Make a list of the lines from these poems which you would include in a "Dictionary of Quotations." (You might do this for Robinson and Amy Lowell, also.)

Metrical Terms

BLANK VERSE: "Mending Wall" and "The Death of the Hired Man" are written in blank verse. Blank verse — do not confuse it with free verse — is a metrical form found in some of the noblest poems of the English language (Shakespeare's plays, for instance, and Milton's *Paradise Lost*). You will certainly want to understand the meaning of this term.

Blank verse is verse written in unrhymed iambic pentameter. Let's see what this definition means. Lines of poetry are divided into "feet," with one accented syllable to every "foot." The *iambic* foot consists of two syllables, an unaccented followed by an accented (te TUM). This is the most commonly used foot in English poetry. To indicate the number of feet to a line, the ancient Greeks have supplied us with some technical terms: one foot, *monometer;* two feet, *dimeter;* three, *trimeter;* four, *tetrameter;* five, *pentameter;* six, *hexameter;* and so on. Fortunately for our memories, these terms, with the exception of *pentameter,* are seldom used.

Iambic pentameter, therefore, is a line of five feet, each foot with two syllables, the second being accented. It is found in sonnets (see p. 262) and in many other stanza forms. *Unrhymed* iambic pentameter is known as blank verse.

Reading blank verse skillfully takes practice. One must not read it in a singsong, and yet one must not lose the rhythm entirely and read it as prose. Select four or five lines from one of Frost's blank-verse poems. First read them with exaggerated accent: "And *gave* him *tea,* and *tried* to *make* him *smoke.*" (You may find some irregularities, of course, as in all good poetry.) Then practice reading the lines freely to bring out both meaning and rhythm. Now read them to the class and let your classmates criticize your rendering.

Edgar Lee Masters
1869–1950

Imagine a book of poetry being a " best seller "! That is what happened in 1915 when *Spoon River Anthology* appeared in the bookshops. Here was something new in poetry, a realistic, often brutally frank series of American portraits. Masters was an Illinois lawyer who had been writing poetry for years without attracting attention. Too much of his verse had been merely a poor imitation of Poe and the English poets whom he had studied. Finally, at the suggestion of a friend he turned his attention to his own surroundings and created a masterpiece. Through the reading of the *Greek Anthology,* a collection of ancient poems, he conceived the idea of a series of epitaphs on the inhabitants of a fictitious Illinois town, Spoon River, written by the dead themselves.

Reading this book is like being present at the Day of Judgment, when the dead arise and the truth about their lives is set free. All the experiences of village life are here represented, the good and the bad crowded together, the joys and hopes recorded, the bitternesses and ironies, the misunderstandings and mysteries revealed. The names of the men and women one forgets, but can one ever again look upon a cemetery in a small town, or even upon the town itself, without repeopling it in imagination with many of the lives depicted here?

Anne Rutledge is the only actual historical character among those who follow. She will be remembered as the sweetheart of Lincoln's early life, lost to him through death.

LUCINDA MATLOCK

I went to the dances at Chandlerville,
And played snap-out at Winchester.
One time we changed partners,
Driving home in the moonlight of middle June,
And then I found Davis.   5
We were married and lived together for seventy years,
Enjoying, working, raising the twelve children,
Eight of whom we lost
Ere I had reached the age of sixty.
I spun, I wove, I kept the house, I nursed the sick,   10
I made the garden, and for holiday
Rambled over the fields where sang the larks,
And by Spoon River gathering many a shell,
And many a flower and medicinal weed —
Shouting to the wooded hills, singing to the green valleys.   15
At ninety-six I had lived enough, that is all,
And passed to a sweet repose.
What is this I hear of sorrow and weariness,
Anger, discontent, and drooping hopes?
Degenerate sons and daughters,   20
Life is too strong for you —
It takes life to love Life.

"Lucinda Matlock" from *Spoon River Anthology* by Edgar Lee Masters. Reprinted by permission of the author.

MRS. GEORGE REECE

To this generation I would say:
Memorize some bit of verse of truth or
  beauty.
It may serve a turn in your life.
My husband had nothing to do
With the fall of the bank — he was only
  cashier.   5
The wreck was due to the president,
  Thomas Rhodes,
And his vain, unscrupulous son.
Yet my husband was sent to prison,
And I was left with the children,
To feed and clothe and school them.
And I did it, and sent them forth   11
Into the world all clean and strong,
And all through the wisdom of Pope,
  the poet:
" Act well your part, there all the honor
  lies."°

14. The line is from "The Essay on Man" by
the English poet Alexander Pope (1688–1744).
It is the second line of a couplet:
"Honor and shame from no condition rise;
Act well your part, there all the honor lies."

GEORGE GRAY

I have studied many times
The marble which was chiseled for
  me —
A boat with a furled sail at rest in a
  harbor.
In truth it pictures not my destination
But my life.   5
For love was offered me, and I shrank
  from its disillusionment;
Sorrow knocked at my door, but I was
  afraid;
Ambition called to me, but I dreaded
  the chances.
Yet all the while I hungered for mean-
  ing in my life
And now I know that we must lift the
  sail   10
And catch the winds of destiny
Wherever they drive the boat.

To put meaning in one's life may end in
  madness,
But life without meaning is the torture
Of restlessness and vague desire —   15
It is a boat longing for the sea and yet
  afraid.

ANNE RUTLEDGE

Out of me unworthy and unknown
The vibrations of deathless music:
" With malice toward none, with char-
  ity for all."°
Out of me the forgiveness of millions
  toward millions,
And the beneficent face of a nation   5
Shining with justice and truth.
I am Anne Rutledge who sleep beneath
  these weeds,
Beloved in life of Abraham Lincoln,
Wedded to him, not through union,
But through separation.   10
Bloom forever, O Republic,
From the dust of my bosom!

3. From Lincoln's Second Inaugural Address.
See page 645.

JOHN HORACE BURLESON

I won the prize essay at school
Here in the village,
And published a novel before I was
  twenty-five.
I went to the city for themes and to en-
  rich my art;
There married the banker's daughter,   5
And later became president of the
  bank —
Always looking forward to some leisure
To write an epic novel of the war.
Meanwhile friend of the great, and
  lover of letters,
And host to Matthew Arnold° and to
  Emerson.   10

10. **Matthew Arnold:** a noted English writer
and lecturer, much entertained in America.

"Mrs. George Reece," "George Gray," "Anne Rutledge," and "John Horace Burleson" from *Spoon River Anthology* by Edgar Lee Masters. Reprinted by permission of the author.

An after-dinner speaker, writing essays
For local clubs. At last brought here —
My boyhood home, you know —
Not even a little tablet in Chicago
To keep my name alive.   15
How great it is to write the single line:
"Roll on, thou deep and dark blue
Ocean, roll!"°

17. **"Roll on ... roll"**: one of the most frequently quoted lines written by the English poet Lord Byron.

SILENCE

None of the many volumes of poetry which Masters published after *Spoon River Anthology* was as powerful, but in *Songs and Satires* (1916) is to be found one poem which ranks with his best. Among the many moments of silence listed, don't overlook the bits of wisdom about artists, and the aged — and the dead.

I have known the silence of the stars
    and of the sea,
And the silence of the city when it
    pauses,
And the silence of a man and a maid,
And the silence for which music alone
    finds the word,
And the silence of the woods before the
    winds of spring begin,   5
And the silence of the sick
When their eyes roam about the room.
And I ask: For the depths
Of what use is language?
A beast of the field moans a few times
When death takes its young: 11
And we are voiceless in the presence of
    realities —
We cannot speak.

A curious boy asks an old soldier
Sitting in front of the grocery store,   15
"How did you lose your leg?"
And the old soldier is struck with si-
    lence,
Or his mind flies away

Because he cannot concentrate it on
    Gettysburg.
It comes back jocosely   20
And he says, "A bear bit it off."
And the boy wonders, while the old sol-
    dier
Dumbly, feebly, lives over
The flashes of guns, the thunder of
    cannon,
The shrieks of the slain,   25
And himself lying on the ground,
And the hospital surgeons, the knives,
And the long days in bed.
But if he could describe it all
He would be an artist.   30
But if he were an artist there would be
    deeper wounds
Which he could not describe.

There is the silence of a great hatred,
And the silence of a great love,
And the silence of a deep peace of
    mind,   35
And the silence of an embittered friend-
    ship.
There is the silence of a spiritual crisis,
Through which your soul, exquisitely
    tortured,
Comes with visions not to be uttered
Into a realm of higher life,   40
And the silence of the gods who under-
    stand each other without speech.
There is the silence of defeat.
There is the silence of those unjustly
    punished;
And the silence of the dying whose hand
Suddenly grips yours.   45
There is the silence between father and
    son,
When the father cannot explain his life,
Even though he be misunderstood for
    it.

There is the silence that comes between
    husband and wife,
There is the silence of those who have
    failed;   50
And the vast silence that covers
Broken nations and vanquished leaders.

"Silence" from *Songs and Satires* by Edgar Lee Masters. Reprinted by permission of the author.

There is the silence of Lincoln,
Thinking of the poverty of his youth.
And the silence of Napoleon   55
After Waterloo.
And the silence of Jeanne d'Arc
Saying amid the flames, " Blessèd Jesus " —
Revealing in two words all sorrow, all hope.
And there is the silence of age,   60
Too full of wisdom for the tongue to utter it
In words intelligible to those who have not lived
The great range of life.

And there is the silence of the dead.
If we who are in life cannot speak   65
Of profound experiences,
Why do you marvel that the dead
Do not tell you of death?
Their silence shall be interpreted
As we approach them.   70

For Discussion of Masters

1. Which of the persons in the poems represent the following things in life: apparent failure, but real success; courage; cowardice; a full and satisfying experience? Which do you admire most? least?

2. Although the three women have totally different lives, what one thing do they all have in common?

3. In " Silence," the poet gives many illustrations of moments of silence. Can you add others? What is meant by lines 31 and 32? What does he say of " the silence of the dead "?

4. Try writing an epitaph for yourself or someone else in the manner of *Spoon River Anthology*. Consult the book itself for other epitaphs, particularly " Dorcas Gustine," " Jacob Goodpasture," " Fiddler Jones," and " Emily Sparks."

Metrical Terms

FREE VERSE: All the poems by Masters in this book are written in *free verse*. This is a term which has already been called to your attention as one of the " new rhythms " of the Imagists (see p. 263). *Free* verse has neither rhyme nor regular meter. It is not right, however, to say that free verse has no rhythm at all. Free verse is not merely prose printed to look like poetry. Though it has no *regular* metrical rhythm, there are accented and unaccented syllables carefully arranged by the poet to give a rhythmical effect.

Carl Sandburg
1878–

When Carl Sandburg's *Chicago Poems* was published in 1916, it met with much violent opposition. Sandburg glossed over nothing in singing of his Chicago, wicked, crooked, and brutal; and many were repelled by the book's raw, thumping language and its frankness. But, as Louis Untermeyer pointed out, " Sandburg was only brutal when dealing with brutality; beneath his toughness he was one of the tenderest of living poets." By 1950, when the publication of his *Complete Poems* was a major literary event, Carl Sandburg had come to be regarded as one of the deans of American poetry, and those who knew his warmly understanding personality found it difficult to realize that he had once been considered a crude literary radical.

Born in Galesburg, Illinois, of Swedish stock, Sandburg went briefly to Lombard College. But he received most of his education in the College of Hard Work, where he took courses in a dozen different states by being a barbershop porter, a theatrical sceneshifter, a truck handler, a potter's apprentice, a hotel dishwasher, a construction worker on a railroad, a harvest hand, a soldier, and a janitor. At present, he lives on a farm in North Carolina.

From the beginning, Whitman was Sandburg's master. From Whitman he learned complete freedom of poetic form and a desire to face life boldly and rejoice in it. Like Whitman, too, Sandburg is a poet of the common man; he glorifies the city worker, as in *Smoke and Steel* (1920), and the multiple voice of democracy. The folk songs of the people have long intrigued him; he often sings to the accompaniment of his guitar the ballads in his collection *The American Songbag*. And he has written the greatest biography of America's democratic hero, Abraham Lincoln (see p. 213).

CHICAGO

The title piece in *Chicago Poems* was first published in *Poetry, a Magazine of Verse*. At that time it won a prize as "the best poem written by a citizen of the United States during the year." It was the foundation stone of Sandburg's fame.

> Hog Butcher for the World,
> Toolmaker, Stacker of Wheat,
> Player with Railroads and the Nation's Freight Handler;
> Stormy, husky, brawling,
> City of the Big Shoulders: 5

They tell me you are wicked and I believe them, for I have seen your painted
    women under the gas lamps luring the farmboys.
And they tell me you are crooked and I answer: Yes, it is true I have seen the gun-
    man kill and go free to kill again.
And they tell me you are brutal and my reply is: On the faces of women and chil-
    dren I have seen the marks of wanton hunger.
And having answered so I turn once more to those who sneer at this my city, and I
    give them back the sneer and say to them:
Come and show me another city with lifted head singing so proud to be alive and
    coarse and strong and cunning.   10
Flinging magnetic curses amid the toil of piling job on job, here is a tall bold slug-
    ger set vivid against the little soft cities;
Fierce as a dog with tongue lapping for action, cunning as a savage pitted against
    the wilderness,
> Bareheaded,
> Shoveling,
> Wrecking,   15
> Planning,
> Building, breaking, rebuilding,

"Chicago" from *Chicago Poems* by Carl Sandburg. Reprinted by permission of Henry Holt and Company, Inc.

Under the smoke, dust all over his mouth, laughing with white teeth,
Under the terrible burden of destiny laughing as a young man laughs,
Laughing even as an ignorant fighter laughs who has never lost a battle,   20
Bragging and laughing that under his wrist is the pulse, and under his ribs the
    heart of the people,
Laughing!
Laughing the stormy, husky, brawling laughter of Youth, half-naked, sweating,
    proud to be Hog Butcher, Toolmaker, Stacker of Wheat, Player with Rail-
    roads, and Freight Handler to the Nation.

CLEAN CURTAINS

"Clean Curtains" is from Sandburg's *Smoke and Steel*. The conflict between the clean curtains and the dust is, of course, symbolic of a much more important conflict in city life. Note the effective repetition of "dust" in the fourth line.

New neighbors came to the corner house at Congress and Green Streets.

The look of their clean white curtains was the same as the rim of a nun's bonnet.

One way was an oyster-pail factory, one way they made candy, one way paper boxes, strawboard cartons.

The warehouse trucks shook the dust of the ways loose and the wheels whirled dust — there was dust of hoof and wagon wheel and rubber tire — dust of police and fire wagons — dust of the winds that circled at midnight and noon listening to no prayers.

"O mother, I know the heart of you," I sang passing the rim of a nun's bonnet — O white curtains — and people clean as the prayers of Jesus here in the faded ramshackle at Congress and Green.   5

Dust and the thundering trucks won — the barrages of the street wheels and the lawless wind took their way — was it five weeks or six the little mother, the new neighbors, battled and then took away the white prayers in the windows?

BUTTONS

The effect of this, as in so many of Sandburg's poems, lies in a single sharp contrast, the parenthesis in lines 7–8 startling one like a flashback in a moving picture. The scene is World War I, but the poet's mental picture was probably reinforced by memories of his own experiences as a soldier during the Spanish-American War.

I have been watching the war map slammed up for advertising in front of the newspaper office.
Buttons — red and yellow buttons — blue and black buttons — are shoved back and forth across the map.

A laughing young man, sunny with freckles,
Climbs a ladder, yells a joke to somebody in the crowd,
And then fixes a yellow button one inch west   5
And follows the yellow button with a black button one inch west.

(Ten thousand men and boys twist on their bodies in a red soak along a river edge,
Gasping of wounds, calling for water, some rattling death in their throats.)
Who would guess what it cost to move two buttons one inch on the war map here
    in front of the newspaper office where the freckle-faced young man is laugh-
    ing to us?

PRAYERS OF STEEL

The " prayers of steel " are those of any person who wishes to build a new and better world. Don't miss the soaring symbol in the last line.

Lay me on an anvil, O God.
Beat me and hammer me into a crow-
  bar.
Let me pry loose old walls.
Let me lift and loosen old foundations.

Lay me on an anvil, O God.   5
Beat me and hammer me into a steel
  spike.
Drive me into the girders that hold a
  skyscraper together.
Take red-hot rivets and fasten me into
  the central girders.
Let me be the great nail holding a skyscraper through the blue nights into
  white stars.

GRASS

In contrast to " Buttons," on the preceding page, this poem shows the healing power of nature over war. Note the unique way in which this idea is suggested. The five battles mentioned were those involving the greatest loss of human life in the Napoleonic wars, the War between the States, and World War I.

      Pile the bodies high at Austerlitz and Waterloo.
      Shovel them under and let me work —
         I am the grass; I cover all.

      And pile them high at Gettysburg
      And pile them high at Ypres° and Verdun.   5
      Shovel them under and let me work.
      Two years, ten years, and passengers ask the conductor:
         What place is this?
         Where are we now?

         I am the grass.   10
         Let me work.

     5. Ypres (ē'pr'. Popularly, wĭ'pĕrz).

"Prayers of Steel" and "Grass" from *Cornhuskers* by Carl Sandburg. Reprinted by permission of Henry Holt and Company, Inc.

FOG

This poem, in contrast to most of Sandburg's poems, shows his ability to treat a subject with delicacy and beauty.

The fog comes
on little cat feet.

It sits looking
over harbor and city
on silent haunches   5
and then moves on.

NOCTURNE IN A DESERTED BRICKYARD

Stuff of the moon
Runs on the lapping sand
Out to the longest shadows
Under the curving willows,
And round the creep of the wave line,
Fluxions of yellow and dusk on the waters   6
Make a wide dreaming pansy of an old
pond in the night.

THE COPPERFACES, THE RED MEN

Carl Sandburg's volume of poetry *The People, Yes* (1936) is a "carryall of American folk tales, catch-phrases, tall stories, gossip, and history." It opens with a modern version of the story of the Tower of Babel in the Bible, and the rest of the book is really the babel of voices arising from all parts of our nation and from all conditions of people. Reading this book gives one somewhat the same sensations as turning the dial of a radio and hearing different voices come from hither and yon out of the air. The verse is without set form; the units of thought have no titles, only numbers; there is no continuity of thought. But the total impression is that one has heard, in the language of the people themselves, the composite voice of America. The portion from section 51 printed here is typical.

The copperfaces, the red men, handed us tobacco,
the weed for the pipe of friendship,
also the bah-tah-to, the potato, the spud.
Sunflowers came from Peruvians in ponchos.
Early Italians taught us of chestnuts,   5
walnuts and peaches being Persian mementos,
Siberians finding for us what rye might do,
Hindus coming through with the cucumber,
Egyptians giving us the onion, the pea,
Arabians handing advice with one gift: 10
"Some like it, some say it's just spinach."
        To the Chinese we have given
        kerosene, bullets, Bibles
and they have given us radishes, soy beans, silk,
poems, paintings, proverbs, porcelain, egg foo yong,   15
gunpowder, Fourth of July firecrackers, fireworks,
and labor gangs for the first Pacific railways.

Now we may thank these people
or reserve our thanks
and speak of them as outsiders   20
and imply the request,
"Would you just as soon get off the earth?"
holding ourselves aloof in pride of distinction
saying to ourselves this costs us nothing
as though hate has no cost   25
as though hate ever grew anything worth growing.
Yes we may say this trash is beneath our notice
or we may hold them in respect and affection
as fellow creepers on a commodious planet
saying, "Yes you too you too are people."   30

The People, Yes!

Coster from Rapho-Guillumette

FREEDOM IS A HABIT

In this, one of his most recent poems, Sandburg has some wise things to say about freedom. You will need to consider each statement carefully — first, to be sure you know what the poet means; second, to decide whether or not you agree with him.

Freedom is a habit
and a coat worn
some born to wear it
some never to know it.
Freedom is cheap   5
or again as a garment
is so costly
men pay their lives
rather than not have it.
Freedom is baffling: 10
men having it often
know not they have it
till it is gone and
they no longer have it.
What does this mean?   15
Is it a riddle?
Yes, it is first of all
in the primers of riddles.
To be free is so-so:
you can and you can't: 20
walkers can have freedom
only by never walking
away their freedom:
runners too have freedom
unless they overrun: 25
eaters have often outeaten
their freedom to eat
and drinkers overdrank
their fine drinking freedom.

For Discussion of Sandburg

1. What was your feeling toward Chicago after reading Sandburg's poem? If Chicago is a " tall bold slugger," what sort of person would best represent Boston? Hollywood? Miami? your own city or town?

2. What is the basic thought in this part of section 51 of *The People, Yes?* Do you personally consider any group of people " outsiders "? What does Sandburg mean by the cost of hate? Where in this poem do you find examples of colloquial, every-day speech? of slang?

3. Explain the " riddle " in " Freedom Is a Habit."

4. Point out the poems in which Sandburg makes use of symbols. Make a list of all common objects which he uses as symbols, and another list of the truths they symbolize.

5. Where do you find examples of Sandburg's " brutal " use of language? where of delicacy of language? Which do you think he handles more adroitly?

6. How would you contrast Frost's and Sandburg's views of people? of nature? What similarities do you find between them?

7. Let a group of students interested in folk music prepare a program from the material in Sandburg's *The American Songbag.* Part of it might be a mock radio broadcast with unidentified speaking voices contributing parts of *The People, Yes.* Choral reading of passages from the latter would also add to the program.

For Your Vocabulary

FIGURATIVE LANGUAGE — COMPARISONS: To make us see Chicago as he sees it, Sandburg compares his city to a " tall bold slugger " who is " fierce as a dog," " cunning as a savage," and " laughing as an ignorant fighter." This use of comparisons is to be found in not only Sandburg's, but all poetry. It is the most common device poets use to create vivid pictures or images. If the comparison is expressed by means of *like* or *as,* it is called a *simile* (" people clean as the prayers of Jesus "). If the comparison is implied, it is called a *metaphor* (" The fog comes on little cat feet "). If the comparison gives the attributes of a human being to an inanimate object, it is called a *personification* (" the moon is a lovely lady "). However, *metaphor* is often used as a general term covering all kinds of comparisons.

Find other examples of metaphorical language in Sandburg's poems. For instance, to what things does he compare freedom in " Freedom Is a Habit "? Find striking metaphors in the works of other poets in this book. Try to create a fresh, striking comparison to express your impression of a person, place, or object.

Vachel Lindsay
1879–1931

Vachel Lindsay was our modern American troubadour. He believed that poetry is made not for the eye, but for the ear; and he spent part of his life journeying up and down the land singing his songs, much as did the ballad singers in the days of knights and feudal castles. Often he made dignified lecture tours from city to city or college to college; but sometimes he threw convention to the winds, and set off afoot across country with nothing to pay his way except his little pamphlet, *Rhymes to Be Traded for Bread*. Because Lindsay was essentially a singer, his poems must be chanted aloud in the Lindsay manner, or much of their appeal is lost. To help the reader, in many of his longer poems he supplied directions for reading aloud.

After graduating from high school in Springfield, Illinois, Vachel Lindsay attended Hiram College and art schools in Chicago and New York. Shortly he was back in his home town, preaching his gospel of beauty and campaigning against civic unrighteousness and ugliness in his privately printed, weekly *War Bulletin*. " Ugliness," he said, " is a kind of misgovernment." Lindsay wrote many beautiful rhymes for children. He developed " poem games " to which children dance, needing no other instrument to keep the rhythm except the human voice. He set to word-music the lives of picturesque and vivid Americans — old Andrew Jackson, William Jennings Bryan, John Brown, Johnny Appleseed, Alexander Campbell. But his poetry is too various to be divided into neat little pigeonholes. He was a modern minstrel who sang in all keys. The poems below are from his *Collected Poems*.

ABRAHAM LINCOLN WALKS AT MIDNIGHT
(*In Springfield, Illinois*)

Masters, Sandburg, and Lindsay — all Illinois poets — have written about Abraham Lincoln in some form. Lindsay felt an especially close bond to Abraham Lincoln because he was brought up in Springfield, Lincoln's home town, and the Lincoln family was close to his own family traditions. The following poem, written during World War I, has become one of the most familiar of the many poems of that day. Since an assured peace has not yet come to the world, it still has its significant message.

"Abraham Lincoln Walks at Midnight" from *Collected Poems* by Vachel Lindsay. Reprinted by permission of The Macmillan Company, publishers.

It is portentous, and a thing of state
That here at midnight, in our little town
A mourning figure walks, and will not
rest,
Near the old courthouse pacing up and
down,

Or by his homestead, or in shadowed
yards   5
He lingers where his children used to
play,
Or through the market, on the well-
worn stones
He stalks until the dawn stars burn
away.

A bronzed, lank man! His suit of ancient black,
A famous high top hat and plain worn
shawl   10
Make him the quaint great figure that
men love,
The prairie lawyer, master of us all.

He cannot sleep upon his hillside now.
He is among us: — as in times before!
And we who toss and lie awake for
long   15
Breathe deep, and start, to see him pass
the door.

His head is bowed. He thinks on men
and kings.
Yea, when the sick world cries, how can
he sleep?
Too many peasants fight, they know not
why,
Too many homesteads in black terror
weep.   20

The sins of all the war lords burn his
heart.
He sees the dreadnoughts scouring every main.
He carries on his shawl-wrapped shoulders now
The bitterness, the folly, and the pain.

He cannot rest until a spirit dawn   25
Shall come; — the shining hope of Europe free:
The league of sober folk, the workers'
earth,
Bringing long peace to Cornland, Alp,
and Sea.

It breaks his heart that kings must murder still,
That all his hours of travail here for
men   30
Seem yet in vain. And who will bring
white peace
That he may sleep upon his hill again?

ON THE BUILDING
OF SPRINGFIELD

Lindsay hoped profoundly that in its
development his own town of Springfield
would heed the call of beauty and satisfy
the needs of the intellect and the spirit.
His repeated preachments against mere
materialism were given scant attention by
his fellow townsmen during his lifetime.
In recent years, however, Springfield has
awakened to its possibilities as a national
shrine because of its association with Lincoln's life, and great projects for beautify-
ing the town have been completed. There
is now just outside the town a large artificial lake, spanned by a beautiful, many-
arched bridge named the Vachel Lindsay
Bridge. At one end of it stands a bust of
the poet.

Let not our town be large, remembering
   That little Athens was the Muses'
   home;
That Oxford rules the heart of London
   still,
   That Florence gave the Renaissance
   to Rome.

Record it for the grandson of your son —
   A city is not builded in a day: 6

"On the Building of Springfield" from *Collected Poems* by Vachel Lindsay. Reprinted by permission of The Macmillan Company, publishers.

The Vachel Lindsay Memorial stands at one end of the bridge, also named after him, which spans Springfield Lake, outside Springfield, Illinois. (Brown Brothers)

Our little town cannot complete her soul
   Till countless generations pass away.

Now let each child be joined as to a church
   To her perpetual hopes, each man ordained;   10
Let every street be made a reverent aisle
   Where Music grows, and Beauty is unchained.

Let Science and Machinery and Trade
   Be slaves of her, and make her all in all —
Building against our blatant restless time   15
   An unseen, skillful, medieval wall.

Let every citizen be rich toward God.
   Let Christ, the beggar, teach divinity —
Let no man rule who holds his money dear.
   Let this, our city, be our luxury.   20

We should build parks that students from afar
   Would choose to starve in, rather than go home,

Fair little squares, with Phidian° ornament,
   Food for the spirit, milk and honeycomb.

Songs shall be sung by us in that good day —   25
   Songs we have written — blood within the rhyme
Beating, as when old England still was glad,
   The purple, rich, Elizabethan° time.

.   .   .   .

Say, is my prophecy too fair and far?
   I only know, unless her faith be high,
The soul of this our Nineveh° is doomed,   31
   Our little Babylon° will surely die.

Some city on the breast of Illinois
   No wiser and no better at the start,

23. **Phidian** (fĭd′ĭ·ăn): Phidias was the greatest of the ancient Greek sculptors. 28. **Elizabethan** (ê·lĭz·á·bē′thăn): pertaining to the flourishing of poetry and drama during the reign of Queen Elizabeth of England in the late sixteenth century. 31. **Nineveh** (nĭn′ĕ·vĕ): capital of ancient Assyria, which finally fell before the conquering Persians. 32. **Babylon** (băb′ĭ·lŏn): capital of Babylonia, which suffered a fate similar to that of Nineveh.

By faith shall rise redeemed, by faith
    shall rise   35
    Bearing the Western glory in her
      heart.

The genius of the Maple, Elm, and Oak,
    The secret hidden in each grain of
      corn,
The glory that the prairie angels sing
    At night when sons of Life and Love
      are born,   40

Born but to struggle, squalid and alone,
    Broken and wandering in their early
      years.
When will they make our dusty streets
    their goal,

Within our attics hide their sacred
    tears?

When will they start our vulgar blood
    athrill   45
With living language — words that set
    us free?
When will they make a path of beauty
    clear
Between our riches and our liberty?

We must have many Lincoln-hearted
    men.
A city is not builded in a day.   50
And they must do their work, and come
    and go
While countless generations pass
    away.

THE LEADEN-EYED

    Lindsay was ever a crusader; he was no believer in " art for art's sake " alone. His pen was always ready to support " causes," to encourage civic improvements, or — as in " The Leaden-Eyed " — to protest against the world's wrongs.

Let not young souls be smothered out before
They do quaint deeds and fully flaunt their pride.
It is the world's one crime its babes grow dull,
Its poor are ox-like, limp and leaden-eyed.

Not that they starve, but starve so dreamlessly,   5
Not that they sow, but that they seldom reap,
Not that they serve, but have no gods to serve,
Not that they die, but that they die like sheep.

For Discussion of Lindsay

1. How many of the causes for Lincoln's unrest in " Abraham Lincoln Walks at Midnight " still exist in the world? Give specific instances.

2. Why does Lindsay think it is not necessary for a town to be large in order to be influential? Which small towns in this country have attained a nationwide reputation?

3. Just what is meant by " leaden-eyed "? What does Lindsay say is " the world's one crime "? Explain clearly the contrast in each of the four lines of the second stanza of " The Leaden-Eyed." Compare this poem with Edwin Markham's famous poem, " The Man with the Hoe " (p. 734).

4. No better material can be found for effective choral reading than the poems of Vachel Lindsay. Before trying them, however, separate the high, low, and medium voice groups so that the leader can use them much as the director of a choir uses the singing voices. Some Lindsay poems offering opportunity for choral reading are " The Santa Fe Trail," " John Brown," " The Chinese Nightingale," " The Daniel Jazz," and the famous " The Congo."

Joyce Kilmer
1886–1918
Aline Kilmer
1888–1941

Joyce Kilmer exuded energy in all he did as reporter, journalist, magazine writer, and soldier in World War I. He was born in New Brunswick, New Jersey, and attended Rutgers and Columbia universities. He married Aline Murray in 1908. In 1913, both the Kilmers embraced the Faith, and until his death in France with the Fighting Sixty-Ninth, Joyce Kilmer glowed in the conscious appreciation of this gift. While Joyce Kilmer was not granted time to deepen his poetic talents, some of his longer poems show power and maturity. His writings include *Trees and Other Poems* (1915), *Main Street and Other Poems* (1917), and *Dreams and Images* (1917), an anthology which he edited.

Of the five Kilmer children, Michael and Rose died young, and Kenton, Deborah, and Christopher were reared by their widowed mother.

Mrs. Kilmer published little, content to let her name rest on her few volumes, *Candles That Burn* (1919) and *Selected Poems* (1929). Her sons follow the family tradition. Kenton edits a poetry column in the Washington *Post,* and is a reference librarian at the Library of Congress; while Christopher fought with the Sixty-Ninth Regiment in World War II. Deborah is a Benedictine nun.

CITIZEN OF THE WORLD

JOYCE KILMER

No longer of Him be it said
" He hath no place to lay His head."

In every land a constant lamp
Flames by His small and mighty camp.

There is no strange and distant place   5
That is not gladdened by His face.

And every nation kneels to hail
The splendor shining through Its veil.

Cloistered beside the shouting street,
Silent, He calls me to His feet.   10

Imprisoned for His love of me
He makes my spirit greatly free.

And through my lips that uttered sin
The King of Glory enters in.

LOVE'S LANTERN (*For Aline*)

JOYCE KILMER

Because the road was steep and long
  And through a dark and lonely land,
God set upon my lips a song
  And put a lantern in my hand.

Through miles of weary miles of night   5
  That stretch relentless in my way
My lantern burns serene and white,
  An unexhausted cup of day.

O golden lights and lights like wine,
  How dim your boasted splendors are.
Behold this little lamp of mine;   11
  It is more starlike than a star!

SANCTUARY   ALINE KILMER

God has builded a house with a low lintel,
And in it He has put all manner of things.
Follow the clue through the mazes that lead to His door,
Look in! look in! see what is there for our finding.
Peace is there like a pearl, and rest and the end of seeking;   5
Light is there and refreshment, but there shall be more.
There we shall find for our use wide beautiful wings,
Ecstasy, solitude, space. And for those who have been too lonely
The love of friends, the warmth of a homely fire.
O never grieve again for the piteous ending   10
Of loveliness that could not be made to last!
There all bright passing beauty is held forever,
Free from the sense of tears, to be loved without regret.
There we shall find at their source music and love and laughter,
Color and subtle fragrance and soft incredible textures: 15
Be sure we shall find what our weary hearts desire.
If we are tired of light there shall be velvet darkness
Falling across long fields, with stars, and a low voice calling,
Calling at last the word we thought would never be spoken.

But we, being hard and foolish and proud and mortal,   20
Are slow to bend and enter that humble portal.

EXPERIENCE   ALINE KILMER

Deborah danced, when she was two,
As buttercups and daffodils do;
Spirited, frail, naïvely bold,
Her hair a ruffled crest of gold,
And whenever she spoke, her voice went singing   5
Like water up from a fountain springing.

But now her step is quiet and slow;
She walks the way primroses go;
Her hair is yellow instead of gilt;
Her voice is losing its lovely lilt,   10
And in place of her wild delightful ways
A quaint precision rules her days.

For Deborah now is three, and oh,
She knows so much that she did not know.

For Discussion of the Kilmers

1. Pick out the paradoxes — the apparent contradictions — in " Citizen of the World." Why do you think this is an effective tribute to the Blessed Sacrament?

2. What evidence in " Love's Lantern " shows you that Joyce Kilmer was an exuberant person?

3. In Aline Kilmer's " Sanctuary " she compares Heaven to a house with a low door. List all the things she finds by stooping and looking in. Why are we so slow to respond to the opportunity described in " Sanctuary "?

4. How did Deborah look and act when she was two? What was some of the knowledge she gained?

5. What similarities and differences do you find between the poems of Joyce and Aline Kilmer?

6. Joyce Kilmer's most famous poem is " Trees." You can obtain recordings of this poem set to music.

James Weldon Johnson
1871–1938

An unusually varied career marked the life of the Negro poet, James Weldon Johnson. He was born in Jacksonville, Florida. After receiving his master's degree from Atlanta University, he was principal of a high school, studied and practiced law, collaborated with his brother in writing light opera, spent seven years in Venezuela and Nicaragua as United States Consul, and translated a Spanish grand opera, *Goyescas*, which was produced at the Metropolitan Opera House in New York. From 1916 to 1930 he was secretary of the National Association for the Advancement of Colored People.

His collections of Negro poetry and Negro spirituals were influential in arousing public appreciation of these rich veins of literature. Among his own writings, *God's Trombones* (1927), from which the following poem is taken, has always made an especial appeal. Supposedly a series of seven Negro sermons, these poems are deeply imbued with the vigorous rhythm and colorful imagery that give Negro folk songs their distinctive quality.

THE CREATION
A Negro Sermon

And God stepped out on space,
And He looked around and said,
" *I'm lonely —*
I'll make me a world."
As far as the eye of God could see   5
Darkness covered everything,
Blacker than a hundred midnights
Down in a cypress swamp.

Then God smiled,
And the light broke,   10
And the darkness rolled up on one side,
And the light stood shining on the other,
And God said, " *That's good!* "

Then God reached out and took the light in His hands,
And God rolled the light around in His hands,   15
Until He made the sun;

And He set that sun a-blazing in the heavens.
And the light that was left from making the sun
God gathered up in a shining ball
And flung against the darkness,   20
Spangling the night with the moon and stars.
Then down between
The darkness and the light
He hurled the world;
And God said, ' *That's good!* "   25

Then God Himself stepped down —
And the sun was on His right hand,
And the moon was on His left;
The stars were clustered about His head,
And the earth was under His feet.   30
And God walked, and where He trod

His footsteps hollowed the valleys out
And bulged the mountains up.

Then He stopped and looked and saw
That the earth was hot and barren.   35
So God stepped over to the edge of the
  world
And He spat out the seven seas;
He batted His eyes and the lightnings
  flashed;
He clapped His hands and the thunders
  rolled;
And the waters above the earth came
  down,   40
The cooling waters came down.

Then the green grass sprouted,
And the little red flowers blossomed,
The pine tree pointed his finger to the
  sky,
And the oak spread out his arms;   45
The lakes cuddled down in the hollows
  of the ground,
And the rivers ran down to the sea;
And God smiled again,
And the rainbow appeared,
And curled itself around His shoulder.

Then God raised His arm and He waved
  His hand   51
Over the sea and over the land,
And He said, "Bring forth! Bring
  forth!"
And quicker than God could drop His
  hand,
Fishes and fowls   55
And beasts and birds
Swam the rivers and the seas,
Roamed the forests and the woods,
And split the air with their wings,
And God said, "That's good!"   60

Then God walked around
And God looked around
On all that He had made.
He looked at His sun,
He looked at His moon,   65
And He looked at His little stars;
He looked on His world

With all its living things,
And God said, "I'm lonely still."

Then God sat down   70
On the side of a hill where He could
  think;
By a deep, wide river He sat down;
With His head in His hands,
God thought and thought,
Till He thought, "I'll make me a man!"

Up from the bed of the river   76
God scooped the clay;
And by the bank of the river
He kneeled Him down;
And there the great God Almighty,   80
Who lit the sun and fixed it in the sky,
Who flung the stars to the most far cor-
  ner of the night,
Who rounded the earth in the middle of
  His hand —
This Great God,
Like a mammy bending over her baby,
Kneeled down in the dust   86
Toiling over a lump of clay
Till He shaped it in His own image;
Then into it He blew the breath of life,
And man became a living soul.   90
Amen. Amen.

For Discussion of Johnson

1. Pick out words and phrases which
give an especially poetic quality to the
story of creation. Compare this poem with
the first chapter of Genesis to find likenesses
and differences.

2. By what means does the poet give to
God a marked personality? If you have
read or seen the play Green Pastures (revived on Broadway in 1951), compare the
picturing of God and the universe in the
two pieces of literature.

3. What differences in form and purpose
do you see between this "sermon" and a
spiritual? To what kind of musical setting
would the sermon lend itself? How would
the music itself have to differ from that of a
spiritual?

4. What resemblance is there between
the poetry of Johnson and that of Lindsay?

Sara Teasdale
1884–1933

The chronicle of outward actions in the life of Sara Teasdale is of little importance compared with the inner expression of thought and imagination found in her poems. She was born and educated in St. Louis, traveled extensively, and later lived in New York City. All her volumes are filled with delicate lyrics like the following samples — elusive little flashes of emotion caught and molded for us like tiny figures in ivory. They are coins for the memory, such as she describes in the first poem.

THE COIN

Into my heart's treasury
  I slipped a coin
That time cannot take
  Nor a thief purloin —
Oh, better than the minting   5
  Of a gold-crowned king
Is the safe-kept memory
  Of a lovely thing.

BARTER

Life has loveliness to sell —
  All beautiful and splendid things,
Blue waves whitened on a cliff,
  Climbing fire that sways and sings,
And children's faces looking up   5
Holding wonder like a cup.

Life has loveliness to sell —
  Music like a curve of gold,
Scent of pine trees in the rain,   9
  Eyes that love you, arms that hold,
And for your spirit's still delight,
Holy thoughts that star the night.

Spend all you have for loveliness,
  Buy it and never count the cost,   14
For one white singing hour of peace
  Count many a year of strife well lost,
And for a breath of ecstasy
Give all you have been or could be.

THE LONG HILL

I must have passed the crest a while
    ago
And now I am going down —
Strange to have crossed the crest and
    not to know,
  But the brambles were always catch-
    ing the hem of my gown.

All the morning I thought how proud I
    should be   5
  To stand there straight as a queen,
Wrapped in the wind and the sun with
    the world under me —
  But the air was dull; there was little I
    could have seen.

"The Coin" from *Flame and Shadow* by Sara Teasdale. Reprinted by permission of The Macmillan Company, publishers.
"Barter" from *Love Songs* by Sara Teasdale. Reprinted by permission of The Macmillan Company, publishers.
"The Long Hill" from *Flame and Shadow*, by Sara Teasdale. Reprinted by permission of The Macmillan Company, publishers.

It was nearly level along the beaten
   track
   And the brambles caught in my
     gown —   10
But it's no use now to think of turning
   back,
   The rest of the way will be only go-
    ing down.

LEAVES

One by one, like leaves from a tree,
All my faiths have forsaken me;
But the stars above my head
Burn in white and delicate red,
And beneath my feet the earth   5
Brings the sturdy grass to birth.
I who was content to be
But a silken-singing tree,
But a rustle of delight
In the wistful heart of night —   10
I have lost the leaves that knew
Touch of rain and weight of dew.
Blinded by a leafy crown
I looked neither up nor down —
But the leaves that fall and die   15
Have left me room to see the sky;
Now for the first time I know
Stars above and earth below.

BEAUTIFUL PROUD SEA

Careless forever, beautiful proud sea,
  You laugh in happy thunder all alone,
You fold upon yourself, you dance your
    dance
    Impartially on drift-weed, sand, or
     stone.

You make us believe that we can outlive
    death,   5
  You make us for an instant, for your
    sake,
Burn, like stretched silver of a wave,
  Not breaking, but about to break.

For Discussion of Teasdale

1. What contrasting moods do you find
in this group of poems? What great satisfactions in life does the poet voice? Where
do you find sadness or wistfulness?

2. In " Barter " does the line, " Spend
all you have for loveliness," mean to spend
money or something else? Justify your answer from the rest of the poem.

3. " The Long Hill " and " Leaves " are
little allegories. What do the hill and the
leaves represent in life? What situations
can you imagine calling forth the feeling
expressed in these and other poems in the
group?

4. In " Beautiful Proud Sea," to what
things does the poet compare the open sea?

Types of Lyric Poetry

Sara Teasdale's poems, like those of most
American poets, are *lyrics*. As was noted
on page 262, narrative and dramatic poems tell stories, but lyric poetry expresses
the poet's thoughts or feelings. Most lyric
poems are known simply as lyrics, but
some are further classified as sonnets,
songs, odes, or elegies — and there are numerous other categories.

The *sonnet* has already been discussed
on page 262. If you are interested in other
lyric poems written in definite rhyme and
stanza patterns, you might investigate the
ballade, the *limerick*, the *rondeau*, the *trio-
let*, and the *villanelle*.

The *song* is a lyric clearly intended for
singing purposes, or one which inspired
some composer to write a melody for it.
(All lyrics, however, are musical in form;
the word *lyric* comes from the same Greek
stem as does *lyre*, a musical instrument.)
For instance, every Holy Week you will
hear featured on the radio a beautiful musical version of Lanier's " A Ballad of
Trees and the Master " (p. 690). If a song
is of a religious bent, it becomes a hymn.
In Part Two you will find two hymns, Emerson's " The Concord Hymn " (p. 555) and
Whittier's " The Eternal Goodness " (p.
496).

The *ode* is a sustained poem of exalted
mood written to celebrate a particular oc-

casion or scene. It is often irregular in metrical form and may be divided into several parts. Sidney Lanier's "The Marshes of Glynn" (p. 691) is an ode.

The *elegy* is a mournful poem on death. The usual tone of an elegy is one of quiet dignity and restraint. Similar to it is the *dirge*, or funeral song. It is questionable whether poems with the welcoming attitude of Whitman's "The Carol of Death"

(p. 701) or the earnest plea of Lowell's "The Dead in Europe" (p. 320) could properly be called elegies. Frost's "The Death of the Hired Man" (p. 270) is an unusual type of elegy worked out through dialogue. Similar to the elegy and yet different from it is the *epitaph*, or inscription for the dead, of which Masters had made such surprising use in his *Spoon River Anthology* (p. 275).

Elinor Wylie
1885–1928

Elinor Wylie (wife of the American poet William Rose Benét) possessed a great sensitiveness to beauty which she displayed in poems that are highly finished technically yet always bear the mark of her personal feeling. This following group of poems selected from her four volumes of poetry shows both the gay agility of her mind and her fondness for stating thoughts indirectly. The meaning is lying there just

under the surface, but sometimes is missed if the poem is read too quickly or carelessly.

"Sea Lullaby" has a quality of cruelty, reflecting the cruelty sometimes found in nature. "Nonsense Rhyme" is quite the opposite of its title. "Velvet Shoes" and "Pretty Words" show the artist's highly developed senses of touch and hearing as well as of sight.

SEA LULLABY

The old moon is tarnished
With smoke of the flood,
The dead leaves are varnished
With color like blood,

A treacherous smiler   5
With teeth white as milk,
A savage beguiler
In sheathings of silk,

The sea creeps to pillage,
She leaps on her prey;   10
A child of the village
Was murdered today.

She came up to meet him
In a smooth golden cloak,
She choked him and beat him   15
To death, for a joke.

Her bright locks were tangled,
She shouted for joy,
With one hand she strangled
A strong little boy.   20

Now in silence she lingers
Beside him all night
To wash her long fingers
In silvery light.

NONSENSE RHYME

Whatever's good or bad or both
Is surely better than the none;
There's grace in either love or loathe;
Sunlight, or freckles on the sun.

The worst and best are both inclined   5
To snap like vixens at the truth;
But O beware the middle mind
That purrs and never shows a tooth!

Beware the smooth ambiguous smile
That never pulls the lips apart;   10
Salt of pure and pepper of vile
Must season the extremer heart.

A pinch of fair, a pinch of foul,
And bad and good make best of all;
Beware the moderated soul   15
That climbs no fractional inch to fall.

Reason's a rabbit in a hutch,
And ecstasy's a werewolf's ghost;
But, O, beware the nothing-much
And welcome madness and the most!   20

VELVET SHOES

Let us walk in the white snow
    In a soundless space;
With footsteps quiet and slow,
    At a tranquil pace,
    Under veils of white lace.   5

I shall go shod in silk,
    And you in wool,
White as a white cow's milk,
    More beautiful
    Than the breast of a gull.   10

We shall walk through the still town
    In a windless peace;
We shall step upon white down,
    Upon silver fleece,
    Upon softer than these.   15

We shall walk in velvet shoes:
    Wherever we go
Silence will fall like dews
    On white silence below.
    We shall walk in the snow.   20

PRETTY WORDS

Poets make pets of pretty, docile words:
I love smooth words, like gold-enameled
    fish
Which circle slowly with a silken swish,
And tender ones, like downy-feathered
    birds:
Words shy and dappled, deep-eyed deer
    in herds,   5
Come to my hand, and playful if I wish,
Or purring softly at a silver dish,
Blue Persian kittens, fed on cream and
    curds.

I love bright words, words up and sing-
    ing early;
Words that are luminous in the dark,
    and sing;   10
Warm lazy words, white cattle under
    trees;
I love words opalescent, cool, and
    pearly,
Like midsummer moths, and honeyed
    words like bees,
Gilded and sticky, with a little sting.   5

For Discussion of Wylie

1. Select phrases or figures of speech which show the poet's tendency to introduce an unexpected, even startling idea; her love of the fantastic image; her appeal to the senses, especially of sound and touch.

2. Read "Sea Lullaby" aloud to bring out the sounds that create a distinct mood and suggest the motion of the sea. Why does the picture of the sea seem more sinister than if the poet had described a destructive storm?

3. Explain the "sense" of "Nonsense Rhyme." Do you agree with her choice between the extremes and the middle course? An informal debate on the subject might interest the class.

4. There is a good musical setting of "Velvet Shoes" by the composer Randall Thompson. Try to get a recording of the song to play in class. How does the music enhance the mood of the poem?

5. Can you find words in any of these poems which illustrate the kind the poet professes to love in "Pretty Words," especially the kind described in the last line?

For Your Vocabulary

FIGURATIVE USE OF WORDS: Freshness and vividness are two of Elinor Wylie's marked traits, and both are associated with figures of speech. "Sea Lullaby" is an excellent example of personification, with the sea spoken of as a person, and vividly described. Note how the various descriptions personify the sea and then how clearly they picture the real sea. Start off with "creeps to pillage . . . leaps on her prey." Can you see the varying movement of water along the shore? What pictures do you get from the following phrases:

in a smooth golden cloak
choked him and beat him to death
her bright locks were tangled
she shouted for joy
to wash her long fingers in silvery light

The other poems abound in figurative use of language. See how many descriptive comparisons you can locate. Give the full attention of your imagination to each word or phrase, and you will get the meaning vividly, as if you had turned a spotlight on it for a moment.

Alan Seeger
1888–1916

Already several young poets have achieved wide recognition for their portrayal of experiences in World War II. Peter Viereck and Karl Shapiro — both represented in this book — have captured in verse the fateful thoughts, the boredom, the heightened emotions of wartime. Three such young men in World War I wrote memorable war poetry in the few brief months before they lost their lives in battle. The first is Rupert Brooke, gifted English poet; the second is a Canadian, John McCrae, author of "In Flanders Fields"; the third is an American poet, Alan Seeger. Like many other young men who loved France, he enlisted in the Foreign Legion, which saw almost continuous service throughout the long struggle. Alan Seeger died in action in July, 1916, fulfilling the prophecy expressed in this, his best-known poem.

I HAVE A RENDEZVOUS WITH DEATH

I have a rendezvous with Death
At some disputed barricade,
When Spring comes back with rustling
  shade
And apple blossoms fill the air —
I have a rendezvous with Death   5
When Spring brings back blue days
  and fair.

It may be he shall take my hand
And lead me into his dark land
And close my eyes and quench my
  breath —
It may be I shall pass him still.   10
I have a rendezvous with Death
On some scarred slope of battered
  hill,
When Spring comes round again this
  year
And the first meadow flowers appear.

God knows 'twere better to be deep   15
Pillowed in silk and scented down,
Where Love throbs out in blissful sleep,
Pulse nigh to pulse and breath to breath,
Where hushed awakenings are dear. . . .
But I've a rendezvous with Death   20
At midnight in some flaming town,
When Spring trips north again this
  year,
And I to my pledged word am true,
I shall not fail that rendezvous.

For Discussion of Seeger

1. Be sure you know what the word
rendezvous means.
2. Name the three places where Seeger
thinks the rendezvous may have to be kept.
3. What is Seeger's attitude toward war?
Why might it be especially tragic for a poet
to have to die in spring? Point out some
proof of this in the poem.
4. Read other poems written by young
soldiers of both World Wars.

"I Have a Rendezvous with Death" by Alan Seeger. Reprinted by permission of Charles Scribner's Sons.

Theatre Arts

A scene from T. S. Eliot's The Cocktail Party. *Alec Guiness as the psychiatrist, Sir Harcourt-Reilly, interviews two clients.*

T. S. Eliot

1888–

Along with Robert Frost and Carl Sandburg, Thomas Stearns Eliot is one of the most celebrated living American poets. Unlike them, however, he does not command a large popular audience, but his influence on the younger poets of our day has been greater than theirs.

Eliot was born in St. Louis, Missouri, but his family's background and his own interests drew him toward the East. He was graduated from Harvard, then studied at the Sorbonne in Paris and became a Rhodes scholar at Oxford. After 1913 he considered London his home, and in 1927 he became a naturalized British subject. His more recent works have been critical essays and poetic dramas, including *Murder in the Cathedral* (1935) and *The Cocktail Party*, which was a hit on Broadway in 1950. He received the Nobel Prize for literature in 1948.

When Eliot published *The Waste Land* in 1922, it puzzled and even angered readers. In it they found lines packed with obscure references (Eliot even furnished a set of footnotes for this long poem!), with abrupt shifts of thought and mood, and with various symbols and images that have a personal meaning for the poet but are not always clear to the reader. Moreover, it was a bleak and despairing poem; it reflected a tortured mind completely frustrated by a meaningless world. This same sense of barrenness and frustration appears in *The Hollow Men* (1925), which is printed here. Yet, many readers find in this poetry both profound ideas and beautiful, often musical, language.

THE HOLLOW MEN

" The Hollow Men " is one of the most famous poems in modern literature — and one of the most difficult. Don't expect to get all, or even part, of its meaning in one or two readings. Read the poem through once or twice at least to get the *feel* of it. Notice some of the striking phrases (" rats' feet over broken glass," " this is cactus land," " valley of dying stars ") and sense the mood of despair they convey. Then reread it with particular attention to the footnotes.

The ideas in the poem belong to a particular period following World War I when some American writers — who were called representatives of " the lost generation " — felt that life was empty and meaningless. They had been disillusioned by the horrors of the war and were repelled by the money-seeking, cynical attitudes of American society in the 1920's. Eliot suggests here that modern men are " hollow " — without faith or hope or usefulness; he thinks they live in a " twilight kingdom," where civilization is dying.

It is good to know that " The Hollow Men " does not represent Eliot's present views. His more recent poetry expresses a religious faith that is hopeful and courageous. He has, in fact, become one of the foremost religious poets in modern literature.

Mistah Kurtz — he dead.

    *A penny for the Old Guy.**

I

We are the hollow men
We are the stuffed men
Leaning together
Headpiece filled with straw. Alas!
Our dried voices, when   5
We whisper together
Are quiet and meaningless
As wind in dry grass
Or rats' feet over broken glass
In our dry cellar   10

Shape without form, shade without color,
Paralyzed force, gesture without motion;°

Those who have crossed
With direct eyes, to death's other Kingdom°
Remember us — if at all — not as lost   15
Violent souls, but only
As the hollow men
The stuffed men.

II

Eyes I dare not meet in dreams
In death's dream kingdom   20
These do not appear:
There, the eyes are
Sunlight on a broken column
There, is a tree swinging
And voices are   25
In the wind's singing
More distant and more solemn
Than a fading star.

Let me be no nearer
In death's dream kingdom   30
Let me also wear
Such deliberate disguises
Rat's coat, crowskin, crossed staves
In a field
Behaving as the wind behaves   35
No nearer —

Not that final meeting
In the twilight kingdom

III

This is the dead land
This is cactus land   40
Here the stone images
Are raised, here they receive
The supplication of a dead man's hand°
Under the twinkle of a fading star.

Is it like this   45
In death's other kingdom
Waking alone
At the hour when we are
Trembling with tenderness
Lips that would kiss   50
Form prayers to broken stone.

IV

The eyes are not here
There are no eyes here
In this valley of dying stars
In this hollow valley   55
This broken jaw of our lost kingdoms

In this last of meeting places
We grope together
And avoid speech
Gathered on this beach of the tumid river   60

Sightless, unless
The eyes reappear
As the perpetual star°

---

* **Mistah Kurtz:** a character in Joseph Conrad's novel *Heart of Darkness*, a cultivated philosopher who dies unremembered in the African jungle. **Old Guy:** this is a cry used by children on Guy Fawkes day in England to obtain handouts, much as is done in America on Halloween. 12. These are descriptions, or suggestions, of modern man's lack of power and usefulness. 14. That is, the dead who stare (**with direct eyes**). **Death's other kingdom** implies that this life is a kind of death also.

43. Men pray (**supplication**) to outworn tradition (**stone images**). In the next stanza the poet says that men desire the vigor and warmth of life (**would kiss**) but can only pray fearfully, because of their lack of faith. 63. That is, men will be sightless unless they regain their faith (**eyes reappear as the perpetual star**).

Multifoliate rose
Of death's twilight kingdom   65
The hope only
Of empty men.

V

Here we go round the prickly pear
Prickly pear prickly pear
Here we go round the prickly pear   70
At five o'clock in the morning.°

Between the idea
And the reality
Between the motion
And the act   75
Falls the Shadow°
      For Thine is the Kingdom

Between the conception
And the creation
Between the emotion   80
And the response
Falls the Shadow
      Life is very long

Between the desire
And the spasm   85
Between the potency
And the existence
Between the essence
And the descent
Falls the Shadow   90
      For Thine is the Kingdom

For Thine is
Life is
For Thine is the

This is the way the world ends   95
This is the way the world ends
This is the way the world ends
Not with a bang but a whimper.

71. This is, of course, a familiar nursery rhyme. Contrasted with the Lord's Prayer line that follows (**For Thine is the Kingdom**), the nursery rhyme suggests the meaninglessness of modern life. **Prickly pear** is desert cactus and thus appropriately substituted for the usual "mulberry bush." 76. Once again the poet indicates man's lack of power and usefulness. This stanza and the two that follow say that man has lost the power to achieve, to accomplish, to build; always the **Shadow** of lost faith and failure falls between what he seeks and what he obtains.

For Discussion of Eliot

1. The mood of this poem is clear without special study. To get the thought requires some digging. With the help of the footnotes, decide on a topic for each numbered section. Then try to state in simple words the idea the poet expresses about each topic.

2. Do you agree with Eliot's thinking when he wrote this poem or with that of the later Eliot, who has become a poet of profound religious faith? What should a man have in place of a " headpiece filled with straw "? What gives meaning to man and to life?

3. What prominent men today would you class as " hollow men "? What prominent men seem to disprove Eliot's estimate of mankind?

4. Compare " The Hollow Men " with Shakespeare's famous lines in *Macbeth:*

    " Out, out, brief candle!
Life's but a walking shadow, a poor player
That struts and frets his hour upon the
    stage
And then is heard no more. It is a tale
Told by an idiot, full of sound and fury,
Signifying nothing."

Which poet better expressed the *idea* that life is meaningless? Which poet better created a *mood* of frustration and despair?

For Your Vocabulary

WORDS TO EXPRESS MOOD: Eliot's chief purpose in " The Hollow Men " is to create a mood of frustration, emptiness, and despair. To do this he uses some memorable phrases such as

" Shape without form, shade without color,
Paralyzed force, gesture without motion."

Analyze the thought of each of those four phrases.

Another telling choice of words is the substitution of *prickly pear* for *mulberry bush.* Just how does this add to the mood? How does the repetition of " Falls the Shadow " affect the reader? Point out other words and phrases which effectively contribute to the mood. What is the effect of the last line?

Edna St. Vincent Millay
1892–1950

Edna St. Vincent Millay was born in Rockland, Maine, and her early life was spent in New England. When she was nineteen she wrote " Renascence," a poem so remarkable that she was at once heralded as a coming poet. This poem was the title piece in her first volume, published in 1917, the same year that she left Vassar College. After that she lived for a time in Greenwich Village in New York, where she wrote stories and was associated with Eugene O'Neill and the Washington Square Players. All in all, she published ten volumes of poetry; several short plays in verse;

and *The King's Henchman*, a libretto for the opera by Deems Taylor. This is a notable attempt to establish the hitherto undeveloped form of grand opera in America.

Miss Millay's flowing melody is evident in her short lyrics. In her earlier poems one finds a kind of lyric wistfulness and an exuberance which makes them probably her most important writing. " God's World," from her first volume of poetry, is " Renascence " in miniature, reflecting the breathless awe of romantic youth, overwhelmed by the magic beauty of an autumn day.

GOD'S WORLD

O world, I cannot hold thee close
  enough!
  Thy winds, thy wide gray skies!
  Thy mists that roll and rise!
Thy woods, this autumn day, that ache
  and sag
And all but cry with color! That gaunt
  crag   5
To crush! To lift the lean of that black
  bluff!
World, world, I cannot get thee close
  enough!

Long have I known a glory in it all,
  But never knew I this;
  Here such a passion is   10
As stretcheth me apart. Lord, I do fear
Thou'st made the world too beautiful
  this year.

My soul is all but out of me — let fall
No burning leaf; prithee, let no bird
  call.

THE SPRING AND THE FALL

This is a more sober poem than " God's World." Youthful exuberance has been subdued by experience and disillusionment.

In the spring of the year, in the spring
  of the year,
I walked the road beside my dear.
The trees were black where the bark
  was wet.
I see them yet, in the spring of the year.
He broke me a bough of the blossoming
  peach   5

That was out of the way and hard to
reach.

In the fall of the year, in the fall of the
year,
I walked the road beside my dear.
The rooks went up with a raucous trill.
I hear them still, in the fall of the year.
He laughed at all I dared to praise,   11
And broke my heart, in little ways.

Year be springing or year be falling,
The bark will drip and the birds be
calling.
There's much that's fine to see and
hear   15
In the spring of a year, in the fall of a
year.
'Tis not love's going hurts my days,
But that it went in little ways.

ON HEARING A SYMPHONY
BY BEETHOVEN

This beautiful sonnet is one of Edna
Millay's most successful poems, a wonderful tribute to the power of music. The
world, which once held for the poet beauty
almost too great to be borne, has been
made unendurable for her by mankind,
" the spiteful and the stingy and the rude."
But Beethoven's music puts them momentarily under a spell, as in a fairy tale. She
responds to the symphony with the same
passionate surrender with which the
younger poet held out her aching arms to
" God's world." And the music does not
fail her. For a moment, at least (one " tranquil blossom on the tortured stem "), it
gives her an insight into the meaning and
direction of life.

Sweet sounds, oh, beautiful music, do
not cease!
Reject me not into the world again.
With you alone is excellence and peace,
Mankind made plausible, his purpose
plain.
Enchanted in your air benign and
shrewd,   5
With limbs a-sprawl and empty faces
pale,
The spiteful and the stingy and the rude
Sleep like the scullions in the fairy tale.
This moment is the best the world can
give:
The tranquil blossom on the tortured
stem.   10
Reject me not, sweet sounds! oh, let me
live,
Till Doom espy my towers and scatter
them,
A city spellbound under the aging sun.
Music my rampart, and my only one.

For Discussion of Millay

1. What mood does Miss Millay try to
express in " God's World "? Try to find
other poems on autumn expressing different moods. What mood does autumn most
commonly arouse in you?

2. How do you account for the change
of attitude toward autumn in " The Spring
and Fall "? What happened to the poet?

3. Point out some effective figures of
speech in " On Hearing a Symphony by
Beethoven." Give in your own words the
meaning of the last four lines. What " rampart " do you have against those things
that would destroy your faith and peace
of mind?

Metrical Terms

REPETITION OF SOUNDS: *Rhyme* is repetition of the same sound at the end of two
or more words. What is the rhyme in the
fourth line of each stanza of " The Spring
and the Fall "?

Alliteration is the repetition of consonants in two or more words. Often the
alliteration occurs at the beginning of
matching words. How many examples can
you find in the first stanza of " God's
World "?

Sister Mary Madeleva,
C.S.C.
1887–

In the crowded schedule of a busy college president and teacher, Sister Mary Madeleva has found time to write a number of exquisite lyrics that reflect her warmth and her interest in life. Born Mary Evaline Wolff, of a German pioneering family in Cumberland, Wisconsin, she grew up loving the out-of-doors as well as study. She first attended the University of Wisconsin, but changed to St. Mary's College, Notre Dame. Here, under the guidance of the Sisters of the Holy Cross, her vocation flowered, and she joined the Congregation while still a student. After her profession she taught at St. Mary's, departing in 1919 to teach in Utah and California. She was president of the College of St. Mary-of-the-Wasatch, Salt Lake City, and at present is president of St. Mary's College, Notre Dame.

Sister Madeleva's first volume, *Knights Errant and Other Poems*, was published in 1923. *Chaucer's Nuns and Other Essays* followed in 1925. Her *Selected Poems* was brought out in 1939. She has been president of the Catholic Poetry Society of America. The influence of Father O'Donnell (see p. 265), whose friendship she valued in her early years at Notre Dame, shines in her quatrains. In her work as teacher, writer, and administrator, she has contributed largely to Catholic letters.

POSSESSION

I cannot chant the angels' hymn
As did the hosts of seraphim.

I cannot even cross the wild
As shepherds did, to find the Child.

I cannot shine, a living star,   5
To guide grave magi from afar.

I have no incense, myrrh, or gold
For gift as had the kings of old.

In all the world there is nowhere
A place so poor, a spot so bare,   10

Save the rude cave at Bethlehem town
Where Christ, my Savior, laid Him
   down.

For that I am like that mean stall
I may possess Him most of all.

CANDLELIGHT

Day has its sun,
And night the stars,
But God has candlelight.

Upon the world's great candlestick He
   sets
The little taper of yourself ashine,   5
And when the sun has sputtered out
And all the stars are dead,
Your immortality may flame and burn
Across His infinite immensity forever.

"Possession" and "Candlelight" from *Selected Poems* by Sister M. Madeleva. Reprinted by permission of The Macmillan Company.

Wherefore He will sometime blow out
  the sun,   10
And snuff the stars,
Preferring candlelight.

For Discussion of Sister Madeleva

1. Do you think the poet regrets her
poverty in " Possession "? What do the
last two lines mean? Do you agree with
the idea? What is poverty of spirit?

2. Humility makes one recognize his
limitations. Point out evidences of humility in the poem. Could it be used as a
preparation for Holy Communion? Why?

3. What is the mood of the poet in
" Candlelight "? What appreciation of the
individual soul do you get from the poem?

Why should God " prefer candlelight "?

4. You have already discussed free verse
(see p. 278). Do you think its use is effective in " Candlelight "? Comment on the
appropriateness of the very simple language and rhythm in " Possession." This
poem is written in *couplets* — two consecu-
tive lines that rhyme. Write a couplet
using the same meter as this poem.

For Your Vocabulary

FIGURATIVE USE OF WORDS: Sister Madeleva looks at things from the inside out.
Using the theme of the soul as the light of
our life, how does she develop the metaphor of the candle and the candlestick?
How is her use of verbs in " Candlelight "
effective in strengthening this image?

Stephen Vincent Benét
1898–1943

Stephen Vincent Benét was born in Bethlehem, Pennsylvania, where his father, an
army officer, was stationed, but much of
his boyhood was spent at posts in California and Georgia. He belonged to a remarkable literary family. His brother, William
Rose Benét, was a well-known critic and
poet; his sister, Laura, is a novelist. His
wife, Rosemary, collaborated with him on
A Book of Americans, charming light-verse
portrayals of famous men. Elinor Wylie
was his sister-in-law.

Before graduating from Yale in 1919,
Stephen Benét had published two volumes
of verse, and within ten years he published
several more volumes, two novels, and
won both *The Nation's* poetry prize and a
Pulitzer Prize, the latter for *John Brown's
Body.* This great poem of the War between
the States sold more than one hundred

thousand copies within a few months and
made Benét a national figure. His interest
in the old battles had been early awakened
by books handed down from several West
Point graduates in his own family. Then,
too, his own varied experience from North
to South gave him sympathetic insight into
the lives of those on both sides.

Stephen Benét's deep feeling for our
past also showed itself in his ballads, revealing different facets of American life,
and in his short stories, like " The Devil
and Daniel Webster." At the start of
World War II, he had turned his talent to
writing a radio drama. His early death at
the age of forty-five was mourned as a
calamity to American letters. His versatil-
ity in both fiction and poetry reminds one
of Poe, who also died at the height of his
powers.

THE BALLAD OF
WILLIAM SYCAMORE

(1790–1871)

My father, he was a mountaineer,
His fist was a knotty hammer;
He was quick on his feet as a running
    deer,
And he spoke with a Yankee stammer.

My mother, she was merry and brave,
And so she came to her labor,   6
With a tall green fir for her doctor grave
And a stream for her comforting neigh-
    bor.

And some are wrapped in the linen fine,
And some like a godling's scion;   10
But I was cradled on twigs of pine
In the skin of a mountain lion.

And some remember a white, starched
    lap
And a ewer with silver handles;
But I remember a coonskin cap   15
And the smell of bayberry candles.

The cabin logs, with the bark still rough,
And my mother who laughed at trifles,
And the tall, lank visitors, brown as
    snuff,
With their long, straight squirrel rifles.

I can hear them dance, like a foggy
    song,   21
Through the deepest one of my slum-
    bers,
The fiddle squeaking the boots along
And my father calling the numbers.

The quick feet shaking the puncheon
    floor,   25
And the fiddle squealing and squealing,
Till the dried herbs rattled above the
    door
And the dust went up to the ceiling.

There are children lucky from dawn to
    dusk,
But never a child so lucky!   30
For I cut my teeth on "Money Musk"°
In the Bloody Ground of Kentucky!

When I grew tall as the Indian corn,
My father had little to lend me,
But he gave me his great, old powder
    horn   35
And his woodsman's skill to befriend
    me.

With a leather shirt to cover my back,
And a redskin nose to unravel
Each forest sign, I carried my pack
As far as a scout could travel.   40

Till I lost my boyhood and found my
    wife,
A girl like a Salem clipper°!
A woman straight as a hunting knife
With eyes as bright as the Dipper!

We cleared our camp where the buffalo
    feed,   45
Unheard-of streams were our flagons;
And I sowed my sons like the apple
    seed
On the trail of the Western wagons.

They were right, tight boys, never sulky
    or slow,
A fruitful, goodly muster.   50
The eldest died at the Alamo.°
The youngest fell with Custer.°

The letter that told it burned my hand.
Yet we smiled and said, "So be it!"

31. "Money Musk": an old dance tune.
42. Salem clipper: Salem, Massachusetts, was
one of the chief seaports in the days of the clipper
ships. 51. Alamo (ăl′á·mō): an old Spanish mission, used as a fort when, in 1836, a garrison
of Texans were slaughtered by the Mexicans.
52. Custer: General George Custer, famous Indian fighter, who between 1866 and 1876 was
sent to quell uprisings in various parts of the
West.

But I could not live when they fenced
the land,   55
For it broke my heart to see it.

I saddled a red, unbroken colt
And rode him into the day there;
And he threw me down like a thunder-
bolt
And rolled on me as I lay there.   60

The hunter's whistle hummed in my ear
As the city men tried to move me,
And I died in my boots like a pioneer
With the whole wide sky above me.

Now I lie in the heart of the fat, black
soil,   65
Like the seed of a prairie thistle;
It has washed my bones with honey and
oil
And picked them clean as a whistle.

And my youth returns, like the rains of
Spring,   69
And my sons, like the wild geese flying;
And I lie and hear the meadowlark sing
And I have much content in my dying.

Go play with the towns you have built
of blocks,
The towns where you would have bound
me!
I sleep in my earth like a tired fox,   75
And my buffalo have found me.

THE MOUNTAIN
WHIPPOORWILL

(Or, How Hillbilly Jim Won
the Great Fiddlers' Prize)

A GEORGIA ROMANCE

Up in the mountains, it's lonesome all
the time,
(Sof' win' slewin' thu' the sweet-potato
vine).

Up in the mountains, it's lonesome for a
child,
(Whippoorwills a-callin' when the sap
runs wild).

Up in the mountains, mountains in the
fog,   5
Everythin's as lazy as an old houn' dog.

Born in the mountains, never raised a
pet,
Don't want nuthin' an' never got it yet.

Born in the mountains, lonesome-born,
Raised runnin' ragged thu' the cockle-
burrs and corn.   10

Never knew my pappy, mebbe never
should.
Think he was a fiddle made of moun-
tain-laurel wood.

Never had a mammy to teach me pretty-
please.
Think she was a whippoorwill, a-skitin'
thu' the trees.

Never had a brother ner a whole pair of
pants,   15
But when I start to fiddle, why, yuh got
to start to dance!

Listen to my fiddle — Kingdom Come —
Kingdom Come!
Hear the frogs a-chunkin' " Jug o' rum,
Jug o' rum! "
Hear that mountain whippoorwill be
lonesome in the air,
An' I'll tell yuh how I traveled to the Es-
sex County Fair.   20

Essex County has a mighty pretty fair,
All the smarty fiddlers from the South
come there.

Elbows flyin' as they rosin up the bow
For the First Prize Contest in the Georgia Fiddlers' Show.

Old Dan Wheeling, with his whiskers
in his ears,   25
Kingpin fiddler for nearly twenty years.

Big Tom Sargent, with his blue wall-
eye,
An' Little Jimmy Weezer that can make
a fiddle cry.

All sittin' roun', spittin' high an' struttin'
proud,
(Listen, little whippoorwill, yuh better
bug yore eyes!)   30
Tun-a-tun-a-tunin' while the jedges told
the crowd
Them that got the mostest claps 'd win
the bestest prize.

Everybody waitin' for the first tweedle-
dee,
When in comes a-stumblin' — hillbilly
me!

Bowed right pretty to the jedges an' the
rest,   35
Took a silver dollar from a hole inside
my vest,

Plunked it on the table an' said,
" There's my callin' card!
An' anyone that licks me — well, he's
got to fiddle hard! "

Old Dan Wheeling, he was laughin' fit
to holler,
Little Jimmy Weezer said, " There's one
dead dollar! "   40

Big Tom Sargent had a yaller-toothy
grin,
But I tucked my little whippoorwill
spang underneath my chin,
An' petted it an' tuned it till the jedges
said, " Begin! "

Big Tom Sargent was the first in line;
He could fiddle all the bugs off a sweet-
potato vine.   45
He could fiddle down a possum from a
mile-high tree,

He could fiddle up a whale from the
bottom of the sea.

Yuh could hear hands spankin' till they
spanked each other raw,
When he finished variations on " Turkey in the Straw."

Little Jimmy Weezer was the next to
play;   50
He could fiddle all night, he could fid-
dle all day.

He could fiddle chills, he could fiddle
fever,
He could make a fiddle rustle like a
lowland river.

He could make a fiddle croon like a
lovin' woman.
An' they clapped like thunder when
he'd finished strummin'.   55

Then came the ruck of the bobtailed
fiddlers,
The let's-go-easies, the fair-to-middlers.

They got their claps an' they lost their
bicker,°
An' they all settled back for some more
corn licker.

An' the crowd was tired of their no-
'count squealing,   60
When out in the center steps Old Dan
Wheeling.

He fiddled high and he fiddled low,
(Listen, little whippoorwill; yuh got to
spread yore wings!)
He fiddled and fiddled with a cherry-
wood bow.
(Old Dan Wheeling's got bee honey in
his strings.)   65

He fiddled the wind by the lonesome
moon.
He fiddled a most almighty tune.

58. **lost their bicker:** failed.

He started fiddling like a ghost.
He ended fiddling like a host.

He fiddled north an' he fiddled south,
He fiddled the heart right out of yore
mouth. 71

He fiddled here an' he fiddled there.
He fiddled salvation everywhere.

*When he was finished, the crowd cut
loose.*
*(Whippoorwill, they's rain on yore
breast.)* 75
*An' I sat there wonderin' "What's the
use?"*
(Whippoorwill, fly home to yore nest.)

But I stood up pert an' I took my bow,
An' my fiddle went to my shoulder, so.

An' — they wasn't no crowd to get me
fazed° — 80
But I was alone where I was raised.

Up in the mountains, so still it makes
yuh skeered.
Where God lies sleepin' in his big white
beard.

An' I heard the sound of the squirrel in
the pine,
An' I heard the earth a-breathin' thu'
the long nighttime. 85

They've fiddled the rose, and they've
fiddled the thorn,
But they haven't fiddled the mountain
corn.

They've fiddled sinful an' fiddled moral,
But they haven't fiddled the breshwood
laurel.

They've fiddled loud, and they've fiddled still, 90
But they haven't fiddled the whippoorwill.

80. fazed: embarrassed.

I started off with a *dump-diddle-dump,*
(Oh, hell's broke loose in Georgia!)
Skunk cabbage growin' by the bee-gum
stump,
(Whippoorwill, yo're singin' now!) 95

My mother was a whippoorwill pert,
My father, he was lazy,
But I'm hell broke loose in a new store
shirt
To fiddle all Georgia crazy.
Swing yore partners — up an' down the
middle! 100
Sashay now — oh, listen to that fiddle!
Flapjacks flippin' on a red-hot griddle,
An' hell broke loose,
Hell broke loose,
Fire on the mountains — snakes in the
grass. 105
Satan's here a-bilin' — oh, Lordy, let him
pass!
Go down Moses, set my people free;
Pop goes the weasel thu' the old Red
Sea!
Jonah sittin' on a hickory bough,
Up jumps a whale — an' where's yore
prophet now? 110
Rabbit in the pea patch, possum in the
pot,
Try an' stop my fiddle, now my fiddle's
gettin' hot!
Whippoorwill, singin' thu' the mountain
hush,
Whippoorwill, shoutin' from the burn-
in' bush, 114
Whippoorwill, cryin' in the stable door,
Sing tonight as yuh never sang before!
Hell's broke loose like a stompin' moun-
tain shoat,
Sing till yuh bust the gold in yore
throat!
Hell's broke loose for forty miles aroun',
Bound to stop yore music if yuh don't
sing it down. 120
Sing on the mountains, little whippoor-
will,
Sing to the valleys, an' slap 'em with a
hill,
For I'm struttin' high as an eagle's quill,
An' hell's broke loose,

Hell's broke loose,   125
Hell's broke loose in Georgia!

They wasn't a sound when I stopped
    bowin',
(*Whippoorwill, yuh can sing no more.*)
But, somewhere or other, the dawn was
    growin',
(*Oh, mountain whippoorwill!*)   130

An' I thought, " I've fiddled all night an'
    lost,
Yo're a good hillbilly, but yuh've been
    bossed."

So I went to congratulate old man Dan,
— But he puts his fiddle into my han' —
An' then the noise of the crowd began!

PORTRAIT OF A
SOUTHERN LADY

(FROM *John Brown's Body*)

John Brown's Body, truly a remarkable
book, is the first serious attempt in poetry
to present an impartial view of the War
between the States. Instead of telling his
story in a continuous narrative, the author
has taken a number of representative characters, some real, some fictional, and has
placed them in scenes that were significant
of the trend of the war. The scene shifts
rapidly from one group to another, but a
connected thread of plot within each group
maintains the reader's interest throughout.
The metrical form also shifts. Some parts
are in blank verse, some in free verse, some
in pure lyrical form. This sketch of Mary
Lou Wingate, the lady of the plantation,
is presented with the firm vigor and occasional satirical flash of the rhymed couplet.

Mary Lou Wingate, as slightly made
And as hard to break as a rapier blade.
Bristol's daughter and Wingate's bride,
Never well since the last child died   4
But staring at pain with courteous eyes.
When the pain outwits it, the body dies,

Meanwhile the body bears the pain.
She loved her hands and they made her
    vain,
The tiny hands of her generation
That gathered the reins of the whole
    plantation;   10
The velvet sheathing the steel demurely
In the trained, light grip that holds so
    surely.

She was at work by candlelight,
She was at work in the dead of night,
Smoothing out troubles and healing
    schisms   15
And doctoring phthisics and rheuma-
    tisms,
Guiding the cooking and watching the
    baking,
The sewing, the soap- and candle-mak-
    ing,
The brewing, the darning, the lady-
    daughters,
The births and deaths in the Negro
    quarters,   20
Seeing that Suke had some new, strong
    shoes
And Joe got a week in the calaboose,
While Dicey's Jacob escaped a whip-
    ping
And the jelly bag dripped with its prop-
    er dripping,
And the shirts and estrangements were
    neatly mended,   25
And all of the tasks that never ended.

Her manner was gracious but hardly
    fervent
And she seldom raised her voice to a
    servant.
She was often mistaken, not often blind;
And she knew the whole duty of wom-
    ankind,   30
To take the burden and have the power
And seem like the well-protected flow-
    er,
To manage a dozen industries
With a casual gesture in scraps of ease,
To hate the sin and to love the sinner

The pride and dignity of the South

And to see that the gentlemen got their
    dinner   36
Ready and plenty and piping hot
Whether you wanted to eat or not.
And always, always, to have the charm
That makes the gentlemen take your
    arm   40
But never the bright, unseemly spell
That makes strange gentlemen love too
    well,
Once you were married and settled
    down
With a suitable gentleman of your own.

And when that happened, and you had
    bred   45
The requisite children, living and dead,
To pity the fool and comfort the weak
And always let the gentlemen speak,
To succor your love from deep-struck
    roots
When gentlemen went to bed in their
    boots,   50
And manage a gentleman's whole plan-
    tation
In the manner befitting your female
    station.

This was the creed that her mother
    taught her
And the creed that she taught to every
    daughter.
She knew her Bible — and how to flirt
With a swansdown fan and a brocade
    skirt.   56
For she trusted in God but she liked for-
    malities
And the world and heaven were both
    realities.
— In heaven, of course, we should all
    be equal,
But, until we came to that golden se-
    quel,   60
Gentility must keep to gentility
Where God and breeding had made
    things stable,
While the rest of the cosmos deserved
    civility
But dined in its boots at the second
    table.

This view may be reckoned a trifle nar-
    row,   65
But it had the driving force of an arrow,
And it helped Mary Lou to stand up
    straight,
For she was gentle, but she could hate
And she hated the North with the hate
    of Jael°
When the dry hot hands went seeking
    the nail,   70
The terrible hate of women's ire,
The smoky, the long-consuming fire.
The Yankees were devils, and she could
    pray,
For devils, no doubt, upon Judgment
    Day,
But now in the world, she would hate
    them still   75
And send the gentlemen out to kill.

The gentlemen killed and the gentle-
    men died,
But she was the South's incarnate pride
That mended the broken gentlemen   79
And sent them out to the war again,
That kept the house with the man away
And baked the bricks where there was
    no clay,
Made courage from terror and bread
    from bran
And propped the South on a swans-
    down fan
Through four long years of ruin and
    stress,   85
The pride — and the deadly bitterness.

69. **Jael:** a woman of Biblical times who
killed the captain of the Canaanites by driving a nail through his forehead while he slept (see
Judges 4:15–22).

For Discussion of Benét

The Ballad of William Sycamore

1. Pick out details that show Sycamore
to have been a typical American in the
early days of the opening of the West.
What is his feeling toward cities and a
settled land?

2. Point out some of the strikingly original phrases in this poem, especially those
relating to Sycamore's death and burial.

3. Look up further details of the fight at the Alamo and the exploits of Custer, referred to in this ballad.

4. Read others of Benét's excellent ballads in *A Book of Americans* written in collaboration with his wife, Rosemary.

The Mountain Whippoorwill

1. Picture in your own words the scene of the story, the appearance of the characters, and the speaker himself.

2. Why are certain lines put in italics? Wherein does the story use the dramatic devices of contrast, suspense, climax? What gives any public competition a dramatic flavor? How does the method of judging this contest compare with any you have witnessed or heard on the radio or television? Is the outcome of the contest more or less effective by being told so briefly?

3. Where in the poem do you feel that the poet is consciously building up sound effects? How do they compare in manner and effectiveness with Vachel Lindsay's? Would this poem lend itself to choral reading, as suggested for Lindsay's poems? How would you adapt it as a radio play?

4. By pointing out specific examples of idioms, figures of speech, details of nature, conceptions of Bible characters, superstitions, and so forth, show how the poet creates the local color of the unsophisticated mountain folk.

Portrait of a Southern Lady

1. Make a list of the main characteristics of Mary Lou Wingate. Have you known anyone like her? Does she fit your previous idea of the lady of a plantation before the war? If you have read *Gone with the Wind* or have seen it in the movies, point out ways in which Mary Lou Wingate and Scarlett O'Hara are alike and unalike.

2. What elements of old plantation life have passed away forever? Which remain in somewhat modified form?

Types of Narrative Poetry

These selections from Benét illustrate three major types of narrative poetry: the ballad, the metrical tale, and the epic.

A *ballad* is a brief story in verse that is intended to be sung. The old folk ballads of England and Scotland, like " Barbara Allen " and the Robin Hood ballads, grew out of generations of singing by the common people, and we may still see the process going on in our American folklore. But other ballads are literary creations by a single writer, such as Lowell's " The Courtin' " (p. 580) and Benét's " The Ballad of William Sycamore " (p. 306). Typical " ballad measure " is the four-line stanza with alternate rhymes, and three or four beats (or feet) to a line. Is Benét's poem in typical ballad measure? Compare it with Whittier's " Skipper Ireson's Ride " (p. 494).

A *metrical* tale is a somewhat longer narrative poem corresponding to the prose short story. Metrical tales abound in American literature, especially in the works of Longfellow and Whittier. Longfellow's *Tales of a Wayside Inn* are probably the best-known examples. Compare Lowell's " The Vision of Sir Launfal " (p. 584) with Benét's " The Mountain Whippoorwill " in terms of their use of a refrain, their stanza length, and adaptability to singing.

Epics are long narrative poems celebrating in dignified style the deeds of a hero. Great classical epics, like the *Iliad* by Homer and the *Aeneid* by Virgil, glorify the mythical heroes of Greece and Rome. Among the European nations we find great national *folk epics* among the common people in the early days before printing — stories that grew by word-of-mouth retelling from one bard to another. Among these are the French *Song of Roland* and the English *Beowulf*. Europeans have also produced some great *literary epics,* each the work of a single author, such as Milton's *Paradise Lost.* From Asia come the *Shah Namah* of Persia and the *Ramayana* and the *Mahabharata* of India. In America, Longfellow tried to create an epic of the American Indian in the *Song of Hiawatha,* using the unusual meter of the *Kalevala,* the great epic poem of Finland. Benét's *John Brown's Body* is epical in scope, but it lacks a single great hero, and it sacrifices the unity of the epic by frequent abrupt changes of meters. However, it is the nearest approach to a great epic yet produced by an American. Its unflagging pace makes it exciting reading. Why not get a copy from the library and sample this book-length poem?

Archibald MacLeish
1892–

Archibald MacLeish was born in Glencoe, Illinois, in what he describes as a wooden château overlooking Lake Michigan. He was graduated from Yale and was in France during World War I. After the war, MacLeish attended Harvard Law School and practiced law for three years, but gave it up in 1923, from which time he dates the real beginning of his life. He settled his family in headquarters in France for five years, and they traveled as far as Iran. After 1928 he was back in this country living on a farm and writing poetry. His long poem on the Spanish conquest of the New World, *Conquistador*, won him a Pulitzer Prize for 1933 and a national reputation. In 1939 President Roosevelt appointed him Librarian of Congress, and later he became an Assistant Secretary of State. He now teaches literature and writing at Harvard.

As his career indicates, MacLeish is not a poet in an " ivory tower," away from the problems of the world. Many of his poems, like those in *Public Speech* and *Land of the Free,* concern social issues.

His radio dramas, like *Air Raid* and *The Fall of the City,* are exciting pictures of the dangerous times preceding and during World War II.

IT IS A STRANGE THING — TO BE AN AMERICAN

(FROM *American Letter*)

It is a strange thing — to be an American.
It is strange to sleep in the bare stars and to die
On an open land where few bury before us:
(From the new earth the dead return no more).
It is strange to be born of no race and no people.   5
In the old lands they are many together. They keep
The wise past and the words spoken in common.
They remember the dead with their hands, their mouths dumb.
They answer each other with two words in their meeting.
They live together in small things. They eat   10
The same dish, their drink is the same and their proverbs.
Their youth is like. They are like in their ways of love.
They are many men. There are always others beside them.
Here it is one man and another and wide
On the darkening hills the faint smoke of the houses.   15
Here it is one man and the wind in the boughs.

Therefore our hearts are sick for the south water.
The smell of the gorse comes back to our night thought.
We are sick at heart for the red roofs and the olives;
We are sick at heart for the voice and the footfall. . . .   20

Therefore we will not go though the sea call us.

This, this is our land, this is our people,
This that is neither a land nor a race. We must reap
The wind here in the grass for our soul's harvest:
Here we must eat our salt or our bones starve.   25
Here we must live or live only as shadows.
This is our race, we that have none, that have had
Neither the old walls nor the voices around us,
This is our land, this is our ancient ground —
The raw earth, the mixed bloods and the strangers,   30
The different eyes, the wind, and the heart's change.
These we will not leave though the old call us.
This is our country-earth, our blood, our kind.

FROM LAND OF THE FREE

One of MacLeish's most original books is *Land of the Free,* an experimental combination of impressive photographs and free verse. Opposite pages of pictures showing dispossessed farm people of the " dust bowl " is a running commentary which he calls a " sound track." The concluding lines of this " sound track " are printed below.

The poem was written in the 1930's when many areas suffered from land erosion, and families were forced to leave worn-out farms. The poet says that the story of American freedom is the story of the westward movement of the pioneers — always onward to more land. And then he wonders if, now that the land is all settled, there may not be a new meaning to American liberty. It is worth thinking about.

We wonder whether the dream of American liberty
Was two hundred years of pine and hardwood
And three generations of the grass

And the generations are up: the years over

We don't know   5

It was two hundred years from the smell of the tidewater
Up through the Piedmont: on through the piney woods:
Till we came out
With our led calves and our lean women
In the oak openings of Illinois   10

It was three generations from the oak trees —
From the islands of elm and the islands of oak in the prairie —
Till we heeled out with our plows and our steel harrows
On the grass-drowned reef bones of the Plains

"Four score and seven years" said the Orator   15

We remember it differently: we remember it
Kansas: Illinois: Ohio: Connecticut.
We remember it Council Bluffs: St. Louis:
Wills Creek: the Cumberland: Shenandoah —
The long harangues of the grass in the wind are our histories   20

We tell our freedom backward by the land
We tell our past by the gravestones and the apple trees

We wonder whether the great American dream
Was the singing of locusts out of the grass to the west and the
West is behind us now: 25
The west wind's away from us:

We wonder if the liberty is done:
The dreaming is finished

We can't say

We aren't sure   30

Or if there's something different men can dream
Or if there's something different men can mean by
Liberty

Or if there's liberty a man can mean that's
Men: not land   35

We wonder

We don't know

We're asking

For Discussion of MacLeish

1. In "It Is a Strange Thing" what kinds of differences between America and Europe are brought out? What effect do these differences have upon the attitude of the American toward his country? Can you give specific examples to show that the tie to the new land is stronger than the tie to the old home across the water?

2. Would you say that "Land of the Free" is pessimistic or hopeful? What new direction does MacLeish suggest for the next chapters in the story of American freedom? What lines might remind you of Katherine Lee Bates's "America the Beautiful" and its "patriot dream" of "alabaster cities, undimmed by human tears"?

3. How does "Land of the Free" relate to the DeVoto article on page 153? In what way was the open land of the frontier a kind of freedom for Americans?

4. Look back over the poets in this section to see which ones have specifically expressed attachment to our country, or aspirations for America. In Part Two, the spirit of America is expressed by older literature — work that helped to build in the minds of more recent writers the concept of what America stands for.

NEW VOICES IN POETRY

During the past decade the American literary scene has rumbled with arguments over the "new" poetry — and they are still to be heard wherever readers or writers congregate. In a way, the disputes remind one of the keen opposition (and support) that Edgar Lee Masters and Carl Sandburg aroused with their realistic poetry during World War I.

But today the issue is different. Now some readers and critics complain that the ultra-modern poetry is difficult to understand, often unintelligible. They argue that T. S. Eliot and many much younger poets write for themselves and each other, rather than for the common reader, that they pack their poems with obscure references and twisted phrases that mean little to most readers. Yet many readers defend the "new" poets and point out that new styles in poetry have always aroused opposition — yet after a time become accepted. Also, it is said, this is a complicated age we live in and it produces a more complicated poetry than previous times.

So run the arguments. You will have a chance here to read samples from six contemporary poets. The poems that follow are not by any means the most difficult of modern poems (they have been selected with the opposite in mind), but they furnish you with a good taste of writing today. Perhaps you will want to compare and contrast them with the twentieth-century poets you have just finished reading. Remember, these are, in a real sense, the poems and the poets of your own day.

Thomas Merton   1915–

Thomas Merton (Father Mary Louis, O.C.S.O.) has described his life in his best-selling autobiography, *The Seven Storey Mountain.* He entered the Cistercian Abbey of Our Lady of Gethsemani in Kentucky in 1941, and was ordained in 1949.

A steadily deepening stream of prose and poetry has flowed from his pen. His books include *Seeds of Contemplation* and *The Tears of the Blind Lions,* both published in 1949. In the selection "My New Freedom," on page 223, he reveals how easily and almost instinctively he turns to verse as a means of expression.

A cosmopolite prior to his entrance into the monastery, Merton seems destined to influence largely the revival of spiritual values current in American letters. In

"The Trappist Abbey: Matins" he links his two loves, nature and vocation. "The Reader" catches the welling peace of the cloister. "The Candlemas Procession," a lyrical outburst of joy in his own calling, expresses a truth for all of us.

THE TRAPPIST ABBEY: MATINS

(Our Lady of Gethsemani, Kentucky)

When the full fields begin to smell of sunrise
And the valleys sing in their sleep,
The pilgrim moon pours over the solemn darkness
Her waterfalls of silence,
And then departs, up the long avenue of trees.   5

The stars hide, in the glade, their light, like tears,
And tremble where some train runs, lost,
Baying in eastward mysteries of distance,
Where fire flares, somewhere, over a sink of cities.

Now kindle in the windows of this ladyhouse, my soul,   10
Your childish, clear awakeness:
Burn in the country night
Your wise and sleepless lamp.
For, from the frowning tower, the windy belfry,
Sudden the bells come, bridegrooms,   15
And fill the echoing dark with love and fear.

Wake in the windows of Gethsemani, my soul, my sister,
For the past years, with smoky torches, come,
Bringing betrayal from the burning world
And bloodying the glade with pitch flame.   20

Wake in the cloisters of the lonely night, my soul, my sister,
Where the apostles gather, who were, one time, scattered,
And mourn God's blood in the place of His betrayal,
And weep with Peter at the triple cock-crow.

THE READER

Lord, when the clock strikes
Telling the time with cold tin
And I sit hooded in this lectern

Waiting for the monks to come,
I see the red cheeses, and bowls   5
All smile with milk in ranks upon their
    tables.

Light fills my proper globe
(I have won light to read by
With a little, tinkling chain)

And the monks come down the cloister
With robes as voluble as water.   11
I do not see them but I hear their waves.

It is winter, and my hands prepare
To turn the pages of the saints:
And to the trees Thy moon has frozen on
  the windows   15
My tongue shall sing Thy Scripture.

Then the monks pause upon the step
(With me here in this lectern
And Thee there on Thy crucifix)
And gather little pearls of water on their
  fingers' ends   20
Smaller than this my psalm.

THE CANDLEMAS PROCESSION

    Lumen
    Ad revelationem gentium. *

    Look kindly, Jesus, where we come,
    New Simeons, to kindle,
    Each at Your infant sacrifice his own life's candle.

    And when Your flame turns into many tongues,
    See how the One is multiplied, among us, hundreds!   5
    And goes among the humble, and consoles our sinful kindred.

    It is for this we come,
    And, kneeling, each receive one flame:
    Ad revelationem gentium.

    Our lives, like candles, spell this simple symbol: 10

    Weep like our bodily life, sweet work of bees,
    Sweeten the world, with your slow sacrifice.
    And this shall be our praise:
    That by our glad expense, our Father's will
    Burned and consumed us for a parable.   15

    Nor burn we now with brown and smoky flames, but bright
    Until our sacrifice is done,
    (By which not we, but You are known)
    And then, returning to our Father, one by one,
    Give back our lives like wise and waxen lights.   20

* ***Lumen Ad revelationem gentium:*** A Light to the revelation of the Gentiles (Luke 2:32).

Robert Lowell   1917–

In 1947, Robert Traill Spence Lowell could well have been named "the year's most honored poet." He received the Pulitzer Prize for his volume, *Lord Weary's Castle,* a grant from the National Institute of Arts and Letters, and a Guggenheim Fellowship. The great grand-nephew of James Russell Lowell, and a distant cousin

of Amy Lowell, he is the third of this
famous Massachusetts family to make his
name in American letters. He attended
Harvard and Kenyon College, Ohio, where
he received his B.A. in 1940.

Lowell uses conventional poetic rhythms
and meters to express the tension of his
thought, often employing satire to show
how far from the Christian ideal the world
has strayed. In " The Dead in Europe " he
voices horror of the mass civilian bomb-
ings; in " Our Lady of Walsingham " he
recalls the famous medieval shrine of Our
Lady in England.

THE DEAD IN EUROPE

After the planes unloaded, we fell down
Buried together, unmarried men and women;
Not crown of thorns, not iron, not Lombard crown,
Not grilled and spindle spires pointing to heaven
Could save us. Raise us, Mother, we fell down   5
Here hugger-mugger in the jellied fire:
Our sacred earth in our day was our curse.

Our Mother, shall we rise on Mary's day
In Maryland, wherever corpses married
Under the rubble, bundled together? Pray   10
For us whom the blockbusters marred and buried;
When Satan scatters us on Rising-day,
O Mother, snatch our bodies from the fire:
Our sacred earth in our day was our curse.

Mother, my bones are trembling and I hear   15
The earth's reverberations and the trumpet
Bleating into my shambles. Shall I bear,
(O Mary!) unmarried man and powder-puppet,
Witness to the Devil? Mary, hear,
O Mary, marry earth, sea, air and fire;   20
Our sacred earth in our day is our curse.

OUR LADY OF WALSINGHAM

There once the penitents took off their shoes
And then walked barefoot the remaining mile;
And the small trees, a stream and hedgerows file
Slowly along the munching English lane,
Like cows to the old shrine, until you lose   5
Track of your dragging pain.
The stream flows down under the druid tree,
Shiloah's whirlpools gurgle and make glad
The castle of God. Sailor, you were glad
And whistled Sion by that stream. But see: 10

Our Lady, too small for her canopy,
Sits near the altar. There's no comeliness
At all or charm in that expressionless
Face with its heavy eyelids. As before,
This face, for centuries a memory,   15
Non est species, neque decor,°
Expressionless, expresses God: it goes
Past castled Sion. She knows what God knows,
Not Calvary's Cross nor crib at Bethlehem
Now, and the world shall come to Walsingham.   20

16. *Non . . . decor:* There is no beauty in Him, nor comeliness (Isaias 53:2).

Sister Mary Jeremy,
O.P.

Sister Mary Jeremy is a fitting representative of the many talented Sisters writing today. Born in Chicago, she attended there the St. Thomas the Apostle High School and the Teachers College. She pursued graduate work at Yale University and the University of Chicago, where she won the John Billings Fiske Prize for poetry. Her poetry has appeared in numerous magazines, and she has published one volume, *Dialogue with an Angel* (1949). At present, she is a member of the English faculty of Rosary College, River Forest, Illinois.

Compression of thought and depth of feeling mark much of Sister Jeremy's work. In "The Departure" you will note the quiet tone in obvious contrast to the sorrow and loss the death has caused. Remember that the poet is talking to a deeply religious, resourceful person who has just died.

THE DEPARTURE

What you took with you no one knew —
The night was cold for setting forth,
The wet leaves stirred without a sound
Till the wind wheeled and galloped
   north.
We listened, but the rain came on   5
And no one knew when you had gone.

Between our pity and the grief
That would not break itself in words
What holiest of signs should pass?
The sea of swords, the hill of glass   10
That every questing princess knows
Were waiting in the dark for you —
You would remember what to do.

But meanwhile lonely clamors rose
Chilling the heart with prophecy   15
Till your remembered silences
Allured them to tranquillity:
As if a star should leave a wake
Of peace above a stricken land,
Saying beyond some ravaged hill,   20
"This world small-spinning in God's
   hand
Is His dear jewel still."

Jessica Powers

Jessica Powers' first volume of poetry was published in 1939 by Clifford Laube on his own Monastine Press. In 1941, she was received into the Order of Discalced Carmelites, and now, as Sister Miriam of the Holy Spirit, resides in the Carmel of the Mother of God, in Milwaukee.

Sister Miriam's most recent volume is *The Place of Splendor* (1946). She is a

"The Departure" from *Dialogue with an Angel* by Sister Mary Jeremy. Reprinted by permission of The Devin-Adair Company.

vice-president of the Catholic Poetry Society of America. Her poetry shows a luminous devotion to the Holy Spirit, and a deep strain of human pity. In " The Moment After Suffering " she analyzes the peace, strength, and wisdom we can gather from mental or physical pain. In " Doxology " she exults in the omnipresence of God. Notice the striking figures of speech in this short poem.

THE MOMENT AFTER SUFFERING

Time's cupped hands hold
No place so lenient, so calm as this,
The moment after suffering; it is like
A sunlit clearing after densest wood,
Bright by antithesis.   5
One sits upon a stump to get one's bearing
And to admire such evidence of day.
Thicket and tangle, creatures of the darkness
Obscurely take their leave and slink away.
One feeds upon a succulent rich wisdom   10
That to the mind's surprise has naught to do
With late abjection; it is revelation
God-fathered, heaven-new.
Oh, there are woods, of course — long forest stretches
Of wide inhabited darkness to be crossed,   15
Hunger and pain, the stir of unnamed creatures,
An imminent certainty of being lost.
But even that eludes this meditation
Or if intrusive brings yet more release.
One muses as to what it will be like   20
To step at last from final forest into
The infinite meadows of unending peace,
A place all light and yet not lighted by
The harsh obtrusive sun that walks our sky,
Light that the soul assimilates until   25
Not witness but participant it stands,
Taking of Godhead its amazing fill.

DOXOLOGY

God fills my being to the brim
With floods of His immensity.
I drown within a drop of Him
Whose sea-bed is infinity.

The Father's Will is everywhere   5
For chart and chance His precept keep.

There are no beaches to His care
Nor cliffs to pluck me from His deep.

The Son is never far from me
For presence is what love compels.   10
Divinely and incarnately
He draws me where His mercy dwells.

"The Moment After Suffering" by Jessica Powers from *The Commonweal*, January 14, 1949. Reprinted by permission of the author and *The Commonweal*.
"Doxology" from *The Place of Splendor* by Jessica Powers. Reprinted by permission of the author.

And lo, myself am the abode
Of Love, the Third of the Triune,
The primal Sweep and Surge of God   15
And my eternal Claimant soon!

Praise to the Father and the Son
And to Their Spirit! May I be,
O Water, Wave, and Tide in One,
Thine animate doxology.   20

Gwendolyn Brooks   1917–

Gwendolyn Brooks was graduated from Chicago's Englewood High School in 1934 and from Wilson Junior College in 1936. Upon leaving college she engaged in newspaper, magazine, and general office work. As Mrs. Henry Blakely she is a housewife and mother of one son. Miss Brooks's poetry has appeared in numerous magazines and anthologies. She has published two volumes, *A Street in Bronzeville* (1945) and *Annie Allen* (1949). For the latter she was given the Pulitzer Prize for poetry, becoming the first Negro woman to win this coveted award.

In this incisive poem, "Truth," she points out that man, although he often prays and hopes for the truth, is sometimes so terrified by the luminous reality of things that he prefers the falsely comforting shadows. See if you agree with her.

TRUTH

And if sun comes
How shall we greet him?
Shall we not dread him,
Shall we not fear him
After so lengthy a   5
Session with shade?

Though we have wept for him,
Though we have prayed
All through the night-years —
What if we wake one shimmering morn-
     ing to   10
Hear fierce hammering
Of his firm knuckles
Hard on the door?

Shall we not shudder? —
Shall we not flee   15
Into the shelter, the dear thick shelter
Of the familiar
Propitious haze?
Sweet is it, sweet is it
To sleep in the coolness   20
Of the snug unawareness.

The dark hangs heavy
Over the eyes.

For Discussion of New Voices in Poetry

1. What is the Matins hour? In Merton's poem, why is the moon called "pilgrim"? To what do the bells call the monks? Why do they spell "love and fear"?

2. What is the general mood of "The Reader"? What does "The Candlemas Procession" symbolize? How does the poet link it with our lives?

3. What detail of "The Dead in Europe" seems particularly striking to you? How do you interpret the last line of each stanza? What does the reference "In Maryland" mean? Why does the poet invoke Our Blessed Mother?

4. Tell the story of Our Lady of Walsingham. What is the Biblical reference in *non est species neque decor*? How can the "expressionless" still "express" God?

5. What aspects of nature are emphasized in "The Departure"? How did the bereaved feel at the death? What recollections of the dead person soothed their fears?

6. Describe the poet's feeling in "The Moment After Suffering." What is the

wisdom learned? What is represented by the forest? the meadows?

7. You are very familiar with the Lesser Doxology. Can you name the Greater? What is the poet praising in " Doxology "? Do you think this is an apt title?

8. In Gwendolyn Brooks's poem, what does the sun represent? Why does she think that people will fear the sun?

For Your Vocabulary

EMOTIONAL EFFECTS THROUGH WORDS: In these poems you will have ample opportunity to study and practice the use of language in creating emotional effects. In Merton's " The Trappist Abbey: Matins " pick out the words and phrases that show his feeling toward nature and toward city life. Notice the sharp picture of the monastery refectory Merton gives in " The Reader." We learn the place, the time, the food, the season, the reading material, the sense of God's presence. Reread the poem to appreciate the details that paint a pic-ture and create a mood.

Lowell emphasizes the confusion and suffering of " The Dead in Europe." Pick out the words that show the horror of the bombing. By what device does the poet create a sense of mounting urgency of the prayer?

ALLUSIONS: " Our Lady of Walsingham " has many Biblical allusions. What does " Shiloah's whirlpools " stand for? (Do you recall that Thomas Merton titled his history of the Trappists *The Waters of Siloe?* Why?) What does Sion mean?

FIGURATIVE USE OF LANGUAGE: Notice how lyrically one simile is used throughout " The Candlemas Procession." Pick out all the allusions to candles. What is the metaphor in " Doxology "? How is it sustained throughout the poem? In " Truth " why is the personification of the second stanza arresting? What do these lines mean? What does the " dear thick shelter " in the third stanza suggest? Identify as many figures of speech as you can in each of these poems.

LIGHT VERSE

For a mood of lighthearted gaiety the rhythm of verse is often more effective than prose. Many of our major poets have written light verse of great charm and wit; and there is another group of versifiers who do not pretend to write serious poetry, but who have a gift for turning a clever phrase and bringing a laugh. Many of them have been newspaper columnists with a following of daily readers. Others have built a wide reputation through repeated successes as magazine contributors.

In the following group of verses you will find great variety — hearty humor, clever " society verse," the surprise ending, the caricature, the humor based on a neat juggling of words or meters or even the absence of capitals and punctuation marks! There are no questions for discussion in this little section. Just enjoy the verses, and — if the spirit moves you — try the fun of writing some light verse of your own.

Arthur Guiterman 1871–1943

Arthur Guiterman was undoubtedly one of our best writers of light humorous verse. The gay swing of his lines is always furthered by the neatness with which the right word falls into the right place. He is the master of the unexpected. Since there is often question as to the pronunciation of his name, he once wrote a little verse to say that his name rhymes not with "cuter man" or "brighter man," but with "fitter man." Two of his many volumes of verse are *The Laughing Muse* and *Chips of Jade*. Whether or not you like Welsh rabbit, you will enjoy untangling the literary and gustatory allusions in "The Rabbit of Wales."

THE RABBIT OF WALES

My riddle's a joy in a world of despair;
A cousin, they say, of the merry March hare;
He flourishes most at three hundred degrees;
His cradle's a toast and his mother's a cheese;
A troublesome, bubblesome, sweet little beast,   5
His fragrant "enough" is as good as a feast
(For who that is mortal may grapple with two!);
When hot he's ambrosia, when cold he is glue;
He never had fur, features, feathers, or scales.
The answer? Of course! 'Tis the Rabbit of Wales.   10

When Arthur ruled Britain with scepter and sword,
There came to the king at the festival board
A wizard unrivaled in magical spell
Hight Morgan ap something in F-double-L.
"Brave knights and fair ladies," he said, "you perceive   15
There's nothing concealed in the pocket or sleeve."
Then, "Hey, presto, change!" from the helm of King Lot
He drew forth the viand all smoking and hot.
"This marvel," quoth he, "to the men of the dales
Of Rheidol, is known as the Rabbit of Wales."   20

Then reveled those lordlings, and when it beseemed,
Betook them to slumber; and soothly, they dreamed
Of gryphons and dragons and giants and things,
Of heathen enchanters and Saracen kings,
Of boars that had tushes full twenty rods long,   25
Of jousts that were bloody and strokes that were strong.
So when of the quests that these knights undertook
You read as reported in Malory's book,
Remember that they who unfolded such tales
Had banqueted free on the Rabbit of Wales.   30

"The Rabbit of Wales" from *Lyric Laughter* by Arthur Guiterman, published by E. P. Dutton and Company. Reprinted by permission of the publishers.

He lives through the ages, more soothing than silk,
As potent as porter, as gentle as milk.
Eternally young, he has heightened disport
In hovel and palace, in tavern and court.
When Jonson and Herrick made feasts at the Sun,   35
The Boar, and the Mermaid, of them he was one.
He frolicked with Shakespeare, with Chaucer and Gower,
With magical Merlin and Owen Glendower;
They find in the primal Devonian shales
The fossil remains of the Rabbit of Wales.   40

When tables are snowy, and heavenward roll
The violet smoke-wreaths that comfort the soul,
He comes from the regions of skillets and spits
Upborne on the platter of rubicund Fritz.
How blithely he bubbles, how sweetly he steams,   45
How mellow, how yellow, how tender he seems!
Acclaim him with rapture, receive him with glee
As well as with mustard piquant as may be,
And drink his repose in the ripest of ales
" Waes hael " to the rantipole Rabbit of Wales.   50

Don Marquis

1878–1937

Like many of our humorists, Don Marquis had the gift of creating a vivid humorous character; but, unlike most of them, his fame rests on several widely differing types rather than on just one. One of his most amusing creations is " archy the cockroach " of the newspaper office. archy has the soul of a free-verse poet. His innate longing for expression impels him to use the typewriter at night to communicate to " the boss "; but, as he cannot work the shift key, there are no capital letters and no punctuation marks in his effusions. He also has difficulty with the mechanism for making a new line, and so his " poems " look most peculiar. archy's comments on current affairs, and his accounts of the vagaries of his friends, like mehitabel, the alley cat, delighted readers of Marquis's column in the New York *Sun* for many years.

FREDDY THE RAT PERISHES

listen to me there have
been some doings here since last
i wrote there has been a battle
behind that rusty typewriter cover
in the corner   5
you remember freddy the rat well
freddy is no more but
he died game the other
day a stranger with a lot of
legs came into our little circle a tough
    looking kid   10
he was with a bad eye

who are you said a thousand legs
if i bite you once
said the stranger you won t ask
again he he° little poison tongue said

15. **he he:** derisive laughter; not a misprint, as one might at first glance suppose. This " poem " makes one realize how much punctuation helps us understand the relationship between words.

Some of the best present-day American humorists are the cartoonists whose work appears in popular magazines. On this page are drawings by two outstanding cartoonists, George Price and Charles Addams.

"I don't know—I've just felt miserable all day."

"George! George! Drop the keys!"

(Above) *Cartoon by George Price reproduced by permission. Copr. 1943 The New Yorker Magazine, Inc.*

(Left) *Cartoon by Charles Addams reproduced by permission. Copr. 1948 The New Yorker Magazine, Inc.*

the thousand legs who gave you hydro-
   phobia   16
i got it by biting myself said
the stranger i m bad keep away
from me where I step a weed dies
if i was to walk on your forehead it
   would   20
raise measles and if
you give me any lip i ll do it

they mixed it then
and the thousand legs succumbed
well we found out this fellow   25
was a tarantula he had come up from
south america in a bunch of bananas
for days he bossed us life
was not worth living he would stand in
the middle of the floor and taunt   30
us ha ha he would say where i
step a weed dies do
you want any of my game i was
raised on red pepper and blood i am
so hot if you scratch me i will light 35
like a match you better
dodge me when i m feeling mean and
i don t feel any other way i was nursed
on a tabasco bottle if i was to slap
your wrist in kindness you   40
would boil over like job° and heaven
help you if i get angry give me
room i feel a wicked spell coming on

last night he made a break at freddy
the rat keep your distance   45
little one said freddy i m not
feeling well myself somebody poisoned
   some
cheese for me i m as full of
death as a drugstore i
feel that i am going to die anyhow   50
come on little torpedo come on don t
   stop
to visit and search then they
went at it and both are no more please

41. **boil over like job**: Job, a character in the
Bible, was afflicted with boils. See Job 2:7.

throw a late edition on the floor i want
   to
keep up with china we dropped freddy
off the fire escape into the alley with 56
military honors

                   archy

Franklin P. Adams

1881–

Franklin Pierce Adams, usually known as
F. P. A., is one of our foremost humorists
today. He maintains a high standard of
humor and writes with the utmost sincerity. He loves to play a joke on his
reader by ending a poem with an unexpectedly simple and naïve conclusion. For
instance, one of his poems describes how
some may sing of the surging sea, others
of the open road, others of the bursting
bomb, and so on, leading the reader to
anticipate a climax that will show the author's own preference. But, instead, the
last line is: "And they all may sing of
whatever they like, as far as I'm concerned." In the following poem he again
plays a simple trick on the reader — or
does he?

THOSE TWO BOYS

When Bill was a lad he was terribly bad.
   He worried his parents a lot;
He'd lie and he'd swear and pull little
   girls' hair;
   His boyhood was naught but a blot.

At play and in school he would fracture
   each rule —   5
   In mischief from autumn to spring;
And the villagers knew when to man-
   hood he grew
   He would never amount to a thing.

When Jim was a child he was not very
   wild;   9
He was known as a good little boy;
He was honest and bright and the
   teachers' delight —
To his father and mother a joy.

All the neighbors were sure that his
   virtue'd endure,
That his life would be free of a spot;
They were certain that Jim had a great
   head on him   15
And that Jim would amount to a lot.

And Jim grew to manhood and honor
   and fame
And bears a good name;
While Bill is shut up in a dark prison
   cell —
You never can tell.   20

Dorothy Parker

1893–

Dorothy Parker has a gift for satirical verse
that places her in a class by herself. She
has been described as " a delicate little
thing of great beauty and charm, who
writes and says the most cutting things
with a lamblike air that would melt the
heart of an iron statue." She is noted for
her last lines, which are often like a pin-
prick to a toy balloon.

Mrs. Parker was born in New Jersey,
and educated in private schools and a convent. Between 1916 and 1920 she was on
the staff first of *Vogue*, then of *Vanity Fair*,
now out of existence. Since 1920 she has
been a free-lance writer, and half a dozen
books have come from her pen. The best-
known are *Enough Rope*, *Sunset Gun*,
Death and Taxes. In 1929 she won the
O. Henry Memorial short story award. Her
book of short stories is called *Here Lies*.

RÉSUMÉ

Suicide is no laughing matter, but even
a serious-minded person could hardly forbear smiling at this oft-quoted bit, a satire
on the gloomy, disillusioned writings of
the 1920's.

Razors pain you;
Rivers are damp;
Acids stain you;
And drugs cause cramp.
Guns aren't lawful;   5
Nooses give;
Gas smells awful;
You might as well live.

ONE PERFECT ROSE

A single flow'r he sent me, since we met.
All tenderly his messenger he chose;
Deephearted, pure, with scented dew
   still wet —
One perfect rose.

I knew the language of the floweret;   5
" My fragile leaves," it said, " his heart
   inclose."
Love long has taken for his amulet
One perfect rose.

Why is it no one ever sent me yet   9
One perfect limousine, do you suppose?
Ah no, it's always just my luck to get
One perfect rose.

THE CHOICE

He'd have given me rolling lands,
   Houses of marble, and billowing
     farms,
Pearls, to trickle between my hands,
   Smoldering rubies, to circle my arms.
You — you'd only a lilting song,   5
   Only a melody, happy and high,

You were sudden and swift and strong —
  Never a thought for another had I.

He'd have given me laces rare,
  Dresses that glimmer with frosty
    sheen,   10

Shining ribbons to wrap my hair,
  Horses to draw me, fine as a queen.
You — you'd only to whistle low,
  Gaily I followed wherever you led.
I took you, and I let him go —   15
  Somebody ought to examine my head!

Ogden Nash   1902–

If you read *The New Yorker* and *The Saturday Evening Post,* you have doubtless enjoyed many times the humorous verse of Ogden Nash. Now a resident of Baltimore, he was born in Rye, New York.

His writing certainly gives the impression that he has had long practice at it, and that he writes with the greatest ease. His name is particularly associated with a certain irregular prose-poetry rhythm, which, like a ride over a rough road in a springless wagon, shakes a laugh out of you at unexpected moments. Another of Nash's characteristics is his original conception of the kinds of words and line lengths that can be made to rhyme with each other.

YOU BET TRAVEL IS BROADENING

Doctors tell me that some people wonder who they are, they don't know if they
    are Peter Pumpkin-eater or Priam,
But I know who I am.
My identity is no mystery to unravel,
Because I know who I am, especially when I travel.
I am he who lies either over or under the inevitable snores,   5
I am he who the air conditioning is in conflict with whose pores,
I am he whom the dear little old ladies who have left their pocketbooks on the
    bureau at home invariably approach,
And he whom the argumentative tippler oozes in beside though there are thirty
    empty seats in the coach.
I am he who finds himself reading comics to somebody else's children while the
    harassed mother attends to the youngest's needs,
Ending up with candy bar on the lapel of whose previously faultless tweeds.   10
I am he in the car full of students celebrating victory with instruments saxophonic
    and ukulelean,
And he who, speaking only English, is turned to for aid by the non-English-speak-
    ing alien.
I am he who, finding himself the occupant of one Pullman space that has been sold
    twice, next finds himself playing Santa,
Because it was sold the second time to an elderly invalid, so there is no question
    about who is going to sit in the washroom from Philadelphia to Atlanta.
I guess I am he who if he had his own private car   15
Would be jockeyed into sharing the master bedroom with a man with a five-cent
    cigar.

For Further Reading of Poetry

The best way for high-school students to become acquainted with the many excellent poets of the present is to read widely in the anthologies here listed.

COLLECTIONS OF POETRY

Ciardi, John, *Mid-Century American Poets* (Twayne, 1950)

Davis, M. G., *The Girls' Book of Verse* (Lippincott, 1922)

Drinkwater, John, H. S. Canby, and W. R. Benét, *Twentieth Century Poetry* (Houghton Mifflin, 1929)

Fish, H. D., *The Boys' Book of Verse* (Lippincott, 1923)

Gordon, Marjory, and M. B. King, *Verse of Our Day* (Appleton, 1931)

Hohn, Max T., *Stories in Verse* (Odyssey, 1943)

Lieberman, Elias, *Poems for Enjoyment* (Harper, 1943)

Matthiessen, F. O., *The Oxford Book of American Verse* (Oxford, 1950)

Monroe, Harriet, and A. C. Henderson, *The New Poetry* (Macmillan, 1932)

Rittenhouse, Jessie, *The Little Book of American Poets* (Houghton Mifflin, 1915)

Rittenhouse, Jessie, *The Little Book of Modern Verse* (3 vols.) (Houghton Mifflin, 1913, 1919, 1947)

Rodman, Selden, *A New Anthology of Modern Poetry* (Random House, 1938)

Rodman, Selden, *100 American Poems* (New American Library, 1948)

Schauffler, R. H., *The Poetry Cure* (Dodd, Mead, 1927)

Smith, Arthur James M., *Book of Canadian Poetry* (University of Chicago Press, 1948)

Stevenson, Burton, *Home Book of Verse*, 8th ed. (Holt, 1949)

Untermeyer, Louis, *Modern American Poetry*, mid-century ed. (Harcourt, Brace, 1950)

Untermeyer, Louis, *Modern British Poetry*, mid-century ed. (Harcourt, Brace, 1950)

Untermeyer, Louis, *This Singing World* (Harcourt, Brace, 1923)

Untermeyer, Louis, *Yesterday and Today* (Harcourt, Brace, 1947)

Williams, Oscar, *A Little Treasury of Modern Poetry* (Scribner, 1946)

COLLECTIONS OF LIGHT VERSE

Daly, T. A., *A Little Book of American Humorous Verse* (McKay, 1926)

Wells, Carolyn, *Book of Humorous Verse* (Garden City, 1947)

White, E. B., and K. S. White, *A Subtreasury of American Humor* (prose and poetry) (Coward, McCann, 1941)

Culver

Modern Drama

GOING to the theater has long been a favorite entertainment of Americans. As important works of literature, however, American plays have only come into their own in modern times. Especially in the last quarter century, with playwrights like Eugene O'Neill, Thornton Wilder, Robert E. Sherwood, Elmer Rice, and Tennessee Williams, our drama has made distinguished contributions to world literature.

Yet early Americans loved a play as well as anyone else. Even among the Colonial Puritans, drama was presented under the soothing title "Moral Dialogues," and in the more worldly Southern colonies both Charleston and Williamsburg had real theaters long before the Revolution. New York and Philadelphia were active theatrical centers before 1776 and they took the lead during the early days of the nation. As settlers pushed into the interior of the continent, traveling companies of actors rode the stagecoaches and canal boats to take their plays to the western settlements. Other companies built theaters on river boats and made circuits of the larger landings. Later, when rail transportation linked all parts of the country, every town of any size had its "Opera House" where road shows played during "the season."

Your grandparents may possibly remember when the local "Opera House" was converted to a motion picture theater and the new mass-produced drama became available every week end, soon every day. What a wonder it was when the movies learned to talk and then took on the colors of real life! By the time most Americans had a choice of several screen dramas within easy driving distance every afternoon and evening, the magic of the vacuum tube had brought radio plays right into the home, available with the twist of a knob. Finally television added sight to the sound of broadcast drama. But no matter how many other kinds of entertainment are put on the air, plays remain high favorites.

You might reasonably expect that movies and radio and television would have shoved stage drama right off the map. But it has not worked out that way. On the contrary, the theater is still strong, with lights sparkling out the announcements of new offerings on Broadway, repertory theaters active in dozens of cities, and each season's hits going on the road to play to the whole country.

The demand extends to printed drama, too. Any list of new books includes many collections and single plays. Radio may be partly responsible for the rising demand, for it has taught people that words alone, without sight, can convey effectively what they see in a stage performance. And since plays on the stage or over radio and television are given at set times, they may or may not fit in with other activities, while the printed words in a book are always there, ready for the reader's leisure hours. That is why, even with drama all around us, on the stage, on the screen, and in the air, more and more printed plays are welcomed by enthusiastic readers.

Guide to Reading Drama

As you read a play you may feel that here is something quite different from other literature. In one way that is true. For every other type of literature is written to be read. Drama is not. It is written for actors to present before a listening and watching audience. All that actors, stage manager, designers, costumers, and director do to bring a play to full life must be done by the reader himself.

Even though it is presented in a different manner, a play is still a story, and all the skills you have developed in reading fiction will help you in reading plays. There are special skills in addition. Understanding the purpose and method of dialogue is one main skill you will want to develop in reading drama. Later, we'll consider a second major skill: keeping your imagination alert.

Following the Story in Dialogue

The story of a play is told entirely through dialogue. The playwright's direct comments and descriptions are therefore confined to the stage directions.

From the opening directions of a play you learn the setting and the cast of characters. Then you launch yourself on the dialogue that sweeps you along at the tempo of actual living. It is as if you had become invisible and then dropped into the midst of a group of people busy about some interesting affairs of their own. You watch and listen to them to find out what sort of people they are and what they are up to. But you have one great advantage. If you eavesdropped on people in real life, you might hang around for quite a while without discovering just what was going on. But in a play the nonessentials are trimmed away and every word counts to make the characters' problems and attitudes clear to the audience as quickly as possible.

First of all, the dialogue identifies the characters for you. The first few speeches made by a character — or by someone else speaking to him or about him — gives you clues to his nature.

Second, dialogue reveals the *relationship* of the characters to one another. It is this relationship that usually reveals the situation on which the play is based. The characters want something, or fear something, or in some other way conflict with one another. Whatever the exact nature of the situation is, you feel a certain tension: a problem exists and must be settled before the play can end.

A third function of dialogue is to carry the story along: it is the wheels on which the plot moves. Most often, you will have no difficulty in following the course of action, but if you do, pause a moment to ask yourself: who is trying to achieve a definite purpose? what is that purpose? what opposition is he meeting? what desires of other characters are in conflict with his desire? Answering these questions to yourself, you will be prepared for decisive moments, when one side or the other gains an advantage and pushes ahead. Most important of all, you will share the emotions of the characters as they achieve success or meet with defeat.

That brings up the fourth special function of dialogue — to stimulate the audience to emotions and ideas. The dialogue of a play helps to set its *tone*, whether it is humorous or gloomy, happy or tragic. Since a dramatist cannot address his audience directly, his characters must say for him whatever feelings or ideas he wishes to convey to the audience. Look, then, for speeches that establish the tone of the play and seem to express its main theme.

Understanding these four uses of dialogue (this is a good time to review them), you can take a second look at any line that puzzles you and discover just why it is in the play. For you can be sure that in the limited space of a play, every speech must serve one or more of these four purposes.

Using Your Imagination

Too many people think that it takes an effort to get imagination to work. Not at all. What it wants is only a chance, a proper share of your attention. If you don't believe that, try an experiment with the description of a scene in *The Ghost Patrol,* which you will soon read. What kind of city street is the main setting? The stage directions say: " The street is in a fairly poor but respectable neighborhood of old brownstone houses." Is it a well scrubbed, tidy street, or a littered, dirty one, or something in between? Is it a street where children play? Is it a forbidding-looking, shadowy place or a warm and friendly place? The stage directions alone cannot tell you what to visualize; you must also take into account the general tone of the play and the nature of the people in it. You need not have lived on such a street, or even have lived in a city, to let your imagination fill in the details of the scene.

The same imagination that fills in a scene for your mental eyes works for your ears as well. You not only see a character, expanding the brief descriptive phrases to make a whole person, but you also hear the tone of his voice and the inflections of his words. Try your imaginative powers on the characters you will soon meet in the following plays. Does the person speak in a loud, shrill voice, or a quiet, subdued one? Is his voice confident or hesitant? As you read each additional line of a play you get a clearer impression of the characters, until you seem to be hearing the words spoken, not merely looking at them on a page. To hear the sounds for the words, your imagination must get inside the character and share the feeling or motive that impels him to each speech.

This process is going on all the time while you read. The reader of drama is a full partner of the playwright. While you are the audience, enjoying the performance, your imagination is busily skipping about doing the work of a whole theatrical company. With a lively imagination, you get a good show.

SINCLAIR LEWIS
1885-1951

The Ghost Patrol

Adapted for Television by William Kendall Clarke

Let's begin our acquaintance with modern American drama with the newest member of the family, the television play. Television drama is fortunately able to make use of the most effective techniques of older types. Like the stage play, it uses settings and actions as well as dialogue to present a story. Like the movies, it can move freely from scene to scene without interruption and can alternate long and short shots to get intimate effects that would be impossible across the footlights. Like the radio play, it must rely on themes of broad appeal that will interest the far-flung, infinitely varied audience that gathers around receiving sets. Another point of kinship with radio drama is the constant need for a great number of new plays to fill the broadcasting schedules. Under the pressure of this need, writers often adapt plays from already published novels and stories. That is how a television play was made of *The Ghost Patrol*, which was first a short story written by the eminent novelist Sinclair Lewis.

Sinclair Lewis was the first American to receive the Nobel Prize for distinction in literature. The award came in recognition of his hard-hitting novels satirizing the dullness and pettiness and hypocrisy in American life. Beginning with *Main Street* (1920), Lewis broadened his harsh picture with *Babbitt* (1922), *Arrowsmith* (1925), his most popular book, and *Dodsworth*

(1929). Yet he wrote of American failings not as a critical outsider but as an ardent American. He was intensely devoted to the best American ideals and fiercely indignant over any cheap compromise with their satisfactory achievement. Lewis knew his America well. Born in Sauk Center, Minnesota, he went east to college. After his graduation from Yale, he traveled back and forth across the country, observing all kinds of life as he took a bewildering variety of jobs. His novels have their settings in small towns as well as cities, and depict businessmen and professional men alike.

The great distinction of Lewis's style is his ability to catch the rhythms and idioms of American speech. That quality was certain to attract scouts for new dramatic material for televizing. For good dialogue is the life of any play. In *The Ghost Patrol*, which reveals Lewis in a mellow, sympathetic mood, you will meet people who express themselves in distinctly individual, highly flavored language.

Reading a Television Play

As in reading a play designed for the stage, you must limber up your imagination. Try to see in your mind's eye the scene of the action and the appearance and varying gestures of the characters. In order to visualize the play, it will be helpful to run over a few of the common staging directions used in television productions. Here they are:

CUT TO means to shift from one scene to another without any transition. In television there are several cameras used simultaneously, so that the shift is made from one camera to another.

DISSOLVE TO means to let one scene gradually fade into a succeeding one.

OFF. When someone speaks *off* he is not visible through the camera at the moment, although he is usually somewhere on the scene.

RIDE OVER. A speaker who starts his speech before the preceding speaker has finished is *riding over.*

AD-LIB means to speak at random and in no particular order.

FADE-OUT is the gradual disappearance of the image from the screen.

Characters

IRATE CITIZEN. A man in his mid-thirties who speaks with a New York accent in a loud and indignant voice.

SERGEANT. A typical, middle-aged, experienced policeman, tall, with an imposing build, a "tough" but kindly face.

LIEUTENANT. About the same age, build, and appearance as the SERGEANT, but with more hair.

NICK SAVARESE. A patrolman in his mid-twenties. He is good-looking — dark-haired, tall, and slender — and he is aware of this, but not so much as to be objectionable.

DAN DORGAN, known as "Pop" around the neighborhood. A short, stocky, ex-patrolman in his sixties, with gray hair, a mustache, a cocky expression, and twinkling eyes.

EFFIE. A pretty girl in her early twenties.

ZOLLIE. A boy of about seventeen. He is slim, of medium height, and looks like his sister, EFFIE, though his face is sometimes marred by a resentful expression.

MRS. TEDESCO. A slender woman of about thirty-five, with an accent that echoes her native Italy.

MRS. BERNSTEIN. Short, stout, pleasant, and dark-haired.

MATTIE GILLESPIE. Anything but the typical pawnshop keeper, she looks more like a small-town shopkeeper or librarian. She is tall and angular, with a precise, controlled expression that often softens into a pleasant smile.

BEN. A small-time crook, short, tough, and undersized. He talks out of the side of his mouth, as if he had seen too many gangster movies.

LOUIS. A dark-haired boy of five or six years.

A VARIED NEIGHBORHOOD CROWD.

ACT I

SCENE: *The Ninth Precinct Station, New York City, present day.*

This is a drab room with the SERGEANT'S *desk sitting high on a platform in the center, surrounded by a low wooden railing. A flag stands at the left of the desk. In front of the railing and at the right is a long wooden table flanked by a few uncomfortable chairs. Doors at left and right — the right one leads outdoors, the left one leads to an office and a locker room. Along the left wall is a washbasin and a bulletin board with Men Wanted signs posted on it.*

SERGEANT O'CONNOR *is seated behind the desk. Standing before him is an* IRATE CITIZEN.

IRATE CITIZEN. I'm a citizen — I pay my taxes — I've got a right to be heard.

SERGEANT. You got the voice for it too. Let me get this straight. You're blowing your top because your stolen car came home safe and sound. Is that it?

IRATE CITIZEN. With a tankful of gas it didn't have when they stole it. And a good wash job on it, *and* the dent in the fender straightened out.

SERGEANT. And you're complaining?

IRATE CITIZEN. Durn right I am. Investigator comes from the insurance company — there's my stolen car sitting at the curb. How do I explain that? No report from you guys — where it was found, who stole it, who found it — nothing.

[*He turns to* LIEUTENANT, *who enters from his office left.*]

IRATE CITIZEN. My brother-in-law saw two hoodlums drive up, three o'clock this morning, with a cop in the back seat. They get out, leave the car in front of my house, and the cop marches them off. Now, that's no way to run a Police Department.

SERGEANT. All right — all right. The Lieutenant won't be needing lessons from you on how to run his business. If you ask me, I think your brother-in-law borrowed the car off you, and he's trying to push the blame over on somebody else.

IRATE CITIZEN. Listen, now — !

LIEUTENANT (*has been examining record on* SERGEANT's *desk*). Take it easy. The Sergeant has your complaint here. We'll look into the matter.

IRATE CITIZEN. Yeah. I'll bet you will! (*He strides off, muttering*) Servants of the people — humph!

LIEUTENANT. Well, O'Connor — looks like our Ghost Patrol's at work again.

[*Cut to* NICK *entering from direction of locker room, buttoning his coat. He winces at the word "ghost."*]

SERGEANT (*off*). If Sonny Boy here was to keep an eye out for catching the *ghost* instead of the pretty *girl* on his beat, maybe we'd be getting a little more respect from the citizens.

LIEUTENANT. How about it, Nick? You've had the beat five months now. When are you going to show some action? Or maybe you like sharing your beat with a ghost.

NICK. Don't worry, Lieutenant. I'll get to the bottom of this.

SERGEANT. Have you thought now, maybe it's gremlins [1] we got?

LIEUTENANT. Whatever it is, it don't look good for the Ninth Precinct. People in the Forest Park neighborhood are saying they don't need the police — they get more help from the Ghost Patrol.

NICK. It's just another sign of their disrespect for the Law. Anything that makes us look foolish, makes them feel important.

LIEUTENANT. We looked foolish, all right, when that shoemaker's kids turned up out of nowhere, after we searched the whole district with a fine comb. Middle of the night they show up here — fed and scrubbed — each one with a lollipop in his hand.

SERGEANT. And saying they dassn't run away again, for the policeman who caught them, made 'em swear it upon the Bible.

LIEUTENANT. And there was that burglar he caught and tied to a lamppost, with the loot in a neat little bundle beside him.

SERGEANT. I tell you, Lieutenant, we ought to be putting the Ghost on the payroll, if we had any conscience at all.

NICK. Well, have your fun. The fact

[1] gremlins: During World War II, delays or breakdowns in war production and military operations were sometimes humorously attributed to "little people" or gremlins.

Television cameras move in for a close-up during one of the police station scenes in The Ghost Patrol. *(Kenyon and Eckhardt)*

remains — there's mighty little trouble on my beat, and maybe *I've* got something to do with it.

SERGEANT. *That's* the question, Nick, my boy. Is it you what's keeping the peace, or some common upstart of a spook? (*The phone rings on* SERGEANT's *desk and he picks it up.*) Ninth Precinct — Sergeant O'Connor speaking —

[*Cut to* LIEUTENANT *drawing* NICK *aside.*]

LIEUTENANT. Nick, there's someone I want you to watch out for. A kid by the name of Zollie Ferrara.

NICK. Ferrara?

LIEUTENANT. Know him?

NICK. No, but the name's familiar. We got more Ferraras than Smiths on my beat.

LIEUTENANT. Zollie's a bad one. He gave us a lot of trouble before we sent him up to reform school three years ago.

NICK. If he makes trouble on my beat, he'll be back there in a hurry.

LIEUTENANT. He's been out now for a few months, but he didn't come home till yesterday. He may be up to something. A tough brat like that can undermine a whole neighborhood.

NICK. Right, sir. I'll keep an eye open for Mr. Ferrara. (*He goes off.*)

SERGEANT (*calling after* NICK). While you're at it, keep both eyes open, and see if you can spot that ghost!

Dissolve to DORGAN's *basement apartment. This is a room in an old brown-*

stone house. The furnishings are old-fashioned, well kept but also well worn, as one might expect to find them in a bachelor's apartment. At the center of the rear wall is a marble fireplace (not used) with a clock and various orna-ments on the mantel, and above it is a group picture of policemen. A dingy, patterned carpet covers the floor, and in the center of it is a heavy round table with straight chairs around it. Along the left wall is a long high win-dow in front of which stand bird cages. Off center are a brass bed (never en-tirely visible) and a clothes tree, on which DORGAN's *uniform jacket hangs prominently.*

DORGAN *is seen pouring wine for* EF-FIE *and* ZOLLIE FERRARA. ZOLLIE *is sullen.*

DORGAN. I been saving this wine for a special occasion. As soon as Effie told me you was home, I got the bottle down and I dusted it off. Well — here's to your welcome home, lad.

[DORGAN *and* EFFIE *hold their glasses to-ward* ZOLLIE, *but he puts his down and turns away.*]

EFFIE. Zollie, please. Pop Dorgan is your friend.

ZOLLIE. Oh, sure. He did me a great favor, getting me sent to reform school.

DORGAN. I thought you'd get off on probation. Did I know you'd go up be-fore Judge Scanlon?

ZOLLIE. I never picked up that rock first. The other side started it.

DORGAN. I warned you plenty of times. And finally you gave someone a con-cussion with that rock you threw.

ZOLLIE. Big Mike would have done a lot worse to me —

DORGAN. That's not the point. You did wrong. And still they should never have sent you to reform school. Even I can see that. Maybe sometimes that swift chariot of the law acts more like a steam roller —

ZOLLIE. I'm flat, I know that. That's

no health resort, that school. And if you'll excuse me, I'll skip that drink —

EFFIE. Zollie, please.

DORGAN. It's all right, Effie, if he doesn't feel like celebrating.

ZOLLIE. What's the use of kidding my-self? I got nothing to celebrate.

DORGAN. You're home, son, and you've got a good sister who loves you and wants to help you.

ZOLLIE. I gotta have a job. And you know how much chance I have of get-ting one.

EFFIE. You only just got home yester-day.

ZOLLIE. But I got out of reform school four months ago. And four months is a long time when you're knocking around, begging for a job. You think it feels good to come crawling back without a dime? You think I want to live off my sister?

DORGAN. We know you don't want to do that, Zollie. But you've got to be pa-tient a bit. You'll be getting work.

ZOLLIE. And then what? You wanta know something? I had *three* jobs since I got out. And I worked hard. So what? Soon as they catch wise that I been to reform school, they throw me out on my ear. Three times it happened to me.

EFFIE (*goes to* ZOLLIE *and puts her arms around him*). Don't, Zollie. Don't get so angry.

DORGAN. There's no use in crying over the past. What we've got to do now is get you a job with someone who knows your record, and still is willing to give you a chance. I've got to help you.

ZOLLIE. No one'll do that!

DORGAN. Effie, did you think of speak-ing to your boss? Maybe he'd put Zol-lie in the shipping department.

EFFIE. Well, I — I could ask.

ZOLLIE. Yeah — that's a great idea. She'll get herself fired for being in the same family as me.

DORGAN (*brightening suddenly*). What would you say to taking a job with Mattie?

ZOLLIE. In the pawnshop?

DORGAN. Sure. It's a good steady business, and you can learn the trade from a master. There's nobody knows the pawnbroking game better than Mattie Gillespie.

EFFIE. Oh, Pop — do you think Mattie would do it?

DORGAN. I'm dang near *sure* of it.

ZOLLIE. What makes you think she'll want to take a chance on me?

DORGAN. Never you mind. She's a good woman that doesn't sit in judgment on anybody. (*He winks.*) Besides, there's not much Mattie Gillespie wouldn't do to please me. I'll speak to her tonight.

ZOLLIE. Gosh, Pop —

EFFIE. Oh, thank you, Pop. Zollie and I appreciate it. You're always so good to everyone —

DORGAN (*rides over last few words*). And now that we've settled our worries, there's no reason why we can't have that drink. To your success in the new job, which Mattie Gillespie is giving you, though she doesn't know it yet!

[*They all drink.*]

You're only a lad, with your whole life ahead of you. Plenty of time to make your sister and your Grandma proud of you.

ZOLLIE. Yeah — I know. That's the kind of talk they kept handing us in reform school. (*He wanders toward bird cages and, taking some crumbs from his pockets, feeds birds.*)

EFFIE (*pleadingly*). Zollie!

ZOLLIE. Well — I'm willing to try. All I'm asking for is a decent break.

DORGAN. And that's what you're going to get. (*He goes to* ZOLLIE *and speaks confidentially as he takes a little purse from his pocket, removes two dollar bills and some silver from the purse, leaving himself only two coins.*) If you want, we can arrange a little loan until you get your first pay.

ZOLLIE. I don't want it.

DORGAN. You need it — take it!

ZOLLIE. All right! But I'll pay you back next week. In the meantime, there's somebody I gotta see —

EFFIE (*trying to detain him*). Grandma expects you home for supper, Zollie.

ZOLLIE. Okay. I'll only be a minute.

EFFIE. But —

[ZOLLIE *starts off. Cut to close-up of* EFFIE *looking after him with a worried frown. Sound of door opening and closing.*]

DORGAN (*off*). Now don't go worrying yourself about him. He's a good boy.

[*Medium close-up of* DORGAN *and* EFFIE.]

EFFIE. He's been seeing Ben since he got back. If he starts going around with that old gang he'll get into trouble again.

DORGAN. No, Effie. You mustn't feel that way. A boy like Zollie needs loving and understanding. But more 'n that, right now he needs trusting. You got to trust him. You know, Effie, I've never had a bad conscience about anyone in my life except Zollie. I ran him in and he got sent to reform school. If I'd really been on the ball, I should have handled it better.

EFFIE. He goes around with a chip on his shoulder —

DORGAN. He's got a mean feeling toward policemen. But he'll get over that. Supposing he should have a policeman for a close relative some day —

EFFIE. Why, Pop Dorgan! I don't know what you mean.

DORGAN. You don't? (*Then, as if imparting a secret*) I mean Nick. You know — Nick. That handsome young policeman who's walking my old beat, and sparking Miss Effie Ferrara with a high degree of regularity.

EFFIE (*goes to bird cages and pretends to be engrossed with birds*). We're just friends — that's all.

DORGAN. Mighty good friends, I'd say. Why, the mention of his name makes your eyes swim and your cheeks turn red.

EFFIE. Well, I — I like him. I mean — he's very nice — and —

DORGAN. And he's a member of the Force. Don't be forgetting that! You're a fine girl, Effie — entitled to the best — but no girl can do better than to hook up with the Police Department.

EFFIE (*laughing*). Well, Nick hasn't asked me to marry him yet.

DORGAN. I don't doubt for a minute he will, and I don't doubt for another minute what your answer'll be. And there's one more doubt I haven't got.

EFFIE. What's that, Mr. Dorgan?

DORGAN. That you'll be a good wife to him — the kind a policeman needs — never forgetting that his duty and his loyalty belongs to the Force, first and last.

EFFIE (*teasing*). Does the Police Department come before his wife, too?

DORGAN (*seriously*). Well, now — I wouldn't say that. But it would be a cruel thing to ask a man to choose between the two.

EFFIE (*laughing*). I'll try to remember that.

DORGAN. There's no higher service a man can perform than upholding the law of the land. I gave the best that was in me for forty-five years, and proud to have the privilege of doing it. It's my only sorrow that they retired me and took my beat away. (*He turns away and, bending over a bird cage, forces a little whistle. There is a silence.*)

EFFIE. Uh — Pop —

DORGAN. What is it, lassie?

EFFIE. Nick doesn't know about Zollie.

[*He looks at her questioningly.*]

I just never mentioned I had a brother. Nick comes from such a nice family — his sister is a schoolteacher. I guess I was sort of ashamed to tell him.

DORGAN. You listen to me, Effie. It isn't your shame, or Zollie's shame. It's a shame on society — and maybe on the Force and on me, when a boy gets himself into trouble, and we can't straighten it out by ourselves, without sending him away.

EFFIE. I hope Nick feels like that.

DORGAN. Why wouldn't he? And when he sees what a fine boy Zollie is, he'll be glad to have him for a brother-in-law.

EFFIE. You really think so? (*She pauses to listen to the sound of a whistle, then draws* DORGAN'S *attention to the shadow that passes the sidewalk-level windows.*) It's Nick! I'll see you tomorrow, Pop.

DORGAN. Now don't you worry yourself about Zollie. I'm talking to Mattie about that job tonight.

[*She gives him a quick kiss and hurries out. He looks after her, beaming.*]

Dissolve to street. The street is in a fairly poor but respectable neighborhood of old brownstone houses that were once family homes but now are converted into apartments or rooming houses. The action of the play is concentrated at one end of the block, on which is a single house and, at the corner, MATTIE GILLESPIE'S *pawnshop. The pawnshop is quite small; it has only a door (on the curb side) and a single, small-paned window crowded with odds and ends — loving cups, watches, tennis rackets, etc. In front of the window, on the sidewalk, is a bench, somewhat the worse for wear, on which* MATTIE *sits and entertains visitors.*

The house where several of the characters live is surrounded by an iron railing, and there are stairs leading up to the half-glassed front door. Because it is summer, the windows are open.

MRS. TEDESCO *leans out of a second-floor window, watering plants in her*

*window box, and also any of the flower
pots she can reach on the fire escape.*
MRS. BERNSTEIN *comes on from left.*

MRS. BERNSTEIN (*waves and calls out
as she comes to door of pawnshop*).
Hey, Mattie! Whatsa matter you didn't
show up last night? Twice I got Bingo.

[MATTIE *appears in doorway of pawnshop.*]

MATTIE. Me and Dan Dorgan went to
the moving pictures.

MRS. BERNSTEIN. Aha! Before we know
it, you'll be getting engaged. Am I right,
Mrs. Tedesco?

MRS. TEDESCO. Mattie and Mr. Dorgan? It could be.

MATTIE. Well, Dan's a good man, and
he's lonesome as all get out, with nothing to keep him busy.

MRS. BERNSTEIN. They never shoulda
made him retire from the police force
when they did, right in the prime of
his life.

MATTIE. He needs someone to keep
him company. But I don't know about
marrying him.

[*A man walks into the pawnshop and*
MATTIE *turns to go in, then stops,
turns back to* MRS. BERNSTEIN.]

He's got a batch of birds living with
him. All that chirping would drive me
crazy. (*She exits into shop.*)

MRS. BERNSTEIN. Why are you sitting
home on such a nice day?

MRS. TEDESCO. I stay here — I think
maybe someone is come about the dog.

MRS. BERNSTEIN. You didn't find it yet?

MRS. TEDESCO (*shaking her head sadly*). Didn't find.

MRS. BERNSTEIN. Ah, that's a shame.
Your little boy must be brokenhearted.

MRS. TEDESCO. He don't eat nothing.
All the time he's crying he wants his
dog.

[BEN *approaches house, then stands on
steps, whistling.*]

MRS. BERNSTEIN. Tsk! tsk! Everybody's
got troubles. You heard what happened

to Mr. Brodsky's sister? Wait! I can't
yell it out. I'll come up.

[*She hurries up the steps and into the
house.* MRS. TEDESCO *ducks from sight.*
BEN *waits, whistling, casually moving
in a small space as he looks over the
pawnshop with assumed indifference.
After a moment,* ZOLLIE *strolls on
from right.*]

BEN. What's the good word, kid?

ZOLLIE. Nothing. I don't know yet,
Ben.

BEN. What's Dorgan doing — stalling?
Didn't you say he was going to talk to
Mattie last night?

[ZOLLIE *shrugs.*]

Listen, you got to get busy, kid. Put a
firecracker under the old man. He gets
you this job — you and me'll pull a fast
one.

ZOLLIE. Maybe I don't want to pull a
fast one.

BEN. Scared?

ZOLLIE. No, I just —

BEN. We got nothing to worry about.
With you on the inside, it'll be a cinch.

ZOLLIE. Yeah, yeah.

BEN. Ain't I giving you half? What's
eating you?

ZOLLIE. Nothing!

BEN. So start acting like you're alive,
or I'll count you out on the deal! Y'hear?
I'm going over to the club, and soon as
you find out from Dorgan if you got
the job, you come and let me know.

ZOLLIE (*blurts out*). I already got the
job! Dorgan asked her and she said yes.

BEN. So what are you holding me off
for, you little sneak? You want to pull it
without me?

ZOLLIE. No! I —

BEN (*interrupting*). Fifty-fifty ain't
enough for you? You got to have it all
to yourself!

ZOLLIE. No! I don't want any of it. I
ain't going to steal from Mattie. I ain't
going to steal from anyone. So leave me
alone, will you?

BEN. Why, you yellow little crumb — wasting my time for nothing. That's what I get for trying to help you. I ought to —

[*He breaks off abruptly as the customer leaves the pawnshop and* MATTIE *comes out and sits on the chair.*]

MATTIE (*jovially, as she settles down with a bottle of soda pop*). Well, Zollie! Resting up for tomorrow?

[*He forces a sickly grin.*]

I got plenty for you to do in there. Going to take everything off the shelves they're setting on, and rearrange 'em — first time in twenty years! That was a real good idea Dan Dorgan had — you coming to work for me.

[BEN *suddenly looks down the street to the right, and, after one last look of disdain toward* ZOLLIE, *walks off quickly, left.*]

ZOLLIE. Yeah. Thanks a lot, Mrs. Gillespie, for giving me the job.

MATTIE. I told you this morning, Zollie, you don't have to thank me. I'm not *giving* you anything. You're going to work and earn whatever you get. And I'm glad to have you.

[*She drinks from the bottle of pop and* ZOLLIE *moves toward the stairs.* EFFIE *and* NICK *walk on from right.*]

EFFIE. Hello, Zollie. (*Then, with pretended nonchalance*) This is Nick — Nick, Zollie.

[*They acknowledge the introduction,* NICK *studying* ZOLLIE *suspiciously.*]

ZOLLIE (*airily*). Say, I got that job, Effie.

EFFIE. Oh, that's wonderful!

ZOLLIE (*with a self-conscious glance at* NICK). I start in tomorrow . . . Well, see you later.

[*As he goes up the steps, he passes a small boy,* LOUIS, *who is on his way down.* ZOLLIE *exits into house.*]

EFFIE (*eager to avoid any questions about* ZOLLIE). Did you find your dog, Louis?

[LOUIS, *fighting back tears, shakes head "No."*]

Oh, that's too bad. Nick, Louis hasn't found his little dog yet. Isn't it a shame?

NICK (*grunts, preoccupied*). Mmp.

EFFIE (*to* LOUIS). And he didn't have a license, did he?

[LOUIS *shakes his head, glancing up at* NICK *fearfully.* EFFIE *pats* LOUIS's *head and addresses* NICK.]

No wonder he's so worried —

NICK (*to* LOUIS, *absently, his mind elsewhere*). Well, that's what happens when you disobey the law. Didn't I tell you to get him a license?

[LOUIS's *lips tremble. With a great effort he controls his tears and walks off slowly, calling in a quavery voice*]

LOUIS. Here, Bozo — here, Bozo —

EFFIE (*looking after* LOUIS). Poor kid.

NICK (*cutting in*). Who's your friend?

EFFIE. My friend?

[NICK *looks up at door through which* ZOLLIE *exited, and* EFFIE *follows his glance.*]

Oh, Zollie! That's my brother . . . He — he's been away. (*Then brightly, to cover her embarrassment*) Well, so long Nick. See you tonight. (*She runs up stairs, exits through door.*)

NICK (*dumbfounded, stares after her, then mutters to himself*). Ferrara — Zollie Ferrara!

Dissolve to DORGAN's *basement apartment.* DORGAN *is alone, cleaning up aft-*

er supper. He wears a clean, starched apron. As he clears the table he examines each item to be sure it needs washing. He hesitates over a piece of silver, finally wipes it carefully in his apron, and puts it with the " clean things." He puts clean paper on the floor of the bird cages, whistling a tune that is easily recognizable as " A Policeman's Lot Is Not a Happy One." He whistles right at the birds, but they won't whistle back.

DORGAN. Ah, I don't blame you for not wanting to learn that silly tune. "A policeman's lot is not a happy one." No one ever spoke or sang a greater lie. A policeman's lot is just about the happiest one in the world. At least it was for me. I was never lonely, for I had a beat to walk, people to talk to, quarrels to settle, young folk to lecture, old folk to comfort. And the best record in the entire city. When I was on the force, there was never a window broken or a thief at large. Only poor Zollie suffered and that was not truly my fault. (*He starts whistling again and then in pantomime walks around the room, twirling an imaginary night stick, nodding as if to friends and acquaintances. There should be something almost Chaplinesque about this scene. Funny and wistful at the same time, the little man dressed in a little brief authority. But* DORGAN *comes back to earth. When he speaks again, it is with a more forceful note.*) Law and Order. Law and Order. That's what they cried for when I first came on the Force and that's what they're crying for now. Always they said there weren't enough policemen or there weren't enough jails or some other such highfalutin nonsense. For the human spirit is sometimes a lawless spirit and if the truth were known, it could be said that we all dwell in cages and beat our wings vainly against the bars. What we all want is a little more kindness and understanding instead of more

policemen and clean, shiny jails. But we got the jails and instead of policemen on the beat at night, they put out those nice, shiny patrol cars with the two-way radios and for a while everybody was happy. But somehow the patrol cars weren't the answer. After they retired old Dorgan, the crimes increased, especially at night. And now they say, "Put the policeman back on the beat, that's the only answer to the crime wave." But they don't send for old Dorgan. Oh, no. He's on the shelf. (*He winks.*) Or that's what they think anyhow! Law and Order. Law and Order. If that's what they want, that's what they'll get and no nonsense about the taxpayer's money! (DORGAN *walks over to his uniform, which is hanging on the clothes tree, and with reverent care starts to brush it. He is interrupted by the whine of a dog, and goes to a box in the far corner of the room, picking up an envelope from the bureau on his way.*) There's no need to cry, laddie. (*He stoops, and when he rises he is holding a dog. He shows the dog the envelope.*) See that? My pension! Money in the pocket, laddie. Tomorrow we'll get you a shiny new license tag, and take you home to your master. From now on, the two of you can face the dog catcher without blinking an eye. (*He pats the dog and places him in the box.*) And no more running away. Do you hear me, you rascal? Now eat your supper and be a nice quiet laddie. It's time for the birds to be sleeping and they don't like any unnecessary noise. (*He puts cover over bird cages.*) Good night. Sleep peaceful. (*He dances a little jig as he puts on the uniform coat, looks admiringly at himself; then after a glance at the clock, shakes his head.*) Too early to go on patrol yet. (*A frayed spot on the sleeve catches his notice. He takes off coat, gets needle and thread, puts on spectacles, adjusts lamp, and carefully, tenderly, darns frayed spot.*)

*Dissolve to street. It is midnight.
The pawnshop is shuttered. Light
comes from a solitary street lamp, off.*
NICK *and* EFFIE *stroll on, romantically
enthralled with each other. They halt
near the steps, and kiss, then look at
each other wordlessly.*

EFFIE. Good night. (*They kiss, then*)
Someone might see us.

NICK. Who cares? We're engaged,
aren't we?

[*She nods happily.*]

And we want everyone to know it, don't
we?

[*She nods demurely.*]

Tomorrow we'll go down to Hillman's
and pick out a diamond ring.

EFFIE. Nick — you know — we could
be engaged without a diamond ring.
I'm not crazy about jewelry. You could
save the money toward buying a house.
We want a house, don't we, in a good
neighborhood?

NICK. We'll have the ring and the
house too. Don't you worry. We're going to have the best of everything. You
won't be living on a patrolman's pay for
long.

EFFIE. Oh, we can manage fine on
your salary.

NICK. It's all right for a beginning,
Effie, but I'm looking ahead. I'm not
going to plod along in harness all my
life, just to get a pat on the back from
the Department. No, Sir! The Department is going to do things for *me*. A
fellow can make a real career for himself on the Force, if he plays it smart.
And he can do it honestly.

EFFIE. I guess it's good to be ambitious. But I think I could be happy with
things exactly the way they are.

NICK. Not me. I want to be something
more than just a cop.

EFFIE. Why, Nick! What's wrong with
being a cop? I'm proud that you have a
job where you can do so much to help
people, and protect them, and keep
them from making mistakes. Folks depend on you, and that's important.

NICK. My job is to enforce the law,
not play Santa Claus. It boils down to
this, honey: The lawbreaker is my enemy and I got to get him before he
gets me. The more arrests I make, the
better my record looks. That's the thing
that counts.

EFFIE. You don't mean that, Nick. It
doesn't sound like you.

NICK (*taking her in his arms*). A girl
can't understand these things. And this
is no time to talk business.

[*She smiles demurely and he gives her
a little kiss.*]

Effie, do you want your Grandma to
live with us after we're married?

EFFIE. I don't know —

NICK. Well, I don't think you can depend on your brother to take care of
her.

EFFIE. Oh, he's crazy about Grandma.
He's always thinking of little things to
do for her.

NICK. That's not what I mean, Effie.
After all he's a kid with a record.

EFFIE. (*She looks into his eyes, then,
flushing*) Oh . . . But he's going to be
all right now, Nick. Zollie's really a good
boy. Don't forget he was only a kid
when that happened, and — and now
he's got a job and everything — I'm sure
he'll *want* to help with Grandma.

NICK. What kind of a job has he got?
Who's he working for?

EFFIE. Mattie Gillespie — right next
door here in the pawnshop, starting tomorrow. He'll behave now, Nick. I
know he will. You should've seen how
happy he was when Mattie hired him.
He's going to be her assistant, and she's
going to teach him the business.

[NICK *listens, frowning, and somewhat withdrawn.*]

Maybe he ought to go to night school and learn bookkeeping. What do you think?

NICK (*absently*). Maybe he ought to get a job out of town.

EFFIE. He's my brother and he stays where I am.

NICK. (*His attention fully on her now, he kisses her.*) Oh, I didn't mean anything.

EFFIE. I certainly hope you didn't.

[*She flounces off, turns, and runs up the steps and into the house.* NICK *looks after her a moment, then turns and walks off. The street is empty. In the distance a tower clock strikes one. A shadow passes before the street lamp. In a moment* BEN *slips on the scene, heading for the pawnshop. He busies himself at the door — it opens — he is inside. Then another shadow approaches. It is* DORGAN *in his uniform. He, too, enters the pawnshop. There is a startled outcry from within, sharp sounds of a struggle, some gun shots, then a crash as a counter upsets. Lights flare on in the shop, windows fly up, heads appear, as* NICK, *returning, dashes into the shop. As heads leave windows, people crowd into the street in various stages of night-dress, choking the door of the pawnshop.*]

VOICES (*ad-libbing*). What is it? What happened? . . . heard a shot. Look out — he's coming out. That's Savarese. Get back and let him come out.

[*The crowd separates a little, unblocking doorway, and* NICK *appears with a handcuffed, dazed, and badly bruised* BEN *in his grasp.*]

NICK (*to crowd*). All right, break it up. Come on — do you hear me?

[MATTIE *appears behind him, tying the sash of her bathrobe.*]

MATTIE (*yelling at* BEN). A fine mess you made of my shop! (*to* NICK) There were two of them, officer! Someone jumped out of my window, and ran down the alley.

NICK (*reacts sharply*). Better check your stock and give us a description of anything that's missing.

[*He moves away with* BEN, *and the people crowd around* MATTIE *to get the details. Camera leaves them to follow* NICK *as he comes toward steps of house.* EFFIE *is standing there.*]

EFFIE. Nick? Are you all right?

NICK (*in a quiet voice, scrutinizing her*). Where's your brother?

EFFIE. Why — why — upstairs, asleep, I suppose.

NICK. Sure. Everybody in the neighborhood's awake — only Zollie. Zollie's asleep in his bed like a little angel.

EFFIE. What do you mean, Nick?

NICK. This punk wasn't alone in that pawnshop. Someone went out of the rear window in a hurry!

[*He brushes past her, towing* BEN *off as* EFFIE *stares after him.*]

Dissolve to Ninth Precinct Station. NICK *is standing over* BEN, *who is slouched sullenly in a chair at the table, handcuffed.*

NICK (*embarrassed*). Yup. Like I said in my report, Lieutenant: Ben was lying on the floor, out cold, with a pair of handcuffs on him.

LIEUTENANT. What do you say, Ben? Who jumped you?

BEN. A cop.

LIEUTENANT (*indicating* NICK). Was it this officer here?

BEN. No.

LIEUTENANT. Who was it?

[BEN *shrugs and doesn't answer.*]

NICK. He claims he didn't get a look at his face.

SERGEANT (*joins group, police blotter in hand. To* LIEUTENANT, *referring to blotter*). Now here's a queer thing, Lieutenant. The pawnshop is right next door to where Zollie Ferrara lives.

[*Cut to close-up of* NICK, *looking very uncomfortable.*]

LIEUTENANT (*off*). Zollie Ferrara, huh? . . . Ben, you were a pal of Zollie's before we sent him away to reform school, weren't you?

BEN. Yeh.

LIEUTENANT. Have you seen him since he got back?

BEN. Yeh.

LIEUTENANT. Was he in on this job with you?

BEN. Maybe he was, and maybe he wasn't.

NICK (*making up his mind after a brief struggle with himself*). More likely he *was*, Lieutenant.

[*Cut to medium shot of* LIEUTENANT, SERGEANT, *looking at* NICK *questioningly.*]

I checked up on the kid, found out he got a job with — with Mattie Gillespie. He was supposed to start working in the pawnshop tomorrow.

LIEUTENANT. Now *that's* an interesting piece of information. How about it, Ben? Come on, open your mouth.

[BEN *opens his mouth in a yawn.*]

Get Zollie down here, Nick.

[NICK *looks at* LIEUTENANT *indecisively.*]

What are you waiting for?

NICK. It's two o'clock, Lieutenant. I figured on bringing him in, in the morning. His family is — is — his grandmother's an old woman, and his sister would — I — I wanted to question him quietly.

LIEUTENANT. I want to talk to him *now*, Savarese — if he hasn't skipped town already. Go and bring the kid in.

NICK. Yes, sir. There's another thing, Lieutenant. I found this badge next to Ben (*He pulls a badge out of his pocket.*) — in the pawnshop. (*He hands over badge to* LIEUTENANT, *who stares at it.*)

LIEUTENANT. Go along now — pick up Zollie like I told you to.

[NICK *exits, then* LIEUTENANT *looks at badge again.*]

This is Patrolman Dan Dorgan's badge. The Chief himself pinned it on Dorgan more than nine years ago.

SERGEANT. He was mighty proud of that badge, Lieutenant. I never thought it would end up in the hockshop.

LIEUTENANT. Poor Dorgan! Not even his honor badge to remind him that he was once a policeman!

[FADE-OUT]

For Discussion of Act I

1. The title and the opening scene lead straight into the first question of the play: Who is the "ghost patrol"? You might have expected solving this mystery to be the main thread of the whole play, yet you surely know the answer by the end of Act I. Who is he? What happenings and speeches reveal his identity?

2. Think of three fresh elements of suspense — uncompleted or unfinished situations — that lead you on to the next act. Identify the conflicting forces in each situation.

3. Explain the meaning of "Cut to . . ." "Dissolve to . . ." "Ad-lib." How do the close-up shots help in presenting the story effectively?

4. Describe the personality of each of the characters in Act I. Select members of the class whose voices are suited to the parts and have them read aloud some of the best scenes. Discuss the interpretation of key lines.

5. Does the tone established in the first part of the play lead you to expect a happy or an unhappy outcome? How is this tone built up?

ACT II

The street. It is morning. MATTIE is sitting on bench in front of her store, with a bottle of pop in her hand. MRS. BERNSTEIN is standing with one foot on the steps, bags of groceries in her arms. The neighborhood is alive with the excitement of last night's events. People are hanging about, discussing the robbery and peering into the pawnshop.

MRS. BERNSTEIN. Well, I'm telling you, I woke up with such a jump when I heard those shots. My heart! Tsk!

MATTIE. Your heart! It's my place was burgled.

MRS. BERNSTEIN. Such excitement we didn't have around here since — I don't know when. (She moves over to bench and settles for a chat.)

MRS. TEDESCO (leans companionably out of window). All night I don't sleep. First is the shooting. Soon as it get quiet, police come and take Zollie away; then Zollie's grandma start in to crying. Mamma mia! I feel so bad for the old lady it make me cry too.

MRS. BERNSTEIN. It's terrible about that Zollie, ain't it? A shame for his family.

MATTIE. The funny part of it is I gave the kid a job.

MRS. BERNSTEIN. No fooling!

MATTIE. Yep. He was supposed to start working for me today — this very morning.

MRS. BERNSTEIN (unaware that the door has opened and EFFIE is coming down stairs). It's a good thing he got caught! You woulda had a crook working right in your store and you wouldn't even realize.

EFFIE (standing defiantly on stairs). Don't you dare call my brother a crook!

[MRS. BERNSTEIN, startled, utters a little exclamation.]

He was asleep when the whole thing happened.

MRS. BERNSTEIN (embarrassed). Excuse me, darling. I didn't mean to hurt your feelings. I — I only thought — he musta done something. The police pulled him out of bed to take him to the station house — I thought —

EFFIE. They didn't pull him out of bed. He went willingly. They just wanted him to answer some questions. That's all — just answer some questions.

MRS. BERNSTEIN. Sure. I'm sorry I said anything. Believe me, I could kick myself. (Then, as she hurries up stairs) My Davy is right. He always tells me I talk too much.

[She exits through door into house, and MRS. TEDESCO retreats from window.]

MATTIE. Now don't you go taking it so hard, Effie. Things'll straighten out.

EFFIE (tearfully). It's just that everyone takes it for granted that Zollie is a thief.

MATTIE. Here comes your officer friend. Maybe he has some good news for you.

[EFFIE turns, goes right of stairs to meet NICK, who comes on right.]

EFFIE (agitated). Where is Zollie? What's going to happen to him? Are they going to let him go?

NICK. I don't know, Effie. It depends on Zollie. If he keeps on the way he's acting now, he'll end up in serious trouble.

EFFIE. Why? What do you mean?

NICK. He's behaving like a stubborn brat. We can't get anything out of him. He keeps insisting he's innocent — he doesn't know anything.

EFFIE. What do you want him to say?

NICK. Effie, he's got to come clean.

Clamming up like this, he'll only make it worse for himself. You better come down and reason with the kid — get him to talk.

EFFIE. You mean tell him to say what you want to hear! It couldn't be true that he's innocent, could it? Of course not. You arrested him, and that's another good mark on your record — and that's all that matters to you.

[*He puts his hand on her arm, but she pushes him away sharply.*]

It's your fault that Zollie's in trouble.

NICK. You know that's not so.

EFFIE. I know that you came in the middle of the night and arrested my brother.

NICK. Now look here, Effie. Brother or no brother, it's my job to enforce the law. I can't let my personal feelings interfere with my duty.

EFFIE. I don't think you *have* any feelings!

NICK (*controlling his anger*). Effie, listen. I didn't come here to argue with you. I need your help.

EFFIE. My help! For what? To get ahead faster on the Force?

[*She stalks off and he looks after her in frustrated silence.*]

Dissolve to DORGAN'S *basement apartment. It is morning. The room is empty, bed neatly made, covers off bird cages, box in the corner empty. There is a sharp rap on the door, then another. After a moment the door opens:* LIEUTENANT *and* SERGEANT *enter with* PATROLMAN. *Their mood is sober.*

SERGEANT. Hello?

[*They look about.*]

Nobody home.

LIEUTENANT. I'm not sorry.

[*They advance into the room uncomfortably.*]

SERGEANT (*admiringly*). Will you look at the menagerie.

PATROLMAN. That's an aviary, Sergeant.

SERGEANT. That it is. Well, be getting about your business, Nielson.

[PATROLMAN *makes a brief, routine inspection of the room as* SERGEANT *and* LIEUTENANT *look about bleakly.* LIEUTENANT *goes to the coat tree where* DORGAN'S *uniform hangs.*]

LIEUTENANT. His uniform. (*He examines the spot from which the badge was torn, observes mended places on the sleeve, sighs, then turns away.*)

PATROLMAN. He's a pretty old man, Dorgan — isn't he?

LIEUTENANT. Be careful you don't say that where he can hear you.

SERGEANT (*to* PATROLMAN). You shoulda seen the battle he put up when it came time to retire him. He claimed he could out-run, out-shoot, and out-fight any man on the Force. Finally the Commissioner says to him, "Dorgan, it'll cause hard feelings and be a reflection on the Department if I let you stay on past the age limit where other fellers have to retire." That persuaded him.

LIEUTENANT (*smiling reminiscently*). Retired just a little more than a year ago, didn't he?

SERGEANT. Fourteen months, I'd say.

LIEUTENANT. Well, locate Dorgan and bring him in, Sergeant.

SERGEANT. Yes, sir.

[*With a nod to* PATROLMAN *and* SERGEANT, LIEUTENANT *goes off.* SERGEANT *shakes his head dolefully.*]

Dissolve to the street. MATTIE *is in the doorway of her pawnshop.* LOUIS *is amusing himself by trying to work the windshield wiper on a car parked nearby. He glances up as* DORGAN *enters left, carrying dog, and comes to electric attention.*

LOUIS. Bozo! (*He snatches the dog out of* DORGAN's *arms and races up the stairs and into the house, yelling*) Ma! Ma!

[MATTIE, *in doorway of pawnshop, hands on hips, shakes her head disapprovingly.* DORGAN *crosses to her.*]

DORGAN. (*Grinning, he mimics her, shaking his head.*) Now what are you complaining about?

[*She continues to shake her head and he does the same, as they sit down together on the bench.*]

MATTIE. Found his dog and brought it back, and look at the gratitude you get. Not so much as a thank you.

DORGAN. The look on his face was thank you enough for me.

MATTIE (*fondly*). That isn't the point, you dumb cop. Kids gotta learn manners or they grow up wild.

DORGAN. I can see you never were a boy, Mattie. A youngster Joe's age doesn't have patience for the politenesses. When you get a little older, like you and me, there's not so much to occupy you — so you fill up time with a lot of polite talk, like (*He bows elaborately*): Good morning, Mrs. Gillespie, and how is the pawnshop business? . . . with burglars and whatnot giving you aggravation? . . . Now, when I was younger, I'd've skipped all that, picked you up under my arm, thrown you into my Model T, and took you for a ride in the park.

MATTIE. If you ask me, Dan, you're young enough and sassy enough to do it today.

DORGAN (*on guard*). Maybe, maybe —

but not *foolish* enough. I got some sensible maturity on me now, and I think of the consequences of my acts.

MATTIE. All the consequences I can think of is, you wouldn't be able to use your arm for a week, except maybe for feeding them silly birds of yours.

DORGAN. Those birds are fine noble creatures. They got character and intelligence, and they don't give me any aggravation.

MATTIE. I don't like birds. They're always looking sideways. (*She imitates a bird.*) I like a creature that looks you straight in both eyes.

DORGAN (*slaps her on the back*). You got your virtues, Mattie, even if you do keep 'em hidden out of sight. I hear how you caught a burglar singlehanded last night — conked him on the head with one of those saxophones, until he yelled for the police to come and save him.

MATTIE (*suddenly serious*). Dan —

DORGAN. Eh?

MATTIE. I kinda hate to tell you, but you'd find out soon enough, anyways —

DORGAN. What are you talking about?

MATTIE. Zollie. They think he was in on the burglary.

DORGAN. That's a lot of crazy nonsense.

MATTIE. Well, they got him down at the station house. Took him there last night.

DORGAN (*stunned for a moment*). But the boy had nothing to do with it.

LOUIS (*as he comes out of the house*). Pop Dorgan! Pop, Bozo's got a license on him.

DORGAN (*preoccupied*). Sure, lad, every dog has got to have a license — that's the law.

LOUIS. Where'd he get it from?

DORGAN. Why, I took him over to the license bureau and let him pick it out for himself.

LOUIS. I don't want nobody to buy Bozo's tag but me. (*He holds out his hand with some nickels and pennies in*

A dramatic moment from The Ghost Patrol. *Mattie, backed up by Mrs. Bernstein, confronts Nick and the captive Ben. (Kenyon and Eckhardt)*

it.) I been saving up — is this enough?

DORGAN. You keep that, lad, and save some more, so you can buy him his next tag when the time rolls around. This one was on me.

LOUIS (*puts money slowly into his pocket, assuming a nonchalant expression to hide his gratitude*). Well, okay. (*Then, bursting*) Thanks a lot, Pop! — Gee! thanks! (*He runs off.*)

DORGAN. See that, Mattie? He was grateful all right. But it's a durn sight easier to say "thank you for passing the salt" than "thank you for saving my life" . . . Well, I gotta go down to the station house and do something about Zollie. (*He is about to leave, when —*)

SERGEANT (*off*). Good morning, Pop.

[*He comes on with* PATROLMAN.]

We been combing the neighborhood searching for you.

DORGAN. Well, now that you found me, I got something to tell you. You had no business arresting Zollie Ferrara. That boy had nothing to do with the burglary last night. What's the big idea pulling him in?

SERGEANT. The Lieutenant, now, must've had good reason to believe —

DORGAN. No reason! No sir, no reason at all! You're down on the boy, is all the reason you had. I'm telling you he's innocent, and I'm going to have a talk with the Lieutenant.

SERGEANT. That's a fine idea, Pop. We'll take a little walk over to headquarters now.

[*They go.* MATTIE *stares after them as a curious neighbor pauses.*]

MATTIE (*to curious neighbor*). The nerve of them cops, calling Dan Dorgan "Pop" like he was an old man!

LOUIS. Did they arrest him, Mrs. Gillespie?

MATTIE. I don't know; I don't like it. . . .

LOUIS (to MRS. BERNSTEIN, who walks on). They arrested Mr. Dorgan.

MRS. BERNSTEIN. What!

[Voices get louder and more excited.]

MATTIE. The Sergeant from the Precinct comes along with another cop, and picks him up in front of my very eyes.

MRS. BERNSTEIN. A bunch of mashiginas! They don't know who to arrest next!

LOUIS (yelling to someone out of sight). Mr. Dorgan got arrested!

MRS. TEDESCO (appearing at window). Whatsa matter? What happen?

LOUIS. They arrest- MATTIE. Couple of
ed Pop Dorgan!   cops took Dan Dor-
                   gan away.

[People begin to gather, attracted by the commotion.]

LOUIS (to everyone who comes on). They arrested Pop Dorgan.

MRS. BERNSTEIN. He wouldn't kill a fly, that man.

[EFFIE comes on from left.]

First your brother and now Mr. Dorgan.

EFFIE. What do you mean?

LOUIS. They arrested Mr. Dorgan.

MATTIE. Took him down to the station house, Effie.

EFFIE. What for?

MATTIE. Who knows what for!

MRS. TEDESCO. Said he kill someone.

EFFIE. Pop Dorgan! They must be crazy!

MRS. BERNSTEIN. I'll get my nephew who's a lawyer.

MATTIE. I'll stand up for him in any court!

THE CROWD (general ad-libs). Yeah! Me too! He's no murderer! Pop Dorgan

never broke the law. Locking up a man like him.

[Indignation has reached the boiling point. Voices are angry, a dog is barking.]

MATTIE (topping them all). We'll show 'em they can't get away with any shenanigans like this. . . .

Dissolve to Ninth Precinct Station. SERGEANT O'CONNOR is at desk. NICK sits on edge of table, ZOLLIE is nearby. LIEUTENANT is pacing the floor as DORGAN berates him.

DORGAN. Lieutenant, Zollie had no part in the robbery. And it's a shame and a disgrace to be taking a boy out of his bed to arrest him when he's done nothing. I grant you he got into mischief when he was a youngster, but he's a good boy now and you got to give him a chance to go straight, or —

LIEUTENANT (riding over the last few words). Never mind about Zollie. You better start worrying about how you can defend yourself.

DORGAN. Defend myself?

LIEUTENANT. Several things. Did you or did you not overcome a man by physical force last night in the pawnshop?

DORGAN. Sure I did. As would any self-respecting policeman under the circumstances.

LIEUTENANT. And did you or did you not patrol the streets in a policeman's uniform?

DORGAN. Begging your pardon, sir, it is nobody's uniform but my own, the same one I was fitted for at Harrison's five years ago. Can you mean to tell me I have no right to be wearing it?

LIEUTENANT. You have no right to impersonate a policeman.

DORGAN. Impersonate a policeman? I

am a policeman. That's what I been these forty-seven years and nobody ever questioned it before now.

[LIEUTENANT *controls his exasperation. Phone rings and, glad of the diversion, he turns to listen as the* SERGEANT *picks it up.*]

SERGEANT. Ninth Precinct. Sergeant O'Connor. . . . Okay. We're ready for him. (*To* LIEUTENANT) They're bringing Ben over from the lockup, Lieutenant.

LIEUTENANT. Good. (*To* ZOLLIE) Maybe you'll have more to say when your pal gets here.

DORGAN. Ben is no pal of Zollie's, Lieutenant. A passing acquaintance, maybe. There's the difference of night and day between the two. That Ben is a mean fellow, always picking on younger lads and leading 'em into trouble. It's going to be easier to keep the peace on my beat now, with him gone.

LIEUTENANT. Dorgan! You were retired fourteen months ago. It is no longer necessary for you to keep the peace on your beat (*He corrects himself hastily*) — on *that* beat! It's Nick's job now.

DORGAN. Well, I don't bother him and he don't bother me. It's *my* beat, Lieutenant, but if the Department sees fit to assign Nick — okay — orders are orders.

LIEUTENANT. Of course. Orders are orders. We agree on that, don't we?

DORGAN. Yes, sir.

LIEUTENANT. And didn't the Department *order* you to retire?

DORGAN. Oh, they meant no harm by it. Just their way of saying, "Dorgan, we want you to take things a little easy." Nevertheless, I got to take care of my beat, sir. Folks count on me. And the Force wouldn't want me to neglect my duties.

LIEUTENANT. You *are not a member* of the Force, Dorgan! And you are breaking the law when you pretend you are!

DORGAN (*almost in tears*). I don't want to contradict you, Lieutenant. But my name is Patrolman Dan Dorgan and I am still on the payroll. The pension check comes regular as clock work, and I'm of the firm opinion that there is no crime in my doing something to earn it.

LIEUTENANT. You are, hmm?

DORGAN. Yes, sir.

LIEUTENANT. Look, Dorgan, if you keep on with this line of talk, you're going to convince me you're — well, not a responsible person. Do you know what that means?

[DORGAN *frowns.*]

This is a rather serious matter.

NICK. Uh — Lieutenant, it isn't necessary to — I mean, we don't have to make charges against Mr. Dorgan, do we?

LIEUTENANT. Why — what have you got in mind?

NICK. Well, he hasn't done any harm. His intentions were good and everything he did turned out for the best. And —

LIEUTENANT. Go on, Nick. Get it off your chest.

NICK. Well, maybe making an arrest isn't always the best solution. Like with Zollie — I jumped to some pretty quick conclusions on account of his past record. And now I realize I had a whole wrong attitude toward him. And, gosh, Lieutenant, what I'm trying to say is, there's a human side to things you've got to consider. You can't always stick to the letter of the law.

[*During the above,* EFFIE *enters, also* MATTIE, LOUIS, MRS. TEDESCO, MRS. BERNSTEIN, *and several neighbors. They stand quietly, listening to* NICK's *words.*]

Maybe Mr. Dorgan did do a couple of things not strictly according to the book, but it's all wrong to condemn a good guy like him on a technicality.

MATTIE. And it's a pity the Police Department doesn't spend its time going after those crooked politicians instead of honest men like Dan Dorgan.

SERGEANT (*coming forward*). Sh! Mrs.

EFFIE. We can only stay a minute, Pop.

DORGAN. Where'd Zollie disappear to?

EFFIE. He ran ahead to tell Grandma everything's all right.

[*She puts her arms around* DORGAN'S *neck.*]

Oh, Pop, you were wonderful at the station house. And Nick too — I was so proud the way you spoke up! And did you notice Zollie, when the Sergeant shook hands with him? How dignified he acted?

DORGAN. Ah, that Zollie's going to grow into a fine man. You wait and see.

[ZOLLIE *enters.*]

Speak of the devil!

EFFIE. Did you see Grandma?

ZOLLIE. Yeah. She said she knew it would come out all right — she was in church all day, praying for me.

EFFIE. Did you tell her about Pop?

ZOLLIE. Yeah, but she couldn't make it out. She don't understand how one cop can arrest another cop.

[*They all laugh.*]

She wants both of you to come for dinner tomorrow night — she's going to make a big bunch of spaghetti.

NICK. Sure thing.

DORGAN. I'll save up my appetite.

EFFIE. It'll be a sort of celebration.

DORGAN. And we've got plenty to celebrate. What do you say, Zollie?

ZOLLIE. Sure. I wanted to tell you, Pop — thanks for sticking up for me in front of everybody.

DORGAN. I was only telling the truth about you, son. I think you and the Police Department are going to get along fine from now on.

NICK. Sure we will.

DORGAN. My boy, you understand, it's no reflection on you, me wanting to keep my beat.

NICK. You don't have to worry about your beat any more, Mr. Dorgan. I'm going to try to take care of it just as you did.

DORGAN. I think you're the man who can do it. (DORGAN *beams as* NICK, EFFIE, *and* ZOLLIE *leave.*)

Dissolve to DORGAN'S *basement apartment.* DORGAN *enters, looking suddenly downcast. He sighs, and, glancing at the uniform on the hanger, goes to the birds and talks to them.*

DORGAN. What am I going to do now, eh? The coat's perfectly good and *I'm* perfectly good, and that bunch at the station house wants to put us out of business. Not that I don't respect their authority, and the Force usually knows what it's doing, but they're forgetting one thing: *I'm a lot older* than they are, and I know how things should be run. (*He sighs.*) Ah, well, I don't want any more trouble like I had today. (*He takes honor badge from his pocket, goes to coat tree, and pins badge in its proper place on coat, in the official manner of the Commissioner.*) Patrolman Dan Dorgan, you're a durn old fool, who's wore out your welcome. We got no more use for you on the Force. (*He shakes hands with the sleeve of the coat. Then he blows his nose, takes uniform off hanger, folds it, and puts it carefully away in chest. Before he has a chance to close the chest, there is a knock at the door and he opens it to admit* MATTIE.) Well, now, it's an unexpected honor when the great lady comes to visit the humble policeman.

MATTIE. Dan Dorgan, you're no humble policeman. Will you kindly get it through your skull you are no more a policeman at *all* — no more than I'm a great lady.

DORGAN. Thank you! Thank you **very**

much indeed! Going over on their side, and I thought you were a real friend, those things you said about me to the Lieutenant.

MATTIE. But it doesn't *matter* about your not being a cop official-like, with a uniform and a beat. Folks'll still come to Dan Dorgan when they need to be helped. Only difference is, you won't have to go out *looking* for trouble. (*She turns and looks at the birds.*) Well, if they aren't the cutest things. I thought you had canaries.

DORGAN (*sulking*). The accuracy of a woman!

MATTIE. Will you look at those pretty feathers! Tweet tweet. Hello, birdies. Don't they sing?

DORGAN. They do not. Can't you tell the difference between a canary and a finch?

MATTIE. And all this time I thought you had a bunch of birds singing their heads off the whole day long. Why these are real nice. I wouldn't mind having 'em around one bit.

DORGAN. Mattie Gillespie, there's something I want to know: What was it you whispered to the Lieutenant?

MATTIE. I said all you need to keep you out of mischief is some good reason for staying home nights.

DORGAN. And could him or you think of something good enough to take the place of my duty and my career?

MATTIE. Dan Dorgan, if you had an ounce of romantic feeling in you, *you'd* have thought of it yourself, before now.

[*She looks him in the eye and he blinks a few times, then nods in resignation. Then he goes to the chest and sighs as he looks at the coat.*]

DORGAN (*to the coat*). I'll be saying good-by to you, since there's a conspiracy to keep us apart.

MATTIE. Why, Dan! It's more than a year since I saw you wearing that. Here, put it on — I never could resist a man in uniform. (*She helps him into*

it.) Oh, but you look grand! Why don't you keep it out, and wear it evenings around the house?

DORGAN. But if I've ceased being a policeman — ?

MATTIE. Dan, we know better than that, don't we?

[*They grin at each other.*]

It's been in my mind for years to marry a cop.

DORGAN. And law or no law, you're not a woman to lightly change your mind. But listen now! around the house only! for I'll have no reason to be spending my evenings elsewhere.

[*They laugh together.*]

[THE END]

For Discussion of the Complete Play

1. In what way had Dorgan broken the law? How did he justify his actions? Even though Dorgan's intent was good, what was the *potential* danger in his actions?

2. Did the rallying of the neighbors influence the Lieutenant's decision not to prosecute Dorgan, or did it merely give him a good excuse for dismissing the charges? Discuss the value of prompt expression of public opinion.

3. How did Nick's attitude toward his job change? Give three reasons for the change. In what ways did the play change your own opinion about the qualities that make a good policeman?

4. Look up the passage on page 345 in which Dorgan discusses the role of a policeman. Arrange an informal debate on the question of crime prevention. How does Dorgan contrast jails to policemen? What does he think is lacking in modern radio-car patrolling? How does knowing people well help prevent crime?

5. Why was it hard for Zollie to re-establish himself as a respected member of the community? What help did he need? What does your own community do to help solve the problem of juvenile delinquency? What more could it do?

6. What action of Ben's showed him at

his worst? What do you think should be done with him?

7. Describe the future you foresee for Mattie and Dorgan. Will Dorgan be happy? How does Mattie suggest a way that Dorgan can keep up his work in the community?

8. How many widely popular themes can you discover in this television play?

Imagine a family of four or five members — you decide their ages — around the television set, and tell why this play might appeal to each one. Write in play form the conversation on this topic after the play ends. Describe each member of the family briefly and then take care to have each person talk in an individual fashion suitable to his age and sex.

Our Town

THORNTON WILDER
1897–

It is a curious fact about the theater that the greatest successes are usually those plays that desert the currently popular patterns and bring genuine novelty to the stage. Such a play is Thornton Wilder's *Our Town*, which brought out the " Standing Room Only " signs on Broadway, won a Pulitzer Prize in 1938, won wide acclaim in a film version, and has remained a national favorite ever since.

Wilder had early established a reputation for originality with a series of experimental short plays and a remarkable novel, *The Bridge of San Luis Rey*. The latter won a Pulitzer Prize in 1928, and when *Our Town* duplicated the triumph ten years later the author became the only writer to win that coveted honor in both fields.

Wilder's early life and education followed a winding trail. Born in Madison, Wisconsin, he started his schooling in California; continued it in China where his father was stationed for eight years in government service; and attended college at Oberlin in Ohio and at Yale. During 1920 he was a graduate student at the American Academy in Rome. Afterward he taught for a time. For thirty years he has devoted

himself almost entirely to writing. Today he is recognized as perhaps the most versatile American man of letters.

Conventional ways of doing things evidently have little charm for Wilder. His writings abound in original plans and fresh approaches. Perhaps you have read *The Happy Journey*, one of his popular one-act plays in which a few chairs represent an automobile and the action takes place during a tour which is imaginatively created on a bare stage. His latest Broadway play, *The Skin of Our Teeth* (1942), telescopes time from the Stone Age to tomorrow in the life of one family. His latest book, a study of Julius Caesar called *The Ides of March* (1948) is apparently a collection of contemporary documents including letters from Caesar himself — but Wilder composed them all.

Knowing this about the author, you will not expect *Our Town* to follow any familiar pattern. And how right you will be! First of all, he has moved the Stage Manager out before the audience and made him a performer in the drama; the Manager becomes an on-stage director who can shift time back and forth as easily as he shifts the scene with a wave of his hand and a couple of sentences. There are no stage sets for the scenes and only a few simple objects are used as properties. You will not lose your bearings, however, for the Stage Manager calls your attention to every shift of scene. He does more than that, though. He also talks directly to the audience and explains his purpose in selecting certain people and events to represent the life in the town of Grover's Corners. The handling of the story in this play is as unusual as the method of presentation. By its very nature drama thrives on tension and excitement, and most plays are deliberately designed to provide a full measure of both. Wilder chooses to warm the hearts of his audience rather than to set their spines tingling. When the Stage Manager makes the exact nature of this purpose clear for you, you get into the swing of the play and share the pleasure all America has taken in it.

Characters

STAGE MANAGER	WALLY WEBB	SIMON STIMSON
DR. GIBBS	EMILY WEBB	MRS. SOAMES
JOE CROWELL, JR.	PROFESSOR WILLARD	CONSTABLE WARREN
HOWIE NEWSOME	MR. WEBB	SI CROWELL
MRS. GIBBS	WOMAN IN THE BALCONY	SAM CRAIG
MRS. WEBB	TALL MAN AT BACK	JOE STODDARD
GEORGE GIBBS	OF AUDITORIUM	PEOPLE OF THE TOWN
REBECCA GIBBS	LADY IN A BOX	

The entire play takes place in Grover's Corners, New Hampshire, 1901 to 1913.

ACT I

No curtain. No scenery. The audience, arriving, sees an empty stage in half-light.

Presently the STAGE MANAGER, *hat on and pipe in mouth, enters and begins placing a table and several chairs downstage left, and a table and chairs downstage right. " Left " and " right " are from the point of view of the actor facing the audience. " Up " is toward the back wall.*

As the house lights go down, he has finished setting the stage and, leaning against the right proscenium pillar, watches the late arrivals in the audience. When the auditorium is in complete darkness, he speaks.

STAGE MANAGER. This play is called *Our Town.* It was written by Thornton Wilder; produced and directed by A——— [or: produced by A———; directed by B———]. In it you will see Miss C———, Miss D———, Miss E———, and Mr. F———, Mr. G———, Mr. H———, and many others.

The name of the town is Grover's Corners, New Hampshire — just across the Massachusetts line: longitude forty-two degrees, forty minutes; latitude seventy degrees, thirty-seven minutes.

The first act shows a day in our town. The day is May 7, 1901. The time is just before dawn.

[*A rooster crows.*]

The sky is beginning to show some streaks of light over in the east there, behind our mount'in. The morning star always gets wonderful bright the minute before it has to go. (*He stares at it for a moment, then goes upstage.*)

Well, I'd better show you how our town lies. Up here (*that is, parallel with the back wall*) is Main Street. Way back there is the railway station;

tracks go that way. Polish Town's across the tracks and some Canuck families. (*Toward the left*) Over there is the Congregational Church; across the street's the Presbyterian. Methodist and Unitarian are over there. Baptist is down in the holla' by the river. Catholic Church is over beyond the tracks.

Here's the Town Hall and Post Office combined; jail's in the basement. Bryan once made a speech from these steps here. Along here's a row of stores. Hitching posts and horse blocks in front of them. First automobile's going to come along in about five years — belonged to Banker Cartwright, our richest citizen . . . lives in the big white house up on the hill.

Here's the grocery store and here's Mr. Morgan's drugstore. Most everybody in town manages to look into those two stores once a day. Public school's over yonder. High school's still farther over. Quarter of nine mornings, noontimes, and three o'clock afternoons, the hull town can hear the yelling and screaming from those schoolyards. (*He approaches the table and chairs downstage right.*)

This is our doctor's house — Doc Gibbs's. This is the back door.

[*Two arched trellises are pushed out, one by each proscenium pillar.*]

There's some scenery for those who think they have to have scenery. There's a garden here. Corn . . . peas . . . beans . . . hollyhocks . . . heliotrope . . . and a lot of burdock. (*Crosses the stage.*)

In those days our newspaper come out twice a week — the Grover's Corners *Sentinel* — and this is Editor Webb's house. And this is Mrs. Webb's garden. Just like Mrs. Gibbs's, only it's got a lot of sunflowers, too. Right here — big butternut tree.

[*He returns to his place by the right proscenium pillar and looks at the audience for a minute.*]

Nice town, y'know what I mean? Nobody very remarkable ever come out of it — s'far as we know. The earliest tombstones in the cemetery up there on the mountain say 1670, 1680 — they're Grovers and Cartwrights and Gibbses and Herseys — same names as are around here now.

Well, as I said, it's about dawn. The only lights on in town are in a cottage over by the tracks where a Polish mother's just had twins. And in the Joe Crowell house, where Joe Jr.'s getting up so as to deliver the paper. And in the depot, where Shorty Hawkins is gettin' ready to flag the five forty-five for Boston.

[*A train whistle is heard. The* STAGE MANAGER *takes out his watch and nods.*]

Naturally, out in the country — all around — they've been lights on for some time, what with milkin's and so on. But town people sleep late.

So — another day's begun. There's Doc Gibbs comin' down Main Street now, comin' back from that baby case. And here's his wife comin' downstairs to get breakfast. Doc Gibbs died in 1930. The new hospital's named after him. Mrs. Gibbs died first — long time ago, in fact. She went out to visit her daughter, Rebecca, who married an insurance man in Canton, Ohio, and died there — pneumonia — but her body was brought back here. She's up in the cemetery there now, in with a whole mess of Gibbses and Herseys — she was Julia Hersey 'fore she married Doc Gibbs in the Congregational Church over there.

In our town we like to know the facts about everybody. . . . That's Doc Gibbs. And there comes Joe Crowell, Jr., delivering Mr. Webb's *Sentinel*.

[DR. GIBBS *has been coming along Main Street from the left. At the point where he would turn to approach his house, he stops, sets down his — imaginary — black bag, takes off his hat, and rubs his face with fatigue, using an enormous handkerchief.* MRS. GIBBS *has entered her kitchen, gone through the motions of putting wood into a stove, lighting it, and preparing breakfast. Suddenly,* JOE CROWELL, JR., *starts down Main Street from the right, hurling imaginary newspapers into doorways.*]

JOE CROWELL, JR. Morning, Doc Gibbs.

DR. GIBBS. Morning, Joe.

JOE CROWELL, JR. Somebody been sick, Doc?

DR. GIBBS. No. Just some twins born over in Polish Town.

JOE CROWELL, JR. Do you want your paper now?

DR. GIBBS. Yes, I'll take it. Anything serious goin' on in the world since Wednesday?

JOE CROWELL, JR. Yessir. My schoolteacher, Miss Foster, 's getting married to a fella over in Concord.

DR. GIBBS. I declare. How do you boys feel about that?

JOE CROWELL, JR. Well, of course, it's none of my business — but I think if a person starts out to be a teacher, she ought to stay one.

DR. GIBBS. How's your knee, Joe?

JOE CROWELL, JR. Fine, Doc. I never think about it at all. Only like you said, it always tells me when it's going to rain.

DR. GIBBS. What's it telling you today? Goin' to rain?

JOE CROWELL, JR. No, sir.

DR. GIBBS. Sure?

JOE CROWELL, JR. Yessir.

DR. GIBBS. Knee ever make a mistake?

JOE CROWELL, JR. No, sir.

[JOE *goes off.* DR. GIBBS *stands reading his paper.*]

STAGE MANAGER. Here comes Howie Newsome delivering the milk.

[HOWIE NEWSOME *comes along Main Street, passes* DR. GIBBS, *comes down the center of the stage, leaves some bottles at* MRS. WEBB's *back door, and crosses the stage to* MRS. GIBBS's.]

HOWIE NEWSOME. Git-ap, Bessie. What's the matter with you? . . . Morning, Doc.

DR. GIBBS. Morning, Howie.

HOWIE NEWSOME. Somebody sick?

DR. GIBBS. Pair of twins over to Mrs. Goruslawski's.

HOWIE NEWSOME. Twins, eh? This town's gettin' bigger every year.

DR. GIBBS. Going to rain, Howie?

HOWIE NEWSOME. No, no. Fine day — that'll burn through. Come on, Bessie.

DR. GIBBS. Hello, Bessie. (*He strokes her.*) How old is she, Howie?

HOWIE NEWSOME. Going on seventeen. Bessie's all mixed up about the route ever since the Lockharts stopped takin' their quart of milk every day. She wants to leave 'em a quart just the same — keeps scolding me the hull trip.

[*He reaches* MRS. GIBBS's *back door. She is waiting for him.*]

MRS. GIBBS. Good morning, Howie.

HOWIE NEWSOME. Morning, Mrs. Gibbs. Doc's just comin' down the street.

MRS. GIBBS. Is he? Seems like you're late today.

HOWIE NEWSOME. Yes. Somep'n went wrong with the separator. Don't know what 'twas.

[*He goes back to Main Street, clucks for Bessie, and goes off right.* DR. GIBBS *reaches his home and goes in.*]

MRS. GIBBS. Everything all right?

DR. GIBBS. Yes. I declare — easy as kittens.

MRS. GIBBS. Bacon'll be ready in a minute. Set down and drink your coffee. Child-*run!* Child-*run!* Time to get up. George! Rebecca! . . . You can catch a couple hours' sleep this morning, can't you?

DR. GIBBS. Hm! . . . Mrs. Wentworth's coming at eleven. Guess I know what it's about, too. Her stummick ain't what it ought to be.

MRS. GIBBS. All told, you won't get more'n three hours' sleep. Frank Gibbs, I don't know what's goin' to become of you. I do wish I could get you to go away some place and take a rest. I think it would do you good.

MRS. WEBB. Emileeee! Time to get up! Wally! Seven o'clock!

MRS. GIBBS. I declare, you got to speak to George. Seems like something's come over him lately. He's no help to me at all. I can't even get him to cut me some wood.

DR. GIBBS. Is he sassy to you?

MRS. GIBBS. No. He just whines! All he thinks about is that baseball — George! Rebecca! You'll be late for school.

DR. GIBBS. M-m-m. . . .

MRS. GIBBS. George!

DR. GIBBS. George, look sharp!

GEORGE'S VOICE. Yes, Pa!

DR. GIBBS (as he goes off the stage). Don't you hear your mother calling you?

MRS. WEBB. Walleee! Emileee! You'll be late for school! Walleee! You wash yourself good or I'll come up and do it myself.

REBECCA GIBBS'S VOICE. Ma! What dress shall I wear?

MRS. GIBBS. Don't make a noise. Your father's been out all night and needs his sleep. I washed and ironed the blue gingham for you special.

REBECCA. Ma, I hate that dress.

MRS. GIBBS. Oh, hush up with you.

REBECCA. Every day I go to school dressed like a sick turkey.

MRS. GIBBS. Now, Rebecca, don't be impossible. You always look *very* nice.

REBECCA. Mamma, George's throwing soap at me.

MRS. GIBBS. I'll come up and slap the both of you — that's what I'll do.

[*A factory whistle sounds. The children enter and take their places at the breakfast tables:* EMILY *and* WALLY WEBB; GEORGE *and* REBECCA GIBBS.]

STAGE MANAGER. We've got a factory in our town too — hear it? Makes blan-

kets. Cartwrights own it and it brung 'em a fortune.

MRS. WEBB. Children! Now I won't have it. Breakfast is just as good as any other meal and I won't have you gobbling like wolves. It'll stunt your growth — that's a fact. Put away your book, Wally.

WALLY. Aw, Ma!

MRS. WEBB. You know the rule's well as I do — no books at table. As for me, I'd rather have my children healthy than bright.

EMILY. I'm both, Mamma; you know I am. I'm the brightest girl in school for my age. I have a wonderful memory.

MRS. WEBB. Eat your breakfast.

WALLY. I'm bright, too, when I'm looking at my stamp collection.

MRS. GIBBS. I'll speak to your father about it when he's rested. Seems to me twenty-five cents a week's enough for a boy your age. I declare I don't know how you spend it all.

GEORGE. Aw, Ma — I gotta lotta things to buy.

MRS. GIBBS. Strawberry phosphates — that's what you spend it on.

GEORGE. I don't see how Rebecca comes to have so much money. She has more'n a dollar.

REBECCA (*spoon in mouth, dreamily*). I've been saving it up gradual.

MRS. GIBBS. Well, dear, I think it's a good thing every now and then to spend some.

REBECCA. Mamma, do you know what I love most in the world — do you? Money!

MRS. GIBBS. Eat your breakfast.

[*The school bell is heard.*]

CHILDREN. Mamma, there's first bell. . . . I gotta hurry. . . . I don't want any more.

MRS. WEBB. Walk fast, but you don't have to run. Wally, pull up your pants at the knee. Stand up straight, Emily.

MRS. GIBBS. Tell Miss Foster I send

her my best congratulations. Can you remember that?

REBECCA. Yes, Ma.

MRS. GIBBS. You look real nice, Rebecca. Pick up your feet.

ALL. Good-by.

[*The children from the two houses join at the center of the stage and go up to Main Street, then off left.* MRS. GIBBS *fills her apron with food for the chickens and comes down to the footlights.*]

MRS. GIBBS. Here, chick, chick, chick, . . . No, go away, you. Go away. . . . Here, chick, chick, chick. What's the matter with *you?* Fight, fight, fight — that's all you do. Hm . . . *you* don't belong to me. Where'd you come from? (*She shakes her apron.*) Oh, don't be so scared. Nobody's going to hurt you.

[MRS. WEBB *is sitting by her trellis, stringing beans.*]

Good morning, Myrtle. How's your cold?

MRS. WEBB. Well, it's better; but I told Charles I didn't know as I'd go to choir practice tonight. Wouldn't be any use.

MRS. GIBBS. Just the same, you come to choir practice, Myrtle, and try it.

MRS. WEBB. Well, if I don't feel any worse than I do now I probably will. While I'm resting myself, I thought I'd string some of these beans.

MRS. GIBBS (*rolling up her sleeves as she crosses the stage for a chat*). Let me help you. Beans have been good this year.

MRS. WEBB. I've decided to put up forty quarts if it kills me. The children say they hate 'em, but I notice they're able to get 'em down all winter. (*Pause*)

MRS. GIBBS. Now, Myrtle. I've got to tell you something, because if I don't tell somebody I'll burst.

MRS. WEBB. Why, Julia Gibbs!

MRS. GIBBS. Here, give me some more

of those beans. Myrtle, did one of those secondhand furniture men from Boston come to see you last Friday?

MRS. WEBB. No-o.

MRS. GIBBS. Well, he called on me. First I thought he was a patient wantin' to see Dr. Gibbs. 'N he wormed his way into my parlor, and, Myrtle Webb, he offered me three hundred and fifty dollars for Grandmother Wentworth's highboy, as I'm sitting here!

MRS. WEBB. Why, Julia Gibbs!

MRS. GIBBS. He did! That old thing! Why, it was so big I didn't know where to put it, and I almost give it to Cousin Hester Wilcox.

MRS. WEBB. Well, you're going to take it, aren't you?

MRS. GIBBS. I don't know.

MRS. WEBB. You don't know — three hundred and fifty dollars! What's come over you?

MRS. GIBBS. Well, if I could get the Doctor to take the money and go away some place on a real trip I'd sell it like that. Myrtle, ever since I was *that* high I've had the thought that I'd like to see Paris, France. I suppose I'm crazy.

MRS. WEBB. Oh, I know what you mean. How does the Doctor feel about it?

MRS. GIBBS. Well, I did beat about the bush a little and said that if I got a legacy — that's the way I put it — I'd make him take me somewhere.

MRS. WEBB. M-m-m. . . . What did he say?

MRS. GIBBS. You know how he is. I haven't heard a serious word out of him ever since I've known him. No, he said, it might make him discontented with Grover's Corners to go traipsin' about Europe; better let well enough alone, he says. Every two years he makes a trip to the battlefields of the Civil War; and that's enough treat for anybody, he says.

MRS. WEBB. Well, Mr. Webb just *admires* the way Dr. Gibbs knows everything about the Civil War. Mr. Webb's a good mind to give up Napoleon and move over to the Civil War, only Dr. Gibbs being one of the greatest experts in the country just makes him despair.

MRS. GIBBS. It's a fact! Dr. Gibbs is never so happy as when he's at Antietam or Gettysburg. The times I've walked over those hills, Myrtle, stopping at every bush and pacing it all out, like we was going to buy it.

MRS. WEBB. Well, if that secondhand man's really serious about buyin' it, Julia, you sell it. And then you'll get to see Paris, all right.

MRS. GIBBS. Oh, I'm sorry I mentioned it. Only it seems to me that once in your life before you die you ought to see a country where they don't talk and think in English and don't even want to.

[*The* STAGE MANAGER *returns to the center of the stage.*]

STAGE MANAGER. That'll do. That'll do. Thank you very much, ladies.

[MRS. GIBBS *and* MRS. WEBB *gather up their things, return into their homes, and disappear.*]

Now we're going to skip a few hours in the day at Grover's Corners. But before we go on, I want you to know some more things about the town — all kinds of things. So I've asked Professor Willard of our State University to come down here and sketch in a few details of our past history — kind of scientific account, you might say. Is Professor Willard here?

[PROFESSOR WILLARD, *a rural savant, pince-nez on a wide satin ribbon, enters from the right with some notes in his hand.*]

May I introduce Professor Willard of our university. A few brief notes, thank you, Professor — unfortunately our time is limited.

PROFESSOR WILLARD. Grover's Corners . . . let me see . . . Grover's Corners

lies on the old Archeozoic [1] granite of the Appalachian range. I may say it's some of the oldest land in the world. We're very proud of that. A shelf of Devonian basalt [2] crosses it with vestiges of Mesozoic shale,[3] and some sandstone outcroppings; but that's all more recent: two hundred, three hundred million years old. Some highly interesting fossils have been found — I may say unique fossils — two miles out of town, in Silas Peckham's cow pasture. They can be seen at the museum in our university at any time. . . . Did you wish the meteorological conditions?

STAGE MANAGER. Thank you. We would.

PROFESSOR WILLARD. The mean precipitation is forty inches. The mean annual temperature is forty-three degrees, ranging between one hundred two degrees in the shade and thirty-eight degrees below zero in winter. The . . . the . . . uh . . .

STAGE MANAGER. Thank you, Professor. And have you Professor Gruber's notes on the history of human life here?

PROFESSOR WILLARD. Hm . . . yes . . . anthropological data. Early Amerindian stock. Cotahatchee [4] tribes . . . no evidence before the tenth century of this era . . . hm . . . now entirely disappeared . . . possible traces in three families. Migration toward the end of the seventeenth century of English brachycephalic [5] blue-eyed stock . . . for the most part. Since then some influx of Slav and Mediterranean types. . . .

STAGE MANAGER. And the population, Professor Willard?

[1] **Archeozoic** (är′kĕ·ō·zō′ĭk): formed in the earliest era of geological history.

[2] **Devonian basalt** (dĕ·vō′nĭ·ăn bȧ·sôlt′): very old rock of volcanic origin.

[3] **Mesozoic shale** (mĕs′·ō·zō′ĭk shāl): another type of rock formed very early in the world's history.

[4] **Cotahatchee** (kŏ·tȧ·hă′chē).

[5] **brachycephalic** (brăk′ĭ·sĕ·făl′ĭk): short-headed, or broad-headed.

PROFESSOR WILLARD. Within the town limits, 2,640. The postal district brings in 507 more. Mortality and birth rates are constant; by MacPherson's gauge, 6.032.

STAGE MANAGER. Thank you *very* much, Professor. We're all very much obliged to you, I'm sure.

PROFESSOR WILLARD. Not at all, sir; not at all.

STAGE MANAGER. This way, Professor, and thank you again.

[*Exit* PROFESSOR WILLARD.]

Now the political and social report: Editor Webb. . . . Oh, Mr. Webb?

[MRS. WEBB *appears at her back door.*]

MRS. WEBB. He'll be here in a minute. . . . He just cut his hand while he was eatin' an apple.

STAGE MANAGER. Thank you, Mrs. Webb.

MRS. WEBB. Charles! Everybody's waitin'. (*Exit*)

STAGE MANAGER. Mr. Webb is publisher and editor of the Grover's Corners *Sentinel*. That's our local paper, y'know.

[MR. WEBB *enters from his house, pulling on his coat. His finger is bound in a handkerchief.*]

MR. WEBB. Hm. . . . I don't have to tell you that we're run here by a board of selectmen. All males vote at the age of twenty-one. Women vote indirect. We're lower middle-class, sprinkling of professional men . . . ten per cent illiterate laborers. Politically, we're eighty-six per cent Republicans; six per cent Democrats; four per cent Socialists; rest, indifferent. Religiously, we're eighty-five per cent Protestants; twelve per cent Catholics; rest, indifferent. Do you want the poverty and insanity statistics?

STAGE MANAGER. Thank you, no. Have you any comments, Mr. Webb?

MR. WEBB. Very ordinary town, if you ask me. Little better behaved than most. Probably a lot duller. But our young people here seem to like it well enough: ninety per cent of 'em graduating from high school settle down right here to live — even when they've been away to college.

STAGE MANAGER. Thank you, Mr. Webb. Now, is there anyone in the audience who would like to ask Editor Webb anything about the town?

WOMAN IN THE BALCONY. Is there much drinking in Grover's Corners?

MR. WEBB. Well, ma'am, I wouldn't know what you'd call *much*. Satiddy nights the farm hands meet down in Ellery Greenough's stable and holler some. Fourth of July I've been known to taste a drop myself — and Decoration Day, of course. We've got one or two town drunks, but they're always having remorses every time an evangelist comes to town. No, ma'am, I'd say likker ain't a regular thing in the home here, except in the medicine chest. Right good for snake bite, y'know — always was.

TALL MAN AT BACK OF AUDITORIUM. Is there no one in town aware of —

STAGE MANAGER. Come forward, will you, where we can all hear you — what were you saying?

TALL MAN. Is there no one in town aware of social injustice and industrial inequality?

MR. WEBB. Oh, yes, everybody is — somethin' terrible. Seems like they spend most of their time talking about who's rich and who's poor.

TALL MAN. Then why don't they do something about it?

MR. WEBB. Well, we're ready to listen to everybody's suggestion as to how you can see that the diligent and sensible'll rise to the top and the lazy and quarrelsome sink to the bottom. We'll listen to anybody. Meantime, until that's settled, we try to take care of those that can't help themselves, and those that can we leave alone. Are there any more questions?

The stage is set for breakfast at the Gibbses' and the Webbs'. (Culver)

LADY IN A BOX. Oh, Mr. Webb? Mr. Webb, is there any culture or love of beauty in Grover's Corners?

MR. WEBB. Well, ma'am, there ain't much — not in the sense you mean. Come to think of it, there's some girls that play the piano at high-school commencement; but they ain't happy about it. Yes, and I see where my daughter's been made to read *The Merchant of Venice* over to the school. Seems all pretty remote to 'em, y'know what I mean. No, ma'am, there isn't much culture; but maybe this is the place to tell you that we've got a lot of pleasures of a kind here: we like the sun comin' up over the mountain in the morning, and we all notice a good deal about the birds. We pay a lot of attention to them, and trees and plants. And we watch the change of the seasons: yes, everybody knows about them. But those other things — you're right, ma'am — there ain't much. *Robinson Crusoe* and the Bible; and Handel's " Largo," we all know that; and Whistler's " Mother " — those are just about as far as we go.

LADY IN A BOX. So I thought. Thank you, Mr. Webb.

STAGE MANAGER. All right! All right! Thank you, everybody.

[MR. WEBB *retires.*]

We'll go back to the town now. It's middle of the afternoon. All 2,642 have had their dinners, and all the dishes have been washed. There's an early-afternoon calm in our town: a buzzin' and a hummin' from the school buildings; only a few buggies on Main Street — the horses dozing at the hitching posts; you all remember what it's like. Doc Gibbs is in his office, tapping people and making them say " Ah." Mr. Webb's cuttin' his lawn over there; one man in ten thinks it's a privilege to push his own lawn mower.

No, sir. It's later than I thought.

There are the children coming home from school already.

[EMILY WEBB *comes sedately down Main Street, carrying some schoolbooks. There are some signs that she is imagining herself to be a lady of striking elegance. Her father's movements to and fro with the lawn mower bring him into her vicinity.*]

EMILY. I *can't*, Lois. I've got to go home and help my mother. I *promised.*

MR. WEBB. Emily, walk simply. Who do you think you are today?

EMILY. Papa, you're terrible. One minute you tell me to stand up straight, and the next minute you call me names. I just don't listen to you. (*She gives him an abrupt kiss.*)

MR. WEBB. Golly, I never got a kiss from such a great lady before.

[*He goes out of sight.* EMILY *leans over and picks some flowers by the gate of her house.* GEORGE GIBBS *comes careening down Main Street. He is throwing a ball up to dizzy heights and waiting to catch it again. This sometimes requires his taking six steps backward.*]

GEORGE. Excuse me, Mrs. Forrest.

STAGE MANAGER (*as* MRS. FORREST). Go out and play in the fields, young man. You got no business playing baseball on Main Street.

GEORGE. Awfully sorry, Mrs. Forrest. . . . Hello, Emily.

EMILY. H'lo.

GEORGE. You made a fine speech in class.

EMILY. Well . . . I was really ready to make a speech about the Monroe Doctrine, but at the last minute Miss Corcoran made me talk about the Louisiana Purchase instead. I worked an awful long time on both of them.

GEORGE. Gee, it's funny, Emily. From my window up there I can just see your head nights when you're doing your homework over in your room.

EMILY. Why, can you?

GEORGE. You certainly do stick to it, Emily. I don't see how you can sit still that long. I guess you like school.

EMILY. Well, I always feel it's something you have to go through.

GEORGE. Yeah.

EMILY. I don't mind it really. It passes the time.

GEORGE. Yeah. . . . Emily, what do you think? We might work out a kinda telegraph from there to there; and once in a while you could give me a kinda hint or two about one of those algebra problems. I don't mean the answers, Emily, of course not . . . just some little hint. . . .

EMILY. Oh, I think *hints* are allowed. So-ah — if you get stuck, George, you whistle to me; and I'll give you some hints.

GEORGE. Emily, you're just naturally bright, I guess.

EMILY. I figure that it's just the way a person's born.

GEORGE. Yeah. But, you see, I want to be a farmer, and my Uncle Luke says whenever I'm ready I can come over and work on his farm and if I'm any good I can just gradually have it.

EMILY. You mean the house and everything?

[*Enter* MRS. WEBB.]

GEORGE. Yeah. Well, thanks. . . . I better be getting out to the baseball field. Thanks for the talk, Emily. . . . Good afternoon, Mrs. Webb.

MRS. WEBB. Good afternoon, George.

GEORGE. So long, Emily.

EMILY. So long, George.

MRS. WEBB. Emily, come and help me string these beans for the winter. George Gibbs let himself have a real conversation, didn't he? Why, he's growing up. How old would George be?

EMILY. I don't know.

MRS. WEBB. Let's see. He must be almost sixteen.

EMILY. Mamma, I made a speech in class today and I was very good.

MRS. WEBB. You must recite it to your father at supper. What was it about?

EMILY. The Louisiana Purchase. It was like silk off a spool. I'm going to make speeches all my life. . . . Mamma, are these big enough?

MRS. WEBB. Try and get them a little bigger if you can.

EMILY. Mamma, will you answer me a question, serious?

MRS. WEBB. Seriously, dear — not serious.

EMILY. Seriously. Will you?

MRS. WEBB. Of course, I will.

EMILY. Mamma, am I good-looking?

MRS. WEBB. Yes, of course you are. All my children have got good features; I'd be ashamed if they hadn't.

EMILY. Oh, Mamma, that's not what I mean. What I mean is: Am I *pretty?*

MRS. WEBB. I've already told you, yes. Now that's enough of that. You have a nice, young, pretty face. I never heard of such foolishness.

EMILY. Oh, Mamma, you never tell us the truth about anything.

MRS. WEBB. I *am* telling you the truth.

EMILY. Mamma, were *you* pretty?

MRS. WEBB. Yes, I was, if I do say it. I was the prettiest girl in town next to Mamie Cartwright.

EMILY. But, Mamma, you've got to say *some*thing about me. Am I pretty enough . . . to get anybody . . . to get people interested in me?

MRS. WEBB. Emily, you make me tired. Now stop it. You're pretty enough for all normal purposes. Come along now and bring that bowl with you.

EMILY. But, Mamma, you're no help at all.

STAGE MANAGER. Thank you. Thank you! That'll do. We'll have to interrupt again here. Thank you, Mrs. Webb; thank you, Emily.

[MRS. WEBB *and* EMILY *withdraw.*]

There are some more things we've got to explore about this town. This time we're going to go about it in another way: we're going to look back on it from the future. I'm not going to tell you what became of these two families we're seeing most of, because the rest of the play will tell you about them. But take some of these others.

Take Joe Crowell, Jr. Joe was a very bright fellow. He graduated with honors and got a scholarship to Boston Tech — M.I.T., that is. But the war broke out, and Joe died in France. All that education for nothing.

Howie Newsome's still delivering milk at Grover's Corners. He's an old man now, has a lot of help; but he still delivers it himself. Says he gets the feel of the town that way. Carries all the accounts in his head; never has to write down a word.

Mr. Morgan's drugstore ain't the same — it's all citified. Mr. Morgan retired and went to live in San Diego, California, where his daughter married a real-estate man, name of Kerby. Mr. Morgan died there in 1935 and was buried in a lot of palm trees. Kinda lost his religion at the end and took up New Thought or something. They read some newfangled poetry over him and cremated him. The New Hampshire in him sort of broke down in him in that climate, seems like.

The Cartwrights got richer and richer. The house is closed most of the year. They're off eating big dinners in hotels now — in Virginia Hot Springs and Miami Beach. They say the winters are cold here. I see where they've become 'Piscopalians.

The Cartwright interests have just begun building a new bank in Grover's Corners — had to go to Vermont for the marble, sorry to say. And they've asked a friend of mine what they should put in the cornerstone for people to dig up a thousand years from now. Of course, they've put in a copy of the New York

Times and a copy of Mr. Webb's *Sentinel*. We're kind of interested in this, because some scientific fellas have found a way of painting all that reading matter with a kind of glue — silicate glue — that'll make it keep a thousand, two thousand, years. We're putting in a Bible . . . and the Constitution of the United States and a copy of William Shakespeare's plays. What do you say, folks? What do you think? Y'know — Babylon once had two million people in it, and all we know about 'em is the names of the kings and some copies of wheat contracts and . . . the sales of slaves. Yes, every night all those families sat down to supper, and the father came home from his work, and the smoke went up the chimney — same as here. And even in Greece and Rome all we know about the real life of the people is what we can piece together out of the joking poems and the comedies they wrote for the theater back then. So I'm going to have a copy of this play put in the cornerstone and the people a thousand years from now'll know a few simple facts about us — more than the Treaty of Versailles and the Lindbergh flight. See what I mean?

Well — you people a thousand years from now — in the provinces north of New York at the beginning of the twentieth century, people et three times a day: soon after sunrise, at noon, and at sunset. Every seventh day, by law and by religion, was a day of rest, and all work came to a stop. The religion at that time was Christianity. I guess you have some other records about Christianity. The domestic setup was marriage: a binding relation between a male and one female that lasted for life. Christianity strictly forbade killing; but you were allowed to kill animals, and you were allowed to kill human beings in war and government punishings. I guess we don't have to tell you about the government and business forms, because that's the kind of thing people seem to hand down first of all. Let me see now if there's anything else. Oh, yes — at death people were buried in the ground just as they are.

So, friends, this is the way we were in our growing up and in our marrying and in our doctoring and in our living and in our dying. Now we'll return to our day in Grover's Corners: A lot of time has gone by. It's evening. You can hear choir practice going on in the Congregational Church. All the children are at home doing their schoolwork. The day is running down like a tired clock.

[*A choir partially concealed in the orchestra pit has begun singing " Blest Be the Tie That Binds."* SIMON STIMSON *stands directing them. Two ladders have been pushed onto the stage; they serve as indication of the second story in the Gibbs and Webb houses.* GEORGE *and* EMILY *mount them, and apply themselves to their schoolwork.* DR. GIBBS *has entered and is seated in his kitchen, reading.*]

SIMON STIMSON. Now look here, everybody. Music come into the world to give pleasure. Softer! Softer! Get it out of your heads that music's only good when it's loud. You leave loudness to the Methodists. You couldn't beat 'em, even if you wanted to. Now again. Tenors!

GEORGE. Hssst! Emily!

EMILY. Hello.

GEORGE. Hello!

EMILY. I can't work at all. The moonlight's so *terrible*.

GEORGE. Emily, did you get the third problem?

EMILY. Which?

GEORGE. The *third?*

EMILY. Why, yes, George — that's the easiest of them all.

GEORGE. I don't see it. Emily, can you give me a hint?

EMILY. I'll tell you one thing: the answer's in yards.

GEORGE. In yards! How do you mean?

EMILY. In *square* yards.

GEORGE. Oh . . . in square yards.

EMILY. Yes, George, don't you see?

GEORGE. Yeah.

EMILY. In square yards of *wallpaper*.

GEORGE. Wallpaper — oh, I see. Thanks a lot, Emily.

EMILY. You're welcome. My, isn't the moonlight *terrible?* And choir practice going on. I think if you hold your breath you can hear the train all the way to Contookuck. Hear it?

GEORGE. M-m-m. What do you know!

EMILY. Well, I guess I better go back and try to work.

GEORGE. Good night, Emily. And thanks.

EMILY. Good night, George.

SIMON STIMSON. Before I forget it: How many of you will be able to come in Tuesday afternoon and sing at Fred Hersey's wedding? Show your hands. That'll be fine; that'll be right nice. We'll do the same music we did for Jane Trowbridge's last month. . . . Now we'll do " Art thou weary; art thou languid?" It's a question, ladies and gentlemen, make it talk. Ready.

DR. GIBBS. Oh, George, can you come down a minute?

GEORGE. Yes, Pa. (*He descends the ladder.*)

DR. GIBBS. Make yourself comfortable, George; I'll only keep you a minute. George, how old are you?

GEORGE. I? I'm sixteen, almost seventeen.

DR. GIBBS. What do you want to do after school's over?

GEORGE. Why, you know, Pa, I want to be a farmer on Uncle Luke's farm.

DR. GIBBS. You'll be willing, will you, to get up early and milk and feed the stock . . . and you'll be able to hoe and hay all day?

GEORGE. Sure, I will. What are you . . . what do you mean, Pa?

DR. GIBBS. Well, George, while I was in my office today I heard a funny sound. . . . And what do you think it was? It was your mother chopping wood. There you see your mother — getting up early, cooking meals all day long, washing and ironing; and still she has to go out in the back yard and chop wood. I suppose she just got tired of asking you. She just gave up and decided it was easier to do it herself. And you eat her meals and put on the clothes she keeps nice for you, and you run off and play baseball — like she's some hired girl we keep around the house but that we don't like very much. Well, I knew all I had to do was call your attention to it. Here's a handkerchief, son. George, I've decided to raise your spending money twenty-five cents a week. Not, of course, for chopping wood for your mother, because that's a present you give her, but because you're getting older — and I imagine there are lots of things you must find to do with it.

GEORGE. Thanks, Pa.

DR. GIBBS. Let's see — tomorrow's pay-day. You can count on it. Hmm. Probably Rebecca'll feel she ought to have some more too. Wonder what could have happened to your mother. Choir practice never was as late as this before.

GEORGE. It's only half-past eight, Pa.

DR. GIBBS. I don't know why she's in that old choir. She hasn't any more voice than an old crow. . . . Traipsin' around the streets at this hour of the night. . . . Just about time you retired, don't you think?

GEORGE. Yes, Pa.

[GEORGE *mounts to his place on the ladder. Laughter and good nights can be heard on stage left and presently* MRS. GIBBS, MRS. SOAMES, *and* MRS. WEBB *come down Main Street. When they arrive at the center of the stage, they stop.*]

MRS. SOAMES. Good night, Martha. Good night, Mr. Foster.

MRS. WEBB. I'll tell Mr. Webb; I *know*

he'll want to put it in the paper.

MRS. GIBBS. My, it's late!

MRS. SOAMES. Good night, Irma.

MRS. GIBBS. Real nice choir practice, wa'n't it? Myrtle Webb! Look at that moon, will you! Tsk-tsk-tsk. Potato weather, for sure.

MRS. SOAMES. Naturally I didn't want to say a word about it in front of those others, but now we're alone — really, it's the worst scandal that ever was in this town!

MRS. GIBBS. What?

MRS. SOAMES. Simon Stimson!

MRS. GIBBS. Now, Louella!

MRS. SOAMES. But, Julia! To have the organist of a church drink and drunk year after year. You know he was drunk tonight.

MRS. GIBBS. Now, Louella. We all know about Mr. Stimson, and we all know about the troubles he's been through, and Dr. Ferguson knows too; and if Dr. Ferguson keeps him on there in his job, the only thing the rest of us can do is just not to notice it.

MRS. SOAMES. Not to notice it! But it's getting worse.

MRS. WEBB. No, it isn't, Louella. It's getting better. I've been in that choir twice as long as you have. It doesn't happen anywhere near so often. . . . My, I hate to go to bed on a night like this. I better hurry. Those children'll be sitting up till all hours. Good night, Louella. (*She hurries downstage, enters her house, and disappears.*)

MRS. GIBBS. Can you get home safe, Louella?

MRS. SOAMES. It's as bright as day. I can see Mr. Soames scowling at the window now. You'd think we'd been to a dance the way the menfolk carry on.

[*Repeated good nights.* MRS. GIBBS *arrives at her home.*]

MRS. GIBBS. Well, we had a real good time.

DR. GIBBS. You're late enough.

MRS. GIBBS. Why, Frank, it ain't any later 'n usual.

DR. GIBBS. And you stopping at the corner to gossip with a lot of hens.

MRS. GIBBS. Now, Frank, don't be grouchy. Come out and smell my heliotrope in the moonlight.

[*They stroll out arm in arm along the footlights.*]

Isn't that wonderful? What did you do all the time I was away?

DR. GIBBS. Oh, I read — as usual. What were the girls gossiping about tonight?

MRS. GIBBS. Well, believe me, Frank — there is something to gossip about.

DR. GIBBS. Hmm! Simon Stimson far gone, was he?

MRS. GIBBS. Worst I've ever seen him. How'll that end, Frank? Dr. Ferguson can't forgive him forever.

DR. GIBBS. I guess I know more about Simon Stimson's affairs than anybody in this town. Some people ain't made for small-town life. I don't know how that'll end; but there's nothing we can do but just leave it alone. Come, get in.

MRS. GIBBS. No, not yet. . . . Oh, Frank, I'm worried about you.

DR. GIBBS. What are you worried about?

MRS. GIBBS. I think it's my duty to make plans for you to get a real rest and change. And if I get that legacy, well, I'm going to insist on it.

DR. GIBBS. Now, Julia, there's no sense in going over that again.

MRS. GIBBS. Frank, you're just *unreasonable!*

DR. GIBBS. Come on, Julia, it's getting late. First thing you know you'll catch cold. I gave George a piece of my mind tonight. I reckon you'll have your wood chopped for awhile anyway. No, no, start getting upstairs.

MRS. GIBBS. Oh, dear. There's always so many things to pick up, seems like. You know, Frank, Mrs. Fairchild always locks her front door every night. All those people up that part of town do.

DR. GIBBS. They're all getting citified, that's the trouble with them. They haven't got nothing fit to burgle and everybody knows it.

[*They disappear.* REBECCA *climbs up the ladder beside* GEORGE.]

GEORGE. Get out, Rebecca. There's only room for one at this window. You're always spoiling everything.

REBECCA. Well, let me look just a minute.

GEORGE. Use your own window.

REBECCA. I did; but there's no moon there. . . . George, do you know what I think, do you? I think maybe the moon's getting nearer and nearer and there'll be a big 'splosion.

GEORGE. Rebecca, you don't know anything. If the moon were getting nearer, the guys that sit up all night with telescopes would see it first and they'd tell about it, and it'd be in all the newspapers.

REBECCA. George, is the moon shining on South America, Canada, and half the whole world?

GEORGE. Well — prob'ly is.

[*The* STAGE MANAGER *strolls on.*]

STAGE MANAGER. Nine-thirty. Most of the lights are out. No, there's Constable Warren trying a few doors on Main Street. And here comes Editor Webb, after putting his newspaper to bed.

MR. WEBB. Good evening, Bill.

CONSTABLE WARREN. Evenin', Mr. Webb.

MR. WEBB. Quite a moon!

CONSTABLE WARREN. Yepp.

MR. WEBB. All quiet tonight?

CONSTABLE WARREN. Simon Stimson is rollin' around a little. Just saw his wife movin' out to hunt for him, so I looked the other way — there he is now.

[SIMON STIMSON *comes down Main Street from the left, only a trace of unsteadiness in his walk.*]

MR. WEBB. Good evening, Simon. . . . Town seems to have settled down for the night pretty well. . . .

[SIMON STIMSON *comes up to him and pauses a moment.*]

Good evening. . . . Yes, most of the town's settled down for the night, Simon. . . . I guess we better do the same. Can I walk along a ways with you?

[SIMON STIMSON *continues on his way without a word and disappears at the right.*]

Good night.

CONSTABLE WARREN. I don't know how that's goin' to end, Mr. Webb.

MR. WEBB. Well, he's seen a peck of trouble, one thing after another. . . . Oh, Bill . . . if you see my boy smoking cigarettes, just give him a word, will you? He thinks a lot of you, Bill.

CONSTABLE WARREN. I don't think he smokes no cigarettes, Mr. Webb. Leastways, not more'n two or three a year. He don't belong to that crowd that hangs out down by the gully.

MR. WEBB. Hm. . . . I hope not. Well, good night, Bill.

CONSTABLE WARREN. Good night, Mr. Webb. (*Exit*)

MR. WEBB. Who's that up there? Is that you, Myrtle?

EMILY. No, it's me, Papa.

MR. WEBB. Why aren't you in bed?

EMILY. I don't know. I just can't sleep yet, Papa. The moonlight's so *won*-derful. And the smell of Mrs. Gibbs's heliotrope. Can you smell it?

MR. WEBB. Hm. . . . Yes. Haven't any troubles on your mind, have you, Emily?

EMILY. *Troubles*, Papa. *No.*

MR. WEBB. Well, enjoy yourself, but don't let your mother catch you. Good night, Emily.

EMILY. Good night, Papa.

[MR. WEBB *crosses into the house, whistling " Blest Be the Tie That Binds," and disappears.*]

REBECCA. I never told you about that letter Jane Crofut got from her minister when she was sick. The minister of her church in the town she was in before she came here. He wrote Jane a letter and on the envelope the address was like this. It said: Jane Crofut, The Crofut Farm, Grover's Corners, Sutton County, New Hampshire, United States of America.

GEORGE. What's funny about that?

REBECCA. But listen, it's not finished: the United States of America, Continent of North America, Western Hemisphere, the Earth, the Solar System, the Universe, the Mind of God — that's what it said on the envelope.

GEORGE. What do you know!

REBECCA. And the postman brought it just the same.

GEORGE. What do you know!

STAGE MANAGER. That's the end of the first act, friends. You can go and smoke now, those that smoke.

For Discussion of Act I

1. How soon do you realize that the Stage Manager is not an ordinary character in a play? Would you say he was even an ordinary human being? Discuss. What is the first hint that he intends to take liberties with time?

2. Compare the description of the scenes in *The Ghost Patrol* with the description the Stage Manager uses to give the setting for this play. How do they differ? What advantages does each method have?

3. Find the speech which explains the purpose of the play. Does the first act achieve this purpose? What sort of happenings filled this act? List some of them. Were any unusual? What appeal do they have for an audience?

4. Does the admission that Grover's Corners pays little attention to social injustice on the one hand, or culture and beauty on the other, affect your attitude toward the town? Recall the evidences of " culture " Editor Webb lists as typical of his town. Are they familiar to you?

5. In a play intended simply to picture the life of a town, you do not expect the plot to be prominent, but Act I presents several situations that hold promise of future action. What are they? What guesses can you make about future developments arising from these situations?

6. What different relationships between members of families or between neighbors have been presented in this act? How do the parents handle their children's failings or foolishness? Explain whether the Webb and Gibbs families are being *contrasted* or *paralleled* in the play.

7. The end of the act in a play always has special significance. Why does the author choose Rebecca's item about the peculiarly addressed letter to end this one?

ACT II

The tables and chairs of the two kitchens are still on the stage. The ladders have been withdrawn. The STAGE MANAGER *has been at his accustomed place, watching the audience return to its seats.*

STAGE MANAGER. Three years have gone by. Yes, the sun's come up over a thousand times. Summers and winters have cracked the mountains a little bit more, and the rains have brought down some of the dirt. Some babies that weren't even born before have begun talking regular sentences already; and a number of people who thought they were right young and spry have noticed that they can't bound up a flight of stairs like they used to, without their heart fluttering a little. Some older sons are sitting at the head of the table, and some people I know are having their meat cut up for them.

All that can happen in a thousand days. Nature's been pushing and contriving in other ways, too: a number of young people fell in love and got married. Yes, the mountain got bit away a few fractions of an inch, millions of gallons of water went by the mill, and here and there a new home was set up under a roof. Almost everybody in the world gets married. You know what I mean? In our town there aren't hardly any exceptions. Most everybody in the world climbs into their graves married.

The first act was called " The Daily Life." This act is called " Love and Marriage." There's another act coming after this; I reckon you can guess what that's about.

So it's three years later. It's 1904. It's July 7, just after high-school commencement. That's the time most of our young people jump up and get married. Soon as they've passed their last examinations in solid geometry and Cicero's orations, looks like they suddenly feel themselves fit to be married.

It's early morning. Only this time it's been raining. It's been pouring and thundering. Mrs. Gibbs's garden, and Mrs. Webb's here — drenched. All those bean poles and pea vines — drenched. All yesterday over there on Main Street the rain looked like curtains being blown along. Hm . . . it may begin again any minute.

There! You can hear the five-forty-five for Boston. And here comes Howie Newsome delivering the milk. And there's Si Crowell delivering the papers like his brother before him. You remember about his brother — all that education he's going to get and that'll be wasted? And there's Mrs. Gibbs and Mrs. Webb come down to make breakfast, just as though it were an ordinary day. I don't have to point out to the women in my audience that those ladies they see before them, both those ladies cooked three meals a day — one of 'em for twenty years, the other for forty — and no

summer vacation. They brought up two children apiece, washed, cleaned the house — and never a nervous breakdown. Never thought themselves hard-used, either.

It's like what one of those Middle West poets said: You've got to love life to have life, and you've got to have life to love life.[1] . . . It's what they call a vicious circle.

[SI CROWELL *has entered, hurling imaginary newspapers into doorways.* HOWIE NEWSOME *has come along Main Street with* BESSIE.]

HOWIE NEWSOME. Git-ap, Bessie.

SI CROWELL. Morning, Howie.

HOWIE NEWSOME. Morning, Si. Anything in the papers I ought to know?

SI CROWELL. Nothing much, except we're losing about the best baseball pitcher Grover's Corners ever had.

HOWIE NEWSOME. Reckon he was. He's been standing off the whole of south New Hampshire singlehanded, looks like.

SI CROWELL. He could hit and run bases, too.

HOWIE NEWSOME. Yep. Mighty fine ball player. . . . Bessie! I guess I can stop and talk if I've a mind to!

SI CROWELL. I don't see how he could give up a thing like that just to get married. Would you, Howie?

HOWIE NEWSOME. Can't tell, Si. Never had no talent that way.

[CONSTABLE WARREN *enters. They exchange good mornings.*]

You're up early, Bill.

CONSTABLE WARREN. Seein' if there's anything I can do to prevent a flood. River's been risin' all night.

HOWIE NEWSOME. Si Crowell's all worked up here about George Gibbs's retiring from baseball.

CONSTABLE WARREN. Yes, sir; that's the way it goes. Back in eighty-four we

[1] See "Lucinda Matlock," page 275. Does he quote the exact words? Is the meaning accurate?

had a player, Si — even George Gibbs couldn't touch him. Name of Hank Todd. Went down to Maine and become a parson. Wonderful ball player. . . . Howie, how did the weather look to you?

HOWIE NEWSOME. No, 'tain't bad. Think maybe it'll clear up for good.

[CONSTABLE WARREN *and* SI CROWELL *continue on their way.* HOWIE NEWSOME *brings the milk first to* MRS. GIBBS's *house. She meets him by the trellis.*]

MRS. GIBBS. Good morning, Howie. Do you think it's going to rain again?

HOWIE NEWSOME. Morning, Mrs. Gibbs. It rained so heavy, I think maybe it'll clear up.

MRS. GIBBS. Certainly hope it will.

HOWIE NEWSOME. How much did you want today?

MRS. GIBBS. I guess I'll need three-a-milk and two-a-cream, Howie. I'm going to have a house full of relations.

HOWIE NEWSOME. My wife says to tell you we both hope they'll be very happy, Mrs. Gibbs. Know they *will.*

MRS. GIBBS. Thanks a lot, Howie. Tell your wife I hope she gits there to the wedding.

HOWIE NEWSOME. Yes, she'll be there; she'll be there if she kin. (*He crosses to* MRS. WEBB's *house.*) Morning, Mrs. Webb.

MRS. WEBB. Oh, good morning, Mr. Newsome. I told you four quarts of milk, but I hope you can spare me another.

HOWIE NEWSOME. Yes'm . . . and the two of cream.

MRS. WEBB. Will it rain all day, Mr. Newsome?

HOWIE NEWSOME. No'm. Just sayin' to Mrs. Gibbs as how it may lighten up. Mrs. Newsome told me to tell you as how we hope they'll both be very happy, Mrs. Webb. Know they *will.*

MRS. WEBB. Thank you, and thank Mrs. Newsome; and we hope to see you all at the wedding.

HOWIE NEWSOME. Yes, Mrs. Webb. We

hope to git there. Couldn't miss that. Chck! Bessie!

[*Exit* HOWIE NEWSOME. DR. GIBBS *descends in his shirt sleeves, and sits down at his breakfast table.*]

DR. GIBBS. Well, Ma, the day has come. You're losin' one of your chicks.

MRS. GIBBS. Frank Gibbs, don't you say another word. I feel like crying every minute. Sit down and drink your coffee.

DR. GIBBS. The groom's up shaving himself. Whistling and singing, like he's glad to leave us. Every now and then he says " I do " to the mirror, but it don't sound convincing to me.

MRS. GIBBS. I declare I don't know how he'll get along. I've arranged his clothes and seen to it he's put warm things on — Frank, they're too young! Emily won't think of such things. He'll catch his death of cold within a week. . . . Here's something I made for you.

DR. GIBBS. Why, Julia Hersey! French toast!

MRS. GIBBS. 'Tain't hard to make, and I had to do something.

DR. GIBBS. I remember my wedding morning, Julia.

MRS. GIBBS. Now don't start that, Frank Gibbs. I tell you I can't stand it.

DR. GIBBS. I was the scaredest young fella in the State of New Hampshire. I thought I'd made a mistake for sure. And when I saw you comin' down that aisle I thought you were the prettiest girl I'd ever seen, but the only trouble was that I'd never seen you before. There I was in the Congregational Church marryin' a total stranger.

MRS. GIBBS. And how do you think I felt! . . . Did you hear Rebecca stirring about upstairs?

DR. GIBBS. Only morning in the year she hasn't been managing everybody's business. She's shut up in her room. I got the impression that maybe she's crying.

MRS. GIBBS. Good Lord! This has got

to stop. . . . Rebecca! Rebecca! Everything's getting cold down here.

[GEORGE *comes rattling down the stairs, very brisk.*]

GEORGE. Good morning, everybody. Only five more hours to live. (*Makes the gesture of cutting his throat.*)

MRS. GIBBS. Where are you going?

GEORGE. Just stepping across the grass to see my girl.

MRS. GIBBS. Now, George! You take an umbrella, or I won't let you out of this house.

GEORGE. Aw, Ma. It's just a *step!*

MRS. GIBBS. From tomorrow on you can kill yourself in all weathers; but while you're in my house you live wisely, thank you. There are your overshoes right there in the hall. And here's an umbrella.

GEORGE. Aw, Ma!

MRS. GIBBS. Maybe Mrs. Webb isn't used to callers at seven in the morning. Take a cup-a-coffee first.

GEORGE. Be back in a minute. (*He crosses the stage, leaping over the puddles.*) Good morning, Mother Webb.

MRS. WEBB. Goodness! You frightened me! Now, George, you can come in a minute out of the wet, but you know I can't ask you in.

GEORGE. Why not?

MRS. WEBB. George, you know's well as I do: the groom can't see his bride on his wedding day, not until he sees her in church.

GEORGE. Aw! That's just a superstition.

[*Enter* MR. WEBB.]

MR. WEBB. Good morning, George.

GEORGE. Mr. Webb, you don't believe in that superstition, do you?

MR. WEBB. There's a lot of common sense in some superstitions, George.

MRS. WEBB. Millions have folla'd it, George, and you don't want to be the first to fly in the face of custom.

GEORGE. How is Emily?

MRS. WEBB. She hasn't waked up yet. I haven't heard a sound out of her.

GEORGE. Emily's *asleep!*

MRS. WEBB. No wonder! We were up till all hours, sewing and packing. I'll tell you what I'll do; you set down here a minute with Mr. Webb and drink this cup of coffee, and I'll go upstairs and see she doesn't come down and surprise you. There's some bacon, too; but don't be long about it.

[*Exit* MRS. WEBB. *Embarrassed silence.*]

MR. WEBB. Well, George, how are you?

GEORGE. Oh, fine. I'm fine. (*Pause*) Mr. Webb, what sense could there be in a superstition like that?

MR. WEBB. Well, you see, on her wedding morning a girl's head's apt to be full of . . . clothes and things like that. Don't you think that's probably it?

GEORGE. Ye-e-s. I never thought of that.

MR. WEBB. A girl's apt to be a mite nervous on her wedding day. (*Pause*)

GEORGE. I wish a fellow could get married without all that marching up and down.

MR. WEBB. Well, every man that's ever lived has felt that way about it, George; but it hasn't done much good. It's the women that have built up weddings, my boy. From now on they have it pretty much as they like. . . . All those good women standing shoulder to shoulder making sure that the knot's tied in a mighty public way.

GEORGE. But . . . you *believe* in it, don't you, Mr. Webb?

MR. WEBB. Oh, yes; oh, yes. Don't you misunderstand me, my boy. Marriage is a wonderful thing — wonderful thing. And don't you forget that, George.

GEORGE. No, sir. Mr. Webb, how old were you when you got married?

MR. WEBB. Well, you see, I'd been to college and I'd taken a little time to get settled. But Mrs. Webb — she wasn't much older than what Emily is. Oh, age hasn't much to do with it, George — not compared to other things.

GEORGE. What were you going to say, Mr. Webb?

MR. WEBB. Oh, I don't know — was I going to say something? (*Pause*) George, I was thinking the other night of some advice my father gave me when I got married. Charles, he said, Charles, start out early showing who's boss, he said. Best thing to do is to give an order, even if it don't make sense; just so she'll learn to obey And he said: If anything about your wife irritates you — her conversation, or anything — just get up and leave the house. That'll make it clear to her, he said. And, ah, yes! he said never, *never* let your wife know how much money you have, never.

GEORGE. Well, Mr. Webb . . . I don't think I could . . .

MR. WEBB. So I took the opposite of my father's advice and I've been happy ever since. And let that be a lesson to you, George, never to ask advice on personal matters. . . . George, are you going to raise chickens on your farm?

GEORGE. What?

MR. WEBB. Are you going to raise chickens on your farm?

GEORGE. Uncle Luke's never been much interested, but I thought —

MR. WEBB. A book came into my office the other day, George, on the Philo System of raising chickens. I want you to read it. I'm thinking of beginning in a small way in the back yard, and I'm going to put an incubator in the cellar —

[*Enter* MRS. WEBB.]

MRS. WEBB. Charles, are you talking about that old incubator again? I thought you two'd be talking about things worth while.

MR. WEBB. Well, Myrtle, if you want to give the boy some good advice, I'll go upstairs and leave you alone with him.

MRS. WEBB. Now, George, I'm sorry, but I've got to send you away so that Emily can come down and get some breakfast. She told me to tell you that she sends you her love, but that she doesn't want to lay eyes on you. So good-by, George.

[GEORGE *crosses the stage to his own home and disappears.*]

MR. WEBB. Myrtle, I guess you don't know about that older superstition.

MRS. WEBB. What do you mean, Charles?

MR. WEBB. Since the cave men: the groom shouldn't be left alone with his father-in-law on the day of the wedding, or near it. Now don't forget that!

STAGE MANAGER. Thank you. Thank you, everybody. Now I have to interrupt again here. You see, we want to know how all this began — this wedding, this plan to spend a lifetime together. I'm awfully interested in how big things like that begin. You know how it is. You're twenty-one or twenty-two, and you make some decisions; then whisssh! you're seventy. You've been a lawyer for fifty years, and that white-haired lady at your side has eaten over fifty thousand meals with you. How do such things begin?

George and Emily are going to show you now the conversation they had when they first knew that . . . that . . . as the saying goes . . . they were meant for one another. But before they do it I want you to try and remember what it was like when you were young, when you were fifteen or sixteen. For some reason it is very hard to do: those days when even the little things in life could be almost too exciting to bear. And particularly the days when you were first in love; when you were like a person sleep-walking, and you didn't quite see the street you were in and didn't quite hear everything that was said to you. You're just a little bit crazy. Will you remember that, please?

Now they'll be coming out of high school at three o'clock. George has just been elected president of the junior class; and, as it's June, that means he'll be president of the senior class all next

year. And Emily's just been elected secretary and treasurer. I don't have to tell
you how important that is. (*He places
a board across the backs of two chairs,
parallel to the footlights, and places two
high stools behind it. This is the counter
of* MR. MORGAN's *drugstore.*) All ready!

[*Emily, carrying an armful of imaginary
schoolbooks, comes along Main Street
from the left.*]

EMILY. I can't, Louise. I've got to go
home. Good-by. . . . Oh, Earnestine!
Earnestine! Can you come over tonight
and do algebra? I did the first and third
in study hall. No, they're not hard. But,
Earnestine, that Caesar's awful hard. I
don't see why we have to do a thing
like that. Come over about seven. Tell
your mother you *have* to. G'by. . . .
G'by, Helen. G'by, Fred.

[GEORGE, *also carrying books, catches up
with her.*]

GEORGE. Can I carry your books home
for you, Emily?

EMILY (*coldly*). Thank you. (*She
gives them to him.*)

GEORGE. Excuse me a minute, Emily.
. . . Say, Bob, get everything ready. I'll
be there in a quarter of an hour. If I'm a
little late, start practice anyway. And
give Herb some long high ones. His eye
needs a lot of practice. Seeya later.

EMILY. Good-by, Lizzy.

GEORGE. Good-by, Lizzy. . . . I'm awfully glad you were elected, too, Emily.

EMILY. Thank you.

[*They have been standing on Main
Street, almost against the back wall.*
GEORGE *is about to take the first steps
toward the audience when he stops
again.*]

GEORGE. Emily, why are you mad at
me?

EMILY. I'm not mad at you.

GEORGE. You . . . you treat me so
funny.

EMILY. Well, I might as well say it
right out, George. I don't like the whole
change that's come over you in the last
year. I'm sorry if that hurts your feelings, but I've just got to tell the truth
and shame the devil.

GEORGE. I'm awfully sorry, Emily.
Wha-a-what do you mean?

EMILY. Well, up to a year ago I used
to like you a lot. And I used to watch
you as you did everything . . . because
we'd been friends so long . . . and then
you began spending all your time at
baseball . . . and you never even spoke
to anybody any more; not even to your
own family you didn't . . . and, George,
it's a fact, you've got awful conceited
and stuck-up, and all the girls say so.
They may not say so to your face, but
that's what they say about you behind
your back; and it hurts me to hear them
say it, but I've got to agree with them
a little. I'm sorry if it hurts your feelings
. . . but I can't be sorry I said it.

GEORGE. I . . . I'm glad you said it,
Emily. I never thought that such a thing
was happening to me. I guess it's hard
for a fella not to have faults creep into
his character.

[*They take a step or two in silence, then
stand still in misery.*]

EMILY. I always expect a man to be
perfect, and I think he should be.

GEORGE. Oh . . . I don't think it's possible to be perfect, Emily.

EMILY. Well, my father is and, as far
as I can see, your father is. There's no
reason on earth why you shouldn't be,
too.

GEORGE. Well, Emily . . . I feel it's
the other way round. That men aren't
naturally good, but girls are. Like you
and your mother and my mother.

EMILY. Well, you might as well know
right now that I'm not perfect. It's not
as easy for a girl to be perfect as a man,
because we girls are more nervous. Now
I'm sorry I said all that about you. I
don't know what made me say it.

GEORGE. No, no — I guess if it's the

truth you ought to say it. You stick to it, Emily.

EMILY. I don't know if it's the truth or not. And I suddenly feel that it isn't important at all.

GEORGE. Emily, would you like an ice-cream soda, or something, before you go home?

EMILY. Well, thank you. . . . I would.

[*They come into the drugstore and seat themselves on the stools.*]

STAGE MANAGER (*as* MR. MORGAN). Hello, George. Hello, Emily. What'll you have? Why, Emily Webb, what've you been crying about?

GEORGE (*groping for an explanation*). She . . . she just got an awful scare, Mr. Morgan. She almost got run over by that hardware-store wagon. Everybody always says that Tom Huckins drives like a crazy man.

STAGE MANAGER. Here, take a drink of water, Emily. You look all shook up. . . . There! Now, what'll you have?

EMILY. I'll have a strawberry phosphate, thank you, Mr. Morgan.

GEORGE. No, no. You go and have an ice-cream soda with me, Emily. Two strawberry ice-cream sodas, Mr. Morgan.

STAGE MANAGER (*working the faucets*). Yes, sir. I tell you, you've got to look both ways before you cross Main Street these days. Gets worse every year. There are a hundred and twenty-five horses in Grover's Corners this minute I'm talking to you. State inspector was in here yesterday. And now they're bringing in these auto-mobiles, the best thing to do is to just stay home. Why, I can remember the time when a dog could lie down all day in the middle of Main Street and nothing would come to disturb him. . . . Yes, Miss Ellis; be with you in a minute. . . . Here are your sodas. Enjoy 'em. (*He goes off.*)

EMILY. They're so expensive.

GEORGE. No, no — don't you think of that. We're celebrating. First, we're celebrating our election. And then do you know what else I'm celebrating?

EMILY. No.

GEORGE. I'm celebrating because I've got a friend who tells me all the things that ought to be told me.

EMILY. George, *please* don't think of that. I don't know why I said it. It's not true. You're —

GEORGE. No, you stick to it, Emily. I'm glad you spoke to me like you did. But you'll see: I'm going to change so quick — you bet I'm going to change. And, Emily, I want to ask you a favor.

EMILY. What?

GEORGE. Emily, if I go away to State Agriculture College next year, will you write me a letter once in a while?

EMILY. I certainly will. I certainly will, George. (*Pause*) It certainly seems like being away three years you'd get out of touch with things.

GEORGE. No, no. I mustn't do that. You see, I'm not only going to be just a farmer. After awhile, maybe, I'll run for something to get elected. So your letters'll be very important to me; you know, telling me what's going on here and everything. . . .

EMILY. Just the same, three years is a long time. Maybe letters from Grover's Corners wouldn't be so interesting after a while. Grover's Corners isn't a very important place when you think of all New Hampshire; but I think it's a very nice town.

GEORGE. The day wouldn't come when I wouldn't want to know everything that's happening here. I know *that's* true, Emily.

EMILY. Well, I'll try to make my letters interesting. (*Pause*)

GEORGE. Y'know, Emily, whenever I meet a farmer I ask him if he thinks it's important to go to agricultural school to be a good farmer.

EMILY. Why, George —

GEORGE. Yeah, and some of them say that it's even a waste of time. You can get all those things, anyway, out of the pamphlets the government sends out.

And Uncle Luke's getting old — he's about ready for me to start in taking over his farm tomorrow, if I could.

EMILY. My!

GEORGE. And, like you say, being gone all that time . . . in other places and meeting other people . . . If anything like that can happen, I don't want to go away. I guess new people aren't any better than old ones. I'll bet they almost never are. Emily, I feel that you're as good a friend as I've got. I don't need to go and meet the people in other towns.

EMILY. But, George, maybe it's very important for you to go and learn all that about cattle judging and soils and those things. And if you're going into politics, maybe you ought to meet people from other parts of the state . . . of course, I don't know.

GEORGE (*after a pause*). Emily, I'm going to make up my mind right now. I won't go. I'll tell Pa about it tonight.

EMILY. Why, George, I don't see why you have to decide right now. It's a whole year away.

GEORGE. Emily, I'm glad you spoke to me about that . . . that fault in my character. And what you said was right; but there was *one* thing wrong in it, and that was when you said that for a year I wasn't noticing people, and . . . you, for instance. Listen, Emily . . . you say you were watching me when I did everything. . . . Why, I was doing the same about you all the time. Why, sure — I always thought about you as one of the chief people I thought about. I always made sure where you were sitting on the bleachers, and who you were with. And we've always had lots of talks . . . and joking, in the halls; and they always meant a lot to me. Of course, they weren't as good as the talk we're having now.

George and Emily make an important discovery. (Culver)

Lately I'd been noticing that you'd been acting kind of funny to me; and for three days I've been trying to walk home with you, but something's always got in the way. Yesterday I was standing over against the wall waiting for you, and you walked home with Miss Corcoran.

EMILY. George! . . . Life's awful funny! How could I have known that? Why, I thought —

GEORGE. Listen, Emily, I'm going to tell you why I'm not going to agricultural school. I think that once you've found a person that you're very fond of . . . I mean a person who's fond of you, too — at least enough to be interested in your character . . . Well, I think that's just as important as college is, and even more so. That's what I think.

EMILY. I think it's awfully important, too.

GEORGE. Emily.

EMILY. Yes, George.

GEORGE. Emily, if I improve and make a big change . . . would you be . . . I mean, could you be . . .

EMILY. I . . . I am now; I always have been. (*Pause*)

GEORGE. So I guess this is an important talk we've been having.

EMILY. Yes.

GEORGE (*taking a deep breath and straightening his back*). Wait just a minute and I'll take you home. (*He rises and goes to the* STAGE MANAGER, *who appears and comes toward him.*) Mr. Morgan, I'll have to go home and get the money to pay you for this. It'll only take me a minute.

STAGE MANAGER. What's that? George Gibbs, do you mean to tell me —

GEORGE. Yes, but I had reasons, Mr. Morgan. Look, here's my gold watch to keep until I come back with the money.

STAGE MANAGER. That's all right. Keep your watch. I'll trust you.

GEORGE. I'll be back in five minutes.

STAGE MANAGER. I'll trust you ten years, George — not a day more. . . . Got all over your shock, Emily?

EMILY. Yes, thank you, Mr. Morgan. It was nothing.

GEORGE (*taking up the books from the counter*). I'm ready.

[*They walk in grave silence down the stage, turn, and pass through the trellis at the Webbs's back door and disappear.*]

STAGE MANAGER. Thank you, Emily. Thank you, George. . . . Now before we go on to the wedding, there are still some more things we ought to know about this — about this marriage. I want to know some more about how the parents took it; but what I want to know most of all is — oh, you know what I mean — what Grover's Corners thought about marriage, anyway. You know's well as I do: people are never able to say right out what they think of money, or death, or fame, or marriage. You've got to catch it between the lines; you've got to *over*hear it.

Oh, Doctor! Mrs. Gibbs!

[*They appear at their side of the stage and exchange a glance of understanding with him. The* STAGE MANAGER *lays across two chairs the same plank that served as a drugstore counter, and it has now become* MRS. GIBBS's *ironing board.* DR. GIBBS *sits down in a rocker and smokes.* MRS. GIBBS *irons a moment in silence, then goes to the foot of the stairs.*]

MRS. GIBBS (*calling*). Rebecca! It's time you turned out your light and went to sleep. George, you'd better get some sleep, too.

REBECCA'S VOICE. Ma, I haven't finished my English.

MRS. GIBBS. What? Well, I bet you haven't been working, Rebecca. You've been reading that Sears Roebuck catalogue, that's what you've been doing. All right, I'll give you ten more minutes. If you haven't finished by then, you'll just have to fail the course and be a disgrace to your father and me. . . . George, what are you doing?

GEORGE'S VOICE (*hurt*). I'm doing history.

MRS. GIBBS. Well, you'd better go to bed. You're probably sleeping at the desk as it is. (*She casts an amused eye at her husband and returns to her ironing.*)

DR. GIBBS. I had a long talk with the boy today.

MRS. GIBBS. Did you?

DR. GIBBS. I tell you, Mrs. G., there's nothing so terrifying in the world as a son. The relation of a father to a son is the confounded awkwardest — I always come away feeling like a soggy sponge of hypocrisy.

MRS. GIBBS. Well, a mother and a daughter's no picnic, let me tell you.

DR. GIBBS. George is set on it: he wants to marry Emily soon as school's out and take her right on to the farm. (*Pause*) He says he can sit up nights and learn agriculture from government pamphlets, without going to college for it.

MRS. GIBBS. He always was crazy about farming. Gets that from my people.

DR. GIBBS. At a pinch I guess he could start in farming; but I swear I think he's too young to get married. Julia, he's just a green, half-grown kid. He isn't ready to be a family man.

MRS. GIBBS. No, he ain't. You're right. But he's a good boy and I wouldn't like to think of him being alone out there . . . coming into town Satiddy nights, like any old farm hand, tuckered out from work and looking for excitement. He might get into bad ways. It wouldn't be enough fun for him to come and sit by our stove, and holding hands with Emily for a year mightn't be enough either. He might lose interest in her.

DR. GIBBS. Hm.

MRS. GIBBS. Frank, I' been watching her. George is a lucky boy when you think of all the silly girls in the world.

DR. GIBBS. But, Julia, George *married*. That great, gangling, selfish nincompoop.

MRS. GIBBS. Yes, I know. (*She takes up a collar and examines it.*) Frank, what do you do to your collars? Do you gnaw 'em? I never saw such a man for collars.

DR. GIBBS. Julia, when I married you, do you know what one of my terrors was in getting married?

MRS. GIBBS. Pshaw! Go on with you!

DR. GIBBS. I was afraid we weren't going to have material for conversation more'n'ld last us a few weeks. I was afraid we'd run out and eat our meals in silence. That's a fact. You and I've been conversing for twenty years now without any noticeable barren spells.

MRS. GIBBS. Well, good weather, bad weather, 'tain't very choice but I always manage to find something to say. (*Pause*)

DR. GIBBS. What do you think? What do you think, Julia? Shall we tell the boy he can go ahead and get married?

MRS. GIBBS. Seems like it's up to us to decide. Myrtle and Charles Webb are willing. They think it's a good idea to throw the young people into the sea and let 'm sink or swim, as soon as they're ready.

DR. GIBBS. What does that mean? Must we decide right now? This minute?

MRS. GIBBS. There you go putting the responsibility on me!

DR. GIBBS. Here it is, almost April. . . . I'll go up and say a word to him right now before he goes to bed. (*He rises.*) You're sure, Julia? You've nothing more to add?

MRS. GIBBS (*stops ironing a moment*). I don't know what to say. Seems like it's too much to ask, for a big outdoor boy like that to go and get shut up in classrooms for three years. And once he's on the farm he might just as well have a companion, seeing he's found a fine girl like Emily. . . . People are meant to live two-by-two in this world. . . . Yes, Frank, go up and tell him it's all right.

[DR. GIBBS *crosses and is about to call when* MRS. GIBBS, *her hands on her cheeks, staring into the audience, speaks in sharp alarm.*]

Wait a minute! Wait a minute! (*Then, resuming her ironing*) No — go and tell him.

DR. GIBBS. Why did you stop then, Julia?

MRS. GIBBS. Oh, you know: I thought of all those times we went through in the first years when George and Rebecca were babies — you walking up and down with them at three in the morning, the whooping cough, the time George fell off the porch. You and I were twenty-five years old, and more. It's wonderful how one forgets one's troubles, like that. . . . Yes, Frank, go upstairs and tell him. It's worth it.

DR. GIBBS. Yes, they'll have a lot of troubles, but that's none of our business. Let'm. Everybody has a right to his own troubles. You ought to be present, Julia — important occasion like that. I'll call him. . . . George! Oh, George!

GEORGE'S VOICE. Yes, Pa.

DR. GIBBS. Can you come down a minute? Your mother and I want to speak to you.

GEORGE. Yeah, sure.

MRS. GIBBS (*putting her arm through her husband's*). Lord, what fool I am; I'm trembling all over. There's nothing to tremble about.

STAGE MANAGER. Thank you! Thank you! . . . Now we're ready to go on with the wedding.

[*While he talks, the actors remove the chairs and tables and trellises from the Gibbs and Webb homes. They arrange the pews for the church in the back of the stage. The congregation will sit facing the back wall. The aisle of the church is in the middle of the scene. A small platform is placed against the back wall; on this the* STAGE MANAGER *as minister can stand.*]

There are a lot of things to be said about a wedding; there are a lot of thoughts that go on during a wedding. We can't get them all into one wedding, naturally, and especially not into a wedding at Grover's Corners, where they're awfully plain and short. In this wedding I play the minister. That gives me the right to say a few more things about it.

For a while now, the play gets pretty serious. Y'see, some churches say that marriage is a sacrament. I don't quite know what that means, but I can guess. Like Mrs. Gibbs said a few minutes ago: People were made to live two-by-two. This is a good wedding, but people are so put together that even at a good wedding there's a lot of confusion way down deep in people's minds; and we thought that that ought to be in our play, too.

The real hero of this scene isn't on the stage at all, and you know who that is. It's like what one of those European fellas said: Every child born into the world is nature's attempt to make a perfect human being. Well, we've seen nature pushing and contriving for some time now. We all know that nature's interested in quantity; but I think she's interested in quality, too — that's why I'm in the ministry. Maybe she's trying to make another good governor for New Hampshire. And don't forget the other witnesses at this wedding — the ancestors. Millions of them. Most of them set out to live two-by-two, also. Millions of them.

Well, that's all my sermon. 'Twan't very long, anyway.

[*The organ starts playing Handel's " Largo." The congregation streams into the church and sits in silence.* MRS. WEBB, *on the way to her place, turns back and speaks to the audience.*]

MRS. WEBB. I don't know why on earth I should be crying. I suppose there's nothing to cry about. It came over me at breakfast this morning; there was Emily eating her breakfast as she's done for seventeen years, and now she's going off to eat it in someone else's house. I suppose that's it. And Emily! She suddenly said: I can't eat another mouthful, and she put her head down on the table and *she* cried.

[*The choir starts singing " Love Divine, All Love Excelling."* GEORGE, *coming through the audience, has reached the stage. He stares at the congregation a moment, then takes a few steps of withdrawal toward the right proscenium pillar.*]

GEORGE (*darkly, to himself*). I wish I were back at school. . . . I don't want to get married.

[*His mother has left her seat and come toward him. She stops, looking at him anxiously.*]

MRS. GIBBS. George, what's the matter?

GEORGE. Ma, I don't want to grow *old*. Why's everybody pushing me so?

MRS. GIBBS. Why, George . . . you wanted it.

GEORGE. Why do I have to get married at all? Listen, Ma, for the last time I ask you —

MRS. GIBBS. No, no, George . . . you're a man now.

GEORGE. Listen, Ma, you never listen to me. All I want to do is to be a fella. Why do —

MRS. GIBBS. George! If anyone should hear you! Now stop. Why, I'm ashamed of you!

GEORGE (*passing his hand over his forehead*). What's the matter? I've been dreaming. Where's Emily?

MRS. GIBBS. Gracious! You gave me such a turn.

GEORGE. Cheer up, Ma. What are you looking so funny for? Cheer up; I'm getting married.

MRS. GIBBS. Let me catch my breath a minute.

GEORGE. Now, Ma, you save Thursday nights. Emily and I are coming over to dinner every Thursday night . . . you'll see. Ma, what are you crying for? Come on, we've got to get ready for this.

[*In the meantime* EMILY, *in white and wearing her wedding veil, has come through the audience and mounted on to the stage. She, too, draws back when she sees the congregation in the church. The choir begins " Blest Be the Tie That Binds."*]

EMILY. I never felt so alone in my whole life. And George over there, looking so . . . I *hate* him. I wish I were dead. Papa! Papa!

MR. WEBB (*leaving his seat in the pews and coming toward her anxiously*). Emily! Emily! Now don't get upset.

EMILY. But, Papa, I don't want to get married.

MR. WEBB. Sh-sh — Emily. Everything's all right.

EMILY. Why can't I stay for a while just as I am? Let's go away.

MR. WEBB. No, no, Emily. Now stop and think.

EMILY. Don't you remember that you used to say — all the time you used to say that I was *your* girl. There must be lots of places we can go to. Let's go away. I'll work for you. I could keep house.

MR. WEBB. Sh. . . . You mustn't think of such things. You're just nervous, Emily. Now, now — you're marrying the best young fellow in the world. George is a fine fellow.

EMILY. But, Papa —

MR. WEBB. George! George!

[MRS. GIBBS *returns to her seat.* GEORGE *hears* MR. WEBB *and looks up.* MR. WEBB *beckons to him. They move to the center of the stage.*]

I'm giving away my daughter, George. Do you think you can take care of her?

GEORGE. Mr. Webb, I want to . . . I want to try. Emily, I'm going to do my best. I love you, Emily. I need you.

EMILY. Well, if you love me, help me. All I want is someone to love me.

GEORGE. I will, Emily.

EMILY. If ever I'm sick or in trouble, that's what I mean.

GEORGE. Emily, I'll try. I'll try.

EMILY. And I mean for ever. Do you hear? For ever and ever.

[*They fall into each other's arms. The March from* Lohengrin *is heard.*]

MR. WEBB. Come, they're waiting for us. Now you know it'll be all right. Come, quick.

[GEORGE *slips away and takes his place beside the* STAGE MANAGER-CLERGYMAN. EMILY *proceeds up the aisle on her father's arm.*]

STAGE MANAGER. Do you, George, take this woman, Emily, to be your wedded wife, to have . . .

[MRS. SOAMES *has been sitting in the last row of the congregation. She now turns to her neighbors and speaks in a shrill voice.*]

MRS. SOAMES. Perfectly lovely wedding! Loveliest wedding I ever saw. Oh, I do love a good wedding, don't you? Doesn't she make a lovely bride?

GEORGE. I do.

STAGE MANAGER. Do you, Emily, take this man, George, to be your wedded husband . . .

MRS. SOAMES. Don't know *when* I've seen such a lovely wedding. But I always cry. Don't know why it is, but I always cry. I just like to see young people happy, don't you? Oh, I think it's lovely.

[*The ring. The kiss. The stage is suddenly arrested into silent tableau.*]

STAGE MANAGER (*his eyes on the distance, says to the audience*). I've married two hundred couples in my day. Do I believe in it? I don't know. M____ marries N____. Millions of them. The cottage, the gocart, the Sunday afternoon drives in the Ford, the first rheu-

matism, the grandchildren, the second rheumatism, the deathbed, the reading of the will — Once in a thousand times it's interesting. Well, let's have Mendelssohn's " Wedding March "!

[*The organ picks up the March. The bride and groom come down the aisle, radiant but trying to be very dignified.*]

MRS. SOAMES. Aren't they a lovely couple? Oh, I've never been to such a nice wedding. I'm sure they'll be happy. I always say *happiness*, that's the great thing! The important thing is to be happy.

[*The bride and groom reach the steps leading into the audience. A bright light is thrown upon them. They descend into the auditorium and run up the aisle joyously.*]

STAGE MANAGER. That's all the second act. Ten minutes' intermission, folks.

For Discussion of Act II

1. What effect is achieved by having the second act open with the same people and the same activities as the first?

2. How does the rainy wedding day fit the shifting moods of the characters most concerned?

3. How would you describe the personalities of George and Emily? Notice that the dramatist takes care to make each a realistic person, with failings as well as virtues. What failings does each display? What strengths of character?

4. Does the conversation between Emily and George after school help you to understand " how all this began," as the Stage Manager says? Why had Emily resented George's absorption in baseball? Do they seem to realize what a serious step they are approaching? Find lines that show that they do, and others that make them sound young and inexperienced. What are some of the things they keep saying are important?

5. Why do both the parents and the young couple have spells of reluctance to

go on with the wedding? What had been Dr. Gibbs's own terror about getting married? What is your understanding of his statement that " everybody has a right to his own troubles "?

6. Why does the Stage Manager say that this is a " good " wedding? What does Mrs. Soames think of it? What do *you* think of Mrs. Soames? Be careful to give her credit for her good qualities.

7. What titles does the Stage Manager give the first two acts? How do these titles support the purpose of the play? What is your own guess for the title of Act III?

ACT III

During the intermission the audience has seen the actors arranging the stage. On the right-hand side, a little right of the center, ten or twelve ordinary chairs have been placed in three openly spaced rows facing the audience. These are graves in the cemetery.

Toward the end of the intermission the actors enter and take their places. The front row contains, toward the center of the stage, an empty chair; then MRS. GIBBS *and* SIMON STIMSON. *The second row contains, among others,* MRS. SOAMES. *The third row has* WALLY WEBB. *The dead sit in a quiet without stiffness and in a patience without listlessness.*

The STAGE MANAGER *takes his accustomed place and waits for the house lights to go down.*

STAGE MANAGER. This time nine years have gone by, friends — summer, 1913. Gradual changes in Grover's Corners. Horses are getting rarer. Farmers coming into town in Fords. Chief difference is in the young people, far as I can see. They want to go to the moving pictures all the time. They want to wear clothes like they see there . . . want to be citified. Everybody locks their house doors now at night. Ain't seen any burglars in town yet, but everybody's heard about 'em. But you'd be surprised, though — on the whole, things don't change much at Grover's Corners.

Guess you want to know what all these chairs are here fur. Smarter ones have guessed it already. I don't know how you feel about such things, but this certainly is a beautiful place. It's on a hilltop — a windy hilltop — lots of sky, lots of clouds, often lots of sun and moon and stars. You come up here on a fine afternoon and you can see range on range of hills — awful blue they are — up there by Lake Sunapee and Lake Winnipesaukee . . . and way up, if you've got a glass, you can see the White Mountains and Mt. Washington — where North Conway and Conway is. And, of course, our favorite mountain, Mt. Monadnock's right here — and all around it lie these towns — Jaffrey, 'n East Jaffrey, 'n Peterborough, 'n Dublin; and (*then, pointing down in the audience*) there, quite a ways down, is Grover's Corners.

Yes, beautiful spot up here. Mountain laurel and li-lacks. I often wonder why people like to be buried in Woodlawn and Brooklyn when they might pass the same time up here in New Hampshire. Over in that corner (*pointing to stage left*) are the old stones — 1670, 1680. Strong-minded people that come a long way to be independent. Summer people walk around there laughing at the funny words on the tombstones . . . it don't do any harm. And genealogists come up from Boston — get paid by city people for looking up their ancestors. They want to make sure they're Daughters of the American Revolution and of the *Mayflower*. . . . Well, I guess that don't do any harm, either. Wherever you come near the human race, there's layers and layers of nonsense.

Over there are some Civil War vet-

erans too. Iron flags on their graves.
. . . New Hampshire boys . . . had a
notion that the Union ought to be kept
together, though they'd never seen more
than fifty miles of it themselves. All they
knew was the name, friends — the
United States of America. The United
States of America. And they went and
died about it.

This here is the new part of the cemetery. Here's your friend, Mrs. Gibbs.
'N let me see — Here's Mr. Stimson,
organist at the Congregational Church.
And over there's Mrs. Soames, who enjoyed the wedding so — you remember?
Oh, and a lot of others. And Editor
Webb's boy, Wallace, whose appendix
burst while he was on a Boy Scout trip
to Crawford Notch. Yes, an awful lot
of sorrow has sort of quieted down up
here. People just wild with grief have
brought their relatives up to this hill.
We all know how it is. And then time
. . . and sunny days . . . and rainy
days . . . 'n snow . . . tz-tz-tz. We're
all glad they're in a beautiful place, and
we're coming up here ourselves when
our fit's over. This certainly is an important part of Grover's Corners. A lot of
thoughts come up here, night and day,
but there's no post office.

Now I'm going to tell you some things
you know already. You know'm as well
as I do, but you don't take'm out and
look at'm very often. I don't care what
they say with their mouths — everybody
knows that *something* is eternal. And it
ain't houses, and it ain't names, and it
ain't earth, and it ain't even the stars
. . . everybody knows in their bones
that *something* is eternal, and that something has to do with human beings. All
the greatest people ever lived have been
telling us that for five thousand years,
and yet you'd be surprised how people
are always losing hold of it. There's
something way down deep that's eternal
about every human being. (*Pause*) You
know as well as I do that the dead don't
stay interested in us living people for

very long. Gradually, gradually, they
let hold of the earth . . . and the ambitions they had . . . and the pleasures
they had . . . and the things they suffered . . . and the people they loved.
They get weaned away from earth.
That's the way I put it — weaned away.
Yes, they stay here while the earth part
of 'em burns away, burns out; and all
that time they slowly get indifferent to
what's goin' on in Grover's Corners.

They're waitin'. They're waitin' for
something that they feel is comin'. Something important and great. Aren't they
waitin' for the eternal part in them to
come out clear? Some of the things
they're going to say maybe'll hurt your
feelings — but that's the way it is:
mother 'n daughter . . . husband 'n
wife . . . enemy 'n enemy . . . money
'n miser — all those terribly important
things kind of grow pale around here.
And what's left? What's left when memory's gone, and your identity, Mrs.
Smith? (*He looks at the audience a minute, then turns to the stage.*)

Well! There are some *living* people.
There's Joe Stoddard, our undertaker,
supervising a new-made grave. And here
comes a Grover's Corners boy, that left
town to go out West.

[JOE STODDARD *has hovered about in the
background.* SAM CRAIG *enters left,
wiping his forehead from the exertion.
He carries an umbrella and strolls
front.*]

SAM CRAIG. Good afternoon, Joe Stoddard.

JOE STODDARD. Good afternoon, good
afternoon. Let me see now: Do I know
you?

SAM CRAIG. I'm Sam Craig.

JOE STODDARD. Gracious sakes' alive!
Of all people! I should'a knowed you'd
be back for the funeral. You've been
away a long time, Sam.

SAM CRAIG. Yes, I've been away over
twelve years. I'm in business out in Buffalo now, Joe. But I was in the East

when I got news of my cousin's death, so I thought I'd combine things a little and come and see the old home. You look well.

JOE STODDARD. Yes, yes, can't complain. Very sad, our journey today, Samuel.

SAM CRAIG. Yes.

JOE STODDARD. Yes, yes. I always say I hate to supervise when a young person is taken. I see you brought your umbrella. It's going to rain and make it sadder still, seems like. They'll be here in a few minutes now. I had to come here early today — my son's supervisin' at the home.

SAM CRAIG (reading stones). Old Farmer McCarty. I used to do chores for him — after school. He had the lumbago.

JOE STODDARD. Yes, we brought Farmer McCarty here a number of years ago now.

SAM CRAIG (staring at MRS. GIBBS's knees). Why, this is my Aunt Julia. . . . I'd forgotten that she'd . . . of course, of course.

JOE STODDARD. Yes, Doc Gibbs lost his wife two, three years ago . . . about this time. And today's another pretty bad blow for him, too.

MRS. GIBBS (to SIMON STIMSON, in an even voice). That's my sister Carey's boy, Sam — Sam Craig.

SIMON STIMSON. I'm always uncomfortable when they're around.

MRS. GIBBS. Simon.

SIMON STIMSON. They and their nonsense and their idiotic glee at being alive.

MRS. GIBBS. Simon, be patient.

SAM CRAIG. Do they choose their own verses much, Joe?

JOE STODDARD. No . . . not usual. Mostly the bereaved pick a verse.

SAM CRAIG. Doesn't sound like Aunt Julia. There aren't many of those Hersey sisters left now. Let me see. Where are — I wanted to look at my father's and mother's . . .

JOE STODDARD. Over there with the Craigs. . . . Avenue F.

SAM CRAIG (reading SIMON STIMSON's epitaph). He was organist at church, wasn't he? Hm, drank a lot, we used to say.

JOE STODDARD. Nobody was supposed to know about it. He'd seen a peck of trouble. Those musical fellas ain't like the rest of us, I reckon. (Behind his hand) Took his own life, y'know?

SAM CRAIG. Oh, did he?

JOE STODDARD. Hung himself in the attic. They tried to hush it up, but of course it got around. His wife's just married Senator Barstow. Many a time I've seen her, eleven o'clock at night, goin' around the streets huntin' for her husband. Think o' that! Now she's married to Senator Barstow over at Manchester. He chose his own epy-taph. You can see it there. It ain't a verse exactly.

SAM CRAIG. Why, it's just some notes of music! What is it?

JOE STODDARD. Oh, I wouldn't know. It was wrote up in the Boston papers at the time.

SAM CRAIG. Joe, what did she die of?

JOE STODDARD. Who?

SAM CRAIG. My cousin.

JOE STODDARD. Oh, didn't you know? Had some trouble bringing a baby into the world. Let's see, today's Friday — 'twas almost a week ago now.

SAM CRAIG (putting up his umbrella). Did the baby live?

JOE STODDARD (raising his coat collar). No. 'Twas her second, though. There's a little boy 'bout four years old.

SAM CRAIG. The grave's going to be over there?

JOE STODDARD. Yes, there ain't much more room over here among the Gibbses, so they're opening up a whole new Gibbs section over by Avenue B. You'll excuse me now. I see they're comin'.

THE DEAD (not lugubrious, and strongly New England in accent). Rain'll do a lot of good. . . . Yes, reckon things were gettin' downright parched. Don't look like it's goin' to last long, tho'. . . . Lemuel, you remember the floods of seventy-nine? Carried away all the bridges but one.

[*From left to right, at the back of the stage, comes a procession. Four men carry a casket, invisible to us. All the rest are under umbrellas. One can vaguely see* DR. GIBBS, GEORGE, *the* WEBBS, *etc. They gather about a grave in the back center of the stage, a little to the left of center.*]

MRS. SOAMES. Who is it, Julia?

MRS. GIBBS (*without raising her eyes*). My daughter-in-law, Emily Webb.

MRS. SOAMES (*a little surprised, but no emotion*). Well, I declare! The road up here must have been awful muddy. What did she die of, Julia?

MRS. GIBBS. In childbirth.

MRS. SOAMES. Childbirth. (*Almost with a laugh*) I'd forgotten all about that! My, wasn't life awful (*with a sigh*) and wonderful.

SIMON STIMSON (*with a sideways glance*). Wonderful, was it?

MRS. GIBBS. Simon! Now, remember!

MRS. SOAMES. I remember Emily's wedding. Wasn't it a lovely wedding! And I remember her reading the class poem at graduation exercises. Emily was one of the brightest girls ever graduated from high school. I've heard Principal Wilkins say so time after time. I called on them at their new farm just before I died. Perfectly beautiful farm.

A WOMAN FROM AMONG THE DEAD. It's on the same road we lived on.

A MAN AMONG THE DEAD. Yes, just near the Elks' picnic grounds. Remember, Joe? By the lake where we always used to go Fourth of July? Right smart farm.

[*They subside. The group by the grave start singing "Blest Be the Tie That Binds."*]

A WOMAN AMONG THE DEAD. I always liked that hymn. I was hopin' they'd sing a hymn.

A MAN AMONG THE DEAD. My wife — my second wife — knows all the verses of about every hymn there is. It just beats the Dutch — she can go through them all by heart.

[*Pause. Suddenly* EMILY *appears from among the umbrellas. She is wearing a white dress. Her hair is down her back and tied by a white ribbon like a little girl's. She comes slowly, gazing wonderingly at* THE DEAD, *a little dazed. She stops halfway and smiles faintly.*]

EMILY. Hello.

VOICES AMONG THE DEAD. Hello, Emily. H'lo, M's. Gibbs.

EMILY. Hello, Mother Gibbs.

MRS. GIBBS. Emily.

EMILY. Hello. (*The hymn continues.* EMILY *looks back at the funeral. She says dreamily*) It's raining.

MRS. GIBBS. Yes. . . . They'll be gone soon, dear. Just rest yourself.

[EMILY *sits down in the empty chair by* MRS. GIBBS.]

EMILY. It seems thousands and thousands of years since I . . . How stupid they all look. They don't have to look like that!

MRS. GIBBS. Don't look at them now, dear. They'll be gone soon.

EMILY. Oh, I wish I'd been here a long time. I don't like being new here. . . . How do you do, Mr. Stimson?

SIMON STIMSON. How do you do, Emily.

[EMILY *continues to look about her with a wan and wondering smile, but for a moment her eyes do not return to the funeral group. As though to shut out from her mind the thought of that group, she starts speaking to* MRS. GIBBS *with a touch of nervousness.*]

EMILY. Mother Gibbs, George and I have made that farm into just the best place you ever saw. We thought of you all the time. We wanted to show you

" Suddenly Emily appears from among the umbrellas." (*Culver*)

the new barn and a great long ce-ment drinking fountain for the stock. We bought that out of the money you left us.

MRS. GIBBS. I did?

EMILY. Don't you remember, Mother Gibbs — the legacy you left us? Why, it was over three hundred and fifty dollars.

MRS. GIBBS. Yes, yes, Emily.

EMILY. Well, there's a patent device on this drinking fountain so that it never overflows, Mother Gibbs, and it never sinks below a certain mark they have there. It's fine. (*Her voice trails off, and her eyes return to the funeral group.*) It won't be the same to George without me, but it's a lovely farm. (*Suddenly she looks directly at* MRS. GIBBS.) Live people don't understand, do they?

MRS. GIBBS. No, dear — not very much.

EMILY. They're sort of shut up in little boxes, aren't they? I feel as though I knew them last a thousand years ago. . . . My boy is spending the day at Mrs. Carter's. (*She sees* MR. CARTER *among* THE DEAD.) Oh, Mr. Carter, my little boy is spending the day at your house.

MR. CARTER. Is he?

EMILY. Yes, he loves it there. . . . Mother Gibbs, we have a Ford, too. Never gives any trouble. I don't drive, though. Mother Gibbs, when does this feeling go away? Of being . . . one of *them?* How long does it . . .

MRS. GIBBS. Sh! dear. Just wait and be patient.

EMILY (*with a sigh*). I know. . . . Look, they're finished. They're going.

MRS. GIBBS. Sh. . . .

[*The umbrellas leave the stage.* DR. GIBBS *comes over to his wife's grave*

and stands before it a moment. EMILY
looks up at his face. MRS. GIBBS *does
not raise her eyes.*]

EMILY. Look! Father Gibbs is bringing some of my flowers to you. He looks
just like George, doesn't he? Oh, Mother
Gibbs, I never realized before how troubled and how . . . how in the dark live
persons are. From morning till night
that's all they are — troubled.

[DR. GIBBS *goes off.*]

THE DEAD. Little cooler than it was.
. . . Yes, that rain cooled it off a little.
Those northeast winds always do the
same thing, don't they? If it isn't a rain,
it's a three-day blow. . . . Reckon it may
clear up before night; often does.

[*A patient calm falls on the stage. The*
STAGE MANAGER *appears at his proscenium pillar, smoking.* EMILY *sits up
abruptly, with an idea.*]

EMILY. But, Mother Gibbs, one can
go back; one can go back there again
. . . into living. I feel it. I know it. Why,
just then for a moment I was thinking
about . . . about the farm . . . and
for a minute I *was* there, and my baby
was on my lap as plain as day.

MRS. GIBBS. Yes, of course you can.

EMILY. I can go back there and live
all those days over again . . . why not?

MRS. GIBBS. All I can say is, Emily,
don't.

EMILY (*taking a few steps toward the*
STAGE MANAGER). But it's true, isn't it?
I can go and live . . . back there . . .
again.

STAGE MANAGER. Yes, some have tried
— but they soon come back here.

MRS. GIBBS. Don't do it, Emily.

MRS. SOAMES. Emily, don't. It's not
what you think it'd be.

EMILY. But I won't live over a sad
day. I'll choose a happy one — I'll choose
the day I first knew that I loved George.
Why should that be painful?

[*They are silent. Her question turns to*
the STAGE MANAGER.]

STAGE MANAGER. You not only live it,
but you watch yourself living it.

EMILY. Yes?

STAGE MANAGER. And as you watch it,
you see the thing that they — down
there — never know. You see the future.
You know what's going to happen afterward.

EMILY. But is that — painful? Why?

MRS. GIBBS. That's not the only reason
why you shouldn't do it, Emily. When
you've been here longer, you'll see that
our life here is our hope that soon we'll
forget all that, and think only of what's
ahead, and be ready for what's ahead.
When you've been here longer, you'll
understand.

EMILY (*softly*). But, Mother Gibbs,
how can I ever forget that life? It's all
I know. It's all I had.

[MRS. GIBBS *does not answer.*]

Mr. Stimson, did you go back?

SIMON STIMSON (*sharply*). No.

EMILY. Did you, Mrs. Soames?

MRS. SOAMES. Oh, Emily. It isn't wise.
Really, it isn't. All we can do is just warn
you. It won't be what you expect.

EMILY (*slowly*). But it's a thing I
must know for myself. I'll choose a happy day, anyway.

MRS. GIBBS. No. At least, choose an unimportant day. Choose the least important day in your life. It will be important enough.

EMILY (*to the* STAGE MANAGER). Then
it can't be since I was married, or since
the baby was born. I can choose a birthday at least, can't I? . . . I choose my
twelfth birthday.

STAGE MANAGER. All right. February
11, 1899. A Tuesday. . . . Do you want
any special time of day?

EMILY. Oh, I want the whole day.

STAGE MANAGER. We'll begin at dawn.
You remember it had been snowing for
several days; but it had stopped the

night before, and they had begun clearing the roads. The sun's coming up.

EMILY (*with a cry*). There's Main Street. . . . Why, that's Mr. Morgan's drugstore before he changed it! . . . And there's the livery stable. (*She walks toward the back of the stage.*)

STAGE MANAGER. Yes, it's 1899. This is fourteen years ago.

EMILY. Oh, that's the town I knew as a little girl. And, look, there's the old white fence that used to be around our house. Oh, I'd forgotten that! Oh, I love it so! Are *they* inside?

STAGE MANAGER. Yes, your mother'll be coming downstairs in a minute to make breakfast.

EMILY (*softly*). Will she?

STAGE MANAGER. And you remember: your father had been away for several days; he came back on the early-morning train.

EMILY. No . . .

STAGE MANAGER. He'd been back to his college to make a speech — in western New York, at Clinton.

EMILY. Look! There's Howie Newsome. There's our policeman. But he's *dead*; he *died*.

[*The* STAGE MANAGER *retires to his corner. The voices of* HOWIE NEWSOME, CONSTABLE WARREN, *and* JOE CROWELL, JR., *are heard at the left of the stage.*]

HOWIE NEWSOME. Whoa, Bessie! Bessie! . . . Morning, Bill.

CONSTABLE WARREN. Morning, Howie.

HOWIE NEWSOME. You're up early.

CONSTABLE WARREN. Been rescuin' a party; darn near froze to death, down by Polish Town thar. Got drunk and lay out in the snowdrifts. Thought he was in bed when I shook'm.

EMILY. Why, there's Joe Crowell.

JOE CROWELL, JR. Good morning, Mr. Warren. Morning, Howie.

[MRS. WEBB *has appeared in her kitchen, but* EMILY *does not see her until she calls.*]

MRS. WEBB. Chil-*dren!* Wally! Emily! . . . Time to get up.

EMILY. Mamma, here I am! Oh, how young Mamma looks! I didn't know Mamma was ever that young. Oh!

MRS. WEBB. You can come and dress by the kitchen fire, if you like; but hurry.

[HOWIE NEWSOME *has entered along Main Street and brings the milk to* MRS. WEBB's *door.*]

Good morning, Mr. Newsome. Whhhh — it's cold.

HOWIE NEWSOME. Ten below by my barn, Mrs. Webb.

MRS. WEBB. Think of it! Keep yourself wrapped up. (*She takes her bottles in, shuddering.*)

EMILY (*with an effort*). Mamma, I can't find my blue hair ribbon anywhere.

MRS. WEBB. Just open your eyes, dear, that's all. I laid it out for you special — on the dresser, there. If it were a snake, it would bite you.

EMILY. Yes, yes. . . . (*She puts her hand on her heart.*)

[MR. WEBB *comes along Main Street, where he meets* CONSTABLE WARREN.]

MR. WEBB. Good morning, Bill.

CONSTABLE WARREN. Good morning, Mr. Webb. You're up early.

MR. WEBB. Yes, just been back to my old college in New York State. Been any trouble here?

CONSTABLE WARREN. Well, I was called up this mornin' to rescue a Polish fella — darn near froze to death he was.

MR. WEBB. We must get it in the paper.

CONSTABLE WARREN. 'Twan't much.

EMILY (*whispers*). Papa.

[MR. WEBB *shakes the snow off his feet and enters his house.*]

MR. WEBB. Good morning, Mother.

MRS. WEBB. How did it go, Charles?

MR. WEBB. Oh, fine, I guess. I told'm a few things.

MRS. WEBB. Did you sit up on the train all night?

MR. WEBB. Yes. Never could sleep on a Pullman anyway.

MRS. WEBB. Charles, seems to me — we're rich enough so that you could sleep in a train once in a while.

MR. WEBB. Everything all right here?

MRS. WEBB. Yes — can't think of anything that's happened, special. Been right cold. Howie Newsome says it's ten below over to his barn.

MR. WEBB. Yes? Well, it's colder than that at Hamilton College. Students' ears are falling off. It ain't Christian. . . . Paper have any mistakes in it?

MRS. WEBB. None that I noticed. Coffee's ready when you want it.

[*He starts upstairs.*]

Charles! Don't forget; it's Emily's birthday. Did you remember to get her something?

MR. WEBB (*patting his pocket*). Yes, I've got something here.

MRS. WEBB. Goodness sakes! I hope she likes what I got for her. I hunted hard enough for it. Children! Hurry up! Hurry up!

MR. WEBB. Where's my girl? Where's my birthday girl? (*He goes off left.*)

MRS. WEBB. Don't interrupt her now, Charles. You can see her at breakfast. She's slow enough as it is. Hurry up, children! It's seven o'clock. Now, I don't want to call you again.

EMILY (*softly, more in wonder than in grief*). I can't bear it. They're so young and beautiful. Why did they ever have to get old? Mama, I'm here. I'm grown up. I love you all, everything. . . . I can't look at everything hard enough. There's the butternut tree. (*She wanders up Main Street.*) There's Mr. Morgan's drugstore. And there's the high school, for ever and ever and ever. And there's the Congregational Church, where I got married. Oh, dear. Oh, dear. Oh, dear!

[*The STAGE MANAGER beckons partially to her. He points to the house. She says a breathless " yes " and goes to the house.*]

Good morning, Mamma.

MRS. WEBB (*at the foot of the stairs, kissing her in a matter-of-fact way*). Well, now, dear, a very happy birthday to my girl and many happy returns. There are some surprises waiting for you on the kitchen table.

EMILY. Oh, Mamma, you *shouldn't* have. (*She throws an anguished glance at the STAGE MANAGER.*) I can't — I can't.

MRS. WEBB (*facing the audience, over her stove*). But birthday or no birthday, I want you to eat your breakfast good and slow. I want you to grow up and be a good strong girl. (*She goes to the stairs and calls.*) Wally! Wally, wash yourself good. Everything's getting cold down here. (*She returns to the stove with her back to EMILY.*)

[*EMILY opens her parcels.*]

That in the blue paper is from your Aunt Carrie, and I reckon you can guess who brought the post-card album. I found it on the doorstep when I brought in the milk. George Gibbs must have come over in the cold pretty early . . . right nice of him.

EMILY (*to herself*). Oh, George! I'd forgotten that.

MRS. WEBB. Chew that bacon slow. It'll help keep you warm on a cold day.

EMILY (*beginning softly but urgently*). Oh, Mamma, just look at me one minute as though you really saw me. Mamma, fourteen years have gone by. I'm dead. You're a grandmother, Mamma. I married George Gibbs, Mamma. Wally's dead, too. Mamma, his appendix burst on a camping trip to North Conway. We felt just terrible about it — don't you remember? But, just for a moment now we're all together. Mamma, just for a moment we're happy. Let's look at one another.

MRS. WEBB. That in the yellow paper is something I found in the attic among your grandmother's things. You're old enough to wear it now, and I thought you'd like it.

EMILY. And this is from you. Why, Mamma, it's just lovely and it's just what I wanted. It's beautiful! (*She flings her arms around her mother's neck.*)

[*Her mother goes on with her cooking, but is pleased.*]

MRS. WEBB. Well, I hoped you'd like it. Hunted all over. Your Aunt Norah couldn't find one in Concord, so I had to send all the way to Boston. (*Laughingly*) Wally has something for you, too. He made it at manual-training class, and he's very proud of it. Be sure you make a big fuss about it. Your father has a surprise for you, too; don't know what it is myself. Sh — here he comes.

MR. WEBB (*off stage*). Where's my girl? Where's my birthday girl?

EMILY (*in a loud voice to the* STAGE MANAGER). I can't. I can't go on. Oh! Oh. It goes so fast. We don't have time to look at one another. (*She breaks down, sobbing.*)

[*At a gesture from the* STAGE MANAGER, MRS. WEBB *disappears.*]

I didn't realize. So all that was going on and we never noticed. Take me back — up the hill — to my grave. But first — wait! One more look. Good-by, good-by, world. Good-by, Grover's Corners . . . Mamma and Papa. Good-by to clocks ticking . . . and Mamma's sunflowers. And food and coffee. And new-ironed dresses and hot baths . . . and sleeping and waking up. Oh, earth, you're too wonderful for anybody to realize you. (*She looks toward the* STAGE MANAGER *and asks, abruptly, through her tears*) Do any human beings ever realize life while they live it — every, every minute?

STAGE MANAGER. No. (*Pause*) The saints and poets, maybe — they do some.

EMILY. I'm ready to go back. (*She returns to her chair beside* MRS. GIBBS.) Mother Gibbs, I should have listened to you. Now I want to be quiet for a while. . . . Oh, Mother Gibbs, I saw it all. I saw your garden.

MRS. GIBBS. Did you, dear?

EMILY. That's all human beings are! Just blind people.

MRS. GIBBS. Look, it's clearing up. The stars are coming out.

EMILY. Oh, Mr. Stimson, I should have listened to them.

SIMON STIMSON (*with mounting violence; bitingly*). Yes, now you know. Now you know! That's what it was to be alive. To move about in a cloud of ignorance, to go up and down trampling on the feelings of those . . . of those about you. To spend and waste time as though you had a million years. To be always at the mercy of one self-centered passion or another. Now you know — that's the happy existence you wanted to go back and see. Did you shout to 'em? Did you call to 'em?

EMILY. Yes, I did.

SIMON STIMSON. Now you know them as they are: in ignorance and blindness.

MRS. GIBBS (*spiritedly*). Simon Stimson, that ain't the whole truth and you know it.

[THE DEAD *have begun to stir.*]

THE DEAD. Lemuel, wind's coming up, seems like. . . . Oh, dear, I keep remembering things tonight. . . . It's right cold for June, ain't it?

MRS. GIBBS. Look what you've done, you and your rebellious spirit stirring us up here. . . . Emily, look at that star. I forget its name.

THE DEAD. I'm getting to know them all, but I don't know their names. My boy, Joel, was a sailor — knew 'em all. He'd set on the porch evenings and tell 'em all by name. Yes, sir, it was wonderful. A star's mighty good company. Yes, yes. Yes, 'tis.

SIMON STIMSON. Here's one of *them* coming.

THE DEAD. That's funny. 'Taint no time for one of them to be here. Goodness sakes.

EMILY. Mother Gibbs, it's George.

MRS. GIBBS. Sh, dear. You just rest yourself.

EMILY. It's George.

[GEORGE *enters from the left and slowly comes toward them.*]

A MAN FROM AMONG THE DEAD. And my boy, Joel, who knew the stars — he used to say it took millions of years for that speck o' light to git to the earth. Don't seem like a body could believe it, but that's what he used to say — millions of years.

ANOTHER. That's what they say.

[GEORGE *flings himself on* EMILY's *grave.*]

THE DEAD. Goodness! That ain't no way to behave! He ought to be home.

EMILY. Mother Gibbs?

MRS. GIBBS. Yes, Emily?

EMILY. They don't understand much, do they?

MRS. GIBBS. No, dear, not very much.

[*The* STAGE MANAGER *appears at the right, one hand on a dark curtain which he slowly draws across the scene. In the distance a clock is heard striking the hour very faintly.*]

STAGE MANAGER. Most everybody's asleep in Grover's Corners. There are a few lights on. Shorty Hawkins, down at the depot, has just watched the Albany train go by. And at the livery stable somebody's setting up late and talking. . . . Yes, it's clearing up. There are the stars — doing their old, old crisscross journeys in the sky. Scholars haven't settled the matter yet, but they seem to think there are no living beings up there. They're just chalk . . . or fire. Only this one is straining away, straining away all the time to make something of itself. The strain's so bad that every sixteen hours everybody lies down and gets a rest. (*He winds his watch.*) Hm. . . . Eleven o'clock in Grover's Corners. . . . You get a good rest, too. Good night.

[THE END]

For Discussion of Act III

1. Now that you have read Act III, what title would you give it? As you think back to the opening of the play, do you see any special significance in the case the doctor had been attending?

2. Was the general tone of the birthday scene much like others earlier in the play? Did it have the same emotional effect on you? Why, or why not?

3. In a full-length play, the chief characters usually undergo some change in attitude or thinking during the course of the play. Between the beginning and the end of *Our Town* what changes do you notice in Emily and George? in other characters? What caused the changes?

4. The introductory note explained to the reader the significance of the people sitting in rows of chairs. What is the first explanation that a theater audience would get? Why is this representation of the dead in a cemetery easier to accept in Act III than it would have been in the opening scene of the play?

5. Have you ever thought that poetry about death and immortality is unnecessarily obscure? Read the Stage Manager's speech on this subject (p. 388). Is the thought poetic? Does it lose effectiveness from being simply expressed?

6. In a novel written earlier than *Our Town*, Wilder tells a short incident about a man who, like Emily, was permitted after his death to go back to earth for one day — the least eventful day in his life. He soon begged to be allowed to rejoin the dead because he " saw that the living, too, are dead and that we can only be said to be alive in those moments when our hearts are conscious of our treasure." Is this the same effect that Emily's return had on her, or a different one? Find Emily's own sad comment on earthly life and compare the two. Do you think reading the play will make you a little more aware of the many

little kindnesses, the unnoticed good in your own life?

7. In his final speech, what does the Stage Manager imply is the trouble with this world? How are his last words a particularly appropriate ending for the play?

For a Review of the Complete Play

1. Why has the dramatist limited the incidents he presents to simple happenings that occur frequently? How would extraordinary or melodramatic incidents conflict with the basic purpose of the play? Where in the first act does the Stage Manager state exactly what he is trying to show?

2. How would you describe the dialogue in this play? Is it unusual or ordinary? How does it fit the tone and subject matter of the play as a whole? Recall some remarks in the play that you have heard many, many times.

3. The Stage Manager is difficult to describe, but all the other characters can be identified in a phrase. Go down the list of characters on page 360 and describe each one in a few words. Compare your descriptions with those of your classmates, and discuss differences. Can you find similar characters in your own community?

4. How would the people in Grover's Corners get along with the people of the Vermont valley described in the essay " Nothing Ever Happens "? Are their ways and lives markedly similar to or different from those of the city people in *The Ghost Patrol*? Explain.

5. In a review of *Our Town* one critic said, " In the day of great language in the theater paint and canvas were missing. Great language cannot hold its own against the weight of papier-mâché . . . It is because there are no painted houses that audiences see so clearly the beauty of [Wilder's] language. It is because there is no canvas hill on the stage that Mr. Wilder has the opportunity to give us eternity." Do you agree? Find passages of " great language " that take the place of paint and canvas.

6. Critics had a field day discussing Wilder's creation of the Stage Manager when this play was first presented. He was called a variation on the Property Man in Chinese drama and on the Chorus in Greek drama. Look up both in an encyclopedia and decide what the Stage Manager has in common with them and how he is different. Wilder himself said the Stage Manager is simply a carry-over from the technique of the novel, and thus a kind of storyteller. He can also be compared to a narrator in a radio play. Which explanation do you find most satisfactory?

7. If you were to choose a " Stage Manager " in this pattern to supervise a play about your own home town or city, what sort of person would you select? Write an opening speech for the Stage Manager about your own community, presenting two families whose lives would be as typical as those of the Webbs and the Gibbses in Grover's Corners.

8. You may have thought that sparkling, witty lines make the best dramatic dialogue. In fact, faithful realism may be a surer source of enjoyment. Review lines in *Our Town* which are entertaining because they sound so much like real people talking. Then write in dramatic form some typical happening in your community, such as a morning scene in your own home, or a conversation among your fellow students about a common school event. Be careful to keep a realistic tone and keep the humor good-natured. After hearing all the episodes read aloud, select several that can be put together to make an assembly program on " Our Town " or " Our School."

For Your Vocabulary

WORD ORIGINS: Are you aware that the source of the word *algebra* is an Arabic word meaning " bone-setting " or " reunion of broken parts "? Thus, *algebra* is an appropriate name for the mathematical process of reduction and comparison by equations.

Many words have interesting origins. *Comedy* comes from a Greek word meaning " an ode sung at a festal procession." *Tragedy* originally meant " goat song," and probably was so called because the singer was clad in goat skins. (You will understand these words better if you look up a brief history of early Greek drama.)

Some other words with interesting origins are: *carnival, capricious, digit, lunatic*. Look up the derivation of each.

PAUL GALLICO
1897–

The Snow Goose

Adapted for Radio by William A. Bacher and Malcolm Meacham

Paul Gallico's short story *The Snow Goose* is a minor classic of World War II literature. Published in 1941, it is still in print after ten years, and the dramatic adaptation of it is one of the most distinguished radio plays ever produced. The play's appeal lies not only in its strong emotional impact on readers of all ages, but also in the stirring message it tells about wartime England. Paul Gallico himself is familiar with England and now lives there in a small country village. For many years after his graduation from Columbia University in 1921, he was one of our leading sports writers. His book *Farewell to Sport* contains some hard-hitting, colorful sports talk that is distinctively American.

While television has grown by leaps and bounds in recent years it has not entirely supplanted the media from which it was born — movies and radio. Radio drama, as a matter of fact, still thrives, and has much to teach writers of television plays. Radio introduced special problems for the playwright. Since it depends entirely on sound, a radio play must make full and flexible use of sound effects and music to suggest action and to create mood. Since there is no stage and no scenery, radio plays often take the opportunity to move about in time and place with a freedom unknown in other dramatic types. In the play that follows, you will observe another device which radio dramatists have used skillfully: the narrator. A narrator can give to the play the smoothness of a good short story in addition to the liveliness of dramatic presentation in key scenes.

Characters

NARRATOR

PHILIP RHAYADER [1]	BANDY
FRITHA	SMITHERS
PRIVATE POTTEN	ARTILLERYMAN

[*Orchestra full into title theme and then down under.*]

NARRATOR. This is the story of a man — a lonely man — whose body was warped, but whose heart was filled with love for

[1] **Rhayader** (rā′à·dēr).

wild and hunted things. He was ugly to look upon, but he created great beauty. It is about him, and a child who came to know him and see beyond the grotesque form that housed him to what lay within, that this story is told.

[*Orchestra swells slightly and modulates to theme of the marsh — low, cold, barren.*]

The Great Marsh lies on the Essex coast between the village of Chelmbury and the ancient Saxon fishing hamlet of Wickaeldroth.[1] It is one of the last wild places of England, desolate, utterly lonely, and made lonelier by the calls and cries of the wild fowl that make their homes in the marshlands and saltings.

[*Low effect held off mike . . . cries and calls of scattered wild fowl . . . hold clear a few seconds.*]

Hard by one of the winding arms of the little River Aelder [2] runs the embankment of an old sea wall. At low water, the ruins of an old abandoned lighthouse show above the wall.

[*Orchestra moods with effect of water washing up against the lighthouse . . . hold a few seconds.*]

In the late spring of 1930, young Philip Rhayader came to live at the lighthouse. He was a painter of birds and nature, who, for reason, had withdrawn from all human society. For he was a hunchback and his left arm was crippled, thin and bent at the wrist, like the claw of a bird . . . and he had found this a world in which he could not take part as other men.

[*Orchestra into mood from Sibelius'* [3] *" The Swan of Tuonela."* [4]]

He was a friend to all things wild, and all wild things repaid him with their friendship. Each fall, the wild geese would come winging down the coast from Iceland and Spitsbergen in great skeins that darkened the sky and filled the air with the rushing noise of their passage (*effect of joyous return of birds with record added*) . . . barking and whooping and honking in the autumn sky, to circle the landmark of the old light and drop to earth nearby to be his guests again — birds that he well re-

[1] **Wickaeldroth** (wĭk′ăl·drôth).
[2] **Aelder** (äl′dĕr).
[3] **Sibelius** (sĭ·bā′lĭ·ŏŏs).
[4] **Tuonela** (tōō·ŏ·nā′lá).

membered and recognized from the previous year.

This made Rhayader happy. And he did not seem to mind so much that the natives looked askance at his misshapen body and dark visage.

But one November afternoon, three years after Rhayader had come to the Great Marsh, a child approached the lighthouse studio by means of the sea wall. In her arms she carried a burden. (*Orchestra in with slender theme for the girl.*) She was no more than twelve, slender, dirty, nervous and timid as a bird, but beneath the grime as eerily beautiful as a marsh fairy. She was desperately frightened of the ugly man she had come to see, but greater than her fear was the legend that this ogre who lived in the lighthouse had magic that could heal injured things. For in her arms was a large white bird, and it was quite still. (*Orchestra mood changes.*) There were stains of blood on its whiteness and on her kirtle where she had held it to her. . . .

RHAYADER (*deep, gentle*). What is it, child? (*Orchestra softly out.*)

FRITHA. I found it, sir. It's hurted. I found it in t' marsh where hunters had been. Can 'ee heal it, sir?

RHAYADER. Yes, yes — we will try. Come, you shall help me.

NARRATOR. There were scissors and bandages and splints on a shelf, and he was marvelously deft. The child watched, fascinated. He bandaged the wing close to the body, and made a splint for the shattered leg.

FRITHA. What — what is it, sir?

RHAYADER. It's a snow goose from Canada. Terrible storms must have driven her far off her course. I have never seen one here before. We will call her the "Lost Princess." In a few days she will be feeling much better. See?

NARRATOR. He reached into his pocket and produced a handful of grain. The snow goose nibbled at it. (*Effect of laughter under line.*) The child laughed with delight — then suddenly caught her breath with alarm as the full import of where she was pressed in upon her, and, without a word, she turned and fled out of the door. . . .

RHAYADER. Wait, wait!

NARRATOR. The girl was already fleeing down the sea wall, but she paused at his voice and looked back.

RHAYADER (*calling*). What is your name, child?

FRITHA (*from a little distance*). Fritha.

RHAYADER (*calling*). Where do you live?

FRITHA. Wi' t' fisherfolk at Wickaeldroth.

RHAYADER. Will you come back tomorrow, or the next day, to see how the Princess is getting along?

[*Orchestra softly back to her theme.*]

NARRATOR. She paused, and Rhayader thought of the wild water birds caught motionless in that split second of alarm before they took their flight. But her thin voice came back to him.

FRITHA (*off*). Ay!

NARRATOR. And then she was gone, with her fair hair streaming out behind her.

[*Orchestra swells to hold few seconds . . . and fades out under.*]

The goose mended rapidly, and the child Fritha became a frequent visitor. Until one day in June, the snow goose, with the others, answered the strong call of the breeding grounds, climbed into the sky in ever widening circles, and vanished.

[*Into opening theme, cold and lonely.*]

With the departure of the snow goose ended the visits of Fritha to the lighthouse. And that summer, out of his memory Rhayader painted a picture of a slender, grime-covered child, her fair hair blown by a November storm, who bore in her arms a wounded white bird.

[*Orchestra swells slightly and then we hear from distance the theme of the snow goose fading in again.*]

But in mid-October, the miracle occurred. Above the sea and tide, he heard a clear high note (*bird call*) and saw a white-pinioned dream that circled the lighthouse once, then dropped to earth and came waddling forward importantly to be fed. It was the snow goose. When next Rhayader went to the village, he left a message with the postmistress:

RHAYADER. Tell Fritha, who lives with the fisherfolk at Wickaeldroth, that the Lost Princess has returned.

NARRATOR. And three days later, Fritha, taller, still tousled and unkempt, came shyly to the lighthouse to visit the Lost Princess.

[*Orchestra into low music, distant, ominous.*]

Time passed. The world outside boiled and seethed and rumbled with the eruption that was soon to break forth. But it had not touched them. Every year, the snow goose would disappear in the spring — and with her, Fritha — for it seemed that when the snow goose was gone, some kind of a bar was up between them, and she did not come to the lighthouse. (*Orchestra out.*)

And then one fall, in answer to the message left for her with the postmistress, Fritha reappeared at the lighthouse, and Rhayader, with a shock, realized that she was a child no longer.

[*Orchestra swells into her theme developed.*]

In the spring of 1940, the birds migrated early from the Great Marsh. The whine and roar of the bombers and the thudding explosions frightened them. Fritha and Rhayader stood shoulder to shoulder on the sea wall and watched them go; she, tall, slender, free as air, and hauntingly beautiful; he, dark, grotesque, his massive bearded head raised to the sky, his glowing dark eyes watching the geese form their flight tracery . . . and suddenly . . .

FRITHA (*excitedly*). Look, Philip, look!

NARRATOR. Rhayader followed her eyes. The snow goose had taken flight, her giant wings spread, but she was flying low. Once, twice, she circled the lighthouse . . . then dropped to earth again in the enclosure and commenced to feed.

FRITHA (*marveling.*) She be'ent goin', Philip! The Princess be goin' to stay!

RHAYADER (*shaken*). Ay, she'll stay. She will never go away again. This is her home now — of her own free will.

NARRATOR. And Fritha was suddenly conscious of the fact that she was frightened (*orchestra into minor treatment of love theme*) and the things that frightened her were in Rhayader's eyes — the longing and the loneliness — and the deep, welling unspoken things that he could not speak, because of what he felt himself to be — misshapen and grotesque.

And the woman in her bade her take flight from something she was not yet capable of understanding.

[*Orchestra swells softly and back to theme of the marsh.*]

It was more than three weeks before she returned to the lighthouse. She came back, she told herself, only to see the snow bird. But she found Philip loading supplies into his little sailboat, which she had often seen him handle with such skill — and a great fear, she knew not why, came into her heart.

[*Orchestra modulates to sea music with counterpoint of war music.*]

FRITHA (*terrified*). Philip — ye be goin' away?

NARRATOR. Forgotten was the snow goose. Rhayader paused in his work to greet her, and there was something in his face, a glow and a look, that she had never seen there before.

RHAYADER (*great suppressed excitement*). Fritha! I am glad you came. Yes, I must go away . . . a little trip. . . . I will come back.

FRITHA. Where must ye go?

NARRATOR. Words came tumbling from Rhayader now. He must go to Dunkirk. A hundred miles across the Channel. A British army was trapped there on the sands, awaiting destruction at the hands of the advancing Germans. The port was in flames. He had heard it in the village where he had gone for supplies. In answer to the Government's call, every tug and fishing boat or power launch that could propel itself was heading across the Channel, to haul the men off the beaches to the transports and destroyers that could not reach the shallows. His little boat could take six men at a time; in a pinch seven . . .

[*Orchestra softly out.*]

FRITHA (*terrified*). Philip! Must 'ee go? You'll not come back. Why must it be 'ee?

RHAYADER. I must, my dear, I must! Men are huddled on the beaches like hunted birds, Fritha, like the wounded and hunted birds we used to find and bring to the sanctuary. They are lost and storm-driven and harried like the Lost Princess you found and brought to me out of the marshes many years ago, and we healed her. They need help, as our wild creatures have needed help, and this is why I must go. It is something that I can do. Yes, I can. For once — for once I can be a man and play my part.

[*Orchestra back to her theme.*]

NARRATOR. And as Fritha stared at Rhayader he no longer seemed ugly or misshapen or grotesque, but very beautiful. Things were turmoiling in her own soul, crying to be said, and she did not know how to say them.

FRITHA. I'll come with 'ee, Philip.

RHAYADER. No. Your place in the boat would cause a soldier to be left behind, and another and another. I must go alone. Will you look after the birds until I return, Fritha?

FRITHA. I will . . . and God speed you, Philip. (*So low we can hardly hear her*) God speed you.

[*Orchestra softly into theme of departure to slowly build.*]

NARRATOR. Fritha stood on the sea wall and watched the sail gliding into the sea.

[*Swan theme blends with departure theme.*]

Suddenly, from the darkness behind her, there came a rush of wings and something swept past her in the air. In the night she saw the flash of white wings and the thrust-forward head of the snow goose. It rose and cruised over the lighthouse once (*call of the snow goose*) then headed out toward where Rhayader's sail was slanting in the gaining breeze, and flew above him in slow, wide circles. . . . "Watch o'er him. Watch o'er him," Fritha whispered.

[*Orchestra up passionately and fades off with a last call of the snow goose far off.*]

NARRATOR. Now the story becomes fragmentary . . . it has been gathered from many sources and many people. Some of it comes from men who have looked upon strange and violent scenes.

[*Orchestra in softly; slight suggestion of war.*]

One of the fragments comes in the words of a man on leave who told it in the public room of the Crown and Arrow, an East Chapel pub. . . .

PRIVATE POTTEN (*fading in*). A goose, a bloomin' goose, so 'elp me.

BANDY (*disbelieving*). Garn . . .

POTTEN. A goose it was. Jock 'ere, seen it same as me. It came flyin' down outa the muck an' stink an' smoke of Dunkirk

that was over'ead. It was white, wiv black wings, an' it circles us like a bloomin' dive bomber. Jock, 'ere, 'e sez, "We're done for. It's the hangel of death a-come for us."

[*Orchestra quick swell to gradually develop into war theme.*]

SMITHERS. Garn, I sez, it's a ruddy goose, come over from 'ome wiv a message from Churchill, an' 'ow are we henjoyin' the bloomin' bathin'. It's a omen, that's what it is, a bloomin' omen. We'll get out of this yet, my lad.

[*Orchestra quick swell to war music and sound effects full and then down.*]

ARTILLERYMAN (*fading in over effect*). A goose . . . a bloomin' goose, so 'elp me. We was roastin' on the beach between Dunkirk and Lapanny, an' offshore is the *Kentish Maid,* a ruddy excursion scow, waitin' to take us off. When a Stuka dives on her . . . and a destroyer comes up an' says, "No, ye don't" to the Stuka with ack-acks and pom-poms, but another Jerry dives on the destroyer, and 'its 'er. Coo, did she go up! She burned before she sunk, an' the smokes come driftin' in, all yellow and black, an' out of it comes this bloomin' goose, a-circlin' around us, trapped on the beach. . . .

[*Call of goose fading in, leading* RHAYADER *theme in with it.*]

A bloomin' omen, I says! An' then 'e comes.

BANDY. 'Oo comes?

[RHAYADER's *theme in full.*]

ARTILLERYMAN. 'Im — that saved the lot of us. Into the shallows 'e sailed, as cool as you please, in a bloomin' little sailboat . . . through a boil of machine-gun bullets and divin' Stukas, never givin' 'em no mind, 'e didn't . . . sailin' between the shells right past the burnin' destroyer, a little dark man wiv a beard, a bloomin' claw for a 'and, and a 'ump on 'is back.

[*War music . . . bombers . . . whining shells in strong behind . . . wash and splash of waves and through it all like an organpoint comes the repeated call of the snow goose.*]

RHAYADER (*through effect . . . slightly off*). I can take seven at a time!

ARTILLERYMAN. An' we waded out to where 'e was . . . the goose conkin' all the time . . . 'im at the tiller lookin' up an' grinnin' at 'er, like 'e knows 'er a lifetime. 'E brings us out to the *Kentish Maid* and turns around and goes back for another load. 'E makes trips all afternoon an' all night, too, because the bloody light of Dunkirk burnin' was light enough to see by.

[*Battle begins to let up.*]

I don't know how many trips 'e made, but 'e brought us all off that particular stretch of 'ell, without the loss of a man. An' then 'e sails back toward Dunkirk, an' the bird wiv 'im, flying around the boat like a white hangel against the smoke . . . (*Fades on line.*)

[*Orchestra swells up full and then softly down to signify the end of the battle.*]

I never did find out what become of 'im, or 'oo 'e was — 'im wiv the 'ump an' 'is little sailboat. A bloomin' good man 'e was, that chap.

NARRATOR. Those were a few fragments of the story. There was just one more.

[*Orchestra swells softly and back to Fritha theme.*]

Fritha had remained alone at the lighthouse, wandering through the storerooms and examining the wonderful paintings within them. Among these, she found the picture that Rhayader had painted of her from memory so many years ago when she was still a child, and the things she saw in it stirred her as nothing ever had before, for much of Rhayader's soul had gone into it. She knew that Rhayader would not return.

[*Orchestra into snow goose theme coming in stronger and stronger and stronger under.*]

And so when she heard the high-pitched, well-remembered note of the snow goose cries from the heaven, it brought no instant of false hope to her heart . . . but the sight, the sound, and the solitude surrounding her broke the dam within her and released the surging, overwhelming truth of her love, let it well forth in tears.

[*The love theme comes up full and tragic but triumphant, built upon the snow goose theme.*]

But the snow goose did not come to earth this time. It only skimmed low, then soared up again, flew in a wide, graceful spiral around the old lighthouse, and then began to climb. But Fritha did not see the snow goose.

[*Chorus joins softly . . . ascending.*]

She saw the soul of Rhayader taking farewell of her before departing forever. She stretched her arms up into the sky and stood on tiptoe, crying, " Godspeed! Godspeed! Philip! "

[*Orchestra and singers up full to finish. And then hold strings for epilogue.*]

NARRATOR (*almost like a commentator*). Early the next morning a German pilot on a dawn raid mistook the old abandoned lighthouse for an active military objective, dived on it, a screaming steel hawk, and blew it and all it contained into oblivion.

[*Orchestra sneaks into original bleak theme.*]

And the sea moved in to cover it over. (*Scattered cries of wild sea gulls.*) And now nothing was left to break the utter desolation — nothing was left but the frightened gulls that wheeled and soared and mewed their plaint over the place that once had been.

[*Orchestra fades out leaving only the plaintive cries of the sea gulls . . . hold few seconds.*]

[THE END]

For Discussion of the Play

1. What emotions did you experience as you read this play? Review various parts of the story and explain what emotion was aroused by each. America's latest winner of the Nobel Prize for literature, William Faulkner, said in accepting the award that it is the writer's privilege to help his fellow man by "lifting his heart, by reminding him of the courage and honor and hope and pride and compassion and pity and sacrifice which have been the glory of his past." Which of these emotions did you experience in reading *The Snow Goose*?

2. Compare the Narrator in this play with the Stage Manager in *Our Town*. What is the chief difference between them? Which type of storyteller do you prefer in a play? How does each one make his play especially suitable for reading? Discuss the possibilities, or difficulties, of producing *The Snow Goose* on television.

3. Why is this really the story of the snow goose, rather than of Fritha and Rhayader, or of Dunkirk? Check the many ways in which the goose is the real center of the story.

4. What did the snow goose bring to Rhayader that he had missed before? Why did he glory more than most men would in the help he could give at Dunkirk?

5. Music is not just an added attraction in the play, but a vital part of the story. What function does the music serve that the stage setting usually serves? What does it do for the play that scenery could not do? You can get a recording of "The Swan of Tuonela," used for the snow goose theme. What music would you suggest for Fritha's theme? for the marshes?

For Further Reading of Drama

BEFORE 1915

Collections

A　Cerf, Bennett, and V. H. Cartmell, *S. R. O.* (The Most Successful Plays in the History of the American Stage) (Doubleday, 1944)

B　Clark, B. H., *Favorite American Plays of the 19th Century* (Princeton University Press, 1943)

C　Halline, A. G., *American Plays* (American Book, 1935)

D　Moses, M. J., *Representative Plays by American Dramatists,* 3 vols. (Dutton, 1925, 1926)

E　Moses, M. J., *Representative American Dramas* (Little, Brown, 1941)

F　Quinn, A. H., *Representative American Plays* (Appleton, 1938)

Individual Plays

(Capital letters after the titles refer to collections listed above, in which the plays may be found.)

Belasco, David, *The Return of Peter Grimm,* D Vol. III, F; *The Girl of the Golden West,* E

Fitch, Clyde, *The City,* E; *The Moth and the Flame,* D Vol. III; *The Girl with the Green Eyes,* F

Gillette, William, *Secret Service,* F

Irving, Washington, *Rip Van Winkle,* dram. by Joseph Jefferson, A, F; dram. by C. Burke, D Vol. III

Stowe, Harriet Beecher, *Uncle Tom's Cabin,* dram. by A. E. Thomas, A; dram. by G. L. Aiken, D Vol. III

Thomas, Augustus, *In Mizzoura,* D Vol. I, F; *The Witching Hour,* E

MODERN

Collections

(See also A–F listed above.)

G　Cartmell, V. H., and Bennett Cerf, *Famous Plays of Crime and Detection* (Blakiston, 1946)

H　Cerf, Bennett, and V. H. Cartmell, *Sixteen Famous American Plays* (Garden City, 1946)

I　Clark, B. H., and W. H. Davenport, *Nine Modern American Plays* (Appleton, 1951)

J　Coe, Kathryn, and W. H. Cordell, *Pu-*

litzer Prize Plays, 1918–1934 (Random House, 1940)

K Cordell, R. A., *Representative Modern Plays* (Nelson, 1929)

L Gassner, John, *Twenty-five Best Plays of the Modern American Theatre*, revised ed. (Crown, 1949)

M Gassner, John, *Best Plays of the Modern American Theatre*, second series (Crown, 1947)

N Hatcher, Harlan H., *Modern American Drama*, revised ed. (Harcourt, Brace, 1949)

O Nagelberg, M. M., *Drama in Our Time* (Harcourt, Brace, 1948)

Individual Plays

Anderson, Maxwell, *High Tor*, I; *Winterset*, F, N

Barry, Philip, *Holiday*, E; *The Philadelphia Story*, M; *You and I*, C

Cohan, G. M., *Seven Keys to Baldpate*, G

Connelly, Marc, *The Green Pastures*, E, H, J

Crothers, Rachel, *Expressing Willie*, K

Davis, Owen, *Icebound*, C, J

Gale, Zona, *Miss Lulu Bett*, J

Glaspell, Susan, *Alison's House*, J

Green, Paul, *In Abraham's Bosom*, J

Hart, Moss, and G. S. Kaufman, *The Man Who Came to Dinner*, H

Howard, Sidney, *The Silver Cord*, F; and Paul de Kruif, *Yellow Jack*, O

Kaufman, G. S., and Marc Connelly, *Dulcy*, E; *Beggar on Horseback*, K, L; Kaufman and Morris Ryskind, *Of Thee I Sing*, J

Kelly, George, *The Show-Off*, E; *Craig's Wife*, J, L

Kesselring, Joseph, *Arsenic and Old Lace*, A, M

Kingsley, Sidney, *Dead End*, H; *Men in White*, J; *The Patriots*, M

Lindsay, Howard, and Russel Crouse, *Life with Father*, H

Miller, Arthur, *All My Sons*, N

Nichols, Anne, *Abie's Irish Rose*, A

O'Neill, Eugene, *Beyond the Horizon*, F, J; *The Hairy Ape*, I, L

Rice, Elmer, *Street Scene*, I, J, L

Riggs, Lynn, *Green Grow the Lilacs*, I

Rinehart, M. R., and Avery Hopwood, *The Bat*, G

Rodgers, Richard, and Oscar Hammerstein, *Oklahoma!* A

Saroyan, William, *The Time of Your Life*, H, M, N

Sherwood, Robert, *Abe Lincoln in Illinois*, I, M, O; *The Petrified Forest*, H; *The Road to Rome*, L

Thurber, James, and Elliott Nugent, *The Male Animal*, M

Van Druten, John, *I Remember Mama*, M

SHORT PLAYS
Collections

Baker, G. P., *Yale One-Act Plays* (French, 1934)

Cerf, Bennett, and V. H. Cartmell, *Thirty Famous One-Act Plays* (Modern Library, 1949)

French, S., *One-Act Plays for Stage and Study* (series of ten) (French)

Goldstone, G. A., *One-Act Plays* (Allyn, 1926)

Griffith, F. J., and J. Mersand, *Modern One-Act Plays* (Harcourt, Brace, 1950)

Isaacs, E. J. R., *Plays of American Life and Fantasy* (Coward-McCann, 1929)

Knickerbocker, E. V., *Short Plays*, revised ed. (Holt, 1949)

Kozlenko, William, *American Scenes* (Day, 1941)

Mayorga, Margaret, *The Best One-Act Plays of 1937*, etc. (series continues annually) (Dodd, Mead)

Shay, Frank, and P. Loving, *Fifty Contemporary One-Act Plays* (World, 1946)

Shay, Frank, *Fifty More Contemporary One-Act Plays* (Appleton, 1928)

Webber, J. P., and H. H. Webster, *Short Plays for Junior and Senior High Schools* (Houghton Mifflin, 1925)

Zachar, I., and R. A. Kimball, *Plays as Experience* (Odyssey, 1944)

RADIO AND TELEVISION PLAYS
Collections

Barnouw, E., *Radio Drama in Action* (Farrar and Rinehart, 1945)

Corwin, Norman, *Thirteen by Corwin* (Holt, 1942)

Fitelson, H. W., *Theatre Guild on the Air* (Rinehart, 1947)

Kaufman, William I., *Best Television Plays of the Year* (Merlin, 1950)

Lass, A. H., *et al.*, *Plays from Radio* (Houghton Mifflin, 1948)

Oboler, Arch, *Oboler Omnibus* (Duell, 1945)

PART TWO

The Growth of American Literature

THE COLONIAL TIME

THE MAKING OF A NATION

THE FLOWERING OF THE
EAST, PARTS ONE AND TWO

THE WESTWARD MOVEMENT

TIME OF CHANGE

AMERICAN LITERATURE
IN THE MODERN WORLD

The Reverend John Cotton, 1584–1652, by an unknown artist. (Connecticut Historical Society)

The Colonial Time

N O OTHER great country has ever had its beginnings so fully recorded. Two Icelandic sagas (long story-poems) tell how Leif Ericson, the Norse sea captain, landed about 1000 A.D. on a coast which we believe to have been the coast of New England. Four hundred and ninety-two years after Ericson's voyage, Columbus kept a full diary. We know how much he was paid — about three hundred dollars a year — and how much his first trip to America cost — about seven thousand dollars. We also know it was a fine April morning when the first colonists landed in Virginia. The strawberries were uncommonly large and tasty, and the Indians came bringing gifts (although later they came with tomahawks). We know this because almost as soon as men landed in America they began to write books about it.

A Different Beginning for a National Literature

Spanish missionaries working out of Mexico and Cuba had produced catechisms, grammars, and prayer books in Indian dialects as early as 1550, and the first book written in America in English was being printed (in England) less than fifteen months after the first permanent settlement at Jamestown, Virginia, in 1607. The first printing press in the colonies was operating in 1638, only eight years after the settlement on Massachusetts Bay, near what is now Boston. Nothing could show more clearly one great difference between American literature and other national literatures of the world.

English literature, French, Spanish, Greek literatures, all began long before the printing press was invented. They began with folklore and minstrel ballads and children's rhymes, handed down by word of mouth for generations.

But America and American literature were born in the glare of publicity. Ours was the first great national literature that began after the invention of mechanical printing. In the year 1300 it cost a prince three thousand dollars to have a single copy of a book made as a gift to his fiancée. In 1608, three thousand dollars printed a large edition of a book about Virginia; and five hundred dollars would equip a print shop. Settlers came to America bringing libraries with them. They sent back notes on America to be made into books and put into other libraries. In effect, American literature was a going concern from the hour of the first permanent settlement.

It was, of course, a *colonial* literature, a part of English literature. The story of American literature is a story of how the new people on the new continent gradually changed colonial writings into a national literature that was distinctively and unmistakably their own.

The Records of a Young Country

For the most part, the writings that have come down to us from the Colonial century are not great literature. They are, rather, the records of a young country.

When present-day explorers land on Antarctica or some other distant and mysterious place, what do we want to know about it? Two things, probably — what is the place like, and what were the experiences of those that landed. That is exactly what Europeans first wanted to know about America, and therefore much of the early American writing is in the form of accounts of life in the new land, written for the folks back home. Some of these accounts were good enough to last, and even today they preserve for us the thrill and excitement of those early years.

We sometimes forget that our early Colonial writers were living a great adventure. In these days when airplanes span the ocean between dinner and breakfast, it is hard to remember that in the early years of Colonial America many a ship unloaded as many dead passengers as live ones! The trip to America was desperately hard. Journey's end had nothing more to offer than uncommon diseases, unprepared-for hardships, hostile savages, and whatever could be won, by hard work and co-operation, from a wilderness. This is the adventurous life which America's earliest literature recorded.

Our early writers did not write wholly about their hardships, however. They also wrote about their hopes. Many an immigrant family looked at the seacoast of America and imagined a land which the endless wars of the Old World could not disturb; a land where their husbands and sons would be free from the fear of being impressed into the army; a land where they would be free to work for themselves, if they wished, with a fair chance of living comfortably; a land where they could worship freely in the way they felt they should; a land where they could live in friendship among people who believed as they did, and where they could freely speak and print and learn. In other words, the America of the Four Freedoms.

Diaries of the Times

YOU CAN read the adventures and hopes of the early Americans in hundreds of journals and diaries. All the missionaries wrote detailed reports of their labors, and many also kept private journals of their own. You will read three diary excerpts — one by a New Englander, one by a Southerner, and one by a French missionary.

The New Englander, Mrs. Sarah Kemble Knight, was herself an illustration of the freedom of opportunity in the New World. She knew enough

about business to be called to New York to help settle an estate. She kept a vivid record of a horseback trip to New York in 1704. Another diarist was a Southerner, an aristocrat, owner of a great estate, head of one of the most famous families of Virginia, the Byrds.

He was far removed from the first log huts at Jamestown. He lived in a mansion at Westover, and had been educated in England. You will notice his polished style of writing, his easy use of Latin, his easy contempt of lower classes. Father Vivier,[1] a French Jesuit, brought to the New World the culture of his religious training in the Old. Reading all three, you will get a bird's-eye view of the American scene in the eighteenth century.

But our early colonists left us a record which probably resulted in more books than all other kinds of writing combined. This was the record of their religious life and thoughts. Because this part of our Colonial literature was so important, we had better take a look at how religious ideas and practices developed in the American colonies.

Religious Freedom in the Colonies

The first public building that went up, almost invariably in New England and often so in the South, was the church. The first freedom that American colonists won for themselves was religious freedom.

Yet religious freedom, like every other freedom, was a hard-won right. There was more religious freedom in America than in any part of the Old World, but there was by no means complete tolerance in Colonial times. If we understand that, we are in position to

[1] Vivier (vē′vyā′).

understand one of the great truths of history — that freedom does not suddenly come into existence. It cannot even be legislated; it has to develop, and be fought for and slowly won.

A great many settlers came to America in those first years seeking religious freedom and finding it. But they were seeking freedom *for themselves* — not for all men! This is not surprising, because the colonists had been brought up in the tradition of a state church. A large part of them came to America because they did not like the state church. But as soon as they were settled in a place where they would be free from constraint and persecution, they wanted at once to make *their own religion* the state church of the new colony.

The first colony guaranteeing religious freedom was Catholic Maryland (1634). (The Puritan government revoked this right in 1654, and the Catholics were themselves deprived of protection under the law.) Later, Rhode Island and Pennsylvania granted religious toleration. More and more islands of safety were found for minority groups. By the time we had become a nation, the American people were willing to write into the first article of the Bill of Rights: " Congress shall make no law respecting an establishment of religion, or prohibiting the free exercise thereof."

The Puritans and Their Literature

The state religion of New England was known as the Puritan religion. We are going to give special attention to the Puritans because they wrote so much of our Colonial literature. In fact, the seventeenth century has been called the Puritan century of American literature.

We must be careful not to get a mistaken idea of the Puritans. We know, from stories and pictures, that they wore plain, severe clothes, and long faces; the pictures show them that way. We know they listened to three-hour sermons, meditated for long periods on damnation, hanged witches, and frightened their children with threats of hellfire. Those are the stories that have come down to us. Yet those stories and those pictures must be something less than the whole truth, for no such people could have done all the Puritans did.

What the Puritans Were Really Like

Let us look at the Puritans again. They were great fighters. More than one of their Indian wars ended with the complete extermination of the Indian tribe involved. They were brave and tough. The very fact that they chose to remain in cold, rocky New England, rather than migrate to the warmer, more fertile colonies farther south, tells us something about them. They were hard-working. They had to be, to make a living off the rugged land where they settled. They became shrewd businessmen. They found a wilderness in New England and built it up into a manufacturing center that competed with the old country. They built ships and sailed them on the seven seas.

They were uncommonly literate. New England colonies were the first to develop adequate school systems. They founded the first college (Harvard, in 1636), the first printing press (in 1638), the first newspaper (*Publick Occurrences*, founded in 1690). The first noteworthy colonial scientists were Puritans. The Puritan clergy were some of the most learned men in the world. One of them, Cotton Mather, published more than four hundred books.

Were they long-faced? Maybe, but they could enjoy themselves on the right occasion: read the account of their first Thanksgiving. The suspicion grows that the long-faced Puritans of our pictures wore the stern faces that come from competence and vigilance rather than gloomy temperament.

How about the long sermons? They had them. There is no doubt of that. And ushers kept the children awake by tapping their heads with long poles wielded from the back of the church. That is true. But the Puritans felt it was especially important to stay awake in church, for the church had a special importance in their lives.

The Church as a Center of Puritan Life

The church did certain jobs in those days which have since been given to other institutions. For a while, it took the place of the newspaper. It provided an occasion for men to pass on to others the current news. Sometimes a town crier stood outside the church and shouted the news. The church was usually an educational center. It was also a government center. The Puritans thought of their government as a theocracy — in which people were governed by the word of God — and the ministers had an influence which few American religious leaders have had since their time.

Another reason for the church's importance was that it played a very dra-

matic part in Puritan life. The Puritans believed that because of Adam's sin in the Garden of Eden, mankind was consigned to hell. Jesus's sacrifice had modified and softened that sentence, so that only *some* persons were doomed. But these were doomed forever. Hell was, therefore, a very real place to the Puritans and a very exciting idea. Puritan writers and preachers described every level, almost every foot, of hell — the fire and the ice and the tortures, and the men and women who were already suffering there. To put it in a way that would probably shock the Puritans, hell was the most interesting subject matter they knew. A sermon like Jonathan Edwards's "Sinners in the Hands of an Angry God" was the most exciting experience of the week for them. In a sense, it took the place of theater and moving picture, even of reading matter.

What the Puritans Wrote and Read

Now, what kind of literature did these remarkable people leave us?

For one thing, schoolbooks. Early American schoolbooks were likely to be religious. *The New England Primer*, the Bible, and the Psalter were for fifty years the only textbooks used in elementary schools in New England. The primer was one of the most widely sold and perhaps most influential of all American books. Millions of school children began to learn their alphabet by memorizing the most fundamental of all truths to the Puritans: " In Adam's fall, we sinned all."

The Puritans did not write much poetry. But there was among them at least one poet whose writing still competes with that of later Americans. His name was Edward Taylor. He lived quietly in New England, and was never famous or even well known in his lifetime. In fact, not until our own day have Americans realized how good a poet he was.

The most common form of Puritan literature was the sermon. In the following pages you will read a selection by the most famous preacher of early America, Jonathan Edwards.

Jonathan Edwards, the Last Puritan

Edwards was the last of a famous group of Puritan preachers. There is a tradition in folk tales that the greatest hero is always the last of the line. So it was with Jonathan Edwards, who was born in 1703, when already the govern-

mental influence of the Puritan ministers was nearly dead. He was a fine scientist; sometime you will enjoy reading his description of the flying spider, which showed the most accurate observation of spiders up to that time. He was the greatest philosopher of the Puritans, and his long *Treatise on Freedom of the Will* won a world-wide reputation. No one could write more beautifully of God and holiness and righteous men. On the other hand, no one could preach more terrifyingly of hell. But he came too late. A century earlier he might have been the greatest man in the colonies. As it was, he preached in a small community in western Massachusetts. Finally called to the presidency of Princeton, with a chance to mold that college along the lines of his thinking, he died of smallpox at the age of fifty-four.

Edwards died at the end of a century and a half of American growth. The colonies had developed greater freedom of worship and more freedom of opportunity than the mother country. Now their development was no longer in a colonial direction. Every step was toward political freedom, and American literature kept pace.

The Painted History
of the
Delaware Indians

Little did the first European settlers in America realize that the illiterate savages they found here had a form of literature of their own. The early Indians did not have a phonetic written language but, like primitive peoples the world over, they created poems that were passed on from person to person, generation to generation, by word of mouth. These poems celebrated tribal heroes or great events or, like the one that follows, attempted to depict the creation of man and the beginnings of the race. Some Indian stories and poems were cast into picture writing, most of which has long since been destroyed. The most complete record to survive the ages is the Wallam Olum (painted history) of the Delaware Indians, which consists of 184 symbols, or glyphs, as they are called. This record begins with the creation of the world, then describes a great flood, and the various wanderings and wars of the tribe. The traditional chants, of which the glyphs were meant to be reminders, had pronounced rhythm, often rhyme, and were undoubtedly accompanied by primitive dances. This, together with its imaginative ideas, justifies calling the painted history a form of poetry. It is, in a very special sense, the first native American writing.

ON THE CREATION

 At first sea water covered all the land.

 Above the water in the mist was the God-creator.

 He caused to be much water, great land, many clouds, the wide sky.

 He caused to be the sun and moon and stars.

 Winds blew hard, clearing the deep water and making it run off.

 Light shone and an island appeared.

 Then he created the first beings, also angels, also souls.

 Afterward he created the man-being, ancestor of man.

 He gave to man the first mother of men.

 Fishes he gave to man, and turtles and beasts and birds.

 But an evil spirit created bad beings, black snakes and monsters.

 At first all beings were friends together.

 But then, while secretly on earth, the snake-god led men to worship evil.

 Wickedness, crime, unhappiness, thus came to the world.

For Discussion of the Painted History

1. How many points of similarity can you find between the Indian account of the creation and the one in the Bible? Let one student read the account of the creation in Genesis, another that in Greek mythology, another that in Norse mythology, and report to the class the points of likeness and difference that they discover.

2. The glyphs are supposed to have some connection with the gesture language used by the Indians. Which of those given here strongly suggest a gesture to be made with hands or arms?

3. What familiar symbols of things or beings can you discover in this "history"? If any member of the class is of Oriental background and knows some of the Japanese or Chinese ideographs, get him to explain the symbols in some of them.

4. As further background, obtain a short history of the Delaware Indians.

The Bay Psalm Book

Twenty years after the landing of the Pilgrims, the first book was printed in America (1640). *The Bay Psalm Book* was so called because it was used throughout the Massachusetts Bay Colony. It shows that the early Puritans were less interested in literary style than in having a translation of the Psalms that would fit hymn tunes used in their services. This is evident when one compares Psalm I in *The Bay Psalm Book* with the same psalm in the Holy Bible, "The Lot of the Just and the Wicked." Notice the difference in the rhythm, and in the choice and order of words.

THE BAY PSALM BOOK

O Blessed man, that in th' advice of
  wicked doeth not walk;
nor stand in sinners way, nor sit in
  chayre of scornfull folk,

But in the law of Jehovah,
  is his longing delight:
and in his law doth meditate, by day
  and eke by night.

And he shall be like to a tree
  planted by water rivers:
that in his season yields his fruit,
  and his leaf never withers.

And all he doth, shall prosper well,
  the wicked are not so:
but they are like unto the chaffe,
  which winde drives to and fro.

Therefore shall not ungodly men,
  rise to stand in the doome,
nor shall the sinners with the just,
  in their assemblie come.

For of the righteous men, the Lord
  acknowledgeth the way:
but the way of the ungodly men,
  shall utterly decay.

THE HOLY BIBLE

The Lot of the Just and the Wicked

1. Blessed is the man who follows not the counsel of the wicked, nor walks in the way of sinners, nor sits in the company of the insolent;

2. But his delight is in the law of the Lord, and on that law he meditates day and night.

3. And he is like a tree planted near running waters, which brings forth its fruit in due season, and whose leaves do not wither, and whatsoever he does, prospers.

4. Not so the wicked, not so; but they are like chaff scattered by the wind.

5. Therefore, the wicked shall not stand in judgment, nor sinners in the council of the just.

6. For the Lord tends the way of the just, but the way of the wicked shall perish.

The New England Primer

For more than a hundred years Puritan children received their first schooling from *The New England Primer*. Since the chief purpose of education at that time was to enable people to read the Bible, it was natural that the alphabet rhymes chanted by the children should be based on Bible stories. The little pictures (not counting the primitive Indian signs) are the earliest examples of what we call today "visual education." Besides the alphabet, the *Primer* contained the catechism and several prayers, including "Now I lay me down to sleep." The *Primer* is believed to have been in existence by 1688; this selection is from the 1727 edition.

A — In ADAM's Fall We finned all.

B — Heaven to find, The Bible Mind.

C — Chrift crucify'd For finners dy'd.

D — The Deluge drown'd The Earth around.

E — ELIJAH hid By Ravens fed.

F — The judgment made FELIX afraid.

G — As runs the Glass, Our Life doth pass.

H — My Book and Heart Must never part.

I — JOB feels the Rod, Yet bleffes GOD.

K — Proud Korah's troop Was fwallowed up

L — LOT fled to *Zoar*, Saw fiery Shower On *Sodom* pour.

M — MOSES was he Who *Israel's* Hoft Led thro' the Sea.

N — NOAH did view The old world & new

O — Young OBADIAS, DAVID, JOSIAS All were pious.

P — PETER deny'd His Lord and cry'd.

Q — Queen ESTHER fues And faves the *Jews*.

R — Young pious RUTH Left all for Truth.

S — Young SAM'L dear The Lord did fear.

T — Young TIMOTHY Learnt fin to fly.

U — VASTHI for Pride, Was fet afide.

W — Whales in the Sea, GOD's Voice obey.

X — XERXES did die, And fo muft I.

Y — While youth do chear Death may be near.

Z — ZACCHEUS he Did climb the Tree Our Lord to fee.

Edward Taylor
1646?–1729

HUSWIFERY

It is odd that a Puritan poet should become news two hundred years after his death, but that is what happened to Edward Taylor. Not until 1937 did his writings come to light. Scholars were surprised by the superior quality of these long-hidden religious poems. The reason for the burial of Edward Taylor's talent was that he had directed his heirs never to publish any of his writings; but after the last descendants died, all personal reasons for withholding the poems were long past. Taylor, a young English schoolmaster, came to Boston in 1668 and entered Harvard College to prepare for the ministry. He was called to Westfield, a village a hundred miles southwest of Boston, where fifteen persons wished to organize a church. Here he stayed for the rest of his life as both pastor and physician to the town.

Edward Taylor's poetry shows that he was well read in the best English poets of the seventeenth century. In that day poets delighted in the use of a "conceit," that is, a somewhat artificial figure of speech carried out in great detail. In some poems, for example, Taylor compares Christ's love for humanity to a garden exhaling sweet odors, a pipe conveying a life-giving liquid, and a mint in which God coins his image. The following poem (modernized in spelling) begins with the figure of the spinning wheel, especially appropriate in a day when that simple machine was found in every kitchen. The entire process of weaving, dyeing, and making garments is then covered as part of good "housewifery." Notice how each detail represents the human being as merely some part of the implements or the raw material, upon which the spirit of God must act in order to produce a devoted life "clothed for glory."

Make me, O Lord, thy Spinning Wheel complete;
    Thy Holy Word my Distaff° make for me.
Make mine Affections thy Swift Flyers° neat,
    And make my Soul thy holy Spool to be.
My Conversation make to be thy Reel,   5
    And reel the yarn thereon spun of thy Wheel.

Make me thy Loom then, knit therein this Twine:
    And make thy Holy Spirit, Lord, wind quills:°
Then weave the Web thyself. The yarn is fine.
    Thine Ordinances make my Fulling Mills.°   10
Then dye the same in Heavenly Colors Choice,
All pink with Varnished Flowers of Paradise.

2. **Distaff** (dǐs'tȧf): the staff for holding the raw wool. 3. **Flyers:** twirling parts for twisting the thread. 8. **quills:** the bobbins on which the yarn was wound before weaving. 10. **Fulling Mills:** mills where the cloth was cleansed and thickened.

Then clothe therewith mine Understanding, Will,
    Affections, Judgment, Conscience, Memory;
My Words and Actions, that their shine may fill   15
    My ways with glory and thee glorify.
Then mine apparel shall display before ye
That I am Clothed in Holy robes for glory.

Jonathan Edwards
1703–1758

SINNERS IN THE HANDS
OF AN ANGRY GOD

A local historian wrote that when Jonathan Edwards, the last great Puritan minister, delivered the sermon from which this excerpt was taken, " there was heard such a breathing of distress and weeping, that the preacher was obliged to speak to the people and desire silence that he might be heard." Edwards's delivery is said to have been forceful, but not violent; and his other writings show him to have been of a gentle nature. The Puritan conception of hell, as described in Edwards's powerful language, was terrifying.

THE God that holds you over the pit of Hell much as one holds a spider or some loathsome insect over the fire, abhors you, and is dreadfully provoked; his wrath toward you burns like fire; he looks upon you as worthy of nothing else but to be cast into the fire; he is of purer eyes than to bear to have you in his sight; you are ten thousand times so abominable in his eyes as the most hateful and venomous serpent is in ours. You have offended him infinitely more than ever a stubborn rebel did his

prince: and yet it is nothing but his hand that holds you from falling into the fire every moment. 'Tis ascribed to nothing else, that you did not go to Hell the last night; that you was [1] suffered to awake again in this world after you closed your eyes to sleep and there is no other reason to be given why you have not dropped into Hell since you arose in the morning, but that God's hand has held you up. There is no other reason to be given why you ha'n't gone to Hell since you have sat here in the house of God, provoking his pure eyes by your sinful wicked manner of attending his solemn worship. Yea, there is nothing else that is to be given as a reason why you don't this very moment drop down into Hell.

O sinner! Consider the fearful danger you are in. 'Tis a great furnace of wrath, a wide and bottomless pit, full of the fire of wrath, that you are held

---

[1] **you was:** This construction was often used in eighteenth-century writing, and was not considered illiterate, as it is now. See similar construction on page 420.

over in the hand of that God whose wrath is provoked and incensed as much against you as against many of the damned, in Hell. You hang by a slender thread, with the flames of divine wrath flashing about it, and ready every moment to singe it and burn it asunder; and you have no interest in any Mediator, and nothing to lay hold of to save yourself, nothing to keep off the flames of wrath, nothing of your own, nothing that you ever have done, nothing that you can do, to induce God to spare you one moment.

It is *everlasting* wrath. It would be dreadful to suffer this fierceness and wrath of Almighty God one moment; but you must suffer it to all eternity: there will be no end to this exquisite, horrible misery. When you look forward you shall see a long forever, a boundless duration before you, which will swallow up your thoughts and amaze your soul; and you will absolutely despair of ever having any deliverance, any end, any mitigation, any rest at all; you will know certainly that you must wear out long ages, millions of millions of ages, in wrestling and conflicting with this almighty, merciless vengeance; and then when you have so done, when so many ages have actually been spent by you in this manner, you will know that all is but a point to what remains. So that your punishment will indeed be infinite. Oh, who can express what the state of a soul in such circumstances is! All that we can possibly say about it gives but a very feeble, faint representation of it; it is inexpressible and inconceivable: for " who knows the power of God's anger? "

THUNDER AND LIGHTNING

The many-sided Jonathan Edwards was one of our earliest American scientific observers. From his *Notes on Natural Science*, this analysis of the causes of thunder and lightning shows his inquiring mind. It is interesting to note that while Edwards studied the principles of lightning, his contemporary, Benjamin Franklin, made his famous experiments with kite and key to bring lightning under man's control.

A comparison of this essay with the preceding sermon shows clearly how a writer's purpose influences the tone of a particular piece of writing.

IT is remarkable of thunder how long one part of the sound will be heard after another, when it is evident that the sound is made all in an instant by the lightning, which continues no longer. This arises from the length of the stream of lightning, whereby one part is a great deal farther from us than another, so that the sound is a great while coming successively. Hence it is that in claps of thunder that are near us, the first noise that we hear seems to be very near the earth, and then it seems to go further and further from us, and the last will be a murmuring up in the clouds; for although the noise that was made in the clouds, and the noise near the earth, was made together as at an instant, yet that in the clouds is much farther, and therefore is longer coming, and is a much lower sound when it sounds.

The rapid vibration of the air jars and jumbles, breaks and condenses the bubbles of the cloud; whence it is that, soon after hard claps of thunder, rain falls in greater plenty.

I regard thunder as a meteor by far the most wonderful and least explicable of any whatsoever. . . .

Lightning seems to be this: An almost infinitely fine, combustible matter that floats in the air, that takes fire by a sudden and mighty fermentation that is some way promoted by the cool and moisture, and perhaps attraction, of the clouds. By this sudden agitation, this fine floating matter is driven forth with

A

B

SEVENTEENTH-CENTURY

houses and their furnishings, whether brought from Europe or made in New England, were characterized by simplicity, utility, and sturdiness. (a) Parson Capen House, Topsfield, Mass., built 1683 (Library of Congress). (b) Stephen Daye Press, first printing press in the colonies (Vt. Historical Society). (c) Chair-table (Metropolitan Museum of Art). (d) Miniature model of New England kitchen (Art Institute of Chicago).

C

D

a mighty force one way or other, which-ever way it is directed, by the circum-stances and temperature of the circum-jacent air; for cold and heat, density and rarity, moisture and dryness has al-most an infinitely strong influence upon the fine particles of matter. This fluid matter, thus projected, still fermenting to the same degree, divides the air as it goes, and every moment receives a new impulse by the continued fermen-tation; and as its motion received its di-rection, at first, from the different tem-perature of the air, on different sides, so its direction is changed, according to the temperature of the air it meets with, which renders the path of the lightning so crooked.

For Your Vocabulary

BASE-WORD: Jonathan Edwards says that "sinners in the hands of an angry God" must despair of any *mitigation* of their hard lot (p. 420), of that lot's ever becom-ing milder. We use several related words with the same base-word, which means "mild, soft." How would it be a *mitigating* circumstance in a burglary, for example, if the offender was a man who stole only food to feed a starving family? What kind of crime would an *unmitigated* offense be?

WORD DISTINCTION: In this same sermon, notice the use of several powerful words of similar, though not identical, meaning. "You are ten thousand times so *abominable* in his eyes as the most *hateful* and *venom-ous* serpent is in ours." How do these words differ in meaning? Why is each appropri-ate in its exact position in this sentence? Extend your vocabulary by noting the slight differences in meaning between these words and *antipathy* and *repugnance*, both of which are commonly used in writing.

For Discussion of Puritan Literature

Religious Books

1. The three ministers who edited *The Bay Psalm Book* said in the preface: " God's altar needs not our polishings, for we have respected rather a plain translation, than to smooth our verses with the sweetness of any paraphrase, and so have attended con-science rather than elegance." How is their aim revealed in *The Bay Psalm Book* ver-sion of Psalm I? What changes in word-ing decrease effectiveness? Why? Find some changes that increase effectiveness. *The Bay Psalm Book* has rhyme but loses some pleasant alliteration (see p. 303). Find examples.

2. What was the positive and valuable contribution of the Puritans to the Ameri-can spirit? Point out places where it is ev-ident in these selections. Are Puritan atti-tudes active in your community today?

3. Can you name other famous Ameri-can schoolbooks besides *The New England Primer?* What did most of the early " read-ers " have in common with the *Primer?*

Edward Taylor

1. To be sure you understand Edward Taylor's use of the " conceit," list in two columns first the implements and raw ma-terials used in clothmaking, and opposite each in the second column the spiritual comparison made by the poet. For exam-ple:

Distaff, a solid	The Bible, a solid
foundation for	foundation for
the wool	the spirit

Why would this comparison make a strong impression on Taylor's parishioners?

Jonathan Edwards

1. Why were Puritan sermons likely to be exciting? Would you like to hear Ed-wards Sunday after Sunday? Why, or why not? Which kind of religious teaching do you think does the most good: that of striving and hope, as in Taylor's poem; or that of fear and punishment, as in Ed-wards's sermon?

2. Does Edwards's explanation of thun-der and lightning seem clear to you? Is it an acceptable explanation to a modern sci-entist? If you don't know, ask your physics teacher.

3. Select an appropriate adjective to describe the tone of Edwards's sermon and another to describe the tone of the essay. What was his purpose in each selection? How does the tone suit the purpose in each case?

Sarah Kemble Knight
1666–1727

FROM HER JOURNAL

Today airplanes make swift round trips between Boston and New York. One can eat breakfast in Boston, attend to a full day's business in New York, and return home for dinner. But in 1704 when Mrs. Sarah Kemble Knight wished to make a similar business trip, it took her five months. There were no airplanes then, no railroad trains, not even stagecoaches. She traveled on horseback. On every page of the journal she kept on this trip one finds evidence of her keen observation and lively imagination. Capable and energetic as she was, it is no wonder that she felt free to sit in judgment on less able fellow Americans she met along the way. (In these selections the author's original spelling and capitalization have been preserved.)

STRANGE CUSTOMS OF CONNECTICUT

Saturday, Oct. 7th, wee sett out early in the Morning, and being something unacquainted with the way, having ask't it of some wee mett, they told us wee must Ride a mile or two and turne down a Lane on the Right hand; and by their Direction wee Rode on but not Yet comeing to the turning, we mett a Young fellow and ask't him how farr it was to the Lane which turn'd down towards Guilford. Hee said wee must Ride a little further, and turn down by the Corner of uncle Sams Lott. My Guide vented his Spleen at the Lubber; and we soon after came into the Rhode, and keeping still on, without any thing further Remarkebell, about two a clock afternoon we arrived at New Haven,

where I was received with all Posible Respects and civility. Here I discharged Mr. Wheeler with a reward to his satisfaction, and took some time to rest after so long and toilsome a Journey; And I inform'd myselfe of the manners and customs of the place, and at the same time employed myselfe in the afair I went there upon.

They are Govern'd by the same Laws as wee in Boston, (or little differing,) thr'out this whole Colony of Connecticot, And much the same way of Church Government, and many of them good, Sociable people, and I hope Religious too: but a little too much Independant in their principalls, and, as I have been told, were formerly in their Zeal very Riggid in their Administrations towards such as their Lawes made Offenders, even to a harmless Kiss or Innocent merriment among Young People. Whipping being a frequent and counted an easy Punishment, about which, as other Crimes, the Judges were absolute in their Sentences. Their Diversions in this part of the Country are on Lecture days [1] and Training days mostly: on the former there is Riding from town to town.

And on training dayes The Youth divert themselves by Shooting at the Target, as they call it, (but it very much resembles a pillory,) where hee that hitts neerest the white has some yards

---

[1] **Lecture days:** Thursdays were so called because of the regular midweek religious lecture.

of Red Ribbin presented him, which being tied to his hattband, the two ends streeming down his back, he is Led away in Triumph, with great applause, as the winners of the Olympiack Games.[1] They generally marry very young: the males oftener as I am told under twentie than above; they generally make public wedings, and have a way something singular (as they say) in some of them, viz. Just before Joyning hands the Bridegroom quitts the place, who is soon followed by the Bridesmen, and as it were, dragg'd back to duty — being the reverse to the former practice among us, to steal Mrs. Bride.

There are great plenty of Oysters all along by the sea side, as farr as I Rode in the Collony, and those very good. And they Generally lived very well and comfortably in their famelies. But too Indulgent (especially the farmers) to their slaves: sufering too great familiarity from them, permitting them to sit at Table and eat with them, (as they say to save time,) and into the dish goes the black as freely as the white hand. They told me that there was a farmer lived nere the Town where I lodgd who had some difference with his slave, concerning something the master had promised him and did not punctualy perform; which caused some hard words between them; But at length they put the matter to Arbitration and Bound themselves to stand to the award of such as they named — which done, the Arbitrators Having heard the Allegations of both parties, Order the master to pay 40s[2] to black face, and acknowledge his fault. And so the matter ended: the poor master very honestly standing to the award.

There are every where in the Towns as I passed, a Number of Indians the Natives of the Country, and are the most salvage of all the salvages of that kind that I had ever Seen: little or no care taken (as I heard upon enquiry) to make them otherwise. They have in some places Landes of their owne, and Govern'd by Law's of their own making; — they marry many wives and at pleasure put them away, and on the least dislike or fickle humor, on either side, saying *stand away* to one another is a sufficient Divorce. And indeed those uncomely *Stand aways* are too much in Vougue among the English in this [Indulgent Colony] as their Records plentifully prove, and that on very trivial matters, of which some have been told me, but are not proper to be Related by a Female pen, tho some of that foolish sex have had too large a share in the story.

If the natives commit any crime on their own precincts among themselves, the English takes no Cognezens[3] of. But if on the English ground, they are punishable by our Laws. They mourn for their Dead by blacking their faces, and cutting their hair, after an Awkerd and frightfull manner; But can't bear You should mention the names of their dead Relations to them: they trade most for Rum, for which they'd hazzard their very lives; and the English fit them Generally as well, by seasoning it plentifully with water.

They give the title of merchant to every trader; who Rate their Goods according to the time and spetia[4] they pay in: viz. Pay, mony, Pay as mony, and trusting. *Pay* is Grain, Pork, Beef, &c. at prices sett by the General Court that Year; *mony* is pieces of Eight, Ryalls,[5] or Boston or Bay shillings (as

---

[1] **Olympiack Games:** The Greeks held great athletic festivals every four years, beginning in 776 B.C., at Olympia. It is from these that the modern Olympic games take their name.

[2] **40s:** 40 shillings. A shilling is equal to twelve pence (12d). In early America, its value fluctuated from one colony to another.

[3] **Cognezens:** cognizance. In other words, the English pay no attention to these crimes.

[4] **spetia:** specie; coin.

[5] **pieces of Eight:** Spanish dollars containing eight reals (**Ryalls**), worth ninety-six cents.

they call them,) or Good hard money, as sometimes silver coin is termed by them; also Wampom, vizt. Indian beads which serves for change. *Pay as mony* is provisions, as aforesaid one Third cheaper then as the Assembly or General Court sets it; and *Trust* as they and the merchant agree for time.

Now, when the buyer comes to ask for a comodity, sometimes before the merchant answers that he has it, he sais, *is Your pay redy?* Perhaps the Chap Reply's Yes: what do You pay in? say's the merchant. The buyer having answered, then the price is set; as suppose he wants a sixpenny knife, in pay it is 12*d* – in pay as money eight pence, and hard money its own price, viz. 6*d*. It seems a very Intricate way of trade and what Lex Mercatoria[1] had not thought of.

Being at a merchants house, in come a tall country fellow, with his alfogeos[2] full of Tobacco; for they seldom Loose their Cudd, but keep Chewing and Spitting as long as they're eyes are open, – he advanc't to the midle of the Room, makes an Awkward Nodd, and spitting a Large deal of Aromatick Tincture, he gave a scrape with his shovel like shoo, leaving a small shovel full of dirt on the floor, made a full stop, Hugging his own pretty Body with his hands under his arms, Stood staring rown'd him, like a Catt let out of a Baskett. At last, like the creature[3] Balamm Rode on, he opened his mouth and said: have You any Ribinen for Hatbands to sell I pray? The Questions and Answers about the pay being past, the Ribin is bro't and opened. Bumpkin Simpers, cryes its confounded Gay I vow; and beckning to the door, in comes Jone Tawdry[4] drop-

ping about 50 curtsees, and stands by him: hee shows her the Ribin. *Law, You,* sais shee, *its right Gent,[5] do You take it, tis dreadfully pretty.* Then she enquires, *have you any hood silk I pray?* Which being brought and bought, *Have You any thred silk to sew it with* says shee, which being accommodated with they Departed. They Generaly stand after they come in a great while speachless, and sometimes dont say a word till they are askt what they want, which I impute to the Awe they stand in of the merchants, who they are constantly almost Indebted too; and must take what they bring without Liberty to choose for themselves; but they serve them as well, making the merchants stay long enough for their pay.

We may observe here the great necessity and bennifitt both of Education and Conversation; for these people have as Large a portion of mother witt, and sometimes a Larger, than those who have bin brought up in Citties; But for want of emprovements, Render themselves almost Ridiculos, as above. I should be glad if they would leave such follies, and am sure all that Love Clean Houses (at least) would be glad on't too.

They are generaly very plain in their dress, throuout all the Colony, as I saw, and follow one another in their modes; that You may know where they belong especially the women, meet them where you will.

Their Chief Red Letter day is St. Election,[6] which is annually Observed according to Charter, to choose their Govenr: a blessing[7] they can never be thankfull enough for, as they will find, if ever it be their hard fortune to loose

---

[1] Lex Mercatoria (mûr·kȧ·tō′rĭ·ȧ): the law of merchants.

[2] alfogeos (ăl·fō′jĭ·ōs): Spanish saddlebags; here used humorously for cheeks.

[3] creature: a famous ass in the Bible (Num. 22:21–33), which could speak.

[4] Jone Tawdry: humorous name for a country girl.

[5] Gent: a rustic abbreviation for genteel or elegant.

[6] St. Election: a humorous way of indicating that an election was as religiously observed as a saint's day in a Catholic country.

[7] blessing: In Massachusetts the governor was appointed by the king, to the great dissatisfaction of that colony.

it. The present Governor in Conecticott is the Honorable John Winthrop Esq. A Gentleman of an Ancient and Honourable Family, whose Father was Govenor here sometime before, and his Grand father had bin Govr of the Massachusetts. This gentleman is a very curteous and afable person, much Given to Hospitality, and has by his Good services Gain'd the affections of the people as much as any who had bin before him in that post.

HARDSHIPS OF TRAVEL

Decr. 6th. Being by this time well Recruited and rested after my Journy, my business lying unfinished by some concerns at New York depending thereupon, my Kinsman, Mr. Thomas Trowbridge of New Haven, must needs take a Journy there before it could be accomplished, I resolved to go there in company with him, and a man of the town which I engaged to wait on me there. Accordingly, Dec. 6th we set out from New Haven, and about 11 the same morning came to Stratford ferry; which crossing, about two miles on the other side Baited our horses and would have eat a morsell ourselves, But the Pumpkin and Indian mixt Bred had such an Aspect, and the Barelegg'd Punch so awkerd or rather Awful a sound, that we left both, and proceeded forward, and about seven at night come to Fairfield, where we met with good entertainment and Lodg'd; and early next morning set forward to Norowalk, from its halfe Indian name *Northwalk,* when about 12 at noon we arrived, and Had a Dinner of Fryed Venison, very savoury. Landlady wanting some pepper in the seasoning, bid the Girl hand her the spice in the little *Gay* cupp on the shelfe. From hence we Hasted towards Rye, walking and Leading our Horses neer a mile together, up a prodigios high Hill; and so Riding till about nine at night, and there arrived and took up our Lodgings at an ordinary,[1] which a French family kept. Here being very hungry, I desired a fricasee which the Frenchman undertakeing, mannaged so contrary to my notion of Cookery, that I hastned to Bed superless; And being shewd the way up a pair of stairs which had such a narrow passage that I had almost stopt by the Bulk of my Body; But arriving at my apartment found it to be a little Lento[2] Chamber furnisht amongst other Rubbish with a High Bedd and a Low one, a Long Table, a Bench and a Bottomless chair, — Little Miss went to scratch up my Kennell[3] which Russelled as if shee'd bin in the Barn amongst the Husks, and supose such was the contents of the tickin — nevertheless being exceedingly weary, down I laid my poor Carkes[4] (never more tired) and found my Covering as scanty as my Bed was hard. Annon I heard another Russelling noise in The Room — called to know the matter — Little miss said shee was making a bed for the men; who, when they were in Bed, complained their leggs lay out of it by reason of its shortness — my poor bones complained bitterly not being used to such Lodgings, and so did the man who was with us; and poor I made but one Grone, which was from the time I went to bed to the time I Riss, which was about three in the morning, Setting up by the Fire till Light, and having discharged our ordinary[5] which was as dear as if we had had far Better fare — wee took our leave of Monsieur and about seven in the morn come to New Rochell a french town, where we had a good Breakfast. And in the strength of that about an how'r before sunsett got to York. Here I applyd myself to Mr. Burroughs, a merchant to

[1] **ordinary:** inn.
[2] **Lento:** a lean-to room, or one under a low, sloping roof.
[3] **scratch up my Kennell:** humorous for shake up my mattress.
[4] **Carkes:** carcass.
[5] **discharged our ordinary:** paid the bill.

whom I was recommended by my Kinsman Capt. Prout, and received great
Civilities from him and his spouse, who
were now both Deaf but very agreeable
in their Conversation, Diverting me
with pleasant stories of their knowledge
in Brittan from whence they both come.

For Your Vocabulary

DIFFERENCES IN SPELLING: You could
scarcely read the psalm from *The Bay
Psalm Book* and the selection from Mrs.
Knight's *Journal* without being impressed
by the difference between seventeenth-
century and modern spelling. *Chayre,
winde, chaffe, shoo, bennifitt, farr, midle,*
are only a few of the many words which

look queer to us. Point out other differences in spelling.

On the whole, do you think modern
spelling is an improvement? How would
you judge whether spelling has improved?
What makes one spelling preferable to another? Which spelling in each of the following groups do you prefer, and why:
*catalog, catalogue; color, colour; gray,
grey; night, nite; plough, plow; program,
programme; shew, show; tho, though;
traveler, traveller?* What is meant by
"spelling reform"? What are the advantages and disadvantages of "reformed
spelling"? In this connection someone may
wish to look up the famous playwright
G. B. Shaw's views on the subject and the
bequest in his will to assist spelling reform.

William Byrd
1674–1744

A HISTORY OF THE DIVIDING LINE

Colonel William Byrd represents the early
Southern aristocrat at his finest. He inherited wealth and a handsome estate; with
his European education he encouraged cultural interests and built up the best private library in Virginia. One of his public
services was to oversee the running of a
definite boundary line between Virginia
and North Carolina to prevent recurring
disputes. The line stands to this day. The
notes taken on this expedition he later ex-
panded into a "history," but they were
not printed until almost a hundred years
after his death. Colonel Byrd's keen observations and vivid descriptions may be compared with those of Sarah Kemble Knight,

but you will notice that his point of view
toward society is different, and his smooth,
witty style is that of a more cultivated
writer.

CAMP LIFE

March 12 [*1728*]. . . . Our landlord [1]
had a tolerable good house and clean
furniture, and yet we could not be
tempted to lodge in it. We chose rather
to lie in the open field, for fear of growing too tender. A clear sky, spangled
with stars, was our canopy which, be-

[1] landlord: a plantation owner named Bal-
lance.

ing the last thing we saw before we fell asleep, gave us magnificent dreams. The truth of it is, we took so much pleasure in that natural kind of lodging that I think at the foot of the account mankind are great losers by the luxury of feather beds and warm apartments.

The curiosity of beholding so new and withal so sweet a method of encamping, brought one of the senators of North Carolina to make us a midnight visit. But he was so very clamorous in his commendations of it that the sentinel, not seeing his quality, either through his habit or behavior, had like to have treated him roughly.

After excusing the unseasonableness of his visit, and letting us know he was a Parliament man, he swore he was so taken with our lodging that he would set fire to his house as soon as he got home and teach his wife and children to lie, like us, in the open field.

THE DISMAL SWAMP

March 14. Before nine of the clock this morning, the provisions, bedding, and other necessaries were made up into packs for the men to carry on their shoulders into the Dismal. They were victualed for eight days at full allowance, nobody doubting but that would be abundantly sufficient to carry them through that inhospitable place; nor indeed was it possible for the poor fellows to stagger under more. As it was, their loads weighed from sixty to seventy pounds, in just proportion to the strength of those who were to bear them.

'Twould have been unconscionable to have saddled them with burthens heavier than that, when they were to lug them through a filthy bog which was hardly practicable with no burthen at all. Besides this luggage at their backs, they were obliged to measure the distance, mark the trees, and clear the way for the surveyors every step they went. It was really a pleasure to see with how

much cheerfulness they undertook, and with how much spirit they went through all this drudgery. For their greater safety, the commissioners took care to furnish them with Peruvian bark, rhubarb, and hipocoacanah,[1] in case they might happen, in that wet journey, to be taken with fevers or fluxes.

Although there was no need of example to inflame persons already so cheerful, yet, to enter the people with better grace, the author and two more of the commissioners accompanied them half a mile into the Dismal. The skirts of it were thinly planted with dwarf reeds and gall bushes but, when we got into the Dismal itself, we found the reeds grew there much taller and closer and, to mend the matter, was so interlaced with bamboo briers that there was no scuffling through them without the help of pioneers. At the same time, we found the ground moist and trembling under our feet like a quagmire, insomuch that it was an easy matter to run a ten-foot pole up to the head in it, without exerting any uncommon strength to do it.

Two of the men, whose burthens were the least cumbersome, had orders to march before with their tomahawks and clear the way, in order to make an opening for the surveyors. By their assistance we made a shift to push the line half a mile in three hours, and then reached a small piece of firm land about one hundred yards wide standing up above the rest like an island. Here the people were glad to lay down their loads and take a little refreshment, while the happy man whose lot it was to carry the jug of rum began already, like Aesop's bread-carriers,[2] to find it grow a good deal lighter.

After reposing about an hour, the

---

[1] **hipocoacanah:** an herb now known as ipecac.

[2] **Aesop's bread-carriers:** According to the fable the man who wanted the lightest burden on the journey was laughed at for choosing the bread, which was the heaviest; but by night the bread had all been distributed and he had only the empty basket to carry.

commissioners recommended vigor and constancy to their fellow travelers, by whom they were answered with three cheerful huzzas in token of obedience. This ceremony was no sooner over but they took up their burthens and attended the motion of the surveyors who, though they worked with all their might, could reach but one mile farther, the same obstacles still attending them which they had met with in the morning.

However small this distance may seem to such as are used to travel at their ease, yet our poor men, who were obliged to work with an unwieldy load at their backs, had reason to think it a long way; especially in a bog where they had no firm footing, but every step made a deep impression, which was instantly filled with water. At the same time they were laboring with their hands to cut down the reeds, which were ten feet high, their legs were hampered with the briers. Besides, the weather happened to be very warm, and the tallness of the reeds kept off every friendly breeze from coming to refresh them. And, indeed, it was a little provoking to hear the wind whistling among the branches of the white cedars, which grew here and there amongst the reeds, and at the same time not have the comfort to feel the least breath of it.

In the meantime the three commissioners returned out of the Dismal the same way they went in and, having joined their brethren, proceeded that night as far as Mr. Wilson's.

This worthy person lives within sight of the Dismal, in the skirts whereof his stocks range and maintain themselves all the winter, and yet he knew as little of it as he did of *Terra Australis Incognita*.[1] He told us a Canterbury tale [2] of

[1] *Terra Australis Incognita:* unknown southern land, such as Byrd's descendant, Rear Admiral Richard E. Byrd, has lately explored.

[2] **Canterbury tale:** here, an incredible tale. The *Canterbury Tales* are famous old stories re-

a North Briton whose curiosity spurred him a long way into this great desert, as he called it, near twenty years ago, but he having no compass, nor seeing the sun for several days together, wandered about till he was almost famished; but at last he bethought himself of a secret his countrymen make use of to pilot themselves in a dark day.

He took a fat louse out of his collar and exposed it to the open day on a piece of white paper which he brought along with him for his journal. The poor insect, having no eyelids, turned himself about till he found the darkest part of the heavens, and so made the best of his way toward the north. By this direction he steered himself safe out, and gave such a frightful account of the monsters he saw and the distresses he underwent, that no mortal since has been hardy enough to go upon the like dangerous discovery.

NORTH CAROLINA PLANTATION LIFE

March 25. . . . In the meantime, we who stayed behind had nothing to do but to make the best observations we could upon that part of the country. The soil of our landlord's plantation, though none of the best, seemed more fertile than any thereabouts, where the ground is near as sandy as the deserts of Africa, and consequently barren. The road leading from thence to Edenton, being in distance about twenty-seven miles, lies upon a ridge called Sandy Ridge, which is so wretchedly poor that it will not bring potatoes.

The pines in this part of the country are of a different species from those that grow in Virginia: their bearded leaves are much longer and their cones much larger. Each cell contains a seed of the size and figure of a black-eyed pea, which, shedding in November, is

counted in verse by the first great English poet, Chaucer. The reference shows Byrd's literary education.

*Westover, on the bank of the James River, was built along classic lines.
William Byrd inherited this dignified brick house from his father, and re-
modeled it to suit his own life of ordered leisure. (Library of Congress)*

very good mast for hogs, and fattens them in a short time.

The smallest of these pines are full of cones, which are eight or nine inches long, and each affords commonly sixty or seventy seeds. This kind of mast has the advantage of all other by being more constant, and less liable to be nipped by the frost or eaten by the caterpillars. The trees also abound more with turpentine, and consequently yield more tar than either the yellow or the white pine; and for the same reason make more durable timber for building. The inhabitants hereabouts pick up knots of lightwood in abundance, which they burn into tar, and then carry it to Norfolk or Nansimond for a market. The tar made in this method is the less valuable because it is said to burn the cordage, though it is full as good for all other uses as that made in Sweden and Muscovy.[1]

Surely there is no place in the world where the inhabitants live with less labor than in North Carolina. It approaches nearer to the description of Lubberland [2] than any other, by the great felicity of the climate, the easiness of raising provisions, and the slothfulness of the people.

Indian corn is of so great increase that a little pains will subsist a very large family with bread, and then they may have meat without any pains at all, by the help of low grounds, and the great variety of mast that grows on the high land. The men for their parts, just

[1] **Muscovy:** Russia.

[2] **Lubberland:** a paradise for lazy fellows. The following comments on the natives show the antipathy between the aristocratic Virginians and the small farmers of North Carolina, who were largely former servants.

like the Indians, impose all the work upon the poor women. They make their wives rise out of their beds early in the morning, at the same time that they lie and snore till the sun has run one-third of his course and dispersed all the unwholesome damps. Then, after stretching and yawning for half an hour, they light their pipes, and, under the protection of a cloud of smoke, venture out into the open air; though, if it happens to be never so little cold, they quickly return shivering into the chimney corner. When the weather is mild, they stand leaning with both their arms upon the cornfield fence, and gravely consider whether they had best go and take a small heat at the hoe: but generally find reasons to put it off till another time.

Thus they loiter away their lives, like Solomon's sluggard [1] with their arms across, and at the winding up of the year scarcely have bread to eat.

To speak the truth, 'tis a thorough aversion to labor that makes people file off to North Carolina, where plenty and warm sun confirm them in their disposition to laziness for their whole lives.

[1] **Solomon's sluggard:** King Solomon said, "Go to the ant, thou sluggard; consider her ways, and be wise" (Prov. 6:6).

Jesuit Relations

LETTER FROM FATHER VIVIER OF THE SOCIETY OF JESUS

The *Jesuit Relations*, the official account of the activity of the French Jesuits in the New World, extends from 1611 to 1716. The annual reports of the missionaries in various parts of New France were sent to the superiors in Quebec or Montreal. These, in turn, sent home detailed reports of conditions that prevailed in the New World, as well as expert maps and accounts of explorations and discoveries. To the body of the *Relations* are appended private journals and letters, like the following one, that describe the American scene.

Father Louis Vivier was born in 1714 and entered the Society of Jesus in 1731. Eighteen years later, he came to the Illinois territory, was stationed at Kaskaskia until 1753, and died at Vincennes in 1756, during the French and Indian War.

Among the ILLINOIS,[1]
November 17, 1750.

MY REVEREND FATHER,
The peace of Our Lord.
I accept with pleasure the proposal which you make me. The slight merits

[1] **Illinois:** a tribe of Indians inhabiting the region in and near the present state of Illinois. The other tribes mentioned in Father Vivier's letter were to be found at various places in the Mississippi Valley.

"Letter from Father Vivier" from *The Jesuit Relations and Allied Documents,* published by Burrows Brothers. Reprinted by permission of the publishers.

I may acquire by my labors I consent willingly to share with you, on the assurance that you give me of assisting me with your holy prayers. I gain too much from this association not to be desirous of entering into it with all my heart.

There is another point which you desire, and on which I will satisfy you; and that is, the description of our Missions. We have three in this quarter: one consisting of Savages; one of French; and a third, partly of French and partly of Savages.

The first is composed of over six hundred Illinois, all baptized excepting five or six; but the brandy sold by the French, especially by the soldiers, in spite of the King's repeated prohibitions, and that which is sometimes distributed to them under the pretext of maintaining them in our interest, has ruined this Mission, and has caused the majority of them to abandon our holy Religion. The Savages — and especially the Illinois, who are the gentlest and most tractable of men — become, when intoxicated, madmen and wild beasts. Then they fall upon one another, stab with their knives, and tear one another. Many have lost their ears, and some a portion of their noses, in these tragic encounters. The greatest good that we do among them consists in administering baptism to dying children. I usually reside in this Mission of Savages with Father Guienne, who acts as my Master in the study of the Illinois language.

The French Cure under Father Vattrin's charge is composed of more than four hundred French people, of all ages, and more than two hundred and fifty Negroes. The third Mission is seventy leagues from here. It is much smaller; Father Meurin has charge of it. The remainder of our Louisiana Mission consists of a residence at New Orleans, where the Superior-general of the Mission resides with another of our Fathers, and two Brethren. We have there a considerable settlement, which is in very good condition. The revenues of this settlement, added to the pensions given us by the King, supply the needs of the Missionaries.

When the Mission is sufficiently provided with laborers (who in this Colony should be twelve in number), one is maintained among the Akansas, another among the Tchactas and a third among the Alibamons. Reverend Father Baudouin, the present Superior-general of the Mission, formerly resided among the Tchactas; he dwelt eighteen years among those barbarians. . . . Father Moran was among the Alibamons some years ago. . . . At present we have no one among the Akansas. Such, my Reverend Father, is the state of our Mission. The remainder of my letter will be a short description of this country. . . .

The mouth of the Mississippi lies on the 29th degree of north latitude. The King maintains a small garrison there, and also a Pilot to meet vessels and bring them into the river. The multitude of islands and of banks — not of sand, but of mud — which fill it, make its entrance very difficult for those who have never been there. The question is, to find the channel; and there is only one Pilot who is accustomed to the place and knows it thoroughly. Vessels experience difficulty in ascending the Mississippi. Besides the fact that the tide of the sea is not felt in it, it winds continually; so that it is necessary either to tow, or to have at one's command wind from all points of the compass. From the twenty-ninth to the thirty-first degree of latitude, it did not seem to me wider than the Seine in front of Rouen, but it is infinitely deeper. As one ascends, it becomes wider, but is shallower in proportion. Its length from the North to the South is known to be more than seven hundred leagues. According to the reports of the latest travelers, its source — which is more than three hundred leagues to the North of the

Illinois — is formed by the discharge of some lakes and swamps.

Mississippi, in the Illinois language, means "the great river." It seems to have usurped that name from the Missouri. Before its junction with that river, the Mississippi is of no great size. Its current is slight, while the Missouri is wider, deeper, more rapid, and takes its rise much farther away. Several rivers of considerable size empty into the Mississippi; but the Missouri alone seems to pour into it more water than all these rivers together. Here is the proof of it: the water of most — I might say, of all — of the rivers that fall into the Mississippi is only passably good, and that of several is positively unwholesome; that of the Mississippi itself, above its junction with the Missouri, is not of the best; on the contrary, that of the Missouri is the best water in the world. Now that of the Mississippi, from its junction with the Missouri to the sea, becomes excellent; the water of the Missouri must therefore predominate. The first travelers who came through Canada discovered the Mississippi; that is the reason why the latter has acquired the name of "great," at the expense of the glory of the other.

Both banks of the Mississippi are bordered, throughout nearly the whole of its course, by two strips of dense forests, the depth of which varies more or less from half a league to four leagues. Behind these forests the country is more elevated, and is intersected by plains and groves, wherein the trees are almost as thinly scattered as in our public promenades. This is partly due to the fact that the Savages set fire to the prairies toward the end of the autumn, when the grass is dry; the fire spreads everywhere and destroys most of the young trees. This does not happen in the places nearer the river, because, the land being lower, and consequently more watery, the grass remains green longer, and is less suscepti-

ble to the attacks of fire.

The plains and forests contain wild cattle, which are found in herds; deer, elk, and bears; a few tigers; numbers of wolves, which are much smaller than those of Europe, and much less daring; wildcats; wild turkeys and pheasants; and other animals, less known and of smaller size. This river, with all those that flow into it, as well as the lakes, — of which there are a great number, but which, individually, are quite small in extent, — are the abode of beavers; of a prodigious number of ducks, of three kinds; of teal, bustards, geese, swans, snipe; and of some other aquatic birds, whose names are unknown in Europe, to say nothing of the fish of many kinds in which they abound.

It is only at fifteen leagues above the mouth of the Mississippi that one begins to see the first French settlements, as the land lower down is not habitable. They are situated on both sides of the river as far as the Town. The lands throughout this extent, which is fifteen leagues, are not all occupied; many await new settlers. New Orleans, the Metropolis of Louisiana, is built on the east bank of the river; it is of medium size, and the streets are in straight lines; some of the houses are built of brick, and others of wood. It is inhabited by French, Negroes, and some Savages who are slaves; all these together do not, it seemed to me, number more than twelve hundred persons. . . .

Ascending the river, one finds French settlements above as well as below New Orleans. The most notable establishment is a small German Colony, ten leagues above it. La Pointe coupée [1] is thirty-five leagues from the German settlement. A palisaded fort has been built there, in which a small garrison is maintained. There are sixty residences, spread over an extent of five or six

_____

[1] **La Pointe coupée:** a point on the west bank of the Mississippi, northwest of Baton Rouge.

leagues, along the west bank of the river. Fifty leagues from La Pointe coupée are the Natchez. . . .

One hundred leagues above the Natchez are the Akansas, a savage Nation of about four hundred warriors. We have near them a fort with a garrison, where the convoys ascending to the Illinois stop to rest. There were some settlers there but in the month of May, 1748, the Chicachats, our irreconcilable foes, aided by some other barbarians, suddenly attacked the post; they killed several persons, and carried off thirteen into captivity. The rest escaped into the fort, in which there were at the time only a dozen soldiers. They made an attempt to attack it, but no sooner had they lost two of their people than they retreated. Their Drummer was a French deserter from the Akansas garrison itself. . . .

The Illinois are on the parallel of 38 degrees 15 minutes of latitude. The climate, which is very different from that of New Orleans, is almost similar to that of France; the great heats make themselves felt there a little earlier and more intensely; but they are neither so constant nor so lasting. The severe cold comes later. In winter, when the North wind blows, ice forms on the Mississippi sufficiently thick to bear the heaviest carts; but such cold weather does not last long. The winter here is an alternation of severe cold and quite mild weather, according as the winds blow from the North or from the South; and they succeed each other with fair regularity. This alternation is very injurious to the fruit trees. The weather may be very mild, a little warm even, as early as mid-February; the sap ascends in the trees, which become covered with blossoms; then a wind from the North springs up, and destroys the brightest hopes.

The soil is fertile, and vegetables of all kinds would grow in it almost as well as in France, if they were cultivated with care. Nevertheless wheat, as a rule, yields only from five to eightfold; but it must be observed that the lands are tilled in a very careless manner, and that they have never been manured during the thirty years while they have been cultivated. This poor success in growing wheat is due still more to the heavy fogs and too sudden heats. But, on the other hand, maize — which in France is called Turkish corn — grows marvelously; it yields more than a thousandfold; it is the food of domestic cattle, of the slaves, and of most of the natives of the country, who eat it as a treat. The country produces three times as much food as can be consumed in it. Nowhere is game more abundant; from mid-October to the end of March the people live almost entirely on game, especially on the wild ox and deer.

The horned cattle have multiplied exceedingly; most of them cost nothing, either for care or for food. The working animals graze on a vast common around the village; others, in much larger numbers, which are intended for breeding, are shut up throughout the year on a peninsula over ten leagues in extent, formed by the Mississippi and the river of the Tamarouas. These animals, which are seldom approached, have become almost wild, and artifice must be employed in order to catch them. If a habitant needs a pair of oxen, he goes to the peninsula. When he sees a bull large enough to be trained, he throws a handful of salt to him, and stretches out a long rope with a noose at the end; then he lies down. The animal which is eager for salt, draws near; as soon as its foot is in the noose the man on the watch pulls the rope, and the bull is captured. The same is done for horses, calves, and colts; this is all that it costs to get a pair of oxen or of horses. Moreover, these animals are not subject to any diseases; they live a long time, and, as a rule, die only of old age.

. . . There are several salt-springs in

this country, one of which, two leagues from here, supplies all the salt consumed in the surrounding country, and in many posts which are dependencies of Canada. There are mines without number, but as no one is in a position to incur the expense necessary for opening and working them, they remain in their original condition. Certain individuals content themselves with obtaining lead from some of these, because it lies almost at the surface of the ground. They supply this country, all the Savage Nations of the Missouri and Mississippi, and several posts of Canada. . . .

For the rest, this country is of far greater importance than is imagined. Through its position alone, it deserves that France should spare nothing to retain it. . . . By founding a solid establishment here, prepared to meet all these troubles, the King would secure the possession of the most extensive and the finest country in north America. To be convinced of this one has but to glance at the well-known map of Louisiana, and to consider the situation of the Illinois country and the multitude of Nations against whom the post usually serves as a barrier. . . .

For Discussion of the Diarists

1. What conditions in Connecticut did Mistress Knight find inferior to those in Massachusetts, and what others did she find preferable? On the whole, would you consider her tolerant or intolerant? Discuss the difficulties of travel in her day. Have we any comparable difficulties today? If so, what?

2. Find evidences of Byrd's energy, his sense of humor, his London education. What passage shows most clearly how far his own life had changed from pioneer conditions?

3. Outline briefly the missions Father Vivier describes. What conditions among the Illinois does he deplore? Which river

impressed him more — the Mississippi or the Missouri? Why? What indications does he give that this area would become the farm belt of the United States? What does he think of the future of his mission?

Reading on the Colonial Time

Adams, R. G., *Gateway to American History* (Little, Brown, 1927)

Bailey, C. S., *Pioneer Art in America* (Viking, 1944)

Bridenbaugh, Carl, *Cities in the Wilderness* (Ronald, 1938)

Calverton, V. F., *The Awakening of America*, Vol. I (Day, 1939)

Chitwood, O. P., *History of Colonial America* (Harper, 1948)

Coleman, R. V., *The First Frontier* (Scribner, 1948)

Dulles, F. R., *America Learns to Play* (first three chapters) (Appleton, 1940)

Eaton, J., *Lone Journey* (Roger Williams) (Harcourt, Brace, 1944)

Gould, M. E., *The Early American House* (McBride, 1949)

Gray, E. J., *Penn* (Viking, 1938)

Halsey, R. T. H., and E. Tower, *Homes of Our Ancestors* (Garden City, 1937)

Knowlton, D. C., and C. M. Gill, *When We Were Colonies* (American Book, 1934)

Langdon, W. C., *Everyday Things in American Life*, 2 vols. (Scribner, 1937–1941)

Phelan, T. P., *Catholics in Colonial Days* (Kenedy, 1935)

Rawson, M. N., *Of the Earth Earthy* (early handicrafts) (Dutton, 1937)

Rawson, M. N., *When Antiques Were Young* (Dutton, 1931)

Wertenbaker, T. J., *The Golden Age of Colonial Culture* (New York University Press, 1942)

Wright, L. B., *Atlantic Frontier* (Knopf, 1947)

COLLECTIONS OF SOURCE MATERIALS

Beston, H., *American Memory* (Farrar and Rinehart, 1937)

Cairns, W. B., *Early American Writers* (Macmillan, 1909)

Hart, A. B., and A. B. Chapman, *How Our Grandfathers Lived* (Macmillan, 1902)

*The interior of Independence Hall in Philadelphia, with the Liberty Bell
(Armstrong Roberts)*

The Making of a Nation

THE United States was born in the eighteenth century. The colonies that had been separate and concerned with their individual problems now united to face common problems — first to fight a war for independence, then to build a national government. And the voices and the writing of this growing America began to be heard and seen far beyond American shores.

In bustling eighteenth century America, people had little occasion to use literature for anything other than a tool. Literature had to do a job — like the ax that cut the forest, or the clipper that carried the goods. Literature's job in the first Colonial century had been to tell the people back home about the new world, to preserve the record of momentous events, to keep the people devout and God-fearing. Later the job was to alert the people to the political abuses of their governors, and still later to rouse the people to revolt and to encourage them during cold winters and military defeat. After the Revolution, the job of literature was to present and weigh all the conflicting ideas of how a new nation should be made, and to reconcile these ideas in documents which would last far into the future.

The American Genius for Political Writing

The best brains of the colonies were going into tasks like these, and that is why few imaginative and purely literary writings — like poems, stories, and novels of high quality — were written in America before 1800. But there is one shelf of early writings that today we would hardly trade for the most elegant poems or stories ever written on the continent. That is the shelf of political essays, speeches, and public documents written in America between 1750 and 1800. Perhaps the American talent is for politics and mechanics, rather than art; some people have said so. Whatever the reason, American talent, American thinking, and American energy combined in those years to produce documents that were read with admiration by the whole world. Franklin, Adams, Paine, Jefferson, Washington — none of them except Franklin and Paine professional writers — became world figures in a way that few of our poets and novelists have. Perhaps the greatest tribute ever paid them was spoken on the floor of the very body they attacked most vigorously, the British Parliament. Lord Chatham said there:

> When your Lordships look at the papers transmitted to us from America; when you consider their decency, firmness, and wisdom, you cannot but respect their cause and wish to make it your own. . . . For solidity of reasoning, force of sagacity, and wisdom of conclusion, under such a difficult body of circumstances, no nation or body of men can stand in preference to the general congress at Philadelphia.

The New American

ONE man represented, better than any other, the new kind of American who was emerging in the eighteenth century as the new country developed.

William Byrd and Jonathan Edwards were strong men, admirable men. But they were English colonials living on the continent of America. In a later time, Ralph Waldo Emerson, Abraham Lincoln, Mark Twain, and Thomas A. Edison were likewise strong and admirable men — and anywhere in the world they would have been recognized as Americans. Somewhere between those groups of men the colonial type fell away and the American type emerged. Exactly where and when we cannot tell, but we do know who it was that stood forth before all the world as the unmistakable representative of the new type, the American. He was Benjamin Franklin.

Benjamin Franklin: His Life Reflects the Times

Look at Franklin's life for a moment. He lived for eighty-four years. Everything about his long life is symbolic of what was happening in the colonies. He was born in Boston, the throne of Puritanism, but Puritan religion slipped easily from him. The best way to serve God, Franklin said, is in doing good to His other children. He illustrates the change that was coming over the northern colonies. The Puritan, the typical New Englander of the seventeenth century, was passing off the stage; the Yankee, the shrewd, kindly businessman, the typical New Englander of the eighteenth century, was replacing him.

When Franklin was twelve he went to work as an apprentice in his brother's newspaper print shop. His choice of trade was itself prophetic, because the power of the press was just beginning to be felt: without the press, there could have been no revolution in 1775; without it, the colonists could never have been ready for independent existence. The trade brought Franklin into contact with books, news, ideas. It took him to Philadelphia. It took him to England for two years when he was eighteen. That is a kind of symbol, too. William Byrd went to England for education; but Franklin went for business. Business was his schoolmaster. He came back from England, cosmopolitan and successful, at the age of twenty, and settled, not in Boston, the great theological town, but in Philadelphia, the great center of business.

Franklin as Citizen and Scientist

Franklin's career in Philadelphia symbolizes, too, the widening interest in culture and science in the eighteenth century. When he was barely twenty-one Franklin started a debating and so-

cial club called the Junto — the forerunner of all our businessmen's luncheon clubs. Most of its meetings were concerned with civic affairs, and from them came many of the progressive ideas that went into making Philadelphia a great city. The first public library in the colonies was one result of these ideas. Franklin was instrumental in founding the academy that grew into the University of Pennsylvania. As postmaster of Philadelphia, and later postmaster-general of all the colonies, he provided good mail service. He encouraged publishing, and himself issued books, newspapers, and magazines. *The Saturday Evening Post* traces its ancestry to one of his magazines. He had immense faith in science, which, he thought, was the vehicle by which the New World could outstrip the old. Someone asked him what good the balloon, just invented, could possibly do. "What good is a newborn baby?" he asked. He became something of a genius at adapting the newborn babies of science to practical use. He invented a better stove for the drafty colonial homes. He developed bifocal glasses.

He drew lightning down from the skies along his kite string, and proved it no different from laboratory electricity. From this experiment, he developed the lightning rod.

Franklin as a Political Figure

It was inevitable that Franklin should be drawn into political service. When he was thirty, he was made clerk of the general assembly of Pennsylvania. He became an assemblyman, and people looked toward him as the best practical intellect in the colony. They began to push more and more jobs at him. "Get Franklin to do it," they would say. He took on the task of representing Pennsylvania at the intercolonial congress, the job of trying to get redress at the English court for Pennsylvania's grievances. He had hardly come back when the situation grew worse again, and the clamor grew, "Call in Franklin." Back to England he went, for eleven years.

When the war came, they called in Franklin again, this time to get the aid of France and other countries unfriendly to England. No ambassador in Europe ever did a better job. Which would have been the greater loss — Franklin in Europe or Washington in the field — no man knows, but without either one of them the war might well have been lost. Franklin helped negotiate the peace treaty, came home to be president of Pennsylvania, and served, at the age of eighty-one, as his state's venerable delegate to the Constitutional Convention.

Franklin as Writer

It is easy to forget, in the glory of his public achievement, that Franklin was a writer. If he had never been a scientist, or a statesman, or a public man, or a businessman, he would still get into histories as a writer. He was not the greatest of our literary men, but he was a good one. His *Autobiography*, parts of which you will read in this book, is one of the classics of our literature. His most popular writing in his own time was *Poor Richard's Almanac*. He published his first almanac when he was only twenty-six. The booklet represented to all the world America's homely wisdom, humor, and way with words. It was the first book from the colonies that seemed to the readers of Europe anything more than a colonial book. Its circulation was fabulous, and anyone who could read English was likely to be repeating, "Poor Richard Says":

God helps them that help themselves.

Keep thy shop and thy shop will keep thee.

Early to bed, and early to rise,
Will make a man healthy, wealthy, and wise.

Franklin also wrote essays and short magazine pieces, a series of witty and graceful bagatelles for the courtiers and

ladies of France, some political documents, and a great many remarkable letters.

He was the first great American humorist. The European countries recognized something original in his humor. They blinked, then roared, when

Franklin told them solemnly of the "great leap of the whale over Niagara." They liked him the more for chuckling at himself in his autobiography. They respected him for the wit with which he exploded every sentence of "Rules by Which a Great Empire May Be Reduced to a Small One" like a whipcrack over the faces of the statesmen of England.

A Typically American Combination of Qualities

A remarkable and versatile man! Perhaps no other American can equal his record. And it is a peculiarly American record. What were the qualities that made it so American? One was his extraordinary grasp of practical affairs, side by side with an idealism that never let him quit trusting in man or in the future of the colonies. That combination of practicality and idealism goes all through American history from Franklin's time on. Franklin could be at once a shrewd businessman and a devoted public servant, a merchant and an artist, a hard bargainer and a generous friend. He had little eye for the past, but a high interest in the future. He was a living example of freedom of opportunity. He had a typically American faith in and grasp of practical science. And he had an American sense of humor.

The French statesman Turgot composed a Latin epitaph on Franklin which was translated, "He snatched the lightning from the heavens and the scepter from the hands of tyrants."

When Franklin was born (1706) Puritan power was at its height, and Jonathan Edwards, greatest of the Puritan preachers, was only three years old. When Franklin died (1790), Edwards had been dead thirty-two years, Puritanism was dead as a political force, national independence had been won, and Washington was President.

Benjamin Franklin
1706–1790

FROM AUTOBIOGRAPHY

Franklin's *Autobiography*, written late in life, is an account of his life up to 1757, portraying his weakness frankly and his strength with no false modesty. The first section, written in the form of a letter to his son, is especially direct, simple, and interesting. It shows clearly the difference between Franklin, the great disciple of common sense, and his Puritan forebears, who listened to long sermons in the attempt to discover whether they were among the chosen of God. Franklin, on the contrary, calmly decided for himself what virtues were desirable, and planned the systematic acquisition of them. While you may protest that what he achieved was not the virtuous but the expedient, you must remember that the self-control he advocated is an excellent foundation for a supernatural edifice.

PROJECT OF ARRIVING AT MORAL PERFECTION

In truth, I found myself incorrigible with respect to Order; and now I am grown old, and my memory bad, I feel very sensibly the want of it. But, on the whole, though I never arrived at the perfection I had been so ambitious of obtaining, but fell far short of it, yet I was, by the endeavor, a better and a happier man than I otherwise should have been if I had not attempted it; as those who aim at perfect writing by imitating the engraved copies, though they never reach the wished-for excellence of those copies, their hand is mended by the endeavor.

It may be well my posterity should be informed that to this little artifice, with the blessing of God, their ancestor owed the constant felicity of his life, down to his seventy-ninth year, in which this is written. What reverses may attend the remainder is in the hand of Providence; but, if they arrive, the reflection on past happiness enjoyed ought to help his bearing them with more resignation. To Temperance he ascribes his long-continued health, and what is still left to him of a good constitution; to Industry and Frugality, the early easiness of his circumstances and acquisition of his fortune, with all that knowledge that enabled him to be a useful citizen, and obtained for him some degree of reputation among the learned; to Sincerity and Justice, the confidence of his country, and the honorable employs it conferred upon him; and to the joint influence of the whole mass of the virtues, even in the imperfect state he was able to acquire them, all that evenness of temper, and that cheerfulness in conversation, which makes his company still sought for, and agreeable even to his younger acquaintance. I hope, therefore, that some of my descendants may follow the example and reap the benefit.

It will be remarked that, though my scheme was not wholly without religion, there was in it no mark of any of the distinguishing tenets of any particular sect. I had purposely avoided them; for, being fully persuaded of the utility and excellency of my method, and that it might be serviceable to people in all religions, and intending some time or other to publish it, I would not have anything in it that should prejudice anyone, of any sect, against it. I purposed writing a little comment on each virtue, in which I would have shown the advantages of possessing it, and the mischiefs attending its opposite vice; and I should have called my book *The Art of Virtue,* because it would have shown the means and manner of obtaining virtue, which would have distinguished it from mere exhortation to be good, that does not instruct and indicate the means, but is like the apostle's man of verbal charity, who, without showing to the naked and hungry how or where they might get clothes or victuals, only exhorted them to be fed and clothed. — James 2:15–16.

But it so happened that my intention of writing and publishing this comment was never fulfilled. I did, indeed, from time to time, put down short hints of the sentiments, reasonings, etc., to be made use of in it, some of which I have still by me; but the necessary close attention to private business in the earlier part of my life, and public business since, have occasioned my postponing it; for, it being connected in my mind with *a great and extensive project* that required the whole man to execute, and which an unforseen succession of employs prevented my attending to, it has hitherto remained unfinished.

In this piece it was my design to explain and enforce this doctrine, that vicious actions are not hurtful because they are forbidden, but forbidden because they are hurtful, the nature of man alone considered; that it was, therefore, everyone's interest to be virtuous who wished to be happy even in this world; and I should, from this circumstance (there being always in the world a number of rich merchants, nobility, states, and princes, who have

need of honest instruments for the management of their affairs, and such being so rare), have endeavored to convince young persons that no qualities were so likely to make a poor man's fortune as those of probity and integrity.

My list of virtues contained at first but twelve; but a Quaker friend having kindly informed me that I was generally thought proud; that my pride showed itself frequently in conversation; that I was not content with being in the right when discussing any point, but was overbearing and rather insolent, of which he convinced me by mentioning several instances; I determined endeavoring to cure myself, if I could, of this vice or folly among the rest, and I added Humility to my list.

I cannot boast of much success in acquiring the *reality* of this virtue, but I had a good deal with regard to the *appearance* of it. I made it a rule to forbear all direct contradiction to the sentiments of others, and all positive assertion of my own. I even forbade myself, agreeably to the old law of our Junto,[1] the use of every word or expression in the language that imported a fixed opinion, such as *certainly, undoubtedly,* etc., and I adopted, instead of them, *I conceive, I apprehend,* or *I imagine* a thing to be so or so; or *it so appears to me at present.* When another asserted something that I thought an error, I denied myself the pleasure of contradicting him abruptly, and of showing immediately some absurdity in his proposition; and in answering I began by observing that in certain cases or circumstances his opinion would be right, but in the present case there *appeared* or *seemed* to me some difference, etc. I soon found the advantage of this change in my manner; the conversations I engaged in went on more pleasantly. The modest way in which I proposed my opinions procured them a readier re-

[1] **Junto:** name of the debating society organized by Franklin.

BENJAMIN FRANKLIN — VERSATILE AMERICAN

(Right) *Franklin, the scholarly gentleman, in a painting by an eighteenth-century artist (Bettmann Archive)*

(Left) *Franklin, the diplomat, feted at the French court, as depicted in an old print (Library of Congress).* (Below left) *A copy of* Poor Richard's Almanack *with a pair of Franklin's spectacles and a typesetter's stick he used (From* Holiday, *copyright 1951 by the Curtis Publishing Co.).* (Below right) *The Franklin stove (Metropolitan Museum of Art).*

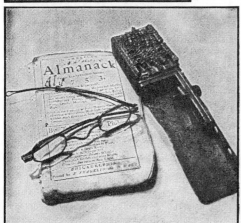

ception and less contradiction; I had less mortification when I was found to be in the wrong, and I more easily prevailed with others to give up their mistakes and join with me when I happened to be in the right.

And this mode, which I at first put on with some violence to natural inclination, became at length so easy and so habitual to me that perhaps for these fifty years past no one has ever heard a dogmatical expression escape me. And to this habit (after my character of integrity) I think it principally owing that I had early so much weight with my fellow citizens when I proposed new institutions, or alterations in the old, and so much influence in public councils when I became a member; for I was but a bad speaker, never eloquent, subject to much hesitation in my choice of words, hardly correct in language, and yet I generally carried my points.

In reality, there is, perhaps, no one of our natural passions so hard to subdue as *pride*. Disguise it, struggle with it, beat it down, stifle it, mortify it as much as one pleases, it is still alive, and will every now and then peep out and show itself; you will see it, perhaps, often in this history; for, even if I could conceive that I had completely overcome it, I should probably be proud of my humility.

SAYINGS OF POOR RICHARD

A standard way for a Colonial printer to eke out his income was to publish an almanac, a descriptive calendar of the year, giving information about such matters as the times of sunrise and sunset, movements of tides, and eclipses. All this information was much the same in any almanac. But a difference existed in the little "fillers" with which the editor rounded out the pages. Franklin's "fillers" in *Poor Richard's Almanac* were memorable "sayings" and bits of practical advice that made his almanac a household favor-

ite for twenty-five years and made Poor Richard immortal. He borrowed freely from the wisdom of the ages, but often he rephrased the maxims and used homely metaphors that had rich meaning for his readers. Few men have used figures of speech to better advantage. As you read these sayings, be sure you get the underlying meaning in such figures as "A small leak will sink a great ship."

Title page of "Poor Richard's Almanack." (Culver)

1. Experience keeps a dear school, but a fool will learn in no other.

2. Hunger is the best pickle.

3. Love your neighbor; yet don't pull down your hedge.

4. If a man empties his purse into

his head, no man can take it away from him. An investment in knowledge always pays the best interest.

5. Three may keep a secret if two of them are dead.

6. Tart words make no friends; a spoonful of honey will catch more flies than a gallon of vinegar.

7. Glass, china, and reputation are easily cracked and never well mended.

8. Fish and visitors smell in three days.

9. One today is worth two tomorrows.

10. A truly great man will neither trample on a worm nor sneak to an emperor.

11. He that riseth late must trot all day, and shall scarce overtake his business at night; while laziness travels so slowly that poverty soon overtakes him. Drive thy business. Let it not drive thee.

12. A little neglect may breed mischief; for want of a nail the shoe was lost; for want of a shoe the horse was lost; for want of a horse the rider was lost; for want of the rider the battle was lost.

13. If you would know the value of money, go and try to borrow some; he that goes a-borrowing goes a-sorrowing.

14. He that composes himself is wiser than he that composes books.

15. He that is of the opinion that money will do everything may well be suspected of doing everything for money.

16. If a man could have half his wishes he would double his troubles.

17. Creditors have better memories than debtors.

18. 'Tis hard for an empty bag to stand upright.

19. A lie stands on one leg, truth on two.

20. The sleeping fox catches no poultry.

21. A plowman on his legs is higher than a gentleman on his knees.

22. When the well's dry, we know the worth of water.

23. A small leak will sink a great ship.

24. 'Tis easier to build two chimneys than to keep one in fuel.

25. Now that I have a sheep and a cow everybody bids me good morrow.

26. Silks and satins, scarlet and velvet, put out the kitchen fire.

27. By diligence and perseverance the mouse ate the cable in two.

28. At a great penny-worth pause awhile. Many are ruined by buying bargains.

29. If you would have a faithful servant and one that you like, serve yourself.

30. Sloth, like rust, consumes faster than labor wears; the used key is always bright.

31. Handle your tools without mittens; remember, the cat in gloves catches no mice.

32. He that hath a trade hath an estate. At the workingman's house hunger looks in, but dare not enter.

For Discussion of Franklin

Project of Arriving at Moral Perfection

1. Which of Franklin's virtues seems to you the hardest to attain? the easiest? the most worth while? What is the chief defect of his list of virtues?

2. Why did humility come last on Franklin's list? How did it affect his method of carrying on an argument? How did this lesson affect his later career? What do you think of his method? Would you use it yourself? Is it widely practiced?

3. Why does the whole discussion belong to an age of Yankee common sense rather than to the late Puritan period typified by Edwards' sermon?

4. What practical value is there in this selection for you?

Sayings of Poor Richard

1. Which maxims say literally what they mean? Which express their ideas through a figure of speech?

2. Paraphrase or explain the meaning

of those in the second group. Which group makes the more vivid impression on you? Memorize those maxims you like best.

3. Write a few figurative maxims of your own, using modern things as comparisons (radio-listening, air travel, and so on). Or tell briefly of some personal experience, ending your talk with a quotation from Poor Richard.

For Your Vocabulary

PERSUASIVE WORDS: Franklin found that he could attain at least the " appearance of humility " and thus win arguments by using certain soothing or persuasive words and phrases and by avoiding others, which he calls dogmatical (we'd say dogmatic). He lists two or three dogmatic words (*certainly, undoubtedly*) and a few persuasive phrases (*I imagine, it so appears to me*). What words of each type can you add to those mentioned by Franklin? Have two students conduct an argument before the class, one using positive, dogmatic assertions and contradictions, the other using persuasive words and phrases. Let half the listeners record the words and phrases *to avoid*, the other half the words and phrases *to employ*.

Voices of the Revolution

IN THE third quarter of the eighteenth century the colonies were feeling their strength and chafing against what seemed to them unjust restrictions and punishments imposed by the mother country. The voices of righteous anger rose from the newspapers and pamphlets of the Atlantic seaboard like the voices of the Old Testament prophets. And a thrilling thing happened to American writing. Lawyers, printers, newspaper reporters, farmers took advantage of the newly-founded newspapers and magazines to talk to their fellow Americans. Under the inspiration of the fight for freedom, they raised the level of their writing above the tone of law brief, newspaper report, letter to the editor, and political speech — raised it to the level of important literature.

Political Writers and Orators

We can mention only a few of these political writers who were the voices of the American Revolution.

One of them was *James Otis*, the lawyer who led the battle in Massachusetts against the writs of assistance which allowed British soldiers to search any home they wished. A man's house is his castle, Otis argued. He made that apply to the whole colonial relation to England.

There were *John* and *Samuel Adams*. John was the lawyer, orator, and writer of polished essays. Samuel was one of the great propagandists of his time. The papers were filled with his shrewd, angry arguments, usually under assumed names, but all designed, as he said, to " keep the enemy in the wrong."

There was *John Dickinson*, the Pennsylvania gentleman farmer who was asked to draft many of the important documents of the Continental Congress, and who set forth the American arguments with great dignity and persuasiveness in a series of published letters " from an American farmer in Pennsylvania to the inhabitants of the British colonies."

Patrick Henry, the Most Famous Orator

Some colonists, like *Patrick Henry*, made their contributions in oratory, which the newspapers picked up and spread. Henry became famous when he arose in the Virginia assembly in 1765 to fight the Stamp Act. This law taxed legal documents, newspapers, pamphlets, and periodicals, and therefore hampered the most articulate men in the colonies — the lawyers, editors, and pamphleteers. Henry told the house in

his speech against that act: "Caesar had his Brutus; Charles the First his Cromwell; and George the Third — may profit by their example!" You are familiar, of course, with his battle cry, "Give me liberty or give me death!" which was in one of his speeches ten years later.

Thomas Paine Puts the War into Words

But of all the voices of the Revolution, no writer had more to do with furthering the American cause than did Thomas Paine. Paine was born in England and came to America only in 1774, in time to help administer the final blow to those colonists who opposed the revolution.

He came to America for one reason only: because he believed in the rights of man, as Jefferson later stated them

in the Declaration, and he sought to do everything possible to maintain and extend them. He was as nearly a professional revolutionary as the Americans had on their side. Furthermore, he could write so the people would read. His pen, they said, trailed fire and blood.

He wrote *Common Sense* in 1776. The time for appealing to Britain was past. The time had come to talk to the people of America and tell them plainly what they had to do. Nobody could do this better than Paine. "I challenge the warmest advocate of reconciliation," he wrote, "to show a single advantage that this continent can reap by being connected with Great Britain. . . . There is something absurd in supposing a continent to be perpetually governed by an island." *Common Sense* sold one hundred thousand copies inside three months. Paine believed what he wrote. He enlisted in the Continental army as a private. In the face of the first defeats, he wrote another piece, which he called simply *The Crisis*. It began with a sentence like a trumpet call: "These are the times that try men's souls." Washington ordered it read to all his troops.

Paine returned to Europe in his last years, living in France. He later wrote vigorously in defense of the French Revolution and consequently was criticized by some Americans for his radical views.

Thomas Jefferson, the Greatest Voice of the Age

Thomas Jefferson, when he was only thirty-three, wrote the greatest piece of literature to come out of the Revolution, the Declaration of Independence. No document of such paramount importance could be written entirely by one man; Jefferson had suggestions from Franklin and others. The final product rang like a clarion. Yet it was simply written. The argument was that man has certain rights, which no government may interfere with; the British government had interfered with those rights in the cases listed; therefore, the only recourse of the colonies was to declare themselves independent of Britain and fight for independence if necessary. You will, of course, read the Declaration carefully. It is not only one of the noblest political documents of all time; it is the heart of the argument for political freedom.

In his later career, Jefferson stood before the country as the greatest champion of the right of the people to control government. "I am not one of those who fear the people," he told the Americans who talked about King Mob; and he said again and again in one phrase or other, "I know no safe depository of the ultimate powers of society but the people themselves." In Jefferson's thinking, political freedom was closely entwined with freedom to worship according to conscience, and freedom to learn. Three of the accomplishments he was most proud of are therefore celebrated in the epitaph which he himself composed for his gravestone:

HERE WAS BURIED
THOMAS JEFFERSON
AUTHOR OF THE DECLARATION
OF AMERICAN INDEPENDENCE,
OF THE STATUTE OF VIRGINIA
FOR RELIGIOUS FREEDOM,
AND FATHER OF THE UNIVERSITY
OF VIRGINIA

The New Nation

After independence was won, there came the most dangerous period of all. You have seen such a period yourself in the years after World War II. You have seen with what mutual suspicion nations face each other, and how every issue must be debated in order to lessen fears, objections, and misunderstandings and to arrive at the best possible compromise. Something very much like that was taking place after the Revolution when the thirteen colonies were trying to write a constitution and make a nation. There was long debate and argument and compromise, and for a while people doubted that the colonies would ever succeed in getting together. But

they did, and the government they created has long ago proved its worth and their wisdom.

The Federalist Papers Defend the Constitution

You ought to remember the name of one classic of political writing that was produced during the period when the new Constitution was being drafted, the *Federalist* papers. They were a series of essays discussing the form that the new government should take, and offering a defense of the proposed Constitution. Hamilton, Madison, and Jay collaborated in writing them, and they helped to focus the thinking of the colonists.

Washington Expresses the American Idea

George Washington, inevitably, was the first President. He could have been the first king, but he declined a crown. He served two terms, saw the country well started, and retired to Mount Vernon on the Potomac. When he left the capital, he wrote an address of kindly advice — as the father of his country might be expected to do. Part of it is reprinted in the following pages. As you read it over you will realize what a long road the country had walked in a century. How strange and inapplicable Washington's phrases would have sounded in 1696: "The unity of government . . . is a main pillar of your real independence . . . The basis of our political systems is the right of the people to make and alter their constitutions of government. . . . the power and the right of the people to establish government . . ."

It is undoubtedly true that the germ of political freedom was in the colonies from the moment the settlers arrived there, but it is also true, as John Adams said, that the real revolution was in the minds of Americans rather than on the battlefield. Somewhere in the years before 1796, the American people came to hold such ideas of political freedom as Washington expressed, and as you will read in the selections that follow. That was the revolution.

Patrick Henry
1736–1799

SPEECH IN THE VIRGINIA CONVENTION

Patrick Henry was one of the Virginians who were convinced that the colonists must resort to armed resistance. On March 23, 1775, he delivered the following speech before the House of Burgesses. This body had reassembled after being dissolved by the royal governor, and a resolution had been proposed that "Virginia be immediately put into a posture of defense." The opposition within the House was strong and influential, for the rich planters feared a popular uprising even more than oppression from the crown.

Imagine yourself one of the men torn between the momentous choices that confronted the burgesses at this fateful session. Picture the rawboned, six-foot lawyer from the western foothills rising to make his impassioned appeal. Yet he could not with mere emotional force sway this assembly of the ablest men in the colony. Follow his reasoning as he lays a solid foundation of facts for each appeal to pride and patriotism. Then you will understand why he moved his audience to choose rebellion rather than further submission.

Mr. President:

No man thinks more highly than I do of the patriotism, as well as abilities, of the very worthy gentlemen who have just addressed the house. But different men often see the same subject in different lights; and, therefore, I hope it will not be thought disrespectful to those gentlemen, if, entertaining as I do opinions of a character very opposite to theirs, I shall speak forth my sentiments freely, and without reserve. This is no time for ceremony. The question before the house is one of awful moment to this country. For my own part, I consider it as nothing less than a question of freedom or slavery. And in proportion to the magnitude of the subject ought to be the freedom of the debate. It is only in this way that we can hope to arrive at truth, and fulfill the great responsibility which we hold to God and our country. Should I keep back my opinions at such a time, through fear of giving offense, I should consider myself as guilty of treason toward my country, and of an act of disloyalty toward the Majesty of Heaven, which I revere above all earthly kings.

Mr. President, it is natural to man to indulge in the illusions of hope. We are apt to shut our eyes against a painful truth, and listen to the song of that siren till she transforms us into beasts. Is this the part of wise men, engaged in a great and arduous struggle for liberty? Are we disposed to be of the number of those who having eyes see not, and having ears hear not, the things which so nearly concern their temporal salvation? For my part, whatever anguish of spirit it may cost, I am willing to know the whole truth; to know the worst and to provide for it.

I have but one lamp by which my feet are guided, and that is the lamp of experience. I know of no way of judging of the future but by the past. And judging by the past, I wish to know what there has been in the conduct of the British ministry for the last ten years to justify those hopes with which gentlemen have been pleased to solace themselves and the house? Is it that insidious smile with which our petition has been lately received? Trust it not, sir; it will prove a snare to your feet. Suffer not yourselves to be betrayed with a kiss. Ask yourselves how this gracious reception of our petition comports with those warlike preparations which cover our waters and darken our land. Are fleets and armies necessary to a work of love and reconciliation? Have we shown ourselves so unwilling to be reconciled that force must be called in to win back our love? Let us not deceive ourselves, sir. These are the implements of war and subjugation — the last arguments to which kings resort.

I ask gentlemen, sir, what means this martial array, if its purpose be not to force us to submission? Can gentlemen assign any other possible motive for it? Has Great Britain any enemy in this quarter of the world, to call for all this accumulation of navies and armies? No, sir, she has none. They are meant for us: they can be meant for no other. They are sent over to bind and rivet upon us those chains which the British ministry have been so long forging.

And what have we to oppose to them? Shall we try argument? Sir, we have been trying that for the last ten years. Have we anything new to offer upon the subject? Nothing. We have held the subject up in every light of which it is capable; but it has been all in vain. Shall we resort to entreaty and humble supplication? What terms shall we find which have not been already exhausted? Let us not, I beseech you, sir, deceive ourselves longer.

Sir, we have done everything that could be done to avert the storm which is now coming on. We have petitioned; we have remonstrated; we have supplicated; we have prostrated ourselves before the throne and have implored its interposition to arrest the tyrannical hands of the ministry and Parliament.

Patrick Henry makes a speech in the Virginia House of Burgesses in Williamsburg — a scene from the documentary film, Bill of Rights. *Although Henry's famous " Give me liberty or give me death!" speech was made before the House of Burgesses at St. John's Church, Richmond, he was a frequent speaker here, where many issues affecting the American colonies were hotly argued. (Metro-Goldwyn-Mayer)*

Our petitions have been slighted; our remonstrances have produced additional violence and insult; our supplications have been disregarded; and we have been spurned with contempt from the foot of the throne! In vain, after these things, may we indulge the fond hope of peace and reconciliation. There is no longer any room for hope. If we wish to be free, if we mean to preserve inviolate those inestimable privileges for which we have been so long contending, if we mean not basely to abandon the noble struggle in which we have been so long engaged, and which we have pledged ourselves never to abandon until the glorious object of our contest shall be obtained — we must fight! I repeat it, sir, we must fight! An appeal to arms and to the God of Hosts is all that is left us!

They tell us, sir, that we are weak — unable to cope with so formidable an adversary. But when shall we be stronger? Will it be the next week, or the next year? Will it be when we are totally disarmed, and when a British guard shall be stationed in every house? Shall we gather strength by irresolution and inaction? Shall we acquire the means of effectual resistance by lying supinely on our backs, and hugging the delusive phantom of hope until our enemies shall have bound us hand and foot? Sir, we are not weak, if we make a proper use of those means which the God of nature hath placed in our power. Three millions of people, armed in the holy cause of liberty, and in such a country as that which we possess, are invincible by any force which our enemy can send against us. Besides, sir, we shall not fight our battles alone. There is a just God who presides over the destinies of nations, and who will raise up friends to fight our battles for us. The battle, sir, is not to the strong alone; it is to the vigilant, the active, the brave. Besides, sir, we have no election. If we were base enough to desire it, it is now too late to retire from the contest. There is no retreat but in submission and slavery! Our chains are forged! their clanking may be heard on the plains of Boston! The war is inevitable — and let it come! I repeat it, sir, let it come!

It is in vain, sir, to extenuate the matter. Gentlemen may cry, Peace, Peace — but there is no peace. The war is actually begun! The next gale that sweeps from the north will bring to our ears the clash of resounding arms! Our brethren are already in the field! Why stand we here idle? What is it that gentlemen wish? What would they have? Is

life so dear, or peace so sweet, as to be purchased at the price of chains and slavery? Forbid it, Almighty God! I know not what course others may take; but as for me, give me liberty or give me death!

For Discussion of Henry

1. How did the orator take pains to insure the good will and attention of the opposition at the beginning of his speech? What strong reason did he give for opposing their views?

2. What common human emotion does Henry brand as the " song of that siren "? What is meant by this phrase? From Henry's speech can you construct the arguments of the opposition? What facts does he cite to undermine these arguments?

3. Why did Henry urge immediate action without delay? What facts does he cite to support this course? Do you agree that delay would have made the task of the colonists more difficult? Why?

4. Before his stirring emotional conclusion, Henry gives reasons why the colonists may hope for victory. Review them. Are they sound arguments?

Thomas Paine

1737–1809

THE CRISIS

Patrick Henry's oratory had its effect upon the Virginia House of Burgesses; but it was Thomas Paine who most effectively persuaded men in all the colonies that they could no longer be Americans and, at the same time, British subjects.

Paine's tract *Common Sense* effectively spread the plea to sever connections with the mother country; within six months of its publication the Declaration of Independence was signed. Then, after the first days of the war brought one discouragement after another to the Americans, Paine again fortified them with a stirring pamphlet, *The Crisis,* part of which you may read here. The opening sentence is one of the great phrases of our American tradition.

THESE are the times that try men's souls. The summer soldier and the sunshine patriot will, in this crisis, shrink from the service of their country; but he that stands it *now,* deserves the love and thanks of man and woman. Tyranny, like hell, is not easily conquered; yet we have this consolation with us, that the harder the conflict, the more glorious the triumph. What we obtain too cheap, we esteem too lightly: it is dearness only that gives everything its value. Heaven knows how to put a proper price upon its goods, and it would be strange indeed if so celestial an article as *freedom* should not be highly rated. Britain, with an army to enforce her tyranny, has declared that she has a right, not only to *tax,* but " to *bind* us in *all cases whatsoever* "; and if being bound in that manner is not slavery, then there is not such a thing as slavery upon earth. Even the expression is impious, for so unlimited a power can belong only to God.

I have as little superstition in me as any man living, but my secret opinion has ever been, and still is, that God Almighty will not give up a people to military destruction, or leave them unsupportedly to perish, who have so earnestly and so repeatedly sought to avoid the calamities of war by every decent method which wisdom could invent. Neither have I so much of the infidel in me as to suppose that He has relinquished the government of the world and given us up to the care of devils; and, as I do not, I cannot see on what grounds the king of Britain can look up to heaven for help against us.

I once felt all that kind of anger which a man ought to feel against the mean principles that are held by the Tories. A noted one, who kept a tavern at Amboy, was standing at his door, with as pretty a child in his hand, about eight or nine years old, as ever I saw, and after speaking his mind as freely as he thought was prudent, finished with this unfatherly expression. " Well! give me peace in my day." Not a man lives on the continent but fully believes that a separation must some time or other finally take place, and a generous parent should have said, " If there must be trouble, let it be in my day, that my child may have peace "; and this single reflection, well applied, is sufficient to awaken every man to duty. Not a place upon earth might be so happy as America. Her situation is remote from all the wrangling world, and she has nothing to do but to trade with them. A man can distinguish himself between temper and principle, and I am as confident as I am that God governs the world, that America will never be happy till she gets clear of foreign dominion. Wars, without ceasing, will break out till that period arrives, and the continent must in the end be conqueror; for though the flame of liberty may sometimes cease to shine, the coal can never expire.

The heart that feels not now, is dead; the blood of his children will curse his cowardice who shrinks back at a time when a little might have saved the whole and made them happy. I love the man that can smile in trouble, that can gather strength from distress and grow brave by reflection. 'Tis the business of little minds to shrink; but he whose heart is firm, and whose conscience approves his conduct, will pursue his principles unto death. My own line of reasoning is to myself as straight and clear as a ray of light. Not all the treasures of the world, so far as I believe, could have induced me to support an offensive war, for I think it murder; but if a thief breaks into my house, burns and destroys my property, and kills or threatens to kill me, or those that are in it, and to "bind me in all cases whatsoever" to his absolute will, am I to suffer it? What signifies it to me, whether he who does it is a king or a common man; my countryman or not my countryman; whether it be done by an individual villain or an army of them? If we reason to the root of things, we shall find no difference; neither can any just cause be assigned why we should punish in the one case and pardon in the other.

For Discussion of Paine

1. What does Paine mean by "the summer soldier and the sunshine patriot"?

2. What statement by the British government does he consider a clear example of tyranny?

3. What answer does Paine have for the timid person who is afraid of England's might? For the one who says, "Give me peace in my day"? For the one who believes all war is wrong?

4. If you had been an undecided citizen of that day, which would have moved you more strongly to action — Patrick Henry or Thomas Paine? Why?

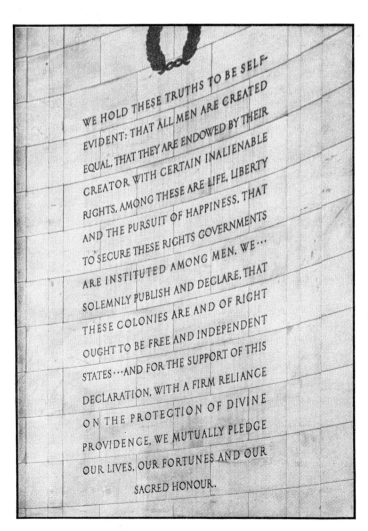

The leading writers of eighteenth-century America were politically-minded. The eloquent words of the Declaration of Independence which appear on the interior of the Jefferson Memorial in Washington, D.C., symbolize the spirit of the founders of our government. (Ewing Galloway)

Thomas Jefferson
1743–1826

THE DECLARATION
OF INDEPENDENCE

Before July 4, 1776, when the Second Continental Congress adopted the Declaration of Independence written by Thomas Jefferson with assistance from a committee including John Adams and Benjamin Franklin, many Americans had only a general idea of the new way of life toward which they struggled. With the publication of this immortal document, their faith was crystallized in words of beauty and power. The formal declaration of separation from England was at the time the main part of the document. But today the preliminary statement of belief in human rights and their fulfillment in government is most stirring. It is the finest expression of the American ideal ever formulated. It was a rallying cry to contemporaries. It has been a lasting inspiration to all Americans of later ages. Do not let your familiarity with the rolling phrases lull you into skimming lightly over their meaning. Think through every word of it. Today the Declaration is as important as ever before in our history.

W
HEN, in the course of human events, it becomes necessary for one people to dissolve the political bands which have connected them with another, and to assume among the powers of the earth the separate and equal station to which the laws of nature and of nature's God entitle them, a decent respect to the opinions of mankind requires that they should declare the causes which impel them to the separation.

We hold these truths to be self-evident: that all men are created equal, that they are endowed by their Creator with certain inalienable rights, that among these are life, liberty, and the pursuit of happiness. That to secure these rights, governments are instituted among men, deriving their just powers from the consent of the governed. That whenever any form of government becomes destructive of these ends it is the right of the people to alter or abolish it, and to institute a new government, laying its foundation on such principles, and organizing its powers in such form, as to them shall seem most likely to effect their safety and happiness. Prudence, indeed, will dictate that governments long established should not be changed for light and transient causes; and accordingly all experience hath shown that mankind are more disposed to suffer, while evils are sufferable, than to right themselves by abolishing the forms to which they are accustomed. But when a long train of abuses and usurpations, pursuing invariably the same object, evinces a design to reduce them under absolute despotism, it is their right, it is their duty, to throw off such government, and to provide new guards for their future security. Such has been the patient sufferance of these colonies; and such is now the necessity which constrains them to

A

B

FURNITURE AND DRESS STYLES IN THE EIGHTEENTH CENTURY

were still patterned on those of Europe, although native American craftsmen were gaining reputations for fine work. (a) Supper room in the Governor's Palace, Williamsburg, Virginia (Colonial Williamsburg, Inc.). (b) Lady's silk brocade dress made in England (Museum of City of New York). (c) Painted settee by English cabinetmaker, Sheraton (Index of American Design, National Gallery of Art). (d) Silver teapot designed by Paul Revere in Boston (Metropolitan Museum of Art).

C

D

E

F

(e) *Mt. Vernon, home of George Washington on the Potomac River, Virginia (Armstrong Roberts).* (f) *Highboy, Queen Anne style, probably made in Connecticut, early eighteenth century (Index of American Design, National Gallery of Art).* (g) *Elegant coach of James Beekman, New York City. Made in France about 1770. (New York Historical Society).*

G

alter their former systems of government. The history of the present King of Great Britain is a history of repeated injuries and usurpations, all having in direct object the establishment of an absolute tyranny over these states. To prove this let facts be submitted to a candid world.

[Here follows a long list of injustices suffered by the Colonies.]

In every stage of these oppressions we have petitioned for redress in the most humble terms: Our repeated petitions have been answered only by repeated injuries.

A prince whose character is thus marked by every act which may define a tyrant, is unfit to be the ruler of a free people.

Nor have we been wanting in attentions to our British brethren. We have warned them from time to time of attempts by their legislature to extend an unwarrantable jurisdiction over us. We have reminded them of the circumstances of our emigration and settlement here. We have appealed to their native justice and magnanimity and we have conjured them by the ties of our common kindred to disavow these usurpations which would inevitably interrupt our connection and correspondence. They too have been deaf to the voice of justice and of consanguinity. We must, therefore, acquiesce in the necessity which denounces our separation and hold them, as we hold the rest of mankind, enemies in war, in peace, friends.

We, therefore, the representatives of the United States of America, in General Congress assembled, appealing to the Supreme Judge of the world for the rectitude of our intentions, do, in the name, and by the authority of the good people of these Colonies, solemnly publish and declare that these United Colonies are and of right ought to be free and independent States; that they are absolved from all allegiance to the British Crown, and that all political connection between them and the State of Great Britain is and ought to be totally dissolved; and that as free and independent States, they have full power to levy war, conclude peace, contract alliances, establish commerce, and to do all other acts and things which independent States may of right do.

And for the support of this declaration, with a firm reliance on the protection of Divine Providence, we mutually pledge to each other our lives, our fortunes, and our sacred honor.

For Discussion of Jefferson

1. What frequently-quoted phrases do you find here? Is it true that all men are created equal? In what sense did the writers of this document mean " equal"?

2. What part of this document might the Southern states have quoted to justify their secession from the Union?

3. Quote passages which remind the British that the colonists had attempted to settle their differences by other means than revolution.

4. What beliefs and policies of present-day totalitarian governments are in direct conflict with the truths expressed in the Declaration?

5. Get a copy of the constitution of the United Nations and compare statements of fundamental principles with those expressed in the Declaration. Do you believe the UN is working toward an extension of these principles to the whole world? Support your answer with definite information.

For Your Vocabulary

WORDS OFTEN CONFUSED: The Declaration says that " it is the right of the people . . . to institute a new government . . . [that] shall seem most likely to *effect* their safety and happiness." Did you read that word *effect* correctly? Or did you misread it to mean *affect?* In general use, *effect* is a noun and *affect* a verb: things which *affect* us have an *effect* on us. The verb *effect,* as used here, however, has a quite different meaning: " to bring to pass." What does it mean to *effect* safety and happiness? What does it mean to *affect* these conditions? Some other words often similarly confused are: *accept, except; al-* *lusion, illusion; contemptible, contemptu-* *ous; credible, creditable; imply, infer.* Use each of these pairs in sentences to show that you understand their meaning. Can you think of other words often confused?

Francis Hopkinson
1737–1791

THE BATTLE OF THE KEGS

As with other wars, the Revolution had its lighter side. The soldiers had their camp and marching songs, the most famous of which is " Yankee Doodle." Satire was a popular weapon of the literary men of the day, and they lost no opportunity to make the enemy appear ridiculous. The author of " The Battle of the Kegs " was a Philadelphia lawyer who had signed the Declaration of Independence and helped to draft the Articles of Confederation. He was also an accomplished musician, and perhaps the best Colonial composer.

Hopkinson's own note to this poem says: " The ballad was occasioned by a real incident. Certain machines, in the form of kegs, charged with gunpowder, were sent down the river to annoy the British shipping, then at Philadelphia. The danger of these machines being discovered, the British manned the wharfs and shipping, and discharged their small arms and cannons at everything they saw floating in the river during the ebb tide."

Gallants, attend, and hear a friend
  Trill forth harmonious ditty:
Strange things I'll tell, which late befell
  In Philadelphia city.

'Twas early day, as poets say,   5
  Just when the sun was rising,
A soldier stood on a log of wood
  And saw a thing surprising.

As in amaze he stood to gaze,
  The truth can't be denied, sir,   10
He spied a score of kegs or more
  Come floating down the tide, sir.

A sailor, too, in jerkin blue,
  This strange appearance viewing,
First damned his eyes, in great sur-
    prise,   15
  Then said, " Some mischief's brewing:

" These kegs, I'm told, the rebels hold,
  Packed up like pickled herring;
And they're come down to attack the
    town,
  In this new way of ferrying."   20

The soldier flew, the sailor too,
  And scared almost to death, sir,
Wore out their shoes to spread the news,
  And ran till out of breath, sir.

Now up and down throughout the town
  Most frantic scenes were acted;   26

And some ran here and others there,
    Like men almost distracted.

Some fire cried, which some denied,
    But said the earth had quakèd;   30
And girls and boys, with hideous noise,
    Ran through the streets half naked.

Sir William,° he, snug as a flea,
    Lay all this time a-snoring,
Nor dreamed of harm, as he lay warm,
    [The Yankees quite ignoring].   36

Now in a fright he starts upright,
    Awaked by such a clatter;
He rubs his eyes and boldly cries,
    "For God's sake, what's the matter?"

At his bedside he then espied   41
    Sir Erskine at command, sir:
Upon one foot he had one boot,
    An t'other in his hand, sir.

"Arise, arise!" Sir Erskine cries;   45
    "The rebels, more's the pity,
Without a boat are all afloat
    And ranged before the city.

"The motley crew, in vessels new,
    With Satan for their guide, sir,   50
Packed up in bags, or wooden kegs,
    Come driving down the tide, sir.

"Therefore prepare for bloody war:
    These kegs must all be routed
Or surely we despised shall be,   55
    And British courage doubted."

The royal band now ready stand,
    All ranged in dread array, sir,
With stomachs stout, to see it out,
    And make a bloody day, sir.   60

The cannons roar from shore to shore,
    The small arms make a rattle;
Since wars began, I'm sure no man
    E'er saw so strange a battle.

33. **Sir William:** Sir William Howe, the British commander.

The rebel dales, the rebel vales,   65
    With rebel trees surrounded,
The distant woods, the hills and floods,
    With rebel echoes sounded.

The fish below swam to and fro,
    Attacked from every quarter: 70
"Why, sure," thought they, "the devil's
    to pay
'Mongst folks above the water."

The kegs, 'tis said, though strongly
    made
Of rebel staves and hoops, sir,   74
Could not oppose their powerful foes,
    The conquering British troops, sir.

From morn till night these men of
    might
Displayed amazing courage,
And when the sun was fairly down
    Retired to sup their porridge.   80

An hundred men, with each a pen,
    Or more, upon my word, sir,
It is most true would be too few
    Their valor to record, sir.

Such feats did they perform that day
    Against those wicked kegs, sir,   86
That years to come, if they get home,
    They'll make their boasts and brags,
    sir.

For Discussion of Hopkinson

1. What caused the false alarm in the story? How is the idea of panic made vivid? How are the British made to appear ridiculous? Why would this tale especially please the Americans during the dark days when the war seemed going against them?

2. This poem is written in typical ballad measure. What can you learn of the ballad form by studying the rhyme scheme and number of accents to a line?

3. What is satire? How effective do you consider it as a weapon? Where else in your reading have you encountered satire? Write a short satire in ballad measure, or in prose, if you prefer, attacking something you dislike.

Alexander Hamilton
1757–1804

SPEECH IN DEFENSE OF THE CONSTITUTION

The speech below, one of many made by Hamilton in favor of ratification of the Constitution, was delivered on June 21, 1788, before the New York State Legislature. Through the force of Hamilton's logic and oratory the sixty-five legislators — forty-six of whom were Antifederalists — were persuaded to ratify by a majority of three. The speech answers the objection that the proposed Constitution did not prevent the "aristocrats" from gaining control of the government.

The sentiments expressed are typical of Hamilton's political philosophy. In American political tradition the term "Hamiltonian" has come to characterize a belief in government by a selected group of the "best people," the more intelligent, the more wealthy, the more able, as contrasted with "Jeffersonian," which denotes confidence in democratic government by the whole people. Jefferson was the leading liberal of his day; Hamilton, the leading conservative.

SIR, we hear constantly a great deal which is rather calculated to awake our passions, and create prejudices, than to conduct us to the truth, and teach us our real interests. I do not suppose this to be the design of the gentlemen. Why, then, are we told so often of an aristocracy? For my part, I hardly know the meaning of this word, as it is applied. If all we hear be true, this government is really a very bad one. But who are the aristocracy among us?

Where do we find men elevated to a perpetual rank above their fellow citizens, and possessing powers entirely independent of them? The arguments of the gentlemen only go to prove that there are men who are rich, men who are poor, some who are wise, and others who are not; that, indeed, every distinguished man is an aristocrat. This reminds me of a description of the aristocrats I have seen in a late publication styled the *Federal Farmer*. The author reckons in the aristocracy all governors of states, members of Congress, chief magistrates, and all officers of the militia. This description, I presume to say, is ridiculous. The image is a phantom. Does the new government render a rich man more eligible than a poor one? No. It requires no such qualification. It is bottomed on the broad and equal principle of your state constitution.

Sir, if the people have it in their option to elect their most meritorious men, is this to be considered as an objection? Shall the Constitution oppose their wishes and abridge their most invaluable privilege? While property continues to be pretty equally divided, and a considerable share of information pervades the community, the tendency of the people's suffrages will be to elevate merit even from obscurity. As riches increase and accumulate in few hands, as luxury prevails in society, virtue will be in a greater degree considered as only a graceful appendage of wealth, and the tendency of things will be to depart from the republican standard. This is the real disposition of human nature: it is what neither the honorable member nor myself can correct; it is a common misfortune, that awaits our state constitution as well as all others.

There is an advantage incident to large districts of election, which perhaps the gentlemen, amidst all their apprehensions of influence and bribery, have not adverted to. In large districts, the corruption of the electors is much more difficult; combinations for the purposes of intrigue are less easily formed; factions and cabals are little known. In a small district, wealth will have a more complete influence, because the people in the vicinity of a great man are more immediately his dependents, and because this influence has fewer objects to act upon. It has been remarked that it would be disagreeable to the middle class of men to go to the seat of the new government. If this be so, the difficulty will be enhanced by the gentleman's proposal. If his argument be true, it proves that the larger the representation is, the less will be your chance of having it filled. But it appears to me frivolous to bring forward such arguments as these. It has answered no other purpose than to induce me, by way of reply, to enter into discussion, which I consider as useless, and not applicable to our subject.

It is a harsh doctrine that men grow wicked in proportion as they improve and enlighten their minds. Experience has by no means justified us in the supposition that there is more virtue in one class of men than in another. Look through the rich and the poor of the community, the learned and the ignorant. Where does virtue predominate? The difference indeed consists, not in the quantity, but kind, of vices which are incident to various classes; and here the advantage of character belongs to the wealthy. Their vices are probably more favorable to the prosperity of the state than those of the indigent, and partake less of moral depravity.

After all, sir, we must submit to this idea, that the true principle of a republic is that the people should choose whom they please to govern them. Representation is imperfect in proportion as the current of popular favor is checked. This great source of free government, popular election, should be perfectly pure and the most unbounded liberty allowed. Where this principle is adhered to; where, in the organization of the government, the legislative, executive, and judicial branches are rendered distinct; where, again, the legislature is divided into separate houses, and the operations of each are controlled by various checks and balances, and, above all, by the vigilance and weight of the state governments — to talk of tyranny and the subversion of our liberties is to speak the language of enthusiasm. This balance between the national and state governments ought to be dwelt on with peculiar attention, as it is of the utmost importance. It forms a double security to the people. If one encroaches on their rights, they will find a powerful protection in the other. Indeed, they will both be prevented from overpassing their constitutional limits, by a certain rivalship, which will ever subsist between them. I am persuaded that a firm union is as necessary to perpetuate our liberties as it is to make us respectable; and experience will probably prove that the national government will be as natural a guardian of our freedom as the state legislatures themselves.

For Discussion of Hamilton

1. What does Hamilton think is the great advantage of a balance between the national and state governments? How does our form of government provide for " checks and balances "?

2. Have the prophecies Hamilton made come to pass? Do you agree or disagree with his argument? Discuss.

3. Contrast the political philosophies of Hamilton and Jefferson. Which is more nearly embodied in the Constitution?

4. Read the Bill of Rights. What fundamental liberties are guaranteed in this part of the Constitution? Does the Constitution protect the rights of those who would criticize and seek to change the form of government it establishes? Discuss this in the light of present-day events.

5. The Preamble to the Constitution is well worth memorizing: " We, the people of the United States, in order to form a more perfect Union, establish justice, insure domestic tranquility, provide for the common defense, promote the general welfare, and secure the blessings of liberty to ourselves and our posterity, do ordain and establish this Constitution for the United States of America."

For Your Vocabulary

CAPITAL LETTERS: When Hamilton spoke of departing from the *" republican* standard " he meant the standards of a republic. If he had meant the standards of the Republican party (not in existence in his day), he would have said *" Republican* standards." There is a similar difference between a *democrat* and a *Democrat.* (By the way, what is the difference in definition between a *democracy* and a *republic?* You may need to refer to a dictionary for help in this. Note the interesting origin of the two words.)

Capital letters function in the meanings of other words. What is the difference between *catholic* interests and *Catholic* interests? between a *communist* and a *Communist?* between a *mason* and a *Mason?* between going *south* and going *South?* Can you give any other words whose meaning is changed by capitalization?

George Washington
1732-1799

FAREWELL ADDRESS

September 17, 1796

In the fall of 1796 Washington decided that the relatively secure condition of America, external as well as internal, justified his leaving the public scene to retire to Mount Vernon. To notify his fellow citizens of his resolution not to be a candidate for a third term as President, he published in a Philadelphia newspaper the famous document now known as " Washington's Farewell Address." Few other state papers have been so frequently reprinted as this

so-called address. Small wonder it is that the parting advice of one who had been the pre-eminent leader of a military, economic, and political struggle should be sought again and again as successive questions of policy have arisen. Every American should know and understand the principles stated in this famous document by the father of our country. In the following selected passages you will find statements of these basic principles, which he himself designated as " some sentiments, which are the result of much reflection, of

This statue of Washington, flanked by Robert Morris (left) *and Haym Salomon* (right), *both of whom played important roles in the Revolution, stands in Chicago, dedicated to the ideal of good citizenship.* (*Ewing Galloway*)

no inconsiderable observation, and which appear to me all-important to the permanency of your felicity as a people."

The headings inserted by the editors at the beginnings of the paragraphs will give you the main points. Dig out for yourself the advice Washington offers his fellow countrymen on each topic. You will need to use the glossary to understand some of the words. But before you seek that assistance, try to figure out the meaning of each difficult word from its context. Then check with the glossary to see how near you came to the definition.

Preserve Liberty

INTERWOVEN as is the love of liberty with every ligament of your hearts, no recommendation of mine is necessary to fortify or confirm the attachment.

Protect National Unity

The unity of government, which constitutes you one people, is a main pillar of your real independence, the support of your tranquillity at home, your peace abroad; of your safety; of your prosperity; of that very liberty which you so highly prize. The name of America, which belongs to you, in your national capacity, must always exalt the just pride of patriotism, more than any appellation derived from local discriminations. One of the expedients of party to acquire influence, within particular districts, is to misrepresent the opinions and aims of other districts. You cannot shield yourselves too much against the jealousies and heartburnings which spring from these misrepresentations.

Obey the Law

The basis of our political systems is the right of the people to make and to alter their constitutions of government. But the constitution which at any time exists, till changed by an explicit and authentic act of the whole people, is sacredly obligatory upon all. The very idea of the power and the right of the people to establish government presupposes the duty of every individual to obey the established government.

Beware of Easy Changes in Government

Toward the preservation of your government, and the permanency of your present happy state, it is requisite, not only that you steadily discountenance irregular opposition to its acknowledged authority, but also that you resist with care the spirit of innovation upon its principles, however specious the pretexts. Remember that facility in changes, upon the credit of mere hypothesis and opinion, exposes to perpetual change, from the endless variety of hypothesis and opinion; and remember, especially, that, for the efficient management of your common interests, in a country so extensive as ours a government of as much vigor as is consistent with the perfect security of liberty is indispensable. Liberty itself will find in such a government . . . its surest guardian.

Beware of Political Party Spirit

Let me warn you in the most solemn manner against the baneful effects of the spirit of party generally. The disorders and miseries which result gradually incline the minds of men to seek security and repose in the absolute power of an individual; and sooner or later the chief of some prevailing faction, more able or more fortunate than his competitors, turns this disposition to the purposes of his own elevation, on the ruins of public liberty.

Preserve Checks and Balances

The necessity of reciprocal checks in the exercise of political power, by dividing and distributing it into different depositories, and constituting each the guardian of the public weal against invasions by the others, has been evinced by experiments ancient and modern, some of them in our country and under our own eyes. To preserve them must be as necessary as to institute them. If, in the opinion of the people, the distribution or modification of the constitutional powers be in any particular wrong, let it be corrected by an amendment in the way which the Constitution designates.

Cherish Religion and Morality

Of all the dispositions and habits which lead to political prosperity, religion and morality are indispensable supports. In vain would that man claim the tribute of patriotism who should labor to subvert these great pillars of human happiness, these firmest props of the duties of men and citizens. The mere politician, equally with the pious man, ought to respect and cherish them. A volume could not trace all their connections with private and public felicity.

Promote Education

Promote, as an object of primary importance, institutions for the general diffusion of knowledge. In proportion as the structure of a government gives force to public opinion, it is essential that public opinion should be enlightened.

Cherish Public Credit

As a very important source of strength and security, cherish public credit.

Avoid Permanent Alliances

Observe good faith and justice toward all nations; cultivate peace and harmony with all. The nation which indulges toward another an habitual hatred or an habitual fondness is in some degree a slave. It is a slave to its animosity or to its affection, either of which is sufficient to lead it astray from its duty and its interest.

The great rule of conduct for us, in regard to foreign nations, is, in extending our commercial relations, to have with them as little political connection as possible. Europe has a set of primary interests, which to us have none, or a remote relation. Hence she must be engaged in frequent controversies, the causes of which are essentially foreign to our concerns. Hence, therefore, it must be unwise in us to implicate ourselves by artificial ties, in the ordinary vicissitudes of her politics or the ordinary combinations and collisions of her friendships and enmities. Our detached and distant situation invites and enables us to pursue a different course. Why forego the advantages of so peculiar a situation? It is our true policy to steer clear of permanent alliances with any portion of the foreign world. Even our commercial policy should hold an equal and impartial hand; neither seeking nor granting exclusive favors or preferences, constantly keeping in view that it is folly in one nation to look for disinterested favors from any other; that it must pay with a portion of its independence for whatever it may accept under that character.

For Discussion of Washington

1. See if you can recall without reference to the text the topics on which Washington offered advice. Group them under two main headings for the whole selection. Try this also for Hamilton's speech on page 461.

2. To understand this address fully you must recognize the difference between the United States in Washington's day and in your own. Compare conditions in such matters as boundaries, population, industries, transportation, communication, political parties; compare the state of international relations in the world in the eighteenth century with that in the twentieth. In the light of changed conditions, which parts of Washington's advice do you think apply today, and which do not? This question affords good subject matter for reports and informal debates.

3. Compare the style of this speech with the sharp, terse sentences of Patrick Henry (p. 449) and with the simplicity of Lincoln's phrasing (pp. 643–47). How is the style of an address intended for oral delivery likely to differ from that of one intended to be read?

For Your Vocabulary

VOCABULARY CHECK: The following short test on the words in the *Farewell Address* is similar to those now being given in branches of the armed services. Take it with your book open so that you can refer to the words in context.

So as not to mark up your book, make an answer sheet with two columns. Head one column SAME and the other column OPPOSITE. Then number from 1 to 10. For each word listed below there will be one word which has either the same or the opposite meaning. Choose this word and put it in the proper column on the answer sheet.

1. *tranquillity* at home *a.* prosperity; *b.* peace; *c.* poverty; *d.* strength

2. any *appellation* *a.* name; *b.* revenue; *c.* happiness; *d.* consolation

3. *explicit* act *a.* implied; *b.* unjust; *c.* hard to explain; *d.* thoughtless

4. *subvert* the power *a.* mismanage; *b.* bless; *c.* overthrow; *d.* wield

5. *discountenance* opposition *a.* destroy; *b.* curse; *c.* confuse; *d.* encourage

6. *facility* in changes *a.* tyranny; *b.* originality; *c.* difficulty; *d.* goodness

7. *baneful* effects *a.* stupid; *b.* similar; *c.* not easily explained; *d.* ruinous

8. public *weal*   *a.* notice; *b.* prosperity; *c.* punishment; *d.* performance

9. *indispensable supports*   *a.* costly; *b.* unnecessary; *c.* desirable; *d.* healthy

10. *disinterested favors*   *a.* uninteresting; *b.* large; *c.* expensive; *d.* unselfish

Reading on the Making of a Nation

SOURCE MATERIALS

Hart, A. B. and Mabel Hill, *Camps and Firesides of the Revolution,* revised ed. (Macmillan, 1922)

Lawson, Robert, *Watchwords of Liberty* (famous slogans and their origin) (Little, Brown, 1943)

Van Doren, Carl, *The Patriotic Anthology* (Doubleday, 1941)

Van Doren, C. C. and C. L. Carmer, *American Scriptures* (Boni and Gaer, 1946)

GENERAL DISCUSSIONS OF THE REVOLUTION

Bates, E. S., *American Faith* (Norton, 1940)

Commager, H. S. and A. Nevins, *Heritage of America* (Little, Brown, 1949)

Miller, J. C., *Origins of the American Revolution* (Little, Brown, 1943)

Monaghan, F., *Heritage of Freedom* (Princeton University Press, 1948)

Umbreit, K. B., *The Founding Fathers* (Harper, 1941)

Van Doren, C. C., *The Great Rehearsal* (Viking, 1948)

BIOGRAPHY

JOHN ADAMS. Bowen, Catherine D., *John Adams* (Little, Brown, 1950)

ETHAN ALLEN. Dean, S. W., *He Fought for Freedom* (Macrae Smith, 1940)

AARON BURR. Carroll, Mary, *The Man Who Would Not Wait* (Longmans, 1941); Lewis, Addison, *The Gadfly* (Book Paths, 1948)

BENJAMIN FRANKLIN. Maurois, André, *Franklin, the Life of an Optimist* (Didier, 1945); Meadowcroft, E. L., *Benjamin Franklin* (Crowell, 1941);

Nicolay, Helen, *Boys' Life of Benjamin Franklin* (Appleton, 1935)

ALEXANDER HAMILTON. Nicolay, Helen, *Boys' Life of Alexander Hamilton* (Century, 1929); Schachner, Nathan, *Alexander Hamilton* (Appleton, 1946); Smertenko, J. J., *Alexander Hamilton, Man of Action* (Messner, 1941)

PATRICK HENRY. Axelrod, Jacob, *Patrick Henry, the Voice of Freedom* (Random House, 1947)

THOMAS JEFFERSON. Written for young people: Daugherty, Sonia: *The Way of an Eagle* (Oxford, 1941); Nicolay, Helen, *Boys' Life of Thomas Jefferson* (Appleton, 1933). Written for adults: Malone, Dumas, *Jefferson the Virginian* (Little, Brown, 1948); Padover, S. K., *Complete Jefferson* (Duell, 1943)

JOHN PAUL JONES. Ellsberg, Edward, *I Have Just Begun to Fight* (Dodd, Mead, 1942); Johnson, G. W., *First Captain* (Coward-McCann, 1947); Lorenz, L., *John Paul Jones* (U. S. Naval Institute, 1943); Thomson, V., *Knight of the Seas* (Liveright, 1939)

FRANCIS SCOTT KEY. Holland, R. S., *Freedom's Flag* (Macrae Smith, 1943)

LAFAYETTE. Eaton, Jeanette, *Young Lafayette* (Houghton Mifflin, 1932); Nicolay, Helen, *Boys' Life of Lafayette* (Harper, 1920)

ISRAEL PUTNAM. Dean, L. W., *Old Wolf* (Farrar and Rinehart, 1942)

PAUL REVERE. Canfield, D. F., *Paul Revere and the Minute Men* (Landmark, 1950); Forbes, Esther, *America's Paul Revere* (simplified form of her standard work) (Houghton Mifflin, 1946); Rogers, F. and A. Beard, *Paul Revere* (Stokes, 1943)

GEORGE WASHINGTON. Freeman, Douglas S., *George Washington* (Scribner, 1948); Nicolay, Helen, *Boys' Life of Washington* (Century, 1932); Niles, B. R., *Martha's Husband* (McGraw-Hill, 1951)

MARTHA WASHINGTON. Desmond, Alice, *Martha Washington, Our First Lady* (Dodd, Mead, 1942)

For fiction, see list of novels, page 129. For historical reference, see also general reference list, page 253.

The clipper ship Benjamin F. Packard, *built in Bath, Maine. She carried lumber from the Pacific Northwest around Cape Horn, and brought tea from China and wool from Australia.* (Ewing Galloway)

The Flowering of the East

Part One

WHO reads an American book?" an English critic asked scornfully in an Edinburgh magazine. "Or goes to an American play?" he added. "Or looks at an American picture or statue? What does the world yet owe to American physicians or surgeons? What new substances have their chemists discovered? What constellations have been discovered by the telescopes of Americans? What have they done in mathematics?"

That was in 1820. By and large, the English critic was right. Two hundred and thirteen years after the first permanent English settlement, there was yet no real American literature. The originality of America had not yet expressed itself in great artists; it had expressed itself in frontier scouts and statesmen and practical men of affairs. America had not created fine art; it had created at first strong colonies, and then a free nation.

The Hundred Years' Growth

The exciting thing about the American story is how, in the hundred years after 1820, Americans made that kind of critic eat his words.

In 1820 there was very little to show. Fifty years later there was already a long shelf of books by distinguished American writers — Irving, Cooper, Bryant, Poe, Hawthorne, Whittier, Emerson, Thoreau, Lincoln, Longfellow, Holmes, Lowell, Prescott, Parkman, Melville, Whitman. Within another fifty years, in 1920, an American writer, Mark Twain, had received world-wide acclaim such as rarely has been given any man of letters. And Europe was reading by American electric lights, flying in a device developed by the Ohio Wright brothers, hiring a Johns Hopkins professor of surgery to be an Oxford professor, hearing about a new American device called radio broadcasting, and looking to the President of the United States to lead the world to peace.

All that in one hundred years! How did it happen? We don't know exactly. If we knew how to make Edisons and Twains we would make more of them. But we can look back and see some reasons why American art, science, and literature suddenly flowered after 1800.

The Time and Place for Literature

For one thing, Americans now had time. There had been very little time for art and literature when the colonists were trying to hold on to a little strip of land between sea and forest, fighting Indians and hunger and distance. There had been very little time while they were fighting for political freedom and planning a constitution and government. Literature is not written on the frontier. There isn't time for it. There is time only to keep alive, and build, and plan for a future that will give later generations more time and opportunity.

But in the nineteenth century the frontier was rolling far to the West, pouring its riches back to the East. The East had to make the machinery to settle the West. The East had to put up the supplies for western migration. The East had to finance a transportation system for the whole country. And so, while the frontier pushed west, large cities and rich states grew on the eastern seaboard. A literary movement seems to need cities, where men can gather and talk and argue, where theaters and museums and art galleries flourish, and where publishers and editors can have their headquarters. So, in the nineteenth century, New York, Boston, and Charleston, South Carolina, became centers of literary and artistic production, with smaller centers all around them.

America's Literary Independence

Moreover, the time was ripe. The freedoms for which Americans had been fighting for two centuries had been won. The nation was independent, and was feeling its muscles proudly like an adolescent boy. A spirit of adventure and accomplishment was in the air. The feeling was something like the Elizabethan Age of England, when Drake had beaten back the Spanish Armada, English ships were sailing to every coast in the world and bringing back wealth and knowledge, and men like Shakespeare were writing in London. The States had won their first war, they were winning the West and sending out ships and goods to all the world, they were growing rich and powerful, and they were proud of being a nation, proud of being Americans. In fact, writers began to be as excited over literary freedom as other Americans had been over freedom of religion and political freedom. They argued that American literature had been a colonial literature too long; now it should stand forth as a true national literature in its own right. American writers, too, should declare independence of Europe. They should write like Americans, not like Englishmen.

And so all the hard-won freedom, the new prosperity and leisure, the idealism, the new national pride, the vigor that had formerly been drained off by the fight for other freedoms — all this flowered in America's first great age of literature.

> *Irving and Cooper*

The Flowering of New York

THE first flowering was in New York. From its very beginning, New York had been cosmopolitan. As early as 1643, a Dutch settler reported, eighteen languages were being spoken there. It was a natural port of entry; and, as industry grew around it in the eighteenth century, it became the great funnel through which much of American export was poured into ships bound for Europe and Asia. Some parts of it looked like a little country town, with streets following old cowpaths through what later became the financial district, and pigs running wild over the lawns and roadways. But Broadway was straight and wide. And great things were being done. By 1800, a cabinet-maker named Duncan Phyfe had a little shop near the foot of Broadway where he was making furniture that today brings fabulous sums and is often duplicated. By 1800, a fur-trader named John Jacob Astor was building a business that connected New York with every part of the continent. The town at the end of the Oregon Trail, where the

Columbia River meets the Pacific, was named after him, Astoria. From the beginning New Yorkers were good businessmen. The first evidence was the purchase of all of Manhattan Island from the Indians for twenty-four dollars.

In the eighteenth century New York had been a little brick town at the lower end of Manhattan Island, where men talked like Englishmen and gathered in coffeehouses consciously patterned after London coffeehouses. But now it was changing. It was becoming different from anything Europe had seen: a melting pot for the races of Europe, an example of the American qualities of shrewdness and enterprise, a center for American thinkers and writers.

Among those early New York writers, the ones who achieved greatest fame were Washington Irving and James Fenimore Cooper.

Washington Irving

Washington Irving was not born to a professional or literary family, as so many European writers were; his father was a hardware merchant, and Washington was trained, like many another middle-class American boy, for law and business. But by one of the chances that make literature, he was never attracted enough by law to practice it. He was attracted more by a trip to Europe than by the opportunities of New York politics, and when he got to Europe the hardware firm he left behind went bankrupt. So he turned to writing to support himself, and became one of the first professional writers in America.

Irving a Writer in the English Style

American literature in his time had not yet declared full literary independence, though it was moving toward it. Irving looked toward Europe more than toward the West. He spent twenty of his first fifty years in Europe. His writing was not much different from the writing of the kindly, urbane humorists and essayists who wrote in England during the eighteenth century. Indeed, he was a curiosity to the English not because he wrote differently from them, but because as an American he could write so well. " It has been a matter of marvel to my European readers that a man from the wilds of America should express himself in tolerable English," he reported, with tongue in cheek. " I was looked upon as something new and strange in literature; a kind of demisavage with a feather in his hand instead of on his head; and there was a curiosity to hear what such a being had to say about civilized society."

Everybody liked the " demisavage." He was lovable, sociable, a good storyteller, playful, witty, fond of gay parties (his social life as a young man became something of a legend in New York), sentimental enough to treasure anything old, romantic enough to be interested in anything strange or distant. He was a kind humorist, not a bitter one. He laughed with, rather than at, his subjects, and he wrote of experiences he was fond of and wanted to share with his readers.

Irving a Portrayer of Three Civilizations

As we look back over his life, we can see that he was profoundly moved by three geographical areas, three civilizations, of which only one was American.

That one was, of course, the New York where he grew up — the city that was growing from an old Dutch town into a melting-pot city, and the Hudson valley that was already so rich in memory and legend. As a matter of fact, Irving himself did a lot to hasten that change in New York City by writing one book, his first one, *A History of New York by Diedrich Knickerbocker*. It was a comic parody on a certain pompous history of the city that glorified the Dutch ancestry of its social leaders. The original book has been forgotten, but Irving's parody lives on, and nobody dared be very pompous about the old Dutch settlers after Irving had set the whole English-speaking world chuckling at his hilarious caricatures of the solid Dutch burghers.

Even more important than New York City to Irving was the old Hudson valley. He made his first trip up the valley in 1800, and on that trip he saw Sleepy Hollow and Rip Van Winkle's Catskills. Later he often went squirrel hunting in Sleepy Hollow. When he came back from his seventeen-year stay in Europe, he bought a house near Tarrytown, and was buried at last in Sleepy Hollow cemetery. Probably he loved no other place on earth so much as that Hudson valley country, and perhaps none of his writing will last longer than the stories he wrote about it — " Rip Van Winkle " and " The Legend of Sleepy Hollow."

But two parts of Europe competed with the Hudson valley for his affection. They were England and Spain. He went to England in 1815 (the first news he heard on shore was that Napoleon had been defeated). He traveled through England, France, and Italy like a pilgrim, reveling in the old buildings, the legends, the unfamiliar scenes, and the gracious living. He felt at home in this kind of life, much more at home certainly than he felt in most parts of America. As he traveled he kept a notebook of what he saw and heard. In 1820, the same year in which the *Edinburgh Review* critic had asked, " Who reads an American book? " he published the best of his notes in England as *The Sketch Book*, and even the *Edinburgh Review* hastened to pay tribute to it. For this book was as good as the best English travel sketches. It was graceful, genial, humorous, urbane. Not even the English had written better about their old inns and their countryside.

Irving's last, and in some respects greatest, love was Spain. He resurrected its romantic old history and legends in *The Conquest of Granada* and the tales of *The Alhambra*, and studied its records for his biography of Columbus. He served four years as American minister to Spain, and was deeply fond of that country and the memories it held.

Irving as a Gentleman in Literature

In his later years he tried to move in the direction of the younger American writers who were depicting their own country. He went to the West and wrote a journal of his trip over the great plains. He wrote, for the Astors, a book on Astoria. He wrote a vigorous reply to European criticism, called " English Writers on America." His last long work was a biography of Washington. But none of these was equal to *The Sketch Book*, the Hudson valley stories, or the tales of Spain. The center of his interest and sympathy was nearer England than Astoria.

His place in our literary tradition is not as a leader of a new national literature, but as the first great exponent of polite literature in a new country. He opened European eyes to us, but he had no particular message. As he himself said, " I have attempted no lofty theme, nor sought to look wise and learned. . . . I have preferred addressing myself to the feeling and fancy of the reader more than to his judgment." He was a gentleman in literature, a genial, kindly, dignified practitioner of the best informal prose he had learned from the old country.

Irving was born (1783) at the end of the Revolution, and died (1859) just before the War between the States. When he was born, only one major American writer was living — Franklin. When he died, all the great writers of the Eastern Flowering had published.

James Fenimore Cooper

Cooper was different in many important ways from Irving. Unlike Irving's graceful style, Cooper's style of writing was rough, sometimes crude. Unlike Irving's mellow humor, Cooper's mood was intensely serious, sometimes too serious for his own good. A better sense of humor would have helped him through some of his troubles in later life.

Irving went to England as a pilgrim; Cooper went as a critic. And yet he learned his lessons too. He learned from novelists like Sir Walter Scott the skill of telling a rousing adventure story. He learned from other Europeans a rather sentimental respect for his own country: for the " noble Indian " and for nature and manners " unspoiled " by civilization.

Cooper's Background on the Frontier

His New York was not like Irving's New York. Irving's was the old Dutch city and the romantic Hudson. Cooper's was the Finger Lake country of central New York State, where his father founded Cooperstown and lived as the master of many square miles of rich land. In Cooper's time this was not very far from the frontier. The Iroquois lived thereabouts, and some of the first stories the boy Cooper heard were of the Indian wars and the pioneer scouts. As Irving " collected " old inns, cathedrals, and ghost stories, so Cooper gathered tales of the frontier, the sea, and the making of America.

As Irving was brought up for business, so Cooper was expected to succeed his father as a gentleman farmer. But coincidences came to the rescue of American literature, even as they had in the case of Irving. Cooper's training did not develop as expected. He didn't like Yale, and Yale didn't like him; they parted company before graduation. Then he shipped to sea and would have made a career in the navy if his father's death and his own marriage had not required his return to civilian life at Cooperstown. For eight years he did the work expected of him — caring for his father's estate. Then occurred the greatest coincidence of all. He decided, on a wager, to try to write a book. He said he could write one as good as the English novel he was reading. The result was a novel, imitative and unoriginal,

of which he was heartily ashamed later. But it did one priceless service for generations of Americans; it got Cooper interested in writing fiction.

Cooper's Novels of the Frontier and the Sea

That first experiment taught him another thing — that he should write about subject matter he knew. So he

turned to the stories about the making of America that he had heard since boyhood, to the stories of the frontier, and to his own experiences at sea. The first of these books came out only a year after his experimental novel, in 1821. It was *The Spy*, an exciting novel of the Revolution, in which George Washington himself was a character. In 1823 he published *The Pioneers*, a frontier novel, in which he introduced a character whom almost every young American knows — Natty Bumppo, or Leatherstocking, the scout modeled after Daniel Boone.

The next year he published his first sea book, *The Pilot*, which he wrote to prove that a man who had been to sea could write about the ocean better than Sir Walter Scott, who was only a landsman. (Cooper was never one to avoid a controversy!) Now the critic in the *Edinburgh Review* might well reconsider his question, "Who reads an American book?" because throughout England readers were poring over Cooper's stories of Harvey Birch (*The Spy*), Leatherstocking (*The Pioneers*), and Long Tom Coffin (*The Pilot*). When *The Last of the Mohicans* came out in 1826, there could have been no doubt that American books were read.

The Leatherstocking Tales

His later novels fell into the three classes just named — the Leatherstocking frontier series, romances of American history like *The Spy*, and sea stories like *The Pilot*. The Leatherstocking series are the best-known. These exciting romances show all of Cooper's strengths and weaknesses as a novelist. They are roughly written. The women in the books — Cooper usually calls them "females" — sometimes strike us as funny, because Cooper goes to such lengths to keep them socially proper and well groomed; a woman fleeing from Indians in the forest still maintains the manners of a Cooperstown drawing room. The historic characters, too, are more like statues than men. Sometimes we feel that he is too sentimental over "the poor Indian."

But against those qualities we can name great and good ones. The books are vital, real, exciting. A few leading characters are really great characters, and some of the scenes are deeply moving. What American boy or girl will ever forget the ending of *The Last of the Mohicans,* or the character of Natty Bumppo, who said, "The only book I read, or care about reading, is the one which God has opened here before us, his creatures, in the noble forest, broad lakes, rolling rivers, blue skies, and the wind, and tempests, and sunshine and other glorious marvels of the land"?

Cooper was born the year Washington became President (1789) and died in 1851, when Americans were streaming into California and when the Fugitive Slave Law was good for an argument almost anywhere in the country.

Washington Irving
1783–1859

THE DEVIL AND TOM WALKER

Imagine yourself a guest at Sunnyside, Irving's home. You are near Sleepy Hollow, and from the windows you may look out over the Hudson River. You have just finished dinner, and before a blazing and crackling log fire you lean back in an easy chair and wait for your host to tell a story. There are no telephones, no radios to interrupt; no train will roar past toward Albany or New York City. In his charming old-school manner, pausing now and then to chuckle with you at some queer twist of the yarn, Irving weaves his story with the artistry of a master storyteller. Last night, perhaps, it was a colorful legend of old Spain with a little of the flavor of the Arabian Nights, but tonight he spins a story as American as are the characters of Rip Van Winkle and Ichabod Crane. He takes his time about the telling. Don't interrupt him or hurry him; a long, pleasant evening is before you.

A FEW miles from Boston in Massachusetts, there is a deep inlet, winding several miles into the interior of the country from Charles Bay, and terminating in a thickly wooded swamp or morass. On one side of this inlet is a beautiful dark grove; on the opposite side the land rises abruptly from the water's edge into a high ridge, on which grow a few scattered oaks of great age and immense size. Under one of these gigantic trees, according to old stories, there was a great amount of treasure buried by Kidd the pirate. The inlet allowed a facility to bring the money in a boat secretly and at night to the very foot of the hill; the elevation of the place permitted a good lookout to be kept that no one was at hand; while the remarkable trees formed good landmarks by which the place might easily be found again. The old stories add, moreover, that the Devil presided at the hiding of the money, and took it under his guardianship; but this, it is well known, he always does with buried treasure, particularly when it has been ill-gotten. Be that as it may, Kidd never returned to recover his wealth; being shortly after seized at Boston, sent out to England, and there hanged for a pirate.

About the year 1727, just at the time that earthquakes were prevalent in New England, and shook many tall sinners down upon their knees, there lived near this place a meager, miserly fellow, of the name of Tom Walker. He had a wife as miserly as himself: they were so miserly that they even conspired to cheat each other. Whatever the woman could lay hands on, she hid away; a hen could not cackle but she was on the alert to secure the new-laid egg. Her husband was continually prying about to detect her secret hoards, and many and fierce were the conflicts that took place about what ought to have been common property. They lived in a forlorn-looking house that stood alone, and had an air of starvation. A few straggling savin [1] trees, emblems of sterility, grew near it; no smoke ever curled from its chimney; no traveler stopped at its door. A miserable horse, whose ribs were as articulate as the bars of a gridiron, stalked about a field where a thin carpet of moss, scarcely covering the ragged beds of pudding stone, tantalized and balked his hunger; and sometimes he would lean his head over the fence, look piteously at the passer-by, and seem to petition deliverance from this land of famine.

The house and its inmates had altogether a bad name. Tom's wife was a tall termagant, fierce of temper, loud of tongue, and strong of arm. Her voice was often heard in wordy warfare with her husband; and his face sometimes showed signs that their conflicts were not confined to words. No one ventured, however, to interfere between them. The lonely wayfarer shrunk within himself at the horrid clamor and clapper-clawing, eyed the den of discord askance, and hurried on his way, rejoicing, if a bachelor, in his celibacy.

One day that Tom Walker had been to a distant part of the neighborhood, he took what he considered a short cut homeward, through the swamp. Like most short cuts, it was an ill-chosen route. The swamp was thickly grown with great gloomy pines and hemlocks,

[1] savin (săv′ĭn): a North American juniper or red cedar.

The Hudson valley was the setting for several of Washington Irving's most famous stories. This old print shows the vista down the river just above West Point, in the 1830's. (*Old Print Shop, New York*)

some of them ninety feet high, which made it dark at noonday, and a retreat for all the owls of the neighborhood. It was full of pits and quagmires, partly covered with weeds and mosses, where the green surface often betrayed the traveler into a gulf of black, smothering mud; there were also dark and stagnant pools, the abodes of the tadpole, the bullfrog, and the water snake; where the trunks of pines and hemlocks lay half drowned, half rotting, looking like alligators sleeping in the mire.

Tom had long been picking his way cautiously through this treacherous forest; stepping from tuft to tuft of rushes and roots, which afforded precarious footholds among deep sloughs; or pacing carefully, like a cat, along the prostrate trunks of trees; startled now and then by the sudden screaming of the bittern, or the quacking of a wild duck rising on the wing from some solitary pool. At length he arrived at a firm piece of ground, which ran out like a peninsula into the deep bosom of the swamp. It had been one of the strongholds of the Indians during their wars with the first colonists. Here they had thrown up a kind of fort, which they had looked upon as almost impregnable, and had used as a place of refuge for their squaws and children. Nothing remained of the old Indian fort but a few embankments, gradually sinking to the level of the surrounding earth, and already overgrown in part by oaks and other forest trees, the foliage of which formed a contrast to the dark pines and hemlocks of the swamp.

It was late in the dusk of evening when Tom Walker reached the old fort, and he paused there awhile to rest himself. Anyone but he would have felt unwilling to linger in this lonely, melancholy place, for the common people had a bad opinion of it, from the stories handed down from the time of the Indian wars, when it was asserted that the savages held incantations here, and made sacrifices to the evil spirit.

Tom Walker, however, was not a man to be troubled with any fears of the kind. He reposed himself for some time on the trunk of a fallen hemlock, listening to the boding cry of the tree toad, and delving with his walking staff into a mound of black mold at his feet. As he turned up the soil unconsciously, his staff struck against something hard. He raked it out of the vegetable mold and lo! a cloven skull, with an Indian tomahawk buried deep in it, lay before him. The rust on the weapon showed the time that had elapsed since this deathblow had been given. It was a dreary memento of the fierce struggle that had taken place in this last foothold of the Indian warriors.

"Humph!" said Tom Walker, as he gave it a kick to shake the dirt from it.

"Let that skull alone!" said a gruff voice. Tom lifted up his eyes, and beheld a great black man seated directly opposite him, on the stump of a tree. He was exceedingly surprised, having neither heard nor seen anyone approach; and he was still more perplexed on observing, as well as the gathering gloom would permit, that the stranger was neither Negro nor Indian. It is true he was dressed in a rude half-Indian garb, and had a red belt or sash swathed round his body; but his face was neither black nor copper-color, but swarthy and dingy, and begrimed with soot, as if he had been accustomed to toil among fires and forges. He had a shock of coarse black hair, that stood out from his head in all directions, and bore an ax on his shoulder.

He scowled for a moment at Tom with a pair of great red eyes.

"What are you doing on my grounds?" said the black man, with a hoarse growling voice.

"Your grounds!" said Tom, with a sneer, "no more your grounds than mine; they belong to Deacon Peabody."

"Deacon Peabody be d——d," said the stranger, "as I flatter myself he will be, if he does not look more to his own sins and less to those of his neighbors. Look yonder, and see how Deacon Peabody is faring."

Tom looked in the direction that the stranger pointed, and beheld one of the great trees, fair and flourishing without, but rotten at the core, and saw that it had been nearly hewn through, so that the first high wind was likely to blow it down. On the bark of the tree was scored the name of Deacon Peabody, an eminent man, who had waxed wealthy by driving shrewd bargains with the Indians. He now looked around, and found most of the tall trees marked with the name of some great man of the colony, and all more or less scored by the ax. The one on which he had been seated, and which had evidently just been hewn down, bore the name of Crowninshield; and he recollected a mighty rich man of that name, who made a vulgar display of wealth, which it was whispered he had acquired by buccaneering.

"He's just ready for burning!" said the black man, with a growl of triumph. "You see I am likely to have a good stock of firewood for winter."

"But what right have you," said Tom, "to cut down Deacon Peabody's timber?"

"The right of a prior claim," said the other. "This woodland belonged to me long before one of your white-faced race put foot upon the soil."

"And pray, who are you, if I may be so bold?" said Tom.

"Oh, I go by various names. I am the wild huntsman in some countries; the black miner in others. In this neighborhood I am known by the name of the black woodsman. I am he to whom the red men consecrated this spot, and in honor of whom they now and then roasted a white man, by way of sweet-smelling sacrifice. Since the red men have been exterminated by you white savages, I amuse myself by presiding at the persecutions of Quakers and Anabaptists; [1] I am the great patron and prompter of slave dealers, and the grand master of the Salem witches."

"The upshot of all which is that, if I mistake not," said Tom, sturdily, "you are he commonly called Old Scratch."

"The same, at your service!" replied the black man, with a half-civil nod.

Such was the opening of this interview, according to the old story; though it has almost too familiar an air to be credited. One would think that to meet with such a singular personage, in this wild, lonely place, would have shaken any man's nerves; but Tom was a hard-minded fellow, not easily daunted, and he had lived so long with a termagant wife that he did not even fear the Devil.

It is said that after this commencement they had a long and earnest conversation together, as Tom returned homeward. The black man told him of great sums of money buried by Kidd the pirate, under the oak trees on the high ridge, not far from the morass. All these were under his command, and protected by his power, so that none could find them but such as propitiated his favor. These he offered to place within Tom Walker's reach, having conceived an especial kindness for him; but they were to be had only on certain conditions. What these conditions were may be easily surmised, though Tom never disclosed them publicly. They must have been very hard, for he required time to think of them, and he was not a man to stick at trifles when money was in view. When they had reached the edge of the swamp, the stranger paused.

[1] **Anabaptists:** a religious sect which arose in Switzerland in 1523. Its members were subject to persecution because of their opposition to infant baptism.

"What proof have I that all you have been telling me is true?" said Tom. "There's my signature," said the black man, pressing his finger on Tom's forehead. So saying, he turned off among the thickets of the swamp, and seemed, as Tom said, to go down, down, down, into the earth, until nothing but his head and shoulders could be seen, and so on, until he totally disappeared.

When Tom reached home, he found the black print of a finger burnt, as it were, into his forehead, which nothing could obliterate. The first news his wife had to tell him was the sudden death of Absalom Crowninshield, the rich buccaneer. It was announced in the papers with the usual flourish, that "a great man had fallen in Israel."

Tom recollected the tree which his black friend had just hewn down, and which was ready for burning. "Let the freebooter roast," said Tom, "who cares!" He now felt convinced that all he had heard and seen was no illusion.

He was not prone to let his wife into his confidence; but as this was an uneasy secret, he willingly shared it with her. All her avarice was awakened at the mention of hidden gold, and she urged her husband to comply with the black man's terms, and secure what would make them wealthy for life. However Tom might have felt disposed to sell himself to the Devil, he was determined not to do so to oblige his wife; so he flatly refused, out of the mere spirit of contradiction. Many and bitter were the quarrels they had on the subject; but the more she talked, the more resolute was Tom not to be damned to please her.

At length she determined to drive the bargain on her own account and, if she succeeded, to keep all the gain to herself. Being of the same fearless temper as her husband, she set off for the old Indian fort toward the close of a summer's day. She was many hours absent. When she came back, she was reserved and sullen in her replies. She spoke something of a black man, whom she had met about twilight hewing at the root of a tall tree. He was sulky, however, and would not come to terms: she was to go again with a propitiatory offering, but what it was she forbore to say.

The next evening she set off for the swamp, with her apron heavily laden. Tom waited and waited for her, but in vain; midnight came, but she did not make her appearance: morning, noon, night returned, but still she did not come. Tom now grew uneasy for her safety, especially as he found she had carried off in her apron the silver teapot and spoons, and every portable article of value. Another night elapsed, another morning came, but no wife. In a word, she was never heard of more.

What was her real fate nobody knows, in consequence of so many pretending to know. It is one of those facts which have become confounded by a variety of historians. Some asserted that she lost her way among the tangled mazes of the swamp, and sank into some pit or slough; others, more uncharitable, hinted that she had eloped with the household booty, and made off to some other province; while others surmised that the tempter had decoyed her into a dismal quagmire, on the top of which her hat was found lying. In confirmation of this, it was said a great black man, with an ax on his shoulder, was seen late that very evening coming out of the swamp, carrying a bundle tied in a checked apron, with an air of surly triumph.

The most current and probable story, however, observes that Tom Walker grew so anxious about the fate of his wife and his property that he set out at length to seek them both at the Indian fort. During a long summer's afternoon he searched about the gloomy place, but no wife was to be seen. He called her name repeatedly, but she was no-

where to be heard. The bittern alone responded to his voice, as he flew screaming by; or the bullfrog croaked dolefully from a neighboring pool. At length, it is said, just in the brown hour of twilight, when the owls began to hoot, and the bats to flit about, his attention was attracted by the clamor of carrion crows hovering about a cypress tree. He looked up, and beheld a bundle tied in a checked apron and hanging in the branches of the tree, with a great vulture perched hard by, as if keeping watch upon it. He leaped with joy; for he recognized his wife's apron, and supposed it to contain the household valuables.

"Let us get hold of the property," said he, consolingly to himself, "and we will endeavor to do without the woman."

As he scrambled up the tree, the vulture spread its wide wings, and sailed off, screaming, into the deep shadows of the forest. Tom seized the checked apron, but, woeful sight! found nothing but a heart and liver tied up in it!

Such, according to this most authentic old story, was all that was to be found of Tom's wife. She had probably attempted to deal with the black man as she had been accustomed to deal with her husband; but though a female scold is generally considered a match for the Devil, yet in this instance she appears to have had the worst of it. She must have died game, however; for it is said Tom noticed many prints of cloven feet deeply stamped about the tree, and found handfuls of hair, that looked as if they had been plucked from the coarse black shock of the woodman. Tom knew his wife's prowess by experience. He shrugged his shoulders, as he looked at the signs of a fierce clapperclawing. "Egad," said he to himself, "Old Scratch must have had a tough time of it!"

Tom consoled himself for the loss of his property with the loss of his wife, for he was a man of fortitude. He even felt something like gratitude toward the black woodman, who, he considered, had done him a kindness. He sought, therefore, to cultivate a further acquaintance with him, but for some time without success; the old blacklegs played shy, for, whatever people may think, he is not always to be had for calling for; he knows how to play his cards when pretty sure of his game.

At length, it is said, when delay had whetted Tom's eagerness to the quick, and prepared him to agree to anything rather than not gain the promised treasure, he met the black man one evening in his usual woodman's dress, with his ax on his shoulder, sauntering along the swamp, and humming a tune. He affected to receive Tom's advances with great indifference, made brief replies, and went on humming his tune.

By degrees, however, Tom brought him to business, and they began to haggle about the terms on which the former was to have the pirate's treasure. There was one condition which need not be mentioned, being generally understood in all cases where the Devil grants favors; but there were others about which, though of less importance, he was inflexibly obstinate. He insisted that the money found through his means should be employed in his service. He proposed, therefore, that Tom should employ it in the black traffic; that is to say, that he should fit out a slave ship. This, however, Tom resolutely refused; he was bad enough in all conscience; but the Devil himself could not tempt him to turn slave trader.

Finding Tom so squeamish on this point, he did not insist upon it, but proposed, instead, that he should turn usurer; the Devil being extremely anxious for the increase of usurers, looking upon them as his peculiar people.

To this no objections were made, for it was just to Tom's taste.

"You shall open a broker's shop in Boston next month," said the black man.

"I'll do it tomorrow, if you wish," said Tom Walker.

"You shall lend money at two per cent a month."

"Egad, I'll charge four!" replied Tom Walker.

"You shall extort bonds, foreclose mortgages, drive the merchants to bankruptcy — "

"I'll drive them to the D——l," cried Tom Walker.

"You are the usurer for my money!" said blacklegs with delight. "When will you want the rhino?"[1]

"This very night."

"Done!" said the Devil.

"Done!" said Tom Walker.

So they shook hands and struck a bargain.

A few days' time saw Tom Walker seated behind his desk in a counting-house in Boston.

His reputation for a ready-moneyed man, who would lend money out for a good consideration, soon spread abroad. Everybody remembers the time of Governor Belcher,[2] when money was particularly scarce. It was a time of paper credit. The country had been deluged with government bills; the famous Land Bank[3] had been established; there had been a rage for speculating; the people had run mad with schemes for new settlements; for building cities in the wilderness; land jobbers went about with maps of grants, and townships, and El Dorados,[4] lying nobody knew where, but which everybody was ready to purchase. In a word, the great speculating fever which breaks out every now and then in the country had raged to an alarming degree, and everybody was

[1] rhino: money.

[2] Belcher: Jonathan Belcher was governor of Massachusetts from 1730 to 1741.

[3] Land Bank: a system by which the province advanced money on mortgages on land.

[4] El Dorados (dō·rä′dōz): literally, "the golden"; hence, any places of fabulous riches.

dreaming of making sudden fortunes from nothing. As usual the fever had subsided; the dream had gone off, and the imaginary fortunes with it; the patients were left in doleful plight, and the whole country resounded with the consequent cry of " hard times."

At this propitious time of public distress did Tom Walker set up as usurer in Boston. His door was soon thronged by customers. The needy and adventurous, the gambling speculator, the dreaming land jobber, the thriftless tradesman, the merchant with cracked credit, in short, everyone driven to raise money by desperate means and desperate sacrifices hurried to Tom Walker.

Thus Tom was the universal friend of the needy, and acted like a " friend in need "; that is to say, he always exacted good pay and good security. In proportion to the distress of the applicant was the highness of his terms. He accumulated bonds and mortgages, gradually squeezed his customers closer and closer: and sent them at length, dry as a sponge, from his door.

In this way he made money hand over hand; became a rich and mighty man, and exalted his cocked hat upon 'Change.[1] He built himself, as usual, a vast house, out of ostentation; but left the greater part of it unfinished and unfurnished, out of parsimony. He even set up a carriage in the fullness of his vainglory, though he nearly starved the horses which drew it; and as the ungreased wheels groaned and screeched on the axletrees, you would have thought you heard the souls of the poor debtors he was squeezing.

As Tom waxed old, however, he grew thoughtful. Having secured the good things of this world, he began to feel anxious about those of the next. He thought with regret on the bargain he

[1] 'Change: Exchange, the place where merchants, brokers, bankers, etc., meet to do business.

had made with his black friend, and set his wits to work to cheat him out of the conditions. He became, therefore, all of a sudden, a violent churchgoer. He prayed loudly and strenuously, as if heaven were to be taken by force of lungs. Indeed, one might always tell when he had sinned most during the week, by the clamor of his Sunday devotion. The quiet Christians who had been modestly and steadfastly traveling Zionward were struck with self-reproach at seeing themselves so suddenly outstripped in their career by this new-made convert. Tom was as rigid in religious as in money matters; he was a stern supervisor and censurer of his neighbors, and seemed to think every sin entered up to their account became a credit on his own side of the page. He even talked of the expediency of reviving the persecution of Quakers and Anabaptists. In a word, Tom's zeal became as notorious as his riches.

Still, in spite of all this strenuous attention to forms, Tom had a lurking dread that the Devil, after all, would have his due. That he might not be taken unawares, therefore, it is said he always carried a small Bible in his coat pocket. He had also a great folio Bible on his countinghouse desk, and would frequently be found reading it when people called on business; on such occasions he would lay his green spectacles in the book, to mark the place, while he turned round to drive some usurious bargain.

Some say that Tom grew a little crackbrained in his old days, and that, fancying his end approaching, he had his horse new-shod, saddled and bridled, and buried with his feet uppermost; because he supposed that at the last day the world would be turning upside down; in which case he should find his horse standing ready for mounting, and he was determined at the worst to give his old friend a run for it. This, however, is probably a mere

" Sunnyside," the rambling vine-covered house in Tarrytown, New York, where Irving settled down for the last years of his life, and where he died in 1859. (Brown Brothers)

old wives' fable. If he really did take such a precaution, it was totally superfluous; at least so says the authentic old legend, which closes this story in the following manner.

One hot summer afternoon in the dog days, just as a terrible black thundergust was coming up, Tom sat in his countinghouse, in his white linen cap and India silk morning gown. He was on the point of foreclosing a mortgage, by which he would complete the ruin of an unlucky land speculator for whom he had professed the greatest friendship. The poor land jobber begged him to grant a few months' indulgence. Tom had grown testy and irritated, and refused another day.

"My family will be ruined, and brought upon the parish," said the land jobber.

"Charity begins at home," replied Tom; "I must take care of myself in these hard times."

"You have made so much money out of me," said the speculator.

Tom lost his patience and his piety. "The Devil take me," said he, "if I have made a farthing!"

Just then there were three loud knocks at the street door. He stepped out to see who was there. A black man was holding a black horse, which neighed and stamped with impatience.

"Tom, you're come for," said the black fellow, gruffly. Tom shrank back, but too late. He had left his little Bible at the bottom of his coat pocket, and his big Bible on the desk buried under the mortgage he was about to foreclose: never was sinner taken more unawares. The black man whisked him like a child into the saddle, gave the horse the lash, and away he galloped, with Tom on his back, in the midst of the thunderstorm. The clerks stuck their pens behind their ears, and stared after him from the windows. Away went Tom Walker, dashing down the streets; his white cap bobbing up and down; his morning gown fluttering in the wind, and his steed striking fire out of the pavement at every bound. When the clerks turned to look for the black man, he had disappeared.

Tom Walker never returned to foreclose the mortgage. A countryman, who lived on the border of the swamp, reported that in the height of the thunder-gust he had heard a great clattering of hoofs and a howling along the road, and running to the window caught sight of a figure, such as I have described, on a horse that galloped like mad across the fields, over the hills, and down into the black hemlock swamp toward the old Indian fort; and that shortly after a thunderbolt falling in that direction seemed to set the whole forest in a blaze.

The good people of Boston shook their heads and shrugged their shoulders, but had been so much accustomed to witches and goblins, and tricks of the Devil, in all kinds of shapes, from the first settlement of the colony, that they were not so much horrorstruck as might have been expected. Trustees were appointed to take charge of Tom's effects. There was nothing, however, to administer upon. On searching his coffers, all his bonds and mortgages were found reduced to cinders. In place of gold and silver, his iron chest was filled with chips and shavings; two skeletons lay in his stable instead of his half-starved horses, and the very next day his great house took fire and was burnt to the ground.

Such was the end of Tom Walker and his ill-gotten wealth. Let all griping money brokers lay this story to heart. The truth of it is not to be doubted. The very hole under the oak trees, whence he dug Kidd's money, is to be seen to this day; and the neighboring swamp and old Indian fort are often haunted in stormy nights by a figure on

horseback, in morning gown and white cap, which is doubtless the troubled spirit of the usurer. In fact, the story has resolved itself into a proverb, and is the origin of that popular saying, so prevalent throughout New England, of "The Devil and Tom Walker."

For Discussion of Irving

1. What parts of this story made you laugh aloud or chuckle to yourself? How would you characterize Irving's humor? Give some examples to illustrate your answer.

2. If you like this story, what would be your reply to someone who did not like it "because it is so impossible and could never have happened"?

3. Count up the familiar expressions which Irving has made concrete in this story, such as "The Devil would have his due."

4. Compare this story with "The Devil and Daniel Webster" (p. 96) as to its point, its general tone, and the picture of the Devil. Bargaining with the Devil is a familiar theme in world literature. Some class members should report on the similarity of Irving's story to Marlowe's play *Faustus*, Goethe's poem and Gounod's opera, *Faust*.

For Your Vocabulary

CONTEXT: In "The Devil and Tom Walker" you discovered that a *usurer* is one who charges extravagantly high interest on loans. Most states now have laws against *usury*. To *extort* is to wring something out of a person by fear or threats. Who urged Tom to turn usurer and extort bonds (p. 481)? What kinds of criminals would you call *extortioners*? *Avarice* is a greedy desire for money or gain, which drove Tom's wife to her death (p. 479). *Parsimony* is extreme dislike of parting with money once gained — excessive economy in spending. How is the meaning of this word illuminated in context (p. 482)? Compare *parsimony* with *frugality*, which Benjamin Franklin listed as a trait he wanted to acquire. What economies do you consider only *frugal*, not *parsimonious*?

Bryant and Whittier

William Cullen Bryant

THERE were American poets before the nineteenth century, as you know from reading Edward Taylor. But William Cullen Bryant was the first American poet to achieve recognition in his own time. As Irving had proved to Europeans that grace and humor might be found in American writing, and as Cooper had proved that Americans could write exciting fiction, so Bryant demonstrated that first-rate lyric poetry might likewise be produced in the country of the coonskin cap and the wigwam.

"Thanatopsis" Bryant's Youthful Creation

Lyric poets are usually young men. When they grow older they often turn to writing philosophical or narrative poetry, or drama; not many of them can prolong the lyric fire beyond forty. Bryant wrote his greatest poem when he was in his teens, and all his major poetry before he was forty.

The great poem is "Thanatopsis." The story of how it came to be published is still worth telling — how Bryant's father found it in his son's desk (the youth was just twenty-three, and had apparently written it some years before), and how he took it to the editor of the *North American Review*, who said in astonishment, "No one on this side of the Atlantic is capable of writing such verses." Proof was demanded and furnished; the poem was published in 1817.

Bryant rewrote the beginning and added the end of it later, but the central part of the poem stands now as it was written by a teen-age boy in western Massachusetts. The *North American Review* asked for more poems. Bryant produced "To a Waterfowl," which he had written in 1815, when he was twenty-one.

Closeness to Nature and God

What kind of young man wrote poetry like that? Bryant was born and grew up in the Berkshire Hills of Massachusetts and sometimes prayed for the gift of expression to match the beauty of nature around him. Nature was always a great part of Bryant's life. Moreover, he was one of the first American poets to feel that they should write about *American* nature. Perhaps earlier poets had not looked carefully at their own birds and trees and flowers. Whatever the reason, they wrote about the same ones the English poets did. It took Bryant to get the English skylark out of American poetry and the native bobolink in!

Bryant was a thoughtful, meditative boy, brought up by parents who were of Puritan descent. Suspected of being in ill health, he tended toward melancholy and was in turn fond of the more melancholy English poets. Nature usually led him to reflect on life and death. Like the English romantic poet Wordsworth, he felt that God was closely identified with nature, and nature with goodness, so that when he wrote about flowers and trees he had no difficulty in changing the subject to ethics or morals or religion. That was the mood in which he wrote the austere and beautiful poem "Thanatopsis."

In these days of large cities and television and fast automobiles, it is sometimes hard for us to understand how these writers of the Eastern Flowering

— Bryant, Whittier, Thoreau, and Emerson, among others — felt about nature. We can understand how they liked to walk in the woods and fields, but it is hard for us to appreciate their feeling that living close to nature was much like living close to God, and that thinking about nature was much like thinking about religion. As one modern cynic has said, that view of nature is hidden today behind billboards.

A Poet Becomes a Public Writer

Bryant could not afford to go to college. He read law in a lawyer's office, and later was admitted to the bar, but

turned to journalism and went to New York as a writer and editor. He became editor of the New York *Evening Post*. As he grew older and his poetic output decreased, however, his influence as a vigorous and liberal editor grew. He started as a political conservative, but came over soon to the side of "the common man" and supported Jackson. He opposed all class legislation, and urged Lincoln to free the slaves sooner than he did. He made the *Post* a paper of high literary quality, and its editorial columns an example of the dignified public service a paper can render in a democracy.

But every afternoon when he could get away from work he escaped from his office in the city to the open countryside where he could hear the bobolink, the rustle of cornfields, and the swish of trees that American poets seemed never to have heard before his time. And whether the editorial work he did in maturity or the poetry he wrote as a young man will ultimately be considered the greater contribution to the good of his countrymen, who can now say?

Bryant was born (1794) just after the death of Franklin. He lived until 1878, when Edison was using electricity, in which Franklin had been so much interested, to light homes and cities.

John Greenleaf Whittier

Bryant and Whittier were born and grew up within a hundred miles of each other in the hills of Massachusetts. Both had a deep feeling for nature, wrote simple, dignified poetry, both were editors and held firm political convictions. But all of Bryant's well-known poetry came early in life; most of Whittier's, late. Although Bryant was only thirteen years older, "Thanatopsis," was actually published forty-nine years before Whittier's best-known poem, *Snow-Bound*. The two men reversed their life patterns. Bryant wrote his poetry first and then moved into journalism and politics; Whittier got his journalism and politics over first, and then concentrated on poetry.

The Editor, Pamphleteer, and Politician

To most of us who think of Whittier as the venerable poet of *Snow-Bound*, "Maud Muller," "The Barefoot Boy," and "In School-Days," it comes as a shock to realize that for two-thirds of his life he was a fiery abolitionist who fought mobs, political opponents, intolerance, and poverty — a man to whom poetry was only a pleasant avocation or a propaganda tool.

There is something very engaging about the picture of this young Quaker, saying " thee " and " thou," behaving with the sweetness and modesty characteristic of his sect, yet burning with the inner hatred of slavery and willing to fight when aroused, with any weapons at hand, for what he believed. He wrote an antislavery pamphlet so vigorous that it closed the door on what had looked like a promising political career. (The abolitionist cause was not popular then, even in the North.) As editor of the *Pennsylvania Freeman,* he aroused so much opposition with abolitionist editorials that a mob burned and sacked his office. He became a contributing editor of the journal that published *Uncle Tom's Cabin.* He wrote moving antislavery lyrics, and in one of the sternest poems in the language, " Ichabod," he denounced Daniel Webster for compromising with the proslavery faction. Never wealthy, he actually suffered from poverty in early years, but still gave his money freely for the cause he believed in. That is the Whittier whose portrait seldom gets into the books — the man of civic indignations, the champion of the underdog, the flashing-eyed, firm-chinned reformer.

The Simple, Unpretentious Poet

Yet his stature as a poet began to be evident even through the smoke screen of his political activity. He became a contributor to the *Atlantic Monthly,* along with Lowell, Emerson, Longfellow, Holmes, and the other great New Englanders. He was hailed by many as the best American balladist, for poems like " Skipper Ireson's Ride." And when the War between the States was over, he lived quietly in a white frame house at Amesbury, Massachusetts, grew his white beard, and wrote warm, reminiscent poems like *Snow-Bound.*

His house at Amesbury was something like his poetry — simple, unpretentious, a real American house. It was the kind of a house in which one might expect to see the warm, kind family life he so often writes about. Perhaps he is most often remembered thus, for the purity and deep spiritual quality of his poetry and the sweetness of his nature, rather than for his turbulent early years. And yet you will never understand Whittier if you take only one side of him. You can quote Whittier himself on that. Against his half-regretful admission that he had not always done his best by poetry —

" And one there was, a dreamer born,
   Who with a mission to fulfill,
Had left the Muses' haunts to turn
   The crank of an opinion mill. . . ."

against that you can quote his defiant challenge: " I set a higher value on my name as appended to the Anti-Slavery Declaration of 1833 than on the title page of any book! " Both voices are Whittier.

Whittier was born (1807) the year Fulton's steamboat ran on the Hudson and died (1892) in the year that the long distance telephone came into use.

William Cullen Bryant
1794–1878

[handwritten: pantheism God + nature creator + creation]

THANATOPSIS *

This is the poem that Bryant wrote in his teens, perhaps the first great poem written in America. The dignity of its blank verse and the power of its expression are truly remarkable, coming from so young a writer. Unless you have thoroughly mastered the reading of blank verse (see p. 274), you may need to give this poem several readings before you can appreciate its excellence. Read it through first for meaning, paying particular attention to the punctuation; then, when what Bryant has to say has become clear to you, try to add the dignified rhythm of the verse and the balanced beauty of the words.

To him who in the love of Nature holds
Communion with her visible forms, she speaks
A various language; for his gayer hours
She has a voice of gladness, and a smile
And eloquence of beauty, and she glides
Into his darker musings, with a mild   6
And healing sympathy, that steals away
Their sharpness, ere he is aware. When thoughts
Of the last bitter hour come like a blight
Over thy spirit, and sad images   10
Of the stern agony, and shroud, and pall,
And breathless darkness, and the narrow house,
Make thee to shudder and grow sick at heart —
Go forth, under the open sky, and list

To Nature's teachings, while from all around —   15
Earth and her waters, and the depths of air —
Comes a still voice — Yet a few days,° and thee
The all-beholding sun shall see no more
In all his course; nor yet in the cold ground,
Where thy pale form was laid, with many tears,   20
Nor in the embrace of ocean, shall exist
Thy image. Earth, that nourished thee, shall claim
Thy growth, to be resolved to earth again,
And, lost each human trace, surrendering up
Thine individual being, shalt thou go
To mix forever with the elements,   26
To be a brother to the insensible rock
And to the sluggish clod, which the rude swain
Turns with his share,° and treads upon. The oak
Shall send his roots abroad, and pierce thy mold.   30

Yet not to thine eternal resting place
Shalt thou retire alone, nor couldst thou wish
Couch more magnificent. Thou shalt lie down

---

* **Thanatopsis** (thăn·à·tŏp′sĭs): a view of death (Greek).

17. **Yet a few days:** This is the first line to be retained from the original poem. The opening couplets of the earlier version were dropped. 29. **share:** plowshare.

With patriarchs of the infant world —
    with kings,
The powerful of the earth — the wise,
    the good,   35
Fair forms, and hoary seers of ages past,
All in one mighty sepulcher. The hills
Rock-ribbed and ancient as the sun —
    the vales
Stretching in pensive quietness be-
    tween;   39
The venerable woods — rivers that move
In majesty, and the complaining brooks
That make the meadows green; and,
    poured round all,
Old Ocean's gray and melancholy
    waste —
Are but the solemn decorations all
Of the great tomb of man. The golden
    sun,   45
The planets, all the infinite host of
    heaven,
Are shining on the sad abodes of death,
Through the still lapse of ages. All that
    tread
The globe are but a handful to the
    tribes
That slumber in its bosom — Take the
    wings   50
Of morning, pierce the Barcan° wilder-
    ness,
Or lose thyself in the continuous woods
Where rolls the Oregon,° and hears no
    sound,
Save his own dashings — yet the dead
    are there;
And millions in those solitudes, since
    first   55
The flight of years began, have laid
    them down
In their last sleep — the dead reign
    there alone.
So shalt thou rest, and what if thou
    withdraw
In silence from the living, and no friend
Take note of thy departure? All that
    breathe   60

51. **Barcan:** pertaining to Barca, a district
in North Africa on the Mediterranean coast.
53. **Oregon:** now known as the Columbia River,
between Oregon and Washington.

Will share thy destiny. The gay will
    laugh
When thou art gone, the solemn brood
    of care
Plod on, and each one as before will
    chase
His favorite phantom; yet all these shall
    leave
Their mirth and their employments,
    and shall come   65
And make their bed with thee.° As the
    long train
Of ages glides away, the sons of men,
The youth in life's green spring, and he
    who goes
In the full strength of years, matron and
    maid,
The speechless babe, and the gray-
    headed man —   70
Shall one by one be gathered to thy
    side,
By those who in their turn shall follow
    them.

So live, that when thy summons
    comes to join
The innumerable caravan, which moves
To that mysterious realm, where each
    shall take   75
His chamber in the silent halls of death,
Thou go not, like the quarry slave at
    night,
Scourged to his dungeon, but, sustained
    and soothed
By an unfaltering trust, approach thy
    grave,
Like one who wraps the drapery of his
    couch   80
About him, and lies down to pleasant
    dreams.

66. **And make their bed with thee:** This was
the end of the original poem.

TO A WATERFOWL

When Bryant as a young man was li-
censed to practice law, he was confronted
by the problem of where to open his office.
One December while tramping over the
hills to consider the town of Plainfield,

Massachusetts, he felt particularly depressed by the uncertainty of his future. On his way he happened to see a bird in flight. As his biographer, John Bigelow, describes it, " He watched the lone wanderer until it was lost in the distance. He then went on with new strength and courage. When he reached the house where he was to stop for the night, he immediately sat down and wrote the lines ' To a Waterfowl ' . . ."

In the poem Bryant writes as if he were still tramping across the countryside. He addresses these lines to the bird, as he sees it pass between him and the setting sun. As you read, try to put yourself in his place, try to feel within yourself the change from depression to " new strength and courage."

Whither, midst falling dew,
While glow the heavens with the last
    steps of day,
Far, through their rosy depths, dost
    thou pursue
Thy solitary way?

Vainly the fowler's eye   5
Might mark thy distant flight to do thee
    wrong,
As, darkly seen against the crimson sky,
Thy figure floats along.

Seek'st thou the plashy brink
Of weedy lake, or marge of river wide,
Or where the rocking billows rise and
    sink   11
On the chafed oceanside?

There is a Power whose care
Teaches thy way along the pathless
    coast —
The desert and illimitable air —   15
Lone wandering, but not lost.

All day thy wings have fanned,
At that far height, the cold, thin atmosphere,
Yet stoop not, weary, to the welcome
    land,
Though the dark night is near.   20

And soon that toil shall end;
Soon shalt thou find a summer home,
    and rest,
And scream among thy fellows; reeds
    shall bend,
Soon, o'er thy sheltered nest.

Thou'rt gone, the abyss of heaven
Hath swallowed up thy form; yet, on
    my heart   26
Deeply hath sunk the lesson thou hast
    given,
And shall not soon depart.

He who, from zone to zone,
Guides through the boundless sky thy
    certain flight,   30
In the long way that I must tread alone,
Will lead my steps aright.

TO THE FRINGED GENTIAN

Simple as this little poem is, it is one of the favorites among Bryant's poetry. It illustrates two of his marked characteristics. First he brought to the poetry of English-speaking people the freshness of the American scene. No one before him had written about gentians — or goldenrod, or prairies, " for which," he said, " the speech of England has no name." Second, he frequently put a short lesson at the end of a poem — the moral tag, as it is often called. This was the fashion of his day, though now much frowned upon by the modern poet.

Thou blossom bright with autumn dew,
And colored with the heaven's own
    blue,
That openest when the quiet light
Succeeds the keen and frosty night,

Thou comest not when violets lean   5
O'er wandering brooks and springs unseen,
Or columbines, in purple dressed,
Nod o'er the ground-bird's hidden nest.

The fringed gentian
(*Gottscho-Schleisner*)

Thou waitest late and com'st alone,
When woods are bare and birds are
    flown,   10
And frosts and shortening days portend
The aged year is near his end.

Then doth thy sweet and quiet eye
Look through its fringes to the sky,
Blue — blue — as if that sky let fall   15
A flower from its cerulean° wall.

I would that thus, when I shall see
The hour of death draw near to me,
Hope, blossoming within my heart,
May look to heaven as I depart.   20

16. **cerulean** (sẻ·rōō′lẻ·ăn): azure, blue.

ABOLITION RIOTS

The other side of Bryant's writing may
be seen in this vigorous and courageous
editorial which appeared in the New York
Evening Post on August 8, 1836. Already
the lines were being drawn for the coming
struggle over the slavery question; already

reason was yielding to force on this great
issue. Bryant understood the real danger
of mob violence to free institutions, and in
this editorial he courageously defended
the rights of the unpopular abolitionists to
the freedom of the press.

As you follow Bryant's argument, keep
an outline of it in your mind. You might
even jot down on paper his main points,
to be sure you have understood them.

A MEETING of the people of Cincinnati have proclaimed the right of
silencing the expression of unpopular
opinions by violence. We refer our readers to the proceedings of an anti-aboli-
tion meeting lately held in that city.
They will be found in another part of
this paper.

The Cincinnati meeting, in the concluding resolution offered by Wilson N.
Brown and adopted with the rest, declare in so many words that, if they
cannot put down the abolitionist press

by fair means, they will do it by foul; if they cannot silence it by remonstrance, they will silence it by violence; if they cannot persuade it to desist, they will stir up mobs against it, inflame them to madness, and turn their brutal rage against the dwellings, the property, the persons, the lives of the wretched abolitionists and their families. In announcing that they will put them down by force all this is included. Fire, robbery, and bloodshed are the common excesses of an enraged mob. There is no extreme of cruelty and destruction to which, in the drunkenness and delirium of its fury, it may not proceed. The commotions of the elements can as easily be appeased by appeals to the quality of mercy as these commotions of the human mind; the whirlwind and the lightning might as well be expected to pause and turn aside to spare the helpless and innocent as an infuriated multitude.

If the abolitionists must be put down, and if the community are of that opinion, there is no necessity of violence to effect the object. The community have the power in their own hands; the majority may make a law declaring the discussion of slavery in a certain manner to be a crime, and imposing penalties. The law may then be put in force against the offenders, and their mouths may be gagged in due form and with all the solemnities of justice.

What is the reason this is not done? The answer is ready. The community are for leaving the liberty of the press untrammeled; there is not a committee that can be raised in any of the state legislatures north of the Potomac who will report in favor of imposing penalties on those who declaim against slavery; there is not a legislature who would sanction such a report; there is not a single free state the people of which would sustain a legislature in so doing. These are facts, and the advocates of mob law know them to be so.

Who are the men that issue this invitation to silence the press by violence? Who but an insolent, brawling minority, a few noisy fanatics, who claim that their own opinions shall be the measure of freedom for the rest of the community, and who undertake to overawe a vast, pacific majority by threats of wanton outrage and plunder? These men are for erecting an oligarchy of their own and riding roughshod over the people and the people's rights. They claim a right to repeal the laws established by the majority in favor of the freedom of the press. They make new laws of their own, to which they require that the rest of the community shall submit, and, in case of a refusal, they threaten to execute them by the ministry of a mob. There is no tyranny or oppression exercised in any part of the world more absolute or more frightful than that which they would establish. So far as we are concerned, we are determined that this despotism shall neither be submitted to nor encouraged. In whatever form it makes its appearance, we shall raise our voice against it. We are resolved that the subject of slavery shall be as it ever has been — as free a subject of discussion and argument and declamation as the difference between whiggism and democracy, or the difference between the Arminians and the Calvinists.[1] If the press chooses to be silent on the subject, it shall be the silence of perfect free will, and not the silence of fear. We hold that this combination of the few to govern the many by the terror of illegal violence is as wicked and indefensible as a conspiracy to rob on the highway. We hold it to be the duty of good citizens to protest against it whenever and wherever it shows itself, and to resist it, if necessary, to the death.

[1] the Arminians and the Calvinists: two groups of Protestants, followers of Arminius, a Hollander, and Calvin, a Swiss, who differed from each other in theological ideas.

For Discussion of Bryant

Thanatopsis

1. According to the first stanza, what different messages does nature have for us? Give some specific examples from your own experience of how nature has affected your mood or changed your thought.

2. Contrast the two views of death in lines 17–30 and 31–72. Does the idea of the companionship of the dead seem consoling to you? According to the poet, in what spirit should one approach death?

3. Recall the four elements of nature that Bryant stresses in his description of the earth. What is the chief difference between these and the subjects of the short poems?

4. Does " Thanatopsis " in any way reveal that it is the work of a teen-age youth? Do you think that Bryant depended more on his reading than on experience in writing the poem?

5. Does this poem express belief in a life after death? Read carefully before answering; there has been considerable difference of opinion on this point.

Shorter Poems

1. Point out the stanzas containing each of the three parts of " To a Waterfowl ": the picture seen by the poet, his meditation about the bird, and his application of his thoughts to his own life.

2. Find lines that show that the poet put himself in the bird's place, and that he felt its sensations. In view of the circumstances under which this poem was written, do you like or dislike the " moral tag "?

3. If you had never seen the flower, what details about it would you learn from " To the Fringed Gentian "?

4. Find a scientific description of a gentian in an encyclopedia or a botany text. What does a poem give that a scientific description fails to give, and vice versa? Show the function of each type of writing in our understanding of nature.

5. If you are especially interested in nature poetry, now is a good time to start making a collection of poems you particularly like, for Bryant affords many examples. Perhaps you would like to specialize in bird or flower poetry. Some students have been interested in collecting poems on death.

Abolition Riots

1. How would you restate Bryant's argument in outline form? What are his main points? his conclusion?

2. What instances of mob violence have you read about recently? What was the issue at stake, and how was it finally affected by the rioting or mob action? What do you think of Bryant's implication that men resort to mob violence only when they cannot obtain laws to accomplish their purpose?

3. From what personal impulses, quite apart from the larger issues, might someone join a mob? Analyze " mob psychology." Could you resist the invitation to join a mob? Discuss.

4. What important sentence from Patrick Henry's speech (p. 449) might Bryant appropriately have quoted in this editorial?

5. Bring to class an editorial from a current newspaper or magazine which strikes you as having persuasive power. Try to find one on the subject of freedom of speech or of the press. Compare the arguments with Bryant's.

For Your Vocabulary

BASE-WORDS: When conflict and argument over government arise, men frequently employ words descriptive of types of government. You know some using the ending -cracy, from the Greek word for rule or power — democracy, or rule by the people, and aristocracy, or rule by only the " best " people. Bryant expresses his alarm (p. 492) at the threat of an oligarchy, rule by only a few, who are not necessarily the best. The ending -archy, like -cracy, means " rule," but this word part occurs also at the beginning of words like archbishop, a bishop with special ruling powers. The term oligarchy is used most often in criticism or attack, aristocracy in approval or praise. The same ending occurs in patriarchs in " Thanatopsis " (l. 34), a word designating the fathers or older men who ruled early tribes. Do you know the exact meaning of more familiar terms built on these same base-words — plutocracy, autocracy, monarchy, anarchy?

John Greenleaf Whittier
1807–1892

SKIPPER IRESON'S RIDE

When Whittier was a young man at Haverhill Academy, a schoolmate from Marblehead told him the story of Skipper Ireson and the old song which had been derisively hurled at him by the women of Marblehead. Many years after, Whittier turned the story into the following ballad, one of the most popular of the many ballads he wrote on American legends and historical incidents. But more than twenty years after he had written it, Whittier discovered from a *History of Marblehead* that Ireson had really been an innocent victim. He had taken the punishment in silence rather than betray his mutinous crew, who refused to stop for the sinking ship lest their valuable catch of cod be spoiled. Whittier thanked the author of the history for clearing the matter up, saying, " I certainly would not do injustice to anyone, dead or living."

Of all the rides since the birth of time,
Told in story or sung in rhyme —
On Apuleius' Golden Ass,°
Or one-eyed Calendar's horse of brass,°
Witch astride of a human hack,   5
Islam's prophet on Al-Borák° —
The strangest ride that ever was sped

3. **Apuleius'** (ăp′û·lē′yŭs) **Golden Ass**: Apuleius, a Roman writer of the second century A.D., told the adventures of a young man turned into an ass. 4. **one-eyed Calendar's horse of brass**: Whittier's memory of the Arabian Nights was somewhat confused. The Calendar and the brass horse that could fly were in two different stories. 6. **Al-Borák**: the winged horse with human face that carried Mohammed to heaven.

Was Ireson's, out from Marblehead!
Old Floyd Ireson, for his hard heart,
Tarred and feathered and carried in
a cart   10
By the women of Marblehead!

Body of turkey, head of owl,
Wings adroop like a rained-on fowl,
Feathered and ruffled in every part,
Skipper Ireson stood in the cart.   15
Scores of women, old and young,
Strong of muscle, and glib of tongue,
Pushed and pulled up the rocky lane,
Shouting and singing the shrill refrain:
" Here's Flud Oirson, fur his horrd
horrt,   20
Torr'd an' futherr'd an' corr'd in a
corrt
By the women o' Morble'ead! "

Wrinkled scolds with hands on hips,
Girls in bloom of cheek and lips,
Wild-eyed, free-limbed, such as chase
Bacchus round some antique vase,   26
Brief of skirt, with ankles bare,
Loose of kerchief and loose of hair,
With conch shells blowing and fish
horns' twang,
Over and over the Maenads° sang: 30
" Here's Flud Oirson, fur his horrd
horrt,
Torr'd an' futherr'd an' corr'd in a
corrt
By the women o' Morble'ead! "

30. **Maenads** (mē′nădz): nymphs who followed Bacchus, Greek god of wine; hence, excited or frenzied women.

Small pity for him! — He sailed away
From a leaking ship in Chaleur Bay° —
Sailed away from a sinking wreck,   36
With his own town's people on her
    deck!
"Lay by! lay by!" they called to him.
Back he answered, "Sink or swim!
Brag of your catch of fish again!"   40
And off he sailed through the fog and
    rain!
    Old Floyd Ireson, for his hard heart,
    Tarred and feathered and carried in
        a cart
    By the women of Marblehead!

Fathoms deep in dark Chaleur   45
That wreck shall lie forevermore.
Mother and sister, wife and maid,
Looked from the rocks of Marblehead
Over the moaning and rainy sea —
Looked for the coming that might not
    be!   50
What did the winds and the sea birds
    say
Of the cruel captain who sailed away? —
    Old Floyd Ireson, for his hard heart,
    Tarred and feathered and carried in
        a cart
    By the women of Marblehead.   55

Through the street, on either side,
Up flew windows, doors swung wide;
Sharp-tongued spinsters, old wives gray,
Treble lent the fish horn's bray.
Sea-worn grandsires, cripple-bound,
Hulks of old sailors run aground,   61
Shook head, and fist, and hat, and cane,
And cracked with curses the hoarse re-
    frain:
    "Here's Flud Oirson, fur his horrd
        horrt,
    Torr'd an' futherr'd an' corr'd in a
        corrt   65
    By the women o' Morble'ead!"

Sweetly along the Salem road
Bloom of orchard and lilac showed.

35. **Chaleur** (shá·lōōr′) **Bay:** in the Gulf of
St. Lawrence.

Little the wicked skipper knew
Of the fields so green and the sky so
    blue.   70
Riding there in his sorry trim,
Like an Indian idol glum and grim,
Scarcely he seemed the sound to hear
Of voices shouting far and near:
    "Here's Flud Oirson, fur his horrd
        horrt,   75
    Torr'd an' futherr'd an' corr'd in a
        corrt
    By the women o' Morble'ead!"

"Hear me, neighbors!" at last he
    cried —
"What to me is this noisy ride?
What is the shame that clothes the
    skin   80
To the nameless horror that lives with-
    in?
Waking or sleeping, I see a wreck,
And hear a cry from a reeling deck!
Hate me and curse me — I only dread
The hand of God and the face of the
    dead!"   85
    Said old Floyd Ireson, for his hard
        heart,
    Tarred and feathered and carried in
        a cart
    By the women of Marblehead!

Then the wife of the skipper lost at sea
Said, "God has touched him! why
    should we!"   90
Said an old wife mourning her only
    son,
"Cut the rogue's tether and let him
    run!"
So with soft relentings and rude excuse,
Half scorn, half pity, they cut him
    loose,
And gave him a cloak to hide him in,
And left him alone with his shame and
    sin.   96
    Poor Floyd Ireson, for his hard heart,
    Tarred and feathered and carried in
        a cart
    By the women of Marblehead!

THE ETERNAL GOODNESS

Written in 1865 just at the close of the War between the States, this is generally considered the finest of Whittier's religious poems. The version given here omits a few stanzas. The poem was addressed to those who held the "iron creeds" of the Puritans: that God as a stern judge would severely punish the wicked, and was therefore to be feared. Whittier believed that if hate and revenge were wrong in human beings, they would also be wrong in God. If God is good, He must therefore be a God of love and mercy.

O friends! with whom my feet have
    trod
The quiet aisles of prayer,
Glad witness to your zeal for God
    And love of man I bear.

I trace your lines of argument;   5
    Your logic linked and strong
I weigh as one who dreads dissent,
    And fears a doubt as wrong.

But still my human hands are weak
    To hold your iron creeds: 10
Against the words ye bid me speak
    My heart within me pleads.

Who fathoms the Eternal Thought?
    Who talks of scheme and plan?
The Lord is God! He needeth not   15
    The poor device of man.

I walk with bare, hushed feet the
    ground
Ye tread with boldness shod;
I dare not fix with mete and bound°
    The love and power of God.   20

Ye praise His justice; even such
    His pitying love I deem:
Ye seek a king; I fain would touch
    The robe that hath no seam.°

Ye see the curse which overbroods   25
    A world of pain and loss;
I hear our Lord's Beatitudes°
    And prayer upon the cross.

More than your schoolmen teach, with-
    in
Myself, alas! I know: 30
Too dark ye cannot paint the sin,
    Too small the merit show.

I bow my forehead to the dust,
    I veil mine eyes for shame,
And urge, in trembling self-distrust,
    A prayer without a claim.   36

I see the wrong that round me lies,
    I feel the guilt within;
I hear, with groan and travail-cries,
    The world confess its sin.   40

Yet, in the maddening maze of things,
    And tossed by storm and flood,
To one fixed trust my spirit clings;
    I know that God is good!

Not mine to look where cherubim   45
    And seraphs may not see,
But nothing can be good in Him
    Which evil is in me.

The wrong that pains my soul below
    I dare not throne above;   50
I know not of His hate, — I know
    His goodness and His love. . . .

I long for household voices gone,
    For vanished smiles I long,
But God hath led my dear ones on,   55
    And He can do no wrong.

I know not what the future hath
    Of marvel or surprise,
Assured alone that life and death
    His mercy underlies. . . .   60

I know not where His islands lift
    Their fronded palms in air;
I only know I cannot drift
    Beyond His love and care. . . .

19. **mete and bound:** definite boundaries (legal term). 24. **the robe . . . no seam:** the robe worn by Christ just before His Crucifixion.

27. **Beatitudes** (bḗ·ăt′ĭ·tūdz): Sermon on the Mount, found in Matt. 5.

SNOW–BOUND A *Winter Idyll* *

After the close of the war, with the question of slavery settled, Whittier's mind turned more toward personal reminiscence. Being a bachelor, he had lived in closer touch with the family of his boyhood than he might otherwise have done. These home ties had recently been broken by the death of his mother and elder sister, and later his younger sister, Elizabeth. No one was left now but his brother Matthew and himself. What more natural than that he should write a memorial poem dedicated to the old household?

The poem was published in 1866 and was immediately hailed as the greatest American pastoral poem. It is printed here in a shortened version. As this poem is written in very simple language, its oral reading is an enjoyable classroom activity.

The sun that brief December day
Rose cheerless over hills of gray,
And, darkly circled, gave at noon
A sadder light than waning moon.
Slow tracing down the thickening sky
Its mute and ominous prophecy,   6
A portent seeming less than threat,
It sank from sight before it set.
A chill no coat, however stout,
Of homespun stuff could quite shut
    out,   10
A hard, dull bitterness of cold,
    That checked, mid-vein, the circling
    race
    Of lifeblood in the sharpened face,
The coming of the snowstorm told.
The wind blew east: we heard the roar
Of Ocean on his wintry shore,   16
And felt the strong pulse throbbing
    there
Beat with low rhythm our inland air.

Meanwhile we did our nightly chores —
Brought in the wood from out of doors,
Littered the stalls, and from the mows
Raked down the herd's-grass for the
    cows;   22

* *Idyll:* a poem or story which is a "little picture" of some pastoral, or country, scene.

Heard the horse whinnying for his corn;
And, sharply clashing horn on horn,
Impatient down the stanchion rows   25
The cattle shake their walnut bows;
While, peering from his early perch
Upon the scaffold's pole of birch,
The cock his crested helmet bent
And down his querulous challenge sent.

Unwarmed by any sunset light   31
The gray day darkened into night,
A night made hoary with the swarm
And whirl-dance of the blinding storm,
As zigzag, wavering to and fro,   35
Crossed and recrossed the wingèd
    snow:
And ere the early bedtime came
The white drift piled the window frame,
And through the glass the clothesline
    posts   39
Looked in like tall and sheeted ghosts.

So all night long the storm roared on:
The morning broke without a sun;
In tiny spherule traced with lines
Of Nature's geometric signs,
In starry flake and pellicle,   45
All day the hoary meteor fell;
And, when the second morning shone,
We looked upon a world unknown,
On nothing we could call our own.
Around the glistening wonder bent   50
The blue walls of the firmament,
No cloud above, no earth below —
A universe of sky and snow!
The old familiar sights of ours
Took marvelous shapes; strange domes
    and towers   55
Rose up where sty or corncrib stood,
Or garden wall, or belt of wood;
A smooth white mound the brush pile
    showed,
A fenceless drift what once was road;
The bridle post an old man sat   60
With loose-flung coat and high cocked
    hat;
The wellcurb had a Chinese roof;°

62. wellcurb had a Chinese roof: Whittier explained, when asked how this could be, that a board had been placed across the curb to hold the bucket and that this gave the roof effect.

And even the long sweep, high aloof,
In its slant splendor, seemed to tell
Of Pisa's leaning miracle.°   65

A prompt, decisive man, no breath
Our father wasted: " Boys, a path! "
Well pleased, (for when did farmer boy
Count such a summons less than joy?)
Our buskins° on our feet we drew;   70
  With mittened hands, and caps drawn
    low,
    To guard our necks and ears from
      snow,
We cut the solid whiteness through.
And, where the drift was deepest, made
A tunnel walled and overlaid   75
With dazzling crystal: we had read
Of rare Aladdin's° wondrous cave,
And to our own his name we gave,
With many a wish the luck were ours
To test his lamp's supernal powers.   80
We reached the barn with merry din,
And roused the prisoned brutes within.
The old horse thrust his long head out,
And grave with wonder gazed about;
The cock his lusty greeting said,   85
And forth his speckled harem led;
The oxen lashed their tails, and hooked,
And mild reproach of hunger looked;
The hornèd patriarch of the sheep,   89
Like Egypt's Amun° roused from sleep,
Shook his sage head with gesture mute,
And emphasized with stamp of foot.

All day the gusty north wind bore
The loosening drift its breath before;
Low circling round its southern zone,
The sun through dazzling snow-mist
    shone.   96
No church bell lent its Christian tone
To the savage air, no social smoke
Curled over woods of snow-hung oak.
A solitude made more intense   100

65. Pisa's (pē′zäz) leaning miracle: a famous
slanting tower in Pisa, Italy. 70. buskins: a
name for heavy boots derived from the high-
heeled boots worn by ancient Greek actors.
77. Aladdin: the youth in the Arabian Nights
who discovered great treasure in a cave through
the power of a magical lamp. 90. Egypt's Amun:
an Egyptian god frequently represented with
a ram's head, usually spelled Amon or Ammon.

By dreary-voicèd elements,
The shrieking of the mindless wind,
The moaning tree boughs swaying
  blind,
And on the glass the unmeaning beat
Of ghostly finger tips of sleet.   105
Beyond the circle of our hearth
No welcome sound of toil or mirth
Unbound the spell, and testified
Of human life and thought outside.
We minded that the sharpest ear   110
The buried brooklet could not hear,
The music of whose liquid lip
Had been to us companionship,
And, in our lonely life, had grown
To have an almost human tone.   115

As night drew on, and, from the crest
Of wooded knolls that ridged the west,
The sun, a snow-blown traveler, sank
From sight beneath the smothering
  bank,   119
We piled with care our nightly stack
Of wood against the chimney back —
The oaken log, green, huge, and thick,
And on its top the stout backstick;
The knotty forestick laid apart,   124
And filled between with curious art
The ragged brush; then, hovering near,
We watched the first red blaze appear,
Heard the sharp crackle, caught the
  gleam
On whitewashed wall and sagging
  beam,
Until the old, rude-furnished room   130
Burst, flowerlike, into rosy bloom;
While radiant with a mimic flame
Outside the sparkling drift became,
And through the bare-boughed lilac
  tree
Our own warm hearth seemed blazing
  free.   135
The crane and pendent trammels
  showed,
The Turks' heads° on the andirons
  glowed;
While childish fancy, prompt to tell
The meaning of the miracle,

137. Turks' heads: the design of the top of
the andiron resembled a Turkish cap.

Whispered the old rhyme: "*Under the*
tree 140
When fire outdoors burns merrily,
There the witches are making tea."

The moon above the eastern wood
Shone at its full; the hill range stood
Transfigured in the silver flood, 145
Its blown snows flashing cold and keen,
Dead white, save where some sharp ra-
vine
Took shadow, or the somber green
Of hemlocks turned to pitchy black
Against the whiteness at their back.
For such a world and such a night 151
Most fitting that unwarming light,
Which only seemed where'er it fell
To make the coldness visible.

Shut in from all the world without, 155
We sat the clean-winged hearth° about,
Content to let the north wind roar
In baffled rage at pane and door,
While the red logs before us beat
The frost line back with tropic heat;
And ever, when a louder blast 161
Shook beam and rafter as it passed,
The merrier up its roaring draft
The great throat of the chimney
laughed;
The house dog on his paws outspread
Laid to the fire his drowsy head, 166
The cat's dark silhouette on the wall
A couchant tiger's seemed to fall;
And, for the winter fireside meet,
Between the andirons' straddling feet,
The mug of cider simmered slow, 171
The apples sputtered in a row,
And, close at hand, the basket stood
With nuts from brown October's wood.

What matter how the night behaved?
What matter how the north wind raved?
Blow high, blow low, not all its snow
Could quench our hearthfire's ruddy
glow. . . .

156. **clean-winged hearth:** A turkey wing was
used for a hearth broom.

We sped the time with stories old, 179
Wrought puzzles out, and riddles told,
Or stammered from our schoolbook lore
" The Chief of Gambia's golden shore."°

. . .

THE FATHER

Our father rode again his ride
On Memphremagog's° wooded side;
Sat down again to moose and samp 185
In trapper's hut and Indian camp. . . .
We shared the fishing off Boar's Head,°
The chowder on the sand beach made,
Dipped by the hungry, steaming hot,
With spoons of clamshell from the pot.
We heard the tales of witchcraft old, 191
And dream and sign and marvel told
To sleepy listeners as they lay
Stretched idly on the salted hay,
Adrift along the winding shores, 195
When favoring breezes deigned to blow
The square sail of the gundalow,°
And idle lay the useless oars.

THE MOTHER

Our mother, while she turned her
wheel
Or ran the new-knit stocking heel, 200
Told how the Indian hordes came down
At midnight on Cocheco° town,
And how her own great-uncle bore
His cruel scalp-mark to fourscore.
Recalling, in her fitting phrase, 205
So rich and picturesque and free,
(The common unrhymed poetry
Of simple life and country ways),
The story of her early days — 209
She made us welcome to her home;
Old hearths grew wide to give us room;
We stole with her a frightened look
At the gray wizard's conjuring-book,

182. "**The Chief of Gambia's golden shore**":
a line from a popular poem of the day called
"The African Chief." This shows the interest
in antislavery in Whittier's boyhood. 184. **Memphremagog** (mĕm′frĕ·mä′gŏg): a lake between
Vermont and Canada. 187. **Boar's Head:** a point
on the coast north of Salisbury, Massachusetts.
197. **gundalow:** a variant of *gondola*, a heavy,
flat-bottomed barge or boat. 202. **Cocheco** (kŏ-
chē′kō): Indian name for Dover, New Hampshire.

The fame whereof went far and wide
Through all the simple countryside; 215
We heard the hawks at twilight play,
The boat horn on Piscataqua,°
The loon's weird laughter far away;
We fished her little trout brook, knew
What flowers in wood and meadow
    grew, 220
What sunny hillsides autumn-brown
She climbed to shake the ripe nuts
    down,
Saw where in sheltered cove and bay
The ducks' black squadron anchored
    lay, 224
And heard the wild geese calling loud
Beneath the gray November cloud. . . .

THE UNCLE

Our uncle,° innocent of books,
Was rich in lore of fields and brooks,
The ancient teachers never dumb
Of Nature's unhoused lyceum. 230
In moons and tides and weather wise,
He read the clouds as prophecies,
And foul or fair could well divine,
By many an occult hint and sign,
Holding the cunning-warded keys° 235
To all the woodcraft mysteries;
Himself to Nature's heart so near
That all her voices in his ear
Of beast or bird had meanings clear. . . .
A simple, guileless, childlike man, 240
Content to live where life began;
Strong only on his native grounds,
The little world of sights and sounds
Whose girdle was the parish bounds. . . .

THE AUNT

Next, the dear aunt,° whose smile of
    cheer 245
And voice in dreams I see and hear —
The sweetest woman ever Fate
Perverse denied a household mate,

Who, lonely, homeless, not the less
Found peace in love's unselfishness, 250
And welcome wheresoe'er she went,
A calm and gracious element,
Whose presence seemed the sweet in-
    come
And womanly atmosphere of home —
Called up her girlhood memories, 255
The huskings and the apple bees,
The sleigh rides and the summer sails,
Weaving through all the poor details
And homespun warp of circumstance
A golden woof-thread of romance. . . .

THE ELDER SISTER

There, too, our elder sister° plied 261
Her evening task the stand beside;
A full, rich nature, free to trust,
Truthful and almost sternly just,
Impulsive, earnest, prompt to act, 265
And make her generous thought a fact,
Keeping with many a light disguise
The secret of self-sacrifice.
O heart sore tried! thou hast the best
That Heaven itself could give thee —
    rest, 270
Rest from all bitter thoughts and things!
  How many a poor one's blessing went
  With thee beneath the low green tent
Whose curtain never outward swings!

THE YOUNGER SISTER

As one who held herself a part 275
Of all she saw, and let her heart
  Against the household bosom lean,
Upon the motley-braided mat
Our youngest° and our dearest sat. . . .
The chill weight of the winter snow 280
  For months upon her grave has lain;
And now, when summer south winds
    blow
  And brier and harebell bloom again,

217. **Piscataqua** (pĭs·kăt′à·kwà): a river in Maine. The rhyme shows that Whittier gave it a rustic pronunciation. 227. **Our uncle:** Moses, the bachelor brother of Whittier's father. 235. **cunning-warded keys:** keys with notches nicely adjusted to fit different locks. 245. **the dear aunt:** Aunt Mercy, his mother's sister, who always made her home with the Whittiers.

261. **elder sister:** Mary, who died five years before the poem was written. She was Mrs. Jacob Caldwell of Haverhill. 279. **Our youngest:** Elizabeth, the unmarried sister, who kept house for Whittier until she died about a year before the poem was written. As she too possessed some poetic gift, the brother and sister were most congenial, and the poet's mourning for her is feelingly expressed.

I tread the pleasant paths we trod,
I see the violet-sprinkled sod   285
Whereon she leaned, too frail and weak
The hillside flowers she loved to seek,
Yet following me where'er I went
With dark eyes full of love's content.
The birds are glad; the brier rose fills
The air with sweetness; all the hills   291
Stretch green to June's unclouded sky;
But still I wait with ear and eye
For something gone which should be
    nigh,
A loss in all familiar things,   295
In flower that blooms, and bird that
    sings. . . .

THE SCHOOLMASTER

Brisk wielder of the birch and rule,
The master of the district school
Held at the fire his favored place;
Its warm glow lit a laughing face   300
Fresh-hued and fair, where scarce ap-
    peared
The uncertain prophecy of beard.
He teased the mitten-blinded cat,
Played cross pins on my uncle's hat,
Sang songs, and told us what befalls   305
In classic Dartmouth's° college halls.
Born the wild Northern hills among,
From whence his yeoman father wrung
By patient toil subsistence scant,
Not competence and yet not want,   310
He early gained the power to pay
His cheerful, self-reliant way;
Could doff at ease his scholar's gown
To peddle wares from town to town;
Or through the long vacation's reach
In lonely lowland districts teach,   316
Where all the droll experience found
At stranger hearths in boarding round,
The moonlit skater's keen delight,
The sleigh drive through the frosty
    night,   320
The rustic party, with its rough
Accompaniment of blindman's buff,
And whirling plate, and forfeits paid,
His winter task a pastime made.
Happy the snow-locked homes wherein

306. **Dartmouth:** a well-known New Hampshire college.

He tuned his merry violin,   326
Or played the athlete in the barn,
Or held the good dame's winding yarn,
Or mirth-provoking versions told
Of classic legends rare and old,   330
Wherein the scenes of Greece and Rome
Had all the commonplace of home,
And little seemed at best the odds
'Twixt Yankee peddlers and old gods.
    . . .

At last the great logs, crumbling low,
Sent out a dull and duller glow,   336
The bull's-eye watch that hung in view,
Ticking its weary circuit through,
Pointed with mutely warning sign
Its black hand to the hour of nine.   340
That sign the pleasant circle broke:
My uncle ceased his pipe to smoke,
Knocked from its bowl the refuse gray
And laid it tenderly away;
Then roused himself to safely cover   345
The dull red brands with ashes over.
And while, with care, our mother laid
The work aside, her steps she stayed
One moment, seeking to express
Her grateful sense of happiness   350
For food and shelter, warmth and
    health,
And love's contentment more than
    wealth,
With simple wishes (not the weak,
Vain prayers which no fulfillment seek,
But such as warm the generous heart,
O'erprompt to do with Heaven its
    part)   356
That none might lack, that bitter night,
For bread and clothing, warmth and
    light.

Within our beds awhile we heard
The wind that round the gables roared,
With now and then a ruder shock,   361
Which made our very bedsteads rock.
We heard the loosened clapboards
    tossed,
The board nails snapping in the frost;
And on us, through the unplastered
    wall,   365
Felt the light-sifted snowflakes fall.

But sleep stole on, as sleep will do
When hearts are light and life is new;
Faint and more faint the murmurs grew,
Till in the summerland of dreams   370
They softened to the sound of streams,
Low stir of leaves, and dip of oars,
And lapsing waves on quiet shores.

Next morn we wakened with the shout
Of merry voices high and clear;   375
And saw the teamsters drawing near
To break the drifted highways out.
Down the long hillside treading slow
We saw the half-buried oxen go,   379
Shaking the snow from heads uptossed,
Their straining nostrils white with frost.
Before our door the straggling train
Drew up, an added team to gain.
The elders threshed their hands a-cold,
    Passed, with the cider mug, their
        jokes   385
    From lip to lip; the younger folks
Down the loose snowbanks, wrestling,
    rolled,
Then toiled again the cavalcade
    O'er windy hill, through clogged ra-
        vine,
    And woodland paths that wound be-
        tween   390
Low drooping pine boughs winter-
    weighed.
From every barn a team afoot,
At every house a new recruit,
Where, drawn by Nature's subtlest law,
Haply the watchful young men saw   395
Sweet doorway pictures of the curls
And curious eyes of merry girls,
Lifting their hands in mock defense
Against the snowball's compliments,
And reading in each missive tossed   400
The charm with Eden never lost.

We heard once more the sleigh bells'
    sound;
    And, following where the teamsters
        led,
The wise old Doctor went his round,
Just pausing at our door to say,   405
In the brief autocratic way
Of one who, prompt at Duty's call,

Was free to urge her claim on all,   408
    That some poor neighbor sick abed
At night our mother's aid would need.
For, one in generous thought and deed,
    What mattered in the sufferer's sight
    The Quaker matron's inward light,
The Doctor's mail of Calvin's creed?°
All hearts confess the saints elect   415
    Who, twain in faith, in love agree,
And melt not in an acid sect
    The Christian pearl of charity!

So days went on: a week had passed
Since the great world was heard from
    last.   420
The Almanac we studied o'er,
Read and reread our little store
Of books and pamphlets, scarce a score;
One harmless novel, mostly hid
From younger eyes, a book forbid,   425
And poetry (or good or bad,
A single book was all we had). . . .

At last the floundering carrier bore
The village paper to our door.   429
Lo! broadening outward as we read,
To warmer zones the horizon spread;
In panoramic length unrolled
We saw the marvels that it told. . . .

Welcome to us its week-old news,
Its corner for the rustic Muse,   435
    Its monthly gauge of snow and rain,
Its record, mingling in a breath
The wedding bell and dirge of death;
Jest, anecdote, and lovelorn tale,
The latest culprit sent to jail;   440
Its hue and cry of stolen and lost,
Its vendue° sales and goods at cost,
    And traffic calling loud for gain.
We felt the stir of hall and street,
The pulse of life that round us beat;
The chill embargo of the snow   446
Was melted in the genial glow;
Wide swung again our ice-locked door,
And all the world was ours once more!

414. **Calvin's creed:** The doctor was a Presbyterian, a sect founded by Calvin. **442. vendue**
(věn'dū): auction.

A

IN THE EARLY 1800'S
there was a burst of cultural activ-
ity, centering around three cities,
New York, Boston, and Charleston.
Trade with the Orient flourished,
the Empire style influenced archi-
tecture, furniture, and dress. (a)
Broadway and Bowling Green,
N.Y., about 1826 (Stokes Collec-
tion, N.Y. Public Library). (b)
Dinnerware imported from Can-
ton, China, about 1838 (Essex In-
stitute).

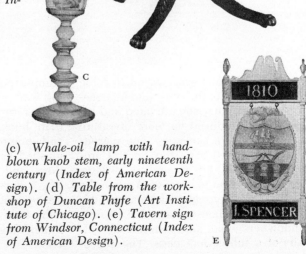

D

C

B

(c) *Whale-oil lamp with hand-*
blown knob stem, early nineteenth
century (Index of American De-
sign). (d) Table from the work-
shop of Duncan Phyfe (Art Insti-
tute of Chicago). (e) Tavern sign
from Windsor, Connecticut (Index
of American Design).

E

For Discussion of Whittier

Skipper Ireson's Ride

1. What details make you feel the spirit of the women? Why did they finally let the skipper go? His speech is imaginary; in reality he said nothing during the ride. Does Whittier's addition make a more effective poem? Why or why not?

2. Read a modern version in "The True Story of Skipper Ireson" by Charles Buxton Going (to be found in Hohn's *Stories in Verse*). Point out differences in the two versions. Which do you like better as a poem? Why?

3. If possible, show pictures of the quaint town of Marblehead or have a description given in class by someone who has been there.

4. Write in prose or verse a legend or old settler's tale of the early days of your own community.

The Eternal Goodness

1. Sum up in a few sentences the main thought of this poem. In what way does it show that Whittier was a Quaker?

2. What contrast is there between the thinking of Whittier and that of the "friends" addressed? With which side do you agree?

3 Compare Whittier's Quaker thinking with the Puritan thinking of Edwards.

4. Select lines that are often quoted or that you think are well suited to quotation. Memorize some of these.

Snow-Bound

1. Point out some of the details that make the forecast of snow and the storm itself especially vivid. Select figures of speech that add to the imaginative quality of the description.

2. Debate the advantages and disadvantages of living in a snowy country.

3. Describe the various members of the group around the fire. Each character may be taken by a different student for description in class. Select the character best liked by the class. Which ones do you think Whittier describes most sympathetically?

4. Compare the amusements of the evening with those which would probably entertain a modern family. How does the reading matter compare with that in your home?

5. Put the conversation around the fire into dramatic form that could be acted in class. For contrast, the conversation of a modern family group might be put on as part of the same program.

6. Find other poems on snow and frost, such as "The Snow-Storm," by Ralph W. Emerson; "A Snow Storm," by Henry van Dyke; "Snow Shower," by Bryant; "Snow Song," by Lucy Larcom; "An Arctic Night," by Fridtjof Nansen; "To a Snowflake," by Francis Thompson; "An Old-Fashioned Snow Storm," by Warner; "The Frost Spirit," by Whittier. How do these compare with *Snow-Bound* in effectiveness of description?

Edgar Allan Poe

POE was the first great writer to come out of the South. Why should a section of the country so cultivated and literate have produced no more literature than it did? We can guess one reason: no city (except Charleston, South Carolina) attracted artists and publishers. There was no Boston or New York in the South. It was a country of broad plantations, stately houses, and aristocratic landowners who administered the affairs of a subservient class. The arts of administration, law, and graceful living were encouraged more than the art of literature. "We produce men, rather than books," a Southerner once said, and pointed to the long and distinguished list of Southern statesmen, soldiers, and jurists, headed by Washington, Jefferson, Lee, and John Marshall. Yet no section of the country in the first half of the nineteenth century was producing books more distinguished than Poe's.

Poe's Turbulent, Short Life

"The great intellect with the sad heart," Edwin Markham called Poe. "The great talent with the sad life," would be another way to put it. Poe was born in Boston of a Southern family who were in a traveling company of actors. Two years later his parents were dead. He was supported by a wealthy Richmond family, the Allans, who gave him his middle name. Attractive, brilliant, erratic, the young Poe never got along very well with anybody who imposed restraint on him. He often quarreled with his foster father. The Allans took him to England for five years, then sent him to the University of Virginia. He spent a wild year there, for he moved in a set with whom drinking and gambling were fashionable, and Poe never did anything by halves. When he lost twenty-five hundred dollars in a card game, he was taken out of the University and put into Mr. Allan's business. That didn't work either. He had an unhappy love affair and didn't like his job. He ran away. Later he enlisted as a soldier under an assumed name. Mr. Allan rescued him from that and had him appointed to West Point, but Poe was dismissed within a year. Thereafter he had to go it alone.

The rest of the story is not pretty. He was a brilliant editor, and made the *Southern Literary Messenger* the outstanding magazine of the South, but lost his editorship as he lost so many other situations, because he drank too much and didn't keep schedules. He married his thirteen-year-old cousin, and thereafter lived mostly in Philadelphia and New York, fighting poverty, in and out of editorial jobs, taking care of his child wife when she developed tuberculosis, depending more and more upon drink to make him forget his troubles, but always writing brilliantly.

His wife died, only twenty-four years old. Two years later he himself was found dying in a Baltimore street. No one knew what had happened to him. He was dead at forty, when most writers are ready to begin their solidest work.

A Versatile Literary Genius

What Poe did in his few years — in spite of some of the greatest handicaps ever set in the way of a man's writing — was astonishing. Forget his life, for a moment, and add up his literary score: He wrote better poetry, better short stories, better criticism than had been written in America up to his time. During the Flowering of the East some people excelled in one of these fields (like Bryant and Whittier in poetry, or Irving and Hawthorne in stories), and some in two (like Emerson and Lowell, in poetry and criticism), but nobody else was able to be a top man in *three*. And Poe did all this in twenty years, between 1829 and his death in 1849. Emerson, Longfellow, Lowell, Whittier, Bryant, Whitman had literary careers of nearly fifty years. Poe burned like a short candle, but no light burned brighter.

Poe the Literary Critic

Almost alone among his great contemporaries, Poe did not hesitate to criticize contemporary writers. Great or small, he put them under the microscope. He gave them such an examination as writers had never before had from an American critic. In cutting out their bad spots, as an editor, he could be as impersonal as a surgeon. He allowed no patriotism, no pleas or threats, to stand in the way of his judgment. "As for American letters," he said, "plain speaking about them is simply the one thing needed." He gave them what they needed.

In brilliant essays, he put forth his theory of criticism. The purpose of writing, he said, is "pleasure, not truth." The object of poetry is "the rhythmical creation of beauty." The well-made story or poem will have every word, every sound contributing to the effect the writer wants to achieve.

Poe the Poet and Story Writer

His own fiction and poetry brilliantly exemplified his theory. Just as he was an artist in the emotional effect of fiction, so he was an artist in the sound

effect of verse. He could make the bells ring in words. He could make readers shiver from the very sound of a poem. He could put together words so that they had the beauty of a Persian tapestry, and merely to hear the words without thinking of their meaning was an esthetic experience.

No other American of his time left so many stories that are still part of our common reading, part of our heritage, and part of the world's heritage, too.

Some of his enduring stories are detective tales, like "The Gold Bug." Poe was the first great writer of mystery and detective stories, preceding the Englishmen Robert Louis Stevenson and A. Conan Doyle by many years. He had a hard, sharp mind which would have made him a great lawyer if his interests had gone that way.

Others are stories of horror and magic, like "The Fall of the House of Usher" and "The Tell-Tale Heart." No one has ever succeeded in getting more cold chills into a few thousand words than Poe. He built his stories like a modern streamlined airplane, with the very first sentence on the theme, and every other sentence pointed straight to the effect he wanted to make.

Two Sides: Reality and Unreality

In both stories and poems you will notice an interesting characteristic of Poe — he was not "local." Bryant wrote about the flowers around him, Whittier about the people of Massachusetts, and Cooper about the American forest and frontier. But Poe wrote often as though he had never seen Richmond or New York. He set most of his stories and poems in an unreal, imaginary world where he could paint any kind of setting he wanted, or in Paris or a distant island where people couldn't check on the accuracy of his details. He didn't care about details of setting. He cared about what kind of emotional effect his writings had on the reader.

Those are the two sides of Poe — first, the hard, logical intellect that led him to write the detective stories and made him a ruthless but brilliant critic, and, second, the sense of unreality and magic that led him to create a world of his own and write poetry in which sound was sometimes more important than sense.

An Artist for the Sake of Art

Poe had no particular message for his readers. He was not a moral writer, like Hawthorne or Bryant. As Lowell said, his heart "somehow seems all squeezed out by the mind." He was an artist for the sake of art — for the sake of making a beautiful poem or story, every word of which would be pointed toward a single effect on the reader. You will notice that his stories and poems usually deal with love, beauty, and death. Those were his three themes, and he used them over and over. He was not concerned with explaining them, advising about them, or discussing the social problems they created. He was concerned with the literary effect he could make out of them. That was the way in which he differed most from his New England contemporaries. Artist in form and sound and in the power of creating emotion, he stopped short of message and moral.

Poe was born in the year (1809) when Jefferson finished his term as President, and died in the year of the great gold rush (1849). He was the only American writer of his time to excel as a critic, a poet, and a short story writer.

Edgar Allan Poe
1809–1849

TO HELEN

·This is one of the earliest poems by Poe, inspired by his youthful admiration for the mother of one of his school friends. He later identified her as "the first purely ideal love of my soul." Lines 9–10 of this poem are very famous and are frequently quoted.

Helen, thy beauty is to me
  Like those Nicean° barks of yore,
That gently, o'er a perfumed sea,
  The weary, wayworn wanderer bore
  To his own native shore.   5

2. **Nicean** (nĭ·sē′ăn): pertaining to Nicea, a town of Asia Minor. Poe probably had no reason for referring to this town especially, but chose the word for its sound and its suggestion of a picturesque ancient ship.

On desperate seas long wont to roam,
  Thy hyacinth° hair, thy classic face,
Thy naiad° airs have brought me home
  To the glory that was Greece
  And the grandeur that was Rome.

Lo! in yon brilliant window niche   11
  How statuelike I see thee stand,
The agate lamp within thy hand!
  Ah, Psyche,° from the regions which
  Are Holy Land!   15

7. **hyacinth:** a favorite adjective for hair in the old Greek epics was "hyacinthine," usually meaning beautiful and curling. 8. **naiad** (nā′ăd): in Greek mythology, a water nymph. 14. **Psyche** (sī′kē): the Greek word for "soul" or "mind," derived from the myth of the Greek maiden beloved of Cupid. Poe uses the word again in "Ulalume," page 512.

THE BELLS

All of Poe's verse is remarkably melodious, but "The Bells" approaches magic. It is probably the purest "sound" poem in the English language. Here Poe reproduces the tonal effects of the bells, largely by a choice of words that approximate their actual sound. This device is called *onomatopoeia* (ŏn′ŏ·măt′ŏ·pē′yȧ), the use of a word whose sound suggests its meaning.

Any poem is best read aloud, but this one *must* be. The rolling l's and r's and the resonant m's and n's, linked with the vowel sounds that imitate the timbre of the various metals, set the bells to ringing as you speak the words. That is the magic that Poe works in this poem.

I

Hear the sledges with the bells,
  Silver bells!
What a world of merriment their melody foretells!
  How they tinkle, tinkle, tinkle,
    In the icy air of night!   5
While the stars, that oversprinkle
All the heavens, seem to twinkle
    With a crystalline delight;
  Keeping time, time, time,
  In a sort of runic° rhyme,   10
To the tintinnabulation that so musically wells
  From the bells, bells, bells, bells,
    Bells, bells, bells —
  From the jingling and the tinkling
    of the bells.

II

Hear the mellow wedding bells,
  Golden bells!   16
What a world of happiness their harmony foretells!
  Through the balmy air of night
  How they ring out their delight!
    From the molten-golden notes,
    And all in tune,   21

10. **runic** (rōō′nĭk): pertaining to runes, letters in an ancient alphabet, used in the writing of ancient Teutonic poetry; hence, strange, magical.

    What a liquid ditty floats
  To the turtledove that listens, while
    she gloats
    On the moon!
Oh, from out the sounding cells,
What a gush of euphony voluminously
    wells!   26
    How it swells!
    How it dwells
  On the future! how it tells
  Of the rapture that impels   30
To the swinging and the ringing
  Of the bells, bells, bells,
Of the bells, bells, bells, bells,
    Bells, bells, bells —
To the rhyming and the chiming of the
    bells!   35

III

Hear the loud alarum bells,
  Brazen bells!
What a tale of terror, now, their turbulency tells!
  In the startled ear of night
  How they scream out their affright!
    Too much horrified to speak,   41
    They can only shriek, shriek,
    Out of tune,
In a clamorous appealing to the mercy
    of the fire,
In a mad expostulation with the deaf
    and frantic fire,   45
  Leaping higher, higher, higher,
  With a desperate desire,
  And a resolute endeavor
  Now — now to sit or never,
By the side of the pale-faced moon.
  Oh, the bells, bells, bells!   51
  What a tale their terror tells
    Of despair!
  How they clang, and clash, and
    roar!
What a horror they outpour   55
On the bosom of the palpitating air!
  Yet the ear, it fully knows,
    By the twanging
    And the clanging,
  How the danger ebbs and flows;
Yet the ear distinctly tells,   61
    In the jangling

And the wrangling,
How the danger sinks and swells —
By the sinking or the swelling in the an-
　　　ger of the bells,　　　65
　Of the bells,
　Of the bells, bells, bells, bells,
　　Bells, bells, bells —
In the clamor and the clangor of the
　　bells!

IV

Hear the tolling of the bells,　　70
　　Iron bells!
What a world of solemn thought their
　　monody° compels!
　In the silence of the night
　How we shiver with affright
At the melancholy menace of their
　　tone!　　　75
　For every sound that floats
　From the rust within their throats
　　Is a groan.
And the people — ah, the people,
They that dwell up in the steeple,
　　All alone,　　　81
And who tolling, tolling, tolling
　In that muffled monotone,
Feel a glory in so rolling　　84

On the human heart a stone —
They are neither man nor woman,
They are neither brute nor human,
　They are ghouls:°
And their king it is who tolls;
And he rolls, rolls, rolls,　　90
　Rolls
　A paean from the bells;
And his merry bosom swells
　With the paean of the bells,
And he dances, and he yells:　　95
Keeping time, time, time,
In a sort of runic rhyme,
　To the paean of the bells,
　　Of the bells:
Keeping time, time, time,　　100
In a sort of runic rhyme,
　To the throbbing of the bells,
Of the bells, bells, bells —
　To the sobbing of the bells;
Keeping time, time, time,　　105
　As he knells, knells, knells,
In a happy runic rhyme,
　To the rolling of the bells,
Of the bells, bells, bells:
　To the tolling of the bells,　　110
Of the bells, bells, bells, bells,
　　Bells, bells, bells —
To the moaning and the groaning of
　　the bells.

72. monody (mŏn′ô·dĭ): a type of music carried by one voice. In ancient Greek times a
monody was sung as a dirge or funeral song;
hence, the word suggests sorrow and tragedy.

88. ghouls (gōolz): imaginary evil creatures
reputed to rob graves and eat the corpses.

THE RAVEN

Poe had very definite beliefs on the nature of poetry — that its essence should be
beauty and that sadness was the mood
most in keeping with poetic beauty. Therefore, he said, there was no subject more
fitting for poetry than the death of a beautiful woman. Some persons have thought
that " The Raven " grew out of Poe's sorrow for the death of his own wife; but, unfortunately for that theory, the poem was
published almost two years before his wife
died. Notice again Poe's almost uncanny
power over the sounds of words. Here he
uses particularly internal rhyme (words at
the middle and end of the same line) and
repetition.

Once upon a midnight dreary, while I pondered, weak and weary,
Over many a quaint and curious volume of forgotten lore —
While I nodded, nearly napping, suddenly there came a tapping,
As of someone gently rapping, rapping at my chamber door.
" 'Tis some visitor," I muttered, " tapping at my chamber door:　　5
　Only this and nothing more."

Ah, distinctly I remember it was in the bleak December,
And each separate dying ember wrought its ghost upon the floor.
Eagerly I wished the morrow; — vainly I had sought to borrow
From my books surcease of sorrow — sorrow for the lost Lenore,   10
For the rare and radiant maiden whom the angels name Lenore:
    Nameless here forevermore.

And the silken sad uncertain rustling of each purple curtain
Thrilled me — filled me with fantastic terrors never felt before;
So that now, to still the beating of my heart, I stood repeating,   15
" 'Tis some visitor entreating entrance at my chamber door,
Some late visitor entreating entrance at my chamber door:
    This it is and nothing more."

Presently my soul grew stronger; hesitating then no longer,
" Sir," said I, " or Madam, truly your forgiveness I implore;   20
But the fact is I was napping, and so gently you came rapping,
And so faintly you came tapping, tapping at my chamber door,
That I scarce was sure I heard you " — here I opened wide the door —
    Darkness there and nothing more.

Deep into that darkness peering, long I stood there wondering, fearing,   25
Doubting, dreaming dreams no mortal ever dared to dream before;
But the silence was unbroken, and the stillness gave no token,
And the only word there spoken was the whispered word, " Lenore? "
This I whispered, and an echo murmured back the word, " Lenore ":
    Merely this and nothing more.   30

Back into the chamber turning, all my soul within me burning,
Soon again I heard a tapping somewhat louder than before.
" Surely," said I, " surely that is something at my window lattice;
Let me see, then, what thereat is, and this mystery explore:
Let my heart be still a moment and this mystery explore: 35
    'Tis the wind and nothing more."

Open here I flung the shutter, when, with many a flirt and flutter,
In there stepped a stately Raven of the saintly days of yore.
Not the least obeisance made he; not a minute stopped or stayed he;
But, with mien of lord or lady, perched above my chamber door,   40
Perched upon a bust of Pallas° just above my chamber door:
    Perched, and sat, and nothing more.

Then this ebony bird beguiling my sad fancy into smiling
By the grave and stern decorum of the countenance it wore —
" Though thy crest be shorn and shaven, thou," I said, " art sure no craven,   45
Ghastly grim and ancient Raven wandering from the nightly shore:
Tell me what thy lordly name is on the night's Plutonian° shore! "
    Quoth the Raven, " Nevermore."

41. Pallas (păl′ăs): Pallas Athene, Greek goddess of wisdom, called Minerva by the Romans.
47. Plutonian (ploō·tō′nĭ·ăn): referring to Pluto, the god who in Greek mythology presided over the regions of the dead.

Much I marveled this ungainly fowl to hear discourse so plainly,
Though its answer little meaning — little relevancy bore;   50
For we cannot help agreeing that no living human being
Ever yet was blessed with seeing bird above his chamber door,
Bird or beast upon the sculptured bust above his chamber door,
      With such name as "Nevermore."

But the Raven, sitting lonely on the placid bust, spoke only   55
That one word, as if his soul in that one word he did outpour.
Nothing further then he uttered, not a feather then he fluttered,
Till I scarcely more than muttered — "Other friends have flown before;
On the morrow *he* will leave me, as my hopes have flown before."
      Then the bird said, "Nevermore."   60

Startled at the stillness broken by reply so aptly spoken,
"Doubtless," said I, "what it utters is its only stock and store,
Caught from some unhappy master whom unmerciful disaster
Followed fast and followed faster till his songs one burden bore:
Till the dirges of his hope that melancholy burden bore   65
      Of 'Never — nevermore.'"

But the Raven still beguiling all my fancy into smiling,
Straight I wheeled a cushioned seat in front of bird and bust and door;
Then, upon the velvet sinking, I betook myself to linking
Fancy unto fancy, thinking what this ominous bird of yore,   70
What this grim, ungainly, ghastly, gaunt, and ominous bird of yore
      Meant in croaking "Nevermore."

This I sat engaged in guessing, but no syllable expressing
To the fowl whose fiery eyes now burned into my bosom's core;
This and more I sat divining, with my head at ease reclining   75
On the cushion's velvet lining that the lamplight gloated o'er,
But whose velvet violet lining with the lamplight gloating o'er
      She shall press, ah, nevermore!

Then, methought, the air grew denser, perfumed from an unseen censer
Swung by seraphim whose footfalls tinkled on the tufted floor.   80
"Wretch," I cried, "thy God hath lent thee — by these angels he hath sent thee
Respite — respite and nepenthe° from thy memories of Lenore!
Quaff, oh quaff this kind nepenthe, and forget this lost Lenore!"
      Quoth the Raven, "Nevermore."

"Prophet!" said I, "thing of evil — prophet still, if bird or devil!   85
Whether tempter sent, or whether tempest tossed thee here ashore,
Desolate yet all undaunted, on this desert land enchanted —
On this home by horror haunted — tell me truly, I implore:
Is there — *is* there balm in Gilead?° — tell me — tell me, I implore!"
      Quoth the Raven, "Nevermore."   90

82. nepenthe (nē·pĕn'thĕ): a drug that destroys pain and brings forgetfulness. **89. balm in Gilead** (gĭl'ė·ăd): a healing lotion made in Gilead, a part of ancient Palestine (see Jer. 8:22). It has become a common expression meaning relief from affliction.

"Prophet!" said I, "thing of evil — prophet still, if bird or devil!
By that heaven that bends above us, by that God we both adore,
Tell this soul with sorrow laden if, within the distant Aidenn,°
It shall clasp a sainted maiden whom the angels name Lenore:
Clasp a rare and radiant maiden whom the angels name Lenore!"   95
    Quoth the Raven, "Nevermore."

"Be that word our sign of parting, bird or fiend!" I shrieked, upstarting:
"Get thee back into the tempest and the night's Plutonian shore!
Leave no black plume as a token of that lie thy soul hath spoken!
Leave my loneliness unbroken! quit the bust above my door!   100
Take thy beak from out my heart, and take thy form from off my door!"
    Quoth the Raven, "Nevermore."

And the Raven, never flitting, still is sitting, still is sitting
On the pallid bust of Pallas just above my chamber door;
And his eyes have all the seeming of a demon's that is dreaming,   105
And the lamplight o'er him streaming throws his shadow on the floor:
And my soul from out that shadow that lies floating on the floor
    Shall be lifted — nevermore!

93. **Aidenn** (ā′dĕn): from the Arabic for Eden.

ULALUME *

Here is a poem that actually did follow the death of Poe's wife. It was published before the first anniversary of her death, at a time when Poe suffered a critical illness. It suggests a deeply despairing and almost disordered mind. Do not try to understand the exact meaning of every line, for it has baffled even the critics. Read it rather for the remarkable creation of a mood and the sonorous roll of the lines.

The skies they were ashen and sober;
    The leaves they were crispèd and
        sere —
    The leaves they were withering and
        sere;
It was night in the lonesome October
    Of my most immemorial year;   5
It was hard by the dim lake of Auber,°
    In the misty mid-region of Weir —

It was down by the dank tarn of Auber,
    In the ghoul-haunted woodland of
        Weir.

Here once, through an alley Titanic°
    Of cypress,° I roamed with my
        Soul —   11
    Of cypress, with Psyche, my Soul.
These were days when my heart was
      volcanic
    As the scoriac rivers that roll —
    As the lavas that restlessly roll   15
Their sulfurous currents down Yaanek
    In the ultimate climes of the pole,
That groan as they roll down Mount
      Yaanek
    In the realms of the boreal pole,

Our talk had been serious and sober,
    But our thoughts they were palsied
      and sere,   21

* **Ulalume** (ū′lá·lōōm′). 6, 7, 16. **Auber** (ō′bĕr) ... **Weir** (wēr) ... **Yaanek** (yä′nĕk): These are all imaginary names made up by Poe for their sound and suggestive effect.

10. **Titanic** (tī·tăn′ĭk): referring to the Titans, a race of giants in Greek mythology. Here it suggests vastness. 11. **cypress**: a tree symbolizing mourning because it is so frequently planted in graveyards.

Our memories were treacherous and
  sere,
For we knew not the month was Octo-
  ber,
And we marked not the night of the
  year —
(Ah, night of all nights in the year!)
We noted not the dim lake of Auber 26
(Though once we had journeyed
  down here),
Remembered not the dank tarn of Au-
  ber,
Nor the ghoul-haunted woodland of
  Weir.

And now, as the night was senescent
  And star dials pointed to morn, 31
  As the star dials hinted of morn,
At the end of our path a liquescent
  And nebulous luster was born,
Out of which a miraculous crescent 35
  Arose with a duplicate horn —
Astarte's° bediamonded crescent
  Distinct with its duplicate horn.

And I said — " She is warmer than
  Dian:°   39
She rolls through an ether of sighs,
  She revels in a region of sighs:
She has seen that the tears are not dry
  on
  These cheeks, where the worm never
  dies,
And has come past the star of the
  Lion°   44
  To point us the path to the skies —
To the Lethean° peace of the skies:
  Come up, in despite of the Lion,
  To shine on us with her bright eyes:
Come up through the lair of the Lion,
  With love in her luminous eyes." 50

But Psyche, uplifting her finger,
  Said — " Sadly this star I mistrust,

Her pallor I strangely mistrust:
Oh, hasten! — oh, let us not linger!
Oh, fly — let us fly! — for we must."
In terror she spoke, letting sink her 56
  Wings till they trailed in the dust;
In agony sobbed, letting sink her
  Plumes till they trailed in the dust,
Till they sorrowfully trailed in the
  dust.   60

I replied — " This is nothing but dream-
  ing:
  Let us on by this tremulous light!
  Let us bathe in this crystalline light!
Its sibylic° splendor is beaming
  With hope and in beauty tonight: 65
  See, it flickers up the sky through the
  night!
Ah, we safely may trust to its gleaming,
  And be sure it will lead us aright:
We safely may trust to a gleaming
  That cannot but guide us aright, 70
Since it flickers up to heaven through
  the night."

Thus I pacified Psyche and kissed her,
  And tempted her out of her gloom,
And conquered her scruples and
  gloom;
And we passed to the end of the vista,
  But were stopped by the door of a
  tomb,   76
  By the door of a legended tomb;
And I said — " What is written, sweet
  sister,
  On the door of this legended tomb? "
She replied — " Ulalume — Ulalume —
  'Tis the vault of thy lost Ulalume! "

Then my heart it grew ashen and
  sober   82
  As the leaves that were crispèd and
  sere,
  As the leaves that were withering and
  sere,
And I cried — " It was surely October
  On *this* very night of last year 86

---

37. **Astarte** (ăs·tär′tĕ): the Phoenician goddess of the moon. 39. **Dian**: Diana, the Roman
goddess of the moon. 44. **Lion**: a northern constellation pictured as a lion. 46. **Lethean** (lē′thē-
ăn for the rhythm, but usually lē·thē′ăn): referring to Lethe, the river of forgetfulness in the
Greek regions of the dead.

64. **sibylic** (sĭ·bĭl′ĭk): pertaining to a sibyl,
in Greek mythology a prophetess. Here, for
the meter, the accent must be put on the first
syllable.

That I journeyed — I journeyed down
here,
That I brought a dread burden down
here:
On this night of all nights in the year,
Ah, what demon has tempted me
here?   90
Well I know, now, this dim lake of
Auber —
This misty mid-region of Weir —
Well I know, now, this dank tarn of
Auber,
This ghoul-haunted woodland of
Weir."

ANNABEL LEE

This and "The Raven" are probably
the two best-known poems by Poe. Annabel Lee is probably Poe's wife, Virginia,
though the story has an old ballad or fairy-
tale style. In reading this poem aloud, notice its rising and falling effects. Don't
overlook the crescendos in the ninth line
and in the whole fifth stanza. The lyrical
last stanza is the calm after the storm.

It was many and many a year ago,
In a kingdom by the sea,
That a maiden there lived whom you
may know
By the name of Annabel Lee;
And this maiden she lived with no oth-
er thought   5
Than to love and be loved by me.

She was a child and *I* was a child,
In this kingdom by the sea;
But we loved with a love that was more
than love,
I and my Annabel Lee;   10
With a love that the wingèd seraphs of
heaven
Coveted her and me.

And this was the reason that, long ago,
In this kingdom by the sea,
A wind blew out of a cloud, chilling
My beautiful Annabel Lee;   16

So that her highborn kinsmen came
And bore her away from me,
To shut her up in a sepulcher
In this kingdom by the sea.   20

The angels, not half so happy in heaven,
Went envying her and me;
Yes, that was the reason (as all men
know,
In this kingdom by the sea)
That the wind came out of the cloud by
night,   25
Chilling and killing my Annabel Lee.

But our love it was stronger by far than
the love
Of those who were older than we,
Of many far wiser than we;   29
And neither the angels in heaven above,
Nor the demons down under the sea,
Can ever dissever my soul from the soul
Of the beautiful Annabel Lee:

For the moon never beams, without
bringing me dreams
Of the beautiful Annabel Lee;   35
And the stars never rise, but I feel the
bright eyes
Of the beautiful Annabel Lee;
And so, all the night-tide, I lie down by
the side
Of my darling, my darling, my life and
my bride
In her sepulcher there by the sea,
In her tomb by the sounding sea.   41

For Discussion of Poe's Poems

The Bells

1. Observe carefully the use of the liquid consonants — l, m, n. What other consonants appear with notable frequency?
What difference can you note in the use of
vowels for the different bells? How does
this selection of vowels and consonants affect the general mood and sound of the
four different sections?

2. Find good examples of onomatopoeic
words. What definition for *tintinnabulation*
can you give? What is the dictionary definition? Find also examples of alliteration

(*runic rhyme*) and the effective repetition of words and phrases.

3. This poem provides an opportunity to examine some words commonly used to describe musical sounds. *Euphony* appears in line 26. How does its meaning differ from *cacophony?* Look up the words *assonance* and *dissonance.* How would you apply their meaning to this poem? to music?

The Raven

1. What atmosphere and mood are established at the very beginning of the poem? From the few effective details given, picture to yourself the kind of room in which this story is set.

2. What in the Raven's manner makes the poem unusually weird and depressing? Of what in life is the Raven a symbol?

3. Find striking examples throughout of Poe's devices: internal rhyme, alliteration, and repetition.

4. To increase your vocabulary, make sure you know these words: *surcease* (10), *fantastic* (14), *obeisance* (39), *mien* (40), *decorum* (44), *relevancy* (50), *ominous* (70), *censer* (79), *seraphim* (80).

Ulalume

1. How do the time of year, the time of night, and the surroundings of nature all contribute to the mood of the poem? How does the moonlight betray the false hope that the poet had placed in it? What warning had he that the place was not a good one to be in?

2. What mood is suggested by the very sound of the name *Ulalume?* Look up the word *ululate* in the dictionary to find its present meaning and derivation. Does this throw any added light on Poe's choice of the name?

3. Select lines or passages in which the sound particularly appeals to you. For melodious flow and sound effects how do you think this poem compares with "The Bells," "The Raven," and "Annabel Lee"?

4. Poe chose words for their sound, yet their meaning is exact also. What difference is there between *withering* and *sere* (3)? What is the relation between *volcanic* and *scoriac* (13–14)? How do *senescent* and *liquescent* (30, 33) differ in meaning? *nebulous* and *luminous* (34, 50)?

Annabel Lee

1. Compare this with the other two poems on the death of a beautiful woman — "The Raven" and "Ulalume" — in terms of emotional appeal, simplicity of style, and use of sound effects. Which of the three do you prefer? For what reasons?

Choral Reading

Poe's poems lend themselves particularly well to choral reading by the class or part of the class. If you wish to try this, here are a few simple directions: Divide your voices according to high, medium, and low voices, somewhat as in a singing choir. Vary the effects of the reading by having certain passages read by a single voice or a single range of voices in contrast to passages read by the entire group. "The Bells" is a good poem to begin with as the differences are so obvious, beginning with the high voices and dropping to the low voices. Vary the volume as well as the pitch. Some passages may be read lightly; others, with the emphasis of the entire chorus. Have a leader direct the reading, and see what interesting voice music you can produce.

THE PIT AND THE PENDULUM

The short story is considered an American contribution to world literature. For this distinction Poe is mainly to be credited. He created singlehanded the detective story; he established a pattern for the usual form of the short story in his own stories; and his is the first critical definition of the short story as we know it today. Poe said that a story writer deliberately conceives "a certain unique or single *effect* to be wrought out" and "then combines such incidents as may best aid him in establishing his preconceived effect." He believed that "in the whole composition there should be no word written, of which the tendency, direct or indirect, is not to the one pre-established design." A short story, then, is all of a piece, and must be short in order to keep its single effect. "The idea of the tale has been presented unblemished, because undisturbed: and this is an end unattainable by the novel." Poe carried out his definition in his own stories: they are brief and create a single effect maintained from the opening sentence to the end. Observe these qualities in the two following stories.

The first story has as a setting the Spanish Inquisition, a court established by the Church in the sixteenth century to prosecute heresy. It soon passed from religious to secular control, becoming an instrument of political power, notorious for its cruel treatment of accused persons. Poe found in this situation the elements of horror.

But Poe is not concerned with informing us about the historical facts of the Inquisition, or about the accusations against the prisoner. He thrusts us at once into the mind of the prisoner as he hears his death sentence pronounced. Never throughout the story does the reader leave that mind, and so he actually feels the horror that overwhelms the prisoner. But to feel the horror of a Poe story requires more imagination than to feel that of a mystery movie or radio play. You yourself must supply from the words the sights and sounds that create the horror.

I WAS sick — sick unto death with that long agony; and when they at length unbound me, and I was permitted to sit, I felt that my senses were leaving me. The sentence — the dread sentence of death — was the last of distinct accentuation which reached my ears. After that, the sound of the inquisitorial voices seemed merged in one dreamy indeterminate hum. It conveyed to my soul the idea of *revolution* — perhaps from its association in fancy with the burr of a mill-wheel. This only for a brief period; for presently I heard no more. Yet, for a while, I saw; but with how terrible an exaggeration! I saw the lips of the black-robed judges. They appeared to me white — whiter than the sheet upon which I trace these words — and thin even to grotesqueness; thin with the intensity of their expression of

firmness — of immovable resolution — of stern contempt of human torture. I saw that the decrees of what to me was fate were still issuing from those lips. I saw them writhe with a deadly locution. I saw them fashion the syllables of my name; and I shuddered because no sound succeeded. I saw, too, for a few moments of delirious horror, the soft and nearly imperceptible waving of the sable draperies which enwrapped the walls of the apartment. And then my vision fell upon the seven tall candles upon the table. At first they wore the aspect of charity, and seemed white slender angels who would save me; but then, all at once, there came a most deadly nausea over my spirit, and I felt every fiber in my frame thrill as if I had touched the wire of a galvanic battery, while the angel forms became meaningless specters, with heads of flame, and I saw that from them there would be no help. And then there stole into my fancy, like a rich musical note, the thought of what sweet rest there must be in the grave. The thought came gently and stealthily, and it seemed long before it attained full appreciation; but just as my spirit came at length properly to feel and entertain it, the figures of the judges vanished, as if magically, from before me; the tall candles sank into nothingness; their flames went out utterly; the blackness of darkness supervened; all sensations appeared swallowed up in a mad rushing descent as of the soul into Hades. Then silence, and stillness, and night were the universe.

I had swooned; but still will not say that all of consciousness was lost. What of it there remained I will not attempt to define, or even to describe; yet all was not lost. In the deepest slumber — no! In delirium — no! In a swoon — no! In death — no! even in the grave all *is not* lost. Else there is no immortality for man. . . .

These shadows of memory tell, indistinctly, of tall figures that lifted and bore me in silence down — down — still down — till a hideous dizziness oppressed me at the mere idea of the interminableness of the descent. They tell also of a vague horror at my heart, on account of that heart's unnatural stillness. Then comes a sense of sudden motionlessness throughout all things; as if those who bore me (a ghastly train!) had outrun, in their descent, the limits of the limitless, and paused from the wearisomeness of their toil. After this I call to mind flatness and dampness; and then all is *madness* — the madness of a memory which busies itself among forbidden things.

Very suddenly there came back to my soul motion and sound — the tumultuous motion of the heart, and, in my ears, the sound of its beating. Then a pause in which all is blank. Then again sound, and motion, and touch — a tingling sensation pervading my frame. Then the mere consciousness of existence, without thought — a condition which lasted long. Then, very suddenly, *thought,* and shuddering terror, and earnest endeavor to comprehend my true state. Then a strong desire to lapse into insensibility. Then a rushing revival of soul and a successful effort to move. And now a full memory of the trial, of the judges, of the sable draperies, of the sentence, of the sickness, of the swoon. Then entire forgetfulness of all that followed; of all that a later day and much earnestness of endeavor have enabled me vaguely to recall.

So far, I had not opened my eyes. I felt that I lay upon my back, unbound. I reached out my hand, and it fell heavily upon something damp and hard. There I suffered it to remain for many minutes, while I strove to imagine where and *what* I could be. I longed, yet dared not to employ my vision. I dreaded the first glance at objects around me. It was not that I feared to look upon things horrible, but that I grew aghast lest there should be *nothing* to see. At length, with a wild desperation at heart, I quickly unclosed my eyes. My worst thoughts, then, were confirmed. The blackness of eternal night encompassed me. I struggled for breath. The intensity of the darkness seemed to oppress and stifle me. The atmosphere was intolerably close. I still lay quietly, and made effort to exercise my reason. I brought to mind the inquisitorial proceedings, and attempted from that point to deduce my real condition. The sentence had passed; and it appeared to me that a very long interval of time had since elapsed. Yet not for a moment did I suppose myself actually dead. Such a supposition, notwithstanding what we read in fiction, is altogether inconsistent with real existence — but where and in what state was I? The condemned to death, I knew, perished usually at the *autos-da-fé,*[1] and one of these had been held on the very night of the day of my trial. Had I been remanded to my dungeon, to await the next sacrifice, which would not take place for many months? This I at once saw could not be. Victims had been in immediate demand. Moreover, my dungeon, as well as all the condemned cells at Toledo, had stone floors, and light was not altogether excluded.

A fearful idea now suddenly drove the blood in torrents upon my heart, and for a brief period, I once more relapsed into insensibility. Upon recovering, I at once started to my feet, trembling convulsively in every fiber. I thrust my arms wildly above and around me in all directions. I felt nothing; yet dreaded to move a step, lest I should be impeded by the walls of a *tomb.* Perspiration burst from every pore, and stood in cold big beads upon my forehead. The agony of suspense grew at length intolerable, and I cautiously

[1] *autos-da-fé* (ô′tôz·dà·fā′): literally, acts of faith; a term used during the Inquisition for the execution or burning of heretics.

moved forward, with my arms extended, and my eyes straining from their sockets, in the hope of catching some faint ray of light. I proceeded for many paces; but still all was blackness and vacancy. I breathed more freely. It seemed evident that mine was not, at least, the most hideous of fates.

And now, as I still continued to step cautiously onward, there came thronging upon my recollection a thousand vague rumors of the horrors of Toledo. Of the dungeons there had been strange things narrated — fables I had always deemed them — but yet strange, and too ghastly to repeat, save in a whisper. Was I left to perish of starvation in this subterranean world of darkness; or what fate, perhaps even more fearful, awaited me? That the result would be death, and a death of more than customary bitterness, I knew too well the character of my judges to doubt. The mode and the hour were all that occupied or distracted me.

My outstretched hands at length encountered some solid obstruction. It was a wall, seemingly of stone masonry — very smooth, slimy, and cold. I followed it up; stepping with all the careful distrust with which certain antique narratives had inspired me. This process, however, afforded me no means of ascertaining the dimensions of my dungeon; as I might make its circuit, and return to the point whence I set out, without being aware of the fact, so perfectly uniform seemed the wall. I therefore sought the knife which had been in my pocket, when led into the inquisitorial chamber; but it was gone; my clothes had been exchanged for a wrapper of coarse serge. I had thought of forcing the blade in some minute crevice of the masonry, so as to identify my point of departure. The difficulty, nevertheless, was but trivial; although, in the disorder of my fancy, it seemed at first insuperable. I tore a part of the hem from the robe and placed the fragment at full length, and at right angles to the wall. In groping my way around the prison, I could not fail to encounter this rag upon completing the circuit. So, at least, I thought; but I had not counted upon the extent of the dungeon, or upon my own weakness. The ground was moist and slippery. I staggered onward for some time, when I stumbled and fell. My excessive fatigue induced me to remain prostrate; and sleep soon overtook me as I lay.

Upon awaking, and stretching forth an arm, I found beside me a loaf and a pitcher with water. I was too much exhausted to reflect upon this circumstance, but ate and drank with avidity. Shortly afterward, I resumed my tour around the prison, and with much toil, came at last upon the fragment of the serge. Up to the period when I fell I had counted fifty-two paces, and upon resuming my walk, I had counted forty-eight more — when I arrived at the rag. There were in all, then, a hundred paces; and, admitting two paces to the yard, I presumed the dungeon to be fifty yards in circuit. I had met, however, with many angles in the wall, and thus I could form no guess at the shape of the vault; for vault I could not help supposing it to be.

I had little object — certainly no hope — in these researches; but a vague curiosity prompted me to continue them. Quitting the wall, I resolved to cross the area of the enclosure. At first I proceeded with extreme caution, for the floor, although seemingly of solid material, was treacherous with slime. At length, however, I took courage, and did not hesitate to step firmly; endeavoring to cross in as direct a line as possible. I had advanced some ten or twelve paces in this manner, when the remnant of the torn hem of my robe became entangled between my legs. I stepped on it, and fell violently on my face.

In the confusion attending my fall, I

did not immediately apprehend a somewhat startling circumstance, which yet, in a few seconds afterward, and while I still lay prostrate, arrested my attention. It was this: my chin rested upon the floor of the prison, but my lips and the upper portion of my head, although seemingly at a less elevation than the chin, touched nothing. At the same time my forehead seemed bathed in a clammy vapor, and the peculiar smell of decayed fungus arose to my nostrils. I put forward my arm, and shuddered to find that I had fallen at the very brink of a circular pit, whose extent, of course, I had no means of ascertaining at the moment. Groping about the masonry just below the margin, I succeeded in dislodging a small fragment, and let it fall into the abyss. For many seconds I hearkened to its reverberations as it dashed against the sides of the chasm in its descent; at length there was a sullen plunge into water, succeeded by loud echoes. At the same moment there came a sound resembling the quick opening, and as rapid closing of a door overhead, while a faint gleam of light flashed suddenly through the gloom, and as suddenly faded away.

I saw clearly the doom which had been prepared for me, and congratulated myself upon the timely accident by which I had escaped. Another step before my fall, and the world had seen me no more. And the death just avoided was of that very character which I had regarded as fabulous and frivolous in the tales respecting the Inquisition. To the victims of its tyranny, there was the choice of death with its direst physical agonies, or death with its most hideous moral horrors. I had been reserved for the latter. By long suffering my nerves had been unstrung, until I trembled at the sound of my own voice, and had become in every respect a fitting subject for the species of torture which awaited me.

Shaking in every limb, I groped my way back to the wall; resolving there to perish rather than risk the terrors of the wells, of which my imagination now pictured many in various positions about the dungeon. In other conditions of mind I might have had courage to end my misery at once by a plunge into one of these abysses; but now I was the veriest of cowards. Neither could I forget what I had read of these pits — that the *sudden* extinction of life formed no part of their most horrible plan.

Agitation of spirit kept me awake for many long hours; but at length I again slumbered. Upon arousing, I found by my side, as before, a loaf and a pitcher of water. A burning thirst consumed me, and I emptied the vessel at a draught. It must have been drugged; for scarcely had I drunk, before I became irresistibly drowsy. A deep sleep fell upon me — a sleep like that of death. How long it lasted, of course, I know not; but when, once again, I unclosed my eyes, the objects around me were visible. By a wild sulfurous luster, the origin of which I could not at first determine, I was enabled to see the extent and aspect of the prison.

In its size I had been greatly mistaken. The whole circuit of its walls did not exceed twenty-five yards. For some minutes this fact occasioned me a world of vain trouble; vain indeed! for what could be of less importance, under the terrible circumstances which environed me, than the mere dimensions of my dungeon? But my soul took a wild interest in trifles, and I busied myself in endeavors to account for the error I had committed in my measurement. The truth at length flashed upon me. In my first attempt at exploration I had counted fifty-two paces, up to the period when I fell; I must then have been within a pace or two of the fragment of serge; in fact, I had nearly performed the circuit of the vault. I then slept, and upon awaking, I must have returned upon my steps — thus supposing the circuit nearly double what it actually was. My confusion of mind prevented me from observing that I began my tour with the wall to the left, and ended it with the wall to the right.

I had been deceived, too, in respect to the shape of the enclosure. In feeling my way I had found many angles, and thus deduced an idea of great irregularity; so potent is the effect of total darkness upon one arousing from lethargy or sleep! The angles were simply those of a few slight depressions, or niches, at odd intervals. The general shape of the prison was square. What I had taken for masonry seemed now to be iron, or some other metal, in huge plates, whose sutures or joints occasioned the depression. The entire surface of this metallic enclosure was rudely daubed in all the hideous and repulsive devices to which the charnel superstition of the monks has given rise. The figures of fiends in aspects of menace, with skeleton forms, and other more really fearful images, overspread and disfigured the walls. I observed that the outlines of these monstrosities were sufficiently distinct, but that the colors seemed faded and blurred, as if from the effects of a damp atmosphere. I now noticed the floor, too, which was of stone. In the center yawned the circular pit from whose jaws I had escaped; but it was the only one in the dungeon.

All this I saw indistinctly and by much effort: for my personal condition had been greatly changed during slumber. I now lay upon my back, and at full length, on a species of low framework of wood. To this I was securely bound by a long strap resembling a surcingle.[1] It passed in many convolutions about my limbs and body, leaving at liberty only my head and my left arm to such extent that I could, by dint of much exertion, supply myself with food from an earthen dish which lay by my

[1] surcingle (sûr′sĭng·g'l): a belt or girth used to fasten something to a horse's back.

side on the floor. I saw, to my horror, that the pitcher had been removed. I say to my horror; for I was consumed with intolerable thirst. This thirst it appeared to be the design of my persecutors to stimulate, for the food in the dish was meat pungently seasoned.

Looking upward, I surveyed the ceiling of my prison. It was some thirty or forty feet overhead, and constructed much as the side walls. In one of its panels a very singular figure riveted my whole attention. It was the painted figure of Time as he is commonly represented, save that, in lieu of a scythe, he held what, at a casual glance, I supposed to be the pictured image of a huge pendulum such as we see on antique clocks. There was something, however, in the appearance of this machine which caused me to regard it more attentively. While I gazed directly upward at it (for its position was immediately over my own) I fancied that I saw it in motion. In an instant afterward the fancy was confirmed. Its sweep was brief, and of course slow. I watched it for some minutes, somewhat in fear, but more in wonder. Wearied at length with observing its dull movement, I turned my eyes upon the other objects in the cell.

A slight noise attracted my notice, and, looking to the floor, I saw several enormous rats traversing it. They had issued from the well, which lay just within view to my right. Even then, while I gazed, they came up in troops, hurriedly, with ravenous eyes, allured by the scent of the meat. From this it required much effort and attention to scare them away.

It might have been half an hour, perhaps even an hour (for I could take but imperfect note of time), before I again cast my eyes upward. What I then saw confounded and amazed me. The sweep of the pendulum had increased in extent by nearly a yard. As a natural consequence, its velocity was also much greater. But what mainly disturbed me was the idea that it had perceptibly *descended*. I now observed — with what horror it is needless to say — that its nether extremity was formed of a crescent of glittering steel, about a foot in length from horn to horn; the horns upward, and the under edge evidently as keen as that of a razor. Like a razor also, it seemed massy and heavy, tapering from the edge into a solid and broad structure above. It was appended to a weighty rod of brass, and the whole *hissed* as it swung through the air.

I could no longer doubt the doom prepared for me by monkish ingenuity in torture. My cognizance of the pit had become known to the inquisitorial agents — *the pit* whose horrors had been destined for so bold a recusant [1] as myself — *the pit*, typical of hell, and regarded by rumor as the ultima Thule [2] of all their punishments. The plunge into this pit I had avoided by the merest of accidents, and I knew that surprise, or entrapment into torment, formed an important portion of all the grotesquerie of these dungeon deaths. Having failed to fall, it was no part of the demon plan to hurl me into the abyss; and thus (there being no alternative) a different and a milder destruction awaited me. Milder! I half smiled in my agony as I thought of such application of such a term.

What boots it to tell of the long, long hours of horror more than mortal, during which I counted the rushing vibrations of the steel! Inch by inch — line by line — with a descent only appreciable at intervals that seemed ages — down and still down it came! Days passed — it might have been that many days passed — ere it swept so closely over me as to fan me with its acrid

[1] **recusant** (rĕk'ů·zănt): one who refuses to comply with some established regulation.
[2] **ultima Thule** (ŭl'tĭ·má thū'lĕ): the northernmost part of the habitable world; hence, most extreme example.

breath. The odor of the sharp steel forced itself into my nostrils. I prayed — I wearied heaven with my prayer for its more speedy descent. I grew frantically mad, and struggled to force myself upward against the sweep of the fearful scimitar. And then I fell suddenly calm, and lay smiling at the glittering death, as a child at some rare bauble.

There was another interval of utter insensibility; it was brief; for, upon again lapsing into life there had been no perceptible descent in the pendulum. But it might have been long; for I knew there were demons who took note of my swoon, and who could have arrested the vibration at pleasure. Upon my recovery, too, I felt very — oh, inexpressibly sick and weak, as if through long inanition. Even amid the agonies of that period, the human nature craved food. With painful effort I outstretched my left arm as far as my bonds permitted, and took possession of the small remnant which had been spared me by the rats. As I put a portion of it within my lips, there rushed to my mind a half-formed thought of joy — of hope. Yet what business had *I* with hope? It was, as I say, a half-formed thought — man has many such which are never completed. I felt that it was of joy — of hope; but I felt also that it had perished in its formation. In vain I struggled to perfect — to regain it. Long suffering had nearly annihilated all my ordinary powers of mind. I was an imbecile — an idiot.

The vibration of the pendulum was at right angles to my length. I saw that the crescent was designed to cross the region of the heart. It would fray the serge of my robe — it would return and repeat its operations — again — and again. Notwithstanding its terrifically wide sweep (some thirty feet or more) and the hissing vigor of its descent, sufficient to sunder these very walls of iron, still the fraying of my robe would be all that, for several minutes, it would accomplish. And at this thought I paused. I dared not go farther than this reflection. I dwelt upon it with a pertinacity of attention — as if, in so dwelling, I could arrest *here* the descent of the steel. I forced myself to ponder upon the sound of the crescent as it should pass across the garment — upon the peculiar thrilling sensation which the friction of cloth produces on the nerves. I pondered upon all this frivolity until my teeth were on edge.

Down — steadily down it crept. I took a frenzied pleasure in contrasting its downward with its lateral velocity. To the right — to the left — far and wide — with the shriek of a damned spirit; to my heart with the stealthy pace of the tiger! I alternately laughed and howled as the one or the other idea grew predominant.

Down — certainly, relentlessly down! It vibrated within three inches of my bosom! I struggled violently, furiously, to free my left arm. This was free only from the elbow to the hand. I could reach the latter, from the platter beside me, to my mouth, with great effort, but no farther. Could I have broken the fastenings above the elbow, I would have seized and attempted to arrest the pendulum. I might as well have attempted to arrest an avalanche!

Down — still unceasingly — still inevitably down! I gasped and struggled at each vibration. I shrunk convulsively at its every sweep. My eyes followed its outward or upward whirls with the eagerness of the most unmeaning despair; they closed themselves spasmodically at the descent, although death would have been a relief, oh! how unspeakable! Still I quivered in every nerve to think how slight a sinking of the machinery would precipitate that keen, glistening ax upon my bosom. It was *hope* that prompted the nerve to quiver — the frame to shrink. It was *hope* — the hope that triumphs on the rack — that whispers to the death-condemned even in the dungeons of the Inquisition.

I saw that some ten or twelve vibrations would bring the steel in actual contact with my robe, and with this observation there suddenly came over my spirit all the keen, collected calmness of despair. For the first time during many hours — or perhaps days — I *thought*. It now occurred to me that the bandage, or surcingle, which enveloped me, was *unique*. I was tied by no separate cord. The first stroke of the razorlike crescent athwart any portion of the band, would so detach it that it might be unwound from my person by means of my left hand. But how fearful, in that case, the proximity of the steel! The result of the slightest struggle how deadly! Was it likely, moreover, that the minions of the torturer had not foreseen and provided for this possibility? Was it probable that the bandage crossed my bosom in the track of the pendulum? Dreading to find my faint, and, as it seemed, my last hope frustrated, I so far elevated my head as to obtain a distinct view of my breast. The surcingle enveloped my limbs and body close in all directions — *save in the path of the destroying crescent.*

Scarcely had I dropped my head back into its original position, when there flashed upon my mind what I cannot better describe than as the unformed half of that idea of deliverance to which I have previously alluded, and of which a moiety only floated indeterminately through my brain when I raised food to my burning lips. The whole thought was now present — feeble, scarcely sane, scarcely definite — but still entire. I proceeded at once, with the nervous energy of despair, to attempt its execution.

For many hours the immediate vicinity of the low framework upon which I lay, had been literally swarming with rats. They were wild, bold, ravenous; their red eyes glaring upon me as if they waited but for motionlessness on my part to make me their prey. "To what food," I thought, "have they been accustomed in the well?"

They had devoured, in spite of all my efforts to prevent them, all but a small remnant of the contents of the dish. I had fallen into an habitual seesaw, or wave of the hand about the platter: and, at length, the unconscious uniformity of the movement deprived it of effect. In their voracity the vermin frequently fastened their sharp fangs in my fingers. With the particles of the oily and spicy viand which now remained, I thoroughly rubbed the bandage wherever I could reach it; then, raising my hand from the floor, I lay breathlessly still.

At first the ravenous animals were startled and terrified at the change — at the cessation of movement. They shrank alarmedly back; many sought the well. But this was only for a moment. I had not counted in vain upon their voracity. Observing that I remained without motion, one or two of the boldest leaped upon the framework, and smelt at the surcingle. This seemed the signal for a general rush. Forth from the well they hurried in fresh troops. They clung to the wood — they overran it, and leaped in hundreds upon my person. The measured movement of the pendulum disturbed them not at all. Avoiding its strokes they busied themselves with the anointed bandage. They pressed — they swarmed upon me in ever accumulating heaps. They writhed upon my throat; their cold lips sought my own; I was half stifled by their thronging pressure; disgust, for which the world has no name, swelled my bosom, and chilled, with a heavy clamminess, my heart. Yet one minute, and I felt that the struggle would be over. Plainly I perceived the loosening of the bandage. I knew that in more than one place it must be already severed. With a more than human resolution I lay *still*.

Nor had I erred in my calculations —

nor had I endured in vain. I at length felt that I was *free*. The surcingle hung in ribands from my body. But the stroke of the pendulum already pressed upon my bosom. It had divided the serge of the robe. It had cut through the linen beneath. Twice again it swung, and a sharp sense of pain shot through every nerve. But the moment of escape had arrived. At a wave of my hand my deliverers hurried tumultuously away. With a steady movement — cautious, sidelong, shrinking, and slow — I slid from the embrace of the bandage and beyond the reach of the scimitar. For the moment, at least, *I was free*.

Free! — and in the grasp of the Inquisition! I had scarcely stepped from my wooden bed of horror upon the stone floor of the prison, when the motion of the hellish machine ceased and I beheld it drawn up, by some invisible force, through the ceiling. This was a lesson which I took desperately to heart. My every motion was undoubtedly watched. Free! — I had but escaped death in one form of agony, to be delivered unto worse than death in some other. With that thought I rolled my eyes nervously around on the barriers of iron that hemmed me in. Something unusual — some change which, at first, I could not appreciate distinctly — it was obvious, had taken place in the apartment. For many minutes of a dreamy and trembling abstraction, I busied myself in vain, unconnected conjecture. During this period, I became aware, for the first time, of the origin of the sulfurous light which illumined the cell. It proceeded from a fissure, about half an inch in width, extending entirely around the prison at the base of the walls, which thus appeared, and were, completely separated from the floor. I endeavored, but of course in vain, to look through the aperture.

As I arose from the attempt, the mystery of the alteration in the chamber broke at once upon my understanding.

I have observed that, although the outlines of the figures upon the walls were sufficiently distinct, yet the colors seemed blurred and indefinite. These colors had now assumed, and were momentarily assuming, a startling and most intense brilliancy, that gave to the spectral and fiendish portraitures an aspect that might have thrilled even firmer nerves than my own. Demon eyes, of a wild and ghastly vivacity, glared upon me in a thousand directions, where none had been visible before, and gleamed with the lurid luster of a fire that I could not force my imagination to regard as unreal.

Unreal! — Even while I breathed there came to my nostrils the breath of the vapor of heated iron! A suffocating odor pervaded the prison! A deeper glow settled each moment in the eyes that glared at my agonies! A richer tint of crimson diffused itself over the pictured horrors of blood. I panted! I gasped for breath! There could be no doubt of the design of my tormentors — oh! most unrelenting! oh! most demoniac of men! I shrank from the glowing metal to the center of the cell. Amid the thought of the fiery destruction that impended, the idea of the coolness of the well came over my soul like balm. I rushed to its deadly brink. I threw my straining vision below. The glare from the enkindled roof illumined its inmost recesses. Yet, for a wild moment, did my spirit refuse to comprehend the meaning of what I saw. At length it forced — it wrestled its way into my soul — it burned itself in upon my shuddering reason. — Oh! for a voice to speak! — oh! horror! — oh! any horror but this! With a shriek, I rushed from the margin, and buried my face in my hands — weeping bitterly.

The heat rapidly increased, and once again I looked up, shuddering as with a fit of the ague. There had been a second change in the cell — and now the change was obviously in the *form*. As before, it was in vain that I, at first, endeavored to appreciate or understand what was taking place. But not long was I left in doubt. The Inquisitorial vengeance had been hurried by my twofold escape, and there was to be no more dallying with the King of Terrors. The room had been square. I saw that two of its iron angles were now acute — two, consequently, obtuse. The fearful difference quickly increased with a low rumbling or moaning sound. In an instant the apartment had shifted its form into that of a lozenge.[1] But the alteration stopped not here — I neither hoped nor desired it to stop. I could have clasped the red walls to my bosom as a garment of eternal peace. "Death," I said, "any death but that of the pit!" Fool! might I have not known that *into the pit* it was the object of the burning iron to urge me? Could I resist its glow? or, if even that, could I withstand its pressure? And now, flatter and flatter grew the lozenge, with a rapidity that left me no time for contemplation. Its center, and of course, its greatest width, came just over the yawning gulf. I shrank back — but the closing walls pressed me resistlessly onward. At length for my seared and writhing body there was no longer an inch of foothold on the firm floor of the prison. I struggled no more, but the agony of my soul found vent in one loud, long, and final scream of despair. I felt that I tottered upon the brink — I averted my eyes —

There was a discordant hum of human voices! There was a loud blast as of many trumpets! There was a harsh grating as of a thousand thunders! The fiery walls rushed back! An outstretched arm caught my own as I fell, fainting, into the abyss. It was that of General Lasalle.

The French army had entered Toledo. The Inquisition was in the hands of its enemies.

---

[1] **lozenge** (lŏz′ĕnj): a diamond-shaped figure.

" Sundry citizens of this good land, meaning well, and hoping well, prompted by a certain something in their nature, have trained themselves to do service in various Essays, Poems, Histories, and books of Art, Fancy, and Truth."

ADDRESS OF THE AMERICAN COPY-RIGHT CLUB.

WILEY AND PUTNAM'S

LIBRARY OF AMERICAN BOOKS.

NO. VIII.

THE RAVEN AND OTHER POEMS.

BY

EDGAR A. POE.

NEW YORK AND LONDON.

WILEY AND PUTNAM, 161 BROADWAY: 6 WATERLOO PLACE.

Price, Thirty-one Cents.

Poe's " The Raven " was first published in 1845 in the paper cover shown here. It was priced at thirty-one cents. Today a good copy of this edition is worth as much as $1500. (N.Y. Public Library)

THE TELL–TALE HEART

This story is shorter than " The Pit and the Pendulum " but an even greater test of Poe's skill, for the cause of the horror comes from *within* the man's mind rather than being imposed from the outside. This is no story for a nervous person to read at night. Poe is trying to make you feel horror at the insanity which leads to murder.

You can read this story in less than half an hour. Choose a time when you are sure to be free from interruption. Breaking into the story would be as unfair to Poe as interrupting a violinist playing a beautiful sonata. Each requires your complete and unbroken attention to accomplish his purpose.

TRUE! — nervous — very, very dreadfully nervous I had been and am; but why *will* you say that I am mad? The disease had sharpened my senses — not destroyed — not dulled them. Above all was the sense of hearing acute. I heard all things in the heaven and in the earth. I heard many things in hell. How, then, am I mad? Hearken! and observe how healthily — how calmly I can tell you the whole story.

It is impossible to say how first the idea entered my brain; but once conceived, it haunted me day and night. Object there was none. Passion there was none. I loved the old man. He had never wronged me. He had never given me insult. For his gold I had no desire. I think it was his eye! yes, it was this! He had the eye of a vulture — a pale blue eye, with a film over it. Whenever it fell upon me, my blood ran cold; and so by degrees — very gradually — I made up my mind to take the life of the old man, and thus rid myself of the eye forever.

Now this is the point. You fancy me mad. Madmen know nothing. But you should have seen *me*. You should have seen how wisely I proceeded — with what caution — with what foresight —

with what dissimulation I went to work! I was never kinder to the old man than during the whole week before I killed him. And every night, about midnight, I turned the latch of his door and opened it — ah, so gently! And then, when I had made an opening sufficient for my head, I put in a dark lantern, all closed, closed, so that no light shone out, and then I thrust in my head. Oh, you would have laughed to see how cunningly I thrust it in! I moved it slowly — very, very slowly, so that I might not disturb the old man's sleep. It took me an hour to place my whole head within the opening so far that I could see him as he lay upon his bed. Ha! — would a madman have been so wise as this? And then, when my head was well in the room, I undid the lantern cautiously — oh, so cautiously — cautiously (for the hinges creaked) — I undid it just so much that a single thin ray fell upon the vulture eye. And this I did for seven long nights — every night just at midnight — but I found the eye always closed; and so it was impossible to do the work; for it was not the old man who vexed me, but his Evil Eye. And every morning, when the day broke, I went boldly into the chamber, and spoke courageously to him, calling him by name in a hearty tone, and inquiring how he had passed the night. So you see he would have been a very profound old man, indeed, to suspect that every night, just at twelve, I looked in upon him while he slept.

Upon the eighth night I was more than usually cautious in opening the door. A watch's minute hand moves more quickly than did mine. Never, before that night, had I *felt* the extent of my own powers — of my sagacity. I could scarcely contain my feelings of triumph. To think that there I was, opening the door, little by little, and he not even to dream of my secret deeds or thoughts. I fairly chuckled at the idea; and perhaps he heard me; for he moved on the bed suddenly, as if startled. Now you may think that I drew back — but no. His room was as black as pitch with the thick darkness (for the shutters were close fastened, through fear of robbers), and so I knew that he could not see the opening of the door, and I kept pushing it on steadily, steadily.

I had my head in, and was about to open the lantern, when my thumb slipped upon the tin fastening, and the old man sprang up in bed, crying out, " Who's there? "

I kept quite still and said nothing. For a whole hour I did not move a muscle, and in the meantime I did not hear him lie down. He was still sitting up in the bed listening — just as I have done, night after night, hearkening to the death watches [1] in the wall.

Presently I heard a slight groan, and I knew it was the groan of mortal terror. It was not a groan of pain or of grief — oh, no! — it was the low stifled sound that arises from the bottom of the soul when overcharged with awe. I knew the sound well. Many a night, just at midnight, when all the world slept, it has welled up from my own bosom, deepening, with its dreadful echo, the terrors that distracted me. I say I knew it well. I knew what the old man felt, and pitied him, although I chuckled at heart. I knew that he had been lying awake ever since the first slight noise, when he had turned in his bed. His fears had been ever since growing upon him. He had been trying to fancy them causeless, but could not. He had been saying to himself — " It is nothing but the wind in the chimney — it is only a mouse crossing the floor," or " It is merely a cricket which has made a single chirp." Yes, he had been trying to comfort himself with these suppositions: but he had found all in

[1] **death watches:** insects that make a ticking sound, regarded by the superstitious as prophesying death.

vain. *All in vain;* because Death, in approaching him, had stalked with his black shadow before him, and enveloped the victim. And it was the mournful influence of the unperceived shadow that caused him to feel — although he neither saw nor heard — to *feel* the presence of my head within the room.

When I had waited a long time, very patiently, without hearing him lie down, I resolved to open a little — a very, very little crevice in the lantern. So I opened it — you cannot imagine how stealthily, stealthily — until at length a single dim ray, like the thread of the spider, shot from out the crevice and fell full upon the vulture eye.

It was open — wide, wide open — and I grew furious as I gazed upon it. I saw it with perfect distinctness — all a dull blue, with a hideous veil over it that chilled the very marrow in my bones; but I could see nothing else of the old man's face or person: for I had directed the ray as if by instinct, precisely upon the damned spot.

And have I not told you that what you mistake for madness is but overacuteness of the senses? — now, I say, there came to my ears a low, dull, quick sound, such as a watch makes when enveloped in cotton. I knew *that* sound well, too. It was the beating of the old man's heart. It increased my fury, as the beating of a drum stimulates the soldier into courage.

But even yet I refrained and kept still. I scarcely breathed. I held the lantern motionless. I tried how steadily I could maintain the ray upon the eye. Meantime the hellish tattoo of the heart increased. It grew quicker and quicker, and louder and louder every instant. The old man's terror *must* have been extreme! It grew louder, I say, louder every moment! — do you mark me well? I have told you that I am nervous: so I am. And now at the dead hour of the night, amid the dreadful silence of that old house, so strange a noise as this excited me to uncontrollable terror. Yet, for some minutes longer I refrained and stood still. But the beating grew louder, louder! I thought the heart must burst. And now a new anxiety seized me — the sound would be heard by a neighbor! The old man's hour had come! With a loud yell, I threw open the lantern and leaped into the room. He shrieked once — once only. In an instant I dragged him to the floor, and pulled the heavy bed over him. I then smiled gaily, to find the deed so far done. But, for many minutes, the heart beat on with a muffled sound. This, however, did not vex me; it would not be heard through the wall. At length it ceased. The old man was dead. I removed the bed and examined the corpse. Yes, he was stone, stone dead. I placed my hand upon the heart and held it there many minutes. There was no pulsation. He was stone dead. His eye would trouble me no more.

If still you think me mad, you will think so no longer when I describe the wise precautions I took for the concealment of the body. The night waned, and I worked hastily, but in silence. First of all I dismembered the corpse. I cut off the head and the arms and the legs.

I then took up three planks from the flooring of the chamber, and deposited all between the scantlings. I then replaced the boards so cleverly, so cunningly, that no human eye — not even *his* — could have detected anything wrong. There was nothing to wash out — no stain of any kind — no blood spot whatever. I had been too wary for that. A tub had caught all — ha! ha!

When I had made an end of these labors, it was four o'clock — still dark as midnight. As the bell sounded the hour, there came a knocking at the street door. I went down to open it with a light heart — for what had I *now* to fear? There entered three men, who introduced themselves, with perfect suavity, as officers of the police. A shriek had been heard by a neighbor during the night; suspicion of foul play had been aroused; information had been lodged at the police office, and they (the officers) had been deputed to search the premises.

I smiled — for *what* had I to fear? I bade the gentlemen welcome. The shriek, I said, was my own in a dream. The old man, I mentioned, was absent in the country. I took my visitors all over the house. I bade them search — search *well*. I led them, at length, to *his* chamber. I showed them his treasures, secure, undisturbed. In the enthusiasm of my confidence, I brought chairs into the room, and desired them *here* to rest from their fatigues, while I myself, in the wild audacity of my perfect triumph, placed my own seat upon the very spot beneath which reposed the corpse of the victim.

The officers were satisfied. My *manner* had convinced them. I was singularly at ease. They sat, and while I answered cheerily, they chatted of familiar things. But, erelong, I felt myself getting pale and wished them gone. My head ached, and I fancied a ringing in my ears: but still they sat and still chatted. The ringing became more distinct — it continued and became more distinct; I talked more freely to get rid of the feeling; but it continued and gained definiteness — until, at length, I found that the noise was *not* within my ears.

No doubt I now grew *very* pale — but I talked more fluently, and with a heightened voice. Yet the sound increased — and what could I do? It was *a low, dull, quick sound — much such a sound as a watch makes when enveloped in cotton.* I gasped for breath — and yet the officers heard it not. I talked more quickly — more vehemently; but the noise steadily increased. I arose and argued about trifles, in a high key and with violent gesticulations; but the noise steadily increased. Why *would* they not be gone? I paced the floor to and fro with heavy strides, as if excited to fury by the observations of the men — but the noise steadily increased. Oh, now, what *could* I do? I foamed — I raved — I swore! I swung the chair upon which I had been sitting, and grated it upon the boards, but the noise arose over all and continually increased. It grew louder — louder — *louder!* And still the men chatted pleasantly, and smiled. Was it possible they heard not? Almighty power! — no, no! They heard! they suspected! — they *knew!* — they were making a mockery of my horror! — this I thought, and this I think. But anything was better than this agony! Anything was more tolerable than this derision! I could bear those hypocritical smiles no longer! I felt that I must scream or die! and now — again! — hark! louder! louder! louder! *louder!*

" Villains! " I shrieked, " dissemble no more! I admit the deed! — tear up the planks! here, here! — it is the beating of his hideous heart! "

For Discussion of Poe's Stories

The Pit and the Pendulum

1. What words in the first sentence set the tone for this story? Describe the three visual images that make up the prisoner's impression of the trial.

2. How does Poe make the prisoner's period of unconsciousness seem especially real? Compare it with any experience of your own in fainting or only falling asleep, and returning to consciousness.

3. Describe the changes that took place in the method of torture. How do they illustrate the point made in the story that the inquisitors practiced mental as well as physical tortures?

4. What evidence was there that the prisoner was being watched by his tormentors?

5. Suggest situations you have read about which would make good backgrounds for a horror story. What differences would you find in the way these conditions would be described in a newspaper account and in a short story as Poe would have written it?

The Tell-Tale Heart

1. Point out details by which Poe builds up the feeling of horror to an almost unbearable climax.

2. How do the two opposing forces in this story differ from those in " The Pit and the Pendulum "?

3. When did you first suspect that the speaker is mad? When were you certain of his insanity? How does the fact that the story is told in the first person increase its effectiveness?

4. What have you learned about human nature from reading these two stories? Does Poe's analysis of fear in the human mind seem correct, judging from your own experience or from your other reading?

5. To see other sides of Poe's skill read a tale based on deduction and reasoning, such as " The Gold Bug " or " The Purloined Letter." Stories of strange uncanny beauty are " The Masque of the Red Death," " Ligeia," and " The Fall of the House of Usher." Other masterpieces depicting mental unbalance are " The Cask of Amontillado " and " The Black Cat."

For Your Vocabulary

WORDS TO PRODUCE ATMOSPHERE: Poe is a master at choosing words that produce atmosphere, particularly an atmosphere of horror. In the first paragraph of " The Pit and the Pendulum " we find *sick, death, agony, torture, shuddered, delirious horror, sable draperies, deadly nausea, meaningless specters, silence, stillness,* and *night.* Find other paragraphs in both of Poe's stories that are rich in words that produce the desired atmosphere.

The opening paragraph of " The Fall of the House of Usher " is considered a masterpiece in the creation of an atmosphere of gloom. Look up the story and point out the words like *dull, dark, soundless, oppressively,* and *shades.* Write a paragraph of your own using as many of these words as possible. Perhaps you can even add to Poe's list.

Hawthorne and Melville

Nathaniel Hawthorne

POE and Hawthorne stand together as the greatest American writers of the short story in their century. They were both interested in the dark and mysterious places of life, in magic and the supernatural. But their differences tell more about them than their similarities.

Poe was not concerned with local settings; Hawthorne was intensely local. New England was in everything he wrote. In fact, the origin of his dark temperament was local. He grew up in Salem, where the pictures of the great Puritans still hung, and the witchcraft scare was still remembered. His house had an ancestral curse on it, and a ghost that was alleged to haunt the yard. His mother took to her room on the day she heard of her husband's death on a distant voyage in a Salem clipper, and there is a legend that she was never seen to emerge until the day she died, nor did anyone else enter the room. When Hawthorne graduated from Bowdoin, he came back home, and lived several years like a recluse. For a time he had his meals left outside the door of his room, and only in the dark of the evening did he emerge to take a walk — alone — through Salem.

Puritan Ancestry and Dark Legends

No town was so full of dark legends as old Salem: skeletons in closets; blood on the walls; houses that poisoned their occupants; old wives living in darkness with the ghosts of their husbands; bodies that walked from graves; men condemned to wander the hills until doomsday; the Devil himself meeting his faithful followers at midnight in the woods. In dark old Salem people told such legends and half believed them; it was hard to tell where reality stopped and fancy started.

Those were the conditions under which Hawthorne served a twelve-year apprenticeship as a writer, sitting in his attic bedroom, looking out the

window to see the ghost in the yard, and writing the stories suggested to him by the old legends and by his surroundings. It is not surprising that he did not grow up to be the kind of writer Irving became in the gay literary fellowship of New York and London.

Hawthorne's Later Life

He left Salem when he was thirty-five and lived away from it for most of the rest of his life. He was fortunate in his friends. George Bancroft, the historian, then in charge of the Boston customhouse, gave him a job and made possible his departure from Salem.

During his last years in Salem, Hawthorne met Sophia Peabody, a beautiful girl from a remarkable family. Her sister Mary later married Horace Mann, and her unmarried sister, Elizabeth, became well known as an educator and writer. Calling on the Peabody sisters, Hawthorne grew more and more at ease in society. When he and Sophia were married, they went to Concord to live in the Old Manse, and there, happy with his friends and his family, Hawthorne wrote many of his best stories. (You will learn about the famous literary town of Concord in reading about the second period of the Flowering of the East.) Then President Franklin Pierce, his old college mate, made Hawthorne consul to Liverpool. He was abroad for seven years and traveled widely, getting especial pleasure (and literary inspiration) from his visits to Italy. Thus Hawthorne's horizons broadened from the gabled house in Salem, yet it is true that the atmosphere of his early years darkened his stories even in later life.

Hawthorne a Psychological Writer

The external facts about Hawthorne's life are not so important as the things that happened to him inside, what he was thinking and why. He wasn't a man of action; he was a man of thought.

And so were the men in his stories. Poe, on the other hand, cared little about what his characters were thinking, about their struggles with guilt or with society. Poe treated his people almost like puppets, moving them wherever he needed them to give the effect he wanted to get from the story. But to Hawthorne the most important part of the story was what his characters were thinking, how they worked out their moral problems, how they answered the questions he posed for them.

Another way to put that difference is to say that Poe was a writer concerned with form, Hawthorne a writer concerned with ideas. Poe wanted to make a perfect work of art; Hawthorne wanted to find out how his characters thought and what made them act as they did.

Characters with Moral Problems

Hawthorne's best stories refuse to stand on the shelves. They walk like people. We know his characters, and almost feel we should help them work out their problems. They are burdened down with problems, all of them. The darkness of old Salem hangs over them. The characters in his fine novel, *The Scarlet Letter,* are involved in a triangle situation which forces them to answer such questions as "What is sin? How can it be expiated? What happens when man takes it upon himself to punish sin?" One of his finest stories, "Ethan Brand," deals with a man's effort to discover the unpardonable sin. Even when he wrote *The Marble Faun,* a fantasy about a statue in Rome, it became a study of the effect of sin on one's conscience. The problems in his stories are like his own problems. The problem of sin and guilt and conscience is his heritage from the Puritans. His brooding, shy nature, his turning inward, his interest in the dark places of the human mind are his heritage from old Salem.

Our heritage from Hawthorne is a group of the finest American stories (such as "The Great Stone Face," "Rappaccini's Daughter," "Ethan Brand," and the one in this book) and four novels of which *The Scarlet Letter* and *The House of the Seven Gables* are best known and most read.

Hawthorne was born (1804) in the year when Lewis and Clark started on their expedition into the unexplored Northwest. He died (1864) as the War between the States drew near a close.

Herman Melville

There was something about Melville, Hawthorne, and Poe that led them always to seek the dark places of life. But Melville went even farther in that dark quest than the others. If they were exciting, he could be more exciting. If they were intense and mysterious, he could be more so. If they lived extraordinary lives, he lived a still more extraordinary one. For there was never another man quite like Melville in American literature. And, to make his record still more unusual, it took Americans three-quarters of a century to realize that he had written a great book.

He was born in New York and grew up in the Hudson valley — so far, like Irving and Cooper, but there the likeness ends. His boyhood was shadowed over by the declining fortunes of his family and the death of his father. He was unhappy, he was poor, he worried about his widowed mother and his five brothers. He went to work in a bank when he was seventeen, then tried schoolteaching, finally did what many a boy did in those days of clipper ships — ran away to sea.

It was a short trip, but thereafter he could never quite get the sea out of his blood or sea stories out of his mind. Three more years of schoolteaching, and then he went to sea again — this time on a whaler out of one of those New England fishing ports from which, in those days, men departed almost daily for every corner of the earth. He sailed when he was only twenty-one. He came back when he was twenty-five. Into those years he packed enough adventure to last a lifetime.

When his slow ship reached the Marquesas Islands in the south central Pacific, he deserted. He wandered several days in a wilderness and came to a kind of tropical paradise which few white men had ever seen and which was hardly changed by civilization. He lived four months with the natives (whom he suspected of being cannibals), watched their dances and feasts, compared their primitive life with the civilization he had known. But he discovered that after a man had tasted " the fatal draught of civilization " he could never be wholly content even in those idyllic surroundings. An Australian whaling crew visited the cannibal islands. Melville sailed away with them.

It was 1844 when he came back to Boston harbor. He had left as a boy, come back as a man. He had faced death, suffered, met with danger, seen and felt deep emotions, observed life as different from his own as any could possibly

be. Above all, he had come to know the sea.

He wrote a book called *Typee*. It was a picture of the life he had seen on the South Pacific islands. In his lifetime, it was his most popular book. It brought him the sum of four hundred dollars.

He wrote *Omoo* and several books about Pacific island life and whaling experiences. They were less popular than *Typee,* and he had trouble making ends meet. In debt to his publishers, he still found money to take a little house in the Berkshire Hills of Massachusetts. There he moved his family and settled down to write what he felt would be his great book.

Moby Dick *an Epic Novel of the Sea*

He wrote a story of a great white whale named Moby Dick, and of Ahab, a sea captain who had lost a leg to the whale and had dedicated the rest of his life to hunting and killing Moby Dick. *Moby Dick* is an exciting adventure story — the greatest whaling story ever written. But it is much more than that. The men on the ship are so real that a reader thinks of them as persons rather than characters. And the whale is no ordinary creature. It becomes a kind of symbol for natural forces, and the hunt is an allegory for man's struggle with nature. A sense of mystery broods over the book — mysterious predictions, magical sights and sounds, strange and inexplicable happenings — as though Melville were trying to take his readers into the mystery of life itself. And through the whole book roars the sea. No American has ever put on paper so much of the feeling of the sea, its strength and mystery, poetry and beauty, danger and cruelty. Perhaps no American book ever written has in it so much sustained excitement, so much elemental terror and beauty. When critics write of it today they fall back on the words " symphony " or " epic," because it has the grandeur and freedom of music, and the sweep of heroic poetry.

Melville's Rediscovery and Rise to Fame

As sometimes happens in the history of literature, this masterpiece fell flat with the readers of its own time. His next book was even less successful. He struggled for a while with poverty and ill health, then gave up writing as a career, and found a job in the New York customhouse. Not till long after he died, in fact not until about 1920, was *Moby Dick* rediscovered. Then new editions were called for, people began to seek it on library shelves, and critics gave it the praise it deserves as one of the two or three greatest American novels. Nowadays other Melville books and stories are also receiving attention and acclaim. His short novel *Benito Cereno* is often reprinted, and *Billy Budd* has been made into a Broadway play, as well as an opera.

Melville had the same life span as Lowell (1819–1891). He was born in the year the first steamboat crossed the Atlantic. He died when trains had spanned the continent, the automobile had been patented, and electric railways were in operation.

Nathaniel Hawthorne
1804–1864

DR. HEIDEGGER'S EXPERIMENT

theme.

Youth + Old age.

Everyone at one time or another asks himself: " If I had my life to live over, how would I change it? Would I profit by experience? " It's a fascinating question, and in this story Hawthorne provides some fascinating answers to it. The story, which appeared in Hawthorne's first successful book, *Twice-Told Tales,* is a fantasy built around the idea of the Fountain of Youth, thought by early Spanish explorers to be located in Florida. By reading it you can observe in short space some of the ideas with which Hawthorne is concerned in many of his other stories. There is the idea of scientific experiment, which took strong hold of popular fancy in a century of marvelous scientific discovery. There is also the problem of the effect of sin in its various forms upon human nature. You can easily see that Hawthorne was studying right and wrong in human conduct, in contrast to Poe, who was interested in artistic effects without concern for moral problems.

T HAT very singular man, old Dr. Heidegger, once invited four venerable friends to meet him in his study. There were three white-bearded gentlemen, Mr. Medbourne, Colonel Killigrew, and Mr. Gascoigne, and a withered gentlewoman, whose name was the Widow Wycherly. They were all melancholy old creatures, who had been unfortunate in life, and whose greatest misfortune it was that they were not long ago in their graves. Mr. Medbourne, in the vigor of his age, had been a prosperous merchant, but had lost his all by a frantic speculation, and was now little better than a mendicant. Colonel Killigrew had wasted his best years, and his health and substance, in the pursuit of sinful pleasures, which had given birth to a brood of pains, such as the gout, and divers other torments of soul and body. Mr. Gascoigne was a ruined politician, a man of evil fame, or at least had been so till time had buried him from the knowledge of the present generation, and made him obscure instead of infamous. As for the Widow Wycherly, tradition tells us that she was a great beauty in her day; but, for a long while past, she had lived in deep seclusion, on account of certain scanda-lous stories which had prejudiced the gentry of the town against her. It is a circumstance worth mentioning that each of these three old gentlemen, Mr. Medbourne, Colonel Killigrew, and Mr. Gascoigne, were early lovers of the Widow Wycherly, and had once been on the point of cutting each other's throats for her sake. And, before proceeding further, I will merely hint that Dr. Heidegger and all his four guests were sometimes thought to be a little beside themselves — as is not unfrequently the case with old people, when worried either by present troubles or woeful recollections.

" My dear old friends," said Dr. Heidegger, motioning them to be seated, " I am desirous of your assistance in one of those little experiments with which I amuse myself here in my study."

If all stories were true, Dr. Heidegger's study must have been a very curious place. It was a dim, old-fashioned chamber, festooned with cobwebs, and besprinkled with antique dust. Around the walls stood several oaken bookcases, the lower shelves of which were filled with rows of gigantic folios and black-letter quartos, and the upper with little parchment-covered duodecimos.[1] Over the central bookcase was a bronze bust of Hippocrates,[2] with which, according to some authorities, Dr. Heidegger was accustomed to hold consultations in all difficult cases of his practice. In the obscurest corner of the room stood a tall and narrow oaken closet, with its door ajar, within which doubtfully appeared a skeleton. Between two of the bookcases hung a looking glass, presenting its high and dusty plate within a tarnished gilt frame. Among many won-

[1] **folios:** large books, from twelve to about twenty inches in height. **quartos:** volumes about nine and one-half by twelve and one-half inches. **duodecimos** (dū′ō·děs′ĭ·mōz): small volumes, about five by eight inches.

[2] **Hippocrates** (hĭ·pŏk′rà·tēz): an ancient Greek physician (460?–377? B.C.), often called the father of medicine.

derful stories related of this mirror, it was fabled that the spirits of all the doctor's deceased patients dwelt within its verge, and would stare him in the face whenever he looked thitherward. The opposite side of the chamber was ornamented with the full-length portrait of a young lady, arrayed in the faded magnificence of silk, satin, and brocade, and with a visage as faded as her dress. Above half a century ago, Dr. Heidegger had been on the point of marriage with this young lady; but, being affected with some slight disorder, she had swallowed one of her lover's prescriptions, and died on the bridal evening. The greatest curiosity of the study remains to be mentioned; it was a ponderous folio volume, bound in black leather, with massive silver clasps. There were no letters on the back, and nobody could tell the title of the book. But it was well known to be a book of magic; and once, when a chambermaid had lifted it, merely to brush away the dust, the skeleton had rattled in its closet, the picture of the young lady had stepped one foot upon the floor, and several ghastly faces had peeped forth from the mirror; while the brazen head of Hippocrates frowned, and said, " Forbear! "

Such was Dr. Heidegger's study. On the summer afternoon of our tale a small round table, as black as ebony, stood in the center of the room, sustaining a cut-glass vase of beautiful form and elaborate workmanship. The sunshine came through the window, between the heavy festoons of two faded damask curtains, and fell directly across this vase; so that a mild splendor was reflected from it on the ashen visages of the five old people who sat around. Four champagne glasses were also on the table.

" My dear old friends," repeated Dr. Heidegger, " may I reckon on your aid in performing an exceedingly curious experiment? "

Now Dr. Heidegger was a very strange old gentleman, whose eccentricity had become the nucleus for a thousand fantastic stories. Some of these fables, to my shame be it spoken, might possibly be traced back to my own veracious self; and if any passages of the present tale should startle the reader's faith, I must be content to bear the stigma of a fiction monger.

When the doctor's four guests heard him talk of his proposed experiment, they anticipated nothing more wonderful than the murder of a mouse in an air pump, or the examination of a cobweb by the microscope, or some similar nonsense, with which he was constantly in the habit of pestering his intimates. But, without waiting for a reply, Dr. Heidegger hobbled across the chamber and returned with the same ponderous folio, bound in black leather, which common report affirmed to be a book of magic. Undoing the silver clasps, he opened the volume and took from among its black-letter pages a rose, or what was once a rose, though now the green leaves and crimson petals had assumed one brownish hue, and the ancient flower seemed ready to crumble to dust in the doctor's hands.

" This rose," said Dr. Heidegger, with a sigh, " this same withered and crumbling flower, blossomed five and fifty years ago. It was given me by Sylvia Ward, whose portrait hangs yonder; and I meant to wear it in my bosom at our wedding. Five and fifty years it has been treasured between the leaves of this old volume. Now, would you deem it possible that this rose of half a century could ever bloom again? "

" Nonsense! " said the Widow Wycherly, with a peevish toss of her head. " You might as well ask whether an old woman's wrinkled face could ever bloom again."

" See! " answered Dr. Heidegger.

He uncovered the vase and threw the faded rose into the water which it contained. At first, it lay lightly on the sur-

The old town of Salem, Massachusetts, was renowned for its shipping activity and made notorious by its seventeenth-century witch trials. The House of the Seven Gables in Salem is the setting of Hawthorne's famous novel, and is still a landmark. (Essex Institute)

face of the fluid, appearing to imbibe none of its moisture. Soon, however, a singular change began to be visible. The crushed and dried petals stirred and assumed a deepening tinge of crimson, as if the flower were reviving from a deathlike slumber; the slender stalk and twigs of foliage became green; and there was the rose of half a century, looking as fresh as when Sylvia Ward had first given it to her lover. It was scarcely full blown; for some of its delicate red leaves curled modestly around its moist bosom, within which two or three dewdrops were sparkling.

"That is certainly a very pretty deception," said the doctor's friends; carelessly, however, for they had witnessed greater miracles at a conjurer's show; "pray how was it effected?"

"Did you never hear of the 'Fountain of Youth'?" asked Dr. Heidegger, "which Ponce de Leon,[1] the Spanish

<hr>

[1] **Ponce de Leon** (pŏns dĕ lē'ŭn): Spanish discoverer of Florida (1460?–1521).

adventurer, went in search of two or three centuries ago?"

"But did Ponce de Leon ever find it?" said the Widow Wycherly.

"No," answered Dr. Heidegger, "for he never sought it in the right place. The famous Fountain of Youth, if I am rightly informed, is situated in the southern part of the Floridian peninsula, not far from Lake Macaco. Its source is overshadowed by several gigantic magnolias, which, though numberless centuries old, have been kept as fresh as violets by the virtues of this wonderful water. An acquaintance of mine, knowing my curiosity in such matters, has sent me what you see in the vase."

"Ahem!" said Colonel Killigrew, who believed not a word of the doctor's story; "and what may be the effect of this fluid on the human frame?"

"You shall judge for yourself, my dear colonel," replied Dr. Heidegger; "and all of you, my respected friends, are welcome to so much of this admirable fluid as may restore to you the bloom of youth. For my own part, having had much trouble in growing old, I am in no hurry to grow young again. With your permission, therefore, I will merely watch the progress of the experiment."

While he spoke, Dr. Heidegger had been filling the four champagne glasses with the water of the Fountain of Youth. It was apparently impregnated with an effervescent gas, for little bubbles were continually ascending from the depths of the glasses, and bursting in silvery spray at the surface. As the liquor diffused a pleasant perfume, the old people doubted not that it possessed cordial and comfortable properties; and though utter skeptics as to its rejuvenescent power, they were inclined to swallow it at once. But Dr. Heidegger besought them to stay a moment.

"Before you drink, my respectable old friends," said he, "it would be well that, with the experience of a lifetime to direct you, you should draw up a few general rules for your guidance, in passing a second time through the perils of youth. Think what a sin and shame it would be, if, with your peculiar advantages, you should not become patterns of virtue and wisdom to all the young people of the age!"

The doctor's four venerable friends made him no answer, except by a feeble and tremulous laugh; so very ridiculous was the idea that, knowing how closely repentance treads behind the steps of error, they should ever go astray again.

"Drink, then," said the doctor, bowing. "I rejoice that I have so well selected the subjects of my experiment."

With palsied hands, they raised the glasses to their lips. The liquor, if it really possessed such virtues as Dr. Heidegger imputed to it, could not have been bestowed on four human beings who needed it more woefully. They looked as if they had never known what youth or pleasure was, but had been the offspring of Nature's dotage, and always the gray, decrepit, sapless, miserable creatures who now sat stooping round the doctor's table, without life enough in their souls or bodies to be animated even by the prospect of growing young again. They drank off the water, and replaced their glasses on the table.

Assuredly there was an almost immediate improvement in the aspect of the party, not unlike what might have been produced by a glass of generous wine, together with a sudden glow of cheerful sunshine brightening over all their visages at once. There was a healthful suffusion on their cheeks, instead of the ashen hue that had made them look so corpselike. They gazed at one another and fancied that some magic power had really begun to smooth away the deep and sad inscriptions which Father Time had been so long engraving on their brows. The Widow Wycherly adjusted her cap, for she felt almost like a woman again.

"Give us more of this wondrous water!" cried they, eagerly. "We are younger — but we are still too old! Quick — give us more!"

"Patience, patience!" quoth Dr. Heidegger, who sat watching the experiment with philosophic coolness. "You have been a long time growing old. Surely, you might be content to grow young in half an hour! But the water is at your service."

Again he filled their glasses with the liquor of youth, enough of which still remained in the vase to turn half the old people in the city to the age of their own grandchildren. While the bubbles were yet sparkling on the brim, the doctor's four guests snatched their glasses from the table, and swallowed the contents at a single gulp. Was it delusion? Even while the draught was passing down their throats, it seemed to have wrought a change on their whole systems. Their eyes grew clear and bright; a dark shade deepened among their silvery locks, they sat around the table, three gentlemen of middle age, and a woman, hardly beyond her buxom prime.

"My dear widow, you are charming!" cried Colonel Killigrew, whose eyes had been fixed upon her face, while the shadows of age were flitting from it like darkness from the crimson daybreak.

The fair widow knew, of old, that Colonel Killigrew's compliments were not always measured by sober truth; so she started up and ran to the mirror, still dreading that the ugly visage of an old woman would meet her gaze. Meanwhile, the three gentlemen behaved in such a manner as proved that the water of the Fountain of Youth possessed some intoxicating qualities; unless, indeed, their exhilaration of spirits were merely a lightsome dizziness caused by the sudden removal of the weight of years. Mr. Gascoigne's mind seemed to run on political topics, but whether relating to the past, present, or future could not easily be determined, since the same ideas and phrases have been in vogue these fifty years. Now he rattled forth full-throated sentences about patriotism, national glory, and the people's right; now he muttered some perilous stuff or other, in a sly and doubtful whisper, so cautiously that even his own conscience could scarcely catch the secret; and now, again, he spoke in measured accents, and a deeply deferential tone, as if a royal ear were listening to his well-turned periods. Colonel Killigrew all this time had been trolling forth a jolly bottle song, and ringing his glass in symphony with the chorus, while his eyes wandered toward the buxom figure of the Widow Wycherly. On the other side of the table, Mr. Medbourne was involved in a calculation of dollars and cents, with which was strangely intermingled a project for sup-

plying the East Indies with ice, by harnessing a team of whales to the polar icebergs.

As for the Widow Wycherly, she stood before the mirror curtsying and simpering to her own image, and greeting it as the friend whom she loved better than all the world beside. She thrust her face close to the glass, to see whether some long-remembered wrinkle or crow's-foot had indeed vanished. She examined whether the snow had so entirely melted from her hair that the venerable cap could be safely thrown aside. At last, turning briskly away, she came with a sort of dancing step to the table.

"My dear old doctor," cried she, "pray favor me with another glass!"

"Certainly, my dear madam, certainly!" replied the complaisant doctor; "see! I have already filled the glasses."

There, in fact, stood the four glasses, brimful of this wonderful water, the delicate spray of which, as it effervesced from the surface, resembled the tremulous glitter of diamonds. It was now so nearly sunset that the chamber had grown duskier than ever; but a mild and moonlike splendor gleamed from within the vase, and rested alike on the four guests and on the doctor's venerable figure. He sat in a high-backed, elaborately-carved oaken armchair, with a gray dignity of aspect that might have well befitted that very Father Time, whose power had never been disputed, save by this fortunate company. Even while quaffing the third draught of the Fountain of Youth, they were almost awed by the expression of his mysterious visage.

But, the next moment, the exhilarating gush of young life shot through their veins. They were now in the happy prime of youth. Age, with its miserable train of cares and sorrows and diseases, was remembered only as the trouble of a dream, from which they had joyously awaked. The fresh gloss of the soul, so early lost, and without which the world's successive scenes had been but a gallery of faded pictures, again threw its enchantment over all their prospects. They felt like new-created beings in a new-created universe.

"We are young! We are young!" they cried exultingly.

Youth, like the extremity of age, had effaced the strongly-marked characteristics of middle life, and mutually assimilated them all. They were a group of merry youngsters, almost maddened with the exuberant frolicsomeness of their years. The most singular effect of their gaiety was an impulse to mock the infirmity and decrepitude of which they had so lately been the victims. They laughed loudly at their old-fashioned attire, the wide-skirted coats and flapped waistcoats of the young men, and the ancient cap and gown of the blooming girl. One limped across the floor like a gouty grandfather; one set a pair of spectacles astride of his nose, and pretended to pore over the black-letter pages of the book of magic; a third seated himself in an armchair, and strove to imitate the venerable dignity of Dr. Heidegger. Then all shouted mirthfully, and leaped about the room. The Widow Wycherly — if so fresh a damsel could be called a widow — tripped up to the doctor's chair, with a mischievous merriment in her rosy face.

"Doctor, you dear old soul," cried she, "get up and dance with me!" And then the four young people laughed louder than ever, to think what a queer figure the poor old doctor would cut.

"Pray excuse me," answered the doctor quietly. "I am old and rheumatic, and my dancing days were over long ago. But either of these gay young gentlemen will be glad of so pretty a partner."

"Dance with me, Clara!" cried Colonel Killigrew.

"No, no, I will be her partner!" shouted Mr. Gascoigne.

"She promised me her hand, fifty years ago!" exclaimed Mr. Medbourne.

They all gathered round her. One caught both her hands in his passionate grasp — another threw his arm about her waist — the third buried his hand among the glossy curls that clustered beneath the widow's cap. Blushing, panting, struggling, chiding, laughing, her warm breath fanning each of their faces by turns, she strove to disengage herself, yet still remained in their triple embrace. Never was there a livelier picture of youthful rivalship, with bewitching beauty for the prize. Yet, by a strange deception, owing to the duskiness of the chamber, and the antique dresses which they still wore, the tall mirror is said to have reflected the figures of the three old, gray, withered grandsires ridiculously contending for the skinny ugliness of a shriveled grandam.

But they were young: their burning passions proved them so. Inflamed to madness by the coquetry of the girl-widow, who neither granted nor quite withheld her favors, the three rivals began to interchange threatening glances. Still keeping hold of the fair prize, they grappled fiercely at one another's throats. As they struggled to and fro, the table was overturned, and the vase dashed into a thousand fragments. The precious Water of Youth flowed in a bright stream across the floor, moistening the wings of a butterfly, which, grown old in the decline of summer, had alighted there to die. The insect fluttered lightly through the chamber, and settled on the snowy head of Dr. Heidegger.

"Come, come, gentlemen! — come, Madam Wycherly," exclaimed the doctor, "I really must protest against this riot."

They stood still and shivered; for it seemed as if gray Time were calling them back from their sunny youth, far down into the chill and darksome vale of years. They looked at old Dr. Heidegger, who sat in his carved armchair, holding the rose of half a century, which he had rescued from among the fragments of the shattered vase. At the motion of his hand, the four rioters resumed their seats; the more readily, because their violent exertions had wearied them, youthful though they were.

"My poor Sylvia's rose!" ejaculated Dr. Heidegger, holding it in the light of the sunset clouds; "it appears to be fading again."

And so it was. Even while the party were looking at it, the flower continued to shrivel up, till it became as dry and fragile as when the doctor had first thrown it into the vase. He shook off the few drops of moisture which clung to its petals.

"I love it as well thus as in its dewy freshness," observed he, pressing the withered rose to his withered lips. While he spoke, the butterfly fluttered down from the doctor's snowy head, and fell upon the floor.

His guests shivered again. A strange chillness, whether of the body or spirit they could not tell, was creeping gradually over them all. They gazed at one another, and fancied that each fleeting moment snatched away a charm, and left a deepening furrow where none had been before. Was it an illusion? Had the changes of a lifetime been crowded into so brief a space, and were they now four aged people, sitting with their old friend, Dr. Heidegger?

"Are we grown old again, so soon?" cried they, dolefully.

In truth they had. The Water of Youth possessed merely a virtue more transient than that of wine. The delirium which it created had effervesced away. Yes! they were old again. With a shuddering impulse, that showed her a woman still, the widow clasped her skinny hands before her face, and wished that the coffin lid were over it, since it could be no longer beautiful.

"Yes, friends, ye are old again," said Dr. Heidegger, "and lo! the Water of Youth is all lavished on the ground. Well — I bemoan it not; for if the fountain gushed at my very doorstep, I would not stoop to bathe my lips in it — no, though its delirium were for years instead of moments. Such is the lesson ye have taught me!"

But the doctor's four friends had taught no such lesson to themselves. They resolved forthwith to make a pilgrimage to Florida, and quaff at morning, noon, and night, from the Fountain of Youth.

For Discussion of Hawthorne

1. Considering the point of the story, why do the characters have to be the kind that one could not admire?

2. Did their actions after drinking the magic liquid impress you as funny or sad? Explain your reaction.

3. What is Hawthorne's answer to the question on which the story hinges: Would we live our lives differently if we could live them over? Do you agree with his conclusion? What value is there in considering a situation which could not happen?

For Your Vocabulary

CONNOTATION: Dr. Heidegger and his guests are remarkable for their advanced age. By taking full account of their actions and characters as a context, you can master some richly descriptive words to deal with old age. Note the *connotation* of each of the words; that is, the pictures or ideas it suggests in addition to its literal, direct meaning. The guests are *palsied*, or trembling and shaking from age and weakness (p. 537). They are *decrepit*, weak and feeble with age (p. 537). But the good doctor himself, who has grown old gracefully, deserves the term *venerable*, applied ironically to the whole group (p. 534). He is worthy of respect for the wisdom he has acquired with his years. What connotation does each of the following words have for you: *ancient, antique, archaic, obsolete, senile?*

Herman Melville
1819–1891
FROM MOBY DICK

CAPTAIN AHAB

Moby Dick is the story of the fateful voyage of the *Pequod,* a whaling ship commanded by the magnificent figure, Captain Ahab. Throughout the novel Captain Ahab relentlessly pursues the white whale that had years before taken off his leg and made a " poor pegging lubber of him." In the following selection from Chapters 28 and 36 of the book, Melville introduces Captain Ahab to the reader and relates the incident in which he stirs up the crew to be on the alert for his enemy.

Among the crew of the *Pequod,* a strange collection of interesting characters are the officers: *Starbuck,* the first mate; *Stubb,* the second mate; *Flask,* the third mate; the harpooners: *Tashtego,* an Indian from Gay Head on Martha's Vineyard; *Daggoo,* a Negro of gigantic size and strength; and *Queequeg,* " a native of Kokovoko, an island far away to the West and South." (" It is not shown on any map," Melville says; " true places never are.") The teller of the story is a young sailor who joins the crew on this final voyage. At the start he says, " Call me Ishmael," a name symbolizing the " wanderer," since it is the name of the outcast son of Abraham in the Bible.

From this short selection you will not feel the epic sweeping scope of *Moby Dick,* but you will sense the book's excitement and the poetic beauty of Melville's style.

For several days after leaving Nantucket, nothing above hatches was seen of Captain Ahab. The mates regularly relieved each other at the watches, and for aught that could be seen to the contrary, they seemed to be the only commanders of the ship; only they sometimes issued from the cabin with orders so sudden and peremptory, that after all it was plain they but commanded vicariously.[1] Yet, their supreme lord and dictator was there, though hitherto unseen by any eyes not permitted to penetrate into the now sacred retreat of the cabin.

Every time I ascended to the deck from my watches below, I instantly gazed aft to mark if any strange face was visible; for my first vague disquietude touching the unknown captain, now in the seclusion of the sea became almost a perturbation.[2] . . . Now, it being Christmas when the ship shot from out her harbor, for a space we had biting Polar weather, though all the time running away from it to the southward; and by every degree and minute of latitude which we sailed, gradually leaving that merciless winter, and all its intolerable weather behind us. It was one of those less lowering,[3] but still gray and gloomy enough mornings of

[1] **vicariously** (vĭ·kâr′ĭ·ŭs·lĭ): not directly; through something else.

[2] That is, at first he was vaguely uneasy about the captain but now at sea he had become almost seriously alarmed.

[3] **lowering** (lou′ẽr·ing): darkening, threatening a storm.

the transition, when with a fair wind the ship was rushing through the water with a vindictive sort of leaping and melancholy rapidity, that as I mounted to the deck at the call of the forenoon watch, so soon as I leveled my glance toward the taffrail, foreboding shivers ran over me. Reality outran apprehension; Captain Ahab stood upon his quarter-deck.

There seemed no sign of common bodily illness about him, nor of the recovery from any. He looked like a man cut away from the stake, when the fire has overrunningly wasted all the limbs without consuming them, or taking away one particle from their compacted aged robustness. His whole high, broad form seemed made of solid bronze, and shaped in an unalterable mold, like Cellini's cast Perseus.[1] Threading its way out from among his gray hairs, and continuing right down one side of his tawny scorched face and neck, till it disappeared in his clothing, you saw a slender rodlike mark, lividly whitish. It resembled that perpendicular seam sometimes made in the straight, lofty trunk of a great tree, when the upper lightning tearingly darts down it, and without wrenching a single twig, peels and grooves out the bark from top to bottom ere running off into the soil, leaving the tree still greenly alive, but branded. Whether that mark was born with him, or whether it was the scar left by some desperate wound, no one could certainly say. By some tacit consent, throughout the voyage little or no allusion was made to it, especially by the mates. But once an old Gay Head Indian among the crew superstitiously asserted that not till he was full forty years old did Ahab become that way branded, and then it came upon him, not in the fury of any mortal fray, but

[1] Cellini's cast Perseus: a famous statue by Benvenuto Cellini (băn·vȧ·nōō′tŏ chĕ·lē′nĕ) (1500–1571) of Perseus holding the Gorgon's snaky-haired l ead.

in an elemental strife at sea. . . .

So powerfully did the whole grim aspect of Ahab affect me, and the livid brand which streaked it, that for the first few moments I hardly noted that not a little of this overbearing grimness was owing to the barbaric white leg upon which he partly stood. It had previously come to me that this ivory leg had at sea been fashioned from the polished bone of the sperm whale's jaw. "Aye, he was dismasted off Japan," said the old Gay Head Indian once; "but like his dismasted craft, he shipped [2] another mast without coming home for it. He has a quiver of 'em."

I was struck with the singular posture he maintained. Upon each side of the *Pequod*'s quarter-deck, and pretty close to the mizzen shrouds, there was an auger hole, bored about half an inch or so, into the plank. His bone leg steadied in that hole, one arm elevated, and holding by a shroud, Captain Ahab stood erect, looking straight out beyond the ship's ever-pitching prow. There was an infinity of firmest fortitude, a determinate, unsurrenderable willfulness, in the fixed and fearless, forward dedication of that glance. Not a word he spoke; nor did his officers say aught to him; though by all their minutest gestures and expressions, they plainly showed the uneasy, if not painful, consciousness of being under a troubled master-eye. And not only that, but moody stricken Ahab stood before them with a crucifixion in his face, in all the nameless regal overbearing dignity of some mighty woe.

Ere long, from his first visit in the air, he withdrew into his cabin. But after that morning, he was every day visible to the crew, either standing in his pivot-hole, or seated upon an ivory stool he had, or heavily walking the deck. As the sky grew less gloomy, indeed, began to grow a little genial, he be-

[2] shipped: took aboard, obtained.

came still less and less a recluse; as if, when the ship had sailed from home, nothing but the dead wintry bleakness of the sea had then kept him so secluded. And, by and by, it came to pass, that he was almost continually in the air; but, as yet, for all that he said, or perceptibly did, on the at last sunny deck, he seemed as unnecessary there as another mast. But the *Pequod* was only making a passage now, not regularly cruising; nearly all whaling preparatives needing supervision the mates were fully competent to, so that there was little or nothing, out of himself, to employ or excite Ahab, now, and thus chase away, for that one interval, the clouds that layer upon layer were piled upon his brow, as ever all clouds choose the loftiest peaks to pile themselves upon.

Nevertheless, ere long, the warm, warbling persuasiveness of the pleasant holiday weather we came to, seemed gradually to charm him from his mood. For, as when the red-cheeked dancing girls, April and May, trip home to the wintry, misanthropic woods, even the barest, ruggedest, most thunder-cloven old oak will at least send forth some few green sprouts, to welcome such gladhearted visitants; so Ahab did, in the end, a little respond to the playful allurings of that girlish air. More than once did he put forth the faint blossom of a look, which, in any other man, would have soon flowered out in a smile. . . .

One morning shortly after breakfast, Ahab, as was his wont, ascended the cabin-gangway to the deck. There most sea captains usually walk at that hour, as country gentlemen, after the same meal, take a few turns in the garden.

Soon his steady, ivory stride was heard, as to and fro he paced his old rounds, upon planks so familiar to his tread that they were all over dented, like geological stones, with the peculiar

mark of his walk. Did you fixedly gaze, too, upon that ribbed and dented brow, there also, you would see still stranger footprints — the footprints of his one unsleeping, ever-pacing thought.

But on the occasion in question, those dents looked deeper, even as his nervous step that morning left a deeper mark. And, so full of his thought was Ahab, that at every uniform turn that he made, now at the mainmast and now at the binnacle, you could almost see that thought turn in him as he turned, and pace in him as he paced; so completely possessing him, indeed, that it all but seemed the inward mold of every outer movement.

"D'ye mark him, Flask?" whispered Stubb; "the chick that's in him pecks the shell. 'Twill soon be out."

The hours wore on — Ahab now shut up within his cabin; anon, pacing the deck, with the same intense bigotry of purpose [1] in his aspect.

It drew near the close of day. Suddenly he came to a halt by the bulwarks, and inserting his bone leg into the auger hole there, and with one hand grasping a shroud, he ordered Starbuck to send everybody aft.

"Sir!" said the mate, astonished at an order seldom or never given on shipboard, except in some extraordinary case.

"Send everybody aft," repeated Ahab. "Mastheads, there! come down!"

When the entire ship's company were assembled, and with curious and not wholly unapprehensive faces were eyeing him, for he looked not unlike the weather horizon when a storm is coming up, Ahab, after rapidly glancing over the bulwarks, and then darting his eyes among the crew, started from his standpoint, and as though not a soul were nigh him resumed his heavy turns upon the deck. With bent head and

---

[1] **bigotry** (bĭg'ŭt·rĭ) **of purpose**: almost frenzied singlemindedness; bigotry means exclusion of other beliefs or ideas.

544
half-
unm
ing
ly w
have
pose
But
paus
"Y
wha
"S
sive
voic
"(
prov
anim
ques
then
"/
"1
"/
men
"/
M
ly g
tena
whil
ousl
it w
excit
ques
Bu
Aha
hole
shro
gras
"/
hear
wha
oun
brig
teen
Star
W
mer
ly r
skirt

¹ s
varia

"And he have one, two, tree — oh! good many iron in him hide, too, Captain," cried Queequeg disjointedly, "all twiske-tee be-twisk, like him — him — " faltering hard for a word, and screwing his hand round and round as though uncorking a bottle — "like him — him —"

"Corkscrew!" cried Ahab, "aye, Queequeg, the harpoons lie all twisted and wrenched in him; aye, Daggoo, his spout is a big one, like a whole shock of wheat, and white as a pile of our Nantucket wool after the great annual sheep-shearing; aye, Tashtego, and he fantails like a split jib in a squall. Death and devils! men, it is Moby Dick ye have seen — Moby Dick — Moby Dick!"

"Captain Ahab," said Starbuck, who, with Stubb and Flask, had thus far been eyeing his superior with increasing surprise, but at last seemed struck with a thought which somewhat explained all the wonder. "Captain Ahab, I have heard of Moby Dick — but it was not Moby Dick that took off thy leg?"

"Who told thee that?" cried Ahab; then pausing, "Aye, Starbuck; aye, my hearties all round; it was Moby Dick that dismasted me; Moby Dick that brought me to this dead stump I stand on now. Aye, aye," he shouted with a terrific, loud, animal sob, like that of a heart-stricken moose; "Aye, aye! it was that accursed white whale that razeed me; made a poor pegging lubber of me for ever and a day!" Then tossing both arms, with measureless imprecations he shouted out: "Aye, aye! and I'll chase him round Good Hope, and round the Horn, and round the Norway Maelstrom, and round perdition's flames before I give him up. And this is what ye have shipped for, men! to chase that white whale on both sides of land, and over all sides of earth, till he spouts black blood and rolls fin out. What say ye, men, will ye splice hands on it, now? I think ye do look brave."

"Aye, aye!" shouted the harpooners

and seamen, running closer to the excited old man: "A sharp eye for the white whale; a sharp lance for Moby Dick!"

"God bless ye," he seemed to half sob and half shout. "God bless ye, men."

For Discussion of Melville

1. Point out passages that contain striking figures of speech. In what two ways is Captain Ahab compared to a tree? How does Melville describe the marks of the peg leg on the deck?

2. In what specific ways did Ahab play upon the crew's emotions to make them eager for the capture of Moby Dick? What do you think of the psychology he employed?

3. Look again at the description of Moby Dick. What details and comparisons seem particularly effective to you? How do you know that capture of the white whale is an obsession with Captain Ahab? Would a whaler ordinarily be satisfied with a single whale? Someone might wish to report to the class on whaling, by reading either *Moby Dick* or reference books.

4. You will want to read the whole story of *Moby Dick*, at least in a shortened form (Max T. Hohn's abridgment is a particularly good one). *Typee* and *Omoo* are excellent adventure stories of the sea also.

For Your Vocabulary

NAUTICAL TERMS: No story of the sea, like *Moby Dick*, is fully enjoyable unless the reader masters some of the large nautical vocabulary employed. Even such a short selection as the one in this book contains a number of nautical terms: *hatches, aft, starboard, taffrail, mizzen shroud, binnacle, bulwarks, jib, razeed*. And perhaps a genuine landlubber would need help on some of the more common terms: *mate, watch, cabin, quarter-deck, prow, mainmast*. How many of these terms do you already know? Perhaps each member of the class can be made responsible for a clear explanation of one term. Or perhaps some sailing enthusiast can explain them all.

Reading on the Flowering of the East, Part One

LITERATURE OF THE PERIOD

Fiction

Irving, Washington, *The Sketch Book:* "Rip Van Winkle," "The Spectre Bridegroom," "The Legend of Sleepy Hollow"; *Bracebridge Hall:* "The Stout Gentleman"; *The Alhambra:* "The Legend of the Moor's Legacy," "The Legend of the Two Discreet Statues," "The Legend of the Three Beautiful Princesses"; *Tales of a Traveler:* "The Adventure of My Uncle," "The Bold Dragoon"

Cooper, James Fenimore, *The Spy, The Pilot, The Deerslayer, The Last of the Mohicans*

Poe, Edgar Allan, "The Black Cat," "The Cask of Amontillado," "A Descent into the Maelstrom," "The Fall of the House of Usher," "The Gold Bug," "MS. Found in a Bottle," "The Masque of the Red Death," "Murders in the Rue Morgue," "The Purloined Letter"

Hawthorne, Nathaniel, *Twice-Told Tales:* "The Ambitious Guest," "The Gray Champion," "Mr. Higginbotham's Catastrophe," "Lady Eleanore's Mantle," "The Wedding Knell," "The Minister's Black Veil"; *Mosses from an Old Manse:* "The Birthmark," "Drowne's Wooden Image," "Rappaccini's Daughter"; *The Snow Image:* "The Great Stone Face," "Ethan Brand"; *Best of Hawthorne*, ed. by Mark Van Doren (Ronald Press, 1951)

Melville, Herman, *Moby Dick, Typee, Omoo, Billy Budd*

Poetry

Bryant, William Cullen, "Robert of Lincoln," "The Death of the Flowers," "A Forest Hymn," "June," "The Yellow Violet," "Song of Marion's Men," "The Battlefield," "Hymn of the City," "Abraham Lincoln"

Whittier, John Greenleaf, "Maud Muller," "Barbara Frietchie," "Barclay of Ury," "The Angels of Buena Vista," "The Pipes of Lucknow," "The Trailing Arbutus," "Laus Deo," "Dear Lord and Father of Mankind"

Poe, Edgar Allan, "To One in Paradise," "Lenore," "The Haunted Palace," "Israfel," "The City in the Sea," "Eldorado," "A Dream within a Dream," "To Annie"

Nonfiction

Irving, Washington, *Diedrich Knickerbocker's History of New York; The Sketch Book:* "English Writers on America," "Rural Life in England," "Five Christmas Sketches," "Stratford-on-Avon"; *Bracebridge Hall:* "Family Servants," "An Old Soldier," "May-Day Customs," "Popular Superstitions"; *The Alhambra:* "The Palace of the Alhambra," "The Hall of Ambassadors," "The Court of Lions," "A Fête in the Alhambra"

BOOKS ABOUT THE PERIOD

Brooks, Van Wyck, *The World of Washington Irving* (Dutton, 1944)

Brooks, Van Wyck, *The Flowering of New England* (Dutton, 1936)

On Individual Authors

IRVING. Benét, Laura, *Washington Irving, Explorer of American Legend* (Dodd, Mead, 1944)

POE. Allen, Hervey, *Israfel* (Rinehart, 1949); Benét, Laura, *Young Edgar Allan Poe* (Dodd, Mead, 1941); Fagin, Nathan B., *Histrionic Mr. Poe* (Johns Hopkins Press, 1949); Quinn, A. H., *Edgar Allan Poe* (Appleton, 1941)

HAWTHORNE. Hawthorne, Hildegarde, *A Romantic Rebel* (by his granddaughter) (Appleton, 1932); Tharp, Louise Hall, *The Peabody Sisters of Salem* (Little, Brown, 1950)

MELVILLE. Leyda, Jay, *The Melville Log* (a sourcebook of Melville material) (Harcourt, Brace, 1951)

There are detailed biographies of these authors by numerous writers of an earlier day, and in series such as American Men of Letters, and American Writers.

The home of Henry Wadsworth Longfellow on Brattle Street in Cambridge.
(Devaney)

The Flowering of the East
Part Two

THE Flowering of the East reached its greatest heights in the twenty-five years before the War between the States.

Those twenty-five years — 1836 to 1861 — were some of the most exciting in American literature. And yet if any of us had been studying American literature in 1836 we should probably have had no idea of what was about to happen.

The best-known American writers then were Irving and Cooper. They had just returned from long residences in Europe; the greater part of their productive careers was behind them. Bryant had written "Thanatopsis" more than twenty years before 1836; he was a busy newspaper editor in New York. There were a few promising young writers in sight. One of them was Poe, who was editing a literary magazine in Richmond in 1836, but had not yet published the stories and poems for which we chiefly remember him. Hawthorne had published one book, which only a few people had read. Emerson published his first book, a small volume called *Nature*, in 1836, but it attracted little attention. Lowell and Thoreau were undergraduates at Harvard; Longfellow had just been appointed to the Harvard faculty.

That was the way things looked in 1836: the best-known writers along toward the end of their literary careers, a few promising youngsters on the horizon, and writers like Emerson, Hawthorne, Longfellow, Thoreau, and Lowell virtually unknown. And then the dam burst!

Hardly a year after that failed to produce a memorable addition to American literature. Hawthorne's first volume of *Twice-Told Tales* and Emerson's first widely read essay came in 1837. Longfellow published "A Psalm of Life" in 1838, a volume of poems in 1839, and his first highly successful volume in 1841. Lowell's first book of poems came in 1840, and Emerson's first book of essays in 1842. Almost every year brought an important contri-

549

bution by Poe. You needn't try to remember all these dates, but you can readily imagine yourself back in the America of a century ago amid this outpouring of literature. Imagine yourself finding Poe's *The Raven and Other Poems* in the bookstores in 1845; Longfellow's poem *Evangeline* in 1847; Lowell's political satires, *The Biglow Papers,* in 1848; Parkman's story of *The Oregon Trail* in 1849; Hawthorne's most famous novel, *The Scarlet Letter,* in 1850; Melville's greatest novel, *Moby Dick,* in 1851; and so on, every year.

If you could have had your choice of a place to watch this literary movement a hundred years ago, you would certainly have chosen Boston, because Boston was the center of it. Those were the great literary years of Boston. Never since those years has any American city produced so large a proportion of the distinguished authors of its time as did Boston during the Flowering of the East.

When we speak of Boston, of course, we are including the towns around it — Cambridge, Salem, Concord, among others. All of these towns had their little groups of authors. In many respects, the most remarkable of these was Concord, and we are going to talk first about the writers of Concord. But if you had gone to Concord, Massachusetts, a century ago, you would have seen nothing remarkable about its appearance. It lies in low hills, near Boston. Its church spires rise out of avenues of trees. It has a common, or town park, and its typical houses are simple and dignified and white. Just like the rest of New England, you might say. And yet, by chance or by design, this town for a generation was such a center of lofty thinking, good talk, and good writing as few towns anywhere have been at any time.

Emerson and Thoreau

The Flowering of New England: Concord

ONE hundred years ago there was an annual series of lectures in Concord, and the speakers were all local residents. It was one of the most distinguished lyceum series in America. The speakers included Emerson, the poet and essayist; Thoreau, the great writer about nature; Alcott, the philosopher; Margaret Fuller, the critic and social reformer; and many others — all from Concord. In almost any house in town you could hear stimulating talk. So famous was the Concord talk that tickets were sometimes sold for "Conversations," and people came from afar to hear two or three of the town's eminent citizens sit on a platform and talk with each other about anything that happened to be on their minds.

It was to Concord that Hawthorne came as a promising young writer. He moved into a famous house, the Old Manse, where Emerson's grandfather had once lived and where Emerson himself lived before he built his own home. Here Hawthorne wrote his book of tales *Mosses from an Old Manse*. It was at Concord that *The Dial*, perhaps the most intellectual magazine in America, was edited. The Transcendentalists, the best-known American philosophic group of their time, were centered there, with Emerson as their leader and Alcott, Thoreau, and Margaret Fuller among the members. (You needn't try to define Transcendentalism now, but you might remember the slogan by which the movement was known, because it fits so perfectly the pattern of their life in Concord — "Plain living and high thinking.")

Physically it was a quiet town but intellectually it was an exciting town, for almost any week might bring another essay by Emerson, another tale by Hawthorne, another of Thoreau's nature descriptions, another issue of *The Dial*. Any week might bring distinguished visitors from this country or abroad to see the literary men of Concord. Perhaps nowhere else in America have men ever quite equaled the combination of leisurely, contemplative living and white-hot intellectual excitement which was Concord in its flowering period.

Ralph Waldo Emerson

The greatest man in Concord and possibly the most influential literary figure in America was Emerson. He was different from any literary man we have met so far in this account of American writers. He was a poet, and a good one, but his influence did not rest on his poetry, as did Whittier's, for instance.

He was an essayist, and a good one, but we remember the essays less than the striking quotations from them. Although as a thinker his ideas were often muddled and his conclusions frequently illogical, yet his influence on a generation of American writers was tremendous.

Boston, Harvard, the Ministry

Hundreds of New England youngsters spent their first twenty years almost exactly as Emerson spent his. He was born in Boston, of a preacher's family. Boston, like Concord, was a country town; he used to lead the family cow to pasture on Boston Common. He went to Harvard, graduated just below the middle of his class, gave his classmates the impression of being retiring, not socially inclined, calm and restrained, but "a man in quest of something."

In quest of something he was. He tried schoolteaching for a few years, then changed over to the family profession and entered divinity school. At twenty-six he was pastor of one of the most famous churches in Boston.

But that was not the answer either; he found he could not believe in the ritual of the church, and resigned. He rejected Catholicism without investigation. He read great books and sought out famous scholars and thinkers. He wanted an answer to the problems he could not solve; he wanted an intellectual foundation on which he could base his life. And the more he consulted other men, the more he read books, the more he became convinced that no one could help him, that he had to find the road himself.

Emerson's Philosophy: Transcendentalism

So he saved a little money and went to Europe, and in Paris, one July day in 1833, he found what he wanted. He was in the museum of natural history, looking at the ferns and flowers. Suddenly a feeling he had often had when walking through the woods or beside Walden Pond came back to him, but clearer than ever before. It was simply this — that all living things are related, that there is a common element in man and in all nature. He called the common force he perceived in all living things the Oversoul. To Emerson it was the same as life, goodness, and truth.

This concept closely approached that of the pagan pantheists. Emerson made no attempt to justify his position in a logical manner. He relied on intuition and inspiration. This reliance on intuition and inspiration was to become the Trancendentalist trademark. On such a flimsy and vague basis Emerson built his philosophy. He stated it in a series of essays when he returned to Concord.

Emerson's Message: *Confidence and Self-Reliance*

If Emerson had lived a little later, he might have described the Oversoul as an electric current. All living things draw their currents from this central source. When a poet plugs in, the current flows through him as poetry. When a philosopher plugs in, it flows through him as wisdom. In the hands of an artist it is the source of beauty.

The Oversoul existed in Homer's time even as it does today, Emerson said. And if Homer, the blind Greek poet of three thousand years before, had access to it, men of today have just as good access. That was the idea Emerson needed. For he now saw clearly that it was no longer necessary to go back to other times or to far countries for wisdom or truth. It was no longer necessary for Americans to humble themselves before the great traditions of Europe, the great names of distant places or past ages. For the truth is here today! The truth is free for the seeking! The truth is within man and within nature — if man will only have the good sense to perceive it.

That was Emerson's message. He put it in ringing phrases that men still remember and quote. "The sun shines today also!" he said, and "Build therefore your own world!" and "Trust thyself: every heart vibrates to that iron string!" It was an optimistic point of view. It avoided the sense of guilt that lay over men like Hawthorne and Bryant. His message, however, was a disappointment to those who looked to him for a deeper spirituality and a more convincing philosophy of life.

Emerson's Influence: *American Independence in Letters*

The rest of Emerson's story is very simple: he preached his belief to ever-widening circles. He lived in Concord, enjoying the friendship of his fellow townsmen, who looked on him more as a neighbor than as a great national figure. But he left Concord occasionally to lecture over a wide area. Three times he crossed the frozen Mississippi on foot to lecture, and late in life he gave a series of talks in California. He published a number of books of essays. He made little money; in fact, he is said never to have received a royalty check for a book of his until he was past fifty. But he had enough income to live in Concord. He had friends, great friends, good enough friends to rebuild his house for him when it burned down. And he had the satisfaction of shocking many of his countrymen into wiser thinking, as for instance the day when he stood on the platform in Harvard's main auditorium to speak on the subject of "The American Scholar," and told his audience: "We have listened too long to the courtly muses of Europe. . . . We will walk on our own feet . . . we will speak our own minds." Some of the scholars in his audience were shocked, but the younger men went away feeling, as later critics felt, that they had heard a declaration of American *intellectual* independence comparable to Jefferson's declaration of political independence.

He had satisfactions like these, and he had the satisfaction of helping young men in whom he believed to start their careers — Thoreau, for instance, and Whitman, whom you will read about later in this volume. Before he died, his ringing phrases and his thin, serene, intelligent face became known all over America as those of a prophet.

Emerson was born (1803) three years after Washington's death, and died (1882) in the year of Franklin Roosevelt's birth. In the year of Emerson's birth, Jefferson bought the Mississippi valley from France. By the time of his death, that land — three quarters of a million square miles — was almost entirely settled.

Henry David Thoreau

The picture we remember of Thoreau is the one Emerson painted. "He knew the country like a fox or a bird, and passed through it as freely by paths of his own," Emerson said. "Under his arm he carried an old music book to press plants; in his pocket, his diary and pencil, a spyglass for birds, microscope, jackknife, and twine. He wore a straw hat, stout shoes, strong gray trousers, to brave scrub oaks and smilax, and to climb a tree for a hawk's or a squirrel's nest. He waded into the pool for the water plants, and his strong legs were no insignificant part of his armor."

One Side of Thoreau: Love of Nature

It is a true picture, according to all we can find out. That is the Thoreau who built a ten- by fifteen-foot hut beside Walden Pond for twenty-nine dollars, and managed to live in solitude and off the bounty of nature. That is the Thoreau who paddled up and down the Concord and Merrimac rivers and kept a delightful journal of what he saw and heard. That is the Thoreau who knew every bird and flower, who always knew where to find an Indian arrowhead, who introduced the city-bred Emerson to the names and habits of wild things. That is the Thoreau who loved nature and went to school to it, and let its inspiration blow through him like the wind through an aeolian harp.

Another Side of Thoreau: Dissenter in Society

But it is not the whole Thoreau. It is not the Thoreau who was described by his neighbors as "a very stubborn and opinionated young man." For among the Concord men, Thoreau was the great arguer, the great dissenter. He argued against the eating of meat, the drinking of alcoholic liquor, the institution of marriage, and the established church. But most of all, he argued against the government.

There is no inconsistency between the Thoreau who loved nature and the Thoreau who refused to pay some of his taxes. Thoreau believed in the simple life. He felt that business and government and civilized institutions got in the way of simple living. While at Harvard, he upheld the thesis that man should work only the seventh day, and keep the other six free for a real " Sabbath of the soul," for getting close to nature and for thinking. He was especially irritated when the government asked him to pay money for activities of which he did not approve — the Mexican war, for instance, and the enforcement of slavery. He went to jail for that refusal, and when Emerson asked him, " Henry, what are you doing in there? " he looked sternly out through the bars and replied, " What are you doing *out there?* "

Walden *Reflects Thoreau's Independence*

Thoreau's ideas had little impact in his own time. The quality that made Emerson a preacher or teacher in all his lectures and writings was somehow left out of Thoreau. He cared little what others believed, and was content with his own problems, his own code, and his own studies of nature. Other men might have been lonely, but Thoreau was never lonely with nature. Other men might have felt the obligation to reform their fellow men or at least to share their discoveries, but Thoreau believed, " I came into the world, not chiefly to make this a good place to live in, but to live in it, be it good or bad."

He wrote with little eye to publication, piled up journals and notes and essays which were never seen until he died. When his book *A Week on the Concord and Merrimack Rivers* was published, it sold very poorly, and Thoreau later remarked that he had a library of eight hundred volumes — seven hundred written by himself! Nobody has ever written a book about

the simple life that is more delightful than *Walden,* which describes the year he lived beside Walden Pond for about twenty-seven cents a week. Nobody has ever written more vividly of such natural scenes as he did in his famous " Battle of the Ants." Few men have written more explosive documents than his essay on " Civil Disobedience," in which he argued, in effect, for individual secession whenever a citizen found himself hampered by his government or not in agreement with it. But the dynamite was hidden during his lifetime,

and the challenge of his ideas was not widely known until he died.

Thoreau went from Harvard College to Concord village and lived there except for brief intervals until he died — at the age of forty-four, of the old New England scourge, tuberculosis. He seldom felt the need to travel, the urge for wider experience, the attraction of a more complex and ancient society. He had the open book of nature to study, the Harvard College library, when necessary, and the society of the good men of Concord. " I have traveled much," he said, " — in Concord! "

Thoreau was born (1817) just before the first steamship crossed the Atlantic, and died (1862) shortly after the first Atlantic cable had been laid. When he was born, only Irving of the great Easterners had published. When he died, all of them were well known, but Mark Twain, the first great writer of the West, had not yet published.

Ralph Waldo Emerson
1803–1882

THE CONCORD HYMN

Today at Concord you can see a graceful stone bridge and at one end, through the trees, the famous bronze statue of the Minute Man. At the base of the statue is the first stanza of "The Concord Hymn." More than a century ago, on July 4, 1837, Ralph Waldo Emerson stood at this bridge and read his poem on the dedication of the original monument commemorating the Battle of Concord, which opened the American Revolution.

Oliver Wendell Holmes thought this the most complete and faultless of Emerson's poems. Today it is regarded as one of the classics of American literature. Try to imagine the occasion for which it was written and to sense the determination of Emerson and his Concord neighbors that the battle of 1775 should be remembered "when, like our sires, our sons are gone." Emerson's poem turned the trick; the "shot heard round the world" is indeed immortal.

By the rude bridge that arched the flood,
  Their flag to April's breeze unfurled,
Here once the embattled farmers stood,
  And fired the shot heard round the world.

The foe long since in silence slept; 5
  Alike the conqueror silent sleeps;
And Time the ruined bridge has swept
  Down the dark stream which seaward creeps.

On this green bank, by this soft stream,
  We set today a votive stone; 10

That memory may their deed redeem,
  When, like our sires, our sons are gone.

Spirit, that made those heroes dare
  To die and leave their children free,
Bid Time and Nature gently spare 15
  The shaft we raise to them and thee.

THE RHODORA *

On Being Asked, Whence Is the Flower?

Chancing upon a pretty woodland flower, Emerson realized that some persons might ask the reason for the existence of this purple blossom, whose "charm is wasted on the earth and sky." For such persons the poet had a memorable answer. This poem, like all of Emerson's poems, gives you something worth thinking about.

In May, when sea winds pierced our solitudes,
I found the fresh rhodora in the woods,
Spreading its leafless blooms in a damp nook,
To please the desert and the sluggish brook.
The purple petals, fallen in the pool,

* Rhodora (rō·dō′rȧ): a shrub commonly found in New England, having large clusters of pink flowers shading into purple, which come out before the leaves in early spring. The original Greek meaning of the word is "rose."

Made the black water with their beau-
ty gay; 6
Here might the redbird come his
plumes to cool,
And court the flower that cheapens his
array.
Rhodora! if the sages ask thee why
This charm is wasted on the earth and
sky, 10
Tell them, dear, that if eyes were made
for seeing,
Then Beauty is its own excuse for be-
ing.
Why thou wert there, O rival of the
rose!
I never thought to ask, I never knew:
But, in my simple ignorance, suppose
The selfsame Power that brought me
there brought you. 16

COMPENSATION

Emerson wrote two short poems and one
long essay (p. 563) on this subject. The
idea of balance in human life — night and
day, good and evil, action and repose —
was a favorite of his. Here he shows that
moments of gaiety and moments of loneliness come to all men, at different times.
Over a long period they balance up.

Why should I keep holiday
When other men have none?
Why but because, when these are gay,
I sit and mourn alone?

And why, when mirth unseals all
tongues, 5
Should mine alone be dumb?
Ah! late I spoke to silent throngs,
And now their hour is come.

FORBEARANCE

Here Emerson says that he would like
to have for his friend anyone who can forbear or refrain from certain selfish or foolish practices. To understand the "forbearance" advocated in the second stanza will
require some thought.

Hast thou named all the birds without
a gun?
Loved the wood rose, and left it on its
stalk?
At rich men's tables eaten bread and
pulse?°
Unarmed, faced danger with a heart of
trust?

And loved so well a high behavior, 5
In man or maid, that thou from speech
refrained,
Nobility more nobly to repay?
O, be my friend, and teach me to be
thine!

3. **pulse**: the seeds of peas, beans, or similar
vegetables.

VOLUNTARIES III

The long poem "Voluntaries" contains
five unconnected stanzas, each treating of
some act of the will in relation to the
struggles of life. The third one of these is
the most easily understood and the best
known. It sounds as if it might have been
written during World War II. The last four
lines, which are the heart of the poem, are
frequently quoted.

In an age of fops and toys,
Wanting wisdom, void of right,
Who shall nerve heroic boys
To hazard all in Freedom's fight —
Break sharply off their jolly games, 5
Forsake their comrades gay
And quit proud homes and youthful
dames
For famine, toil, and fray?
Yet on the nimble air benign
Speed nimbler messages, 10
That waft the breath of grace divine
To hearts in sloth and ease.

So nigh is grandeur to our dust,
So near is God to man,
When duty whispers low, *Thou must,*
The youth replies, *I can.*   16

EACH AND ALL

Here is a poem that expresses Emerson's belief that all things in nature are bound together in a " perfect whole." The theme is found in lines 11–12:

> " All are needed by each one;
> Nothing is fair or good alone."

In the first stanza the poet shows how unaware men may be of their interdependence, of the fact that " all are needed by each one." In the second, third, and fourth stanzas he carries this idea into the field of beauty and shows by three striking examples that " nothing is fair or good alone," that things are best in their original setting. In the last stanza, he says that for a time he believed that beauty was a mere childish delusion; however, he finally realized that beauty exists not in any single object but is part of nature's grand design — " the perfect whole."

Little thinks, in the field, yon red-
    cloaked clown,
Of thee from the hilltop looking down;
The heifer that lows in the upland farm,
Far-heard, lows not thine ear to charm;
The sexton, tolling his bell at noon,   5
Deems not that great Napoleon
Stops his horse, and lists with delight,
Whilst his files sweep round yon Alpine
    height;
Nor knowest thou what argument
Thy life to thy neighbor's creed has
    lent.   10

All are needed by each one;
Nothing is fair or good alone.
I thought the sparrow's note from heav-
    en,
Singing at dawn on the alder bough;
I brought him home, in his nest, at
    even;   15

He sings the song, but it cheers not
    now,
For I did not bring home the river and
    sky —
He sang to my ear — they sang to my
    eye.

The delicate shells lay on the shore;
The bubbles of the latest wave   20
Fresh pearls to their enamel gave,
And the bellowing of the savage sea
Greeted their safe escape to me.
I wiped away the weeds and foam,   24
I fetched my sea-born treasures home;
But the poor, unsightly, noisome things
Had left their beauty on the shore
With the sun and the sand and the wild
    uproar.

The lover watched his graceful maid,
As 'mid the virgin train she strayed,   30
Nor knew her beauty's best attire
Was woven still by the snow-white
    choir.
At last she came to his hermitage,
Like the bird from the woodlands to
    the cage —
The gay enchantment was undone,   35
A gentle wife, but fairy none.

Then I said, " I covet truth;
Beauty is unripe childhood's cheat;
I leave it behind with the games of
    youth " —
As I spoke, beneath my feet   40
The ground pine curled its pretty
    wreath,
Running over the club-moss burrs;
I inhaled the violet's breath;
Around me stood the oaks and firs;
Pine cones and acorns lay on the
    ground;   45
Over me soared the eternal sky,
Full of light and of deity;
Again I saw, again I heard,
The rolling river, the morning bird —
Beauty through my senses stole;   50
I yielded myself to the perfect whole.

For Discussion of Emerson's Poems

1. For each poem write a good sentence or two to show the main point Emerson makes. In general, how do these poems differ from Poe's?

2. In "The Concord Hymn" what is meant by "the shot heard round the world"? What appeal is made in the last stanza? Why is *hymn* a suitable word to describe this poem?

3. Compare "The Concord Hymn" with Lincoln's "Gettysburg Address" (see p. 644). What similarities and differences were there in the occasions? in the appeals made at the end?

4. What evidence can you find in these poems that Emerson, as well as Bryant, was a lover of nature? Which two poems of this group discuss the meaning of beauty? Is there any difference in their treatment of this theme?

5. If you are collecting poems on flowers, compare the ideas that different flowers have suggested to different poets: the

rhodora to Emerson, the fringed gentian to Bryant, the daffodil to Wordsworth, the dandelion to Lowell, and so on.

6. As you observe your own life and that of others, do you find compensation such as Emerson describes? other kinds of compensation?

7. Why do you think Emerson admired a person who displayed the qualities found in "Forbearance"? Are these some of the qualities you would seek in a friend? If not, make your own list of qualities.

8. What does "Voluntaries III" show of Emerson's attitude toward youth? How was youth's response illustrated in World War II? What examples can you give of sacrifice of self to duty in time of peace?

9. What does "Each and All" say about the unconscious influence of one person on another, especially in lines 9 and 10? Point out examples of loss of charm through loss of environment or setting. Can you give examples from your own experience? How does this poem illustrate Emerson's belief in the Oversoul?

GIFTS

Emerson's essays reveal the main trends of his thought: his search for interpretations of life and his concern for moral problems. A swift glance at the titles will show this. "Friendship," "Love," "Self-Reliance," "Heroism," "Character," "Manners," "Compensation" — each treats of some quality of human life with a sincerity and wisdom that have won for their author a reputation as sage and prophet. In the essay "Gifts" Emerson tries to influence the reader to "high thinking" on the matter of giving and receiving gifts.

Most of Emerson's essays were originally composed as lectures, but more important for today's reader to understand is the fact that they were composed from his *Journals*. As a young man Emerson began the habit of jotting down his random reflections in journals, and over the years these many volumes became a treasure store of carefully worded ideas. When he wrote an essay, Emerson went to the journals and collected from them his many different expressions on the subject. The result is that Emerson's essays contain

striking, memorable sentences one after another, each highly polished in style and containing a thought in itself. It will help you in reading these essays if you will remember that Emerson's unit of thought is generally the sentence — not the paragraph, as with most writers. You should read slowly and think about each sentence.

> Gifts of one who loved me —
> 'Twas high time they came;
> When he ceased to love me,
> Time they stopped for shame.

IT is said that the world is in a state of bankruptcy, that the world owes the world more than the world can pay, and ought to go into chancery, and be sold. I do not think this general insolvency, which involves in some sort all the population, to be the reason of the difficulty experienced at Christmas and New Year, and other times, in bestowing gifts; since it is always so pleasant

The Minute Man overlooks the famed bridge at Concord. On his pedestal is carved the first stanza of Emerson's poem, "The Concord Hymn." (Devaney)

to be generous, though very vexatious to pay debts. But the impediment lies in the choosing. If, at any time, it comes into my head that a present is due from me to somebody, I am puzzled what to give, until the opportunity is gone. Flowers and fruits are always fit presents — flowers, because they are a proud assertion that a ray of beauty outvalues all the utilities of the world. These gay natures contrast with the somewhat stern countenance of ordinary nature; they are like music heard out of a workhouse. Nature does not cocker [1] us; we are children, not pets; she is not fond; [2] everything is dealt to us without fear or favor, after severe universal laws. Yet these delicate flowers look like the frolic and interference of love and beauty. Men used to tell us that we love flattery, even though we are not deceived by it, because it shows that we are of importance enough to be courted. Something like that pleasure, the flowers give us: what am I to whom these sweet hints are addressed? Fruits are acceptable gifts, because they are the flower of commodities, and admit of fantastic values being attached to them. If a man should send to me to come a hundred miles to visit him, and should set before me a basket of fine summer fruit, I should think there was some proportion between the labor and the reward.

For common gifts, necessity makes pertinences and beauty every day, and one is glad when an imperative leaves him no option, since if the man at the door has no shoes you have not to consider whether you could procure him a paintbox. And as it is always pleasing to see a man eat bread, drink water, in the house or out of doors, so it is always a great satisfaction to supply these first wants. Necessity does everything well. In our condition of universal dependence, it seems heroic to let the petitioner be the judge of his necessity, and to give all that is asked, though at great inconvenience. If it be a fantastic desire, it is better to leave to others the office of punishing him. I can think of many parts I should prefer playing to that of the Furies. [3]

Next to things of necessity, the rule for a gift, which one of my friends prescribed, is, that we might convey to some person that which properly belonged to his character, and was easily associated with him in thought. But our tokens of compliment and love are for the most part barbarous. Rings and other jewels are not gifts, but apologies for gifts. The only gift is a portion of thyself. Thou must bleed for me. Therefore the poet brings his poem; the shepherd, his lamb; the farmer, corn; the miner, a gem; the sailor, coral and shells; the painter, his picture; the girl, a handkerchief of her own sewing. This is right and pleasing, for it restores society in so far to its primary basis, when a man's biography is conveyed in his gift, and every man's wealth is an index of his merit. But it is a cold, lifeless business when you go to the shops to buy me something which does not represent your life and talent, but a goldsmith's. This is fit for kings, and rich men who represent kings, and a false state of property, to make presents of gold and silver stuffs, as a kind of symbolical sin-offering, or payment of blackmail.

The law of benefits is a difficult channel, which requires careful sailing, or rude boats. It is not the office of a man to receive gifts. How dare you give them? We wish to be self-sustained. We do not quite forgive a giver. The hand that feeds us is in some danger of being bitten. We can receive anything from love, for that is a way of receiving it from ourselves; but not from anyone who assumes to bestow. We sometimes hate the meat which we eat, because

---

[1] **cocker:** spoil, coddle.
[2] **fond:** foolishly tender.

[3] **Furies:** in Greek mythology, beings who punished the wicked.

there seems something of degrading dependence in living by it.

Brother, if Jove to thee a present make,
Take heed that from his hands thou nothing take.

We ask the whole. Nothing less will content us. We arraign society, if it do not give us, besides earth and fire and water, opportunity, love, reverence, and objects of veneration.

He is a good man who can receive a gift well. We are either glad or sorry at a gift, and both emotions are unbecoming. Some violence, I think, is done, some degradation borne, when I rejoice or grieve at a gift. I am sorry when my independence is invaded, or when a gift comes from such as do not know my spirit, and so the act is not supported; and if the gift pleases me overmuch, then I should be ashamed that the donor should read my heart, and see that I love his commodity and not him. The gift, to be true, must be the flowing of the giver unto me, correspondent to my flowing unto him. When the waters are at a level, then my goods pass to him, and his to me. All his are mine, all mine his. I say to him, "How can you give me this pot of oil, or this flagon of wine, when all your oil and wine is mine?" Which belief of mine this gift seems to deny. Hence the fitness of beautiful, not useful things for gifts. This giving is flat usurpation, and therefore when the beneficiary is ungrateful, as all beneficiaries hate all Timons,[1] not at all considering the value of the gift, but looking back to the greater store it was taken from, I rather sympathize with the beneficiary than with the anger of my lord Timon. For the expectation of gratitude is mean, and is continually punished by the total insensibility of the obliged person. It is a

[1] Timon, the leading character in Shakespeare's play *Timon of Athens*, spent his entire fortune on lavish gifts and was then spurned by those who had flattered him.

great happiness to get off without injury and heartburning from one who has had the ill luck to be served by you. It is a very onerous business, this of being served, and the debtor naturally wishes to give you a slap. A golden text for these gentlemen is that which I so admire in the Buddhist, who never thanks, and who says, " Do not flatter your benefactors."

The reason of these discords I conceive to be that there is no commensurability between a man and any gift. You cannot give anything to a magnanimous person. After you have served him, he at once puts you in debt by his magnanimity. The service a man renders his friend is trivial and selfish, compared with the service he knows his friend stood in readiness to yield him, alike before he had begun to serve his friend, and now also. Compared with that good will I bear my friend, the benefit it is in my power to render him seems small. Besides, our action on each other, good as well as evil, is so incidental and at random, that we can seldom hear the acknowledgments of any person who would thank us for a benefit without some shame and humiliation. We can rarely strike a direct stroke, but must be content with an oblique one; we seldom have the satisfaction of yielding a direct benefit, which is directly received. But rectitude scatters favors on every side without knowing it, and receives with wonder the thanks of all people.

I fear to breathe any treason against the majesty of love, which is the genius and god of gifts, and to whom we must not affect to prescribe. Let him give kingdoms or flower leaves indifferently. There are persons from whom we always expect fairy tokens; let us not cease to expect them. This is prerogative, and not to be limited by our municipal rules. For the rest, I like to see that we cannot be bought and sold. The best of hospitality and of generosity is also not in the will, but in fate. I find that I am not much to you; you do not need me; you do not feel me; then am I thrust out of doors, though you proffer me house and lands. No services are of any value, but only likeness. When I have attempted to join myself to others by services, it proved an intellectual trick — no more. They eat your service like apples, and leave you out. But love them, and they feel you, and delight in you all the time.

SELECTIONS FROM OTHER EMERSON ESSAYS

Since Emerson's essays are rather rambling in construction, one can gain from individual paragraphs an understanding of his point of view, and a vivid impression of the great thoughts which have stirred the minds of men and women for a century.

FROM " NATURE "

IT SEEMS as if the day was not wholly profane in which we have given heed to some natural object. The fall of snowflakes in a still air, preserving to each crystal its perfect form; the blowing of sleet over a wide sheet of water, and over plains; the waving rye field; the mimic waving of acres of houstonia,[1] whose innumerable florets whiten and ripple before the eye; the reflections of trees and flowers in glassy lakes; the musical steaming odorous south wind, which converts all trees to wind harps; the crackling and spurting of hemlock in the flames; or of pine logs, which yield glory to the walls and faces in the sitting room — these are the music and pictures of the most ancient religion. . . . We can find these enchantments without visiting the Como Lake, or the Madeira Islands. . . . In

every landscape, the point of astonishment is the meeting of the sky and the earth, and that is seen from the first hillock as well as from the top of the Alleghenies. The stars at night stoop down over the brownest, homeliest common with all the spiritual magnificence which they shed on the Campagna,[2] or on the marble deserts of Egypt. . . . The difference between landscape and landscape is small, but there is great difference in the beholders. . . . Nature cannot be surprised in undress. Beauty breaks in everywhere.

FROM " MANNERS "

THE gentleman is a man of truth, lord of his own actions, and expressing that lordship in his behavior, not in any manner dependent and servile either on persons, or opinions, or possessions. Beyond this fact of truth and real force, the word denotes good nature or benevolence; manhood first and then gentleness. The popular notion certainly adds a condition of ease and fortune; but that is a natural result of personal force and love, that they should possess and dispense the goods of the world. In times of violence every eminent person must fall in with many opportunities to approve [3] his stoutness and worth; therefore every man's name that emerged at all from the mass in the feudal ages, rattles in our ear like a flourish of trumpets. But personal force never goes out of fashion. That is still paramount today, and in the moving crowd of good society, the men of valor and reality are known, and rise to their natural place. The competition is transferred from war to politics and trade, but the personal force appears readily enough in these new arenas. . . . My gentleman gives the law where

---

[1] **houstonia** (hoos·tō′nĭ·à): a low, slender plant named for Dr. Houston, a naturalist.

[2] **Campagna** (käm·pä′nyä): the countryside surrounding Rome.

[3] **approve:** prove.

he is; he will outpray saints in chapel, outgeneral veterans in the field, and outshine all courtesy in the hall. He is good company for pirates, and good with academicians.

FROM "FRIENDSHIP"

A FRIEND is a person with whom I may be sincere. Before him I may think aloud. I am arrived at last in the presence of a man so real and equal that I may drop even those undermost garments of dissimulation, courtesy, and second thought, which men never put off, and may deal with him with the simplicity and wholeness with which one chemical atom meets another. Sincerity is the luxury allowed, like diadems and authority, only to the highest rank, *that* being permitted to speak truth, as having none above it to court or conform unto. Every man alone is sincere. At the entrance of a second person, hypocrisy begins. We parry and fend the approach of our fellow man by compliments, by gossip, by amusements, by affairs. We cover up our thought from him under a hundred folds. . . . Almost every man we meet requires some civility, requires to be humored — he has some fame, some talent, some whim of religion or philanthropy in his head that is not to be questioned, and which spoils all conversation with him. But a friend is a sane man who exercises not my ingenuity but me. My friend gives me entertainment without requiring me to stoop, or to lisp, or to mask myself. A friend therefore is a sort of paradox in nature. I who alone am, I who see nothing in nature whose existence I can affirm with equal evidence to my own, behold now the semblance of my being, in all its height, variety, and curiosity, reiterated in a foreign form; so that a friend may well be reckoned the masterpiece of nature.

FROM "COMPENSATION"

THE same dualism underlies the nature and condition of man. Every excess causes a defect; every defect an excess. Every sweet hath its sour; every evil its good. Every faculty which is a receiver of pleasure has an equal penalty for its abuse. It is to answer for its moderation with its life. For every grain of wit there is a grain of folly. For everything you have missed, you have gained something else; and for everything you gain, you lose something. If riches increase, they are increased that use them. If the gatherer gathers too much, nature takes out of the man what she puts into his chest; swells the estate, but kills the owner. Nature hates monopolies and exceptions. The waves of the sea do not more speedily seek a level from their loftiest tossing than the varieties of condition tend to equalize themselves. There is always some leveling circumstance that puts down the overbearing, the strong, the rich, the fortunate, substantially on the same ground with all others. . . .

The farmer imagines power and place are fine things. But the President has paid dear for his White House. It has commonly cost him all his peace, and the best of his manly attributes. To preserve for a short time so conspicuous an appearance before the world, he is content to eat dust before the real masters who stand erect behind the throne. Or do men desire the more substantial and permanent grandeur of genius? Neither has this an immunity. He who by force of will or of thought is great and overlooks thousands, has the responsibility of overlooking. With every influx of light comes new danger. Has he light? He must bear witness to the light, and always outrun that sympathy which gives him such keen satisfaction, by his fidelity to new revelations of the incessant soul.

FROM "SELF-RELIANCE"

THERE is a time in every man's education when he arrives at the conviction that envy is ignorance; that imitation is suicide; that he must take himself for better, for worse, as his portion; that though the wide universe is full of good, no kernel of nourishing corn can come to him but through his toil bestowed on that plot of ground which is given him to till. The power which resides in him is new in nature, and none but he knows what he can do, nor does he know until he has tried. Not for nothing one face, one character, one fact, makes much impression on him, and another none. This sculpture in the memory is not without pre-established harmony. The eye was placed where one ray should fall, that it might testify of that particular ray. We but half express ourselves and are ashamed of that divine idea which each of us represents. . . .

Society everywhere is in conspiracy against the manhood of every one of its members. Society is a joint-stock company, in which the members agree, for the better securing of his bread to each shareholder, to surrender the liberty and culture of the eater. The virtue in most request is conformity. Self-reliance is its aversion. It loves not realities and creators, but names and customs.

Whoso would be a man must be a nonconformist. He who would gather immortal palms must not be hindered by the name of goodness, but must explore if it be goodness. Nothing is at last sacred but the integrity of your own mind. Absolve you to yourself, and you shall have the suffrage of the world. . . .

What I must do is all that concerns me, not what the people think. This rule, equally arduous in actual, and in intellectual life, may serve for the whole distinction between greatness and meanness. It is the harder because you will always find those who think they know what is your duty better than you know it. It is easy in the world to live after the world's opinion; it is easy in solitude to live after our own; but the great man is he who in the midst of the crowd keeps with perfect sweetness the independence of solitude.

The civilized man has built a coach, but has lost the use of his feet. He is supported on crutches, but lacks so much support of muscle. He has got a fine Geneva watch, but he has lost the skill to tell the hour by the sun. A Greenwich nautical almanac he has, and so, being sure of the information when he wants it, the man in the street does not know a star in the sky. The solstice he does not observe; the equinox he knows as little; and the whole bright calendar of the year is without a dial in his mind.

FAMOUS QUOTATIONS
FROM EMERSON

Like Franklin, Emerson has contributed many wise sayings that have passed into our common stock of quotations. But the essential difference between the two men is easily seen when one rereads the sayings of Poor Richard on page 444, and then turns immediately to these which follow. Emerson supplies the qualities of idealism and high aspiration which were lacking in Franklin's plain common sense.

1. Hitch your wagon to a star.
— "Civilization"

2. 'Tis man's perdition to be safe, when for the truth he ought to die.
— "Sacrifice"

3. For what avail the plow or sail, Or land or life, if freedom fail?
— "Boston"

4. Nothing great was ever achieved without enthusiasm.
— "Circles"

5. The reward of a thing well done is to have done it.
— "New England Reformers"

6. The true test of a civilization is, not the census, nor the size of cities, nor the crops — no, but the kind of man the country turns out.   — "Civilization"

7. The ornament of a house is the friends who frequent it.
— "Domestic Life"

8. What you *are* stands over you the while, and thunders so that I cannot hear what you say to the contrary.
— "Social Aims"

9. Every man alone is sincere. At the entrance of a second party, hypocrisy begins.   — "Friendship"

10. Shallow men believe in luck.
— "Conduct of Life"

11. Great men are they who see that spiritual is stronger than any material force, that thoughts rule the world.
— "Progress of Culture"

12. [One of the most popular quotations attributed to Emerson is, oddly enough, not to be found among his printed writings in the form it commonly takes, but the *idea* behind it appears in his *Journals*.]

I trust a good deal to common fame as we all must. If a man has good corn, or wood, or boards, or pigs to sell, or can make better chairs or knives, crucibles or church organs than anybody else, you will find a broad, hard-beaten road to his house, though it be in the woods.

[And here it is in briefer form as you have probably heard it:]

If you write a better book, or preach a better sermon, or build a better mousetrap than your neighbor, the world will make a beaten track to your door.

For Discussion of Emerson's Essays

Gifts

1. Why does Emerson think that flowers and fruits are always fit presents? Does he approve of giving necessaries? jewelry? handkerchiefs? Under what circumstances do you think he would approve or disapprove of the following as gifts: a check, winter underwear, a gold bracelet, a photograph, an embroidered lunch cloth, a corsage bouquet, a book of poetry, a necktie?

2. What difficulties does he see in receiving gifts? In the light of this essay what criticisms can you make of some of our common practices in Christmas giving? Do you disagree with Emerson on any point? If so, what?

3. What is meant by "We do not quite forgive a giver"?

Selections from Other Essays

1. How many ideas expressed in Emerson's poems are echoed in his essays?

2. Name two or three persons prominent in public life today who you think could be called gentlemen according to Emerson's definition. Name two or three who could not. Defend your answers.

3. What difference is there between a friend as Emerson defines one and a friend in the common use of the word — an acquaintance? Do you think that most school friendships stand the test of Emerson's definition?

4. Would you agree with Emerson that there are *always* compensations in life? Give illustrations to prove your point.

5. By what kind of people is Emerson's message of self-reliance most needed? Do you feel that it is needed in your high school? Is it needed generally in the country today? Support your points by examples.

6. What dangers would there be to society if Emerson's words on self-reliance were taken too literally? From what you know of Emerson do you think he is approving lawbreaking? Why or why not?

7. Compare the selections from "Self-Reliance" with the poem "Each and All." Do they conflict in their main points?

8. In "Self-Reliance" Emerson reveals his attitude toward timesaving and laborsaving devices. Is there any merit in his idea? What effect would adoption of his

attitude have on material progress and improvement?

9. Discuss the meanings of the famous quotations, and whether or not you think they are borne out in your experience. What single sentences do you find in any of the paragraphs from his essays which might be added to the list of famous quotations? From the entire group memorize those you think particularly valuable.

10. Write a short contrast between Franklin and Emerson illustrating their differences in point of view as shown in the quotations from each writer.

11. Consider, not necessarily for class discussion but in your own mind, ways in which any of Emerson's ideas might enter into your own attitudes or actions.

12. If you have found the paragraphs from the essays challenging, try reading the essays in their complete form. Others which might interest you are " Experience," " Character," " Politics," " Heroism," " Love," " The American Scholar." If you find the essays too difficult, you might enjoy *The Heart of Emerson's Journals*, where you will find bits of his philosophy interspersed with the daily happenings of his life.

For Your Vocabulary

BASE-WORDS: This is a good time to review the word part *bene-* meaning " good." Emerson uses three words built on it — *benign*, good in the sense of " kindly " and " gracious " (p. 556); *beneficiary*, the one who *benefits* (p. 561); and *benevolence*, the quality of wishing others good fortune (p. 562). A *benevolent* person may take action as a *benefactor* to make the good come to pass. There are parallel words with the base-word *male-* which means " evil." With this preparation, try to define *malevolence* and *malediction*. (Do you know exactly what a *benediction* is?) How would a *malign* person differ from a *malefactor?*

CONTEXT: Check *insolvency* in context (p. 558). The preceding sentence states the idea clearly. The *in-* here means " not." What is a *solvent* business firm?

Henry David Thoreau

1817–1862

FROM WALDEN

REFLECTIONS

Man's struggle to get possession of things to make life easier and pleasanter is as old as the human race. The struggle to keep *things* from swamping him is almost as old. Many great writers down through the ages have warned us that the surest way to have an empty life is to fill it with *things.* When you are young and still want many things, this warning is not so impressive. It is only when the edge is worn off the delight of possession and the possessions take up more and more of your time and attention that you begin to see the charms of the simple life.

Walden is one of the greatest accounts in literature of an experiment with the simple life. It was only an experiment. Thoreau was no hermit. He learned what he wanted to know — what is real living? — and went back to his usual village life, wiser and happier.

What Thoreau enthusiasts cherish most

A small stretch of shoreline at Walden Pond as it looks today. (Charles Phelps Cushing)

is not whole passages of description and narrative but brilliant short statements that catch and hold a truth as if in the beam of a spotlight. Here are some of them. If you think them through, you may achieve the happy compromise and never be hedged in by your material possessions, but enjoy the simpler pleasures of life. Or, fifteen or twenty years from now, when you find things closing in on you until you cannot tell whether you are living at all, some short observation of Thoreau's can work like a charm to bring balance and sanity back into your life. That is why Thoreau has grown steadily in popularity as life has grown more complex.

M̲ost of the luxuries, and many of the so-called comforts of life are not only not indispensable, but positive hindrances to the elevation of mankind.

Every morning was a cheerful invitation to make my life of equal simplicity, and I may say innocence, with Nature herself. I have been as sincere a worshiper of Aurora [1] as the Greeks. I got up early and bathed in the pond; that was a religious exercise, and one of the best things which I did.

To him whose elastic and vigorous thought keeps pace with the sun, the day is a perpetual morning. It matters not what the clocks say or the attitudes and labors of men. Morning is when I am awake and there is a dawn in me. Moral reform is the effort to throw off sleep. Why is it that men give so poor an account of their day if they have not been slumbering? They are not such poor calculators. If they had not been overcome with drowsiness, they would have performed something. The millions are awake enough for physical labor; but only one in a million is awake enough for effective intellectual exertion, only one in a hundred millions to

---

[1] Aurora: the goddess of morning; the personification of dawn.

---

a poetic or divine life. To be awake is to be alive. I have never yet met a man who was quite awake. How could I have looked him in the face?

I went to the woods because I wished to live deliberately, to front only the essential facts of life, and see if I could not learn what it had to teach, and not, when I came to die, discover that I had not lived. I did not wish to live what was not life, living is so dear; nor did I wish to practice resignation, unless it was quite necessary. I wanted to live deep and suck out all the marrow of life, to live so sturdily and Spartanlike as to put to rout all that was not life, to cut a broad swath and shave close, to drive life into a corner and reduce it to its lowest terms, and, if it proved to be mean, why then to get the whole and genuine meanness of it and publish its meanness to the world; or, if it were sublime, to know it by experience and be able to give a true account of it in my next excursion.

Still we live meanly, like ants; though the fable tells us that we were long ago changed into men; like pygmies we fight with cranes; it is error upon error, and clout upon clout, and our best virtue has for its occasion a superfluous and evitable wretchedness. Our life is frittered away by detail.

Simplify, simplify. Instead of three meals a day, if it be necessary eat but one; instead of a hundred dishes, five; and reduce other things in proportion.

Why should we live with such hurry and waste of life? We are determined to be starved before we are hungry. Men say that a stitch in time saves nine, and so they take a thousand stitches today to save nine tomorrow. As for *work*, we haven't any of any consequence. We have the Saint Vitus's dance, and cannot possibly keep our heads still.

When we are unhurried and wise, we perceive that only great and worthy things have any permanent and absolute existence, that petty fears and petty pleasures are but the shadow of the reality. This is always exhilarating and sublime.

Let us spend one day as deliberately as Nature, and not be thrown off the track by every nutshell and mosquito's wing that falls on the rails. Let us rise early and fast, or break fast, gently and without perturbation; let company come and let company go, let the bells ring and the children cry — determined to make a day of it.

Time is but the stream I go a-fishing in. I drink at it; but while I drink I see the sandy bottom and detect how shallow it is. Its thin current slides away, but eternity remains.

If the day and the night are such that you greet them with joy, and life emits a fragrance like flowers and sweet-scented herbs, is more elastic, more starry, more immortal — that is your success.

THE BATTLE OF THE ANTS

With both time and desire to observe nature in all her forms, Thoreau made good use of his life in the woods to watch and record the animal life about him. Together with Audubon, the student of birds, he was the first of a large group of American nature writers. Not quite a scientific naturalist like many of his successors, Thoreau enlivened his accounts with bits of philosophy and humor. One of the best-known parts of *Walden* is this vividly told battle of the ants.

I T IS remarkable how many creatures live wild and free though secret in the woods, and still sustain themselves in the neighborhood of towns, suspected by hunters only. How retired the otter manages to live here! He grows to be four feet long, as big as a small boy, perhaps without any human being getting a glimpse of him. I formerly saw the raccoon in the woods behind where my house is built, and probably still heard their whinnering at night. Commonly I rested an hour or two in the shade at noon, after planting, and ate my lunch, and read a little by a spring which was the source of a swamp and of a brook, oozing from under Brister's Hill, half a mile from my field. The approach to this was through a succession of descending grassy hollows, full of young pitch pines, into a larger wood about the swamp. There, in a very secluded and shaded spot, under a spreading white pine, there was yet a clean, firm sward to sit on. I had dug out the spring and made a well of clear gray water, where I could dip up a pailful without roiling it, and thither I went for this purpose almost every day in midsummer, when the pond was warmest. Thither, too, the woodcock led her brood, to probe the mud for worms, flying but a foot above them down the bank, while they ran in a troop beneath; but at last, spying me, she would leave her young and circle round and round me, nearer and nearer till within four or five feet, pretending broken wings and legs, to attract my attention, and get off her young, who would already have taken up their march, with faint, wiry peep, single file through the swamp, as she directed. Or I heard the peep of the young when I could not see the parent bird. There too the turtledoves sat over the spring, or fluttered from bough to bough of the soft white pines over my head; or the red squirrel, coursing down the nearest bough, was particularly familiar and inquisitive. You only need sit still long enough in some attractive spot in the woods that all its inhabitants may exhibit themselves to you by turns.

I was witness to events of a less peaceful character. One day when I went out to my woodpile, or rather my pile of stumps, I observed two large ants, the one red, the other much larger, nearly half an inch long, and black, fiercely contending with one another. Having once got hold they never let go, but struggled and wrestled and rolled on the chips incessantly. Looking farther, I was surprised to find that the chips were covered with such combatants, that it was not a *duellum* [1] but a *bellum*,[2] a war between two races of ants, the red always pitted against the black, and frequently two red ones to one black. The legions of these Myrmidons [3] covered all the hills and vales in my woodyard, and the ground was already strewn with the dead and dying, both red and black. It was the only battle which I have ever witnessed, the only battlefield I ever trod while the battle was raging; internecine war; the red republicans on the one hand, and the black imperialists on the other. On every side they were engaged in deadly combat, yet without any noise that I could hear, and human soldiers never fought so resolutely. I watched a couple that were fast locked in each other's embraces in a little sunny valley amid the chips, now at noonday prepared to fight till the sun went down, or life went out. The smaller red champion had fastened himself like a vise to his adversary's front, and through all the tumblings on that field never for an instant ceased to gnaw at one of his feelers near the root, having already caused the other to go by the board; while the stronger black one dashed him from side to side, and, as I saw on looking nearer, had already divested him of several of his members. They fought with more pertinacity than bulldogs. Neither mani-

fested the least disposition to retreat. It was evident that their battle cry was "Conquer or die." In the meanwhile there came along a single red ant on the hillside of this valley, evidently full of excitement, who either had dispatched his foe, or had not yet taken part in the battle; probably the latter, for he had lost none of his limbs; whose mother had charged him to return with his shield or upon it. Or perchance he was some Achilles,[4] who had nourished his wrath apart, and had now come to avenge or rescue his Patroclus. He saw this unequal combat from afar — for the blacks were nearly twice the size of the red — he drew near with rapid pace till he stood on his guard within half an inch of the combatants; then, watching his opportunity, he sprang upon the black warrior, and commenced his operations near the root of his right foreleg, leaving the foe to select among his own members; and so there were three united for life, as if a new kind of attraction had been invented which put all other locks and cements to shame. I should not have wondered by this time to find that they had their respective musical bands stationed on some eminent chip, and playing their national airs the while, to excite the slow and cheer the dying combatants. I was myself excited somewhat even as if they had been men. The more you think of it, the less the difference. And certainly there is not the fight recorded in Concord history, at least, if in the history of America, that will bear a moment's comparison with this, whether for the numbers engaged in it, or for the patriotism and heroism displayed. . . .

I took up the chip on which the three I have particularly described were struggling, carried it into my house, and

---

[1] *duellum*: duel.

[2] *bellum*: war.

[3] **Myrmidons**: followers of Achilles in the Trojan War. The word originally meant "ant-men."

[4] **Achilles**: Greek hero, represented in the *Iliad* as sulking in his tent over a hurt to his pride; but when his best friend, Patroclus, is killed, he forgets his wrath and re-enters the battle in his desire for vengeance.

placed it under a tumbler on my window sill, in order to see the issue. Holding a microscope to the first-mentioned red ant, I saw that, though he was assiduously gnawing at the near foreleg of his enemy, having severed his remaining feeler, his own breast was all torn away, exposing what vitals he had there to the jaws of the black warrior, whose breastplate was apparently too thick for him to pierce; and the dark carbuncles of the sufferer's eyes shone with ferocity such as war only could excite. They struggled half an hour longer under the tumbler, and when I looked again the black soldier had severed the heads of his foes from their bodies, and the still living heads were hanging on either side of him like ghastly trophies at his saddlebow, still apparently as firmly fastened as ever, and he was endeavoring with feeble struggles, being without feelers and with only the remnant of a leg, and I know not how many other wounds, to divest himself of them; which at length, after half an hour more, he accomplished. I raised the glass, and he went off over the window sill in that crippled state. Whether he finally survived that combat, and spent the remainder of his days in some Hôtel des Invalides,[1] I do not know; but I thought that his industry would not be worth much thereafter. I never learned which party was victorious, nor the cause of the war; but I felt for the rest of that day as if I had had my feelings excited and harrowed by witnessing the struggle, the ferocity and carnage, of a human battle before my door.

Kirby and Spence[2] tell us that the battles of ants have long been celebrated and the dates of them recorded, though they say that Huber is the only modern author who appears to have witnessed them. "Aeneas Silvius," they say, "after giving a very circumstantial account of one contested with great obstinacy by a great and small species on the trunk of a pear tree, adds that 'this action was fought in the pontificate of Eugenius the Fourth, in the presence of Nicholas Pistoriensis, an eminent lawyer, who related the whole history of the battle with the greatest fidelity.' A similar engagement between great and small ants is recorded by Olaus Magnus, in which the small ones, being victorious, are said to have buried the bodies of their own soldiers, but left those of their giant enemies a prey to the birds. This even happened previous to the expulsion of the tyrant Christiern the Second from Sweden." The battle which I witnessed took place in the Presidency of Polk, five years before the passage of Webster's Fugitive Slave Bill. . . .

For Discussion of Thoreau

Reflections

1. Why did Thoreau go to the woods to live? Find the paragraph where he explains his purpose clearly. Pick out the statement that you think gives the best reason for his experiment.

2. What are some of Thoreau's objections to the way most people live? What reason does he usually give for his objections? Which objections do you agree with? disagree with? Examine the personal reasons that lead you to disagree. Can you imagine reaching a stage in life when you would agree with him on the same points? Think of your own favorite ways of passing time away. Which ones simply pass the time? Which ones involve growth in understanding and enjoyment of life?

3. For a clever description of the changed appearance of Walden today, see E. B. White's essay "Walden" in One Man's Meat. Also, compare Thoreau's ideas on things with the famous Wordsworth sonnet "The World Is Too Much with Us."

[1] **Hôtel des Invalides:** famous veterans' hospital in Paris.

[2] **Kirby and Spence:** English naturalists of the early nineteenth century. Huber was a Swiss naturalist of the same time. Aeneas Silvius Piccolomini (1405–1464) became Pope Pius II in 1458.

The Battle of the Ants

1. Make a list of all the different living creatures that Thoreau has observed as indicated in this selection. Do his observations seem to you wide or limited? accurate or faulty?

2. How does the author make the ants seem human? How does he show his familiarity with history? with writings on natural science?

3. When Thoreau records so exactly the time of his observation of the battle of the ants, do you think he is being serious or facetious?

> ## Longfellow and Lowell

The Flowering of New England: Boston

"How do you endure this constant praise of Boston?" a New Yorker once asked a prominent Bostonian around 1850. The Bostonian answered, "We suspect it is true."

Maybe it was. Boston was what the historians call the "culture town" of the Eastern Flowering. It was the source of ideas, the gathering place of thinkers and writers. Include with Boston its suburban Cambridge and its close neighbor Concord, and you have a center which for high thinking and good writing has never yet been equaled in America.

Boston was a flourishing business center gathered around the harbor and the Hill. Clippers from all over the world came into the harbor, and the countinghouses and stores stood on narrow, twisting streets around the harbor. On the Hill stood the gold-domed statehouse as a symbol of the ordered freedom for which Massachusetts Bay had always stood. Cambridge was a few miles away across the Charles River — a little country town with graceful homes and Harvard College. Concord was but twenty miles away on the Boston turnpike.

The Literary Hub of the East

Where else in America was so much being written? Visitors who came to Boston and the towns around it wrote back home that everyone seemed to be writing a book! Any day a Boston publisher might put in his sales window Emerson's new essay, Longfellow's new volume of poetry, Francis Parkman's new history. Any day a new magazine like the *Atlantic Monthly* (founded in Boston in 1857) might appear. Every few weeks a remarkable club met in Boston. Some of its members were Emerson, the philosopher; the poets Lowell, Longfellow, and Whittier; the historians Prescott and Motley; the novelist Hawthorne; the humorist Holmes; and many others including the best-known critics and scientists of that time in America. All its members were from the three towns that formed the literary hub of the East.

The Spring, Summer, and Autumn of New England's Flowering

Culture towns, the historians tell us, go through seasons like the earth. Boston had its springtime, in the 1840's, when everything was new and fresh and vigorous. It had a summer, in the 1850's, when the town was most productive and sure of itself. It had an autumn, after the War between the States, when some of the early vigor was gone and new ideas were more likely to come from New York or the West.

Boston no longer occupies such a commanding position in American literature as it did. Other great centers have arisen. But when you think of Boston today and of the tourists who go there to see *old* Boston — Bunker Hill and Faneuil Hall and the Old North Church and Paul Revere's shop — remember that in the years between 1840 and 1880 people were going there to see *new* Boston, the *new* books, the *newest* things in American thought, the newest and most popular writers.

Henry Wadsworth Longfellow

It was Longfellow who finally answered the question, "Who reads an American book?" His books sold in the millions during his lifetime. Every school child who knew English knew some of Professor Longfellow's poetry. In Europe, Poe was more highly praised and imitated, but Longfellow was more read. No other American poet has been so much translated as he.

A Youthful Success and a Long, Honored Life

He was a Portland, Maine, boy, a Bowdoin graduate and a classmate of Hawthorne's. On commencement day he had a singular piece of good luck. His college gave him a six hundred dollar fellowship, told him to go to Europe and prepare himself to teach modern languages. That was the first of a number of trips abroad, and it was the first step in his path toward the distinguished Harvard professorship of modern languages, to which he succeeded in 1836, at the phenomenal age of twenty-nine.

He was a good teacher. For eighteen years he made the great books of Europe live for Harvard undergraduates. Then he resigned his professorship to have more time for the musical and pol-

ished poetry which the whole world was beginning to read.

He had two great personal sorrows, when his first wife died suddenly, and when his second wife was burned to death. Travel in Europe was probably the greatest thing that happened to him. He went there frequently and he read its literature always. He lived in beautiful Craigie House in Cambridge, which had been Washington's headquarters during part of the Revo-

lution. He lived quietly and serenely, surrounded by literary friends, and by the most literate community he could have found to live in. As a man and as a poet he was widely beloved and honored, and his death at seventy-five was mourned by both the Old World and the New.

Longfellow's Poetry: Abundance and Variety

Longfellow left a great deal of poetry, probably more than any other American. Only a small portion of it is top-notch; not all of it is considered as good today as his admirers in his own time said it was. Poetic reputations have a way of going by extremes. In Longfellow's time he was extravagantly praised; after he died, his reputation snapped back like a rubber band, and it became fashionable to be scornful about his poems. Now we are beginning to reach an equilibrium, and we can see that he wrote some very fine poetry indeed, and that he left a number of poems which will be in our poetic heritage for as long as we can foresee.

How can one describe Longfellow's poetry? It was, for one thing, always perfectly smoothed and finished and joined, in the same artful way a statue is worked over by a fine sculptor. It was musical and melodious. It had a twilight shade, a mood of melancholy, wistfulness, a longing toward the past. It was poetry of peace and serenity, rather than of war and change. It was poetry which sometimes echoed European writers, and could only have been written by a man who had read widely and well.

But perhaps the best way to describe it is to remind ourselves of some of the poems he left:

Poems of the simple life and homely ethics — "The Village Blacksmith," "A Psalm of Life," "Excelsior," "The Arrow and the Song," and "The Children's Hour."

Melodious lyrics — "Hymn to the Night," "The Day Is Done," and "My Lost Youth."

Thoughtful and challenging poems — "The Arsenal at Springfield," "The Jewish Cemetery at Newport," "Morituri Salutamus," "The Building of the Ship," and some vigorous antislavery poems.

Historical tales and ballads — "Paul Revere's Ride," "The Wreck of the Hesperus," and Tales of a Wayside Inn.

Some of the best poetic translations ever made, like the Divine Comedy, which he translated from Dante's Italian.

Some of the finest sea poetry ever written in America, of which "The Tide Rises, the Tide Falls" is an example.

A number of fine sonnets, like the one in this book.

Some of the best long narrative poetry written by an American — The Song of Hiawatha, his free rendering of Indian legends and history in literary epic form; Evangeline, the story of the Acadians told in epic verse; and The Courtship of Miles Standish, a chapter out of New England history which he retold with insight and loving care.

Longfellow was born (1807) in the same year as Whittier, and died (1882) in the same year as Emerson. When he was born, the exciting new invention was the steam engine. When he died, the exciting new development was the use of electricity.

James Russell Lowell

Lowell succeeded Longfellow as professor of modern languages at Harvard. He lived all his life in Cambridge near Longfellow's Craigie House, in the beautiful ancestral home of the Lowells, called Elmwood. He traveled widely and was as well read as Longfellow in French, Spanish, German, and Italian literature. His library was quite as well lined as Longfellow's.

A Man of Civic Conscience and Many Interests

But if you try to describe Lowell in terms of book-lined studies and college professorships, you will go far astray. For he was a man of public affairs with a civic conscience.

He described himself with uncanny insight in A Fable for Critics:

There is Lowell, who's striving Parnassus to climb
With a whole bale of isms tied together with rhyme . . .
The top of the hill he will ne'er come nigh reaching
Till he learns the distinction 'twixt singing and preaching.

The truth is, he simply had too many interests to give the kind of attention to poetry that Longfellow gave. There is an interesting thing about the three poems of his which you will read in this book; they were all published in book form in the same year, 1848, when Lowell was not quite thirty. It was not until the sixties that he again challenged people with his poetry on the War between the States, culminating with the noble " Ode Recited at the Commemoration of the Living and Dead Soldiers of Harvard University."

Lowell as Social and Literary Critic

While Longfellow was singing himself into the hearts of people, Lowell was addressing himself to their minds on a series of public questions: abolition, temperance, woman suffrage, the Mexican War, the War between the States. He wrote about politics and foreign affairs, and was his country's representative at the courts of Spain and England. In fact, he was not chiefly a poet at all. As Longfellow was the poet of the Boston flowering, so Lowell was the critic.

As social critic, Lowell wrote with a robust humor, a homely common sense that reminded people of Franklin. People read *The Biglow Papers* — the alleged work of a shrewd, little-schooled New England farmer named Hosea Biglow — in somewhat the same spirit as they had read *Poor Richard*. And under this literary mask, Lowell managed to communicate a lot of homespun wisdom about what the government was and was not doing.

As literary critic, he wrote on many of the great writers of the world. His criticism was suave, urbane, based on wide reading. It gave the impression that Lowell was trying to arbitrate among the previous critics, trying to find the middle road, trying to show his readers a safe, well-rounded viewpoint. Even his sparkling *A Fable for Critics* has this viewpoint. As a critic, Poe was more brilliant, more erratic, more original; Lowell was safer, more balanced. Poe was more penetrating; Lowell, broader.

Lowell as Editor and Friend of Writers

Lowell became the first editor of the *Atlantic Monthly,* founded in 1857, in the midsummer of literary New England. It carried the finest fruits of the literary flowering. Perhaps no magazine attracted more distinguished contributors in its first years — Emerson, Thoreau, Holmes, Lowell, Longfellow, Parkman, and all the rest of that Boston-Concord-Cambridge group. Later Lowell became editor of the *North American Review,* and his service to American writers in these two editorships was great.

Perhaps Lowell scattered his energies too much. Perhaps he could never decide — as he suggested in *A Fable for Critics* — whether to be a poet or a reformer. But he was a good citizen and a good writer, and one of the best informed and most versatile members of the whole remarkable New England group.

Lowell was born (1819) two years later than Thoreau, four years before Parkman. He died (1891) two years before Parkman, twenty-nine years after Thoreau. The frontier was between the Alleghenies and the Mississippi when he was born. When he died there was no longer any open frontier in the United States.

Henry Wadsworth Longfellow
1807–1882

HYMN TO THE NIGHT

Although Longfellow is best known and perhaps best loved for his simple poems in simple patterns, he was also master of more elaborate verse forms and of a stately manner for solemn subjects. This poem, first published in *Voices of the Night* four years after the death of the poet's first wife, displays both qualities.

'Ασπασίη, τρίλλιστος *

I heard the trailing garments of the Night
　Sweep through her marble halls!
I saw her sable skirts all fringed with light
　From the celestial walls!

I felt her presence, by its spell of might,
　Stoop o'er me from above;　　　　6
The calm, majestic presence of the Night,
　As of the one I love.

I heard the sounds of sorrow and delight,
　The manifold, soft chimes,　　　10
That fill the haunted chambers of the Night,
　Like some old poet's rhymes.

From the cool cisterns of the midnight air
　My spirit drank repose; rest recline

* 'Ασπασίη, τρίλλιστος (ăs′pȧ·zē′ȧ, trĭl′ĭs·tŏs): "Welcome, thrice prayed for . . ." *Iliad*, Book viii.

The fountain of perpetual peace flows there —　　　　　　　　15
　From those deep cisterns flows.

O holy Night; from thee I learn to bear
　What man has borne before!
Thou layest thy finger on the lips of Care,
　And they complain no more.　　20

Peace! Peace! Orestes-like° I breathe this prayer!
　Descend with broad-winged flight,
The welcome, the thrice-prayed for, the most fair,
　The best-beloved Night!

21. Orestes-like: Orestes (ȯ·rĕs′tēz) was a youth in Greek literature who prayed to Athena for peace from the pursuit of the Furies.

THE TIDE RISES, THE TIDE FALLS

From boyhood Longfellow loved the sea. In this poem you will feel the long swing of the tides and hear the wash of waves. Part of the fascination of the sea is its mystery, and appropriately Longfellow weaves into the poem the shadowy outlines of a story that leave questions in your mind.

The tide rises, the tide falls,
The twilight darkens, the curlew calls;
Along the sea sands damp and brown
The traveler hastens toward the town,
　And the tide rises, the tide falls.　　5

Darkness settles on roofs and walls,
But the sea, the sea in the darkness calls;
The little waves, with their soft white hands,
Efface the footprints in the sands,
    And the tide rises, the tide falls. 10

The morning breaks; the steeds in their stalls
Stamp and neigh as the hostler calls;
The day returns, but nevermore
Returns the traveler to the shore,
    And the tide rises, the tide falls. 15

THE ARSENAL AT SPRINGFIELD

This impressive plea for peace was written long before the War between the States. It still has a real message for the modern world.

This is the Arsenal.° From the floor to ceiling,
    Like a huge organ, rise the burnished arms;
But from their silent pipes no anthem pealing
    Startles the villages with strange alarms.

Ah! what a sound will rise, how wild and dreary,   5
    When the death angel touches those swift keys!
What loud lament and dismal Miserere°
    Will mingle with their awful symphonies!

I hear even now the infinite fierce chorus,
    The cries of agony, the endless groan,   10
Which, through the ages that have gone before us,
    In long reverberations reach our own.

On helm and harness rings the Saxon hammer,
    Through Cimbric° forest roars the Norseman's song,
And loud, amid the universal clamor,   15
    O'er distant deserts sounds the Tatar° gong.

I hear the Florentine,° who from his palace
    Wheels out his battle bell with dreadful din,
And Aztec° priests upon their teocallis°
    Beat the wild war drums made of serpent's skin;   20

The tumult of each sacked and burning village;
    The shout that every prayer for mercy drowns;
The soldiers' revels in the midst of pillage;
    The wail of famine in beleaguered towns;

The bursting shell, the gateway wrenched asunder,   25
    The rattling musketry, the clashing blade;

1. **Arsenal** (är′sĕ·năl): a building where weapons are stored. This one is in Springfield, Massachusetts. 7. **Miserere** (mĭz′ĕ·rē′rĕ): the first word in the Latin version of the Psalm beginning "Have mercy upon me, O Lord!" 14. **Cimbric** (sĭm′brĭk): referring to the Cimbri, a tribe of Norsemen destroyed by the Romans. 16. **Tatar** (tä′tĕr): The Tatars, a race of savage Orientals, swept over Asia and most of Europe in the thirteenth century. 17. **Florentine** (flŏr′ĕn·tēn): The soldiers of Florence, Italy, in medieval times actually wheeled a great bell out into the battlefield. 19. **Aztec**: a native race of Mexicans, found and later practically exterminated by the Spaniards. **teocallis** (tē′ō·kăl′ĭz): flat-topped pyramids of worship.

And ever and anon, in tones of thunder,
  The diapason of the cannonade.

Is it, O man, with such discordant noises,
  With such accursèd instruments as these,   30
Thou drownest Nature's sweet and kindly voices,
  And jarrest the celestial harmonies?

Were half the power that fills the world with terror,
  Were half the wealth bestowed on camps and courts,
Given to redeem the human mind from error,   35
  There were no need of arsenals nor forts:

The warrior's name would be a name abhorrèd!
  And every nation, that should lift again
Its hand against a brother, on its forehead
  Would wear forevermore the curse of Cain!°   40

Down the dark future, through long generations,
  The echoing sounds grow fainter and then cease;
And like a bell, with solemn, sweet vibrations,
  I hear once more the voice of Christ say, " Peace! "

Peace! and no longer from its brazen portals   45
  The blast of War's great organ shakes the skies!
But beautiful as songs of the immortals,
  The holy melodies of love arise.

40. **Cain:** a son of Adam and Eve who was cursed because he slew his brother Abel (Gen. 4).

THE SHIP OF STATE

The closing lines of " The Building of the Ship " have become part of the body of America's patriotic literature. In this long poem the author describes the careful building of a great sailing vessel, which is to be named the *Union* because on the day of its completion the old master builder will give his daughter in marriage to the young craftsman. In the conclusion of the poem, which is given here, the poet addresses the country itself as the Ship of State. In 1849, when the poem was published, the Union of States had already been threatened by dissension between the North and the South. There is still significance for the present generation in this solemn dedication to the Union.

Thou, too, sail on, O Ship of State!
Sail on, O *Union*, strong and great!
Humanity with all its fears,
With all the hopes of future years,
Is hanging breathless on thy fate!   5
We know what Master laid thy keel,
What Workmen wrought thy ribs of steel,
Who made each mast, and sail, and rope,
What anvils rang, what hammers beat,
In what a forge, and what a heat   10
Were shaped the anchors of thy hope!
Fear not each sudden sound and shock,
'Tis of the wave and not the rock;
'Tis but the flapping of the sail,
And not a rent made by the gale!   15
In spite of rock and tempest's roar,
In spite of false lights on the shore,
Sail on, nor fear to breast the sea!
Our hearts, our hopes, are all with thee,
Our hearts, our hopes, our prayers, our tears,   20
Our faith triumphant o'er our fears,
Are all with thee — are all with thee!

DIVINA COMMEDIA I

Longfellow was the first of several American poets to excel in writing sonnets. The one that follows was the poet's introduction to his translation of the great Italian epic, Dante's *Divine Comedy*. He had undertaken this monumental task as a refuge from his grief over the tragic death of his second wife. The sonnet form has fourteen lines and in one type of sonnet there is a distinct division of thought between the first eight lines and the last six. In this sonnet watch for the division between the two parts, and notice that the picture presented in the first part is carried over as a figure of speech in the second.

Oft have I seen at some cathedral door
  A laborer, pausing in the dust and heat,
  Lay down his burden, and with reverent feet
  Enter, and cross himself, and on the floor
Kneel to repeat his paternoster° o'er; 5
  Far off the noises of the world retreat;
  The loud vociferations of the street
  Become an undistinguishable roar.
So, as I enter here from day to day,
  And leave my burden at this minster° gate   10
  Kneeling in prayer, and not ashamed to pray,
The tumult of the time disconsolate,
  To inarticulate murmurs dies away,
  While the eternal ages watch and wait.

5. **paternoster** (pä'tĕr·nŏs'tĕr): the Lord's Prayer. 10. **minster:** church. Here used figuratively for Dante's *Divine Comedy*.

For Discussion of Longfellow

1. Point out words or lines in " Hymn to the Night " which refer to the poet's recent bereavement; others which have a soothing effect upon the spirit; others which show his knowledge of ancient literature.

2. What picture of the sea is suggested by the rhythm of the opening lines of " The Tide Rises, the Tide Falls " and by the refrain? Describe the mood of the poem. How do you interpret the references to the erased footprints and the traveler who returns no more?

3. In " The Arsenal at Springfield " show how an impression of sound or music is carried throughout the poem. In what two ways is the organ a fitting instrument with which to compare the arsenal? What different ages and parts of the world are brought into the survey of war sounds? How does this review of other times, other places strengthen Longfellow's point? What great plea does he make for peace?

4. Write an additional stanza to this poem to follow line 28, describing modern aerial warfare. Sum up the various attempts to establish world peace since Longfellow's day. What is the outlook at present?

5. In " The Ship of State " explain what you think is meant by the Master and the Workmen. Give some examples from American history of what the poet might have had in mind to represent the anvils, hammers, forge, and so on. What events just prior to 1849, when the poem was published, might have been referred to in " sudden sound and shock," " rock and tempest's roar," " false lights on the shore "?

6. This entire passage is a fine example of *analogy*. Explain the meaning of this word by specific reference to the passage. Compare the dedication at the end with that at the conclusion of Lincoln's Gettysburg Address (p. 644). The entire stanza deserves memorization.

7. Summarize the thought of " Divina Commedia I " in two sentences, one for the octave (first eight lines) and one for the sestet (last six lines). Find two phrases that hint at the sorrow in the poet's life. In what ways do you suppose the effort of translation helped Longfellow forget this sorrow more than reading alone would have done?

8. Review requirements for the form of the sonnet on page 262. Is Longfellow's a perfect sonnet? Why is the sonnet pattern a greater challenge to a poet than that of a long narrative poem?

James Russell Lowell
1819–1891

THE COURTIN'

Lowell was one of the first American poets to write successfully in dialect. He created Hosea Biglow, an illiterate but shrewd New England farmer, to give vent to his feelings on the Mexican War situation in 1848. *The Biglow Papers* have immortalized the Yankee twang. To add to the humor, the papers were supposed to have been edited by a minister, Homer Wilbur, Esq., in whose elaborate footnotes Lowell satirized pedantic learning. A second series of *The Biglow Papers* during the War between the States expressed in homely fashion the ideas of New Englanders concerning the progress of the war. Many parts of *The Biglow Papers* are crowded with references unintelligible to readers of today, but some of the verses will continue to delight young people for years to come. Among these "The Courtin'" is usually the favorite.

Zekle crep' up, quite unbeknown,
  An' peeked in thru the winder,
An' there sot Huldy all alone,
  'ith no one nigh to hender.

Agin' the chimbly crooknecks hung, 5
  An' in amongst 'em rusted
The ole queen's-arm° thet gran'ther
    Young
  Fetched back frum Concord busted.

The wannut logs shot sparkles out
  Towards the pootiest, bless her! 10
An' leetle fires danced all about
  The chiny on the dresser.

    7. **ole queen's-arm:** old musket.

The very room, coz she wuz in,
  Looked warm frum floor to ceilin',
An' she looked full ez rosy agin 15
  Ez th' apples she wus peelin'.

She heerd a foot an' knowed it, tu,
  A-raspin' on the scraper —
All ways to once her feelin's flew
  Like sparks in burnt-up paper. 20

He kin' o' l'itered on the mat,
  Some doutfle o' the sekle;
His heart kep' goin' pitypat,
  But hern went pity Zekle.

An' yit she gin her cheer a jerk 25
  Ez though she wished him furder,
An' on her apples kep' to work,
  Parin' away like murder.

"You want to see my Pa, I s'pose?"
  "Wal, no; I come designin' —" 30
"To see my Ma? She's sprinklin' clo'es
  Agin tomorrer's i'nin'."

He stood a spell on one foot fust,
  Then stood a spell on t'other.
An' on which one he felt the wust 35
  He couldn't ha' told ye, nuther.

Sez he, "I'd better call agin";
  Sez she, "Think likely, *Mister*";
The last word pricked him like a pin,
  An' — wal, he up an' kist her. 40

When Ma bimeby upon 'em slips,
  Huldy sot pale ez ashes,
All kind o' smily round the lips
  An' teary round the lashes.

Her blood riz quick, though, like the
  tide   45

  Down to the Bay o' Fundy.
An' all I know is they wuz cried°
  In meetin', come nex' Sunday.

47. they wuz cried: The banns (that is, the announcement of their approaching marriage) were read in church.

A FABLE FOR CRITICS

Lowell was the most respected literary critic of his day, turning out essays on both American and foreign books and authors. Yet it is a poem that most interestingly shows his talent for detecting the strength and weakness in writers of his own day. *A Fable for Critics* is a long poem of over one thousand lines in rhymed couplets, addressed — as was the fashion — to Apollo, the god of poetry and art. In the selection that follows, Lowell wittily describes a number of writers who are represented in this book even pointing out his own vulnerable spot. You have already read selections by most of them and can compare your impressions with his.

[*Emerson*] There comes Emerson first, whose rich words, every one,
Are like gold nails in temples to hang trophies on,
Whose prose is grand verse, while his verse, the Lord knows,
Is some of it pr——. No, 'tis not even prose;
I'm speaking of meters; some poems have welled   5
From those rare depths of soul that have ne'er been excelled.
They're not epics, but that doesn't matter a pin,
In creating, the only hard thing's to begin;
A grass blade's no easier to make than an oak,
If you've once found the way, you've achieved the grand stroke. . . .   10

[*Bryant*] There is Bryant, as quiet, as cool, and as dignified,
As a smooth silent iceberg, that never is ignified,
Save when by reflection 'tis kindled o' nights
With a semblance of flame by the chill northern lights.
He may rank (Griswold° says so) first bard of your nation,   15
(There's no doubt that he stands in supreme iceolation,)
Your topmost Parnassus° he may set his heel on,
But no warm applauses come, peal following peal on —
He's too smooth and too polished to hang any zeal on. . . .
If he stir you at all, it is just, on my soul,   20
Like being stirred up with the very North Pole. . . .

[*Whittier*] There is Whittier, whose swelling and vehement heart
Strains the strait-breasted drab of the Quaker apart,
And reveals the live man, still supreme and erect,
Underneath the bemummying wrappers of sect;   25

15. Griswold: American critic and editor of Lowell's day who was represented in the poem as leading the poets up to Apollo. **17. Parnassus** (pär·năs′ŭs): mountain in Greece, sacred to Apollo and the Muses.

There was ne'er a man born who had more of the swing
Of the true lyric bard and all that kind of thing;
And his failures arise (though he seems not to know it)
From the very same cause that has made him a poet —
A fervor of mind which knows no separation   30
'Twixt simple excitement and pure inspiration. . . .
Then his grammar's not always correct, nor his rhymes,
And he's prone to repeat his own lyrics sometimes,
Not his best, though, for those are struck off at white heats
When the heart in his breast like a trip hammer beats,   35
And can ne'er be repeated again any more
Than they could have been carefully plotted before. . . .

[*Hawthorne*] There is Hawthorne, with genius so shrinking and rare
That you hardly at first see the strength that is there;
A frame so robust, with a nature so sweet,   40
So earnest, so graceful, so solid, so fleet,
Is worth a descent from Olympus° to meet;
'Tis as if a rough oak that for ages had stood,
With his gnarled bony branches like ribs of the wood,
Should bloom after cycles of struggle and scathe,°   45
With a single anemone trembly and rathe.°. . .
When Nature was shaping him, clay was not granted
For making so full-sized a man as she wanted,
So, to fill out her model, a little she spared
From some finer-grained stuff for a woman prepared,   50
And she could not have hit a more excellent plan
For making him fully and perfectly man. . . .

[*Poe and Longfellow*] There comes Poe, with his raven, like Barnaby Rudge,°
Three fifths of him genius and two fifths sheer fudge,
Who talks like a book of iambs and pentameters,°   55
In a way to make people of common sense damn meters,
Who has written some things quite the best of their kind,
But the heart somehow seems all squeezed out by the mind,
Who — but heyday! What's this? Messieurs Mathews° and Poe,
You mustn't fling mud balls at Longfellow so,   60
Does it make a man worse that his character's such
As to make his friends love him (as you think) too much?
Why, there is not a bard at this moment alive
More willing than he that his fellows should thrive;
While you are abusing him thus, even now   65
He would help either one of you out of a slough;
You may say that he's smooth and all that till you're hoarse,
But remember that elegance also is force;

42. **Olympus:** mountain in Greece, home of the gods. 45. **scathe:** misfortune. 46. **rathe:** early
in the season. 53. **Barnaby Rudge:** a crazed youth in Dickens's novel of that name, who had a pet
raven; Poe had his poem "The Raven." 55. **iambs and pentameters:** See page 274, for explanation of these metrical terms. 59. **Mathews:** an editor and critic of the time who, like Poe, wrote
severe criticism of Longfellow.

Lowell House at Harvard University, with its Georgian tower, bears the name of one of the many illustrious literary figures who were associated with Harvard in the nineteenth century. (Harvard News Bureau)

After polishing granite as much as you will,
The heart keeps its tough old persistency still;   70
Deduct all you can, *that* still keeps you at bay;
Why, he'll live till men weary of Collins and Gray.°. . .

[*Holmes*] There's Holmes, who is matchless among you for wit,
A Leyden jar° always full charged, from which flit
The electrical tingles of hit after hit;   75
In long poems 'tis painful sometimes, and invites
A thought of the way the new telegraph writes,
Which pricks down its little sharp sentences spitefully,
As if you'd got more than you'd title to rightfully,
And you find yourself hoping its wild father lightning   80
Would flame in for a second and give you a fright'ning. . . .

[*Lowell*] There is Lowell, who's striving Parnassus to climb
With a whole bale of *isms* tied together with rhyme;
He might get on alone, spite of brambles and boulders,
But he can't with that bundle he has on his shoulders.   85
The top of the hill he will ne'er come nigh reaching
Till he learns the distinction 'twixt singing and preaching;
His lyre has some chords that would ring pretty well,
But he'd rather by half make a drum of the shell,
And rattle away till he's old as Methusalem,°   90
At the head of a march to the last new Jerusalem.

72. **Collins and Gray:** well-known English poets of the eighteenth century. 74. **Leyden** (lī'děn)
jar: an electricity condenser which can give strong shocks. 90. **Methusalem** (mē·thū'zě·lĕm):
Methuselah, oldest man in the Bible (Gen. 5:27).

THE VISION OF SIR LAUNFAL

Published the same year as the first series of *The Biglow Papers*, yet entirely different from them in treatment, is *The
Vision of Sir Launfal*, probably the best-
known and most-quoted poem by Lowell.

The author's own note of explanation is
helpful:

" According to the mythology of the ro-
mancers, the San Greal, or Holy Grail, was
the cup out of which Jesus partook of the
Last Supper with his disciples. It was
brought into England by Joseph of Ari-
mathea, and remained there, an object
of pilgrimage . . . for many years in
the keeping of his lineal descendants. It
was incumbent upon those who had charge
of it to be chaste in thought, word, and
deed; but one of the keepers having brok-
en this condition, the Holy Grail disap-

peared. From that time it was a favorite
enterprise of the knights of Arthur's court
to go in search of it. Sir Galahad was at
last successful in finding it, as may be read
in the seventeenth book of the *Romance of
King Arthur*. Tennyson has made Sir Galahad the subject of one of the most exquisite of his poems. The plot (if I may give
that name to anything so slight) of the following poem is my own, and to serve its
purposes, I have enlarged the circle of
competition in search of the miraculous
cup in such a manner as to include, not
only other persons than the heroes of the
Round Table, but also a period of time
subsequent to the supposed date of King
Arthur's reign."

The form of this poem is somewhat involved. Its two parts are each preceded by

a " prelude." You must be sure to recognize the vision within the two parts of the story itself. The vision begins in Part One and goes right on through Part Two (excluding the second " prelude "). Sir Launfal goes to sleep, dreams, and awakens the next morning. The main body of the poem is his dream, in which he first appears as a young man and then as " an old, bent man, worn out and frail."

PRELUDE TO PART FIRST

[In this introductory section, Lowell philosophizes — like an organist musing over the keys — on various subjects, ending with the joy and solace to be found in nature, particularly in the spring. Beginning with line 33, the poet, like the organist, pulls out all stops and lets his ideas roll forth on this theme.]

Over his keys the musing organist,
  Beginning doubtfully and far away,
First lets his fingers wander as they list,
  And builds a bridge from Dreamland
    for his lay:
Then, as the touch of his loved instru-
  ment   5
  Gives hope and fervor, nearer draws
    his theme,
First guessed by faint, auroral flushes
  sent
  Along the wavering vista of his dream.

Not only around our infancy°
Doth Heaven with all its splendors
  lie;   10
Daily, with souls that cringe and plot,
We Sinais° climb and know it not.
Over our manhood bend the skies;
  Against our fallen and traitor lives
The great winds utter prophecies;   15
  With our faint hearts the mountain
    strives;

Its arms outstretched, the druid° wood
  Waits with its benedicite;°
And to our age's drowsy blood
  Still shouts the inspiring sea.   20

Earth gets its price for what Earth gives
  us;
  The beggar is taxed for a corner to
    die in,
The priest hath his fee who comes and
  shrives us,
  We bargain for the graves we lie in;
At the devil's booth are all things sold,
Each ounce of dross costs its ounce of
  gold;   26
For a cap and bells° our lives we pay,
Bubbles we buy with a whole soul's
  tasking:
'Tis Heaven alone that is given away,
'Tis only God may be had for the ask-
  ing;   30
No price is set on the lavish summer;
June may be had by the poorest comer.

And what is so rare as a day in June?
  Then, if ever, come perfect days;   34
Then Heaven tries earth if it be in tune,
  And over it softly her warm ear lays;
Whether we look, or whether we listen,
We hear life murmur, or see it glisten;
Every clod feels a stir of might,
  An instinct within it that reaches and
    towers,   40
And groping blindly above it for light,
  Climbs to a soul in grass and flowers.
The flush of life may well be seen
  Thrilling back over hills and valleys;
The cowslip startles in meadows green,
  The buttercup catches the sun in its
    chalice,   46
And there's never a leaf or a blade too
  mean
  To be some happy creature's palace;
The little bird sits at his door in the sun,
  Atilt like a blossom among the leaves,

---

9. Not . . . infancy: The English poet Wordsworth had written, "Heaven lies about us in our infancy!" Lowell asserted that Heaven was not limited to our infancy. 12. Sinais (sī′nīz): Mount Sinai was the place where God gave Moses the Ten Commandments (Exod. 19). Here it symbolizes communion with Heaven.

17. druid: ancient Celtic priest who held the oak sacred and worshiped in the woods. 18. benedicite (bĕn′ē-dĭs′ĭ-tē): blessing. 27. cap and bells: the jingling headdress of a king's jester; in other words, mere superficial pleasures.

And lets his illumined being o'errun 51
  With the deluge of summer it receives;
His mate feels the eggs beneath her
  wings,
And the heart in her dumb breast flut-
  ters and sings;
He sings to the wide world, and she to
  her nest — 55
In the nice ear of Nature which song is
  the best?

Now is the high tide of the year,
  And whatever of life hath ebbed
  away
Comes flooding back with a ripply
  cheer
  Into every bare inlet and creek and
  bay; 60
Now the heart is so full that a drop
  overfills it;
We are happy now because God wills it;
No matter how barren the past may
  have been,
'Tis enough for us now that the leaves
  are green;
We sit in the warm shade and feel right
  well 65
How the sap creeps up and the blossoms
  swell;
We may shut our eyes, but we cannot
  help knowing
That skies are clear and grass is grow-
  ing.
The breeze comes whispering in our
  ear
That dandelions are blossoming near,
  That maize has sprouted, that streams
  are flowing, 71
That the river is bluer than the sky,
That the robin is plastering his house
  hard by;
And if the breeze kept the good news
  back,
For other couriers we should not lack;
  We could guess it all by yon heifer's
  lowing — 76
And hark! how clear bold chanticleer,
Warmed with the new wine of the year,
  Tells all in his lusty crowing!

Joy comes, grief goes, we know not how;
Everything is happy now, 81
  Everything is upward striving;
'Tis as easy now for the heart to be true
As for grass to be green or skies to be
  blue —
'Tis the natural way of living. 85
Who knows whither the clouds have
  fled?
  In the unscarred heaven they leave
  no wake;
And the eyes forget the tears they have
  shed,
  The heart forgets its sorrow and ache;
The soul partakes the season's youth, 90
  And the sulfurous rifts of passion and
  woe
Lie deep 'neath a silence pure and
  smooth,
  Like burnt-out craters healed with
  snow.
What wonder if Sir Launfal now 94
Remembered the keeping of his vow?

PART FIRST

I

"My golden spurs now bring to me,
  And bring to me my richest mail,
For tomorrow I go over land and sea
  In search of the Holy Grail.
Shall never a bed for me be spread, 100
Nor shall a pillow be under my head,
Till I begin my vow to keep;
Here on the rushes° will I sleep,
And perchance there may come a vision
  true
Ere day create the world anew." 105
  Slowly Sir Launfal's eyes grew dim;
  Slumber fell like a cloud on him,
And into his soul the vision flew.

II

[Sir Launfal's vision, or dream, begins
in this section.]

The crows flapped over by twos and
  threes;

---

103. **rushes:** This is inside the castle, not outside. The floors were covered with rushes.

In the pool drowsed the cattle up to
    their knees; 110
  The little birds sang as if it were
  The one day of summer in all the
    year;
And the very leaves seemed to sing on
    the trees;
The castle alone in the landscape lay
Like an outpost of winter, dull and
    gray; 115
'Twas the proudest hall in the North
    Countree,
And never its gates might opened be
Save to lord or lady of high degree;
Summer besieged it on every side,
But the churlish stone her assaults de-
    fied; 120
She could not scale the chilly wall,
Though around it for leagues her pavil-
    ions tall
Stretched left and right,
Over the hills and out of sight.
  Green and broad was every tent, 125
  And out of each a murmur went
Till the breeze fell off at night.

III

The drawbridge dropped with a surly
    clang,
And through the dark arch a charger
    sprang,
Bearing Sir Launfal, the maiden
    knight,° 130
In his gilded mail, that flamed so bright
It seemed the dark castle had gathered
    all
Those shafts the fierce sun had shot
    over its wall
  In his siege of three hundred sum-
    mers long,
And, binding them all in one blazing
    sheaf, 135
  Had cast them forth; so, young and
    strong,
And lightsome as a locust leaf,
Sir Launfal flashed forth in his un-
    scarred mail,
To seek in all climes for the Holy Grail.

130. maiden knight: one who has not been in
battle.

IV

It was morning on hill and stream and
    tree, 140
  And morning in the young knight's
    heart;
Only the castle moodily
Rebuffed the gifts of the sunshine free,
  And gloomed by itself apart; 144
The season brimmed all other things up
Full as the rain fills the pitcher plant's
    cup.

V

As Sir Launfal made morn through the
    darksome gate,
  He was 'ware of a leper, crouched by
    the same,
Who begged with his hand and moaned
    as he sate; 149
And a loathing over Sir Launfal came.
The sunshine went out of his soul with
    a thrill,
  The flesh 'neath his armor 'gan shrink
    and crawl,
And midway its leap his heart stood still
  Like a frozen waterfall; 154
For this man, so foul and bent of stature,
Rasped harshly against his dainty na-
    ture,
And seemed the one blot on the sum-
    mer morn —
So he tossed him a piece of gold in
    scorn.

VI

The leper raised not the gold from the
    dust:
" Better to me the poor man's crust, 160
Better the blessing of the poor,
Though I turn me empty from his door;
That is no true alms which the hand can
    hold;
He gives nothing but worthless gold
  Who gives from a sense of duty; 165
But he who gives but a slender mite,
And gives to that which is out of sight,
  That thread of the all-sustaining
    Beauty
Which runs through all and doth all
    unite —

...e hand cannot clasp the whole of his
  alms,   170
...ie heart outstretches its eager palms,
...or a god goes with it and makes it
  store
...o the soul that was starving in darkness before."

PRELUDE TO PART SECOND

[The vision is interrupted by another
prelude, in which a winter scene — in contrast to the previous summer scene — is depicted. At the end Sir Launfal appears as
an old man.]

Down swept the chill wind from the
  mountain peak,
From the snow five thousand summers
  old;   175
On open wold and hilltop bleak
  It had gathered all the cold,
And whirled it like sleet on the wanderer's cheek;
It carried a shiver everywhere
From the unleafed boughs and pastures
  bare;   180
The little brook heard it and built a roof
'Neath which he could house him, win-
  terproof;
All night by the white stars' frosty
  gleams
He groined his arches and matched his
  beams;   184
...ender and clear were his crystal spars
...the lashes of light that trim the stars;
...sculptured every summer delight
...is halls and chambers out of sight;
...etimes his tinkling waters slipped
...n through a frost-leaved forest
  crypt,   190
...ng sparkling aisles of steel-stemmed
  trees
Bending to counterfeit a breeze;
Sometimes the roof no fretwork knew
But silvery mosses that downward grew;
Sometimes it was carved in sharp relief   195
With quaint arabesques of ice-fern leaf;
Sometimes it was simply smooth and
  clear

For the gladness of heaven to shine
  through, and here
He had caught the nodding bulrush
  tops
And hung them thickly with diamond
  drops,   200
That crystaled the beams of moon and
  sun,
And made a star of every one.
No mortal builder's most rare device
Could match this winter palace of ice;
'Twas as if every image that mirrored
  lay   205
In his depths serene through the sum-
  mer day,
Each fleeting shadow of earth and sky,
  Lest the happy model should be lost,
Had been mimicked in fairy masonry
  By the elfin builders of the frost.   210

Within the hall are song and laughter;
  The cheeks of Christmas glow red and
  jolly;
And sprouting is every corbel° and
  rafter
  With lightsome green of ivy and
  holly;
Through the deep gulf of the chimney
  wide   215
Wallows the Yule log's roaring tide;
The broad flame pennons droop and
  flap
  And belly and tug as a flag in the
  wind;
Like a locust shrills the imprisoned sap,
  Hunted to death in its galleries blind;
And swift little troops of silent sparks,
Now pausing, now scattering away as
  in fear,   222
Go threading the soot forest's tangled
  darks
  Like herds of startled deer.
But the wind without was eager and
  sharp,   225
Of Sir Launfal's gray hair it makes a
  harp,
  And rattles and wrings
  The icy strings,

213. **corbel** (kôr′bĕl): bracket.

Singing, in dreary monotone,
A Christmas carol of its own,   230
Whose burden still, as he might guess,
Was " Shelterless, shelterless, shelter-
  less! "
The voice of the seneschal° flared like
  a torch
As he shouted the wanderer away from
  the porch,
And he sat in the gateway and saw all
  night   235
The great hall fire, so cheery and bold,
Through the window slits of the castle
  old,
Build out its piers of ruddy light
Against the drift of the cold.

PART SECOND

I

There was never a leaf on bush or
  tree,   240
The bare boughs rattled shudderingly;
The river was dumb and could not
  speak,
  For the weaver Winter its shroud had
    spun;
A single crow on the treetop bleak
  From his shining feathers shed off the
    cold sun;   245
Again it was morning, but shrunk and
  cold,
As if her veins were sapless and old,
And she rose up decrepitly
For a last dim look at earth and sea.

II

Sir Launfal turned from his own hard
  gate,   250
For another heir in his earldom sate;
An old, bent man, worn out and frail,
He came back from seeking the Holy
  Grail;
Little he recked of his earldom's loss;
No more on his surcoat was blazoned
  the cross,   255
But deep in his soul the sign he wore,
The badge of the suffering and the poor.

  233. **seneschal** (sĕn'ĕ·shăl): steward.

III

Sir Launfal's raiment thin and spare
Was idle mail 'gainst the barbèd air,
For it was just at the Christmas time;
So he mused, as he sat, of a sunnier
  clime,   261
And sought for a shelter from cold and
  snow
In the light and warmth of long ago;
He sees the snakelike caravan crawl
O'er the edge of the desert, black and
  small,   265
Then nearer and nearer, till, one by
  one,
He can count the camels in the sun,
As over the red-hot sands they pass
To where, in its slender necklace of
  grass,
The little spring laughed and leaped in
  the shade,   270
And with its own self like an infant
  played,
And waved its signal of palms.

IV

" For Christ's sweet sake, I beg an
  alms " —
The happy camels may reach the spring,
But Sir Launfal sees naught save the
  gruesome thing,   275
The leper, lank as the rain-blanched
  bone,
That cowers beside him, a thing as lone
And white as the ice isles of Northern
  seas
In the desolate horror of his disease.

V

And Sir Launfal said, "I behold in
  thee   280
An image of Him who died on the tree.
Thou also hast had thy crown of thorns,
Thou also hast had the world's buffets
  and scorns,
And to thy life were not denied
The wounds in the hands and feet and
  side.   285
Mild Mary's Son, acknowledge me;
Behold, through him, I give to Thee! "

VI

Then the soul of the leper stood up in
 his eyes
  And looked at Sir Launfal, and
  straightway he
Remembered in what a haughtier guise
 He had flung an alms to leprosie, 291
When he girt his young life up in
 gilded mail
And set forth in search of the Holy
 Grail.
The heart within him was ashes and
 dust;
He parted in twain his single crust, 295
He broke the ice on the streamlet's
 brink,
And gave the leper to eat and drink.
'Twas a moldy crust of coarse, brown
 bread,
 'Twas water out of a wooden bowl —
Yet with fine wheaten bread was the
 leper fed, 300
  And 'twas red wine he drank with his
  thirsty soul.

VII

As Sir Launfal mused with a downcast
 face,
A light shone round about the place;
The leper no longer crouched at his side,
But stood before him glorified, 305
Shining and tall and fair and straight
As the pillar that stood by the Beautiful
 Gate° —
Himself the Gate° whereby men can
Enter the temple of God and Man.

VIII

His words were shed softer than leaves
 from the pine, 310
And they fell on Sir Launfal as snows on
 the brine,
That mingle their softness and quiet in
 one
With a shaggy unrest they float down
 upon;

307. the Beautiful Gate: a gate of the Temple
at Jerusalem (Acts 3:2). 308. Himself the Gate:
Christ said, "I am the door." The leper had become Christ.

And the voice that was calmer than si-
 lence said,
" Lo, it is I, be not afraid! 315
In many climes, without avail,
Thou hast spent thy life for the Holy
 Grail;
Behold, it is here — this cup which thou
Didst fill at the streamlet for Me but
 now;
This crust is My body broken for thee;
This water His blood that died on the
 tree; 321
The Holy Supper° is kept, indeed,
In whatso we share with another's need;
Not what we give, but what we share,
For the gift without the giver is bare;
Who gives himself with his alms feeds
 three, 326
Himself, his hungering neighbor, and
 Me."

IX

[The vision ends and Sir Launfal is
brought back to reality.]

Sir Launfal awoke as from a swound;
" The Grail in my castle here is found!
Hang my idle armor up on the wall;
Let it be the spider's banquet hall; 331
He must be fenced with stronger mail
Who would seek and find the Holy
 Grail."

X

The castle gate stands open now,
 And the wanderer is welcome to the
 hall 335
As the hangbird is to the elm-tree
 bough;
No longer scowl the turrets tall,
The Summer's long siege at last is o'er;
When the first poor outcast went in at
 the door,
She entered with him in disguise, 340
And mastered the fortress by surprise;
There is no spot she loves so well on
 ground,

322. Holy Supper: The Last Supper, wherein
Christ instituted the Holy Eucharist, and so
gave Himself to mankind.

She lingers and smiles there the whole
    year round;
The meanest serf on Sir Launfal's land
Has hall and bower at his command;
And there's no poor man in the North
    Countree   346
But is lord of the earldom as much as he.

For Discussion of Lowell

The Courtin'

1. Be sure that you understand the dialect. Any words or phrases that are not clear should be restated in standard English. What does a dialect poem lose when translated into standard English?

2. Point out details that are typical of an old-fashioned New England kitchen. If possible, find pictures of such kitchens with their open fireplaces.

3. Point out bits of humor either in the actions of the characters or in the poet's choice of words.

A Fable for Critics

1. The most natural way to study *A Fable for Critics* is to discuss whether Lowell's comments seem justified from what you have read by these authors. If you disagree with his impression of any of them, try to discover whether he was wrong or whether you have not yet read enough by that author to judge his work as a whole.

2. Point out good examples of Lowell's wit. Find some examples of puns. Can you justify the use of puns in this type of poem? Where does exaggerated rhyme add to the humor?

3. Are the authors on the whole treated sympathetically or satirically? If you had been any of these men, would you have felt angry at Lowell's comments on you? Discuss the individual authors.

4. The manner of this poem is not hard to parody. Try writing "A Fable for Teachers," "A Fable for Students," or another poem of humorous brief comments on familiar persons or types.

The Vision of Sir Launfal

PRELUDE TO PART FIRST

1. How does the organist compare with the poet approaching his theme? with you, writing a theme for school? Why are the first ideas called " auroral flushes "?

2. What proof does the poet give that we have contacts with Heaven all through our lives? What kind of things must we pay for and what things are given away in this world?

3. In the famous description of the June day, pick out the details that suggest awakening and teeming life. How would you answer the question in line 56? What is the effect of such a day upon a person?

PART FIRST

4. Look up the part played by the vigil in the training of a knight in E. M. Tappan's *When Knights Were Bold*, or a similar book on knighthood.

5. Describe the way Sir Launfal appears in the vision as he goes forth on his quest. You would enjoy reading a similar description of Sir Lancelot in Tennyson's " The Lady of Shalott," Part III.

6. Why did the leper reject Sir Launfal's gift?

PRELUDE TO PART SECOND

7. Note the words and phrases you think especially vivid in the description of winter. Give examples from your own observation of how the frost mimics the images of summer, and see Emerson's poem " The Snow-Storm " for comparison.

8. Explain the tradition of the Yule log and other medieval Christmas customs which have come down to our own day. See Irving's " Christmas Sketches " in *The Sketch Book*.

9. Point out the various figures of speech the poet uses in describing the great hall fire.

PART SECOND

10. Part Second is in direct contrast to Part First. See how many points of contrast you can find.

11. Why does the leper accept Sir Launfal's gift this time? What miraculous transformation takes place? Explain the speech of the transformed leper in your own words.

12. What effect did the vision have on Sir Launfal? on life in the castle? Do you think life for the poor and needy of his realm became any easier? Why?

For Your Vocabulary

FIGURATIVE USE OF WORDS: The contrast of summer and winter in *The Vision of Sir Launfal* is created by listing details of summer and winter scenes. But the impression of the inhospitable castle is achieved by figurative use of words that usually name unlikable human traits. The *churlish* stone defied the assaults of the summer (l. 120). A *churl* is a rude, bad-tempered person. The drawbridge dropped with a *surly* clang (l. 128). The castle *moodily rebuffed* the gifts of sunshine (ll. 142–43), refused bluntly to meet a friendly advance. After Sir Launfal has learned sympathy for his fellow men, the turrets no longer *scowl*. By such figurative use of single words the castle is given as definite a personality as a human being, and not a likable being, either.

With this good example of the method fresh in your mind, try writing a brief paragraph, such as would be used in a story, describing a house that has a distinctive feeling — a simple but friendly, happy house; or a stiffly formal house. Think of words to describe the personality you want to give it, and then use them figuratively as you provide factual details. Try to get some verbs, some nouns, and some adjectives among your key words.

Oliver Wendell Holmes

HOLMES was a physician and a professor of medicine at Harvard. He practiced medicine from the day he hung out his shingle at the age of twenty-seven (saying, as he later claimed, "the smallest fevers gratefully received") and taught at Harvard until he was seventy-four. In his own time he was known as the author of an important medical article on puerperal fever, which saved many lives, and as the author of fiction which applied medical knowledge to social problems.

The Writer of Light Verses

The picture we remember of Holmes, however, is of the man who lived in the gracious house on Beacon Street beside the Charles River. This was the gay, laughing Holmes, the witty Holmes who was the favorite guest at all the best Boston dinners, the Holmes who was as interested in horse races and prize fights as in lectures and music, the Holmes who was a loyal friend of all the Boston writers and many others, and above all the Holmes who would come to a dinner or a meeting with an appropriate poem written for the occasion.

When he graduated from Harvard, Holmes was asked to give the class poem. It was a kind of foreshadowing

of what was to come, for in later years he wrote an endless series of class poems, alumni poems, dinner poems, commemorative poems. No one could do this kind of thing quite so well; no one would do it so gladly and graciously and with such a light touch. So throughout his life he was in demand as a writer of occasional verses. He had no equal in that field in Europe or America.

A few times he dropped the playful mood and wrote out of deep and sincere feeling. That was how we got "Old Ironsides" and "The Chambered Nautilus." And sometimes his humor was just the right touch for an important subject, as for instance in "The Deacon's Masterpiece," which describes the breakdown of the old Puritan order in New England.

The Conversationalist and Essayist

Even more than as a poet or a physician, Holmes was renowned in Boston as a conversationalist — the man whose presence would make any dinner a success, the man whose talk crackled with electric sparks, or as Lowell said,

> "A Leyden jar always full charged, from which flit
> The electrical tingles of hit after hit."

It is hard for us to preserve that talent of Holmes. The nearest we can come to it is to read some of the conversational essays he published in the *Atlantic Monthly* and in book form as *The Autocrat of the Breakfast Table.*

Holmes was born (1809) about the same time as Whittier, Longfellow, and Poe, but outlived them all (dying in 1894). During his lifetime the country grew from around five million to about seventy million people.

Oliver Wendell Holmes
1809–1894

OLD IRONSIDES

When Holmes was just twenty-one, he gained for himself permanent fame, and for the United States the preservation of a historic relic, by writing "Old Ironsides." This poem was a vigorous protest against the destruction of the frigate *Constitution,* which had defeated the *Guerrière* in the War of 1812. At first published in the Boston *Advertiser,* the verses were later copied in newspapers and scattered on broadsides all over the country. Such indignation was aroused that the ship was saved and became an object of great interest in the Charlestown Navy Yard, just outside of Boston. In 1928, because of its rotting timbers, it was taken apart and carefully restored. It was soon afterward declared a national memorial.

Ay, tear her tattered ensign down!
  Long has it waved on high,
And many an eye has danced to see
  That banner in the sky;
Beneath it rung the battle shout,   5
  And burst the cannon's roar —
The meteor of the ocean air
  Shall sweep the clouds no more.

Her decks, once red with heroes' blood.
    Where knelt the vanquished foe,   10
When winds were hurrying o'er the
        flood,
    And waves were white below,
No more shall feel the victor's tread,
    Or know the conquered knee —
The harpies of the shore shall pluck   15
    The eagle of the sea!

Oh, better that her shattered hulk
    Should sink beneath the wave;
Her thunders shook the mighty deep,
    And there should be her grave;   20
Nail to the mast her holy flag,
    Set every threadbare sail,
And give her to the god of storms,
    The lightning and the gale!

MY AUNT

This and the next poem, "The Last
Leaf," were first published when Holmes
was twenty-two years old. In both of them
youth smiles at the older generation.

My aunt! my dear unmarried aunt!
    Long years have o'er her flown;
Yet still she strains the aching clasp
    That binds her virgin zone;
I know it hurts her — though she looks
    As cheerful as she can;   6
Her waist is ampler than her life,
    For life is but a span.

My aunt! my poor deluded aunt!
    Her hair is almost gray;   10
Why will she train that winter curl
    In such a springlike way?
How can she lay her glasses down,
    And say she reads as well,
When through a double convex lens
    She just makes out to spell?   16

Her father — Grandpapa! forgive
    This erring lip its smiles —
Vowed she should make the finest girl
    Within a hundred miles;   20

He sent her to a stylish school;
    'Twas in her thirteenth June;
And with her, as the rules required,
    " Two towels and a spoon."

They braced my aunt against a board,
    To make her straight and tall;   26
They laced her up, they starved her
        down,
    To make her light and small;
They pinched her feet, they singed her
        hair,
    They screwed it up with pins —   30
O never mortal suffered more
    In penance for her sins.

But when my precious aunt was done,
    My grandsire brought her back;
(By daylight, lest some rabid youth   35
    Might follow on the track;)
" Ah! " said my grandsire, as he shook
    Some powder in his pan,°
" What could this lovely creature do
    Against a desperate man! "   . 40

Alas! nor chariot, nor barouche,
    Nor bandit cavalcade,
Tore from the trembling father's arms
    His all-accomplished maid.
For her how happy had it been!   45
    And Heaven had spared to me
To see one sad, ungathered rose
    On my ancestral tree.

38. **powder in his pan:** gunpowder in the hollow lock by which old guns were primed.

THE LAST LEAF

This poem was suggested to Holmes by
the appearance of old Major Thomas Melville, grandfather of Herman Melville, author of *Moby Dick*. It is interesting to
know that the portrait of the old man and
the suit of clothes described in the poem
are both preserved in the Old Boston Statehouse museum.

I saw him once before,
    As he passed by the door,
        And again

Louisburg Square in Boston, elegant center of New England's literary and cultural aristocracy of the nineteenth century. (Ewing Krainin from Frederic Lewis)

The pavement stones resound
As he totters o'er the ground   5
    With his cane.

They say that in his prime,
Ere the pruning knife of Time
    Cut him down,
Not a better man was found   10
By the crier on his round
    Through the town.

But now he walks the streets,
And he looks at all he meets
    Sad and wan,   15
And he shakes his feeble head,
That it seems as if he said,
    " They are gone."

The mossy marbles rest
On the lips that he has prest   20
    In their bloom,
And the names he loved to hear
Have been carved for many a year
    On the tomb.

My grandmamma has said —   25
Poor old lady, she is dead
    Long ago —
That he had a Roman nose,
And his cheek was like a rose
    In the snow.   30

But now his nose is thin,
And it rests upon his chin
    Like a staff,
And a crook is in his back,
And a melancholy crack   35
    In his laugh.

I know it is a sin
For me to sit and grin
    At him here;
But the old three-cornered hat,   40
And the breeches, and all that,
    Are so queer!

And if I should live to be
The last leaf upon the tree
    In the spring,   45

Let them smile, as I do now,
At the old forsaken bough
    Where I cling.

THE HEIGHT OF THE RIDICULOUS

Here is another example of Holmes's humor. Be sure you catch the pun in line 16.

I wrote some lines once on a time
    In wondrous merry mood,
And thought, as usual, men would say
    They were exceeding good.

They were so queer, so very queer,   5
    I laughed as I would die;
Albeit, in the general way,
    A sober man am I.

I called my servant, and he came;
    How kind it was of him   10
To mind a slender man like me,
    He of the mighty limb!

" These to the printer," I exclaimed,
    And, in my humorous way,
I added (as a trifling jest),   15
    " There'll be the devil to pay."

He took the paper, and I watched,
    And saw him peep within;
At the first line he read, his face
    Was all upon the grin.   20

He read the next; the grin grew broad,
    And shot from ear to ear;
He read the third; a chuckling noise
    I now began to hear.

The fourth; he broke into a roar;   25
    The fifth; his waistband split;
The sixth; he burst five buttons off,
    And tumbled in a fit.

Ten days and nights, with sleepless eye,
    I watched that wretched man,   30
And since, I never dare to write
    As funny as I can.

THE BOYS

Dr. Holmes's wit and engaging personality made him highly popular in Boston
as an after-dinner speaker and writer of
poems for special occasions. Probably the
best known of these poems is "The Boys,"
written for the thirtieth reunion of his own
Harvard class of 1829, a class famous for
the notable men it produced.

Has there any old fellow got mixed with the boys?
If there has, take him out, without making a noise.
Hang the almanac's cheat and the catalogue's spite!
Old time is a liar! We're twenty tonight!

We're twenty! We're twenty! Who says we are more?   5
He's tipsy — young jackanapes! — show him the door!
"Gray temples at twenty?" — Yes! *white* if we please;
Where the snowflakes fall thickest there's nothing can freeze!

Was it snowing I spoke of? Excuse the mistake!
Look close — you will not see a sign of a flake!   10
We want some new garlands for those we have shed —
And these are white roses in place of the red.

We've a trick, we young fellows, you may have been told,
Of talking (in public) as if we were old —
That boy we call "Doctor," and this we call "Judge";   15
It's a neat little fiction — of course it's all fudge.

That fellow's the "Speaker" — the one on the right;
"Mr. Mayor," my young one, how are you tonight?
That's our "Member of Congress," we say when we chaff;
There's the "Reverend" What's his name? — don't make me laugh.   20

That boy with the grave mathematical look
Made believe he had written a wonderful book,
And the Royal Society thought it was *true!*
So they chose him right in; a good joke it was, too!

There's a boy, we pretend, with a three-decker brain,   25
That could harness a team with a logical chain;
When he spoke for our manhood in syllabled fire,
We called him "The Justice," but now he's "The Squire."

And there's a nice youngster of excellent pith —
Fate tried to conceal him by naming him Smith;°   30
But he shouted a song for the brave and the free —
Just read on his medal, "My country," "of thee!"

---

30. **Smith:** Samuel Francis Smith, author of "America." Note that he is the only classmate
called by name; and he is probably the only one whose name has ever been heard by the average
high-school student of today. Anyone who is curious to identify the others can find them listed
in the footnotes of the Cambridge edition of Holmes's poems.

You hear that boy laughing? — You think he's all fun;
But the angels laugh, too, at the good he has done;
The children laugh loud as they troop to his call,   35
And the poor man that knows him laughs loudest of all!

Yes, we're boys — always playing with tongue or with pen —
And I sometimes have asked — Shall we ever be men?
Shall we always be youthful, and laughing, and gay,
Till the last dear companion drops smiling away?   40

Then here's to our boyhood, its gold and its gray!
The stars of its winter, the dews of its May!
And when we have done with our life-lasting toys,
Dear Father, take care of thy children, *the boys!*

THE CHAMBERED NAUTILUS

Dr. Holmes was not merely "a funny man." This poem, which he preferred above all his writings and by which he hoped to be remembered, is one of the best-loved poems of aspiration in our national literature. He caught his idea from the shell of the nautilus, of which he had several specimens. In *The Autocrat of the Breakfast Table,* where this poem was originally published, the author describes "the ship of pearl" as "a series of enlarging compartments successively dwelt in by the animal that inhabits the shell, which is built in a widening spiral." The name "nautilus," meaning sailor, grew out of the old belief that the little creature sailed by the gauzy wings which are really its tentacles.

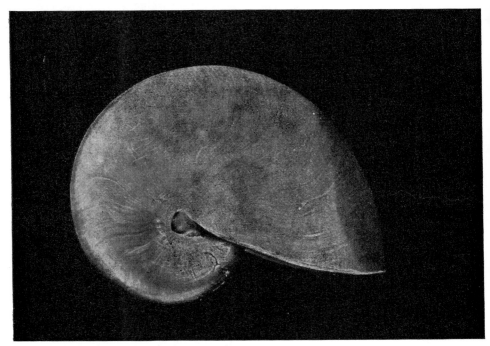

The chambered nautilus, the "ship of pearl" of Holmes's poem. (American Museum of Natural History)

This is the ship of pearl, which, poets
  feign,
  Sails the unshadowed main —
  The venturous bark that flings
On the sweet summer wind its purpled
  wings
In gulfs enchanted, where the Siren°
  sings,   5
  And coral reefs lie bare,
Where the cold sea maids rise to sun
  their streaming hair.

Its webs of living gauze no more unfurl;
  Wrecked is the ship of pearl!
  And every chambered cell,   10
Where its dim dreaming life was wont
  to dwell,
As the frail tenant shaped his growing
  shell,
  Before thee lies revealed —
Its irised ceiling rent, its sunless crypt
  unsealed!

Year after year beheld the silent toil 15
  That spread his lustrous coil;
  Still, as the spiral grew,
He left the past year's dwelling for the
  new,
Stole with soft step its shining archway
  through,
  Built up its idle door,   20
Stretched in his last-found home, and
  knew the old no more.

Thanks for the heavenly message
  brought by thee,
  Child of the wandering sea,
  Cast from her lap, forlorn!
From thy dead lips a clearer note is
  born   25
Than ever Triton° blew from wreathèd
  horn!
  While on mine ears it rings,

Through the deep caves of thought I
  hear a voice that sings:

Build thee more stately mansions, O my
  soul,
  As the swift seasons roll!   30
  Leave thy low-vaulted past!
Let each new temple, nobler than the
  last,
Shut thee from heaven with a dome
  more vast,
  Till thou at length art free,
Leaving thine outgrown shell by life's
  unresting sea!   35

For Discussion of Holmes

1. Do you recall why the nickname
" Old Ironsides " was given to the *Constitution?* Who are called the " harpies of the
shore "? What were three possible fates for
the vessel? Which did Holmes advocate?
Which came about finally?

2. Look up the history of the *Constitution,* especially its fight with the *Guerrière.*

3. How are " My Aunt " and " The Last
Leaf " similar in tone? What clearly indicates that they were written in Holmes's
youth? Do the poems seem disrespectful?
What thoughts on the relations between
youth and age do they awaken in you?

4. How did the education of " my aunt "
differ from that of a girl today? What
change has come about in the position and
interests of unmarried women since
Holmes's day?

5. Pick out from the humorous poems
words, phrases, or rhymes which seem to
snap into the right place with the suddenness and appropriateness that we call wit.

6. In the vein of " The Boys " write a
prophecy for your class thirty years hence.

7. Point out phrases or lines in " The
Chambered Nautilus " that show the delicate beauty of the shell. Study the picture
on page 598 and, if possible, bring a nautilus shell to class to see just how it is
formed. Express in your own words the
comparison made by the poet between the
shell and man's life.

8. " The Chambered Nautilus " has been
made into a beautiful cantata by John S.
Fearis. It is not too hard for high-school
glee clubs.

---

5. **Siren:** In classical mythology the sirens
were sea nymphs near the west coast of Italy
who lured mariners to their death by singing
enchanting songs. **26. Triton** (trī′tŏn): ancient
sea god whose lower part resembled a fish. He
is usually represented as blowing a trumpet made
of a sea shell.

The New England Historians

THE art of writing history flourished in New England alongside the arts of poetry, fiction, and criticism. For the first time in America, a group of historians appeared who were able to reproduce the dramatic quality of the past, yet record accurately the facts of that past. At least four of these historians wrote books that were as widely read as novels or books of verse. George Bancroft wrote an exciting and emotional *History of the United States;* John Lothrop Motley wrote the dramatic history of Holland in its fight with Spain (*The Rise of the Dutch Republic* and *The History of the United Netherlands*); William Hickling Prescott wrote the glamorous story of early Spanish conquests in the New World (including *The Conquest of Peru* and *The Conquest of Mexico*); and Francis Parkman wrote a monumental series of books on the long battle of England and France for North America.

Francis Parkman

Of these four, it is Parkman who now stands out from the others. He was Boston born, Harvard educated. His first great interests were the frontier and Indians, and in 1846 he took a trip over the Oregon Trail to see what the West looked like and how the red man really lived. He wrote a memorable book about this trip (*The Oregon Trail*). But he began to have a wider view of his job. The real story of the American forest and frontier before the Revolution, he decided, was the story of the battle of France and England for the continent. On this topic he wrote a series of remarkable histories under the title *France and England in North America.* No one before Parkman had ever seen the history of the continent in such a dramatic focus.

History Written under Handicaps

Parkman proved to all later generations that history might be both scholarly and dramatic. He proved it the hard way. For almost all his adult life he was a semi-invalid and nearly blind. He had to go through thousands of pages of documents, many of them in manuscript form, many in French or Spanish. When his eyes were unequal to the task, he had to get somebody to read to him. The reader was usually a high-school girl who knew no foreign language and pronounced all the words like English. Poor Parkman had therefore to guess what the words really were, and then to remember the points and references he wanted to use, and finally to dictate his own book, often without the use of notes or text. The fact that he triumphed over these obstacles and successfully completed a monumental work of writing bears witness to the strength of the literary devotion which men held in those great years of the Eastern Flowering.

Parkman was born (1823) when men were still trying to perfect the steam engine for factory and transportation use. When he died (1893) the automobile, phonograph, telephone, and electric light had been invented.

Francis Parkman
1823–1893

LE JEUNE[1] AND
THE HUNTERS

One of the most glorious pages in the history of Mother Church was written by the heroic Jesuit missionaries, who faced almost unbelievable hardships and difficulties, to bring the Cross to the New World. They built a line of missions stretching over one thousand miles through the wilderness of Canada and the northern reaches of the United States. In the field of exploration, the names of Father Jacques Marquette and Father Louis Hennepin will always occupy a prominent place.

In *The Jesuits in North America,* Francis Parkman pays tribute to this heroism. In spite of the religious prejudice so common at that time, Parkman could not help pausing in admiration at the unstinted self-sacrifice of the Jesuit missionaries. The following is his account of Father Paul Le Jeune's first journey into the wilderness. Many regard this selection as the finest piece of Parkman's writing. Pay close attention to the simple but effective style.

O N A morning in the latter part of October, Le Jeune embarked with the Indians, twenty in all, men, women, and children. No other Frenchman was of the party. Champlain bade him an anxious farewell, and commended him to the care of his red associates, who had taken charge of his store of biscuit, flour, corn, prunes, and turnips, to which, in an evil hour, his friends had persuaded him to add a small keg of

[1] **Le Jeune** (lĕ zhŭn).

wine. The canoes glided along the wooded shore of the Island of Orleans, and the party landed, toward evening, on the small island immediately below. Le Jeune was delighted with the spot, and the wild beauties of the autumnal sunset.

His reflections, however, were soon interrupted. While the squaws were setting up their bark lodges, and Mestigoit was shooting wild fowl for supper, Pierre returned to the canoes, tapped the keg of wine, and soon fell into the mud, helplessly drunk. Revived by the immersion, he next appeared at the camp, foaming at the mouth, threw down the lodges, overset the kettle, and chased the shrieking squaws into the woods. His brother Mestigoit rekindled the fire, and slung the kettle anew; when Pierre, who meanwhile had been raving like a madman along the shore, reeled in a fury to the spot to repeat his former exploit. Mestigoit anticipated him, snatched the kettle from the fire, and threw the scalding contents in his face. " He was never so well washed before in his life," says Le Jeune; " he lost all the skin of his face and breast. Would to God his heart had changed also! " He roared in his frenzy for a hatchet to kill the missionary, who therefore thought it prudent to spend the night in the neighboring woods. Here he stretched himself on the earth, while a charitable squaw covered him with a sheet of birch bark. "Though my bed," he writes, "had not been made up since the creation of the world, it was not hard enough to prevent me from sleeping."

Such was his initiation into Indian winter life. Passing over numerous adventures by water and land, we find the party, on the twelfth of November, leaving their canoes on an island, and wading ashore at low tide over the flats to the southern bank of the St. Lawrence. As two other bands had joined them, their number was increased to forty-five persons. Now, leaving the river behind, they entered those savage highlands whence issue the springs of the St. John [1] — a wilderness of rugged mountain ranges, clad in dense, continuous forests, with no human tenant but this troop of miserable rovers, and here and there some kindred band, as miserable as they. Winter had set in, and already dead Nature was sheeted in funereal white. Lakes and ponds were frozen, rivulets sealed up, torrents encased with stalactites of ice; the black rocks and the black trunks of the pine trees were beplastered with snow, and its heavy masses crushed the dull green boughs into the drifts beneath. The forest was silent as the grave.

Through this desolation the long file of Indians made its way, all on snowshoes, each man, woman, and child bending under a heavy load, or dragging a sledge, narrow, but of prodigious length. They carried their whole wealth with them, on their backs or on their sledges — kettles, axes, bales of meat, if such they had, and huge rolls of birch bark for covering their wigwams. The Jesuit was loaded like the rest. The dogs alone floundered through the drifts unburdened. There was neither path nor level ground. Descending, climbing, stooping beneath halffallen trees, clambering over piles of

[1] St. John: a river flowing through Maine and eastern Canada.

prostrate trunks, struggling through matted cedar swamps, threading chill ravines, and crossing streams no longer visible, they toiled on till the day began to decline, then stopped to encamp. Burdens were thrown down, and sledges unladen. The squaws, with knives and hatchets, cut long poles of birch and spruce saplings; while the men, with snowshoes for shovels, cleared a round or square space in the snow, which formed an upright wall three or four feet high, enclosing the area of the wigwam. On one side, a passage was cut for an entrance, and the poles were planted around the top of the wall of snow, sloping and converging. On these poles were spread the sheets of birch bark; a bearskin was hung in the passageway for a door; the bare ground within and the surrounding snow were covered with spruce boughs; and the work was done.

This usually occupied about three hours, during which Le Jeune, spent with travel, and weakened by precarious and unaccustomed fare, had the choice of shivering in idleness, or taking part in a labor which fatigued, without warming, his exhausted frame. The sorcerer's wife was in far worse case. Though in the extremity of a mortal sickness, they left her lying in the snow till the wigwam was made — without a word, on her part, of remonstrance or complaint. Le Jeune, to the great ire of her husband, sometimes spent the interval in trying to convert her; but she proved intractable, and soon died unbaptized.

Thus lodged, they remained so long as game could be found within a circuit of ten or twelve miles, and then, subsistence failing, removed to another spot. Early in the winter, they hunted the beaver and the Canada porcupine; and, later, in the season of deep snows, chased the moose and the caribou.

Put aside the bearskin, and enter the hut. Here, in a space some thirteen feet square, were packed nineteen savages, men, women, and children, with their dogs, crouched, squatted, coiled like hedgehogs, or lying on their backs, with knees drawn up perpendicularly to keep their feet out of the fire. Le Jeune, always methodical, arranges the grievances inseparable from these rough quarters under four chief heads — Cold, Heat, Smoke, and Dogs. The bark covering was full of crevices, through which the icy blasts streamed in upon him from all sides; and the hole above, at once window and chimney, was so large, that, as he lay, he could watch the stars as well as in the open air. While the fire in the midst, fed with fat pine knots, scorched him on one side, on the other he had much ado to keep himself from freezing. At times, however, the crowded hut seemed heated to the temperature of an oven. But these evils were light, when compared to the intolerable plague of smoke. During a snowstorm, and often at other times, the wigwam was filled with fumes so dense, stifling, and acrid, that all its inmates were forced to lie flat on their faces, breathing through mouths in contact with the cold earth. Their throats and nostrils felt as if on fire; their scorched eyes streamed with tears; and when Le Jeune tried to read, the letters of his breviary seemed printed in blood. The dogs were not an unmixed evil, for, by sleeping on and around him, they kept him warm at night; but, as an offset to this good service, they walked, ran, and jumped over him as he lay, snatched the food from his birchen dish, or, in a mad rush at some bone or discarded morsel, now and then overset both dish and missionary.

Sometimes of an evening he would leave the filthy den, to read his breviary in peace by the light of the moon. In the forest around sounded the sharp crack of frost-riven trees; and from the horizon to the zenith shot up the silent meteors of the northern lights, in whose fitful flashings the awe-struck Indians beheld the dancing of the spirits of the dead. The cold gnawed him to the bone; and, his devotions over, he turned back shivering. . . .

Of the three brothers who had invited him to join the party, one, we have seen, was the hunter, Mestigoit; another, the sorcerer; and the third, Pierre, whom, by reason of his falling away from the Faith, Le Jeune always mentions as the Apostate. He was a weak-minded young Indian, wholly under the influence of his brother the sorcerer, who, if not more vicious, was far more resolute and wily. From the antagonism of their respective professions, the sorcerer hated the priest, who lost no opportunity of denouncing his incantations, and who ridiculed his perpetual singing and drumming as puerility and folly. The former, being an indifferent hunter, and disabled by a disease which he had contracted, depended for subsistence on his credit as a magician; and in undermining it Le Jeune not only outraged his pride, but threatened his daily bread. He used every device to retort ridicule upon his rival. At the outset, he had proffered his aid to Le Jeune in his study of the Algonquin; and, like the Indian practical jokers of Acadia [1] in the case of Father Biard, palmed off upon him the foulest words in the language as the equivalent of things spiritual. Thus it happened, that, while the missionary sought to explain to the assembled wigwam some point of Christian doctrine, he was interrupted by peals of laughter from men, children, and squaws. And now, as Le Jeune took his place in the circle, the sorcerer bent upon him his malignant eyes, and began that course of rude bantering which filled to overflowing the cup of the Jesuit's woes. All took their cue from him, and

[1] **Acadia** (*à·kā′dĭ·à*): original name for Nova Scotia.

made their afflicted guest the butt of their inane witticisms. "Look at him! His face is like a dog's!" – "His head is like a pumpkin!" – "He has a beard like a rabbit's!" The missionary bore in silence these and countless similar attacks; indeed, so sorely was he harassed, that, lest he should exasperate his tormentor, he sometimes passed whole days without uttering a word.

Le Jeune, a man of excellent observation, already knew his red associates well enough to understand that their rudeness did not of necessity imply ill will. The rest of the party, in their turn, fared no better. They rallied and bantered each other incessantly, with as little forbearance and as little malice as a troop of unbridled schoolboys. No one took offence. To have done so would have been to bring upon one's self genuine contumely. This motley household was a model of harmony. True, they showed no tenderness or consideration toward the sick and disabled; but for the rest, each shared with all in weal or woe: the famine of one was the famine of the whole, and the smallest portion of food was distributed in fair and equal partition. Upbraidings and complaints were unheard; they bore each other's foibles with wondrous equanimity; and while persecuting Le Jeune with constant importunity for tobacco, and for everything else he had, they never begged among themselves.

When the fire burned well and food was abundant, their conversation, such as it was, was incessant. They used no oaths, for their language supplied none – doubtless because their mythology had no beings sufficiently distinct to swear by. Their expletives were foul words, of which they had a superabundance, and which men, women, and children alike used with a frequency and hardihood that amazed and scandalized the priest.

There was one point touching which Le Jeune and his Jesuit brethren had as yet been unable to solve their doubts. Were the Indian sorcerers mere impostors, or were they in actual league with the Devil?

Thus prone to believe in the immediate presence of the nether powers, Le Jeune watched the sorcerer with an eye prepared to discover in his conjurations the signs of a genuine diabolic agency. His observations, however, led him to a different result; and he could detect in his rival nothing but a vile compound of impostor and dupe. The sorcerer believed in the efficacy of his own magic, and was continually singing and beating his drum to cure the disease from which he was suffering. Toward the close of the winter, Le Jeune fell sick, and in his pain and weakness nearly succumbed under the nocturnal uproar of the sorcerer, who hour after hour sang and drummed without mercy – sometimes yelling at the top of his throat, then hissing like a serpent, then striking his drum on the ground as if in a frenzy, then leaping up, raving about the wigwam, and calling on the women and children to join him in singing. Now ensued a hideous din; for every throat was strained to the utmost, and all were beating with sticks or fists on the bark of the hut to increase the noise, with the charitable object of aiding the sorcerer to conjure down his malady, or drive away the evil spirit that caused it.

He had an enemy, a rival sorcerer, whom he charged with having caused by charms the disease that afflicted him. He therefore announced that he should kill him. As the rival dwelt at Gaspé,[1] a hundred leagues off, the present execution of the threat might appear difficult; but distance was no bar to the vengeance of the sorcerer. Ordering all the children and all but one of the women to leave the wigwam, he seated himself, with the woman who remained, on the

[1] **Gaspé** (gàs·pā'): a peninsula in the province of Quebec.

ground in the center, while the men of the party, together with those from other wigwams in the neighborhood, sat in a ring around. Mestigoit, the sorcerer's brother, then brought in the charm, consisting of a few small pieces of wood, some arrowheads, a broken knife, and an iron hook, which he wrapped in a piece of hide. The woman next rose, and walked around the hut, behind the company. Mestigoit and the sorcerer now dug a large hole with two pointed stakes, the whole assembly singing, drumming, and howling meanwhile with a deafening uproar. The hole made, the charm, wrapped in the hide, was thrown into it. Pierre, the Apostate, then brought a sword and a knife to the sorcerer, who, seizing them, leaped into the hole, and with furious gesticulation hacked and stabbed at the charm, yelling with the whole force of his lungs. At length he ceased, displayed the knife and sword stained with blood, proclaimed that he had mortally wounded his enemy, and demanded if none present had heard his death cry. The assembly, more occupied in making noises than in listening for them, gave no reply, till at length two young men declared that they had heard a faint scream, as if from a great distance; whereat a shout of gratulation and triumph rose from all the company.

There was a young prophet, or diviner, in one of the neighboring huts, of whom the sorcerer took counsel as to the prospect of his restoration to health. The divining lodge was formed, in this instance, of five or six upright posts planted in a circle and covered with a blanket. The prophet ensconced himself within; and after a long interval of singing, the spirits declared their presence by their usual squeaking utterances from the recesses of the mystic tabernacle. Their responses were not unfavorable; and the sorcerer drew much consolation from the invocations of his brother impostor. . . .

Le Jeune, robbed of his sleep by the ceaseless thumping of the sorcerer's drum and the monotonous cadence of his medicine songs, improved the time in attempts to convert him. "I began," he says, "by evincing a great love for him, and by praises, which I threw to him as a bait whereby I might catch him in the net of truth." But the Indian, though pleased with the Father's flatteries, was neither caught nor conciliated.

Nowhere was his magic in more requisition than in procuring a successful chase to the hunters — a point of vital interest, since on it hung the lives of the whole party. They often, however, returned empty-handed; and for one, two, or three successive days no other food could be had than the bark of trees or scraps of leather. So long as tobacco lasted, they found solace in their pipes, which seldom left their lips. "Unhappy infidels," writes Le Jeune, "who spend their lives in smoke, and their eternity in flames!"

As Christmas approached, their condition grew desperate. Beavers and porcupines were scarce, and the snow was not deep enough for hunting the moose. Night and day the medicine drums and medicine songs resounded from the wigwams, mingled with the wail of starving children. The hunters grew weak and emaciated; and as after a forlorn march the wanderers encamped once more in the lifeless forest, the priest remembered that it was the eve of Christmas. "The Lord gave us for our supper a porcupine, large as a sucking pig, and also a rabbit. It was not much, it is true, for eighteen or nineteen persons; but the Holy Virgin and St. Joseph, her glorious spouse, were not so well treated, on this very day, in the stable of Bethlehem."

On Christmas Day, the despairing hunters, again unsuccessful, came to pray succor from Le Jeune. Even the Apostate had become tractable, and the famished sorcerer was ready to try the efficacy of an appeal to the deity of his rival. A bright hope possessed the missionary. He composed two prayers, which, with the aid of the repentant Pierre, he translated into Algonquin. Then he hung against the side of the hut a napkin which he had brought with him, and against the napkin a crucifix and a reliquary, and, this done, caused all the Indians to kneel before them, with hands raised and clasped. He now read one of the prayers, and required the Indians to repeat the other after him, promising to renounce their superstitions and obey Christ, whose image they saw before them, if He would give them food and save them from perishing. The pledge given, he dismissed the hunters with a benediction. At night they returned with game enough to relieve the immediate necessity. All was hilarity. The kettles were slung, and the feasters assembled. Le Jeune rose to speak, when Pierre, who having killed nothing was in ill humor, said, with a laugh, that the crucifix and the prayer had nothing to do with their good luck; while the sorcerer, his jealousy reviving as he saw his hunger about to be appeased, called out to the missionary, "Hold your tongue! You have no sense!" As usual, all took their cue from him. They fell to their repast with ravenous jubilation, and the disappointed priest sat dejected and silent.

Repeatedly, before the spring, they were thus threatened with starvation. Nor was their case exceptional. It was the ordinary winter life of all those Northern tribes who did not till the soil, but lived by hunting and fishing alone. The desertion or the killing of the aged, sick, and disabled, occasional cannibalism, and frequent death from famine were natural incidents of an existence which during half the year was but a desperate pursuit of the mere necessaries of life under the worst conditions of hardship, suffering, and de-basement.

At the beginning of April, after roaming for five months among forests and mountains, the party made their last march, regained the bank of the St. Lawrence, and waded to the island where they had hidden their canoes. Le Jeune was exhausted and sick, and Mestigoit offered to carry him in his canoe to Quebec. This Indian was by far the best of the three brothers, and both Pierre and the sorcerer looked to him for support. He was strong, active, and daring, a skillful hunter, and a dexterous canoe man. Le Jeune gladly accepted his offer; embarked with him and Pierre on the dreary and tempestuous river; and, after a voyage full of hardship, during which the canoe narrowly escaped being ground to atoms among the floating ice, landed on the Island of Orleans, six miles from Quebec. The afternoon was stormy and dark, and the river was covered with ice, sweeping by with the tide. They were forced to encamp. At midnight the moon had risen, the river was comparatively unencumbered, and they embarked once more. The wind increased, and the waves tossed furiously. Nothing saved them but the skill and courage of Mestigoit. At length they could see the rock of Quebec towering through the gloom, but piles of ice lined the shore, while floating masses were drifting down on the angry current. The Indian watched his moment, shot his canoe through them, gained the fixed ice, leaped out, and shouted to his companions to follow. Pierre scrambled up, but the ice was six feet out of the water, and Le Jeune's agility failed him. He saved himself by clutching the ankle of Mestigoit, by whose aid he gained a firm foothold at the top, and for a moment, the three voyagers, aghast at the narrowness of their escape, stood gazing at each other in silence.

It was three o'clock in the morning when Le Jeune knocked at the door of his rude little convent on the St. Charles; and the Fathers, springing in joyful haste from their slumbers, embraced their long-absent Superior with ejaculations of praise and benediction.

For Discussion of Parkman

1. "History without geography is the romance of nowhere." Locate on a map the section in which Father Le Jeune spent the winter. The footnotes about the St. John River and Gaspé will aid you.

2. The interest in Parkman's account is heightened by the struggle between the priest and the sorcerer. What is the source of the conflict? How does the sorcerer try to undermine the priest's influence? What is the result of the conflict?

For Your Vocabulary

WORD ORIGINS: In the selection you will find Algonquin words, such as *wigwam*. Try to locate other words of Indian origin. Explain the derivation of the following: *immersion, missionary, diabolic, sorcerer, incantation, mythology.*

Reading on the Flowering of the East, Part Two

LITERATURE OF THE PERIOD

Poetry

Emerson, Ralph Waldo, "The Humblebee," "The Snow-Storm," "The Romany Girl," "The Problem," "The Test," "A Fable," "Terminus," "Brahma"

Thoreau, Henry David, "A Prayer," "Independence"

Longfellow, Henry Wadsworth, "My Lost Youth," "A Psalm of Life," "The Wreck of the Hesperus," "The Skeleton in Armor," "The Old Clock on the Stairs," "The Discoverer of the North Cape," *Evangeline, The Courtship of Miles Standish, Tales of a Wayside Inn, The Song of Hiawatha*

Lowell, James Russell, "The First Snowfall," "She Came and Went," "The Changeling," "To a Dandelion," "The Fatherland," "Stanzas on Freedom," "The Present Crisis," "Commemoration Ode" (especially stanza VI on Lincoln),

"Rhoecus"

Holmes, Oliver Wendell, "The Deacon's Masterpiece," "How the Old Horse Won the Bet," "To an Insect," "The Voiceless," "Dorothy Q.," "Homesick in Heaven"

Many interesting lesser poets of the period may be read in Jessie Rittenhouse's *Little Book of American Poets* (Houghton, Mifflin, 1915).

Nonfiction

Emerson, Ralph Waldo. See study suggestions, pages 565–66.

Thoreau, Henry David, *Walden, The Portable Thoreau,* ed. by Carl Bode (Viking, 1947)

Parkman, Francis, *The Oregon Trail, Pioneers of France in the New World, La Salle and the Discovery of the Great West, Montcalm and Wolfe, A Half Century of Conflict, The Battle for North America,* ed. by John Tebbel (Doubleday, 1948)

ON INDIVIDUAL AUTHORS

EMERSON. Hawthorne, Hildegarde, *Youth's Captain* (Longmans, 1935); Hoeltje, H. H., *The Sheltering Tree* (Duke University Press, 1943)

THOREAU. Canby, H. S., *Thoreau* (Houghton Mifflin, 1943); Hawthorne, Hildegarde, *Concord's Happy Rebel* (Longmans, 1940); Kane, Henry B., *Thoreau's Walden* (Knopf, 1946); Robbins, R. W., *Discovery at Walden* (the author, R.F.D. 1, Concord, Massachusetts, 1947); Whicher, G. F., *Walden Revisited* (Rinehart, 1945)

LONGFELLOW. Thompson, L. R., *Young Longfellow* (Macmillan, 1939)

LOWELL. Beatty, R. C., *James R. Lowell* (Vanderbilt University Press, 1942)

HOLMES. Hawthorne, Hildegarde, *The Happy Autocrat* (Longmans, 1938); Tilton, Eleanor M., *The Amiable Autocrat* (Schuman, 1947)

PARKMAN. Wade, M., *Francis Parkman, Heroic Historian* (Viking, 1942)

There are detailed biographies of these authors by numerous writers of an earlier day, and in series such as American Men of Letters and American Writers.

Emigrants crossing the Rocky Mountains, as romantically depicted in a print by the famous lithograph firm of Currier and Ives. (Culver)

The Westward Movement

WHILE in the East cities were growing and culture was broadening, another movement of importance was taking place in the nation. It was the movement west. The great books were being written in the East, but the great history was being made beyond the Alleghenies.

At the end of the Revolution, the United States owned the country as far west as the Mississippi, but Maine was still a frontier. The Allegheny Mountains stood like a huge dam, a few hundred miles from the seacoast, holding the tide of settlement from flowing west.

And then the dam broke! When the last shot was fired at the redcoats, it seemed as though the whole country turned its back on Europe and climbed up the Alleghenies for a look at the West. They cut ribbons of clear land through the thick Allegheny forests. They streamed over Daniel Boone's road into Kentucky, keeping a sharp eye open for Indians behind the trees. They made an ox road over the Pennsylvania mountains to Fort Pitt, where they built barges and sailed away into the fertile plain country, singing " Hi-O, away we go, Floating down the river on the O-hi-O! " They dug the Erie Canal and sailed along the Great Lakes to what looked like good farm land. The whole irresistible tide of human migration burst through the dam and rolled toward the Mississippi.

The Advancing Frontier

The young men bought themselves coonskin caps, and oiled their flintlock guns, and rode Indian ponies out to seek adventure. Or they bought a Conestoga wagon with the canvas top looking so much like a sail that people began to call it a prairie schooner. They traded guns and flour and big silver coins for a pair of oxen, and rumbled off in their big Conestogas to find a homestead.

And not only the men. Their wives and babies rode along in the Conestoga. Their big boys walked along beside the oxen or cantered up and down on a pony, looking for buffalo. Their mothers and grandmothers came along west, hardly complaining when the wagon jiggled on the rough trail and made them drop a stitch in their knitting or patching. Whole families, whole communities moved west. They carried with them their strong faith. Groups of priests went west to take up where the French and Spanish missionaries had left off, and the pioneer sisters followed to found schools and hospitals in the American wilderness.

For the United States, Thomas Jefferson bought the whole western half of the Mississippi valley and sent Lewis and Clark to see what lay in the mysterious distances to the west. Zebulon Pike (his name is on Pikes Peak) went to look at the upper Mississippi and the mountain country of the Southwest. Jedediah Smith found a way over the dry lands and the desert to the Southwest. They came back with stories of snowy mountains, herds of buffalo, and rich soil. And hardly were their reports in the newspapers when covered wagons began to follow the trails they had blazed.

Pioneer Life and Literature

This was not like traveling through the plains country east of the Mississippi. As soon as a caravan left the Missouri River it was in a high dry plain, which was as boundless and unmarked as the sea, and on which the six-foot prairie grass blew in waves like sea water. In fact, the prairies reminded people of the sea — storms were like sea storms, and starting on the trail was like sailing out of port. Once out, a man was on his own. Civilization fell away. It was man against nature. He had to protect himself, feed himself, find his way. He even had to navigate, sometimes, as though he were at sea. Farther west, he had to face wild animals, and deserts where the temperature went up to one hundred and thirty and it was sixty miles between waterholes. To move from the Missouri to the good western land took about four months,

if the caravan was lucky. Many a caravan never got there. Many a settler, many a child, ended his trip in a shallow grave just far enough off the trail so that wagons would not run over it.

People Filling the Land

A party of fur traders made a discovery — a natural gateway through the Rockies at South Pass in Wyoming. And then, in 1848, men began to whisper a wild rumor that had supposedly started in California. Gold had been found at Sutter's Mill!

In 1849 the human tide that flowed west was like a Mississippi flood. In the late forties and the fifties, the Oregon Trail, the great route to all the West, was worn smooth for half a mile wide, in some places, and even today you can see where the trail ran, because the land was so pounded down by the feet of oxen that prairie grass and prickly pear will hardly grow there. In those years, so many people, so many families, went to the West that there was an almost constant cloud of dust above the trail.

The men in Washington who kept our census records marked carefully on the map where the frontier seemed to be from year to year. They followed it through Ohio, Indiana, and Illinois, into Iowa and Missouri in the thirties, then on its big jump across the dry plains to the western slopes. They put down a neat row of figures:

Year	Size of country in sq. mi.	Population	People per sq. mi.
1790	867,980	3,929,881	4.5
1850	2,944,337	23,191,876	7.9
1900	2,974,159	75,994,575	25.6

They estimated that in 1900 there were more than eight times as many people in the West alone as had been in the whole country in 1800. People were moving westward, not only within the country, but from Europe to America. Millions of immigrants — Germans, Irish, and still later Scandinavians — were swelling the population.

But the real story is men, not numbers. The American people found trails that had once been buffalo paths to the salt licks. Indians had used those trails. And then the white scouts came cautiously over them. Fur traders came, hard on the heels of the scouts. And close behind them came the settlers, the great wave of brave adventurous people from the East and from Europe. Into the wilderness they brought the church, the law, the newspaper, trade and manufacturing, and all the precious freedoms won along the Atlantic seaboard. In a hundred years they took the bare face of a continent, three million square miles, and built a nation on it.

What the Frontier Meant to America

The westward-rolling frontier, more than anything else, made Americans different from Europeans. And since books are made by men, it helped make American books different from European books.

Here are some of the characteristics the frontier developed in men.

Frontiersmen were *self-reliant, practical, ingenious.* They had to be. There were no garages, repairmen, doctors, advisers to consult. Even today, many Americans are better at practical than abstract problems. When surprised Europeans during World War II called the Americans who invaded Normandy "an army of mechanics," they were paying tribute to the same practicality Americans learned on the frontier.

They were *optimistic, confident,* sometimes *cocky.* They were looking toward the future, not the past; making history, not reading it. They could always get a new start in the West if they needed to.

They were *democratic.* No other political philosophy except democracy could possibly have come out of the American frontier. Frontiersmen looked on each other as equals; they faced the same hazards, took the same risks, fought for the same rewards. They didn't believe in "classes" and special privileges. They were used to governing themselves.

Finally, they had a *sense of humor.* They liked to throw back their heads and laugh loudly. The tall tales of America grew — bigger and bigger — on the frontier. If you will look closely at the ways and ideas of Americans today, you will find these things still strong in them.

It was noticed in the East that the frontier roughened manners. But it was also noticed that out of the West came a vitality and freshness and strength which swept into American thinking and writing.

The Frontier in Literature

Great writers, great books, did not come at once from the frontier. Great novels and poems come from the eddies, not the main streams of history. There isn't time in the midst of a great event to write great fiction or poetry about it. Sometime later, when history has passed by, writers have time to think about what has happened and leisure to write about it.

Frontiersmen didn't have time to write. They were too busy clearing their acres, keeping night watches against Indians, setting traps in the mountains.

When frontiersmen did write, it was usually letters or a diary, or a description of the new scenes for folks back home (like Dame Shirley's letters from the California mines). Sometimes an Easterner like Francis Parkman went out to the frontier and returned home to write an excellent piece of reportage about it (like *The Oregon Trail*). The sea was a road to the frontier, too, and one Easterner, Richard Henry Dana, Jr., sailing round the cape to California,

caught the spirit of that frontier in a book called *Two Years before the Mast.* Mostly, though, the records of the frontiersmen have had to be restudied and retold as literature in our time by men like Stanley Vestal.

Western Humor

The frontiersman's real contribution to literature was his kind of humor. Sitting before the campfire, he loved to spin tales. He would keep a straight face, but his stories were as incredible as the Western country, his imagination as boundless as the prairie, his subject matter as fantastic as the boiling springs in which a man could cook a trout twenty feet from the icy stream where he caught it. The stories were not modest; they were often slapstick, and they did not use drawing-room language. Language itself bowed to the demands of Western storytellers. When ordinary words were not sufficient, the frontiersmen coined new ones — "tetotaciously," "exfluncted," "obfliscated," "bodayciously."

A group of newspaper columnists first put Western humor into print and made the East familiar with it. One of the most popular of these frontier humorists was Artemus Ward, a Maine man who wrote for the Cleveland *Plain Dealer*, telling side-splitting tales in the most outrageous spelling ever devised by man. The spelling was part of his pose. He pretended to be the proprietor of a wax-figure show, and the droll deadpan stories of his adventures were as exaggerated as the best frontier storyteller could have wished. President Lincoln once startled his cabinet by reading Artemus Ward aloud to them. It was his way to relax and break the almost unbearable tension of the war years.

Indian Folk Literature

All too often we forget that the first Americans were the Indians. You will see as you read about life on the Western frontier that their culture was varied. Some tribes led a desperate, hand-to-mouth existence little better than that of the animals around them. But the proud, mounted Indians of the plains and the pueblo-dwellers of the Southwest found time for the development of legends and songs of real charm. Here are selections of folk literature from two of the more advanced tribes.

SONG OF THE SKY LOOM
Tewa Indian Song

In the settled life of the Pueblo Indians of the Southwest, weaving was a highly developed art. Weaving terms often figured in their speech. To the Tewas, for instance, the small desert rain characteristic of that part of the country, with its showers visibly threading their way downward, looked like the loom on which they wove their blankets. They called such showers the "sky loom." Any rain was a blessing in their parched land. This song is a prayer for one of the little desert rains.

O our Mother the Earth. O our Father the Sky,
Your children are we, and with tired backs
We bring you the gifts you love.
Then weave for us a garment of brightness;
May the warp° be the white light of morning,   5

5. **warp:** the threads lengthwise in a loom, crossed by the **weft** (l. 6), the filling thread carried by the shuttle.

May the weft be the red light of evening,
May the fringes be the falling rain,
May the border be the standing rainbow.
Thus weave for us a garment of brightness,
That we may walk fittingly where birds
sing,   10
That we may walk fittingly where grass
is green,
O our Mother the Earth, O our Father
the Sky.

THE SHARPENED LEG
Cheyenne Indian Story

Most of the stories told by the American
Indians are either religious or heroic, but
a few verge on the humorous. The humor
in this little tale told by the Cheyennes,
one of the superior tribes of Plains Indians,
is at the expense of the white men they
encountered in early frontier days.

THERE was a man whose leg was
pointed, so that by running and
jumping against trees he could stick in
them. By saying "naiwatoutawa," he
brought himself back to the ground. On
a hot day he would stick himself against
a tree for greater shade and coolness.
However, he could not do this trick
more than four times. Once while he
was doing this, White Man came to
him, crying, and said, "Brother, sharpen
my leg!" The man replied, "That is
not very hard. I can sharpen your leg."
White Man stood on a large log, and
the other, with an ax, sharpened his leg,
telling him to hold still bravely. The
pain caused the tears to come from his
eyes.

When the man had sharpened his
leg, he told him to do the trick only
four times a day and to keep count in
order not to exceed this number. White
Man went down toward the river, singing. Near the bank was a large tree;
toward this he ran, then jumped and
stuck in it. Then he called himself back
to the ground. Again he jumped, this
time against another tree; but now he
counted one, thinking in this way to
get the better of the other man. The
third time, he counted two. The fourth
time, birds and animals stood by; and
he was proud to show his ability, and
jumped high, and pushed his leg in up
to the knee. Then coyotes, wolves, and
other animals came to see him; some of
them asked how he came to know the
trick and begged him to teach it to
them, so they could stick to trees at
night.

He was still prouder now; and for the
fifth time he ran and jumped as high as
he could, and half his thigh entered the
tree. Then he counted four. Then he
called to get to the ground again. But he
stuck. He called out all day; he tried to
send the animals to the man who had
taught him. He was fast in the tree for
many days, until he starved to death.

For Discussion of Indian Literature

1. Why did the Pueblo Indians regard
the earth as their mother, the sky as their
father? How is the picture of a loom developed by various images in the poem?
Where else in this book have you found
weaving used as a poetic figure of speech?

2. What is the attitude of White Man
toward the Indians in "The Sharpened
Leg"? of the Indians toward White Man?
Do you think the overconfidence of white
men sometimes gave the Indians a realistic
basis for such stories? Why?

3. Were these tribes more or less advanced than the Ogillallahs Parkman visited? Give specific reasons for your answer.

4. Can you find out from history or local
old-timers what Indians once lived in your
locality? How advanced was their way of
life?

5. You can read more Indian songs in
The Winged Serpent, edited by Margot
Astrov, and more narratives in *Pueblo In-
dian Folk Stories,* collected by Charles F.
Loomis.

Ivy Bolton

1879–

THE GROWTH
OF THE MISSIONS

News of the discovery of gold in California in 1848 drew thousands of people to the Pacific coast. Some made the trip by sea, others braved the dangers of the overland route. When they reached their destination, they found a civilization that had been flourishing for almost a century.

A great deal of the credit for the highly civilized state of the Indians must be given to Father Junípero [1] Serra, a Franciscan priest, who founded his first mission at San Diego in 1769. Despite the hazards of hostile Indians, epidemics, and near-starvation in the wilderness, Father Serra founded many of the great missions of California and brought Christianity to thousands of savages in a fierce new world.

Handicapped by a snake bite on his leg which never healed, he walked through the wildest parts of Mexico and California converting the Indians. His ability to bear pain and hardship astonished and captivated the savages. His faith and unfailing sense of humor sustained him until his missions were secure. Father Serra built a line of nine missions, laying the foundations of great cities — San Francisco, Los Angeles, Santa Barbara, and Monterey.

Ivy Bolton's interest in Indians and pioneers was fostered by her father, an authority on Indian lore and Indian problems. Of the subject of her biography she states: "In Father Serra I found an opportunity to write the story of a real person, a pioneer who feared nothing, who ignored his handicaps and carried on in the face of disappointments because God had called him to a mighty work."

[1] **Junípero** (ho͞o·nē′på·rò).

"THE churches and the schools are the center of our missions, my brothers," Father Serra said. "Our own monasteries can wait; we can get along with what we have, but the churches and schools must be erected properly and of lasting material, for we build for the future."

He was not talking to the Spanish authorities now, but to those who shared his responsibilities, the Father Guardians of the missions who came together at San Carlos at Carmel-by-the-Sea for rest, refreshment, and counsel.

Some of them had doubted Father Serra's wisdom when at Monterey he had not built San Carlos close to the barracks. He had separated the mission at once, seeking carefully until he had found this quiet spot on the Carmel River at a considerable distance from the place the military authorities had chosen.

"Is it safe?" some of them had asked. "You do not know the Indians of Monterey, my father."

"We did not come to California to avoid risks," Father Serra had answered. "What we came to do was to win Indians, and *that* we cannot do on top of a barracks."

Today the visitors saw the outcome of the plan. Down out of sight — though not out of sound — was the fort, surrounded by barracks and small houses for the carpenters, blacksmiths, and other craftsmen. Innumerable small huts had been erected for the muleteers, the servants, and the Indians brought from Mexico.

"Already the settlement is growing," Father Crespi told the visitors. "The *San Antonio* and other ships make this their first port and each boat brings new arrivals for the settlement. Here we are alone. The Indians come to us and we can train them as we will."

Today everyone was willing to follow Father Serra's way. All the missions were outside the settlement and the plan now was to spread out, to reclaim land and make the missions to some extent self-supporting.

No one put in a plea for new monastic quarters. Though personal comforts were reduced to a minimum and the dwellings of the friars were still the flimsy shacks first erected, everyone knew that the poorest hut and the least convenient was Father Serra's own. They knew that he would always lead the way himself. . . .

Father Serra watched his guests depart the next day. How good God was to send him helpers such as these, he thought.

He stood there smiling as he watched the busy mission that was his own. The pile of stone for the church was growing, though the Indians were slow workers. Some of the younger men were plowing and a group of older ones were gathered about Father Crespi as he talked to them of the things of God.

Over at one corner, Indian women were cooking over a wood fire, making their chia[1] seed porridge and acorn bread. Others were fashioning the tamales[2] that even the Spaniards liked. They were about the shape and size of an orange, black and a little greasy, flavored with almonds.

It was not hard to teach the women, Father Serra mused. They were eager to learn — and the young married men were not too difficult. But something would have to be planned for the older lads who abhorred school and who spent their time in idleness and mischief. There must be something that they would like. Just now Father Serra did not know what.

The children were Father Serra's closest friends. They were forlorn little things, very much neglected till they were old enough to be of some use. Father Serra had been horrified when he found that the chiefs were willing to give the children away, not only the girls but boys, too, in exchange for pieces of cloth and old iron hoops. A battered hat was worth a lad of eleven.

Father Serra had gone to the rescue and now every mission had its school which rang with the laughter of little boys who romped and raced, who picked up the Spanish tongue with ease and responded loyally to that of which they had so little — love.

As soon as Father Serra came in sight they ran to him, climbing all over him and settling down at his feet while he told them stories or listened to their tales. They loved the touch of his hand in blessing upon their heads, and the most coveted of honors was to serve his Mass.

"They are our hope," Father Serra would say when a new young father came to him in despair because the class of small boys had suddenly vanished out of the window and departed. "They probably saw a squirrel or a bird. They will come back, my son. Be patient."

Yes, little by little, things were growing. It had not been easy to teach the Indians better ways of living. "Why build a house of adobe?"[3] one would

---

[1] **chia** (chē′ä): a plant growing in southwestern United States.

[2] **tamales** (tá·mä′lěz): a Mexican dish made of crushed maize mixed with minced meat, heavily seasoned.

[3] **adobe** (á·dō′bĭ): chunks of earth dried in the sun to be used as bricks.

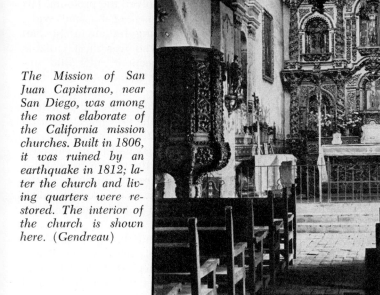

The Mission of San Juan Capistrano, near San Diego, was among the most elaborate of the California mission churches. Built in 1806, it was ruined by an earthquake in 1812; later the church and living quarters were restored. The interior of the church is shown here. (Gendreau)

ask. " It would have to be cleaned from time to time." The easiest way to clean a shack roofed with boughs was to burn it down and start afresh. Nor was there need to hurry about rebuilding. The summer nights were comfortable out of doors.

Only the rule that proper houses must be built on the mission lands or mission grants made any Indian consent to such waste of time and energy. But now some wanted to be with the fathers and had made a beginning.

It was some weeks later when he visited San Diego that Father Serra solved the problem of employment for the older lads. The flocks and herds of the mission had grown. Now the problem was how to look after them.

" We will make our own vaqueros [1] or cowboys," Father Serra decided.

There was an abundance of horses. Wild herds roamed the valleys and the

¹ **vaqueros** (vä·kâr′ōz): a Spanish word for herdsmen.

plains in such numbers that they were frequently a menace to the home farms and ranches, for in drought they invaded the pastures. Some of these were poor stock but there were good bands among them, mares and stallions that had drifted off from the expeditions and had inhabited some secluded place.

Riding was a new idea to the California Indians. They liked horse meat — and the herds would have been hunted down if they had not found it almost impossible to catch up with them. It took time and patience to teach them new ideas on the subject.

Father Serra chose his older lads carefully. It was a coveted honor to be enrolled in the class of the vaqueros and meant that there were tests to be made. A lad must be honest, fearless, and willing to obey and learn before he could have the opportunity.

The enrolled boy received a blanket, a new loincloth, and a serge blouse.

He had much to study and many a

hard tumble before he was allowed to ride the range. Next he had to make a lasso, a task not too difficult for him, and to learn to coil it and throw it with accuracy. He was taught to brand animals and herd them. Only then could he join the others in hunting the wild horses and bringing them in to tame.

To blindfold and saddle a wild horse and then keep a seat on the back of the bucking, rearing creature was a hard task, but still more astonishing was the gentling, the stroking of neck and throat, then talking to the frightened pony till he knew his master.

"We have found the way, my sons," Father Serra would say when he visited his missions and saw the pastures where the cattle grazed with the Indian lads caring for them.

It was not easy to be a good herdsman. There were real dangers surrounding the animals. The grizzly bear was a formidable antagonist and would come creeping down to carry off sheep and cattle if the herdsmen were not alert. Still more to be dreaded was the snarling puma with its sudden spring on cattle and men alike. The bobcat and the coyote took heavy toll at first till the Indians learned that the lasso was a weapon which could be cast and used to drag the snarling, fighting wild beasts out of harm's way.

"To make herdsmen of these Indians is pure folly," the soldiers and their comandantes would grumble. "They are worthless, useless, lazy, and also liars."

Sometimes it seemed as if they were right. To have so many calves and good beef cattle at one's disposal in the far pastures, near the home which was so poor and where one's own people lived from hand to mouth, was a sore temptation and one which often proved irresistible. There were unauthorized feasts in the villages at first, and the puma and the bear also kept high festival while the herdsman joined the family party. The friars found that they must count every animal themselves when they returned home.

It was not Father Serra but one of the other friars who solved the problem. His solution was spoken of far and wide. There was a young Indian in the San Diego Mission who was most capable and alert, an excellent rider and unafraid. Wherever a horse would take him he would go, and onlookers held their breath as they watched him leap the streams and the crevasses which no one else would attempt.

He fought pumas and bears valiantly and successfully, though his adventures were apt to enlarge themselves in the telling. Altogether, he was considered an excellent vaquero until he got near his own territory.

Then they found that he came back with fewer calves each day, and it was a very depleted herd that came back in two months. Proof was sought for and secured.

The boy was very penitent. Also he was dismayed. His horse and all his equipment belonged to the mission. If he was dismissed for this behavior he would have to go back to tilling the land, a task that he abhorred.

He took himself to the Father Guardian and poured out the whole story of his sins. He was going to be better. He was going to be the most reliable of vaqueros after this. He would tell no lies; he would never take anything that was not his — ever again.

The Father Guardian viewed his penitence with an effort to keep a stern and forbidding face.

"I could send you right away from us for all this, my son," he said at last. "We have done it before. No, do not weep. We may be able to give you another chance. First, you must prove all this reformation. Go to the mission school tomorrow, and when you have learned to read and write you may come back to me and we will see."

"Not ride? Not go to the pastures?

Not tend the cattle? " the penitent cried in dismay.

" If you want to do those things again and are really sorry for robbing us, go and learn," said the Father Guardian firmly.

" I will go," the boy said sadly and made his way to the mission school and introduced himself as a pupil to the Father Master, who received him without enthusiasm.

Six long weary weeks — and oh, how long they were! — as he toiled at a desk, making endless pothooks with a pen clamped in his hand like a dagger or a knife. He spent hours trying to discover why A was not B and what C had to do with the matter anyway. Intellectual work was never the outstanding gift of the vaquero.

It was a sadder, wiser, and very forlorn Indian boy who sought the Father Guardian six weeks later. " I am nothing but a wild Indian," the boy said wearily. " Oh, Father, let me go back to the herds. I will be the most honest Indian you ever had. The pothooks look worse every day and A and B and C grow more confusing. I will never steal again — I will tell the truth, always, always."

The Father Guardian thought for a few minutes. " I will give you one more chance, my son," he said at last, trying not to laugh when the lad leaped into the air with a shout which resembled a war whoop.

" I suppose we had better keep that lad in the home pastures from now on," the young brother farmer said diffidently the next evening, but the Father Guardian shook his head.

" Send him everywhere and especially near his own people," he answered. " That lad will not steal again."

He did not, though it involved bitter misunderstandings with his own family. In the years that followed he loved to tell the story of how the fathers had made him trustworthy.

The story of his punishment had a far-reaching effect. It roused laughter now and then, but a sorely tempted vaquero would think twice before he allowed himself or his friends to steal.

An hour or two in the stocks, even a day or so in prison might be worth while, but pothooks and A and B and C — most decidedly not.

They were a wild and fearless set, these vaquero lads, but the fathers won them. Father Serra and his friars understood them, and there were fewer and fewer complaints as the years went on. The Spanish soldiers eyed the cowboys with astonishment as they came in to own up frankly about something that had gone amiss — my own fault, Father — was generally the end of the report.

The way was not all sunshine. There were many failures and disappointments when long hours of toil seemed to have gone for nothing. The old people were difficult, dull, and always unpredictable. Worst of all, they had a way of picking up their families and belongings and disappearing overnight to some new hunting ground.

It was small wonder that sometimes the friars grew weary and discouraged and begged to go home to Mexico City and the regular life there.

Discouragement was the hardest thing for Father Serra to understand. He could see good in the most worthless material. He never faltered on his way for pain, fatigue, unkindness, and danger. It took long years for him to learn to be patient with weaker men, but from the time he became the head of the missions he managed to acquire sympathy with the discouraged and was quick to discover if the reason for depression was inability, illness, or a real need of change and rest.

To all the friars, as well as to himself, the rule was the same. " No service is too great, no service is too small, if it helps to win Christ's people," said Father Serra.

A

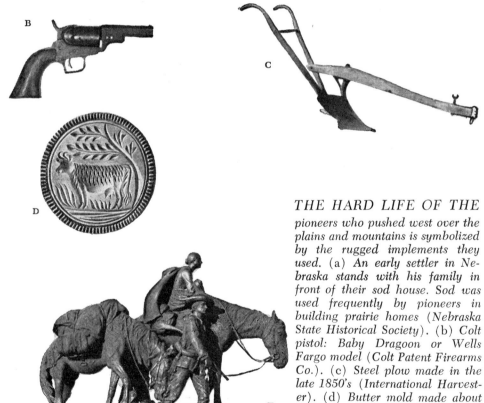

B

C

D

E

THE HARD LIFE OF THE

pioneers who pushed west over the plains and mountains is symbolized by the rugged implements they used. (a) *An early settler in Nebraska stands with his family in front of their sod house. Sod was used frequently by pioneers in building prairie homes (Nebraska State Historical Society). (b) Colt pistol: Baby Dragoon or Wells Fargo model (Colt Patent Firearms Co.). (c) Steel plow made in the late 1850's (International Harvester). (d) Butter mold made about 1855 (Index of American Design). (e) "Pioneer Mother," statue by Phimister Proctor, which stands in Kansas City, Missouri (Armstrong Roberts).*

F

G

(f) *Conestoga wagon — the "prairie schooner" (Black Star). (g) Navaho Indian blanket (Heye Foundation). (h) Scales for weighing gold, used in the California Gold Rush (Index of American Design). (i) "F Street, Denver," in an old print dated 1866. A variety of vehicles and several different kinds of draft-animals can be seen on this unpaved street with its wooden sidewalks (Old Print Shop).*

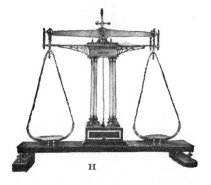

H

I

For Discussion of Bolton

1. Faith and sacrifice comprised the secret of Father Serra's success as a missioner. Check over the selection and recall incidents that reveal his faith and readiness to make sacrifices.

2. In building the missions, Father Serra insisted that they be separated from the military barracks. Explain the reason for his insistence on this point.

3. The living quarters of the friars were of secondary importance in the plan for the missions. Why is this truly a missionary tradition?

4. Obtain an atlas or a gazetteer from your school library. Turn to the list of the towns and cities of California. How many can you find that are named after the saints or the mysteries of our religion?

Richard
Henry Dana, Jr.
1815–1882
FROM TWO YEARS BEFORE THE MAST

FROM THE FORECASTLE

While daring trappers and explorers were opening the overland way across the continent, Yankee ships were making the hard voyage to reach the Pacific Coast by sea. One of the early sailors was Richard Henry Dana, Jr. When he had to leave Harvard because of failing eyesight, Dana shipped as an ordinary seaman on a vessel bound from Boston around Cape Horn to California and back. After his return he wrote the famous *Two Years before the Mast* (1840) with the avowed purpose of telling of life at sea not from the point of view of the officers, but from the point of view of the common sailor. He was concerned over the tyranny and brutal treatment that sailors had to endure, as you can see from his account of the captain's behavior in this selection. In the following passage we find the young sailor suffering from an infected tooth on top of the usual rigors of sea life.

Friday, July 1. We were now nearly up to the latitude of Cape Horn; and having over forty degrees of easting to make, we squared away the yards before a strong westerly gale, shook a reef out of the fore topsail, and stood on our way, east by south, with the prospect of being up with the cape in a week or ten days. As for myself, I had had no sleep for forty-eight hours; and the want of rest, together with constant wet and cold, had increased the swelling, so that my face was nearly as large as two, and I found it impossible to get my mouth open wide enough to eat. In this state the steward applied to the captain for some rice to boil for me, but he only got a — "No! d—— you! Tell him to eat salt junk and hard bread, like the rest of them." This was, in truth, what I expected. However, I did not starve; for Mr. Brown, who was a man as well as a sailor and had always been a good friend to me, smuggled a pan of rice into the galley, and told the cook to boil it for me, and not let the "old man" see it. Had it been fine weather, or in port, I should have gone below and lain by until my face got well; but in such weather as this, and shorthanded as we were, it was not for me to desert my post; so I kept on deck, and stood my watch and did my duty as well as I could.

Monday, July 4. This was "Independence Day" in Boston. What firing of guns, and ringing of bells, and rejoicings of all sorts, in every part of our country! The ladies (who have not gone down to Nahant for a breath of cool air and sight of the ocean) walking the streets with parasols over their heads, and the dandies in their white pantaloons and silk stockings! What quantities of ice cream have been eaten, and how many loads of ice brought into the city from a distance and sold out by the lump and the pound!

The smallest of the islands which we saw today would have made the fortune of poor Jack, if he had had it in Boston; and I dare say he would have had no objection to being there with it. This, to be sure, was no place to keep the Fourth of July. To keep ourselves warm, and the ship out of the ice, was as much as we could do. Yet no one forgot the day; and many were the wishes and conjectures and comparisons, both serious and ludicrous, which were made among all hands. The sun shone bright as long as it was up, only that a scud of black clouds was ever and anon driving across it. At noon we were in latitude 54° 27′ S., and longitude 85° 5′ W., having made a good deal of easting, but having lost in our latitude by the heading off of the wind. Between daylight we saw thirty-four ice islands of various sizes; some no bigger than the hull of our vessel, and others apparently nearly as large as the one that we first saw. At 4:00 P.M. (it was then quite dark)

all hands were called, and sent aloft, in a violent squall of hail and rain, to take in sail. We had now all got on our "Cape Horn rig," thick boots, southwesters coming down over our necks and ears, thick trousers and jackets, and some with oilcloth suits over all. Mittens, too, we wore on deck; but it would not do to go aloft with them, as, being wet and stiff, they might let a man slip overboard, for all the hold he could get upon a rope: so we were obliged to work with bare hands, which, as well as our faces, were often cut with the hailstones, which fell thick and large. Our ship was now all cased with ice — hull, spars, and standing rigging; and the running rigging so stiff that we could hardly bend it so as to belay it, or, still less, take a knot with it; and the sails frozen. One at a time (for it was a long piece of work and required many hands) we furled the courses, mizzen topsail, and fore-topmast staysail; and close-reefed the fore and main topsails; and hove the ship to under the fore, with the main hauled up by the clewlines and buntlines and ready to be sheeted home if we found it necessary to make sail to get the windward of an ice island. A regular lookout was then set, and kept by each night. It blew hard the whole time, and there was an almost constant driving of either rain, hail, or snow. In addition to this, it was "as thick as muck" and the ice was all about us.

The captain was on deck nearly the whole night, and kept the cook in the galley, with a roaring fire, to make coffee for him, which he took every few hours, and once or twice gave a little to his officers; but not a drop of anything was there for the crew. The captain, who sleeps all the daytime and comes and goes at night as he chooses, can have his brandy and water in the cabin, and his hot coffee at the galley; while Jack, who has to stand through everything and work in wet and cold, can have nothing to wet his lips or warm his stomach. This was a "temperance ship," by her articles, and, like too many such ships, the temperance was all in the forecastle. The sailor, who only takes his one glass as it is dealt out to him, is in danger of being drunk; while the captain, upon whose self-possession and cool judgment the lives of all depend, may be trusted with any amount to drink at his will.

But this is not doubling Cape Horn. Eight hours of the night our watch was on deck, and during the whole of that time we kept a bright lookout: one man on each bow, another in the bunt of the foreyard, the third mate on the scuttle, one man on each quarter, and another always standing by the wheel. The chief mate was everywhere, and commanded the ship when the captain was below. When a large piece of ice was seen in our way, or drifting near us, the word was passed along, and the ship's head turned one way and another; and sometimes the yards squared or braced up. There was little else to do than to look out, and we had the sharpest eyes in the ship on the forecastle. The only variety was the monotonous voice of the lookout forward — "Another island!" — "Ice ahead!" — "Ice on the lee bow!" — "Hard up the helm!" — "Keep her off a little!" — "Stead-y!"

In the meantime the wet and cold had brought my face into such a state that I could neither eat nor sleep; and though I stood it out all night, yet, when it became light, I was in such a state that all hands told me I must go below, and lie by for a day or two, or I should be laid up for a long time. When the watch was changed I went into the steerage, and took off my hat and comforter, and showed my face to the mate, who told me to go below at once, and stay in my berth until the swelling went down, and gave the cook orders to make a poultice for me, and said he would speak to the captain.

I went below and turned in, covering myself over with blankets and jackets, and lay in my berth nearly twenty-four hours, half asleep and half awake, stupid from the dull pain.

It was a dreadful night for those on deck. A watch of eighteen hours, with wet and cold and constant anxiety, nearly wore them out; and when they came below at nine o'clock for breakfast, they almost dropped asleep on their chests, and some of them were so stiff that they could with difficulty sit down. Not a drop of anything had been given them during the whole time (though the captain, as on the night that I was on deck, had his coffee every four hours), except that the mate stole a potful of coffee for two men to drink behind the galley, while he kept a lookout for the captain. Every man had his station and was not allowed to leave it; and nothing happened to break the monotony of the night, except once setting the main topsail to run clear of a large island to leeward which they were drifting fast upon. Some of the boys got so sleepy and stupefied that they actually fell asleep at their posts; and the young third mate, Mr. Hatch, whose post was the exposed one of standing on the fore scuttle, was so stiff, when he was relieved, that he could not bend his knees to get down. By a constant lookout and a quick shifting of the helm, as the islands and pieces came in sight, the ship went clear of everything but a few small pieces, though daylight showed the ocean covered for miles.

At daybreak it fell a dead calm; and with the sun the fog cleared a little and a breeze sprung up from the westward, which soon grew into a gale. We had now a fair wind, daylight, and comparatively clear weather; yet, to the surprise of everyone, the ship continued hove-to. "Why does not he run?" "What is the captain about?" was asked by everyone; and from questions it soon grew into complaints and mur-

murings. When the daylight was so short, it was too bad to lose it, and a fair wind, too, which everyone had been praying for. As hour followed hour, and the captain showed no sign of making sail, the crew became impatient, and there was a good deal of talking and consultation together on the forecastle. They had been beaten out with the exposure and hardship, and impatient to get out of it; and this unaccountable delay was more than they could bear in quietness, in their excited and restless state. Some said the captain was frightened — completely cowed by the dangers and difficulties that surrounded us, and was afraid to make sail — while others said that in his anxiety and suspense he had made a free use of brandy and opium, and was unfit for his duty.

The carpenter, who was an intelligent man, and a thorough seaman, and had great influence with the crew, came down into the forecastle and tried to induce them to go aft and ask the captain why he did not run, or request him, in the name of all hands, to make sail. This appeared to be a very reasonable request, and the crew agreed that if he did not make sail before noon they would go aft. Noon came, and no sail was made. A consultation was held again; and it was proposed to take the ship from the captain and give the command of her to the mate, who had been heard to say that if he could have his way the ship would have been half the distance to the cape before night — ice or no ice. And so irritated and impatient had the crew become that even this proposition, which was open mutiny, was entertained; and the carpenter went to his berth, leaving it tacitly understood that something serious would be done if things remained as they were many hours longer. When the carpenter left, we talked it all over and I gave my advice strongly against it. Another of the men, too, who had known something of the kind attempt-

ed in another ship by a crew who were dissatisfied with their captain, and which was followed with serious consequences, was opposed to it. Stimson, who soon came down, joined us, and we determined to have nothing to do with it. By these means the crew were soon induced to give it up for the present, though they said they would not lie where they were much longer without knowing the reason.

I still remained in my berth, fast recovering, yet not well enough to go safely on deck. And I should have been perfectly useless; for, from having eaten nothing for nearly a week, except a little rice which I forced into my mouth the last day or two, I was as weak as an infant. To be sick in a forecastle is miserable indeed. It is the worst part of a dog's life, especially in bad weather. The forecastle, shut up tight to keep out the water and cold air; the watch either on deck or asleep in their berths; no one to speak to; the pale light of the single lamp, swinging to and fro from the beam, so dim that one can scarcely see, much less read, by it; the water dropping from the beams and carlines and running down the sides, and the forecastle so wet and dark and cheerless, and so lumbered up with chests and wet clothes, that sitting up is worse than lying in the berth. These are some of the evils. Fortunately I needed no help from anyone, and no medicine; and if I had needed help, I don't know where I should have found it. Sailors are willing enough; but it is true, as is often said, no one ships for nurse on board a vessel. Our merchant ships are always undermanned; and if one man is lost by sickness, they cannot spare another to take care of him. A sailor is always presumed to be well, and if he's sick he's a poor dog. One has to stand his wheel, and another his lookout; and the sooner he gets on deck again the better.

Accordingly, as soon as I could possibly go back to my duty, I put on my thick clothes and boots and southwester and made my appearance on deck. I had been but a few days below, yet everything looked strangely enough. The ship was cased in ice — decks, sides, masts, yards, and rigging. Two close-reefed topsails were all the sail she had on, and every sail and rope was frozen so stiff in its place that it seemed as though it would be impossible to start anything. Reduced, too, to her topmasts, she had altogether a most forlorn and crippled appearance. The sun had come up brightly; the snow was swept off the decks and ashes thrown upon them so that we could walk, for they had been as slippery as glass. It was, of course, too cold to carry on any ship's work, and we had only to walk the deck and keep ourselves warm. The wind was still ahead, and the whole ocean, to the eastward, covered with islands and field ice.

At four bells the order was given to square away the yards, and the man who came from the helm said that the captain had kept her off to N.N.E. What could this mean? The wildest rumors got adrift. Some said that he was going to run out of the ice and cross the Pacific, and go home round the Cape of Good Hope. Soon, however, it leaked out, and we found that we were running for the Straits of Magellan. The news soon spread through the ship, and all tongues were at work talking about it. No one on board had been through the straits; but I had in my chest an account of the passage of the ship A. J. Donelson, of New York, through those straits a few years before. The account was given by the captain, and the representation was as favorable as possible. It was soon read by everyone on board, and various opinions pronounced. The determination of our captain had at least this good effect: it gave us something to think and talk about, made a break in our life, and diverted our minds from the monotonous dreariness of the prospect before us. Having made a fair wind of it, we were going off at a good rate and leaving the thickest of the ice behind us. This, at least, was something.

Having been long enough below to get my hands well warmed and softened, the first handling of the ropes was rather tough; but a few days hardened them. And as soon as I got my mouth open wide enough to take in a piece of salt beef and hard bread, I was all right again.

For Discussion of Dana

1. What evidence does Dana cite to prove that the distinction between captain and crew was exaggerated and unfair? What do you know of shipboard working conditions today? What safeguards now exist for merchant sailors?

2. What details does Dana give that make you feel keenly the bitter cold in which the sailors worked? How does the sailors' hatred of the cold play a part in the drama aboard ship? What recollections of the sailors intensify their unhappy situation?

3. Imagine yourself to be an adventurous young American of the 1830's or 1840's. Write a letter to your family explaining why you have decided to make a trip by sea. Put in definite details to show that you have considered the hardships of the journey before making up your mind.

4. For more information about the actual life of a sailor, read all of *Two Years before the Mast*.

For Your Vocabulary

NAUTICAL TERMS IN CONTEXT: As in the *Moby Dick* selection on page 541, you probably notice a number of nautical terms. How many of these were you able to define from context: *topsail, galley, hull, spars, belay, rigging, furled, hove-to, leeward*? What actions are described in the following phrases: " squared away the yards," " stood on our way," " hove the ship to under the fore," " make sail "?

Louise Amelia Clappe
1819-1906
FROM THE SHIRLEY LETTERS

A GOLD RUSH MINING CAMP

Most people who lived through the Gold Rush days in the mining camps of California were too busy with pick and shovel to notice carefully the life around them, much less write about it. But the young wife of a doctor in one of the mushrooming settlements, Mrs. Louise Amelia Knapp (Smith) Clappe, left the digging to others and used her pen to work a different kind of gold mine, a veritable gold mine of information about life in the camps. She had promised to give her sister back in New England a complete and truthful account of the strange new world she was living in, and she succeeded remarkably in a series of letters. Her keen eye took in every detail of the camp on Rich Bar, and her lively pen recorded the whole picture.

Somehow an early California magazine secured and printed copies of the letters under the pen name " Dame Shirley." For over seventy years the " Shirley Letters " lay hidden in files, known only to a few enthusiasts. Recently they have been collected and published. Now readers far and wide have discovered that the author gives them just what the subtitle promises, " A Trip into the Mines." The letters are distinctly feminine. Dame Shirley wrote in the refined vocabulary and style cultivated by gentlewomen of her day. More important, she noted and recorded trifles that men would never have thought worthy of comment.

Rich Bar,
East Branch of the North Fork
of Feather River,
September 20, 1851

I INTEND today, dear M., to be as disagreeably statistical and as praiseworthily matter-of-factish as the most dogged utilitarian could desire. I shall give you a full, true, and particular account of the discovery, rise, and progress of this place, with a religious adherence to *dates,* which will rather astonish your unmathematical mind. But let me first describe the spot, as it looked to my wondering and unaccustomed eyes. Remember, I had never seen a mining district before; and had

just left San Francisco, amid whose flashy-looking shops and showy houses the most of my time had been spent, since my arrival into the Golden State. Of course, to me, the coup d'œil [1] of Rich Bar was charmingly fresh and original. Imagine a tiny valley, about eight hundred yards in length and, perhaps, thirty in width (it was measured for my especial information), apparently hemmed in by lofty hills, almost perpendicular, draperied to their very summits with beautiful fir trees; the blue-bosomed " Plumas," or Feather River I suppose I must call it, undulat-

[1] coup d'œil (kōō dû'y): a brief survey, as at one glance.

"A Gold Rush Mining Camp" from *The Shirley Letters, from the California Mines,* edited by Carl I. Wheat, published by Alfred A. Knopf, Inc.

ing along their base, and you have as good an idea as I can give you of the *locale* of " Barra Rica," [1] as the Spaniards so prettily term it.

In almost any of the numerous books written upon California, no doubt you will be able to find a most scientific description of the origin of these " Bars." I must acknowledge, with shame, that my ideas on the subject are distressingly vague. I could never appreciate the poetry or the humor of making one's wrists ache by knocking to pieces gloomy looking stones, or in dirtying one's fingers by analyzing soils, in a vain attempt to fathom the osteology, or anatomy, of our beloved earth; though my heart is thrillingly alive to the faintest shade of color, and the infinite variety of styles in which she delights to robe her ever-changeful and ever-beautiful *surface*. In my unscientific mind the *formations* are without form and void; and you might as well talk Chinese to me, as to embroider your conversation with the terms " hornblende," " mica," " limestone," " slate," " granite," and " quartz," in a hopeless attempt to enlighten me as to their merits. The dutiful diligence with which I attended course after course of lectures on geology by America's greatest illustrator of that subject, arose rather from my affectionate reverence for our beloved Dr. H., [2] and the fascinating charm which his glorious mind throws round every subject which it condescends to illuminate, than to any interest in the dry science itself. It is, therefore, with a most humiliating consciousness of my geological deficiencies, that I offer you the only explanation which I have been able to obtain from those most learned in such matters here.

I gather from their remarks that these bars are formed by deposits of earth, rolling down from the mountains, crowding the river aside, and occupying a portion of its deserted bed. If my definition is unsatisfactory, I can but refer you to some of the aforesaid works upon California.

Through the middle of Rich Bar runs the street, thickly planted with about forty tenements; among which figure round tents, square tents, plank hovels, log cabins, etc., — the residences, varying in elegance and convenience from the palatial splendor of " The Empire," [3] down to a " local habitation," formed of pine boughs, and covered with old calico shirts.

Today I visited the " Office "; the only one on the river. I had heard so much about it from others, as well as from F., [4] that I really *did* expect something extra. When I entered this imposing place, the shock to my optic nerves was so great that I sank, helplessly, upon one of the benches which ran, divanlike, the whole length (ten feet!) of the building, and laughed till I cried. There was, of course, no floor; a rude nondescript in one corner, on which was ranged the medical library, consisting of half a dozen volumes, did duty as a table. The shelves, which looked like sticks snatched hastily from the woodpile and nailed up without the least alteration, contained quite a respectable array of medicines. The white canvas window stared everybody in the face, with the interesting information painted on it, in perfect grenadiers of capitals, that this was Dr. ——'s office.

At my loud laugh (which, it must be confessed, was noisy enough to give the

---

[1] Barra Rica (bä′rá rē′ká): Spanish for "Rich Bar."

[2] Dr. H.: the noted geologist and scholar, Dr. Edward Hitchcock, who for many years taught chemistry and geology at Amherst College.

[3] The Empire, Rich Bar's "hotel," had a combination saloon and general store, a parlor, and four bedrooms, all lined with brightly colored calico.

[4] Her husband, Dr. Fayette Clappe, whose office is here described.

whole street assurance of the presence of a woman), F. looked shocked, and his partner looked prussic acid. To him (the partner, I mean — he hadn't been out of the mines for years), the "Office" was a thing sacred and set apart for an almost admiring worship. It was a beautiful, architectural ideal, embodied in pine shingles and cotton cloth. Here, he literally "lived, and moved, and had his being," his bed and his board. With an admiration of the fine arts, truly praiseworthy, he had fondly decorated the walls thereof with sundry pictures from Godey, Graham and Sartain's Magazines, among which, fashion plates with imaginary monsters sporting miraculous waists, impossible wrists and fabulous feet, largely predominated.

During my call at the office, I was introduced to one of the *finders* of Rich Bar — a young Georgian, who afterward gave me a full description of all the facts connected with its discovery. This unfortunate had not spoken to a woman for two years; and in the elation of his heart at the joyful event, he rushed out and invested capital in some excellent champagne, which I, on Willie's principle of "doing in Turkey as the Turkies do," assisted the company in drinking to the honor of my own arrival. I mention this, as an instance that nothing can be done in California without the sanctifying influence of the *spirit;* and it generally appears in a much more "questionable shape" than that of sparkling wine. Mr. H. informed me, that on the twentieth of July, 1850, it was rumored at Nelson's Creek — a mining station situated at the Middle Fork of the Feather River, about eighty miles from Marysville — that one of those vague "Somebodies" — a near relation of the "They Says" — had discovered mines of a remarkable richness in a northeasterly direction, and about forty miles from the first-mentioned place. Anxious and immediate search

was made for "Somebody," but, as our Western brethren say, he "wasn't thar!" But his absence could not deter the miners when once the golden rumor had been set afloat. A large company packed up their goods and chattels, generally consisting of a pair of blankets, a frying pan, some flour, salt pork, brandy, pickax, and shovel, and started for the new Dorado. They "traveled, and traveled, and traveled," as we used to say in the fairy stories, for nearly a week in every possible direction, when one evening, weary and discouraged, about one hundred of the party found themselves at the top of that famous hill, which figures so largely in my letters, whence the river can be distinctly seen. Half of the number concluded to descend the mountain that night, the remainder stopping on the summit until the next morning. On arriving at Rich Bar, part of the adventurers camped there, but many went a few miles further down the river. The next morning two men turned over a large stone, beneath which they found quite a sizable piece of gold. They washed a small panful of the dirt, and obtained from it two hundred and fifty-six dollars. Encouraged by this success, they commenced staking off the legal amount of ground allowed to each person for mining purposes; and, the remainder of the party having descended the hill, before night the entire bar was "claimed." In a fortnight from that time, the two men who found the first bit of gold had each taken out six thousand dollars. Two others took out thirty-three pounds of gold in eight hours; which is the best day's work that has been done on this branch of the river; the largest amount ever taken from one panful of dirt was fifteen hundred dollars. In little more than a week after its discovery, five hundred men had settled upon the bar for the summer. Such is the wonderful alacrity with which a mining town is built. Soon after was discovered on the same side of the river — about half a mile apart, and at nearly the same distance from this place — the two bars, "Smith" and "Indian," both very rich; also another, lying across the river, just opposite Indian, called "Missouri Bar." There are several more, all within a few miles of here, called "Frenchman's," "Taylor's," "Brown's," "The Junction," "Wyandott" and "Muggin's." But they are at present of little importance as mining stations.

Those who worked in these mines during the fall of 1850 were extremely fortunate; but, alas! the Monte [1] fiend ruined hundreds! Shall I tell you the fate of two of the most successful of these gold hunters? From poor men, they found themselves at the end of a few weeks, absolutely rich. Elated with their good fortune, seized with a mania for Monte, in less than a year, these unfortunates — so lately respectable and intelligent — became a pair of drunken gamblers. One of them at this present writing, works for five dollars a day and boards himself out of that; the other actually suffers for the necessaries of life — a too common result of scenes in the mines.

There were but few that dared to remain in the mountains during the winter for fear of being buried in the snow; of which at that time they had a most vague idea. I have been told that in these sheltered valleys it seldom falls to the depth of more than a foot, and disappears almost invariably within a day or two. Perhaps there were three hundred that concluded to stay; of which number, two-thirds stopped on Smith's Bar, as the labor of mining there is much easier than it is here. Contrary to the general expectation, the weather was delightful until about the middle of March; it then commenced storming, and continued to snow and rain incessantly for nearly three weeks. Supposing that the rainy season had passed, hundreds had arrived on the river during the previous month. The snow, which fell several feet in depth on the mountains, rendered the trail impassable and entirely stopped the pack trains; provisions soon became scarce, and the sufferings of these unhappy men were, indeed, extreme. Some adventurous spirits, with true Yankee hardihood, forced their way through the snow to the Frenchman's ranch, and packed flour *on their backs,* for more than forty miles! The first meal that arrived sold for three dollars a pound. Many subsisted for days on nothing but barley, which is kept here to feed the pack-mules on. One unhappy individual who could not obtain even a little barley, for love or money, and had eaten nothing for three days, forced his way out to the Spanish rancho fourteen miles distant, and in less than an hour after his arrival, had devoured *twenty-seven* biscuit and a corresponding quantity of other eatables, and, of course, drinkables to match. Don't let this account alarm you. There is no danger of another famine here. They tell me that there is hardly a building in the place that has not food enough in it to last its occupants for the next two years; besides, there are two or three well-filled groceries in town.

For Discussion of The Shirley Letters

1. Describe the general layout of the town. What buildings were worthy of special note? Try to obtain pictures of Gold Rush days which will help illustrate this account. What kinds of boom towns are still to be found occasionally in America?

2. How was Rich Bar discovered? How soon after the first trace of gold was found was the entire bar staked? What happened to the fortunes some of the discoverers amassed?

3. Why was Dame Shirley moved to laughter when she first saw her husband's

[1] **Monte** (mǒn′tå): a Spanish and Spanish-American gambling game played with a Spanish pack of cards.

office? What testimony does she give that the medical supplies were not so inadequate as the furnishings?

4. What details did the writer record that a man would not have noticed? Recall some comments that might be attributed to a New England background rather than to usual feminine interests. Would you call Dame Shirley strait-laced? Why, or why not?

For Your Vocabulary

" OLOGIES ": " Shirley " says she has never desired " to fathom the *osteology* . . .

of our beloved earth." A little later she speaks of attending lectures on *geology*. Both of these words contain *-logy*, which means " science." *Osteology* is the science dealing with bones. (What is an *osteopath?*) *Geology* is the science which treats of the history of the earth as recorded in rocks. (Compare it with *geography*.) So many sciences have names ending in *-ology* that sciences and theories and philosophies are sometimes humorously referred to as *ologies*. What is the meaning of *biology, philology, theology, zoology, genealogy, mineralogy?* (Note the spelling of the last two.)

Artemus Ward
1834–1867

A BUSINESS LETTER

As the frontier grew into pioneer communities and then into towns, newspapers were established. Now the West had a voice, and Western humor laughed aloud in the special columns that soon became a feature of the papers. The most popular columnists, far from echoing the cultured style of Eastern journals, made capital of the crude vernacular of the frontier. Many wrote in dialect. Artemus [1] Ward (as Charles Farrar Browne signed his column), one of the most widely popular, went further and used outrageous misspelling as an additional source of fun. The audience he addressed was not in the parlors of Boston but in the circle sitting on cracker boxes around the stove in country stores. The group of humorists he represents are called " The Crackerbox Philosophers." They de-

serve the full title, for along with fun, they served up shrewd observations on their communities. You can see the Yankee keenness for getting on in the world in this letter. The sideshow described here is a fiction which Ward carried on in his column in the Cleveland *Plain Dealer*.

To the Editor of the —

Sir. — I'm movin' along — slowly along — down tords your place. My show at present consists of three moral Bares, a Kangaroo (a amoozin little Raskal — 'twould make you larf yerself to deth to see the little cuss jump up and squeal), wax figgers of G. Washington, Gen. Taylor, John Bunyan, Capt. Kidd, and Dr. Webster in the act of killin' Dr. Parkman, besides several miscellanyus moral

---

[1] Artemus (är'tĕ·mŭs).

wax statoots of celebrated piruts & murderers, &c., ekalled by few & exceld by none. Now, Mr. Editor, scratch orf a few lines sayin' how is the show bizness down to your place. I shall have my hanbills dun at your offiss. Depend upon it. I want you should git my hanbills up in flamin' stile. Also, git up a tremenjus excitement in yr. paper 'bowt my onparaleld Show. We must fetch the public somhow. We must wurk on their feelins. Cum the moral on 'em strong. If it's a temperance community, tell 'em I sined the pledge fifteen minutes arter Ise born, but on the contery, ef your peple take their tods, say Mister Ward is as Jenial a feller as we ever met, full of conwivIality, & the life an sole of the Soshul Bored. Take, don't you? If you say anythin' abowt my show, say my snaiks is as harmliss as the newborn Babe. What a interestin' study it is to see a zewolOgical animil like a snaik under perfeck subjection! My Kangaroo is the most larfable little cuss I ever saw. All for 15 cents. I am anxyus to skewer your infloounce. I repeet in regard to them hanbills, that I shall git 'em struck orf up to your printin' offiss. My perliteral sentiments agree with yourn exactly. I know thay do, becawz I never saw a man whoos didn't.

Respectively yures,

A. Ward.

P.S. — You scratch my back & Ile scratch your back.

For Discussion of Ward

1. Like all satire, this letter merely exaggerates practices which all readers knew existed. What are some of them? Interpret the postscript.

2. How does the spelling add to the humorous effect? What words in this letter are spelled according to a backwoods pronunciation?

3. Can you understand why this letter would have appealed to Abraham Lincoln, considering his upbringing and his personality?

The War between the States

THE westward movement cannot be understood fully unless we take into account the War between the States. It is possible that a settlement between North and South could have been reached if it had not been for their competition to win over the West to one side or the other. And once the war was over, the wearied, depleted peoples of both sides turned westward for a new start. The West boomed as never before.

Not much of the literature we read today came out of the years between 1861 and 1865. But the War between the States has entered into our feeling and thinking, and become a part of our heritage, in a way that few other events have. It has been the subject of many books and poems since 1865, and in a sense it has gone into every book written in America since then, because it has become a part of every American.

Never was a war undertaken with less willingness or with heavier hearts. This was a war between states that had fought side by side for independence. This was brother against brother. Many Northerners believed sincerely that slavery was morally wrong and degrading, and were infuriated that "the land of the free" should also be the land of slavery. Many Southerners believed just as sincerely that slavery was necessary to the best way of life; they pointed to the achievements of Greece when Athens had four slaves to every free man; and they were infuriated at the thought that Northerners should set themselves up as judges over the South. And some Northerners and Southerners alike, though they opposed slavery, preferred slower, more gradual means of ending it than the immediate action proposed by the fiery Abolitionists.

The Issues at Stake

The issues were both old and complicated. From the first, the South had developed into a country of broad plantations owned by a leisurely, cultivated aristocracy. There were few factories, few large cities. The country lived on what it grew and on what it got from the cotton it sent abroad for sale. The North, on the other hand, early developed cities, manufacturing centers, financiers. Its agriculture was in farms, rather than plantations; the owner and his family tilled the farm; and the hired workers, if any, sat at the family table and were called "help." These two sections naturally came to have different needs and to feel differently about political questions. The North wanted a strong federal government and a high tariff to protect its manufactures and its wage scale. The South preferred a localized government by states, and a low tariff which would encourage trade and make the most of its cheap labor.

It was the West that really pushed the older sections into war. We have come to see now that the War between the States was really one chapter in the settling of the West. Both sections needed the wealth of the West. The North did not want the slave lands extended. The South felt it should not be excluded from a part of the continent it had helped to gain. When the South talked of secession, the northern states along the Mississippi River talked of union because they did not want customhouses blocking their outlet to the Gulf of Mexico. The statesmen of the East arranged compromise after compromise — one slave state for one free state, one free state for one slave state. But the situation grew more and more explosive. Some of the Western states began to take things into their own hands — Kansas with John Brown, for example, and California, which announced calmly that it was going to be a free state regardless of what anybody else said. It became apparent, as Lincoln said, that "the union cannot permanently exist half slave and half free." The election of 1860 laid the fire, and the attack on Fort Sumter supplied the spark. The South seceded, and the North went to war.

The final issue, once war came, was whether states had the right to secede, rather than the question of slavery. We realize now that slavery was like a wolf which the South held by the ears and could neither hold indefinitely nor let go. We realize also that emancipation did not solve the racial problem underlying slavery, and that emancipation and the war together kept the South poor for decades. Some men in 1860 and 1861 were merely hot-headed. Others, like Lincoln and Lee, saw the gravity of the problems and foresaw some of the results. They went to war sadly and with foreboding.

Before peace came again, nearly half a million soldiers died. Beautiful cities were burned. Northern resources were drained. The South was impoverished.

The War between the States (1861–65) came, on the average, about two-thirds through the careers of Emerson, Longfellow, Lowell, Whittier, and Holmes. Poe and Irving were already dead. Thoreau and Hawthorne died during the war. Whitman had just begun his career. Mark Twain had not yet published.

Two Great Americans

No chapter in our national history has so wrung our hearts, so deeply moved and stirred us. And yet there was surprisingly little important literature written about the war until much later. There were some great songs, like " The Battle Hymn of the Republic." A little later there were fine poems, like Lowell's " Commemoration Ode," and Timrod's " Ode."

But great chapters of history do not make great books until later; they make great men! The War between the States gave us at least two men who are among our greatest.

Lee: Leader of the South

One of them was Robert E. Lee, soldier, born of a soldier's family, father of soldiers. When the war began, he was offered the command of the Northern army, but he stayed with his state and his South. He was more than a general;

he was a great leader. When the time came to admit the war was lost and say farewell to his troops, he turned all his energies to helping Southerners return to the American family of states, bury their bitterness, and look ahead, not back. He represented all the chivalry of the South, all the daring and bravery and resourcefulness that Europe had learned to expect of Americans, all the humanity and regard for his men that might be expected of any greathearted gentleman. He was not a brilliant writer, but he wrote with clarity and character. Historians have disagreed on some of the details, but they have agreed that he was one of the most distinguished of Americans, one of the finest products of the society that made Washington and Jefferson.

Lincoln: Champion of Union

The other man of the war, Abraham Lincoln, was the product of a different society, and important to us not only because of his greatness but because he represents a new kind of American and a new America. He was a Westerner, and could have come from no other part of the country. He had been a poor boy and a rail-splitter and he had lived on the frontier. He was lean and awkward, ill at ease with a teacup or small talk. His second Secretary of War called him a " gorilla," although later the Secretary changed his mind and said that the President was the greatest and kindest of leaders. He had been a lawyer in the back country, and had a way of saying things shrewdly, briefly, and cutting right to the heart of the matter. He had an exuberant sense of humor, although he was a sad man, and he loved to drive home a point with a story. He was warmhearted and kindly, but tough — in doing what he believed in. He was practical and earthy and homespun, and he could write sentences that shouted and sang. He was the first great American out of the West. And as the Yankee Franklin was the typical American of the eighteenth century, and Ralph Waldo Emerson of Concord was the leading thinker of the Eastern Flowering, so Abraham Lincoln stood forth to all the world as the man of this new America that was growing behind the frontier.

Lincoln the Writer

He was a fine writer as well as a great man. Or perhaps it was that the greatness of the man transferred itself to many of the speeches, state papers, and letters he wrote. Some of them are in this book: his solemn, modest farewell to his home-town friends when he left to become inaugurated as President; his masterly constructive rebuke to General Hooker; his letter of sympathy to the woman who had given her sons in battle; his address at Gettysburg which was so short that almost nobody who heard it realized he had heard one of the great masterpieces of all oratory; and his second inaugural address, looking forward to the tasks of reuniting the country, which an assassin's bullet kept him from undertaking.

Abraham Lincoln was born (1809) in the same year as Poe, and just after Emerson, Hawthorne, and Longfellow. He was killed (1865) one year after Hawthorne's death, seventeen years before Emerson and Longfellow died.

When Lincoln was born, Jefferson was still President, the country was about 1,700,000 square miles in area, and had seventeen states. When he died, the area was over three million square miles, and the states numbered thirty-six.

Negro Spirituals

Out of the dark days of their slavery Negroes wrought one of the richest groups of songs America has produced. Into their religious songs they poured their troubles in this world and their hope for happiness in the next. Together with the Western cowboy ballads, the Negro spirituals are the most important folk literature produced in America: they grew out of the land and are completely native to it. The mellow harmonies and the moving sincerity of the spirituals have won them a high place in popular favor and in the repertory of great concert singers. You can best appreciate the great beauty of these songs by listening to recordings such as Marian Anderson's. But you can make them most real by imagining, as you read, the slaves picking cotton in the fields, or loading the heavy bales on barges, with one rich voice singing out the varying lines and the whole company coming in on the refrain. Then you will understand why the troubles of this life, "this heavy load," come into the songs so often. The following spirituals have more stanzas than those given here.

NOBODY KNOWS DE TROUBLE I SEE

No-bod-y knows de trou-ble I see, No-bod-y knows but

Je-sus— No-bod-y knows de trou-ble I see, Glo-ry, hal-le-

lu-jah! Oh, No-bod-y knows de trou-ble I see,

No-bod-y knows but Je-sus— No-bod-y knows de trou-ble I see,

Glo-ry, hal-le-lu-jah! Some-times I'm up Some-times I'm down,

Oh, yes, Lord; Some-times I'm al-mos' to de groun'—

Oh, yes, Lord. Al-tho' you see me goin' 'long so,

Oh, yes, Lord: I have my tri-als here be-low—

Oh, yes, Lord. Oh! No-bod-y knows de trou-ble I see,

No-bod-y knows but Je-sus— No-bod-y knows de

slower

trou-ble I see, Glo-ry, hal-le-lu-jah!

LET MY PEOPLE GO!

When Is-rael was in E-gypt's land Let my peo-ple go, Op-

pressed so hard they could not stand, Let my peo-ple go.

Go down Mos-es, 'Way down in E-gypt's land,—

Tell— ole— Pha - raoh, To let my peo-ple

go. O let my peo-ple go.—

2. Thus saith the Lord, bold Moses said,
Let my people go!
If not I'll smite your first-born dead;
Let my people go!

3. No more shall they in bondage toil,
Let my people go!
Let them come out with Egypt's spoil,
Let my people go!

For Discussion of Negro Spirituals

1. Why was Moses a favorite Biblical character with the slaves? What lines would they sing thinking of themselves rather than the Israelites? Why did they sing a generalized complaint like "Nobody knows de trouble I see" instead of describing the troubles?

2. Can you recall other spirituals that are mournful recitations of the troubles of this world?

3. What is the usual theme of those spirituals that have a hopeful mood, in contrast to the two given here? "Deep River" and "Swing Low, Sweet Chariot" are typical of this group.

4. Try to obtain a recording of spirituals sung by famous Negro singers, notably, Roland Hayes and Marian Anderson.

Glimpses of Lee

FROM THE ROBERT E. LEE READER

The military leader of the South was not a literary man. We have little from his pen except letters and routine military papers. To discover why he inspired such extraordinary devotion we must go to the writings of others. In the recently published *The Robert E. Lee Reader*, Stanley F. Horn has collected significant letters from Lee's hand and memoirs by those who knew the man, as well as passages from later biographies and studies. Of the three selections from the *Reader* given here, the first is a letter showing with what a heavy heart Lee approached the great struggle between the states. The second reveals the restrained dignity with which he met defeat. The third shows Lee, as president of Washington College (later called Washington and Lee) at Lexington, Virginia, continuing his efforts to help the South bury the bitterness of war and rebuild its shattered institutions. Mr. Horn, a historian of the Confederacy, links the sections with his own explanatory comments.

I. LETTER TO HIS SON,
BY ROBERT E. LEE

In common with most professional soldiers, Lee took no active part and little interest in political affairs. His letters during the latter part of 1860, however, showed how greatly he was disturbed by the widening breach between the North and South. His political philosophy is well expressed in a letter he wrote to his son on January 23, 1861, from Fort Mason:

I RECEIVED Everett's "Life of Washington" which you sent me, and enjoyed its perusal. How his spirit would be grieved could he see the wreck of his mighty labors! I will not, however, permit myself to believe, until all ground of hope is gone, that the fruit of his noble deeds will be destroyed, and that his precious advice and virtuous example will so soon be forgotten by his countrymen. As far as I can judge by the papers, we are between a state of anarchy and civil war. May God avert both of these evils from us! I fear that mankind will not for years be sufficiently Christianized to bear the absence of restraint and force. I see that four states [1] have declared themselves out of the Union; four more will apparently follow their example. Then, if the border states are brought into the gulf of revolution, one-half of the country will be arrayed against the other. I must try and be patient and await the end, for I can do nothing to hasten or retard it.

The South, in my opinion, has been aggrieved by the acts of the North, as you say. I feel the aggression and am willing to take every proper step for redress. It is the principle I contend for, not individual or private benefit. As an American citizen, I take great pride in my country, her prosperity and institutions, and would defend any state if her rights were invaded. But I can anticipate no greater calamity for the country than a dissolution of the Union. It would be an accumulation of all the evils we complain of, and I am willing to sacrifice everything but honor for its preservation. I hope, therefore, that all constitutional means will be exhausted before there is a resort to force. Secession is nothing but revolution. The framers of our Constitution never exhausted so much labor, wisdom and forbearance in its formation, and surrounded it with so many guards and securities, if it was intended to be broken by every member of the confederacy at will. It was intended for "perpetual union," so expressed in the preamble, and for the establishment of a government, not a compact, which can only be dissolved by revolution or the consent of all the people in convention

[1] So. Carolina, Mississippi, Florida, Alabama.

assembled. It is idle to talk of secession. Anarchy would have been established, and not a government, by Washington, Hamilton, Jefferson, Madison, and the other patriots of the Revolution. . . . Still, a Union that can only be maintained by swords and bayonets, and in which strife and civil war are to take the place of brotherly love and kindness, has no charm for me. I shall mourn for my country and for the welfare and progress of mankind. If the Union is dissolved, and the government disrupted, I shall return to my native state and share the miseries of my people; and save in defense will draw my sword on none.

II. LEE'S RETURN TO RICHMOND, BY DOUGLAS SOUTHALL FREEMAN

His army surrendered, paroled, and dispersed, Lee's military responsibilities were at an end and he could now return home — or, at least, he could return to Richmond where his wife and daughters were now living. Like many another Confederate soldier, he had no home now.[2]

Dr. Freeman provides a moving account of the defeated commander's return to Richmond from Appomattox.[3]

Quietly and unceremoniously he left his last headquarters on the 12th and started home. With him rode Taylor, Marshall and Cooke, the last-named sick and in an ambulance lent by the Federals. They took with them their headquarters wagon and General Lee's old ambulance, which Britt drove. Colonel Venable started with them but parted company very soon, as his route to reach his family in Prince Edward County was different from theirs. . . .

[2] **home:** The Lee family home, Arlington, had been confiscated by the Federal government, and years later became the Arlington national cemetery.

[3] **Appomattox** (ăp'ô·măt'ŭks): in Virginia, where Lee surrendered to General Grant.

"Lee's Return to Richmond," reprinted from Volume IV of *R. E. Lee, a Biography* by Douglas Southall Freeman; copyright 1935 by Charles Scribner's Sons; used by permission of the publishers.

The worst of the strain was over now. Rest had begun to restore the nerves of the men, who had scarcely relaxed from the time they left Petersburg until they surrendered. They already had exhausted the fighting and its outcome as a theme of conversation, and as they went homeward through the budding trees, away from the sounds of rumbling wagon trains and marching columns, they talked freely and of many things, but little of the war. When Lee did speak of the struggle and its outcome, his thought, as always, was of those around him rather than of himself. He urged the young officers to go home, to take whatever work they could find, and to accept the conditions necessary for their participation in the government.

In some way the news of Lee's coming spread ahead of him. Women hastened to cook provisions and brought them out to the road, where they waited for him. "These good people are kind, too kind," he is reported to have said. "Their hearts are as full as when we began our first campaigns in 1861. They do too much — more than they are able to do — for us." His only concern over food was about some oats he had procured for Traveler,[1] and was afraid someone else might take. As the day wore on, Traveler cast a shoe and became lame. Lee soon stopped at Flanagan's Mill, Cumberland County, where he spent the night under the friendly roof of Madison Flanagan. The mount was shod that night and was ready for the road the next morning. . . .

The company was swelled that morning by the arrival of Rooney Lee [2] and the General's nephew, John Lee. Riders and vehicles soon got under way — there were twenty horses altogether — and went down the River road, through Powhatan and Chesterfield counties. As they neared the capital of the dying Confederacy, in the midst of a gloomy spring downpour, General Lee and two of his officers went ahead of the wagons and of the ambulances. Ere long they reached Manchester, which was then a separate municipality on the south bank of James River, opposite Richmond. While the rain was at its heaviest he passed in the town the home of a Baptist minister who chanced to see the General, and later wrote of the scene in these moving words: "His steed was bespattered with mud, and his head hung down as if worn by long traveling. The horseman himself sat his horse like a master; his face was ridged with self-respecting grief; his garments were worn in the service and stained with travel; his hat was slouched and spattered with mud and only another unknown horseman rode with him, as if for company and for love. Even in the fleeting moment of his passing by my gate, I was awed by his incomparable dignity. His majestic composure, his rectitude and his sorrow were so wrought and blended into his visage and so beautiful and impressive to my eyes that I fell into violent weeping. To me there was only one where this one was. . . ."

The streets through which General Lee rode in Manchester cut off his view of Richmond until he was close to the James River, which he had made renowned in military history. Then he could see how deep and how hideous were the scars on the face of the city. Both bridges were gone: a line of Federal pontoons afforded the only crossing. Nearly the whole waterfront had been consumed in the fire of April 2–3 that had followed the evacuation. Arsenal, factories, flouring mills, tobacco warehouses, stores, dwellings — all were destroyed. . . .

Arriving in front of his house, he turned his horse over to one of the men

---

[1] Traveler: Lee's favorite horse.
[2] Rooney Lee: the general's second son, William Henry Fitzhugh Lee, called "Rooney" by his father.

attending the wagons. The heartbroken civilians of Richmond, widows, old men, maidens, thronged him as the soldiers had at Appomattox. They wanted to speak to him and to shake his hand, and if that was impossible, at the least to touch his uniform. He grasped as many outstretched palms as he could. In a moment, with his emotions strained almost to tears, he made his way to the iron gate, and up the granite steps. Bowing again to the crowd, he entered the house and closed the door. The cheers of the crowd died out, and it began to scatter. His marching over and his battles done, Robert E. Lee unbelted his sword forever.

III. LEE IN LATER LIFE, BY GAMALIEL BRADFORD

The far-reaching effects of Lee's attitude in defeat, of his teaching and example to the students under his guidance, of his paradoxical plucking of the flower of success from the thistle of failure, is beautifully expressed by Gamaliel Bradford.

In point of fact, he was creating, or re-creating, a great nation still. His patience, his courage, his attitude toward the past, his attitude toward the future, his perfect forgiveness, his large magnanimity, above all, his hope, were reflected in the eager hearts about him, and from them spread wide over the bruised and beaten South, which stood so sorely in need of all these things.

I have already referred to the immense importance of his general influence in bringing about reconciliation and peace. It is almost impossible to overestimate this. We have the high Northern evidence of Grant: "All the people except a few political leaders in the South will accept whatever he does as right and will be guided to a great extent by his example." Perhaps nothing will better illustrate the passionate testimony of Southerners than a simple

anecdote. A Confederate soldier told General Wise that he had taken the oath of allegiance to the United States. "You have disgraced the family," said Wise. "General Lee told me to do it." "Oh, that alters the case. Whatever General Lee says is all right, I don't care what it is." Does not the knowledge of these things double the pathos of that profoundly pathetic sentence in one of Lee's last letters? "Life is indeed gliding away and I have nothing of good to show for mine that is past. I pray I may be spared to accomplish something for the benefit of mankind and the honor of God." If he had accomplished nothing, what shall be said of some of us?

Yet, in spite of all this, it must be admitted that Lee's life will always be regarded as a record of failure. And it is precisely because he failed that I have been interested to make this study of him.

Success is the idol of the world, and the world's idols have been successful. Washington, Lincoln, Grant, were doubtless very great. But they were successful. Who shall say just how far that element of success enters into their greatness? Here was a man who remains great, although he failed. America in the twentieth century worships success, is too ready to test character by it, to be blind to those faults success hides, to those qualities that can do without it. Here was a man who failed grandly, a man who said that "human virtue should be equal to human calamity," and showed that it could be equal to it, and so, without pretense, without display, without self-consciousness, left an example that future Americans may study with profit as long as there is an America.

A young sophomore was once summoned to the president's office and gently admonished that only patience and industry would prevent the failure

"Lee in Later Life," reprinted from Lee, the American by Gamaliel Bradford, published by Houghton Mifflin Company.

that would inevitably come to him through college and through life.

"But, General, you failed," remarked the sophomore, with the inconceivable ineptitude of sophomores.

"I hope that you may be more fortunate than I," was the tranquil answer.

Literature can add nothing to that.

For Discussion of Lee

1. What beliefs did Lee hold about secession? Judging from this letter, what were his reasons for deciding finally to uphold the secessionists? Recall a passage showing his devotion to his native state.

2. Find evidence that Lee was still a hero to the South, despite his defeat. Discuss how it is possible for a man to be great though a failure. What can we learn from Lee in the hour of his defeat?

3. What incidents in Lee's trip home show the attitude of the people toward him? Compare his homecoming with that of some other great American general. In what ways were they alike? In what ways different?

4. What qualities and attitudes of Lee does Bradford mention as being helpful in restoring the South?

5. Would you call Lee's life a success or a failure? What standards do you have for deciding such a question?

For Your Vocabulary

EFFECTIVE PHRASES: Were you specially struck with the phrase, "*the inconceivable ineptitude of sophomores*"? Just what does this phrase mean? What is meant by *sophomoric* behavior? Find in the dictionary the meaning of the two Greek words that make up *sophomore* and explain how the word came to have its modern meaning. Name other words containing the base-word *soph*.

The use of exactly the right word is a mark of effective writing. In the stories of Lee there are some well-chosen adjectives: *perpetual* union, *self-respecting* grief, *incomparable* dignity, *tranquil* answer. What does each phrase mean?

Abraham Lincoln
1809–1865

It would be difficult to imagine a greater contrast in background than we find between Lee and Lincoln. Lee grew up in the cultured setting of a Virginia plantation, won honors at West Point, and went into an assured military career. Lincoln grew up in the backwoods, struggled to educate himself by the light from an open fireplace, and knew hard days in the beginning of his law practice in Illinois. Both received the highest confidence and honor, first of their own sections and finally of the whole nation. It takes both these men to represent the America of their day. It was Lincoln who set down in simple words the truest statement America has of the trials and griefs and triumphant faiths of the time. These brief selections from his speeches and letters show his gift for speaking and writing simply, honestly, and yet with the profound wisdom and nobility of a truly great nature.

FAREWELL AT SPRINGFIELD

When Lincoln left Springfield, Illinois, in 1861, he seemed to realize that fate might never let him return. His departure has been described by Carl Sandburg in *Abraham Lincoln: the Prairie Years:* " A cold drizzle of rain was falling on the morning of February 11 when Lincoln and his party of fifteen were to leave Springfield on the eight-o'clock at the Great Western Railway station. Chilly gray mist hung the circle of the prairie horizon. A short little locomotive with a flat-topped smokestack stood puffing with a baggage car and special passenger car hitched on; a railroad president and superintendent were on board. A thousand people crowded in and around the brick station, inside of which Lincoln was standing, and one by one came hundreds of old friends, shaking hands, wishing him luck and Godspeed, all faces solemn. Even Judge David Davis, weighing 350 pounds, wearing a new white silk hat, was a serious figure.

" A path was made for Lincoln from the station to his car; hands stretched out for one last handshake. He hadn't intended to make a speech; but on the platform of the car, as he turned and saw his home people, he took off his hat, stood perfectly still, and looked almost as he had at the Bowling Green burial services when tears had to take the place of words. He raised a hand for silence. They stood with hats off. Then he said slowly, amid the soft gray drizzle from the sky ":

FRIENDS, no one who has never been placed in a like position can understand my feelings at this hour nor the impressive sadness I feel at this parting. For more than a quarter of a century I have lived among you, and during all that time I have received nothing but kindness at your hands. Here I have lived from my youth till now I am an old man. Here the most sacred trusts of earth were assumed; here all my children were born and one of them lies buried. To you, dear friends, I owe all that I have, all that I am. All the strange checkered past seems to crowd now upon my mind. Today I leave you; I go to assume a task more difficult than that which devolved upon General Washington. Unless the great God who assisted him shall be with and aid me, I must fail. But if the same omniscient mind and the same Almighty arm that directed and protected him shall guide and support me, I shall not fail; I shall succeed. Let us all pray that the God of our fathers may not forsake us now. To Him I commend you all. Permit me to ask that with equal sincerity and faith you will all invoke His wisdom and guidance for me. With these few words I must leave you — for how long I know not. Friends, one and all, I must now bid you an affectionate farewell.

Carl Sandburg continues:

" Bells rang, there was a grinding of wheels, and the train moved and carried Lincoln away from Springfield. The tears were not yet dry on some faces when the train had faded into the gray to the east.

" Some of the crowd said afterward that Lincoln, too, was in tears, that tears ran down his face as he spoke that morning.

" And one of the crowd said there were no tears on Lincoln's face. ' But he had a face with dry tears,' said this one. ' He was a man who often had dry tears.' "

LETTER TO GENERAL JOSEPH HOOKER

During 1862 the Northern army had suffered several defeats, and Lincoln had had to remove both General McClellan and General Burnside. The man that he put in command of the Army of the Potomac over the protests of Secretary Stanton and General Halleck was General Joseph Hooker, who had served under both of his predecessors and had criticized both with great frankness. The day after the appointment Lincoln sent General Hooker this remarkable letter, which shows his directness, fearlessness, and understanding of men. It administers a rebuke at the same time that it shows confidence and offers encouragement.

I HAVE placed you at the head of the Army of the Potomac. Of course I have done this upon what appear to me to be sufficient reasons, and yet I think it best for you to know that there are some things in regard to which I am not quite satisfied with you. I believe you to be a brave and skillful soldier, which, of course, I like. I also believe you do not mix politics with your profession, in which you are right. You have confidence in yourself, which is a valuable, if not an indispensable, quality. You are ambitious, which, within reasonable bounds, does good rather than harm; but I think that during General Burnside's command of the army you have taken counsel of your ambition, and thwarted him as much as you could, in which you did a great wrong to the country and to a most meritorious and honorable brother officer. I have heard, in such way as to believe it, of your recently saying that both the army and the government needed a dictator. Of course it was not for this, but in spite of it, that I have given you the command. Only those generals who gain successes can set up dictatorships. What I now ask of you is military success, and I will risk the dictatorship. The government will support you to the utmost of its ability, which is neither more nor less than it has done and will do for all commanders. I much fear that the spirit which you have aided to infuse into the army, of criticizing their commander and withholding confidence from him, will now turn upon you. I shall assist you as far as I can to put it down. Neither you nor Napoleon, if he were alive again, could get any good out of an army while such a spirit prevails in it. And now, beware of rashness, but with energy and sleepless vigilance go forward and give us victories.

LETTER TO MRS. BIXBY

It is characteristic of Lincoln that he found time amid his care and heavy responsibility to write this personal letter to a mother mourning her sons lost for the cause of the Union. Characteristic, too, is the fact that he expressed in the letter feelings many people had experienced but few had found words for.

I HAVE been shown in the files of the War Department a statement of the Adjutant-General of Massachusetts that you are the mother of five sons who have died gloriously on the field of battle. I feel how weak and fruitless must be any words of mine which should attempt to beguile you from the grief of a loss so overwhelming. But I cannot refrain from tendering to you the consolation that may be found in the thanks of the Republic they died to save. I pray that our heavenly Father may assuage the anguish of your bereavement, and leave you only the cherished memory of the loved and lost, and the solemn pride that must be yours to have laid so costly a sacrifice upon the altar of freedom.

GETTYSBURG ADDRESS

November 19, 1863

Carl Sandburg has given you a full account (p. 213) of the circumstances under which this brief address was first given. You read it then to place it in its original setting. Read it now to fill in your understanding of the man and his way of thinking.

FOUR score and seven years ago our fathers brought forth on this continent a new nation, conceived in liberty, and dedicated to the proposition that all men are created equal.

Now we are engaged in a great civil war, testing whether that nation, or any

Richmond, Virginia, was devastated during the War between the States. Matthew Brady, master photographer of that era, recorded the desolate scene in 1865. (U.S. Army)

nation so conceived and so dedicated, can long endure. We are met on a great battlefield of that war. We have come to dedicate a portion of that field as a final resting place for those who here gave their lives that that nation might live. It is altogether fitting and proper that we should do this.

But in a larger sense we cannot dedicate, we cannot consecrate, we cannot hallow this ground. The brave men, living and dead, who struggled here have consecrated it far above our poor power to add or detract. The world will little note nor long remember what we say here, but it can never forget what they did here. It is for us, the living, rather, to be dedicated here to the unfinished work which they who fought here have thus far so nobly advanced. It is rather for us to be here dedicated to the great task remaining before us — that from these honored dead we take

increased devotion to that cause for which they gave the last full measure of devotion; that we here highly resolve that these dead shall not have died in vain; that this nation, under God, shall have a new birth of freedom; and that government of the people, by the people, and for the people, shall not perish from the earth.

SECOND INAUGURAL ADDRESS

March 4, 1865

The morning of Lincoln's second inauguration was cold and stormy, but at noon the sun came out as the procession moved with dignity from the White House. Numbers of wounded soldiers were conspicuous in the great throng. The following comment upon the address was made by the London *Spectator* after the President's death: " We cannot read it without a renewed conviction that it is the noblest political document known to history, and should have for the nation and the statesmen he left behind him something of a sacred and almost prophetic character." This speech and the Gettysburg Address are inscribed on opposite walls of the beautiful Lincoln Memorial at Washington.

FELLOW COUNTRYMEN: At this second appearing to take the oath of the presidential office, there is less occasion for an extended address than there was at the first. Then a statement, somewhat in detail, of a course to be pursued, seemed fitting and proper. Now, at the expiration of four years, during which public declarations have been constantly called forth on every point and phase of the great contest which still absorbs the attention and engrosses the energies of the nation, little that is new could be presented. The progress of our arms, upon which all else chiefly depends, is as well known to the public as to myself; and it is, I trust, reasonably satisfactory and encouraging to all. With high hope for the future, no prediction in regard to it is ventured.

On the occasion corresponding to this four years ago, all thoughts were anxiously directed to an impending civil war. All dreaded it — all sought to avert it. While the inaugural address was being delivered from this place, devoted altogether to saving the Union without war, insurgent agents were in the city seeking to destroy it without war — seeking to dissolve the Union, and divide effects, by negotiation. Both parties deprecated war; but one of them would make war rather than let the nation survive; and the other would accept war rather than let it perish. And the war came.

One-eighth of the whole population were colored slaves, not distributed generally over the Union, but localized in the southern part of it. These slaves constituted a peculiar and powerful interest. All knew that this interest was, somehow, the cause of the war. To strengthen, perpetuate, and extend this interest was the object for which the insurgents would rend the Union, even by war; while the government claimed no right to do more than to restrict the territorial enlargement of it.

Neither party expected for the war the magnitude or the duration which it has already attained. Neither anticipated that the cause of the conflict might cease with, or even before, the conflict itself should cease. Each looked for an easier triumph and a result less fundamental and astounding. Both read the same Bible, and pray to the same God; and each invokes His aid against the other. It may seem strange that any men should dare to ask a just God's assistance in wringing their bread from the sweat of other men's faces; but let us judge not, that we be not judged.[1] The prayers of both could not be answered — that of neither has been answered fully.

The Almighty has his own purposes. "Woe unto the world because of offenses! for it must needs be that offenses come; but woe to the man by whom the offense cometh."[2] If we shall suppose that American slavery is one of those offenses which, in the province of God, must needs come, but which, having continued through His appointed time, He now wills to remove, and that He gives to both North and South this terrible war, as the woe due to those by whom the offense came, shall we discern therein any departure from those divine attributes which the believers in a living God always ascribe to Him? Fondly do we hope — fervently do we pray — that this mighty scourge of war may speedily pass away. Yet, if God wills that it continue until all the wealth piled by the bondman's two hundred and fifty years of unrequited toil shall

[1] judge not . . . judged: Matt. 7:1.
[2] woe . . . cometh: Matt. 18:7.

be sunk, and until every drop of blood drawn with the lash shall be paid by another drawn with the sword, as was said three thousand years ago, still it must be said, " The judgments of the Lord are true and righteous altogether." [1]

With malice toward none; with charity for all; with firmness in the right, as God gives us to see the right, let us strive on to finish the work we are in; to bind up the nation's wounds; to care for him who shall have borne the battle, and for his widow and his orphan — to do all which may achieve and cherish a just and lasting peace among ourselves, and with all nations.

For Discussion of Lincoln

1. Many qualities of Lincoln are reflected in this series of brief utterances. Find passages that show his humility; his

[1] **The judgments . . . altogether:** Ps. 18.9.

consideration of others; his insistence on the right; his devoutness; his heavy sense of responsibility to the nation as commander in chief.

2. It is now recognized that Lincoln's death was an even greater loss to the South than to the North. What course would he have taken with the defeated Confederacy? Which of his ideals for reunion was imperfectly achieved?

3. One of Lincoln's gifts was the ability to put into simple words the profound feelings that often defeat attempts at expression. Find passages that have become part of the creed of our nation.

4. Do you find any points of resemblance between Lincoln and Lee? What was the greatest difference between the two men? In what ways did Lincoln represent the West? With the possible exception of Napoleon, more books have been written about Lincoln than any other human figure. Can you think of several reasons why this should be so? What makes Lincoln seem to most people to be a complicated character?

Abram Ryan
1838–1886

THE CONQUERED BANNER

Love for the South and love for Religion were the dominant themes of Father Ryan's life and poetry. Born in Norfolk, Virginia, of Irish extraction, he shared his parents' devotion to their native land. The War between the States erupted shortly after his ordination, and he joined the Confederate forces as chaplain, serving during the entire conflict. He saw the devastation of the South, and shared the defeat and dejection of its people. " The Conquered Banner " written at a single

sitting, tells you what he thought of the " Stars and Bars."

Furl that banner, for 'tis weary;
Round its staff 'tis drooping dreary;
　Furl it, fold it — it is best;
For there's not a man to wave it,
And there's not a sword to save it,　　5
And there's not one left to lave it
In the blood which heroes gave it,
And its foes now scorn and brave it;
　Furl it, hide it — let it rest!

" The Conquered Banner " from *Poems: Patriotic, Religious, Miscellaneous* by Abram J. Ryan. Reprinted by permission of P. J. Kenedy and Sons.

Take that banner down! 'tis tattered;   10
Broken is its staff and shattered;
And the valiant hosts are scattered
    Over whom it floated high.
Oh, 'tis hard for us to fold it,
Hard to think there's none to hold it,   15
Hard that those that once unrolled it
    Now must furl it with a sigh!

Furl that banner — furl it sadly!
Once ten thousands hailed it gladly,
And ten thousands wildly, madly,   20
    Swore it should forever wave;
Swore that foeman's sword should never
Hearts like theirs entwined dissever,
Till that flag should float forever
    O'er their freedom or their grave!   25

Furl it! for the hands that grasped it,
And the hearts that fondly clasped it,
    Cold and dead are lying low;
And that banner — it is trailing,
While around it sounds the wailing   30
    Of its people in their woe.

For, though conquered, they adore it,
Love the cold, dead hands that bore it,
Weep for those who fell before it,

Pardon those who trailed and tore it;   35
And oh, wildly they deplore it,
    Now to furl and fold it so!

Furl that banner! True, 'tis gory,
Yet 'tis wreathed around with glory,
And 'twill live in song and story,   40
    Though its folds are in the dust!
For its fame on brightest pages,
Penned by poets and by sages,
Shall go sounding down the ages —
    Furl its folds though now we must.   45

Furl that banner, softly, slowly!
Treat it gently — it is holy,
    For it droops above the dead.
Touch it not — unfold it never;
Let it droop there, furled forever,   50
    For its people's hopes are fled!

For Discussion of Ryan

1. From this poem indicate Father Ryan's attitude toward the Southern cause, the Southern army, and its defeat.

2. What principal emotions mark this poem? What war issues are echoed in it? How does he think posterity will treat the Southern cause? Was he right?

The Postwar West

BEFORE we consider the West after the War between the States, let us be sure we do not lose sight of our literary timetable. The development of the West *was parallel in time to the literary flowering of the East*. Within the same general period, 1800 to 1880, literature was produced in both the East and West, though the literary flowering of the West came later in the period. After 1880 we can think of American literature as a single piece, without dividing it into East and West.

Settlement of the West

The West, in 1865 and the years following, was more than ever a land of opportunity. The Homestead Law made it possible for anyone to own land simply by " squatting " on it. And how the settlers poured in! Half a million came in one year — later, a million. Those who could not speak English tied tags on their coats and allowed themselves to be shipped and unloaded like baggage. Miners explored the mountains and sieved the creek sand. Cattlemen sought out the water holes. Farmers crowded the cattlemen. By 1890, settlements were so close together that the census bureau could no longer chart a frontier line. The 1890 census solemnly reported that the frontier was at an end.

But by that time the century of Western settlement had put the blood of every race into the American melting pot. It had given the characteristics of its life to American customs and American thinking. And it had breathed its vigor into a few excellent writers.

Folk Literature of the West

The men who were taking up the last open sections of land and making miles of prairie into ranges for the great cattle industry of the West had little more time for literary writing than had the early trappers and gold-seekers who came before them. But now men were more numerous, and out of the companionship of camp and settlement there grew the folk literature of the West. Around the fire behind the chuckwagon out on the range cowboys sang of their day in the saddle, leaving behind them a wealth of ballads such as " All Day on the Prairie." And the early homesteaders who broke fresh ground on the treeless plains left a record of their hardships in songs like " The Little Old Sod Shanty."

Western humor still roared on its boisterous way, finding its fullest expression in tall-tale heroes like Pecos Bill of the cattle range and Paul Bunyan of the lumbering camps. Nothing was ordinary about these tall tales — any more than the West was ordinary. The men could "walk like an ox, run

like a fox, swim like an eel, make love like a mad bull " — that was Davy Crockett's boast. Paul Bunyan could carry water for the Minnesota lakes, build the Black Hills, and use a full-grown pine tree for a toothpick. In the lumbering camps growing thicker and thicker as the new settlements clamored for building materials, every evening in the bunkhouse added new feats to this astonishing saga.

Bret Harte and Local Color

A different kind of Western writing is illustrated by Bret Harte. Harte was an Easterner who went to California and dug literary gold out of the hills. He learned the customs, the language, the setting, the adventures of the Western miners and prospectors, and then put them into fiction. He wrote half a dozen memorable stories, and went back East, with a guarantee of $10,000 a year, to write for the *Atlantic Monthly*.

Harte wrote about the quaint and interesting aspects of the West, the ways in which it was different from other parts of the country. All over the country there was this same interest in localities — what was quaint or interesting or different about this place as compared to others? In New Orleans, George W. Cable was discovering the Creoles. In Virginia, Thomas Nelson Page was writing about the romance of the old plantation mansions. In Georgia, Joel Chandler Harris was retelling the charming folklore of the Negro. In Tennessee, Mary Murfree had discovered the mountaineers. In New England, Sarah Orne Jewett and Mary Wilkins Freeman; in Kentucky, James Lane Allen; in the Middle West, Edward Eggleston — all these recorded the quaint and distinctive " local color " of their regions.

These authors wrote stories in which the *setting* was as important as the characters or action; they wrote about places as well as people, and often they used local dialects to give their stories an authentic atmosphere. You will discover that the local color of the California mining camps is one of the chief elements in Bret Harte's story "The Outcasts of Poker Flat."

The West's First Great Writer

Mark Twain blew into American literature like a fresh wind off the prairies. As Lincoln had brought the spirit of the West into our statesmanship, so Mark Twain put it into our books.

There were many things alike in those two Westerners. They both came out of log cabins, frontier experiences, and boyhood years sparse with education. They were simple men, and unaffected. They came awkwardly, bashfully to the cultured East, and they had the same ability first to inspire ridicule (Lincoln was called a gorilla, and Mark Twain a ruffian) and then to inspire love. Both were fond of a good story, and told it well. They had the same boisterous Western humor, covering up the same thoughtful sadness. They both were intensely American. Europeans had marveled at how much like cultured Europeans were Longfellow and Lowell, but they exclaimed at how unlike Europe-

ans, how American, were Lincoln and Mark Twain. As Lowell called Lincoln

"New birth of our new soil,
The first American!"

so a later historian wrote of Mark Twain: "Here at last was an authentic American — a native writer thinking his own thoughts, using his own eyes, speaking his own dialect — everything European fallen away." But the path of one of these Americans led to the White House and death at fifty-six, when his real greatness was just beginning to be understood; and the path of the other led through a series of adventures to a series of triumphs which made him one of the best-known, best-loved men alive; and when he died at seventy-five the whole world mourned.

Mark Twain on the Mississippi

His real name was Samuel Clemens, and he grew up in Hannibal, Missouri, on the west bank of the Mississippi. In those days a pageant of the frontier passed up and down the river, and every steamboat carried men who were either going to or returning from great events and exciting adventures. Sam Clemens lived the boyhood of Tom Sawyer and Huck Finn, playing pranks, swimming in the river, exploring the cave in the hill, listening to the slaves, the pilots, the frontiersmen. When he was old enough, he learned to set type in his brother's print shop, and helped put out a weekly newspaper. But the river life was more glamorous, and he apprenticed himself to one of the most famous pilots on the river. He had to learn every foot of a constantly changing river, by day and by night, from St. Louis to New Orleans. He tells about it in one of the selections in this book.

He learned to be a pilot and a good one, in the days when pilots were highly paid and envied. But the war closed down the river trade. He enlisted in the

Southern militia, and served a few weeks. What happened to him shouldn't have happened to a comic opera soldier. Before his little squad could even find the Confederate army, he had sprained his ankle, gone hungry awhile, and been nearly captured by U. S. Grant. That

was enough war for Sam. When his older brother was named secretary to the new Territory of Nevada, he piled into the overland stage and went along as his assistant.

Mark Twain in the Mining West

Nevada was a new kind of frontier for him. He had soaked up the legends and the color of the river frontier, but this wild and woolly Far West was a different thing. He loved it. He prospected for silver, and came within an hour of owning one of the biggest lodes in Nevada. He wrote for the rough and ready newspapers of the silver frontier, and got so well into the spirit of things that he had to leave suddenly for California when a two-gun man started looking all over Nevada for him. In San Francisco he became a star reporter and a peerless storyteller. He spent many an evening swapping stories with Artemus Ward; and San Franciscans still prize legends of the parties Clemens, Ward, and their hearty friends used to have, usually ending near dawn with Clemens leading the rest in a game of follow-the-leader, jumping from roof to roof down the steep hills of San Francisco.

Mark Twain around the World

That was in the 1860's. Toward the end of that decade three things happened that changed the whole course of young Clemens's life. In the first place, he sent a story to a New York magazine. It was a story he had heard from prospectors in California, called "The Jumping Frog." He sent it off, and never expected to hear of it again, but Easterners read it and chuckled and then laughed broadly, and sent a hurry call to find out who was this Westerner, Clemens. That was the first thing. The second was an assignment from one of the San Francisco papers to go to the Hawaiian Islands (Sandwich Islands, they were called then) and write signed articles on what he saw. When he returned, some of his cronies persuaded him to give a public lecture on his experiences. The articles had been good, but the lecture was like nothing else ever heard in San Francisco. The audience held its sides and rolled in the aisles. The very walls shook with the laughter. The echoes traveled as far as the eastern seaboard, and invitations came addressed to "a man named Clemens" inviting him to come east and lecture on the Sandwich Islands.

And those two events helped make the third. Samuel Clemens went east with his slow Western drawl, his inimitable art of storytelling, his long mustaches and his stock of Western anecdotes, and got a chance to go on a cruise to Europe and the Mediterranean. He was to write back letters to American newspapers. A publisher gathered them together under the title *Innocents Abroad,* and Samuel Clemens signed the good strong pen name derived from his experience as a river pilot, Mark Twain. The book swept America, just as the story and the lectures had. This was something new, something fresh. Most Americans had gone to Europe as pilgrims to marvel; Mark

Twain had gone to Europe with the Western "show me" attitude. He poked fun alike at the traditions of ancient Europe and the gullibility of American tourists. He played pranks in Rome, and bet money with Egyptians on foot races up the pyramids. He forgot to be sentimental and had an uproarious time, and wrote a best seller.

Mark Twain in the Literary East

From that time on, Mark Twain's career was patterned. He married an Eastern girl, and lived most of his writing years in the East. He wrote successful book after successful book. He became a bosom friend of several Eastern writers and met the honored old men Emerson, Lowell, and Holmes. He made a lot of money, and lived in great houses. But he remained always as unaffectedly Western, as impulsive and lovable as he had ever been. Once he went to see General Grant, and found him near death and penniless, working on his memoirs. He gave the old man $75,000, and published his memoirs for him. Altogether, the General and his widow made $400,000 from that book, through Mark Twain. But Mark Twain himself was not so lucky. He lost a good deal of money in publishing, a good deal more in trying to perfect a typesetting machine which printers had urgently needed ever since Gutenberg. If he had backed the Mergenthaler Linotype, he might have become a millionaire. But he backed the wrong inventor, and his firm went bankrupt. He refused to take advantage of the bankruptcy laws, assumed the entire debt himself, and set off, at the age of sixty, on a world-wide lecture tour and a three-year program of writing to repay the debt.

He paid it all, and lived fifteen years more, honored in his own country and abroad, his flowing white hair, drooping white mustaches, and bright blue eyes better known all over the world than the face of many a king.

Mark Twain the Writer

He lived and wrote in the East, yet wrote like a Westerner and usually of the West. *Tom Sawyer* and *Huckleberry Finn* are novels based on his own boyhood. *Life on the Mississippi* is about his river and his days as a pilot. *Roughing It* is about his years in the Far West. *A Connecticut Yankee* is about King Arthur's Court, but it is a burlesque in the lighthearted style of *Innocents Abroad. Personal Recollections of Joan of Arc* was one of his own favorites. In his last ten years he produced a different kind of book, a book that many people could not believe Mark Twain had written. The laughing Mark Twain had become a bitter, satirical Mark Twain, and they couldn't believe it. But as Mark Twain himself said in early years, that was merely the other side of the coin. Scratch a humorist, and you find a sad man. In those last years, Mark Twain put into books the disillusionment and harsh atheism he had hidden under his laughter. That is why *The Man Who Corrupted Hadleyburg, The Mysterious Stranger*, and *What Is Man?* came as a shock after the earlier and more famous books.

By the time he wrote those late books the temper of the West was changing. Some of the optimism had gone. Most of the good land was settled, the mines were appropriated, and many men were finding that they had settled on land too dry for good farming. It was the end of the frontier, the natural reaction after a period of great optimism and hope, and Mark Twain reflected some of the change.

But the earlier, happier books are the ones by which we are likely to remember him. In a sense which would not be true of many other American authors, those books *are* Mark Twain. There was very little artifice in them. As Howells said, "Of all the literary men I have ever known, he was the most unliterary . . ." The books are the man. They are his slow Western drawl, his wholesomeness and health and lack of affectation, his manner of bringing realities and absurdities together and then keeping a straight face as though he had not the slightest idea that anything he said might be convulsing readers from New York to Calcutta.

When Mark Twain was born (1835), Andrew Jackson was President. When he died (1910), Theodore Roosevelt had just gone out of office. When he was born, Emerson had not yet published. When he died, E. A. Robinson had been publishing books of verse for ten years.

Folk Literature of the Frontier

ALL DAY ON THE PRAIRIE
Texas Cowboy Song
arranged by David Guion

Cowboys built up a body of songs second in number only to the Negro spirituals. The cowboy had two reasons for singing. He sang to pass the time away, in camp with his fellows, or riding herd, or covering his range alone. He also found that singing helped with his work. The wistful songs of the homes far away were useful on night herd duty, because slow, sad tunes quieted the cattle as the rider circled them on the bedding ground. The complaints of the hardships of his life — a universally favorite topic — were the basis of ballads sung to relieve the dusty job of prodding up the laggards, or "drags," at the end of the trail herd, the high points of the refrain coming up to a yell as a rope flicked at a slow calf, "Whoopee ti yi yo, git along, little dogies." Rarer are the songs like "All Day on the Prairie," in which the singer expresses his joy in the self-reliant outdoor life of riding range.

All day on the prairie in the saddle I ride,
Not even a dog, boys, to trot by my side.
My fire I must kindle with chips° gathered round,
And boil my own coffee without being ground.

I wash in a pool, dry on a toesack;°   5
I carry my wardrobe all on my back;
For want of an oven I cook in a pot,
And sleep on the ground for want of a cot.

3. **chips:** pieces of dried dung, the only fuel available on the treeless prairies. 5. **toesack:** a coarse sack such as those used for grain, made of jute or hemp fiber.

And then, if my cooking is not so complete,
You cannot blame me for wanting to
eat,   10
But show me a man, boys, that sleeps
more profound
Than this big cowpuncher who sleeps
on the ground.

My ceiling's the sky, boys, my floor is
the grass,
My music's the lowing of herds as they
pass;
My books are the rivers, my sermons
the stones,   15
My parson's a wolf on his pulpit of
bones.

THE LITTLE OLD SOD SHANTY: Pioneer Ballad

In *The American Songbag* Carl Sandburg printed this ballad from the prairies
with an explanatory introduction:

"A little girl from western Nebraska,
home again after a trip to the East, was
asked, 'What is the East?' She answered,
'The East is where trees come between you
and the sky.' Early settlers noticed log
cabins were scarcer as timberland thinned
out going farther west. On the windy, open
prairies of the Great Plains, the best house
to be had in short order was of sod. A
cellar was dug first; long slices of turf were
piled around the cellar lines; wooden cross-
poles held the sod roof. Ceilings went high
or low: tall men put roofs farther from the
ground than short men did. In timber
country farther east they sang 'The Little
Old Log Cabin in the Lane'; its tune was
familiar to the lonely 'sodbuster' who
made this song about his dwelling — in a
region where rivers are sometimes a half
mile wide and a half inch deep."

I am look-ing rath-er seed-y now while hold-ing down my
Yet I rath-er like the no-vel-ty of liv-ing in this

claim, And my vict-uals are not al-ways of the best;—
way, Though my bill of fare is al-ways rath-er tame,—

—— And the mice play shy-ly round me as I nes-tle down to
—— But I'm hap py as a clam on the land of Un-cle

rest, In my lit-tle old sod shan-ty in the West.
Sam, In my lit-tle old sod shan-ty on my claim.

From *The American Songbag* by Carl Sandburg, copyright, 1927, by Harcourt, Brace and Company, Inc.

Refrain

The hing-es are of leath-er and the win-dows have no glass, While the board roof lets the howl-ing bliz-zards in,— And I hear the hun-gry ki-yote as he slinks up through the grass, Round my lit-tle old sod shan-ty on my claim.—

2. O when I left my Eastern home, a bachelor so gay,
   To try and win my way to wealth and fame,
   I little thought that I'd come down to burning twisted hay
   In the little old sod shanty on my claim.
   My clothes are plastered o'er with dough, I'm looking like a fright,   5
   And everything is scattered round the room,
   But I wouldn't give the freedom that I have out in the West
   For the table of the Eastern man's old home.

3. Still I wish that some kindhearted girl would pity on me take,
   And relieve me from the mess that I am in;
   The angel, how I'd bless her if this her home she'd make   10
   In the little old sod shanty on my claim.
   And we would make our fortunes on the prairies of the West,
   Just as happy as two lovers we'd remain;
   We'd forget the trials and troubles we endured at the first,
   In the little old sod shanty on our claim.

4. And if kindly fate should bless us with now and then an heir,
   To cheer our hearts with honest pride of fame,
   O then we'd be contented for the toil that we had spent
   In the little old sod shanty on our claim.
   When time enough had lapsed and all of those little
   To noble man- and womanhood had grown,
   It wouldn't seem half so lonely as around us we
   And see the little old sod shanty on our claim

For Discussion of Folk Ballads

All Day on the Prairie

1. Does the cowboy seem to complain about the comforts that he lacks, or is he proud of getting along without them? Support your answer with quotations from the song.

2. Literary quotations often crop up in cowboy songs, because reading aloud was a favorite pastime for the group around the campfire or in the bunkhouse at night. This ballad contains an echo of Shakespeare's lines in *As You Like It:*

" And this our life exempt from public haunt
Finds tongues in trees, books in the running brooks,
Sermons in stones, and good in everything."

(Act II, Sc. i, ll. 15–17)

Does the cowboy singer find his life just as attractive? What new touches from his own environment does he add?

The Little Old Sod Shanty

1. Give a detailed description of the little old sod shanty. What special disadvantages does it have? What is the settler's one wish? Do you think he will get it? Will he be happy if he does?

2. Is the tone of the poem as a whole cheerful or plaintive? What does the tune contribute to the mood?

James Stevens

1892–

AN AMERICAN HERCULES

The Northwestern lumber camps gave American folklore the fabulous hero of tall tales, Paul Bunyan. James Stevens worked for many months in lumber camps in Washington, Oregon, and Idaho before retelling the best stories about the giant logger in his book *Paul Bunyan.* In " An American Hercules " Mr. Stevens has written especially for *Adventures in American Literature* an account of the way the Paul Bunyan legend developed, giving as an example of the stories a hitherto unrecorded ... of typical flavor. Picture the proper ... g for the tale, as Mr. Stevens describes ...he introduction to his book:

Paul Bunyan bunkhouse service is to hear, when it is spontaneous and in a proper setting; preferably around a big heated stove in the winter, when the wind is howling through crackling boughs outside and the pungent smell of steaming wool drifts down from the drying lines above the stove. When a vasty spirit of the woods really moves the meeting, a noble and expansive ecstasy of the soul is exhibited."

Draw up your chair, stranger.

PAUL BUNYAN, the mythical hero of the lumberjacks, is the supreme figure of American folklore. Paul was a Herculean logger who combed his

'can Hercules" by James Stevens. Reprinted by permission of the author.

Paul Bunyan and Babe, his blue ox, tower over local citizens on the prairie outside Bemidji, in northwestern Minnesota. Tales spun by lumberjacks in this region claim that the legendary hero scooped out Lake Superior with his bare hands to make a reservoir for quenching his thirst and that his chore boy, carrying water to him in the north woods from the reservoir, made Minnesota's thousands of lakes with his footprints. (The Bemidji Pioneer)

beard with a young pine tree; who skidded his timber with Babe the Blue Ox, a creature so vast that he measured forty-two ax handles and a plug of chewing tobacco between the horns; who operated a camp cookhouse where the flapjack griddle was greased by twenty-four Arabs — imported from the Sahara Desert because they could stand the heat — skating to and fro with slabs of bacon strapped to their feet; who tamed the Mississippi when it was young and wild by building river corrals and driving the river through their gates (the Great Lakes remain as evidence of this feat); who ruled the American country in the period when it was only a timberland. This epoch, according to the best authorities, began with the Winter of the Blue Snow and ended with the Spring the Rain Came Up from China.

Here, indeed, is a full-bodied myth. The Paul Bunyan stories have been told in American logging camps since 1840. They are unquestionably of Canadian origin. There was a Paul Bunyan who won fame in the Papineau Rebellion of 1837. There is no evidence that the beginnings of the stories are beyond him. The other materials and characters of the myth were developed out of the magic of bunkhouse nights; when the workday in the woods, or on the iced road, or on the drive, was done; when the camp men, isolated from all life but that of the woods, had no other outlet for their fancies than the creation of romances about their own life.

Thus Paul Bunyan; Babe the Blue Ox; Johnny Inkslinger, the timekeeper who figured with a fountain pen fed by hose lines from twenty-four barrels of ink; Hels Helson, the Big Swede and bull of the woods, who muddied the Missouri River forever with one spring bath; and many smaller characters — such as Hot Biscuit Slim, the cook; Shanty Boy, the bard; and Big Ole, the blacksmith — have been celebrated in logging camps from Bangor, Maine, to Portland, Oregon. The tall tale, the "whopper," is not confined, of course, to the lumber camps. It appears with the earliest accounts of the Appalachian pioneers. It is forever present in the best writings of Mark Twain. Other mythical heroes have won a certain fame, such as Tony Beaver of the Virginia mountains and Pecos Bill, the Southwestern *vaquero* who once straddled a cyclone and rode it to a finish. But the myth of Paul Bunyan stands alone, possessing, as it does, its own time, place, and people.

The stories are told in this manner:

Supper is over in the logging camp, and the after-supper period of smoking and quiet is also done. A murmur of talk about the day's work rises from the gang around the heating stove. There is a strong smell of steaming wool from the drying lines. Blue pipe smoke drifts through the mellow light of the Rochester burners. A gust of frosty air blows in whenever the bunkhouse door is opened. Some logger ventures the opinion that this will be the hardest winter this part of the country has ever known. Weather talk runs on until someone states solemnly that "the weather ain't what she used to be. Gettin' old now, the weather is. Take the Year of the Two Winters, in Paul Bunyan's time. Yes, sir. Then. That year two winters come all at once. —"

Then there is a contest to see who can tell the tallest tale about cold weather in the day of Paul Bunyan.

Or it is a summer night, and the loggers are circling a smudge fire outside the bunkhouse. Mosquitoes swarm up from the swamp below camp. So mosquito stories are in order. Any man is free to invent new Paul Bunyan yarns himself, or he can repeat the stories heard from other bards. Occasionally some bard is so inspired that his creation is never forgotten, and becomes a permanent addition to the Paul Bunyan myth. Such is the story of the mammoth mosquitoes and their amazing experiences with Bum and Bill, Paul Bunyan's battling bees.

Here is the story.

It was in the Year of the Dry Summer that Paul Bunyan's loggers first encountered mosquitoes. That was the season Paul Bunyan invented thunder. Day after day, week after week, month after month, the great hero-leader of the loggers toiled through experiments with all the sounds he could imagine.

Just as cows, pigs, dogs, hens, and ducks could be called, so could clouds be called, thought Paul Bunyan. Seventeen thousand various kinds of calls the great logger tried that summer before he hit on the sound of thunder. Then his labors were rewarded. Paul Bunyan had not thundered once before a stray cloud rolled up from the west. He thundered on, and by midnight so many clouds had gathered that the Dry Summer ended in a downpour that was a deluge instead of a rain. Ever since that parched season the weather has used the thunder which Paul Bunyan invented for it.

But Paul Bunyan had other troubles during this wretched summer. Time and again he had to quit his important labor of trying out sounds that would call up clouds, and attend to small bothers, plagues, and worries. The most troublesome of all these troubles was the invasion of mosquitoes.

The mammoth mosquitoes came from the Tall Wolf country. There the tribe had experienced a devastating famine. For the larger it grew, the smaller became the tribe of tall wolves, the mammoth mosquitoes' natural prey. Eventually the last tall wolf was gone, and only a small company of female mosquitoes was left from the once vast and powerful insect tribe. These females were forced by hunger into migration. They were ready to fall and perish from exhaustion when they reached Paul Bunyan's loggers, who, stripped to the waist, were at work even on this, the hottest of the Dry Summer's days.

Paul Bunyan was afar from his loggers at the moment, pondering deeply on the problem of calling up the clouds. He failed to notice when the ring of axes and the drone of saws were hushed. Not until agonizing yells arose from his loggers did the hero-leader realize that a new trouble had come to camp. Then he saw that his men were struggling for their lives all through the timber five

miles away. Two strides and one leap, and Paul Bunyan was on the scene of battle.

Many of his loggers were already white and faint from loss of blood, and the others were hacking desperately with their axes at the dodging, diving mosquitoes. Two of the mammoth winged females were sprawled lifelessly over some pine logs. Others had paused in the fight to bind up their split bills. The battle raged on.

Paul Bunyan was so stirred with wrath at the sight that he unloosed a yell of astonishment and anger. The loggers, of course, were all lifted off their feet and then hurled to the ground by the force of that cyclonic voice; and the mammoth mosquitoes instantly took advantage of this and plunged on the loggers with bloodthirsty hums. Each one held down seven or more men at once and prepared to feast.

For a moment Paul Bunyan was in a panic. He thought of smashing the mosquitoes with smacks of his hand but that would have crushed the loggers underneath. With a mighty effort, the great logger collected his wits. He had to think fast, and he did. Paul Bunyan was that kind of man. And at once he acted.

What he did was to call for Babe the Blue Ox, whose ears were so far from his muzzle that he couldn't hear himself snort. As he approached, Babe saw what was needed for the emergency. He did not wait for orders. Without even a glance at Paul, the Blue Ox did a squads rightabout, halted, straightened out his tail, and began to flirt the mosquitoes off the prone loggers with swishes of his huge tail brush. In one minute every frustrated mosquito was humming angrily in the air and the saved loggers were galloping for the protection of the bunkhouses. There they remained. All night the ravenous mammoth mosquitoes maintained a deafening and ominous hum over the bunkhouses. Paul Bunyan listened. He figured and planned, the ideas for sounds to call clouds forgotten for the moment. At dawn Paul Bunyan had a satisfying idea. He called for Johnny Inkslinger, his timekeeper and man of science.

"Johnny," said Paul, "you need a vacation."

"Yes, sir, Mr. Bunyan," said Johnny, but not very enthusiastically; for if there was anything he hated it was to leave his figures, his grand fountain pen and ink barrels.

"A vacation," Paul Bunyan repeated firmly. "So a vacation you shall take. A hunting vacation, Johnny. I'm going to send you bee hunting."

"Mr. Bunyan," said Johnny Inkslinger, "I am a good hunter and I like to hunt. Why, once I found a moose who had died of old age, found his moldering bones, I did, and I tracked him to his birthplace. How's that for hunting, Mr. Bunyan?" said Johnny proudly. But then he looked doubtful. "I don't know about hunting bees, though, Mr. Bunyan."

"You must not only hunt bees, Johnny. You must trap 'em and tame 'em."

"Now, Mr. Bunyan, that's asking a lot," protested Johnny Inkslinger. "I never did claim to be a bee trapper, or a bee tamer, either. Why pick on me, Mr. Bunyan?"

"Don't question orders, Johnny," said Paul Bunyan, kindly but sternly. "You pack up now for a vacation in the Mastodonic Clover country. Once there, hunt, trap, and tame the two fightingest, savagest, irritablest, cantankerousest bees you can find. Then trot 'em home to camp."

"Trot 'em, Mr. Bunyan?"

"Trot 'em, Johnny. Trot the bees."

"Yes, sir," said Johnny; and with a will, for he was sentimental about obeying orders.

When Johnny Inkslinger was sent by Paul Bunyan to do anything, he did it.

So he wasn't a day in the Mastodonic Clover country until he had hunted down, trapped, and tamed — as nearly as two such fighting, savage, irritable, and cantankerous bees could be tamed — the two famous battling bees, Bum and Bill. Johnny tamed the two bees so that they allowed him to chain their wings to their bodies. They also trusted him with their stingers, which he put in his knapsack. Then Johnny Inkslinger put calked boots on the bees' hind feet, trotted them out of the clover country, trotted them on over hill and dale, trotted them all the way to camp, just as Paul Bunyan had ordered.

Paul Bunyan had a great hive ready for the two warriors. When their wings were unchained, Bum and Bill took off their calked boots, stretched their legs, ate a hearty meal of lump sugar, and turned in for a refreshing sleep. The next morning they buzzed for their stingers at sunup and showed in other ways that they were eager for battle. Paul Bunyan himself led them to the woods, for Johnny Inkslinger insisted on getting back to his figures at once.

Logging had been continued under the tail of Babe the Blue Ox. For three days he had been swishing the ravenous mammoth mosquitoes away from the loggers. He was so tail-weary that he welcomed Bum and Bill, the battling bees, with a joyful moo that shivered the timber for miles. The bees answered with buzzes of rage, and it required all of Paul Bunyan's bee-taming art to convince the fighting bees that Babe was a friend and not the enemy. Bum and Bill were still buzzing suspicion when they sighted the actual foe. Then, with a battle cry that sounded like the rasping roar of a band saw, Bum and Bill lit out in a beeline and charged in an irresistible attack. In seventeen seconds the bodies of seventeen mammoth mosquitoes crashed down into the timber, shattering scores of great pines into splinters. A thunderous hum of fear sounded from the survivors. They flew off in a panic. Pursued and pursuers vanished in the haze of the Dry Summer, which smothered the forest. Soon the hums of fear and the buzzes of rage were only faint murmurs among the far trees. Paul Bunyan's teeth shone through his beard in a smile of triumph.

"Yay, Babe!" he commanded the Blue Ox.

The logging went on.

Paul Bunyan brushed his hands and praised the saints that this mosquito trouble had been so easily ended. Then he returned to his great task of trying out sounds which would call up clouds. The labor engrossed the great logger to such a degree that the mosquito invasion vanished from his thoughts. He also forgot the two big battling bees who had driven the invaders from the logging camp. But Johnny Inkslinger did not forget. Often he raised his head from his books and held his fountain pen poised in the air, while the hose lines from the ink barrels gushed an inky flood to the office floor. This Johnny Inkslinger did not notice in such moments, for he was remembering his grand success as a bee hunter, a bee trapper, and a bee tamer. It was one of the proudest memories of his life.

And often Johnny Inkslinger wondered what had become of the bees he had tamed, what had happened to the female mammoth mosquitoes Bum and Bill had driven from the camp. Weeks had passed, and still there was not a hum from the mosquitoes or a buzz from the bees.

Then, during such a moment of wondering and remembering, Johnny Inkslinger heard a sound from the distance that was nothing but a buzz-hum. He ran out of the office and peered into the heat haze. A small, dark cloud seemed to be moving toward the camp. Johnny watched and waited. The cloud grew larger. As it approached the loggers in the woods, Johnny saw that the cloud was a vast swarm of giant insects. They hovered over the loggers for an instant, then dived without circling. And again agonizing yells rolled up from the timber and smote Paul Bunyan's ears.

"What's happened down there?" Paul Bunyan shouted.

"The mosquitoes have come back!" said Johnny Inkslinger.

"It's a new kind, then," said Paul Bunyan, coming on the run and calling Babe the Blue Ox. "Look at 'em. They're bees!"

"They're mosquitoes," said Johnny. "Look at their bills!"

"But look at their stingers!"

"Sure enough," said Johnny Inkslinger, almost dumb with astonishment. "Why — why — Mr. Bunyan — they — "

"Look at 'em!" yelled Paul Bunyan. "Why, they got bills in front and stingers behind, and they're getting the loggers going and coming! You know what's happened? Those two bees have married the mosquitoes, that's what! And these are the offspring! Bills in front and stingers behind! Yay, Babe!"

And on Paul galloped with Babe the Blue Ox, who soon got his tail brush to working and let the loggers escape to the bunkhouses. But these mammoth insects which were half mosquito and half bee wouldn't be denied. They attacked the bunkhouses. One would stick his bill under one side of a shake on a bunkhouse roof, and his stinger under the other side; and then he would flap his wings until he had ripped off the shake; and the loggers would have to stand guard with pike poles and peavies [1] to keep the savage insects from coming at them through the ripped roofs. Paul Bunyan saw that he needed to act quick. So he spent another night in figuring and planning. And, just as usual, he had a grand idea at daylight. He called for Johnny Inkslinger.

[1] **peavies:** poles with iron points and movable iron hooks.

"Johnny," said Paul Bunyan, "we are going to carry sugar."

"Yes, Mr. Bunyan."

"We are going to throw some rafts together, Johnny, and then we are going to load the rafts with all the sugar in camp. After that we are going to rope the rafts together and have Babe the Blue Ox tow the whole raft fleet out into the middle of Lake Michigan."

Johnny Inkslinger never batted an eye. He knew the great logger too well to think that any of his ideas were foolish. So Johnny went to work without a word; and by noon the rafts were built, loaded, and roped together. Paul hitched Babe to the head raft of the fleet.

"Yay, Babe," he commanded.

And the Blue Ox bowed his neck, lumbered off, and straight to the center of Lake Michigan he towed the raftloads of sugar. Johnny Inkslinger stayed on shore. He watched and waited. Soon he saw all the mosquito-bees flying out over the lake after the rafts. Then Johnny Inkslinger realized what Paul Bunyan was up to.

"Oh, ain't he got a brain, though?" said Johnny Inkslinger worshipfully. "Oh, but ain't Paul Bunyan got a brain?"

And a brain Paul Bunyan certainly had. For he had figured that the bee blood in the hybrid insects would send them after the sugar. And he had figured that their mosquito blood would make them fill their stomachs till they were stuffed. And Paul Bunyan knew the weight of sugar. . . .

Sure enough, the mosquito-bees glutted themselves on sugar till they could hardly fly. Then Paul Bunyan started Babe on a run for the shore. The stuffed insects tried to follow. But lower and lower they flew; and soon, with anguished buzz-hums, they all sank into the waters of the great lake; and that was the last of them.

The camp of Paul Bunyan was never again troubled by mammoth mosquitoes, or by mammoth mosquito-bees, either. Bum and Bill at last returned to camp, and gave every appearance of being ashamed of themselves. Paul Bunyan did not reproach them, but gave them a home in a furnished hive; and thereafter Bum and Bill occupied themselves solely with making honey for the loggers' flapjacks. Their fighting days were done.

History does not state the fate of the female mammoth mosquitoes. Some authorities advance the idea that they flew to Asia. They point to the elephant to prove their contention. The elephant, they assert, is descended from the mammoth mosquito of Paul Bunyan's time. Other authorities ridicule this idea, asserting that the elephant is too small to be a descendant of the mammoth mosquito.

All such ideas and contentions are guesswork, however. And guesswork has no place in the history of Paul Bunyan.

For Discussion of Tall Tales

1. Can you understand why life on the frontier made tall tales especially popular there? If you know other folk heroes of amazing power, like Pecos Bill, the cowboy, and John Henry, the railroad worker, compare their exploits with Paul Bunyan's.

2. Even with the fun and exaggeration, you can learn something about logging camps and how they operated from tales of Paul Bunyan. What information did you pick up?

3. Telling tall tales has always been a favorite American diversion. Your own neighborhood has its pet "whoppers." Write out one of them — or make up a fresh one of your own. Or take James Stevens's *Paul Bunyan*, J. C. Bowman's *Pecos Bill*, or Margaret Prescott Montague's *Tony Beaver* for one of your outside reading assignments. If you prefer short stories, try Mark Twain's great yarn, "The Jumping Frog."

Bret Harte
1836-1902

THE OUTCASTS OF POKER FLAT

At a certain stage in the development of the literature of the West a subtle change took place. Writers began to emphasize the "local color" of the West and to write stories and accounts of Western life with a romantic appeal. Bret Harte's skill with plot and suspense would have made his stories popular in any day. But to understand the way they swept the country back in the 1860's and 70's, imagine yourself an Easterner full of curiosity about the wild, rough life in the West. Then you will notice how he fills his stories with the sort of details and atmosphere in setting and in characterization that build up "local color."

As Mr. John Oakhurst, gambler, stepped into the main street of Poker Flat on the morning of the twenty-third of November, 1850, he was conscious of a change in its moral atmosphere since the preceding night. Two or three men, conversing earnestly together, ceased as he approached, and exchanged significant glances. There was a Sabbath lull in the air, which, in a settlement unused to Sabbath influences, looked ominous.

Mr. Oakhurst's calm, handsome face betrayed small concern in these indications. Whether he was conscious of any predisposing cause was another question. "I reckon they're after somebody," he reflected; "likely it's me." He returned to his pocket the handkerchief with which he had been whipping away the red dust of Poker Flat from his neat boots, and quietly discharged his mind of any further conjecture.

In point of fact, Poker Flat was "after somebody." It had lately suffered the loss of several thousand dollars, two valuable horses, and a prominent citizen. It was experiencing a spasm of virtuous reaction, quite as lawless and ungovernable as any of the acts that had provoked it. A secret committee had determined to rid the town of all improper persons. This was done permanently in regard to two men who were then hanging from the boughs of a sycamore in the gulch, and temporarily in the banishment of certain other objectionable characters. I regret to say that some of these were ladies. It is but due to the sex, however, to state that their impropriety was professional, and it was only in such easily established standards of evil that Poker Flat ventured to sit in judgment.

Mr. Oakhurst was right in supposing that he was included in this category. A few of the committee had urged hanging him as a possible example and a sure method of reimbursing themselves from his pockets of the sums he had won from them. "It's agin justice," said Jim Wheeler, "to let this yer young man from Roaring Camp — an entire stranger — carry away our money." But a crude sentiment of equity residing in the breasts of those who had been fortunate enough to win from Mr. Oakhurst overruled this narrower local prejudice.

Mr. Oakhurst received his sentence with philosophic calmness, nonetheless coolly that he was aware of the hesitation of his judges. He was too much of a gambler not to accept fate. With him life was at best an uncertain game, and he recognized the usual percentage in favor of the dealer.

A body of armed men accompanied the deported wickedness of Poker Flat to the outskirts of the settlement. Besides Mr. Oakhurst, who was known to be a coolly desperate man, and for whose intimidation the armed escort was intended, the expatriated party consisted of a young woman familiarly known as " The Duchess "; another who had won the title of " Mother Shipton "; and " Uncle Billy," a suspected sluice robber and confirmed drunkard. The cavalcade provoked no comments from the spectators, nor was any word uttered by the escort. Only when the gulch which marked the uttermost limit of Poker Flat was reached, the leader spoke briefly and to the point. The exiles were forbidden to return at the peril of their lives.

As the escort disappeared, their pent-up feelings found vent in a few hysterical tears from the Duchess, some bad language from Mother Shipton, and a Parthian [1] volley of expletives from Uncle Billy. The philosophic Oakhurst alone remained silent. He listened calmly to Mother Shipton's desire to cut somebody's heart out, to the repeated statements of the Duchess that she would die in the road, and to the alarming oaths that seemed to be bumped out of Uncle Billy as he rode forward. With the easy good humor

characteristic of his class, he insisted upon exchanging his own riding horse, " Five-Spot," for the sorry mule which the Duchess rode. But even this act did not draw the party into any closer sympathy. The young woman readjusted her somewhat draggled plumes with a feeble, faded coquetry; Mother Shipton eyed the possessor of Five-Spot with malevolence, and Uncle Billy included the whole party in one sweeping anathema. [2]

The road to Sandy Bar — a camp that, not having as yet experienced the regenerating influences of Poker Flat, consequently seemed to offer some invitation to the emigrants — lay over a steep mountain range. It was distant a day's severe travel. In that advanced season the party soon passed out of the moist, temperate regions of the foothills into the dry, cold, bracing air of the Sierras. The trail was narrow and difficult. At noon the Duchess, rolling out of her saddle upon the ground, declared her intention of going no farther, and the party halted.

The spot was singularly wild and impressive. A wooded amphitheater, surrounded on three sides by precipitous cliffs of naked granite, sloped gently toward the crest of another precipice that overlooked the valley. It was, undoubtedly, the most suitable spot for a camp, had camping been advisable. But Mr. Oakhurst knew that scarcely half the journey to Sandy Bar was accomplished, and the party were not equipped or provisioned for delay. This fact he pointed out to his companions curtly, with a philosophic commentary on the folly of " throwing up their hand before the game was played out." But they were furnished with liquor, which in this emergency stood them in place of food, fuel, rest, and prescience. In spite of his remonstrances, it was not long before they were more or less un-

---

[1] **Parthian:** The Parthians were an ancient people who shot their arrows while fleeing.

[2] anathema (*a·năth'ē·ma*): a curse.

der its influence. Uncle Billy passed rapidly from a bellicose state into one of stupor, the Duchess became maudlin, and Mother Shipton snored. Mr. Oakhurst alone remained erect, leaning against a rock, calmly surveying them.

Mr. Oakhurst did not drink. It interfered with a profession which required coolness, impassiveness, and presence of mind, and, in his own language, he "couldn't afford it." As he gazed at his recumbent fellow exiles, the loneliness begotten of his pariah trade, his habits of life, his very vices, for the first time seriously oppressed him. He bestirred himself in dusting his black clothes, washing his hands and face, and other acts characteristic of his studiously neat habits, and for a moment forgot his annoyance. The thought of deserting his weaker and more pitiable companions never perhaps occurred to him. Yet he could not help feeling the want of that excitement which, singularly enough, was most conducive to that calm equanimity for which he was notorious. He looked at the gloomy walls that rose a thousand feet sheer above the circling pines around him, at the sky ominously clouded, at the valley below, already deepening into shadow; and, doing so, suddenly he heard his own name called.

A horseman slowly ascended the trail. In the fresh, open face of the newcomer Mr. Oakhurst recognized Tom Simson, otherwise known as "The Innocent," of Sandy Bar. He had met him sometime before over a "little game," and had, with perfect equanimity, won the entire fortune — amounting to some forty dollars — of that guileless youth. After the game was finished, Mr. Oakhurst drew the youthful speculator behind the door and thus addressed him: "Tommy, you're a good little man, but you can't gamble worth a cent. Don't try it over again." He then handed him his money back, pushed him gently from the room, and so made a devoted slave of Tom Simson.

There was a remembrance of this in his boyish and enthusiastic greeting of Mr. Oakhurst. He had started, he said, to go to Poker Flat to seek his fortune. "Alone?" No, not exactly alone; in fact (a giggle), he had run away with Piney Woods. Didn't Mr. Oakhurst remember Piney? She that used to wait on the table at the Temperance House? They had been engaged a long time, but old Jake Woods had objected, and so they had run away, and were going to Poker Flat to be married, and here they were. And they were tired out, and how lucky it was they had found a place to camp, and company. All this the Innocent delivered rapidly, while Piney, a stout, comely damsel of fifteen, emerged from behind the pine tree, where she had been blushing unseen, and rode to the side of her lover.

Mr. Oakhurst seldom troubled himself with sentiment, still less with propriety; but he had a vague idea that the situation was not fortunate. He retained, however, his presence of mind sufficiently to kick Uncle Billy, who was about to say something, and Uncle Billy was sober enough to recognize in Mr. Oakhurst's kick a superior power that would not bear trifling. He then endeavored to dissuade Tom Simson from delaying further, but in vain. He even pointed out the fact that there was no provision, nor means of making a camp. But, unluckily, the Innocent met this objection by assuring the party that he was provided with an extra mule loaded with provisions, and by the discovery of a rude attempt at a log house near the trail. "Piney can stay with Mrs. Oakhurst," said the Innocent, pointing to the Duchess, "and I can shift for myself."

Nothing but Mr. Oakhurst's admonishing foot saved Uncle Billy from bursting into a roar of laughter. As it was, he felt compelled to retire up the canyon until he could recover his gravity. There he confided the joke to the tall pine trees, with many slaps of his leg, contortions of his face, and the usual profanity. But when he returned to the party, he found them seated by a fire — for the air had grown strangely chill and the sky overcast — in apparently amicable conversation. Piney was actually talking in an impulsive girlish fashion to the Duchess, who was listening with an interest and animation she had not shown for many days. The Innocent was holding forth, apparently with equal effect, to Mr. Oakhurst and Mother Shipton, who was actually relaxing into amiability. "Is this yer a d——d picnic?" said Uncle Billy, with inward scorn, as he surveyed the sylvan group, the glancing firelight, and the tethered animals in the foreground. Suddenly an idea mingled with the alcoholic fumes that disturbed his brain. It was apparently of a jocular nature, for he felt impelled to slap his leg again and cram his fist into his mouth.

As the shadows crept slowly up the mountain, a slight breeze rocked the tops of the pine trees and moaned through their long and gloomy aisles. The ruined cabin, patched and covered with pine boughs, was set apart for the ladies. As the lovers parted, they unaffectedly exchanged a kiss, so honest and sincere that it might have been heard above the swaying pines. The frail Duchess and the malevolent Mother Shipton were probably too stunned to remark upon this last evidence of simplicity, and so turned without a word to the hut. The fire was replenished, the men lay down before the door, and in a few minutes were asleep.

Mr. Oakhurst was a light sleeper. Toward morning he awoke benumbed and cold. As he stirred the dying fire, the wind, which was now blowing strongly, brought to his cheek that which caused the blood to leave it — snow!

He started to his feet with the intention of awakening the sleepers, for there was no time to lose. But, turning to where Uncle Billy had been lying, he found him gone. A suspicion leaped to his brain, and a curse to his lips. He ran to the spot where the mules had been tethered — they were no longer there. The tracks were already rapidly disappearing in the snow.

The momentary excitement brought Mr. Oakhurst back to the fire with his usual calm. He did not waken the sleepers. The Innocent slumbered peacefully, with a smile on his good-humored, freckled face: the virgin Piney slept beside her frailer sisters as sweetly as though attended by celestial guardians; and Mr. Oakhurst, drawing his blanket over his shoulders, stroked his mustaches and waited for the dawn. It came slowly in a whirly mist of snowflakes that dazzled and confused the eye. What could be seen of the landscape appeared magically changed. He looked over the valley, and summed up the present and future in two words, "Snowed in!"

A careful inventory of the provisions, which, fortunately for the party, had been stored within the hut, and so escaped the felonious fingers of Uncle Billy, disclosed the fact that with care and prudence, they might last ten days longer. "That is," said Mr. Oakhurst *sotto voce* [1] to the Innocent, "if you're willing to board us. If you ain't — and perhaps you'd better not — you can wait till Uncle Billy gets back with provisions." For some occult reason, Mr. Oakhurst could not bring himself to disclose Uncle Billy's rascality, and so offered the hypothesis that he had wandered from the camp and had accidentally stampeded the animals. He dropped a warning to the Duchess and Mother Shipton, who of course knew the facts of their associate's defection. "They'll find out the truth about us *all* when they find out anything," he added

---

[1] *sotto voce* (sŏt'tŏ vō'chä): in an undertone (Italian).

significantly, "and there's no good frightening them now."

Tom Simson not only put all his worldly store at the disposal of Mr. Oakhurst, but seemed to enjoy the prospect of their enforced seclusion. "We'll have a good camp for a week, and then the snow'll melt, and we'll all go back together." The cheerful gaiety of the young man and Mr. Oakhurst's calm infected the others. The Innocent, with the aid of pine boughs, extemporized a thatch for the roofless cabin, and the Duchess directed Piney in the rearrangement of the interior with a taste and tact that opened the blue eyes of that provincial maiden to their fullest extent. "I reckon now you're used to fine things at Poker Flat," said Piney. The Duchess turned away sharply to conceal something that reddened her cheeks through their professional tint, and Mother Shipton requested Piney not to "chatter." But when Mr. Oakhurst returned from a weary search for the trail, he heard the sound of happy laughter echoed from the rocks. He stopped in some alarm, and his thoughts first naturally reverted to the whisky, which he had prudently cached. "And yet it don't somehow sound like whisky," said the gambler. It was not until he caught sight of the blazing fire through the still blind storm, and the group around it, that he settled to the conviction that it was "square fun."

Whether Mr. Oakhurst had cached his cards with the whisky as something debarred the free access of the community, I cannot say. It was certain that, in Mother Shipton's words, he "didn't say 'cards' once" during that evening. Haply the time was beguiled by an accordion, produced somewhat ostentatiously by Tom Simson from his pack. Notwithstanding some difficulties attending the manipulation of this instrument, Piney Woods managed to pluck several reluctant melodies from its keys, to an accompaniment by the Innocent on a pair of bone castanets. But the crowning festivity of the evening was reached in a rude camp-meeting hymn, which the lovers, joining hands, sang with great earnestness and vociferation. I fear that a certain defiant tone and Covenanters' [1] swing to its chorus, rather than any devotional quality, caused it speedily to infect the others, who at last joined in the refrain:

"I'm proud to live in the service of the Lord,
And I'm bound to die in His army."

The pines rocked, the storm eddied and whirled above the miserable group, and the flames of their altar leaped heavenward, as if in token of the vow.

At midnight the storm abated, the rolling clouds parted, and the stars glittered keenly above the sleeping camp. Mr. Oakhurst, whose professional habits had enabled him to live on the smallest possible amount of sleep, in dividing the watch with Tom Simson somehow managed to take upon himself the greater part of that duty. He excused himself to the Innocent by saying that he had "often been a week without sleep." "Doing what?" asked Tom. "Poker!" replied Oakhurst sententiously. "When a man gets a streak of luck, he don't get tired. The luck gives in first. Luck," continued the gambler reflectively, "is a mighty queer thing. All you know about it for certain is that it's bound to change. And it's finding out when it's going to change that makes you. We've had a streak of bad luck since we left Poker Flat — you come along, and slap, you get into it, too. If you can hold your cards right along you're all right. For," added the gambler, with cheerful irrelevance,

"I'm proud to live in the service of the Lord,
And I'm bound to die in His army."

[1] **Covenanters:** in seventeenth-century Scotland, adherents of the Presbyterian Covenant to resist the rule of the Anglican Church.

The third day came, and the sun, looking through the white-curtained valley, saw the outcasts dividing their slowly decreasing store of provisions for the morning meal. It was one of the peculiarities of that mountain climate that its rays diffused a kindly warmth over the wintry landscape, as if in regretful commiseration of the past. But it revealed drift on drift of snow piled high around the hut — a hopeless, uncharted, trackless sea of white lying below the rocky shores to which the castaways still clung. Through the marvelously clear air the smoke of the pastoral village of Poker Flat rose miles away. Mother Shipton saw it, and from a remote pinnacle of her rocky fastness hurled in that direction a final malediction. It was her last vituperative attempt, and perhaps for that reason was invested with a certain degree of sublimity. It did her good, she privately informed the Duchess. "Just you go out there and cuss, and see." She then set herself to the task of amusing "the child," as she and the Duchess were pleased to call Piney. Piney was no chicken, but it was a soothing and original theory of the pair thus to account for the fact that she didn't swear and wasn't improper.

When night crept up again through the gorges, the reedy notes of the accordion rose and fell in fitful spasms and long-drawn gasps by the flickering campfire. But music failed to fill entirely the aching void left by insufficient food, and a new diversion was proposed by Piney — storytelling. Neither Mr. Oakhurst nor his female companions caring to relate their personal experiences, this plan would have failed too, but for the Innocent. Some months before he had chanced upon a stray copy of Mr. Pope's ingenious translation of the *Iliad*. He now proposed to narrate the principal incidents of that poem — having thoroughly mastered the argument and fairly forgotten the words —

in the current vernacular of Sandy Bar. And so for the rest of that night the Homeric demigods again walked the earth. Trojan bully and wily Greek wrestled in the winds, and the great pines in the canyon seemed to bow to the wrath of the son of Peleus.[1] Mr. Oakhurst listened with great satisfaction. Most especially was he interested in the fate of "Ashheels," as the Innocent persisted in denominating the "swift-footed Achilles."

So, with small food and much of Homer and the accordion, a week passed over the heads of the outcasts. The sun again forsook them, and again from leaden skies the snowflakes were sifted over the land. Day by day closer around them drew the snowy circle, until at last they looked from their prison over drifted walls of dazzling white, that towered twenty feet above their heads. It became more and more difficult to replenish their fires, even from the fallen trees beside them, now half hidden in the drifts. And yet no one complained. The lovers turned from the dreary prospect and looked into each other's eyes, and were happy. Mr. Oakhurst settled himself coolly to the losing game before him. The Duchess, more cheerful than she had been, assumed the care of Piney. Only Mother Shipton — once the strongest of the party — seemed to sicken and fade. At midnight on the tenth day she called Oakhurst to her side. "I'm going," she said, in a voice of querulous weakness, "but don't say anything about it. Don't waken the kids. Take the bundle from under my head, and open it." Mr. Oakhurst did so. It contained Mother Shipton's rations for the last week, untouched. "Give 'em to the child," she said, pointing to the sleeping Piney. "You've starved yourself," said the gambler. "That's what they call it," said the woman querulously, as she lay down

[1] son of Peleus (pē′lūs): Achilles (á·kĭl′ēz), the hero of the *Iliad*.

again, and, turning her face to the wall, passed quietly away.

The accordion and the bones were put aside that day, and Homer was forgotten. When the body of Mother Shipton had been committed to the snow, Mr. Oakhurst took the Innocent aside, and showed him a pair of snowshoes, which he had fashioned from the old packsaddle. "There's one chance in a hundred to save her yet," he said, pointing to Piney; "but it's there," he added, pointing toward Poker Flat. "If you can reach there in two days she's safe." "And you?" asked Tom Stimson. "I'll stay here," was the curt reply.

The lovers parted with a long embrace. "You are not going, too?" said the Duchess, as she saw Mr. Oakhurst apparently waiting to accompany him. "As far as the canyon," he replied. He turned suddenly and kissed the Duchess, leaving her pallid face aflame, and her trembling limbs rigid with amazement.

Night came, but not Mr. Oakhurst. It brought the storm again and the whirling snow. Then the Duchess, feeding the fire, found someone had quietly piled beside the hut enough fuel to last a few days longer. The tears rose to her eyes, but she hid them from Piney.

The women slept but little. In the morning looking into each other's faces, they read their fate. Neither spoke, but Piney, accepting the position of the stronger, drew near and placed her arm around the Duchess's waist. They kept this attitude for the rest of the day. That night the storm reached its greatest fury, and, rending asunder the protecting vines, invaded the very hut.

Toward morning they found themselves unable to feed the fire, which gradually died away. As the embers slowly blackened, the Duchess crept closer to Piney, and broke the silence of many hours: "Piney, can you pray?" "No, dear," said Piney simply. The Duchess, without knowing exactly why, felt relieved, and, putting her head upon Piney's shoulder, spoke no more. And so reclining, the younger and purer pillowing the head of her soiled sister upon her virgin breast, they fell asleep.

The wind lulled as if it feared to waken them. Feathery drifts of snow, shaken from the long pine boughs, flew like white-winged birds, and settled about them as they slept. The moon through the rifted clouds looked down upon what had been the camp. But all human stain, all trace of earthly travail, was hidden beneath the spotless mantle mercifully flung from above.

They slept all that day and the next, nor did they waken when voices and footsteps broke the silence of the camp. And when pitying fingers brushed the snow from their wan faces, you could scarcely have told from the equal peace that dwelt upon them which was she that had sinned. Even the law of Poker Flat recognized this, and turned away, leaving them still locked in each other's arms.

But at the head of the gulch, on one of the largest pine trees, they found the deuce of clubs pinned to the bark with a bowie knife. It bore the following, written in pencil in a firm hand:

BENEATH THIS TREE
LIES THE BODY
OF
JOHN OAKHURST
WHO STRUCK A STREAK OF BAD LUCK
ON THE 23D OF NOVEMBER, 1850,
AND
HANDED IN HIS CHECKS
ON THE 7TH DECEMBER, 1850.

And pulseless and cold, with a Derringer by his side and a bullet in his heart, though still calm as in life, beneath the snow lay he who was at once the strongest and yet the weakest of the outcasts of Poker Flat.

For Discussion of Harte

1. What typically Western circumstances form the basis of this story? Why had the citizens' committee suddenly decided to clean up Poker Flat? What was the argument for merely banishing Oakhurst instead of hanging him?

2. Which characters do you consider to be realistic? How was Oakhurst different from the typical mining-camp gambler? Why did he not drink? Is this detail realistic or romantic? Can you detect any instances where Harte exaggerated his story in order to build up its Western atmosphere, its local color?

3. Explain the last statement in the story, that Oakhurst "was at once the strongest and yet the weakest of the outcasts of Poker Flat."

4. One of Harte's assets was his humor. What evidence of it do you find in this story (which is one of his more serious ones)? Which characters furnish the humor?

5. It is known that Bret Harte studied Dame Shirley's letters for background material for his stories. What elements in the letter you read (p. 627) could have been used for this story? How do the accounts differ? Compare the purposes of the two writers.

6. For comparison of this story with one about a genuine Western desperado and the vigilantes' handling of him, read Chapter XI of Mark Twain's *Roughing It.*

For Your Vocabulary

CONTEXT: The outcasts take their expulsion in different ways that reveal their dispositions and characters, and Harte has some choice words to describe their reactions. With a whole story for context, you can master their meaning easily. One of the party is *bellicose,* inclined to "go to war" (how does this word differ from *belligerent?*). Another is *maudlin,* or tearfully emotional, a state often associated, as in this case, with drunkenness. Only one of them meets the crisis with *equanimity,* a calm, even state of mind. Think about the meaning of each word, and see if you can recall without looking back in the story which character's reaction it described. Check up if you need to. The words are used on page 665.

Mark Twain

1835–1910

A LIGHTNING PILOT

In this selection from *Life on the Mississippi,* Twain has already made one trip up the river in training to become a pilot, jotting down notes on all the landmarks a pilot had to know if he was to bring his boat through in safety. Those notes are in the "book" he refers to. Mr. Bixby is the master pilot who has agreed to "teach him the river" for a fee of five hundred dollars. The price may not seem too high when you see Mr. Bixby in action and realize the quality of training the money went for.

"A Lightning Pilot" from *Life on the Mississippi* by Mark Twain. Reprinted by permission of Harper & Brothers.

WHEN I returned to the pilothouse St. Louis was gone, and I was lost. Here was a piece of river which was all down in my book, but I could make neither head nor tail of it; you understand, it was turned around. I had seen it when coming upstream, but I had never faced about to see how it looked when it was behind me. My heart broke again, for it was plain that I had got to learn this troublesome river *both ways*.

The pilothouse was full of pilots, going down to "look at the river." What is called the "upper river" (the two hundred miles between St. Louis and Cairo, where the Ohio comes in) was low; and the Mississippi changes its channel so constantly that the pilots used to always find it necessary to run down to Cairo to take a fresh look, when their boats were to lie in port a week; that is, when the water was at a low stage. A deal of this "looking at the river" was done by poor fellows who seldom had a berth and whose only hope of getting one lay in their being always freshly posted and therefore ready to drop into the shoes of some reputable pilot, for a single trip, on account of such pilot's sudden illness or some other necessity. And a good many of them constantly ran up and down inspecting the river, not because they ever really hoped to get a berth, but because (they being guests of the boat) it was cheaper to "look at the river" than stay ashore and pay board. In time these fellows grew dainty in their tastes, and only infested boats that had an established reputation for setting good tables. All visiting pilots were useful, for they were always ready and willing, winter or summer, night or day, to go out in the yawl and help buoy the channel or assist the boat's pilots in any way they could. They were likewise welcomed because all pilots are tireless talkers, when gathered together, and as they talk only about the river they are always understood and are always interesting. Your true pilot cares nothing about anything on earth but the river, and his pride in his occupation surpasses the pride of kings.

We had a fine company of these river inspectors along this trip. There were eight or ten, and there was abundance of room for them in our great pilothouse. Two or three of them wore polished silk hats, elaborate shirt fronts, diamond breastpins, kid gloves, and patent-leather boots. They were choice in their English, and bore themselves with a dignity proper to men of solid means and prodigious reputation as pilots. The others were more or less loosely clad, and wore upon their heads tall felt cones that were suggestive of the days of the Commonwealth.[1]

I was a cipher in this august company, and felt subdued, not to say torpid. I was not even of sufficient consequence to assist at the wheel when it was necessary to put the tiller hard down in a hurry; the guest that stood nearest did that when occasion required — and this was pretty much all the time, because of the crookedness of the channel and the scant water. I stood in a corner, and the talk I listened to took the hope all out of me. One visitor said to another:

"Jim, how did you run Plum Point, coming up?"

"It was in the night, there, and I ran it the way one of the boys on the *Diana* told me; started out about fifty yards above the woodpile on the false point, and held on the cabin under Plum Point till I raised the reef — quarter less twain — then straightened up for the middle bar till I got well abreast the old one-limbed cottonwood in the bend, then got my stern on the cottonwood, and head on the low place above the point, and came through a-booming — nine and a half."

"Pretty square crossing, ain't it?"

[1] **Commonwealth:** the period 1649 to 1660 in English history when the Puritans were in power. Their characteristic headgear was a tall, cylindrical hat with a broad brim.

"Yes, but the upper bar's working down fast."

Another pilot spoke up and said:

"I had better water than that, and ran it lower down; started out from the false point — mark twain [1] — raised the second reef abreast the big snag in the bend, and had quarter less twain."

One of the gorgeous ones remarked:

"I don't want to find fault with your leadsmen, but that's a good deal of water for Plum Point, it seems to me."

There was an approving nod all around as this quiet snub dropped on the boaster and "settled" him. And so they went on talk-talk-talking. Meantime the thing that was running in my mind was, "Now, if my ears hear aright, I have not only to get the names of all the towns and islands and bends, and so on, by heart, but I must even get up a warm personal acquaintanceship with every old snag and one-limbed cottonwood and obscure woodpile that ornaments the banks of this river for twelve hundred miles; and more than that, I must actually know where these things are in the dark, unless these guests are gifted with eyes that can pierce through two miles of solid blackness. I wish the piloting business was in Jericho and I had never thought of it."

At dusk Mr. Bixby tapped the big bell three times (the signal to land) and the captain emerged from his drawing room in the forward end of the "texas" [2] and looked up inquiringly. Mr. Bixby said:

"We will lay up here all night, Captain."

"Very well, sir."

That was all. The boat came to shore and was tied up for the night. It seemed to me a fine thing that the pilot could do as he pleased, without asking so

[1] mark twain: the leadsman's cry for two fathoms of water, safe depth for the boat.

[2] "texas": the structure at the front of the boat which housed the officers' quarters and the pilothouse.

grand a captain's permission. I took my supper and went immediately to bed, discouraged by my day's observations and experiences. My late voyage's notebooking was but a confusion of meaningless names. It had tangled me all up in a knot every time I had looked at it in the daytime. I now hoped for respite in sleep; but no, it reveled all through my head till sunrise again, a frantic and tireless nightmare.

Next morning I felt pretty rusty and low-spirited. We went booming along, taking a good many chances, for we were anxious to "get out of the river" (as getting out to Cairo was called) before night should overtake us. But Mr. Bixby's partner, the other pilot, presently grounded the boat, and we lost so much time getting her off that it was plain the darkness would overtake us a good long way above the mouth. This was a great misfortune, especially to certain of our visiting pilots, whose boats would have to wait for their return, no matter how long that might be. It sobered the pilothouse talk a good deal. Coming upstream, pilots did not mind low water or any kind of darkness; nothing stopped them but fog. But downstream work was different; a boat was too nearly helpless, with a stiff current pushing behind her; so it was not customary to run downstream at night in low water.

There seemed to be one small hope, however: if we could get through the intricate and dangerous Hat Island crossing before night, we could venture the rest; for we would have plainer sailing and better water. But it would be insanity to attempt Hat Island at night. So there was a deal of looking at watches all the rest of the day, and a constant ciphering upon the speed we were making. Hat Island was the eternal subject; sometimes hope was high and sometimes we were delayed in a bad crossing, and down it went again. For hours all hands lay under the burden of this suppressed excitement; it was even communicated to me, and I got to feeling so solicitous about Hat Island, and under such an awful pressure of responsibility, that I wished I might have five minutes on shore to draw a good, full, relieving breath and start over again. We were standing no regular watches. Each of our pilots ran such portions of the river as he had run when coming upstream, because of his greater familiarity with it; but both remained in the pilothouse constantly.

An hour before sunset Mr. Bixby took the wheel, and Mr. W. stepped aside. For the next thirty minutes every man held his watch in his hand and was restless, silent, and uneasy. At last somebody said, with a doomful sigh:

" Well, yonder's Hat Island — and we can't make it."

All the watches closed with a snap; everybody sighed and muttered something about its being " too bad, too bad " — " ah, if we could *only* have got here half an hour sooner! " — and the place was thick with the atmosphere of disappointment. Some started to go out but loitered, hearing no bell tap to land. The sun dipped behind the horizon; the boat went on. Inquiring looks passed from one guest to another; and one who had his hand on the doorknob and had turned it waited, then presently took away his hand and let the knob turn back again. We bore steadily down the bend. More looks were exchanged, and nods of surprised admiration — but no words. Insensibly the men drew together behind Mr. Bixby, as the sky darkened and one or two dim stars came out. The dead silence and sense of waiting became oppressive. Mr. Bixby pulled the cord, and two deep, mellow notes from the big bell floated off on the night. Then a pause, and one more note was struck. The watchman's voice followed, from the hurricane deck:

" Labboard lead, there! Stabboard [1] lead! "

The cries of the leadsmen began to rise out of the distance, and were gruffly repeated by the word passers on the hurricane deck.

" M-a-r-k three! M-a-r-k three! Quarter less three! Half twain! Quarter twain! M-a-r-k twain! Quarter less— "

Mr. Bixby pulled two bell ropes, and was answered by faint jinglings far below in the engine room, and our speed slackened. The steam began to whistle through the gauge cocks. The cries of the leadsmen went on — and it is a weird sound, always, in the night. Every pilot in the lot was watching now, with fixed eyes, and talking under his breath. Nobody was calm and easy but Mr. Bixby. He would put his wheel down and stand on a spoke, and as the steamer swung into her (to me) utterly invisible marks — for we seemed to be in the midst of a wide and gloomy sea — he would meet and fasten her there. Out of the murmur of half-audible talk, one caught a coherent sentence now and then — such as:

" There; she's over the first reef all right! "

After a pause, another subdued voice:

" Her stern's coming down just *exactly* right, by *George!* "

" Now she's in the marks; over she goes! "

Somebody else muttered:

" Oh, it was done beautiful — *beautiful!* "

Now the engines were stopped altogether, and we drifted with the current. Not that I could see the boat drift, for I could not, the stars being all gone by this time. This drifting was the dismalest work; it held one's heart still. Presently I discovered a blacker gloom than that which surrounded us. It was the head of

[1] **Labboard . . . Stabboard** " (lä'bôrd, stä'bôrd): larboard, or left, and starboard, or right. Calling for soundings on both sides of the boat showed that they were in a tight spot.

the island. We were closing right down upon it. We entered its deeper shadow, and so imminent seemed the peril that I was likely to suffocate; and I had the strongest impulse to do *something*, anything, to save the vessel. But still Mr. Bixby stood by his wheel, silent, intent as a cat, and all the pilots stood shoulder to shoulder at his back.

" She'll not make it! " somebody whispered.

The water grew shoaler and shoaler, by the leadsman's cries, till it was down to:

"Eight and a half! E-i-g-h-t feet! E-i-g-h-t feet! Seven and — "

Mr. Bixby said warningly through his speaking tube to the engineer:

" Stand by, now! "

" Ay, ay, sir! "

"Seven and a half! Seven feet! *Six* and — "

We touched bottom! Instantly Mr. Bixby set a lot of bells ringing, shouted through the tube, " *Now*, let her have it — every ounce you've got! " then to his partner, " Put her hard down! Snatch her! Snatch her! " The boat rasped and ground her way through the sand, hung upon the apex of disaster a single tremendous instant, and then over she went! And such a shout as went up at Mr. Bixby's back never loosened the roof of a pilothouse before!

There was no more trouble after that. Mr. Bixby was a hero that night; and it was some little time, too, before his exploit ceased to be talked about by rivermen.

Fully to realize the marvelous precision required in laying the great steamer in her marks in that murky waste of water, one should know that not only must she pick her intricate way through snags and blind reefs, and then shave the head of the island so closely as to brush the overhanging foliage with her stern, but at one place she must pass almost within arm's reach of a sunken

and invisible wreck that would snatch the hull timbers from under her if she should strike it, and destroy a quarter of a million dollars' worth of steamboat and cargo in five minutes, and maybe a hundred and fifty human lives into the bargain.

The last remark I heard that night was a compliment to Mr. Bixby, uttered in soliloquy and with unction by one of our guests. He said:

" By the Shadow of Death, but he's a lightning pilot! "

ACROSS THE PLAINS BY STAGECOACH

You remember that the War between the States interrupted Mark Twain's career as a river pilot. Now we go with him on his journey to Nevada in 1867 with his older brother, the newly appointed secretary of that Territory. The statutes and the unabridged dictionary that are so troublesome in the stagecoach are the new secretary's equipment for his office. In *Roughing It*, from which this selection is taken, Mark Twain gives a rich account of his experiences in the Far West.

B Y EIGHT o'clock everything was ready, and we were on the other side of the river.[1] We jumped into the stage, the driver cracked his whip, and we bowled away and left " the States " behind us. It was a superb summer morning, and all the landscape was brilliant with sunshine. There was a freshness and breeziness, too, and an exhilarating sense of emancipation from all sorts of cares and responsibilities, that almost made us feel that the years we had spent in the close, hot city, toiling and slaving, had been wasted and thrown away. We

[1] river: the Missouri. The fact that at this time the land west of the State of Missouri had not yet been admitted to statehood explains the next sentence.

"Across the Plains by Stagecoach" from *Roughing It* by Mark Twain. Reprinted by permission of Harper & Brothers.

were spinning along through Kansas, and in the course of an hour and a half we were fairly abroad on the great Plains. Just here the land was rolling — a grand sweep of regular elevations and depressions as far as the eye could reach — like the stately heave and swell of the ocean's bosom after a storm. And everywhere were cornfields, accenting with squares of deeper green this limitless expanse of grassy land. But presently this sea upon dry ground was to lose its " rolling " character and stretch away for seven hundred miles as level as a floor!

Our coach was a great swaying and swinging stage, of the most sumptuous description — an imposing cradle on wheels. It was drawn by six handsome horses, and by the side of the driver sat the " conductor," the legitimate captain of the craft; for it was his business to take charge and care of the mails, baggage, express matter, and passengers.

We three were the only passengers this trip. We sat on the back seat, inside. About all the rest of the coach was full of mailbags — for we had three days' delayed mails with us. Almost touching our knees, a perpendicular wall of mail matter rose up to the roof. There was a great pile of it strapped on top of the stage, and both the fore and hind boots [1] were full. We had twenty-seven hundred pounds of it aboard, the driver said — " a little for Brigham, and Carson, and 'Frisco, but the heft of it for the Injuns, which is powerful troublesome 'thout they get plenty of truck to read." But as he just then got up a fearful convulsion of his countenance which was suggestive of a wink being swallowed by an earthquake, we guessed that his remark was intended to be facetious, and to mean that we would unload the most of our mail matter somewhere on the Plains and leave it to the Indians, or whosoever wanted it.

[1] boots: leather compartments for baggage at each end of the coach.

We changed horses every ten miles, all day long, and fairly flew over the hard level road. We jumped out and stretched our legs every time the coach stopped, and so the night found us still vivacious and unfatigued. . . .

About an hour and a half before daylight we were bowling along smoothly over the road — so smoothly that our cradle only rocked in a gentle, lulling way that was gradually soothing us to sleep, and dulling our consciousness — when something gave way under us. We were dimly aware of it, but indifferent to it. The coach stopped. We heard the driver and conductor talking together outside, and rummaging for a lantern, and swearing because they could not find it — but we had no interest in whatever had happened, and it only added to our comfort to think of those people out there at work in the murky night, and we snug in our nest with the curtains drawn. But presently, by the sounds, there seemed to be an examination going on, and then the driver's voice said:

" By George, the thorough brace is broke! "

This startled me broad awake — as an undefined sense of calamity is always apt to do. I said to myself: " Now, a thorough brace is probably part of a horse; and doubtless a vital part, too, from the dismay in the driver's voice. Leg, maybe, and yet how could he break his leg waltzing along such a road as this? No, it can't be his leg. That is impossible unless he was reaching for the driver. Now, what can be the thorough brace of a horse, I wonder? Well, whatever comes, I shall not air my ignorance in this crowd, anyway."

Just then the conductor's face appeared at a lifted curtain, and his lantern glared in on us and our wall of mail matter. He said:

" Gents, you'll have to turn out a spell. Thorough brace is broke."

We climbed out into a chill drizzle, and felt ever so homeless and dreary. When I found that the thing they called a "thorough brace" was the massive combination of belts and springs which the coach rocks itself in, I said to the driver:

"I never saw a thorough brace used up like that, before, that I can remember. How did it happen?"

"Why, it happened by trying to make one coach carry three days' mail — that's how it happened," said he. "And right here is the very direction [1] which is wrote on all the newspaper bags which was to be put out for the Injuns for to keep 'em quiet. It's most uncommon lucky becuz it's so nation dark I should 'a' gone by unbeknowns if that air thorough brace hadn't broke."

I knew that he was in labor with another of those winks of his, though I could not see his face, because he was bent down at work; and wishing him a safe delivery, I turned to and helped the rest get out the mail sacks. It made a great pyramid by the roadside when it was all out. When they had mended the thorough brace we filled the two boots again, but put no mail on top, and only half as much inside as there was before. The conductor bent all the seat backs down, and then filled the coach just half full of mailbags from end to end. We objected loudly to this for it left us no seats. But the conductor was wiser than we, and said a bed was better than seats, and moreover this plan would protect his thorough braces. We never wanted any seats after that. The lazy bed was infinitely preferable. I had many an exciting day, subsequently, lying on it, reading the statutes and the dictionary, and wondering how the characters would turn out.

The conductor said he would send back a guard from the next station to take charge of the abandoned mailbags,

___
[1] direction: address.

and we drove on.

It was now just dawn; and as we stretched our cramped legs full length on the mail sacks, and gazed out through the windows across the wide wastes of greensward clad in cool powdery mist, to where there was an expectant look in the eastern horizon, our perfect enjoyment took the form of a tranquil and contented ecstasy. The stage whirled along at a spanking gait, the breeze flapping curtains and suspended coats in a most exhilarating way; the cradle swayed and swung luxuriously, the pattering of the horses' hoofs, the cracking of the driver's whip, and his "Hi-yi! g'lang!" were music; the spinning ground and the waltzing trees appeared to give us a mute hurrah as we went by, and then slack up and look after us with interest, or envy, or something; and as we lay and smoked the pipe of peace and compared all this luxury with the years of tiresome city life that had gone before it, we felt that there was only one complete and satisfying happiness in the world and we had found it.

After breakfast, at some station whose name I have forgotten, we three climbed up on the seat behind the driver, and let the conductor have our bed for a nap. And by and by, when the sun made me drowsy, I lay down on my face on top of the coach, grasping the slender iron railing and slept for an hour or more. That will give one an appreciable idea of those matchless roads. Instinct will make a sleeping man grip a fast hold of the railing when the stage jolts, but when it only swings and sways, no grip is necessary. Overland drivers and conductors used to sit in their places and sleep thirty or forty minutes at a time, on good roads, while spinning along at the rate of eight or ten miles an hour. I saw them do it, often. There was no danger about it; a sleeping man *will* seize the irons in time when the coach jolts. These men were hard-worked, and it was not possible for them to stay awake all the time. . . .

MARK TWAIN AND THE MISSISSIPPI

(Below) *Two young adventurers poling down the river on a raft, in a scene from* The Adventures of Mark Twain. (*Culver*)

(Above) *Twain on one of his many journeys.* (*Bettmann*) (Below) *In* The Adventures of Huckleberry Finn, *two types of river craft pass.* (*Metro-Goldwyn-Mayer*)

As the sun went down and the evening chill came on, we made preparation for bed. We stirred up the hard leather letter sacks, and the knotty canvas bags of printed matter (knotty and uneven because of projecting ends and corners of magazines, boxes, and books). We stirred them up and redisposed them in such a way as to make our bed as level as possible. And we *did* improve it, too, though after all our work it had an upheaved and billowy look about it, like a little piece of a stormy sea. Next we hunted up our boots from odd nooks among the mailbags where they had settled, and put them on. Then we got down our coats, vests, pantaloons, and heavy woolen shirts, from the arm loops where they had been swinging all day, and clothed ourselves in them — for there being no ladies either at the stations or in the coach, and the weather being hot, we had looked to our comfort by stripping to our underclothing, at nine o'clock in the morning.

All things being now ready, we stowed the uneasy dictionary where it would lie as quiet as possible, and placed the water canteen and pistols where we could find them in the dark. Then we smoked a final pipe, and swapped a final yarn; after which we put the pipes, tobacco, and bag of coin in snug holes and caves among the mailbags, and then fastened down the coach curtains all around and made the place as "dark as the inside of a cow," as the conductor phrased it in his picturesque way. It was certainly as dark as any place could be — nothing was even dimly visible in it. And finally we rolled ourselves up like silkworms, each person in his own blanket, and sank peacefully to sleep.

Whenever the stage stopped to change horses, we would wake up, and try to recollect where we were — and succeed — and in a minute or two the stage would be off again, and we likewise. We began to get into country, now, threaded here and there with little streams. These had high steep banks on each side, and every time we flew down one bank and scrambled up the other, our party inside got mixed somewhat. First we would all be down in a pile at the forward end of the stage, nearly in a sitting posture, and in a second we would shoot to the other end, and stand on our heads. And we would sprawl and kick, too, and ward off corners and ends of mailbags that came lumbering over us and about us; and as the dust arose from the tumult, we would all sneeze in chorus, and the majority of us would grumble and probably say some hasty thing like: "Take your elbow out of my ribs! — Can't you quit crowding?"

Every time we avalanched from one end of the stage to the other, the unabridged dictionary would come too; and every time it came it damaged somebody. One trip it "barked" the Secretary's elbow; the next trip it hurt me in the stomach, and the third it tilted Bemis's nose up till he could look down his nostrils — he said. The pistols and coin soon settled to the bottom, but the pipes, pipestems, tobacco, and canteens clattered and floundered after the dictionary every time it made an assault upon us, and aided and abetted the book by spilling tobacco in our eyes, and water down our backs.

Still, all things considered, it was a very comfortable night. It wore gradually away, and when at last a cold gray light was visible through the puckers and chinks in the curtains, we yawned and stretched with satisfaction, shed our cocoons, and felt that we had slept as much as was necessary. By and by as the sun rose up and warmed the world, we pulled off our clothes and got ready for breakfast. We were just pleasantly in time, for five minutes afterward the driver sent the weird music of his bugle winding over the grassy solitudes, and presently we detected a low hut or two in the distance. Then the rattling of the coach, the clatter of our six horses' hoofs, and the driver's crisp commands awoke to a louder and stronger emphasis, and we went sweeping down on the station at our smartest speed. It was fascinating — that old overland stagecoaching.

THE PONY EXPRESS

In a little while all interest was taken up with stretching our necks and watching for the " pony-rider " — the fleet messenger who sped across the continent from St. Joe to Sacramento, carrying letters nineteen hundred miles in eight days! Think of that for perishable horse and human flesh and blood to do! The pony-rider was usually a little bit of a man, brimful of spirit and endurance. No matter what time of the day or night his watch came on, and no matter whether it was winter, or summer, raining, snowing, hailing, or sleeting, or whether his " beat " was a level straight road or a crazy trail over mountain crags and precipices, or whether it led through peaceful regions or regions that swarmed with hostile Indians, he must be always ready to leap into the saddle and be off like the wind! There was no idling-time for a pony-rider on duty. He rode fifty miles without stopping, by daylight, moonlight, starlight, or through the blackness of darkness, just as it happened. He rode a splendid horse that was born for a racer and fed and lodged like a gentleman; kept him at his utmost speed for ten miles, and then as he came crashing up to the station where stood two men holding fast a fresh, impatient steed, the transfer of rider and mailbag was made in the twinkling of an eye, and away flew the eager pair and were out of sight before the spectator could get hardly the ghost of a look.

Both rider and horse went " flying light." The rider's dress was thin, and fitted close; he wore a " roundabout " and a skullcap, and tucked his pantaloons into his boot-tops like a race-rider. He carried no arms — he carried nothing that was not absolutely necessary, for even the postage on his literary freight was worth *five dollars a letter*. He got but little frivolous correspondence to carry — his bag had business letters in it, mostly. His horse was stripped of all unnecessary weight, too. He wore a little wafer of a racing saddle, and no visible blanket. He wore light shoes, or none at all. The little flat mail pockets strapped under the rider's thighs would each hold about the bulk of a child's primer. They held many and many an important business chapter and newspaper letter, but these were written on paper as airy and thin as gold leaf, nearly, and thus bulk and weight were economized. The stagecoach traveled about a hundred to a hundred and twenty-five miles a day (twenty-four hours), the pony-rider about two hundred and fifty. There were about eighty pony-riders in the saddle all the time, night and day, stretching in a long scattering procession from Missouri to California, forty flying eastward, and forty toward the west, and among them making four hundred gallant horses earn a stirring livelihood and see a deal of scenery every single day in the year.

We had had a consuming desire from the beginning, to see a pony-rider, but somehow or other all that passed us and all that met us managed to sneak by in the night, and so we heard only a whiz and a hail, and the swift phantom of the desert was gone before we could get our heads out of the windows. But now we were expecting one along every moment, and would see him in broad daylight. Presently the driver exclaims:

" *Here he comes!* "

Every neck is stretched further, and every eye strained wider. Away across the endless dead level of the prairie a black speck appears against the sky, and it is clear that it moves. Well, I should think so! In a second or two it becomes a horse and rider, rising and falling, rising and falling — sweeping toward us nearer and nearer — growing more and more distinct, more and more sharply defined — nearer and still nearer, and the flutter of the hoofs comes faintly to the ear — another instant a whoop and a hurrah from our upper deck, a wave of the rider's hand, but no reply, and man and horse burst past our excited faces and go swinging away like a belated fragment of a storm!

So sudden is it all, and so like a flash of unreal fancy, that but for the flake of white foam left quivering and perishing on a mail sack after the vision had flashed by and disappeared, we might have doubted whether we had seen any actual horse and man at all.

TAMING A GUIDE

Some years after the stagecoach trip Sam Clemens had achieved a reputation as a reporter — " commentator " would describe him better — that resulted in his being sent on a luxury cruise to write back accounts of the experience for American newspapers. Here, at last, in *Innocents Abroad,* Western humor collided with the culture of Europe. Perhaps the guides drew his fire particularly because their business was to hold fast to the wonders and shrines of the past, while Mark Twain's curiosity led him off on such contemporary subjects as the scarcity of soap and the novel mechanics of European windows.

IN THIS place I may as well jot down a chapter concerning those necessary nuisances, European guides. Many a man has wished in his heart he could do without his guide; but knowing he could not, has wished he could get some amusement out of him as a remuneration for the affliction of his society. We accomplished this latter matter, and if our experience can be made useful to others they are welcome to it.

Guides know about enough English to tangle everything up so that a man can make neither head nor tail to it. They know their story by heart — the history of every statue, painting, cathedral, or other wonder they show you. They know it and tell it as a parrot would — and if you interrupt and throw them off the track, they have to go back and begin again. All their lives long they are employed in showing strange things to foreigners and listening to their bursts of admiration. It is human nature to take delight in exciting admiration. It is what prompts children to say " smart " things, and do absurd ones, and in other ways " show off " when company is present. It is what makes gossips turn out in rain and storm to go and be the first to tell a startling bit of news. Think, then, what a passion it becomes with a guide, whose privilege it is, every day, to show to strangers wonders that throw them into perfect ecstasies of admiration! He gets so that he could not by any possibility live in a soberer atmosphere. After we discovered this we *never* went into ecstasies any more — we never admired anything — we never showed any but impassible [1] faces and stupid indifference in the presence of the sublimest wonders a guide had to display. We had found their weak point. We have made good use of it ever since. We have made some of those people savage, at times, but we have never lost our own serenity.

The doctor asks the questions, generally, because he can keep his countenance, and look more like an inspired idiot, and throw more imbecility into the tone of his voice than any man that lives. It comes natural to him.

The guides in Genoa are delighted to secure an American party, because Americans so much wonder, and deal

---

[1] **impassible:** impassive, without expression.

"Taming a Guide" from *Innocents Abroad* by Mark Twain. Reprinted by permission of Harper & Brothers.

so much in sentiment and emotion before any relic of Columbus. Our guide there fidgeted about as if he had swallowed a spring mattress. He was full of animation, full of impatience. He said:

"Come wis me, genteelmen! — come! I show you ze letter-writing by Christopher Colombo! — write it himself! — write it wis his own hand! — come!"

He took us to the municipal palace. After much impressive fumbling of keys and opening of locks, the stained and aged document was spread before us. The guide's eyes sparkled. He danced about us and tapped the parchment with his finger:

"What I tell you, genteelmen. Is it not so? See! handwriting Christopher Colombo! write it himself!"

We looked indifferent, unconcerned. The doctor examined the document very deliberately, during a painful pause. Then he said without any show of interest:

"Ah — Ferguson — what — what did you say was the name of the party who wrote this?"

"Christopher Colombo! ze great Christopher Colombo!"

Another deliberate examination.

"Ah — did he write it himself, or — or how?"

"He write it himself! — Christopher Colombo! he's own handwriting, write by himself!"

Then the doctor laid the document down and said:

"Why, I have seen boys in America only fourteen years old that could write better than that."

"But zis is ze great Christo — "

"I don't care who it is! It's the worst writing I ever saw. Now you mustn't think you can impose on us because we are strangers. We are not fools by a good deal. If you have got any specimens of penmanship of real merit, trot them out! — and if you haven't, drive on!"

We drove on. The guide was consid-

erably shaken up, but he made one more venture. He had something which he thought would overcome us. He said:

"Ah, genteelmen, you come wis me! I show you beautiful, oh, magnificent bust of Christopher Colombo! — splendid, grand, magnificent."

He brought us before the beautiful bust — for it *was* beautiful — and sprang back and struck an attitude:

"Ah, look, genteelmen! — beautiful, grand — bust, Christopher Colombo! — beautiful bust, beautiful pedestal!"

The doctor put up his eyeglasses — procured for such occasions:

"Ah — what did you say this gentleman's name was?"

"Christopher Colombo! — ze great Christopher Colombo!"

"Christopher Colombo — the great Christopher Colombo. Well, what did *he* do?"

"Discover America! — discover America, oh, ze devil!"

"Discover America. No — that statement will hardly wash. We are just from America ourselves. We heard nothing about it. Christopher Colombo — pleasant name — is — is he dead?"

"Oh, *corpo di Baccho!* [1] — three hundred year!"

"What did he die of?"

"I do not know! — I cannot tell."

"Smallpox, think?"

"I do not know, genteelmen! — I do not know *what* he die of."

"Measles, likely?"

"Maybe — maybe — I do *not* know — I think he die of somethings."

"Parents living?"

"Im-posseeble!"

"Ah — which is the bust and which the pedestal?"

"Santa Maria! — *zis* ze bust! — *zis* ze pedestal!"

"Ah, I see, I see — happy combination — very happy combination indeed.

[1] *corpo di Baccho!* (kôr′pŏ dē bä′kō): body of Bacchus, an exclamation of exasperation.

Is — is this the first time this gentleman was ever on a bust? " [1]

That joke was lost on the foreigner — guides cannot master the subtleties of the American joke.

We have made it interesting for this Roman guide. Yesterday we spent three or four hours in the Vatican again, that wonderful world of curiosities. We came very near expressing interest, sometimes — even admiration — it was very hard to keep from it. We succeeded though. Nobody else ever did in the Vatican museums. The guide was bewildered — nonplussed. He walked his legs off, nearly, hunting up extraordinary things, and exhausted all his ingenuity on us, but it was a failure; we never showed any interest in anything. He had reserved what he considered his greatest wonder till the last — a royal Egyptian mummy, the best-preserved in the world, perhaps. He took us there. He felt so sure, this time, that some of his old enthusiasm came back to him:

" See, genteelmen! — Mummy! Mummy! "

The eyeglasses came up as calmly, as deliberately as ever.

" Ah, — Ferguson — what did I understand you to say the gentleman's name was? "

" Name? — he got no name! — Mummy! — 'Gyptian mummy! "

" Yes, yes. Born here? "

" No! 'Gyptian mummy! "

" Ah, just so. Frenchman, I presume? "

" No! — not Frenchman, not Roman! — born in Egypta! "

" Born in Egypta. Never heard of Egypta before. Foreign locality likely. Mummy — Mummy. How calm he is — how self-possessed. Is, ah — is he dead? "

" Oh, *sacré bleu*, been dead three thous' year! "

---

[1] **on a bust:** slang for "on a spree."

The doctor turned on him savagely:

" Here, now, what do you mean by such conduct as this! Playing us for Chinamen because we are strangers and trying to learn! Trying to impose your vile, secondhand carcasses on *us!* — thunder and lightning, I've a notion to — to — if you've got a nice *fresh* corpse, fetch him out! — or, by George, we'll brain you! "

We make it exceedingly interesting for this Frenchman. However, he has paid us back, partly, without knowing it. He came to the hotel this morning to ask if we were up, and he endeavored as well as he could to describe us, so that the landlord would know which persons he meant. He finished with the casual remark that we were lunatics. The observation was so innocent and so honest that it amounted to a very good thing for a guide to say.

For Discussion of Mark Twain

A Lightning Pilot

1. Can you understand why the apprentice pilot was discouraged at first? What did he have to learn? Why did both classes of visiting pilots add to his discouragement?

2. The pilot was the chief of a busy team on a steamboat. What part did each one play?

3. Make a chart showing the course Mr. Bixby followed to bring his boat safely past the island. Some of the hazards are vaguely located, but most are very definite.

4. Why did Mark Twain quit a profession that so fascinated him?

Across the Plains by Stagecoach

1. Describe the stagecoach in which the brothers made their trip, and the system of shifting horses and drivers. What was the " conductor's " job?

2. What were the chief hardships of the trip? Why did the passengers enjoy the trip? What bit of comfort did they enjoy that passengers on modern means of transportation cannot indulge in?

3. What details of the pony express rider's costume and equipment show the

straining for all possible speed? Explain how the pony express system operated.

Taming a Guide

1. What was the tourists' only real grudge against the guides? Why did they get tired of the guides' spiels? What was the policy Mark Twain's group took to pester the guides? Why was the doctor chosen as spokesman?

2. What passages reveal that Mark Twain was actually interested in and appreciative of the historical treasures of Europe?

Reading on the Westward Movement

INFORMAL HISTORY

Chapman, Arthur, *The Pony Express* (Burt, 1936)

Dick, Everett, *The Story of the Frontier* (Tudor, 1947)

Dobie, J. Frank, *Apache Gold and Yaqui Silver* (Little, Brown, 1939)

Duffus, R. L., *The Sante Fe Trail* (Tudor)

Garland, Hamlin, *The Book of the American Indian* (Harper, 1923)

Hough, Emerson, *The Story of the Cowboy* (Grosset, 1925)

Hulbert, A. B., *Forty-Niners* (Little, Brown, 1949)

LaFarge, Oliver, *As Long as the Grass Shall Grow* (Alliance, 1940)

Magaret, Helene, *Giant in the Wilderness* (Bruce, 1952)

Paine, R. D., *Ships and Sailors of Old Salem* (Lauriat, 1923)

Sabin, E. L., *Gold-Seekers of '49* (Lippincott, 1939)

Saxon, Lyle, *Fabulous New Orleans* (Crager, 1950)

Schauinger, J. H., *Cathedrals in the Wilderness* (Bruce, 1952)

Segale, Sister Blandina, *At the End of the Santa Fe Trail* (Bruce, 1948)

Vestal, Stanley, *Warpath* (Random House, 1948)

FICTION

Adams, Andy, *The Log of a Cowboy* (Houghton Mifflin, 1931)

Cable, G. W., *Old Creole Days* (Heritage, 1943)

Ferber, Edna, *Cimarron* (Grosset, 1943)

Ferber, Edna, *Showboat* (Grosset)

Guthrie, A. B., *The Big Sky* (Sloane, 1949)

Guthrie, A. B., *The Way West* (Sloane, 1950)

Hough, Emerson, *North of '36* (Grosset, 1941)

James, Will, *Home Ranch* (World, 1945)

James, Will, *Smoky* (Scribner, 1929)

Lane, R. W., *Let the Hurricane Roar* (Longmans)

Lane, R. W., *Free Land* (World)

Page, Elizabeth, *Wagons West* (Farrar and Rinehart, 1939)

Richter, Conrad, *The Sea of Grass* (Grosset, 1943)

White, Stewart Edward, *Stampede* (Sun Dial, 1943)

NARRATIVE POEMS

Benét, Stephen Vincent, *John Brown's Body* (Oxford, 1944)

Neihardt, J. G., *The Song of Jed Smith* (Macmillan, 1941)

FOLKLORE

Bowman, J. C., *Pecos Bill* (Whitman, 1937)

Chaplin, Henry, *The Adventures of Johnny Appleseed* (Grosset, 1938)

Lomax, John A., *Cowboy Songs* (Macmillan, 1938)

Lomax, John A., *Songs of the Cattle Trail and Cow Camp* (Macmillan, 1919)

Lummis, C. F., *Pueblo Indian Folk-Stories* (Century, 1910)

BIOGRAPHY

Bradford, Gamaliel, *Confederate Portraits* (Houghton Mifflin, 1914)

Bradford, Gamaliel, *Union Portraits* (Houghton Mifflin, 1916)

Bruce, H. A. B., *Daniel Boone and the Wilderness Road* (Macmillan, 1910)

Dobie, J. Frank, *A Vaquero of the Brush Country* (Little, Brown, 1943)

Rourke, Constance, *Davy Crockett* (Harcourt, Brace, 1934)

Saxon, Lyle, *Lafitte the Pirate* (Appleton, 1931)

Siringo, Charles A., *A Texas Cowboy* (Sloane, 1950)

Vestal, Stanley, *Kit Carson* (Houghton Mifflin, 1931)

Vestal, Stanley, *Sitting Bull* (Houghton Mifflin, 1932)

Enormous freight yards at Houston, Texas, a crossroad for transcontinental traffic, symbolize America's transition to a fully industrialized society. (Ewing Galloway)

Time of Change

WRITERS rarely think of themselves as belonging to a literary "movement." They write what they think, the best way they can write it, and let other people worry about whether they express the ideas or contribute to the style of a particular group. Certainly Mark Twain or Walt Whitman couldn't have said whether he belonged to a literary movement or didn't.

Yet when we look back over several centuries of literature we tend to see writers in groups. We notice that a group of writers write in the same way or about the same basic themes and ideas. When these groups are large and clearly distinguished from other groups, we sometimes say they represent a literary movement. Keep in mind, however, that more than one movement may be in progress at the same time. Remember that there are no high fences or sharp border lines between movements. Remember also that at times the "new" writers sound no newer than the "old" ones.

It is clear to us now, as we look back, that a literary movement was beginning to take shape in this country in the years after the War between the States. This period, with its new literary directions, we call the Time of Change.

The Directions of Change

What were these new directions? You may find it easier to recognize than to define them. You will easily see the difference between the mellow, cultured Longfellow and the rebellious Whitman, the dreamy Poe and the angry Hamlin Garland, the kindly humor of Irving and the bitter humor of Ambrose Bierce, the gentle Bryant writing about flowers and birds and the worried Markham writing about the working man. These later writers wrote about subjects which the earlier ones did not often choose to touch. They had different attitudes toward the world around them and different ways of saying what they had to say.

Looking back now, it seems clear to us that Longfellow and his contemporaries belong in one literary movement, and Garland and his contemporaries in another. You may want to remember that we sometimes call the literary age of Longfellow the American Romantic Movement, and the literary age of Garland and his contemporaries the American Realistic Movement, but you will not need just now to go into the exact meaning literary historians give those terms.

But remember that a change was taking place in the country, and that literature always reflects a change of that kind. The period between the Revolution and the War between the States was a kind of youth and springtime for America, and the literature too had a springtime flavor. After the war, spring was over. The country had to face the hard realities that come with growing up. And the literature mirrored the new problems, attitudes, responsibilities, experiments.

New Directions in Poetry

Lanier and Dickinson

New directions were evident in poetry before they appeared in fiction. Sidney Lanier helped lead the way. Lanier was the South's greatest poet after Poe. As with most other Southern writers, his career was tragically interrupted by the War between the States. He was only fifteen when it started, but he entered the blockade-running service so necessary to the South's survival. Captured, imprisoned by the Northern army, he developed tuberculosis. He lived only sixteen years after the war's end. In that time he wrote poems of a lyrical and musical nature, and of deep feeling and keen imagination. The "newness" of his poetry consisted largely in his experiments with musical patterns in verse. It is not surprising, therefore, to note the fact that he was a distinguished musician as well as poet. He was one of the great symphony orchestra flutists of his time, and one of the ablest interpreters of music in poetry.

Emily Dickinson was writing poems in Amherst, Massachusetts, during the same years that Lanier was writing in the South, but only a handful of her

poems were published in her lifetime. She lived a quiet, retiring life and literally hid her great talent. The reason why she did so is still rather mysterious, but it apparently involved an unfortunate love affair. Whatever the reason, she confined herself almost entirely to her immediate family. She sat at her desk and scribbled poems, on envelopes, on scratch paper, on anything that happened to be handy, with no thought of publishing them. Baking a cake for a friend, she might send it along with a brief verse written on the wrapper. When her literary executors found these scraps, some years after Emily's death, they got one of the great thrills of American literary history. For it was soon realized that she was one of the great poets of her time. As simple and direct as a child, she had a fresh and original way of putting an idea, a way of using words as sharply and exactly as a surgeon's knife, and a penetrating

insight into the reasons why people act as they do. In our time, rather than hers, she has become one of the most widely read of American poets.

One reason why she seems to belong to our time rather than to the nineteenth century is the intensely personal quality of her poetry. Notice how often the first-person pronoun occurs in her poems, how often they tell what "I" think or say or see. In this respect she was less like Bryant, Whittier, Longfellow, or Poe, than like certain poets of the twentieth century, such as Edna St. Vincent Millay and Elinor Wylie.

Walt Whitman and the Birth of Modern Poetry

But the poet who was the chief nonconformist, the chief innovator of the new era, was Walt Whitman.

By birth and experience Whitman was as Eastern as any of the writers of the Eastern flowering, and yet all his life he was in revolt against the kind of poetry they wrote. In his own time there was some question whether he could properly be called a poet at all, but of all the nineteenth-century Eastern group he had the most influence on later poets.

Whitman's Self-Education

He was born on a Long Island farm, but moved to Brooklyn when he was very young. Unlike most of the Eastern writers he did not have the advantage of four years at Harvard or Yale. In fact, he left school at twelve. Thereafter he was his own schoolmaster, and he gave himself a hard course.

He began with a print shop — like Benjamin Franklin and so many other writers. He worked for several newspapers, because they gave him a chance to write and, more important, to meet and observe people. He tried schoolteaching for a while, went back to the newspaper business, and got to be editor of the Brooklyn *Eagle*. The publisher didn't like his editorials and fired him. But Whitman went on with his self-education.

By this time he had decided a fundamental question about the education he was giving himself. He had decided that the chief subject in his self-taught school would have to be *people*. He wanted to understand people, and felt he could do that only by talking to them, seeing how they live, finding out how they think and feel. If he could understand other people he could come nearer understanding himself, and that, he felt, was the chief purpose of education. So he spent many an afternoon and holiday walking through the New York harbor district and the markets, talking to anyone who would talk to him, watching and listening. He rode the ferry across the Hudson again and again, merely to observe the many kinds of people on it. He traveled to New Orleans, came back, tried managing a bookshop, tried running a print shop, tried building and selling houses — all the while studying people, getting his ideas in order, getting ready to write.

None of the earlier Eastern writers had ever learned to write that way. Most of them had gone to a university, read great books, gone to Europe, associated with great literary men. But Whitman had hardly seen a university or a literary man. He had prepared himself to write by learning about ordinary men.

Leaves of Grass

Then in 1855 he printed a book called *Leaves of Grass*. He said it was poetry, but some people were dubious. It had very few rhymes and none of the elegance and niceties of the regular verse that respectable poets like Longfellow, Holmes, and Lowell wrote. It had long free-verse lines, which might have sounded all right given aloud as chants or declamations, but looked very queer in print. And then — such subject matter!

It was certainly the most unusual book of poetry published in America in the nineteenth century. Whitman himself said:

"Camerado, this is no book;
Who touches this, touches a man."

There was nothing literary, nothing traditional about the book. It *was* a man. It was a man's thoughts and feelings. It was a glorification of man: not of a Greek god, not of an ideal man, but of an ordinary average man; not of man in a dress suit, but of man in overalls at work. Be proud of your muscles, your health, your vigor, said Whitman. Be strong, be natural. You are just as much a part of nature as a leaf of grass.

Not many people read the book. Of those who did, more than half were not interested or didn't understand, and most of the others were a little shocked.

But a few of the readers of the book were excited. Emerson got a free copy and wrote Whitman, " I greet you at the beginning of a great career! " Whitman was a newspaperman and knew the value of advertising; he used Emerson's sentence to advertise his book. Emerson's enthusiasm later cooled, but he sent Thoreau to see Whitman when the latter went to Boston, and gradually a

little circle of live minds began to appreciate this unusual poet.

The literary history of Whitman is the history of *Leaves of Grass*. All his life he wrote that one book over. It grew in length, changed in contents, mellowed, but still was the same book, the result of a man's self-schooling in the university of life. That schooling went on as long as Whitman lived. The War between the States was a great university for him. Whitman worked in hospitals during that war, taking care of the wounded. His experiences moved him deeply, added deep and solemn notes to his writing. Two of his best poems deal with the death of Lincoln. After the war he traveled about the country, gave lectures on a few occasions, and wrote other books, one of them a prose work declaring his thoughts on America's democratic system. He never made much money; in fact, he was sometimes in want. As an old man the "good gray poet" settled down in a house in Camden, New Jersey, and went on reading, listening, walking the docks and the slum streets, talking long hours with friends — and rewriting *Leaves of Grass.*

Whitman's Message to Americans

We have become used to free verse now and know that Whitman's verse is not barbarous, as some of his contemporaries said it was. We know he wrote some of the truest poetry ever written in America. And we remember him for two messages he put again and again into his poems and his criticism.

One of these we have already mentioned: Be in love with life. Don't be afraid of it; don't be ashamed of being a part of nature. Be strong, be natural. Be proud that you are related to every living thing, and don't set yourself apart from other living things because you use a fork and eat from a plate.

The other message was somewhat like Emerson's "The sun shines today also." The past is dead, said Whitman. You can get some of it from books. But don't mourn the past — live today! The best way to wisdom is to study the people around you, the common people, the poor people. Don't be snobbish; don't scorn the average man around you. For these average men here in America have the "fullest potential known to history." There is no limit to what can be done in America if Americans will only believe in themselves and their country.

Walt Whitman was born (1819) in the same year as Lowell and two years after Thoreau, and he died (1892) in the same year as Whittier. When he was born, Irving was beginning to publish "The Sketch Book." When he died, Edwin Arlington Robinson was beginning to write poems.

Sidney Lanier
1842–1881

In many ways Sidney Lanier is a conventional poet. He writes of love and death and man's feeling of the presence of God in the natural world. His verses usually have the familiar patterns of rhythm and rhyme. To that extent he is much like the poets of the early half of the century. But even in his nature poems there are echoes of the world of work and care and strife that characterized the period after the war. A word here, a phrase there, reminds you that he wrote in later, more complex times than those which shaped Longfellow, Lowell, Emerson, and Holmes. There is a new richness in his rhythm and melody. He believed that with proper care for the pure sound of words, poetry could become a kind of music of its own.

This blending of old elements with new ones makes Lanier truly a poet of transition, and a good writer with whom to introduce the "Time of Change."

SONG OF THE CHATTAHOOCHEE

Two great loves of Lanier's were for music and for the outdoor scenes of his native Georgia. In this poem he combines the two as he describes the swift course of a river with word music that echoes the dashing and rippling of the water. The description shows the beauties that tempt the river to linger, while the rhythm expresses the urgency that impels it toward the plain. All the devices that make melody in poetry — alliteration, rhyme, repetition — have their share in creating the music of this most popular of all Lanier's poems.

Out of the hills of Habersham,
  Down the valleys of Hall,
I hurry amain to reach the plain,
Run the rapid and leap the fall,
Split at the rock and together again,   5
Accept my bed, or narrow or wide,
And flee from folly on every side
With a lover's pain to attain the plain
  Far from the hills of Habersham,
  Far from the valleys of Hall.   10

All down the hills of Habersham,
  All through the valleys of Hall,
The rushes cried, *Abide, abide,*
The willful waterweeds held me thrall,
The laving laurel turned my tide,   15
The ferns and the fondling grass said
    Stay,
The dewberry dipped for to work delay,
And the little reeds sighed, *Abide,*
    abide,
  Here in the hills of Habersham,
  Here in the valleys of Hall.   20

High o'er the hills of Habersham,
  Veiling the valleys of Hall,
The hickory told me manifold
Fair tales of shade, the poplar tall
Wrought me her shadowy self to hold,
The chestnut, the oak, the walnut, the
    pine,   26

Overleaning, with flickering meaning
    and sign,
Said, *Pass not, so cold, these manifold*
  Deep shades of the hills of Haber-
    sham,
  These glades in the valleys of Hall.

And oft in the hills of Habersham,   31
  And oft in the valleys of Hall,
The white quartz shone, and the smooth
    brook-stone
Did bar me of passage with friendly
    brawl,
And many a luminous jewel lone   35
— Crystals clear or a-cloud with mist,
Ruby, garnet, and amethyst —
Made lures with the lights of streaming
    stone
  In the clefts of the hills of Haber-
    sham,
  In the beds of the valleys of Hall.   40

But oh, not the hills of Habersham,
  And oh, not the valleys of Hall
Avail: I am fain for to water the plain.
Downward the voices of Duty call —
Downward, to toil and be mixed with
    the main   45
The dry fields burn, and the mills are to
    turn,
And a myriad flowers mortally yearn,
And the lordly main from beyond the
    plain
  Calls o'er the hills of Habersham,
  Calls through the valleys of Hall.   50

A BALLAD OF TREES AND THE MASTER

Strong religious feeling appears in many of Lanier's poems. This is a striking and original conception of Christ's experience in the Garden of Gethsemane. Vividly and memorably the poet's imagination makes us see the Biblical story in a new light. The poem has several musical settings and is often sung by church choirs.

Into the woods my Master went,
Clean forspent, forspent.
Into the woods my Master came,
Forspent with love and shame.
But the olives they were not blind to
    Him,   5
The little gray leaves were kind to
    Him:
The thorn tree had a mind to Him
When into the woods He came.

Out of the woods my Master went,
And He was well content.   10
Out of the woods my Master came,
Content with death and shame.
When Death and Shame would woo
    Him last,
From under the trees they drew Him
    last:
'Twas on a tree they slew Him — last
When out of the woods He came.   16

THE MARSHES OF GLYNN

A glance down the page will reveal that this is not a poem of regular lines and set pattern. The poetry Lanier created to express the beauty of the seaside marshes is not the neat melody of a song but the flowing sweep of a symphony. A song composed of short, regular lines could portray a carefully laid out garden, but not the wild magnificence of the marshes.

Long descriptive passages preface each statement of the feelings the marshes stir in the poet. To help you follow the thought, marginal notes guide you to the main point of each section. Using these notes to keep the thought development clear, you can enjoy fully the imagery and melody of each descriptive passage and share the moods that lead the poet from weariness and doubt to serene confidence.

This is not an easy poem, but it is a great one. You will want to study it carefully. Read it slowly the first time to understand it. Then read it again more rapidly, preferably aloud, to blend music and imagery, mood and thought, into one splendid poetic experience.

Glooms of the live oaks, beautiful-braided and woven
With intricate shades of the vines that myriad-cloven
Clamber the forks of the multiform boughs —
    Emerald twilights —
    Virginal shy lights,   5
Wrought of the leaves to allure to the whisper of vows,
When lovers pace timidly down through the green colonnades
Of the dim sweet woods, of the dear dark woods,
    Of the heavenly woods and glades,
That run to the radiant marginal sand-beach within   10
    The wide sea-marshes of Glynn —

The poet addresses the deep tangled shadows amid the live oaks, seeing in them a retreat for lovers,

Beautiful glooms, soft dusks in the noonday fire —
Wildwood privacies, closets of lone desire,
Chamber from chamber parted with wavering arras of leaves —
Cells for the passionate pleasure of prayer for the soul that
    grieves,   15

and seeing in them a quiet retreat for prayer and solitary thought.

Pure with a sense of the passing of saints through the wood,
Cool for the dutiful weighing of ill with good —

O braided dusks of the oak and woven shades of the vine,
While the riotous noonday sun of the June day long did shine
Ye held me fast in your heart and I held you fast in mine; 20
But now when the noon is no more, and riot is rest,
And the sun is await at the ponderous gate of the West,
And the slant yellow beam down the wood-aisle doth seem
Like a lane into heaven that leads from a dream —
Ay, now, when my soul all day hath drunken the soul of the oak,
And my heart is at ease from men, and the wearisome sound of the
  stroke 26
  Of the scythe of time, and the trowel of trade is low,
  And belief overmasters doubt, and I know that I know,
  And my spirit is grown to a lordly great compass within,
That the length and the breadth and the sweep of the marshes of
  Glynn 30
Will work me no fear like the fear they have wrought me of yore
When length was fatigue, and when breadth was but bitterness
  sore,
And when terror and shrinking and dreary unnamable pain
Drew over me out of the merciless miles of the plain —

Oh, now, unafraid, I am fain to face 35
  The vast sweet visage of space.
To the edge of the wood I am drawn, I am drawn,
Where the gray beach glimmering runs, as a belt of the dawn,
  For a mete and a mark
  To the forest-dark — 40
    So:
Affable live oak, bending low —
Thus — with your favor — soft, with a reverent hand,
(Not lightly touching your person, Lord of the land!)
Bending your beauty aside, with a step I stand 45
On the firm-packed sand,
    Free
By a world of marsh that borders a world of sea.

  Sinuous southward and sinuous northward the shimmering
    band
  Of the sand-beach fastens the fringe of the marsh to the folds
    of the land. 50
Inward and outward to northward and southward the beach-lines
  linger and curl
As a silver-wrought garment that clings to and follows the firm
  sweet limbs of a girl.
Vanishing, swerving, evermore curving again into sight,
Softly the sand-beach wavers away to a dim gray looping of light.

Through the heat of a June day he has relaxed in the shadows.

At evening he is rested from the cares of the world and strong against fear, no longer weary and afraid of great spaces.

So he steps out confidently from the protecting woods to the open sweep of the marshes.

He rejoices in the wide panorama of curving marshes and sea.

And what if behind me to westward the wall of the woods stands
    high?   55
The world lies east: how ample, the marsh and the sea and the
    sky!
A league and a league of marsh-grass, waist-high, broad in the
    blade,
Green, and all of a height, and unflecked with a light or a shade,
Stretch leisurely off, in a pleasant plain,
To the terminal blue of the main.   60
Oh, what is abroad in the marsh and the terminal sea?
    Somehow my soul seems suddenly free   *His soul is freed*
From the weighing of fate and the sad discussion of sin,   *of its care by the*
By the length and the breadth and the sweep of the marshes of *sweeping views.*
    Glynn.

Ye marshes, how candid and simple and nothing withholding and
    free   65   *The marshes*
Ye publish yourselves to the sky and offer yourselves to the sea! *seem open, serene*
Tolerant plains, that suffer the sea and the rains and the sun,   *and confident,*
Ye spread and span like the catholic man who hath mightily *like a man who*
    won   *has won greatness*
God out of knowledge and good out of infinite pain   *of soul after*
And sight out of blindness and purity out of a stain.   70 *suffering and is*
                                                          in harmony with
                                                          God.

Armstrong Roberts

" Glooms of the live oaks, beautiful-braided and woven
With intricate shades of the vines that myriad-cloven . . ."

As the marsh-hen secretly builds on the watery sod,
Behold I will build me a nest on the greatness of God:
I will fly in the greatness of God as the marsh-hen flies
In the freedom that fills all the space 'twixt the marsh and the
    skies:
By so many roots as the marsh-grass sends in the sod   75
I will heartily lay me a-hold on the greatness of God:
Oh, like to the greatness of God is the greatness within
The range of the marshes, the liberal marshes of Glynn.

The poet resolves to find refuge and strength in the greatness of God, which he senses in the greatness of the marshes.

And the sea lends large, as the marsh: lo, out of his plenty the sea
Pours fast: full soon the time of the flood-tide must be: 80
Look how the grace of the sea doth go
About and about through the intricate channels that flow
    Here and there,
        Everywhere,
Till his waters have flooded the uttermost creeks and the low-lying
    lanes,   85
And the marsh is meshed with a million veins,
That like as with rosy and silvery essences flow
    In the rose-and-silver evening glow.
        Farewell, my lord Sun!
The creeks overflow; a thousand rivulets run   90
'Twixt the roots of the sod; the blades of the marsh-grass stir;
Passeth a hurrying sound of wings that westward whir;
Passeth, and all is still; and the currents cease to run;
And the sea and the marsh are one.

The sea comes in with the rising tide, and the sun goes down.

How still the plains of the waters be!   95
The tide is in his ecstasy;
The tide is at his highest height;
    And it is night.

And now from the Vast of the Lord will the waters of sleep
Roll in on the souls of men,   100
But who will reveal to our waking ken
The forms that swim and the shapes that creep
    Under the waters of sleep?
And I would I could know what swimmeth below when the tide
    comes in   104
On the length and the breadth of the marvelous marshes of Glynn.

As the tide comes over the marshes, so sleep rolls over men. The poet broods over the mysterious force of life beneath the surfaces of tide and sleep.

For Discussion of Lanier

Song of the Chattahoochee

1. Observe how neatly this poem is organized, with the second, third, and fourth stanzas each offering a different kind of temptation to linger. Name a topic for each stanza. Do these stanzas describe different parts of the river's course?

2. Why must the river rush on to the plain? No direct moral is expressed, but the last stanza suggests a comparison with man's life. What is it?

3. Make a chart of the rhymed words in one stanza to show how intricate the pattern is. Be sure to show the internal

rhymes (a word in the center of a line rhyming with the end word). Do all the stanzas follow the same pattern? Find examples of alliteration. Do most of the lines contain alliteration? What are the slight variations in the refrain at the end of each stanza? Why is this variation more effective than identical refrains would be?

4. Read Tennyson's " The Brook," with which " Song of the Chattahoochee " is often compared. How are the poems alike? How different? Which rhythm do you prefer? Which thought?

5. Place names of Indian origin, like " Chattahoochee," are often flowing and musical. Are there any in your state that would fit into poems? Try putting several of them together to make musical lines. In this connection, you will enjoy reading Benét's poem " American Names."

A Ballad of Trees and the Master

1. Why was Christ " forspent " when He went into the woods? Why was He " content with death and shame " when He came out of the woods? How is the repeated mention of trees brought to a climax at the end?

The Marshes of Glynn

1. What are your chief impressions of the wooded parts of the marshes? What mood did they create in the poet? Find clues to the source of the weariness and fear from which he fled to the woods.

2. State your dominant impression of the grassy plain beyond the woods. What pictures remain in your mind? What resolve formed in the poet's mind as he looked over the wide stretches?

3. Describe the coming in of the tide. How is sleep like a tide sweeping over the souls of men? What do you think the poet means by " the forms that swim and the shapes that creep under the waters of sleep "?

4. Find passages that have a particularly musical sound. Give examples of internal rhyme and alliteration that contribute to the music.

5. Which type of poetic music do you like better, the irregular flow of this poem or the strict rhythmic pattern of " Song of the Chattahoochee "? How can you account for your preference? Can you cite other poems you have read in this book that fall into one or the other of these types?

Emily Dickinson
1830–1886

Emily Dickinson's poems are all short, but not because she had little to say. Don't let the simple words and few lines trick you into thinking the meaning is slight or trivial.

Like so many modern poets (whom she resembles much more than poets of her own century), she packed meaning into a terse style. These poems have remarkable power to startle the mind and challenge the imagination. Like skyrockets, they explode in your mind in a star-shower of suggested thoughts.

Emily Dickinson was hardly at all concerned with the pressures or problems of society. The poet's relation to other people is rarely suggested. But she constantly explored and expressed her deepest thoughts and feelings, and that may account for the fact that she never published her writings.

I'M NOBODY

I'm nobody! Who are you?
  Are you nobody, too?
Then there's a pair of us — don't tell!
  They'd banish us, you know.

How dreary to be somebody!   5
  How public like a frog
To tell your name the livelong day
  To an admiring bog!

A WORD

A word is dead
When it is said,
  Some say.
I say it just
Begins to live   5
  That day.

TO MAKE A PRAIRIE

To make a prairie it takes a clover
And one bee —
One clover, and a bee,
And reverie.
The reverie alone will do   5
If bees are few.

THE STORM

It makes Emily Dickinson seem startlingly modern to know that a new volume of her hitherto unpublished poems came out in 1945. A careful reading of this *Bolts of Melody*, as it is called, shows that her best work had been gleaned in the earlier volume, but nevertheless the amazing freshness and originality of her imagery is still there, as this little poem shows.

Like rain it sounded till it curved,
And then I knew 'twas wind;
It walked as wet as any wave
But swept as dry as sand.

When it had pushed itself away   5
To some remotest plain
A coming as of hosts was heard —
That was indeed the rain!

It filled the wells, it pleased the pools,
It warbled in the road,   10
It pulled the spigot from the hills
And let the floods abroad;

It loosened acres, lifted seas,
The sites of centers stirred,
Then like Elijah° rode away   15
Upon a wheel of cloud.

15. **Elijah** (ė·lī′já): For this Bible story see II Kings 2:9–12.

AN ALTERED LOOK
ABOUT THE HILLS

An altered look about the hills;
A Tyrian° light the village fills;
A wider sunrise in the dawn;
A deeper twilight on the lawn;
A print of a vermilion foot;   5
A purple finger on the slope;
A flippant fly upon the pane;
A spider at his trade again;
An added strut in chanticleer;
A flower expected everywhere;   10
An ax shrill singing in the woods;
Fern odors on untraveled roads —
All this and more I cannot tell,
A furtive look you know as well,
And Nicodemus' mystery°   15
Receives its annual reply.

2. **Tyrian** (tĭr′ĭ·ăn): Ancient Tyre (tĭr) was famous for its manufacture of purple dye.
15. **Nicodemus'** (nĭk·ô·dē′mŭs) mystery: John 3: 1 ff. Nicodemus' question was "How can a man be born again?" What is the "annual reply"?

THE TRUTH IS STIRLESS

The truth is stirless. Other force
May be presumed to move.
This then is best for confidence —
When oldest cedars swerve

And oaks unclinch their fists,   5
And mountains feeble lean,
How excellent a body
That stands without a bone!

How vigorous a force
That holds without a prop!   10
Truth stays herself, and every man
That trusts her, boldly up.

HOW HAPPY IS THE LITTLE STONE

How happy is the little stone
That rambles in the road alone,
And doesn't care about careers,
And exigencies never fears;
Whose coat of elemental brown   5
A passing universe put on;
And independent as the sun,
Associates or glows alone,
Fulfilling absolute decree
In casual simplicity.   10

I NEVER SAW A MOOR

I never saw a moor,
   I never saw the sea;
Yet know I how the heather looks,
   And what a wave must be.

I never spoke with God,   5
   Nor visited in heaven;
Yet certain am I of the spot
   As if the chart were given.

THE SOUL SELECTS HER OWN SOCIETY

An experience of Emily Dickinson's girlhood colored her whole life and may have been responsible for the retired existence she lived. While on a visit to Philadelphia (as her niece tells the story) she fell in love with a young man and he with her. The tragedy was that he was already married. Emily's decision was that they must never see each other again. Except to her devoted sister-in-law she never referred directly to this painful experience. But some of her poems, like the next two, seem to be based upon it.

The soul selects her own society,
   Then shuts the door;
On her divine majority
   Obtrude no more.

Unmoved, she notes the chariot's pausing   5
   At her low gate;
Unmoved, an emperor is kneeling
   Upon her mat.

I've known her from an ample nation
   Choose one;   10
Then close the valves of her attention
   Like stone.

MY LIFE CLOSED TWICE

My life closed twice before its close;
   It yet remains to see
If Immortality unveil
   A third event to me,

So huge, so hopeless to conceive,   5
   As these that twice befell.
Parting is all we know of heaven,
   And all we need of hell.

WE NEVER KNOW
HOW HIGH

We never know how high we are
   Till we are called to rise;
And then, if we are true to plan,
   Our statures touch the skies.

The heroism we recite   5
   Would be a daily thing,
Did not ourselves the cubits warp
   For fear to be a king.

For Discussion of Emily Dickinson

1. For each poem write in a sentence or
two the thoughts that are suggested to you
but not directly expressed in the poem.
Compare these suggested ideas with those
your classmates get from the same poems.
How would you explain the fact that different readers will often make different interpretations?

2. Judging from this group of poems,
what were Emily Dickinson's chief interests? Are they usual ones for a poet? What
can you gather about her ideas on society?
religion? nature?

3. What reflections of her own life did
you discover? of her experience with love?

4. Did you notice that the poet takes
liberties with the usual idea of rhyme?
What do you think she considered more
important than rhyme?

5. Emily Dickinson's figures of speech
are particularly interesting. How many can
you find in this group of poems?

6. Few poets offer more attractions to
a browsing reader. Get a volume of her
poems and go on an exploring expedition.

Walt Whitman
1819–1892

All of the poems that follow are taken
from *Leaves of Grass,* a book that is unique
in literary history. The last edition of this
book is sometimes called the Deathbed
Edition (1891–92), because the poet revised it shortly before his death. Poems
written when he was in his thirties appear
alongside some written when he was approaching seventy. Taken altogether, they
express the changing thoughts and feelings of a complex and fascinating individual over the course of a lifetime.

To understand the sensation the poetry
of Walt Whitman created when it first appeared, wipe from your mind all you know
of modern free verse. That came later.

Read these poems against the background
of the poetry you found in "The Flowering of the East." That was the only kind
of poetry Americans knew before Whitman. Those of you who love regular
rhythm and rhyme may agree with the
early critics that this is not poetry at all.
But if you respond to long, swinging
rhythms that seem to grow out of what
the poet is saying, you will approve of
Whitman's innovations. If you like poetry
to spread out and touch the whole realm
of human life, you will find him as exciting
as did a few readers in his own day who
realized that here was a man who would
change the course of American poetry.

ONE'S–SELF I SING

This little poem is the first selection in
Leaves of Grass. It expresses Whitman's belief that in writing frankly and honestly of
himself, he spoke for all men.

One's-self I sing, a single separate person,
Yet utter the word Democratic, the word En-Masse.

Of physiology from top to toe I sing,
Not physiognomy alone nor brain alone is worthy for the Muse,
    I say the Form complete is worthier far,   5
The Female equally with the Male I sing.

Of Life immense in passion, pulse, and power,
Cheerful, for freest action formed under the laws divine,
The Modern Man I sing.

SHUT NOT YOUR DOORS

This poem is also from the first part of
Leaves of Grass, and it declares Whitman's
faith that his book brings something new
to mankind. He declares his poetry is not
intended to add to men's knowledge, but to
express their wordless feelings.

Shut not your doors to me proud libraries,
For that which was lacking on all your well-fill'd shelves,
    Yet needed most, I bring,
Forth from the war emerging, a book I have made,
The words of my book nothing, the drift of it everything,
A book separate, not link'd with the rest nor felt by the intellect,
But you ye untold latencies will thrill to every page.

I HEAR AMERICA SINGING

Here you meet the people Whitman
knew and loved best, his ordinary fellow
Americans. This is the way he loved to
think of them — busy, strong, and happy,
each singing his own particular song as he
went about his daily work.

I hear America singing, the varied carols I hear,
Those of mechanics, each one singing his as it should be blithe and strong,
The carpenter singing his as he measures his plank or beam,
The mason singing his as he makes ready for work, or leaves off work,
The boatman singing what belongs to him in his boat, the deck hand singing on
    the steamboat deck,   5
The shoemaker singing as he sits on his bench, the hatter singing as he stands,

The woodcutter's song, the plowboy's on his way in the morning, or at noon inter-
mission or at sundown,
The delicious singing of the mother, or of the young wife at work, or of the girl
sewing or washing,
Each singing what belongs to him or her and to none else,
The day what belongs to the day — at night the party of young fellows, robust,
friendly, 10
Singing with open mouths their strong melodious songs.

MANNAHATTA

Whitman loved the old Indian names. His native Long Island he preferred to call Paumanok, and his exuberant affection for his city needed a more musical title than " New York." He found a satisfactory name in the Indian word Mannahatta, which has been preserved in the modern term Man-hattan.

I was asking for something specific and perfect for my city,
Whereupon lo! upsprang the aboriginal name.

Now I see what there is in a name, a word, liquid, sane, unruly, musical, self-
sufficient,
I see that the word of my city is that word from of old,
Because I see that word nested in nests of water bays, superb, 5
Rich, hemmed thick all around with sailships and steamships, an island sixteen
miles long, solid-founded,
Numberless crowded streets, high growths of iron, slender, strong, light, splendidly
uprising toward clear skies,
Tides swift and ample, well loved by me, toward sundown,
The flowing sea-currents, the little islands, larger adjoining islands, the heights,
the villas,
The countless masts, the white shore-steamers, the lighters, the ferryboats, the
black sea-steamers well modeled, 10
The downtown streets, the jobbers' houses of business, the houses of business of
the ship merchants and money brokers, the river streets,
Immigrants arriving, fifteen or twenty thousand in a week,
The carts hauling goods, the manly race of drivers of horses, the brown-faced
sailors,
The summer air, the bright sun shining, and the sailing clouds aloft,
The winter snows, the sleigh bells, the broken ice in the river, passing along up or
down with the flood tide or ebb tide, 15
The mechanics of the city, the masters, well formed, beautiful-faced, looking you
straight in the eyes,
Trottoirs° thronged, vehicles, Broadway, the women, the shops and shows,
A million people — manners free and superb — open voices — hospitality — the
most courageous and friendly young men,
City of hurried and sparkling waters! city of spires and masts!
City nested in bays! my city! 20

17. **trottoirs** (trŏ·twär′): sidewalks (French).

BEAT! BEAT! DRUMS!

The terrific upheaval that war brings into civilian life has rarely been more vividly pictured than in this poem. The irregularity of the rhythm serves to emphasize the general chaos, with the drums beating like the throbbing of a quickened pulse.

Beat! beat! drums! — blow! bugles! blow!
Through the windows — through doors — burst like a ruthless force,
Into the solemn church, and scatter the congregation,
Into the school where the scholar is studying;
Leave not the bridegroom quiet — no happiness must he have now with his bride,
Nor the peaceful farmer any peace, plowing his field or gathering his grain,   6
So fierce you whir and pound, you drums — so shrill you bugles blow.

Beat! beat! drums! — blow! bugles! blow!
Over the traffic of cities — over the rumble of wheels in the streets;
Are beds prepared for sleepers at night in the houses? no sleepers must sleep in
    those beds,   10
No bargainers' bargains by day — no brokers or speculators — would they continue?
Would the talkers be talking? would the singer attempt to sing?
Would the lawyer rise in the court to state his case before the judge?
Then rattle quicker, heavier drums — you bugles wilder blow.

Beat! beat! drums! — blow! bugles! blow!   15
Make no parley — stop for no expostulation,
Mind not the timid — mind not the weeper or prayer,
Mind not the old man beseeching the young man,
Let not the child's voice be heard, nor the mother's entreaties,
Make even the trestles to shake the dead where they lie awaiting the hearses,   20
So strong you thump O terrible drums — so loud you bugles blow.

THE CAROL OF DEATH

It is natural that a man of Whitman's elemental vigor should have been greatly attracted by the personality of Abraham Lincoln. Of all the poets who have paid tribute to him, none has sounded the note of personal grief at his death more feelingly than Whitman. You have doubtless known for years his short poem, " O Captain! My Captain! " He gave full expression to his grief in the long poem " When Lilacs Last in the Dooryard Bloomed." In the following selection from this poem he finds consolation in the carol of a " graybrown bird " among " the ghostly pines." " And the voice of my spirit," he wrote, " tallied the song of the bird."

Come lovely and soothing death,
Undulate round the world, serenely arriving, arriving,
In the day, in the night, to all, to each,
Sooner or later delicate death.

Praised be the fathomless universe,   5
For life and joy, and for object and knowledge curious,
And for love, sweet love — but praise! praise! praise!
For the sure-enwinding arms of cool-enfolding death.

Dark mother always gliding near with soft feet,
Have none chanted for thee a chant of fullest welcome?   10
Then I chant it for thee, I glorify thee above all,
I bring thee a song that when thou must indeed come, come unfalteringly.

Approach strong deliveress,
When it is so, when thou hast taken them I joyously sing the dead,
Lost in the loving floating ocean of thee,   15
Laved in the flood of thy bliss O death.

From me to thee glad serenades,
Dances for thee I propose saluting thee, adornments and feastings for thee,
And the sights of the open landscape and the high-spread sky are fitting,
And life and the fields, and the huge and thoughtful night.   20

The night in silence under many a star,
The ocean shore and the husky whispering wave whose voice I know,
And the soul turning to thee O vast and well-veiled death,
And the body gratefully nestling close to thee.

Over the treetops I float thee a song,   25
Over the rising and sinking waves, over the myriad fields and the prairies wide,
Over the dense-packed cities all and the teeming wharves and ways,
I float this carol with joy, with joy to thee O death.

A NOISELESS PATIENT SPIDER

Whitman wrote often of man's physical strengths and sensations, but he was also keenly alive to man's spirit. Here he compares the yearnings of a human soul to a " gossamer thread " flung out by a spider starting to spin its web.

A noiseless patient spider,
I marked where on a little promontory it stood isolated,
Marked how to explore the vacant vast surrounding,
It launched forth filament, filament, filament, out of itself,
Ever unreeling them, ever tirelessly speeding them.   5

And you O my soul where you stand,
Surrounded, detached, in measureless oceans of space,
Ceaselessly musing, venturing, throwing, seeking the spheres to connect them,
Till the bridge you will need be formed, till the ductile anchor hold,
Till the gossamer thread you fling catch somewhere, O my soul.   10

Gendreau

"... the husky whispering wave whose voice I know"

ON THE BEACH AT NIGHT

The longing of the soul for something beyond itself, which you found in the preceding poem, has here grown into a triumphant faith. Here Whitman declares his faith in a divine, immortal power that is greater than the earth or universe: "Something there is," he says, "that shall endure longer than sun or any revolving satellite."

Notice that here the meaning is conveyed by the use of symbols. As the child watches the night sky, the poet makes us understand a larger meaning in what she sees.

This is one of the finest of Whitman's lyrics, combining his tenderness toward children, his breathless descriptions of nature, and his strong sense of faith.

On the beach at night,
Stands a child with her father,
Watching the east, the autumn sky.

Up through the darkness,
While ravening clouds, the burial clouds, in black masses spreading,   5
Lower sullen and fast athwart and down the sky,
Amid a transparent clear belt of ether yet left in the east,
Ascends large and calm the lord-star Jupiter,
And nigh at hand, only a very little above,
Swim the delicate sisters the Pleiades.°   10
From the beach the child holding the hand of her father,
Those burial clouds that lower victorious soon to devour all,
Watching, silently weeps.

Weep not, child,
Weep not, my darling,   15
With these kisses let me remove your tears,
The ravening clouds shall not long be victorious;
They shall not long possess the sky, they devour the stars only in apparition,
Jupiter shall emerge, be patient, watch again another night, the Pleiades shall
    emerge,
They are immortal, all those stars both silvery and golden shall shine out again,
The great stars and the little ones shall shine out again, they endure,   21
The vast immortal suns and the long-enduring pensive moons shall again shine.

Then dearest child mournest thou only for Jupiter?
Considerest thou alone the burial of the stars?
Something there is   25
(With my lips soothing thee, adding I whisper,
I give thee the first suggestion, the problem and indirection),
Something there is more immortal even than the stars,
(Many the burials, many the days and nights, passing away,)
Something that shall endure longer even than lustrous Jupiter,   30
Longer than sun or any revolving satellite,
Or the radiant sisters the Pleiades.

10. **Pleiades** (plē′ya·dēz): the cluster of stars called "The Seven Sisters."

From the preceding poems you have gained an idea of the range of Whitman's interests as well as of his characteristic attitudes. See what further illustrations of these qualities you can discover as you read the last three poems.

WHEN I HEARD THE LEARN'D ASTRONOMER

When I heard the learn'd astronomer,
When the proofs, the figures, were ranged in columns before me,
When I was shown the charts and diagrams, to add, divide, and measure them,
When I sitting heard the astronomer where he lectured with much applause in the
    lecture room,
How soon unaccountable I became tired and sick,   5
Till rising and gliding out I wandered off by myself,
In the mystical moist night air, and from time to time,
Looked up in perfect silence at the stars.

For Discussion of Whitman

1. The first four poems build up an accurate impression of the subjects that primarily interested Whitman. List them in your own words. Which of the interests did he share with such poets as Longfellow, Lowell, and Whittier? Which ones were new in American poetry?

2. In what ways does Whitman's use of meter and line and stanza patterns differ from more conventional poetry? What connection do you see between his poetic style and the usual themes or subjects of his poetry?

3. How does the picture of American life in " I Hear America Singing " seem to fit our times? Are all these types of people still to be found in America? What other types would you add to bring the picture up to date?

4. Compare Whitman's picture of New York with cities you know. What details give a definitely " city " effect and would not be true of a small town?

5. In what way is the rhythm of " Beat! Beat! Drums! " appropriate to the picture in this poem? Illustrate your answer with mention of specific lines. What effects of war upon civilian life are especially emphasized? Which of the effects mentioned seem to you the most devastating?

6. Is the tone of " The Carol of Death " prevailingly mournful or consoling? Compare this view of death with that in " Thanatopsis " (p. 488).

7. In " On the Beach at Night " why did the child weep when the clouds came up over the stars? What did the stars and clouds symbolize, or stand for, in the child's mind? How did the poet comfort and reassure her?

8. Why do you think Whitman is often called " the poet of democracy "? Point out evidence from these poems of his democratic beliefs and ideas. In this respect, what modern poets does he remind you of?

9. One of Whitman's special attractions is his gift for magnificent short descriptive phrases. Collect a series of such phrases from these poems, dealing with a sufficient variety of subjects to give an accurate impression of his interests.

For Your Vocabulary

MOOD WORDS: Whitman depends heavily upon the choice of words and phrases to create the mood of a poem, since he does not employ the aid of rhyme or meter. Notice in " Beat! Beat! Drums! " how he adds to the effective repetition of the opening line with many forceful phrases: *burst* like a *ruthless force, scatter* the congregation, so *fierce* you *whir* and *pound,* so *shrill* you bugles blow. Point out the " mood words " in the rest of this poem.

In " The Carol of Death," how do words like *lovely* and *soothing* death, *undulate* round the world, and *serenely* arriving, create a different kind of mood? Analyze the use of words to create mood, similarly, in " On the Beach at Night " (how is the word *lower* used there?), and " The Carol of Death."

John Bannister Tabb

1845–1909

John Bannister Tabb began a lifelong friendship with Sidney Lanier when both were prisoners. As a boy in his teens, fresh from his parents' luxurious plantation in Virginia, he became a blockade runner in the Confederate Navy. He was captured during the war and spent some time in Point Lookout Prison in Maryland, where he met Lanier. After the war he thought seriously of becoming an Anglican clergyman, but in 1872, after investigation and prayer, he entered the Catholic Church. He made his theological studies at St. Charles College, Ellicott City, Maryland, where he was ordained in 1884, and where he spent the rest of his life as a teacher of English.

Father Tabb compiled his own textbook, which he entitled *Bone Rules or Skeleton of English Grammar,* and prefaced it with a characteristic dedication — " My pupils, active and passive, perfect and imperfect, past, present, and future (in whatever mood they may be)." His lectures were famous for lively wit, apt illustration, and occasional cartoons drawn on the blackboard. Father Tabb drew his best inspiration from common objects, which he interpreted in a highly original way. He usually connected his natural theme to a scriptural allusion by means of a single sustained metaphor. While few of his themes are, strictly speaking, religious, all of his work has religious undertones.

FATHER DAMIEN

O God, the cleanest offering
   Of tainted earth below,
Unblushing to thy feet we bring —
   " *A leper white as snow!* "

CHRIST THE MENDICANT

A stranger, to His own
He came; and one alone,
   Who knew not sin,
His lowliness believed,
And in her soul conceived   5
   To let Him in.

He naked was, and she
Of her humanity
   A garment wove.

He hungered; and she gave,   10
What most His heart did crave,
    A Mother's love.

STABAT MATER

The star that in his splendor hid her
        own,
    At Christ's Nativity,
Abides — a widowed satellite — alone,
    On tearful Calvary.

LANIER'S FLUTE

When palsied at the pool of thought
    The Poet's words were found,
Thy voice the healing Angel brought
    To touch them into sound.

A CHRISTMAS CRADLE

Let my heart the cradle be
Of Thy bleak Nativity!
Tossed by wintry tempests wild,
If it rock Thee, Holy Child,
Then, as grows the outer din,   5
Greater peace shall reign within.

MY MEDIATOR

" None betwixt God and me? "
" Behold, my neighbor, thee,
Unto His lofty throne
He makes my stepping stone."

For Discussion of Tabb

1. Recall the story of Father Damien.
Point out the paradox in the poem.

2. To whom is the poet referring in
" Christ the Mendicant "? What do you
think of this unusual reference to the In-
carnation?

3. Do you think " Stabat Mater " is a
good title for that poem?

4. What is the Gospel story behind the
allusions in " Lanier's Flute " ?

5. Explain the Christian attitude toward suffering shown in " A Christmas
Cradle."

6. If you enjoyed these poems, you will
find delight in reading Father Tabb's
" Taxgatherer," " An Autumn Leaf," and
" December."

For Your Vocabulary

METRICAL TERMS: A *quatrain* is a four-
line stanza, usually with alternate rhyme.
Compression of thought is an essential
element of a good quatrain. Pick out all
the figures of speech you recognize in
these poems. How do they illustrate Father Tabb's intensity?

James
Whitcomb Riley
AND Eugene Field

While Lanier and Dickinson and Whitman
were exploring new frontiers in poetry,
other poets were capturing a large audience by writing about incidents and scenes
and characters everyone could understand
and enjoy. Among the most popular of

these poets were Eugene Field and James Whitcomb Riley, both Midwestern newspapermen who understood public taste and found themselves sympathetic with it. Many of their poems gained a permanent hold on the affections of American readers. Who has not read " The Gingham Dog and the Calico Cat " and " Wynken, Blynken, and Nod " by Field? What American youngster has not met and loved Little Orphant Annie and The Raggedy Man in Riley's poems?

Here are two samples of the verses that won countless Americans to the reading of poetry. The first is in the Hoosier dialect often used by Riley.

WHEN THE FROST IS ON THE PUNKIN

JAMES WHITCOMB RILEY   1849–1916

When the frost is on the punkin and the fodder's in the shock,
And you hear the kyouck and gobble of the struttin' turkey cock,
And the clackin' of the guineys, and the cluckin' of the hens,
And the rooster's hallylooyer as he tiptoes on the fence;
O, it's then the time a feller is a-feelin' at his best,   5
With the risin' sun to greet him from a night of peaceful rest,
As he leaves the house, bareheaded, and goes out to feed the stock,
When the frost is on the punkin and the fodder's in the shock.

They's something kindo' harty-like about the atmusfere
When the heat of summer's over and the coolin' fall is here —   10
Of course we miss the flowers, and the blossums on the trees,
And the mumble of the hummin'birds and buzzin' of the bees;
But the air's so appetizin'; and the landscape through the haze
Of a crisp and sunny morning of the airly autumn days
Is a pictur' that no painter has the colorin' to mock —   15
When the frost is on the punkin and the fodder's in the shock.

The husky, rusty russel of the tossels of the corn,
And the raspin' of the tangled leaves, as golden as the morn;
The stubble in the furries — kindo' lonesomelike, but still
A-preachin' sermuns to us of the barns they growed to fill;   20
The strawstack in the medder, and the reaper in the shed;
The hosses in theyr stalls below — the clover overhead! —
O, it sets my hart a-clickin' like the tickin' of a clock,
When the frost is on the punkin and the fodder's in the shock!

Then your apples all is gethered, and the ones a feller keeps   25
Is poured around the cellar floor in red and yeller heaps;
And your cider makin's over, and your wimmern folks is through
With theyr mince and apple butter, and theyr souse and sausage, too!
I don't know how to tell it — but ef sich a thing could be
As the Angels wantin' boardin', and they'd call around on *me* —   30
I'd want to 'commodate 'em — all the whole indurin' flock —
When the frost is on the punkin and the fodder's in the shock!

LITTLE BOY BLUE

EUGENE FIELD 1850–1895

The little toy dog is covered with dust,
But sturdy and staunch he stands;
The little toy soldier is red with rust,
And his musket molds in his hands.
Time was when the little toy dog was
new   5
And the soldier was passing fair;
And that was the time when our Little
Boy Blue
Kissed them and put them there.

" Now don't you go till I come," he said,
"And don't you make any noise! "
So toddling off to his trundle bed,   11
He dreamt of the pretty toys;
And, as he was dreaming, an angel song
Awakened our Little Boy Blue —
Oh! the years are many, the years are
long,   15
But the little toy friends are true!

Ay, faithful to Little Boy Blue they
stand,
Each in the same old place,
Awaiting the touch of a little hand,
The smile of a little face;   20
And they wonder, as waiting the long
years through,
In the dust of that little chair,
What has become of our Little Boy
Blue
Since he kissed them and put them
there.

For Discussion of Field and Riley

1. Why would these poems strike a responsive chord in thousands of readers? State the theme of each in general terms to show that it would have wide appeal.

2. Be sure you can interpret Riley's dialect to get the meaning, especially in words like " hallylooyer," " furries," " medder." What is meant by " Hoosier " dialect? How does the dialect add to the flavor of the poem?

3. How does autumn make the poet feel? Does it affect you the same way? What are the special signs of autumn in your environment?

4. Though " Little Boy Blue " is about a child, it is definitely a poem for adults. Why? What is your own reaction to keeping mementos of a dead child just as he left them?

5. Try to analyze the reasons why Field and Riley are lesser poets than Dickinson or Whitman. Does wide popularity ensure greatness for a poet? Can you name any that are both popular and great?

Social Consciousness and The Rise of Realism

The Machine Age and Social Consciousness

Literature always reflects what is happening in the country where it is written. In the Time of Change it reflected the spirit of an age of science and invention, machines, industry, and cities. It reflected the quick, and sometimes harsh, changes that were taking place in American life. In place of the simple society of the earlier part of the century — cultured and well-ordered in the East, vigorous and optimistic in the West — Americans now lived under complex conditions.

The American West was an area greatly in need of machines. Everything in the West was on such a vast scale — the farms so large, the mineral deposits so great, the distances so overwhelming — that, from the beginning of settlement until today, the West has called for machinery to supplement the work of men. And the practical, inventive Americans have responded by devising machines powerful and wonderful enough to compete with nature itself.

Inventions Multiply America's Power

The list of American mechanical inventions between the Revolution and 1900 is little short of miraculous. The list includes, among others, the cotton gin, the telegraph, the typewriter, the telephone, the phonograph, the electric light, the automobile, the linotype, the motion picture, and the airplane. Thanks to inventions like these, and especially to the discovery of new sources of power — first the steam engine, then the internal combustion engine and the dynamo — the country was able to multiply its human muscles many times. It could send materials by fast transportation or transmit power along wires. Thus it was able to reach out into far corners of the continent and take advantage of rich natural resources which otherwise would have been closed to human use. All over the country, factories began to stick their smokestacks into the sky.

Mass Production and Big Business Change Society

The master craftsmen of the industrial East were giving way to unskilled labor in the mass-production methods of factories. The gay West, where individual miners, trappers, and settlers could once strike it rich, was now being taken over by big operators and gigantic companies. As Paul Revere, the master silversmith, was the symbol of the old East, and Kit Carson, the footloose scout, a symbol of the old West, so the big men of this new America were Andrew Carnegie, who made steel, John D. Rockefeller, who pumped petroleum, Commodore Vanderbilt, who owned railroads, and J. P. Morgan, whose money power extended into a dozen different industries.

The outlook for an individual operator was not so good as it had been a few decades before. The country had gone *big* business. Furthermore, by 1880, there was an inevitable reaction against the optimism and hope of the early West. The trouble lay in the fact that America was no longer a land of opportunity in the same way it had been. Theodore Roosevelt explained that, when he wrote about the coal strikes. "A few generations ago,"

he said, "an American workman could have saved money, gone west, and taken up a homestead. Now the free lands were gone. In earlier days a man who began with pick and shovel might have come to own a mine. That outlet too was now closed, as regards the immense majority." In other words, the pots of gold were farther away. There was little chance to get a fresh start somewhere else. Farmers could not so easily give up their dry lands and find homesteads elsewhere. Wage earners could not so easily quit their jobs and start in business for themselves. They had to stay where they were and face it out.

America Faces a New Frontier

That meant that they were facing a different kind of frontier — not a geographic one, but a social and economic frontier. There were still plenty of gains to be won, but they were not land and wealth but rather improved working conditions, housing conditions, better wages, lower prices, sanitation, schooling. Investigators were shocked to find that in some of the great industrial cities men were working and dwelling in conditions fully as bad as those they had left behind in Europe. There was plenty of money, plenty of natural resources, plenty of wonderful machines in the country, and still many families were poorly fed, poorly housed, poorly clothed, poorly paid, unhealthy, dissatisfied. In the face of this discovery, many writers became "socially conscious." That is, they began to write of social injustices, of the unpleasant things that industrial civilization was doing to the working classes, and of the various ways in which American civilization in the late nineteenth century was falling short of its high promise.

The Rise of Realism

In literature this social consciousness helped bring about realism. Now, there is nothing fancy or mysterious about literary realism. It is simply the feeling on the part of an author that a thing worth writing about must be a *real* thing. You will see how different this is from preceding literary fashions if you will recall Poe's misty, magic scenery, Cooper's idealized "noble savage," and the way in which Mark Twain described Tom Sawyer and Huck Finn laughing through life from one adventure to another. None of that for these new realistic writers! Let's forget the misty and glamorous past, people were saying. Let's quit writing about men who never existed — the ideal men, the unbeatable men, the Paul Bunyans. Let's write about the ordinary man, the average man, the little man. Let's tell about his defeats as well as his victories; his disappointments, his moments of weariness and discouragement, as well as his high moments.

One of the new writers, William Dean Howells, said: Let's be "simple, natural, and honest"; if a man is a bore, let's show him as a bore; let's not pick out the one moment in his life when he acts like a hero. Our governments, our business, our economic lives aren't perfect; let's show them as they are. That was the spirit in which men like Howells, James, Garland, and Norris began to write fiction.

William Dean Howells

Howells (1837–1920) grew up in Ohio, and as a young man, went to work for Columbus newspapers, wrote a campaign biography of Lincoln, served a political appointment as American consul in Venice, and then returned to the United States to settle in Boston when that city was still the center of American literary life.

Successor to the Old Tradition

He went to Boston in 1866, twenty-nine years old, like a pilgrim. He went to see James Russell Lowell, because Lowell was editor of the *Atlantic Monthly,* in which Howells had published a poem. Lowell liked the young man, and within a few years Howells was living in Cambridge. Howells fitted well into the old literary group. He catered to the vanities and the foibles of the great and elderly New Englanders. He was young, likable, talented, a good critic.

It was logical that Howells should eventually inherit the editorship of the *Atlantic Monthly.* Yet when it became evident that the center of publishing and writing was passing to New York, Howells moved there, as an editor and writer. When Holmes, Longfellow, and Lowell were the greatest names in American literature, he was their close friend in Boston. When Mark Twain became the best-known American writer, Howells was his bosom friend in New York. He had a talent for being in the right place at the right time.

Forerunner of the New Realism

But that is not to say that he rode on other men's reputations. He did very well by himself. He was an excellent editor, and his own books, when they were put together at the end of his sixty years of writing, totaled nearly one hundred volumes. Thirty-six of them were novels, and of these you will want to read at least *The Rise of Silas Lapham* and *A Modern Instance* some day. Some of them were plays, some travel books, some criticism, several delightful pictures of his literary friends and acquaintances. He knew almost everyone worth knowing in American literature in his time, and he had a fine eye for character and appearance.

Howells himself wrote the best account of the method of realism by which he pictured American life fully and honestly. " The sincere observer of man," he said, " will not desire to look upon his heroic or occasional phases, but will seek him in his habitual moods of vacancy and tiresomeness. . . . It will not do to lift either houses or men *far* out of the average; they become spectacles, ceremonies; they cease to have charm, to have character."

Thomas Bailey Aldrich

Thomas Bailey Aldrich (1836–1907), who succeeded Howells as editor of the *Atlantic Monthly,* was another writer who represents the transition from romantic to realistic fiction. Aldrich is famous for his children's book, *The Story of a Bad Boy,* which was perhaps the first realistic treatment of a boy in American literature, appearing seventeen years before Mark Twain's *Tom Sawyer.* But Aldrich, a romanticist at heart, was prouder of well-turned stories like " A Struggle for Life," which you will soon read, and " Marjorie Daw," which popularized surprise endings; and of his long, elegant poems, with their Oriental, romantic settings.

Henry James

Like Howells, Henry James went east to write. But whereas Howells had been born in Ohio and went to Boston, James (1843–1916) was born in New York and educated at Harvard, and went to Europe. He traveled to Geneva, Paris, Bonn, London, and everywhere else a wealthy and cultivated family might want to send a brilliant son. James finally settled down to write in Europe. Most of his adult life was spent there, and finally he became a British subject, as a protest against his native country's slowness in taking part in World War I.

Realism Applied to the Upper Classes

He agreed with Howells in the thought that the fiction worth writing is realistic fiction, and that one should write about people in ordinary moments, rather than in heroic or unusual moments. Unlike Howells, though, he had little experience with the average American. His acquaintances were of the upper classes, and especially of the wealthy international families. One problem interested him above all others: he would write about an American in European society, or a European in American society, and analyze the troubles resulting from each one's failure to understand the other's society.

Realism as a Study of People's Minds

Henry James had one great skill, perhaps above any other novelist who ever wrote in America. He had the ability to get into a character's mind and show what he was thinking and how he was reacting. The realism he sought was the realism of the *mind.* The more he dug for those treasures, the more subtle, involved, complicated his books became. Someone said that whereas his brother, the great psychologist William James, made psychology as interesting as novels, Henry James made novels as difficult as psychology.

Some of James's best-known novels are *The American, Daisy Miller, The Portrait of a Lady,* and *The Ambassadors.* All of these illustrate his favorite theme of contrasting European and American characters. He also wrote over a hundred short stories, including the famous ghost story, "The Turn of the Screw."

Hamlin Garland

Hamlin Garland as a writer illustrates both the rise of realism and the growth of social consciousness in fiction.

Like both Howells and James he went east to write, but with a different background. He was a "son of the Middle Border" (that was the title he gave to his best-known book), born in Wisconsin, brought up mostly in Iowa and South Dakota. He sold a claim in Dakota for enough money to take him to Boston. Three years later he came back to visit the prairies where he had grown up. "This was an epoch-making experience for me," he wrote. "My three years in Boston had given me perspective on the life of the prairie farmer. I perceived with new vision the loneliness and drudgery of the farmers' wives. All across northwestern Iowa and up through central Dakota I brooded darkly over the problem presented, and this bitter mood was deepened by the condition in which I found my mother on a treeless farm just above Ordway. It was in this mood of resentment that I began to write."

Stories of Hard Conditions on the Land

The result of that visit was a series of biting stories about unfair living conditions on the prairie, of which "Under the Lion's Paw" is one. He published those stories under the title *Main-Traveled Roads.* Later in life he wrote his autobiographical account of prairie life,

A Son of the Middle Border. All his writing is distinguished by rugged strength, a stern realism, and a conviction that — as he put it — "to spread the reign of justice should everywhere be the design and intent of the artist."

Other Writers of Realism

Other writers too were dealing realistically and vigorously with some of the social and economic problems of the times. You will find in the following

pages two selections suggestive of some of the problems that came with the tremendous immigration from Europe — more than eight million in the single decade between 1901 and 1910. Mary Antin describes some of the feelings of a Russian girl coming to the land of freedom. Thomas A. Daly suggests in his dialect poem some of the problems of the melting pot, where unlike peoles were thrown in together, and the only answer was for all of them to become Americans. Unfortunately that process is not completed yet, as our racial and religious prejudices indicate.

Dramatizing the Problems of Workers

Edwin Markham's eloquent poem, "The Man with the Hoe," made a deep impression in the 1890's because it seemed to typify not only farmers, but all workers. It made people ask questions: Is this the best our land of opportunity can do? Is this what our forefathers dreamed about and foresaw as the future of this new race of men? Is it for this kind of life that we settled the West, dug minerals out of the mountains, and built up industry? Are our workers really like this, and if so what can we do for them? How can we distribute the wealth of the new land so that these men get a better share? How can we use the time so that these men have leisure to be more than working animals? How can we use our huge machines and our great companies for the little man's good? Those were the questions writers were asking, and orators were shouting, at the end of the century.

The last of those questions is the one Finley Peter Dunne ("Mr. Dooley") suggests in his dialect sketch on machinery. Underneath the humor of the sketch is a bitter accusation that all our wonderful new machinery is not really being used for man's good. Is the machine serving man, or man serving the machine? It is a question that echoed up and down the country.

Frank Norris's Novels on Big Business

But perhaps no nineteenth-century novelist indicted and criticized our social system more bitterly than Frank Norris. He wrote two books of three he had planned on a challenging idea, the epic of the wheat. He was going to show how the great natural power of the crop was being perverted by greed and not used for the good of man. His first book, *The Octopus*, was on the theme that the railroads were squeezing out the farmer who raised the wheat. The second book, *The Pit*, showed how the wheat was used for speculation in the Chicago grain pit. Norris's idea was that

nature is bigger than man, that if man didn't use the wheat properly the wheat would ruin him. *The Octopus* ended with the death of the greedy railroad manager who fell into the hold of a grain boat and literally drowned in the wheat. *The Pit* ended with the financial ruin of the man who had sought to corner the grain market. But most Americans didn't wait for *nature* to punish the men who were responsible for bad conditions; they sought new laws and new officeholders.

Crane, Bierce, and Harris

You ought to remember a few other names out of this period in our literature. One of these is Stephen Crane, a brilliant foreign correspondent, novelist, and story writer who died young but left such novels as *The Red Badge of Courage* and *Maggie*, and such memorable short stories as "The Open Boat," which you will surely want to read. Another is Ambrose Bierce, who wrote penetrating short stories based on his war experiences, and some blood-chilling horror stories. A third, Joel Chandler Harris, for twenty years editor of the Atlanta *Constitution*, put the shrewdness, humor, dignity, and common sense of the Negro into his *Uncle Remus* stories. He preserved the Negro folklore and dialect in the collection of Brer Rabbit tales.

Journalist "Muckrakers"

Finally, there was the name of a group and of a kind of writing which hit hard at social ills and inequalities. "Muckraking," it was called; the writers, most of them journalists, were "muckrakers." They were so called because they raked up unsavory facts about some American politicians and businessmen. Upton Sinclair, for instance, told the story of immigrant workers in the Chicago stockyards so vividly and malodorously that he forced the passage of a pure foods law. Lincoln Steffens, whose autobiography is represented in Part One of this book, was also one of the crusading muckraking writers.

Most of these muckraking books and articles came out in the years between 1900 and 1910, when Theodore Roosevelt was waving his big stick at the big business trusts. They were often sensational in their disclosures but they represented hard work and a strong sense of idealism in the writers. The muckraking books accomplished minor reforms, and did a great service in awakening the country to its social problems.

The same social currents and anxieties which presented themselves to American writers when the frontier closed in 1890 have been a part of our literature and a challenge to us all — truly our new frontier — ever since.

Hamlin Garland
1860–1940

UNDER THE LION'S PAW

As the Western lands were taken up, the true frontier came to its end. There was still room for more settlers in the West, but instead of staking a claim to a free government homestead, a newcomer had to trade with men who already held the land. That is the situation in this story.

In some stories the author comments on people and happenings to be sure his readers get the impression he wants them to have. In others, you are an observer without a guide; you must form your own impressions. Hamlin Garland tells his story in the latter way. "This is what happened," he says, in effect. "It's up to you to decide what it means."

IT was the last of autumn and first day of winter coming together. All day long the plowmen on their prairie farms had moved to and fro in their wide level fields through the falling snow, which melted as it fell, wetting them to the skin — all day, notwithstanding the frequent squalls of snow, the dripping, desolate clouds, and the muck of the furrows, black and tenacious as tar.

Under their dripping harness the horses swung to and fro silently, with that marvelous uncomplaining patience which marks the horse. All day the wild geese, honking wildly, as they sprawled sidewise down the wind, seemed to be fleeing from an enemy behind, and with

"Under the Lion's Paw" from *Main-Traveled Roads* by Hamlin Garland, published by Harper & Brothers. Reprinted by permission of the author's estate.

neck outthrust and wings extended, sailed down the wind, soon lost to sight.

Yet the plowman behind his plow, though the snow lay on his ragged greatcoat, and the cold clinging mud rose on his heavy boots, fettering him like gyves, whistled in the very beard of the gale. As day passed, the snow, ceasing to melt, lay along the plowed land, and lodged in the depth of the stubble, till on each slow round the last furrow stood out black and shining as jet between the plowed land and the gray stubble.

When night began to fall, and the geese, flying low, began to alight invisibly in the near cornfield, Stephen Council was still at work "finishing a land." He rode on his sulky plow when going with the wind, but walked when facing it. Sitting bent and cold but cheery under his slouch hat, he talked encouragingly to his four-in-hand.

"Come round there, boys! — Round agin! We got t' finish this land. Come in there, Dan! *Stiddy*, Kate, — stiddy! None o' y'r tantrums, Kittie. It's purty tuff, but got a be did. *Tchk! tchk!* Step along, Pete! Don't let Kate git y'r single-tree on the wheel. *Once* more!"

They seemed to know what he meant, and that this was the last round, for they worked with greater vigor than before.

"Once more, boys, an' then, sez I, oats an' a nice warm stall, an' sleep f'r all."

By the time the last furrow was turned on the land it was too dark to see the house, and the snow was changing to rain again. The tired and hungry man could see the light from the kitchen shining through the leafless hedge, and he lifted a great shout, "Supper f'r a half a dozen!"

It was nearly eight o'clock by the time he had finished his chores and started for supper. He was picking his way carefully through the mud, when the tall form of a man loomed up before him with a premonitory cough.

"Waddy ye want?" was the rather startled question of the farmer.

"Well, ye see," began the stranger, in a deprecating tone, "we'd like t' git in f'r the night. We've tried every house f'r the last two miles, but they hadn't any room f'r us. My wife's jest about sick, 'n' the children are cold and hungry — "

"Oh, y' want 'o stay all night, eh?"

"Yes, sir; it 'ud be a great accom — "

"Waal, I don't make it a practice t' turn anybuddy way hungry, not on sech nights as this. Drive right in. We ain't got much, but sech as it is — "

But the stranger had disappeared. And soon his steaming, weary team, with drooping heads and swinging singletrees, moved past the well to the block beside the path. Council stood at the side of the "schooner" and helped the children out — two little half-sleeping children — and then a small woman with a babe in her arms.

"There ye go!" he shouted jovially, to the children. "*Now* we're all right! Run right along to the house there, an' tell Ma'm Council you wants sumpthin' t' eat. Right this way, Mis' — keep right off t' the right there. I'll go an' git a lantern. Come," he said to the dazed and silent group at his side.

"Mother," he shouted, as he neared the fragrant and warmly lighted kitchen, "here are some wayfarers an' folks who need sumpthin' t' eat an' a place t' snooze." He ended by pushing them all in.

Mrs. Council, a large, jolly, rather coarse-looking woman, took the children in her arms. "Come right in, you little rabbits. 'Most asleep, hey? Now here's a drink o' milk f'r each o' ye. I'll have s'm tea in a minute. Take off y'r things and set up t' the fire."

While she set the children to drinking milk, Council got out his lantern and went out to the barn to help the stranger about his team, where his loud, hearty voice could be heard as it came and went between the haymow and the stalls.

The woman came to light as a small, timid, and discouraged-looking woman, but still pretty, in a thin and sorrowful way.

"Land sakes! An' you've traveled all the way from Clear Lake t'day in this mud! Waal! waal! No wonder you're all tired out. Don't wait f'r the men, Mis' —" She hesitated, waiting for the name.

"Haskins."

"Mis' Haskins, set right up to the table an' take a good swig o' tea whilst I make y' s'm toast. It's green tea, an' it's good. I tell Council as I git older I don't seem to enjoy Young Hyson n'r Gunpowder. I want the reel green tea, jest as it comes off'n the vines. Seems t' have more heart in it, some way. Don't s'pose it has. Council says it's all in m' eye."

Going on in this easy way, she soon had the children filled with bread and milk and the woman thoroughly at home, eating some toast and sweet-melon pickles, and sipping the tea.

"See the little rats!" she laughed at the children. "They're full as they can stick now, and they want to go to bed. Now, don't git up, Mis' Haskins; set right where you are an' let me look after 'em. I know all about young ones, though I'm all alone now. Jane went an' married last fall. But, as I tell Council, it's lucky we keep our health. Set right there, Mis' Haskins; I won't have you stir a finger."

It was an unmeasured pleasure to sit there in the warm, homely kitchen, the jovial chatter of the housewife driving out and holding at bay the growl of the impotent, cheated wind.

The little woman's eyes filled with tears which fell down upon the sleeping baby in her arms. The world was not so desolate and cold and hopeless, after all.

"Now I hope Council won't stop out there and talk politics all night. He's the greatest man to talk politics an' read the *Tribune* — How old is it?"

She broke off and peered down at the face of the babe.

"Two months 'n' five days," said the mother, with a mother's exactness.

"Ye don't say! I want 'o know! The dear little pudzy-wudzy!" she went on, stirring it up in the neighborhood of the ribs with her fat forefinger.

"Pooty tough on 'oo to go gallivant'n' 'cross lots this way —"

"Yes, that's so; a man can't lift a mountain," said Council, entering the door. "Mother, this is Mr. Haskins, from Kansas. He's been eat up 'n' drove out by grasshoppers."

"Glad t' see yeh! — Pa, empty that washbasin 'n' give him a chance t' wash."

Haskins was a tall man, with a thin, gloomy face. His hair was a reddish brown, like his coat, and seemed equally faded by the wind and sun, and his sallow face, though hard and set, was pathetic somehow. You would have felt that he had suffered much by the line of his mouth showing under his thin, yellow mustache.

"Hain't Ike got home yet, Sairy?"

"Hain't seen 'im."

"W-a-a-l, set right up, Mr. Haskins; wade right into what we've got; 'tain't much, but we manage to live on it — she gits fat on it," laughed Council, pointing his thumb at his wife.

After supper, while the women put the children to bed, Haskins and Council talked on, seated near the huge cooking-stove, the steam rising from their wet clothing. In the Western fashion Council told as much of his own life as he drew from his guest. He asked but few questions, but by and by the story of Haskins's struggles and defeat came out. The story was a terrible one, but he told it quietly, seated with his elbows on his knees, gazing most of the time at the hearth.

"I didn't like the looks of the country, anyhow," Haskins said, partly rising and glancing at his wife. " I was ust t' northern Ingyannie, where we have lots o' timber 'n' lots o' rain, 'n' I didn't like the looks o' that dry prairie. What galled me the worst was goin' s' far away acrosst so much fine land layin' all through here vacant."

" And the 'hoppers eat ye four years, hand runnin', did they?"

" Eat! They wiped us out. They chawed everything that was green. They jest set around waitin' f'r us to die t' eat us, too. Heavens! I ust t' dream of em sittin' 'round on the bedpost, six feet long, workin' their jaws. They eat the fork-handles. They got worse 'n' worse till they jest rolled on one another, piled up like snow in winter. Well, it ain't no use. If I was t' talk all winter I couldn't tell nawthin'. But all the while I couldn't help thinkin' of all that land back here that nobuddy was usin' that I ought 'o had 'stead o' bein' out there in that cussed country."

" Waal, why didn't ye stop an' settle here?" asked Ike, who had come in and was eating his supper.

" Fer the simple reason that you fellers wantid ten 'r fifteen dollars an acre fer the bare land, and I hadn't no money fer that kind o' thing."

" Yes, I do my own work," Mrs. Council was heard to say in the pause which followed. " I'm a gettin' purty heavy t' be on m' laigs all day, but we can't afford t' hire, so I keep rackin' around somehow, like a foundered horse. S' lame — I tell Council he can't tell how lame I am, f'r I'm jest as lame in one laig as t' other." And the good soul laughed at the joke on herself as she took a handful of flour and dusted the biscuit-board to keep the dough from sticking.

" Well, I hain't *never* been very strong," said Mrs. Haskins. " Our folks was Canadians an' small-boned, and then since my last child I hain't got up again fairly. I don't like t' complain. Tim has about all he can bear now —

but they was days this week when I jest wanted to lay right down an' die."

" Waal, now, I'll tell ye," said Council, from his side of the stove, silencing everybody with his good-natured roar, " I'd go down and *see* Butler, *anyway*, if I was you. I guess he'd let you have his place purty cheap; the farm's all run down. He's ben anxious t' let t' somebuddy next year. It 'ud be a good chance fer you. Anyhow, you go to bed and sleep like a babe. I've got some plowing t' do, anyhow, an' we'll see if somethin' can't be done about your case. Ike, you go out an' see if the horses is all right, an' I'll show the folks t' bed."

When the tired husband and wife were lying under the generous quilts of the spare bed, Haskins listened a moment to the wind in the eaves, and then said, with a slow and solemn tone,

" There are people in this world who are good enough t' be angels, an' only haff t' die to *be* angels."

II

Jim Butler was one of those men called in the West " land poor." Early in the history of Rock River he had come into the town and started in the grocery business in a small way, occupying a small building in a mean part of the town. At this period of his life he earned all he got, and was up early and late sorting beans, working over butter, and carting his goods to and from the station. But a change came over him at the end of the second year, when he sold a lot of land for four times what he paid for it. From that time forward he believed in land speculation as the surest way of getting rich. Every cent he could save or spare from his trade he put into land at forced sale, or mortgages on land, which were " just as good as the wheat," he was accustomed to say.

Farm after farm fell into his hands, until he was recognized as one of the leading landowners of the county. His mortgages were scattered all over Cedar County, and as they slowly but surely fell in he sought usually to retain the former owner as tenant.

He was not ready to foreclose; indeed, he had the name of being one of the "easiest" men in the town. He let the debtor off again and again, extending the time whenever possible.

"I don't want y'r land," he said. "All I'm after is the int'rest on my money — that's all. Now, if y' want 'o stay on the farm, why, I'll give y' a good chance. I can't have the land layin' vacant." And in many cases the owner remained as tenant.

In the meantime he had sold his store; he couldn't spend time in it; he was mainly occupied now with sitting around town on rainy days smoking and "gassin' with the boys," or in riding to and from his farms. In fishing time he fished a good deal. Doc Grimes, Ben Ashley, and Cal Cheatham were his cronies on these fishing excursions or hunting trips in the time of chickens or partridges. In winter they went to Northern Wisconsin to shoot deer.

In spite of all these signs of easy life Butler persisted in saying he "hadn't enough money to pay taxes on his land," and was careful to convey the impression that he was poor in spite of his twenty farms. At one time he was said to be worth fifty thousand dollars, but land had been a little slow of sale of late, so that he was not worth so much.

A fine farm, known as the Higley place, had fallen into his hands in the usual way the previous year, and he had not been able to find a tenant for it. Poor Higley, after working himself nearly to death on it in the attempt to lift the mortgage, had gone off to Dakota, leaving the farm and his curse to Butler.

This was the farm which Council advised Haskins to apply for; and the next day Council hitched up his team and drove down to see Butler.

"You jest let *me* do the talkin'," he said. "We'll find him wearin' out his pants on some salt barrel somew'ers; and if he thought you *wanted* a place he'd sock it to you hot and heavy. You jest keep quiet; I'll fix 'im."

Butler was seated in Ben Ashley's store telling fish yarns when Council sauntered in casually.

"Hello, But; lyin' agin, hey?"

"Hello, Steve! How goes it?"

"Oh, so-so. Too dang much rain these days. I thought it was goin' t' freeze up f'r good last night. Tight squeak if I get m' plowin' done. How's farmin' with *you* these days?"

"Bad. Plowin' ain't half done."

"It 'ud be a religious idee f'r you t' go out an' take a hand y'rself."

"I don't haff to," said Butler, with a wink.

"Got anybody on the Higley place?"

"No. Know of anybody?"

"Waal, no; not eggsackly. I've got a relation back t' Michigan who's ben hot an' cold on the idee o' comin' West f'r some time. *Might* come if he could get a good layout. What do you talk on the farm?"

"Well, I d' know. I'll rent it on shares or I'll rent it money rent."

"Waal, how much money, say?"

"Well, say ten per cent, on the price — two-fifty."

"Wall, that ain't bad. Wait on 'im till 'e thrashes?"[1]

Haskins listened eagerly to this important question, but Council was coolly eating a dried apple which he had speared out of a barrel with his knife. Butler studied him carefully.

"Well, knocks me out of twenty-five dollars interest."

"My relation'll need all he's got t'

[1] "Wait on 'im till 'e thrashes?": Not expect payment until the first crop of wheat is threshed?

The tranquillity of a Midwest farm as evening falls. (*Monkmeyer*)

git his crops in," said Council, in the same, indifferent way.

"Well, all right; *say* wait," concluded Butler.

"All right; this is the man. Haskins, this is Mr. Butler — no relation to Ben — the hardest-working man in Cedar County."

On the way home Haskins said: "I ain't much better off. I'd like that farm; it's a good farm, but it's all run down, an' so 'm I. I could make a good farm of it if I had half a show. But I can't stock it n'r seed it."

"Waal, now, don't you worry," roared Council in his ear. "We'll pull y' through somehow till next harvest. He's agreed t' hire it plowed, an' you can earn a hundred dollars plowin' an' y' c'n git the seed o' me, an' pay me back when y' can."

Haskins was silent with emotion, but at last he said, "I ain't got nothin' t' live on."

"Now, don't you worry 'bout that. You jest make your headquarters at ol' Steve Council's. Mother'll take a pile o' comfort in havin' y'r wife an' children 'round. Y' see, Jane's married off lately, an' Ike's away a good 'eal, so we'll be darn glad t' have y' stop with us this winter. Nex' spring we'll see if y' can't git a start agin." And he chirruped to the team, which sprang forward with the rumbling, clattering wagon.

"Say, looky here, Council, you can't do this. I never saw —" shouted Haskins in his neighbor's ear.

Council moved about uneasily in his seat and stopped his stammering gratitude by saying: "Hold on, now; don't make such a fuss over a little thing. When I see a man down, an' things all on top of 'm, I jest like t' kick 'em off an' help 'm up. That's the kind of religion I got, an' it's about the *only* kind."

They rode the rest of the way home in silence. And when the red light of the lamp shone out into the darkness of the cold and windy night, and he thought of this refuge for his children and wife, Haskins could have put his arm around the neck of his burly companion and squeezed him like a lover. But he contented himself with saying, " Steve Council, you'll git y'r pay f'r this some day."

" Don't want any pay. My religion ain't run on such business principles."

The wind was growing colder, and the ground was covered with a white frost, as they turned into the gate of the Council farm, and the children came rushing out, shouting, " Papa's come! " They hardly looked like the same children who had sat at the table the night before. Their torpidity, under the influence of sunshine and Mother Council, had given way to a sort of spasmodic cheerfulness, as insects in winter revive when laid on the hearth.

III

Haskins worked like a fiend, and his wife, like the heroic woman that she was, bore also uncomplainingly the most terrible burdens. They rose early and toiled without intermission till the darkness fell on the plain, then tumbled into bed, every bone and muscle aching with fatigue, to rise with the sun next morning to the same round of the same ferocity of labor.

The eldest boy drove a team all through the spring, plowing and seeding, milked the cows, and did chores innumerable, in most ways taking the place of a man.

An infinitely pathetic but common figure — this boy on the American farm, where there is no law against child labor. To see him in his coarse clothing, his huge boots, and his ragged cap, as he staggered with a pail of water from the well, or trudged in the cold and cheerless dawn out into the frosty field behind his team, gave the city-bred visitor a sharp pang of sympathetic pain.

Yet Haskins loved his boy, and would have saved him from this if he could, but he could not.

By June the first year the result of such herculean toil began to show on the farm. The yard was cleaned up and sown to grass, the garden plowed and planted, and the house mended.

Council had given them four of his cows.

" Take 'em an' run 'em on shares. I don't want 'o milk s' many. Ike's away s' much now, Sat'd'ys an' Sund'ys, I can't stand the bother anyhow."

Other men, seeing the confidence of Council in the newcomer, had sold him tools on time; and as he was really an able farmer, he soon had round him many evidences of his care and thrift. At the advice of Council he had taken the farm for three years, with the privilege of re-renting or buying at the end of the term.

" It's a good bargain, an' y' want 'o nail it," said Council. " If you have any kind ov a crop, you c'n pay y'r debts, an' keep seed an' bread."

The new hope which now sprang up in the heart of Haskins and his wife grew almost as a pain by the time the wide field of wheat began to wave and rustle and swirl in the winds of July. Day after day he would snatch a few moments after supper to go and look at it.

" Have ye seen the wheat t'day, Nettie? " he asked one night as he rose from supper.

" No, Tim, I ain't had time."

" Well, take time now. Le's go look at it."

She threw an old hat on her head — Tommy's hat — and looking almost pretty in her thin, sad way, went out with her husband to the hedge.

" Ain't it grand, Nettie? Just look at it."

It was grand. Level, russet here and there, heavy-headed, wide as a lake, and full of multitudinous whispers and gleams of wealth, it stretched away before the gazers like the fabled field of the cloth of gold.

"Oh, I think — I *hope* we'll have a good crop, Tim; and oh, how good the people have been to us!"

"Yes; I don't know where we'd be t'day if it hadn't ben f'r Council and his wife."

"They're the best people in the world," said the little woman, with a great sob of gratitude.

"We'll be in the field on Monday sure," said Haskins, gripping the rail on the fences as if already at the work of the harvest.

The harvest came, bounteous, glorious, but the winds came and blew it into tangles, and the rain matted it here and there close to the ground, increasing the work of gathering it threefold.

Oh, how they toiled in those glorious days! Clothing dripping with sweat, arms aching, filled with briers, fingers raw and bleeding, backs broken with the weight of heavy bundles, Haskins and his man toiled on. Tommy drove the harvester, while his father and a hired man bound on the machine. In this way they cut ten acres every day, and almost every night after supper, when the hand went to bed, Haskins returned to the field shocking the bound grain in the light of the moon. Many a night he worked till his anxious wife came out at ten o'clock to call him in to rest and lunch.

At the same time she cooked for the men, took care of the children, washed and ironed, milked the cows at night, made the butter, and sometimes fed the horses and watered them while her husband kept at the shocking.

No slave in the Roman galleys could have toiled so frightfully and lived, for this man thought himself a free man, and that he was working for his wife and babes.

When he sank into his bed with a deep groan of relief, too tired to change his grimy, dripping clothing, he felt that he was getting nearer and nearer to a home of his own, and pushing the wolf of want a little farther from his door.

There is no despair so deep as the despair of a homeless man or woman. To roam the roads of the country or the streets of the city, to feel there is no rood of ground on which the feet can rest, to halt weary and hungry outside lighted windows and hear laughter and song within — these are the hungers and rebellions that drive men to crime and women to shame.

It was the memory of this homelessness, and the fear of its coming again, that spurred Timothy Haskins and Nettie, his wife, to such ferocious labor during that first year.

IV

"'M, yes; 'm, yes; first-rate," said Butler, as his eye took in the neat garden, the pigpen, and the well-filled barnyard. "You're gitt'n' quite a stock around yeh. Done well, eh?"

Haskins was showing Butler around the place. He had not seen it for a year, having spent the year in Washington and Boston with Ashley, his brother-in-law, who had been elected to Congress.

"Yes, I've laid out a good deal of money durin' the last three years. I've paid out three hundred dollars f'r fenc-in'."

"Um — h'm! I see, I see," said Butler, while Haskins went on:

"The kitchen there cost two hundred; the barn ain't cost much in money, but I've put a lot o' time on it. I've dug a new well, and I — "

"Yes, yes, I see. You've done well. Stock worth a thousand dollars," said Butler, picking his teeth with a straw.

"About that," said Haskins, modestly. "We begin to feel's if we was gitt'n' a home f'r ourselves; but we've worked hard. I tell you we begin to feel it, Mr. Butler, and we're goin' t' begin to ease up purty soon. We've been kind o' plan-nin' a trip back t' *her* folks after the fall plowin's done."

" *Eggs-actly!* " said Butler, who was evidently thinking of something else. " I suppose you've kind o' calc'lated on stayin' here three years more? "

" Well, yes. Fact is, I think I c'n buy the farm this fall, if you'll give me a reasonable show."

" Um — m! What do you call a reasonable show? "

" Well, say a quarter down and three years' time."

Butler looked at the huge stacks of wheat, which filled the yard, over which the chickens were fluttering and crawling, catching grasshoppers, and out of which the crickets were singing innumerably. He smiled in a peculiar way as he said, " Oh, I won't be hard on yeh. But what did you expect to pay f'r the place? "

" Why, about what you offered it for before, two thousand five hundred, or *possibly* three thousand dollars," he added quickly, as he saw the owner shake his head.

" This farm is worth five thousand and five hundred dollars," said Butler, in a careless and decided voice.

" *What!* " almost shrieked the astounded Haskins. " What's that? Five thousand? Why, that's double what you offered it for three years ago."

" Of course, and it's worth it. It was all run down then; now it's in good shape. You've laid out fifteen hundred dollars in improvements, according to your own story."

" But *you* had nothin' t' do about that. It's my work an' my money."

" You bet it was; but it's my land."

" But what's to pay me for all my — "

" Ain't you had the use of 'em? " replied Butler, smiling calmly into his face.

Haskins was like a man struck on the head with a sandbag; he couldn't think; he stammered as he tried to say: " But — I never'd git the use — You'd rob me! More'n that: you agreed — you promised

that I could buy or rent at the end of three years at — "

" That's all right. But I didn't say I'd let you carry off the improvements, nor that I'd go on renting the farm at two-fifty. The land is doubled in value, it don't matter how; it don't enter into the question; an' now you can pay me five hundred dollars a year rent, or take it on your own terms at fifty-five hundred, or — git out."

He was turning away when Haskins, the sweat pouring from his face, fronted him, saying again:

" But *you've* done nothing to make it so. You hain't added a cent. I put it all there myself, expectin' to buy. I worked an' sweat to improve it. I was workin' for myself an' babes — "

" Well, why didn't you buy when I offered to sell? What y' kickin' about? "

" I'm kickin' about payin' you twice f'r my own things — my own fences, my own kitchen, my own garden."

Butler laughed. " You're too green t' eat, young feller. *Your* improvements! The law will sing another tune."

" But I trusted your word."

" Never trust anybody, my friend. Besides, I didn't promise not to do this thing. Why, man, don't look at me like that. Don't take me for a thief. It's the law. The reg'lar thing. Everybody does it."

" I don't care if they do. It's stealin' jest the same. You take three thousand dollars of my money — the work o' my hands and my wife's." He broke down at this point. He was not a strong man mentally. He could face hardship, ceaseless toil, but he could not face the cold and sneering face of Butler.

" But I don't take it," said Butler, coolly. " All you've got to do is to go on jest as you've been a-doin', or give me a thousand dollars down, and a mortgage at ten per cent on the rest."

Haskins sat down blindly on a bundle of oats nearby, and with staring eyes and drooping head went over the situation. He was under the lion's paw. He felt a horrible numbness in his heart and limbs. He was hid in a mist, and there was no path out.

Butler walked about, looking at the huge stacks of grain, and pulling now and again a few handfuls out, shelling the heads in his hands and blowing the chaff away. He hummed a little tune as he did so. He had an accommodating air of waiting.

Haskins was in the midst of the terrible toil of the last year. He was walking again in the rain and the mud behind his plow; he felt the dust and dirt of the threshing. The ferocious husking-time, with its cutting wind and biting, clinging snows, lay hard upon him. Then he thought of his wife, how she had cheerfully cooked and baked, without holiday and without rest.

"Well, what do you think of it?" inquired the cool, mocking, insinuating voice of Butler.

"I think you're a thief and a liar!" shouted Haskins, leaping up. "A blackhearted houn'!" Butler's smile maddened him; with a sudden leap he caught a fork in his hands, and whirled it in the air. "You'll never rob another man, damn ye!" he grated through his teeth, a look of pitiless ferocity in his accusing eyes.

Butler shrank and quivered, expecting the blow; stood, held hypnotized by the eyes of the man he had a moment before despised — a man transformed into an avenging demon. But in the deadly hush between the lift of the weapon and its fall there came a gush of faint, childish laughter and then across the range of his vision, far away and dim, he saw the sun-bright head of his baby girl, as, with the pretty, tottering run of a two-year-old, she moved across the grass of the dooryard. His hands relaxed: the fork fell to the ground; his head lowered.

"Make out y'r deed an' mor'gage, an' git off'n my land, an' don't ye never cross my line again; if y' do, I'll kill ye."

Butler backed away from the man in wild haste, and climbing into his buggy with trembling limbs drove off down the road, leaving Haskins seated dumbly on the sunny pile of sheaves, his head sunk into his hands.

For Discussion of Garland

1. The first section of this story pictures two important elements of life on the Middle Border. Identify each in a descriptive phrase.

2. How did Mrs. Council put the weary travelers at ease as she welcomed them to her kitchen? Do you detect a definite purpose in her chattering on and on?

3. In his fight to make a good life for himself and his family, Haskins had to struggle against distinctly different kinds of obstacles. What were they? Are these enemies still arrayed against farmers?

4. In what different ways did Council help Haskins? Recall passages that proved that Haskins appreciated his kindness. What did Council mean by saying " My religion ain't run on . . . business principles "?

5. Describe the life of the Haskins family while they were trying to get re-established. What did Garland think about " child labor " on the Border farms? How do you know that even a prosperous farmer had to work hard?

6. What did Butler do in making his final trade with Haskins that was unfair? Was Butler within his legal rights? Give arguments for and against the law that improvements made by a tenant belong to the landlord.

7. Explain the significance of the title. How does the phrase occur in the story?

8. Contrast the characters of Council and Butler. Discuss whether Butler should be considered a producer or a nonproducer in society. Did he fulfill a necessary function in the early Midwest? Would he today?

9. To appreciate literary realism, compare this story with " The Outcasts of Poker Flat " (p. 663) as to plot, characters, and the author's purpose. What special satisfaction does each type of story offer? Which do you prefer?

For Your Vocabulary

WORD POWER: An unusual expression in "Under the Lion's Paw" is "a *premonitory* cough," a cough giving warning that someone is present and about to speak. What is a *premonition?* An *admonition?* Do you have *monitors* in your school?

When the man did begin to speak, he spoke "in a *deprecating* tone." It is a tone which seems to say, "I hope you'll excuse me for being so bold, but — " What is the exact definition of *deprecate?*

What is the meaning of *torpidity* (p. 721)? Why is the comparison with insects in winter especially good? What is meant when we say that *hibernating* animals are in a state of *torpor?*

Mary Antin
1881–1949

FIRST IMPRESSIONS OF THE PROMISED LAND

America might be having growing pains during the 1890's, but it was still the promised land to many a European immigrant. What was America like to these eager newcomers? In Mary Antin's autobiographical book, *The Promised Land* (1912), we can rediscover our own country with a little immigrant girl who was just thirteen when she came to Boston from Russia. The eager child whom we find in the following chapter from *The Promised Land* successfully adapted her ways to those of the new country, went through the public schools of Boston, and attended Columbia University. When she was twenty, she married a professor at Columbia.

B Y THE time we joined my father,[1] he had surveyed many avenues of approach toward the coveted citadel of fortune. One of these, heretofore untried, he now proposed to essay, armed with new courage and cheered on by the presence of his family. In partnership with an energetic little man who had an English chapter in his history, he prepared to set up a refreshment booth on Crescent Beach. But while he was completing arrangements at the beach we remained in town, where we enjoyed the educational advantages of a thickly populated neighborhood; namely, Wall Street, in the West End of Boston.

Anybody who knows Boston knows that the West and North Ends comprise the chief tenement districts of Boston, where people who have never lived in the tenements are fond of going sightseeing. He may know all this and yet not guess how Wall Street, in the West End, appears in the eyes of a little im-

[1] **joined my father:** He had been in America for three years before his family came.

Selection from *The Promised Land* by Mary Antin. Reprinted by permission of Houghton Mifflin Company.

migrant from Polotzk. What would the sophisticated sight-seer say about Union Place, off Wall Street, where my new home waited for me? He would say that it is no place at all, but a short box of an alley. Two rows of three-story tenements are its sides, a stingy strip of sky is its lid, a littered pavement is the floor, and a narrow mouth its exit.

But I saw a very different picture on my introduction to Union Place. I saw two imposing rows of brick buildings, loftier than any dwelling I had ever lived in. Brick was even on the ground for me to tread on, instead of common earth or boards. Many friendly windows stood open, filled with uncovered heads of women and children. I thought the people were interested in us, which was very neighborly. I looked up to the topmost row of windows, and my eyes were filled with the May blue of an American sky!

In our days of affluence in Russia we had been accustomed to upholstered parlors, embroidered linen, silver spoons and candlesticks, goblets of gold, kitchen shelves shining with copper and brass. We had feather beds heaped halfway to the ceiling; we had clothespresses dusky with velvet and silk and fine woolen. The three small rooms into which my father now ushered us, up one flight of stairs, contained only the necessary beds, with lean mattresses; a few wooden chairs, a table or two; a mysterious iron structure, which later turned out to be a stove; a couple of unornamental kerosene lamps; and a scanty array of cooking utensils and crockery. And yet we were all impressed with our new home and its furniture. It was not only because we had just passed through our seven lean years, cooking in earthen vessels, eating black bread on holidays, and wearing cotton; it was chiefly because these wooden chairs and tin pans were American chairs and pans that they shone glorious in our eyes. And if

there was anything lacking for comfort or decoration we expected it to be presently supplied — at least, we children did. Perhaps my mother alone, of us newcomers, appreciated the shabbiness of the little apartment and realized that for her there was as yet no laying down of the burden of poverty.

Our initiation into American ways began with the first step on the new soil. My father found occasion to instruct or correct us even on the way from the pier to Wall Street, which journey we made crowded together in a rickety cab. He told us not to lean out of the windows, not to point, and explained the word " greenhorn." We did not want to be " greenhorns," and gave the strictest attention to my father's instructions. I do not know when my parents found opportunity to review together the history of Polotzk in the three years past, for we children had no patience with the subject; my mother's narrative was constantly interrupted by irrelevant questions, interjections, and explanations.

The first meal was an object lesson of much variety. My father produced several kinds of food, ready to eat, without any cooking, from little tin cans that had printing all over them. He attempted to introduce us to a queer, slippery kind of fruit, which he called " banana," but had to give it up for the time being. After the meal he had better luck with a curious piece of furniture on runners, which he called " rocking chair." There were five of us newcomers, and we found five different ways of getting into the American machine of perpetual motion, and as many ways of getting out of it. One born and bred to the use of a rocking chair cannot imagine how ludicrous people can make themselves when attempting to use it for the first time. We laughed immoderately over our various experiments with the novelty, which was a wholesome way of letting off steam aft-

" Steerage," famous photograph taken by Alfred Stieglitz in 1907 on a ship arriving from Europe. (Philadelphia Museum of Art)

er the unusual excitement of the day.

In our flat we did not think of such a thing as storing the coal in the bathtub. There was no bathtub. So in the evening of the first day my father conducted us to the public baths. As we moved along in a little procession, I was delighted with the illumination of the streets. So many lamps, and they burned until morning, my father said, and so people did not need to carry lanterns. In America, then, everything was free, as we had heard in Russia. Light was free; the streets were as bright as a synagogue on a holy day. Music was free; we had been serenaded, to our gaping delight, by a brass band of many pieces, soon after our installation on Union Place.

Education was free. That subject my father had written about repeatedly, as comprising his chief hope for us children, the essence of American opportunity, the treasure that no thief could touch, not even misfortune or poverty. It was the one thing that he was able to promise us when he sent for us; surer, safer than bread or shelter. On our second day I was thrilled with the realization of what this freedom of education meant. A little girl from across the alley came and offered to conduct us to school. My father was out, but we five between us had a few words of English by this time. We knew the word school. We understood. This child, who had never seen us till yesterday, who could not pronounce our names, who was not much better dressed than we, was able to offer us the freedom of the schools of Boston! No application made; no questions asked; no examinations, rulings, exclusions; no machinations; no fees. The doors stood open for every one of us. The smallest child could show us the way.

This incident impressed me more than anything I had heard in advance of the freedom of education in America. It was a concrete proof — almost the thing itself. One had to experience it to understand it.

It was a great disappointment to be told by my father that we were not to enter upon our school career at once. It was too near the end of the term, he said, and we were going to move to Crescent Beach in a week or so. We had to wait until the opening of the schools in September. What a loss of precious time — from May till September!

Not that the time was really lost. Even the interval on Union Place was crowded with lessons and experiences. We had to visit the stores and be dressed from head to foot in American clothing; we had to learn the mysteries of the iron stove, the washboard, and the speaking tube; we had to learn to trade with the fruit peddler through the window, and not to be afraid of the policeman; and, above all, we had to learn English.

The kind people who assisted us in these important matters form a group by themselves in the gallery of my friends. If I had never seen them from those early days till now, I should still have remembered them with gratitude. When I enumerate the long list of my American teachers, I must begin with those who came to us on Wall Street and taught us our first steps. To my mother, in her perplexity over the cookstove, the woman who showed her how to make the fire was an angel of deliverance. A fairy godmother to us children was she who led us to a wonderful country called " uptown," where, in a dazzlingly beautiful palace called a " department store," we exchanged our hateful homemade European costumes, which pointed us out as " greenhorns " to the children on the street, for real American machine-made garments, and issued forth glorified in each other's eyes.

With our despised immigrant clothing we shed also our impossible Hebrew names. A committee of our friends, several years ahead of us in American experience, put their heads together and concocted American names for us all. Those of our real names that had no pleasing American equivalents they ruthlessly discarded, content if they retained the initials. My mother, possessing a name that was not easily translatable, was punished with the undignified nickname of Annie. Fetchke, Joseph, and Deborah issued as Frieda, Joseph, and Dora, respectively. As for poor me, I was simply cheated. The name they gave me was hardly new. My Hebrew name being Maryashe in full, Mashke for short, Russianized into Marya (*Mar-ya*), my friends said that it would hold good in English as *Mary;* which was very disappointing, as I longed to possess a strange-sounding American name like the others.

I am forgetting the consolation I had, in this matter of names, from the use of my surname, which I have had no occasion to mention until now. I found on my arrival that my father was " Mr. Antin " on the slightest provocation, and not, as in Polotzk, on state occasions alone. And so I was " Mary Antin," and I felt very important to answer to such a dignified title. It was just like America that even plain people should wear their surnames on weekdays.

For Discussion of Antin

1. What features of the new environment that were commonplace to Americans seemed wonderful to the newcomers? What evidence can you find that things seemed wonderful not because they were unusually splendid but just because they were American?

2. How did the immigrant family show their great desire to fit into the life of America? How could Americans living abroad win more friends for the United States if they made an equal effort to fit into the life of the country?

3. In what ways does our country lose something by the rapid and complete Americanization of immigrants — by their discarding of their native languages, customs, costumes, etc.? What is the other side to this question? Which side do the young members of immigrant families usually take? Why?

4. Did you find yourself hoping that everyone would be kind to Mary and her family? What experience have you had with newcomers to America? Discuss whether it is enough for a person to be " tolerant " of someone who is " different " from him.

5. Do you believe that immigrants like the Antins made (and will make) just as good citizens as native-born Americans? What can the latter learn from such immigrants that will make them better citizens themselves?

6. See how many immigrants you can think of who achieved success in America in different fields. What did they contribute to our country?

7. To discover how other immigrants have fared in their early days in America, select an autobiography from the reading list " Americans from Other Lands " on page 255. See whether America still seems a land of freedom and opportunity for newcomers.

For Your Vocabulary

SLANG: Mary Antin's father urged her not to be a *greenhorn*. Did you notice that whenever Miss Antin used this slang expression she enclosed it in quotation marks? What do you suppose is the reason for this? Some slang is very effective and finds its way into our accepted usage, but most slang expressions have very temporary popularity. What is your opinion of these slang expressions: *easy mark, nutty, beat it, rough stuff, pinched by a cop?* Discuss whether there is a difference between slang and colloquial English. Is either ever acceptable in literature? Try to find some slang expressions that over the years have become part of acceptable usage. If this sort of study interests you, do some browsing in H. L. Mencken's *The American Language,* a standard work on American usage.

Thomas
Augustine Daly
1871–1948

TWO 'MERICANA MEN

As the immigrants kept coming, foreign accents were heard more and more often in the Eastern cities. Though "broken English" was sometimes ignorantly ridiculed and laughed at, it could also be echoed in a warmhearted, friendly fashion. T. A. Daly, of the Philadelphia *Evening Ledger*, wrote many poems in various dialects, of which the Italian proved most successful. Most Italian words end in vowels, and the Italian learning to speak English tends to adapt English words to the same pattern, making an especially musical dialect. Because of Daly's remarkably clear spelling, the poem is easy to read aloud with the proper accent.

Beeg Irish cop dat walks hees beat
  By dees peanutta stan',
First two, t'ree week w'en we are meet
  Ees call me "Dagoman."
An' w'en he see how mad I gat,   5
  Wheech eesa pleass heem, too,
Wan day he say: "W'at's matter dat,
  Ain't 'Dago' name for you?
Dat's 'Mericana name, you know,
  For man from Eetaly;   10
Eet ees no harm for call you so,
  Den why be mad weeth me?"

First time he talka deesa way
  I am too mad for speak,
But nexta time I justa say: 15
  "All righta, Meester Meeck!"
O! my, I nevva hear bayfore
  Sooch langwadge like he say;

An' he don't look at me no more
  For mebbe two, t'ree day.   20
But pretta soon agen I see
  Dees beeg poleecaman
Dat com' an' growl an' say to me:
  "Hallo, Eyetalian!
Now, mebbe so you gon' deny   25
  Dat dat's a name for you."
I smila back, an' mak' reply:
  "No, Irish, dat'sa true."
"Ha! Joe," he cry, "you theenk dat we
  Should call you 'Merican?"   30
"Dat's gooda 'nough," I say, "for me,
  Eef dat's w'at you are, Dan."

So now all times we speaka so
  Like gooda 'Merican:
He say to me, "Good morna, Joe,"   35
  I say, "Good morna, Dan."

For Discussion of Daly

1. How is this little poem like Mary Antin's narrative of her first months in Boston? How is it different?

2. In what way does the author show his liking and respect for the foreigners in his city? How does he suggest that all Americans were once foreigners? Why are racial or national "nicknames" of the sort used here so offensive?

3. Could this story have been told as well without the dialect? What other dialect poems do you know? Get up a program of class favorites and discuss the effectiveness of the various dialects.

"Two 'Mericana Men" from *Carmina* by Thomas Augustine Daly. Reprinted by permission of Harcourt, Brace and Company, Inc.

Finley Peter Dunne

1867-1936

MR. DOOLEY ON MACHINERY

Another newspaper columnist who used dialect effectively was Finley Peter Dunne of the Chicago *Post,* generally rated the most popular " crackerbox philosopher " between Artemus Ward and Will Rogers. His Mr. Dooley, an Irish saloonkeeper who commented amusingly to his friend Hennessy on what he read in the papers, became such a favorite that nine " Mr. Dooley " books were published between 1898 and 1911. Dunne followed no political party and spoke his mind freely, applying humor and good common sense to widely discussed issues of his day. He had courage, too, for he often championed unpopular figures in the news, and during the muckraking era he criticized reformers as well as the bosses of political machines. In the following piece, Mr. Dooley " debunks " the popular worship of machines and exaggerated faith in mechanical progress. You will find ideas here worth a second — and a third — thought in this day when machines threaten to destroy the men who made them.

Mr. Dooley was reading from a paper. " 'We live,' he says, 'in an age iv wondhers. Niver befure in th' histhry iv th' wurruld has such pro-gress been made.'

"Thrue wurruds an' often spoken. Even in me time things has changed. Whin I was a la-ad Long Jawn Wintworth cud lean his elbows on th' high-est buildin' in this town. It took two months to come here fr'm Pittsburgh on a limited raft an' a stagecoach that run fr'm La Salle to Mrs. Murphy's hotel. They wasn't anny tillygraft that I can raymimber an' th' sthreetcar was pulled be a mule an' dhruv be an engineer be th' name iv Mulligan. We thought we was a pro-grissive people. Ye bet we did. But look at us today. I go be Casey's house tonight an' there it is a fine story-an'-a-half frame house with Casey settin' on th' dure shtep dhrinkin' out iv a pail. I go be Casey's house tomorrah an' it's a hole in th' groun'. I rayturn to Casey's house on Thursdah an' it's a fifty-eight-story buildin' with a morgedge onto it an' they're thinkin' iv takin' it down an' replacin' it with a modhren sthructure. Th' shoes that Corrigan th' cobbler wanst wurruked on fr a week, hammerin' away like a woodpecker, is now tossed out be th' dozens fr'm th' mouth iv a masheen. A cow goes lowin' softly in to Armour's an' comes out glue, beef, gelatin, fertylizer, celooloid, joolry, sofy cushions, hair restorer, washin' sody, soap, lithrachoor, an' bedsprings so quick that while aft she's still cow, for'ard she may be anything fr'm buttons to Pannyma hats. I can go fr'm Chicago to New York in twinty hours; but I don't have to, thank th' Lord. Thirty years ago we thought 'twas marvelous

"Mr. Dooley on Machinery" from *Observations of Mr. Dooley* by Finley Peter Dunne. Reprinted by permission of Harper & Brothers.

to be able to tillygraft a man in Saint Joe an' get an answer that night. Now, be wireless tillygraft ye can get an answer befure ye sind th' tillygram if they ain't careful. Me friend Macroni [1] has done that. Be manes iv his wondher iv science a man on a ship in mid-ocean can sind a tillygram to a man on shore, if he has a confid'rate on board. That's all he needs. Be mechanical science an' thrust in th' op'rator annywan can set on th' shore iv Noofoundland an' chat with a frind in th' County Kerry. [2]

"Yes, sir, mechanical science has made gr-reat sthrides. Whin I was a young man we used to think Hor'ce Greeley was th' gr-reatest livin' American. He was a gran' man, a gran' man with feathers beneath his chin an' specs on his nose like th' windows in a diver's hemlet. His pollyticks an' mine cudden't live in th' same neighborhood, but he was a gran' man all th' same. We used to take th' Cleveland *Plain Daler* in thim days f'r raycreation an' th' New York *Thrybune* f'r exercise. 'Twas considhered a test iv a good-natured Dimmycrat if he cud read an article in th' *Thrybune* without havin' to do th' stations iv th' cross [3] aftherward f'r what he said. I almost did wanst, but they was a line at th' end about a frind iv mine be th' name iv Andhrew Jackson an' I wint out an' broke up a Methodist prayer meetin'. He was th' boy that cud put it to ye so that if ye voted th' Dimmycrat tickit it was jus' th' same as demandin' a place in purgatory. Th' farmers wud plant annything fr'm a rutybaga to a Congressman on his advice. He niver had money enough to buy a hat, but

he cud go to th' Sicrety iv th' Threasury an' tell him who's pitcher to put on th' useful valentines we thrade f'r groceries.

"But if Hor'ce Greeley was alive today where'd he be? Settin' on three inches iv th' edge iv a chair in th' outside office iv me frind Pierpont Morgan [4] waitin' f'r his turn. In th' line is th' Imp'ror iv Germany, th' new cook, th' prisidint iv a railroad, th' cap'n iv th' yacht, Rimbrandt [5] th' painther, Jawn W. Grates, [6] an' Hor'ce. Afther a while th' boy at th' dure says, 'Ye're next, ol' party. Shtep lively, f'r th' boss has had a Weehawken Peerooginy [7] sawed off on him this mornin' an' he mustn't be kep' waitin'.' An' th' iditor goes in. 'Who ar-re ye?' says th' gr-reat man, givin' him wan iv thim piercin' looks that whin a man gets it he has to be sewed up at wanst. 'I'm ye'er iditor,' says Hor'ce. 'Which wan?' says Pierpont. 'Number two hundhred an' eight.' 'What's ye'er spishilty?' 'Tahriff an' th' improvemint iv th' wurruld,' says Hor'ce. 'See Perkins,' says Pierpont, an' th' intherview is over. Now what's made th' change? Mechanical science, Hinnissy. Somewan made a masheen that puts steel billets within th' reach iv all. Hince Charlie Schwab. [8]

"What's it done f'r th' wurruld? says ye. It's done ivrything. It's give us fast ships an' an autymatic hist f'r th' hod, an' small flats an' a taste iv solder in th' peaches. If annybody says th' wurruld ain't betther off thin it was, tell him

---

[1] **Macroni:** Of course he means Marconi (1874–1937), the Italian inventor who put wireless telegraphy on a commercial basis.

[2] **County Kerry:** in southwest Ireland.

[3] **do th' stations iv th' cross:** a humorous reference to the Democratic ire likely to be aroused by the staunchly Republican *Tribune*. The explosive speech of a Democrat that often followed the reading of the paper sometimes merited the Stations of the Cross as a sacramental penance.

[4] **Morgan:** John Pierpont Morgan, Sr. (1837–1913), important American financier.

[5] **Rimbrandt:** Rembrandt (1606–1669), famous Dutch painter, included humorously because Morgan was a great collector of art.

[6] **Jawn W. Grates:** misspelling of John W. Gates, a famous speculator.

[7] **Weehawken Peerooginy:** Perugino (1446–1523) was a famous Italian painter. Weehawken is a town in New Jersey. The combination suggests that Morgan has been cheated in supposing he had purchased an original old master that proved to be only a copy.

[8] **Charlie Schwab:** Charles M. Schwab (1862–1939), president of two steel corporations and other industrial corporations.

that a masheen has been invinted that makes honey out iv pethrolyum. If he asts ye why they ain't anny Shakesperes today, say, 'No, but we no longer make sausages be hand.'

" 'Tis pro-gress. We live in a cinchry iv pro-gress an' I thank th' Lord I've seen most iv it. Man an' boy I've lived pretty near through this wondherful age. If I was proud I cud say I seen more thin Julyus Caesar iver see or cared to. An' here I am, I'll not say how old, still pushin' th' malt acrost th' counther at me thirsty counthrymen. All around me is th' refinemints iv mechanical janius. Instead iv broachin' th' beer kag with a club an' dhrawin' th' beer through a fassit as me Puritan forefathers done, I have that wondher iv invintive science th' beer pump. I cheat mesilf with a cash raygisther. I cut off th' end iv me good cigar with an injanyous device an' pull th' cork out iv a bottle with a conthrivance that wud've made that frind that Hogan boasts about, that ol' boy Archy Meeds,[1] think they was witchcraft in th' house. Science has been a gr-reat blessin' to me. But amidst all these granjoors here am I th' same ol' antiquated combination iv bellows an' pump I always was. Not so good. Time has worn me out. Th' years like little boys with jackknives has carved their names in me top. Ivry day I have to write off something f'r deprecyation. 'Tis about time f'r whoiver owns me to wurruk me off on a thrust. Mechanical science has done ivrything f'r me but help me. I suppose I ought to feel supeeryor to me father. He niver see a high buildin' but he didn't want to. He cudden't come here in five days but he was a wise man an' if he cud've come in three he'd have stayed in th' County Roscommon.[2]

" Th' pa-apers tells me that midical science has kept pace with th' hop-skip-an'-a-jump iv mechanical inginooty. Th' doctors has found th' mikrobe iv ivrything fr'm lumbago to love an' fr'm jandice to jealousy, but if a brick bounces on me head I'm crated up th' same as iv yore an' put away. Rockyfellar can make a pianny out iv a bar'l iv crude ile, but no wan has been able to make a blade iv hair grow on Rockyfellar. They was a doctor over in France that discovered a kind iv a thing that if 'twas pumped into ye wud make ye live till people got so tired iv seein' ye around they cud scream. He died th' nex' year iv premachure ol' age. They was another doctor cud insure whether th' nex' wan wud be a boy or a girl. All ye had to do was to decide wud it be Arthur or Ethel an' lave him know. He left a fam'ly iv unmarredgeable daughters.

" I sometimes wondher whether progress is anny more thin a kind iv a shift. It's like a merry-go-round. We get up on a speckled wooden horse an' th' mechanical pianny plays a chune an' away we go, hollerin'. We think we're thravelin' like th' divvle but th' man that doesn't care about merry-go-rounds knows that we will come back where we were. We get out dizzy an' sick an' lay on th' grass an' gasp, 'Where am I? Is this th' meelin-yum?'[3] An' he says, 'No, 'tis Ar-rchey Road.' Father Kelly says th' Agyptians done things we cudden't do an' th' Romans put up skyscrapers an' aven th' Chinks had tillyphones an' phonygrafts.

" I've been up to th' top iv th' very highest buildin' in town, Hinnissy, an' I wasn't anny nearer Hivin thin if I was in th' sthreet. Th' stars was as far away as iver. An' down beneath is a lot iv us runnin' an' lapin' an' jumpin' about, pushin' each other over, haulin' little sthrips iv ir'n to pile up in little build-

---

[1] **Archy Meeds:** Archimedes (är′kĭ·mē′dēz), a Greek mathematician and inventor (287?–212 B.C.)

[2] **County Roscommon** (rŏs·kŏm′ŭn): in central Ireland.

[3] **meelin-yum:** millennium, the thousand years during which, according to the Book of Revelations, Christ will return to rule on earth.

in's that ar-re called skyscrapers but not be th' sky; wurrukin' night an' day to make a masheen that'll carry us fr'm wan jack-rabbit colony to another an' yellin', 'Pro-gress!' Pro-gress, oho! I can see th' stars winkin' at each other an' sayin', 'Ain't they funny! Don't they think they're playin' the divil!'

"No, sir, masheens ain't done much f'r man. I can't get up anny kind iv fam'ly inthrest f'r a steam dredge or a hydhraulic hist. I want to see skyscrapin' men. But I won't. We're about th' same hight as we always was, th' same hight an' build, composed iv th' same inflamable an' perishyable mateeryal, an exthra hazardous risk, unimproved an' li'ble to collapse. We do make progress, but it's th' same kind Julyus Caesar made an' ivry wan has made befure or since an' in this age iv masheenery we're still burrid be hand."

"What d'ye think iv th' man down in Pinnsylvanya who says th' Lord an' him is partners in a coal mine?" asked Mr. Hennessy, who wanted to change the subject.

"Has he divided th' profits?" asked Mr. Dooley.

For Discussion of Dunne

1. What kinds of machines does Mr. Dooley mention? Have we any still more astonishing machines today?

2. What is his conclusion about the importance of machinery? Do you agree with him? How would you relate Mr. Dooley's ideas to those of Thoreau?

3. Is the Irish dialect as effective as Daly's Italian dialect (p. 730)? Is it as easy to read aloud? What does it contribute to the effect of the article?

4. Do you think you would read "Mr. Dooley" if he were appearing in your daily paper? Why?

Edwin Markham
1852–1940

THE MAN WITH THE HOE

WRITTEN AFTER SEEING MILLET'S WORLD-
FAMOUS PAINTING OF A BRUTALIZED
TOILER IN THE DEEP ABYSS
OF LABOR

During his varied life as farmer, ranch hand, and teacher in Oregon and California, Edwin Markham wrote many poems which won only moderate success up to the time he was forty-seven years old. Then he published "The Man with the Hoe." Coming at a time when there was a great wave of concern about common workers and their hard lot, the poem stirred tremendous interest and made Markham suddenly famous. It has continued to hold a place among the really great American poems. The subtitle explains the origin of the poem. In Millet's [1] painting, Markham saw the figure of "the landless, the soul-blighted workman of the world; the dumb

[1] **Millet** (mĭ·lā').

"The Man with the Hoe," the painting by Millet given a lasting place in literature by Markham's poem. (Art-Lore, Inc.)

creature that has no time to rest, no time to think, no time for the hopes that make us men."

God made man in his own image; in the image of God made He him. — *Genesis.*

Bowed by the weight of centuries he
    leans
Upon his hoe and gazes on the ground,
The emptiness of ages in his face,
And on his back the burden of the
    world.
Who made him dead to rapture and de-
    spair,   5
A thing that grieves not and that never
    hopes,
Stolid and stunned, a brother to the ox?
Who loosened and let down this brutal
    jaw?
Whose was the hand that slanted back
    this brow?
Whose breath blew out the light with-
    in this brain?   10
Is this the thing the Lord God made
    and gave
To have dominion over sea and land;
To trace the stars and search the heav-
    ens for power;
To feel the passion of eternity?
Is this the dream He dreamed who
    shaped the suns   15
And marked their ways upon the an-
    cient deep?

Down all the caverns of hell to their last
    gulf
There is no shape more terrible than
    this —
More tongued with cries against the
    world's blind greed —
More filled with signs and portents for
    the soul —   20
More packed with danger to the uni-
    verse.

What gulfs between him and the sera-
    phim!
Slave of the wheel of labor, what to
    him
Are Plato° and the swing of Pleiades?
What the long reaches of the peaks of
    song,   25
The rift of dawn, the reddening of the
    rose?
Through this dread shape the suffering
    ages look;
Time's tragedy is in that aching stoop;
Through this dread shape humanity be-
    trayed,
Plundered, profaned, and disinherited,
Cries protest to the Powers that made
    the world,   31
A protest that is also prophecy.

24. **Plato** (plā′tō): an ancient Greek philosopher whose idealistic views of man have greatly
influenced the world.

O masters, lords and rulers in all lands,
Is this the handiwork you give to God,
This monstrous thing distorted and soul-
quenched?   35
How will you ever straighten up this
shape;
Touch it again with immortality;
Give back the upward looking and the
light;   38
Rebuild in it the music and the dream;
Make right the immemorial infamies,
Perfidious wrongs, immedicable woes?

O masters, lords and rulers in all lands,
How will the future reckon with this
man?
How answer his brute question in that
hour
When whirlwinds of rebellion shake all
shores?   45
How will it be with kingdoms and with
kings —
With those who shaped him to the thing
he is —
When this dumb Terror shall rise to
judge the world,
After the silence of the centuries?

For Discussion of Markham

1. Point out physical features that create the impression of a crushed being,
hardly human. What are some of the things
in your own life that this man has never
had time or opportunity to enjoy?

2. With what questions does the poem
close? To whom are they addressed?

3. Some critics have said that Millet
never intended to portray such a hopeless
creature, but simply an honest workman
resting. Study the copy of the picture on
page 735 and decide which interpretation
you prefer.

For Your Vocabulary

WORD POWER: Markham stresses the injustice done to the " man with the hoe " in
such words as *profaned* (l. 30) and *perfidious* (l. 41). We *profane* something
when we debase it by wrong or unjust use.
A *fane* is a temple, and the word *profane*
originally meant " before (i.e., outside) the
temple," hence not sacred. What is *profane*
language? What is the difference in connotation between *profane* and *secular*?
From what root is *perfidious* derived?

Frank Norris
1870–1902

FROM THE OCTOPUS

ALL THE TRAFFIC
WILL BEAR

The early struggles of the Western farmers against exorbitant railroad freight rates,
which often took all the profit out of their
farming, form the central theme of *The
Octopus* (1901). In this episode from the
novel we get a clear picture of how a rise

in rates could bring ruin to a farmer, even when he thought he could escape the general fate by raising another crop. All through the book S. Behrman, whom you will shortly meet, personifies the cold, impersonal greed of the railroads that fattened off the struggling farmers.

THE ex-engineer [1] reached the post office in Bonneville toward eleven o'clock; but he did not at once present his notice of the arrival of his consignment at Ruggles's office. It entertained him to indulge in an hour's lounging about the streets. It was seldom he got into town, and when he did he permitted himself the luxury of enjoying his evident popularity. He met friends everywhere, in the post office, in the drugstore, in the barbershop, and around the courthouse. With each one he held a moment's conversation; almost invariably this ended in the same way:

"Come on 'n have a drink."

"Well, I don't care if I do."

And the friends proceeded to the Yosemite bar, pledging each other with punctilious ceremony. Dyke, however, was a strictly temperate man. His life on the engine had trained him well. Alcohol he never touched, drinking instead ginger ale, sarsaparilla and iron — soft drinks.

At the drugstore, which also kept a stock of miscellaneous stationery, his eye was caught by a "transparent slate," a child's toy, where upon a little pane of frosted glass one could trace with considerable elaboration outline figures of cows, plows, bunches of fruit, and even rural water mills that were printed on slips of paper underneath.

"Now, there's an idea, Jim," he observed to the boy behind the soda-water fountain; "I know a little tad that would just about jump out of her skin for that. Think I'll have to take it with me."

[1] ex-engineer: a character named Dyke, who had formerly worked for the railroad.

"How's Sidney getting along?" the other asked, while wrapping up the package.

Dyke's enthusiasm had made of his little girl a celebrity throughout Bonneville.

The ex-engineer promptly became voluble, assertive, doggedly emphatic.

"Smartest little tad in all Tulare County, and more fun! A regular whole show in herself."

"And the hops?" inquired the other.

"Bully," declared Dyke, with the good-natured man's readiness to talk of his private affairs to anyone who would listen. "Bully. I'm dead sure of a bonanza crop by now. The rain came *just* right. I actually don't know as I can store the crop in those barns I built, it's going to be so big. That foreman of mine was a daisy. Jim, I'm going to make money in that deal. After I've paid off the mortgage — you know I had to mortgage, yes, crop and homestead both, but I can pay it off and all the interest to boot, lovely — well, and as I was saying, after all expenses are paid off I'll clear big money, m' son. Yes, sir. I *knew* there was boodle in hops. You know the crop is contracted for already. Sure, the foreman managed that. He's a daisy. Chap in San Francisco will take it all and at the advanced price. I wanted to hang on, to see if it wouldn't go to six cents, but the foreman said, 'No, that's good enough.' So I signed. Ain't it bully, hey?"

"Then what'll you do?"

"Well, I don't know. I'll have a layoff for a month or so and take the little tad and Mother up and show 'em the city — 'Frisco — until it's time for the schools to open, and then we'll put Sid in the seminary at Marysville. Catch on?"

"I suppose you'll stay right by hops now?"

"Right you are, m' son. I know a good thing when I see it. There's plenty others going into hops next season. I set 'em the example. Wouldn't be surprised if it came to be a regular industry here-abouts. I'm planning ahead for next year already. I can let the foreman go, now that I've learned the game myself, and I think I'll buy a piece of land off Quien Sabe and get a bigger crop, and build a couple more barns, and, by George, in about five years' time I'll have things humming. I'm going to make *money*, Jim."

He emerged once more into the street and went up the block leisurely, plant-ing his feet squarely. He fancied that he could feel he was considered of more importance nowadays. He was no longer a subordinate, an employee. He was his own man, a proprietor, an owner of land, furthering a successful enterprise. No one had helped him; he had followed no one's lead. He had struck out unaided for himself, and his success was due solely to his own intelligence, industry, and foresight. He squared his great shoulders till the blue gingham of his jumper all but cracked. Of late, his great blond beard had grown and the work in the sun had made his face very red. Un-der the visor of his cap — relic of his engineering days — his blue eyes twin-kled with vast good nature. He felt that he had made a fine figure as he went by a group of young girls in lawns and muslins and garden hats on their way to the post office. He wondered if they looked after him, wondered if they had heard that he was in a fair way to be-come a rich man.

But the chronometer in the window of the jewelry store warned him that time was passing. He turned about and, cross-ing the street, took his way to Ruggles's office, which was the freight as well as the land office of the P. and S. W. Rail-road.

As he stood for a moment at the count-er in front of the wire partition, waiting for the clerk to make out the order for the freight agent at the depot, Dyke was surprised to see a familiar figure in con-ference with Ruggles himself, by a desk inside the railing.

The figure was that of a middle-aged man, fat, with a great stomach, which he stroked from time to time. As he turned about, addressing a remark to the clerk, Dyke recognized S. Behrman. The banker, railroad agent, and political ma-nipulator seemed to the ex-engineer's eyes to be more gross than ever. His smooth-shaven jowls stood out big and tremulous on either side of his face; the roll of fat on the nape of his neck, sprin-kled with sparse, stiff hairs, bulged out with great prominence. His great stom-ach, covered with a light brown linen vest, stamped with innumerable inter-locked horseshoes, protruded far in ad-vance, enormous, aggressive. He wore his inevitable round-topped hat of stiff brown straw, varnished so bright that it reflected the light of the office win-dows like a helmet; and even from where he stood Dyke could hear his loud breathing and the clink of the hollow links of his watch chain upon the vest buttons of imitation pearl, as his stom-ach rose and fell.

Dyke looked at him with attention. There was the enemy, the representative of the Trust with which Derrick's League was locking horns. The great struggle had begun to invest the com-batants with interest. Daily, almost hourly, Dyke was in touch with the ranchers, the wheat growers. He heard their denunciations, their growls of ex-asperation and defiance. Here was the other side — this placid fat man, with a stiff straw hat and linen vest, who never lost his temper, who smiled affably upon his enemies, giving them good advice, commiserating with them in one defeat after another, never ruffled, never ex-cited, sure of his power, conscious that back of him was the Machine, the co-lossal force, the inexhaustible coffers of a mighty organization, vomiting millions to the League's thousands.

The League was clamorous, ubiqui-tous, its objects known to every urchin on the streets; but the Trust was silent, its ways inscrutable — the public saw only results. It worked on in the dark, calm, disciplined, irresistible. Abruptly Dyke received the impression of the multitudinous ramifications of the colossus. Under his feet the ground seemed mined; down there below him in the dark the huge tentacles went silently twisting and advancing, spreading out in every direction, sapping the strength of all opposition, quiet, gradual, biding the time to reach up and out and grip with a sudden unleashing of gigantic strength.

"I'll be wanting some cars of you people before the summer is out," observed Dyke to the clerk as he folded up and put away the order that the other had handed him. He remembered perfectly well that he had arranged the matter of transporting his crop some months before, but his role of proprietor amused him and he liked to busy himself again and again with the details of his undertaking.

"I suppose," he added, "you'll be able to give 'em to me. There'll be a big wheat crop to move this year, and I don't want to be caught in any car famine."

"Oh, you'll get your cars," murmured the other.

"I'll be the means of bringing business your way," Dyke went on; "I've done so well with my hops that there are a lot of others going into the business next season. Suppose," he continued, struck with an idea, "suppose we went into some sort of pool, a sort of shippers' organization, could you give us special rates, cheaper rates — say a cent and a half?"

The other looked up.

"A cent and a half! Say *four* cents and a half and maybe I'll talk business with you."

"Four cents and a half," returned Dyke; "I don't see it. Why, the regular rate is only two cents."

"No, it isn't," answered the clerk, looking him gravely in the eye, "it's five cents."

"Well, there's where you are wrong, m' son," Dyke retorted genially. "You look it up. You'll find the freight on hops from Bonneville to 'Frisco is two cents a pound for carload lots. You told me that yourself last fall."

"That was last fall," observed the clerk. There was a silence. Dyke shot a glance of suspicion at the other. Then, reassured, he remarked, "You look it up. You'll see I'm right."

S. Behrman came forward and shook hands politely with the ex-engineer.

"Anything I can do for you, Mr. Dyke?"

Dyke explained. When he had done speaking, the clerk turned to S. Behrman and observed respectfully:

"Our regular rate on hops is five cents."

"Yes," answered S. Behrman, pausing to reflect; "yes, Mr. Dyke, that's right — five cents."

The clerk brought forward a folder of yellow paper and handed it to Dyke. It was inscribed at the top "Tariff Schedule No. 8," and underneath these words, in brackets, was a smaller inscription: "*Supersedes No. 7 of Aug. 1.*"

"See for yourself," said S. Behrman. He indicated an item under the head of "Miscellany."

"The following rates for carriage of hops in carload lots," read Dyke, "take effect June 1, and will remain in force until superseded by a later tariff. Those quoted beyond Stockton are subject to changes in tariff arrangements with carriers by water from that point."

In the list that was printed below, Dyke saw that the rate for hops between Bonneville or Guadalajara and San Francisco was five cents.

For a moment Dyke was confused. Then swiftly the matter became clear in his mind. The railroad had raised the freight on hops from two cents to five.

All his calculations as to a profit on his little investment he had based on a freight rate of two cents a pound. He was under contract to deliver his crop. He could not draw back. The new rate ate up every cent of his gains. He stood there ruined.

"Why, what do you mean?" he burst out. "You promised me a rate of two cents and I went ahead with my business with that understanding. What do you mean?"

S. Behrman and the clerk watched him from the other side of the counter.

"The rate is five cents," declared the clerk doggedly.

"Well, that ruins me!" shouted Dyke. "Do you understand? I won't make fifty cents. *Make!* Why, I will *owe* — I'll be — be — That ruins me, do you understand?"

The other raised a shoulder.

"We don't force you to ship. You can do as you like. The rate is five cents."

"Well — but — blast you, I'm under contract to deliver. What am I going to do? Why, you told me — you promised me a two-cent rate."

"I don't remember it," said the clerk. "I don't know anything about that. But I know this: I know that hops have gone up. I know the German crop was a failure and that the crop in New York wasn't worth the hauling. Hops have gone up to nearly a dollar. You don't suppose we don't know that, do you, Mr. Dyke?"

"What's the price of hops got to do with you?"

"It's got *this* to do with us," returned the other with a sudden aggressiveness, "that the freight rate has gone up to meet the price. We're not doing business for our own health. My orders are to raise your rate to five cents, and I think you are getting off easy."

Dyke stared in blank astonishment. For the moment the audacity of the affair was what most appealed to him. He forgot its personal application.

"Great Scott," he murmured, "Great Scott! What will you people do next? Look here. What's your basis of applying freight rates, anyhow?" he suddenly vociferated with furious sarcasm. "What's your rule? What are you guided by?"

But at the words S. Behrman, who had kept silent during the heat of the discussion, leaned abruptly forward. For the only time in his knowledge, Dyke saw his face inflamed with anger and with the enmity and contempt of all this farming element with whom he was contending.

"Yes, what's your rule? What's your basis?" demanded Dyke, turning swiftly to him.

S. Behrman emphasized each word of his reply with a tap of one forefinger on the counter before him:

"All — the traffic — will — bear."

The ex-engineer stepped back a pace, his fingers on the ledge of the counter, to steady himself. He felt himself grow pale; his heart became a mere leaden weight in his chest, inert, refusing to beat.

In a second the whole affair, in all its bearing, went speeding before the eye of his imagination like the rapid unrolling of a panorama. Every cent of his earnings was sunk in this hop business of his. More than that, he had borrowed money to carry it on, certain of success — borrowed of S. Behrman, offering his crop and his little home as security. Once he failed to meet his obligations, S. Behrman would foreclose. Not only would the railroad devour every morsel of his profits, but also it would take from him his home; at a blow he would be left penniless and without a home. What would then become of his mother — and what would become of the little tad? She, whom he had been planning to educate like a veritable lady. For all that year he had talked of his ambition for his little daughter to everyone he met. All Bonneville knew of it. What a mark for gibes he had made of himself: The workingman turned farmer! What a target for jeers — he who had fancied he could elude the railroad! He remembered he had once said the great trust had overlooked his little enterprise, disdaining to plunder such small fry. He should have known better than that. How had he ever imagined the road would permit him to make any money?

Anger was not in him yet; no rousing of the blind, white-hot wrath that leaps to the attack with prehensile fingers moved him. The blow merely crushed, staggered, confused.

He stepped aside to give place to a coatless man in a pink shirt, who entered, carrying in his hands an automatic door-closing apparatus.

"Where does this go?" inquired the man.

Dyke sat down for a moment on a seat that had been removed from a worn-out railway car to do duty in Ruggles's office. On the back of a yellow envelope he made some vague figures with a stump of blue pencil, multiplying, subtracting, perplexing himself with many errors.

S. Behrman, the clerk, and the man with the door-closing apparatus involved themselves in a long argument, gazing intently at the top panel of the door. The man who had come to fix the apparatus was unwilling to guarantee it, unless a sign was put on the outside of the door warning incomers that the door was self-closing. This sign would cost fifteen cents extra.

"But you didn't say anything about this when the thing was ordered," declared S. Behrman. "No, I won't pay it, my friend. It's an overcharge."

"You needn't think," observed the clerk, "that just because you are dealing with the railroad you are going to work us."

Genslinger came in, accompanied by Delaney. S. Behrman and the clerk, abruptly dismissing the man with the door-closing machine, put themselves behind the counter and engaged in conversation with these two. Genslinger introduced Delaney. The buster had a string of horses he was shipping southward. No doubt he had come to make arrangements with the railroad in the matter of stock cars. The conference of the four men was amicable in the extreme.

Dyke, studying the figures on the back of the envelope, came forward again. Absorbed only in his own distress, he ignored the editor and the cowpuncher.

"Say," he hazarded, "how about this? I make out —"

"We've told you what our rates are, Mr. Dyke," exclaimed the clerk angrily. "That's all the arrangement we will make. Take it or leave it." He turned again to Genslinger, giving the ex-engineer his back.

Dyke moved away and stood for a moment in the center of the room, staring at the figures on the envelope.

"I don't see," he muttered, "just what I'm going to do. No, I don't see what I'm going to do at all."

Ruggles came in, bringing with him two other men in whom Dyke recognized dummy buyers of the Los Muertos and Osterman ranchos. They brushed by him, jostling his elbow, and as he went out of the door he heard them exchange jovial greetings with Delaney, Genslinger, and S. Behrman.

Dyke went down the stairs to the street and proceeded onward aimlessly in the direction of the Yosemite House, fingering the yellow envelope and looking vacantly at the sidewalk.

There was a stoop to his massive shoulders. His great arms dangled loosely at his sides, the palms of his hands open.

As he went along, a certain feeling of shame touched him. Surely his predicament must be apparent to every passer-by. No doubt everyone recognized the unsuccessful man in the very way he slouched along. The young girls in lawns, muslins, and garden hats, returning from the post office, their hands full of letters, must surely see in him the type of the failure, the bankrupt.

Then brusquely his tardy rage flamed up. No, it was not his fault; he had made no mistake. His energy, industry, and foresight had been sound. He had been merely the object of a colossal trick, a sordid injustice; a victim of the insatiate greed of the monster, caught and choked by one of those millions of tentacles suddenly reaching up from below, from out the dark beneath his feet, coiling around his throat, throttling him, strangling him, sucking his blood. For a moment he thought of the courts, but instantly laughed at the idea. What court was immune from the power of the monster? Ah, the rage of helplessness, the fury of impotence! No help, no hope — ruined in a brief instant — he a veritable giant, built of great sinews, powerful, in the full tide of his manhood, having all his health, all his wits. How could he now face his home? How could he tell his mother of this catastrophe? And Sidney — the little tad; how could he explain to her this wretchedness — how soften her disappointment? How keep the tears from out her eyes — how keep alive her confidence in him — her faith in his resources?

Bitter, fierce, ominous, his wrath loomed up in his heart. His fists gripped tight together; his teeth clenched. Oh, for a moment to have his hand upon the throat of S. Behrman, wringing the breath from him, wrenching out the red life of him — staining the street with the blood sucked from the veins of the people!

To the first friend that he met, Dyke told the tale of the tragedy, and to the next, and to the next. The affair went from mouth to mouth, spreading with electrical swiftness, overpassing and running ahead of Dyke himself, so that

by the time he reached the lobby of the Yosemite House he found his story awaiting him. A group formed about him. In his immediate vicinity business for the instant was suspended. The group swelled. One after another of his friends added themselves to it. Magnus Derrick joined it, and Annixter.[1] Again and again Dyke recounted the matter, beginning with the time when he was discharged from the same corporation's service for refusing to accept an unfair wage. His voice quivered with exasperation; his heavy frame shook with rage; his eyes were injected, bloodshot; his face flamed vermilion, while his deep bass rumbled throughout the running comments of his auditors like the thunderous reverberation of diapason.

From all points of view the story was discussed by those who listened to him, now in the heat of excitement; now calmly, judicially. One verdict, however, prevailed. It was voiced by Annixter: "You're stuck. You can roar till you're black in the face, but you can't buck against the railroad. There's nothing to be done."

"You can shoot the ruffian; you can shoot S. Behrman," clamored one of the group. "Yes, sir, you can shoot him."

"Poor fool," commented Annixter, turning away.

Nothing to be done. No, there was nothing to be done — not one thing. Dyke, at last alone and driving his team out of the town, turned the business confusedly over in his mind from end to end. Advice, suggestion, even offers of financial aid had been showered upon him from all directions. Friends were not wanting who heatedly presented to his consideration all manner of ingenious plans, wonderful devices. They were worthless. The tentacle held fast. He was stuck.

[1] **Derrick ... Annixter:** men prominent in the league formed to fight the railroad rates, which Norris describes on page 738.

For Discussion of Norris

1. How does the author build up the impression of Dyke's optimism and good spirits in the early part of the narrative? What omen of trouble appears in the story before Dyke actually hears of the rate change?

2. For what purpose in his story did Norris bring in the incident about the door-closing gadget? about the bronco-

buster shipping his horses?

3. What passages refer to the title of the novel from which this selection was taken? Does the comparison strike you as being effective, considering the conditions depicted in this selection?

4. Do you agree with Annixter that there was nothing Dyke could do about his predicament? What is the present-day situation on freight rates — how are shippers protected from exorbitant rates?

Thomas
Bailey Aldrich
1836–1907

A STRUGGLE FOR LIFE

Aldrich is an old friend to those who have met him as Tom Bailey in the delightful pages of *The Story of a Bad Boy*. His famous book is still a favorite with boys everywhere.

Aldrich reminds us that not all the writers of his time made a decided shift to realism. Many writers went on publishing romantic and melodramatic tales. " A Struggle for Life " is such a tale, and it has the added attraction of a surprise ending, a device that Aldrich helped to popularize.

ONE morning last April, as I was passing through Boston Common, which lies pleasantly between my residence and my office, I met a gentleman lounging along The Mall. I am generally preoccupied when walking, and often thread my way through crowded streets without distinctly observing a single soul. But this man's face forced itself upon me, and a very singular face it was. His eyes were faded, and his hair, which he wore long, was flecked with gray. His hair and eyes, if I may say so, were seventy years old, the rest of him not thirty. The youthfulness of his figure, the elasticity of his gait, and the venerable appearance of his head were incongrui-

ties that drew more than one pair of curious eyes toward him. He was evidently an American — the New England cut of countenance is unmistakable — evidently a man who had seen something of the world; but strangely old and young.

Before reaching the Park Street gate, I had taken up the thread of thought which he had unconsciously broken; yet throughout the day this old young man, with his unwrinkled brow and silvered locks, glided in like a phantom between me and my duties.

The next morning I again encountered him on The Mall. He was resting lazily on the green rails, watching two little sloops in distress, which two ragged shipowners had consigned to the mimic perils of the Pond. The vessels lay becalmed in the middle of the ocean, displaying a tantalizing lack of sympathy with the frantic helplessness of the owners on shore. As the gentleman observed their dilemma, a light came into his faded eyes, then died out, leaving them drearier than before. I wondered if he, too, in his time, had sent out ships that drifted and drifted and never came to port; and if these poor toys were to him types of his own losses.

"I would like to know that man's story," I said, half aloud, halting in one of those winding paths which branch off from the quietness of the Pond, and end in the rush and tumult of Tremont Street.

"Would you?" replied a voice at my side. I turned and faced Mr. H——, a neighbor of mine, who laughed heartily at finding me talking to myself. "Well," he added, reflectively, "I can tell you this man's story; and if you will match the narrative with anything as curious, I shall be glad to hear it."

"You know him, then?"

"Yes and no. I happened to be in Paris when he was buried."

"Buried!"

"Well, strictly speaking, not buried; but something quite like it. If you've a spare half-hour," continued my interlocutor, "we'll sit on this bench, and I will tell you all I know of an affair that made some noise in Paris a couple of years ago. The gentleman himself, standing yonder, will serve as a sort of frontispiece to the romance — a full-page illustration, as it were."

The following pages contain the story that Mr. H—— related to me. While he was telling it, a gentle wind arose; the miniature sloops drifted feebly about the ocean; the wretched owners flew from point to point, as the deceptive breeze promised to waft the barks to either shore; the early robins trilled now and then from the newly fringed elms; and

the old young man leaned on the rail in the sunshine, wearily, little dreaming that two gossips were discussing his affairs within twenty yards of him.

Three people were sitting in a chamber whose one large window overlooked the Place Vendôme. M. Dorine, with his back half turned on the other two occupants of the apartment, was reading the *Moniteur*, pausing from time to time to wipe his glasses, and taking scrupulous pains not to glance toward the lounge at his right, on which were seated Mademoiselle Dorine and a young American gentleman, whose handsome face rather frankly told his position in the family. There was not a happier man in Paris that afternoon than Philip Wentworth. Life had become so delicious to him that he shrank from looking beyond today. What could the future add to his full heart? what might it not take away? In certain natures the deepest joy has always something of melancholy in it, a presentiment, a fleeting sadness, a feeling without a name. Wentworth was conscious of this subtle shadow that night, when he rose from the lounge and thoughtfully held Julie's hand to his lip for a moment before parting. A careless observer would not have thought him, as he was, the happiest man in Paris.

M. Dorine laid down his paper and came forward. "If the house," he said, "is such as M. Martin describes it, I advise you to close with him at once. I would accompany you, Philip, but the truth is, I am too sad at losing this little bird to assist you in selecting a cage for her. Remember, the last train for town leaves at five. Be sure not to miss it; for we have seats for M. Sardou's [1] new comedy tomorrow night. By tomorrow night," he added laughingly, "little Julie here will be an old lady — 'tis such an

---

[1] **M. Sardou** (sär·dōō'): Victorien Sardou (1831–1908), popular French dramatist. "M." before all these names stands for *Monsieur* (mĕ·syû'), meaning *Mr.*

age from now until then."

The next morning the train bore Philip to one of the loveliest spots within thirty miles of Paris. An hour's walk through green lanes brought him to M. Martin's estate. In a kind of dream the young man wandered from room to room, inspected the conservatory, the stables, the lawns, the strip of woodland through which a merry brook sang to itself continually; and, after dining with M. Martin, completed the purchase, and turned his steps toward the station, just in time to catch the express train.

As Paris stretched out before him, with its million lights twinkling in the early dusk, and its sharp spires here and there pricking the sky, it seemed to Philip as if years had elapsed since he left the city. On reaching Paris he drove to his hotel, where he found several letters lying on the table. He did not trouble himself even to glance at their superscriptions as he threw aside his traveling surtout for a more appropriate dress.

If, in his impatience to see Mademoiselle Dorine, the cars had appeared to walk, the fiacre which he had secured at the station appeared to creep. At last it turned into the Place Vendôme, and drew up before M. Dorine's residence. The door opened as Philip's foot touched the first step. The servant silently took his cloak and hat, with a special deference, Philip thought; but was he not now one of the family?

"M. Dorine," said the servant slowly, "is unable to see Monsieur at present. He wishes Monsieur to be shown up to the *salon*."

"Is Mademoiselle — "

"Yes, Monsieur."

"Alone?"

"Alone, Monsieur," repeated the man, looking curiously at Philip, who could scarcely repress an exclamation of pleasure.

It was the first time that such a privilege had been accorded him. His interviews with Julie had always taken place in the presence of M. Dorine, or some members of the household. A well-bred Parisian girl has but a formal acquaintance with her lover.

Philip did not linger on the staircase; his heart sang in his bosom as he flew up the steps, two at a time. Ah! this wine of air which one drinks at twenty, and seldom after! He hastened through the softly lighted hall, in which he detected the faint scent of her favorite flowers, and stealthily opened the door of the *salon*.

The room was darkened. Underneath the chandelier stood a slim black casket on trestles. A lighted candle, a crucifix, and some white flowers were on a table nearby. Julie Dorine was dead.

When M. Dorine heard the indescribable cry that rang through the silent house, he hurried from the library, and found Philip standing like a ghost in the middle of the chamber.

It was not until long afterward that Wentworth learned the details of the calamity that had befallen him. On the previous night Mademoiselle Dorine had retired to her room in seemingly perfect health. She dismissed her maid with a request to be awakened early the next morning. At the appointed hour the girl entered the chamber. Mademoiselle Dorine was sitting in an armchair, apparently asleep. The candle had burnt down to the socket; a book lay half open on the carpet at her feet. The girl started when she saw that the bed had not been occupied, and that her mistress still wore an evening dress. She rushed to Mademoiselle Dorine's side. It was not slumber. It was death.

Two messages were at once dispatched to Philip, one to the station at G——, the other to his hotel. The first missed him on the road, the second he had neglected to open. On his arrival at M. Dorine's house, the servant, under the supposition that Wentworth had been advised of Mademoiselle Dorine's death, broke the intelligence with awkward cruelty, by showing him directly to the *salon.*

Mademoiselle Dorine's wealth, her beauty, the suddenness of her death, and the romance that had in some way attached itself to her love for the young American, drew crowds to witness the final ceremonies which took place in the church in the Rue d'Aguesseau.[1] The body was to be laid in M. Dorine's tomb, in the cemetery of Montmartre.

This tomb requires a few words of description. First, there was a grating of filigrained iron; through this you looked into a small vestibule or hall, at the end of which was a massive door of oak opening upon a short flight of stone steps descending into the tomb. The vault was fifteen or twenty feet square, ingeniously ventilated from the ceiling, but unlighted. It contained two sarcophagi; the first held the remains of Madame Dorine, long since dead; the other was new, and bore on one side the letters J. D., in monogram, interwoven with fleurs-de-lis.

The funeral train stopped at the gate of the small garden that enclosed the place of burial, only the immediate relatives following the bearers into the tomb. A slender wax candle, such as is used in Catholic churches, burnt at the foot of the uncovered sarcophagus, casting a dim glow over the center of the apartment, and deepening the shadows which seemed to huddle together in the corners. By this flickering light the coffin was placed in its granite shell, the heavy slab laid over it reverently, and the oaken door revolved on its rusty hinges, shutting out the uncertain ray of sunshine that had ventured to peep in on the darkness.

M. Dorine, muffled in his cloak, threw himself on the back seat of the carriage, too abstracted in his grief to observe that he was the only occupant of the vehicle. There was the sound of wheels grating on the graveled avenue, and then all was silence again in the cemetery of Montmartre. At the main entrance the carriages parted company, dashing off into various streets at a pace that seemed to express a sense of relief. The band plays a dead march going to the grave, but *Fra Diavolo* [2] coming from it.

It is not with the retreating carriages that our interest lies. Nor yet wholly with the dead in her mysterious dream; but with Philip Wentworth.

The rattle of wheels had died out of the air when Philip opened his eyes, bewildered, like a man abruptly roused from slumber. He raised himself on one arm and stared into the surrounding blackness. Where was he? In a second the truth flashed upon him. He had been left in the tomb! While kneeling on the farther side of the stone box, perhaps he had fainted, and in the last solemn rites his absence had been unnoticed.

His first emotion was one of natural terror. But this passed as quickly as it came. Life had ceased to be so very precious to him; and if it were his fate to die at Julie's side, was not that the fulfillment of the desire which he had expressed to himself a hundred times that morning? What did it matter, a few years sooner or later? He must lay down the burden at last. Why not then? A pang of self-reproach followed the thought. Could he so lightly throw aside the love that had bent over his cradle? The sacred name of mother rose involuntarily to his lips. Was it not cowardly to yield up without a struggle the life which he should guard for her sake? Was it not his duty to the living and the dead to face the difficulties of his position, and overcome them if it were within human power?

With an organization as delicate as a woman's, he had that spirit which, however sluggish in repose, can leap with a kind of exultation to measure its strength with disaster. The vague fear of the su-

---

[1] Rue d'Aguesseau (rōō dà·gĕ·sō'): *Rue* means *street*.

[2] *Fra Diavolo* (frà dē·ä'vō·lō): an opera with gay, vivacious music.

pernatural, that would affect most men in a similar situation, found no room in his heart. He was simply shut in a chamber from which it was necessary that he should obtain release within a given period. That this chamber contained the body of the woman he loved, so far from adding to the terror of the case, was a circumstance from which he drew consolation. She was a beautiful white statue now. Her soul was far hence; and if that pure spirit could return, would it not be to shield him with her love? It was impossible that the place should not engender some thought of the kind. He did not put the thought entirely from him as he rose to his feet and stretched out his hands in the darkness; but his mind was too healthy and practical to indulge long in such speculations.

Philip chanced to have in his pocket a box of wax tapers which smokers use. After several ineffectual attempts, he succeeded in igniting one against the dank wall, and by its momentary glare perceived that the candle had been left in the tomb. This would serve him in examining the fastenings of the vault. If he could force the inner door by any means, and reach the grating, of which he had an indistinct recollection, he might hope to make himself heard. But the oaken door was immovable, as solid as the wall itself, into which it fitted airtight. Even if he had had the requisite tools, there were no fastenings to be removed; the hinges were set on the outside.

Having ascertained this, he replaced the candle on the floor, and leaned against the wall thoughtfully, watching the blue fan of flame that wavered to and fro, threatening to detach itself from the wick. "At all events," he thought, "the place is ventilated." Suddenly Philip sprang forward and extinguished the light. His existence depended on that candle!

He had read somewhere, in some account of shipwreck, how the survivors had lived for days upon a few candles

which one of the passengers had insanely thrown into the longboat. And here he had been burning away his very life.

By the transient illumination of one of the tapers, he looked at his watch. It had stopped at eleven — but at eleven that day or the preceding night? The funeral, he knew, had left the church at ten. How many hours had passed since then? Of what duration had been his swoon? Alas! It was no longer possible for him to measure those hours which crawl like snails to the wretched, and fly like swallows over the happy.

He picked up the candle, and seated himself on the stone steps. He was a sanguine man, this Wentworth, but, as he weighed the chances of escape, the prospect did not seem encouraging. Of course he would be missed. His disappearance under the circumstances would surely alarm his friends; they would instigate a search for him; but who would think of searching for a live man in the cemetery of Montmartre? The Prefect of Police would set a hundred intelligences at work to find him; the Seine might be dragged, *les misérables* [1] turned over at the deadhouse; a minute description of him would be in every detective's pocket and he — in M. Dorine's family tomb!

Yet, on the other hand, it was here he was last seen; from this point a keen detective would naturally work up the case. Then might not the undertaker return for the candlestick, probably not left by design? Or, again, might not M. Dorine send fresh wreaths of flowers, to take the place of those which now diffused a pungent, aromatic odor throughout the chamber? Ah! what unlikely chances! But if one of these things did not happen speedily, it had better never happen. How long could he keep life in himself?

With unaccelerated pulse, he quietly cut the half-burned candle into four equal parts. "Tonight," he meditated, "I will eat the first of these pieces; tomor-

[1] *les misérables* (lä mē·zả·rả'bl'): the unfortunates.

row, the second; tomorrow evening, the third; the next day, the fourth; and then — then I'll wait!"

He had taken no breakfast that morning, unless a cup of coffee can be called a breakfast. He had never been very hungry before. He was ravenously hungry now. But he postponed the meal as long as practicable. It must have been near midnight, according to his calculation, when he determined to try the first of his four singular repasts. The bit of white wax was tasteless; but it served its purpose.

His appetite for the time appeased, he found a new discomfort. The humidity of the walls, and the wind that crept through the unseen ventilator, chilled him to the bone. To keep walking was his only resource. A sort of drowsiness, too, occasionally came over him. It took all his will to fight it off. To sleep, he felt, was to die: and he had made up his mind to live.

Very strange fancies flitted through his head as he groped up and down the stone floor of the dungeon, feeling his way along the wall to avoid the sepulchers. Voices that had long been silent spoke words that had long been forgotten; faces he had known in childhood grew palpable against the dark. His whole life in detail was unrolled before him like a panorama; the changes of a year, with its burden of love and death, its sweets and its bitternesses, were epitomized in a single second. The desire to sleep had left him. But the keen hunger came again.

It must be near morning now, he mused; perhaps the sun is just gilding the pinnacles and domes of the city; or, maybe, a dull, drizzling rain is beating on Paris, sobbing on these mounds above me. Paris! It seems like a dream. Did I ever walk in its gay streets in the golden air? Oh, the delight and pain and passion of that sweet human life!

Philip became conscious that the gloom, the silence, and the cold were gradually conquering him. The feverish activity of his brain brought on a reaction. He grew lethargic, he sank down on the steps, and thought of nothing. His hand fell by chance on one of the pieces of candle; he grasped it and devoured it mechanically. This revived him. "How strange," he thought, "that I am not thirsty. Is it possible that the dampness of the walls, which I must inhale with every breath, has supplied the need of water? Not a drop has passed my lips for two days, and still I experience no thirst. That drowsiness, thank Heaven, has gone. I think I was never wide awake until this hour. It would be an anodyne like poison that could weigh down my eyelids. No doubt the dread of sleep has something to do with this."

The minutes were like hours. Now he walked as briskly as he dared up and down the tomb; now he rested against the door. More than once he was tempted to throw himself upon the stone coffin that held Julie, and make no further struggle for his life.

Only one piece of candle remained. He had eaten the third portion, not to satisfy hunger, but from a precautionary motive. He had taken it as a man takes some disagreeable drug upon the result of which hangs safety. The time was rapidly approaching when even this poor substitute for nourishment would be exhausted. He delayed that moment. He gave himself a long fast this time. The half inch of candle which he held in his hand was a sacred thing to him. It was his last defense against death.

At length, with such a sinking at heart as he had not known before, he raised it to his lips. Then he paused, then he hurled the fragment across the tomb, then the oaken door was flung open, and Philip, with dazzled eyes, saw M. Dorine's form sharply outlined against the blue sky.

When they led him out, half-blinded, into the broad daylight, M. Dorine noticed that Philip's hair, which a short time since was as black as a crow's wing, had actually turned gray in places. The man's eyes, too, had faded; the darkness had spoiled their luster.

" And how long was he really confined in the tomb? " I asked, as Mr. H—— concluded the story.

" *Just one hour and twenty minutes!* " replied Mr. H——, smiling blandly.

As he spoke, the little sloops, with their sails all blown out like white roses, came floating bravely into port, and Philip Wentworth lounged by us, wearily, in the pleasant April sunshine.

Mr. H——'s narrative made a deep impression on me. Here was a man who had undergone a strange ordeal. Here was a man whose sufferings were unique. His was no threadbare experience. Eighty minutes had seemed like two days to him! If he had really been immured two days in the tomb, the story, from my point of view, would have lost its tragic element.

After this it was but natural I should regard Mr. Wentworth with deepened interest. As I met him from day to day, passing through the Common with that same abstracted air, there was something in his loneliness which touched me. I wondered that I had not before read in his pale meditative face some such sad history as Mr. H—— had confided to me. I formed the resolution of speaking to him, though with what purpose was not very clear to my mind. One May morning we met at the intersection of two paths. He courteously halted to allow me the precedence.

" Mr. Wentworth — " I began.

He interrupted me.

" My name, sir," he said, in an offhand manner, " is Jones."

" Jo-Jo-Jones! " I gasped.

" Not Joe Jones," he returned coldly, " Frederick."

Mr. Jones, or whatever his name is, will never know, unless he reads these pages, why a man accosted him one morning as " Mr. Wentworth," and then abruptly rushed down the nearest path, and disappeared in the crowd.

The fact is, I had been duped by Mr. H——, who is a gentleman of literary proclivities, and has, it is whispered, become somewhat demented in brooding over the Great American Novel — not yet hatched. He had actually tried the effect of one of his chapters on me!

My hero, as I subsequently learned, is no hero at all, but a commonplace young man who has some connection with the building of that pretty granite bridge which will shortly span the crooked little lake in the Public Garden.

When I think of the cool ingenuity and readiness with which Mr. H—— built up his airy fabric on my credulity, I am half inclined to laugh; though I feel not slightly irritated at having been the unresisting victim of his Black Art.

For Discussion of Aldrich

1. What was the author's purpose in writing this story? How does the story differ in purpose and appeal from a realistic story like " Under the Lion's Paw "?

2. Judging from your own reactions, how successful was the double surprise? There are two tests of a good surprise ending: (*a*) You should not be able to see it coming; (*b*) You should be obliged to admit, on looking back over the story, that all the necessary clues are there.

3. Read the famous " Marjorie Daw " and others of Aldrich's surprise-ending stories. Are you always surprised? What story with a surprise ending can you find in Part One of this volume?

For Your Vocabulary

CONTEXT: Try to define the following words from the context of the story: *incongruities* (p. 743), *dilemma* (p. 744), *interlocutor* (p. 744), *subtle* (p. 744), *surtout* (p. 745), *fiacre* (p. 745), *sarcophagus* (p. 746), *lethargic* (p. 748), *anodyne* (p. 748).

Joel Chandler Harris
1848–1908

MR. FOX GOES
A–HUNTING, BUT MR.
RABBIT BAGS THE GAME

During his childhood in Georgia, Joel Chandler Harris made friends with the elderly Negroes who were no longer able to work in the cotton fields, learning their dialect, and drinking in their folk tales. At thirteen, he became a printer's apprentice to Joseph Addison Turner, a wealthy Georgian planter, who published the *Countryman*. The Turner plantation housed one hundred Negroes, whom Harris soon knew well. During his editorship of the Atlanta *Constitution* after the war, he began to write his Uncle Remus stories to fill the columns of his paper, creating a composite of the old Negroes he had known. These tales were simple but carefully written stories, with local color and dialect that preserved the materials of Negro folklore. Harris married a French-Canadian Catholic, and his family was reared in the Faith. Shortly before his death, he was received into the Church.

A TTER Brer Fox hear 'bout how Brer Rabbit done Brer Wolf," said Uncle Remus, scratching his head with the point of his awl, " he 'low, he did, dat he better not be so brash, en he sorter let Brer Rabbit 'lone. Bimeby dey 'gun ter git kinder familious wid wunner nudder like dey useter, en it got so Brer Fox'd call on Brer Rabbit, en dey'd set up en smoke der pipes, dey would, like no ha'sh feelin's 'd ever rested 'twixt um.

" Las', one day Brer Fox come 'long all rig out, en ax Brer Rabbit fer ter go huntin' wid 'im, but Brer Rabbit, he sorter feel lazy, en he tell Brer Fox dat he got some udder fish fer ter fry. He wuz gone all day, en he had a monstus streak er luck, Brer Fox did, en he bagged a sight er game. Bimeby, to'rds de shank er de evenin', Brer Rabbit sorter stretch hisse'f, he did, en 'low hit's mos' time fer Brer Fox fer ter git 'long home. Den Brer Rabbit, he went'n mounted a stump fer ter see ef he could year Brer Fox comin'. He ain't bin dar long, twel sho' nuff, yer come Brer Fox thoo de woods, singing like he wuz at a frolic. Brer Rabbit, he lipt down off'n de stump, he did, en lay down in de road en make like he dead. Brer Fox he come 'long, he did, en see Brer Rabbit layin' dar. He tu'n 'im over, he did, en 'zamine 'im, en say, sezee:

" ' Dish yer rabbit dead. He look like he bin dead long time. He dead, but he mighty fat. He de fattes' rabbit w'at I ever see, but he bin dead too long. I feard ter take 'im home,' sezee.

"Mr. Fox Goes a-Hunting, but Mr. Rabbit Bags the Game" from *Uncle Remus* by Joel Chandler Harris. Reprinted by permission of the Estate of Joel Chandler Harris.

" Brer Rabbit ain't sayin' nuthin'. Brer Fox, he sorter lick his chops, but he went on en lef' Brer Rabbit layin' in de road. Dreckly he wuz outer sight, Brer Rabbit, he jump up, he did, en run roun' thoo de woods en git before Brer Fox agin. Brer Fox, he come up, en dar lay Brer Rabbit, periently cole en stiff. Atter while he onslung his game-bag, en say ter hisse'f, sezee:

" ' Deze yer rabbits gwine ter was'e. I'll des 'bout leave my game yer, en I'll go back'n git dat udder rabbit,' sezee.

" En wid dat he drapt his game en loped back up de road atter de udder rabbit, en w'en he got outer sight, ole Brer Rabbit, he snatch up Brer Fox game en put out fer home. Nex' time he see Brer Fox, he holler out:

" ' What you kill de udder day, Brer Fox?' sezee.

" Den Brer Fox holler back:

" ' I kotch a han'ful er hard sense, Brer Rabbit,' sezee.

" Den ole Brer Rabbit, he laff, he did, en up en 'spon,' sezee:

" ' Ef I'd a know'd you wuz atter dat, Brer Fox, I'd a loant you some er mine,' sezee."

For Discussion of Harris

1. Why did Brer Rabbit refuse to hunt with Brer Fox? How did he outwit him?
2. What do you think the allegory means? In what ways does the dialect help create the humorous tone of this typical Uncle Remus story?

Reading on the Time of Change

LITERATURE OF THE PERIOD

Poetry

Dickinson, Emily, Complete Poems (Little, Brown, 1924)
Field, Eugene, " Jest 'fore Christmas," " Seein' Things," " Wynken, Blynken and Nod," " The Little Peach," " Casey's Table d'Hote," " Our Two Opinions "
Lanier, Sidney, Selected Poems, ed. by

Stark Young (Scribner, 1947): " Tampa Robins," " From the Flats," " Life and Song," " The Revenge of Hamish "
Markham, Edwin, " Lincoln, the Man of the People," " In a Cornfield," " To Young America," Quatrains
Riley, James Whitcomb, " Little Orphant Annie," " The Raggedy Man," " The Old Swimmin' Hole," " Out to Old Aunt Mary's," " The Old Man and Jim," " Knee-Deep in June," " My Ruthers," " A Life Lesson," " My Fiddle "
Whitman, Walt, Leaves of Grass: " O Captain! My Captain! " " Pioneers! O Pioneers! " " The Prairie Grass Dividing," " For You, O Democracy," " I Saw in Louisiana a Live-Oak Growing," " Salut au Monde! " " Out of the Cradle Endlessly Rocking," " Come Up from the Fields, Father," " As Toilsome I Wander'd Virginia's Woods "

Realistic Fiction

Bierce, Ambrose, " An Occurrence at Owl Creek Bridge," " A Horseman in the Sky "
Crane, Stephen, The Red Badge of Courage, " The Open Boat," " A Little Brown Dog," " The Bride Comes to Yellow Sky "
Garland, Hamlin, Main-Traveled Roads, Other Main-Traveled Roads
Howells, William Dean, The Rise of Silas Lapham, A Modern Instance
James, Henry, Roderick Hudson, The American, Daisy Miller, The Portrait of a Lady, The Bostonians
Norris, Frank, The Octopus, The Pit

ON INDIVIDUAL AUTHORS

DICKINSON. Benét, Laura, Come Slowly, Eden (Dodd, Mead, 1942)
FIELD. Nolan, Jeanette C., The Gay Poet (Messner, 1940)
LANIER. Mims, Edwin, Sidney Lanier (Houghton Mifflin, 1912)
NORRIS. Walker, Franklin, Frank Norris (Doubleday, 1932)
RILEY. Nolan, Jeanette C., James Whitcomb Riley, Hoosier Poet (Messner, 1941)
WHITMAN. Deutsch, Babette, Walt Whitman, Builder for America (Messner, 1941)

Design for modern education: The Memorial Building of the University of Miami, Coral Gables, Florida. (Devaney)

American Literature
in the Modern World

I N Part One of this book there are many selections from the best writers of our own day. At this point, now that you have watched the growth of American literature from its beginnings, we can talk about the modern age. Comments on the modern writers have been placed with their stories, poems, or articles, so that it will not be necessary to discuss the rich American literature of the twentieth century so fully as we have discussed the literature of the nineteenth century.

It would not be possible, in any case, to put these present-day writers and their books into the pattern of history, as we have put the writers and writings of previous centuries. History is like a map. You can make a fairly good rough map of a wooded country by standing on a mountain and looking down over the forest. But if you stand in the midst of the woods, you can see only the few trees around you. Writing history, too, is much easier if you can stand up on the mountain of time.

But it may help you to read and understand these modern American writings if we try to draw out the bare outlines of the twentieth-century pattern, as we see it now from the vantage point of mid-century. At least, we can show some of the ways in which modern books are related to the books and men that have gone before. And let us start by taking a look at the road our literature has traveled since those first American books were written more than three centuries ago.

Our American Heritage: The Seventeenth and Eighteenth Centuries

Americans have sought different kinds of freedom, and their quest has borne different names; but it has been the same quest. The first English-speaking Americans came in order to be free to own land, to profit from their hard work and skill, to be free to worship in public as they saw fit. They carved out a little strip of land between the angry sea and the mysterious forest. There wasn't much literature in that first century; there wasn't time. What was written, mostly, had to be written: letters, records, sermons. But in the process of winning that little strip of coast and fighting for those first freedoms, the settlers began to become Americans, rather than merely colonists. Soon they felt the need of political freedom — the right to make their own laws, elect their own governors, keep their tax money at home. In the fire of revolution and the heat of welding together a new nation, Americans produced their first writing that was as good as any nation had done in the same field — state papers like the Declaration of Independence, and political essays and orations that astonished the courts of Europe. In this time, too, appeared a man whom Europe took to be the first real American, no longer a colonial type but a new product of a new land, Benjamin Franklin.

The Nineteenth Century

Then in the nineteenth century these newly won freedoms flowered in the first great age of American literature, which we have called the Flowering of the East. Up and down the Atlantic coast appeared poets, novelists, and critics of a high order, concerned with cultural and artistic independence. Boston and New York became literary centers comparable to other world cities.

While the books were being written in the East, the frontier plunged westward, in search of elbow room and opportunity, the chance to start fresh and perhaps to get rich quick. On the frontier, as in the first coastal settlements, there was little time for literature, but out of the westward movement emerged certain national characteristics which all the world began to recognize as American. In the midst of the westward movement, Americans had to stop and fight a bloody war to decide certain old differences and to determine what kind of racial and political freedom should be applied to the new West. Out of that war came a leader who was a symbol of both the new West and the American nation, Abraham Lincoln. And out of the later frontier came Mark Twain, the most original and native of our writers up to that time.

The land filled up, and freedom of opportunity built a great industrial civilization across the continent. The frontier passed out of existence as a symbol of opportunity. Pessimism began to replace optimism, and the new spirit gave rise to a realistic tone in fiction and a strong current of social protest. Americans began to see that the frontier open to them was no longer a geographic one, that the freedom they wanted could be attained only by staking out claims on a social and scientific frontier. The questions before the people as the nineteenth century came to an end were how the great scientific advances of the last years could be made to serve man, and how the social and economic life of the nation could be made to bear out the promise of America's first three centuries. In other words, how could the individual best win freedom within the system?

Our American heritage is a tradition of adventurous pioneering on a frontier of freedom. " Freedom's a hard-bought thing," said Stephen Benét. The extraordinary thing is that Americans have always been willing to buy freedom, even with their blood.

That is the tradition in which our great books have been written.

Literature Early in the Twentieth Century

The twentieth century began in literature with a wave of protest against what our developing industrial civilization had done or had failed to do for us.

The beginning years of the century were the period of the muckrakers. Theodore Roosevelt used the name. He applied it to a group of writers, Lincoln Steffens and Upton Sinclair among them, who specialized in investigating and revealing corruption and social injustice. These men pointed out that, fine as our civilization was, it could still be greatly improved in many ways. They pointed to the injustices being done to immigrants, factory workers, and slum dwellers, and called on the country to pioneer on the frontier of social betterment as it had pioneered in setting up a government, settling a continent, and building an industrial system.

Modern Fiction: Realistic and Vigorous

In the last of the nineteenth century, Howells, Crane, and Norris, each in his own way, had been forerunners of modern realism. Fiction now became even more bitter and hard hitting. O. Henry wrote stories of the drabness of city life. Jack London wrote of men who preferred " the call of the wild " to civilization as it stood. Theodore Dreiser wrote of the strong but by no means wholly admirable financiers and tycoons who typified the age. The gay adventures, the happy endings so common in nineteenth-century fiction became less important in the early twentieth century. In their place fiction acquired a strength and vigor that was impressive.

Beginnings of Modern Poetry

In the early years of the century, also, able poets such as Edwin Arlington Robinson wrote unforgettable portraits of the men of the age, and voiced concern lest America be traveling a road that was leading it short of its great destiny. Robinson's early poems were a preview of the remarkable revival of American poetry that took place in the second and third decades of the century.

World War I and Its Aftermath

In 1917, the country responded to its President's call to "keep the world safe for democracy," and plunged with traditional American idealism into a great war. The aftermath was not good for idealism. Our statesmen did not find a suitable political climate in which to set up a League of Nations, and finally our Senate repudiated the League. The country as a whole, once its idealism was spent in war, reacted like a rubber ball bouncing back from a wall.

For the next ten years we forgot internationalism, stayed at home, reminded ourselves that Washington had warned us against "entangling alliances," and enjoyed an economic boom. Those were fabulous years, the 1920's. There was so much wealth in the land that it seemed as though the old frontier promise of a pot of gold might come true for every man.

Fiction of the Twenties

Yet writers warned us that we were building a house on sand. Sinclair Lewis tried to show us that by producing successful and solid men (like those he described in his novels *Babbitt* and *Main Street*) we were not necessarily producing great or happy men. Novelists like Willa Cather wrote about values and ideals that sometimes seemed alien to the 1920's — those of the American pioneers (as in her novel *My Ántonia*) and of the early Catholic fathers on this continent (as in her novel *Death Comes for the Archbishop*).

Some writers like Hemingway turned their backs on the country and went to Europe to write. Hemingway wrote hard, skillful stories, many of them dealing with what some critics called a "lost generation," meaning a generation that had somehow lost touch with the traditions and values in which it had developed.

New Flowering of Poetry and Drama

In the years just before World War I there were signs of a great flowering of poetry and drama. Just as American fiction was winning the attention and respect of readers the world over, some brilliant young writers were making American poetry and drama the foremost of the age. Robert Frost and Carl Sandburg published poetry that burst upon the public like a fireworks display. Robert Frost wrote in more "natural" language than earlier poets had, and to his own time he called attention to some of the beauties and homely virtues of the simple life which the times seemed to be neglecting.

In the 1920's, T. S. Eliot was the forerunner of a group of poets who belonged to the "lost generation" and despaired over the brutality of war; his complex, densely-packed style of poetry was argued over bitterly but it won the admiration of many later poets. Edna St. Vincent Millay, almost as personal in her lyrics as Emily Dickinson had been, wrote poems of great emotional power. Poets like Carl Sandburg and Vachel Lindsay spoke out boldly about common life and, following the example of Walt Whitman before them, put new force into poetry with their free verse.

In drama, too, American writing was exciting, daring, brilliant. Of all the types of literature, drama had been the least distinguished in America's growth; literally, no play of lasting value was produced in the first three centuries. Then came 1915, with Eugene O'Neill and the amateur group known as the Provincetown Players. Writing one-act plays for the most part, the Players at first startled and then won over audiences with their realistic, vigorous drama, and helped launch the "little theater" movement which enrolled amateur writers, players, and producers throughout the country. On Broadway during the twenties, playwright after playwright scored successes which established American drama as a great art. O'Neill analyzed personality in a penetrating fashion in plays like *Strange Interlude,* and he won a Nobel Prize. Thornton Wilder experimented with a stage bare of properties or sets, allowing the characters in a play like *Our Town* to stand out more clearly and familiarly as people.

The End of the Twenties

The 1920's rolled on — speakeasies, Lindbergh, political scandals, Coolidge, new fast automobiles, radio broadcasting, home-brew, people by the hundreds of thousands playing the stock market, prices up to the skies and salaries up with them, and the country so rich and prosperous and dizzy with power that it seemed as though nothing could stop it.

And then, in October, 1929, the bottom dropped out of the stock market. The country reeled like a flabby boxer hit in the stomach. It tried to rally, only to be knocked down again. It said there was nothing to worry about — while banks failed, farmers had their mortgages foreclosed, and city children stood in breadlines. Finally, it simply stood scared and bewildered while all the gingerbread castles of the 1920's crashed into little soggy crumbs.

The 1930's and America's Economic Trial

Then began the third distinct period in this century of ours. It was a period of economic and social thinking, and also a spiritual period, because America was trying to find its way back to the old ideals and goals from which it had turned. The reassuring voice of the President was heard on the radio — in fireside chats, he called them. "The only thing we have to fear is fear itself," he said. The common man, the ordinary

American, deserved a "new deal," he said. We argued about that new deal according to which party we belonged to, but we saw many steps taken along a path writers had talked about ever since the Western frontier closed, the path toward a new American homestead on the economic and scientific frontier.

A Literary Return to Examining America's Roots

It was a stirring time for writers. Many of those who had run away to Europe came back and discovered America all over again. Novelists like Willa Cather tried to show the opportunity and the hardship that America gave her immigrants and missionaries. Others like John Steinbeck tried to show what the depression meant to some of the people. Poets like Stephen Benét and Archibald MacLeish went back into our history and tried to interpret the American dream, the American way, so that the country might get back to it. Dramatists like Thornton Wilder wrote about American life in prose that was almost poetry. A group of talented new poets and story writers arose. One of the most somber and questioning was William Faulkner, who was to win a Nobel Prize in 1950. Two others were Jesse Stuart and William Saroyan, whose work is remarkable for its faith in people. Both of these writers can be regional (Saroyan's region is California, Stuart's is Kentucky) without being self-conscious, as some local colorists were.

World War II and Its Aftermath

As the third decade ended, war drums beat across the world again. The United States was drawn into the conflict, slowly, inevitably. We who had said in the twenties that we would never again fight outside our hemisphere sent our

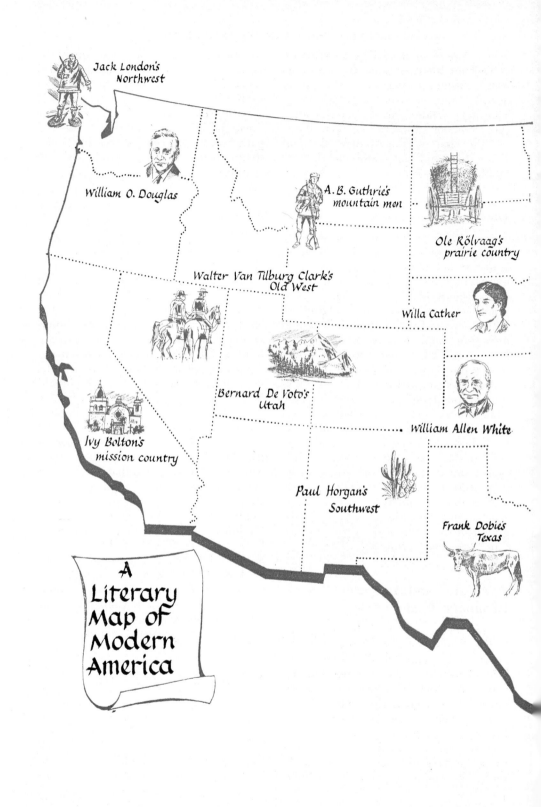

Jack London's Northwest

William O. Douglas

A. B. Guthrie's mountain men

Ole Rölvaag's prairie country

Walter Van Tilburg Clark's Old West

Willa Cather

Bernard De Voto's Utah

William Allen White

Ivy Bolton's mission country

Paul Horgan's Southwest

Frank Dobie's Texas

A Literary Map of Modern America

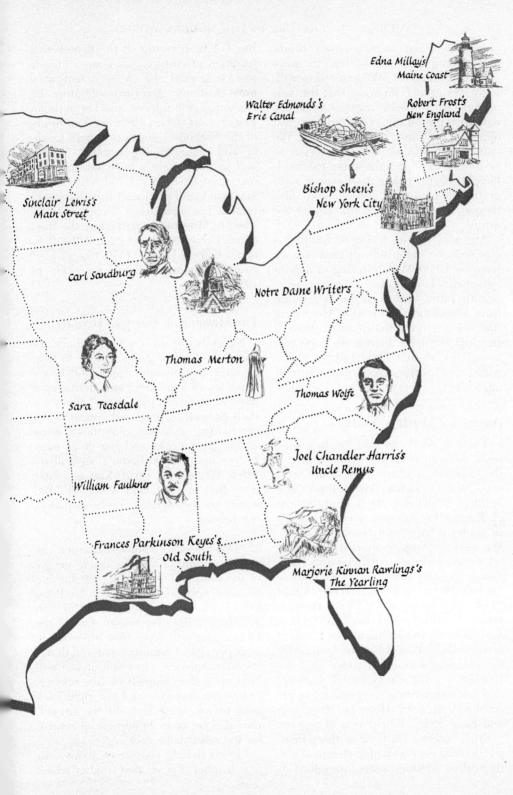

Edna Millay's
Maine Coast

Walter Edmonds's
Erie Canal

Robert Frost's
New England

Sinclair Lewis's
Main Street

Bishop Sheen's
New York City

Carl Sandburg

Notre Dame Writers

Thomas Merton

Sara Teasdale

Thomas Wolfe

Joel Chandler Harris's
Uncle Remus

William Faulkner

Frances Parkinson Keyes's
Old South

Marjorie Kinnan Rawlings's
The Yearling

young men, our airplanes, our bright and shining materials of war to every corner of the globe. We entered unwillingly, yet grimly, knowing that this was a " fight for freedom " against aggressor nations representing everything we had opposed for three hundred years. We won a victory that was too solemn to be glorious in any light sense, too hard-bought to be celebrated except with gratitude to two hundred and fifty thousand dead and with prayers for the future.

And now we are trying to conquer a new frontier, more difficult than any we have yet faced. We are trying to uphold our way of life, our American way, against bitter and powerful opposition from anti-democratic forces. More than that, we are trying to extend the kind of freedom we have known as a people, to nations, so that the countries of the world can live together without fear of aggression.

American Writers Today

There is no doubt that we have had some distinguished American writing in the twentieth century. Five of our writers — Sinclair Lewis, Pearl Buck, and William Faulkner in the field of the novel, Eugene O'Neill in drama, T. S. Eliot in poetry — have won the Nobel Prize. We have a group of short-story writers who may well rank with Poe and Hawthorne. Among them are J. F. Powers, Eudora Welty, Jessamyn West, Albert Eisele, Jean Stafford, and Paul Horgan. Helen C. White and her sister Olive have contributed brilliantly to the field of accurate historical fiction. And in this age of mass communication we have developed to a high level a comparatively new form of writing — reportage, as exemplified in John Hersey's *Hiroshima* and Ernie Pyle's World War II reports.

From modern Catholic authors there has been an ever-widening stream of distinguished writing. Sister Mariella Ga-

ble, O.S.B., carrying on the Benedictine tradition of culture, has done a unique service toward the development of a great Catholic American literature by her unflagging interest and her anthologies of short stories. Professor Leo Brady of the Catholic University is both teacher and prize-winning novelist. Walter and Jean Kerr are a husband and wife team that have taught and written drama, acted, and produced Broadway successes. The Blackfriars Guild, a Little Theatre Movement sparked by the Reverend Urban Nagle, O.P., and the Reverend Gilbert Hartke, O.P., has wielded steady influence since its inception in 1937.

The Meaning of America's Heritage

Never before in our history have we had more need of great writers, to help us see our problems clearly and to remind us of our American heritage of freedom. For in these critical times we shall do well to ponder the meaning of our heritage as it has come down to us in our great books and our great men. No one has put that better than William Allen White, the great Kansas editor who died in 1944, and whose life and words are themselves a precious part of our heritage:

" Don't bemoan your lost frontier," he said in a radio talk to the young people of the country. " It is even now flashing on your horizon. A gorgeous land lies before you, fair and more beautiful than man before has ever known. Out of the laboratories will come new processes to multiply almost infinitely material things for your America — but only if you will hold open the channels of free science, unfettered thought, and the right of a man to use his talents to the utmost, provided he gives honest social returns for the rewards he takes.

" Don't delude yourselves about your new frontier. For on that frontier which will rise over the laboratories you will find the same struggle, the same hardships, the same inequities that your forefathers have found on every frontier since the beginning of time. But don't let that discourage you.

"Finally, remember this: If you hang your horse thieves, if you jail your pirates of finance, and if you, indeed, make your new world worth while, it will be worth while not because of the material richness that the laboratories will bring you. All the regal wealth of this continent was here for countless centuries, before our English-speaking race came to develop the land. But they made it a noble civilization, not because of the fertile soil, the abundant mines, the illimitable forests, but because they, your forebears, transmuted into a livable approximate to a just society the physical blessings of nature — through the social forces that rise out of the humble virtues of man's heart: duty, tolerance, faith, and love. The American pioneers — your forefathers — institutionalized in American government, and somewhat in commerce, and certainly in their way of living, a neighborly consideration of the rights of others. They dedicated the products of our soil, the output of our mines, the wealth of our forests, to the establishment of a government of the people, by the people, and for the people, that the people may not perish from the earth.

"In closing let me say that your heritage is not in these great lovely cities, not this wide and fertile land, not the mountains full of undreamed-of riches. These you may find in other continents.

"What we bequeath to you that is precious are the few simple virtues which have stood us in good stead in the struggle of our generation. We leave you our enthusiasm, our diligence, our zeal for a better world, that were the lodestars of our fathers. As our legatees we assign you our tolerance; our patience; our kindness; our faith, hope, and love — which make for the self-respect of man. These qualities of heart and mind grow out of a conviction that the democratic philosophy as a mode of thinking will lead mankind into a nobler way of life."

General Reference Books on American Literature

Cambridge History of American Literature, ed. by William P. Trent and others, 4 vols. (Macmillan, 1931)

Cowie, Alexander, The Rise of the American Novel (American Book, 1948)

Gardiner, Harold, S.J., Fifty Years of the American Novel (Scribner, 1951)

Gregory, Horace, and Marya Zaturenska, A History of American Poetry, 1900–1940 (Harcourt, Brace, 1946)

Hart, James D., Oxford Companion to American Literature, 2nd ed. (Oxford, 1948)

Millett, Fred B., Contemporary American Authors (Harcourt, Brace, 1940)

Mott, Frank Luther, Golden Multitudes: The Story of Best Sellers in the United States (Macmillan, 1947)

Parrington, V. L., Main Currents in American Thought (Harcourt, Brace, 1939)

Pattee, F. L., The New American Literature, 1890–1930 (Century, 1930)

Pattee, F. L., First Century of American Literature, 1770–1870 (Appleton, 1935)

Perry, Bliss, The American Spirit in Literature (Yale University Press, 1918)

Quinn, Arthur Hobson, ed., The Literature of the American People, An Historical and Critical Survey (Appleton, 1951)

Spiller, Robert E., and others, eds., Literary History of the United States, 3 vols. (Macmillan, 1948)

A Chronology of American History and Literature

THE COLONIAL TIME   1607–1775

Jamestown settled, 1607

First representative assembly in America, 1619

Introduction of Negro slavery in America, 1619

Plymouth settled, 1620

Maryland founded, 1634

Harvard College founded, 1636

First Navigation Act, 1660

First newspaper, 1690

French and Indian Wars, 1754–1763

John Smith's *A True Relation of Virginia,* 1608

Jesuit Relations, 1611–1716

The Bay Psalm Book, 1640

Bradford's *Plymouth Plantation,* 1651

The New England Primer, 1688

Edward Taylor, 1646?–1729

Cotton Mather, 1663–1728

Sarah Kemble Knight, 1666–1727

William Byrd, 1674–1744

Jonathan Edwards, 1703–1758

THE MAKING OF A NATION   1775–1800

Revolution, 1775–1781

Land Ordinance for survey and sale of public lands in Northwest, 1785

Steamboat, 1787

Ratification of Constitution, 1788

First American factory, 1790

First census, 1790

Bill of Rights, 1791

Cotton gin, 1793

War with France on sea, 1798–1800

Patrick Henry's speech, 1775

Declaration of Independence, 1776

Federalist Papers, 1787

Benjamin Franklin, 1706–1790

George Washington, 1732–1799

Thomas Paine, 1737–1809

Charles Carroll, 1737–1832

Thomas Jefferson, 1743–1826

Philip Freneau, 1752–1832

Alexander Hamilton, 1757–1804

THE FLOWERING OF THE EAST   1800–1880

Slave trade prohibited, 1808

War with England, 1812–1815

Key wrote "The Star-Spangled Banner," 1814

Washington Irving, 1783–1859

James Fenimore Cooper, 1789–1851

William Cullen Bryant, 1794–1878

Ralph Waldo Emerson, 1803–1882

Missouri Compromise, 1820

Monroe Doctrine, 1823

Erie Canal completed, 1825

First railroad, 1830

McCormick reaper, 1831

Discovery of process for vulcanizing rubber, 1839

Independent Treasury established, 1840

Atlantic cable, 1858

Telephone invented, 1876

Electric light, 1879

Nathaniel Hawthorne, 1804–1864

William Gilmore Simms, 1806–1870

Henry Wadsworth Longfellow, 1807–1882

John Greenleaf Whittier, 1807–1892

Oliver Wendell Holmes, 1809–1894

Edgar Allan Poe, 1809–1849

Henry David Thoreau, 1817–1862

James Russell Lowell, 1819–1891

Herman Melville, 1819–1891

Francis Parkman, 1823–1893

Louisa May Alcott, 1832–1888

THE WESTWARD MOVEMENT 1800–1880

Louisiana Purchase, 1803

Lewis and Clark expedition, 1804–1806

Florida bought, 1819

Texas annexation, 1845

England concedes Oregon to U.S., 1846

Mexican War, Southwest added, 1848

Gold rush to California, 1849

War between the States, 1861–1865

Emancipation Proclamation, 1863

Alaska bought, 1867

First railroad to Pacific completed, 1869

Pierre de Smet, 1801–1873

Robert E. Lee, 1807–1870

Abraham Lincoln, 1809–1865

Richard Henry Dana, Jr., 1815–1882

Henry Timrod, 1828–1867

Artemus Ward, 1834–1867

Mark Twain, 1835–1910

Bret Harte, 1836–1902

Joaquin Miller, 1839–1913

George Washington Cable, 1844–1925

Lafcadio Hearn, 1850–1904

TIME OF CHANGE 1880–1920

Sherman Antitrust Law, 1890

First American automobile, 1892

Motion picture, 1894

Invention of wireless, 1895

Spanish-American War, 1898

First airplane flight by Wright brothers, 1903

Opening of Panama Canal, 1914

U.S. Proclamation of Neutrality in World War I, 1914

U.S. in World War I, 1917–1918

Walt Whitman, 1819–1892

Emily Dickinson, 1830–1886

Thomas Bailey Aldrich, 1836–1907

William Dean Howells, 1837–1920

Sidney Lanier, 1842–1881

Henry James, 1843–1916

John Bannister Tabb, 1845–1909

Joel Chandler Harris, 1848–1908

James Whitcomb Riley, 1849–1916

Hamlin Garland, 1860–1940

Frank Norris, 1870–1902

Stephen Crane, 1871–1900

THE MODERN AGE 1920–1950's

League of Nations organized, 1920

First radio broadcasting station, 1920

Stock-market crash, 1929

New Deal administration, 1933

E. A. Robinson, 1869–1935

Amy Lowell, 1874–1925

Robert Frost, 1875–

Jack London, 1876–1916

Social Security Act, 1935
Neutrality Act, 1939
Lend-Lease Act, 1941
Atlantic Charter, 1941
U.S. in World War II, 1941–1945
Atomic bomb revealed, 1945
United Nations organized, 1945
European Recovery Program begins, 1948
Atlantic Pact signed, 1949
European Defense Program (SHAPE) organized, 1950
United Nations forces in Korea, 1950
Nationwide television coverage, 1951
Japanese peace treaty signed, 1951

Carl Sandburg, 1878–
Sinclair Lewis, 1885–1951
T. S. Eliot, 1888–
Eugene O'Neill, 1888–
Edna St. Vincent Millay, 1892–1950
Fulton Oursler, 1893–1952
Thornton Wilder, 1897–
William Faulkner, 1897–
Albert Eisele, 1897–1951
Ernest Hemingway, 1898–
E. B. White, 1899–
John Steinbeck, 1902–
Paul Horgan, 1903–
Thomas Merton (Father Louis, O.C.S.O.) 1915–
James Farl Powers, 1917–

About the Editing of This Book

Perhaps more than any other textbook, *Adventures in American Literature* has helped to establish the content and organization of courses in American literature in high schools the country over.

Years of experimenting and experience have shown that the basic organization of the book, which is retained in this edition, is approved by most teachers. The division into Part One, Modern American Literature (twentieth century), and Part Two, The Growth of American Literature (seventeenth through nineteenth centuries), provides for utmost flexibility. Those teachers who prefer a strictly chronological approach may begin with Part Two and complete their course with Part One. The selections and editorial matter are designed to accommodate this arrangement. Those teachers who wish to begin with contemporary writing can begin with Part One. The last section of Part Two, called American Literature in the Modern World, relates earlier literature to contemporary writing, and serves as a bridge between the two main divisions. In the preparation of the Cardinal Newman Edition, the editors have combined a representative selection of Catholic writings of the American past with modern literature, presenting contemporary subjects and ideas that vitally affect the moral and intellectual growth of young people.

In their work on the Cardinal Newman Edition of *Adventures in American Literature*, the editors have tried to apply their own teaching experience at this grade level, as one measure of judging the appropriateness of selections and study materials. They have been fortunate to have the advice of Sister M. Patricia, C.S.J., Diocesan High School Supervisor, Cleveland, Ohio, who read the manuscript, and Brother John Baptist Titzer, C.S.C., School Supervisor, Brothers of the Holy Cross, Notre Dame, Indiana, who read the galleys of this edition. Their assistance is gratefully acknowledged.

AUTHOR AND SELECTION INTRODUCTIONS. In Part Two, the author biographies are given as part of the general literary history, on the assumption that the story of traditional American literature is best told through the lives of its writers. Preceding the selections in Part Two are short introductions whose main function is to provide pre-reading helps for the student. In Part One the author's biography and reading helps are combined in a single introduction to a selection.

STUDY AIDS AND READING LISTS. As in previous editions, the study questions are designed to (1) test the student's comprehension, (2) help him to relate his own experiences and thoughts to those found in his reading, (3) suggest activities and projects that will bring into use all language skills, (4) encourage him to extend his understanding of the selection to other writing and to related fields of music, art, architecture. The illustrations throughout, and especially the handicraft and architecture pictures in Part Two, largely serve to correlate literature with other arts.

VOCABULARY PROGRAM. The vocabulary program of the previous edition has been extended and broadened. Relatively less attention is now given to technical aspects of word building (base-words, prefixes, suffixes) and relatively more to interesting questions of word distinction, definition from context, emotional effects of words, figurative language, and word origins.

FOOTNOTES AND GLOSSARY. Footnotes are provided for foreign words and phrases as well as for archaic, dialectal, or difficult English usages. The glossary at the end of the book includes multiple definitions for those words that have more than one meaning in the text, and this feature, together with the pronunciation scale, makes the glossary directly usable as a dictionary.

The pronunciation system of diacritical marks used throughout the book, both in footnotes and glossary, is based on Webster's New Collegiate Dictionary, 5th ed.

Glossary

Words which have been introduced and discussed in the various *For Your Vocabulary* sections throughout the text are included in this glossary. For definitions and information about these words refer to the specific sections indicated by the page numbers.

A

abased (*à*·bāst′). Lowered; degraded.
abate (*à*·bāt′). To reduce.
abet (*à*·bĕt′). To encourage or support.
abhor (ăb·hôr′). To regard with horror.
abject (ăb′jĕkt). Cast down in spirit.
aboriginal (ăb′ŏ·rĭj′ĭ·năl). Native; original; first.
absolute (ăb′sŏ·lūt). Free from limit or restriction.
abysm (*à*·bĭz″m). A bottomless gulf or space.
abyss (*à*·bĭs′). Any deep immeasurable space or chasm.
academician (*à*·kăd′ĕ·mĭsh′ăn). A person devoted to the study of arts and sciences.
acrid (ăk′rĭd). *See page 196.*
adduce (*ă*·dūs′). To offer as an argument.
adversity (ăd·vûr′sĭ·tĭ). Hardship; ill fortune.
advert (ăd·vûrt′). To turn the mind or attention.
aeolian (ē·ō′lĭ·ăn) **harp.** A box fitted with strings tuned in unison, on which the wind produces musical tones.
affable (ăf′*à*·b'l). Courteous; pleasant.
affect (ă·fĕkt′). *See page 458.*
affinity (*ă*·fĭn′ĭ·tĭ). 1. Relationship. 2. Attraction; mutual liking.
affirmation (ăf′ēr·mā′shŭn). 1. Positive statement of something as true; assertion. 2. Confirmation; ratification.
affluence (ăf′lū·ĕns). Abundance of property.
agility (*à*·jĭl′ĭ·tĭ). Quickness in moving.
ague (ā′gū). A chill; a state of shaking, as with cold.
albeit (ôl·bē′ĭt). Although.
allegation (ăl′ĕ·gā′shŭn). A statement made positively but without proof.
allegory (ăl′ĕ·gō′rĭ). A prolonged metaphor in which a series of actions are symbolic of other actions.
allusion (*ă*·lū′zhŭn). 1. An implied reference; a hint. 2. A reference to something generally familiar.
alpaca (ăl·păk′*à*). 1. A kind of llama with fine, wooly hair, domesticated in Peru.

2. Wool of the alpaca, or a thin cloth made from it.
amain (*à*·mān′). At full speed.
ambrosia (ăm·brō′zhĭ·*à*). 1. In Greek and Roman mythology, the food of the gods. 2. Anything exquisitely gratifying in taste or smell.
amenities (*à*·mĕn′ĭ·tĭz). *See page 18.*
amicable (ăm′ĭ·k*à*·b'l). Peaceable; friendly.
amulet (ăm′û·lĕt). An ornament worn as a charm.
animate (ăn′ĭ·māt). 1. To make alive. 2. To give spirit to; to stimulate.
anomaly (*à*·nŏm′*à*·lĭ). Deviation from the common rule; irregularity.
anon (*à*·nŏn′). Soon.
anonymity (ăn′ŏ·nĭm′ĭ·tĭ). State of having no name.
anticipate (ăn·tĭs′ĭ·pāt). 1. To foresee. 2. To use or introduce ahead of time.
antipathy (ăn·tĭp′*à*·thĭ). Dislike; antagonism.
antithesis (ăn·tĭth′ĕ·sĭs). The direct opposite.
anvil (ăn′vĭl). 1. An iron block on which metal is shaped by hammering. 2. Anything resembling an anvil in shape or use.
apathy (ăp′*à*·thĭ). Indifference to what appeals to feelings or interest.
apex (ā′pĕks). The highest point.
apparition (ăp′*à*·rĭsh′ŭn). Ghost, phantom.
appease (ă·pēz′). 1. To soothe; calm. 2. To satisfy by making concessions or granting demands, often signifying a sacrifice of principle to avoid aggression.
appellation (ăp′ĕ·lā′shŭn). *See page 466.*
append (ă·pĕnd′). To attach as an accessory or supplement.
apprehension (ăp′rē·hĕn′shŭn). Distrust or fear of future evil.
approximate (ă·prŏk′sĭ·mĭt). An approach to a correct estimate; an approximation.
aquatic (*à*·kwăt′ĭk). 1. Living on or in water. 2. Performed on water.
arabesque (ăr·*à*·bĕsk′). A fanciful ornament.
arduous (är′dū·ŭs). Difficult; laborious.
arid (ăr′ĭd). 1. Dry; barren. 2. Lacking in interest.

ā pe, chảotic, bâre, ăt, *à*ttend, ärt, flảsk, *á*top; ēke, mẹrely, ĕlect, ĕcho, prudĕnt, doẽr; ītem, ĭnn, rarĭty; ōde, ŏpaque, fôr, dŏt, lŏft, cŏnfide; so͞on, to͞ok; sour, toil; tūbe, ūnique, tûrn, sŭp, ŭntil.

arraign (ă·rān′). **1.** To call a prisoner before a court. **2.** To accuse.

arras (ăr′ăs). Tapestry.

articulate (är·tĭk′ū·lāt). **1.** Able to speak clearly. **2.** Clear; separate; distinct.

artifice (är′tĭ·fĭs). A trick.

askance (à·skăns′). Sideways; hence, with disdain, envy, or distrust.

assay (ă·sā′). Analysis of an ore or drug.

assiduously (ă·sĭd′ū·ŭs·lĭ). With care and close attention.

assimilate (ă·sĭm′ĭ·lāt). **1.** To make alike. **2.** To appropriate and make part of itself; to absorb.

assonance (ăs′ō·năns). Resemblance of sound in words or syllables.

assurance (ă·shōōr′ăns). **1.** A pledge. **2.** Confidence; self-reliance. **3.** State of being sure; certainty.

astrakhan (ăs′trà·kăn). The long curled fur of a special breed of Russian lambs.

atoll (ăt′ŏl). A coral island or islands consisting of a belt of coral reef surrounding a central lagoon.

attaché (ăt′à·shā′). A member of a diplomatic staff.

audacity (ô·dăs′ĭ·tĭ). Daring; boldness.

aura (ô′rà). A distinctive atmosphere surrounding a person or thing.

auroral (ô·rō′răl). Pertaining to the dawn; rosy; radiant.

austere (ôs·tēr′). **1.** Harsh; bitter. **2.** Severely simple.

avalanche (ăv′à·lánch). Landslide.

avarice (ăv′à·rĭs). Greediness after wealth.

aversion (à·vûr′zhŭn). Dislike.

avidity (à·vĭd′ĭ·tĭ). Extreme greediness.

avocation (ăv′ō·kā′shŭn). A hobby.

B

bagatelle (băg′à·tĕl′). A trifle.

baneful (bān′fŏŏl). *See page 466.*

banter (băn′tẽr). **1.** To ridicule good-naturedly. **2.** Light ridicule; chaff.

barouche (bà·rōōsh′). A four-wheeled carriage.

beguiler (bē·gīl′ẽr). Deluder; deceiver.

beleaguered (bē·lē′gẽrd). Surrounded with an army.

belfry (bĕl′frĭ). A tower, usually one that holds a bell.

bellicose (bĕl′ĭ·kōs). *See page 670.*

belly (bĕl′ĭ). **1.** Abdomen. **2.** To swell or bulge out.

beneficent (bē·nĕf′ĭ·sĕnt). Doing or producing good.

beneficiary (bĕn′ē·fĭsh′ĭ·ẽr′ĭ). *See page 566.*

benevolence (bē·nĕv′ō·lĕns). *See page 566.*

benign (bē·nīn′). *See page 566.*

bilge (bĭlj). Foul water that collects in the bottom of a boat.

billow (bĭl′ō). **1.** A wave or a rolling mass like a wave. **2.** To rise or swell.

bivouac (bĭv′ŏŏ·ăk). To encamp without tents or housing.

bizarre (bĭ·zär′). Odd or eccentric in style.

blatant (blā′tănt). Brawling; noisy.

blithe (blīth). Merry; cheerful; lighthearted.

bonanza (bō·năn′zà). Anything exceptionally rich, yielding a large return in money.

boodle (bōō′d'l). **1.** A collection of persons. **2.** Bribe money; graft.

boreal (bō′rē·ăl). Northern.

boudoir (bōō′dwär). A small private room, especially one belonging to a lady.

bravo (brä′vō). **1.** Well done. **2.** A desperado; a hired assassin.

breeches (brĭch′ĕz). A garment covering the hips and thighs, worn in the eighteenth century.

brief (brēf). A concise statement of a client's case.

broadside (brôd′sīd′). A sheet of paper, especially of large size, printed on one side only.

brocade (brō·kād′). A rich fabric with a raised design, woven usually of silk, silver, or gold.

browse (brouz). **1.** To graze. **2.** Tender shoots, twigs, and leaves fit for food for cattle.

brusque (brŭsk). Abrupt; short in manner.

buffet (bŭf′ĕt). A blow as with a hand; a slap.

burgeoning (bûr′jŭn·ĭng). Sending forth buds; sprouting.

burlesque (bûr·lĕsk′). A mocking imitation.

butte (būt). An isolated hill or small mountain with steep sides.

buxom (bŭk′sŭm). Having health, vigor, and pleasing appearance.

C

cabal (kà·băl′). A number of persons united in some secret design.

cache (kăsh). **1.** A hiding place for stores that are to be recovered later. **2.** To store supplies; to hide.

cacophony (kă·kŏf′ō·nĭ). Harsh or discordant sound.

cadaver (kà·dăv′ẽr). A dead body.

cadence (kā′dĕns). **1.** Rhythm. **2.** A fall of the voice in utterance.

calked (kôk′d). Fitted with a pointed piece of metal projecting downward, to prevent slipping.

calliope (kà·lī′ō·pē). A musical instrument made of whistles operated by keys.

Calvary (kăl′và·rĭ). The place, outside the

---

bar; church; dog; ardŭous; fat; go; hear; jail; key; lame; meat; not; ring; pay; ran; see; shell; ten; there, thick; pastūre; vast; wind; yes; zoo, zh = z in azure.

ancient city of Jerusalem, where Christ was crucified.

canny (kăn'ĭ). **1.** Knowing; clever; shrewd. **2.** Thrifty; frugal.

Canuck (ká·nŭk'). Slang term for a Canadian.

caricature (kăr'ĭ·ká·tūr). A picture or description characterized by exaggeration or distortion.

carrion (kăr'ĭ·ŭn). **1.** Decaying flesh of a dead animal. **2.** Feeding on decaying flesh.

catamount (kăt'á·mount). A wildcat.

catholic (kăth'ō·lĭk). Universal or general.

celestial (sē·lĕs'chăl). Heavenly; divine.

celibacy (sĕl'ĭ·bá·sĭ). State of being unmarried; single life.

censer (sĕn'sēr). A vessel for perfumes, especially one in which incense is burned.

chaff (chàf). **1.** The husks of grain that are separated from the seed by threshing. **2.** Anything light and worthless.

chalice (chăl'ĭs). A sacred vessel, specially blessed, used at Mass; also, a drinking cup.

chancery (chàn'sēr·ĭ). A state of control by the courts pending legal settlement.

chanticleer (chăn'tĭ·klēr). A rooster.

charnel (chär'nĕl). Pertaining to a burial place.

chastity (chăs'tĭ·tĭ). Purity; virtue.

château (shă·tō'). **1.** A feudal castle in France. **2.** A large country house.

chic (shēk). **1.** Striking elegance in style. **2.** Fashionable.

chivalrous (shĭv'ăl·rŭs). **1.** Pertaining to chivalry, the system of knighthood in feudal times. **2.** Having the qualities characteristic of chivalry — courage, courtesy, generosity, and so on.

chronometer (krō·nŏm'ē·tēr). An instrument for measuring time.

churlish (chûr'lĭsh). *See page 592.*

circumjacent (sûr'kŭm·jā'sĕnt). Bordering on every side.

cite (sīt). **1.** To quote as authority; to bring forward for illustration.

clairvoyant (klâr·voi'ănt). Having an unnatural power to see and know things not apparent to an ordinary person.

clapperclaw (klăp'ēr·klô'). To revile; to scold.

clarion (klăr'ĭ·ŭn). A kind of trumpet with clear, shrill tones.

cognizant (kŏg'nĭ·zănt). Aware of from observation.

coincidence (kō·ĭn'sĭ·dĕns). An accidental occurrence of events or ideas at the same time, in a way that seems especially fitting.

collaborate (kŏ·lăb'ō·rāt). **1.** To act jointly. **2.** To co-operate voluntarily.

colleague (kŏl'ēg). An associate, usually in a profession.

colloquial (kŏ·lō'kwĭ·ăl). Acceptable and correct in ordinary, familiar conversation, letters, or informal speeches.

colossus (kō·lŏs'ŭs). Anything of gigantic size.

combustible (kŏm·bŭs'tĭ·b'l). Capable of being burned.

comely (kŭm'lĭ). Pleasing or agreeable to the sight.

commend (kŏ·mĕnd'). **1.** To entrust to one's care. **2.** To recommend. **3.** To praise.

commensurable (kŏ·mĕn'shŏō·rá·b'l). Capable of being exactly measured by the same unit of measure.

commiserating (kŏ·mĭz'ēr·āt·ĭng). Sympathizing.

communal (kŏm'ū·năl). Owned in common; participated in jointly by a whole community.

compass (kŭm'pás). **1.** A device for determining direction. **2.** An enclosed space, limit, or boundary.

complacency (kŏm·plā'sĕn·sĭ). Self-satisfaction.

complaisant (kŏm·plā'zănt). Disposed to please; courteous; obliging.

complement (kŏm'plē·mĕnt). **1.** To supply a lack. **2.** One of two parts which make a whole.

condone (kŏn·dōn'). Pardon; excuse.

confabulation (kŏn·făb'ū·lā'shŭn). Conversation; chat.

confidant (kŏn·fĭ·dănt'). One to whom secrets are confided.

confrontation (kŏn'frŭn·tā'shŭn). Act of meeting face to face, especially hostilely.

conjecture (kŏn·jĕk'tûr). A supposition; a guess.

conjuration (kŏn'jŏō·rā'shŭn). **1.** Practice of magic. **2.** An expression or trick used in practicing magic.

conjure (kŏn·jŏōr'). **1.** To summon a devil by incantation. **2.** To implore earnestly.

connotation (kŏn'ō·tā'shŭn). The suggestive significance of a word apart from its recognized meaning.

consanguinity (kŏn·săng·gwĭn'ĭ·tĭ). Blood relationship.

consistent (kŏn·sĭst'ĕnt). **1.** Having agreement with itself; not contradictory. **2.** Possessing firmness; solid.

constituent (kŏn·stĭt'ū·ĕnt). **1.** A part serving to make up a whole; an element. **2.** One who aids in electing another as his representative in a legislative body.

consummate (kŏn·sŭm'ĭt). To the utmost degree; perfect.

consummation (kŏn'sŭ·mā'shŭn). Bringing to completion; achievement.

āpe, chāotic, bâre, ăt, ăttend, ärt, flásk, átop; ēke, mẹrely, ĕlect, ĕcho, prudĕnt, doēr; ītem, ĭnn, rarĭty; ōde, ŏpaque, fôr, dŏt, lŏft, cŏnfide; sōōn, tŏŏk; sour, toil; tūbe, ûnique, tûrn, sŭp, ŭntil.

contagious (kŏn·tā′jŭs). **1.** Communicable by contact, as disease. **2.** Spreading from one to another.

contumacious (kŏn′tū·mā′shŭs). Rebellious; stubbornly disobedient.

contumelious (kŏn′tū·mē′lĭ·ŭs). *See page 38.*

converge (kŏn·vûrj′). To approach nearer together; to incline toward one point.

convexity (kŏn·vĕk′sĭ·tĭ). Curvature like the exterior of a sphere.

conviviality (kŏn·vĭv′ĭ·ăl′ĭ·tĭ). Jovial fellowship; festivity.

coquetry (kō′kĕ·trĭ). Flirtation.

cordiality (kôr·jăl′ĭ·tĭ). Heartiness; warmth of feeling.

cosmopolite (kŏz·mŏp′ō·līt). One at home in any country.

cosmos (kŏz′mŏs). The universe.

couchant (kouch′ănt). Lying down with the head raised.

coveted (kŭv′ĕt·ĕd). Desired; longed for.

credence (krē′dĕns). Belief.

cresendo (krĕ·shĕn′dō). In music, a gradual increase in sound.

crevasse (krĕ·văs′). *See page 204.*

crevice (krĕv′ĭs). A narrow opening resulting from a crack or split.

crookneck (krŏŏk′nĕk). Either of two varieties of squash with tapering necks.

crypt (krĭpt). A vault partly or wholly underground.

cubit (kū′bĭt). A measure of length (in English measure, 18 inches).

cul-de-sac (kŏŏl′dē·săk′). *See page 204.*

cynic (sĭn′ĭk). *See page 170.*

D

dais (dā′ĭs). Platform.

dear (dēr). Costly; expensive.

debase (dĕ·bās′). To reduce in dignity or value.

debris (dĕ·brē′). Rubbish, especially such as results from destruction; ruins.

decade (dĕk′ād). Ten years.

decorum (dĕ·kō′rŭm). Propriety; good form.

decrepit (dĕ·krĕp′ĭt). *See page 540.*

deduce (dĕ·dūs′). To derive by reasoning.

defalcation (dĕ·făl·kā′shŭn). Misappropriation of money.

defection (dĕ·fĕk′shŭn). Desertion.

deferential (dĕf·ēr·ĕn′shăl). Yielding to the opinion or wishes of another.

deft (dĕft). Skillful.

degenerate (dĕ·jĕn′ēr·ĭt). Degraded; lowered in quality.

deign (dān). To condescend to give.

deity (dē′ĭ·tĭ). A god (capitalized when referring to God).

delusion (dĕ·lū′zhŭn). False belief; misconception.

demean (dĕ·mēn′). **1.** To debase or lower. **2.** To behave or comport (oneself).

denominate (dĕ·nŏm′ĭ·nāt). To give a name to.

denomination (dĕ·nŏm′ĭ·nā′shŭn). **1.** Act of naming. **2.** A category. **3.** A group of individuals called by the same name; a sect.

denude (dĕ·nūd′). To divest of covering; to strip.

depleted (dĕ·plēt′ĕd). Exhausted of its strength or resources.

depravity (dĕ·prăv′ĭ·tĭ). Corruption.

deprecating (dĕp′rĕ·kāt·ĭng). *See page 725.*

derision (dĕ·rĭzh′ŭn). Contemptuous laughter.

derisive (dē·rī′sĭv). Scornful; mocking.

deter (dĕ·tûr′). To turn aside or discourage through fear.

deteriorate (dĕ·tēr′ĭ·ō·rāt). *See page 158.*

dialect (dī′ά·lĕkt). *See page 30.*

diapason (dī′ά·pā′zŭn). An organ stop covering the full range of the instrument.

didactic (dī·dăk′tĭk). Intended for instruction.

dilapidated (dĭ·lăp′ĭ·dāt′ĕd). Fallen into partial ruin or decay.

dirge (dûrj). A lyrical or musical composition expressive of grief.

disapprobation (dĭs′ăp·rō′bā′shŭn). Disapproval.

discountenance (dĭs·koun′tĕ·năns). *See page 466.*

discourse (dĭs′kōrs). **1.** Conversation; orderly speech or writing. **2.** Act of reasoning logically. **3.** To express oneself at length in speech or writing.

disillusionment (dĭs′ĭ·lū′zhŭn·mĕnt). State of being free from illusions; disenchantment.

disinter (dĭs′ĭn·tûr′). To take out of the grave; to dig up.

disinterested (dĭs·ĭn′tēr·ĕs·tĕd). *See page 466.*

dissenter (dĭ·sĕn′tēr). **1.** One who disagrees. **2.** One who separates from an established church.

dissimulation (dĭ·sĭm·û·lā′shŭn). False pretension; deception.

dissipated (dĭs′ĭ·pāt′ĕd). **1.** Scattered. **2.** Wasteful in the pursuit of pleasure.

dissonance (dĭs′ō·năns). A mingling of discordant sounds.

distaff (dĭs′tȧf). **1.** The staff for holding wool or flax in spinning. **2.** Pertaining to women, or work that is traditionally women's.

distraught (dĭs·trôt′). Distracted; very agitated.

divert (dĭ·vûrt′). **1.** To turn aside. **2.** To amuse.

divest (dĭ·vĕst′). **1.** To strip. **2.** To dispossess.

---

bar; church; dog; ardŭous; fat; go; hear; jail; key; lame; meat; not; ring; pay; ran; see; shell; ten; there, thick; pastûre; vast; wind; yes; zoo, zh = z in azure.

divining (dĭ·vīn′ĭng). Foretelling; prophesying.

docile (dŏs′ĭl). Obedient; easy to manage.

doggedly (dŏg′ĕd·lĭ). In a manner stubbornly determined.

dogie (dō′gĭ). A motherless calf in a range herd.

dogmatical (dŏg·măt′ĭ·kăl). *See page 445.*

dotage (dōt′ĭj). Feebleness of mind, resulting from old age.

draught (dráft). A drink.

drone (drōn). **1.** A lazy person. **2.** To make a low, dull sound.

dross (drŏs). **1.** Scum thrown off from molten ore. **2.** Waste matter.

ductile (dŭk′tĭl). Capable of being drawn out or hammered thin.

dupe (dūp). One who is deceived easily.

E

eccentricity (ĕk′sĕn·trĭs′ĭ·tĭ). Oddity; peculiarity.

ecstasy (ĕk′stȧ·sĭ). A state of overmastering feeling, as joy or rapture.

eerily (ē′rĭ·lĭ). In a weird, unearthly manner.

effect (ĕ·fĕkt′). *See page 458.*

effervescent (ĕf′ĕr·vĕs′ĕnt). Bubbling; showing high spirits.

effusion (ĕ·fū′zhŭn). A gushing or unrestrained utterance.

eke (ēk). Also (archaic).

elated (ē·lāt′ĕd). Lifted up in spirit.

elicit (ē·lĭs′ĭt). To draw forth; evoke.

emaciated (ē·mā′shĭ·āt′ĕd). Very thin; lean.

emanation (ĕm′ȧ·nā′shŭn). The act of issuing forth.

emulate (ĕm′ū·lāt). To strive to equal or surpass.

emulsion (ē·mŭl′shŭn). An oily mass in suspension in watery liquids.

engross (ĕn·grōs′). **1.** To take possession of the whole of; monopolize; absorb. **2.** To write in a large hand.

enigma (ē·nĭg′mȧ). Something perplexing; a riddle.

enmity (ĕn′mĭ·tĭ). Hostility; hatred.

ennui (än′wē). *See page 18.*

ensemble (än·sŏm′b′l). A whole; all the parts together or the total effect produced by them.

ensign (ĕn′sīn). **1.** Flag. **2.** (usually ĕn′sĭn) Lowest commissioned officer in the U.S. Navy.

entice (ĕn·tīs′). Allure; tempt; attract.

epitomize (ē·pĭt′ō·mīz). To summarize; to abridge.

equanimity (ē′kwȧ·nĭm′ĭ·tĭ). *See page 670.*

equinox (ē′kwĭ·nŏks). The time when the sun crosses the equator and day and night everywhere are of equal length.

equipage (ĕk′wĭ·pĭj). A carriage.

equity (ĕk′wĭ·tĭ). Fairness in dealing.

erratic (ĕ·răt′ĭk). Having no certain course; wandering.

esoteric (ĕs′ō·tĕr′ĭk). Designed for and understood by only a select group.

espy (ĕs·pī′). To catch sight of.

esthetic (ĕs·thĕt′ĭk). Artistic; pertaining to the love of beauty.

euphony (ū′fō·nĭ). Harmonious sound.

evince (ē·vĭns′). To show.

ewer (ū′ẽr). A type of wide-mouthed jug.

excruciating (ĕks·kroo′shĭ·āt′ĭng). *See page 50.*

exhilarating (ĕg·zĭl′ȧ·rāt′ĭng). Cheering; enlivening.

exhortation (ĕg′zôr·tā′shŭn). Giving of earnest advice.

exhume (ĕks·hūm′). To dig out of the ground.

exigency (ĕk′sĭ·jĕn·sĭ). Special requirement or need of a situation or occasion.

exotic (ĕks·ŏt′ĭk). Introduced from a foreign country.

expatiate (ĕks·pā′shĭ·āt). To wander at will over a subject.

expatriated (ĕks·pā′trĭ·āt·ĕd). Exiled.

expedient (ĕks·pē′dĭ·ĕnt). Conducive to special advantage rather than to what is right.

expiate (ĕks′pĭ·āt). To make amends for.

expletive (ĕks′plē·tĭv). An oath or exclamation.

explicable (ĕks′plĭ·kȧ·b′l). Capable of being explained.

explicit (ĕks·plĭs′ĭt). *See page 466.*

exploit (ĕks·ploit′). **1.** A heroic deed. **2.** To utilize; get the value from.

expostulation (ĕks·pŏs′tū·lā′shŭn). Earnest protest.

expound (ĕks·pound′). **1.** To set forth, as a theory. **2.** To interpret; explain the meaning of.

exquisite (ĕks′kwĭ·zĭt). **1.** Pleasing by reason of beauty. **2.** Of surpassing quality.

extemporize (ĕks·tĕm′pō·rīz). To compose on the spur of the moment without previous planning.

extenuate (ĕks·tĕn′ū·āt). **1.** To weaken. **2.** To represent as less than it appears to be.

extort (ĕks·tôrt′). *See page 484.*

exuberant (ĕg·zū′bẽr·ȧnt). Overflowing with high spirits.

exude (ĕks·ūd′). To discharge through pores.

F

facetious (fȧ·sē′shŭs). Witty; exciting laughter.

facility (fȧ·sĭl′ĭ·tĭ). *See page 466.*

āpe, châotic, bâre, ăt, ăttend, ärt, flásk, ȧtop; ēke, mẽrely, ĕlect, ĕcho, prudĕnt, doẽr; ītem, ĭnn, rarĭty; ōde, ŏpaque, fôr, dŏt, lŏft, cŏnfide; soon, took; sour, toil; tūbe, ūnique, tûrn, sŭp, ŭntil.

fain (fān). Well-pleased; glad.

fathom (făth'ŭm). A measure of length containing six feet, used chiefly in measuring cables, cordage, and depth of water.

feign (fān). To pretend.

felicity (fē·lĭs'ĭ·tĭ). Happiness.

felonious (fē·lō'nĭ·ŭs). Criminal; villainous; traitorous.

fetish (fē'tĭsh). Any object of special devotion.

fidelity (fĭ·dĕl'ĭ·tĭ). Loyalty; faithfulness to a trust.

figuratively (fĭg'ŭr·á·tĭv·lĭ). Not literally; employing a figure of speech.

fillip (fĭl'ĭp). 1. A smart blow. 2. Something serving to rouse or excite.

firmament (fûr'má·mĕnt. The arch of the sky.

flair (flâr). Critical sense; instinctive discernment.

flamboyant (flăm·boi'ănt). Ornate; strikingly colored.

flaunt (flônt). 1. To wave or flutter showily. 2. To display boastfully.

flotsam (flŏt'săm). Anything drifting about on the surface of water.

flux (flŭks). An excessive discharge from the bowels or other part.

fodder (fŏd'ẽr). Food for cattle, horses, and other domestic animals.

foppery (fŏp'ẽr·ĭ). Behavior of a fop or dandy.

forspent (fŏr·spĕnt'). Tired out; exhausted.

fortitude (fŏr'tĭ·tūd). Courageous endurance.

fratricidal (frăt'rĭ·sīd'ăl). With brother killing brother.

freebooter (frē'bōōt'ẽr). One who goes about plundering; a pirate.

frequent (frē·kwĕnt'). To visit often.

frescoed (frĕs'kōd). Painted on walls.

fricassee (frĭk'á·sē'). A dish made of fowls, veal, or other meat cut into pieces and stewed in gravy.

frond (frŏnd). A leaf, especially that of a palm.

frugality (frōō·găl'ĭ·tĭ). Thrift; economy.

furtive (fûr'tĭv). Sly; secret.

futile (fū'tĭl). Useless.

G

gamut (găm'ŭt). An entire range or series.

gaunt (gônt). 1. Haggard. 2. Forbidding; grim.

gentry (jĕn'trĭ). People of education and good breeding.

genus (jē'nŭs). A class, order, kind, sort.

geology (jē·ŏl'ō·jĭ). *See page 631.*

gesticulation (jĕs·tĭk'ū·lā'shŭn). Motion of the body to express an idea.

gibe (jīb). To utter taunting, sarcastic words.

gloom (glōōm). 1. Partial or total darkness. 2. A shady or dark place.

gonad (gŏn'ăd). An essential sexual gland; an ovary or testis.

gondola (gŏn'dô·lá). 1. A long narrow, flat-bottomed boat with a high prow and stern used in the canals of Venice. 2. A railroad car with sides but no top.

gorse (gôrs). A spiny evergreen shrub with yellow flowers.

gossamer (gŏs'á·mẽr). Gauzelike.

gratuitous (grá·tū'ĭ·tŭs). 1. Given without pay. 2. Not called for by the circumstances.

groined (groind). Built so as to form intersecting arches.

gross (grōs). Coarse; unrefined; insensitive.

grotesque (grŏ·tĕsk'). Absurdly distorted.

guileless (gīl'lĕs). Innocent; lacking in deceit.

gullibility (gŭl'lĭ·bĭl'ĭ·tĭ). Tendency to believe anything one is told.

gunnel (gŭn'ĕl). Variation of *gunwale*, that part of a vessel where topsides and deck meet.

gustatory (gŭs'tá·tō·rĭ). Pertaining to taste.

guttural (gŭt'ẽr·ál). Harsh or rasping, as resembling a throat sound.

gyves (jīvz). Shackles on the arms or legs to prevent free action.

H

hallow (hăl'ō). To make holy.

haply (hăp'lĭ). By chance.

harpsichord (härp'sĭ·kôrd). An old-fashioned stringed instrument, forerunner of the piano.

harpy (här'pĭ). A fabulous winged monster which fed on shipwreck victims.

harrow (hăr'ō). A piece of farm machinery used for pulverizing and smoothing the soil.

heft (hĕft). 1. The greater part or bulk. 2. Weight.

Herculean (hûr·kū'lē·ăn). Having extraordidnary strength or size.

hermitage (hûr'mĭ·tĭj). A secluded residence.

heterogeneous (hĕt'ẽr·ō·jē'nē·ŭs). Differing in kind; having unlike qualities.

highboy (hī'boi). A chest of drawers mounted on a tablelike base.

hoary (hōr'ĭ). White with age.

homely (hōm'lĭ). 1. Simple; plain; unpretending. 2. Not pretty.

hostler (hŏs'lẽr). One who takes care of horses.

hyperbole (hī·pûr'bō·lē). *See page 187.*

hypothesis (hī·pŏth'ē·sĭs). Something assumed or conceded merely for the purpose of argument.

---

bar; church; dog; ardúous; fat; go; hear; jail; key; lame; meat; not; ring; pay; ran; see; shell; ten; ᵗhere, thick; pastûre; vast; wind; yes; zoo, zh = z in azure.

I

idiosyncrasies (ĭd'ĭ·ō·sĭng'krȧ·sĭz). Distinctive peculiarities.

idyllic (ī·dĭl'ĭk). Pleasing in natural simplicity.

ignified (ĭg'nĭ·fīd). Set on fire.

illimitable (ĭl·lĭm'ĭt·ȧ·b'l). Not capable of being limited; immeasurable.

immedicable (ĭm·mĕd'ĭ·kȧ·b'l). Incurable.

immemorial (ĭm·mē·mō'rĭ·ăl). Beyond the reach of memory.

immersion (ĭ·mûr'shŭn). 1. The state of being plunged into water. 2. Baptism by submersion in water.

imminent (ĭm'ĭ·nĕnt). Threatening to happen at once; impending.

immortal (ĭ·môr'tăl). 1. Destined to live forever. 2. Not perishable; abiding. 3. A person whose fame is lasting.

impervious (ĭm·pûr'vĭ·ŭs). Not able to be entered into.

impious (ĭm'pĭ·ŭs). Irreverent.

imponderable (ĭm·pŏn'dēr·ȧ·b'l). Incapable of being weighed.

import (ĭm'pōrt). Meaning; significance.

importunity (ĭm'pŏr·tū'nĭ·tĭ). Repeated requesting; persistent urging.

impostor (ĭm·pŏs'tēr). One who imposes on others, often pretending to be what he is not.

impotence (ĭm'pō·tĕns). Weakness.

imprecation (ĭm'prē·kā'shŭn). A curse.

impregnable (ĭm·prĕg'nȧ·b'l). Able to resist attack; unconquerable.

impregnate (ĭm·prĕg'nāt). To infuse particles of another substance into.

impromptu (ĭm·prŏmp'tū). Offhand; done without planning.

inanition (ĭn·ȧ·nĭsh'ŭn). Exhaustion from lack of food.

inanity (ĭn·ăn'ĭ·tĭ). A pointless thing; that which is senseless or without significance.

incandescent (ĭn·kăn·dĕs'ĕnt). 1. Glowing with intense heat; shining; brilliant. 2. Pertaining to a lamp whose light is produced by heat.

incantation (ĭn·kăn·tā'shŭn). The use of spells or charms in magic; sorcery.

incarnate (ĭn·kär'nāt). To embody; to give actual form to.

inception (ĭn·sĕp'shŭn). Beginning.

incinerated (ĭn·sĭn'ēr·āt'ĕd). Burnt to ashes.

incongruity (ĭn'kŏng·grōō'ĭ·tĭ). Lack of conformity or suitability.

inconsequential (ĭn·kŏn'sē·kwĕn'shăl). Irrelevant; unimportant.

incorrigible (ĭn·kŏr'ĭ·jĭ·b'l). Unmanageable; unruly.

incorruptible (ĭn'kŏ·rŭp'tĭ·b'l). 1. Incapable

of being bribed or made bad. 2. A just and upright person.

incumbent (ĭn·kŭm'bĕnt). 1. Imposed as a duty. 2. One holding an office.

indecorum (ĭn'dē·kō'rŭm). Impropriety.

indefatigable (ĭn'dē·făt'ĭ·gȧ·b'l). Incapable of being fatigued; tireless.

indictment (ĭn·dīt'mĕnt). A formal charge of wrongdoing.

indigence (ĭn'dĭ·jĕns). Poverty.

indigenous (ĭn·dĭj·ē·nŭs). Produced naturally; inborn.

indispensable (ĭn'dĭs·pĕn'sȧ·b'l). *See page 466.*

ineptitude (ĭn·ĕpt'ĭ·tūd). *See page 642.*

inequity (ĭn·ĕk'wĭ·tĭ). Injustice.

inert (ĭn·ûrt'). Inactive; sluggish.

inexorable (ĭn·ĕk'sō·rȧ·b'l). Not to be moved by entreaty; relentless.

infallible (ĭn·făl'ĭ·b'l). Not liable to be mistaken; certain.

infamy (ĭn'fȧ·mĭ). Disgrace; evil reputation.

infatuation (ĭn·făt'û·ā'shŭn). State of extravagant passion.

inferno (ĭn·fûr'nō). 1. Hell. 2. Any very hot place.

infidel (ĭn'fĭ·dĕl). An unbeliever.

ingratiate (ĭn·grā'shĭ·āt). To bring into favor; to win favor by efforts to please.

initiative (ĭn·ĭsh'ĭ·ȧ·tĭv). 1. The right or power to produce a new course of action. 2. Self-reliant enterprise; energy displayed in starting action.

innate (ĭn'nāt). Inborn; native; natural.

insatiable (ĭn·sā'shĭ·ȧ·b'l). Incapable of being satisfied.

inscrutable (ĭn·skrōō'tȧ·b'l). Incomprehensible; mysterious.

insensible (ĭn·sĕn'sĭ·b'l). Incapable of feeling or sensation.

insidious (ĭn·sĭd'ĭ·ŭs). Sly; treacherous; doing damage without arousing suspicion.

insinuating (ĭn·sĭn'û·āt'ĭng). 1. Introducing indirectly. 2. Hinting; suggesting.

insolent (ĭn'sō·lĕnt). Haughty and contemptuous; very disrespectful.

insolvency (ĭn·sŏl'vĕn·sĭ). *See page 566.*

insurgent (ĭn·sûr'jĕnt). Rebellious.

integrity (ĭn·tĕg'rĭ·tĭ). 1. Honesty. 2. State of being undivided, in complete harmony with oneself.

integument (ĭn·tĕg'û·mĕnt). A covering.

internecine (ĭn'tēr·nē'sĭn). Involving mutual slaughter; deadly.

intimate (ĭn'tĭ·mĭt). 1. Deep-seated; closely associated. 2. A close friend; a confidant. 3. (ĭn'tĭ·māt). To suggest indirectly; to hint.

intolerable (ĭn·tŏl'ēr·ȧ·b'l). Not to be endured; unbearable.

āpe, chāotic, bâre, ăt, ȧttend, ärt, flȧsk, ȧtop; ēke, mẽrely, ĕlect, ĕcho, prudĕnt, doẽr; ītem, ĭnn, rarĭty; ōde, ŏpaque, fôr, dŏt, lôft, cŏnfide; sōōn, tŏŏk; sour, toil; tūbe, ûnique, tûrn, sŭp, ŭntil.

intractable (ĭn·trăk'tȧ·b'l). Not easily managed or directed; obstinate.

inviolable (ĭn·vī'ô·lȧ·b'l). Incapable of being destroyed.

invocation (ĭn·vō·kā'shŭn). **1.** A calling forth. **2.** A prayer or solemn entreaty.

irate (ī'rāt). Angry; enraged.

irised (ī'rĭst). Colored like the rainbow.

irrelevant (ĭr·rĕl'ē·vȧnt). Unrelated; unessential.

J

jeopardy (jĕp'ẽr·dĭ). Serious danger.

jerkin (jûr'kĭn). A jacket or short coat.

jocosely (jō·kōs'lĭ). In a humorous manner.

joust (jŭst). A combat on horseback between two knights with lances.

jowls (joulz). Cheeks.

K

ken (kĕn). Insight; understanding.

kirtle (kûr't'l). **1.** A man's coat. **2.** A woman's gown.

knouter (nout'ẽr). One who flogs criminals.

L

lacerated (lăs'ẽr·āt'ĭd). Torn; mangled.

laggard (lăg'ẽrd). **1.** A loiterer. **2.** Slow; sluggish.

laureate (lô'rē·āt). **1.** Crowned with laurel as a mark of honor. **2.** Distinguished.

lave (lāv). To wash; bathe.

lectern (lĕk'tẽrn). A reading desk or stand in a church.

lenient (lē'nĭ·ĕnt). **1.** Relaxing, softening. **2.** Mild; not severe.

lethal (lē'thȧl). Deadly; fatal.

lethargy (lĕth'ẽr·jĭ). **1.** Morbid drowsiness. **2.** Indifference.

libel (lī'bĕl). *See page 243.*

librettist (lĭ·brĕt'ĭst). The writer of the text or words of an opera.

lilting (lĭlt'ĭng). **1.** Lively; springy. **2.** Rhythmical.

lintel (lĭn'tĕl). A horizontal beam above a door or window.

liquescent (lĭ·kwĕs'ĕnt). Becoming liquid; melting.

liqueur (lē·kûr'). An alcoholic beverage.

lodestar (lōd'stär'). A star that leads, especially the polestar.

lubber (lŭb'ẽr). A big, clumsy fellow.

luminous (lū'mĭ·nŭs). Shining; brilliant.

lyceum (lī·sē'ŭm). An association providing inspirational lectures, concerts, entertainments.

M

machination (măk'ĭ·nā'shŭn). Artful scheme or plot.

magnanimity (măg'nȧ·nĭm'ĭ·tĭ). Generous and courageous spirit.

magnitude (măg'nĭ·tūd). Greatness.

malady (măl'ȧ·dĭ). Sickness; ailment.

malediction (măl'ē·dĭk'shŭn). A curse.

malevolent (mȧ·lĕv'ô·lĕnt). Wishing evil; malicious.

manifest (măn'ĭ·fĕst). Evident; obvious.

marge (märj). Margin, as of a stream.

marmot (mär'mŭt). A certain short-legged animal with coarse fur, a short bushy tail, and small ears.

mast (màst). Feed for livestock.

maudlin (môd'lĭn). *See page 670.*

maze (māz). A confusing network of paths; a labyrinth.

melodramatic (mĕl'ô·drȧ·măt'ĭk). Sensational; overly romatic or sentimental.

mendicant (mĕn'dĭ·kȧnt). One who lives by alms; a beggar.

menial (mē'nĭ·ȧl). **1.** Low; mean. **2.** A domestic servant.

meridian (mē·rĭd'ĭ·ȧn). Highest point.

meritorious (mĕr·ĭ·tō'rĭ·ŭs). Deserving of reward or honor.

mesquite (mĕs·kēt'). A spiny, deep-rooted shrub.

metaphor (mĕt'ȧ·fẽr). An implied comparison.

mete (mēt). Boundary.

meticulous (mē·tĭk'ū·lŭs). Unduly careful of small details.

mien (mēn). Manner; bearing.

minimum (mĭn'ĭ·mŭm). **1.** The least quantity allowable, opposite of *maximum*. **2.** The lowest amount recorded, as *minimum* temperature.

minion (mĭn'yŭn). A lowly servant; one who does another's bidding without question.

minor (mī'nẽr). **1.** Less; inferior; smaller. **2.** In a type of key that often gives the effect of somberness or weirdness.

mirage (mĭ·räzh'). An optical illusion caused by reflection, usually on heat rays.

moiety (moi'ĕ·tĭ). A part; roughly half.

momentous (mō·mĕn'tŭs). Very important.

monetary (mŏn'ē·tẽr'ĭ). Pertaining to coinage or currency.

monger (mŭng'gẽr). A trader; a dealer.

morass (mō·răs'). A tract of soft, wet ground; marsh.

moribund (mŏr'ĭ·bŭnd). In a dying state.

mortar (môr'tẽr). **1.** A building material. **2.** A strong vessel in which substances are pounded by a pestle.

---

bar; church; dog; ardŭous; fat; go; hear; jail; key; lame; meat; not; ring; pay; ran; see; shell; ten; there, thick; pastūre; vast; wind; yes; zoo, zh = z in azure.

mortification (môr'tĭ·fĭ·kā'shŭn). **1.** Humiliation and chagrin caused by something which wounds one's pride. **2.** Death of bodily tissue.

motley (mŏt'lĭ). Composed of widely varying colors or parts.

muleteer (mū'lĕ·tēr). A driver of mules.

N

naive (nä·ēv'). Simple; unsophisticated.

nebulous (nĕb'ū·lŭs). Cloudy; hazy; misty.

nether (nĕth'ēr). Under.

nocturnal (nŏk·tûr'năl). Pertaining to the night.

nocturne (nŏk'tûrn). **1.** A dreamy musical composition. **2.** A night scene.

noisome (noi'sŭm). Offensive to the senses.

nomenclature (nō'mĕn·klā'tŭr). The system of names used in a particular branch of knowledge or art.

nonchalance (nŏn'shà·lăns). *See page 158.*

nonconformist (nŏn'kŏn·fôr'mĭst). One who does not follow an established pattern.

nondescript (nŏn'dĕ·skrĭpt). **1.** Not easily described. **2.** A person of no particular class.

novocain (nō'vò·kān). A local anesthetic.

O

oasis (ò·ā'sĭs). A fertile spot in a desert.

obeisance (ò·bā'săns). A low bow.

obituary (ò·bĭt'ū·ĕr·ĭ). A notice of death, with a biographical sketch.

obligatory (ŏb·lĭg'à·tō'rĭ). Required.

obliterate (ŏb·lĭt'ĕr·āt). To erase or blot out.

obsolescent (ŏb·sò·lĕs'ĕnt). Going out of use.

obtrusive (ŏb·trōō'sĭv). Pushing forward where unwanted.

occult (ŏ·kŭlt'). **1.** Mysterious. **2.** Pertaining to magic.

odium (ō'dĭ·ŭm). The reproach and discredit attached to something hated.

oligarchy (ŏl'ĭ·gär'kĭ). *See page 493.*

ominous (ŏm'ĭ·nŭs). Foreshadowing evil.

omniscient (ŏm·nĭsh'ĕnt). Knowing everything.

omnivorous (ŏm·nĭv'ò·rŭs). Eating everything.

onerous (ŏn'ĕr·ŭs). Burdensome; oppressive.

opalescent (ō'păl·ĕs'ĕnt). Reflecting an iridescent light; like an opal.

opulent (ŏp'ū·lĕnt). Wealthy.

oracular (ò·răk'ū·lēr). Forecasting the future.

ostentation (ŏs'tĕn·tā'shŭn). Unnecessary show.

osteology (ŏs'tē·ŏl'ò·jĭ). *See page 631.*

P

pacific (pà·sĭf'ĭk). Calm; peace-loving.

paean (pē'ăn). A song of joy, praise, or triumph.

palatial (pà·lā'shăl). Befitting a palace; magnificent.

palisade (păl'ĭ·sād'). **1.** A fence of stakes, for defense. **2.** A line of cliffs.

pall (pôl). A heavy cloth thrown over a coffin.

pallid (păl'ĭd). Deficient in color; pale.

palpable (păl'pà·b'l). *See page 18.*

palsied (pôl'zēd). *See page 540.*

paradox (păr'à·dŏks). A statement seemingly self-contradictory.

paragon (păr'à·gŏn). A model; a type of perfection.

paramount (păr'à·mount). Supreme.

parapet (păr'à·pĕt). **1.** A low barrier, such as a railing, at the edge of a platform or roof. **2.** An elevation of earth or stone, built to protect soldiers.

paraphrase (păr'à·frāz). A restatement of a passage, giving the meaning in another form.

parasitic (păr'à·sĭt'ĭk). Living on other organisms.

pariah (pà·rī'à). **1.** An outcast. **2.** Despised by society.

parody (păr'ò·dĭ). An imitation in a humorous manner.

parsimony (pär'sĭ·mōn'nĭ). *See page 484.*

participant (pär·tĭs'ĭ·pănt). One who shares.

pastoral (pàs'tò·răl). Relating to rural life.

paternal (pà·tûr'năl). Fatherly; pertaining to a father.

patriarch (pā'trĭ·ärk). A person regarded as father or founder of a race, science, religion, etc.

peccadillo (pĕk'à·dĭl'ō). A slight offense; a petty fault.

pedantic (pê·dăn'tĭk). Pertaining to a showy display of learning.

pellicle (pĕl'ĭ·k'l). A thin skin or film.

pensive (pĕn'sĭv). Sadly thoughtful.

perambulation (pēr·ăm'bū·lā'shŭn). Walking about.

perception (pēr·sĕp'shŭn). **1.** Delicate understanding. **2.** Direct acquaintance with anything through the senses.

perdition (pēr·dĭsh'ŭn). Ruin; eternal death.

peremptory (pēr·ĕmp'tō·rĭ). Leaving no chance for refusal or denial.

perfidious (pēr·fĭd'ĭ·ŭs). Guilty of violating a trust.

perfunctory (pēr·fŭngk'tō·rĭ). Done mechanically by way of routine.

peroration (pĕr'ò·rā'shŭn). The final summing up of an argument.

āpe, châotic, bâre, ăt, ăttend, ärt, flăsk, átop; ēke, mĕrely, ĕlect, ĕcho, prudĕnt, doĕr; ītem, ĭnn, rarĭty; ōde, ŏpaque, fôr, dŏt, lŏft, cŏnfide; sōon, tŏŏk; sour, toil; tūbe, ūnique, tûrn, sŭp, ŭntil.

persiflage (pûr'sĭ·fläzh). Flippant jesting; frivolous talk.

personnel (pûr'sŏ·nĕl'). **1.** The body of persons employed in some service. **2.** Of or pertaining to such people.

pertinacity (pûr'tĭ·năs'ĭ·tĭ). Unyielding perseverance.

pertinence (pûr'tĭ·nĕns). A fact related to the matter in hand.

perturbation (pûr'tẽr·bā'shŭn). A state of great alarm or agitation.

perverse (pẽr·vûrs'). Contrary; obstinate in the wrong; willful.

phaeton (fā'ĕ·t'n). A kind of light four-wheeled carriage.

phenomenal (fĕ·nŏm'ĕ·n'l). Exceptional; unusual.

phonetics (fō·nĕt'ĭks). *See page 152.*

phthisic (tĭz'ĭk). Wasting of tissue, as in tuberculosis.

pidgin (pĭj'ĭn). Pidgin English, a jargon of English words arranged according to Chinese usage, spoken in the Far East between natives and foreigners.

pillory (pĭl'ō·rĭ). A device for punishment, consisting of a frame having holes through which the head and hands of an offender were thrust.

piquant (pē'kănt). **1.** Pleasantly sharp. **2.** Engaging; having a lively charm.

pique (pēk). To arouse anger or resentment in; to nettle.

placid (plăs'ĭd). Peaceful; quiet.

plashing (plăsh'ĭng). Splashing.

plausible (plô'zĭ·b'l). Superficially reasonable; fair.

poignant (poin'yănt). *See page 50.*

pontificate (pŏn·tĭf'ĭ·kāt). The term of office of a pope.

pontoon (pŏn·tōōn'). A flat-bottomed boat.

portend (pōr·tĕnd'). To foreshadow; foretell.

portentous (pōr·tĕn'tŭs). **1.** Ominous. **2.** Marvelous.

posterity (pŏs·tẽr'ĭ·tĭ). Offspring or descendants.

posthumous (pŏs'tṳ·mŭs). **1.** Born after the death of the father. **2.** Published after the death of the author.

potency (pō'tĕn·sĭ). Ability to bring about a certain result.

potential (pō·tĕn'shăl). Possible, as opposed to actual.

precarious (prē·kâr'ĭ·ŭs). **1.** Uncertain. **2.** Insecure.

precept (prē'sĕpt). A rule of action or conduct.

predominate (prē·dŏm'ĭ·nāt). To prevail; to rule; to have mastery.

prehensile (prē·hĕn'sĭl). Adapted for seizing.

premonitory (prē·mŏn'ĭ·tō'rĭ). *See page 725.*

prerogative (prē·rŏg'a·tĭv). **1.** A right or privilege. **2.** Of first importance.

prescience (prē'shĭ·ĕns). Foresight; knowledge of future events.

prestidigitator (prĕs'tĭ·dĭj'ĭ·tā'tẽr). One who performs sleight of hand tricks.

prevalent (prĕv'a·lĕnt). Widespread; general.

primeval (prī·mē'văl). Belonging to the first ages of history.

prior (prī'ẽr). **1.** The head of one of the houses of certain religious orders. **2.** Earlier in time; taking precedence in time or importance.

probity (prŏb'ĭ·tĭ). Uprightness; honesty.

prodigious (prō·dĭj'ŭs). Extraordinary in size or degree; huge.

profaned (prō·fānd'). *See page 736.*

progenitor (prō·jĕn'ĭ·tẽr). A forefather.

promenade (prŏm'ĕ·näd). **1.** A place for walking in a public area. **2.** A march opening a formal ball. **3.** A dance given by a school class.

propitiate (prō·pĭsh'ĭ·āt). To render favorable.

proscenium (prō·sē'nĭ·ŭm). The part of the stage in front of the curtain.

prostrate (prŏs'trāt). Stretched out; lying with the body extended.

provocative (prō·vŏk'a·tĭv). Stimulating; serving to arouse.

puerility (pū'ẽr·ĭl'ĭt·ĭ). Childishness; immaturity.

puerperal (pū·ûr'pẽr·ăl). Pertaining to childbirth.

puncheon (pŭn'chŭn). A split log with the face smoothed, used in flooring.

punctilious (pŭngk·tĭl'ĭ·ŭs). Careful; exact in details.

pungence (pŭn'jĕns). Sharpness; keenness of taste or smell.

purchase (pûr'chĭs). *See page 204.*

purgatory (pûr'ga·tō'rĭ). A place or state of temporary punishment.

purloin (pûr·loin'). To steal.

pylon (pī'lŏn). A monumental mass flanking an approach to a bridge.

Q

quagmire (kwăg'mīr'). Soft, wet, miry land.

quarry (kwŏr'ĭ). **1.** The game hunted. **2.** An open excavation, for obtaining stone.

querulous (kwĕr'ṳ·lŭs). Complaining; peevish.

quest (kwĕst). Search; hunt.

quizzical (kwĭz'ĭ·kăl). Bantering; teasing.

R

rabid (răb'ĭd). Furious; raging.

rantipole (răn'tĭ·pōl). Wild; romping.

---

bar; church; dog; ardữous; fat; go; hear; jail; key; lame; meat; not; ring; pay; ran; see; shell; ten; there, thick; pastụre; vast; wind; yes; zoo, zh = z in azure.

rapport (ră·pōrt′). Relation of harmony; accord.

raucous (rô′kŭs). Hoarse; harsh; strident.

receding (rē·sēd′ĭng). Moving back or away.

reciprocal (rē·sĭp′rō·kăl). Shared, felt, or shown by both sides.

recked (rĕk′d). Heeded; regarded.

recluse (rē·klōōs′). A person who lives in seclusion, as a hermit.

reconnaissance (rē·kŏn′ĭ·săns). A preliminary examination or survey.

recruit (rē·krōōt′). 1. To provide with new troops. 2. To restore the vigor or health of.

rectitude (rĕk′tĭ·tūd). Uprightness.

recumbent (rē·kŭm′bĕnt). Lying down; resting.

recusant (rĕk′ū·zănt). One who refuses to comply with some practice, especially in religion.

redress (rē·drĕs′). To set right; to make amends for.

refute (rē·fūt′). To prove to be false.

rehabilitate (rē′hȧ·bĭl′ĭ·tāt). To restore to a former good condition.

rejuvenescent (rē·jōō′vē·nĕs′ĕnt). Renewing youth.

relevancy (rĕl′ē·văn·sĭ). Proper application to matter at hand.

remonstrance (rē·mŏn′străns). Protest; act of urging in opposition.

remuneration (rē·mū′nēr·ā′shŭn). Pay.

rendezvous (rän′dē·vōō). 1. A meeting by appointment. 2. A place appointed for a meeting.

renegade (rĕn′ē·gād). 1. One who leaves his professed religious faith. 2. A traitor.

repertory (rĕp′ēr·tō′rĭ). A list of those pieces which have been rehearsed and are ready for performance.

reprove (rē·prōōv′). To rebuke; to blame.

republican (rē·pŭb′lĭ·kăn). *See page 463.*

requisite (rĕk′wĭ·zĭt). Required by circumstances or nature.

respite (rĕs′pĭt). Interval of rest from labor or pain.

reveille (rĕv′ĕ·lē′). A bugle call summoning soldiers to the day's duties.

reverberation (rē·vûr′bēr·ā′shŭn). The act of being forced back; echoing back and forth.

reverie (rĕv′ēr·ĭ). State of being lost in thought.

ritual (rĭt′ū·ăl). 1. The established form of conducting worship. 2. Any ceremonial code.

roistering (rois′tēr·ĭng). Swaggering.

rubicund (rōō′bĭ·kŭnd). Ruddy; rosy.

ruck (rŭk). Crowd of ordinary persons.

rumination (rōō′mĭ·nā′shŭn). 1. A chewing again of what has been chewed slightly and swallowed. 2. Musing; reflection.

ruthless (rōōth′lĕs). Without pity.

S

sagacity (sȧ·găs′ĭ·tĭ). Keen judgment.

samp (sămp). Coarse hominy.

sanctuary (săngk′tū·ĕr′ĭ). 1. A church or temple. 2. Immunity from law gained by entering a sacred place.

sanguinary (săng′gwĭ·nĕr′ĭ). Bloody.

sardonic (sär·dŏn′ĭk). Sneeringly scornful.

satellite (săt′ĕ·līt). 1. An attendant attached to a powerful person; an associate. 2. In the solar system, a secondary planet or a body that revolves around a larger body.

satire (săt′īr). 1. Wit or sarcasm used to discredit vice or folly. 2. A written work ridiculing human follies.

savor (sā′vēr). *See page 196.*

schism (sĭz′m). Division or separation.

scimitar (sĭm′ĭ·tēr). A curved sword, used chiefly by Moslems.

scion (sī′ŭn). 1. A descendant. 2. *See footnote on page 19.*

scoriac (skō′rĭ·ăk). Full of rock refuse.

scullion (skŭl′yŭn). A kitchen servant.

secular (sĕk′ū·lȧr). 1. Pertaining to nonreligious things; worldly; not sacred. 2. Not bound by monastic vows.

semantics (sē·măn′tĭks). *See page 152.*

senescent (sē·nĕs′ĕnt). Growing old; aged.

sennight (sĕn′īt). A week (archaic).

sensuous (sĕn′shōō·ŭs). Characterized by sense impressions or imagery.

sententiously (sĕn·tĕn′shŭs·lĭ). In a manner emphasizing a meaning or moral.

sepulcher (sĕp′ŭl·kēr). A tomb; a burial vault.

seraphim (sĕr′ȧ·fĭm). Highest order of angels.

sere (sēr). Dried up; withered.

servile (sûr′vĭl). Behaving like a slave.

shoaler (shōl′ēr). More shallow.

shrive (shrīv). To pardon the sins of one confessing them.

sibyl (sĭb′ĭl). Prophetess.

siesta (sĭ·ĕs′tȧ). A short rest, especially at midday.

simultaneous (sī′mŭl·tā′nē·ŭs). Happening at the same time.

singletree (sĭng′g′l·trē′). The pivoted bar to which the traces of a harnessed horse are fixed.

sinister (sĭn′ĭs·tēr). Boding evil; indicating harm or disaster.

sinuous (sĭn′ū·ŭs). Bending in and out; winding.

skein (skān). A twisted loop of yarn or thread.

skepticism (skĕp′tĭ·sĭz′m). A doubting state of mind.

slick (slĭk). A smooth surface of water, as that caused by a film of oil or by the sweep of a ship's stern.

slough (slou). A place of deep mud or mire.

āpe, chăotic, bâre, ăt, ȧttend, ärt, flȧsk, ȧtop; ēke, mẽrely, ĕlect, ĕcho, prudĕnt, doẽr; ītem, ĭnn, rarĭty; ōde, ȯpaque, fôr, dŏt, lŏft, cŏnfide; sōōn, tŏŏk; sour, toil; tūbe, ūnique, tûrn, sŭp, ŭntil.

sluggard (slŭg'ẽrd). A person habitually lazy.

sociology (sō'sĭ·ŏl'ŏ·jĭ). The science of the origin and evolution of society.

solace (sŏl'ĭs). Comfort; consolation.

soliloquy (sŏ·lĭl'ŏ·kwĭ). A monologue; act of talking to oneself.

solstice (sŏl'stĭs). The day on which the sun is farthest from the equator, north or south.

sophomore (sŏf'ŏ·mōr). *See page 642.*

souse (sous). Something steeped in pickle.

sovereignty (sŏv'ẽr·ĭn·tĭ). Supreme political power.

spa (spä). A resort with mineral springs.

specious (spē'shŭs). Plausible, but false.

spherule (sfẽr'ōōl). A little sphere or spherical body.

spleen (splēn). 1. Organ of the body near the stomach. 2. Anger.

sporadic (spŏ·răd'ĭk). Occurring in scattered instances.

squalid (skwŏl'ĭd). Dirty; filthy; poor.

squeamish (skwēm'ĭsh). 1. Dainty; over-nice. 2. Easily nauseated.

squill (skwĭl). A bulbous herb of the lily family.

stalactite (stȧ·lăk'tīt). A deposit of calcium carbonate hanging like an icicle from the roof of a cavern.

stamina (stăm'ĭ·nȧ). Vigor; endurance.

stanchion (stăn'shŭn). An upright bar, brace, or support.

statute (stăt'ūt). A law.

staunch (stônch). 1. To stop the flow of, as blood. 2. Sound; firm. 3. Loyal; steady. *Also spelled* stanch.

stentorian (stĕn·tō'rĭ·ăn). Extremely loud.

sterility (stĕ·rĭl'ĭ·tĭ). Unfruitfulness; barrenness.

stirrup (stĭr'ŭp). A ring attached to the saddle for holding the foot of a horseback rider.

stocks (stŏks). A wooden frame with holes for hands and feet, used to confine prisoners.

stolid (stŏl'ĭd). Dull; not easily excited.

suavity (swä'vĭ·tĭ). Smooth politeness.

subjugation (sŭb'jŏŏ·gā'shŭn). The act of conquering.

subscribe (sŭb·skrīb'). 1. To give consent or agreement by signing. 2. To sign one's name in token of a promise to pay. 3. To write one's name beneath.

subsequently (sŭb'sē·kwĕnt·lĭ). In a manner following in time, order, or place; succeeding; later.

subservient (sŭb·sûr'vĭ·ĕnt). Subordinate; meekly obedient.

subsistence (sŭb·sĭs'tĕns). Means of support; livelihood.

subtle (sŭt''l). 1. Cunningly made. 2. Mentally acute; shrewd.

subvert (sŭb·vûrt'). *See page 466.*

succor (sŭk'ẽr). 1. To go to the aid of; to relieve. 2. Aid; help.

succulence (sŭk'ŭ·lĕns). *See page 197.*

suffice (sŭ·fīs'). To meet or satisfy a need.

sumptuous (sŭmp'tū·ŭs). Luxurious; splendid.

supernal (sū·pûr'năl). Coming from heaven.

supine (sū·pīn'). Lying on the back or with face upward.

supplant (sŭ·plănt'). To overthrow; to take the place of.

supplicate (sŭp'lĭ·kāt). To entreat for; to ask for earnestly and humbly.

surcease (sûr·sēs'). End.

surcoat (sûr'kōt). A cloak worn over armor.

surplice (sûr'plĭs). An outer vestment worn by clergy.

susceptible (sŭ·sĕp'tĭ·b'l). Unresisting; easily affected.

sustain (sŭs·tān'). 1. To support; to hold up from below. 2. To carry on; maintain. 3. To aid; comfort. 4. To suffer; bear. 5. To allow; admit as valid.

suture (sū'tûr). Seam along which two parts are sewed or united.

swain (swān). A young peasant, a rustic.

swivel (swĭv''l). A part that turns to permit the connecting part to rotate.

sylvan (sĭl'văn). Pertaining to the woods.

synthetic (sĭn·thĕt'ĭk). Not genuine; artificial.

T

tangible (tăn'jĭ·b'l). Capable of being touched.

tarn (tärn). Small mountain lake.

tarpaulin (tär·pô'lĭn). Canvas waterproofed with tar or paint used for covering the hatches of ships, boats, etc.

tawny (tô'nĭ). Of a deep tan color.

temporal (tĕm'pŏ·răl). Pertaining to this world.

tenacious (tē·nā'shŭs). Holding fast; strong.

tenet (tĕn'ĕt). An opinion or principle.

tentacle (tĕn'tȧ·k'l). A long, flexible feeler, like the arms of an octopus.

tentative (tĕn·tȧ·tĭv). Experimental.

termagant (tûr'mȧ·gănt). A quarrelsome, scolding woman.

terminal (tûr'mĭ·năl). Pertaining to the end or boundary.

terrain (tĕ·rān'). *See page 143.*

terrestrial (tĕ·rĕs'trĭ·ăl). 1. Earthly. 2. Pertaining to land as distinct from water and air.

tether (tĕth'ẽr). A rope or leash on which an animal is confined to a small range.

texture (tĕks'tûr). 1. The characteristic arrangement of woven threads. 2. The manner of structure of something, as the skin, a painting, etc.

---

bar; church; dog; ardŭous; fat; go; hear; jail; key; lame; meat; not; ring; pay; ran; see; shell; ten; there, thick; pastŭre; vast; wind; yes; zoo, zh = z in azure.

theocracy (thē·ŏk′rȧ-sĭ). Government of a state by the direction of God.

theology (thē·ŏl′ō·jĭ). A system of religious theory.

thicket (thĭk′ĕt). A dense growth of shrubbery.

tiller (tĭl′ēr). A lever used for turning a rudder from side to side.

tome (tōm). A large book.

torpidity (tôr·pĭd′ĭ-tĭ). *See page 725.*

tractable (trăk′tȧ-b′l). Easily led, taught, or controlled.

trammel (trăm′ĕl). **1.** To confine or hamper. **2.** An adjustable pothook for the fireplace crane.

tranquillity (trăn·kwĭl′ĭ-tĭ). *See page 466.*

transcendent (trăn·sĕn′dĕnt). Surpassing; extraordinary.

transient (trăn′shĕnt). Of short duration.

travail (trăv′āl). **1.** Toil. **2.** Agony.

traverse (trăv′ērs). **1.** To pass across. **2.** To survey or study carefully.

treadle (trĕd′′l). A device pressed by the foot to drive a machine.

truculence (trŭk′ū·lĕns). Fierceness.

trundle (trŭn′d′l) **bed.** A low bed which may be pushed under another bed.

tryst (trĭst). An appointment to meet.

tumid (tū′mĭd). Swollen; bursting.

turbid (tûr′bĭd). Having the sediment disturbed; cloudy; not clear.

tycoon (tī·kōōn′). A businessman of unusual wealth and power.

U

ubiquitous (û·bĭk′wĭ·tŭs). Being everywhere at the same time.

ultimate (ŭl′tĭ·mĭt). Most remote in time or space; extreme.

unalienable (ŭn·āl′yĕn·ȧ-b′l). Not to be transferred or taken away.

unconscionable (ŭn·kŏn′shŭn-ȧ-b′l). **1.** Unreasonable. **2.** Not guided by conscience.

unction (ŭngk′shŭn). **1.** Fervent emotion. **2.** Emotional gush.

undulate (ŭn′dū·lāt). To rise and fall as if on waves.

unkempt (ŭn·kĕmpt′). Not combed; tousled.

unmercenary (ŭn·mûr′sē·nĕr·ĭ). Not seeking pay or reward.

unmitigated (ŭn·mĭt′ĭ·gāt′ĕd). Not softened or lessened.

unrequited (ŭn·rē·kwīt′ĕd). Not returned.

unresonant (ŭn·rĕz′ō·nȧnt). Not echoing.

unscrupulous (ŭn·skrōō′pū·lŭs). Unprincipled.

urbane (ûr·bān′). Courteous; polite.

usurer (ū′zhōō·rēr). *See page 484.*

usurpation (ū′zûr·pā′shŭn). Unauthorized exercise of powers belonging to another.

utilitarian (û·tĭl′ĭ·târ′ĭ·ăn). One who believes in usefulness as opposed to beauty or ornamentation.

V

vagrant (vā′grănt). An idle wanderer; a beggar.

venerable (vĕn′ēr·ȧ-b′l). *See page 540.*

vengeless (vĕnj′lĕs). Without revenge.

veracious (vē·rā′shŭs). Truthful.

verge (vûrj). A border or limit.

verger (vûrj′ēr). An official who takes care of the interior of a church building.

veritable (vĕr′ĭ·tȧ-b′l). Authentic; real; true; genuine.

vernacular (vēr·năk′û·lēr). The common mode of speech in a particular locality.

vestige (vĕs′tĭj). A trace, a mark, remains.

vesture (vĕs′tûr). A covering; a garment.

viand (vī′ănd). An article of food.

vicarious (vī·kâr′ĭ·ŭs). Acting as or being a substitute.

vicissitude (vĭ·sĭs′ĭ·tūd). Change of fortune.

vigilance (vĭj′ĭ·lȧns). Watchfulness; caution.

vindication (vĭn′dĭ·kā′shŭn). The act of supporting or maintaining as true or correct, against objections.

visage (vĭs′ĭj). Face.

vivify (vĭv′ĭ·fī). To give life to; animate.

vixen (vĭk′s′n). **1.** A she-fox. **2.** A shrewish, ill-tempered woman.

vociferation (vō·sĭf′ēr·ā′shŭn). Loud outcry.

voluble (vŏl′û·b′l). **1.** Fluent in speech; glib. **2.** Easily rolling or turning.

voracity (vō·răs′ĭ·tĭ). Greediness.

votive (vō′tĭv). Given or done as an act of consecration.

vouchsafe (vouch·sāf′). To grant.

W

wanton (wŏn′tŭn). **1.** Unruly; undisciplined. **2.** Unjustified.

weal (wēl). *See page 466.*

weir (wēr). **1.** A dam. **2.** A fence set in a stream to catch fish.

welkin (wĕl′kĭn). *See page 38.*

werewolf (wēr′wŏŏlf). A person who can assume at will a wolf's shape and appetite.

winch (wĭnch). Any of various machines or instruments to turn or strain something more or less forcibly.

wistaria (wĭs·tā′rĭ·ȧ). *See page 175.*

withal (wĭth·ôl′). Together with this; besides.

wont (wŭnt). Custom; habit; usage.

Y

yawl (yôl). A light boat.

āpe, chȧotic, bâre, ăt, ȧttend, ärt, flȧsk, ȧtop; ēke, mẽrely, ẽlect, ĕcho, prudĕnt, doẽr; ītem, ĭnn; rarĭty; ōde, ŏpaque, fôr, dŏt, lŏft, cŏnfide; sōōn, tŏŏk; sour, toil; tūbe, ūnique, tûrn, sŭp, ŭntil.

Index

From colonial beginnings
our rich and varied literature has grown with the nation.